'TAMING THE TIGER'

The Story of the India General Service Medal 1908-1935

'TAMING THE TIGER'

The Story of the India General Service Medal 1908–1935

by

RICHARD G.M.L. STILES

SAVANNAH

2012

© Richard G. M. L. Stiles and Savannah Publications
First published 2012

Published by Savannah Publications
90 Dartmouth Road, Forest Hill, London SE23 3HZ, UK
British Library Cataloguing in Publication Data

A CIP catalogue record is available from the British Library
ISBN 1 902366 51 4
EAN 9781902366517

Published in the UK by Lightening Source
Cover Design: Reggie Freeman (from a concept by Thérèse Lambert-Stiles)

Also available from the same author:
Mayhem in the Med: A Chronicle of the Cyprus Emergency 1955–1960. (Savannah Publications, 2005 & 2009).

The Law of The Frontier

The tribesman sits on his perch in the mountains and smiles at the soldier who tries
To cheat him of Allah's wine fountains or a free trip to paradise.

He knows that the rifle he clutches can fire like the finger of fate,
He knows that the trigger he touches is his key to the Golden Gate.

At last one day comes an army picquet, by the grace of the Prophet half trained.
They chatter like kids playing cricket as they clamber the rocky terrain.

Their backs are a wonderful target, a snapped disc he thinks at one hundred feet.
So the tribesman draws bead on their leader all brass and blanco and glint.

Three shots echo out in the nullah,
Three shots crack the still air,
Three Tommies drop and cry mother, as their bloodied hands paw at the air.

The tribesman waits not a minute longer.
Away with the speed of a tiger, his feet as swift as a goat.

This is the law of the Frontier. Learn it and learn it again.
The tribesman is no mere hunter, he is a warrior in more than just name.

A soldier who knows how to soldier, not spit or polish or shine.
So learn the law of the Frontier. Be cunning, be quick, be like a tiger.

Abridged By R. G. M. L. Stiles from a work by P Fitzharris, 1935

To:

Kenneth George Stiles
&
Leo Donald Lambert

Both of Whom Served With Honour

~~~~~~~~~~~~

Contents

Preface

This project has been a labour of love for a passion that spans some thirty years or more. When I wrote the original 'Story of the India General Service Medal 1908–1935' (Imperial Press, 1992) while living in the United States during the mid 1980s, I never thought that one day I would be in a position to work with the actual (British Establishment) medal rolls pertaining to this award. Access to these documents at the National Archives, Kew, London has enabled me to quench my thirst for accurate information regarding the identities and entitlements of the, hitherto, elusive 'odd men' for whom the India General Service Medal 1908–1935 is an 'Aladdin's Cave' of opportunity for medal collectors.

Access to these documents over the past five or six years inspired me to research my previous work further and commit to paper a detailed and complete medal roll for the India General Service Medal 1908–1935. My dilemma in doing so was to manage the sheer volume of names on the official roll when combined with the background narrative for each of the twelve campaigns commemorated by the award. My decision was to restrict the army roll to those units present in less than battalion strength (or equivalent). Multi-clasp entitlements, including inter-service transfers, have been researched for each and every recipient albeit any additional clasps won following a transfer to the Indian Establishment are beyond the scope of this work.

The publication of 'Taming the Tiger', The Story of the India General Service Medal 1908–1935 will give interested parties the answers to five key questions pertaining to the award of this medal.

- What circumstances/actions led to the sanction of any given campaign clasp on the India General Service Medal 1908–1935.
- What is the 'Odd Man' entitlement of any given campaign clasp on the India General Service Medal 1908–1935.
- What is the multi-clasp entitlement for all recipients of multi-clasp India General Service Medals 1908–1935.
- How scarce is the regimental or unit entitlement (including the Royal Air Force) for any given campaign clasp(s) on the India General Service Medal 1908–1935.

Finally, as I write this preface, British service personnel continue to be deployed on active duty in Afghanistan. Those with an interest in the subject matter of this book will be aware that, as far as the British Army is concerned, the current conflict could in fact be called the Fourth Afghan War. Therefore I would like to take this opportunity to recognise the hard work, commitment and courage of today's generation of service personnel in a region where so much blood has been spilt before.

Richard G.M.L. Stiles,
Wiltshire
2012

Acknowledgements

'*Taming The Tiger*', *The Story of The India General Service Medal 1908–1935* could not have been realised in its current form without the help, support and encouragement of many individuals. To this end I would like to thank my wife, Therese, for her patience and specific support with photographic illustrations many of which were extracted from a collection assembled by her late father, Leo Lambert USAF (Retd), whilst stationed in Peshawar, Pakistan during the early 1960s. I would also like to thank my son, Morgan, for giving me many hours of help at the National Archives (and elsewhere), writing copious list of names from difficult to read medal rolls and also my daughter Isabelle, for simply being patient and supportive with this work over the years.

Over the course of time I have had contact with just about every museum related to units that participated in one of more of the campaigns commemorated by the India General Service Medal 1908–1935. To list each and every person involved in supplying me with useful information and/or photographs would be impossible. I would, however, like to draw particular attention to the following individuals who so kindly accessed rare items from their museum collections with a view to advising me on the exact naming styles/unit abbreviations employed on seldom seen examples:

Ian Bailey, The Adjutant Generals Corps Museum
Dominique Bignall, The Royal Engineers Museum
Helen Burbage, The Royal Sussex Regiment Museum
Peter Donnelly, The King's Own Royal Regiment Museum
Jeffrey Elson, The Staffordshire Regiment Museum
Emma Halford-Forbes, The Black Watch Museum
Celia Green, Royal Welch Museum,
Capt. Gurung, RHQ (Royal Highland Fusiliers) Royal Regiment of Scotland
Christine Pullen, Royal Green Jackets Museum
Charles Reid, The Gordon Highlanders Museum
Dave Sands, The Worcestershire Regiment Museum
Mark Smith, The Royal Artillery Museum
George Streatfeild, The Soldiers of Gloucestershire Museum
Amy Wergerhoff, The Queen's Own Hussars Museum
Lt. Col. G Wood, RHQ (Royal Scots Borders) Royal Regiment of Scotland.

I would also like to extend my sincere thanks to medal specialist and consultant John Hayward for his invaluable advice on establishing the criteria for measuring the scarcity of any particular example from which I created the tables in the individual medal rolls.

Norman Gooding supplied me with much useful information on female recipients of the India General Service Medal 1908–1935, while Bob Courtney in Australia assisted me greatly by discovering why certain members of the Australian Army qualified for particular clasps as well as advising me on the naming styles used for medals to the Rifle Brigade and the King's Royal Rifle Corps.

R G M L Stiles

~ Fort Jamrud, as shown on the reverse of the
India General Service Medal 1908–1935 ~

~ Fort Jamrud, as depicted in a contemporary photograph ~

BACKGROUND

~ Authorisation ~

A Special Army Order, dated 12th December 1908, sanctioned the institution of the India General Service Medal 1908–1935. Army Order No. 1, dated 1st January 1909, set out further criteria. The medal became the second granted for general service in India during the reign of King Edward VII (the first was the India Medal 1895–1902) and, as such, maintained a continuity of practice pertaining to the award of general service medals for military campaigns on the Indian Sub Continent dating back to the institution of the India Medal 1854–95. Considering the substantial design alterations to the 1895 medal when struck with the image of King Edward (it had previously depicted Queen Victoria) for the Waziristan Campaign of 1901–02, by authority of Army Order No. 43 of 1903, it seems curious that the War Office felt it necessary to strike a completely new medal in 1908.

Originally struck to reward personnel employed under Major General Sir James Willcocks during the Zakka Khel and/or Mohmand Expeditions of 1908, the India General Service Medal 1908–1935 subsequently went on to commemorate a further eleven campaigns before being discontinued upon the death of King George V in 1935. Awards were suspended during the Great War, despite the fact that there were numerous military operations on the Indian frontier between 1914 and 1918 which, in the ordinary course of events, would have been commemorated by the issue of an Indian campaign medal. Instead, the award, where appropriate, of the 1914–15 Star and/or the Allied Victory Medal 1914–19, to accompany the British War Medal, was made. (The British War Medal 1914–20 was awarded to all British personnel deployed to India during the Great War regardless of whether the recipient was engaged in 'active' military operations).

~ Participating Units and Personnel ~

For a complete understanding of the units and personnel involved it is essential to be aware of the changes that were made in 1921 to Indian Army unit designations and titles. Indian Frontier Garrison Artillery Mountain Batteries, for example, were first re-designated 'Pack' Batteries and then subsequently completely renumbered. Therefore, examples of the India General Service Medal 1908–1935 exist named to the same unit but with different designations e.g. 27 Mountain Battery became 27 Pack Battery and then subsequently 107th (Gujarat) Pack Battery. Further radical changes to the Indian Army Order of Battle, including the merging or disbandment of many 'war' raised units, occurred in 1922 and 1923. Reference to the charts listing Indian Army units qualifying for clasps associated with the Frontier Campaigns of 1919–24 at the end of Chapter Three of this book will give clarity to these different designations.

It must be emphasised that many British personnel elected to transfer to the Indian Establishment after 1919. This practice increased in the early 1920s with the creation of new organisational structures, such as the Indian Signal Service and the Indian Army Service Corps. These fledgling units offered adventurous opportunities for short-term secondment from regular British formations. Some personnel transferred to the Indian Political Service or the various Indian Police establishments. Thus, examples of the India General Service Medal 1908–1935 exist with the first award gained in a widely eligible unit but with additional, and sometimes rarer, clasps gained in subsequent organisations and establishments.

A large number of Territorial Force units were sent to India during the early stages of the Great War to facilitate the redeployment of Regular Army formations to active theatres. In total, some 55,000 members of the Territorial Force were eventually deployed in the Sub Continent with many subsequently being sent to Mesopotamia. Some of these units, details of which appear in the appropriate roll at the end of Chapter Three, received the clasp for service in the Third Afghan War (clasp 'AFGHANISTAN N.W.F. 1919') and, in some instances, those for the Waziristan operations of 1919–24 (clasps 'WAZIRISTAN 1919–21' and WAZIRISTAN 1921-24'). These are the only occasions in which Territorial Army forces raised in the United Kingdom received an India General Service Medal. Medals to members of the Auxiliary Forces India are seen on the market from time to time, albeit generally to members of the various AFI railway regiments. Members of the Indian Army Reserve of Officers and Indian Unattached List also qualified for several clasps.

The 'AFGHANISTAN N.W.F. 1919' clasp was the first to be made available to personnel of the Royal Air Force. 'BURMA 1930–32' is the rarest award to the RAF, with a total of only 14 clasps/medals authorised. The clasp 'MAHSUD 1919–20' is usually found in combination with other clasps, but just 4 RAF recipients received it as a single clasp. "WAZIRISTAN 1925', a clasp previously considered unique to the RAF is now known to have been awarded to two Political Officers of the Indian establishment.

No awards have been identified to the Royal Navy or Royal Marines.

Civilian personnel, including medical doctors and female nurses attached to both the British and Indian Establishments, were eligible for the award of the India General Service Medal 1908–1935. With the exception of awards to the Political Department, Indian Police and Frontier Constabulary, examples to named civilian recipients are scarce. The most common clasps awarded to civilians were those for the frontier campaigns of 1919 to 1924.

In common with the 1854 and 1895 series of Indian General Service Medals, the 1908 medal was initially authorised for award in both silver and bronze. The practice of awarding bronze medals to camp followers and civilian non-combatants, such as bearers and domestic servants, ceased after the award of the clasp 'ABOR 1911–12'. Thereafter, all eligible personnel were granted silver medals. Consequently, silver medals from 'AFGHANISTAN N.W.F. 1919' forward exist named to Indian domestic staff serving with British units including the RAF. From 1922, following the structural changes made to the Indian Army Establishment, it was decided that each British infantry battalion would be assigned an 'Indian Platoon' to serve in a support role, such as mule leaders for the battalion's machine gun company. As far as can be determined, medals awarded to personnel of an Indian platoon were named to its parent unit.

~ Design Details ~

Obverse

- 1st Type 1908. Uncrowned bust of King Edward VII in Field Marshal's uniform with legend 'EDWARDVS VII KAISER-I-HIND'. This effigy by George W de Saulles. Genuine examples will include the initials 'DES' in the field below the sovereign's image.

- 2nd Type 1911–1925. Crowned bust of King George V in State Robes with legend 'GEORGIVS V KAISER-I-HIND'. This effigy by Sir Bertram Mackennal. Genuine examples will include the initials 'BM' in the field to the left of the sovereign.

- 3rd Type 1930–1935. Crowned bust of King George V in State Robes with legend 'GEORGIVS . V . D . G. BRITT . OMN . REX . ET . INDIAE . IMP .'. This effigy by Sir Bertram Mackennal. Genuine examples incorporate the initials 'BM' among the folds of the sovereign's robes in the 6 o'clock location.

Reverse

- All issues – one branch of oak and one of laurel beneath a tablet upon which is the word 'INDIA'. Above this, an engraving by Richard Garbe of Fort Jamrud situated at the mouth of the Khyber Pass on the North West Frontier with a view of the Alachi Mountains beyond. Genuine examples incorporate the initials G, with a small R to the centre, beneath the ribbon joining the oak and laurel branches.

Size

- 36mm/1.42 inches in diameter. Collectors should examine any variance to the perfect circumference of any given example. Any 'squaring' of the arc or thinning of the 'rim' may suggest the medal has been renamed.

Claw and Shoulders

- All types of the India General Service Medal 1908–1935 were minted in Calcutta with the suspender attached to the 'piece' by means of a plain shouldered double claw with a central rivet as employed on the 1854 and 1895 India General Service Medals. However, from 'AFGHANISTAN N.W.F. 1919' forward, medals were struck also at the Royal Mint in London for distribution to personnel who had already returned to Home Service duties or had been discharged prior to the medal being issued. Medals minted at the Royal Mint were manufactured with a single 'claw', or 'flange', with ornate scroll shaped shoulders employed to attach the suspender to the 'piece'. The medal roll generally identifies medals awarded to 'individual' British recipients in India with the words 'Issued by the Government of India', or similar description.

Suspender

- Standard 'India' style floreate swivel suspender as employed on the 1854 and 1895 India General Service Medals. These are often 'slack' on medals awarded to members of mounted units. Fixed suspension examples of the Royal Mint issue have been seen bearing the clasp 'AFGHANISTAN N.W.F. 1919'.

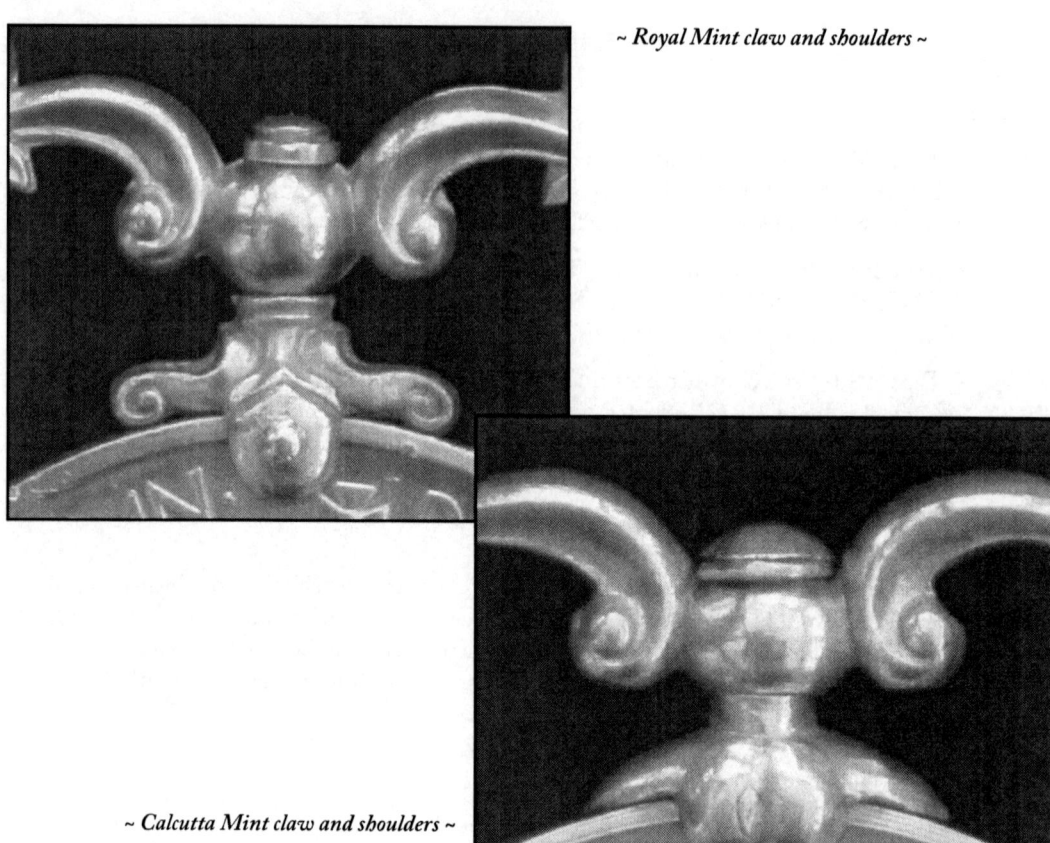

~ Royal Mint claw and shoulders ~

~ Calcutta Mint claw and shoulders ~

Clasps and Naming Styles

- Twelve authorised. (Details of individual clasps shown below).

- All 'MAHSUD 1919–20' and 'WAZIRISTAN 1919–21' combinations examined display the 'MAHSUD 1919–20' clasp nearest to the medal. Any medal bearing a single clasp 'MAHSUD 1919–20' should be carefully examined for evidence of a second clasp having been removed. Genuine single clasp 'MAHSUD 1919–20' medals are scarce. All recipients serving in British units are listed in the rolls following Chapter Three.

- The 'MALABAR 1921–22' clasp and the 'WAZIRISTAN 1919–21' clasp can be in either order. For example, some members of the disbanded Leinster Regiment, who transferred to another unit in 1922, may have qualified for the 'WAZIRISTAN 1919–21' clasp after qualifying for the 'MALABAR 1921–22' clasp.

- Qualification for additional clasps was often sanctioned some time after a recipient had left the service. Such clasps would be generally despatched to the recipient's last known address and were therefore often not attached securely to the medal. At best, these clasps were simply slid into place on the ribbon. The use of the medal rolls contained in this book will aid the identification of recipients who qualified for clasps that have become separated from their host medal.

- The clasp 'WAZIRISTAN 1925' should never be seen in combination with 'WAZIRISTAN 1921–24' due to an 'austerity' ruling published in Air Ministry Order 643/26 dated 2nd December 1926 which required those eligible for both clasps to choose one or the other only.

- The maximum number of clasps won by a soldier in British service was six.

- The maximum number of clasps won by RAF personnel was five.

- Personnel frequently moved from one unit to another thus qualifying for additional clasps on a medal named to the unit in which the first clasp was won. Where possible, such anomalies have been recorded in the rolls contained in this book. Possible subsequent service and qualification for clasps on the Indian Establishment is not recorded.

- Clasps issued during the award parameters of the 1st and/or 2nd types of the India General Service Medal 1908–1935 should never be seen on the 2nd and/or 3rd types.

- Details on hand engraved examples of the first two types can vary slightly. For example, medals to British regiments have been seen with and without the abbreviation 'Bn' before the unit name, while, in some instances, just the letter 'R' is used, instead of the abbreviation 'Regt'.

CLASP	BRITISH AUTHORISATION	NAMING STYLE
NORTH WEST FRONTIER 1908	Army Order No. 2 of 1909	Engraved Large Running Script*
ABOR 1911–12	Army Order No. 308 of 1912	Engraved Large Sloping Script*
AFGHANISTAN N.W.F. 1919	Army Order No. 223 of 1920 amended by No. 434 of 1920 and No. 362 of 1921	Impressed Block Capitals
MAHSUD 1919–20	Army Order No. 361 of 1921 amended by No. 347 of 1922	Impressed Block Capitals
WAZIRISTAN 1919–21	Army Order No. 795 of 1920 amended by Nos. 361 of 1921, Nos. 94 & 347 of 1922, No. 107 & 417 of 1923 and No. 149 of 1927	Impressed Block Capitals
MALABAR 1921–22	Army Order 50 off 1924	Impressed Block Capitals
WAZIRISTAN 1921–24	Army Order 177 of 1925 amended by No. 704 of 1925	Impressed Block Capitals
WAZIRISTAN 1925	Air Ministry Order 255 of 1926	Impressed Block Capitals
NORTH WEST FRONTIER 1930–31	Army Order 94 of 1933 amended by No. 123 of 1933 and No. 15 of 1935	Thin Impressed Block Capitals
BURMA 1930–32	Army Order No. 94 of 1933	Small Impressed Block Capitals
MOHMAND 1933	Army Order 186 of 1934	Small Impressed Block Capitals
NORTH WEST FRONTIER 1935	Army Order No. 51 of 1936 amended by No. 111 of 1936	Thin Impressed Block Capitals

- The (British) Army Orders setting the award criteria for each campaign were generally amended under (British) Indian Army 'Instructions' for the Indian Establishment, for example, Instruction India 795 of 1920 regarding the authorisation of the 'AFGHANISTAN N.W.F. 1919' clasp.

Ribbon

- 32 mm/1.25 inches wide; dark green with a 15mm/0.6-inch central dark blue stripe.

Mentions-in-Despatches

- Recipients of a Mention in Despatches from 11th August 1920 forward were retrospectively permitted to wear the bronze oak leaf emblem on the ribbon following the publication of Command Papers 7035 and 109 dated February and September 1947 respectively.

Miniatures

- In common with most other British campaign medals, miniature versions of the India General Service Medal 1908–1935 were produced for display when wearing either military mess dress or civilian evening dress. Examples were manufactured in Britain, as well as India, consequently a vast number of versions exist of varying quality made from a variety of materials. Miniature medals struck concurrent with the period of general issue of the full size medal was available were produced in silver and are of good quality. Miniatures have been seen with additional unauthorised clasps including 'WAZIRISTAN 1917' and 'MOHMAND 1934'.

~ The Rolls ~

The British Army medal rolls for the India General Service Medal 1908–1935 are available on microfilm at the National Archives, Kew, London in series WO/100/397 forward. (Royal Air Force rolls are to be released into the series AIR 81). The British Army (and some Indian Army) rolls have also been scanned commercially and released on line via subscription.

Using either of these media to search for a specific recipient or to browse a unit entitlement can be complex. Many pages of the original paper roll fell out of sequence during their long years of storage and consequently, when committed to microfilm, numerous chronological errors and order of precedence mistakes were erroneously captured in the data base. Researchers should, therefore, be aware that:

- For any given formation, officers and other rank lists are frequently recorded separately and are therefore stored on separate microfilm reels

- Odd pages from different time periods/campaigns (including the India General Service Medal 1936–1939) can appear in any given run.

- Transferred personnel are often recorded under the unit they were serving in at the time of initial qualification as well as at the time of award. Close examination of the microfilm image will generally identify which is which.

- A 'confirmed' award can be subsequently revoked by a second roll entry.

- Rank and serial number at initial qualification are not always the same as at the time of award. (Where appropriate I have listed both potential serial numbers in the rolls published in this book).

- When browsing a unit on line, it is important to look beyond the 'India specific' search browsers due to several microfilm downloads having been saved among the data bases of earlier campaigns.

In an attempt to bring clarity to all of these complexities, I have examined each and every page of the India General Service Medal 1908–1935 roll held at the National Archives with a view to publishing in this book the following information:

- A full and credible roll of all British Army and Royal Air Force commissioned personnel who qualified for the India General Service Medal 1908–1935 and their relevant campaign clasp combinations. (Officers of the Indian Mountain Artillery and the Indian Sappers and Miners are included because they held commissions in the Royal Artillery and Royal Engineers).

- A full and credible roll of all British Army enlisted personnel who qualified for a clasp while serving with a unit that was present in less than regimental strength – the infamous 'Odd Men'. For example, an entry for '17940 Pte. H Willans', 1st Bn, Duke of Wellington's Regt. is not included because 1st Bn, Duke of Wellington's Regt. qualified for the 'AFGHANISTAN N.W.F. 1919' clasp as an entire battalion and the roll would therefore be 600–700 names long! An entry does exist, however, for '202083 Pte. A D S Morrison', 2/4th Bn, Duke of Cornwall's Light Infantry because only 44 members of the Regiment qualified for the 'AFGHANISTAN N.W.F. 1919' clasp.

- A full and credible roll of all personnel who qualified for more than one clasp while serving with the British Army or Royal Air Force.

When using the rolls published in this book, it is important to note that:

- Double barrelled names are listed in the alphabetical sequence of the second name recorded. This is because it is not always possible to determine from the Medal Roll whether or not any given set of second names is a double barrelled variant or not.

- For most 'Odd Men' entries, the relevant unit abbreviation to be engraved or stamped on the recipient's medal is shown. These abbreviations are noted in the rolls contained within this book. Multiple variations of official abbreviations were available to some units. These have been noted when appropriate. A medal with a different style of unit abbreviation on the edge should be considered with great care.

- For personnel extra regimentally employed, the rolls often show the type of duty and duty station. Where possible this information has been included. Please consult the Glossary for details of unit abbreviations.

- It is beyond the scope of this work to attempt to replicate for the Indian Establishment the details contained herein for the British Army. Every effort has been made, however, to reproduce a credible order of battle for the Indian Establishment after each chapter.

Orders / Decorations And Honours

These have been omitted from the text to maintain simplicity.

Ranks

Where possible, the roll states a recipient's rank at the time of qualification for the India General Service Medal 1908–1935. This is not always an exact science. Acting and temporary ranks are combined in my roll with substantive personnel of the same rank. All Subalterns are grouped as Lieutenants. Non-commissioned ranks are grouped as Company Quartermaster Sergeant / Staff Sergeant / Colour Sergeant, then Quartermaster Sergeant/Sergeant then Lance Sergeant / Corporal and finally Lance Corporal/Private (or unit equivalent designation).

It should be noted that during the early twentieth century (and before) a Brigadier General was considered a temporary (operational) appointment for (full) Colonels and (occasionally) Lieutenant Colonels. (Appointments upon retirement were not unknown). The grade was abolished in 1922 in favour of Colonel Commandant but this was only a short-lived rank. Appointments to (substantive) Brigadiers occurred from 1928 forward.

Casualties

Casualty rolls for those who died have been compiled from a wide variety of sources including returns published in *The Times* of the period; regimental histories, memorials and the medal roll itself. The online search facility of the Commonwealth War Graves Commission has been extremely useful in compiling the list for the period 1919–22. Deaths registered in India on this site have been cross-referenced with the relevant roll to ensure the casualty was a recipient of the India General Service Medal 1908–1935. It has not been possible to list those who were wounded. Deaths have been included for a period of approximately six months after the conclusion of each campaign in the hope that personnel dying from the effects of wounds, injury or disease sustained on active service may be catalogued. It is beyond the scope of this book to attempt to list casualty returns associated with the Indian Establishment although individual identified entries have been included in the text from time to time.

~ Medal Record Cards (WO372) and National Archives Online Research System ~

The Medal Record Cards are archived on the National Archives database in alphabetical sequence by surname. They contain the names of some six million personnel. The online search system requires details of name, serial number and, ideally, unit. It is not possible to search by medal entitlement and, consequently, details of a recipient are required before this verification route can be employed. The last one or two digits of serial numbers are often omitted thus making online searches by serial number difficult. Poor interpretation of the hand writing on the cards, coupled with (perhaps) a lack of subject knowledge on the part of those employed to create the database, has resulted in a large number of online medal record cards identifying a medal recipient against a spurious unit. Examples include 'L/11862 Pte. J Bailey, 21ˢᵗ Lancers' who is shown as being with the '4ᵗʰ Lancers' - a unit that I believe never existed. 'Capt. G L Dunn, Kent Cyclist Bn', is shown as being in the 'East Kent Regt.' '265079 Acting Sergeant W A Elkington, Kent Cyclist Bn' is shown as being in the 'Huntingdonshire Cyclist Bn'. '7870494 Pte D A Hay, 1 Armoured Car Company, Tank Corps' is shown as being in the 'Ammunition Cavalry Company'! The list goes on...

~ Rarity of Clasps~

While 'value' is largely subjective and generally dependent upon desirability, 'rarity' is a more exact science. Lack of previously published detailed research pertaining to the India General Service Medal 1908–1935 has led to a wide variety of (perhaps misleading) assessments in the past. This work is designed to bring clarity to this subject and, as such, challenges many previously held positions.

The following 'range' is used consistently throughout the work to access rarity across 'authorised/ issued' clasps:

No of Recipients	Rarity
1	According to the roll as seen, can be considered Unique
2 – 10	Of the Utmost Rarity
11 – 20	Extremely Rare
21 – 50	Very Rare
51 – 100	Rare
101 – 250	Scarce

*

MAP ONE

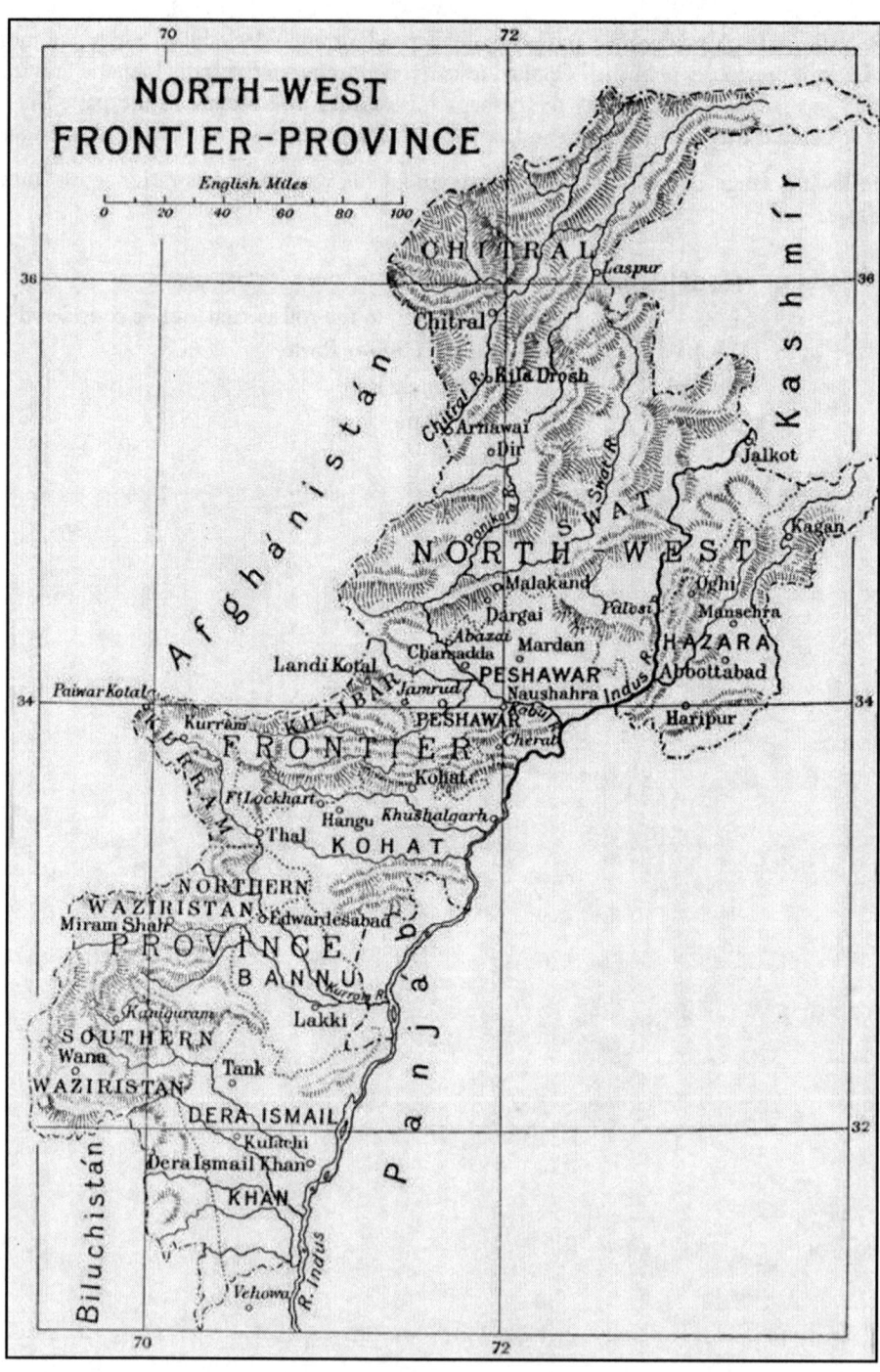

~ *The North West Frontier of India* ~

MAP TWO

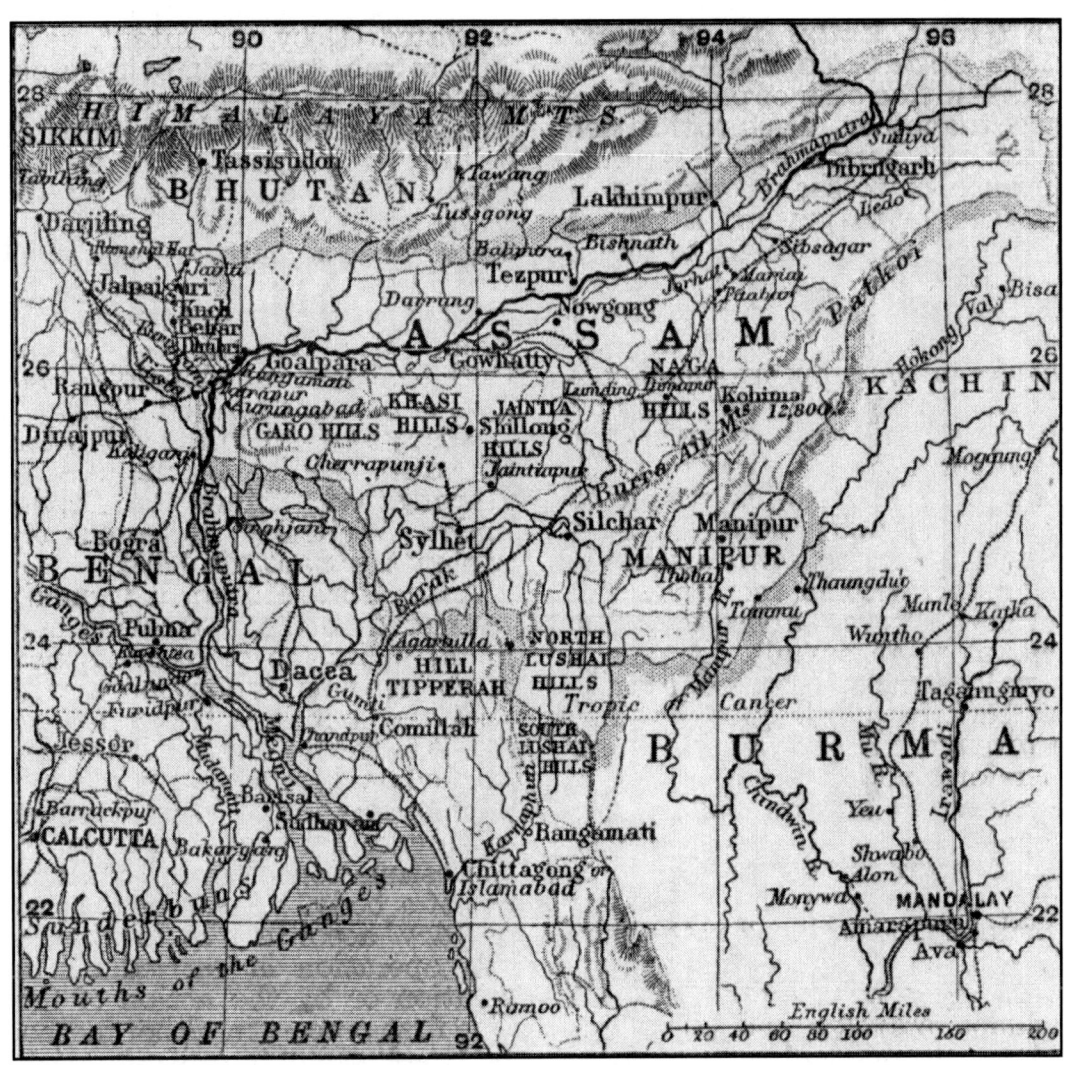

~ North East Indian Frontier and Assam ~

MAP THREE

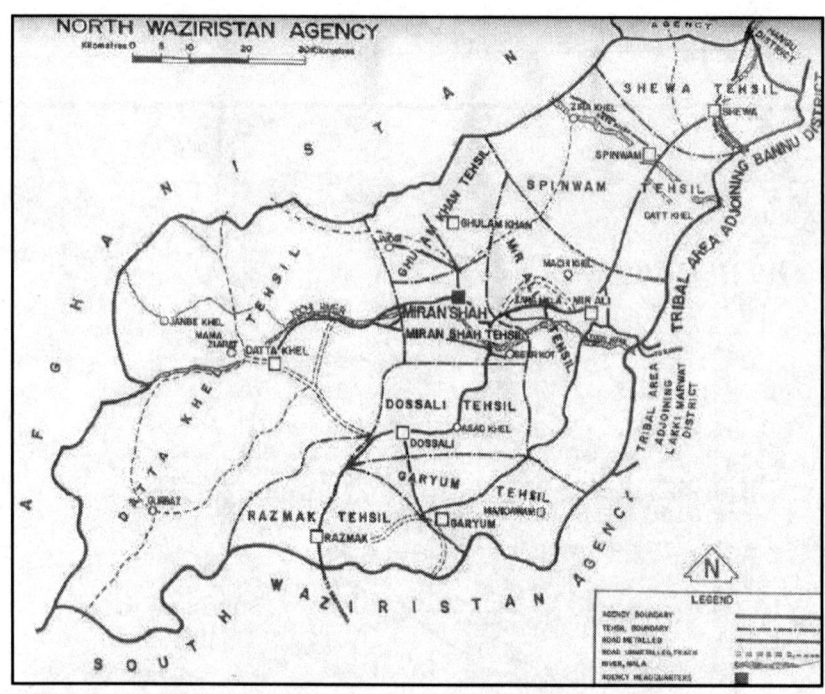

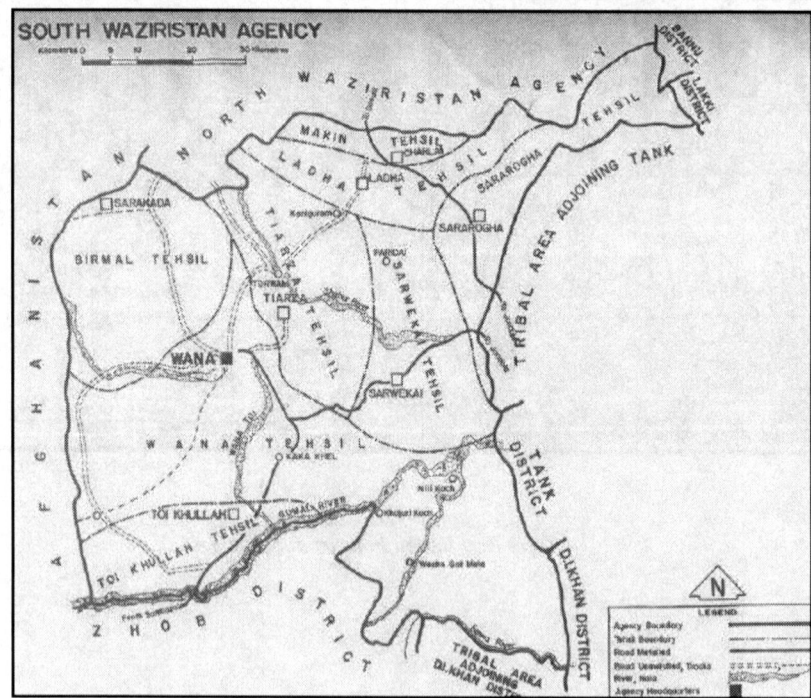

~ Waziristan ~

MAP FOUR

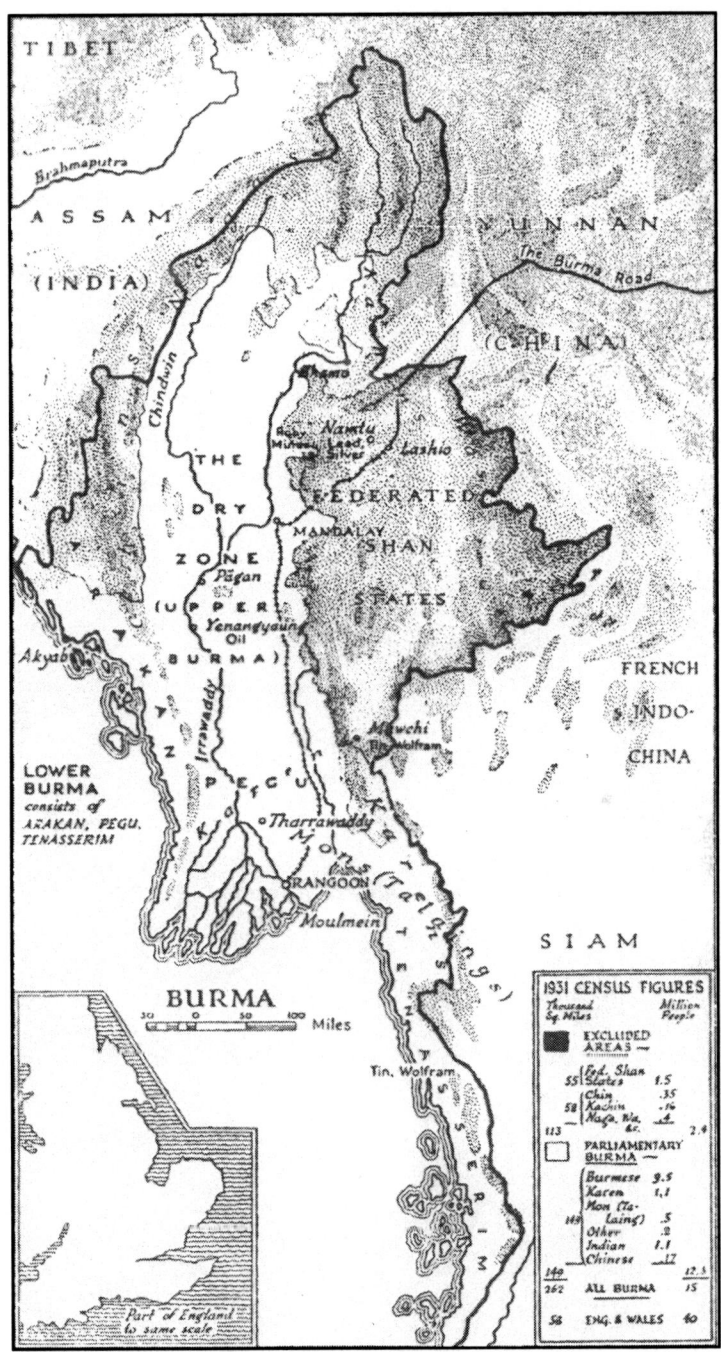

~ *Burma 1930–32* ~

1. NORTH WEST FRONTIER CAMPAIGNS 1908

~ India General Service Medal 1908–1935 ~
NORTH WEST FRONTIER 1908
Issue 1: Calcutta Mint

The clasp 'NORTH WEST FRONTIER 1908' was authorised by Army Order No. 2 of 1909, to reward troops and certain mobilised civilians deployed under the command of Major General Sir J. Willcocks during the Zakka Khel and Mohmand expeditions on the Indian North West Frontier. This was the first clasp awarded with the India General Service Medal 1908–1935. Enrolled camp followers and associated official native non-combatants received bronze medals and clasps.

To qualify for the 'NORTH WEST FRONTIER 1908' clasp, personnel had to satisfy one, or more, of the following requirements:

- Served in the Zakka Khel Expedition with the Bazaar Valley Field Force deploying under the orders of Major General J. Willcocks from Ali Masjid in the Khyber Pass into, or towards, the Bazaar Valley between 14th February 1908 and 1st March 1908 inclusive. Personnel who did not proceed beyond Ali Masjid were not entitled.

- Served on the Mohmand–Peshawar frontier, north of the pontoon bridge across the Swat River at Abazai between 19th April 1908 and 26th April 1908, inclusive.

- Served at Landi Kotal in the Khyber Pass between 2nd May 1908 and 5th May 1908, inclusive.

- Served in the Mohmand Field Force deploying under the orders of Major General J. Willcocks beyond Hafiz Khor, between 12th May 1908 and 31st May 1908, inclusive.

Due to the above criteria, not all mobilised units qualified. Many individuals qualified while serving on detached duties.

~ The Zakka Khel Expedition: February–March 1908 ~

The Zakka Khel formed the southern most 'clan' of the eight sub-divisions of the Afridi people. The tribal homeland of the Zakka Khel was concentrated in the isolated, inhospitable mountains and valleys of Yaghistan in that portion of the North West Frontier Province of India lying beyond the administrative boundary. To the north was the Khyber Pass, to the south were the Safed Koh Mountains, and to the west was Afghanistan, while to the east were Peshawar and British-administered India. The majority of Zakka Khel permanent settlements were located in the western Baazar Valley, an area that extended west from the Kajauri Plain that, in turn, was located to the southwest of Peshawar.

Due to what was interpreted as daring and treacherous behaviour, the Zakka Khel were considered by the British to be one of the most truculent and lawless clans on the Indo-Afghan border. Between 1901 and 1908, they were held responsible for the violent deaths of some 32 British subjects. Kidnap and extortion, especially of merchants travelling the caravan route through the Khyber Pass to and from Peshawar, were a common source of revenue. The Zakka Khel, in common with their fellow Afridi brethren, tended to migrate to the South Maiden Valley of Tirah during the long hot summer season, returning to the Baazar Valley area in the autumn. The Zakka Khel were a thriving community in 1908 and were able to field some 5,000–6,000 well-armed warriors.

Generals Tytler and Maude had clashed with the Zakka Khel during the Second Afghan War of 1878–80. Though initially successful, these engagements were never followed up in earnest by the authorities and further military operations were subsequently deemed necessary. In 1897, a frontier wide uprising occurred and Lieutenant General W.S.A. Lockhart was despatched by the Government of India to quell the situation in what came to be known as the Tirah Campaign. By 1898, most of the North West Frontier tribes had sued for peace. The Zakka Khel, Mahsud and Waziri clans, however,

~ Danger lurked around every twist and turn of the Khyber caravan trail for all travellers ~

continued to oppose British authority. Hence the British established a blockade of the Mahsud and Waziri territory by a military force deployed under the command of Major General C.C. Egerton between 23rd November 1901 and 10th March 1902. (The operation under Major General Egerton was recognised by the award of the India Medal 1895–1902 with clasp 'WAZIRISTAN 1901–2'). Britain's subsequent frontier policy, initially under the direction of the Viceroy, Lord Curzon, thence the Earl of Minto, restricted entry into, or occupation of, recognized tribal homelands lying beyond India's administrative boundary.

The Government of India decreed that from November 1901 only locally raised militia formations, such as the Khyber Rifles or the Kurram Militia, were to be deployed fulltime in tribal regions. Political officers supported by military staff drawn from both the British and British Indian Establishments controlled these militia forces. Regular forces of the British and British Indian Armies were henceforth to be maintained in static garrisons located within British administered territory, from which movable columns could be despatched as and when required. This strategy was facilitated by the constantly improving quality of railway communication throughout the Indian Sub Continent. Indeed, by this juncture, the line from Peshawar extended west as far as Fort Jamrud at the mouth of the Khyber Pass, while the line from Nowshera extended north as far as Dargai via Mardan. In a society, where respect for authority and strength of arms appear to have been closely interlinked, such a policy rapidly resulted in further dilution of British credibility. Consequently, by 1907, the Zakka Khel had grown so confident of their position that Malik Khawas Khan attempted to open independence negotiations with the Khyber Area Political Agent, Lieutenant Colonel Sir George O. Roos-Keppel, during an Afridi Political *jirga* held at Landi Kotal in the Khyber Pass.

Following the Government's swift rejection of this approach, a militant section of the Zakka Khel determined that more 'direct' action would be required to secure their objectives. In October 1907, a group of armed warriors attacked the village of Pubbie near Peshawar in British-administered India. Several members of the Indian Frontier Constabulary were killed during the ensuing clamour. The tribesmen successfully evaded capture and retired in good order back to their homeland. Several Zakka Khel *maliks*, realising such action was unlikely to go unpunished by the British, thereupon declared that should the authorities decide to pursue the raiding party across the administrative boundary, ten British soldiers would perish for every warrior killed.

The *maliks* need not have feared. The local administration failed to sanction a punitive operation and this led directly to a strengthening of Zakka Khel resolve. On 13th November 1907, 50 warriors looted the peaceful agricultural village of Lacho, located some 50 miles south of Peshawar. A few days later, in Kohat District, a Zakka Khel force destroyed the Government Post Office and injured several local villagers – one mortally. When the local militia and Frontier Constabulary eventually arrived on the scene to investigate the incident, the perpetrators sprang an ambush, killing three militiamen and a police sepoy. The Zakka Khel then escaped into the surrounding countryside carrying with them several captured Government issue Lee Enfield rifles.

On 5th January 1908, Malik Multan led a particularly audacious Zakka Khel raid into British-administered India. The tribesmen attacked the town of Jalazai, situated on the Peshawar Nowshera railway, destroying key government buildings and strategic railway infrastructure. This incident was followed up with further attacks including the targeting of the train station at Kacha Garhis, west of Peshawar. British outrage, including petitions by the board of the North West Railway Company, prompted Sir Harold Deane, Chief Commissioner of the North West Frontier Province, to start considering a permanent solution for the protection of British interests within his domain.

29

When some £6,600 worth of precious gems were stolen by the Zakka Khel from a Peshawar City jewellers shop on 28th January 1908, the Secretary of State for India, Lord Morley, gave Chief Commissioner Deane permission to begin planning for immediate punitive action. On 9th February, the Chief Commissioner called a *jirga* of all Afridi clans resident in the non-administered territories of the North West Frontier, with a view to ensuring that the region's tribesmen would not construe any potential military incursion into Zakka Khel territory as a frontier-wide invasion by the British authorities. The Zakka Khel, naturally, refused to attend. Those clans that did present themselves in Peshawar on 12th February insisted that they were opposed to the current climate of tension on the frontier and wished to live in peace with the Government. The Aka Khel, for example, advised Commissioner Deane that their elders had made the Zakka Khel perpetrators of the Jalazai incident abandon much of their 'prize' before fleeing back to the Bazaar Valley across their territory. As anticipated, however, none of the assembled tribesmen was prepared to support British military action as punishment.

Major General J. Willcocks, the recently appointed Commander of the 1st (Peshawar) Division, had already begun planning for a military expedition against the Zakka Khel when Chief Commissioner Deane summoned him to Government House in Peshawar on 10th February 1908. Following the meeting it was determined that a significant force, to be designated the Bazaar Valley Field Force, would be mobilized and deployed forthwith to punish the tribesmen. The force was to be drawn from the 1st (Peshawar) Division and consist of the 1st Infantry Brigade, Brigadier General C.A. Anderson, and the 2nd Infantry Brigade, Major General A.A. Barrett. Operations were to be restricted entirely to the Bazaar Valley and its immediate environs. Despite petitions to the contrary from several prominent British business and middle-ranking officials, there was to be no long-term occupation or annexation of tribal territory. These conditions of war were imposed on General Willcocks by the Secretary of State for India.

BAZAAR VALLEY FIELD FORCE COMMAND & STAFF, FEBRUARY 1908

GOC 1st (Peshawar) Division – Maj. Gen. Sir J Willcocks

1st Division Staff – Brig. Gen. H Mullally

Capt. J Campbell, 1st Bn, Argyll & Sutherland Highlanders....................................Deputy Assistant Quartermaster General, Int
Lt. Col. H J Dundee, Royal Engineers..Chief Engineering Officer
Maj. C L Gregory, 19th Hussars...Deputy Assistant Quartermaster General
Capt. P Howell, Queen's Own Corps of Guides...Provost Marshal
Lt. Col. G O Roos-Keppel..Area Political Officer
Lt. Col. M W Kerin, Royal Army Medical Corps...Senior Medical Officer
Capt. N J C Livingston-Learmouth, 15th Hussars...Aide de Camp
Bvt. Col. A W Money, Royal Field Artillery..Quartermaster General
Capt. S F Muspratt, 12th Cavalry, IA...Intelligence Officer
Capt. A W Peek, 22nd Cavalry, IA..Deputy Assistant Adjutant General
Capt. F T Rich, Royal Engineers..Survey Officer
Maj. G L'H Sanders, Supply & Transport Corps..Divisional Supply Officer
Lt. A J Thompson, Army Veterinary Corps...Senior Veterinary Officer
Capt. A Whatman, 2nd Bn, Somerset Light Infantry...Signals Officer

1st Infantry Brigade – Brig. Gen. C A Anderson

Capt. E E Barwell, 57th Rifles..Deputy Assistant Quartermaster General
Lt. H F Elgee, 1st Bn, South Wales Borders...Orderly Officer
Maj. A F Ferguson Davie, 53rd Sikhs...Signals Officer
Lt. L Forbes, 57th Rifles..Orderly Officer
Maj. R de B James, Army Service Corps...Brigade Supply Officer
Capt. A L Tarver, 124th DCO Baluch Infantry...Deputy Assistant Adjutant General

4 Guns, 22 (Derajat) Mountain Battery, Indian Frontier Artillery
1ˢᵗ Bn, Royal Warwickshire Regiment
53ʳᵈ Sikhs (Frontier Force), 59ᵗʰ Scinde Rifles (Frontier Force) & 2/5ᵗʰ Gurkha Rifles
A&B Sections, No. 1 British Field Hospital, Royal Army Medical Corps
No. 101 Native Field Hospital & A&B Sections, 102 Native Field Hospital, Indian Hospital Corps

2ⁿᵈ Infantry Brigade – Maj. Gen. A A Barret

Maj. H M Allen, 25ᵗʰ Cavalry, IA..Deputy Assistant Adjutant General
Capt. W C W Harrison, Supply & Transport Corps...Brigade Supply Officer
Lt. D K McLeod, Queen's Own Corps of Guides..Signals Officer
Capt. H H Norman, 2ⁿᵈ Bn, Northampton Regiment.................................Deputy Assistant Quartermaster General
Lt. J P Villiers-Stuart, 55ᵗʰ Rifles..Orderly Officer

2 Squadrons, 37ᵗʰ Lancers (Baluch Horse), IA, (Div Tps Attch.)
3 Mountain Battery, Royal Garrison Artillery
1ˢᵗ Bn, Seaforth Highlanders
28ᵗʰ Punjabis, 45ᵗʰ Rattray's Sikhs & 54ᵗʰ Sikhs (Frontier Force)
C&D Sections, No. 1 British Field Hospital, Royal Army Medical Corps
C&D Sections, 102 Native Field Hospital & No. 103 Native Field Hospital, Indian Hospital Corps

3ʳᵈ (Reserve) Infantry Brigade – Brig. Gen. H B Watkis

Capt. H H Holdich*, 1ˢᵗ Scots Guards...Orderly Officer
Maj. G B H Rice, 31ˢᵗ Sikh Pioneers..Brigade Major
Capt. A R B Shuttleworth...Brigade Supply Officer

23 (Peshawar) Mountain Battery, Indian Frontier Artillery
1ˢᵗ Bn, Royal Munster Fusiliers
55ᵗʰ Coke's Rifles (Frontier Force), 1/1ˢᵗ PWO Gurkha Rifles (The Malaun Regiment) & 1/6ᵗʰ Gurkha Rifles

Divisional Troops & Lines of Communication – Col. S F Biddulph, 19ᵗʰ Lancers, IA

Lt. R E Barrow, 38ᵗʰ Dogras..Signals Officer
Lt. W Gibson, 1ˢᵗ Bn, Northumberland Fusiliers..Signals Officer
Lt. R D C McLeod, 19ᵗʰ Lancers, IA..Staff Officer
Lt. D P Sandeman, Queen's Own Corps of Guides...Signals Officer
Maj. G H Stewart, 7ᵗʰ Rajputs..Transport Officer
Lt. A P Wavell*, 2ⁿᵈ Bn, Royal Highlanders...Ammunition Column

2 Squadrons. 19ᵗʰ Lancers, IA
Balance, 22 (Derajat) Mountain Battery, Indian Frontier Artillery
23ʳᵈ Sikh Pioneers, 25ᵗʰ Punjabis & Khyber Rifles Militia
No. 6 Company, 1ˢᵗ Prince of Wales's Own Sappers and Miners
3 Sections, No. 9 Company, 2ⁿᵈ Queen's Own Sappers & Miners
No. 105 Native Field Hospital, Indian Hospital Corps

Depot – Peshawar – Lt. Col. A R Dick, 22ⁿᵈ Cavalry, IA

Maj. H R Blore*, King's Royal Rifle Corps..Deputy Assistant Adjutant & Quartermaster General
Lt. Col. H H Brown*, Royal Army Medical Corps...Senior Medical Officer
Lt. I A Finnis*, Royal Artillery..Ordnance Officer
Maj. H L D Fordyce, Supply & Transport Corps...Brigade Supply Officer
Maj. L A S Hanmer, 21ˢᵗ Cavalry, IA..Railway Transport Officer
Lt. H C Sinnott*, 1ˢᵗ Bn, Royal Warwickshire Regiment.....................................Commanding British Troops Depot
Capt. C J White, 53ʳᵈ Sikhs...Commanding Indian Troops Depot

Note * = Name Not Found On British Medal Roll

A reserve force consisting of the 3ʳᵈ Infantry Brigade, Brigadier General H.B. Watkis, was brought up by rail to a staging area near Nowshera in case the Mohmands, to the north of the Khyber Pass, decided to exploit the situation. Local intelligence had already suggested that Zakka Khel emissaries were actively seeking allies from those peoples living on both sides of the Indo Afghan border to assist

~ View west along the Khyber Pass ~

in their struggle against the British. In all, some 14,600 troops (about 2,000 British and 12,000 Indian Army, including followers) were made available for deployment along with 475 horses, 353 ponies and 4,200 pack mules.

The Bazaar Valley Field Force formed up under the guise of spring field manoeuvres.

*

The manoeuvrability restrictions imposed upon Major General J. Willcocks by the Government of India prevented a direct invasion of the Bazaar Valley along the conventional Bara River route from Peshawar via Fort Jamrud and the eastern Khyber. Access would instead need to be secured from the north. To this end on 13th February 1908, Lieutenant Colonel G.O. Roos-Keppel led several hundred sepoys of the Queen's Own Corps of Guides Infantry, supported by a rifle company of the 2/5th GR, to Landi Kotal in the midst of the Khyber Pass. Later that same day the 1st and 2nd Infantry Brigades came up to Fort Jamrud from Peshawar. The 1st Bn, Royal Warwickshire Regt. immediately established a secure perimeter to the west of the fort. The main force continued its march westward the following day. Upon reaching Lala China, situated within striking distance of the Chora Pass, it was determined that the 2nd Infantry Brigade would establish a forming-up point for the force. The 1st Infantry Brigade arrived some hours later at Fort Ali Masjid, situated half way between Landi Kotal and Fort Maude. (1st Bn, Royal Warwickshire Regt. having left Lieutenant T.V. Barney and 118 other ranks to guard Fort Jamrud, then deployed as the rearguard escorting the baggage train mules of the Supply and Transport Corps). The Bazaar Valley Field Force then established a forward operating base on the Shahgai Heights and a reconnaissance was made of the available routes south into the Bazar Valley via the Chora, Alachie and Bazaar Passes.

*~ Lieutenant Colonel
Sir G O Roos-Keppel ~*

On the night of 15th/16th February 1908, Lieutenant Colonel G.O. Roos-Keppel took two rifle companies of the 2/5th GR, supported by some 700 Khyber Rifles from Landi Kotal, into the mouth of the narrow Bazaar Pass. A steady uninterrupted pace was set and by about 9 a.m. the narrow trail crested its summit. The column continued to advance throughout the morning and occupied the small Zakka Khel settlement at Chinar at about midday. The village was deserted; the inhabitants appeared to have fled east to picquet the Alachi Heights. Lieutenant Colonel Roos-Keppel then advanced east along the Walai stream with a view to securing a rendezvous with Major General J. Willcocks and the 2nd Infantry Brigade at Walai village. Having left Chinar unsecured, the Zakka Khel reoccupied the site shortly thereafter.

The 2nd Infantry Brigade, supported by the balance of the 2/5th GR, advanced from Lala China south, through the snowy Chora Pass to Chora village and beyond, as far as Sarkhum on the border between Din Khel and Zakka Khel territory. An advance was then executed along the Walai stream west towards Lieutenant Colonel G.O. Roos-Keppel at Walai village. Enemy snipers were active and the 2/5th GR were required to picquet the route back towards Chora thus establishing a degree of security for any future deployments from that place. A bivouac was established for the night at the foot of the strategically important Khar Ghundai, the summit of which having previously been secured by the 1st Bn, Seaforth Highlanders. Despite the sighting of picquets at strategic locations, Zakka Khel snipers were active during the ensuing hours of darkness and seven men were shot – two mortally.

Meanwhile, the 1st Infantry Brigade, accompanied by the stores and supplies of the force baggage train, moved laboriously up to Chora and occupied the village. With the position firmly secured, Brigadier General C.A. Anderson deployed 22 (Derajat) Mountain Battery and the 53rd Sikhs to the adjacent fortified 'palace' of Yar Mohammed Khan. The 25th Punjabis and 59th Rifles were subsequently deployed as Lines of Communication defence. The following day, 'G' Company, 1st Bn, Royal Warwickshire Regt., under Major A.Y. Spearman, relieved the 53rd Sikhs, while a further four companies of the regiment reinforced the Lines of Communication forward towards the 2nd Infantry Brigade. The Sappers and Miners thereupon began the task of improving the track to enable Supply and Transport Corps mule teams to begin resupplying the brigade.

The advance on Walai village continued early the following day. Concerted sniper interference from tribesmen, secreted in positions along the crest of the Sara Paial, eventually necessitated an assault in that direction. An attack by sepoys of the 45th Sikhs faltered until reinforced by several rifle companies of the 1st Bn, Seaforth Highlanders supported by shrapnel fire from 3rd Mountain Battery, RGA. With the summit of the Sara Paial secured, henceforth renamed '45th Sikhs Hill', the 1st Infantry Brigade resumed its advance virtually unopposed, whereupon Lieutenant Colonel G.O. Roos-Keppel's command was reunited with the main force.

On 17th February 1908, the 1st and 2nd Infantry Brigades rendezvoused at Walai village and rapid preparations were made to retake Chinar and force the open confrontation that Major General J. Willcocks sought. The RGA Mountain Batteries, equipped with their new 10lb breech-loading field guns, quickly came into action against several Zakka Khel concentrations, thus enabling the infantry to establish a secure form-up position east of Chinar. The going had been tough. The after effects of heavy sleet and snow severely debilitated all the troops deployed. Meanwhile, the 59th Scinde Rifles relieved the various 1st Bn, Royal Warwickshire Regt. picquets along the Walai road.

Early on the morning of 18th February 1908, the 2nd Infantry Brigade broke camp and advanced on Chinar. The 1st Bn, Seaforth Highlanders, supported by the 54th Sikhs, captured the spur feature to the north of the objective under the cover of heavy shellfire courtesy of the mountain batteries. Soon after the initial salvos found their targets, the enemy was observed fleeing across the open valley towards Halwai and the northern slops of the Surghar Mountains. Chinar was captured the following day. No. 6 Field Company, 1 PWO Sappers and Miners, thereupon set about destroying all enemy towers and associated fortifications in the area. The force then retired towards Walai village, covered by 3 Mountain Battery, RGA with 'A' and 'B' Companies, 1st Bn, Royal Warwickshire Regt., Major P.T. Westmoreland, on the right flank and the 2/5th GR, Lieutenant Colonel J.M. Stewart, on the left. The enemy pressed this action hard, resulting in the wounding of three officers and six other ranks. The following day a further expedition to Chinar was conducted to ensure a number of additional structures were razed.

Major General J. Willcocks thereupon focused his attention on Zakka Khel fortifications in the Tsatsobi Pass region at the eastern end of the Bazaar Valley. This manoeuvre also helped prevent enemy warriors from evading retribution by fleeing across the political frontier into Afghanistan. At Khwar and Sarmando, the village watchtowers were blown up by the Sappers and Miners of the 1st Infantry Brigade, while in the Algad Valley, 22 (Derajat) Mountain Battery quickly dispersed a *lashkar* advancing from Halwai, some five miles southwest of Chinar. Though constantly harassed during the withdrawal back to Walai, the brigade suffered no British casualties.

On 20th February 1908, 'A' and 'B' companies, 1st Bn, Royal Warwickshire Regt. relieved the 1st Bn, Seaforth Highlanders on Kwanundi Hill, south of Walai. The balance of the 1st Infantry Brigade was then detailed to destroy the Kwa Caves complex and the village of Samundo. Local intelligence suggested that one of the principal Zakka Khel leaders, a *mullah* by the name of Dandi, had been sighted in Halwai and Brigadier General C.A. Anderson's force was immediately warned off to advance the following day in pursuit. Moving down the Walai Valley, the 1st Bn, Royal Warwickshire Regt., less three companies, deployed on the left flank, the 53rd Sikhs in the centre and the 59th Scinde Rifles on the right flank. Held in reserve was 'F' Company, 1st Bn, Royal Warwickshire Regt. Meanwhile, the 2nd Infantry Brigade, supported by a squadron of the 37th Lancers, IA, reinforced their positions on the Chinar Hills with a view to giving the 1st Infantry Brigade flank support from the east. The 28th Punjabis meanwhile occupied Chinar village.

During the afternoon of 21st February 1908, a party of Zakka Khel penetrated the 2nd Infantry Brigade perimeter killing Major D. Forbes-Sempill, 1st Bn, Seaforth Highlanders and wounding 12 sepoys. The 1st Bn, Royal Warwickshire Regt. eventually captured Halwai, but Dandi had fled into the surrounding mountains. The 2/5th GR then advanced up to Halwai Hill and gave covering fire, while No. 6 Field Company, 1 PWO Sappers and Miners, destroyed the village. The force then fell back on the Chinar Hills, passing through the 28th Punjabis located in Chinar village. Zakka Khel warriors were determined to follow up this withdrawal and within a short space of time the 28th Punjabis, 53rd Sikhs and 59th Rifles became severely pressed. As these units fell back, the 1st Bn, Seaforth Highlanders, and in turn, the Khyber Rifles became engaged.

East of the Chinar Hills, the Zakka Khel broke contact and the force regained the comparative safety of Walai camp shortly before nightfall. Further casualties were incurred on the night of 22nd

February 1908, when the enemy succeeded in infiltrating the perimeter established by the 1st Bn, Royal Warwickshire Regt. A brisk firefight occurred near to the battalion cookhouse (wagon) during which three men were wounded and an Indian sepoy killed. The warriors were eventually driven off into the night with some loss.

BRITISH ARMY ROLL OF HONOUR THE ZAKKA KHEL EXPEDITION 1908			
Date	**Person**	**Unit**	**Type Of Casualty**
16/2/08	22834 Gnr. H Salter	3 Mtn. Bty, Royal Garrison Artillery	Mortally Wounded In Chest
18/2/08	2 Lt. I Mac Fadyean, IAUL	Attached 1st Bn, Seaforth Highlanders	Mortally Wounded In Abdomen
19/2/08	9043 Pte. R Fordyce	'F' Coy, 1st Bn, Seaforth Highlanders	Killed, Shot To Head
21/2/08	Maj. Hon. Forbes Sempill DSO	1st Bn, Seaforth Highlanders	Killed, Shot To Heart
25/2/08	Sgt. Carlyle	1st Bn, Seaforth Highlanders	Dead. Pneumonia
21/3/08	5361 L/Sgt. J Howard	1st Bn, Royal Warwickshire Regt.	Dead. Enteric

A party of Afridi elders, acting on behalf of the Zakka Khel, approached Major General J. Willcocks' operational headquarters in Walai village late on 23rd February 1908. They petitioned the General to grant a two-day ceasefire, during which the mediators pledged to bring in the principle Zakka Khel *maliks* for negotiations. Major General Willcocks found their proposal acceptable and the mediators departed. Subsequently, on 27th February, Lieutenant Colonel G.O. Roos-Keppel escorted some 300 Zakka Khel notables to a *jirga* two miles west of Chinar. Conditions of submission to British authority were tendered by General Willcocks' political advisors culminating in the *maliks* agreeing to a range of terms for relay to Chief Commissioner Deane for approval. These were:

- Future responsibility for Zakka Khel behaviour to be divided amongst the principle Afridi clans.

- All possible future Zakka Khel raids across the administrative boundary into British India to be punished by *jirgas* from the principle Afridi clans.

- In respect of the current situation, the Zakka Khel to pay the Government of India a fine, in rifles, to the value of Rs. 20,000.

Chief Commissioner Dean, having found the proposed terms acceptable, instructed Major General J. Willcocks to begin the evacuation of the Bazaar Valley and return his command to Peshawar cantonment via Ali Masjid. With a severe blizzard closing in on the region, the force struck camp and retraced their steps to Fort Jamrud. On 1st March 1908, the Bazaar Valley Field Force was officially demobilised and returned to Peshawar the following day leaving a small force, comprising the 59th Rifles, with cavalry support, to defend surplice stores stockpiled in the Khyber Pass.

~ The Mohmand Expedition: April–May 1908 ~

The Mohmand tribal homeland was situated in the central northwest region of the North West Frontier Province of India beyond the administrative border. The Kunar River in Afghanistan formed the western boundary of Mohmand influence, with the Khyber Pass and the Swat River, on the Peshawar frontier, forming the southern and eastern boundaries respectively. The Khapak Mountains divided the Mohmand into two distinct sections. To the north of this natural barrier resided the Upper Mohmand, who were fiercely independent and had historically maintained little more than rudimentary contact with the British Government. The Baezai section of this tribe resided mostly on the Afghan side of the frontier, albeit the associated Musa Khel sub clan settled principally in British territory. Located to the north were the Safi and Utman Khel tribal areas. To the southwest were the Khwaezai and in the central area were the Safi. To the east lay the Bajaur sections. South of the Khapak Mountains was the Lower Mohmand region. The Gandab Valley Halamazai dominated this section. Lesser sections comprised the Burnhan and Isa Khel located in the Alimandi Hills between the Gandab Valley and the Swat. The Lower Mohmand maintained generally friendly relations with British India and consequently received Government allowances.

The principle routes into the Mohmand region from Peshawar were along the Gandab Valley, north from Michni through the Karappa and Nahakki Passes, from Fort Shabkadar through the Alimandi Hills north, or from the Malakand Agency through Bajaur and thence south and west. Beyond the fertile river valleys lay a vast barren region of scrub-covered hills upon which the tribesmen eked out a meagre living. Settlements were generally small, characterised by the tall masonry watchtowers seen throughout the frontier region. The views of the village *mullah* were sacrosanct. In common with most frontier tribesmen, the Mohmand maintained strict codes of hospitality and would generally offer asylum to those who sought it.

The Mohmands suffered a serious diminution of manpower during the frontier uprising of 1897–98. Unlike the Zakka Khel, they had been relatively peaceful during the period post 1898 but they reacted negatively to the rigour of Britain's punitive action in the Bazaar Valley during February 1908.

~ Fort Shabkadar 1908 ~

Lashkars were raised in support of the Zakka Khel although none arrived in the Bazaar Valley in time to influence events there. Following the conclusion of the Bazaar Valley campaign, the military authorities decided to reinforce Fort Shabkadar with additional cavalry and infantry formations. Responsibility for this force, which also included 18 Battery, RFA, lay with Lieutenant Colonel V.B. Fane, 21st PAVO Cavalry, IA.

On 3rd April 1908, Brevet. Major A.Y. Spearman, 1st Bn, Royal Warwickshire Regt., accompanied by Lieutenants. F. McCartney and G.F. Waterworth, led a patrol of frontier scouts to Matta Moghal Khel, 23 miles northwest of Peshawar. Here they proceeded to monitor the activities of several Mohmand *lashkars* that had recently crossed into British India from Afghanistan. The Kabul-based Mullah Hazrat Sahib, accompanied by the former Naib Kotal of Jelallabad, the Khan of Girdoo, had actively incited anti British sentiment among the Mohmand for some months. It was now obvious that the Mohmands were preparing to engage in some degree of hostile activity in an attempt to defend their territory from an assumed invasion by the British. When the village of Kamali, located 20 miles northwest of Peshawar, was attacked by a Mohmand war party, the Government appealed to Amir Habibullah of Afghanistan to close the border in an attempt to help stem further incursions. Despite having been welcomed to India on an official visit in January 1907, Habibullah refused to comply.

On 16th April 1908, tribesmen loyal to the British Crown from the Halamazai village of Malik Ghulam Khan succeeded in arresting a wanted Upper Mohmand leader and delivered him up to the British authorities for trial. This betrayal of the Afridi 'blood bond' precipitated a serious inter-tribal feud between Upper and Lower Mohmand sections that soon threatened to plunge the entire region into full-scale war. Chief Commissioner Deane thereupon mobilised the Peshawar-based 1st Bn, Northumberland Fus., and deployed 61 rifles of 'E' Company and eight rifles of 'F' Company to supplement 3 Mountain Battery, RGA and Major A.Y. Spearman's small force of infantry at Matta Moghal Khel. Intelligence gathering patrols continued to be despatched over a wide region but it was not until a sortie, led by Lieutenant W.G.M. Sarel, 1st Bn, Northumberland Fus., drew enemy fire while less that a mile from Matta, that a decision was made to seek further assistance from the Peshawar garrison.

The Station Officers Mess in Peshawar was in the midst of a formal reception in honour of Field Marshal Lord Kitchener of Khartoum, Commander in Chief India, when Major Rawlinson, Deputy Commissioner, North West Frontier Province, alerted the assembled officers of the situation unfolding on the Mohmand–Peshawar Frontier. The festivities drew to an abrupt conclusion with all officers returning to their units with a view to preparing for active duty

On 17th April 1908, Major General J. Willcocks rode up to Fort Shabkadar for an intelligence briefing and physical appreciation of the situation. Later that same day, Major A.Y. Spearman's local scouts, augmented by a draft from 'G' Company, 1st Bn, Royal Warwickshire Regt., deployed to Shabkadar in support of the fort's resident garrison. The following day, this party combined with a detachment of the 59th Scinde Rifles and 28th Punjabis, plus a mounted escort furnished by the 19th Lancers, IA, moved on to the remote post at Garhi Sadar. Major Spearman, however, remained in Shabkadar to liaise with the post commander, Lieutenant Colonel V.B. Fane, 21st PAVO Cavalry, IA.

A cavalry patrol in the foothills near Garhi Sadar drew heavy enemy fire at midday on 19th April 1908, forcing it to retire back on the post. With reports of significantly increasing enemy activity in the area, it was determined to evacuate the entire garrison and fall back on Matta Moghal Khel. Under the cover of darkness, the troops began to retire but it was not long before the flank guards drew fire from the Mohmands. The ensuing firefight caused the pack mules to stampede, spreading confusion

~ Sir Harold Dean,
Chief Commissioner North West Frontier Province

and panic among the ranks. The right flank guard, 28th Punjabis, stood its ground and eventually fought off the attack, but not before the 1st Bn, Royal Warwickshire Regt. lost one man killed and another wounded.

The following day, Brigadier General C.A. Anderson marched the balance of the 1st Bn, Royal Warwickshire Regt. to Fort Shabkadar from Peshawar. Accompanying the battalion were: a section, 80 Battery, RFA; 500 rifles, 1st Bn, Northumberland Fus.; with a balance of 59th Scinde Rifles and 'A' Squadron, 19th Lancers, IA. The main column included: 100 troopers, 21st PAVO Cavalry, IA; 250 rifles, 53rd Sikhs; and 102 rifles, 57th Rifles, under Major F.W.B. Gray. The column marched on to Matta Moghal Khel, where they dug in during the course of 21st April 1908. Meanwhile, a small force of men drawn from 1st Bn, Royal Warwickshire Regt., 28th Punjabis, and 59th Scinde Rifles supported by 25 Sappers and Miners, re-occupied the hastily evacuated position at Garhi Sadar.

In Peshawar, Major General J. Willcocks had by this juncture determined his plan of campaign and orders were issued for the general mobilisation of 1st (Peshawar) Division consisting of the 1st and 2nd Infantry Brigades. The 3rd Infantry Brigade, Brigadier General J.G. Ramsey, was brought up by rail from Nowshera to act as Divisional Reserve. The key objectives for the newly designated Mohmand Field Force were declared to be:

- The destruction of Mohmand concentrations along the Shabkadar–Abazai line.

- Executing a punitive expedition into southern and central Mohmand territory.

- Extending such action as necessary into northern Mohmand.

The artillery at Matta Moghal Khel began to shell enemy concentrations in the hills near Garhi Sadar early on 22nd April 1908. That evening tribesmen counter-attacked and penetrated the post perimeter forcing the troops therein to retire once again. The following day, Brigadier General C.A. Anderson prepared plans to sweep the high ground northwest of Matta. Consequently, at 6 a.m. on 24th April, a significant force deployed from Matta towards the surrounding hills.

At approximately 9 a.m., a Mohmand *lashkar*, numbering some 4,000 men, was observed among the hills to the west of the form-up position. A frontal assault was executed with the 1st Bn, Royal Warwickshire Regt. on the left flank, the 1st Bn, Northumberland Fus. centre and the Indian troops on the right flank. The artillery continued firing until the infantry were within 150 yards of their objective. A fierce firefight then broke out and the bayonet was widely employed before the enemy formation began to collapse and retire in ragged order. By 11 a.m., the troops had carried their objectives and Brigadier General C.A. Anderson signalled a general withdrawal back to Matta. The Mohmands had, however, feigned their retreat and soon began to fire upon the retiring troops. Enemy marksmen quickly found their range. The British force sustained some 53 dead and injured by the time it had regained the relative safety of Matta.

Elsewhere, Major General J. Willcocks moved a column from Fort Shabkadar to secure the Lines of Communication along the Shabkadar road on the main force's left flank south towards the Mohmand villages situated at Shahbaz Khar and Hafiz Khor in the Gandab Valley. This force comprised: 18 Battery, RFA with 1 Section, 22 (Derajat) Mtn. Battery in support; 150 rifles, 'E' Company; 1st Bn, Royal Warwickshire Regt., Capt. G.B. Marriott; 400 rifles, 1st Bn, Seaforth Highlanders; and 150 rifles, 28th Punjabis. Some 500 rifles, Queen's Own Corps of Guides Infantry, recently deployed to Shabkadar from Mardan, remained in the fort as the force reserve. Those occupying the villages were successfully dislodged, but not without loss to the British force. The Political Department interrogated several captured village elders. Intelligence gathered indicated that two Afghan Mohmand *lashkars* were encamped near Ningrahr and Bohai Dag. The *maliks* also advised their interrogators that several leading Afghan *mullahs* were calling on the Safi and Utman Khel peoples to declare *jihad* against the British in support of the Mohmand *lashkars* already deployed.

OPERATIONS MATTA AREA, 24th APRIL 1908

Striking Force:
4 guns, 80 Battery, RFA
2 squadrons, 19th Lancers, IA
1 squadron, 21st Prince Albert Victor's Own Cavalry, IA
300 rifles, 1st Bn, Northumberland Fusiliers
2 companies, 1st Bn, Royal Warwickshire Regiment
150 rifles, 59th Scinde Rifles
230 rifles, 57th Rifles
250 rifles, 53rd Sikhs
Reserve Matta:
balance, 19th Lancers, IA
balance, 21st Lances, IA
270 rifles, 1st Bn, Northumberland Fusiliers
detachment, Sappers & Miners
23rd Sikh Pioneers

Major General J. Willcocks spent much of 25th April 1908 advancing from Matta Moghal Khel north along the Gandab Valley towards Shahbaz Khar. No contact was made. Reconnaissance patrols were deployed beyond Hafiz Kor, but no evidence of enemy activity was observed. During the return to Matta, however, a non-commissioned officer of the 1st Bn, Royal Warwickshire Regt. was accidentally shot dead. On 19th April 1908, reinforcements in the form of 8 Mountain Battery, RGA, marched up to Matta, having deployed earlier from Rawalpindi to Peshawar with the 3rd (Reserve) Brigade.

The deployment of further artillery firepower was fortuitous. On 27th April 1908, an estimated 18,000 Afghan Mohmands crossed into British India from Afghanistan. They divided themselves into two *lashkars*, the larger of which, under Malik Multan of Jalazai fame, deployed towards Landi Kotal in the Khyber Pass, while Mullah Sufi Sahib took the smaller force south into the Upper Bazaar Valley, both sought support from the recently defeated Zakka Khel. The residents of the Bazaar Valley, anxious to avoid breaking the terms of their February 1908 peace treaty, were disinclined to join the Mohmands. They determined instead to send a delegation of elders to the Khyber Political Agent, Lieutenant Colonel G.O. Roos-Keppel, at Landi Kotal, informing him of the situation. Major General J. Willcocks reacted promptly to this important intelligence and, on 3rd May 1908, the 2nd and 3rd Infantry Brigades were deployed by rail from Peshawar into the Khyber Pass area. A base camp was established at Fort Jamrud, with the perimeter secured by the 1st Bn, Royal Munster Fus. and 40th Pathans. Meanwhile, Major General Willcocks rode from Fort Shabkadar to Landi Kotal, (via Peshawar), in order to personally direct operations on the ground. As per his previous brief, a frontier wide uprising had to be prevented at all costs.

The following evening, the isolated Michni–Kandao blockhouse, garrisoned by Subedar Tor Khan and 150 sepoys, Khyber Rifles, came under sustained attack by a strong force of Mohmands. A siege ensued which only lifted after some 18 hours The 3rd Infantry Brigade at Fort Jamrud also came under heavy fire at dawn the same day, leaving several members of the 1st Bn, Royal Munster Fus. injured. By 5 p.m. on 4th May 1908, the 3rd Infantry Brigade was on the move, marching to Landi Kotal via Ali Masjid. The following day the British force advanced against Khargali, some two and a half miles distant. The left flank was composed of 28 (Indian) Mountain Battery, 1st Bn, Royal Munster Fus., 40th Pathans, and two companies, 21st Punjabis. On the right flank were four guns 80 Battery, RFA, Khyber Rifles, two companies, 21st Punjabis, and half a squadron, 19th Lancers, IA. Those occupying

~ Isolated blockhouse on the Momand Line of the type defended by Subedar Tor Khan ~

Khargali defended their position robustly and inflected several casualties upon the British including Major H. Coape-Smith, 11th Lancers (IA), attached 19th Lancers (IA), who was killed. Khargali was eventually captured and the ridge between that place and Landi Kotal secured. The Afghan force was subsequently observed crossing back into Afghanistan and thus was not pursued. Shortly thereafter, the British troops withdrew back to Landi Kotal during which a few isolated enemy snipers succeeded in inflicting several casualties among the ranks.

On 7th May 1908, there having been no evidence of enemy activity for some days in the Khyber area, Major General J Willcocks decided to re-deploy the 3rd Infantry Brigade from Landi Kotal back to Peshawar via Ali Masjid. Within days, however, the Brigade was redirected to a holding position in Nagoman Camp. At this time, the 1st Infantry Brigade began to concentrate at Fort Shabkadar inpreparation for an advance into the Mohmand hinterland. Once plans for this advance had been finalised it was determined that the 3rd Infantry Brigade would be employed on the force's Lines of Communication. Meanwhile, a local Mohmand *jirga* convened at Shabkadar to discuss possible peace options with Major B.D. Blackway, the expedition's Political Officer. Only a few Mohmand clans were inclined to send representatives and consequently the gathering was adjourned until all were prepared to participate. Major Blackway assured the elders from villages that did send representation that they would suffer no further reparations by the military authorities.

MOHMAND FIELD FORCE DISPOSITIONS, 3rd MAY 1908

Fort Landi Kotal:
4 guns, 18 Battery, Royal Field Artillery
21st and 22nd Punjabis, 40th Pathans, Det. Khyber Rifles Militia
Fort Ali Masjid:
2 guns, 18 Battery, Royal Field Artillery
23 (Peshawar) Mountain Battery, Indian Frontier Artillery
1st Bn, Seaforth Highlanders
Infantry of Queen's Own Corps of Guides, detachment of Khyber Rifles Militia
Khyber Movable Column:
15th Ludhiana Sikhs, 19th and 20th Punjabis
Fort Jamrud:
1st Bn, Royal Munster Fusiliers
54th Sikhs (Frontier Force)
Peshawar Area:
19th Lancers, IA
80 Battery, Royal Field Artillery, 3 Mountain Battery, Royal Garrison Artillery
2nd Cable & Telephone Section, 1st Prince of Wales's Own Sappers & Miners
1st Bn, Royal Warwickshire Regiment
45th Rattray's Sikhs
Mohmand Border:
21st Prince Albert Victor's Own Cavalry (Frontier Force), IA
8 Mountain Battery, Royal Garrison Artillery
28 (Indian) Mountain Battery, Indian Frontier Artillery
No. 6 Field Company, 1st Prince of Wales's Own Sappers & Miners
1st Bn, Northumberland Fusiliers
34th Sikh Pioneers
28th Punjabis, 53rd Sikhs (Frontier Force), 55th Cokes Rifles (Frontier Force),
57th Wilde's Rifles (Frontier Force), 59th Scinde Rifles (Frontier Force)
No. 1 British Field Hospital, Royal Army Medical Corps
Nos. 101 & 102 Native Field Hospital, Indian Hospital Corps

Nowshera (Including Malakand Movable Column): 37th Lancers (Baluch Horse), IA 62 and 75 Batteries, Royal Field Artillery 22 (Derajat) Mountain Battery, India Frontier Artillery 1st Bn, West Yorkshire Regiment 30th and 33rd Punjabis, 1/4th Gurkha Rifles
Hasan Abdul: 21 (Kohat) Mountain Battery, Indian Frontier Artillery 1/5th, 2/5th and 1/6th Gurkha Rifles
Mardan: Cavalry of The Queen's Own Corps of Guides
Chitral & Drosh: No. 9 Field Company, 2nd Queen Victoria's Sappers & Miners 1/2nd Gurkha Rifles
Dargai: 82nd Punjabis
Malakand: Det. 37th Lancers (Baluch Horse), IA 52nd Sikhs (Frontier Force)
Note: *Not all above units were actively engaged on operations with the MFF and therefore not all above units qualified for qualified for the clasp 'NORTH WEST FRONTIER 1908'.*

On, or about, 11th May 1908, the Medical Officer of the 1st Bn, Northumberland Fus. was forced to place the battalion in quarantine due to an outbreak of cholera among the men. Accordingly, the 1st Bn, Royal Munster Fus. was moved up to Fort Shabkadar to fill the gap in the order of battle. Almost immediately upon their arrival, however, the 1st Bn, Royal Munster Fus. also began to show signs of infection. Consequently, this battalion was also quarantined under the care of 'A' and 'B' Sections, 7 British Field Hospital, RAMC. Father Looman, Bengal Ecclesiastical Establishment, supplied much needed pastoral care. This turn of events was a set back for Major General J. Willcocks, because the 1st and 2nd Infantry Brigades were now ready to advance into the Mohmand hinterland. Orders were thus given calling for the deployment to Fort Shabkadar of the 1st Bn, West Yorkshire Regt. from Nowshera. Upon its arrival in theatre, the battalion was split into two wings. Five rifle companies plus the machine guns, under Captain W. de S. Cayley, were sent up to Ghalanai leaving the balance of the battalion, under Major J. O'B. Minogue, to deploy to Matta and the Burjina Pass. The 1/4th GR were similarly brought up from Nowshera but they also contracted cholera and were subsequently replaced in the line by 19th Punjabis.

MOHMAND FIELD FORCE COMMAND & STAFF, APRIL 1908

GOC 1st (Peshawar) Division – Maj. Gen. Sir J Willcocks

Divisional Staff:

Maj. A W F Baird, 2nd Bn, Gordon Highlanders	Deputy Assistant Adjutant General
Col. W R Birdwood	Chief Staff Officer
Lt. J M Blair, 2nd Bn, Royal Highlanders	Orderly Officer
Col. J E Dickie, Royal Engineers	Chief Engineering Officer
Lt. Col. H J Dundee, Royal Engineers	Assistant Chief Engineering Officer
Maj. A England, Army Veterinary Corps	Senior Veterinary Officer
Lt. H O B Hood, 8th Rajputs	Supply & Transport Officer
Capt. C Fitz H Lance, 19th Hussars	Provost Marshal
Lt. A P Y Langhorne, Royal Garrison Artillery	Aide de Camp
Bvt. Col. A W Money, Royal Field Artillery	Assistant Adjutant & Quartermaster General

Maj. A Mullally, Supply & Transport Corps...Divisional Transport Officer
Capt. T S Patterson, 19th Hussars...Signals Officer
Capt. A G Stuart, 40th Pathans...Deputy Assistant Quartermaster General
Capt. G R Trotter, 56th Rifles...Deputy Assistant Quartermaster General Int.
Col. H R Whithead, Royal Army Medical Corps...Principle Medical Officer
Lt. Col. A B C Williams, Supply & Transport Corps...Divisional Supply Officer

1st Infantry Brigade – Brig. Gen. C A Anderson

Capt. J A M Bannerman, 1st Bn, R Warwickshire Regiment...Orderly Officer
Capt. E E Barwell, 57th Rifles..Deputy Assistant Quartermaster General
Lt. W Gibson, 1st Bn, Northumberland Fusiliers...Signals Officer
Capt. H N Holden, Viceroy's Bodyguard, AFI..Provost Marshal
Maj. M R de B James, Army Service Corps..Brigade Supply Officer
Capt. H T Moffett, 2nd Bn, Leinster Regiment...Provost Marshal
Capt. A L Tarver, 124th DCO Baluch Infantry...Deputy Assistant Adjutant General

2nd Infantry Brigade – Maj. Gen. A A Barrett

Capt. A H Babington, Supply & Transport Corps..Signals Officer
Capt. A L Tarver, 124th DCO Baluch Infantry...Deputy Assistant Adjutant General
Capt. H J P Brownie, 1/5th GR...Provost Marshal
Capt. J E L Bruce, Royal Field Artillery..Deputy Assistant Adjutant General
Capt. C B Chamley, 1st Bn, Seaforth Highlanders...Brigade Supply Officer
Capt. D A D McVean, 45th Sikhs...Orderly Officer
Capt. H H Norman, 2nd Bn, Northamptonshire Regiment........................Deputy Assistant Quartermaster General

3rd (Reserve) Infantry Brigade – Brig. Gen. J G Ramsey

Capt. W H Beach*, Royal Engineers...Deputy Assistant Quartermaster General
Capt. H J Boyd, 13th Lancers, IA,...Orderly Officer
Maj. A I R Glasfield, 97th Deccan Infantry..Deputy Assistant Adjutant General
Maj. G B H Rice, 32nd Sikh Pioneers..Brigade Major
Lt. H C H O'Brien, 1st Bn Royal Munster Fusiliers...Signals Officer
Lt. W H B Salmon, Supply & Transport Corps..Brigade Supply Officer

Divisional Troops & Lines of Communication – Col. S F Biddulph, 19th Lancers, IA

Maj. W L Amesbury, Supply & Transport Corps...Chief Transport Officer
Lt. F Curtis, 19th L, IA...Assistant Signals Officer
Maj. W Ewbank, Royal Engineers...Field Officer
Capt. M G Heath, Queen's (Royal West Surrey Regiment)...Signals Officer
Lt. R D C McLeod, 19th Lancers, IA...Staff Officer
Lt. F S Paterson, 19th L, IA..Assistant Signals Officer
Capt. F T Rich, Royal Engineers..Survey Officer
Maj. G L'H Sanders, Supply & Transport Corps...Divisional Supply Officer
Maj. G L Saunders, Supply & Transport Corps...Chief Supply Officer
Lt. Col. R G Strange, Royal Field Artillery..Section Commandant
Lt. H B Wood, Supply & Transport Corps..Transport Officer

Base Depot – Lt. Col. A R Dick, 22nd Cavalry, IA

Capt. H J P Brown, 1/5th GR...Railway Transport Officer thence Provost Marshal
Capt. H Clarke*, Royal Artillery...Ordnance Officer
Capt. W G R Farmer*, Royal Artillery...Commander British Troops Depot
Maj. A S Hamilton, 52nd Sikhs...................................Deputy Assistant Adjutant & Quartermaster General
Lt. Col. F P Nicholls*, Royal Army Medical Corps...Senior Medical Officer
Maj. J S Swan, Supply & Transport Corps...Brigade Transport Officer
Maj. E G Vaughan, Supply & Transport Corps...Brigade Supply Officer
Capt. C J White, 53rd Sikhs...Commander Indian Troops Depot

*Note: Names not found on British Army Roll at National Archives

A reconnaissance of Major General E. Elles' 1897 Gandab Valley route into the Mohmand region had been made in the days immediately proceeding 12th May 1908. Intelligence reports indicated that Malik Sarto Fakir, a veteran Mohmand leader from the 1897 troubles, had raised a *lashkar* in the Upper Swat Valley. Other reports suggested that a Kandarhara Safi force was forming up at Laksrai while Khwaezai and Baizai warriors were reported to be blocking the strategic Khapak Pass, at the western end of the Toratigga Valley. Reports, disturbing to the British, came from the Kurram border, indicating that a group of Zakka Khel had decided, after all, to trek north to assist their Mohmand brothers.

The 1st and 2nd Infantry Brigades deployed into the Gandab Valley from Fort Shabkadar early on 13th May 1908, following a collapse in negotiations at the tribal *jirga*. Major General J. Willcocks, who accompanied the 1st Infantry Brigade, established his forward operating headquarters at Dand, where friendly Halamazai agreed to provide fresh supplies of animal fodder for the cavalry, artillery and pack mules. Meanwhile, the 2nd Infantry Brigade advanced to Hafiz Kor. Major General Willcocks, anxious lest the rest of his command succumb to cholera, despatched Brigadier General C.A. Anderson with two squadrons of 21st Cavalry, IA, 55th Coke's Rifles, and infantry from the Queen's Own Corps of Guides, to secure the fresh water reserves in the Kamalai Valley. Some 66 rifles of the 1st Bn, Royal Warwickshire Regt., under Major A.Y. Spearman, thereupon began to organise water replenishment in conjunction with the Supply and Transport Corps. Mules, escorted by members of the 1st Bn, West Yorkshire Regt., brought up further fresh supplies two days later.

On 16th May 1908, the 1st Infantry Brigade deployed up to Kasai. The advancing column implemented a pincer-style manoeuvre with a view to trapping several enemy formations observed the previous day. Meanwhile, the right and centre sections of 8 Mountain Battery, RGA, were sent up Danesh Khel, to the west of the Khapak Pass, to assist the 2nd Infantry Brigade destroy enemy villages situated there. Rumour was rife that Multan himself was in the area but this information was eventually discredited. All key objectives were achieved with little enemy resistance although the subsequent return to camp was followed up by a small *lashkar* of tribesmen. To cover the final stages of the retirement, 8 Mountain Battery, RGA, was obliged to fire some 22 shrapnel rounds. Later the same day the Battery fired a further 40 rounds during the deployment of the Brigade's defensive picquets. These outposts were pressed severely throughout the night by small parties of the enemy.

The following day, a reconnaissance was made of the intended line of advance through the Darwazi Pass towards Botal Gandai. Several more villages were raised to the ground by the Sappers and Miners, action that prompted further robust resistance from the enemy. During the evening of 17th May 1908, the 22nd Punjabis picquet near Darwazagai was heavily attacked. With the post commander dead, a total massacre was prevented only by the heroism of Naik Jehanded, who rallied the survivors until relieved at dawn by 57th and 59th Rifles. Major General J. Willcocks subsequently praised the Punjabi platoon in a despatch addressed to their commanding officer, Lieutenant Colonel C.A. Fowler, dated 19th May 1908.

The further north the force advanced, the more resolute Mohmand resistance became. During the afternoon of 18th May 1908, 500 tribesmen had attacked the Nahakki Valley picquet line. The ensuing battle was contended fiercely, the enemy only retiring after having inflicted some 27 casualties on the British, including three Indian Army officers. The 2nd Infantry Brigade engaged the Khwaezai near Bohai Dag, while on 20th May 1908 at Zanawar, in the Chinar Hills, strong opposition was encountered when members of the 34th Sikh Pioneers, under Major G.E.L. Gilbert, destroyed the village fortifications. The watchtowers at Khan Begkor were also blown.

Meanwhile, Brigadier General C.A. Anderson advanced the 1st Infantry Brigade into Utmanzai territory. Cavalry patrols found the strategically important Umra Killi settlements occupied in force by Dawizai, Utman Khel and Safi warriors. Heavy fighting ensued with right and centre sections of 8 Mountain Battery, RGA, giving close support. The Battery fired over 164 rounds and suffered several casualties from snipers. At dusk, the enemy fled, leaving 57th Rifles and 53rd Sikhs to count over 200 enemy dead strewn among the ruins. Major General J. Willcocks subsequently supplemented the Brigade's losses by re-deploying the 55th Coke's Rifles from the 2nd Infantry Brigade at Nahakki up to Umra Killi. Fatal casualties that day included Lieutenant G.H. Soole, 21st Cavalry, IA and Lieutenant G.F. Archibald, 82nd Punjabis, attached 57th Rifles.

On 21st May 1908, the 2nd Infantry Brigade entered Safi territory and established a camp at Kandahari. Thereupon, Mohmand elders approached this location with a view to entering into peace negotiations with Major General J. Willcocks. Meanwhile, 1st Infantry Brigade moved on to Habibzai where, supported by an additional two guns from 28 (Indian) Mountain Battery, it established a secure location. It then moved on to Lakarai, with the centre section 8 Mountain Battery, RGA, on left flank guard and the left section acting as rear guard. During this advance, 81 rounds were fired. At Shota Khel, large numbers of tribesmen surrendered to the advancing force. At Khurga it was found that enemy snipers were occupying sangars spread across the intended line of advance. Further, a *lashkar* of some 3,000 was observed in what was considered as a hostile formation some miles deeper along the valley. Now 8 Mountain Battery, RGA, was immediately pressed into action to disperse the threat, thus buying the infantry valuable time to focus their efforts on dislodging several enemy snipers. The Battery was successful in dispersing the enemy, but not before they had suffered casualties, including one Indian non-commissioned officer who was killed.

At this juncture, cholera broke out among troops of the 1st Bn, West Yorkshire Regt. at Ghalanai. Lieutenant W. Benson, RAMC, the Battalion Medical Officer, immediately advised Major W. de Cayley to move his command into a quarantine zone three quarters of a mile to the northwest of the main camp. The Indian Army Battalion at Ghalanai did likewise in a southwesterly direction. Unfortunately, this manoeuvre, while partially successful, failed to prevent the deaths of two West Yorkshire Regt. personnel. The 1st Bn, Royal Munster Fus. had, by that juncture, been cholera free for almost two weeks and were instructed to return to Peshawar where they subsequently took the train to Rawalpindi. During the withdrawal, Sergeant Bride fell from one of the many pontoon bridges into the Kabul River and would have drowned had it not been for the swift action of Private J. Green, who dived into the tumult and rescued him. Some time later Private Green was invested with the Royal Humane Societies Medal for Life Saving in respect of this incident.

Few Mohmand clans now remained in the field. Those that did remain hostile continued to suffer extensive reparations as the British force relentlessly advanced deeper into the Upper Mohmand hinterland. The village of Insarai was levelled on 26th May 1908, and 2,000 recalcitrant Utman Khel were dispersed by high explosive shells near Korgha. The 1st Infantry Brigade halted at Mulla Killi on 27th May 1908 and then moved on to Lagham beyond the Gurang Pass. By this time only the Baezai around Khoda Khel remained belligerent. The subjugation of this area was a delicate affair due to the fact it straddled the Indo-Afghan border and the Commander in Chief India, Field Marshal Lord Kitchener, had given Major General J. Willcocks explicate instructions not to cross into Afghan territory. Consequently, great care was taken in the securing of Khoda Khel village and its subsequent destruction by the 34th Sikh Pioneers. Enemy snipers followed up the Army's withdrawal and inflicted several casualties, including Lieutenant W. Young, 67th Punjabis, attached 57th Rifles, who was killed.

This was the Mohmand Field Force's final engagement and, by 31ˢᵗ May 1908, the 1ˢᵗ (Peshawar) Division had begun to cross the administrative border back into British India.

*

BRITISH ARMY ROLL OF HONOUR THE MOHMAND EXPEDITION 1908			
Date	Person	Unit	Type Of Casualty
15/4/1908	4107 Cpl. John Satchwell	1ˢᵗ Bn, Royal Warwickshire Regt.	Killed, GSW Chest
19/4/1908	9138 Pte. R Adams	1ˢᵗ Bn, Royal Warwickshire Regt.	Killed, GSW Abdomen
24-25/4/1908	Lt. G D Martin	1ˢᵗ Bn, Royal Warwickshire Regt.	Mortally Wounded Thigh & Scrotum
24/4/1908	2Lt. A L Hume Spry	1ˢᵗ Bn Royal Warwickshire Regt.	Wounded Abdomen DOW June 18ᵗʰ, 1908
24/4/1908	9513 Pte. S H Morris	1ˢᵗ Bn, Northumberland Fusiliers	Killed, GSW Abdomen
24/4/1908	893 Pte. H G Rose	1ˢᵗ Bn, Northumberland Fusiliers	Killed, GSW Chest
8/5/1908	27749 A Loveland	80 Bty, Royal Field Artillery	Died. Cholera
12/5/1908	7126 Pte. H Glassbrook	1ˢᵗ Bn, Royal Munster Fusiliers	Died. Cholera
13/5/1908	3829 C/Sgt. A Tyler	1ˢᵗ Bn, Royal Munster Fusiliers	Died. Cholera
13/5/1908	5348(5) Sgt. J Noble	1ˢᵗ Bn, Royal Munster Fusiliers	Died. Cholera
13/5/1908	7998 L/Cpl. D Kelleher	1ˢᵗ Bn, Royal Munster Fusiliers	Died. Cholera
13/5/1908	6374 L/Cpl. P Murphy	1ˢᵗ Bn, Royal Munster Fusiliers	Died. Cholera
13/5/1908	4929 Pte. J Bullen	1ˢᵗ Bn, Royal Munster Fusiliers	Died. Cholera
13/5/1908	6217 Pte. M Egan	1ˢᵗ Bn, Royal Munster Fusiliers	Died. Cholera
13/5/1908	7279 Pte. W Gibson	1ˢᵗ Bn, Royal Munster Fusiliers	Died. Cholera
13/5/1908	7581 Pte. J Griffin	1ˢᵗ Bn, Royal Munster Fusiliers	Died. Cholera
13/5/1908	6772 Pte. T Lennehan	1ˢᵗ Bn, Royal Munster Fusiliers	Died. Cholera
13/5/1908	5612 Pte. J McCarthy	1ˢᵗ Bn, Royal Munster Fusiliers	Died. Cholera
13/5/1908	5805 Pte. M Moylen	1ˢᵗ Bn, Royal Munster Fusiliers	Died. Cholera
13/5/1908	8241 Pte. J Parsons	1ˢᵗ Bn, Royal Munster Fusiliers	Died. Cholera
13/5/1908	8303 Pte. E Sellors	1ˢᵗ Bn, Royal Munster Fusiliers	Died. Cholera
14/5/1908	6673 L/Cpl. T Deasy	1ˢᵗ Bn, Royal Munster Fusiliers	Died. Cholera
14/5/1908	5255 Pte. R Balkwill	1ˢᵗ Bn, Royal Warwickshire Regt.	Died. Cholera
14/5/1908	8201 Pte. M Keane	1ˢᵗ Bn, Royal Munster Fusiliers	Died. Cholera
14/5/1908	753(1)6 Pte. M Rabbette	1ˢᵗ Bn, Royal Munster Fusiliers	Died. Cholera
14/5/1908	4518 Pte. H Selfe	1ˢᵗ Bn, Royal Munster Fusiliers	Died. Cholera
14/5/1908	8410 Pte. B Tierney	1ˢᵗ Bn, Royal Munster Fusiliers	Died. Cholera
15/5/1908	5413 Pte. L/Cpl. W Waghorne	1ˢᵗ Bn, Royal Munster Fusiliers	Died. Cholera
15/5/1908	4413 Pte. J Barry	1ˢᵗ Bn, Royal Munster Fusiliers	Died. Cholera
16/5/1908	4987 Pte. P Doran	1ˢᵗ Bn, Royal Munster Fusiliers	Died. Cholera
16/5/1908	7396 Pte. D Greany	1ˢᵗ Bn, Royal Munster Fusiliers	Died. Cholera
16/5/1908	6597 Pte. J Hoare	1ˢᵗ Bn, Royal Munster Fusiliers	Died. Cholera
16/5/1908	7229 Pte. F Holland	1ˢᵗ Bn, Royal Munster Fusiliers	Died. Cholera

16/5/1908	6558 Pte. J Lynch	1st Bn, Royal Munster Fusiliers	Died. Cholera
16/5/1908	6788 Pte. J Walsh	1st Bn, Royal Munster Fusiliers	Died. Cholera
17/5/1908	8104 Pte. H Hissie (Hisee)	1st Bn, Royal Munster Fusiliers	Died. Cholera
17/5/1908	7380 Pte. M O'Sullivan	1st Bn, Royal Munster Fusiliers	Died. Cholera
18/5/1908	4(5)744 Pte. M Jones	1st Bn, Royal Munster Fusiliers	Died. Cholera
18/5/1908	5118 Pte. S Mahoney	1st Bn, Royal Munster Fusiliers	Died. Cholera
19/5/1908	16637 Sgt/Farrier. W Thorpe	8 Mtn. Bty, Royal Garrison Artillery	Died. Septic Poisoning
19/5/1908	5864 Pte. J Murphy	1st Bn, Royal Munster Fusiliers	Died. Cholera
20/5/1908	558 Pte. J Melvin	1st Bn, Royal Warwickshire Regt.	Died. Cholera
20/5/1908	9546 Pte. J White	1st Bn, Seaforth Highlanders	Killed, GSW Head
21/5/1908	6114 Pte. T Plackett	1st Bn, West Yorkshire Regt.	Died. Cholera
21/5/1908	6146 Pte. T Rogerson	1st Bn, West Yorkshire Regt.	Died. Cholera
22/5/1908	6048 Pte. J Doyle	1st Bn, Royal Munster Fusiliers	Died. Cholera
24/5/1908	Maj. N C Mac Lachlan	1st Bn, Seaforth Highlanders	Killed, GSW Head
24/5/1908	4260 L/Sgt. H S Seaton	1st Bn, Royal Warwickshire Regt.	Died. Cholera
25/5/1908	19495 Gnr. F C Walker	3 Mtn Bty, Royal Garrison Artillery	Died Peshawar
26/5/1908	Lt. Barff (Not Identified On Role)	1st Bn, West Yorkshire Regt.	Died. Enteric
26/5/1908	6409 Pte. G Burley	1st Bn, Royal Munster Fusiliers	Died. Cholera
25/5/1908	7885 Pte. G Hartley	1st Bn, Royal Munster Fusiliers	Died. Cholera
2/6/1908	6647 Dmr. A Barrett	1st Bn, Royal Munster Fusiliers	Died. Cholera
6/6/1908	71 Pte. W Holland	1st Bn, Royal Warwickshire Regt.	Died. Cholera
7/6/1908	7875 Pte. F Timmins	1st Bn, Royal Munster Fusiliers	Died. Cholera
13/6/1908	5172 Pte. W Tritton	1st Bn, Royal Warwickshire Regt.	Died.
16/6/1908	1203 Sgt. F W Sharp	3 Mtn Bty, Royal Garrison Artillery	Died.
21/6/1908	832 Pte. A Stone	1st Bn, Royal Warwickshire Regt.	DOW
27/6/1908	21398 Dvr. J Doyle	80 Bty, Royal Field Artillery	Died. Cholera
2/7/1908	3723 Pte. H Pace	1st Bn, Royal Warwickshire Regt.	Died. Cholera
11/7/1908	8462 Pte. W Cooper	1st Bn, Royal Warwickshire Regt.	Died.
26/7/1908	9664 Pte. E Peakman	1st Bn, Royal Warwickshire Regt.	Died.
6/8/1908	Maj. F McDowell[1]	Royal Army Medical Corps	Died
31/8/1908	8788 Pte. W Richardson	1st Bn, Royal Warwickshire Regt.	Died.
9/9/1908	20633 Gnr. H Graham	80 Bty, Royal Field Artillery	Died. Cholera
19/9/1908	455 Pte. W Robertson	1st Bn, Royal Warwickshire Regt.	Died.
15/10/1908	8632 L/Sgt. J Gracie	1st Bn, Royal Warwickshire Regt.	Died.
6/11/1908	5852 Pte. W Smith	1st Bn, Royal Warwickshire Regt.	Died.
26/11/1908	7226 Pte. G Stanford	1st Bn, Royal Warwickshire Regt.	Died
8/12/1908	28159 Dvr. E Powell	80 Bty, Royal Field Artillery	Died.
Unidentified	32229 Gnr. J Armstrong	18 Bty, Royal Field Artillery	Died.
Unidentified	21600 Dvr. W Brown	18 Bty, Royal Field Artillery	Died.
Unidentified	33605 Gnr. J Ford	18 Bty, Royal Field Artillery	Died.
Unidentified	12711 Gnr. T Gelder	18 Bty, Royal Field Artillery	Died.

Unidentified	??452 Dvr. C Jones	18 Bty, Royal Field Artillery	Died.
Unidentified	40181 Gnr. W Roberts	80 Bty, Royal Field Artillery	Died.
Unidentified	25767 Gnr. J Deane	3 Mtn Bty, Royal Garrison Artillery	Died.
Unidentified	6580 Bmdr. F Feeley	3 Mtn Bty, Royal Garrison Artillery	Died
Unidentified	29885 Gnr. D Foley	3 Mtn Bty, Royal Garrison Artillery	Died.
Unidentified	23663 Gnr. G W Handsley	3 Mtn Bty, Royal Garrison Artillery	Died.
Unidentified	70443 Sgt. R Mann	3 Mtn Bty, Royal Garrison Artillery	Died.
Unidentified	Lt. A F Macauley	Royal Engineers	Died
Unidentified	4613 Sgt. A E Dunn	1st Bn, Northumberland Fusiliers	Died.
Unidentified	7173 Pte. H Mundy	1st Bn, Northumberland Fusiliers	Died.
Unidentified	1495 Pte. G Nash	1st Bn, Northumberland Fusiliers	Died.
Unidentified	4716 C/Sgt. J Roberts	1st Bn, Northumberland Fusiliers	Died.
Unidentified	1972 Pte. W Stowell	1st Bn, Northumberland Fusiliers	Died.
Unidentified	2011 Pte. J Twigg	1st Bn, Northumberland Fusiliers	Died.
Unidentified	102 Pte. P Weston	1st Bn, Northumberland Fusiliers	Died.
Unidentified	4698 Pte. A Bellamy	1st Bn, West Yorkshire Regiment	Died.
Unidentified	6256 Pte. A Davis	1st Bn, West Yorkshire Regiment	Died.
Unidentified	7412 Pte. G Ellis	1st Bn, West Yorkshire Regiment	Died.
Unidentified	7856 Pte. W Hardcastle	1st Bn, West Yorkshire Regiment	Died.
Unidentified	7952 Pte. H Hunter	1st Bn, West Yorkshire Regiment	Died.
Unidentified	10338 Pte. R Dingwall	1st Bn, Seaforth Highlanders	Died.
Unidentified	Pte. A Ecclestone	1st Bn, Seaforth Highlanders	Died.
Unidentified	6277 Pte. M Morrison	1st Bn, Seaforth Highlanders	Died.
Unidentified	6049 Sgt. C Parks	1st Bn, Seaforth Highlanders	Died.
Unidentified	4503 Pte. J Smith	1st Bn, Seaforth Highlanders	Died.

NORTH WEST FRONTIER 1908[1] ROLL

BRITISH ESTABLISHMENT
THE ARMY

~ Staff Grade Officers ~
Note a.   *Only Officers of the British Army are listed. Those on the Indian Establishment are beyond the scope of this work.*
Note b.   *Medals named in running script.*

Major Generals: ~ J. Willcocks[1] Cmd., 1 Div
Brigadier Generals: ~ C A Anderson[1] Cmd., 1 Bde & H Mullaly[1] CSO
Colonels: ~ J E Dickie[1] CRE, (Bvt.) A W Money[1] RFA, AA&QMG & H R Whitehead[1] PMO, MFF

THE CAVALRY:

~ 10th (Prince of Wales's Own Royal) Hussars ~
Note a.   *Roll of all personnel identified as eligible.*
Note b.   *Recipients attached Indian Telegraph Department (ITD) unless otherwise shown.*
Note c.   *Medals named in running script: '10th Royal Hussars'.*

Single Clasp	No. Identified	Rarity
North West Frontier 1908[1]	4	Of the Utmost Rarity

Quartermaster Sergeants/Sergeants: ~ 4838 A J Dennis[1] attch. S&TC posted No. 112 NFH
Lance Corporals/Privates: ~ 5252 H J E Evans[1], 5144 H Howard[1] & 5224 W Hughes[1]

~ 12th (Prince of Wales's Royal) Lancers ~
Note a.   *Roll of all personnel identified as eligible.*
Note b.   *Recipient attached Indian Telegraph Department (ITD).*
Note c.   *Medals named in running script, believed: '12th Royal Lancers'*

Single Clasp	No. Identified	Rarity
North West Frontier 1908[1]	1	According to the roll as seen, can be considered Unique

Lance Corporals/Privates: ~ 5114 H Stewart[1]

~ 15th (King's) Hussars ~
Note a.   *Roll of all personnel identified as eligible.*
Note b.   *Recipient served as Aide de Camp (ADC) in the Bazaar Valley Field Force (BVFF).*
Note c.   *Medals named in running script, believed: 15th Hussars'*

Single Clasp	No. Identified	Rarity
North West Frontier 1908[1]	1	According to the roll as seen, can be considered Unique

Captains: ~ N J C Livingstone-Learmouth[1]

~ 19th (Queen Alexandra's Own Royal) Hussars ~

Note a.   *Roll of all personnel identified as eligible.*
Note b.   *Medals named in running script, believed: '19th Royal Hussars'*

Single Clasp	No. Identified	Rarity
North West Frontier 1908[1]	3	Of the Utmost Rarity

Majors: ~ C L G Gregory[1] DA&QMG, BVFF
Captains: ~ C Fitz H Lance[1] PM, MFF & T S Patterson[1] SO, MFF

THE ARTILLERY:

~ Royal Field Artillery ~
Sub Units Identified As Entitled:
18, 62, 75 & 80 Field Batteries
1st Divisional Ammunition Column

Royal Field Artillery: Staff Duties:

Note a.   *Roll of all personnel identified as eligible.*
Note b.   *The roll does not specify Battery affiliation, nor does the 1908 Army List.*
Note c.   *Medals named in engraved running script: 'R.F.A.', Officers may be simply 'R.A.'*

Lieutenant Colonels: ~ R G Strange[1] Cmd., 3 Art Bde
Captains: ~ J E L Bruce[1] DA&QMG, 2 Bde., MFF
Bombardiers: ~ 23270 R Waddle[1] attch. HQ, 3 Art Bde.
Trumpeters: ~ 16050 B Rickwood[1] Tptr, Cmd., 3 Art Bde.

18 Field Battery, Royal Field Artillery

Note a.   *Roll of all personnel identified as eligible.*
Note b.   *Not all serial numbers on roll are legible; missing digits are represented thus: ?*
Note c.   *Medals named in engraved running script: '18th By R.F.A.', Officers may be simply 'R.A.'*

Single Clasp	No. Identified	Rarity
North West Frontier 1908[1]	166	Scarce
Combination Clasps	**No. Identified**	**Rarity**
North West Frontier 1908[1] Abor 1911– 12[2]	1	According to the roll as seen, can be considered Unique

Majors: ~ W G H Manley[1]
Captains: ~ E P Bedwell[1]
Lieutenants: ~ C R Gover[1], J M Ingram[1] & H H Joll[1]
Warrant Officers Class II: ~ (BSM) 42216 J W Humby[1]
Battery Quartermaster Sergeants/Staff Sergeants: ~ (Saddle) 75131 J Monger[1]
Quartermaster Sergeants/Sergeants: ~ (Battery) 15117 A G Arkell[1], 1740 W Cox[1], ?0083 W E Eaton[1], 19425 T H Humphris[1], 87930 H Kent[1], ??570 A Lockyear[1] & 15256 J Tobin[1]
Corporals: ~ 14177 H S Gilbery[1], 88124 F Hayman[1], 16258 R S Mills[1], 22731 G W Shadbolt[1], 7651 P S Smith[1] & (Farrier) 5779 W L Vaughan[1]
Bombardiers: ~ (Act) 18484 A Bithell[1], 26024 J Brabin[1], (Act) 18920 J W Ellis[1], 28646 J Fuller[1], (Act) ???9 E Lemmon[1], (Act) 18963 R Meggison[1], 6533 J Mitchell[1], 32162 H Richards[1], (Act) 42007 F Richardson[1], 13038 G Rolfe[1], 19406 J Stevenson[1], (Act) 19359 E Turner[1], 20465 J Vincent[1] & 577 T Walker[1]

Corporals: ~ 14177 H S Gilbery[1], 88124 F Hayman[1], 16258 R S Mills[1], 22731 G W Shadbolt[1] & 7651 P S Smith[1]

Bombardiers: ~ (Act) 18484 ? Bithell[1], 26024 ? Brabin[1], (Act) 18920 J W Ellis[1], 28646 J Fuller[1], (Act) ???9 E Lemmon[1], (Act) 18963 R Meggion[1], 6533J Mitchell[1], 32162 H Richards[1], (Act) 42007 F Richardson[1], 19406 J Stevenson[1], (Act) 19359 E Turner[1], 20465 J Vincent[1] & 577 T Walker[1]

Gunners/Drivers: ~ 13016 G Aldridge[1], 32734 G Alfrey[1], 23023 J Ampleford[1], 21036 H Anderson[1], 32229 J Armstrong[1], 50371 R Armstrong[1], 36826 P Balls[1], 31412 G Bartlett[1], 6148 J W Bell[1], 33369 A Bennett[1], 22045 E Boult[1], 37556 E Boyd[1], 14808 J Brennon[1], 41112 W Bridgeland[1], 34002 H Brown[1], 23791 J Brown[1], 21600 W Brown[1], 21039 J Burnett[1], 2889 C Cardy[1], 19374 W Clayton[1], 39434 J Collard[1], 30852 R Colville[1], 24711 H Cordner[1], 23012 T Copley[1], 35055 J F Cullane[1], 29092 G Davey[1], 27590 M Davis[1], 97308 W Davis[1], 18972 F Dewar[1], 46701 E Docherty[1], 34230 F Dodd[1], 40815 R Donkin[1], 10671 A Ducker[1], 37562 G Easdon[1], 16440 A Edwards[1], 44712 J Eggleton[1], 22436 W Ellwood[1], 22504 E Evans[1], 22943 R Fakes[1], 25474 A E Felton[1], 99708 P Fitzpatrick[1], 17380 P Flanigan[1], 43888 A G Fletcher[1], 33608 J Ford[1], 32458 A Francis[1], 38338 R Gammie[1], 12711 T Gelder[1], 20444 J Gerrard[1], 19993 J Gilbertson[1], 26105 A Gillieland[1], 18875 R S Gilmour[1], 35709 H Graham[1&2], 26532 G Guymer[1], 32221 F Harding[1], 35444 J Hayde[1], 42555 F Hayler[1], 18942 G Heelbeck[1], 29270 A Heslop[1], 33596 E Higginbotham[1], 33915 P Holmby[1], 33907 H Holton[1], 42610 S Howard[1], 10618 C Hutton[1,] 23014 A Jackson[1], 14038 W Jenkinson[1], 31043 C Jones[1], ??452 C Jones[1], ??4906 G Jones[1], 22494 M Joyce[1], 3897 D Kay[1], ?6857 A King[1], ?1185 J King[1], ??219 A Lamb[1], 41989 R Lamberton[1], ??468 H D Lonergan[1], ??267 W P Lott[1], ???92 J Loveridge[1], ???24 C E Lucas[1], ??738 J MacKay[1], ???2 J Mason[1], ??3392 W McCabe[1], 33374 P McCorkindale[1], ??732 R McDowell[1], 39937 H McIntyre[1], 36790 J Morris[1], ??040 J E A Mould[1], ??983 T Murphy[1], 14879 E Nicklin[1], 20392 P Noden[1], 33375 J O'Neill[1], 30065 A Palmer[1], 4495 R Parker[1], 37605 W Patterson[1], 33379 W Peabody[1], 17514 W Pember[1], 15992 D Pennell[1], 14637 W E Phillips[1], 33520 J Poole[1], 33104 M Pope[1], 20467 J Pringle[1], 42980 A Rastrick[1], 34059 S W Reader[1], 21630 R Reed[1], 12894 H Richmond[1], 31385 T Roan[1], 39302 G Robson[1], 38619 A Rogers[1], 5534 G Rolph[1], 15216 J Rourke[1], 36537 J S Ryrie[1], 39961 W Saunders[1], 46477 F Scorr[1], 21578 W Scott[1], 31393 P Shaw[1], 46741 W Shepherd[1], 33794 A Sheridan[1], 33357 A Stewart[1], 32950 W Steward[1], 46098 C Stone[1], 5028 J Stone[1], 15113 R Totten[1], 32344 S Truelove[1], 28524 W Underwood[1], 41496 R Walker[1], 88493 A Want[1,] 31944 W White[1], 31334 G Wileman[1], 37595 C Wilson[1], 19936 J Wilson[1], 21967 A Wood[1] & 18976 G Woodhouse[1]

Shoeing Smiths: ~ 8644 H B Ledger[1]

Trumpeters: ~ 36656 C R Kilroy[1]

62 Field Battery, Royal Field Artillery

Note a.   *Roll of all personnel identified as eligible.*

Note b.   *Recipients attached 'A' & 'B Sections, No. 1 British Field Hospital (BFH), Royal Army Medical Corps (RAMC), Bazaar Valley Field Force (BVFF).'*

Note c.   *Medals named in running script: '62ⁿᵈ By, R.F.A.'*

Single Clasp	No. Identified	Rarity
North West Frontier 1908[1]	5	Of the Utmost Rarity

Corporals: ~ 23053 H Conlon[1]

Bombardiers: ~ 32227 P Powell[1] & 11055 G Roby[1] as Transport Sergeant

Gunners/Drivers: ~ 28262 G Hurst[1] & 781 F W Joliffe[1]

75 Field Battery, Royal Field Artillery

Note a.   *Roll of all personnel identified as eligible.*

Note b.   *Recipients attached to No.1 Divisional Ammunition Column (DAC), Royal Field Artillery (RFA), Mohmand Field Force (MFF) unless shown otherwise.*

Note c.   *Medals named in running script: '75ᵗʰ By, R.F.A.'*

Single Clasp	No. Identified	Rarity
North West Frontier 1908[1]	7	Of the Utmost Rarity

Corporals: ~ 7583 W Coe[1]

Bombardiers: ~ 38319 S Barr[1] attch. No. 1 BFH, MFF, 32225 H Hutt[1] & 22207 E A McCulloch[1] attch. ITD

Gunners/Drivers: ~ 21030 E Bailey[1], 12763 J R Russell[1] & 44286 E Thompson[1]

80 Field Battery, Royal Field Artillery

Note a.   *Roll of all personnel identified as eligible.*
Note b.   *Medals named in running script: '80[b] By, R.F.A.', Officers may be simply 'R.A.'*

Single Clasp	No. Identified	Rarity
North West Frontier 1908[1]	137	Very Scarce

Captains: ~ F Ashton[1] & H Fawcus[1]

Lieutenants: ~ J Slade Powell[1]

Warrant Officers Class II: ~ (BSM) 35458 D Hill[1]

Battery Quartermaster Sergeants/Staff Sergeants: ~ (Armt) 433 P Heaton[1]

Quartermaster Sergeants/Sergeants: ~ 7999 H Boyd[1], (Saddle) 2915 W Brown[1], (Farrier) 3922 E Campion[1], 65180 A Fisher[1], 74034 J Gower[1] & 7940 H Morgan[1]

Corporals: ~ 3284 F Ashton[1], (Wheeler) 88581 W Hilton[1], 12 P Jewell[1], 31530 J King[1], 2875 F Phipps[1], (Shoeing Smith) 5795 J Reilly[1], 4109 T Sharrock[1], 9656 A Virgin[1] & 87365 J Warboys[1]

Bombardiers: ~ 20309 H Banks[1], 2135 G Blackburn[1], (Act) 31722 A Carter[1], (Act) 35035 W Clarkson[1], 27299 C Crowe[1], 2554 L Forsyth[1], (Act) 32084 W Gwynne[1], 16467 C Lawlor[1], 2195 A Miller[1], (Act) 10694 T Moroney[1], (Act) 12726 F Poolman[1], (Act) 3125 G Reynolds[1] & 6579 A Warner[1]

Gunners/Drivers: ~ 16417 T Allen[1], 43745 J Andrews[1], 43598 H Bailey[1], 19447 J Barnett[1], 97688 J Bell[1], 33452 G Bignell[1], 44431 T Bishop[1], 21079 T Brownlee[1], 40283 J Burkhill[1], 21113 S Burrows[1], 32900 H Caine[1], 45532 R Campbell[1], 46513 H Chandler[1], 32052 T Clarke[1], 32851 M Colgan[1], 45070 W Collett[1], 22871 J Conner[1], 42767 G Cox[1], 18564 J Crawley[1], 36645 A Davis[1], 13159 D Didcock[1], 21398 J Doyle[1], 22364 W Elden[1], 14420 S Eyre[1], 45071 E Fear[1], 14491 H George[1], 18746 M Gerathy[1], 17726 J Gibbs[1], 27347 J Goldsmith[1], 20633 H Graham[1], 24566 R Griffiths[1], 15008 F Grundy[1], 20618 L Hart[1], 16439 J Hastings[1], 19445 C Hayes[1], 19444 A Henderson[1], ?5487 B Hill[1], 14482 H Hill[1], 26382 T Hudson[1], 25438 J Hughes[1], 41268 W Hughes[1], 48945 J Ives[1], 29138 J Jones[1], 43436 J Kenny[1], 23599 W Kerr[1], 29159 M Lacey[1], 21117 K Lennox[1], 23514 J Levenson[1], 28347 S Linnell[1], 27749 A Loveland[1], 20630 G Marchant[1], 22823 M Martin[1], 6559 S Martin[1], 37264 W Marston[1], 89989 G Masters[1], 27477 F Mayhew[1], 21087 J McBride[1], 20092 J McConkey[1], 26121 G McCormick[1], 13959 P McCrudden[1], 17511 J McGowan[1], 8341 W McKerr[1], 31349 W Merger[1], 44993 F Monelle[1], 12755 D Morton[1], 40312 B Moses[1], 20685 J Murphy[1], 32102 P Murphy[1], 20656 J Nicholson[1], 25292 F Norris[1], 18808 G O'Donnell[1], 44328 J Osborne[1], 22267 S Owen[1], 15906 M Fitz-Patrick[1] attch. AVC, 5809 J Peters[1], 33012 J Phillips[1], 21597 R Philpot[1], 28159 E Powell[1], 36549 M Purcell[1], 25471 W Reeves[1], 33027 W Reasson[1], 25488 R Reynolds[1], 16710 E Richardson[1], 3007 W Richardson[1], 44216 J Roberts[1], 40181 W Roberts[1], 16396 W Robinson[1], 19492 J Ryan[1], 18806 H Sanderson[1], 40518 S Shelton[1], 29151 E Shufflebottom[1], 12695 H Smith[1], 15886 T Smith[1], 35598 J Smythe[1], 32060 W Sowerby[1], 22995 J Sowter[1], 26176 J Thompson[1], 40586 W Turner[1], 12437 G Vine[1], 13915 F Walsh[1], 46442 C Whiddett[1] & 47950 E Wilson[1]

Shoeing Smith: ~ 23624 J Reilly[1]

Trumpeters: ~ 34369 A Beer[1]

1st Divisional Ammunition Column, Royal Field Artillery

Note a.   *Roll of all personnel identified as eligible.*
Note b.   *The roll does not specify Battery affiliation; nor does the* 1908 Army list.
Note c.   *Medals named in running script:: 'R.F.A.' or 'R.A.'*

Captains: ~ F C Tyler[1] MFF

Battery Quartermaster Sergeants/Staff Sergeants: ~ 27868 A F Dixon[1] MFF

Batteries Not Identified

Note a.   It has not been possible to trace the Batteries of the following recipients.
Note b.   *Medals named in running script:: 'R.F.A.' or 'R.A.'*

Lieutenants: ~ P S Smith[1&3]

Gunners/Drivers: ~ (1405251) 32566 W J Burrough[1,3,4(L/Sgt.)&6(L/Sgt.)], (1029540) 76691 J Fettis[1,3&6], 75158 A H Hunt[1&3(Bdr.)] & 59283 C A Legge[1&3]

~ Royal Garrison Artillery ~

Sub Units Identified As Being Entitled:
1, 3, 7 & 8 Mountain Batteries
71 (Heavy) Battery & 101 Company

Royal Garrison Artillery Staff Appointments
Note a.   *Roll of all personnel identified as eligible.*
Note b.   *Recipient served as an Aide de Camp (ADC).*
Note c.   *The roll does not specify Battery affiliation, nor does the* 1908 *Army list.*
Note d.   *Medals named in running script: 'R.G.A.'*

Lieutenants: ~ A P Y Langhorne[1] ADC

No. 1 Mountain Battery, Royal Garrison Artillery
Note a.   *Roll of all personnel identified as eligible.*
Note b.   *Recipient attached 23 Mountain Battery, Frontier Garrison Artillery.*
Note c.   *Medals named in running script: 'No 1 Mtn B. R.G.A.'*

Single Clasp	No. Identified	Rarity
North West Frontier 1908[1]	1	According to the roll as seen, can be considered Unique

Lieutenants: ~ M R Strover[1]

No. 3 Mountain Battery, Royal Garrison Artillery
Note a.   *Roll of all personnel identified as eligible.*
Note b.   *The surviving roll is in poor condition rendering the names of several non-commissioned and other rank personnel illegible. Missing digits are represented thus: ?.*
Note c.   *Medals named in running script: 'No 3 Mtn B. R.G.A.'*

Single Clasp	No. Identified	Rarity
North West Frontier 1908[1]	Est. 88	Rare

Combination Clasps	No. Identified	Rarity
North West Frontier 1908[1] Afghanistan N.W.F. 1919[3]	11	Extremely Rare
North West Frontier 1908[1] Afghanistan N.W.F. 1919[3] Mahsud 1919–20[5] Waziristan 1919–21[4]	1	According to the roll as seen, can be considered Unique
North West Frontier 1908[1] Afghanistan N.W.F. 1919[3] Mahsud 1919–20[5] Waziristan 1919–21[4] Waziristan 1921–24[6]	1	According to the roll as seen, can be considered Unique

Majors: ~ F H S Giles[1]
Captains: ~ C F Phipps[1]
Lieutenants: ~ P A F W a Beckett[1], J F King[1], F H Reid[1] & J F Young[1]
Quartermaster Sergeants/Sergeants: ~ 68306 G A Beer[1], (Farrier) 24838 A E Calvert[1], 31873 J Charlton[1], 21822 E J Connolly[1], 10443 ?? Mann[1], 11002 F Pound[1], 1203 F Sharpe[1] & 90627 J Thomas[1]

Corporals: ~ 70542 S A Allen[1], 2671 H W Clark[1], 3276 A Dorman[1], 6162 D Fealy[1] & 28932 F McDonnell[1]

Bombardiers: ~ 9488 H Airey[1], 1675 W Clark[1] attch. ITD, 11989 H A Collis[1&3(WO11)], 7623 G D(i)(e)sborough[1], (Saddle) 34689 H C Dowding[1], 6580 F Feeley[1], 8823 C W Gainsborough[1], 2182 H A Grout[1], 16850 J Gulliver[1], (Act) 15633 F C Jenner[1], 11782 W Lattimer[1], 30342 C Mockford[1&3(Sgt.)], 13359 T Morris[1], 11495 J Oliver[1], 22770 H G Papworth[1], 22949 F Povey[1], 7118 H Purkiss[1], 27763 C W Roberts[1], 6882 C Sawford[1], 17540 G Smith[1], 7745 H Wells[1] & 24646 J T D Wilmott[1]

Gunners: ~ 21470 A A Arnold[1], 20967 G Birch[1], 10104 P Blaylock[1], 64505 E Boxold[1], 13305 A Brookes[1], 23261 E Brown[1], 25793 R B Brown[1], 25766 W Brunt[1], 22972 J Bryans[1], 7297 D Buck[1], 25767 J Deane[1], 3003 M Donohue[1], 17763 I H Doody[1], 23432 J Dooney[1], 23617 T Duck[1&3], 24167 E Duffy[1], 23319 W S Efford[1], 25764 G Everton[1,3,4,5&6], 29385 D Foley[1], 2668 T Gibson[1], 22448 W Glanville[1], 7321 E Glass[1], 8315 F Haines[1], 23663 C W Handley[1], 7108 G L Haselden[1], 8015 H S Hayes[1], 23431 W Humphrey[1], 25020 E A Hurlock[1&3(Sgt.)], 22372 T Ingram[1], 7718 F Jones[1], 7294 ?? Keller[1], 7769 F W Kelly[1], 20062 J Kelly[1], 95083 G Kersey[1], 12399 P Kiernan[1], 20798 P Langstone[1], 74357 T Lawlor[1], 8240 J J Long[1], 24327 G Mayo[1], 12411 J McEwan[1], 25796 S Minogue[1&3], 33589 E Mitchelmore[1], 12226 D Molloy[1&3], 17783 S Morgan[1], 23583 J Moylan[1], 15621 F Mullholland[1], 15176 J Nolan[1], 8717 B O'Neill[1], 22115 T O'Neill[1], 13590 H Paige[1], 22968 G Pearson[1&3(Sgt.)], 34037 A Pelling[1], 9774 A G Pridham[1], 1685 T Reddington[1], 25772 J Reid[1], 8014 F Richards[1], 22834 H T Salter[1], 7631 G C Saville[1], 1595 J Simpson[1&3], 10626 W Smith[1], 22810 S G Springford[1], 25795 T Stevenson[1], 15627 F Stratton[1], 25769 J Teear[1,3,4&5], 4305 C Temple[1], 24321 W Trigwell[1&3], 11453 S Usher[1], 22814 T Wainwright[1], 19495 F C Walker[1], 8111 P Walsh[1], 2187 ? Walsh[1], 7960 J Ward[1], 22837 W Wetton[1&3], 10204 H Wharton[1], 6278 A H Wilcox[1], 21404 G P Williams[1], 15762 C Wilson[1], 19876 A J Wood[1], 8412 C Woodland[1], 7254 R E Wright[1], 23069 A A Wrigley[1], 22971 S Vaughan[1&3] & 4327 E ??????[1]

Trumpeters: ~ 19630 W Ottaway[1] & 16134 E F Tallentire[1]

No. 7 Mountain Battery, Royal Garrison Artillery

Note a.   *Roll of all personnel identified as eligible.*

Note b.   *Recipient attached Indian Telegraph Department (ITD).*

Note c.   *Medals named in running script: 'No 7 Mtn B. R.G.A.'*

Single Clasp	No. Identified	Rarity
North West Frontier 1908[1]	1	According to the roll as seen, can be considered Unique

Gunners: ~ 29182 J Adams[1]

No. 8 Mountain Battery, Royal Garrison Artillery

Note a.   *Roll of all personnel identified as eligible.*

Note b.   *The surviving roll is in very poor condition and at least 44 non-commissioned and other rank names are illegible albeit some serial numbers can be identified. Missing digits are represented thus: ?. Some names have been identified from other sources. These are listed in the roll sequence by rank.*

Note c.   *Medals named in running script: 'No 8 Mtn B. R.G.A.'*

Single Clasp	No. Identified	Rarity
North West Frontier 1908[1]	Est. 104	Scarce
Combination Clasps	**No. Identified**	**Rarity**
North West Frontier 1908[1] Afghanistan N.W.F. 1919[3]	2	Of the Utmost Rarity
North West Frontier 1908[1] Afghanistan N.W.F. 1919[3] Mahsud 1919–20[5] Waziristan 1919–21[4]	1	According to the roll as seen, can be considered Unique

Majors: ~ F W S Stanton[1] & W Strong[1]

Captains: ~ F A Easton[1]

Lieutenants: ~ P R Mitchell[1], W S Nicholson[1] & L N Stephens[1]

Warrant Offices Class II: ~ (BSM) 96373 J Simmonds[1]

Battery Quartermaster Sergeants/Staff Sergeants: ~ (Battery) 92698 H Stock[1]

Quartermaster Sergeants/Sergeants: ~ 3074 ? Elliott[1], 600 O Hennessy[1], 6421 J Holdsworth[1], 12105 A Juniper[1], 5832 E H Millinship[1] & (Farrier) 16637 W Thorpe[1]

Corporals: ~ 7582 A G Pay[1], 8198 A Potier[1], 17974 ? Stewart[1], (Saddler) 2238 T Smyth[1] & 7825 ??? [1]

Bombardiers: ~ (Act) 1301 F Carter[1], (Act) 9757 F Davies[1], 8577 R Haugh[1], 291 (1400252) J Kenneally[1,(3,4&5 WOII)], 6808 A Poole[1], 6506 J W West[1], (Act) 23387 A Wilson[1] & 27692 J A Wood[1]

Gunners: ~ 24932 G Adams[1], 25929 R Alderman[1], 19641 G H Bailey[1], 16571 W Beresford[1], 95906 C P Brewster[1], 24926 N S Bright[1], 15724 R Buckland[1], 22381 J Caldwell[1], 6766 A Cameron[1], 14625 T Carroll[1], 14292 E Carter[1], 95239 G Coinage[1], 11427 F Davenport[1], 17763 H Doody[1], 20858 J Doyle[1], 16736 W H Flambard[1&3(Sgt.)], 18638 ? Ford[1], 18045 L A Grainger[1], 21781 E Gove[1], 18166 D Grant[1], 21587 ? Hall[1], 13203 ? Hampton[1], 11582 G Hankinson[1], 10242 J Harrison[1], 13908 A Harvey[1], 12817 E H Hibbert[1], 22396 W Innerd[1], 24927 E Jennings[1], 22378 D Kelly[1], 9617 W Kirby[1], 74356 T Lawlor[1], 14956 C Milton[1], 8820 P A Mountford[1], 20621 H Mulhall[1], 15621 F Mullholland[1], 6782 R Mullholland[1], 11302 J Murphy[1], 23??4 J O'Neill[1], ?211? ? O'Neill[1], 10784 W Orders[1], 25116 A E Parish[1], 8867 F Peters[1], 13824 J Pilkington[1], 6808 A Pople[1], 24465 W H Portor[1], 25889 H Price[1], 22374 J G Priest[1], 17905 A Pye[1], 7954 J Rease[1], 19095 H Rix[1], 15126 F Sharp[1], 10708 E J Smith[1], 24933 G H Smith[1], 5659 J Smith[1], 19726 S R Stirley[1], 23933 R Thornton[1], 24516 B Vine[1], 8111 P Walsh[1], 20060 J W Watson[1], 17942 A J White[1], 17486 S C Wintle[1], 18087 D Wilson[1], 14184 H Young[1], 21731 ??? [1], 7854[1] ???, 18643 ??? [1], 25795 ??? [1], 11008 ??? [1], 4305 ??? [1], 18637 ???[1], 18148 ??? [1], 7967 ???[1], 9515 ??? [1], 24515 ??? [1], 9202 ??? [1], 30078 ??? [1], 14221 ??? [1] & 7431 ??? [1]

Trumpeters: ~ 24121 P Bock[1&3(Gnr)]

71 Heavy Battery, Royal Garrison Artillery

Note a. *Roll of all personnel identified as eligible.*

Note b. *Recipients served as signallers attached to 1 Brigade (1 Bde) unless otherwise shown.*

Note c. *Medals named in running script: 'No 71 Hvy B. R.G.A.'*

Single Clasp	No. Identified	Rarity
North West Frontier 1908[1]	6	Of the Utmost Rarity

Bombardiers: ~ 7851 C H Kruse[1] & 10181 G Russell[1]

Gunners: ~ 22344 J Bryson[1], 13993 E Carlisle[1] attch. 1 DAC, MFF, 21131 H G H Colenutt[1] & 10222 T Joel[1] attch. 1 DAC, MFF

No. 101 Company, Royal Garrison Artillery

Note a. *Roll of all personnel identified as eligible.*

Note b. *Recipient attached Indian Telegraph Department (ITD).*

Note c. *Medals named in running script: 'R.G.A.'*

Single Clasp	No. Identified	Rarity
North West Frontier 1908[1]	1	According to the roll as seen, can be considered Unique

Gunners: ~ 1189 E Cross[1]

THE INDIAN FRONTIER GARRISON ARTILLERY:

Sub Units Identified As Entitled:
22 (Derajat), 23 (Peshawar), 28 & 31 Indian Mountain Batteries

Note a.   *Roll of all Commissioned personnel identified as eligible.*
Note b.   *The Indian Frontier Garrison Artillery formed part of the Royal Garrison Artillery order of battle. Officers of the Frontier Garrison Artillery held Royal Garrison Artillery commissions.*
Note c.   *Indian Army establishment not included on roll.*
Note d.   *Medals named in running script: Battery details followed by 'R.G.A.'*

Single Clasp	No. Identified	Rarity
North West Frontier 1908[1]	12	**Extremely Rare**

Combination Clasps	No. Identified	Rarity
North West Frontier 1908[1] Afghanistan N.W.F. 1919[3]	1	**According to the roll as seen, can be considered Unique**
North West Frontier 1908[1] Waziristan 1919-21[4], Waziristan 1921–24[6] North West Frontier 1930–31[9]	1	**According to the roll as seen, can be considered Unique**
North West Frontier 1908[1] Waziristan 1921– 24[6]	1	**According to the roll as seen, can be considered Unique**
North West Frontier 1908[1] Waziristan 1921–24[6] North West Frontier 1930–31[9]	1	**According to the roll as seen, can be considered Unique**

Lieutenant Colonels: ~ (Bvt) R W Fuller[1] 28 Mtn Bty
Captains: ~ G G W Corrie[1&3(Lt. Col.)] 23 Mtn Bty, T M Luke[1] 28 Mtn Bty, S W Robinson[1] 28 Mtn Bty & C de Sausmarez[1] 22 Mtn Bty
Lieutenants: ~ E S Allsup[1] 31 Mtn Bty attch. 23 Mtn Bty, J C Bassett[1] 23 Mtn Bty, J H Bateson[1] 23 Mtn Bty, J D Byrne[1] 28 Mtn Bty, D D H Campell[1] 31 Mtn Bty attch. 23 Mtn Bty, S Carwithen[1] 22 Mtn Bty, J H Edmond[1,4(Maj.),6(Maj.)&9(Lt. Col.)] 28 Mtn Bty, N Robertson-Glasgow[1] 22 Mtn Bty, E M Little[1,6(Maj.)&9(Lt. Col.)] 22 Mtn Bty, G L L Mayo[1] 28 Mtn Bty & E le G Whitting[1&6(35 Ind Mtn Bty)] 23 Mtn Bty

THE CORPS OF ROYAL ENGINEERS:

Units Identified As Being Entitled:
1st Prince of Wales's Own Sappers & Miners
2nd Queen's Own Sappers & Miners
Officers attached Military Works Service & Survey of India

Note a.   *Roll of all Royal Engineer personnel identified as eligible.*
Note b.   *Officers of the Indian Army Sappers & Miners and Military Works Service held Royal Engineer commissions.*
Note c.   *Indian Army establishment not included on roll.*
Note d.   *Medals named in running script: 'R.E.' followed by 'No 1 Co. 1st S&M etc'*

Single Clasp	No. Identified	Rarity
North West Frontier 1908[1]	28	**Very Rare**

Combination Clasps	No. Identified	Rarity
North West Frontier 1908[1] Abor 1911–12[2]	1	According to the roll as see, can be considered Unique
North West Frontier 1908[1] Abor 1911–12[2] Afghanistan N.W.F. 1919[3]	1	According to the roll as see, can be considered Unique
North West Frontier 1908[1] Afghanistan N.W.F. 1919[3]	1	According to the roll as see, can be considered Unique
North West Frontier 1908[1] Waziristan 1919 – 21[4]	1	According to the roll as see, can be considered Unique
North West Frontier 1908[1] Waziristan 1921 – 24[6]	1	According to the roll as see, can be considered Unique
North West Frontier 1908[1] Waziristan 1921–24[6] North West Frontier 1930–31[9]	1	According to the roll as see, can be considered Unique

Lieutenant Colonels: ~ H J Dundee[1] CRE, BVFF

Majors: ~ W Ewbank[1] attch. MWS

Captains: ~ W H Breech[1] DA&QMG, 3 Bde., J R E Charles[1&6(Maj. Gen.)] 6 Fld Coy, 1 PWO S&M, A H Cunningham[1] 1 Fld Coy, 1 PWO S&M, E C Tylden-Patterson[1,2(Maj.)&3(Lt. Col.)] 2 Fld Coy, 1 PWO S&M, F T Rich[1] Survey Officer, MFF, A R C Sanders[1] Cbl & Telph Sect, 1 PWO S&M, R B Skinner[1&3(Lt. Col.)] attch. MWS, J F Turner[1] attch. MWS, C M Wagstaff[1,6(Col.)&9(Maj. Gen.)] 9 Fld Coy, 2 QO S&M & H E Winslow[1] attch. MWS

Lieutenants: ~ E C Baker[1] Survey Officer MFF, T P Bassett[1] 9 Fld Coy, 2 QO S&M, A J G Bird[1] 6 Fld Coy, 1 PWO S&M, L V Bond[1] 6 Fld Coy, 1 PWO S&M, E P le Breton[1&2] 9 Fld Coy, 2 QO S&M, A Campbell[1] attch. MWS, B H Fox[1] 6 Fld Coy, 1 PWO S&M, P C S Hobart[1&4(Maj.)] 2 Fld Coy, 1 PWO S&M, E H Kelly[1] 1 Fld Coy, 1 PWO S&M, E J Loring[1] 1 Fld Coy, 1 PWO S&M, A F Macauley[1] 1 Fld Coy, 1 PWO S&M, J A McQueen[1] 9 Fld Coy, 2 QO S&M, G E Sopworth[1] 6 Fld Coy, 1 PWO S&M, T H L Spaight[1] Cbl & Telph Sect, 1 PWO S&M & H W Tomlinson[1] Cbl & Telph Sect, 1 PWO S&M

Company Quartermaster Sergeants/Sergeants: ~ 23804 G H Cornish[1] 1 Fld Coy, 1 PWO S&M, 2615 H Gallagher[1] Cbl & Telph Sect, 1 PWO S&M, 1105 F C Hawkins[1] 6 Fld Coy, 1 PWO S&M, 2411 G B Hewison[1] 6 Fld Coy, 1 PWO S&M & 10284 A P Hoskins[1] 9 Fld Coy, 2 QO S&M

Lance Sergeants/Corporals: ~ 9201 W Hayward[1] 2 Fld Coy, 1 PWO S&M & 9820 J B Paull[1] 1 Fld Coy, 1 PWO S&M

THE INFANTRY:

~ The Queen's (Royal West Surrey Regiment) ~

Note a.   *Roll of all personnel identified eligible.*

Note b.   *Recipient served as Signals Officer (SO), Mohmand Field Force (MFF).*

Note c.   *Medals named in running script: '1ˢᵗ Bn R. W. Surrey R.'*

Single Clasp	No. Identified	Rarity
North West Frontier 1908[1]	1	According to the roll as seen, can be considered Unique

Captains: ~ M G Heath[1]

~ 1st Bn, The Northumberland Fusiliers ~

Note a.   *Roll of all commissioned personnel identified as eligible.*

Note b.   *Non-commissioned and other rank personnel multi-clasp only.*

Note c.   *Battalion to France 14th August 1914. Many personnel entitled to the clasp 'North West Frontier 1908' would have been deployed during World War One and large numbers would have been casualties.*

Note d.   *Medals named in running script: '1st Bn Northd. Fus.'*

Single Clasp	No. Identified	Rarity
North West Frontier 1908[1]	Battalion Strength	Not Rare

Majors: ~ S H Enderby[1] & D Sapte[1] (Cmd.)

Captains: ~ C W Wreford-Brown[1], W Clifford[1], G Coles[1], A C Girdwood[1], E Gordon[1], H R Sandilands[1] & A C Temperley[1]

Lieutenants: ~ I M Bonham-Carter[1], W Gibson[1], C G Maud[1], W Platt[1], E L Salier[1], W G M Sarel[1], B H Selby[1], G O Sloper[1] & E H Staples[1]

~ 1st Bn, The Royal Warwickshire Regiment ~

Note a.   *Roll of all commissioned personnel identified as eligible.*

Note b.   *Non-commissioned and other rank personnel multi-clasp only.*

Note c.   *Battalion believed to be first unit awarded the IGS Medal 1908–35. Medals presented in Peshawar by Maj. Gen. Sir James Willcocks on 24th March 1909.*

Note d.   *Battalion to France 22nd August 1914. Many personnel entitled to clasp 'North West Frontier 1908' would have been deployed during World War One and large numbers would have been casualties.*

Note e.   *Medals named in running script: '1st R. War. R.'*

Single Clasp	No. Identified	Rarity
North West Frontier 1908[1]	Battalion Strength	Not Rare
Combination Clasps	**No. Identified**	**Rarity**
North West Frontier 1908[1] Afghanistan N.W.F. 1919[3]	1	According to the roll as seen, can be considered Unique
North West Frontier 1908[1] Waziristan 1919–21[4] Waziristan 1921–24[6]	1	According to the roll as seen, can be considered Unique
North West Frontier 1908[1] Waziristan 1921–24[6]	1	According to the roll as seen, can be considered Unique

Lieutenant Colonels: ~ F G F Browne[1]

Majors: ~ St. J A Cox[1], (Bvt) A Y Spearman[1], H R Vaughan[1] & P T Westmoreland[1]

Captains: ~ D A L Day[1], B G R Gordon[1], C R MacDonald[1], G B Marriott[1], E J de P O'Kelly[1], A J Poole[1] & A S Toogood[1]

Lieutenants: ~ J A M Bannerman[1], T V Barney[1], H W Dakeyne[1], C E Davies[1], K F Franks[1], C G P Gilliat[1], (QM) T H Harwood[1], J M Lorimer[1], F A Macartney[1], G D Martin[1], C L N Newall[1], A L Hume-Spry[1], C T Tomes[1], G F Waterworth[1] & T N Whaley[1]

Lance Sergeants/Corporals: ~ (1039149) 6230 C M Lee[1&(6 Sgt. RFA)]

Lance Corporals/Privates: ~ 7711 C Groves[1,(4&6 as Sgt. RTC)] & 8918 L Flanner[1&3(Ox&Bucks LI)]

~ 1st Bn, The Lincolnshire Regiment ~

Note a. *Roll of all personnel identified as eligible.*
Note b. *Medals named in running script: '1st Bn Lincolnshire R.'*

Single Clasp	No. Identified	Rarity
North West Frontier 1908[1]	1	According to the roll as seen, can be considered Unique

Lance Corporals/Privates: ~ ? Shields[1]

~ 2nd Bn, The Prince Albert's (Somerset Light Infantry) ~

Note a. *Roll of all personnel identified as eligible.*
Note b. *Recipient served as Signals Officer (SO), Bazaar Valley Field Force (BVFF).*
Note c. *Medals named in running script: '2nd Bn Som. L. I.'*

Single Clasp	No. Identified	Rarity
North West Frontier 1908[1]	1	According to the roll as seen, can be considered Unique

Captains: ~ A B Whatman[1]

~ 1st Bn, The Prince of Wales's Own (West Yorkshire Regiment) ~

Note a. *Roll of all commissioned personnel identified as eligible.*
Note b. *Non-commissioned and other rank personnel multi-clasp only*
Note c. *Battalion split into two 'Wings' during Mohmand operations; officers at Burjina Pass marked thus (*).*
Note d. *Battalion to France 10th September 1914. Many personnel entitled to 'North West Frontier 1908' would have been deployed during World War One and large numbers would have been casualties.*
Note e. *Medals named in running script: '1st W. Y. Regt.'*

Single Clasp	No. Identified	Rarity
North West Frontier 1908[1]	Battalion Strength.	Not Rare

Majors: ~ T P Barrington[1], W de S Cayley[1] (Cmd.), G G Lang[1]* & J O'B Minogue[1]*
Captains: ~ S G Francis[1], M B Riall[1]* & F P Worsley[1]
Lieutenants: ~ E A W Armitage[1], E Grant-Dalton[1]*, G C L Fenton[1]*, M Fisher[1], J A W Foottit[1]*, S T Grigg[1], F H Hawley[1]*, (QM) W H Hill[1], C P Martin[1] Adjt, F H Maylon[1]*, R J McLaren[1], E A Porch[1], E T Welchman[1] & N R Whitaker[1]

~ 2nd Bn, The East Yorkshire Regiment ~

Note a. *Roll of all personnel identified as eligible.*
Note b. *Recipient attached to the Corps of Military Staff Clerks (CMSC), 1 Brigade (1 Bde), Mohmand Field Force (MFF).*
Note c. *Medals named in running script: '2nd E. Y. Regt.'*

Single Clasp	No. Identified	Rarity
North West Frontier 1908[1]	1	According to the roll as seen, can be considered Unique

Lance Sergeants/Corporals: ~ 5796 H D Wilson[1]

~ 1st Bn, The Royal Irish Regiment ~

Note a. *Roll of all personnel identified as eligible.*
Note b. *All officers identified attached 1 Royal Munster Fusiliers.*
Note c. *All non-commissioned and other rank personnel identified attached 'A' and 'B' Sections, No. 7 British Field Hospital (BFH), Royal Army Medical Corps (RAMC), unless shown otherwise.*
Note d. *Medals named in running script: '1ˢᵗ Bn Rl. Irish Regt.'*

Single Clasp	No. Identified	Rarity
North West Frontier 1908[1]	6	Of the Utmost Rarity

Combination Clasps	No. Identified	Rarity
North West Frontier 1908[1] Abor 1911– 12[2]	1	According to the roll as seen, can be considered Unique

Captains: ~ J G A Massy[1]
Lieutenants: ~ A H Caldecott[1] & F C Ferguson[1]
Quartermaster Sergeants/Sergeants: ~ 6415 (E) (M) O'Halloran[1]
Lance Corporals/Privates: ~ 6013 J Flannigan[1], 9127 T E Fisher[1&2] attch. ITD & 5714 A Lydon[1]

~ 1st Bn, The Lancashire Fusiliers ~

Note a. *Roll of all personnel identified as eligible.*
Note b. *Recipient attached 1 West Yorkshire, Burjina Pass detachment.*
Note c. *Medals named in running script: '1ˢᵗ Bn Lan. Fus.'*

Single Clasp	No. Identified	Rarity
North West Frontier 1908[1]	1	According to the roll as seen, can be considered Unique

Lieutenants: ~ R Haworth[1]

~ 1st Bn, The South Wales Borderers ~

Note a. *Roll of all personnel identified as eligible.*
Note b. *Medals named in running script: '1ˢᵗ Bn S. Wales. Bord.'*

Single Clasp	No. Identified	Rarity
North West Frontier 1908[1]	2	Of the Utmost Rarity

Captains: ~ H F Elgee[1] Orderly Officer to Brig. Gen. Anderson
Quartermaster Sergeants/Sergeants: ~ ???? E Lobar[1] attch. S&TC

~ 1st Bn, The Gloucestershire Regiment ~

Note a. *Roll of all personnel identified as eligible.*
Note b. *Names removed from main joint roll but appear on supplementary Regiment specific roll.*
Note c. *All recipients attached 'A' Section, No. 13 British Field Hospital (BFH), Royal Army Medical Corps (RAMC).*
Note d. *Medals named in running script, believed: '1ˢᵗ Bn Glouc. R.'*

Single Clasp	No. Identified	Rarity
North West Frontier 1908[1]	3	Of the Utmost Rarity

Lance Sergeants/Corporals: ~ 5739 E W Woollen[1]
Lance Corporals/Privates: ~ 5984 A H Dowdeswell[1] & 6005 R Dowdeswell[1]

~ 1st Bn, The Royal Sussex Regiment ~

Note a.   *Roll of all personnel identified as eligible.*
Note b.   *Recipient attached Supply & Transport Corps (S&TC).*
Note c.   *Medals named in running script: '1ᵈ Bn R. Sussex R.*

Single Clasp	No. Identified	Rarity
North West Frontier 1908[1]	1	According to the roll as seen, can be considered Unique

Lance Sergeants/Corporals: ~ ???? W Rundle[1]

~ 2nd Bn, The Black Watch (Royal Highlanders) ~

Note a.   *Roll of all personnel identified as eligible.*
Note b.   *All officers attached 1 Seaforth Highlanders unless shown otherwise.*
Note c.   *All non-commissioned and other rank personnel attached Indian Telegraph Department (ITD) unless shown otherwise.*
Note d.   *Medals named in running script > '2ⁿᵈ Bn The Black Watch'*

Single Clasp	No. Identified	Rarity
North West Frontier 1908[1]	7	Of the Utmost Rarity

Captains: ~ J K M Blair[1] Orderly Officer, MFF & J T C Murray[1]
Lieutenants: ~ P A Duff[1] & A P Wavell[1]
Quartermaster Sergeants/Sergeants: ~ 3292 W H Green[1]
Lance Corporals/Privates: ~ ???? H Crawford[1] attch. S&TC & 8204 D Murdoch[1]

~ 1st Bn, The Oxfordshire & Buckinghamshire Light Infantry ~

Note a.   *Roll of all personnel identified as eligible.*
Note b.   *Recipients served as Clerks to the Divisional Signals Officer (DSO), Mohmand Field Force (MFF) unless shown otherwise.*
Note c.   *Medals named in running script: '1ᵈ Bn Oxford L.I.'*

Single Clasp	No. Identified	Rarity
North West Frontier 1908[1]	3	Of the Utmost Rarity

Quartermaster Sergeants/Sergeants: ~ 7768 G H Poxley[1] attch. ITD
Lance Corporals/Privates : ~ 5637 H T Payne[1] & 5637 P H Thomas[1]

~ 2nd Bn, The Northamptonshire Regiment ~

Note a.   *Roll of all personnel identified as eligible.*
Note b.   *Recipient served as Deputy Adjutant & Quartermaster General (DA&QMG), Bazaar Valley Field Force (BVFF).*
Note c.   *Medals named in running script: '2ⁿᵈ Bn Northampt'n. R.'*

Single Clasp	No. Identified	Rarity
North West Frontier 1908[1]	1	According to the roll as seen, can be considered Unique

Captains: ~ H H Norman[1]

~ 1st Bn, The King's (Shropshire Light Infantry) ~

Note a.   *Roll of all personnel identified as eligible.*
Note b.   *Recipient attached 1 West Yorkshire Regiment.*
Note c.   *Medals named in running script: '2nd Bn K.S.L.I.'*

Single Clasp	No. Identified	Rarity
North West Frontier 1908[1]	1	According to the roll as seen, can be considered Unique

Captains: ~ C W Battye[1]

~ 1st Bn, The Duke of Cambridge's Own (Middlesex Regiment) ~

Note a.   *Roll of all personnel identified as eligible.*
Note b.   *Recipient attached 1 West Yorkshire Regiment, Burjina Pass Detachment.*
Note c.   *Medals named in running script.: 1st Bn Midd'x Regt.'*

Single Clasp	No. Identified	Rarity
North West Frontier 1908[1]	1	According to the roll as seen, can be considered Unique

Lieutenants: ~ E R Gibbons[1]

~ 1st Bn, The Highland Light Infantry ~

Note a.   *Roll of all personnel identified as eligible.*
Note b.   *Recipients attached 1 Seaforth Highlanders.*
Note c.   *Medals named in running script: '1st Bn High. L.I.' or '1st Bn H.L.I.'*

Single Clasp	No. Identified	Rarity
North West Frontier 1908[1]	2	Of the Utmost Rarity

Captains: ~ H Stockwell[1]
Lieutenants: ~ G M Knight[1]

~ 1st Bn, The Seaforth Highlanders (Ross-shire Buffs, The Duke of Albany's) ~

Note a.   *Roll of all commissioned personnel identified as eligible.*
Note b.   *Non-commissioned and enlisted personnel multi-clasp only.*
Note c.   *Battalion to France 12th October 1914. Many personnel entitled to the clasp 'North West Frontier 1908' would have been deployed during World War One and large numbers would have been casualties.*
Note d.   *Medals named in running script:: '1st Bn Sea. Highrs.'*

Single Clasp	No. Identified	Rarity
North West Frontier 1908[1]	Bn. Strength	Not Rare
Combination Clasps	**No. Identified**	**Rarity**
North West Frontier 1908[1] Waziristan 1919 - 21[4]	1	According to the roll as seen, can be considered Unique
North West Frontier 1908[1] Waziristan 1919 - 21[4] Waziristan 1921 – 24[6]	1	According to the roll as seen, can be considered Unique

Lieutenant Colonels: ~ A A Spottiswoode[1]
Majors: ~ N C MacLauchlan[1], Hon. D Forbes-Sempill[1] & R S Vanderleur[1]
Captains: ~ K C Buchanan[1], C B Chamley[1], P C L L Daniell[1], C P Doig[1], D A Garden[1], R Horn[1], (QM) D King[1] & H W C Wicks[1]
Lieutenants: ~ F Anderson[1], P H Allamby[1], P W Brodie[1], P C Campbell[1], J Mac A Craig[1], H B Davidson[1], M R Duncan[1], M W Fenton[1], F R C Forsyth[1], F W I V Fraser[1], G O V Gray[1], C H Hopkinson[1], H H Kennedy[1], I C MacFadyen[1], K D M MacLachlan[1], W A A Middleton[1], F T H Mullaly[1], A C Murray[1], C S Narine[1], T J Ponting[1], K Forbes-Robinson[1], J F Russell[1] & R C F Schomberg[1]
Lance Corporals/Privates: ~ 8427 A Brown[1&4] & 7897 A Graham[1,4(RE)&6(R Sigs)]

~ 2nd Bn, The Gordon Highlanders ~

Note a.   Roll of all personnel identified as eligible.
Note b.   All recipients attached 1 Seaforth Highlanders unless shown otherwise.
Note c.   Medals named in running script: '2nd Bn Gord. Highrs.'

Single Clasp	No. Identified	Rarity
North West Frontier 1908[1]	5	Of the Utmost Rarity

Majors: ~ (Bvt) A W F Baird[1] DAAG, MFF
Captains: ~ W W McGregor[1]
Lieutenants: ~ K H Bruce[1] & L Gordon[1]
Quartermaster Sergeants/Sergeants: ~ 5796 R Stewart[1] attch. ITD

~ 1st Bn, The Princess Louise's (Argyll & Sutherland Highlanders) ~

Note a.   Roll of all personnel identified as eligible.
Note b.   Recipient attached 1 Seaforth Highlanders.
Note c.   Medals named in running script, believed: 'A.&S.Highrs.'

Single Clasp	No. Identified	Rarity
North West Frontier 1908[1]	1	According to the roll as seen, can be considered Unique

Captains: ~ J Campbell[1]

~ 2nd Bn, The Prince of Wales's Leinster Regiment (Royal Canadians) ~

Note a.   Roll of all personnel identified as eligible.
Note b.   Recipients served as Orderlies attached 'C' Section, No. 13 British Field Hospital (BFH), Royal Army Medical Corps (RAMC), unless shown otherwise.
Note c.   Medals named in running script, believed: '2nd Bn Leinster R.'

Single Clasp	No. Identified	Rarity
North West Frontier 1908[1]	4	Of the Utmost Rarity

Captains: ~ H T Moffett[1] PM, 2 Bde., MFF
Quartermaster Sergeants/Sergeants: ~ 4417 A Hughes[1]
Lance Corporals/Privates: ~ 6560 W Conway[1] & 7663 E Morrison[1]

~ 1st Bn, The Royal Munster Fusiliers ~

Note a.   *Roll of all commissioned personnel identified as eligible;*

Note b.   *Non-commissioned and other rank personnel multi-clasp only.*

Note c.   *Battalion to Gallipoli April 1915. Many personnel entitled to the clasp 'North West Frontier 1908' would have been deployed during World War One and large numbers would have been casualties.*

Note d.   *Medals named in running script: '1st Rl. M. Fus.'*

Single Clasp	No. Identified	Rarity
North West Frontier 1908[1]	Bn. Strength	Not Rare

Combination Clasps	No. Identified	Rarity
North West Frontier 1908[1] Afghanistan N.W.F. 1919[3]	1	According to the roll as seen, can be considered Unique
North West Frontier 1908[1] Burma 1931 – 32[10]	1	According to the roll as seen, can be considered Unique

Lieutenant Colonels: ~ B St. J le Marchant[1]

Majors: ~ A E O Congdon[1], J K O'Meagher[1] & H E Tizard[1]

Captains: ~ A M Bent[1], A Gorman[1] 'A' Coy & W A Hutchinson[1] 'F' Coy

Lieutenants: ~ C F Aspinall[1], R G Bacon[1], (QM) R T Baxter[1], H E R R Braine[1&10 (Brig. Gen.)] 'G' Coy, H C H O'Brien[1] 'Tpt Officer', J W Considine[1] 'MG Officer', C J S le Cornu[1] 'E' Coy, C D Frost[1] 'B' Coy, G Ireland[1], C H Landey[1], J Latham[1] 'A' Coy, T F O'Malley[1] 'D' Coy, D Pott[1] 'C' Coy & H B T Rye[1]

Lance Corporals/Privates: ~ 6215 J Costello[1&3(Gnr. RGA)]

~ 2nd Bn, The Prince Consort's Own (Rifle Brigade) ~

Note a.   *Roll of all personnel identified as eligible.*

Note b.   *Recipient attached the Corps of Military Staff Clerks (CMSC) as Head Clerk to the Principle Medical Officer (PMO), Mohmand Field Force (MFF).*

Note c.   *Medals named in running script, believed: '2nd Bn Rif. Bde.' or '2nd Bn Rifle Bde.'*

Single Clasp	No. Identified	Rarity
North West Frontier 1908[1]	1	According to the roll as seen, can be considered Unique

Lance Corporals/Riflemen: ~ 8374 H Arnot[1]

THE CORPS:

~ The Army Service Corps ~

Note a.   *Roll of all personnel identified as eligible.*

Note b.   *Medals named in running script: A.S.C.'*

Single Clasp	No. Identified	Rarity
North West Frontier 1908[1]	4	Of the Utmost Rarity

Majors: ~ M R de B James[1] attch. S&TC as BSO, BVFF & MFF

Captains: ~ N G Anderson[1] attch. S&TC as LofC Supply Officer BVFF, H A Douglas[1] attch. S&TC & W A M Welwood[1] Cmdt, 20 MC

~ The Royal Army Medical Corps ~
Units Identified As Being Entitled:
1, 7, & 13 British Field Hospitals
Medical Officers Attached Field Units

Note a. *Roll of all personnel identified as eligible.*
Note b. *Medals named in running script: 'R.A.M.C.'*

Single Clasp	No. Identified	Rarity
North West Frontier 1908[1]	23	Very Rare

Lieutenant Colonels: ~ M W Kerin[1] SMO, BVF, O R A Julian[1] & F H Treherne[1] OC, No. 13 BFH

Majors: ~ E S Clark[1] OC, 'C' & 'D' Sect, No. 1 BFH, MFF, H N Dunn[1] OC, 'A' & 'B' Sect, No. 1 BFH, N Faichnie[1] OC, 'A' & 'B' Sect, No. 7 BFH, F McDowell[1] & F Smith[1] Sanitary Officer, MFF

Captains: ~ C A J A Balck[1] 'A' & 'B' Sect, No. 7 BFH, J G Bell[1] 'C' & 'D' Sect, No. 13 BFH, ? ? Sylvester-Bradley[1], R J Cahill[1] MO, 1 R Warwick, A Chopping[1], A W Gaiter[1] MO, 1 Seaforth, C W O'Brien[1] 'C' & 'D' Sect, No. 1 BFH, BVFF, S B Smith[1] 'A' & 'B' Sect, No. 13 BFH & J A Turnbull[1] 'C' & 'D' Sect, No. 1 BFH

Lieutenants: ~ W Benson[1] MO, 1 West Yorkshire, G de la Cour[1] 'A' & 'B' Sect, No. 1 BFH, C T Edmunds[1] 'C' & 'D' Sections, 1 BFH, D de O'Grady[1] MO, 59th & 57th Rifles, IA, V G Johnson[1] MO, 1 Seaforth & M B H Ritchie[1] MO, 1 R Munster Fus

~ The Army Ordnance Corps ~

Note a. *Roll of all personnel identified as eligible.*
Note b. *Medals named in running script: 'A.O.C.'*

Single Clasp	No. Identified	Rarity
North West Frontier 1908[1]	6	Of the Utmost Rarity

Company Quartermaster Sergeants/Staff Sergeants: ~ (Armt) 844 J Arnold[1] attch. 1 Seaforth, (Armt) 390 F J Battle[1] attch. 18 Bty, RFA, (Armt) 1025 W Benham[1] attch. 1 NF, (Armt) 1030 F Ingram[1] attch. 1 R Munster Fus & (Armt) 912 T McNeill[1] attch. 1 R Warwick

Quartermaster Sergeants/Sergeants: ~ (Armt) 433 P Heaton[1] attch. 80 Bty, RFA

~ The Army Veterinary Corps ~

Note a. *Roll of all personnel identified as eligible.*
Note b. *Medals named in running script: 'A.V.C.'*

Single Clasp	No. Identified	Rarity
North West Frontier 1908[1]	2	Of the Utmost Rarity

Majors: ~ A England[1] SVO, MFF
Lieutenants: ~ A J Thompson[1] SVO, BVF

MISCELLANEOUS:

~ The Corps of Military Staff Clerks~

Note a.   *Roll of all personnel identified as eligible.*
Note b.   *Recipient served on the staff of Headquarters (HQ), 1 Brigade (1 Bde.), Mohmand Field Force (MFF).*
Note c.   *It is unclear whether the Corps of Military Staff Clerks (CMSC) were British or Indian Establishment and for that reason I have included the following personnel in the 'miscellaneous' section of the roll. It is important to note that the Indian Corps of Clerks (ICC) was not formed until 1924 (The Indian Army Corps of Clerks (IACC) from 1934).*
Note d.   *Medals named running script: 'C.M.S.C.'*

Single Clasp	No. Identified	Rarity
North West Frontier 1908[1]	1	According to the roll as seen, can be considered Unique

Sergeants: ~ ??? P Prentice[1]

INDIAN ESTABLISHMENT

Qualifying Units Present (Officers Plus Known Individuals)

The Cavalry:
Commanding Officer Or Single Representative

1st Duke of York's Own Lancers (Skinner's Horse) .... Capt. F F Innes-Lillington attch. S&TC (Only)
5th Cavalry..Capt. H N Holden (Only
7th Hariana Lancers. .... Capt. G G M Wheeler attch. S&TC (Only)
11th King Edward's Own Lancers (Proybyn's Horse)................ Maj. H Coape-Smith attch. 19th Lancers (Fane's Horse) (Only)
12th Cavalry ....Capt. S Muspratt, Intelligence Officer (Only)
13th Duke of Connaught's Lancers (Watson's Horse)...........................Lt. H I Boyd, Orderly Officer 3rd Brigade GOC (Only)
16th Cavalry ....Capt. G A Jamison attch. S&TC (Only)
19th Lancers .... (Fane's Horse) Bvt. Col. S F Biddulph
21st Prince Albert Victor's Own Cavalry (FF)... Bvt. Col. G B Unwin / Lt. Col. V B Fane
22nd Sam Browne's Cavalry (FF) .... Lt. Col. A R Dick Base Cmdt (Only)
23rd Cavalry (FF) ....Indian NCO & Other Rank Individuals
25th Cavalry (FF) ....Maj. H M Allen DAAG (Only)
30th Lancers (Gordon's Horse)..Capt. A R Barnard attch. S&TC (Only)
34th Prince Albert Victor's Own Poona Horse ....Capt. J L Lunham (Only) attch. 57th Rifles
35th Scinde Horse ....Lt. E H Lancaster attch. S&TC (Only)
37th Lancers (Baluch Horse).. Bvt. Col. H T Kenny
The Viceroy's Bodyguard ....Capt. H Napier Holden attch. 5th Cavalry, Provost Marshal 1st Brigade (Only)

The Frontier Garrison Artillery:
22 (Derajat) Mountain Battery FF, 23 (Peshawar) Mountain Battery FF, 28 (Indian) Mountain Battery

The Sappers & Miners:
1st Prince of Wales's Own Sappers & Miners
Nos. 1, 2 & 6 Field Companies Plus Cable & Telephone Section
2nd Queen's Own Sappers & Miners
No. 9 Field Company

Military Works Service

The Pioneers:
Commanding Officer or Single Representative

23rd Sikh Pioneers.. Bvt. Col. A F Hogge
31st Sikh Pioneers .... Maj. G B H Rice (Only)
34th Sikh Pioneers...Maj. G E L Gilbert

The Infantry:
Commanding Officer or Single Representative

Queen's Own Corps of Guides Infantry (Lumsden's) ....Col. G J Younghusband
7th Duke of Connaught's Own Rajputs .... Maj. G H Stewart LofC Transport Officer (Only)
8th Rajputs..Lt. H O B Hood attch. S&TC (Only)
19th Punjabis...Lt. Col. L N Herbert
20th Punjabis..Indian NCO & Other Rank Individuals
21st Punjabis .... Col. P M Carpendale
22nd Punjabis.. Lt. Col. C A Fowler
25th Punjabis ....Lt. Col. A Hamilton
26th Punjabis .... Capt. P S Stoney attch. 54th Sikhs (FF) & Lt. H T C Ivens attch. 54th Sikhs (FF) (2 Only)
28th Punjabis...Bvt. Col. W E Phillips
33rd Punjabis ....Indian NCO & Other Rank Individuals
38th Dogras.....................Capt. M G D Rowlandson attch. 54th Sikhs (FF) & Lt. R E Barrow L of C Signals Officer (2 Only)
40th Pathans ....Lt. Col. G R Crawford
45th Rattray's Sikhs. .... Lt. Col. L C Fryer
47th Sikhs...Capt. C G Ames attch. 57th Wilde's Rifles (FF) (Only)
53rd Sikhs (FF)..Bvt. Col. C J Melliss
54th Sikhs (FF).. Lt. Col. K J Buchanan
55th Coke's Rifles (FF)...Col. C A Nicholls
56th Punjabi Rifles (FF) ....Capt. H A Bickford attch. Khyber Rifles & Capt. G R Trotter DAQMG (Only)
57th Wilde's Rifles (FF) .... Maj. F W B Gray
58th Vaughan's Rifles (Frontier Force)...................................... Capt. R F Findlay attch. 57th Wilde's Rifles (FF) (Only)
59th Scinde Rifles (FF)..Bvt. Col. E W Cunliffe / Lt. Col. R A Curruthers
67th Punjabis ....Lt. M C Cribbon attch. 28th Punjabis PlusLts. W Young & T Luck attch. 54th Sikhs (FF) (3 Only)
82nd Punjabis................ Capt. C T Morris , Lts. G F Archibald, L Reilly & W Rowlandson all attch. 57th Rifles (FF) (4 Only)
84th Punjabis...Lt. J J Hodgson attch. 59th Scinde Rifles (FF) Only
86th Carnatic Infantry..Lt. L A M Jones attch. S&TC (Only)
124th Duchess of Connaught's Own Baluchistan Infantry ....Capt. A L Tarver DAAG, 1st Brigade (Only)
127th Baluch Light Infantry..Capt. P H Dyke attch. S&TC (Only)
1/1st Prince of Wales's Own Gurkha Rifles, (The Malaun Regt.)
1/4th Gurkha Rifles
1/5th Gurkha Rifles (FF)...Capt. H J P Brown (Only) (Provost Marshal)
2/5th Gurkha Rifles (FF)...Lt. Col. J M Stewart
1/6th Gurkha Rifles
2/6th Gurkha Rifles......................Lts. S W Beeman, H M M Hackett, J W B Harte & B C Sparrow attch. 2/5th GR (4 Only)

Militia & Volunteers:
Khyber Rifles, Kurram Militia,
Baluchistan Rifle Volunteers AFI & 24th North West Railway Volunteers, AFI

Indian Corps:
The Supply & Transport Corps: (Including British Officers & NCO's)
Camel Corps
50th Silladar & 51st Government Camel Corps
Mule Corps
1st, 6th, 7th, 8th, 16th, 19th (Cadre), 20th (Cadre), 28th & 29th

The Indian Subordinate Medical Department / The Indian Medical Service
The Army Hospital Corps / The Army Bearer Corps:
101st, 102nd, 103rd, 105th, 112th & 113th Native Field Hospitals

The Indian Army Veterinary Corps:

The Indian Unattached List: (Including British Officers & NCO's)

The Judicary:
Frontier Constabulary & Jail Department

The Telegraph Department:

The Postal Department:

Postmaster K A Appleby

The Indian Ecclesiastical Department:
Rev. C H Looman, RC, Rev. J H McNeill, Rev. C Stewart

The Political & Civil Departments:
Lt. Col. G O Roos-Keppel .... Chief Political Officer BVFF, Political Agent Khyber & Cmdt. Khyber Rifles
Maj. B D Blakeway .... Chief Political Officer
Capt. W J Keen .... Political Officer - Mohmand Border
Mr. E G Gregson .... Political Officer – 1st Brigade
Mr. E B Howell .... Asst. Political Agent Khyber
Mr. J L Maffrey .... Political Officer – 2nd Brigade
Dr. F W De Penning .... Agency Surgeon Khyber

Selected Supernumary Staff

The Media:
Mr. L James, *'The Times'*, Mr. H Newman, *'Reuters'*

(This list may not be exhaustive as some Indian Army supplementary rolls may now be missing)

2. ABOR EXPEDITION
1911–1912

~ India General Service Medal 1908–1935 ~
ABOR 1911–12
Issue 2: Calcutta Mint

The clasp 'ABOR 1911–12' was authorised by Army Order No. 308 of 1912 to reward (primarily) Indian Army troops and certain authorised civil personnel deployed under the command of Major General H. Bower during the Abor Expedition on the Indian North East Frontier. This was the second clasp awarded to the India General Service Medal 1908–1935 and the first to be approved during the reign of King George V. Enrolled camp followers and associated official native non-combatants received bronze medals and clasps.

To qualify for the 'ABOR 1911–12' clasp, personnel had to satisfy the following requirement:

- Served in the Abor Expedition in an official capacity, civil or military, going under the orders of Major General H. Bower, at or beyond the Kobo Base Camp between 6th October 1911 and 20th April 1912, both dates inclusive.

Due to the above criteria, not all mobilised units qualified. Those personnel employed in the concurrent 'civil' expeditions among the adjacent Miri and Mishmi peoples did not qualify.

*

The Abor region was located in the Himalayan Mountain Range of northeast Bengal and Assam. To the north lay Tibet and to the south, beyond the eastern bank of the Brahmaputra River, extended the lush tea producing regions of the Assam hinterland. The East India Company, and thus by default subsequently British India, had acquired much of this area in 1826 upon the conclusion of the First Burmese War. The terrain associated with this remote and, in 1911, largely unexplored area, was highly inhospitable. Successions of densely forested mountain ranges gradually rose higher and higher to form a natural snow-capped frontier landscape. Constantly drenched by some of the most torrential rainfall in the world, deep, impenetrable gorges crisscrossed the mountain slopes from which the headwaters of the mighty Brahmaputra emanated.

Between 1826 and 1911, several officially sanctioned punitive expeditions were conducted against the Abor in retaliation for raids against Assamese farmers and associated European economic interests.

In 1862, the Government of India determined that the hill tribes were not of a mind to succumb to its influences and, consequently, a semi-independent zone was established encompassing the land that lay between the Tibetan border and the rivers Brahmaputra/Lohit. The Bengal Eastern Frontier Regulations of 1873 established both a recognised administered territories boundary and an 'outer' Political Frontier. Further regulations published in May 1900 stated that the undertaking of any expedition beyond the 'inner' boundary required written permission from the Bengal and Assam Provincial Government. In instances where an expedition might cause conflict with either local peoples or adjacent foreign states, permission from the Government of India was required. These travel regulations were further ratified in January 1904.

Other than the regional capital of Sadiya, the principle settlements in northern Assam with a strong British influence in 1911 were Dibrugarh and Ledo. Each of these key locations was served by rail communications stretching back south into the Indian hinterland. The remotest village on the Dibang River officially in British administered territory was Pasighat. Vessels of the River Steamer & India General Inland Steamer Company could, over a period of two weeks, navigate the Brahmaputra from the coastal port of Calcutta north as far as Sadiya, with an intermediate stop at Dibrugarh. Government administration of the region was via Political Agents reporting to the Lieutenant Governor of East Bengal and Assam, Sir Lancelot Hare, based in Shillong. Also located at Shillong was the headquarters of the British Indian Army in the region. An infantry battalion was also maintained at Dibrugarh in conjunction with various widely dispersed posts manned by battalions of both the Lakhimpur and Naga Hills (native) Military Police.

The Abor people were divided into two different groups. The 'Bor' Abors resided between the Dihang and Dibang rivers, while the 'Dobah' Abors occupied the hills west of Sissin, along the ancient Tawang Tract trade route into Tibet. Further east, along the Lohit Valley, resided the Mishmi. To the west were the Miri. Of Mongolian descent, these tribes had little concept that they were considered to be subjects of an Imperial Power and consequently they held in great contempt what (little) local authority the Government of India could muster in the region. Tattooed extensively and with ears pierced by bamboo, the Abor were a fearsome looking people to western eyes. Warriors would wear little in the way of clothing beyond a rudimentary loincloth or *galae*. Bear skin sporrans served as knap sacks. The frequent use of opiates was widespread.

The Abor had an established military tradition and possessed a vast arsenal of spears, long straight swords (*dhaos*) and small bows, with deadly poison-tipped arrows. A few 'antique' firearms, usually of Chinese origin, complemented these armaments. Personal protection consisted of a bamboo helmet, simple bamboo shields and buffalo-hide shoulder yokes. Panj sticks were widely employed in trenches dug around stockades and settlements. Stone chutes were often deployed in ambush positions to seal off the escape route of any would-be attacker. Although principally defensive in nature, Abor field tactics also featured flanking charges. The Abor were organised on the basis of village fiefdoms run by an elected Gam. Feuds between villages were commonplace. This lack of mutual trust and co-operation was to hinder the tribesmen from mounting an effective resistance against the Abor Expeditionary Force.

*

In 1905, the Assistant Political Officer at Sadiya, Mr. Noel Williamson, argued that extensive exploration of the land beyond the administrative boundary should be undertaken. A desire to open up the area to further British development, including the expansion of tea cultivation and forestry exploitation, largely drove this notion. Lord Morley, Secretary of State for India, fiercely opposed this position and official permission for any such venture was withheld. Williamson, however, was determined to ignore this prohobition and during the 1907 and 1908 dry seasons, he ventured up the Lohit River as far as Rima in Mishmi territory. He subsequently mounted an expedition along the Dihang River, north from Sadiya to the Abor settlement at Kebang. The local tribesmen appeared to receive him in a favourable manner and Williamson's party received invitations to visit the area again on future occasions. Indeed Takat Gam, the headman at Kebang, invited him to penetrate the territory further when he next had an opportunity, suggesting the villages of Komsing and Riu as suitable and interesting destinations.

On 6th March 1911, the East Bengal and Assam Provincial Government sought permission from the Government of India to send Williamson on an 'official' expedition to ascertain the current extent of Chinese and Tibetan intrigue north of the 'inner' boundary. A secondary objective was to remind all Abor Gams that a 'poll tax' treaty signed with British India in 1863 was in default and should now be honoured. It was understood by the authorities that the expedition would not deploy from Sadiya until April, by which time provision would have been made to provide the participants with an armed escort of local military police.

Williamson was dismissive of the need for official protection and on 14th March 1911, he set out from Sadiya along the Dibang River accompanied by his friend Dr. Gregorson from Dibrugarh. The expedition details consisted of one native military police orderly, 35 Nepalese baggage coolies, commanded by Sirdar Lal Bahadur, two personal servants, and four Miri scouts. Not far from Kebang, several Abor warriors intercepted Williamson's small party. Takat Gam was now eager to discourage the planned visit to his village due to an outbreak of fever among his people. The meaning of this message was 'lost in translation' and Williamson assumed that the Abor were simply being unfriendly. The expedition thus determined to divert towards the village of Sissin where, on 22nd March, a base camp was

~ Coolies guard a rudimentary baggage cart, 1911 ~

established on the riverbank. At this time, several of the expedition coolies also began to display symptoms of a fever-like illness and consequently when, a week later, Williamson determined to press on towards Komsing to meet Madu Gam, Dr. Gregorson remained in situ to nurse the sick. Before departing Sissin, Williamson decided to send three runners back to Pasighat with a series of official despatches for onward transmission to the authorities in Sadiya.

During their trek back to Pasighat, the Gam of Rotung offered shelter to Williamson's messengers and their Miri scout. Unfortunately, the principle runner decided to mislead his hosts and told them that his satchel contained letters seeking the deployment of a punitive military expedition into Abor territory in revenge for Takat Gam having prevented 'Britain's Imperial Envoy' from visiting Kebang. The local council of Gams took this as a threat to the 'independence' of the Abor nation and murdered the four men forthwith. At Kebang, a war council of Gams was assembled quickly which voted to treat Williamson and his other companions in like fashion. A force of Kebang warriors thereupon went to Sissin, where they attacked Dr. Gregorson's makeshift hospital. (The only survivor was Lal Bahadur, who latter became principle scout to Major General H. Bower). The tribesmen then proceeded directly to Komsing, where Williamson met the same fate on, or about, 31st March 1911. (Some time later foresters working for the Meckla Nadi Saw Mill Company happened upon a handful of dazed and starving coolies, who subsequently claimed to be survivors of the Komsing massacre). Returning to Kebang, the Abor deposed Takat Gam and replaced him with the more aggressive Lomgah Gam.

*

When news of the atrocities committed at Komsing and Sissin reached Dibrugarh on 5th April 1911, the Deputy Commissioner of Lakhimpur, Mr. A.H.W. Bentinck, instructed Captain George Duff-Sutherland-Dunbar, 31st Punjabis, and Commandant of the Lakhimpur Military Police, to deploy a rifle company of his command to Pasighat. Captain A.M. Hutchins, 3rd GR, was ordered to command this expedition and was given strict instructions to gather local intelligence pertaining to Williamson. He was to remain at Pasighat until the conclusion of the monsoon season, at which juncture a full-scale punitive expedition would be mounted. Meanwhile, a Mr. W.C.M. Dundas was appointed to replace Williamson at Sadiya as Assistant Political Officer.

The Indian High Command shortly thereafter instructed the 8th (Lucknow) Division to mobilise the 23rd Infantry Brigade, Major General H. Bower, with a view to mounting a full-scale punitive expedition against the Abor. Initial plans and expenditures for the operation were outlined in Indian Government Paper No.19 of 1911. The total cost was estimated at £147,000. Major General Bower was an experienced frontier campaigner. He immediately recognised that maintaining the integrity of his Lines of Communication in jungle conditions, combined with a high standard of field engineering, would be essential considerations if the mission was to be a success. Although heavy supplies and troops could be deployed into the region by rail and/or river vessel, no direct access to a concentration point on the west bank of the Brahmaputra was possible. After much investigation, Captain O.H.B. Trenchard, RE, selected for development a forest glade known locally as Kobo. This site was located on the north bank of the river about 40 miles upstream from Dibrugarh. The nearest native village to the location was the Miri settlement at Poba.

Once the location of the base camp was announced, the task of concentrating the expedition's resources began in earnest. A military presence in the region was now needed and several trains of the Assam-Bengal Railway Company were employed to deploy the balance of the Lakhimpur and Naga Hills Military Police to Dibrugarh.

ABOR EXPEDITIONARY FORCE STAFF, OCTOBER 1911

23rd (Assam) Brigade – Maj. Gen. H Bower

Capt. H S Becher, 2nd Gurkha Rifles..Provost Marshal
Capt. R L Bignell, 41st Dogras...Treasure Chest Officer
Maj. J Davidson, Indian Medical Service..Assistant Director of Medical Services
Lt. J H Knight, Royal Engineers...Brigade Signals Officer
Capt. W B Hore, 120th Rajputana Infantry..Intelligence Officer
Maj. C A R Hutchinson, 41st Dogras...General Staff Officer 2
Temp. Brig. Gen. D C MacIntyre, IA.........................Base Commander Kobo & Inspector Lines of Communication
Capt. C W F Melville, 9th Hodson's Horse, IA..Staff Surgeon
Capt. L H S Smithers, 17th Infantry (The Loyal Regiment)....................................Orderly Officer & Brigade Major
Capt. O H B Trenchard, Royal Engineers...Survey Officer
Maj. E G Vaughan, Supply & Transport Corps...Brigade Supply Officer
Lt. A B Hay Webb, 5th Gurkha Rifles (Frontier Force)..Water Transport Officer

Meanwhile, in Calcutta, the Provincial Government chartered several river steamers and arranged for all available officers currently on leave to return to their regiments. Initially, only regular army units were to be engaged in the expedition but, after much debate and a petition from the Dibrugarh Tea Planters Association, Major General H. Bower agreed to permit a token presence from the locally raised Assam Valley Light Horse, AFI, to support the regular force. After much deliberation, Captain C L Lovell of the Nokhroy Tea Estate, and a 12-man Vickers Maxim Gun party, were selected for deployment. (The Adjutant of the AVLI, Captain J.R. Hutchison, 38th King George's Own Central India Horse, IA, was additionally employed on detached duties).

At Kobo, the base camp commandant, Colonel D.C.F. Macintyre, S&TC, assigned the Sappers and Pioneers the task of levelling a 600 square yard area of virgin forest. Several elephant teams assisted the troops in their labours by moving heavy materials including uprooted trees and other obstacles. The camp was to be a semi-permanent structure with stockade, watchtowers and a 20-foot deep fresh water well. Landing stages capable of accommodating river steamers and flat barges were constructed and provision was made for the establishment of telephone contact with Dibrugarh.

SHIPPING MOVEMENTS, AUGUST 1911

S.S. Mirani Surg. Capt. C W F Melville, 9th Hodson's Horse 140 all ranks, 'A' Section, 168th Indian Field Ambulance and Hospital Corps. Maj. E C Tylden-Patterson, Royal Engineers No. 1 Coy, 1st King George's Own Bombay Sappers & Miners plus 50 mules
S.S. Battani Maj. E H S Cullen, 32nd Sikh Pioneers 32nd Sikh Pioneers plus 63 mules
S.S. Sherani Col. J Fisher, 1/2nd Gurkha Rifles 1/2nd Gurkha Rifles and 31 Signal Company, Indian Signal Service, Sappers & Miners
S.S. Scinde Naga Carrier Corps from Kokilamukh
S.S. Pagan General Stores and Equipment

On the morning of 7th October 1911, Major General H. Bower and his Staff occupied their new headquarters at Kobo following a delayed voyage up river from Dibrugarh aboard the S.S. *Battani*. Soon thereafter, the remaining units and detached officers arrived on site enabling a period of intensive training in jungle warfare to begin. The mortars were test fired along with two smooth bore 7lb field guns (Castor and Pollux). Of great necessity was the creation, under the direction of Colonel A.E. Woods, Deputy Commissioner Nagar Hills, of an extensive coolie corps for carrying baggage and other supplies. The coolies, recruited from the Nagar and Manipur Hills regions, were no friends of the Abor and, on more than one occasion, they petitioned their officers for the opportunity to be delegated the task of undertaking the force's mission alone, rather than wasting the time of the British.

*

It was determined that the main thrust into Abor territory would be via Pasighat. A detached column would operate simultaneously in order to protect the main force's western flank. This column would advance across country to the River Pobe at Oniyuk and then move upstream to Ledlum. The two columns would eventually converge deep in Abor territory, whereupon the principle Abor Gams responsible for plotting the murders of Williamson and Gregorson, along with their respective settlements, would be subjected to punitive retribution. Thereafter, the plan of campaign was to allow the remaining Abor villages a measure of clemency and to offer them the opportunity to become loyal subjects of the Crown. Upon the conclusion of field operations, survey work was to begin which would include the establishment of a clearly demarcated frontier between British India and adjacent states. Anthropological, botanical and zoological studies were also to be undertaken and, to that end, several scientific observers accompanied the force.

~ Troopers of the Assam Valley Light Horse, Dibrugarh Camp, 1911 ~

Within 48 hours of Major General H. Bower arriving in Kobo, Major A.B. Lindsay, 1/2nd GR, was despatched on a 'path cutting' reconnaissance towards Ledlum. The patrol consisted of two rifle companies 1/2nd GR, one field company 1 KGO Sappers and Miners, one company 32nd Pioneers, 300 coolies and three elephants. A signals section under Lieutenant J.H. Knight, RA (attch. S&M), was also deployed. Initially, the going was straightforward with flat open country and an established well-worn native track to follow. After a few miles, however, the jungle foliage grew dense and almost impenetrable, requiring the use of machetes to hack a way through. Recent torrential rain had flooded vast tracts of land forcing the men to wade waist deep through serpent-infested swamps. Arriving at Oniyuk, it was quickly found that the route up the River Pobe would be impossible to navigate without specialist equipment and that an alternative solution was required. Consequently, the patrol retraced its steps, returning to Kobo on 18th October 1911.

ASSAM VALLEY LIGHT HORSE VICKERS MAXIM GUN DETACHMENT
ABOR EXPEDITIONARY FORCE 1911–1912

Captains: (Surgeon) J M Falkener (Detached) & C L Lovell
Squadron Sergeant Majors: Webster
Sergeants: Davies
Corporals: Ashe
Troopers: Falconer, Floyer, Hardwicke, Henning, Kilgour, Lemon, Middleton, Southon & Whitten
Captain J R Hutchinson, 38th Central India Horse, Adjutant AVLI (Detached)

*

The Ledlum Column deployed from Kobo on 20th October 1911. The force, commanded by Lieutenant Colonel J Fisher, 1/2nd GR, consisted of Mr. J.E. Scott, Assistant Political Officer, two rifle companies 1/2nd GR, one company 32nd Sikh Pioneers, 300 men of the Lakhimpur Military Police, a section from 168th Indian Field Hospital, with Surgeon Captain J.M. Falkner, AFI, in attendance. Fourteen elephants and a Naga Hills coolie corps accompanied the column. Retracing the steps of the earlier reconnaissance patrol, the column quickly advanced as far as Oniyuk. Here a timber stockade was constructed and a section of military police posted as an ongoing deterrent. The following day the troops advanced to Manning via Dora. A forward operating camp was established at Making during the early evening of the third day. Early the following day an Abor ambush was sprung while the troops navigated a narrow track. The attack was fought off successfully, despite the efforts of several enemy archers who released score upon score of poisoned arrows.

Ledlum was occupied on 24th October 1911, whereupon scouts were despatched to local villages requesting all Abor Gams to attend upon Lieutenant Colonel J. Fisher, 1/2nd GR, with a view to negotiating terms of submission. Patrols securing in-depth the Ledlum area advanced towards Mishing on 27th October. Movement in Abor territory was slow and laborious due to the frequency of enemy booby traps and the need to circumnavigate potential ambush positions. One such encounter by a platoon of the 1/2nd GR on the first day of patrolling left two Abor dead and at least three wounded.

The Ledlum Column advanced to Mishing on 2nd November 1911, where once again patrolling in depth occurred. Enemy barricades and stone chutes were located at almost every turn of the jungle trail. The Abor abandoned the majority of defensive stockades long before the Gurkhas arrived. At Dorsing, however, they put up a stout resistance before being overrun by the advancing troops. The destruction of Dorsing was followed up on 9th November with the torching of Kaking and Kharan. During this latter incident, a Naga Hills coolie was killed in action.

Over the following two weeks, Lieutenant Colonel J. Fisher, 1/2nd GR, succeeded in negotiating mutually acceptable terms with the local Gams. Accordingly, on 25th November 1911, he was in a position to offer his column to Major General H. Bower for redeployment. Consequently, the Ledlum Column was transferred to the orbit of the Main Column. Military Police details remained at Mishing and Balek while two rifle companies of the 1/2nd GR and the 32nd Sikh Pioneers were detached in support of the Lines of Communication. The balance of the force made its way to Rotung, where it rendezvoused with the Main Column on 2nd December.

ORBIT, GURKHA RIFLES OFFICERS MESS
ABOR EXPEDIONARY FORCE 1911–1912

1/2nd King Edward's Own Gurkha Rifles (The Sirmoor Rifles) Lieutenant Colonels: J Fisher Majors: A B Lindsay & E H Sweet Captains: H S Becher Provo Marshal, Staff & N C Nicolay Lieutenants: A J H Chope, H F F Marsh, G M McCleverty & A H R Saunders
3rd Queen Alexandra's Own Gurkha Rifles Captains: A M Hutchins
5th Gurkha Rifles (FF) Captains: A M Graham Lieutenants: A B Hay Webb
1/8th Gurkha Rifles Lieutenant Colonels: F Murray Majors: J A Wilson Captains: J F S D Coleridge, D H R Gifford, A L M Molesworth & D S Orchard Lieutenants: ~ G C B Buckland, H R Harington, H Kennedy, M A C Kennedy, H R C Meade & E J Ross

ORBIT, 41st DOGRAS OFFICERS MESS
ABOR EXPEDITIONARY FORCE 1911–1912

Majors: C A R Hutchinson Captains: R L Bignell Lieutenants: E Perry, W Pope, W Rogers, R P Searle & J W Smith

*

The Main Column deployed from Kobo early on 22nd October 1911. The force, commanded directly by Major General H. Bower, was divided into two divisions. Division One, commanded by Lieutenant Colonel F. Murray, 1/8th GR, consisted of five rifle companies 1/8th GR, two companies 32nd Sikh Pioneers, half a field company 1 King George's Own Sappers and Miners, one section 168th Indian Field Hospital, a detachment Telegraph Department, one coolie corps, six elephants and the Assam Brigade Headquarters Staff. Division Two, commanded by Lieutenant Colonel H. Peterson, 32nd Sikh Pioneers, was composed of four companies 32nd Sikh Pioneers, four rifle companies 1/8th GR, half a field company 1 King George's Own Sappers and Miners, a detachment 31 Signals Company, Sappers and Miners, the AVLH maxim gun section, and a coolie corps. Several detachments of the 1/2nd GR and 32nd Sikh Pioneers remained at Kobo under the command of Major H.M.M. Brooke, S&TC.

~ Ghurka riflemen rest after encounter with the enemy ~

ORBIT, SUPPLY & TRANSPORT CORPS
ABOR EXPEDITIONARY FORCE 1911–1912

Majors: E G Vaughan & H M M Brooke
Captains: G W Bond, C Edward Collins, W B Dunlop,
O Greoghegan, C W Hext, H Hail, H Price, M Synge, T Timbrell & C Wildes
Conductors: E Bray, C W Hayman, A Seecombe, C Williams & R Wright
Sub Conductors: ~ H Alexander, E Adams, J Ballin,
W Dacies (attch. Telegraph Dept), P Mason & A Tyler
Deputy Commissary: H W Wilsey
Assistant Commissary: J Foy
Staff Sergeants: A Clegg, J Connaughton, E Cork, E Costello, A Develin,
C J Foinette, C Mackay, F Mitton, T Murray, E Orriss, G King, W Little, J Lynch

Major J.A. Wilson, 1/8th GR, with two rifle companies of his battalion, had been sent out from Kobo the previous day, with a view to securing a campsite for the Main Column on the bank of the Kemi River. This location became known as 6 Mile Camp. From this site, the Main Column advanced, by division, to Pilong and thence across the Mora Lalli River to Lokhpur. Thick jungle, heavy monsoon and jagged outcrops of rock challenged the column every yard of the way. During this section of the march, a falling tree invalided Conductor C. Williams, S&TC. Shortly thereafter, a sepoy of the 32nd Sikh Pioneers became the victim of an accidental shooting. On the 25th October 1911, the column arrived in Pasighat, whereupon contact was made with the Military Police detachment that had been despatched there by river steamer seven months previously. The Military Police were fully expecting the force, having been advised of its imminent arrival by Lieutenant A.B. Hay Webb, 5th GR, who had arrived by water ahead of time direct from Kobo with 46 supply canoes.

The following day, an attempt was made to cut a path up the Dihang towards Jonakmukh. This process took several days, but once achieved the column deployed upstream and established picquets on three high peaks affording views all the way to China, Tibet and back into Assam. Officers were advised that the next objective was to be the capture of Old Rengging, but it soon became apparent that the route in that direction would necessitate significant engineering works. Progress was slowed by the need to advance in skirmish order, with the infantry securing every yard of jungle before the sappers could deploy in support. Eventually the jungle opened out into a series of lightly wooded hills, each of which showed signs of recent cultivation. A forward operating camp was established at Rammi Dambang and patrols were despatched to secure intelligence pertaining to the route ahead.

On 6th November 1911, the column advanced as far as the southern bank of the Dihang tributary known as the Sirpo River. Patrols deployed to confirm the exact location of Old Rengging and secure the surrounding area. One of these formations subsequently captured and then destroyed the principle objective, while a second formation recovered several of Williamson's personal possessions lying abandoned beside a well-trodden path. Reconnaissance observations made from the surrounding hills enabled Major General H. Bower to gain a visual picture of his next objective – the Abor stronghold of Pongging.

By 9th November 1911, the Main Column had established a fortified position on the site of Old Rengging. A makeshift timber stockade was constructed and a platoon of Military Police detailed to provide a garrison. Heavy rains held up further advances towards Pongging, although local patrolling continued. One such patrol had the misfortune to discover the badly dismembered remains of Williamson's three despatch runners and their Miri scout. Physical contact with the enemy was minimal, although it was apparent that the Abor were constantly observing the troops from a safe distance. A weakly defended Telegraph Department work detail was attacked on 12th November with a loss of two coolies killed.

ORBIT, 32nd SIKH PIONEERS OFFICERS MESS
ABOR EXPEDIONARY FORCE 1911–1912

Lieutenant Colonels: H Peterson
Majors: E H S Cullen
Captains: G C Hodgson & H S Mitchell
Lieutenants:
(QM) H W Andrews, A T G Beckham, B Christie, Hon M de Courcy,
C T Daly, I Burn Murdoch, W M Ommaney & N S Taylor

Major General H. Bower received an important signal from Mr. W.T. Ballantine, Assistant Political Officer Sadiya, on 13th November 1911. The message informed the General that Mr. W.C.M. Dundas had been recalled from his travels in the Mishmi region to receive in *jirga* three leading Padam Abor Gams, who had come down to Sadiya from Damro to present a peace proposal to the British authorities. The natives had apparently agreed to provide labour for road construction gangs and to begin paying their poll tax liability. Mr. Dundas subsequently ratified this treaty in person following a treacherous canoe journey from Sadiya up stream to Major General Bower's field headquarters.

Three rifle companies of the 1/8th GR explored the route along the Lelek River towards Rotung on 17th November 1911. While the men crossed a makeshift bridge, an Abor ambush was sprung. Arrows rained down from the cover of the far bank. Most of the projectiles fell harmlessly into the rushing water, but one lodged itself in the thigh of Captain J.R. Hutchison, 38th King George's Own Central India Horse, IA, delivering a potentially lethal dose of poison into the officer's bloodstream. Captain

Hutchinson was invalided back to Dibrugarh for medical treatment and narrowly avoided dying from the effects of septic shock.

Despite this incident, the Main Column pressed on towards Rotung, fording first the River Lelek and then the River Egar, where upon a camp was established on the afternoon of 19th November 1911. When reconnaissance patrols reported the presence of a formidable Abor stockade blocking the path ahead, Major General H. Bower determined that he would view the obstruction himself. Taking 20 riflemen of the 1/8th GR, under Lieutenant G.C.B. Buckland, Major General Bower retraced the steps of his earlier reconnaissance party. This was not a good ploy, for soon thereafter an Abor war party attacked the patrol. Lal Bahadur, survivor of the massacre at Sissin, fell mortally wounded in the chest. A poisoned arrow grazed General Bower's hand but failed to infect him. The use of rock chutes by the Abor prevented the patrol from fighting through the ambush. Consequently, a decision was taken to bring up additional resources and take the assault to the enemy by deploying a flanking manoeuvre against the stockade itself. Riflemen commanded by Lts. G.C.B. Buckland and H. Kennedy executed the attack and carried the obstacle after a sharp firefight. Eighteen Abor corpses were subsequently recovered from the site. The smouldering remains of Rotung were occupied early the following morning.

At Rotung the force halted with a view to replenishing supplies and securing the Lines of Communication back to Old Rengging. Clothing and general equipment required a new issue for all concerned. Hostile jungle vegetation, combined with a constantly damp and humid climate, had reduced most uniforms to rags. Enemy interference with the supply lines was a constant irritancy and frequent contacts were made during ongoing reconnaissance activities resulting in further loses for the Abor. On 29th November 1911, a dishevelled, emaciated looking coolie, claiming to be the personal servant of Dr. Gregorson and a survivor of the Sissin massacre, hailed a Gurkha patrol. The man had suffered many hardships but had somehow managed to survive in the jungle for some eight months. Although extremely frightened, the malnourished coolie managed to provide substantial intelligence including information about a key Abor stronghold located at Kekar Mann Ying, a large rocky feature on the right bank of the Dihang.

ORBIT, INDIAN MEDICAL SERVICE
ABOR EXPEDITIONARY FORCE 1911–1912

| Majors: J Davidson Asst. Director, Medical Services & MO 2nd GR |
| Captains: H B Drake, MO 32nd Sikh Pioneers, T J C Evans, |
| W H Hamilton, J S O'Neill, A T Pridham, MO 8th GR, G C Seymour & F H Stewart |
| Lieutenants: R L Gamlen & J Foy |

Major General H Bower immediately despatched a force under Lieutenant Colonel F. Murray, 1/8th GR, with a view to verifying the intelligence pertaining to Kekar Mann Ying. Advancing via Kalek, the Gurkhas encountered little opposition and a full appreciation of the objective was achieved without loss. Upon returning to Rotung, it was determined that, in order to secure an effective attack, one assault group would be required to first cross to the opposite bank of the Dihang River. This would be a difficult exercise due to the swift, rapid-infested water, some 170 yards wide at its narrowest point.

It took the Sappers and Miners three days to secure a cable from the left bank of the Dihang to the right bank, thus enabling a small force to be pulled across the torrent under cover of darkness and establish a presence on the opposite bank. Their objective was a feature known as Sissin Hill, from where the AVLH Vickers Maxim-Gun detachment would be able to have an unobstructed view of Kekkar Man Ying. Unfortunately, several of the enemy observed the river crossing manoeuvre and, shortly after the party had landed, the Abor launched a determined assault. In the subsequent confusion, two riflemen of 1/2nd GR were killed and several others wounded.

At dawn on 4th December 1911, a heavy mist carpeted the intended line of advance toward Kekar Man Ying. This natural cover enabled Captain D.H.R. Gifford, 1/8th GR, to deploy three rifle companies unobserved into a position on the left flank. Advancing soon thereafter, the main party became exposed to view as the mist lifted. Major General H. Bower quickly brought his field guns and machine guns into action with a view to covering the advance. The going was very tough. Some 50 rock chutes were encountered along a path that in places was only barely 18 inches wide. Nevertheless, by the time the troops had reached the summit of their objective, the Abor had fled leaving behind over 30 dead and dying. Four rifle companies of 1/8th GR immediately pressed on towards Babuk, killing several additional Abor en-route. Meanwhile, the right flank party was ordered to destroy Sissin village before returning to the Main Column.

A general advance was then made along the Dihang River as far as its confluence with the Side River. Here a camp was established for the night of 5th December 1911, prior to a further three-mile trek to Puak. It was estimated that this location was situated halfway between Rotung and the primary expedition objective of Kebang village. Several Abor attacks were repulsed over the following days without loss to the force. Patrols were sent out reconnoitre the route to Kebang and a plan devised to secure this objective. The plan called for Lieutenant Colonel F. Murray, 1/8th GR, to lead a flanking movement to secure the high ground overlooking the village thus enabling Major General H. Bower to launch a frontal assault against the objective. No Abor resistance was encountered and Kebang was torched without loss.

The force then advanced rapidly to the banks of the Yambung River, from whence several reconnaissances were made of Komsing, Yemsing and several other key Abor settlements. Fighting patrols were thereupon despatched to destroy these locations. Most of the objectives were found to have been abandoned, but on 13th December 1911, Lieutenant Colonel F. Murray's party encountered some resistance at Yemsing, culminating in the death of four of the enemy. It was not until 17th December that Lieutenant W.C. Cave-Brown's boat section succeeded in effecting a suitable river crossing to enable patrols to operate in tandem to the main force on the opposite bank of the Dihang River.

The key objective on the right bank of the Dihang was the village of Panggi, which, when approached, immediately despatched peace envoys declaring their innocence regarding the Williamson affair. After much discussion with his Staff, Major General H. Bower determined that if constructive relations were to be achieved a degree of clemency should now be shown to the Abor. Consequently, Panggi avoided destruction on condition that the local Gam despatch envoys to all remaining Abor settlements instructing them to attend a *jirga* under Major General Bower with a view to demonstrating their loyalty to the Crown. The message clearly inferred that only those persons directly involved in the conspiracy to murder Williamson and Gregorson were to be punished.

These conditions were unwelcome and a number of Abor leaders, including the Gam of Jaru, tried to prevent their village councils from adopting any form of appeasement. On more than one occasion, this hardline attitude to the British cost the non-compliant Gam his life. Nevertheless, the majority of Abor did eventually give in, albeit it took the Gams of Kebang and Rotung significantly longer to do so than the others. Fines began to be paid from about 4th January 1912 onwards. A Political Officer recovered Williamson's pocket watch and sent it for onward transmission to his next-of-kin. This capitulation enabled the Abor Expeditionary Force to begin the second phase of its mission. While the survey parties were engaged in the field, Lieutenant Colonel F. Murray, 1/8th GR, led a patrol to Komsing where, following a short memorial service, a cairn commemorating Noel Williamson was unveiled on 10th January 1912. A similar event occurred a few days later near Sissin in respect of the late Dr. Gregorson.

*

The work of the survey teams culminated in 3,500 square miles of previously unexplored territory being committed to a series of maps on a scale of four inches to one mile. To achieve this feat, individual teams advanced beyond the heat of the jungle, far into the snow-capped mountains that lay along the Indo-Tibetan border. The varied flora and fauna were meticulously recorded and photographed. Upon the conclusion of the survey phase, the Abor Expeditionary Force retired in stages back to Kobo, where it was demobilised on 12th May 1912.

To prevent any further unrest in the region, it was determined that a permanent military and police presence should be established. The 538-strong volunteer Assam Valley Light Horse, based at Dibrugarh was further strengthened, while the local (native) Military Police formations were reorganised. These latter units were eventually formed into the Assam Rifles. Additionally, the North East Frontier Tract was reorganised into three subsections with a new, more focused structure of political officers.

BRITISH ARMY ROLL OF HONOUR THE ABOR EXPEDITION 1911–1912			
Date:	**Person:**	**Unit:**	**Type Of Casualty:**
3/12/1911	Capt. A M Hutchins	3rd QAO GR	Died of Pneumonia
8/12/1912	9156 Pte. P J McIntosh	1 HLI	Died

ABOR 1911–12² ROLL

BRITISH ESTABLISHMENT
THE ARMY

~ Staff Grade Officers ~

Note a.   *Only Officers of the British Army are listed. Those on the Indian Establishment are beyond the scope of this work and are thus excluded.*

Note b.   *Medals named in running script.*

None eligible

THE CAVALRY:

~ 1ˢᵗ King's Dragoon Guards ~

Note a.   *Roll of all personnel identified as eligible.*

Note b.   *Recipient attached Indian Telegraph Department (ITD).*

Note c.   *Medals named in running script, believed '1ˢᵗ Dragoon Gds.'*

Single Clasp	No. Identified	Rarity
Abor 1911–12²	1	According to the roll as seen, can be considered Unique

Lance Corporals/Privates: ~ 6205 E Henderson²

~ 17ᵗʰ (Duke of Cambridge's Own) Lancers ~

Note a.   *Roll of all personnel identified as eligible.*

Note b.   *Recipient attached Indian Telegraph Department (ITD).*

Note c.   *Medals named in running script, believed '17ᵗʰ Lancers.'*

Single Clasp	No. Identified	Rarity
Abor 1911–12²	1	According to the roll as seen, can be considered Unique

Lance Corporals/Privates: ~ 6254 F E Wright² .

THE ARTILLERY:

~ The Royal Field Artillery ~

Note a.   *Roll of all personnel identified as eligible.*

Note b.   *Recipients attached Indian Telegraph Department (ITD) unless shown otherwise.*

Note c.   *Medals named in running script, Battery details followed by ' R.F.A.' Officers may be simply 'R.A.'*

Single Clasp	No. Identified	Rarity
Abor 1911–12²	2	Of the Utmost Rarity

Combination Clasps	No. Identified	Rarity
North West Frontier 1908[1] Abor 1911–12[2]	1	According to the roll as seen, can be considered Unique

Lieutenants: ~ J H Knight[2] attch. 31 Signal Coy, S&M as OC
Gunners: ~ 35709 H Graham[1&2] 18 Bty, RFA & 22423 J Sidlow[2] 9 Bty, RFA

THE CORPS OF ROYAL ENGINEERS:

Sub Units Identified As Entitled:
1 King George's Own Sappers & Miners:
No. 1 Field Company & Detachment No. 5 Field Company
Indian Signals Service Sappers & Miners:
Detachment 31 Signals Company
Survey of India

Note a.   *Roll of all Royal Engineer personnel identified as eligible.*
Note b.   *Officers of the Indian Sappers & Miners held Royal Engineer commissions.*
Note c.   *Indian Army establishment not included on roll.*
Note d.   *Medals named in running script 'R.E.' followed by '(No 1 Co. 1ˢᵗ S&M)' (etc)*

Single Clasp	No. Identified	Rarity
Abor 1911–12[2]	10	Of the Utmost Rarity
Combination Clasps	**No. Identified**	**Rarity**
North West Frontier 1908[1] Abor 1911–12[2]	1	According to the roll as seen, can be considered Unique
North West Frontier 1908[1] Abor 1911–12[2] Afghanistan N.W.F. 1919[3]	1	According to the roll as seen, can be considered Unique
Abor 1911–12[2] Mahsud 1919–20[5] Waziristan 1919–21[4]	1	According to the roll as seen, can be considered Unique
Abor 1911–12[2] Waziristan 1921–24[6]	2	Of the Utmost Rarity

Majors: ~ E C Tylden-Patterson [1(Capt),2&3(Lt. Col.)] No. 1 Fld Coy, 1 KGO S&M
Captains: ~ C P Gunter[2] SofI & O H B Trenchard[2] OC SofI
Lieutenants: ~ E B le Breton[1&2] Det No. 5 Fld Coy, 1 KGO S&M, W C Cave-Brown[2] No. 1 Fld Coy, 1 KGO S&M, A F Charter[2] No. 1 Fld Coy, 1 KGO S&M, F S Collin[2] No. 1 Fld Coy, 1 KGO S&M, R Maxwell Everett[2&6(Maj. 3rd S&M)] SofI, J A Field[2] SofI, J F Gray[2] Det No. 5 Fld Coy, 1 KGO S&M, H T Morshead[2,4(Maj.)&5(Maj.)] SofI & G F T Oakes[2] SofI
Warrant Officers Class II: ~ (Act. CSM) 3155 J Eltham[2] No. 1 Fld Coy, 1 KGO S&M
Quartermaster Sergeants/Sergeants: ~ 3536 G Hay[2] No. 1 Fld Coy, 1 KGO S&M
Lance Sergeants/Corporals: ~ 12481 W E Coltham[2&6 (MES)] No. 1 Fld Coy, 1 KGO S&M

THE INFANTRY:

~ 2nd Bn, The King's (Liverpool Regiment) ~

Note a.   *Roll of all personnel identified as eligible.*
Note b.   *Medals named in running script, believed '2nd Bn L'Pool Regt.'*

Single Clasp	No. Identified	Rarity
Abor 1911–12[2]	2	Of the Utmost Rarity

Lance Corporals/Privates : ~ 10865 R Duffey[2] misc attch. & 8000 F Howard[2] attch. ITD

~ 2nd Bn, The East Yorkshire Regiment ~

Note a.   *Roll of all personnel identified as eligible.*
Note b.   *Recipient served as Official Press Correspondent, Abor Expeditionary Force (AEF).*
Note c.   *Medals named in running script '2nd Bn E. Y. Regt.'*

Single Clasp	No. Identified	Rarity
Abor 1911–12[2]	1	According to the roll as seen, can be considered Unique

Captains: ~ F G Poole[2]

~ 1st Bn, The Royal Irish Regiment ~

Note a.   *Roll of all personnel identified as eligible.*
Note b.   *Recipient attached Indian Telegraph Department (ITD).*
Note c.   *Medals named in running script '1st Bn Rl. Irish Regt.'*

Single Clasp	No. Identified	Rarity
North West Frontier 1908[1]	0	None Identified

Combination Clasps	No. Identified	Rarity
North West Frontier 1908[1] Abor 1911–12[2]	1	According to the roll as seen, can be considered Unique

Lance Corporals/Privates: ~ 9127 T E Fisher[1&2]

~ 1st Bn, The Prince of Wales's Volunteers (South Lancashire Regiment) ~

Note a.   *Roll of all personnel identified as eligible.*
Note b.   *Medals named in running script '1st Bn. S. Lan. Regt.'*

Single Clasp	No. Identified	Rarity
Abor 1911–12[2]	1	According to the roll as seen, can be considered Unique

Lance Corporals/Privates: ~ (17080) 6240 P S Mullarkey[2] misc attch.

~ 2nd Bn, The King's (Shropshire Light Infantry) ~
:

Note a. *Roll of all personnel identified as eligible.*
Note b. *Recipient attached Indian Telegraph Department (ITD).*
Note c. *Medals named in running script, believed '2nd Bn. K.S.L.I.'*

Single Clasp	No. Identified	Rarity
Abor 1911–12[2]	1	According to the roll as seen, can be considered Unique

Lance Corporals/Privates: ~ 8240 W H Baker[2]

~ 1st Bn, The Manchester Regiment ~

Note a. *Roll of all personnel identified as eligible.*
Note b. *Recipients attached Indian Telegraph Department (ITD).*
Note c. *Medals named in running script '1st Bn Manch. Regt.'*

Single Clasp	No. Identified	Rarity
Abor 1911–12[2]	2	Of the Utmost Rarity

Lance Corporals/Privates: ~ 9177 J Ogden[2] & 999 W Shaw[2]

~ 1st Bn, The Prince of Wales's (North Staffordshire Regiment) ~

Note a. *Roll of all personnel identified as eligible.*
Note b. *Recipient attached Indian Telegraph Department (ITD).*
Note c. *Medals named in running script '2nd Bn N. Staff. R.'*

Single Clasp	No. Identified	Rarity
Abor 1911–12[2]	1	According to the roll as seen, can be considered Unique

Lance Corporals/Privates: ~ 9247 A Bishop[2]

1st Bn, The York & Lancashire Regiment ~:

Note a. *Roll of all personnel identified as eligible.*
Note b. *Recipient attached Indian Telegraph Department (ITD).*
Note c. *Medals named in running script '1st Bn York & Lanc. R.'*

Single Clasp	No. Identified	Rarity
Abor 1911–12[2]	1	According to the roll as seen, can be considered Unique

Lance Corporals/Privates: ~ 8124 G J Patrick[2]

~ 1st Bn, The Seaforth Highlanders (Ross-Shire Buffs, The Duke of Albany's) ~

Note a.   *Roll of all personnel identified as eligible.*
Note b.   *Recipient attached Indian Telegraph Department (ITD).*
Note c.   *Medals named in running script '1st Bn Sea. Highrs.'*

Single Clasp	No. Identified	Rarity
Abor 1911–12[2]	1	According to the roll as seen, can be considered Unique

Lance Corporals/Privates: ~ 7678 N Aitkin[2]

~ 2nd Bn, The Gordon Highlanders ~

Note a.   *Roll of all personnel identified as eligible.*
Note b.   *Recipient attached Indian Telegraph Department (ITD).*
Note c.   *Medals named in running script '2nd Bn Gord. Highs.'*

Single Clasp	No. Identified	Rarity
Abor 1911–12[2]	1	According to the roll as seen, can be considered Unique

Lance Corporals/Privates: ~ 9166 J McIntosh[2]

~ 2nd Bn, The Connaught Rangers ~

Note a.   *Roll of all personnel identified as eligible.*
Note b.   *Recipient attached Indian Telegraph Department (ITD).*
Note c.   *Medals named in running script, believed '2nd Bn Conn. Rang.'*

Single Clasp	No. Identified	Rarity
Abor 1911–12[2]	1	According to the roll as seen, can be considered Unique

Lance Corporals/Privates: ~ 6266 W Rouse[2]

~ 1st Bn, The Royal Munster Fusiliers ~

Note a.   *Roll of all personnel identified as eligible.*
Note b.   *Recipient attached Indian Telegraph Department (ITD)*
Note c.   *Medals named in running script '1st Bn Rl. M. Fus.'*

Single Clasp	No. Identified	Rarity
Abor 1911–12[2]	1	According to the roll as seen, can be considered Unique

Lance Corporals/Privates: ~ 7065 J Killin[2]

THE CORPS:

~ The Army Ordnance Corps ~

Note a.   *Roll of all personnel identified as eligible.*
Note b.   *Medals named in running script 'A.O.C.'*

Single Clasp	No. Identified	Rarity
Abor 1911–12[2]	4	Of the Utmost Rarity

Warrant Officers Class I: ~ (Condtr) F I Williams[2]
Warrant Officers Class II: ~ (Sub Condtr) H Ward[2]
Company Quartermaster Sergeants/Staff Sergeants: ~ (Armt) 1118 W Smithson[2] attch. IOD
Quartermaster Sergeants/Sergeants: ~ (Stores) ? ? ? E W Guest[2]

MISCELLANEOUS:

~ The Corps of Military Staff Clerks ~

Note a.   *Roll of all personnel identified as eligible.*
Note b.   *It is unclear whether the Corps of Military Staff Clerks (CMSC) were British or Indian Establishment and for that reason I have included the following personnel in the 'miscellaneous' section of the roll. It is important to note that the Indian Corps of Clerks (ICC) was not formed until 1924. (The Indian Army Corps of Clerks (IACC) from 1934).*
Note c.   *Medals named in running script 'C.M.S.C.'*

Single Clasp	No. Identified	Rarity
Abor 1911–12[2]	2	Of the Utmost Rarity

Sergeants: ~ W C S De Knock[2] & A Park[2]

INDIAN ESTABLISHMENT

Qualifying Units Present (Officers Plus Known Individuals)

The Cavalry:
Commanding Officer Or Single Representative
9th Hodson's Horse Surgeon..Capt. C W F Melville, Staff Surgeon (Only)
38th King George's Own Central India Horse.............................Capt. J R Hutchison, Adjt. Assam Valley Light Horse (Only)

The Artillery:
No Presence Identified

The Sappers & Miners:
1st King George's Own Sappers & Miners
No. 1 Field Company & Det. No. 5 Field Company

Indian Signals Service, Sappers & Miners
Det. No. 31 Signal Company

The Pioneers:
32nd Sikh Pioneers...Lt. Col. H Peterson
34th Sikh Pioneers...Capt. J E H Wilson attch. 32nd Sikh Pioneers (Only)
61st Madras Pioneers...Detachment Only

The Infantry:

17th (The Loyal Regiment)..Capt. L H S Smithers, Act. Bde. Maj. (Only)
27th Punjabis..Bronze Example Known
31st Punjabis......................Capt. Sir George Duff-Sutherland-Dunbar, Bart., Cmdt., Lakhimpur Hills Military Police (Only)
41st Dogras..Maj. C A R Hutchinson, GSO2
82nd Punjabis..Capt. W A Power (Only)
120th Rajputana Infantry..Capt. W B Hore, Intelligence Officer (Only)
1/2nd King Edward's Own Gurkha Rifles (The Sirmoor Rifles)..Col. J Fisher
3rd Queen Alexandra's Own Gurkha Rifles...............Capt. A M Hutchins, Asst Cmdt. Lakhimpur Hills Military Police (Only)
5th Gurkha Rifles (FF)...Capt. A M Graham, Cmdt. Lushai Hills Det., Assam MP
5th Gurkha Rifles (FF)..Lt. A B Hay Webb, Water Transport Officer (Only)
1/8th Gurkha Rifles...Lt. Col. F Murray (Later Maj. J A Wilson)

Militia & Volunteers:

The Assam Valley Light Horse...Capt. C L Lovell AFI

The Indian Corps:
The Supply & Transport Corps: (Including British Officers & NCO's)
Mule Corps & Carrier Corps

5 (Cavalry) Brigade Mule Cadre...S/Sgt. J Lynch
26th Mule Corps..Capt. C E Edward Collins

No. 1 Gurkhali Carrier Corps
Nos. 1, 2, 3, 4 & 5 Naga Hills Carrier Corps, (Including Boat Detachment).......Col. A E Woods, Deputy Commissioner, Nagar Hills

The Indian Subordinate Medical Department / The Indian Medical Service
The Army Hospital Corps / The Army Bearer Corps:

'C' Section, 168th Indian Field Hospital...Capt. J S O'Neill
169th Indian Field Hospital
'A' Section, 168th Field Ambulance

The Judiciary, Police & Intelligence
Lushi Hills Bn & Lakhimpur Hills Bn Assam Military Police
Mr. A J Harrison...Intelligence Officer

The Telegraph Department:
Mr. G E O De Smidt...Chief Telegraph Engineer

The Political & Civil Departments:

Capt. F Bailey...Chief Political Officer
Mr. A H W Bentinck Indian Civil Service...Asst. Political Officer
Mr. I H Burkhill...Botanist
Mr. R A Hodgart...Indian Museum
Mr. S W Kemp..Zoologist
Mr. J Needham Indian Civil Service...Asst. Political Officer
Mr. J E Scott...Asst. Political Officer & Commandant Carrier Corps

The Media:
Capt. Poole

3. FRONTIER CAMPAIGNS 1919–1925

~ Afghanistan North West Frontier 1919 ~

~ India General Service Medal 1908–1935 ~
AFGHANISTAN N.W.F. 1919
Issue 2: Calcutta Mint

The 'AFGHANISTAN N.W.F. 1919' clasp was sanctioned by Army Order 223 of 1920, later amended by Army Orders 434 of 1920 and 362 of 1921. The clasp rewarded troops, airmen and certain war-mobilised civilians employed on operations during the Third Afghan War of 1919. Many personnel qualified while on detached duty, or as members of hastily organised sub-formations rushed to the Indo-Afghan frontier from the Indian hinterland, or the Mesopotamian/ Persian theatres, to swell depleted Sub-Continent garrisons.

Following the order for general mobilisation on 5th May 1919, the field army was divided into four principle spheres of operation:

i. The North-West Frontier Force under General A.A. Barrett.

ii. The Baluchistan Force under Lieutenant General R. Wapshare.

iii. The Waziristan Force under Major General N.G, Woodyatt thence Major General S.H. Climo.

iv. The North East Persia Force under Major General W. Malleson.

To qualify for the 'AFGHANISTAN N.W.F. 1919' clasp, personnel had to satisfy one, or more, of the following requirements:

- Served west of the River Indus, exclusive of Sind Province, between 6th May 1919 and 8th August 1919, inclusive.

- Served under the orders of the General Officer Commanding the Baluchistan Force on the East Persian Lines of Communication between 6th May 1919 and 8th August 1919, inclusive.

- Served in North Eastern Persia under the orders of the General Officer Commanding between 6th May 1919 and 8th August 1919, inclusive.

- Served in the Khyber Pass, west of and excluding Fort Jamrud, between 9th August 1919 and 30th September 1919, inclusive.

- Served with the Waziristan Force, including those formations stationed at Dera Ismail Khan, Mianwali, Mari-Indus and Kalabagh, between 9th August 1919 and 30th September 1919, inclusive.

Due to the above criteria, not all mobilised units qualified.

Royal Air Force qualification was based on the criteria above, but inferred service in support of the activities of the field army.

Medals with the 'AFGHANISTAN N.W.F. 1919' clasp were the first of the 1908–35 series minted in both London and Calcutta. Interested parties should refer to the 'claw' on the 'flange' of any given example to determine provenance (see Introduction, page 15). I have seen fixed suspension examples with London Mint 'claws' but have been unable to verify why they exist. Authorised camp followers from this campaign forward received silver medals in line with combatant troops.

The climatic conditions endured by personnel employed on the North West Frontier during the summer of 1919 were extremely harsh. Temperatures were consistently eight to ten degrees centigrade above the daily average leading to significant levels of heat-related stress and sickness. A scarcity of clean water resulted in some 900 disease-related deaths.

Contrary to popular belief, the Third Afghan War was not the RAF's first combative role post World War One. Operations in Persia between 12th November 1918 and 22nd June 1919, during the Arab Revolt, qualified 30 Squadron, RAF, for the (then new) General Service Medal (Army and RAF) 1918–62 with clasp 'S PERSIA'.

*

Following the conclusion of World War One in November 1918, Amir Habibullah of Afghanistan petitioned the Viceroy of India, Lord Chelmsford, for an invitation to the Versailles Peace Conference in France. Many enlightened diplomats felt that this request had merit. Allied politicians were aware that the Amir had withstood both external pressure from the Central Powers and domestic pressure from pro-Ottoman Caliphates to open up a 'fourth front' on the Indian North Western Frontier. This had enabled the release of thousands of British and British Indian Army troops for deployment to operational theatres elsewhere throughout the world. It was also common knowledge that Afghanistan now sought to reverse its dependence upon Britain for foreign policy management, as mandated in the peace terms concluding the Second Afghan War of 1878–89. Whitehall, however, refused to sanction the Amir's request and accordingly, in February 1919, an angry Habibullah threatened to send a delegation direct to the Versailles conference charged with publicising Britain's ingratitude.

While the British Government pondered the Amir's position, Habibullah undertook a hunting expedition to the remote Lagham Valley region of Afghanistan. Accompanying the Amir were his brother, Nashrullah Khan, and the Chief of the Afghan Army General Staff, General Nadir Khan. These influential men had been key supporters of the pro Central Powers faction during the late war. They now sought vengeance against the Amir for squandering a four-year-long window of opportunity to wrestle full independence from Britain. A conspiracy to eliminate Habibullah had existed within the senior Afghan echelons for some time and a convenient accident in the countryside seemed like the

~ Habibullah ~
Amir Of Afghanistan

ideal way to disguise an assassination. Consequently, late on 19th February 1919, the conspirators arranged for the Amir to be murdered while he slept. As soon as news of the Amir's death began to circulate, Nashrullah Khan declared himself the 'rightful' heir to the Afghan throne.

The plot did not go to plan. Amanullah Khan, the Amir's third son and Governor of Kabul, was instead proclaimed his father's legitimate successor and, with the support of the Army, arranged for the arrest of Nashrullah Khan on charges of treason. There was concern in some circles, however, that Amanullah had been complicit in the death of his father. Public opinion deteriorated further when several influential Islamic judges acquitted both Nashrullah Khan and General Nadir Khan following a less than robust inquiry. Acutely aware of growing public distrust, whilst also sensing a potential weakening of British authority throughout the Sub-Continent, Amanullah seized upon an opportunity to unite the 'nation' in a common cause.

*

Capitalising upon growing social disorder and nationalist sentiment in war-weary British India, several influential Afghan *mullahs* had been pressurising the Kabul-based 'Provisional Government of India' to ferment a rebellion against the British Crown in the Punjab region, a region that was a focal area of anti-colonial subversion. Such was the economic suffering in India at this time that it was not hard to ferment unrest, especially among thousands of recently demobilised and largely unemployed Indian Army personnel, as well as an increasingly desperate merchant class. In early April 1919, riots in Delhi, Ahmadabad, Lahore and Amritsar claimed the lives of several Europeans.

Early on 10th April 1919, 1st Bn, South Lancashire Regt. (Prince of Wales Volunteers), supported by a rifle company from the 2/6th Bn, Royal Sussex Regt., was despatched from Lahore to Amritsar, where it was tasked with assisting Brigadier General R.E.H. Dyer in the maintenance of civil order within the increasingly volatile city. A major Sikh religious festival was due to be celebrated at the Jallianwala Bagh on 13th April. Due to the recently passed Rowlett Act banning unauthorised public assembly, any public gathering would be in direct defiance. Thus, when excited crowds began to swarm into Amritsar city centre in expectation of the forthcoming celebrations, they were greeted by a strong force of British and Gurkha troops. The Sikh pilgrims were not intimidated, their antics more devotional than revolutionary. Nevertheless, the order was given for everyone whatever their intention to disperse and return from whence they had come. When the crowd appeared to be hesitant to disperse, Brigadier General Dyer ordered his troops to open fire.

The 'Amritsar Massacre' shook the Empire and cost Brigadier General R.E.H. Dyer his otherwise unblemished reputation. It also left 379 Sikh worshippers dead and over 1,200 injured. Indiscriminate violence in support of the slain Sikhs rapidly erupted throughout the Sub-Continent. Martial law was declared in Lahore on 15th April 1919 following an attack upon 'The Ferozepore Express' train service when several European travellers were injured. Elsewhere, plans were made for the Army to seal off the

North West Frontier provincial capital of Peshawar should the need arise. All militia and police leave was cancelled forthwith.

The British had unwittingly played into Amanullah's hand. It mattered little to the Amir of Afghanistan that Sikhs and not Muslims had perished in Amritsar. The event was simply another example of British arrogance and tyranny. When *jihad* was declared in Kabul in reprisal for the killings, excited crowds eagerly took to the streets calling for the Amir to lead them in holy war to punish the British 'infidel' and set their brothers in India free. The Afghan Army capitalised on these disturbances to deploy forces up tp the Indo-Afghan border under the pretext they were there to prevent 'Indian' nationalist violence from spreading west into Afghanistan.

*

May 1919 found the British military establishment in India ill prepared for a new war. British Indian Army units in the act of demobilising from war service in France, Mesopotamia, Egypt and elsewhere, were in no position to halt the process and deploy back on to active duty. The bulk of the regular British Army garrison had withdrawn from India during the early stages of the First World War, leaving behind only a token force of eight infantry battalions supported by two cavalry regiments and supporting arms. These units had formed a core presence around which a significant number of Territorial Army formations deployed. Experienced regular officers and non-commissioned officers were in short supply due to personnel having transferred to sister battalions deployed in combat zones or new formations such as the Machine Gun Corps, the (Royal) Tank Corps, and even the fledgling Royal Air Force (formed barely a year previously).

BRITISH REGULAR ARMY
CAVALRY & INFANTRY REGIMENTS REMAINING IN INDIA 1914–1918 PERIOD

CAVALRY:
1st King's Dragoon Guards
21st (Empress of India's) Lancers
INFANTRY:
2nd Bn, King's (Liverpool Regt.)
2nd Bn, Somerset Light Infantry
Alexandra, Princess of Wales's Own (Yorkshire Regt.)
1st Bn, Duke of Wellington's (West Riding Regt.)
1st Bn, Royal Sussex Regt.
1st Bn, South Lancashire Regt. (Prince of Wales's Volunteers)
2nd Bn, North Staffordshire Regt.
1st Bn, Durham Light Infantry

Further, by 1919, the Territorial Army troops stationed in India were eager to return home after almost five years of continuous overseas service. Civil employment opportunities and loved ones in Britain were much more appealing than soldiering in the mountains and arid deserts of frontier India. They had volunteered with a view to defending Britain from a European foe, not the Sub-Continent from Afghan intrigue or local unrest. With the repatriation process in full progress, gaps in the war establishment of many units had to be filled hurriedly with spare men either already en-route to demobilisation or from numerous rundown formations unable to function anymore as cohesive organisations. Morale among the volunteers was not good and the threat of mutiny was often not far from the surface. Indeed at one point, some men belonging to Brigadier General W.J. O'Dowda's Brigade, temporarily detrained their transport at Hassan Abdul near Rawalpindi, and waited by the railway tracks for a ride east! Some full strength battalions, such as the 1st Bn, Royal Sussex Regt., were on summer camp, miles from their depots and stores, when war broke out on 6th May.

*

RELATIVE TROOP STRENGTHS AFGHANISTAN NORTH WEST FRONTIER, MAY 1919

BRITISH / INDIAN ARMIES:
North West Frontier Force 1st & 10th Cavalry Brigades (Each with 4 x 13lb Guns, RHA) 1st & 2nd Infantry Brigades, 1st Peshawar Division 3 Frontier Infantry Garrisons - (Kohat, Bannu, and Derajat) Divisional Artillery RFA - 8 x 18lb Guns & 4 x 4.5" Howitzers RGA - 8 x 2.75" Mountain Guns
Khyber Area 6 Cavalry Regiments, 24 Infantry Battalions, 40 Artillery Pieces & 48 Machine Guns Various Irregular Formations
Peshawar Area 4 Infantry Battalions, 14 Artillery Pieces &12 Machine Guns Various Irregular Formations Lines of Communication
AFGHAN ARMY:
Kabul – Jellalabad Area 7 Cavalry Regiments, 31 Infantry Battalions, 92 Artillery Pieces & Assorted Machine Guns
Elsewhere 14 Cavalry Regiments, 44 Infantry Battalions & 188 Artillery Pieces

*

During April 1919, Major Campbell, the officer commanding the Khyber Rifles militia at Fort Landi Kotal in the Khyber Pass, experienced a steep decline in both morale and discipline among his troops. The widespread Afghan-inspired unrest that was infecting the peoples of the entire North West Frontier Province region, coupled with domestic political agitation from, among others, M.K. Ghandi and the Indian Congress Party, posed difficult questions for many locally recruited militiamen. This 'blood bond' was an immensely powerful emotional force, especially when laced with religious fervour. With sepoys deserting on almost a daily basis, General A.A. Barratt, GOC Northern Command, determined that an immediate show of force was required. Consequently, Lieutenant General F. Campbell, Commander 1st (Peshawar) Division, was instructed to deploy the Peshawar Flying Column, consisting of detachments 1/15th Sikhs and 1/9th GR, post haste to Landi Kotal, where they disarmed and disembodied the few remaining members of the Khyber Rifles remaining in post. This small force was supported by signallers drawn from the 2nd Bn, Somerset LI, under Lieutenant F.W. Lias, with one section 6 Mountain Battery, RGA, and a field troop of Sappers and Miners.

On 1st May 1919, Afghan Army scouts observed a British officer accompanied by several sepoys reconnoitring the old caravan oasis at Bagh Springs on the Afghan Khyber border. The sovereignty

*~ The road through the Khyber Pass was
ideal ambush territory ~*

of this small, yet strategically important, feature had been the subject of dispute between British India and Afghanistan for some time. Instead of dismissing the incident as a routine British patrol, the Amir became agitated when advised of the situation and instructed his local commander, General Saleh Muhammad, to take counter measures. On the following day, the Afghan Government formally advised the British Political Agent at Landi Kotal, Abdul Qayyum, that it was their intention to commence the construction of a fortified position at Bagh Springs. In response to this communiqué, Qayyum stated that his masters in Delhi would consider such action a hostile invasion of British Indian territory and that he could not be responsible for any consequences incurred.

General Saleh Muhammad was undaunted by Qayyum's declaration. On 3rd May 1919, 150 Afghan soldiers, with artillery support, occupied the Bagh Springs oasis area. That night a party of local Shinwari tribesmen, acting in collusion with the Afghan military, murdered five Indian coolies based at the water pumping station, located downstream from Bagh on the banks of the Khyber River. When news of this atrocity was circulated, the Viceroy, Lord Chelmsford, immediately asked the Amir to arrest the perpetrators. Amanullah determined instead to reinforce his position at Bagh with three infantry battalions and then proceeded to cut off completely the vital fresh water supply to Fort Landi Kotal.

The various frontier tribes, all of whom had been courted by Kabul to declare *jihad* on Britain for some months, considered such forthright action a strong sign of Afghan intent. Soon thereafter, thousands of Afridi and Waziri warriors began to come down from the mountains and travel to Jellalabad where they joined a mass *jirga* in support of the Afghan regime. The British Government could no longer ignore such overt Afghan confrontation. On 6th May 1919, the Government of India declared war and began the process of general mobilisation. The Third Afghan War had begun.

At noon on 6th May 1919, the balance of the 1st (Peshawar) Division received orders to mobilise for active service. The 1st Infantry Brigade, Brigadier General G.D. Crocker, received orders to deploy immediately to Landi Kotal. The 2nd Bn, Somerset LI, and 8 Mountain Battery, RGA, were detailed to form the vanguard of this manoeuvre. To facilitate their deployment the Peshawar Cantonment Supply and Transport Corps MT Company placed at their disposal 37 thirty-cwt lorries. The advanced guard, under Captain G.N. Molesworth, 2nd Somerset LI, arrived at their objective at 11am on 7th May and proceeded to establish a secure harbour area in which to receive the balance of the brigade. The Brigade Major had furnished Captain Molesworth with a schedule outlining the intended order of march for the units coming up from Peshawar but, when the columns began to arrive on 8th May, the list was found to be incomplete. Much reorganisation of the position had to take place before all of the brigade could be accommodated. Meanwhile, the 2nd Infantry Brigade, Major General S.H. Climo, and the 3rd Infantry Infantry Brigade, Major General A. Skeen, began the process of deploying up to Peshawar by train and thence on to Fort Jamrud and Camp Kacha Garhi respectively.

~ Territorials on the Frontier fight on after demobilisation in other first World War theatres ~

On the morning of 8th May 1919, a reconnaissance of the wider Landi Kotal area was made by 'HQ' and 'B' Companies, 2nd Bn, Somerset LI, supported by 8 Mountain Battery, RGA. The British observed Afghan troops reinforcing their positions far to the west on the Ashrafai Khel heights. Although the Afghans opened fire, the range was too great to inflict casualties on the British patrol. The hostile actions of the Afghans prompted Brigadier General G.D. Crocker to take steps to improve his defensive perimeter. 'A' Company, 2nd Somerset LI, was immediately despatched to picquet an elevated feature some 300 yards south of the Fort. Simultaneously, 150 rifles of the 1/9th GR occupied 'Suffolk Hill', a position to the southwest of Fort Landi Kotal, located only 1,500 yards from the Afghan forward positions at Bagh Springs.

At midnight on 8th May 1919, Brigadier General G D Crocker held a tactical briefing for his senior officers. The assembled personnel reviewed at length growing concerns from the Principal Medical Officer regarding the increasing shortage of fresh water supplies at Landi Kotal. Accordingly, a decision made to recover the waterworks at Bagh Springs early the next day. The battle plan required the 2nd Bn, Somerset LI, less 'A' Company, and a section of 8 Mountain Battery, RGA, to join the 1/9th GR on 'Suffolk Hill'. 77 Howitzer Battery, RFA, and the balance of 8 Mountain Battery, RGA, were to come into action on a knoll north of the Khyber road. Once these troops had been deployed, a strike force, consisting of the 1/15th Sikhs and the 1/11th GR, were to capture the waterworks and then advance left onto the main Afghan positions. 2/123rd Outram's Rifles, recently arrived from Fort Jamrud after a forced march through the night, were to be held in reserve.

1ˢᵗ (PESHAWAR) INFANTRY BRIGADE, 8ᵗ /9ᵗʰ MAY 1919 – BRG. GEN. G D CROCKER

Defensive Dispositions, Landi Kotal:
Two Troops 30ᵗʰ Lancers, IA
One Section, 6 Mountain Battery, Royal Garrison Artillery
'A' Company, 2ⁿᵈ Bn, Somerset Light Infantry
1/9ᵗʰ GR & 1/35ᵗʰ Sikhs
263 Company, Machine Gun Corps Infantry
Striking Force, Landi Kotal:
77 Howitzer Battery, Royal Field Artillery
8 Mountain Battery, Royal Garrison Artillery
2ⁿᵈ Bn, Somerset Light Infantry (less 'A' Company)
1/11ᵗʰ GR (detached from 2ⁿᵈ (Nowshera) Infantry Brigade) & 1/15ᵗʰ Sikhs

Due to the rough terrain, it was difficult for the artillery to bring down effective covering fire in support of the strike force's advance to contact. The noise of the shellfire, however, immediately alerted the enemy to the intentions of the British and the rapid response of the Afghans quickly stifled Brigadier General G.D. Crocker's assault. With little effective cover, the Sikhs and Gurkhas soon began to take casualties. By noon it was determined that the force should be withdrawn back to the safety of Fort Landi Kotal. Too many men had been employed on defensive duties and it was subsequently suggested that the reconnaissance of the forward area had been weak. The RAF successfully salvaged the force some credibility when three BE2C Camel aircraft, operated by 114 Squadron from RAF Kohat, engaged enemy reserve concentrations in and around Fort Dakka situated on the Afghan side of the Khyber frontier.

*

In Peshawar, the civil situation deteriorated rapidly. Anti-British propaganda was widespread. The Afghan postmaster, who had enjoyed a certain degree of diplomatic immunity as an Afghan Political Emissary, was arrested and subsequently deported to Burma. He was charged with inciting an insurrection during a speech in the Bazaar at which leaflets were distributed stating that the Central Powers had resumed the war in Europe and were calling upon Egypt and India to rise up against the British. On 8ᵗʰ May 1919, martial law was declared and the old walled city closed by troops from the 6ᵗʰ Infantry Brigade under Brigadier General G. Christian. 1 KDG, which had arrived in theatre from Meerut earlier that day with the 1ˢᵗ Cavalry Brigade, Brigadier General F.G.H. Davies, secured each of the 16 city gates and supplied mounted patrols around the city perimeter. Additional British reinforcements arrived over the following days. The 1/4ᵗʰ Bn, Queen's Royal Surrey Regt. from Jullundur, was tasked with, among other things, providing security for the North West Railway Bn, AFI, armoured train that ran daily to and fro from Peshawar Cantonment to Fort Jamrud. The security of the immediate Peshawar vicinity was placed under the command of Brigadier General L.W.Y. Campbell of the Sialkot Infanty Brigade, while Lines of Communication 'West' were placed under the control of Brigadier General Lane.

Following the failed assault on Bagh Springs, the military authorities determined to reinforce the Fort Landi Kotal garrison with the 2ⁿᵈ Infantry Brigade from Fort Jamrud. Lieutenant General F. Campbell was anxious to mount a reinvigorated assault in the direction of Bagh, to not only secure much needed access to fresh water supplies and thus combat the growing threat of a cholera outbreak but also, and of equal importance, to ensure that the indigenous peoples understood that the British force was there to 'win'. Otherwise any further failures on the part of the British would be interpreted as signs of weakness thus ensuring greater support for the Afghans.

PESHAWAR INTERNAL SECURITY AREA

Brig. Gen. L W Y Campbell:
1/4th Queen's (Royal West Surrey Regt) & 2/4th (Cumberland and Westmoreland) Bn, Border Regt 37th Dogras (Later to 5th Infantry Brigade) & 3/2nd GR

LINES OF COMMUNICATION 'WEST'

Brig. Gen. Lane:
23rd Cavalry, IA 2/2nd Rajputs & 110th Mahratta LI

On 11th May 1919, senior officers in the Khyber area were presented with a revised battle plan. The 2nd Bn, Somerset LI, less 'B' and 'D' Companies, then in position on 'Suffolk Hill', plus one section 263 Company, MGC, were to move to a spur feature southwest of 'Bright's Hill'. From this location, it was anticipated that enfilade fire could be brought to bear on the forward Afghan lines. The 2nd Infantry Brigade, comprising the 2nd Bn, North Staffordshire Regt., 1/11th GR, 2/11th GR, and 2/123rd Outram's Rifles, were to deploy to the small Frontier Constabulary post at Michni Kando from whence the main assault was to be launched. 4/3rd GR and a portion of 2/1st GR from the 3rd Infantry Brigade, Major General A Skeen, were held in reserve.

~ The British camp at Dakka looking south west across the Kabul River into Afghanistan ~

The day progressed well. The 2nd Bn, North Staffordshire Regt. attacked the Afghan forward positions and, assisted by the 2nd Bn, Somerset LI's covering fire, succeeded in destroying the majority of the enemy's sangars. The 2/11th GR and 2/123rd Outram's Rifles, with 77 Howitzer Battery, RFA, in support, scaled the rocky Kafir Kot and occupied the Afghan positions located there. By mid-afternoon, the 2nd Infantry Brigade was bivouacked in Bagh while the bulk of the Afghan Army was observed retiring west in poor order towards Fort Dakka. Aircraft of 114 Squadron, RAF, followed up the Afghan retreat penetrating beyond the Indo-Afghan border where it accounted for some 30–40 enemy. Shortly thereafter, rumours began to circulate suggesting that General Saleh Muhammad had fled to Jellalabad and that the Afghans had abandoned their strategic position at Dakka.

Later the same day, Brigadier General G.D. Crocker took a composite infantry battalion to reconnoitre Tor Tasppar and the Spinatsuka Hills. Close contact occurred with a large force of Afghan infantry and the British suffered four casualties. Following Brigadier General Crocker's report to Lieutenant General F. Campbell, it was determined that the entire western Khyber should be occupied in depth and an incursion made into Afghanistan, with a view to securing (the now open) Afghan position at Fort Dakka. This location commanded a strategically important position at the junction of the Kabul to Jellalabad and Peshawar roads. Thus, a general advance west from Fort Landi Kotal began on 13th May 1919, with 1/11th GR acting as vanguard. By mid-morning British troops were occupying the hills overlooking the eastern Dakka Plain. The force encountered no opposition and the route ahead appeared deserted. At noon, Fort Jamrud received a signal calling for the cavalry to advance west along the Khyber Pass with a view to lending support to the infantry.

The 1st Cavalry Brigade, Brigadier General F.G.H. Davies, consisting of the 1st KDG, augmented by troopers of the 21st Lancers, 1st Lancers, IA, 33rd Light Cavalry, IA and 'M' Battery, RHA, together with Brigadier General G.M. Baldwin and the 30th Lancers, IA of the 10th Cavalry Brigade, had concentrated at Fort Jamrud on 11th May 1919. Accompanying these men were 15 and 24 Squadrons, MGC Cavalry. Upon receiving the order 'Go Dakka', they did just that, stopping only to water their mounts at Ali Masjid. The objective was secured early that afternoon and by sunset, horse lines had been established on a grassy bank adjacent to the Kabul River at Fort Dakka.

A relative lull in activity now occurred on the Khyber Front during which the Maharajah of Bikaner offered the Government of India the use of his Imperial Service force. The RAF maintained ongoing reconnaissance missions during which several Afghan Army positions were observed high upon the Peiwar Kotal, some 90 miles west of Peshawar. Afghan emissaries, attempting to rally local support in and around Waziristan, suffered a significant setback on 15th May 1919 when the Shaman Khel Mahsuds reported for their annual Government subsidy, preferring British hard cash, rather than Afghan promises of 'liberation'.

The cavalry force at Fort Dakka, not yet under 1st (Peshawar) Division command, appeared intent on whiling away the hours bathing in the Kabul River. The lack of activity caused Lieutenant General F. Campbell much anxiety and, accordingly, on 15th May 1919, he sent Brigadier General G.D. Crocker down to Dakka with HQ details of the 1st Infantry Brigade accompanied by 1/15th Sikhs and 1/19th GR. This action provoked some degree of confusion at Dakka. With three, one star generals present, no-one really knew who was in command! Resolution came swiftly. The following day Brigadier General G.M. Baldwin returned to Peshawar, leaving his command absorbed into the 1st Cavalry Brigade. Brigadier General G.D. Crocker was appointed GOC Dakka area.

Early on 16th May 1919, Lieutenant Colonel C.N. McMullen, 1/15th Sikhs, embarked upon a reconnaissance into the Afghan hinterland west of Fort Dakka with a view to ascertaining the feasibility of 1st (Peshawar) Division's advance upon Kabul. The Battalion, less two rifle companies, was supported by B, C & D Squadrons, 1st KDG, 'M' Battery, RHA and one section of 15 Squadron, MGC Cavalry. Advancing around a bend in the road near Busawal, six miles west of Dakka, the lead squadron of 1st KDG ran into a significant concentration of Afghan troops who were evidently forming up in preparation to recapture Fort Dakka. Strongly outnumbered, the Dragoon Guards had to rely on Horse Artillery support to extricate them from certain destruction. Hotly pursued, the reconnaissance force retired upon Dakka with the loss of one officer and several other ranks killed and wounded.

Meanwhile, separate Afghan force succeeded in securing a vantage point above Fort Dakka and subjected the British positions there to a fusillade of shot and shell. Fortunately, the remainder of the 2nd Infantry Brigade was in the process of moving into the area at that time and consequently by nightfall the situation had been stabilised. It was, however, now essential that the enemy be driven from their positions overlooking Dakka. Accordingly, orders were prepared for a brigade level assault to be delivered at dawn on 17th May 1919, in the direction of 'Stonehenge Hill' and 'Sikh Hill'.

In the attack that followed, the abundance of cavalry available to Brigadier General G.D. Crocker at Dakka was much squandered. As momentum slowed, the 2nd Bn, Somerset LI, should have been committed, their arc in the defensive perimeter taken over by dismounted troopers. There was simply insufficient infantry to conduct an up hill assault against eight Afghan battalions. By 8 a.m., the artillery's ammunition was virtually exhausted and it was not until the late morning that three lorry loads of ordnance was delivered to the frontline from Fort Landi Kotal. Communications were diabolical. Lieutenant General F. Campbell received notification of the planned attack only one hour before the troops crossed the start line! Major General A. Skeen and the 3rd Infantry Brigade were immediately despatched towards Fort Dakka in support of the action. Arriving shortly after midday, the 1st Bn, Yorkshire Regt., deployed to reinforce the right flank attack, while 285 Company, MGC was deployed centre and 2/11th GR was deployed left flank. Confusion remained a serious issue and the force suffered several 'friendly fire' casualties as a result.

ASSAULT FORCE, DAKKA, 17th MAY 1919

2/35th Sikhs, Right Flank - Objective: 'Stonehenge Hill'
1/15th Sikhs, Left Flank - Objective: 'Sikh Hill'
1/9th GR - Support Battalion
2nd Bn, Somerset Light Infantry - Reserve Force

The 17th May 1919 proved to be both long and extremely hot, but, after a difficult fight, the troops eventually secured their objectives. Defeated Afghans fled their posts leaving behind their dead and dying. Fresh sangars were constructed by the British and the force stood-to all night. In recognition of the 2nd Bn, Somerset LI's gallant capture of 'Stonehenge Hill', the feature was renamed 'Somerset Hill'. The troops were relieved on 18th May 1919 and returned to Fort Dakka where preparations were underway to evacuate the town and establish a new base some miles distance at Fort Robat.

The RAF had also been active. A sortie had penetrated Afghanistan, as far west as Jellalabad. Several key structures had been bombed and a military column attacked. Airmen followed up this raid several days later with an attack on Kabul. During this assault Captain D.H.M. Carbery, RAF, struck the Royal Palace forcing the Amir's harem to flee into the street!

On 21st May 1919, Adbur Rahman, an Afghan peace envoy, attempted to open negotiations with the British, but the GOC sent him straight back to Kabul. Cholera broke out in the Khyber area, but the infection was contained and fortunately did not spread far. Activity among the Shinwaris and Mohmands was a constant irritant for the force, with sniping across the Kabul River a daily ordeal. The flow of the Kabul River severely hindered effective follow-up operations against the hostile tribesmen. Consequently, the GOC sought help from the Royal Navy and eventually two small naval launches were delivered to the force to facilitate 'hot pursuit' operations. Foraging parties were constantly searching for food among abandoned local villages. Several booby traps were set by the roadside at Girdi following the discovery of the mutilated corpse of a previously lost Dragoon Guardsman.

*

With the 1st (Peshawar) Division fully committed on the Afghan border, the Lines of Communication from Fort Landi Kotal east towards Peshawar were placed in the care of the 6th Infantry Brigade, 2nd (Rawalpindi) Division, under Brigadier General G. Christian. On 14th May 1919, reinforcements for Landi Kotal left Fort Jamrud escorted by 2/8th GR and 2/34th Sikh Pioneers. 1/61st Sikh Pioneers picqueted the road through the Khyber Pass but hostile local tribesmen had infiltrated the area and what had previously been only occasional sniping soon developed into a major firefight. The troops took several casualties and the convoy was forced to take shelter at Fort Ali Masjid.

On 16th May 1919, the reinforcement column succeeded in fighting its way through to Fort Landi Kotal. Riflemen of 2/8th GR were despatched to 'Orange Patch Ridge', some thousand yards southwest of Ali Masjid, from whence they were able to cover much of the route down to the column's objective. As dusk began to fall, the ridge was evacuated. Tribesmen caught the troops on the move and a rifle company of 2/33rd Punjabis had to be deployed to cover the withdrawal. During the night, several hundred Afghans reoccupied 'Orange Patch Ridge' and began firing on Fort Ali Masjid. Casualties began to be taken by the sheltering troops and consequently Lieutenant Colonel Wall, 2/8th GR, determined to retake the ridge.

The initial assault broke down rapidly. Fortunately, Captain W. Holderness, 1st Bn, Royal Sussex Regt., arrived shortly thereafter with an ammunition convoy from Peshawar. Lieutenant Colonel Wall immediately deployed the convoy escort to support the Gurkhas and Sikhs. Captain Holderness divided his command into two large platoons and formed a skirmish line that then successfully swept the slopes of the ridge. In recognition of this victory 'Orange Patch Ridge' was renamed 'Sussex Ridge'. Tribal aggression steadily intensified during the days following the engagement. To counter this activity General A.A. Barratt deployed the 4th Infantry Brigade, 2nd (Rawalpindi) Division, under Brigadier General E.C. Peebles, to Fort Ali Masjid.

*

Indian Army scouts near Ghalanai in the Gandab Valley observed 1,200 Afghan troops with six artillery pieces supported by an estimated 4,000 Mohmand tribesmen under Mir Sahib Jan Badshab on 19th May 1919. Ghalanai was located some 13 miles northwest of Fort Shabkadar on the former (1901–02) Mohmand Blockade Line. An enemy formation of this magnitude posed a serious threat to the security of Peshawar and the rear area of the Khyber Force. Provision was therefore made to deploy the 44th Infantry Brigade, Brigadier General W.M. Southey, 16th (Lahore) (Reserve) Division, in support of the existing Peshawar Internal Security Area command. The Mohmand warriors subsequently dispersed without a fight, with the Afghans following suit shortly thereafter.

*

In the eastern Khyber region, Malik Yar Mohammad, of the Din Khel Afridis, had demonstrated an increasingly hostile attitude towards the British throughout the Great War period. It was belived that Government subsidies, provided primarily for agricultural improvements, had been diverted to fund the construction of a masonry fort and watchtower at Chora, seven miles southwest of Fort Ali Masjid. The outbreak of hostilities with Afghanistan on 6th May 1919, provided Yar Mohammad with an ideal excuse to pursue his own anti-British objectives.

Initially, the Din Khel Afridi were only able to mounted small-scale operations. During May and June 1919, the Afridis at Chora slowly built up their reserves and, by mid-July, they were in a position to conduct their own operations independent of support from the Afghan Army. Thus on the morning of 18th July, a large *lashkar* descended on the entire Ali Masjid area. The 2/67th Punjabis at Fort Maud, three miles southwest of Fort Ali Masjid, were especially hard-pressed. Urgent signals were despatched seeking relief, but reinforcements did not arrive until the following day when a column from Fort Jamrud came up. This column consisted of one squadron, 30th Lancers, IA, 74 Battery, RFA, one armoured

~ *General Nadir Khan, 1919* ~

motor battery, 222 Company, MGC, 1/61st Sikh Pioneers, 2/61st Sikh Pioneers, and 3/39th Garhwal Rifles. This action prompted the Afridis to withdraw back to Chora where they remained until 13th September when an artillery barrage mounted by 77 Howitzer Battery, RFA, 60 Battery, RFA and 4 Mountain Battery, RGA, succeeded in destroying most of the fortifications located there.

*

The Central Front North encapsulated the Tirah, Kohat and Kuram Valley regions while the Central Front South extended throughout both Northern and Southern Waziristan. Represented extensively throughout this area were the Afridi, Orakzei, Chamkanni, Waziri and Mahsud peoples. Lines of Communication were adequate on this front only so long as the strategically important Kohat Pass and the various east to west railway routes remained open. Troop dispositions on 6th May 1919 consisted primarily of the garrisons at Kohat, Bannu, and Derajat. These regular forces were augmented by the Kurram Militia with its HQ at Parachinar, the North Waziristan Militia with its HQ at Miranshah in the Tochi Valley and the South Waziristan Militia spread thinly across the Jandola to Wana sector. Following the outbreak of war, all forces in the region were brought under the control of Major General N G Woodyatt and styled the Waziristan Force.

TROOP DISPOSITIONS, WAZIRISTAN, 6th MAY 1919

BANNU AREA:
Bannu 31st DCO Lancers, IA (Less 1 Squadron) 1 Section 33 Indian Mountain Battery, Frontier Garrison Artillery 1/103rd Mahratta LI & 3/6th GR (Less Detachment, Kurram Garha) 5 & 6 Armoured Motor Batteries, Machine Gun Corps
Dardoni (Miranshah) 1 Squadron, 31st DCO Lancers, IA 33 Indian Mountain Battery (Less 1 Section) No. 55 Field Company, 1st King George's Own Sappers and Miners 1/41st Dogras & 2/112th Infantry HQ North Waziristan Militia
Kurram Garha Detachment, 3/6th GR
Dispersed Posts and Forts North Waziristan Militia and Frontier Constabulary
DERAJAT AREA:
Dera Ismail Khan 27th Cavalry, IA (Less 1 Squadron) 27 Indian Mountain Battery (Less 1 Section) 7 Armoured Motor Battery, Machine Gun Corps 1/76th Punjabis (Less 2 ½ Companies) & 2/2nd GR
Tank 1 Squadron, 27th Cavalry, IA 1 Section, 27 Indian Mountain Battery 2 Platoons, 1/76th Punjabis
Manzai No. 75 Field Company, 3rd Sappers and Miners 1/66th Punjabis
Jandola, Khirgi, Girni ad Jatta 2 Companies. 1/76th Punjabis Dispersed Posts and Forts Including Wana South Waziristan Militia and Frontier Constabulary

The Waziristan region was a rough parallelogram shaped mountainous area dissected by the (often dry) Gomel and Zhob Rivers. Averaging 100 miles from north to south, Waziristan extended 60 miles or so west from the Indus River to the Indo-Afghan border. To the south lay Baluchistan while to the north and east lay the Kurram, Bannu and Dera Ismail Khan areas.

Facing the Waziristan Force were 14 Afghan infantry battalions drawn from General Nadir Khan's Army of the Khost. Heavily outnumbered, Major General N G Woodyatt prepared plans for the evacuation of all remote militia posts and a general retirement east on key garrisons as and when the Afghans invaded British territory. This strategy would enable a more substantial defensive line to be established. Having already witnessed the disintegration of the Khyber Rifles Militia due to 'divided' loyalties, the ongoing justification for maintaining the existing thinly spread non-regular forces across such a remote region was in doubt anyway. General Nadir Khan's force remained relatively inactive during the early part of May, no doubt waiting for 'victories' in the Khyber region to sap both British morale and manpower.

~ Sepoys parade inside remote desert fort ~

On 21st May 1919, Major General N G Woodyatt received intelligence suggesting that the Afghan military concentration in the Khost region was about to cross into the Upper Tochi area thus threatening the British garrisons at Wana, Miranshah and Thal. As a result, the 67th Infantry Brigade, Brigadier General C.E. Fourkes, was tasked with securing the evacuation of the Upper Tochi militia posts. Mechanised transport was limited and the retiring troops had to destroy vast quantities of valuable stores at each and every location to prevent them falling into enemy hands.

The evacuation of the designated locations began early on 25th May 1919. Brigadier General C.E. Fourkes sent a light column on a circular tour of the threatened region calling at Datta Khel, Tut Narai, Spina Khaisora, Boya, and other small posts along the route. At each stop, the resident garrison was expected to abandon its position and immediately take its place in the evacuation force. News of this plan quickly circulated among local tribesmen and at dusk that day the (now) empty post at Boya was sacked by Waziri warriors. Meanwhile, a hastily formed *lashkar* took to the field with a view to ambushing the retiring troops as they forded the Tochi River. Harassed the entire route to Dardoni, several hundred native militiamen took advantage of the confusion to abandon 'the colours' and swell the ranks of their kinsmen.

Forts Shewa and Spinwam were somewhat more isolated than those previously mentioned and it was determined that a separate relief operation would have to be launched to secure their safe evacuation. Consequently, Lieutenant Colonel B.P. Ellwood, 31st Lancers, IA, was detailed to advance with three mounted squadrons from Khajuri towards the Kaitu River in support of Lieutenant Poulton, NWM, who was in the process of extricating his small command from Shewa and thence on to Spinwam. From Spinwam, an ever-dwindling band of survivors fell back on Idak and subsequently Fort Miranshah. As a result of hostile action, there were several casualties among the retiring troops.

Morale at Fort Miranshah deteriorated rapidly. On 26th May 1919, in an attempt to stabilise the situation there, a rifle company of the 1/41st Dogras deployed from Dardoni in support. The fort gradually became more and more crowded with displaced persons, both military and civil. During the night of 27th/28th May, a mutiny broke out among the militia culminating in a large contingent of rebels, led by Jamadar Tarin, a Tori Khel Waziri, and Subedar Pat, a decorated Madda Khel Waziri, fleeing through a roughly hewn hole in the fort's exterior wall taking with them all of their field kit and a large quantity of ammunition.

On 27th May 1919, Major General N.G. Woodyatt transferred to the command of the 4th (Quetta) Division in relief of Lieutenant General R. Wapshare. Major General S.H. Climo succeeded General Woodyatt in command of the Waziristan Force. This officer held both political and military authority thus enabling him to control directly the various Political Officers present within his sphere of operations.

*

The forced evacuation of military facilities in Northern Waziristan had a profoundly demoralising effect on the hitherto loyal South Waziristan Militia based at Wana and its associated 12 outposts including Nili Kach, Sarwekai, Kharab Kot, Tanai, Khajuri Kach and Toi Khula. Existing intelligence suggested that Afghan deployments were likely to threaten the Wana garrison should the Tochi region be evacuated. Consequently, Major C.G. Crosthwaite, Political Officer in Wana, determined that all militia posts in the immediate region must withdraw back to the relative safety of Fort Sandeman before locals could organize offensive operations against them.

The evacuation of Fort Wana was scheduled for the evening of 26th May 1919. Major G.H. Russell, Officer Commanding SWM, had already despatched Captain H.R. Traill and Lieutenant R.E. Hunt to bring in the garrisons of Karab Kot and Tanai, and remove them to Fort Moghal Kot in the Zhob. Lieutenant A.R. Baker was similarly despatched towards Khajuri Kach with a view to effecting the abandonment of this location, and others in the area. Initially all went well at Wana, but in the late evening seven subadars, mistaking the withdrawal for an act of treachery, seized the fort's keep and opened fire upon their former comrades. Much confusion ensued with more and more sepoys joining the insurrection. An orderly withdrawal was now out of the question. Nevertheless, some 300 loyal troops and their British officers, accompanied by eight heavily-laden camels, managed to fight their way out of the fort and into the desert beyond. During this action, Asstistant Superintendant A.F. Reilly of the Frontier Police was killed.

The column from Fort Wana marched all night hoping for sanctuary at Fort Toi Khula. Arriving at their objective at about 7 a.m. the following morning, it rapidly became evident that the post had already fallen to the enemy. Disengaging from the ensuing firefight, Major G.H. Russell led his men across the Tesh Plain towards Fort Moghal Kot. While crossing the arid Tesh, the column affected a rendezvous with Captain H.R. Traill and the remaining elements of the Karab Kot and Tanai garrisons. There was no sign of Lieutenant A.R. Baker. Harried on both flanks by the enemy, the exhausted men eventually fought their way through to their intended destination. Lieutenant Baker arrived a day later accompanied by seven sowars, all that remained of the Khajuri Kach garrison.

Moghal Kot was unable to accommodate so many additional personnel. Rations were depleted and the demands of the numerous wounded troops and followers made a bad situation intolerable. An immediate withdrawal to the more substantial Zhob Militia post of Mir Ali Khel was determined as the only viable option. Wireless communications with this location had remained intact and a signal was sent requesting the militia located there to advance upon Moghal Kot and picquet the projected line of retirement. The Moghal Kot force began their evacuation early on 30th May 1919. Casualties, including five British officers killed and two wounded out of only eight present, were taken as soon as the lead elements ventured outside the relative safety of the fort's ramparts. An element of panic began to spread with many sepoys breaking ranks and fleeing south into the desert. Only the arrival of a mounted patrol, despatched from Mir Ali Khel in response to the earlier signals seeking assistance, prevented a total massacre.

The security situation throughout Waziristan was now desperate. Dardoni, Miranshah, Idak, Jandola and Saidgi were all in a state of siege from tribesmen while key garrisons such as Wana lay open to Afghan occupation. Though fresh troops were available in Bannu, Major General H. Climo, determined not to commit his reserves until reinforcements from the 43rd Infantry Brigade, Brig. Gen. J.L.J. Clarke, arrived were in position. Simultaneously, the 1/15th Sikhs, 4/39th Garhwal Rifles, and additional firepower from 23 Mountain Battery, FGA, reinforced the main Bannu garrison on 30th May 1919. Once in situ, the plan was to form a relief column to advance along the Tochi Valley. Mahsud tribesmen laying siege to Jandola, would not for the time being be attacked. Meanwhile, in an attempt to restore a sense of fighting spirit, the 67th Infantry Brigade, augmented by some 250 loyal North Waziristan Militia sepoys, broke out of their perimeter at Dardoni and fought a successful, if local, action on 31st May.

The Waziristan Force was withdrawn from the North West Frontier Force order of battle on 1st June 1919, coming instead directly under the orders of the Commander in Chief, India, General C.C. Munro. This decision enabled Major General S.H. Climo to establish his own specific strategy for dealing with the specialist nature of a tribal uprising. Two separate operations were required. Firstly the reoccupation of Northern and Southern Waziristan, Tochi and Wana respectively, and secondly, of equally immediate importance, a show of force was required to hold the Mahsud in check.

In Northern Waziristan, an Afghan thrust into the Kurram Valley region now materialised. The Thal Garrison and its strategic railhead infrastructure were now threatened. Fortunately, the revised command structure for the Waziristan Force now enabled operations in the Kurram to be managed directly from HQ North West Frontier Force by General A.A. Barrett.

*

The Tochi Relief Column advanced from Bannu on 2nd June 1919. Saidgi was relieved later the same day and Khajuri Kach re-occupied without opposition the following morning. A squadron of the 31st Lancers, IA, succeeded in securing Idak on 4th June whereupon wireless communications with the besieged 67th Infantry Brigade in Dardoni were restored. This latter place was relieved a short time latter and the garrison reinforced by the 1/103rd Mahratta Light Infantry. Punitive action was launched against several local tribal villages but much of the force was deployed south to Khirgi in support of Brigadier General P.J. Miles who had been ordered to relieve Jandola.

The Jandola relief column set out from Khirgi on 9th June 1919, securing its objective without a shot fired in anger. Surprisingly, they found the small garrison, commanded by Captain R.C. Anderson, 1/76th Punjabis, in good spirits despite having been besieged for some two weeks with scant water supplies and in temperatures of one hundred and fifteen degrees Fahrenheit. With fresh troops posted, the force retired back to Khirgi two days later.

*

The capture of the Kohat Brigade and Thal Garrison, under Brigadier General Eustace, would have been a prestigious prize for the Afghan Army. Accordingly, two rifle companies the 2/10th Jats, one squadron the 31st Lancers, IA, and one section 33 Mountain Battery, FGA, plus a section of mortars, were despatched from Bannu to Kurram Garhi in order to cover the exposed flank along the projected Afghan line of advance towards Thal. Situated adjacent to the northeastern bank of the Kurram River, Thal consisted of a Bangash Pathan village dominated by a traditionally designed earth and stone fort structure. The garrison could not employ the Kurram River, which generally ran dry during the summer months, as a robust line of defence. There was no outer perimeter area until 26th May 1919, when a defensive line was established incorporating the terminus of the Rawalpindi railway, but excluding the native village, the bazaar and the principle fresh water well. With the town reinforced, nine defensive picquets were constructed. To the north were deployed the 4/39th Garhwal Rifles, to the east the 1/151st Sikhs and to the southwest the 1/109th Infantry, less one rifle company held in reserve. The 3/9th GR maintained an inner defensive line.

The Afghan Army established a forward operating base at Yusuf Khel, three miles west of Thal. The enemy force consisted of 3,000 Afghan regular troops supported by seven 7.5cm German Krupp mountain guns and an undetermined, yet very large, number of local tribesmen under Malik Babrak. When the Afghan artillery opened up on Thal from the Khopianga Ridge early on 27th May 1919, their shells were both accurate and destructive. The British mountain guns were completely outranged. An attempt by the RAF to dislodge the Afghan gunners on 28th May failed.

Afghan infantry soon captured the outskirts of Thal where they secured the main fresh water well. With the town surrounded, Brigadier General Eustace declared Thal to be under a state of siege and sent urgent requests to General A.A. Barrett to affect a relief force. At GHQ North West Frontier Force, General Barrett cancelled his previously planned advance on Jellalabad from the Khyber and instead, diverted the recently arrived 16th (Lahore) Division, Major General W.G.L. Beynon, south towards Thal. On 1st June 1919, a mobile column drawn primarily from the 45th Infantry Brigade, designated the Thal Relief Force, formed up under Brigadier General R.E.H. Dyer at Hangu on the railway line west of Kohat.

~ Thal fort, 1919 ~

THAL RELIEF FORCE, JUNE 1919

Brig. Gen. R E H Dyer:
HQ 45th Infantry Brigade
89 Field Battery – Royal Field Artillery
One Section, 23 Mountain Battery – Frontier Garrison Artillery
1/25th (Cyclist) Bn, London Regiment & One Coy, 2/4th (Cumberland and Westmoreland) Bn, Border Regt
1/69th Punjabis, 2/72nd Punjabis, Two Coys, 57th Rifles, 2/41st Dogras & 3/150th Infantry
Half Section, No. 57 Field Company, 1st King George's Own Sappers and Miners
One Section Pack Wireless, Indian Signal Service

Once in position in front of Thal, Brigadier General R.E.H. Dyer initially engaged several tribal *lashkars* while simultaneously feigning an attack on the more robust Afghan positions. Following a brisk engagement, the tribesmen fell back and were followed up 1/25th Bn, London Regt., 69th Punjabis, 2/41st Dogras and 3/150th Infantry. In an attempt to capture several strategically located elevated positions, a British assault was launched on 2nd June 1919. During this engagement, an Afghan officer approached the British line under a flag of truce with a message for Brigadier General Dyer informing him that the Amir had instructed General Nadir Khan to ceasefire. The gates of Thal were flung open and an RAF aircraft and an armoured car were observed racing to be the first relief inside the Fort.

Early on 3rd June 1919, a small force consisting of one squadron the 37th Lancers, IA, one section 87 Battery, RFA and sixty rifles drawn from both 1/25th Bn, London Regt. and 2/4th Bn, Border Regt., were sent to secure the Afghan position at Yusuf Khel. The camp was deserted. Tonne's of abandoned ordnance and broken military hardware lay strewn around much of which had been looted by local tribesmen.

*

Some contemporary observers dismissed the northern campaign in Chitral State as a mere 'sideshow'. The operations in that region were, however, significant because their conduct preserved the integrity of a British protectorate from an alien aggressor and as a result lent reassurance of British intent to other Princely States on the Sub Continent. The only troops in Chitral during early May 1919 were the 1/11th Rajputs, 23 Mountain Battery, FGA, and one section 2 Queen Victoria's Own Sappers and Miners. These regular forces, supported by the Chitral Scouts Militia, fell under the command of Lieutenant Colonel F.C.S. Sambourne-Palmer. Additionally the Methar of Chitral's Bodyguard was available for deployment should the need arise. Opposing this weak force were three Afghan infantry battalions, eight mountain guns and four machine gun units.

On 12th May 1919, the Afghan Army crossed the Indo Afghan border having received reassurances that the Methar of Chitral was prepared to switch allegiance from the British Crown to Afghanistan. Upon entering Chitral State, the Afghan force captured the militia post at Dokalim. The enemy troops thereupon appeared intent on securing Chitral's second largest town – Kala Drosh. Accordingly, the local British Political Agent, Major Reilly, advanced from Kala Drosh with two companies Chitral Scouts Militia and one company of the Methar's Bodyguard in order to secure the bridge over the Kunar River at Nagar. When news of an Afghan assault on Galapach reached the column, Major Reilly advanced the Scouts post haste with a view to driving off the enemy attack. In the subsequent engagement, the enemy fled the field leaving behind 30 of dead and 40 of their wounded. Following this defeat the Methar reaffirmed his allegiance to the British authorities.

The Afghans made several further incursions into Chitral over the ensuing months. All of these assaults were eventually reversed, although the villages of Arnawai and Dokalim were not surrendered until 22ⁿᵈ January 1922! The loyalty of the Chitral Scouts Militia was refreshing for the Government of India. The record of accomplishment of militia units elsewhere during this period having been quite the reverse.

*

The South Baluchistan Front was some 200 miles in length and consisted primarily of barely inhabited arid scrubland. The region contained few substantial settlements other than Quetta and New Charman. The local tribesmen were not normally of an aggressive disposition to the British Crown. Nevertheless, an Afghan incursion into the area would have been extremely serious due to its proximity to British interests in Persia. Troop dispositions in Baluchistan consisted of the 4th (Quetta) Division at Kitchener Barracks, Lieutenant General R. Wapshare, and one flight 114 Squadron, RAF. Unfortunately the squadron's two BE 2E reconnaissance aircraft been wrecked at Quetta aerodrome on 12th May 1919 and consequently, forward observation of the Afghan Army in this theatre was severely restricted until machines from RAF Sibi could be transferred.

Lieutenant General R. Wapshare's plan of campaign for the Baluchistan Front demanded an aggressive advance against the city of Kandahar located deep inside Afghanistan. This plan of action was subsequently revised by the GOC in order to facilitate an assault against the Afghan fort at Spin Baldak. This ancient structure was located just inside the Afghan frontier some six miles northwest of the British railhead at New Charman. The fort was 250 yards square with reinforced packed earth walls some 30 feet high. A deep dry moat surrounded the entire perimeter.

At this juncture, Major General N.G. Woodyatt assumed command of the 4th (Quetta) Division and by 26th May 1919, after a long march from Quetta over the Khojak Pass, the force had formed up at New Charman with a view to advancing on Spin Baldak. The assault began early the following day with the 1/4th Bn, Royal West Kent Regt. and 1/129th Baluch LI of the 57th Infantry Brigade, Brigadier General J.L.R. Gordon, in the vanguard, supported by 270 Company, Machine Gun Corps and 73 Field Company, 3 Queen Victoria's Own Sappers and Miners. On the right flank was the 11th Infantry Brigade, Major General T.H. Hardy, where 'A' and 'B' Companies, 1st Bn, DWR, were tasked with capturing a feature known as 'Tower Hill'. The 10th Infantry Brigade remained in reserve tasked with defending the artillery lines.

BALUCHISTAN FIELD FORCE

4th QUETTA DIVISION: Initially Lt. Gen. R Wapshare and thence Maj. Gen. N G Woodyatt
12th CAVALRY BRIGADE Lt. Col. H B Birdwood 25th Cavalry, IA & 42ⁿᵈ Cavalry, IA 22 Machine Gun Squadron, Machine Gun Corps Cavalry
10th INFANTRY BRIGADE Brig. Gen. H de C O'Grady 2ⁿᵈ Bn, King's (Liverpool) Regt 281 Company, Machine Gun Corps 3/124th Duchess of Connaught's Baluchi LI & 1/5th Native Infantry

11th INFANTRY BRIGADE
Maj. Gen. T H Hardy
No. 24 Field Company, 3rd Sappers and Miners
1st Bn, Duke of Wellingtons Regt (West Riding)
1/22nd Punjabis, 1/4th GR & 2/10th GR
57th INFANTRY BRIGADE
Brig. Gen. J L R Gordon
No. 73 Field Company, 3rd Sappers and Miners
1/4th Bn, R. West Kent Regt
270 Company, Machine Gun Corps
1/129th Baluchis (Duke of Connaught's Own Light Infantry), 2/119th Infantry & 3/7th GR
DIVISIONAL TROOPS
Royal Field Artillery – 102, 1104 and 1107 Batteries
Royal Garrison Artillery – 4 Mountain Battery
33 Divisional Signal Company
2/23rd Sikh Pioneers
2/153rd Punjabis, 1/97th Deccan Infantry, 3/24th Baluchistan Infantry & Jhind Infantry (Imperial Service)
18th Indian Veterinary Section

The lack of effective aerial reconnaissance capability resulted in a poor appreciation of the terrain. The infantry became bogged down among the sand dunes that lay forward of their start line and soon required extrication by the reserve battalions. Liaison with the RAF proved to be inept and one aircraft bombed the point company of the 1/22nd Punjabis killing five sepoys and wounding ten others. Having regrouped, a second attack eventually secured its objective, despite a flanking attack by a party of enemy who had vacated the structure by a previously undetected exit. By mid afternoon, both the village and the fort were in British hands. Discovered among the ruins were the corpses of 170 enemy combatants. Some 186 Afghans attempted to escape back to Afghanistan. These men were quickly intercepted by the cavalry of 12th Cavalry Brigade under Lieutenant Colonel H.B. Birdwood. The 57th Infantry Brigade was subsequently tasked with securing both the fort and its immediate vicinity while the remaining troops withdrew back to New Charman. Fort Spin Baldak was restored to Afghanistan as part of the peace terms concluding the conflict.

*

Further north, near the confluence of the Gomal and Zhob Rivers, the operational situation was less clear-cut. On the afternoon of 27th May 1919, Major G.H. Russell had arrived at the Zhob Militia post at Moghal Khot with his small band of survivors from Wana. Instructions were immediately sent to the 3/1st GR at Fort Sandeman, some fifty miles further south along the Zhob Valley ordering the troops to take the relevant precautions. When news of the unrest reached the Baluchistan Field Force HQ in Quetta, the GOC made a decision to despatch the 10th Infantry Brigade, Brigadier General H. de C. O'Grady, to the region in order to restore some semblance of order. A small relief column consisting of the Patiala Lancers, the 3/124th Baluchis, the 1/5th LI and one section 281 Company MGC was despatched directly to Fort Sanderman. The force was ambushed at Kapip on 16th June and suffered four officers and 49 other ranks killed before fighting through to their destination. Once the Fort had been secured operations began with a view to punishing local tribes and recovering control of the network of militia posts that had been severely damaged by looters.

*

A cease-fire request from the Afghan Government was delivered to General A.A. Barratt at GHQ NWFF in Peshawar late on 2nd June 1919. The Government of India had already prepared the terms under which they would be willing to enter into discussions with the Afghans. These were as follows:

- All Regular and Irregular Afghan Army units to withdraw to a point at least twenty miles distant from any British or Indian Army units.

- The British and Indian Armies to hold and maintain their current positions.

- The RAF to continue to over fly Afghanistan for the purposes of reconnaissance and monitoring the movement of Afghan military forces.

- The Government of Afghanistan to discourage breaches the cease-fire agreement, especially with regard to the inciting of tribal unrest and insurrection against British rule.

Both adversaries claimed to have won the war. To reinforce the British position on the subject, RAF aircraft were deployed to drop leaflets on native settlements throughout the frontier region emphasising the fact that the Amir had sued for peace first. Unfortunately, article four of the ceasefire terms was not adhered to very robustly. Many minor engagements were fought by the Army throughout June 1919 leading to further casualties among both the British and Indian establishments. Only when the Government of India threatened to formally renew hostilities did the Amir pledge to enforce all of the peace conditions. The Amir also agreed to send delegates to a formal peace conference in Rawalpindi. Ali Ahmed, the Amir's cousin, was selected to lead the four man Afghan delegation, but preparations were protracted and it was not until 24th June that the envoys set out for India from Kabul.

*

~ Afghan delegates arrive for the Peace Conference ~

Despite overtures for peace, an Afghan force occupied the abandoned South Waziristan Militia headquarters at Wana on, or about, 7th June 1919. This action appeared isolated and the British authorities believed this belligerent act could be resolved diplomatically at the forthcoming peace conference. Consequently, due to the ever-growing tribal unrest independent of Afghan leadership, field operations concentrated on dispersing native *lashkars* and exacting punitive retribution. These activities were conducted on the land and from the air. In retaliation for the alleged use of air power against defenceless tribal settlements, Waziri warriors launched an attack against RAF Bannu on the night of 14th July 1919. Troops from the 2/27th Punjabis, deployed on airfield protection duties, eventually succeeded in repulsing this incursion.

Throughout Waziristan, fanatical tribesmen constantly harassed military convoys and road picquets. Numerous casualties were inflected on the Army. Of particular note was the ambush of an 82nd Punjabis patrol on 8th August 1919. This incident consisted of an attack by some 200 Mahsud warriors under Musa Khan and led to the deaths of at least one Indian officer and 19 sepoys. Tribesmen destroyed a section of the Bannu to Kalabagh railway on 25th August 1919. This was followed up two days later by a party of Mahsud who literally cut their way through the wall of Fort Girni and engaged the garrison in a bitter hand-to-hand struggle. The Mahsud later murdered 15 sepoys at the Labour Corps camp near Gambila in the Mianwali region. On 19th September, a group of Mahsud tribesmen in the Derajat region attacked the militia post at Zarkani, killing Major W.G.W. Durham, 27 Light Cavalry, IA, and five sepoys of his command.

*

When Sir A Hamilton, Indian Foreign Secretary, received Ali Ahmed in Rawalpindi, much of the content of the initial peace talks focused on which party would accept responsibility for starting the conflict and which prisoners would be exchanged for whom. A plan to reaffirm the route of the Indo Afghan border was also agreed. Eventually, the question of Afghanistan's future political independence from Britain was tabled. On 6th August 1919, a signal was received from Whitehall agreeing to grant Afghanistan full independence in exchange for the cancellation of any future financial subsidies. Two days later the interested parties signed the Treaty of Rawalpindi and the Third Afghan War was formally concluded. (Operations continued right up to the day the peace treaty was signed. One of the last actions being the cleansing of the Kajauri Plain by Major General Shepherd, of tribesmen intent on interfering with Peshawar).

Qualification for the 'AFGHANISTAN N.W.F. 1919' clasp to the India General Service Medal 1908–1935 terminated at midnight 8th August 1919. Due to the ongoing conflict in Waziristan, an extension to midnight 30th September was granted for troops of the Waziristan Force. Active involvement with the Waziristan Force from 1st October onwards qualified for the additional award of the clasp 'WAZIRISTAN 1919 – 21'.

KOHAT / KURRAM FORCE

28 Indian Mountain Battery
No. 74 Field Company, 3rd Sappers & Miners
44 Divisional Signal Company
4 Armoured Motor Battery
22 Company, MGC Cav
288 Company, MGC
Kurram Militia

COMMAND STRUCTURE, AFGHANISTAN NORTH WEST FRONTIER 1919

Commander North West Frontier Force Gen. A A Barratt	
1st (Peshawar) Division: Lt. Gen. F Campbell	
Brigade Commanders	
Brig. Gen. F G H Davies	1st Cavalry Brigade
Brig. Gen. G D Crocker	1st (Peshawar) Infantry Brigade
Maj. Gen. S H Climo	2nd (Nowshera) Infantry Brigade
Maj. Gen. A Skeen (Later Brig. Gen. R O B Taylor)	3rd (Abbottabad) Infantry Brigade
Brig. Gen. L W Y Campbell	(Sialkot) Infanty Brigade - Peshawar Internal Security Area
Brig. Gen. Lane	Lines of Communication Peshawar Area
2nd (Rawalpindi) Division: Maj. Gen. C M Dobell	
Brigade Commanders	
Brig. Gen. G M Baldwin	10th Cavalry Brigade
Brig. Gen. E C Peebles	4th Infantry Brigade
Brig. Gen. F H Peterson	5th Infantry Brigade
Brig. Gen. G Christian	6th Infantry Brigade
16th (Lahore) Central Reserve Division: Maj. Gen. W G L Benyon	
Brigade Commanders	
Brig. Gen. W M Southey	44th Infantry Brigade
Brig. Gen. R E H Dyer	45th Infantry Brigade
Brig Gen: C G Bruce	46th (Mobile) Infantry Brigade
Baluchistan Field Force:	
4th (Quetta) Division: Lt. Gen. R Wapshare thence Lt. Gen. N G Woodyatt	
Brigade Commanders	
Lt. Col. H B Birdwood	12th Cavalry Brigade
Brig. Gen. H de O'Grady	10th (Quetta) Infantry Brigade
Maj. Gen. T H Hardy	11th Infantry Brigade
Brig. Gen. J L R Gordon	57th Infantry Brigade
Waziristan Force: Maj. Gen. N G Woodyatt thence Maj. Gen. S H Climo	
Brigade Commanders	
Brig. Gen. J L J Clarke	43rd Infantry Brigade
Brig. Gen. C E Fourkes	67th Infantry Brigade

~ Extra Regimentally Employed Personnel ~
Special Service Battalions, Small Seconded Formations and Individuals
'AFGHANISTAN NORTH WEST FRONTIER 1919'

The transition to British peacetime establishments following the conclusion of World War One found the remaining British and Indian Armies stationed in the sub-continent ill prepared for a new confrontation. When hostilities with Afghanistan were declared by Britain in May 1919, it became necessary to draft in any available resource in order to bring deployable units up to war strength. Personnel, especially Territorial Force troops, were diverted from active demobilisation in adjacent theatres, while existing establishments, including Garrison Battalions, provided resources ranging in strength from rifle companies to sections. The deployment of complete individuals was common.

The majority of these 'odd' men were formed into hastily created Special Service Battalions that were deployed as follows:

- Nos. 1–4 / A Pool of reserves to bring existing line battalions up to war establishment. (Note: No. 2 SSB = Railway Duties Establishment)

- Nos. 6, 12, 15, 16 & 18 / Internal security duties in the Indian hinterland.

- No. 17 / Deployed as a line battalion to Southern Waziristan and Baluchistan.

Medals therefore exist to a wide variety of units not otherwise present.

For:

AFGHANISTAN NORTH WEST FRONTIER 1919[3] Roll and Units Present: See 'Combined Frontier Campaigns 1919–1925 Roll', located at the end of Chapter 3

AFGHANISTAN NORTH WEST FRONTIER 1919[3] Known Casualties: See 'Combined Frontier Campaigns 1919–1925 Casualties Roll', located at the end of Chapter 3

~ Mahsud 1919–1920 & Waziristan 1919–1921 ~

~ The India General Service Medal 1908–1935~
MAHSUD 1919-20
WAZIRISTAN 1919-21
Issue 2. Calcutta Mint

The operations in Waziristan and Mahsud were closely inter-related and therefore, for the sake of continuity, it is best to consider the events surrounding both campaigns in the same section.

*

The clasp 'WAZIRISTAN 1919–21' was sanctioned under Army Order No. 361 of 1921, subsequently amended by Army Orders 94 of 1922, 347 of 1922, 107 of 1923 and 149 of 1927. It was instituted to award military personnel and certain war mobilised civilians employed under the command of Major General S.H. Climo engaged in ongoing operations against various elements of the Waziri and Mahsud peoples who were determined to exploit the military and political disruption throughout the Indian North West Frontier emanating from the Third Afghan War 1919. The initial qualifying date for this award, 1st October 1919, ran sequentially with midnight 30th September 1919, the final qualifying date for the clasp 'AFGHANISTAN N.W.F. 1919'.

To be eligible for the 'WAZIRISTAN 1919–21' clasp to the India General Service Medal 1908–1935, Army personnel had to serve on the War Establishment (India) in Northern or Southern Waziristan and satisfy one (or more) of the following criteria:

- Served on the Bannu Line between 1st October 1919 and midnight 27th November 1919 inclusive.

- Served on the Tank Line between 1st October 1919 and midnight 20th December 1921 inclusive.

- Served west of Kharkon Algad between 27th November 1921 and midnight 16th December 1921 inclusive.

- Served in the Zhob region on the posted strength of Forts Brunj Safi, Mir Ali Khel and Mogul Kot between 12th November 1920 and midnight 31st May 1921 inclusive.

Royal Air Force personnel qualified under similar provisions.

*

The clasp 'MAHSUD 1919–20' was sanctioned under Army Order No. 361 of 1921 to reward military personnel and certain war mobilised civilians employed under Major General A. Skeen and engaged with the Derajat Column in the subjugation of the Mahsuds. Initially only formations deployed west of Jandola between 18th December 1919 and 8th April 1920 qualified for the award. In 1922, however, Army Order No. 347 extended eligibility to personnel engaged during the same period along the Takki Zam line north of and including Jandola.

Royal Air Force personnel qualified under similar provisions.

Mahsud territory was totally enclosed by Northern and Southern Waziristan. Consequently, these scarce bars are rarely found singularly, especially to British Army recipients. Single entitlements do exist and reference should be made to the medal roll at the end of this chapter to verify such entitlement.

*

The origins of the Waziristan 1919–21 campaign are reviewed at the start of this chapter. Suffice it to say, a full-scale, anti British frontier rebellion had been fermented amongst the Waziri and Mahsud by Afghan emissaries during the Third Afghan War 1919. By October 1919, this violence required urgent pacification. Much of the unrest had in fact been inspired by the false rumour that Britain had agreed to transfer sovereignty of the Waziristan and the Mahsud regions to Afghanistan during the Rawalpindi Peace negotiations of August 1919.

The 'Waziristan Force' had previously concentrated on breaking up tribal *lashkars* and picqueting the Lines of Communication that stretched back from the remotest fort to Force Headquarters in Dera Ismail Khan. Punitive action focused on demonstrating to local warriors that anti-British behaviour would not be tolerated. By October 1919, Major General S.H. Climo had reversed a number of earlier strategic setbacks. These actions included the relief of the Tochi Forts and operations in the Derajat region leading to the relief of Jandola. Fort Wana, however, remained securely in 'enemy' hands. Here an Afghan force under Colonel Shah Daula became a focal point for tribal elders seeking inspiration and material support for their on-going military campaign against British interests. The British Government determined that the Army should adopt a more aggressive stance following several tribal raids across the Administrative Boundary into the 'settled districts' of British India east of the Indus River. (A report was even commissioned by the CGS India to investigate the possible use of gas ordnance to disperse and incapacitate such tribal activity).

*

On 5th October 1919, the escort to a Sappers and Miners telephone cable section was attacked near Manjhi Post in Wana Waziri territory. Captain C.E. Broughton, 34th Horse, IA attached Bhopal Imperial Service Lancers, and his force comprising three mounted troops plus a platoon drawn from the 1/150th Infantry, were all but massacred. A handful of survivors escaped back to Manjhi where they raised the alarm. That evening a decision was made to deploy a second force to search for wounded survivors and recover the dead. To this end Major J.M.L. Bostock, Bhopal Imperial Service Lancers, was despatched to the scene from Kaur Bridge, accompanied by two rifle companies composed of the 109th Infantry and 3rd Guides Infantry, plus a squadron of his command.

The recovery of the dead was successful, but upon the force's retirement, contact was made with a small party of Waziri who, after exchanging a few desultory shots, dispersed. The cavalry did not

~ Waziri tribesmen 1919-1924 ~

follow up this incident properly and consequently the presence of a large tribal *lashkar* in the area went undetected. Some hours latter an enemy ambush was sprung. The force's rear guard, furnished by a platoon of the 109th Infantry, was quickly cut off and overwhelmed. Frantic attempts to rescue these men failed. The incident culminated in the deaths of three British officers and some 80 sepoys.

In an attempt to seek immediate retribution for this reversal, 16 aircraft of the newly established 1st (Indian) Wing RAF conducted a raid against several Wana Waziri villages on 9th October 1919. This punitive action only went to encourage further confrontation and a week later a large *lashkar* invested Fort Murtaza, while simultaneously severing the water supply to the forts at Jatta and Kaur Bridge. Fortunately, the latter location was at that juncture being used as a concentration point for the Lines of Communication defence force. Consequently, an immediate call to arms resulted in a rapid dispersal of the Waziri warriors as well as the prompt reconnection of the water supply!

Afghan emissaries continued to advise and support anti-British sentiment throughout Waziristan despite their Government's recent defeat in the Third Afghan War. Tribal elders were constantly appealing to General Nadir Khan of the Afghan Army to make good his promise to occupy western Waziristan despite his mandate to comply with the terms of the Rawalpindi Peace Treaty. Thus in early October 1919, General Khan secretly conducted a party of Waziri and Mahsud *maliks* to Kabul for an audience with the Amir. During this meeting, the Amir, not wishing any more conflict with the British, reviewed the terms that were now in effect and advised the tribesmen to return to British territory and make good the peace. This advice was resolutely ignored.

On 21st October 1919, the Indian Army suffered heavy losses during engagements near Girni and Khajuri. During the contact at the latter location Captain H.J. Andrews, IMS, won a posthumous Victoria Cross. Following this incident, it was determined that an increased level of offensive operations would be required to restore the rule of law. Two possible future policies were thus considered. One plan called for the full occupation of the Waziristan region from the Administrative Border up to the Durand Line. This idea was rejected due to lack of adequate manpower combined with the level of financial expenditure required. The second scheme called for the establishment of several large permanent garrisons throughout the region linked by modern metalled roads enabling the rapid deployment of troops by motor vehicle to deal with perceived confrontational behaviour as and when it occurred.

Upon acceptance of the second proposal, the Government of India prepared the following plan of action:

Upper Tochi Posts ~
No attempt to be made to re-occupy until alternative objectives were secured.

Tochi Waziri Tribal Areas ~
Government terms to be announced in *jirga* at Miranshah on 9th November 1919. Troops of the Tochi Column to advance as far as Datta Khel only. 1 (Indian) Wing RAF to be held on constant alert thus facilitating an immediate military response if necessary. Acceptance of all Government terms to be made public by 17th November.

Wana Waziri Tribal Areas ~
Terms to be announced in *jirga* at a later date.

Mahsud Tribal Area ~
Government terms to be announced by Major General S.H. Climo in *jirga* at Khirgi on 3rd November 1919. The decision of the Mahsud to be made public by 11th November. If rejected, punitive measures to be enforced upon the conclusion of operations in Tochi territory.

*

Review of Terms Presented
- The Amir of Afghanistan has not secured from the British any amnesty for lawless behaviour on behalf of the Mahsud or Tochi tribes and none should be sought henceforth.

- The Government to be permitted by local elders to construct metalled roads and station troops in any area deemed necessary without interference or molestation. Local labour to be contracted by the authorities against normal pay scales.

- All British military equipment stolen since 1st May 1919 to be returned to the British Government via local Political Agents or Residents.

- A fine of Rs. 10,000 to be levied against the Mahsud and Rs. 40,000 to be levied against the Tochi Waziri.

- The payment of tribal allowances to be suspended until the Government is satisfied with tribal behaviour and intent.

- A deposit of 200 'local' rifles to be placed with the Political Department as a guarantee of good faith. These rifles to be returned to the tribal authorities once all other terms are complied with.

- Sepoys and Sowars currently posted as 'absent' or 'deserted' from the various regional militia forces to be acquitted of their offences under the military penal code and discharged from their military obligations once their Government Issue rifles are returned.

- Officers and non-commissioned officers deserted from the various Waziristan militia forces to turn themselves in for summary trial or else remain liable to ongoing arrest.

The Tochi Waziri did not agree to subjugate themselves to the terms stipulated by the Government. Consequently, it was decided to advance the Tochi Column, which had been forming up at Miranshah since 8th November 1919 in readiness for such an eventuality, into the Tochi hinterland with a view to forcing the tribesmen into submission. The column was commanded by Major General A Skeen and consisted of the 43rd Infantry Brigade, under Brigadier General G. Gwyn-Thomas, and the 67th Infantry Brigade, under Brigadier General F.G. Lucas. The balance of the Waziristan Force at this time was deployed along the Lines of Communication, some 350 miles in length. The railheads of Bannu in the north and Tank in the south were well protected as was the strategically located Indus River port and joint Army and Royal Air Force Headquarters at Dera Ismail Khan.

RAF support came in the form of No. 1 (Indian) Wing with squadrons divided among aerodromes at Mianwali, Bannu and Tank. The aircraft available were primarily Bristol F2b Fighters, De Havilland 9As and De Havilland 10s.

On 12th November 1919, the Tochi Column began its advance towards Datta Khel. A *lashkar* of Madda Khel Waziri was observed at one stage during the march but no contact occurred. The 'first echelon' occupied their objective without opposition on 14th November, following an RAF bombing sortie that encouraged even the bravest of warriors to retire. Meanwhile, the second and third echelons occupied the villages of Degan and Boya respectively. Two days later a party of Tochi *maliks* was received by Major General S.H. Climo in Data Khel and, in line with the terms recently set out at Miranshah, surrendered (the local area). The RAF was thereupon employed to visit remote renegades and encourage their capitulation!

~ Bristol F2b being turned into the wind for take off ~

COMPOSITION OF THE TOCHI COLUMN, NOVEMBER 1919

Maj. Gen. A Skeen
No. 1 Echelon:
Headquarters Tochi Column
Cavalry
1 & Half Squadrons, 31ˢᵗ D C O Lancers, IA
Artillery
1 Section, RFA Howitzers
35 Indian Mountain Battery
Sappers & Pioneers
No. 55 Field Company, 1ˢᵗ King George's Own Sappers & Miners,
2-61ˢᵗ King George's Own Pioneers
Survey Section
Signals
HQ Section only, No. 40 Divisional Signal Company, No. 16 Pack Wireless Section
Infantry
Northern Waziristan Militia, 3ʳᵈ Queen Victoria's Own Guides Infantry (Scouts)
Ancillary Support Units
Medical, Supply, etc
Lines of Communication Defence
2/21ˢᵗ and 2/76ᵗʰ Punjabis from the 47ᵗʰ Infantry Brigade
& (2/76ᵗʰ Punjabis later transferred to the 68ᵗʰ Infantry Brigade for the Derajat expedition)
67ᵗʰ Infantry Brigade – Brig. Gen. F G Lucas
1/55ᵗʰ Coke's Rifles, 1/103ʳᵈ Mahratta LI, 104ᵗʰ Wellesley's Rifles & 2/112ᵗʰ Infantry
No. 2 Echelon:
Sappers & Pioneers
No. 74 Field Company, 3ʳᵈ Sappers & Miners, 3/34ᵗʰ Royal Sikh Pioneers
Machine Gun Corps
6 Armoured Motor Battery, Motorised Machine Gun Corps
Infantry
2/152ⁿᵈ Punjabis (from 43ʳᵈ Infantry Brigade)
Ancillary Support Units
Medical, Supply, etc
No. 3 Echelon:
Cavalry
Half Squadron, 31ˢᵗ DCO Lancers, IA
Artillery
33 Indian Mountain Battery (less 1 section)
43ʳᵈ Infantry Brigade
4/39ᵗʰ Garhwal Rifles, 57ᵗʰ Wilde's Rifles & 82ⁿᵈ Punjabis
Ancillary Support Units
Medical, Supply, etc

The Government had not received a satisfactory response from the Mahsud. Therefore, with the Tochi situation stabilised, the British force evacuated Datta Khel on 25ᵗʰ November 1919, and withdrew back to Dardoni. The troops were transferred to the newly formed Derajat Column ready for an advance into Mahsud territory and, if necessary, the capture of the tribal 'capital' region that lay along the Makin Valley. The balance of the Waziristan Force maintained their existing positions. Thus, on 27ᵗʰ November, the Derajat Column proceeded to Tank via Bannu where it formed up with its Lines of Communication defence and ancillary units on the Tank–Jandola line. Meanwhile, the RAF had made a series of concerted aerial assaults on Mahsud settlements, penetrating as far as the Makin area, in an attempt to sap the enemy's morale and deter it from engaging with any British advance.

A Mahsud *jirga* opened in Kanigurum on 28th November 1919. The assembled elders were keen to continue to exploit the presence of General Nadir Khan in Jellalabad. The Afghan General, who had previously promised to send significant quantities of supplies across the Afghan boarder into British India, had recently been instructed by the Amir to restrict his intrigues. Nevertheless, Afghan agents attending the Kanigurum *jirga* advised the Mahsud that arms and ammunition would soon be made available. Consequently, and in light of ongoing RAF raids against undefended village settlements, a decision was reached by the Mahsud calling for more concerted and unified action against the British.

*

The plan of campaign for the invasion of the Mahsud region required the advance of the main column on a single front from Jandola. This strategy was designed to force the enemy into concentrating the bulk of its force in a defensive strategy, thus enabling as many warriors as possible to be accounted for in any given engagement. The plan also reduced the complexity of the Lines of Communication. In the mountainous terrain of the Mahsud, any defence required the establishment of frequent semi permanent picquets, each well protected by rock and wire with adequate signals communication between both each other and the main force.

With reconnaissances completed, preparatory work began to secure the first stage of the projected line of advance on 11th December 1919. A small force secured the Spinkai Raghza ridge north of Jandola after which work commenced on improving the existing rough track into something akin to a road. Tribesmen resisted this activity resulting in constant skirmishes and sniping over a three-day period, which accounted for 46 military killed, including 2nd Lieutenant N.D. Douglas, 3rd Queen Victoria's Own Guides. On 17th December, Major General A. Skeen's operational headquarters accompanied the deployment of the 67th Infantry Brigade from Khirgi to Jandola via the River Tank Zam. Later that same day, a strong force of Mahsud closed on Jandola's defensive picquets. Artillery fire failed to contain the attack, the enemy withdrawing only after having been engaged at close quarters by the infantry. This incident resulted in the force losing a further 34 sepoys killed.

On 18th December 1919, the Derajat Column began the advance into Mahsud territory. A small force drawn from the 68th Infantry Brigade, under Brigadier General J.L.R. Gordon, secured the confluence of the Shahur and Tank Zam Rivers while the main column began to clear the Sarkai Ridge with a view to occupying the Palosina Plain, three miles north northwest of Jandola. The skirmish line drove waiting tribesmen down towards the Tank Zam River where the RAF 'encouraged' further retirement west. The engineers established a base camp on level ground adjacent to the river once the plain was safely secured.

The Palosina Plain was dominated by high ground, including a feature christened Mandanna Hill that, if occupied, would give a commanding view of the intended line of advance along the Tank Zam towards the Mahsud settlement at Kotkai. Thus, on 19th December 1919, a force composed of 1/55th Coke's Rifles and 1/103rd Mahratta Light Infantry was detailed to capture the hill and establish a permanent picquet on its summit. Shortly after starting out, however, large numbers of tribesmen swarmed down on the advancing infantry forcing the troops to withdraw in 'ragged' order. Casualties were high. The 1/103rd Mahratta Light Infantry lost Major C. McVeagh, Captain G. Horsburgh and Lieutenant H. le G. Gasper and some 95 Sepoys killed. A further 150 officers and other ranks were wounded. Brigadier General F.G. Lucas, however, successfully executed a brigade level attack against the same objective the following morning. The battalions deployed were 2/19th Punjabis, 1/55th Rifles, 109th Infantry and 2/112th Infantry supported by two sections 55 Field Company, 1st King George's Own

Sappers and Miners plus two companies 3/34th Sikh Pioneers. The Mahsud were overwhelmed but not without loss to the Army including Lieutenant Colonel R.D.G. Churchill, 2/19th Punjabis. During the late afternoon a picquet was established under the direction of Captain A.L. Cuthbert, 2/19th Punjabis. The main force was thereupon withdrawn from the area. With hindsight, this manoeuvre proved to be an unwise decision and within hours, Captain Cuthbert and most of his command were dead.

An attempt to establish command of a second feature, known as Black Hill, met with similar opposition before being finally secured on 25th December 1919. During this operation the 2/19th and 82nd Punjabis, combined with 2/112th Infantry, suffered significant casualties including Lieutenant Colonel H.C.D. Jarrett 2/19th Punjabis and Lt. L.F.C. Arnold RF attached 82nd Punjabis plus 66 sepoys killed. Consequently, a decision was made, calling for these battalions to be withdrawn into the Lines of Communication defences establishment in an attempt to enable them to reorganise. The 4/39th Garhwal Rifles, 2/76th Punjabis and 2/152nd Punjabis were immediately deployed to fill the gap in the order of battle.

Mahsud casualties had been equally significant since the Derajat Column began its advance. To that end, a party of tribal elders requested a meeting with the authorities on, or about, the 27th December 1919. Permission was granted for the *maliks* to assemble for a two-day *jirga* before Major General S. H. Climo in Jandola commencing on 28th December. Most attended the meeting with the notable exception of the Abdullai Mahsud who inhabited a remote area of the Makin Valley region. The terms originally announced in Khirgi on 3rd November were restated to the assembled elders but with extra covenants, including a demand for additional rifles to be surrendered. General Climo also advised the *maliks* that until the sincerity of their capitulation could be measured in full, the advance of the Derajat Column to Makin would continue.

Thus, on 29th December 1919, the 43rd Infantry Brigade advanced from Palosina to Kotkai and remained at that location until 7th January 1920, before being relieved by the 67th Infantry Brigade. During the intervening period, the Lines of Communication back to Jandola were further developed and several permanent picquets established north of Kotkai in readiness for further advances. Most of these activities went unmolested, as per the terms of the recent *jirga*. On 2nd January 1920, however, a position under construction on a feature known as Scrub Hill came under concerted attack from a *lashkar* led by the renegade Malik Fazldin. The picquet guard, furnished by 4/39th Garhwal Rifles, retired with 35 dead, but only after a gallant stand by a section under Lieutenant W.D. Kenny who was subsequently recognised by the award of a posthumous Victoria Cross.

The defeat of Fazldin's *lashkar* at Katkai prompted the Shaman Khel and Mansai Mahsud to surrender and submit to terms. The Nana Khel and Shabi Khel Mahsud remained in the field, however, supported in strength by Wana Waziri drawn from both sides of the Durand Line. Thus, as the Derajat Column advanced towards the strategic Ahnai Tangi Pass, there were still plenty of committed Mahsud available to mount a resolute defence along the projected British line of advance. In an attempt to mitigate the anticipated opposition, on 7th January 1920, Major General S.H. Climo instructed the 43rd Infantry Brigade to secure the east bank of the Tank Zam thus enabling this force to protect the flank of the 67th Infantry Brigade as it advanced to contact along the west bank towards the mouth of the Ahnai Tangi.

Attempts by both Brigades to complete their missions resulted in serious loss of life during operations on both 9th and 10th of January 1920. A more coordinated attack was organised for effect early on 11th January. The 43rd Infantry Brigade, comprising 4/39th Garhwal Rifles, 109th Infantry, 2/152nd Punjabis, supported by two companies of the recently deployed 2/150th Infantry, was to develop an

~ Looking through the narrow Ahnai Tangi Pass - 1920 ~

attack on the Konr Range overlooking the eastern flank of the Ahnai Tangi. The 67th Infantry Brigade, comprised of 1/55th Coke's Rifles, 57th Wilde's Rifles, 2/76th Punjabis and the newly arrived 2/5th GR, was detailed to launch a dawn attack to secure the mouth of the pass. Kotkai was left in control of 2/9th GR which had just marched up from Jandola. This plan was executed successfully, though with some loss. The abandoned militia post near to the mouth of the Ahnai Tangi was reoccupied and picquets established.

AHNAI TANGI TROOP DISPOSITIONS, 14th JANUARY 1920

Advance Guard – Lt. Col. H Herdon, 1/55th Coke's Rifles
1 Section, No. 27 (Indian) Mountain Battery, Detachment No. 38 Divisional Signal Company, HQ Section 1/55th Coke's Rifles, 2 Companies, 2/5th GR
Flank Guard – Lt. Col. J D Crowdy, 2/5th GR (Latter Lt. Col. Chamberlain, 2/76th Punjabis)
2/5th GR (less 2 Companies) (Latter reinforced by 'ad hoc' elements 2/76th Punjabis and 1 Company 2/9th GR)
Main Body – Maj. Gen. A Skeen
1 Troop, 21st Cavalry, IA, 6 Mountain Battery, RGA, (less 1 Section) 27 Indian Mountain Battery (less 2 Sections) No. 55 Field Company, 1st King George's Own Sappers & Miners Photo and Survey Sections, 2nd Queen Victoria's Sappers & Miners. No. 38 Divisional Signal Company (less 1 Section), No. 16 Pack Wireless Station 3/34th Sikh Pioneers 2/76th Punjabis & 2 Companies 109th Infantry
Rear Guard – Maj. A E Mahon, 109th Infantry
109th Infantry (less 2 Companies)
Road Guard From Start Point To Rear Guard – Brig. Gen. F G Lucas
1 Section, 6 Mountain Battery, RGA, 1 Section, 27 (Indian) Mountain Battery 2/9th Gurkha Rifles (latter less 1 Company detached to Flank Guard), 57th Wilde's Rifles

Early on the morning of 14th January 1920, 1/55th Coke's Rifles, supported by two companies 2/5th GR and two guns 27 Mountain Battery, attempted to penetrate the Ahnai Tangi proper. The mission was to probe the extent and intent of the enemy's defensive plan and then secure the route in preparation of the advance of the main column. Meanwhile, a flank guard, composed of the balance of 2/5th GR, set out to secure a feature christened Flathead Left. Heavy enemy sniper fire began to cut into the flanks of both parties and casualties were soon sustained including Major J.D. Crowdy, 2/5th GR, the acting commanding officer of 2/76th Punjabis.

Reinforcements, furnished by 2/9th GR, were deployed to the flank guard in order to enable further elevated positions to be captured and secured. Meanwhile, on the floor of the Ahnai Tangi, the main column had begun its advance even before being given the 'all clear' by the advance guard. Consequently, men, mules and supplies began to form up in the open offering the enemy extensive target opportunities. Anxious not to retire, Major General A Skeen ordered the creation of a makeshift defensive laager area in the shelter of the dry riverbed. This position became known as Asa Khan Camp. Only after the high ground was secured, at the cost of the life of Lieutenant Colonel A. Chamberlain, 1st Duke of York's Own Lancers, IA, attached 2/76th Punjabis, did the pressure on the main force subside.

Intelligence reports later estimated that some 4,000 Mahsud warriors, with Wana Waziri support, had been engaged in the defence of the Ahnai Tangi. Consequently, it is not surprising that Asa Khan Camp remained occupied for five long days before the column broke out onto the Sorarogha plateau beyond. Nine British officers were killed and two wounded, while the Indian ranks suffered two officers and 365 Sepoys killed or wounded. Casualties were not limited to the Indian Army. Tribal marksmen succeeded in shooting down three of the RAF aircraft that had been acting in close support to the force. The aircrews, though injured, evaded capture and were eventually recovered. The enemy subsequently acknowledged some 400 casualties among its ranks. Further investigation suggested that it was principally the decision of the Mahsud to evacuate their wounded that enabled the Derajat Column to resume its advance.

An advance base camp was established on the Sorarogha Plateau and soon, thereafter, the Sappers and Miners constructed a rough airstrip thus enabling the RAF to maintain long-range patrols and reconnaissance sorties deep into the Mahsud hinterland. Foot patrols were constant. On 19th January 1920, the village of Nai Karch was searched. Following the discovery of a severed human head hidden in an earthenware jar, a decision was made to burn the settlement to the ground. Major General A. Skeen decided that ten days worth of stores should be assembled before any further advance on Makin was attempted. Meanwhile, the exhausted main column buried its dead and rested. The 3rd Queen's Own Corps of Guides, which had been attached to the column as reinforcements from the 68th Infantry Brigade at Jandola, spent the respite acclimatising and training with the more 'seasoned' units.

North of the Sorarogha camp, the River Tank Zam cut through the Sarkai Ridge via a deep gorge known as the Barari Tangi. Before any advance along the riverbed could be attempted, it was necessary to capture the steep bluffs dominating the feature. To this end Brigadier Genral F G Lucas advanced with 1/55th Rifles, 2/5th GR and 2/9th GR to secure the highest points on both the left and right flanks. This exercise took two days to accomplish under constant enemy assault, hence numerous casualties were sustained. Had it not been for the ability of the RAF to maintain air to ground support, the death toll would have been far greater.

On 26th January 1920, the 68th Infantry Brigade marched up from Jandola to Kotkai with a view to relieving the 43rd Infantry Brigade as Tank Lines of Communication defences. This manoeuvre enabled the latter brigade to deploy up to Sorarogha in support of the 67th Infantry Brigade. Two days later, under cover of darkness, an assault on the Barari Tangi was launched. The assault took the Mahsud by surprise and they were unable to mount any depth of defence. By nightfall on 28th January 1920, a patrol base had been established just north of the Barari Tangi at Ahmadwan.

BARARI TANGI TROOP DISPOSITIONS, 28th JANUARY 1920

Elevated Flank Guard – Brig. Gen. F G Lucas
1/55th Coke's Rifles, 2/5th GR, 2 Coys, 109th Infantry & 3rd Queen's Own Corps of Guides
Barari Tangi Advance Guard – Brig. Gen. G Gwyn-Thomas
57th Wilde's Rifles & 2/150th Infantry
Flanking Detachment
2 Coys, 4/39th Garhwal Rifles & 2/9th GR

Heavy snow and driving sleet prevented the Derajat Column from engaging in anything more than consolidation operations during the ensuing few days. By 1st February 1920, however, the weather had cleared sufficiently to continue the advance towards the Aka Khel Plateau. The village of Ahmadwan was captured without a shot being fired, followed in quick succession by the villages of Bangwada and Shinkaur. Once again, the cover of darkness was utilised to good effect. (The bulk of the Mahsud defence had withdrawn further north where they converged with a Wana Waziri *lashkar*, supported by Afghan mountain guns, provided by Colonel Shah Daula's force at Fort Wana). All objectives were quickly secured with the loss of ten killed and 19 wounded, including an RAF flight observer. The artillery was used to good effect and the Wana Waziri *lashkar*, forming up at Shin Konr, was dispersed by shellfire. Subsequent reconnaissance flights confirmed direct hits on all of the Afghan gun positions.

Soon after establishing a secure position on the Aka Khel, the weather closed in again. Patrols of 3rd Queen's Own Corps of Guides and 2/5th GR, that had been tasked with securing several sites in preparation for an advance towards Janjal on the Piazha Algad plateau, were forced to seek shelter from the intense cold rather than continue their missions. The blizzard lasted two days. By 7th February 1920, however, the main force had established a new advance camp at Piazha Raghza. Over the following seven days, this location was consolidated along with the Lines of Communication back to Sorarogha.

~ Mules bring up supplies through the Barari Tangi – 1920 ~

Fresh troops in the form of 4/3rd GR were received at this time. Permanent picquets were established, though the decision to site one of these locations in an old Mahsud watchtower resulted in disaster when, on 13th February, the unsound structure collapsed killing 15 sepoys.

The Derajat Column had now penetrated deep into the Mahsud hinterland and the military authorities determined that a campaign of punitive restoration should now be prosecuted against the Mahsud for not having complied with the agreements made in *jirga* at Jandola on 29th December 1919. Consequently, a number of local settlements were destroyed and the inhabitants forced to take shelter in remote caves. Notice was given to the Mahsud that, in light of their decision to ignore the original terms of capitulation, new requirements would now be imposed. The fresh terms stipulated that the principle settlements of both Makin and Kaniguram would be destroyed unless a fine of 200 Government Issue rifles per village be surrendered in advance of the Derajat Column arriving at either location.

On 15th February 1920, the main force left Piazha Raghza and advanced as far as Marobi. The 43rd Infantry Brigade remained in camp to become No. 3 Section, Lines of Communication Defences. The following day, fresh reinforcements arrived in the form of 3/11th GR. Meanwhile, the main column, having established a well-defended fallback position at Marobi, advanced to within two miles of the start of the Makin Valley where it established a patrol base on the east bank of the Tauda China River. Various acts of a punitive nature were then undertaken, some of which drew enemy fire and resultant casualties.

DERAJAT COLUMN

Advance From Piazha Raghza to Makin (Listed in Column of Route)
2/5th GR, 2/9th GR, 4/3rd GR, 1/55th Coke's Rifles, 3rd Queen's Own Corps of Guides, 3/34th Sikh Pioneers, 6 Mountain Battery, RGA, 27 (Indian) Mountain Battery, No. 55 Field Company, 1st King George's Own and Miners, Ancillary Units

Several days passed during which the Mahsud elders in Makin failed to comply with the new terms of submission. Consequently, Major General A. Skeen determined to advance across the Tauda China and lay waste several Makin settlements along with much of the surrounding agricultural area including the large village of Umar Khan. On 19th and 20th February 1920, troops attempted to secure high ground to cover the general advance. Outlaying hamlets were destroyed with loss. Shortly thereafter, elders from Umar Khan approached column headquarters and surrendered 12 Government Issue rifles. This submission was accepted and no further destruction of their property occurred. Elsewhere, across the Makin region, a total of 51 watchtowers and 450 lodge houses were raised to the ground.

With little left to achieve in the Makin area, Major General A. Skeen withdrew his force during the night of 29th February/1st March 1920. Despite operating under the cover of darkness, the retirement of several flank guard picquets was followed up closely by parties of tribesmen. The next objective of the Derajat Column was Kaniguram. *Maliks* from this settlement approached column headquarters at this time with an offer comprising approximately half of the required deposit of Government Issue rifles. This proposed settlement was rejected by the authorities and preparations for the advance continued.

The advance to contact towards Kaniguram via Ladha began early on 3rd March 1920. Sniping was encountered throughout much of the march; however, with every mile traversed it became increasingly clear that no enemy *lashkar* had been assembled to contest the Derajat Column in depth. Ladha was reached later the same day and a patrol base established. Kaniguram was approached on 6th March. A deputation of *maliks* approached the column while it was still half a mile or so from its objective. The elders advised Major General A. Skeen that the balance of their levy was still unavailable despite their attempts to secure a further 100 rifles. Major General Skeen thereupon determined to reconsider his demands. The Mahsud had already lost much of their manpower, as well as infrastructure and cultivated land. The efforts of the *maliks* appeared genuine and thus an extension of time was granted to them for the collection of the fine.

Meanwhile, useful survey work was conducted and the construction begun of a graded road from Kaniguram, back down the Lines of Communication towards Jandola. In April 1919, the weather cleared sufficiently for patrols to visit remote areas to ensure all possible sections of the Mahsud were now well aware of Britain's supremacy in the region. On 6th April, watchtowers were destroyed above Giga Khel, near the Afghan frontier, but the following day a sharp engagement was fought with a party of Wana Waziri. Thirty sepoys were injured in the fire fight, six mortally. Satisfactory levels of fine collected, the force retired back to Ladha where a permanent garrison was established to enable early and rapid response should the Mahsud determine to take up arms again.

With all key objectives accomplished, Major General S.H. Climo ordered Major General A. Skeen to conclude active operations on 7th May 1920.

MAHSUD CAMPAIGN UNIT ORBIT

Derajat Column - Maj. Gen. A Skeen:
Striking Force
Cavalry 1 Squadron (less 1 Troop) & 21st PAVO Cavalry, IA
Artillery 6 Mountain Battery, RGA 27 (Indian) Mountain Battery
Sappers & Miners No. 55 Field Company, 1st King George's Own Sappers & Miners No. 4 Photo Litho Section, 2nd Queen Victoria's Own Sappers & Miners
Signals HQ Section, 38 Divisional Signal Company No. 16 Pack Wireless Station
Pioneers 3/34th Sikh Pioneers
Infantry **43rd Infantry Brigade – Brig. Gen. G Gwyn-Thomas** 4/39th Garhwal Rifles, 57th Wilde's Rifles, 2/76th Punjabis (From 68th Infantry Brigade on 21st December 1919), 82nd Punjabis & 2/152nd Punjabis **67th Infantry Brigade – Brig. Gen. F G Lucas** 1/55th Coke's Rifles, 1/103rd Mahratta LI, 104th Wellesley's Rifles, 109th Infantry (From 68th Infantry Brigade 17th December 1919 in Relief of 104th Wellesley's Rifles), 2/112th Infantry & 2/19th Punjabis (From 68th Infantry Brigade)
Militia Southern Waziristan Militia (100 Scouts)
Number 1 Section – Lines of Communication Darya Khan to Jandola:

Cavalry
16th Cavalry, IA, 21st PAVO Cavalry, IA, (Less 1 Squadron) & 27th Light Cavalry, IA
Artillery
1 Sect, 35 (Indian) Mountain Battery
Machine Gun Corps
6 & 7 Armoured Motor Batteries
Infantry
62nd Infantry Brigade – Brig. Gen. R B Worgan (GOC No. 1 Section)
2/90th Punjabis, 2/94th Infantry, 2/102nd Grenadiers, 2/113th Infantry, 2/127th Baluchis & 2/150th Infantry
Militia
South Waziristan Militia
Supply Units S&TC
119 Brigade Supply Section, Half 395 Bakery Section & Half 396 Butchery Section

Number 2 Section – Lines of Communication Jandola Forward:

Cavalry
1 Troop, 21st PAVO Cavalry, IA
Artillery
35 (Indian) Mountain Battery less 1 Sect.
Sappers & Miners
No. 75 Field Company, 3rd Sappers & Miners
Signals
No. 3 Pack Wireless Station
68th Infantry Brigade – Brig. Gen. J L R Gordon (GOC No. 2 Section)
3rd Queen's Own Corps of Guides (To Derajat Column)
2/19th Punjabis (To Derajat Column)
2/76th Punjabis (To Derajat Column on 21st December 1919)
109th Infantry (To Derajat Column on 17th December 1919)
104th Wellesley's Rifles (From Derajat Column 17th December 1919 Forward)
Supply Units S&TC
No. 37 Brigade Supply Section, Half 395 Bakery Section & Half 396 Butchery Section
Details
Post Machine Guns

Note: The 2/19th Punjabis, 82nd Punjabis, 1/103rd Mahratta Light Infantry and 2/112th Infantry, IA were relieved by the 2/5th Gurkha Rifles (5th January 1920), 2/9th Gurkha Rifles (10th January 1920), 4/3rd Gurkha Rifles (12th February 1920) and 3/11th Gurkha Rifles (16th February 1920)

CASUALTY RETURN FOR DERAJAT COLUMN 11TH DECEMBER 1919–8TH APRIL 1920

	Killed	Missing	Wounded	Total
British Officers	28	1	40	69
British Other Ranks	1		1	1
Indian Officers	15	4	68	87
Indian Other Ranks	323	232	1,574	2,129

*

Following the break up of the Derajat Column, Major General S.H. Climo transferred command of the Waziristan Force to Major General W.S. Leslie. The bulk of the troops assigned to the Waziristan Force, at that juncture, were drawn from the following Infantry Brigades:

• 43 Infantry Brigade – Piazha Plateau to the edge of Ladha

• 62 Infantry Brigade – Jandola to Khirgi

- 63 Infantry Brigade – Khirgi (exclusive) along the Tank Zam River to the northern end of the Ahnai Tangi Pass.

- 67 Infantry Brigade – Ladha area.

The two principle Lines of Communication extending from Force Headquarters at Dera Ismail Khan remained:

- North – Mari Indus Port > Kalabagh > Bannu > Dardoni and thence to Datta Khel following the Tochi River

- South – Mari Indus Port > Kalabagh > Tank > Jandola > Ladha

*

General C.C. Monro, Commander in Chief, India, had paid Major General S.H. Climo an official visit on 26th April 1920. He was acutely aware that the Waziristan Force was suffering from increasing exhaustion and manpower issues. Many of the Indian Army troops engaged on the frontier had been on active service almost continuously since 1915! A decision was therefore taken to reinforce the field army, on rotation, with several reformed British infantry battalions that had recently arrived in India from Britain. The units concerned were 2nd Bn, Queen's (Royal West Surrey Regiment), 2nd Bn, Norfolk Regt, 1st Bn, Royal Welsh Fusiliers and 1st Bn, Border Regt.

These British regiments were ill prepared for active service when ordered to mobilize and deploy west of the Indus into Waziristan. April and May were traditionally training months for British Army troops stationed in India and, consequently, most rifle companies were engaged in manoeuvres far from their 'war stores'. Headquarters formations were under strength and largely undergoing restructure. 'C' Company, 2nd Bn, Norfolk Regt., for example, was stranded in camp at Ranikhet for over two weeks following the deployment of the 67th Infantry Brigade to Ladha.

Beyond Ladha, recalcitrant Mahsud groups remained engaged in active operations against the newly established British presence. Tribesmen in the Makin Valley had largely recovered from earlier operations and consequently, on 10th July 1920, a British column deployed from Ladha with a view to destroying additional Mahsud infrastructure. This column comprised 6 Pack Battery, RGA, 2nd Bn, Norfolk Regt., 2/41st Dogras and 3/11th GR. Enemy opposition to this manoeuvre proved greater than expected and large numbers of Mahsuds closely followed up the retirement back to Ladha. During this operation, the rear guard, furnished by 2/41st Dogras, lost 28 men killed. Contacts diminished significantly following this action.

*

Despite the virtual subjugation of the Mahsud tribes, the Wana Waziri remained belligerent. An unsuccessful attack on the Drazinda Frontier Constabulary Post on 27th September 1920 was followed up a month later during the Hindu feast of Diwali by a better-planned manoeuvre against the garrison at Kaur Bridge. The attacking force comprised warriors from both the Wana Waziri and Mahsud Sections. These men, anticipating a lack of resolute security precautions during the religious celebration, cut their way through the post perimeter wall during the late evening. After securing the wireless room, the enemy went on to kill 41 members of the garrison, including one British officer and two British other ranks. Following this disastrous event, an official inquiry led to a tightening of standard operating procedures.

The Kaur Bridge incident, combined with the continuing presence of Colonel Shah Daula's Afghan garrison at Fort Wana, led the Government of India to decide that the long awaited offensive against the Wana Waziri clans should now take place. Consequently, Major General W.S. Leslie began the task of organising an independent column for operations in Southern Waziristan and the eventual recapture of Wana. This force was designated the Wana Column. As a preamble to the deployment of the Wana Column, terms of capitulation were offered to the principle Wana *maliks* during a *jirga* at Murtaza on 10th October 1920.

*

Review of Terms Presented
- Payment of a fine of Rs. 40,000, of which Rs. 20,000 to be paid to the Government at a second *jirga* at Murtaza on 10th November 1920.

- Surrender of 250 local rifles, 200 of which to be handed in at the *jirga* on 10th November 1920.

- Surrender of all Government Issue rifles stolen since 1st May 1920.

*

A mere handful of Wana Waziri *maliks* assembled in Murtaza for the stipulated *jirga*. Instead, the majority of warriors rallied behind the rebellious Haji Abdul Razak who sought *jihad* rather than peace. Thus, on 12th November 1920, following several RAF bombing sorties, the Wana Column made good its advance from Jandola across Mahsud territory towards Chagmalai at the mouth of the Shahur Tangi gorge. This narrow, three-mile long feature was quickly secured and permanent picquets established to guard the Lines of Communication back towards Jandola.

Meanwhile Haji Abdul Razak ventured north to the Mahsud settlement at Sarwekai seeking support from local elders for additional warriors to be made available to reinforce his *lashkars*. Surprisingly, the Mahsud *maliks* refused and instructed the Wana Waziri leader to retire back into Waziristan. This rejection prompted a few of the assembled Wana Waziri to reconsider their positions. Hence several parties left the field and shortly thereafter, a trickle of reparations began to be deposited with the political authorities. The insignificant nature of these deposits did not deter Major General W.S. Leslie from his mission. Having secured Sarwekai on 15th December 1920, it was determined to hold the 23rd Infantry Brigade, Brigadier General W.F. Bainbridge, in reserve and deploy the 24th Infantry Brigade, Brigadier General O.C. Borrett, with artillery and engineering support in the final advance to Fort Wana.

COMPOSITION OF THE WANA COLUMN, NOVEMBER/DECEMBER 1920

Headquarters Wana Column – Maj. Gen. W S Leslie
Artillery 6 Pack Battery, RGA, 35 (Indian) Pack Battery **Sappers & Pioneers** No. 14 Field Company, 2nd Queen Victoria's Own Sappers & Miners, No. 3 Litho Photography Section, 2nd Queen Victoria's Own Sappers & Miners, 48th Pioneers, 2–61st King George's Own Pioneers, Survey Section **Infantry / Militia / Machine Gun Corps** 6 Company, 11th Machine Gun Battalion, Machine Gun Corps Detachment South Waziristan Militia **Ancillary Support Units** Medical, Supply, etc
23rd Infantry Brigade – Brig. Gen. W F Bainbridge **HQ and Signals Section** **Infantry** 2nd Bn, Queen's (Royal West Surrey Regt) (From 18th Infantry Brigade – Bareilly), 28th Punjabis, 2/30th Punjabis & 1/4th GR
24th Infantry Brigade – Brig. Gen. O C Borrett **HQ and Signals Section** **Infantry** 2nd Bn, Norfolk Regt (From 67th Infantry Brigade – Ladha), 2/41st Dogras, 58th Rifles & 4/3rd GR

No contacts were made by Brigadier General O.C. Borrett's force until 19th December 1920 when patrols reported the presence of a small *lashkar*. The enemy was put to flight following a dawn attack led by 4/3rd GR. Bristol FB2 fighters of 20 Squadron, RAF, followed up the enemy's retirement, enabling the ground troops to make further rapid advances. A patrol base was established at Karab Kot later the same day. (The aircraft employed were, for the first time on frontier operations, fitted with air to ground communicating wireless). Fort Wana was occupied on 22nd December without a shot being fired, the Afghan garrison having fled back across the Durand Line some days previously. The 24th Infantry Brigade celebrated Christmas and New Year in Fort Wana prior to commencing its return to Jandola on 2nd January 1921.

*

A diplomatic mission, led by Secretary H. Dobbs, was despatched to Kabul in early January 1921 to negotiate with the Afghan Government about its future position in regard to the political and material support of frontier tribes along the Durand Line. Raids by resistant Waziri against isolated military posts and supply convoys continued throughout January and February culminating in two fatal engagements in early March near Sarwekai. Following these incidents the military authorities decided to return to Fort Wana and establish permanently held Lines of Communication from that location back to Jandola. The approach of the 'hot' season, however, saw the various British battalions deployed in Waziristan retire from theatre in favour of their (cooler) summer stations.

*

Spring 1921 saw the Waziristan Force significantly overstretched. Troops were thinly deployed among widely dispersed garrisons supported by complex Lines of Communication extending back from Datta Khel, Ladha and Fort Wana. Recalcitrant Waziri and Mahsud remained active and small-scale contacts were a constant irritation. Occasionally, such attacks were more intense in nature. On 6th April 1921, for example, two RIASC supply convoys on the Wana/Jandola line were ambushed while passing each other at Tora Tizha. Following the initial assault, the escort, furnished by 2/41st Dogras and 58th Rifles, supported by 35 Pack Battery, launched a counter attack. The enemy put up a stout resistance and yielded its position at the cost of six sepoys killed and a further 31 wounded. Ambushes along the Shahur Tangi in April and July were also pressed hard by the enemy. In one action at Haider Kach, Sepoy Ishar Singh, of the Lewis Gun detachment, 28th Punjabis, won the Victoria Cross.

In time, most of the remaining hostile tribesmen abandoned their activities and, as autumn 1921 approached, the situation throughout both Waziristan and the Mahsud territories had largely stabilised. On 5th November 1921, a *jirga* of Mahsud *maliks* was advised of Britain's intention to maintain the Mahsud as a tribal region and to reintroduce the payment of annual allowances. A similar declaration was announced to the Wana Waziri on 10th November. It was made clear to those assembled that they were expected to recognise British sovereignty west from the Indus as far as the Durand Line. Further, it was emphasised that Britain had the right to station troops whenever and wherever the Government wished within tribal territory without molestation. Additional financial benefits were offered to the more reliable groups in return for the raising of local Kahassadar militia tasked with securing the military infrastructure and communications throughout the region including the maintenance of the Wana Garrison and the settlement's revised supply line along the Gomel River. Having received a positive response from the various tribal groups, a decision was made to withdraw the regular military presence in Southern Waziristan back to Jandola and beyond. This action was completed in time for Christmas 1921.

WANA COLUMN CASUALTIES NOVEMBER 1920–MARCH 1921

Killed	36
Wounded	65
Died of Wounds	12
Died of Disease	98

COMMAND STRUCTURE, WAZIRISTAN FIELD FORCE 1919–1921

Commander Waziristan Force Maj. Gen. N G Woodyatt Maj. Gen. S H Climo – To May 1921 Temp. Maj. Gen. W S Leslie – From May 1921	
Commander Striking Force Maj. Gen. A Skeen	
Inspector General Of Communications Temp. Brig. Gen. H C Tytler	
Brigade Commanders	
Brig. Gen. W F Bainbridge	23rd Infantry Brigade
Brig. Gen. O C Borrett	24th Infantry Brigade

Brig. Gen. G Gwyn-Thomas	43rd Infantry Brigade
Brig. Gen. T R MacLauchlan	45th Infantry Brigade
Brig. Gen. W C Walton	47th Infantry Brigade
Brig. Gen. R B Worgan	62nd Infantry Brigade
Brig. Gen. F G Lucas	67th Infantry Brigade
Brig. Gen. J L R Gordon	68th Infantry Brigade

~ Waziristan 1921–1924 ~

The clasp 'WAZIRISTAN 1921–24' was sanctioned under Army Order No. 177 of 1925, to reward military and certain civil personnel borne on the War Establishment (India) engaged in ongoing policing and infrastructure development throughout Northern and Southern Waziristan. In late 1921, command of the Waziristan Force transferred from Major General W.S. Leslie to Major General T.G. Matheson. In May 1923, command of the Waziristan Force passed to Major General R.E. Charles. The initial qualifying date for this clasp, 21st December 1921, ran sequentially with midnight 20th December 1921, the final qualifying date for the clasp 'WAZIRISTAN 1919–21'.

To qualify for the 'WAZIRISTAN 1921–24' clasp personnel had to satisfy one (or more) of the following requirements:

- Served on the War Establishment (India) in Northern or Southern Waziristan between 21st December 1921 and 31st March 1924, inclusive.

- Served on the War Establishment (India) in the Civil Districts of Bannu, Dera Ismail Khan or Mianwali (west of the River Indus only) between 21st December 1921 and 31st March 1924, inclusive.

~ India General Service Medal 1908–1935~
WAZIRISTAN 1919–21
WAZIRISTAN 1921–24
Issue 2. Calcutta Mint

- Served on the posted strength of the military posts of Mari Indus or Darya Khan between 21st December 1921 and 31st March 1924, inclusive.

Royal Air Force personnel qualified under similar provisions.

*

Collectors should be aware that the rundown of the British Indian Army, following the conclusion of the Great War, culminated in a major restructure of its entire organisation. The initial stages of this reorganisation principally affected the Indian Artillery and the Indian Signals Service. In 1922 the Indian Cavalry and Infantry arms were restructured leading to the disbandment of some units, the merging of others and the widespread adoption of new regimental titles, details of which appear at the end of this chapter. Medals can therefore be found bearing the 'WAZIRISTAN 1921-1924' clasp with both 'pre' and 'post' reorganisation unit designations. A multi-bar specimen with a pre 'WAZIRISTAN 1921-24' clasp named with a 'post' restructure regimental title or unit designation should be regarded with caution because to all intents and purposes such a medal could only exist if it was a 'late' claim or a replacement for a lost or destroyed medal named in error to the recipient's subsequent unit. For the sake of continuity, post restructure titles are used for Indian Establishment units from this section of the book forward.

*

Royal Air Force support of ground operations during the early stages of operational activity in 1922 was severely hampered by a lack of serviceable aircraft. Extremes of climate during recent harsh winters had damaged much of the fragile fabric cladding to be found on these early machines. Propellers were in short supply, in addition to engine parts and associated spares. Some squadrons attached to No. 1 (Indian) Wing were barely able to maintain a 50 percent operational capability during much of the period under review.

On 17th August 1922, a De Havilland DH9A of No. 27 Squadron, based at RAF Risalpur, suffered total engine failure. In the ensuing crash, Flying Officers Luard and D.C. Duncan were killed. These two officers had recently corresponded with their parents describing the poor mechanical state of the aircraft they had to contend with. When these letters were published in 'The Times' there was public outrage. Questions were raised in both Houses of Parliament and eventually the Air Ministry was forced to despatch a senior Air Officer to investigate the situation.

Air Vice Marshal J. Salmond, RAF, found the alleged problems to be largely as described. Much of the RAF in India was barely operational. During his tour of inspection, one squadron was forced to send a runner into the local village to purchase an inner tube from a native vendor before the Air Vice Marshal's staff car could continue on its journey. Upon returning to London, Air Marshal Salmond ensured that adequate aircraft and spares were sent out to the frontier regions.

*

Government austerity in the post Great War global economic depression resulted in the adoption by the Commander in Chief India, General Lord Rawlinson, of a revised strategy for the ongoing subjugation of tribal areas on the Indian Frontier. A widely dispersed field army with long Lines of Communication requiring constant picqueting was an expensive luxury. The Kahassadar militia system was expanded, while the Northern and Southern Waziristan Militias were disbanded and then reconstituted as the Tochi and Southern Waziristan Scouts respectively. Following the transfer of Fort Wana to a Kahassadar garrison in December 1921, the Waziristan Force focused on defending the Ladha/Tank Zam Line back to Jandola and the Tochi Line back to Bannu. A decision was made calling for the abandonment of Ladha and the creation of a new purpose built military cantonment strategically located in central Waziristan but with easy access to the volatile Mahsud. The military authorities envisaged that radiating out from this site would be a modern, circular road system along which mechanised units could rapidly deploy reinforcements to trouble spots from the railheads at Bannu and Tank. This policy was christened the 'Forward Policy'.

During early 1922, the Waziristan Force underwent a reorganisation in preparation for the launch of the 'Forward Policy'. The 7th Infantry Brigade, under Colonel Commandant H.E. Herdon, at Datta Khel and the 8th Infantry Brigade, under Colonel Commandant C. Prissick, at Bannu were transferred to the command of Major General A. Le G. Jacob, GOC Kohat District, where they formed up with the 5th Infantry Brigade, under Colonel Commandant F.E. Conningham, at Idak to form the Razmak Force. This formation was tasked with the advance to, and establishment of, the proposed new military cantonment. The change in structure enabled Major General T.G. Matheson to focus

~ The completion of the road to Razmak enabled the prosecution of the 'Forward Policy' ~

on the activities of his command, (the 9th Infantry Brigade, under Colonel Commandant H.M.W. Souter, at Ladha, the 10th Infantry Brigade, under Colonel Commandant H.W. Jackson, at Manzai and the 21st Infantry Brigade, under Colonel Commandant W. J. Mitchell, at Sorarogha), plus associated supporting formations and garrisons.

*

For most Waziris and Mahsuds, some benefits accrued from the British 'Forward Policy' – financial inducements, employment, and generally stable conditions. A few groups, principally the Jalal Khel Waziri and the Abdullai Mahsud, remained hostile in the belief that Britain's long-term objective was to bring 'their' society under 'administered' control.

Desolate sniping continued throughout Waziristan following the evacuation of Fort Wana in December 1921. A Tochi Waziri *lashkar* was active in the Datta Khel area over Christmas and into the New Year. RAF operations continued over the Mahsud as often as operationally possible and, on 20th January 1922, the Abdullai Mahsud met in *jirga* to discuss whether to comply with the previously rejected Government terms. Road survey work continued in all areas. By the end of January 1922, however, the frequency of attacks against road survey parties, construction gangs and supply columns began to rise steadily.

AMBUSH CASUALTIES, WAZIRISTAN, JANUARY 1922

1/3rd Madras Regt.	2 Sepoys Killed
5/13th Frontier Force Rifles (Vaughan's)	4 Sepoys Killed
2/15th Punjab Regt.	13 Sepoys Killed

On 4th April 1922, Fort Wana was besieged by a *lashkar* composed of some 2,000 Jalal Khel tribesmen led by the now notorious Haji Abdul Razak. Inspired by the newly installed Wana Political Agent, Naib Tahsildar, the small Kahassadar garrison courageously defended its position for five days. Eventually, RAF fighters operating from Tank, succeeded in breaking up the enemy formation and dispersing the survivors into the surrounding hills. (A decision was subsequently made to reinforce the Wana Khassador garrison with 500 South Waziristan Scouts). A week later, a second party of warriors struck at the remote Fort Zam, mid way between Jandola and Tank. Its intention, as was later discovered, was to interfere with the construction of a dam at the mouth of the Tank River. The attack was pressed home with zeal resulting in several deaths including Captain N. Wodehouse and an Indian subadar.

Open feuds developed between those tribesmen willing to accept British terms and those wishing to remain in the field. When rebel warriors attacked a patrol of the 1/4th Bombay Grenadiers in Tori Khel country, killing an officer and wounding two sepoys, local *maliks* appealed to their Political Agent for protection. The elders duly contacted Mr. Pears, Resident of Waziristan, and a *jirga* of Kabul Khel and Tori Khel elders was scheduled for 12th May 1922. Following protracted negotiation, these elders agreed to the construction of a major military cantonment on the Razmak plateau with associated infrastructure including metalled roads. The new structure was to be completed and occupied in force by 14th January 1923. In return, the *maliks* were given the following safeguards:

- The Government of India to protect the tribes of the Tochi Agency from molestation by rebel elements, especially those originating in the Kurram and Khaisora regions.

- The Government of India to refrain from claiming property rights in the Tochi Agency.

- The Government of India to refrain from the establishment of Frontier Constabulary posts or the application of the Indian Criminal Code in the Tochi Agency.

- Domestic disputes in the region to be settled locally by tribal elders under the terms of established Islamic codes.

The Government favoured the Razmak site because it lay on the boundary between Southern Waziristan and the Mahsud. The level terrain was ideal for ongoing expansion as well as the creation of an RAF landing strip. At an altitude of some 6,000 feet above sea level, the climate on the Razmak plateau was suitable for year round occupation by both British and Indian Army formations.

*

Haji Abdul Razak remained relatively inactive during the latter half of May and throughout June 1922. On 1st July, however, a column of the 81st Local (Transport) Corps was ambushed near Barari Tangi. During this action, Captain R.W. Edmuston was killed and three sepoys wounded. Troops from Sorarogha deployed to the scene as soon as they became aware of the engagement and pursued the enemy warriors for some distance. Several Jalal Khel settlements were subsequently searched by the Army and at least one village razed to the ground in punishment.

The weather rapidly deteriorated towards the end of July 1922 with the onset of the monsoon season. Civil engineering works ground to a virtual halt. The destructive force of flash flooding washed away many recently constructed sections of the Kotkai–Sorarogha portion of the Tank Zam road. Supply convoys were constantly delayed which resulted in supply problems in some more remote locations.

During September 1922, a recalcitrant Mahsud section launched a daring raid across the Indus River into the Dera Ismail Khan district. The village of Kulachi was attacked and three Hindu villagers were kidnapped. Several weeks later, a second Mahsud war party crossed the Indus and penetrated the Mianwali civil district. Peaceful farming communities were again targeted and a number of hostages taken. On this occasion, however, the authorities managed to pursue the attackers and all of the civil captives were subsequently rescued.

Intelligence suggested that some tribal groups, notably the Jalal Khel Waziri and the Abdullai Mahsud, regarded the abandonment of Ladha as a sign of weakening resolve on the part of the British, as opposed to a more efficient firming up of regional control. The fact that stores removed from Ladha for eventual use in Razmak were, because of the existing Lines of Communication, heading in the opposite geographic direction, only went further to reinforce this belief. Consequently, the more Ladha was 'run down' as an operational base, the more confident these groups became. Previous agreements to place Mahsud sponsored Kahassadar posts at Tauda China, Sarwekai and Haidari Kach were rejected now by tribal elders and the incidence of interference with road construction gangs began to increase further. This culminated in an ambush on the Tochi–Razmak road during early December 1922 that resulted in the death of Lieutenant Dickson, RE. Following this incident, further road construction was suspended resulting in serious financial loss to those local groups supplying the labour details.

CHART ILLUSTRATING OFFICIAL RECORDINGS OF TRIBAL AGRESSION WAZIRISTAN 1920–1922			
	1920	**1921**	**1922**
Terrorist Raids	611	391	194
Kidnappings	463	310	148

The RAF was immediately called upon to deliver punitive retribution in relation to the murder of Lieutenant Dickson. However, inclement weather prevented air operations until 17th December 1922 whereupon Nos. 27 and 28 Squadrons launched intensive sweeps of hostile Mahsud areas. This action lasted several days. On 9th January 1923, Royal Artillery gunners shelled several Mahsud settlements. Jalal Khel elders finally agreed to accept British terms on 25th January 1923. As a token of good faith, the tribe released several RAF prisoners, including Flight Officers St. Ledger and A.H. Hearn, who had been held following the shooting down of two aircraft. The Abdullai Mahsud, however, refused to surrender.

*

The creation and deployment of the Razmak Force under Major General A. Le G. Jacob progressed throughout the spring and summer of 1922. Based upon the Bannu railhead, the line of advance was to be along the Tochi road via Thal and over the Razmak Narai Pass. Progress had been slow due to a combination of difficult terrain, poor weather conditions and constant enemy harassment. By the end of the year, however, mechanised transport was able to proceed as far as Damil and the 5th Infantry Brigade had established forward picquets as far as Tamre Oba. The 8th Infantry Brigade protected the Lines of Communication back to Bannu, while 7 Infantry Brigade was held in reserve at Assad Khel.

On 1st January 1923, the 7th Infantry Brigade, less 1st Bn, Border Regt. detached for two days as camel train escort, marched through the 5th Infantry Brigade positions and established a new forward location at Tamre Oba. The Force then advanced to Razani in preparation for the difficult advance through the narrow Narai Pass. Prior to commencing this manoeuvre, the 5th Infantry Brigade was tasked with capturing the strategically important Alexandra Ridge with a view to establishing elevated picquets to cover the progress of the main force. Casualties were sustained by 2/3rd QAO GR following several contacts with small parties of Mahsud tribesmen. Further advances were stalled until the camel track leading to the mouth of the Narai Pass could be widened by the Sappers and Miners. The 7th Infantry Brigade entered the Narai Pass in a heavy snowstorm on 23rd January. No opposition was encountered and, by late evening, the entire force, less Lines of Communication protection, were established (in deep snow) on the Razmak Plateau.

*

The continued aggression of the Abdullai Mahsud prompted Major General T.G. Matheson to seek permission from the CGS, General C Jacob on 9th January 1923, to embark on renewed punitive operations against hostile factions in the Makin Valley. For this operation it was determined that the 9th Infantry Brigade, Colonel Commandant H.M.W. Souter, from Ladha, and the 7th Infantry Brigade, Colonel Commandant H.E. Herdon, from Razmak, would form up at Tauda China and conduct a joint expedition supported by Nos. 27 and 28 Squadrons RAF operating out of RAF Dardoni. It was made clear to the GOC Waziristan Force, however, that this manoeuvre could not influence the planned final evacuation of Ladha. All troops on the Tank Zam line, including the 9th Infantry Brigade, were to be withdrawn back to Jandola by 25th February at the latest.

The two infantry brigades, now designated the Makin Column, rendezvoused on 4th February 1923 at Sorarogha, following the reinforcement of the Line of Communication back to Ladha. Tribesmen fiercely contested this action and the force suffered some 30 casualties during the establishment of a forward operating base and associated forward picquets. Further picquets were established along the projected line of advance the following day. During the operations to secure Split Hill, a picquet of the 2nd Bn, RWF sustained 14 casualties including six killed. By this juncture, however, the enemy were well aware of the military's objective and to that end they withdrew across the Tauda China River with a view to reinforcing their depth of defence in the Makin Valley.

On 6th February 1923, the 7th Infantry Brigade launched a pre dawn assault against several Mahsud villages along the northern Makin escarpment. Opposition was initially light and within hours the settlements of Lali Khel and Mazdakai were ablaze courtesy of 13 Field Company, 2nd Queen Victoria's Sappers and Miners and 3/3rd (Royal) Sikh Pioneers. Meanwhile, the 9th Infantry Brigade delivered similar retribution on the southern escarpment focusing on the villages of Dinour and Kut. Having achieved their primary objectives, the force began to withdraw from the area during the early afternoon. Previously concealed tribesmen now began to follow up the rear platoon of 1/9th GR as they evacuated their position on Vantage Point above Lali Khel. Fortunately, 'B' Company, 1st Bn, Border Regt., had remained in the area and subsequently facilitated the safe withdrawal of the Gurkhas. RAF assistance was sought by the GOC and eventually the two brigades fought their way back to Tauda China for the loss of six men killed and 22 wounded.

Further operations in the Makin region were restricted for several days by sleet and snow combined with intense cold. A break in the weather on 9th February 1923 enabled the 7th Infantry Brigade to penetrate the Mahsud hinterland further and secure positions overlooking the villages of Azdi Khel, Abbas Khel, Vantage Village, and several others. The Tochi Scouts were detached to secure the Brigade's outer flank while the inner flank was secured by the 9th Infantry Brigade. On this occasion, the force concentrated on the destruction of the region's agricultural infrastructure. Once again, the Mahsud followed up the afternoon withdrawal, resulting in British casualties of 12 dead and 14 wounded.

COMPOSITION OF THE RAZMAK FORCE – MAJ. GEN. A Le JACOB

Cavalry and Armoured Cars
16th Light Cavalry, IA
Two Sections, 7 Armoured Car Company, Royal Tank Corps
Artillery (British)
11 Pack Battery, Royal Garrison Artillery,
One Section, 47 (Howitzer) Battery, Royal Field Artillery
Artillery (Indian)
23 Pack Brigade
103 (Peshawar) Pack Battery, 108 (Lahore) Pack Battery & 121 (Nowshera) Pack Battery
Sappers & Pioneers
No. 13 Field Company, Queen Victoria's Own Sappers & Miners,
Nos. 20 & 21 Field Companies, Royal Bombay Sappers & Miners
Survey Section
2/3rd Sikh & 3/3rd (Royal) Sikh Pioneers
Infantry
5th Infantry Brigade - Col. F E Conningham
2/13th Frontier Force Rifles, 1/4th Bombay Grenadiers & 1/5th (Royal) GR
7th Infantry Brigade - Col. H E Herdon
1st Bn, Border Regt,
1/3rd Madras Regiment, 2/3rd QAO GR, 1/9th GR & Tochi Scouts
8th Infantry Brigade – Col. C Prissick
2/7th Rajput Regt (PAV), 4/11 Sikh Regt & 5/10 Baluch Regt (KGO Jacob's Rifles)
Reserve
1/3rd QAO GR & 2/8th GR
Support & Ancillary Services

The villages of Tora Tizha and Dinaur were burnt to the ground the following day. On this occasion, however, tribesmen fought back before the withdrawal commenced which left 2/18th Royal Garhwal Rifles hard pressed on several occasions. Two Ladha based artillery howitzers, which had been brought up to supplement the column's pack artillery batteries, shelled inaccessible sites, such as the Abdullai hamlet of Mandech. By the 12th February 1923, all hostile settlements had been levelled enabling the 9th Infantry Brigade to begin its long withdrawal back to begin its long withdrawal back to Jandola via Ladha. The 7th Infantry Brigade remained in the Makin to oversee the peace process that culminated in a *jirga* at Tauda China on 22nd February. During this assembly Major General T.G. Matheson advised the Abdullai *maliks* that construction of the Sorarogha–Razmak and Jandola–Sarwekai roads would resume post haste and that the enlistment of local Kahassadar to protect said Lines of Communication, with South Waziristan Scout support, was imperative if Government grants were to be reinstated. A second *jirga* opened in Tauda China on 12th March with a view to ensuring all Mahsud *maliks* were aware of Government expectations.

CASUALTIES MAKIN COLUMN, FEBRUARY 1923

British Officers Wounded	6
British Other Ranks Killed	6
British Other Ranks Wounded	17
Indian Other Ranks Killed	36
Indian Other Ranks Wounded	72

By mid March 1923, the new Wana–Sarwekai–Jandola route had been completed to a standard suitable for use by mechanised transport. This state of affairs enabled the GOC to contemplate the withdrawal of the South Waziristan Scouts element of the Fort Wana garrison and their subsequent redeployment to several other posts along the route including Sarwekai. To ensure this manoeuvre was executed without interference from any Tochi Waziri, the 9th Infantry Brigade was deployed west from Jandola to picquet the road. The operation began on 2nd April, and was completed without loss after two weeks. Henceforth, regular contact would be maintained with the Wana Kahassadar garrison by the introduction of a weekly RAF patrol.

FRONTIER SCOUT DISPOSITIONS, APRIL 1924 (RANKED BY POST ESTABLISHMENT)

South Waziristan Scouts
Jandola (HQ Location)
Sarwekai, Sorarogha, Splitoi, Kotkai, Chagmalai and Ahna
Tochi Scouts
Miranshah (HQ Location)
Tamre Oba, Spinwam, Datta Khel, Boya and Idak

*

~ Pack Artilllery on the move, Waziristan early 1920s ~

In April 1923, a party of Waziri warriors, including Ajab Khan, Shahzada Gul Akbar, Sultan Mir and Haider Shah, crossed into the Kohat District with, it would seem, the intention of seeking out a suitable European to kidnap and hold for ransom. Finally, they selected 17-year old Molly Ellis. Unfortunately, the abduction did not go smoothly and during the ensuing struggle at the girl's residence, Major and Mrs. Archibald Ellis were murdered. Molly Ellis was spirited away and held captive in the remote Tirah Mountains. The authorities immediately denounced the kidnapping as a complete outrage, especially when a degree of Afghan complacency was detected.

Lord Montagu of Beaulieu initiated a debate on the 'Ellis affair' in the House of Lords. Many

Peers felt that the murders and kidnapping had been committed in retaliation for recent frontier bombing raids by the RAF in which native women and children had been maimed and killed. The policy of embarking on such missions without warning was reviewed by the Air Ministry soon thereafter. Mrs. Lillian Starr, an envoy selected by the Chief Commissioner of the North West Frontier Province, succeeded in securing the release of Molly Ellis during early May 1923. Accompanied by Rissaldar Moghul Baz Khan, Mrs Starr displayed such courage in her endeavours that she was subsequently awarded the Kaiser-I-Hind Medal in gold.

*

Sporadic sniping continued throughout Waziristan during the remainder of May 1923. There were no serious incidents, however, until 6th June when the village of Maddi, located between Tank and Dera Ismail Khan, fell victim to enemy attack. A patrol of Frontier Constabulary, under Superintendent Perrot, was immediately despatched to the scene whereupon the raiders were pursued for two days before making their escape into Afghanistan. During this operation, one Indian police constable was killed and several were wounded. Among the injured was Mr. W.C. Plumb, Government District Officer.

Organized resistance to the 'Forward Policy' had all but collapsed by mid 1923. A certain degree of lawlessness persisted but this was attributed to criminally inspired behaviour rather than politically inspired violence. July was a fairly peaceful month, the only incident of note being the murder at Piazha Raghza of Lieutenants H. Ross Fairfax and Webster, IA, attached 21 Field Company, Royal Bombay Sappers and Miners. On 7th August, the first motor convoy ran from Razanito to Razmak. The casualty returns for September record the death of three military personnel due to 'enemy' action including Battery Sergeant Major McCubbing, RGA, who was shot by a sniper during a unit inspection by General Lord Rawlinson, the Commander in Chief, India.

~ Mechanised transport overtakes an Indian Infantry Battalion on the march~

Isolated acts of criminal behaviour, such as the murder of Captain and Mrs. Watts, Kurram Militia, continued well into November 1923. Despite such incidents, the Regular Army continued to transfer responsibility for regional 'policing' and infrastructure defence to the militia and the various tribal Kahassadar units. Civil engineering works continued apace in order to bring the new road system to the standard required of heavy motorised convoys. The technical complexity of the projects including the creation of an all weather, metalled road through obstacles including the Barari Tangi, should not be underestimated.

By the beginning of December 1923, the defence of the entire Tank Zam route from Jandola to Razmak had been assigned to the South Waziristan Scouts. The first quarter of 1924 saw continued progress in the development of the new road system and the establishment of the Razmak Cantonment. On 31st March the CGS saw fit to change the military establishment in Waziristan from that of a Field Force on active duty to that of a Military District with separate military and political structures.

With effect from 1st April 1924, the military command in Waziristan passed from HQ Western Command to HQ Northern Command. The period commemorated by the 'WAZIRISTAN 1921–24' clasp to the India General Service Medal 1908–1935 was officially concluded. Two weeks later a routine patrol mounted by the Razmak based 1st Bn, R Berkshire Regt. was engaged in a fierce firefight. The deaths of 5330511 Private C. Cockford and 5330409 Private T. Spokes marked the beginning of a long period official 'peace'.

REGULAR ARMY FORCE DISPOSITIONS, WAZIRISTAN, 1ST APRIL 1924

HQ Waziristan Military District	Dera Ismail Khan
Infantry Brigade Battle Group	Bannu, Gardai, Manzai and Razmak
Other Force Detachment Locations	Damdil, Dardoni, Idak, Mari Indus, Saidgi and Tank

COMMAND STRUCTURE, WAZIRISTAN FIELD FORCE 1921–1924

Commander Waziristan Force Maj. Gen. W S Leslie – To Late 1921 Maj. Gen. T G Matheson – To May 1923 Maj. Gen. R E Charles – From May 1923	
Brigade Commanders	
Col. Cmdt. H M W Souter	9th Infantry Brigade
Col. Cmdt. H W Jackson	10th Infantry Brigade
Col. Cmdt.. W J Mitchell	21st Infantry Brigade
Commander Razmak Force Maj. Gen. A Le G Jacob	
Brigade Commanders	
Col. Cmdt. F E Conningham	5th Infantry Brigade
Col. Cmdt. H E Herdon thence H J P Browne	7th Infantry Brigade
Col. Cmdt. C Prissick	8th Infantry Brigade

	BRITISH ARMY & RAF ROLL OF HONOUR FRONTIER CAMPAIGNS 1919–1924					

Date	Person	Unit	Afghan 19	Waz 19	Mahsd 19	Waz 21
11/05/1919	37170 Pte. A Chapman	2nd Bn, N Staffordshire Regt.	Afghan			
11/05/1919	8778 Cpl. G E Facey	2nd Bn, Som Light Infantry	Afghan			
11/05/1919	8257 Pte. A C George	2nd Bn, Som Light Infantry	Afghan			
11/05/1919	8849 Pte. T Hale	2nd Bn, Som Light Infantry	Afghan			
11/05/1919	48892 Pte. W J Ody	2nd Bn, N Staffordshire Regt.	Afghan			
11/05/1919	37201 Pte. W A Simpson	2nd Bn, N Staffordshire Regt.	Afghan			
12/05/1919	240171 L/Cpl. W Richardson	1st Bn, Yorkshire Regt.	Afghan			
14/05/1919	855206 Cpl. F W Archer	RFA attch. 1 MT Coy	Afghan			
14/05/1919	9496 A/Cpl. G Lunt	2nd Bn, N Staffordshire Regt.	Afghan			
14/05/1919	2 Lt. G H E Sanders	21st Lancers	Afghan			
16/05/1919	62557 Pte. J Bailey	15 Sqn, MGCC	Afghan			
16/05/1919	L/8822 Pte. A Bruce	1st Bn, R Sussex Regt.	Afghan			
16/05/1919	100762 Pte. G Hammond	15 Sqn, MGCC	Afghan			
16/05/1919	5760 Pte. H Hoare	2nd Bn, Som Light Infantry	Afghan			
16/05/1919	D-33639 Pte. A F S Rice	1st King's Dragoon Guards	Afghan			
16/05/1919	H-39762 Pte. J Gorham-Smith	7th Hussars attch. 1st King's Dragoon Guards	Afghan			
16/05/1919	Lt. R I Ward	1st King's Dragoon Guards	Afghan			
17/05/1919	13626 Pte. J Haig	1st King's Dragoon Guards	Afghan			
20/05/1919	D-12314 Pte. J Wark	1st King's Dragoon Guards	Afghan			
24/05/1919	33632 Pte. W Dunn	1st King's Dragoon Guards	Afghan			
27/05/1919	201479 L/Cpl. C J Andrews	1/4th Bn, R West Kent Regt.	Afghan			
27/05/1919	9823 Cpl. W Atkinson	1st Bn, DWR	Afghan			
27/05/1919	200228 Sgt. W Haines	1/4th Bn, R West Kent Regt.	Afghan			
27/05/1919	9551 Pte. G A Thompson	1st Bn, DWR	Afghan			
29/05/1919	201556 Pte. W P Ellis	1/4th Bn, R West Kent Regt.	Afghan			
30/05/1919	Lt. E J Macrostie	25th Bn, London Regt.	Afghan			
02/06/1919	2093 Cpl. J T Roberts	15 Bty, MMGC	Afghan			
05/06/1919	D-334 Pte. H Purchase	1st King's Dragoon Guards	Afghan			
07/06/1919	???? Dvr. T Taylor	77 Bty, RFA	?			
10/06/1919	12226 Gnr. D Molloy	3 Mtn Bty, RGA	Afghan			
12/06/1919	242435 Pte. A A Curtis	1/5th Bn, Hampshire Regt.	Afghan			
13/06/1919	241392 Pte. E J Harris	1/5th Bn, Hampshire Regt.	Afghan			
13/06/1919	241487 Pte. G H E Pearson	1/5th Bn, Hampshire Regt.	Afghan			
14/6/1919	225020 Dvr. C Spruce	102 Bty, RFA	?			
14/06/1919	B/34941 Gnr. D Surridge	4 Mtn Bty, RGA	Afghan			
14/06/1919	L/9803 Pte. E Tidman	1st Bn, R Sussex Regt.	Afghan			
15/06/1919	265703 Pte. E A Birch	1st/1st Kent (Cyclist) Bn	Afghan			
15/06/1919	L/9475 Dmr. J M Penfold	1st Bn, R Sussex Regt.	Afghan			

16/06/1919	32644 Gnr. S Bassett	8 Mtn Bty, RGA	Afghan		
16/06/1919	7177 Pte. S Horton	1st King's Dragoon Guards	Afghan		
16/06/1919	D-19632 Sgt. J Kidd	1st King's Dragoon Guards	Afghan		
16/06/1919	B/74872 Gnr. W Smith	4 Mtn Bty, RGA	Afghan		
19/06/1919	201773 Pte. W Bramble	1/4th Bn, Hampshire Regt. attch 1st Bn, R Sussex Regt.	Afghan		
20/06/1919	200093 Pte. H L Britter	1/4th Bn, R West Kent Regt.	Afghan		
21/06/1919	241929 L/Cpl. W A L Drake	1/5th Bn, Hampshire Regt.	Afghan		
22/06/1919	851079 Gnr. W Hardy	RFA	Afghan		
22/06/1919	51705 Pte. A Matthews	2nd Bn, N Staffordshire Regt.	Afghan		
22/06/1919	8886 Pte. A Payne	2nd Bn, N Staffordshire Regt.	Afghan		
22/06/1919	8439 A/S/Sgt. J H Ryan	2nd Bn, N Staffordshire Regt.	Afghan		
23/06/1919	241935 Sgt. C Cherrett	1/5th Bn, Hampshire Regt.	Afghan		
23/06/1919	119146 Pte. D Waugh	260 Coy, MGC	Afghan		
24/06/1919	51475 Pte. H Cuthbert	2/4th Bn, Border Regt.	Afghan		
01/07/1919	Capt. R J Butler	1st Bn, KOYLI attch. 2nd Bn, Som LI	Afghan		
03/07/1919	265043 A/WO2 C H Lord	1st/1st Kent (Cyclist) Bn	Afghan		
07/07/1919	Matron F M Hall	QAIMNS	?		
08/07/1919	40849 Pte. W Lucas	1/6th Bn, Hampshire Regt. attch. 2/6th Bn, R Sussex Regt.	Afghan		
10/07/1919	D-5561 Pte. G T Mordy	1st King's Dragoon Guards	Afghan		
12/07/1919	TF-267237 A/Sgt. C E Scott	1st Bn, R Sussex Regt.	Afghan		
13/07/1919	175075 Pte. S Cox	260 Coy, MGC	Afghan		
13/07/1919	175068 Pte. P Penn	260 Coy, MGC	Afghan		
14/07/1919	L/11075 Pte. J W Rose	1/4th Bn, R West Kent Regt.	Afghan		
15/07/1919	315261 Pnr. G Page	36 Sig Coy, RE	Afghan		
16/07/1919	29990 Sgt. R I Jones	RAMC	Afghan		
17/07/1919	188097 Gnr. J R Morgan	1 DAC, RFA	Afghan		
18/07/1919	D-35055 Pte. P E Beckett	1st King's Dragoon Guards	Afghan		
18/07/1919	200095 Pte. G Dawson	1/4th Bn, Queen's Regt.	Afghan		
18/07/1919	G/22342 Pte. A Lewin	2/6th Bn, R Sussex Regt.	Afghan		
18/07/1919	61834 Pte. H Mills	RAMC	Afghan		
19/07/1919	102459 Pte. J T Solomon	RAMC	Afghan		
20/07/1919	125072 Pte. G Lomax	260 Coy, MGC	Afghan		
23/07/1919	G/57027 Pte. D Croy	1/9th Bn, Middlesex Regt. attch. 1st Bn, Yorkshire Regt.	Afghan		
23/07/1919	Lt. E H Hare	6th Bn, RDF attch. 1st Bn, Yorkshire Regt.	Afghan		
23/07/1919	202067 Pte. W C Thubron	1st Bn, Yorkshire Regt.	Afghan		
23/07/1919	9320 Sgt. E A Westcott	1st Bn, Yorkshire Regt.	Afghan		
24/07/1919	L/9972 Pte. A S Stoner	1st Bn, R Sussex Regt.	Afghan		
25/07/1919	L/46942 Dvr. J H Padbury	74 Bty, RFA	Afghan		

27/07/1919	L/9360 Pte. H Bray	1st Bn, R Sussex Regt.	Afghan			
07/08/1919	10935 Pte. J H Phillips	2nd Bn, Liverpool Regt.	Afghan			
07/08/1919	174926 Gnr. H L Talbot	4 DAC, RFA	Afghan			
08/08/1919	39475 Pte. H Colman	1st Bn, Yorkshire Regt.	Afghan			
14/08/1919	223462 Gnr. J Waller	74 Bty, RFA	Afghan			
22/08/1919	404283 AM1 W C Weeks	114 Sqn, RAF	Afghan			
01/09/1919	94408 Pte. W Monery	222 Coy, MGC	Afghan			
02/09/1919	19182 Pte. T H Mitchell	2nd Bn, Som Light Infantry	Afghan			
06/09/1919	113963 Pte. A Flathers	263 Coy, MGC	Afghan			
06/09/1919	9603 Pte. E Langbridge	1st Bn, S Lancashire Regt.	Afghan			
07/09/2019	11108 Pte. W B Jones	1/6th Bn, Devon Regt. attch. 1/25th Bn, London Regt.	Afghan			
11/09/1919	M2/166590 Sgt. J Baxter	630 MT Coy, RASC	Afghan			
14/09/1919	201252 A/Cpl. W Thompson	2/4th Bn, Border Regt.	Afghan			
17/09/1919	170420 Gnr. A V Allen	60 Bty, RFA	Afghan			
25/09/1919	124778 Pte. T Arnison	11 Armd Bty, MGC	Afghan			
27/09/1919	D-15969 Pte. F Ormerod	1st King's Dragoon Guards	Afghan			
30/09/1919	200554 Sgt. G Proctor	2/4th Bn, Border Regt.	Afghan			
02/10/1919	200872 Pte. J S Ebbutt	1/4th Bn, Queen's Regt.	Afghan			
26/10/1919	21846 Pte. J Ekin	1st Bn, Yorkshire Regt attch. MGC	Afghan			
26/10/1919	27986 BQMS J A Gould	99 Bty, RFA	Afghan			
03/11/1919	832065 Gnr. R I Callow	38 Bty, RFA	Afghan			
05/11/1919	Capt. G W E Maude	1st Bn, Yorkshire Regt.	Afghan			
07/11/1919	203637 Dvr. P Thewlis	1091 Bty, RFA	Afghan			
17/11/1919	DM2/207458 A/Sgt. R Meldrum	RASC attch. S&TC		Waz		
23/11/1919	121305 SSM J R Whincup	22 Sqn MGC C (Late 21st Lancers)	Afghan			
24/11/1919	L/10867 Pte. J H Linfield	1st Bn, R Sussex Regt.	Afghan			
24/11/1919	5871 S/Sgt. E P Sadler	RGA	?			
28/11/1919	????? L/Cpl. F Howe	2nd Bn, Som LI	?			
5/12/1919	M/36084 Pte. G Matthews	694 (MT) Coy, RASC	?	?		
16/12/1919	8396 Pte. T Gannon	1st Bn, S Lancashire Regt. attch. S&TC	Afghan			
16/12/1919	118372 A/Cpl. F Windibank	270 Coy, MGC	Afghan			
17/12/1919	38241 Cpl. F Dyer	8 Mtn Bty, RGA	Afghan			
18/12/1919	37558 Gnr. E A Tatham	1 Mtn Bty, RGA	?			
21/12/1919	13446 F/Sgt. F Luxford	102 Bty, RFA		?		
31/12/1919	121379 Pte. C H G Park	22 Sqn, MGC C	Afghan			
Unknown	11084 Pte. L Sawyer	1st Bn, DLI	Afghan			
Unknown	9988 Cpl. F Mathews	1st Bn, DLI	Afghan			
Unknown	37595 Cpl. F Ward	RGA	Afghan			
Unknown	105638 Gnr. J W Barty	RGA	Afghan			

Unknown	32756 Gnr. W Burgoyne	RGA	Afghan			
Unknown	8498 Pte. G Ives	1st Bn, Yorkshire Regt.	Afghan			
Unknown	32668 Pte. A Lambert	1st Bn, Yorkshire Regt.	Afghan			
Unknown	8255 Pte. A P Loughran	1st Bn, Yorkshire Regt.	Afghan			
Unknown	8587 Pte. N N Walker	1st Bn, Yorkshire Regt.	Afghan			
Unknown	8781 Pte. H C Wildish	1st Bn, Yorkshire Regt.	Afghan			
Unknown	9625 Pte. E Wood	1st Bn, Yorkshire Regt.	Afghan			
Unknown	Lt. Col. A F Garrett	RE (CRO Peshawar)	Afghan			
Unknown	L/9394 Pte. A Chapman	1st Bn, R Sussex Regt.	Afghan			
Unknown	L/9413 Pte. F W Hellings	1st Bn, R Sussex Regt.	Afghan			
Unknown	L/8644 L/Cpl. G Hook	1st Bn, R Sussex Regt.	Afghan			
Unknown	L/8135 Pte. H Whatmore	1st Bn, R Sussex Regt.	Afghan			
05/01/1920	163859 Pte. C Judson	15 Sqn, MGCC	Afghan			
17/1/1920	227650 Gnr. W Mills	23 Mtn Bty, FGA		?		
05/02/1920	200896 Pte. C Hodge	1/4th Bn, R West Kent Regt.	Afghan			
25/02/1920	Lt. E B Pigott	6 Mtn Bty, RGA			Waz	Mahsd
06/03/1920	35663 Pte. R C Makinson	286 Coy, MGC	Afghan			
10/03/1920	Lt. J B Gibbons	33 Mtn Bty, RGA			Waz	
10/03/1920	33852 L/Bmdr A E Mew	6 Mtn Bty, RGA	Afghan			
15/03/1920	228864 Sdl/S/Sgt. J Savage	1 Mtn Bty, RGA	Afghan			
16/03/1920	240442 A/Cpl. G Surtees	1/5th Bn, E Kent Regt.	Afghan			
20/03/1920	29578 Pte. C Cufflin	1st (G) Bn, HLI attch. 2/6th Bn, R Sussex Regt.	Afghan			
31/03/1920	G/6657 Pte. G Edwards	1st /1st Kent (Cyclist) Bn	Afghan			
01/04/1920	121353 Pte. E N Flynn	22 Sqn, MGCC	Afghan			
20/04/1920	256561 Dvr. H R Eversden	121 (How) Bty, RFA		?		
28/04/1920	64081 Pte. W Cutter	2nd Bn, Lincolnshire Regt. attch. MT Coy, S&TC	Afghan			
21/05/1920	9024 Gnr. D Cornfield	RGA	Afghan			
04/06/1920	???? Pte. D S Vargis	33 DCS, Royal Signals/RE		?		
05/06/1920	73271 Pte. W Debbage	2nd Bn, Norfolk Regt.			Waz	
03/07/1920	73279 Pte. W L Gooch	2nd Bn, Norfolk Regt.			Waz	
04/07/1920	5763534 Pte. F N Harris	2nd Bn, Norfolk Regt.			Waz	
23/07/1920	Gnr. J Lanagan	23 Mtn Bty, FGA		?		
15/09/1920	37893 Gnr. G C Berry	6 Pack Bty, RGA	Afghan		Waz	Mahsd
28/09/1920	????? Gnr. J H Stent	4 DAC, RFA		?		
09/10/1920	4459 Pte. J Lacey	2nd Bn, Queen's Regt.		?		
19/10/1920	Shoe S D R B Potts	102 Bty, RFA		?		
11/11/1920	5763258 Pte. S E Grant	2nd Bn, Norfolk Regt.			Waz	
15/11/1920	22610 S G Springford	1 Mtn Bty, RGA		?		
02/12/1920	7809418 Pte. E Ward	11Bn, MGC		?		

03/01/1921	206598 Gnr. T Malin	1093 Bty, RFA	Afghan			
13/01/1921	Gnr. A Linsell	23 Mtn Bty, FGA		?		
14/02/1921	6078366 Bdsm. J Edwards	2nd Bn, Queen's Regt.		Waz		
04/04/1921	31905 Gnr. A H Marshall	6 Mtn Bty, RGA	Afghan	Waz	Mahsd	
29/04/1921	7577435 Pte. B Ormerod	2nd Bn, RWF				Waz
19/05/1921	1403426/27686 Gnr. G H Kilner	6 Pack Bty, RGA	?	Waz	Mahsd	
26/05/1921	5763070 C/Sgt. F W Morris	2nd Bn, Norfolk Regt.		Waz		
31/05/1921	Bdr. F R Weller	1 Mtn Bty, RGA		?		
13/06/1921	7817761 Pte. J Cooper	5 Armd MB, MGC		Waz		
13/06/1921	5764291 WO2 A Dixon	2nd Bn, Norfolk Regt.		Waz		
23/06/1921	1402391 Bmdr. W G Newland	10 Pack Bty, RGA		Waz		
27/06/1921	Lt. B U Farrell	RASC		Waz		
15/07/1921	1403486/27979 Gnr. M Power	6 Mtn Bty, RGA	Afghan	Waz	Mahsd	
16/07/1921	7811386 Pte. W Pitts	6 Coy, MGC		Waz		
19/07/1921	7811204 Pte. W A R Phillips	6 Coy, MGC		Waz		
05/08/1921	1416647/229015 Gnr. J S C Peake	6 Pack Bty, RGA		Waz		
29/08/1921	7811687 Pte. W Pollitt	6 Coy, MGC		Waz		
07/09/1921	3705 Pte. S Gipp	11th Bn, MGC		Waz		
16/09/1921	6078439 Pte. F G Buckfield	2nd Bn, Queen's Regt.		Waz		
04/10/1921	1041343 Gnr. M Delaney	86 Bty, RFA			?	
05/10/1921	6078449 Pte. G A E Hughes	2nd Bn, Queen's Regt.		Waz		
06/11/1921	L/8591 Pte. T Kitching	5 AMB, MGC (Was) 2nd Bn, N Staffordshire Regt.	Afghan	Waz		
24/11/1921	7817678 Pte. C W Abbott	16 AMB, MGC		Waz		
13/12/1921	4178898 A/WO2 C Rush	2nd Bn, RWF		Waz		Waz
19/12/1921	1403651 Gnr. T H Channon	12 Pack Bty, RGA		Waz		Waz
23/12/1921	1403074 Gnr. A Melville	12 Pack Bty, RGA		Waz		Waz
Unknown	64476 Pte. J McClay	2nd Bn, W Yorkshire Regt		Waz		
Unknown	Capt. F S W Savill-Onley	RASC		Waz		
Unknown	EMT44189 Sgt. J Coombs	RASC (8 MT Coy)		Waz		
Unknown	62065 Gnr. C C Croucher	RGA		Waz		
Unknown	22985 Gnr. F Ballinger	RGA	Afghan	Waz		
Unknown	Lt. A S N Barron	RASC	Afghan	Waz		
15/01/1922	Maj. B V Mair	1st Bn, Manchester Regt.	Afghan			
19/01/1922	4180483 Pte. J Hughes	2nd Bn, RWF		Waz		Waz
30/01/1922	6077356 Pte. W F Doe	2nd Bn, Queen's Regt.		Waz		
03/02/1922	6077413 L/Cpl. A A Webster	2nd Bn, Queen's Regt.		Waz		
08/02/1922	363103 Sgt. J A Hood	31 Sqn, RAF				Waz
14/02/1922	4180235 Pte. E H Longfellow	2nd Bn, RWF		Waz		Waz
12/4/1922	1041367 Gnr. A McNeilly	86 Bty, RFA				?
10/05/1922	4179391 Sgt. D Hanscombe	2nd Bn, RWF				Waz
06/06/1922	???? Gnr. G H Vickery	37 Bty, RFA				?

14/06/1922	6077774 Pte. A Surridge	2nd Bn, Queen's Regt.		Waz		
21/06/1922	20727 Pte. E W A Mealin	1st Bn, Ox & Bucks LI	Afghan	Waz		Waz
23/06/1922	1405265 Gnr. M P Edwards	12 Pack Bty, RGA		Waz		Waz
27/07/1922	1038954 Gnr. P L Parvin	28 Pack Bty, RGA		Waz		
29/07/1922	4182011 L Bowen	2nd Bn, RWF		Waz		Waz
29/07/1922	4180560 C Lloyd	2nd Bn, RWF				Waz
29/07/1922	4179366 F H Tevendale	2nd Bn, RWF		Waz		Waz
05/10/1922	4180491 B Lamb	2nd Bn, RWF				Waz
16/10/1922	M/ 18764 EMT43850 J Sanderson	RASC (25 MT Coy)				Waz
25/10/1922	4180003 Sgt. G Rhodes	2nd Bn, RWF		Waz		Waz
?/12/1922	Lt. Dickson	Royal Engineers		?		Waz
08/01/1923	6076581 L/Cpl. A White	2nd Bn, Queen's Regt.		Waz		
05/02/1923	4179610 CQMS G Grindley	2nd Bn, RWF		Waz		Waz
05/02/1923	5097437 Pte. J Heath	2nd Bn, RWF				Waz
05/02/1923	4114088 Pte. F Johns	2nd Bn, RWF				Waz
05/02/1923	2731111 Pte. B P Murphy	2nd Bn, RWF				Waz
06/02/1923	4181586 Pte. H B Sherriff	2nd Bn, RWF		Waz		Waz
11/02/1923	4681384 F Jennings	9 ACC, RTC				Waz
11/03/1923	4179204 L/Cpl. J R Freegrove	2nd Bn, RWF		Waz		Waz
13/03/1923	3590317 L/Cpl. J Barnett	1st Bn, Border Regt.				Waz
23/03/1923	Capt. J F Carr	28 Mtn Bty, RGA	Afghan			
26/04/1923	7870494 Pte. D A Hay	9 ACC, RTC				Waz
23/05/1923	1404691 Bmdr. T W Tummons	11 Pack Bty, RGA				Waz
08/06/1923	285000 AC1 W I J McManus	5 Sqn, RAF				Waz
26/06/1923	1409134 Gnr. C Gray	12 Pack Bty, RGA		Waz		Waz
01/07/1923	3947089 Pte. W Barton	2nd Bn, RWF		Waz		Waz
09/07/1923	4180507 Pte. F Williams	2nd Bn, RWF				Waz
24/07/1923	3589911 Pte. E A Gough	1st Bn, Border Regt.				Waz
?/7/1923	Lt. H Ross-Fairfax	Royal Engineers		?		Waz
?/7/1923	Lt. X Webster	Royal Engineers		?		Waz
18/08/1923	4180465 Pte. J R Jones	2nd Bn, RWF		Waz		Waz
05/09/1923	M33647 A/Sgt A Clayton	RASC (27 MT Coy)				Waz
09/10/1923	29629 Gnr. A Jorgensen	47 Bty, RFA				?
18/10/1923	4179951 Pte. C J Harris	2nd Bn, RWF		Waz		Waz
18/10/1923	4180055 Pte. E Hope	2nd Bn, RWF		Waz		Waz
19/10/1923	3948730 Pte. T Collins	1st Bn, Welch Regt.				Waz
01/11/1923	1423650/220050 Gnr. E Stewart	Royal Artillery				Waz
12/11/1923	10213 Pte. S G Walter	1st Bn, W Yorkshire Regt.		Waz		
14/11/1923	5488883 Sig. S F Johnson	86 Bty, RFA				?
18/11/1923	3950005 Pte. S White	1st Bn, Welch Regt.				Waz
22/11/1923	4178978 Pte. W Watson	2nd Bn, RWF		Waz		

Date	Number & Name	Unit			
27/11/1923	5095903 Pte. E Caldicote	2ⁿᵈ Bn, R Warwickshire Regt.			Waz
?/12/23	1855258 Sgt. A E Denyer	R SIGS (2 Wireless Coy)			Waz
07/01/1924	7040382 Fus. J Kearns	2ⁿᵈ Bn, RIF			Waz
11/02/1924	4180536 Pte. W T Chance	2ⁿᵈ Bn, RWF	Waz		Waz
19/03/1924	723042 Pte. H Hughson	1ˢᵗ Bn, Welch Regt.			Waz
19/03/1924	5430865 L/Cpl. H A Morton	1ˢᵗ Bn, Berkshire Regt.			Waz
23/03/1924	Lt. C H G Davis	2ⁿᵈ Bn, Queen's Regt.	Waz		Waz
31/03/1924	M18651 Sgt. M White	RASC (18 MT Coy)			Waz
15/04/1924	5330511 Pte. C E Crockford	1ˢᵗ Bn, Berkshire Regt.			Waz
15/04/1924	5330409 Pte. T C Spokes	1ˢᵗ Bn, Berkshire Regt.			Waz
28/04/1924	5329560 Sgt. S W White	1ˢᵗ Bn, Berkshire Regt.			Waz
03/06/1924	3950179 Pte. A S Pomeroy	1ˢᵗ Bn, Welch Regt.			Waz
06/06/1924	3951990 Boy C N Joiner	1ˢᵗ Bn, Welch Regt.			Waz
18/06/1924	726832 Pte. H Hurst	1ˢᵗ Bn, Welch Regt.			Waz
20/06/1924	5329647 Pte. S Clarke	1ˢᵗ Bn, Berkshire Regt.			Waz
26/06/1924	3948132 Sgt. W M Brazel	1ˢᵗ Bn, Welch Regt.			Waz
04/07/1924	5330055 Pte. P J Elliott	1ˢᵗ Bn, Berkshire Regt.			Waz
14/07/1924	EMT44061 Pte. G T Cowley	RASC (10 MT Coy)			Waz
27/07/1924	5328983 Pte. H Slade	1ˢᵗ Bn, Berkshire Regt.			Waz
06/08/1924	5329158 L/Cpl. F F Elliott	1ˢᵗ Bn, Berkshire Regt.			Waz
18/08/1924	4179979 Pte. W H Holcombe	2ⁿᵈ Bn, RWF	Waz		Waz
11/09/1924	7873347 Pte. R Knocker	7 ACC, RTC			Waz
14/09/1924	7871453 Pte. E G Guttridge	9 ACC, RTC			Waz
17/09/1924	1418546 Gnr. E Holland	13 Pack Bty, RGA			Waz
25/11/1924	3948319 Pte. R McKenham	1ˢᵗ Bn, Welch Regt.			Waz
03/12/1924	7870761 Cpl. C Royston	7 ACC, RTC			Waz
Unknown	4180473 Pte. G F West	2ⁿᵈ Bn, RWF			Waz
Unknown	1404119 BSM A McCubbing	12 Pack Bty, RGA	Waz		Waz
Unknown	1422799 Gnr. S Waddell	10 Pack Bty, RGA			Waz
Unknown	Maj. H E Festing	1ˢᵗ Bn, Border Regt.	Waz		Waz
Unknown	3591184 Cpl. E H Busby	1ˢᵗ Bn, Border Regt.			Waz
Unknown	3590833 Pte. F Halliwell	1ˢᵗ Bn, Border Regt.			Waz
Unknown	3590825 L/Cpl. R Slater	1ˢᵗ Bn, Border Regt.			Waz
Unknown	3589707 Pte. T Thompson	1ˢᵗ Bn, Border Regt.			Waz
Unknown	6077837 Pte. C A Carnell	2ⁿᵈ Bn, Queen's Regt.	Waz		Waz
Unknown	1856992 L/Cpl. P E ook	R SIGS ('C' Div)			Waz
Unknown	1856089 F/S/Sgt. W G Aldridge	R SIGS ('G' Div)			Waz
Unknown	7870253 Siglm. T Boyles	R SIGS ('G' Div)			Waz
Unknown	2309731 Siglm. J Murray	R SIGS ('G' Div)			Waz
Unknown	50770 F/Sgt. E J Punchard	11ᵗʰ Hussars attch. R Sigs	Waz		Waz

FRONTIER CAMPAIGNS 1919–1924[3,4,5&6] ROLL

AFGHANISTAN N.W.F. 1919[3], MAHSUD 1919–20[5], WAZIRISTAN 1919–21[4] & WAZIRISTAN 1921–24[6]

BRITISH ESTABLISHMENT
THE ARMY

~ Staff Grade Officers ~

Note a.   *Only Officers of the British Army are listed. Officers of the Indian Establishment are beyond the scope of this work and are thus excluded.*

Note b.   *Medals named in impressed capitals.*

Major Generals: ~ J R E Charles[1(Capt. RE)&6], G Cree[3] DDMS, H P Leader[3], R St. C Lecky[3] & T G Matheson[4&6]

Brigadier Generals: ~ G P Campbell[3,4&5] Chief Engineer & DD Works, C T Caulfeild[3] CRA, 2 Div., G Christian[3] Cmd. 6 Bde., J L J Clarke[3] Cmd. 43 Bde., G D Crocker[3] Cmd. 1 Bde., W E R Dickson[3] IG Coms, C H Fourkes[4], Cmd. 67 Bde. Tochi Col, G G Loch[4] Cmd. 21 & 62 Bde.(s), E C Peebles[3] Cmd. 4 Bde., F W D Quinton[3] & R F Sorsbie[3] CRE, NWFF

Colonels: ~ F R Buswell[3] ADMS, H B Fawcus[3], F W Haswell[3], H R Headlam[4&5] Staff, W E Hudleston[4] Late RAMC, ADMS WFF, A E C Keble[3&4] Late RAMC, E W Larnder[3], G T K Maurice[3], A Rolland[4&6(MES)] MWS, W W Seymour[4&5] Late RB, HQ WFF, A J Turner[6], C M Wagstaff[1(Capt. RE),6&9(Maj. Gen.)] & B Watts[6] Late RAMC

THE CAVALRY

A. The Cavalry of The Line
~ 1st (King's) Dragoon Guards ~

Note a.   *Roll of all commissioned personnel identified as eligible.*

Note b.   *Non-commissioned and other rank personnel multi clasp or non–Afghanistan 1919 single clasp.*

Note c.   *India August 1914. France & Flanders November 1914. India November 1917 thence Iraq from January 1920.*

Note d.   *The double spread eagle insignia, based on the Arms of Court of Austria and the Regiments' former Colonel-in-Chief, Emperor Francis Joseph I, was 'retired' in 1915 in favour of a star design bearing the initials KDG. (An eagle design was re introduced in 1937).*

Note e.   *Battle Honour 'Third Afghan War 1919'.*

Note f.   *Medals named in impressed capitals: '1 K. D. GUARDS.' Some late claims may be named '1- D. GDS.'*

Single Clasp	No. Identified	Rarity
Afghanistan N.W.F. 1919[3]	Regt. Strength	Not Rare
Mahsud 1919–20[5]	0	None Identified
Waziristan 1919–21[4]	0	None Identified
Waziristan 1921–24[6]	0	None Identified
Combination Clasps	No. Identified	Rarity
Mahsud 1919–20[5] Waziristan 1921–21[4]	1	According to the roll as seen, can be considered Unique

Lieutenant Colonels: ~ (Temp) H F Wickham[3] & H J Williams[3]

Majors: ~ R S Spurrier[3]

Captains: ~ W R F Cooper[3], H M Fleming[3], H S Hatfield[3], (QM) A H Haws[3], D L G Carleton-Smith[4&5] Staff, E W H Sprot[3], B M Ward[3] & C E Wilson[3]

Lieutenants: ~ R A S Adair[3] attch. 1 MMG Bty, W G Baker[3], B D J Barnes[3], (E) W P Barrett[3], A Brown[3], F W F Card[3], C G Corner[3], R R Herron[3], B G Holt[3], A Jacques[3], A E Massey[3], R L McCollough[3], J P Moreton[3], G E T Mott[3], W H Muir[3], W S H Parker[3], L G L Peacocke[3], A B H N Richardson[3], R L Green Shields[3], J A Boogle- Smith[3], R Browning Smith[3], J R Spurrier[3], J G E Tiarks[3], J L Waggett[3] & R I Ward[3]

~ 2nd Dragoon Guards (Queen's Bays) ~

Note a.   Roll of all personnel identified as eligible.
Note b.   Recipient attached 'D' Divisional Signals Company (DSC).
Note c.   France & Flanders August 1914. Palestine July 1919 thence India from December 1920. A single composite squadron consisting of one troop 'A' Squadron and three troops 'B' Squadron qualified for the clasp 'MALABAR 1921 – 22'.
Note d.   Medals named in impressed capitals: 'THE BAYS.'

Single Clasp	No. Identified	Rarity
Afghanistan N.W.F. 1919[3]	0	None Identified
Mahsud 1919–20[5]	0	None Identified
Waziristan 1919–21[4]	0	None Identified
Waziristan 1921–24[6]	0	None Identified
Combination Clasps	**No. Identified**	**Rarity**
Waziristan 1919–21[4] Waziristan 1921–24[6]	1	According to the roll as seen, can be considered Unique

Quartermaster Sergeants/Sergeants: ~ (D-1705) 391782 R Kirby[4&6]

~ 3rd (Prince Of Wales') Dragoon Guards ~

Note a.   Roll of all personnel identified as eligible.
Note b.   Recipient served on the staff of Headquarters (HQ), Waziristan Field Force (WFF).
Note c.   Egypt August 1914. France & Flanders October 1914 thence India from December 1919 forward.
Note d.   Amalgamated with 6th Dragoon Guards (Carabineers) in 1922 to form the 3rd Carabineers (Prince of Wales' Dragoon Guards).
Note e.   Medals named in impressed capitals: '3 D. GUARDS.' or '3-D. GDS.'

Single Clasp	No. Identified	Rarity
Afghanistan N.W.F. 1919[3]	0	None Identified
Mahsud 1919–20[5]	0	None Identified
Waziristan 1919–21[4]	1	According to the roll as seen, can be considered Unique
Waziristan 1921–24[6]	0	None Identified

Lance Corporals/Privates: ~ (D-10826) 390131 D Jackson[4]

151

~ 4th (Royal Irish) Dragoon Guards ~

Note a.   *Roll of all personnel identified as eligible.*
Note b.   *Recipient attached 24 Machine Gun Squadron (MG Sqn), Machine Gun Corps Cavalry (MGCC).*
Note c.   *France & Flanders August 1914 forward. India 1921.*
Note d.   *Amalgamated with 7th (Princess Royal's) Dragoon Guards in 1922 to form the 4th/7th Royal Dragoon Guards.*
Note e.   *Medals named in impressed capitals: '4 D. GUARDS.' or '4-D. GDS'*

Single Clasp	No. Identified	Rarity
Afghanistan N.W.F. 1919[3]	1	According to the roll as seen, can be considered Unique
Mahsud 1919–20[5]	0	None Identified
Waziristan 1919–21[4]	0	None Identified
Waziristan 1921–24[6]	0	None Identified

Captains: ~ A Wright[3]

~ 5th (Princess Charlotte of Wales's) Dragoon Guards ~

Note a.   *Roll of all personnel identified as eligible.*
Note b.   *France & Flanders August 1914 forward. Ireland May–October 1919 thence Egypt and Palestine.*
Note c.   *Amalgamated with 6th (Inniskilling) Dragoons in 1922 to form the 5th Inniskilling Dragoon Guards.*
Note d.   *Medals named in impressed capitals: 5 D. GUARDS.' or '5-D GDS.'*

Single Clasp	No. Identified	Rarity
Afghanistan N.W.F. 1919[3]	0	None Identified
Mahsud 1919–20[5]	0	None Identified
Waziristan 1919–21[4]	0	None Identified
Waziristan 1921–24[6]	1	According to the roll as seen, can be considered Unique

Combination Clasps	No. Identified	Rarity
Afghanistan N.W.F. 1919[3] Waziristan 1919–21[4] Waziristan 1921–24[6]	1	According to the roll as seen, can be considered Unique

Majors: ~ (Act) L F Levinson[6] attch. 'B' DSC
Warrant Officers Class II: ~ (SSM) 389397 A T Jones[3,4&6] attch. 'G' DSC

~ 3/6th Dragoon Guards (Carabineers) ~

Note a.   *Roll of all personnel identified as eligible.*
Note b.   *Recipient attached to (and eventually transferred to) the Royal Air Force (RAF) as an Intelligence Officer (IO).*
Note c.   *France & Flanders August 1914 forward. Ireland 1919 to 1921.*
Note d.   *Amalgamated with 3rd (Prince of Wales') Dragoon Guards in 1922 to form 3rd Carabineers (Prince of Wales' Dragoon Guards).*
Note e.   *If medal exists probably named in impressed capitals: '3-6 D. GUARDS.'*

Single Clasp	No. Identified	Rarity
Afghanistan N.W.F. 1919[3]	0	None Identified.
Mahsud 1919–20[5]	0	None Identified.
Waziristan 1919–21[4]	0	None Identified.

Waziristan 1921–24[6]	1	The Medal Record Card states medal issued but returned and re- issued as 'R.A.F.' If still in existence can be considered Unique.

Captains: ~ P F J Kent[6] attch. 28 & 29 Sqns, RAF as IO

~ 3rd (King's Own) Hussars ~

Note a. *Roll of all personnel identified as eligible.*
Note b. *France & Flanders August 1914 forward. Turkey November 1921 to August 1923 thence Egypt.*
Note c. *The Medal Record Cards pertaining to the recipients listed below suggest their medals should be inscribed '7 HRS' and not '3 HRS'! It is not clear which title was used when the medals were issued. Indeed some medals to Hussar Regiments are named simply 'HUSSARS' or 'CORPS OF HUSSARS'. Consequently, these names have additionally been listed in the 7th Hussars roll below.*

Single Clasp	No. Identified	Rarity
Afghanistan N.W.F. 1919[3]	2	If verified, of the Utmost Rarity
Mahsud 1919–20[5]	0	None Identified
Waziristan 1919–21[4]	0	None Identified
Waziristan 1921–24[6]	0	None Identified

Quartermaster Sergeants/Sergeants: ~ H-6708 P V Barrett[3] attch. 1 KDG
Lance Sergeants/Corporals: ~ H-7643 J King[3] attch. 1 CBSS

~ 4th (Queen's Own) Hussars ~

Note a. *Roll of all personnel identified as eligible.*
Note b. *France & Flanders August 1914 forward. India October 1921.*
Note c. *Medals named in impressed capitals: '4 HRS', 'HUSSARS' or 'CORPS OF HUSSARS'.*

Single Clasp	No. Identified	Rarity
Afghanistan N.W.F. 1919[3]	0	None Identified
Mahsud 1919–20[5]	0	None Identified
Waziristan 1919–21[4]	0	None Identified
Waziristan 1921–24[6]	1	According to the roll as seen, can be considered Unique

Lance Sergeants/Corporals: ~ (Act) (H-70231) 536534 E H Wailes[6] attch. 7 Bde. as Clk

~ 5th (Royal Irish) Lancers ~

Note a. *Roll of all personnel identified as eligible.*
Note b. *France & Flanders August 1914 forward. India November 1919.*
Note c. *Amalgamated with 16th (The Queen's) Lancers in 1922 to form the 16th/5th the Queen's Royal Lancers.*
Note d. *Medals named in impressed capitals: '5 LRS.'*

Single Clasp	No. Identified	Rarity
Afghanistan N.W.F. 1919[3]	0	None Identified
Mahsud 1919–20[5]	0	None Identified
Waziristan 1919–21[4]	2	Of the Utmost Rarity
Waziristan 1921–24[6]	0	None Identified

Lieutenant Colonels: ~ H A Cape[4] attch. 2/5 GR & M F McTaggart[4] attch. Gordons

~ 6th (Inniskilling) Dragoons ~

Note a. *Roll of all personnel identified as eligible.*
Note b. *Recipient attached Indian Signal Corps (ISC).*
Note c. *India August 1914. France & Flanders December 1914.*
Note d. *Amalgamated with 5th Dragoon Guards in 1922 to form the 5/6th Dragoon thence, in 1927, the 5th Inniskilling Dragoon Guards.*
Note e. *Medals named in impressed capitals: '6 DNS.'*

Single Clasp	No. Identified	Rarity
Afghanistan N.W.F. 1919[3]	1	According to the roll as seen, can be considered Unique
Mahsud 1919–20[5]	0	None Identified
Waziristan 1919–21[4]	0	None Identified
Waziristan 1921–24[6]	0	None Identified

Quartermaster Sergeants/Sergeants: ~ (Act) D-2696 W Wakefield[3]

~ 7th (Queen's Own) Hussars ~

Note a. *Roll of all personnel identified as eligible.*
Note b. *India August 1914. Mesopotamia November 1917 thence India December 1920 forward.*
Note c. *Medals named in impressed capitals: '7 HRS', 'HUSSARS' or 'CORPS OF HUSSARS'. Medal record card states medals for personnel attached 1 KDG to be named '7 HRS ATT[D] 1/D GDS.' It is not certain as to whether this occurred and I have never seen an example named thus.*

Single Clasp	No. Identified	Rarity
Afghanistan N.W.F. 1919[3]	28	Very Rare
Mahsud 1919–20[5]	0	None Identified
Waziristan 1919–21[4]	3	Of the Utmost Rarity
Waziristan 1921–24[6]	1	According to the roll as seen, can be considered Unique
Combination Clasps	**No. Identified**	**Rarity**
Afghanistan N.W.F. 1919[3] Mahsud 1919–20[5] Waziristan 1919–21[4]	2	Of the Utmost Rarity
Afghanistan N.W.F. 1919[3] Mahsud 1919–20[5] Waziristan 1919–21[4] Waziristan 1921–24[6]	1	According to the roll as seen, can be considered Unique
Afghanistan N.W.F. 1919[3] Waziristan 1919–21[4] Waziristan 1921–24[6]	1	According to the roll as seen, can be considered Unique
Waziristan 1919–21[4] Waziristan 1921–24[6]	1	According to the roll as seen, can be considered Unique

Majors: ~ F L Andrews[3]
Lieutenants: ~ H F Dixson[3,4&5] attch. 39 DSC & R C Jones[3,4,5&6] attch. 38 DSC
Warrant Officers Class I: ~ (Act) H-4638 A B Terry[4] attch. 12 MT Coy, S&TC
Warrant Officers Class II: ~ H-4270 P G Gordon[3] attch. MMP
Squadron Quartermaster Sergeants/Staff Sergeants: ~ (Act) H-5141 B Meehan[3] attch. Gen Mallison Mission & (Farrier) H-45627 H Woodhall[3] attch. IMVS
Quartermaster Sergeants/Sergeants: ~ H-6708 P V Barrett[3] attch. 1 KDG, (Possibly named '3 HRS'), H-5213 R J Cann[3] attch. 6 CBST, (Act) H-27623 P S Crowley[3] attch. 61 PMC, (Act) H-39749 G Hogan[3] attch. 4 Div. Sply Coy, S&TC, H-3151 W R Holland[3] attch. 21 L thence 1 KDG, (Act) H-580 J Irish[3] attch. 10 IMVS, (Act) H-39513 G L Johnson[4] attch. 'C'

Railhead, RTE, (Act) H-27402 F B Penhearow[3] attch. 22 Div. Sply Coy, S&TC, H-5253 F A Randall[3] attch. MMP, (Tmpt) H-3751 B C Ross[3] attch. 3/W Sig Sqn & 532864 B C Saville[3,4&5] attch. 'F' DSC

Lance Sergeants/Corporals: ~ 6209 H Emery[3] attch. 1 KDG, 532965 W A Gidney[3,4&6] attch. 33 DSC, H-7643 J King[3] attch. 1 CBSS, (Possibly named '3 HRS'), H-7402 W Tavener[3] attch. 44 DSC & 376 J Rayne[3] attch. 1 KDG, (Possibly named '1 K D GDS')

Lance Corporals/Privates: ~ H-7418 C S Brown[3] attch. 3 LofC Sig Sqn, 533541 T W Brown[4], H-35715 E J Canty[3] attch. MMP, BFF, 45670 J Chandler[3] attch. 1 KDG, H-7305 A P Cleverly[3] attch. 44 DSC, H-9113 G G Cullis[3] attch. 1 KDG, (532904) H-3647 A V Earl[3] attch. 46 Bde. Sig Sect, H-45679 A E Goddard[3] attch. 1 KDG, 533043 H Green[4&6], 531941 F Nixon[6], H-39762 J Gorham-Smith[3] attch. 1KDG, H-35535 W Stockoe[3] attch. 1 KDG, H-3611 R Strode[3] attch. 36 DSC, 531894 C Swaby[4&6] & H-7153 J R Taylor[3] attch. 15 IMVS

~ 8th (King's Royal Irish) Hussars ~

Note a.　Roll of all personnel identified as eligible.
Note b.　India August 1914. France & Flanders November 1914 forward. India December 1919 thence Iraq October 1920 and Egypt December 1921.
Note c.　Medals named in impressed capitals: '8 HRS', 'HUSSARS' or 'CORPS OF HUSSARS'.

Single Clasp	No. Identified	Rarity
Afghanistan N.W.F. 1919[3]	1	According to the roll as seen, can be considered Unique
Mahsud 1919–20[5]	0	None Identified
Waziristan 1919–21[4]	0	None Identified
Waziristan 1921–24[6]	0	None Identified
Combination Clasps	No. Identified	Rarity
Afghanistan N.W.F. 1919[3] Waziristan 1919–21[4]	1	According to the roll as seen, can be considered Unique
Mahsud 1919–20[5] Waziristan 1919–21[4]	1	According to the roll as seen, can be considered Unique

Lieutenants: ~ W M F Bayliss[3&4(16/5L)] & B H House[4&5]
Lance Sergeants/Corporals: ~ (Act) H-80990 L Rooney[3] attch. 15 MG Sqn, MGCC

~ 13th Hussars ~

Note a.　Roll of all personnel identified as eligible.
Note b.　India August 1914. France & Flanders December 1914, Mesopotamia July 1916 thence Persia 1918.
Note c.　Amalgamated with 18th (Queen Mary's Own) Hussars in 1922 to form the 13th/18th Royal Hussars (Queen Mary's Own).
Note d.　Medals named in impressed capitals: '13 HRS', 'HUSSARS' or 'CORPS OF HUSSARS'. Medal record cards state medals for personnel attached 1 KDG to be named '13 HRS ATTᴰ 1 K.D.G.' It is not certain as to whether this occurred and I have never seen an example named thus.

Single Clasp	No. Identified	Rarity
Afghanistan N.W.F. 1919[3]	13	Extremely Rare
Mahsud 1919–20[5]	0	None Identified
Waziristan 1919–21[4]	0	None Identified
Waziristan 1921–24[6]	0	None Identified

Quartermaster Sergeants/Sergeants: ~ H-4609 E Lowder[3] attch. Armd Train, (Act) H-33903 F Sentence[3] attch. RTE & 281934 S Wardle[3] attch. Armd Train, (From S. Notts Hussars)

Lance Sergeants/Corporals: ~ H-4972 P C J Grahame[3] attch. 1 KDG, H-46230 W Hart[3] attch. 1 KDG, (Possibly named '1 K D GDS'), (Act) H-1200 W Kimberley[3] attch. MMP & (Act) (Saddle) H-7634 A E Richards[3] attch. MMP, BFF

Lance Corporals/Privates: ~ H-7924 E Hider[3] attch. 1 KDG, 3123 G Jelley[3] attch. 1 KDG, H-46234 W T Newton[3] attch. MMP, H-9382 J O'Connor[3] attch. MMP, BFF, H-31959 J Phillips[3] attch. MMP, H-4423 F Walmsley[3] attch. RAMC

~ 14th (King's) Hussars ~

Note a.   *Roll of all personnel identified as eligible.*
Note b.   *India August 1914. Mesopotamia November 1915, Persia January 1918, Mesopotamia December 1918 forward.*
Note c.   *Amalgamated with 20th Hussars in 1922 to form the 14th/20th King's Hussars.*
Note d.   *Medals named in impressed capitals: '14 HRS', 'HUSSARS' or 'CORPS OF HUSSARS'.*

Single Clasp	No. Identified	Rarity
Afghanistan N.W.F. 1919[3]	12	Extremely Rare
Mahsud 1919–20[5]	0	None Identified
Waziristan 1919–21[4]	0	None Identified
Waziristan 1921–24[6]	0	None Identified

Lieutenants: ~ A G Gosnell[3] attch. 1 KDG
Quartermaster Sergeants/Sergeants: ~ H-5880 T Rutter[3] attch. 6 CBST
Lance Sergeants/Corporals: ~ (Act) H-5345 H W Cutler[3] attch. 6 CBST, H-4109 F Hughes[3] attch. 18 IMVS, (Act) H-28730 E M Marsh[3] attch. MMP, H-4410 R Watts[3] attch. MMP & H-10508 F Wilkinson[3] attch. MMP
Lance Corporals/Privates: ~ H-34164 G F Haselgrove[3] attch. MMP, BFF, H-6276 H Smith[3] attch. MMP, 310807 F E Steel[3] attch. 1 KDG, H-36349 T Swales[3] attch. 1 KDG & H-1688 F Wetton[3] attch. 6 CBST

~ 15th (The King's) Hussars ~

Note a.   *Roll of all personnel identified as eligible.*
Note b.   *Recipient attached Headquarters (HQ), 10 Cavalry Brigade (10 Cav Bde).*
Note c.   *France & Flanders August 1914 forward. Ireland September 1919.*
Note d.   *Amalgamated with 19th Royal Hussars (Queen Alexandra's Own) in 1922 to form the King's Royal Hussars.*
Note e.   *Medals named in impressed capitals: '15 HRS', 'HUSSARS' or 'CORPS OF HUSSARS'.*

Single Clasp	No. Identified	Rarity
Afghanistan N.W.F. 1919[3]	1	According to the roll as seen, can be considered Unique
Mahsud 1919–20[5]	0	None Identified
Waziristan 1919–21[4]	0	None Identified
Waziristan 1921–24[6]	0	None Identified

Majors: ~ C Nelson[3]

~ 16th/5th Lancers (From 1922) ~

Note a.   *Roll of all personnel identified as eligible.*
Note b.   *Formed in India on 29th September 1922. To Egypt March 1924.*
Note c.   *Roll shows medals named in impressed capitals: '16-5 LRS.' albeit 'WAZIRISTAN 1919-21' clasp recipients could expect medals to be named '16 LCRS'.*

Single Clasp	No. Identified	Rarity
Afghanistan N.W.F. 1919[3]	0	None Identified
Mahsud 1919–20[5]	0	None Identified
Waziristan 1919–21[4]	1	According to the roll as seen, can be considered Unique
Waziristan 1921–24[6]	3	Of the Utmost Rarity
Combination Clasps	No. Identified	Rarity
Mahsud 1919–20[5] Waziristan 1919–21[4] Waziristan 1921–24[6]	1	According to the roll as seen, can be considered Unique

Squadron Quartermaster Sergeants/Staff Sergeants: ~ 311920 G W Cooper[6] attch. 'B' Corps Sigs
Quartermaster Sergeants/Sergeants: ~ (Act) (L/19761) 314723 D T Cloughley[4,5&6] attch. HQ, 7 Bde., 314964 J W T Hauser[6] attch. MFD & (Act) 7817177 A Kerr[6] attch. LofC Sigs, WFF
Lance Corporals/Privates: ~ (L-18119) 313765 W J Parker[4] attch. HQ, WFF

~ 18th (Queen Mary's Own) Hussars ~

Note a.   *Roll of all personnel identified as eligible.*
Note b.   *France & Flanders August 1914 forward. India December 1919 to 1922.*
Note c.   *Amalgamated in United Kingdom with 13th Hussars in 1922 to form the 13th/18th Royal Hussars (Queen Mary's Own).*
Note d.   *Medals named in impressed capitals: '18 HRS', 'HUSSARS' or 'CORPS OF HUSSARS'.*

Single Clasp	No. Identified	Rarity
Afghanistan N.W.F. 1919[3]	0	None Identified
Mahsud 1919–20[5]	0	None Identified
Waziristan 1919– 21[4]	4	Of the Utmost Rarity
Waziristan 1921–24[6]	0	None Identified
Combination Clasps	No. Identified	Rarity
Mahsud 1919–20[5] Waziristan 1919–21[4]	1	According to the roll as seen, can be considered Unique

Lieutenants: ~ W F Brown[4] attch. MFO, Tank
Squadron Quartermaster Sergeants/Staff Sergeants: ~ (Act) (19177) 537810 A W Knight[4] attch. HQ, WFF
Quartermaster Sergeants/Sergeants: ~ (Act) (H-9659) 537379 J F Ballance[4] attch. HQ, WFF, (Act) H-5011 K J Cottis[4] attch. MDF Tank & (H-47527) 536680 A A Leach[4&5] attch. 3/W Sig Sqn

~ 19th (Queen Alexandra's Own Royal) Hussars ~

Note a.   *Roll of all personnel identified as eligible.*
Note b.   *Recipients attached Headquarters (HQ), Waziristan Field Force (WFF).*
Note c.   *France & Flanders August 1914 forward. India November 1919 to 1922.*
Note d.   *Amalgamated with 15th (The King's Hussars) in 1922 to form the King's Royal Hussars.*
Note e.   *Medals named in impressed capitals: '19 HRS', 'HUSSARS' or 'CORPS OF HUSSARS'.*

Single Clasp	No. Identified	Rarity
Afghanistan N.W.F. 1919[3]	0	None Identified
Mahsud 1919–20[5]	0	None Identified
Waziristan 1919–21[4]	2	Of the Utmost Rarity
Waziristan 1921–24[6]	0	None Identified

Lance Corporals/Privates: ~ 536915 H J Gardiner[4] & 537970 H R Philpott[4]

~ 21ˢᵗ (Empress of India's) Lancers ~

Note a.   *Roll of all personnel identified as eligible.*

Note b.   *India August 1914 forward. United Kingdom 1921.*

Note c.   *Amalgamated with 17ᵗʰ (Duke of Cambridge's Own) Lancers in 1922 to form the 17ᵗʰ/21ˢᵗ Lancers.*

Note d.   *Medals named in impressed capitals: '21 LRS.' Medal Record Cards state that some of the men shown on the roll as attached to 1 KDG should have received medals named '21 LRS ATTᴰ 1 K. D. GDS.'. It is not certain as to whether this occurred and I have never seen an example named thus. Further, many men included on the 21ˢᵗ Lancers roll actually qualified for Afghanistan 1919 while 'cap badged' Corps of Lancers. I have reviewed the Medal Record Card for all personnel on the roll and compiled the list below accordingly. It is evident from the Medal Record Cards that groups exist with the British War Medal, (and where pertinent the Victory Medal), named '21 LRS.' while the India General Service Medal is named 'CORPS OF LANCERS.' This is an ambiguous area and use of both the 21ˢᵗ Lancers roll and the Corps of Lancers roll is advised when researching any given recipient.*

Note e.   *Battle Honour 'Third Afghan War 1919' published in Army Order 27 of March 1924 and subsequently withdrawn by Army Order 246 of 1924.*

Single Clasp	No. Identified	Rarity
Afghanistan N.W.F. 1919[3]	83	Rare
Mahsud 1919–20[5]	0	None Identified
Waziristan 1919– 21[4]	0	None Identified
Waziristan 1921–24[6]	0	None Identified
Combination Clasps	**No. Identified**	**Rarity**
Afghanistan N.W.F. 1919[3] Waziristan 1919–21[4]	1	According to the roll as seen, can be considered Unique
Afghanistan N.W.F. 1919[3] Mahsud 1919–20[5] Waziristan 1919– 21[4]	1	According to the roll as seen, can be considered Unique
Afghanistan N.W.F. 1919[3] North West Frontier 1930–31[9]	1	According to the roll as seen, can be considered Unique

Majors: ~ W A Jones[3,4&5] attch. HQ, WFF

Lieutenants: ~ H Baddeley[3]

Squadron Quartermaster Sergeants/Staff Sergeants: ~ (Act) L-13626 H T Jarratt[3] attch. CMSC

Quartermaster Sergeants/Sergeants: ~ (Act) L-2130 D J Beams[3] attch. HQ, 1 Div., L-355 B W Kelsey[3] attch. ITD & L-13584 T Warren[3] attch. 3 FVS, RAVC

Lance Sergeants/Corporals: ~ (L-1940) L-20234 P Batson[3] attch. S Persian Gendarmerie, L-19982 W Chilton[3] attch. 1 KDG, L-1767 A D Downey[3] attch. 40 DSC, L-20266 T Flower[3] attch. 1 KDG thence Gen Mollison Mission, L-2962 F C Jackson[3] attch. 36 DSC, L-3435 C F Rhoades[3] attch. 1 CBST, (Act) L-11476 W T Tickner[3] attch. 1 MT Coy, S&TC & L-4491 H C Williams[3&4] attch. 40 DSC

Lance Corporals/Privates: ~ L-20364 A Ainsworth[3] attch. 22 MG Sqn, MGCC, L-2410 B H Aldis[3] attch. 44 DSC, L-19137 P W Averies[3] attch. 1 KDG, L/11862 J Bailey[3] attch. 1 KDG, (possibly named '1 KDG'), L-20293 G Bevilacqua[3] attch. 1 KDG, (possibly named '1 KDG'), L-20376 C Beaumont[3] attch. 22 MG Sqn, MGCC, L-11202 A Benson[3] attch. 22 MG Sqn, MGCC, L-19512 P Brown[3] attch. 22 MG Sqn, MGCC, L-19977 N H Canning[3] attch. 22 MG Sqn, MGCC, L-10610 R A Canning[3], L-2447 E A Chalk[3] attch. 22 MG Sqn, MGCC, L-19502 A Davenport[3] attch. 1 KDG, L-11703 G Devlin[3] attch. 1 KDG, L-11808 G Dunkling[3] attch. 1 KDG, L-3565 C R Farrow[3&(9 RAF)] attch. 22 MG Sqn, MGCC, L-1269 G Faulconbridge[3] attch. 1 CBST, L-19973 A Flavell[3] attch. 22 MG Sqn, MGCC, L-20349 A E Foreman[3] attch. 22 MG Sqn, MGCC, L-3489 J A Goodwin[3] attch. 36 DSC, L-20340 G W Gopsill[3] attch. 22 MG Sqn, MGCC, L-20365 J Gray[3] attch. 22 MG Sqn, MGCC, L-12037 P Gregory[3] attch. 22 MG Sqn, MGCC, L-12052 W Griffiths[3] attch. 22 MG Sqn, MGCC, L-11357 J Halden[3] attch. 1 KDG, L-10613 W Harrod[3] attch. 1 KDG, L-9840 E R Haslam[3] attch. 22 MG Sqn, MGCC, L-2087 J Hawke[3] attch. 22 MG Sqn, MGCC, L-19978 H U Hewitt[3] attch. 22 MG Sqn, MGCC, L-19145 W Hindley[3] attch. 1 KDG, L-3430 W C Hockham[3] attch. 36 DSC, L-10873 J Hoddy[3] attch. 22 MG Sqn, MGCC, L-11611 A E Holdstock[3] attch. 22 MG Sqn, MGCC, L-20311 E A S Isworth[3] attch. HQ Risalpur Cav Bde., L-11546 T Jackson[3] attch. 22 MG Sqn, MGCC, L-19505 S T Jones[3] attch. 22 MG Sqn, MGCC, L-19149 H Lindsey[3] attch. 22 MG Sqn, MGCC, L-3438 F W Martin[3] attch. 1 CBST, L-10527 G McCann[3] attch. 22 MG Sqn, MGCC, L-19148 J McGowan[3] attch. 1 KDG, L-11813 N McGrath[3] attch. 1 KDG, L-2265 F J McLaren[3] attch. 36 DSC, L-20397 F J McQueen[3], L-19566 G Meredith[3] attch. 22 MG Sqn, MGCC, L-20900 A J Morgan[3] attch. 1 KDG, L-11816 P Nolan[3] attch. 22 MG Sqn, MGCC, L-11748 J O'Callaghan[3] attch. 22 MG Sqn, MGCC, L-19971 J Owen[3] attch. 22 MG Sqn, MGCC, L-19558 M Power[3] attch. 22 MG

Sqn, MGCC, L-10542 M Reilly[3] attch. 1 KDG, L-19514 H H L Rough[3] attch. 22 MG Sqn, MGCC, L-5607 T Saunders[3] attch. HQ, 1 Cav Bde., L-1433 A H Smith[3] attch. 22 MG Sqn, MGCC, L-19141 G Smith[3] attch. 1 KDG, L-19995 R D Smith[3] attch. 22 MG Sqn, MGCC, L-20334 T W Smith[3] attch. 22 MG Sqn, MGCC, L-19967 A Sparrow[3] attch. 1 KDG, L-19979 W A Spencer[3] attch. 22 MG Sqn, L-19972 G Stannett[3] attch. 22 MG Sqn, MGCC, L-20254 A Strickland[3] attch. 8 CCFA, L-20300 F Stringer[3] attch. 22 MG Sqn, MGCC, L-20369 J W Thornton[3] attch. 22 MG Sqn, MGCC, L-19530 C Vowles[3] attch. 40 DSC, L-10630 H Ward[3] attch. 22 MG Sqn, MGCC, L-3570 G A Watling[3] attch. 36 DSC, L-20351 H Watson[3] attch. 22 MG Sqn, MGCC, L-4080 J F Webb[3] attch. 22 MG Sqn, MGCC, L-11976 W Webster[3] attch. 22 MG Sqn, MGCC, L-20255 H Whitman[3] attch. 22 MG Sqn, MGCC, L-20606 J A Willis[3] attch. 44 DSC, L-816 A Wise[3] attch. MAD 1 PD, L-19503 G H Wright[3] attch. 22 MG Sqn, MGCC & L-1026 H C Young[3] attch. 22 MG Sqn, MGCC

~ The Corps of Dragoons ~

Note a.   *Roll of all personnel identified as eligible.*
Note b.   *Recipient attached 36 Divisional Signal Company (DSC). Parent unit = Royal Dragoons.*
Note c.   *Medals named in impressed capitals: 'CORPS. OF DRAGOONS.'*

Single Clasp	No. Identified	Rarity
Afghanistan N.W.F. 1919[3]	1	According to the roll as seen, can be considered Unique
Mahsud 1919–20[5]	0	None Identified
Waziristan 1919–21[4]	0	None Identified
Waziristan 1921–24[6]	0	None Identified

Warrant Officers Class II: ~ (SSM) D-1563 W J Stewart[3]

~ The Corps of Hussars ~

Note a.   *No recipients identified on roll as being named 'Corps of Hussars' but after cross referencing with Medal Record Cards combined with specimens examined, the following roll can be compiled.*
Note b.   *Recipient attached 44 Divisional Signal Company (DSC). Parent Unit = 7th Hussars.*
Note c.   *Medals named in impressed capitals: 'CORPS. OF HUSSARS.'*

Single Clasp	No. Identified	Rarity
Afghanistan N.W.F. 1919[3]	1	According to the roll as seen, can be considered Unique
Mahsud 1919–20[5]	0	None Identified
Waziristan 1919–21[4]	0	None Identified
Waziristan 1921–24[6]	0	None Identified

Lance Corporals / Privates: ~ H-7652 W M Tate[3]

~ The Corps of Lancers ~

Note a.   *Roll of all personnel identified as eligible.*
Note b.   *All of these personnel were originally included on the 21st Lancers roll and have only been identified as 'Corps of Lancers' following examination of each recipient's Medal Record Card. Experience dictates that it is possible some of the medals belonging to those listed below were actually named: '21 LRS'.*
Note c.   *Medals named in impressed capitals: 'CORPS. OF LANCERS.'*

Single Clasp	No. Identified	Rarity
Afghanistan N.W.F. 1919[3]	27	Very Rare
Mahsud 1919–20[5]	0	None Identified
Waziristan 1919–21[4]	0	None Identified
Waziristan 1921–24[6]	0	None Identified

Squadron Quartermaster Sergeants/Staff Sergeants: ~ (Act) L-20258 H P Stevens[3] attch. HQ, Risalpur Cav Bde.

Lance Sergeants/Corporals: ~ L-13542 T Birch[3] attch. 2 MT Coy, S&TC

Lance Corporals/Privates: ~ L-19128 A Ash[3] attch. 22 MG Sqn, MGCC, L-20623 B Bradley[3] attch. 22 MG Sqn, MGCC, L-19138 J Chambers[3] attch. 22 MG Sqn, MGCC, L-19127 J J Clarke[3] attch. 22 MG Sqn, MGCC, L-2381 G W Clements[3] attch. 22 MG Sqn, MGCC, L-19146 J Crocker[3] attch. 22 MG Sqn, MGCC, L19140 E Crowther[3] attch. 22 MG Sqn, MGCC, L-19136 J Day[3] attch. 22 MG Sqn, MGCC, L-19508 E J Eddy[3] attch. 22 MG Sqn, MGCC, L-19515 J W Evans[3] attch. 22 MG Sqn, MGCC, L-19143 W R Fletcher[3] attch. 22 MG Sqn, MGCC, L-20605 T Goulding[3] attch. 22 MG Sqn, MGCC, L-19549 W Haggas[3] attch. 22 MG Sqn, MGCC, L-19560 G E Heyburn[3] attch. 22 MG Sqn, MGCC, L-19122 J I Howard[3] attch. 22 MG Sqn, MGCC, L-19127 J O'Donnell[3] attch. MMP (aka J J Clarke), L-19142 G S F Olney[3] attch. 22 MG Sqn, MGCC, L-19975 R Peake[3] attch. 22 MG Sqn, MGCC, L-19126 E H Perry[3] attch. 22 MG Sqn, MGCC, L-19550 P Smithson[3] attch. 22 MG Sqn, MGCC, L-19979 J W Stockdale[3] attch. 1 KDG, L-19504 G E Tudman[3] attch. 22 MG Sqn, MGCC, L-19518 W Tupling[3] attch. 22 MG Sqn, MGCC, L-19562 J Venning[3] attch. 22 MG Sqn, MGCC & L-19133 H Wilson[3] attch. 22 MG Sqn, MGCC

~ Reserve Regiment of Cavalry ~

Note a.   *Roll of all personnel identified as eligible.*

Note b.   *Seventeen reserve cavalry regiments were formed in August 1914 to provide support for the first line cavalry formations. A 1917 reorganisation established a new structure with three reserve regiments for the Household Cavalry and four reserve regiments for all others.*

Note c.   *The 2nd Reserve Cavalry Regiment provided (after the 1917 reorganisation) drafts for 3rd, 4th, 7th and 8th Hussars plus the Dorset Yeomanry, 1st & 3rd County of London Yeomanry, South Nottinghamshire Hussars, Oxfordshire Hussars and the Westmorland & Cumberland Yeomanry.*

Note d.   *The 5th Reserve Cavalry Regiment provided (after the 1917 reorganisation) drafts for 10th, 14th, 18th & 20th Hussars plus the Royal Gloucestershire Hussars, Northumberland Hussars, Warwickshire Yeomanry, Worcestershire Yeomanry and (until early 1918) Yorkshire Hussars.*

Note e.   *Medals named in impressed capitals with regiment number followed by: 'R. R. OF CAV.'*

Single Clasp	No. Identified	Rarity
Afghanistan N.W.F. 1919[3]	2	Of the Utmost Rarity
Mahsud 1919–20[5]	0	None Identified
Waziristan 1919–21[4]	0	None Identified
Waziristan 1921–24[6]	0	None Identified

Lieutenants: ~ D C Murphy[3] (2 RR of CAV) attch. 7 Hrs thence 1 KDG & H J T Wilson[3] (5 RR of CAV) attch. 1 KDG

B. THE YEOMANRY

~ Staffordshire Yeomanry (Queen's Own Royal Regt.) ~

Note a.   *Roll of all personnel identified as eligible.*

Note b.   *Recipient attached 2/4 Border Regiment.*

Note c.   *United Kingdom August 1914. Egypt November 1915, Western Frontier Force 1916, Palestine 1917 thence Syria until June 1919.*

Note d.   *Medals named in impressed capitals: 'STAFF. YEO.'*

Single Clasp	No. Identified	Rarity
Afghanistan N.W.F. 1919[3]	1	According to the roll as seen, can be considered Unique
Mahsud 1919–20[5]	0	None Identified
Waziristan 1919–21[4]	0	None Identified
Waziristan 1921–24[6]	0	None Identified

Lieutenants: ~ P A Aitchison[3]

~ Yorkshire Dragoons (Queen's Own) ~

Note a.   *Roll of all personnel identified as eligible.*
Note b.   *United Kingdom August 1914. France & Flanders July 1915 forward.*
Note c.   *Medals named in impressed capitals: 'YORK. DNS.'*

Single Clasp	No. Identified	Rarity
Afghanistan N.W.F. 1919[3]	1	According to the roll as seen, can be considered Unique
Mahsud 1919–20[5]	0	None Identified
Waziristan 1919–21[4]	0	None Identified
Waziristan 1921–24[6]	0	None Identified

Lieutenants: ~ H R C Bennett[3] attch. 630 MT Coy, RASC and thence 28 MAC, RASC

~ Leicestershire Yeomanry (Prince Albert's Own) ~

Note a.   *Roll of all personnel identified as eligible.*
Note b.   *United Kingdom August 1914. France & Flanders November 1914 forward. Broken up by squadron April 1918 with squadrons posted to 4th Hussars, 5th Lancers and 16th Lancers.*
Note c.   *Medals named in impressed capitals: 'LEIC. YEO.'*

Single Clasp	No. Identified	Rarity
Afghanistan N.W.F. 1919[3]	2	Of the Utmost Rarity
Mahsud 1919–20[5]	0	None Identified
Waziristan 1919–21[4]	0	None Identified
Waziristan 1921–24[6]	0	None Identified

Lance Corporals/Privates: ~ 2018 A G Vessey[3] attch. MFP & 255683 W J Stone[3] attch. MMP

~ Northumberland Yeomanry (Hussars) ~

Note a.   *Roll of all personnel identified as eligible.*
Note b.   *United Kingdom August 1914. France & Flanders October 1914 forward.*
Note c.   *Medals named in impressed capitals 'NORTH'D. YEO.'*

Single Clasp	No. Identified	Rarity
Afghanistan N.W.F. 1919[3]	2	Of the Utmost Rarity
Mahsud 1919–20[5]	0	None Identified
Waziristan 1919–21[4]	0	None Identified
Waziristan 1921–24[6]	0	None Identified

Captains: ~ H G C Carr-Ellison[3] attch. 21 L thence HQ, NWFF
Lieutenants: ~ R K F Hurndall[3] attch. 22 MG Sqn, MGCC

~ Denbighshire Yeomanry ~

Note a.   *Roll of all personnel identified as eligible.*
Note b.   *Recipient attached 21st Prince Albert Victor's Own Cavalry (PAVO Cav.), Indian Army (IA).*
Note c.   *United Kingdom August 1914. Egypt April 1915. Dismounted in 1916 and used to form 24th Bn, Royal Welsh Fusiliers.*
Note d.   *Medals named in impressed capitals: 'DENBIGH. YEO.'*

Single Clasp	No. Identified	Rarity
Afghanistan N.W.F. 1919[3]	1	According to the roll as seen, can be considered Unique
Mahsud 1919–20[5]	0	None Identified
Waziristan 1919–21[4]	0	None Identified
Waziristan 1921–24[6]	0	None Identified

Lieutenants: ~ M G Weaver[3]

~ Westmorland and Cumberland Yeomanry ~

Note a.   *Roll of all personnel identified as eligible.*
Note b.   *Recipient attached 15 Machine Gun Squadron (MG Sqn), Machine Gun Corps Cavalry (MGCC).*
Note c.   *United Kingdom August 1914. France & Flanders July 1915. Absorbed into 7th Bn, Border Regiment September 1917.*
Note d.   *Medals named in impressed capitals: 'WEST. & CUMB. YEO.'*

Single Clasp	No. Identified	Rarity
Afghanistan N.W.F. 1919[3]	1	According to the roll as seen, can be considered Unique
Mahsud 1919–20[5]	0	None Identified
Waziristan 1919–21[4]	0	None Identified
Waziristan 1921–24[6]	0	None Identified

Captains: ~ F H Robinson[3]

~ Buckinghamshire Yeomanry (Royal Bucks, Hussars) ~

Note a.   *Roll of all personnel identified as eligible.*
Note b.   *United Kingdom August 1915. Egypt April 1915, Gallipoli August 1915, Mudros November 1915, Egypt November 1915, Palestine 1917. Amalgamated With Berkshire Yeomanry April 1918 to form 'C' Bn, MGC thence to France & Flanders June 1918. United designation changed to 101 Company MGC August 1918.*
Note c.   *Medals named in impressed capitals: 'BUCKS. YEO.'*

Single Clasp	No. Identified	Rarity
Afghanistan N.W.F. 1919[3]	2	Of the Utmost Rarity
Mahsud 1919–20[5]	0	None Identified
Waziristan 1919–21[4]	0	None Identified
Waziristan 1921–24[6]	0	None Identified

Lance Sergeants/Corporals: ~ (Act) 206358 F Hawkins[3] attch. MMP
Lance Corporals/Privates: ~ 206368 T W Leach[3] attch. 1 KDG

~ Gloucestershire Yeomanry (Royal Gloucester Hussars) ~

Note a. *Roll of all personnel identified as eligible.*
Note b. *Recipient attached 1 King's Dragoon Guards.*
Note c. *United Kingdom August 1914. Egypt April 1915, Gallipoli August 1915, Mudros November 1915, Egypt November 1915, Palestine 1917, Syria 1918 to 1919.*
Note d. *Medals named in impressed capitals: 'GLOUC. YEO.'*

Single Clasp	No. Identified	Rarity
Afghanistan N.W.F. 1919[3]	1	According to the roll as seen, can be considered Unique
Mahsud 1919–20[5]	0	None Identified
Waziristan 1919–21[4]	0	None Identified
Waziristan 1921–24[6]	0	None Identified

Lance Corporals/Privates: ~ 235535 W Walkley[3] attch. 1 KDG

~ Hertfordshire Yeomanry (Carabineers) ~

Note a. *Roll of all personnel identified as eligible.*
Note b. *United Kingdom August 1914. Egypt September 1914, Gallipoli August 1915, Mudros November 1915 & Egypt November 1915. Early 1916 Regiment broken up by squadron. 'D' Squadron Mesopotamia March 1916, N. W. Persia April 1918 and India January to August 1919.*
Note c. *'D' Sqn stationed India January to August 1919.*
Note d. *Medals named in impressed capitals: 'HERTS. YEO.'*

Single Clasp	No. Identified	Rarity
Afghanistan N.W.F. 1919[3]	16	Extremely Rare
Mahsud 1919–20[5]	0	None Identified
Waziristan 1919–21[4]	0	None Identified
Waziristan 1921–24[6]	0	None Identified

Lance Corporals/Privates: ~ 106034 J W Bird[3] attch. 1 KDG, 145475 W T Bryant[3] attch. 21 L thence 22 MG Sqn, MGCC, 106098 P H Clark[3] attch. 21 L thence 22 MG Sqn, MGCC, 105858 L Dowse[3] attch. 21 L thence 22 MG Sqn, MGCC, 105992 A C Dunkley[3] attch. 19 IMVS, 106566 W E James[3] attch. 1 KDG, 106570 H Johnson[3] attch. 1 KDG, 106567 A Jones[3] attch. 1 KDG, 106565 J Jones[3] attch. 1 KDG, 105602 R B Martin[3] attch. 1 KDG, 105210 E Roberts[3] attch. 21 L thence 22 MG Sqn, MGCC, 106039 S C Rochester[3] attch. MMP, 105731 W Skinner[3] attch. 1 KDG, 106568 B L J Smith[3] attch. 1 KDG, (Possibly named to KDG) & 106571 W A Taylor[3] attch. 1 KDG
Shoeing Smiths: ~ 106075 T W Tyler[3] attch. 1 KDG

~ 1st County of London Yeomanry (Middlesex Duke Of Cambridge's Hussars) ~

Note a. *Roll of all personnel identified as eligible.*
Note b. *Recipient attached 15 Machine Gun Squadron (MG Sqn), Machine Gun Corps Cavalry (MGCC).*
Note c. *United Kingdom August 1914. Egypt April 1915, Gallipoli August 1915, Mudros November 1915, Egypt November 1915, Salonika November 1916, Egypt June 1917, Palestine 1917 to 1919.*
Note d. *Medals named in impressed capitals: '1 - CO. OF LOND YEO.'*

Single Clasp	No. Identified	Rarity
Afghanistan N.W.F. 1919[3]	1	According to the roll as seen, can be considered Unique
Mahsud 1919–20[5]	0	None Identified
Waziristan 1919–21[4]	0	None Identified
Waziristan 1921–24[6]	0	None Identified

Lieutenants: ~ J W Putnam[3]

~ Surrey Yeomanry (Queen Mary's Regiment) ~

Note a.   *Roll of all personnel identified as eligible.*
Note b.   *United Kingdom August 1914. 'A' & 'B' Squadrons – France and Flanders December1914/January 1915, Salonika December 1915/February 1916. 'C' Squadron Egypt February 1916, Mudros June 1915, Egypt Feb 1916 and France & Flanders March 1916. 'Q' Squadron to South Russia February 1919 to June 1919.*
Note c.   *Medals named in impressed capitals: 'SURR. YEO.'*

Single Clasp	No. Identified	Rarity
Afghanistan N.W.F. 1919[3]	6	Of the Utmost Rarity
Mahsud 1919–20[5]	0	None Identified
Waziristan 1919–21[4]	0	None Identified
Waziristan 1921–24[6]	0	None Identified

Lieutenants: ~ H W Jackson[3] attch. 1 KDG
Lance Corporals/Privates: ~ 46614 H J Beales[3] attch. 22 MG Sqn, MGCC, 46623 W H Clapton[3] attch. 21 L thence 1 KDG, 46622 R Fendell[3] attch. 21 L thence 22 MG Sqn, MGCC, 46616 R Grieff[3] attch. 1 KDG & 46618 W R Howett[3] attch. 21 L thence 22 MG Sqn, MGCC

~ Fife and Forfar Yeomanry ~

Note a.   *Roll of all personnel identified as eligible.*
Note b.   *United Kingdom August 1914. Gallipoli September 1915, Imbros December 1915, Egypt December 1915. December 1916 became 14ᵗʰ Bn, Black Watch.*
Note c.   *Medals named in impressed capitals: 'FIFE & FORFAR YEO.'*

Single Clasp	No. Identified	Rarity
Afghanistan N.W.F. 1919[3]	2	Of the Utmost Rarity
Mahsud 1919–20[5]	0	None Identified
Waziristan 1919–21[4]	0	None Identified
Waziristan 1921–24[6]	0	None Identified

Captains: ~ P R Myburgh[3] attch. 22 MG Sqn, MGCC
Lance Corporals / Privates: ~ 85252 D Peat[3] attch. 21 L thence 22 MG Sqn, MGCC

~ Northamptonshire Yeomanry ~

Note a.   *Roll of all personnel identified as eligible.*
Note b.   *Recipients attached 1 King's Dragoon Guards.*
Note c.   *United Kingdom August 1914. France & Flanders November 1914, Italy November 1917 forward.*
Note d.   *Medals named in impressed capitals: 'NORTH'N. YEO.'*

Single Clasp	No. Identified	Rarity
Afghanistan N.W.F. 1919[3]	3	Of the Utmost Rarity
Mahsud 1919–20[5]	0	None Identified
Waziristan 1919–21[4]	0	None Identified
Waziristan 1921–24[6]	0	None Identified

Lance Corporals/Privates: ~ 145271 U W Bryan[3], 145764 T H H Coulson[3] & 145833 F D MacMain[3]

~ 1st Lovat's Scouts Yeomanry ~

Note a.   *Roll of all personnel identified as eligible.*
Note b.   *Recipient attached 5 Motor Transport Company (MT Coy), Supply & Transport Corps (S&TC).*
Note c.   *United Kingdom August 1914. Gallipoli September 1915, Imbros December 1915 and Egypt December 1915. September 1916 formed 10th Battalion, Cameron Highlanders.*
Note d.   *Medals named in impressed capitals: '1 - LOVAT'S SCTS.'*

Single Clasp	No. Identified	Rarity
Afghanistan N.W.F. 1919[3]	1	According to the roll as seen, can be considered Unique
Mahsud 1919–20[5]	0	None Identified
Waziristan 1919–21[4]	0	None Identified
Waziristan 1921–24[6]	0	None Identified

Lieutenants: ~ J D Mackintosh[3] attch. 5 MT Coy, S&TC

THE TANK CORPS (ROYAL FROM 1922):
Sub Units Identified As Entitled:
No. 1 Armoured Motor Brigade
1, 7, 8, 9 & 10 Armoured Car Companies

Note a.   *Roll of all commissioned personnel identified as eligible.*
Note b.   *Non-commissioned and other rank personnel multi clasp only or non–Afghanistan 1919 / Waziristan series single clasp.*
Note c.   *The Tank Corps was formed in 1917 from the heavy branch of the Machine Gun Corps. It is believed Motorised Machine Gun units remained within the orbit of the MGC until disbandment.*
Note d.   *Non commissioned and other rank personnel numbering appears within the same series as the Machine Gun Corps. Where possible, the personnel listed below have been double-checked from the Medal Roll against their Medal Record Card to give clarity regarding the unit designation likely to be noted on the medal. In some instances, the information on the Medal Record Card is not conclusive.*
Note e.   *Medals to the Corps for the period 1919 until the prefix 'Royal' was granted in 1922 are named in impressed capitals: 'TANK CORPS.'. Thereafter medals named in impressed capitals: 'R. TANK CORPS.'*

Single Clasp	No. Identified	Rarity
Afghanistan N.W.F. 1919[3]	0	None Identified
Mahsud 1919–20[5]	0	None Identified
Waziristan 1919–21[4]	In Strength	Not Rare
Waziristan 1921–24[6]	In Strength	Not Rare
Combination Clasps	**No. Identified**	**Rarity**
Waziristan 1919–21[4] Malabar 1921–22[7]	1	According to the roll as seen, can be considered Unique
Waziristan 1919–21[4] Malabar 1921–22[7] Waziristan 1921–24[6]	3	Of the Utmost Rarity
Waziristan 1919–21[4] Waziristan 1921–24[6]	59	Rare
Waziristan 1919–21[4] Waziristan 1921–24[6] Mohmand 1933[11]	1	According to the roll as seen, can be considered Unique
Waziristan 1919–21[4] North West Frontier 1930–31[9]	1	According to the roll as seen, can be considered Unique
Malabar 1921–22[7] Waziristan 1921–24[6]	5	Of the Utmost Rarity

Waziristan 1921–24[6] North West Frontier 1930–31[9]	3	**Of the Utmost Rarity**
Waziristan 1921–24[6] Mohmand 33[11]	1	**According to the roll as seen, can be considered Unique**
Waziristan 1921–24[6] North West Frontier 1935[12]	3	**Of the Utmost Rarity**

Lieutenant Colonels: ~ E H Wildblood[6] 7 ACC

Majors: ~ R C Apletre[6] 9 ACC, W A Moore[4&6] 10 ACC, (Bvt) E H Kendrick[6] 9 ACC, S P A Rolls[6] Staff, G A Rosser[4,7(8 ACC)&6] 9 ACC & J C Tilly[6] 1 ACC

Captains: ~ V A Gascoyne-Cecil[6] 10 ACC, E C N Custance[6] 9 ACC, H H E Henson[·4&6] 10 ACC, D V Lawson[6] 9 ACC, A McCouh[6] 9 ACC, G W Quin-Smith[6&12] 9 ACC, C H Windrum[6] 1 ACC & E G Worlock[6] 1 ACC

Lieutenants: ~ E G M Adams[6] 1 ACC, W S Bagnall[6] 9 ACC, G H Brooks[6&12(Capt.)] 1 ACC, O E Chapman[6] 9 ACC, I F Clewent[6] 9 ACC, T A B Copestake[6] 1 ACC, L P Crough[6] 1 ACC, G J N Culverwell[4&6] 10 ACC, P Dean[4&6] 10 ACC, R S Evans[4&6] 10 ACC, C Foreman[6], H F B Garrett[6&9(Capt.)] 1 ACC, E Genochio[6] 1 ACC, A E P Hall[6&9(Capt.)] 9 ACC, F A B Jones[4&6] 10 ACC, N A S Jones[4&6] 10 ACC, T A Lakeman[6] 9 ACC, F V Lyons[6] 9 ACC, R L B Maddison[6] 9 ACC, T Ivor Moore[6] 1 ACC, S P H Moorhead[6] 1 ACC, G W Richards[4&6] 1 ACC, H Skinner[6] 9 ACC & S A Young[4&6] 10 ACC

Warrant Officers Class II: ~ 7807349 H Keeble[4&6] 10 ACC

Company Quartermaster Sergeants/Staff Sergeants: ~ 304060 V J Tompkins[4&6] 10 ACC

Quartermaster Sergeants/Sergeants: ~ 7868872 S Bassett[4&6] 10 ACC, 7868009 F H Cossum[4&6] 10 ACC, 1020229 F R Cox[4&6] 10 ACC, 1403632 W Dorrington[4&6] 10 ACC, 3378080 R Dunn[4&6] 10 ACC, (Act) 7815894 W Elliott[4&6] 10 ACC, 7807749 H Homer[4&6] 10 ACC, 1406626 H Lord[4&6] 10 ACC, ?????? (H V, F E, F W G) Trott[4&6] 10 ACC, G Whatmore[4&6] 10 ACC & 1402977 W R Wisken[4&6] 10 ACC

Lance Sergeants/Corporals: ~ 7817768 G R Bummage[4&6] 1 ACC, 7871379 J W Edmonds[4&9(Sgt. 7 ACC)], 7810828 S A Fitzgerald[4&6] 9 ACC, 7871250 J Quigg[6&11(L/Cpl.)], 7211427 B Stanger[4&6] 10 ACC & 2866154 W Walls[4&6] 10 ACC

Lance Corporals/Privates: ~ 7808789 W H F Aylward[4&6] 10 ACC, 7811849 W Barr[7(8 ACC)&6] 10 ACC, (118796) 6451050 A Bergman[4,6&11(L/Cpl. R Sigs)] 10 ACC, 7817354 J Brennan[4&6] 10 ACC, 2876648 F A Britton[4&6] 10 ACC, 4259990 G Brown[4&6] 10 ACC, 7870888 W Burlington[4&6] 10 ACC, 7819462 J E Burns[7(8 ACC)&6] 9 ACC, 7814338 R W Burton[4&7(8 ACC)], 7876421 F Buxton[4&6] 10 ACC, 7870110 A E Church[4&6] 10 ACC, 7814942 C H Clarke[4&6] 10 ACC, 7812214 D Daly[7&6] 9 ACC, 7872533 D J Dawson[4&6] 10 ACC, 7870563 D Ferguson[4&6] 10 ACC, 4682034 E Francis[4&6] 10 ACC, 7810861 J Gardner[4,6&7(8 ACC)] 10 ACC, 7817575 T R Gibbons[4&6] 10 ACC, 7871062 J F Gibson[4,7&6] 9 ACC, 7872009 F W C Hall[4&6] 10 ACC, 7869781 W H Hawtin[4&6] 10 ACC, 7871657 G Jones[4&6] 10 ACC, 7808726 T Kelsey[4&6] 9 ACC, 7870481 J Ladds[4&6] 10 ACC, 7869367 F P Luck[7&6] 9 ACC, 7870537 A Lumsden[4&6] 10 ACC, 3122426 J McInnes[4&6] 10 ACC, 22666 W T Miles[4&6] 10 ACC, 7869030 A Mumford[4&6] 9 ACC, 7006351 J Murphy[4&6] 10 ACC, 7812869 J Osborne[4&6] 10 ACC, 7869208 J H Pemberton[6&9(L/Sgt.)] 7 ACC, 7869381 T Phillips[4&6] 10 ACC, 7807083 A Pountney[4&6] 10 ACC, 1414601 W Pulman[4&6] 10 ACC, 7811248 A Shore[4&6] 10 ACC, 7869746 H H Steward[4&6] 10 ACC, 2203390 H Stewart[6&12(Cpl. 2 LTC)] 7 ACC, 7872089 J N Swift[4&6] 10 ACC, 7816618 C W Taylor[4&6] 10 ACC, 7870275 F Temple[7&6] 9 ACC, 7808615 J Walker[4&6] 10 ACC & 7807130 G Williams[4&6] 10 ACC

THE MACHINE GUN CORPS:
Sub Units Identified As Entitled:
HQ 1 & 10 Armoured Motor Brigades
15, 22, 23, 24 & Detachments 25 Squadrons, Machine Gun Corps, Cavalry
1, 2, 3, 4, 5, 6, 7, 8, 10, 11, 15, 16, 19 & 22 Motorised (Armoured) Machine Gun Batteries
185, 187, 204, 205, 222, 228, 260, 263, 270, 281, 282, 285, 286, 287 & 288 Companies
Machine Gun Corps, Infantry
(Details) 9, 11 (Subsequently 6 Coy) & 12 (Details Only) Machine Gun Battalions
Detachment 17 Ind Div. Machine Gun Battalion

Note a. *Roll of all commissioned personnel identified as eligible.*

Note b. *Non-commissioned and other rank personnel multi clasp only or non-Afghanistan 1919 / Waziristan series single clasp.*

Note c. *The Machine Gun Corps was formed in 1915 with three branches – a. Machine Gun Corps Cavalry, b. Machine Gun Corps Infantry (From May 1918 included Guards Machine Gun Regiment), c. Motorised Machine Gun Service.*

Note d. *The Heavy Machine Gun Corps was formed in 1916 and subsequently became the nucleolus for the creation of the Tank Corps in 1917.*

Note e. *The Machine Gun Corps was disbanded in 1922 with many non-demobilising personnel transferring to the Tank Corps.*

Note f.   *Non-commissioned and other rank numbering appears within the same series as the Tank Corps. Where possible, the personnel listed below have been double-checked from the Medal Roll against their Medal Record Card to give clarity regarding the unit designation likely to be noted on the medal. In some instances, the information on the Medal Record Card is not conclusive.*

Note g.   *Medals named in impressed capitals: 'M.G.C.'*

Single Clasp	No. Identified	Rarity
Afghanistan N.W.F. 1919[3]	In Strength	Not Rare
Mahsud 1919–20[5]	1	According to the roll as seen, can be considered Unique
Waziristan 1919–21[4]	?	Scarce
Waziristan 1921–24[6]	0	Corps Disbanded 1922

Combination Clasps	No. Identified	Rarity
Afghanistan N.W.F. 1919[3] Mahsud 1919–20[5] Waziristan 1919–21[4]	1	According to the roll as seen, can be considered Unique
Afghanistan N.W.F. 1919[3] Mahsud 1919–20[5] Waziristan 1919–21[4] Waziristan 1921–24[6]	1	According to the roll as seen, can be considered Unique
Afghanistan N.W.F. 1919[3] Waziristan 1919–21[4]	7	Of the Utmost Rarity
Afghanistan N.W.F. 1919[3] Waziristan 1919–21[4] Waziristan 1921–24[6]	10	Of the Utmost Rarity
Afghanistan N.W.F. 1919[3] Malabar 1921–22[7]	1	According to the roll as seen, can be considered Unique
Afghanistan N.W.F. 1919[3] Waziristan 1921–24[6]	6	Of the Utmost Rarity
Mahsud 1919–20[5] Waziristan 1919–21[4]	6	Of the Utmost Rarity
Mahsud 1919–20[5] Waziristan 1919–21[4] Waziristan 1921–24[6]	1	According to the roll as seen, can be considered Unique
Waziristan 1919–21[4] Waziristan 1921–24[6]	44	Very Rare

Majors: ~ H A Garstin[3] 15 Sqn, 1 Cav Bde. & J B Saul[3] & M H W Smithers[3] 281 Coy, 4 Quetta Div.

Captains: ~ C O D Anderson[3] 15 MMG Bty, A W Craven[3], (Act) C S Elmslie[3] 4 MMG Bty, KKF, S A Fitkin[3] 22 Sqn, 12 Cav Bde., C W Giffard[3] 22 MG Sqn, 12 Cav Bde. & E Oldham[3] 281 Coy, 4 Div.

Lieutenants: ~ C J Ainslie[3], H T Appleton[3] 260 Coy, 16 Div., P Back[3] 222 Coy, 2 Div., F J Barley[3] 287 Coy, E L Bartleman[3] 205 Coy, F G Bartlett[3] 22 Sqn, 12 Cav Bde , L W S Blackmore[3] 263 Coy, 1 Div., E C Browne[3], H Corson[3] 3 MMG Bty, F G Daniel[3] 288 Coy, R T Donaldson[3] 281 Coy, 4 Div., A W Doubleday[3] 25 MG Sqn, W P Elton[3], C A C Farr[3] 285 Coy, 1 Div., G Fleming[3] 281 Coy, 4 Div., J R Frith[3] 260 Coy, 16 Div., P A T Goodwin[3], R A C Hill[3&4] 260 Coy, 16 Div., E Holden[3] 286 Coy, T H Holland[3], W E Howard[3] 281 Coy, 4 Div., H Jackson[3] 24 Sqn attch. 22 Sqn, 12 Cav Bde., A M Ketley[3] 19 MMG Bty, K A Knight[3] 3 MMG Bty, T Lismore[3] 222 Coy, 2 Div., J A McBride[3] 270 Coy, 57 Bde., A Parr[3] 15 MMG Bty, T O Parry[3] 222 Coy, 2 Div., W M R Pearson[3] 285 Coy, 1 Div., C H Z Piercy[3], H Player[3] 15 Sqn, 1 Cav Bde., J Prentice[3] 270 Coy, 57 Bde., C A Rennie[3] 22 Sqn, 12 Cav Bde., T E Roberts[4], M H Rosher[3] 22 Bty, G W O Saul[3], S V J Scott[3] 1 MMG Bty, J Shaw[3] 288 Coy, 16 Div., G Dornley-Smith[3] 222 Coy, 2 Div., W Stones[3] 24 Sqn attch. 15 Sqn, 1 Cav Bde., F G Sturges[3] 24 Sqn, 10 Cav Bde., H C Treadaway[3] 15 Sqn, 1 Cav Bde., C F Turnbull[3] 285 Coy MGC, 1 Div., G T Turner[3] 19 MG Bty, E P Windsor[3] 22 MMG Bty, G White[3] 281 Coy, 4 Div. & T C Zimmerman[3] 260 Coy, 16 Div.

Warrant Officers Class II: ~ (BSM) 163452 T E Banfield[3,4&5]

Quartermaster Sergeants/Sergeants: ~ (Act) 7810078 R J Blewett[4&6(RTC)], 7809854 E J Hawkins[4&5] attch. 82 Punjabis, IA, (Act) 7808533 C Keeley[4&6] 11 Bn, (7817546) 163367 A C Leggett[3&6(RTC)], (Act) (7817592) 163480 A Parker[4&5] 10 MMG Bty, (Act) (7817517) 147194 G R Pentney[3,(4&6 RTC)], (Fitter), (50770) 7816186 E J Punchard[4&6(R.Sigs)], (7871588) 163453 R A H Spooner[3,(S/Sgt. Tank Corps 4,5&6)] & (Act) 163414 W Thompson[3&4]

Lance Sergeants/Corporals: ~ 7815371 A G Annetts[4&6], 7810785 D C Brown[4&6(RTC)], (Act) (7817709) 200742 A B Hood[4&6] 11 Bn, (7810524) 713970 R Lansdown[3&6(RTC)], (7817807) 163504 L Matthews[3,4&6] & (Act) 7811626 R P Timms[4&6] 11 Bn

Lance Corporals/Privates/Gunners: ~ (7817606) 164086 W Allen[3,(4&6 RTC)], 7814964 W Appleby[4&6] 11 Bn, 7814754 A P Archer[4&6(RTC)], 7808215 A E Baxter[4&6(RTC)], 7814895 J Boylan[4&6] 11 Bn, (7808215) 48770 E J Booker[3,4&6] 22 MG Sqn, MGC, 7809150 E T Booker[4&6] 11 Bn, 7815045 H W Bullers[4&6] 11 Bn, 7808487 J Crawford[4&6] 11 Bn, 158241 M Dunne[3&7(8 ACC RTC)], 7809955 W C Easton[4&6] 11 Bn, 3902925 T G Field[4&6] 11 Bn, 7817910 F C Forrester[4&6] 11 Bn, 7814724 J Frisby[4&6(RTC)], (7817437) 113560 A G Fry[3,4&6(RTC)], 7811379 J J Fullen[4&6] 11 Bn, 28 H N Garstin[4&5] 6 MMG Bty, 119149 M Ging[3&4], 7812244 L A Hand[4&6] 11 Bn, 7811689 E H Hare[4&6(RTC)], (7817710) 200743 F Hayton[4&6] 11 Bn, (7808534) 25734 J Hedley[4&6] 11 Bn, (7817808) 175033 T Hengler[3,4&6], 17562 A W Hicks[5] attch. 104 Rifles, IA, (7817467) 125518 F E Hobday[3,4&6] 11 Bn, 7808409 W Hodge[4&6] 11 Bn, 7817362 W J Hyde[3,4&6] 11 Bn, 123014 W Izzard[3&4], 7811801 P Law[4&6(RTC)], 7808028 F L McBride[4&6(RTC)], 7809295 J McCarthy[4&6(RTC)], 7814968 J McCormack[4&6(RTC)], 7810040 W Middleton[4&6] 11 Bn, 7811638 J F Miller[4&5] 11 Bn, 7817650 W Morphus[4&6(RTC)], 7807219 A W Nicholls[3,4&6(RTC)], 145401 J Oxey[4&5], (7817560) 163406) A Parker[3&4(10 ACC Tank Corps)], 7811717 H Parker[4&6(RTC)], 7817760 F Pickering[4&6] 11 Bn, (7817561) 163408 O Price[3&4(10 ACC Tank Corps)], (7808654) 28893 F Putland[3], 7814986 B O Read[4&6] 11 Bn, 7808117 R Russell[4&6] 11 Bn, 7808404 F Shaw[4&6] 11 Bn, 7808665 A N Showell[4&6(RTC)], 7815385 S Silvester[4&6] 11 Bn, 7815379 C E Smith[4&6] 11 Bn, 7808668 S H Smith[4&6(RTC)], (7809473) 61238 R Spracklen[3&6(Som LI)] attch. 'G' DSC, (7817463) 124644 P G Stead[3&6(7 ACC, RTC)], 7813764 J E Stebbings[4,5&6(RTC)] 11 Bn, 7817648 J Summerfield[4&6] 11 Bn, 145088 H H Taplin[4&6(RTC)], 7817765 F H Trowell[4&6(RTC)], 163565 R Uphill[3&4] 11 AMB, (7817439) 113957 W Watson[3,4&6(RTC)], 191974 J Whitham[3&6(RTC)], 138626 W H Wilson[4&5] 11 Bn, 7811252 F (G) (T) Withers[4&6] 11 Bn & 7811086 W H Woolley[3&6]

THE ARTILLERY:

~ The Royal Horse Artillery ~
Sub Units Identified As Entitled:
'I' Battery – Individuals; 'K' Battery – Individuals; 'M' Battery – Battery Strength'
1st Cavalry Brigade;Ammunition Column;
'A' Ammunition Column

Note a.   *Roll of all personnel identified as eligible.*

Note b.   *All personnel 'M' Battery, Royal Horse Artillery (RHA) unless shown otherwise.*

Note c.   *'M' Battery attached 1 Cavalry Brigade (1 Cav Bde.).*

Note d.   *Medals named in impressed capitals: 'R.A.' According to the roll some individual claims may be named 'R.H.A.' If such specimens exist, it would be contrary to normal practise for the period.*

Single Clasp	No. Identified	Rarity
Afghanistan N.W.F. 1919[3]	167	Scarce
Waziristan 1919– 21[4]	0	None Identified
Mahsud 1919–20[5]	0	None Identified
Waziristan 1921–24[6]	1	According to the roll as seen, can be considered Unique

Majors: ~ R Archer-Houblon[6] 'I' Bty attch. Staff, 9 & 21 Bde.(s) & (Act) S S Lee[3] Cmd.

Captains: ~ D F Aikenhead[3] & D J Hobgen[3]

Lieutenants: ~ E Collard[3], (Temp) C G Harraway[3] & G Lamb[3] attch. 'A' Ammo Col

Warrant Officers Class II: ~ (Temp) 63369 J Merrifield[3]

Battery Quartermaster Sergeants/Staff Sergeants: ~ 25765 D M O'Brien[3] & (Battery) 50255 E W Gilbertson[3] attch. 1 CBAC, RHA

Quartermaster Sergeants/Sergeants: ~ 67889 P C Brotherton[3], 65337 F J Dennis[3], 48499 A L Fitch[3], (Temp) 176900 H A Gatward[3], 38894 W G Harbour[3], 61536 G Jackson[3], 52125 W G Knight[3], 68833 C Millard[3], 53958 T E Perrin[3], 43360 W Pope[3] attch. RE Sigs, (Act) 126710 N K Smith[3] attch. 16 IMVS, 37207 W J Sprunt[3] & 600363 A Urquhart[3]

Corporals: ~ 63089 W G Benham[3], 66239 R Binnington[3], (Act) 51396 J W Foddering[3], 23106 J Hammond[3], 67953 J Hill[3], 67943 T Hill[3], (Act) 65834 H Mumby[3], (Act) 33082 G Musk[3] & (Act) 54711 F T Watson[3]

Bombardiers: ~ 43363 E A Candon[3] attch. 1 CBAC, RHA, 56848 E Dance[3], 40201 A A Hoyle[3], (Act) 60765 G F Mouser[3], 50881 F H Mulholland[3], 51985 A Pothergill[3], (Act) 51717 J Shaw[3], 87937 D Tinson[3] & (Temp) 32926 L Wood[3]

Lance Bombardiers/Gunners /Drivers: ~ 153869 R Abrahams[3], 126705 L Anderson[3], 61401 A E Andrews[3], 54644 J Ashcroft[3], 206191 H Austin[3], 206172 F Baker[3], 59432 S Baker[3], 28422 E W Ball[3] 'K' Bty, 195131 J Bates[3], 21941 F J Baxter[3],

195132 W Baxter[3], 216718 H M Beeby[3], 223921 J W Beevis[3], 47614 M Bennett[3], 223862 B Berg[3], 223852 J Berg[3], 111055 W C J Bloomfield[3], 108312 H A Bolton[3], 140255 A B Bose[3], 65854 T Bridgeland[3] attch. 1 CBAC, RHA, 108186 T C Bridgeman[3], 223861 F Briggs[3], 65709 C W Britton[3], 53943 E W J Brooks[3], 102589 A W Browning[3], 206134 G J Butler[3], 206237 A E Chadwick[3], 53030 E D Chapman[3], 67300 A G Cheverton[3] attch. 1 CBAC, RHA, 99709 A Christmas[3], 68375 G Chiswell[3], 102635 A G Collins[3], 223942 M R Concannon[3], 61740 E Cornish[3], 206177 G Crew[3], 31801 F H Criop[3], 71457 J R Croft[3], 31773 E Dabb[3], 206158 W Damiral[3], 53706 R Dickson[3], 232502 C W Duncombe[3], 53979 J H Dunn[3] attch. 1 CBAC, RHA, 45304 S J Emery[3], 127148 K England[3], 230466 F Evans[3], 224154 F Forester[3], 1021321 J Gibbons[3] attch. 16 IMVS, 49157 J H Gough[3], 140037 L G Grasse[3], 140257 C F W Green[3], 87763 F Green[3], 99524 V A Harris[3], 153731 W N Hay[3], 195117 G Hensley[3], 230473 J Henson[3], 113926 R Hill[3], 176911 W J Hoeltschi[3], 53836 A Hole[3], 79061 F Hollingsworth[3], 87933 E Houghton[3], 223909 A Humphreys[3] attch. 1 CBAC, RHA, 72348 J Hurd[3], 33739 F W Ireland[3], 206031 W F Jack[3], 206215 J Jessiman[3], 65006 R C Johnson[3], 206234 A W Lander[3], 140284 J H Laws[3], 194893 J T J Leonard[3] attch. 1 CBAC, RHA, 224148 R W Leppard[3], 911162 B Logsden[3], 62668 F B Love[3], 76053 C E Madder[3], 195137 L McBride[3], 52580 C G Morgan[3], 62695 F Morley[3], 66406 A Mortlock[3], 19079 T F Nickson[3], 61435 W Pace[3], 6608 F W Page[3], 195141 J H Parr[3] attch. 1 CBAC, RHA, 206035 F Pickett[3], 194934 W D Pike[3], 89347 W L H Quaintance[3], 240513 E Redshaw[3], 240478 H E Reed[3], 67933 H H Richardson[3], 33846 G W Robbins[3], 622330 H Robinson[3], 195119 E Robson[3], 223926 V Sargeant[3], 68711 E A Seeley[3], 196649 A E Shelton[3], 62346 E H Shipperd[3], 88115 B Short[3], 177037 C E Smith[3], 34229 E W D Smith[3], 110939 T H South[3], 62164 G A Stanley[3], 16692 T Stearman[3], 55603 J A Stokes[3], 102604 A L Stratford[3], 126622 A Stroud[3], 205957 A E Summers[3], 223802 C H Swannell[3] attch. 1 CBAC, RHA, 223803 W Swannell[3], 230685 T Swarbrick[3], 119147 J V Symonds[3], 126741 E J Theobald[3], 194840 S T Theobald[3], 223919 L T Tompson[3], 206192 H Tree[3], 194946 J Turner[3], 177003 A Waddy[3], 87745 B A Warren[3] attch. HQ, NWFF, 901554 A G Watkins[3], 126754 W G Wheeler[3], 77212 E Wiese[3], 108316 A Willsher[3], 206130 C J Wren[3], 177032 A Wright[3] & 267667 S H F Wright[3]

Shoeing Smiths: ~ W Smith[3] 'I' Bty attch. R.A. Details Quetta

Trumpeters: ~ 266732 J Darby[3], 90217 J H Eldridge[3] & 45461 C A Villa[3]

~ The Royal Field Artillery ~
Sub Units Identified As Entitled:
HQ's 7, 16 & 21 Artillery Brigades
3, 4, 13, 28, 30, 37, 38, 47, 60, 70, 74, 77, 79, 86, 87, 89, 90
101, 102, 108, 128, 217, 1091, 1093, 1096, 1098, 1104, 1107 & 'Y' Field Batteries
No. 1 Special Section
1, 2, 4 12, 16 & 46 Divisional Ammunition Columns
Cavalry and Infantry Brigade Ammunition Columns

Note a.   *Roll of all commissioned personnel identified as eligible.*

Note b.   *Non-commissioned and other rank personnel multi clasp or non-Afghanistan 1919 / Waziristan single clasp recipients.*

Note c.   *The Royal Field Artillery (RFA) and the Royal Garrison Artillery (RGA) merged in 1924 and re-adopted the simple title 'Royal (Regiment of) Artillery' (RA).*

Note d.   *Medals to the Royal Field Artillery for 'Afghanistan N.W.F. 1919' are named in impressed capitals either: 'R.F.A.' or 'R.A.'. There after the initials 'R.A.' are used consistently.*

Single Clasp	No. Identified	Rarity
Afghanistan N.W.F .1919[3]	In Strength	Not Rare
Mahsud 1919–20[5]	1	According to the roll as seen, can be considered Unique
Waziristan 1919–21[4]	In Strength	Not Rare
Waziristan 1921–24[6]	In Strength	Not Rare
Combination Clasps	**No. Identified**	**Rarity**
North West Frontier 1908[1] Afghanistan N.W.F. 1919[3]	3	Of the Utmost Rarity
North West Frontier 1908[1] Afghanistan N.W.F. 1919[3] Waziristan 1919–21[4] Waziristan 1921–24[6]	1	According to the roll as seen, can be considered Unique

North West Frontier 1908[1] Afghanistan N.W.F. 1919[3] Waziristan 1921–24[6]	1	According to the roll as seen, can be considered Unique
Afghanistan N.W.F. 1919[3] Mahsud 1919–20[5] Waziristan 1919–21[4]	1	According to the roll as seen, can be considered Unique
Afghanistan N.W.F. 1919[3] Mahsud 1919–20[5] Waziristan 1919–21[4] Waziristan 1921–24[6] North West Frontier 1930–31[9]	1	According to the roll as seen, can be considered Unique
Afghanistan N.W.F. 1919[3] Waziristan 1919– 21[4]	4	Of the Utmost Rarity
Afghanistan N.W.F. 1919[3] Waziristan 1919–21[4] Waziristan 1921–24[6]	1	Of the Utmost Rarity
Afghanistan N.W.F. 1919[3] Waziristan 1919–21[4] Waziristan 1921–24[6] Burma 1930–32[10]	1	According to the roll as seen, can be considered Unique
Afghanistan N.W.F. 1919[3] Waziristan 1921–24[6]	2	Of the Utmost Rarity
Afghanistan N.W.F. 1919[3] North West Frontier 1930–31[9]	7	Of the Utmost Rarity
Afghanistan N.W.F. 1919[3] North West Frontier 1935[12]	1	According to the roll as seen, can be considered Unique
Mahsud 1919–20[5] Waziristan 1919–21[4]	4	Of the Utmost Rarity
Waziristan 1919–21[4] Waziristan 1921–24[6]	11	Extremely Rare
Waziristan 1919–21[4] Waziristan 1921–24[6] North West Frontier 1930–31[9]	1	According to the roll as seen, can be considered Unique
Waziristan 1921–24[6] North West Frontier 1930–31[9]	1	According to the roll as seen, can be considered Unique
Waziristan 1921–24[6] North West Frontier 1935[12]	1	According to the roll as seen, can be considered Unique

Lieutenant Colonels: ~ F G T Deshon[3] attch. HQ. 7 Bde., A M Duthie[3] Cmd. 21 Art Bde., BFF, E Flowers[3], H G Martin[3], A M Murray[3] Cmd. 21 Art Bde. BFF, F W Richey[6] Cmd. 21 Pk Art Bde., (Act) J W Renny Tailyour[3] & H de L Walters[4] CRA, WFF & Cmd. 11 Pk Bde.

Majors: ~ (Act) S C M Archibald[3] attch. HQ. 7 Bde., H A Blair[3], C L Bolton[3], F V Budden[3] 1104 Bty, O Cavenagh[3], F H Clarke[4&6] SORA, WFF, L G L Denne[3], D B Hale[3] 38 Bty, P J B Heelas[3] 1104 Bty, F C Hoare[3] 79 Bty, C B Grice-Hutchinson[6], H L Rothwell-Jackson[3] 1107 Bty, R P Landon[3&9], R S Leach[3] 38 Bty, J de B T Lucas[3], B L Marrinier[3&9], R B Miller[3] 1093 Bty, (Act) H L Nathan[4] attch. S&TC, J Pritchard[3] 1091 Bty, H Pybus[3] 1093 Bty, L T Raikes[3], J Stanford[3], F Sutton[4], A Gardner Waterman[3], C H E Wilson[3] 101 Bty & D C Wilson[3]

Captains: ~ H C Allen[3] 79 Bty, R A Archer[3] 38 Bty, G E Barford[3] attch. HQ. 16 Div., D H Behrens[3] attch. E Persian LofC, W J Bell[3&9(Bvt. Lt. Col.)], A L Binney[3], L M Blomenstok[3] 102 Bty, A Bourne[3] 38 Bty, E G Brinkley[3] 38 Bty, D S Carnochan[3] Staff, R Fitz Corfield[3] attch. HQ. 14 Bde., W G C Cockaday[3] 2 DAC, W Cunningham[3] 1107 Bty, F Dodd[3] attch. HQ. 7 Bde., B G Donne[3] 77 Bty, E G Earle[3] 1107 Bty, W W Fahey[3] 4 DAC, W E Flight[3] attch. HQ. 21 Bde. RFA, P F Harrison[4&6] Staff, C H C Johnstone[3] attch. HQ. 7 Bde. RFA, G W Kinnes[3], J Knock[3] attch. IOD, G Leggatt[3], W Mallalieu[3] 89 Bty, TRF, A R Mauger[3] 101 Bty, P Millett[3] 74 Bty, C E A Mouritz[3], J C J Nicol[3], G T Nugee[3], R Reid[3] 74 Bty, R Rose[3], F M Shepherd[3], J N Slater[3] 1098 Bty, J Smith[4] attch. RE, R C B Stillman[3], H G Straker[3] 77 Bty, A H Thompson[3], C H N Young[6] & R A Young[3] Staff (Originally S African Forces)

Lieutenants: ~ W J Abbott[3], R S Aiton[3], H E Ambrose[3], H M Ballenden[3] attch. HQ. 16 Bde., R C Barrett[3] 38 Bty, E O Becher[6], J Blackburn[3] attch. 217 Bde. RFA, F Bosher[3] attch. 27 Mtn Bty, J Botting[3] 16 DAC, A M Bourne[3] 38 Bty, C A Bowden[3] attch. 23 Mtn. Bty, R S Bowman[3], L G N Brearley[3], J H Brown[6] attch. 'B' Corps Sigs, G W K Butcher[3], A E Butler[3] 89 Bty, B A Capell[6],

E H Chard[3], J A R Colam[6], E Collier[3], P A M Court[3] 2 DAC, H W Cracknell[3] attch. 102 ILC, E Darling[6] 70 Bty, R S C T Edge[6] attch. 'D' DSC, F W Euridge[4&5], L T Firbank[6], S H Freeman[3] attch. HQ, 7 Bde., L S Gallagher[4], C B Gray[3], H Harrison[3] 1091 Bty, F A A Hart[3] 89 Bty, TRF, G C Hawker[3], E W Herbert[3], J S Holbrook[4] No. 1 'Special' Sect, J M Holliday[3&4(Capt.)], G W Howes[3] attch. HQ, 21 Bde. RFA, C A Carkeet-James[6] attch. IAOC, J Kells[3], J V Kelly[3], J G King[3], C W Knight[4] attch. 128 Bty, L C Knight[3] 1104 Bty, R Langford[3] attch. HQ, 27 Bde., E W Langhorne[6], W J Lewis[3] attch. 21 Pk Art Bde., W B Little[3], W Loxton[3] 79 Bty, W J Martin[3], E S Mawer[3] 102 Bty, W J McHaffie[3], M J McIntyre[3] attch. 30 Mtn Bty, G A Mills[3] 1 DAC RFA, W A Monaghan[3] 30 Bty, T H Musgrave[3] No. 1 'Special' Sect, J S Neale[3] 1107 Bty, D W D Nicholl[6], C V Oakley[6], E C Ormond[3] attch. 40 DSC, 16 Div., H L Powe[3] 1093 Bty, F H S Pownall[4] 128 Bty, J E Pratt[4] 128 Bty, W Rainford[3], H C F Randolph[6], A J Ridgwell[3] 101 Bty, A J D Ronald[6], D C Sexton[3] attch. HQ, 16 Bde., R W Shepard[3], A N Skinner[6] attch. 31 Sqn, RAF, G M Smart[3], L A Smith[3], P S Smith[1&3], R J Sopwith[3] 77 Bty, C M Spencer[3] 16 DAC, H L G Stewart[4] attch. RASC, E W N Stone[3] 101 Bty, W E Walkers-Symons[4] 3 M Bde., A G Taylor[3] attch. ISC, A T Umfreville[3] 4 DAC, D F Ward[3] 1091 Bty, E P Warner[3] 12 DAC, F J Watson[3] 4 Bty, E G Watt[3], M Wheiton[3&4] & J R Williamson[3] HQ, 7 Bde. & A Wright[3]

Battery Quartermaster Sergeants / Staff Sergeants: ~ (Act) 61822 A Broughton[3&9(25 Bty)] 90 Bty & (Act BQMS) L/21622 C J Kearley[3,4&5] attch. 7 MT Coy, S&TC

Quartermaster Sergeants/Sergeants: ~ (1040961) 59954 M A Collins[3,4&5] attch. IOD, 1039076 L G Cresswell[4&6] 128 Bty, 1017797 W C Crowl[4&6] 70 Bty, 1405815 E Evans[4&6] attch. 'G' DSC, 267663 R Ford[3&4] 74 Bty, 1038448 H Howard[3&6] attch. 'G' DSC, (Act) 44669 A R McDonald[3&4] attch. 1 LofC Sig Sect, (1039070) 910057 J N G Nelson[6&12(WOII)], 1038886 P E Shields[4&6] 128 Bty, (1048955) 853 I H Small[3,4,5,6&(9 CQMS R Sigs)], (Act) (1052126) 54632 A W Smith[5] 86 Bty attch. 20 IMVS, 1038887 R Sutterby[4&6] 70 Bty & (Act) 1049940 A W Usher[3,4&6]

Bombardiers: ~ (1041137) 73549 C E Collins[3&9], 1043816 F C Edlin[4,6&9(Mec/S/Sgt. R.E.)] attch. HQ, WFF, 75158 A H Hunt[1&3] 101 Bty & 73643 G H King[4&6]

Lance Bombardiers/Gunners/Drivers: ~ 189085 R H Butler[4&6], 1043704 W J Denham[4&6] attch. IAOC, (1029540) 76691 J Fettis[1,3&6] 47 Bty, (10318) 910538 F Hamilton[3&6(R Berkshire)], (1028640) 110142 F Hill[3&12(WOII)] 3 Bty, (129235) 7811020 W Jenkins[4&5(attch. 11 Bn MGC)], 59283 C A Legge[1&3] 101 Bty, (138108) 7811357 P Manning[4&5(attch. 11 Bn MGC)], (2313068) 62497 N McCullough[3&9(Cpl. R Sigs)], 1417376 J W Norley[6&9], 137412 C Petherbridge[4&5], (1038999) 295488 W Potter[3,4,6&(10 CQMS R Sigs)] attch. 'G' DSC & 1039062 J A Yates[4&6] 128 Bty

Boys: ~ (1017539) 245667 W F Allen[3&9(WOII)]

~ The Royal Garrison Artillery ~
Sub Units Identified As Entitled:
HQ Heavy Brigade
HQ 1, 2 & 4 British Mountain Brigades
1, 3, 4, 5, 6, 8, 9, 10, 11 & 12 Mountain / Pack Batteries
10 & 13 Medium Batteries
60, 68 & 80 Heavy Batteries
Royal Garrison Artillery Personnel Attached Indian Mountain / Pack Batteries As Shown

Note a. *Roll of all commissioned personnel identified as eligible.*

Note b. *Non-commissioned and other rank personnel multi clasp or non-Afghanistan 1919/Waziristan single clasp recipients.*

Note c. *From 1920 to 1927, the designation 'Pack Battery' replaced the title 'Mountain Battery'. In 1927, the descriptor 'Indian Mountain Battery' was employed for batteries of the Indian Frontier Garrison Artillery Establishment; however, the word 'Indian' was dropped the following year.*

Note d. *Medals to the Royal Garrison Artillery for 'Afghanistan 1919' are named 'R.G.A.'. Personnel who qualified for 'Waziristan 1919–21' prior to the changes in Note 3 above also received medals named 'R.G.A.'. After 1920, medals named 'R.A.'. (FGA awards contained the designation 'P BTY.').*

Note e. *Between 1920 and 1928, the FGA battery numbering system was changed. (Refer to Frontier Garrison Artillery synopsis for detailed breakdown of title development).*

Note f. *For the sake of continuity, where entitlement by battery is identified in the roll below, the 1919 designation has been used. (See note 3 above).*

Note g. *During the period 1919–1921, the Royal Garrison Artillery discontinued the use of the rank designation 'Corporal' and adopted the existing Royal Field Artillery designation 'Bombardier' instead. This decision made necessary the re-mustering of existing Bombardiers as 'Lance Bombardiers'.*

Note h. *The Royal Garrison Artillery and the Royal Field Artillery merged in 1924 and re-adopted the simple title 'Royal (Regiment of) Artillery'. Medals named in impressed capitals: 'R.A.'*

Note i. *The Indian Frontier Garrison Artillery was absorbed into the Royal Artillery in 1924 and remained so until 1939, when they resumed their place in the, (new 1935), Indian (Army) Artillery establishment.*

Note j.   *From 1927 forward to the mid WWII era the initials R.A. were included in any given battery title and further changes were made to battery numbering and designation. Thus, for example, 101 Royal (Kohat) Pack Battery (FF) became 1 Royal (Kohat) Indian Mountain Battery R.A. (FF).*

Single Clasp	No. Identified	Rarity
Afghanistan N.W.F. 1919[3]	In Strength	Not Rare
Mahsud 1919–20[5]	1	According to the roll as seen, can be considered Unique
Waziristan 1919–21[4]	In Strength	Not Rare
Waziristan 1921–24[6]	In Strength	Not Rare
Combination Clasps	*No. Identified*	*Rarity*
North West Frontier 1908[1] Afghanistan N.W.F. 1919[3]	14	Extremely Rare
North West Frontier 1908[1] Afghanistan N.W.F. 1919[3] Mahsud 1919–20[5] Waziristan 1919–21[4]	2	Of the Utmost Rarity
North West Frontier 1908[1] Afghanistan N.W.F. 1919[3] Mahsud 1919–20[5] Waziristan 1919–21[4] Waziristan 1921–24[6]	1	According to the roll as seen, can be considered Unique
North West Frontier 1908[1] Waziristan 1919–21[4] Waziristan 1921–24[6] North West Frontier 1930–31[9]	1	According to the roll as seen, can be considered Unique
North West Frontier 1908[1] Waziristan 1921–24[6]	1	According to the roll as seen, can be considered Unique
North West Frontier 1908[1] Waziristan 1921–24[6] North West Frontier 1930–31[9]	1	According to the roll as seen, can be considered Unique
Afghanistan N.W.F. 1919[3] Waziristan 1919–21[4]	11	Extremely Rare
Afghanistan N.W.F. 1919[3] Mahsud 1919–20[5] Waziristan 1919–21[4]	53	Rare
Afghanistan N.W.F. 1919[3] Mahsud 1919–20[5] Waziristan 1919–21[4] Waziristan 1921–24[6]	37	Very Rare
Afghanistan N.W.F. 1919[3] Mahsud 1919–20[5] Waziristan 1919–21[4] Waziristan 1921–24[6] North West Frontier 1930–31[9]	1	According to the roll as seen, can be considered Unique
Afghanistan N.W.F. 1919[3] Waziristan 1919–21[4] Waziristan 1921–24[6]	8	Of the Utmost Rarity
Afghanistan N.W.F. 1919[3] Waziristan 1921–24[6]	16	Extremely Rare
Afghanistan N.W.F. 1919[3] Malabar 1921–22[7] Waziristan 1921–24[6]	2	Of the Utmost Rarity
Afghanistan N.W.F. 1919[3] North West Frontier 1930–31[9]	3	Of the Utmost Rarity

172

Mahsud 1919–20[5] **Waziristan 1919–21[4]**	4	Of the Utmost Rarity
Mahsud 1919–20[5] **Waziristan 1919–21[4]** **Waziristan 1921–24[6]**	8	Of the Utmost Rarity
Mahsud 1919–20[5] **Waziristan 1919–21[4]** **Waziristan 1921–24[6]** **North West Frontier 1930–31[9]**	1	According to the roll as seen, can be considered Unique
Mahsud 1919–20[5] **Waziristan 1919–21[4]** **Waziristan 1921–24[6]** **North West Frontier 1935[12]**	1	According to the roll as seen, can be considered Unique
Waziristan 1919–21[4] **Waziristan 1921–24[6]**	208	Scarce
Waziristan 1919–21[6] **Malabar 1921–22[7]** **Waziristan 1921–24[6]**	1	According to the roll as seen, can be considered Unique
Waziristan 1919–21[4] **Waziristan 1921–24[6]** **North West Frontier 1930–31[9]**	2	Of the Utmost Rarity
Waziristan 1919–21[4] **Waziristan 1921–24[6]** **Mohmand 1933[11]**	1	According to the roll as seen, can be considered Unique
Waziristan 1919–21[4] **North West Frontier 1930–31[9]**	1	According to the roll as seen, can be considered Unique
Waziristan 1919–21[4] **Mohmand 1933[11]** **North West Frontier 1935[12]**	1	According to the roll as seen, can be considered Unique
Malabar 1921–22[7] **Waziristan 1921–24[6]**	42	Very Rare
Malabar 1921–22[7] **Waziristan 1921–24[6]** **North West Frontier 1930–31[9]**	2	Of the Utmost Rarity
Malabar 1921–22[7] **Waziristan 1921–24[6]** **North West Frontier 1935[12]**	1	According to the roll as seen, can be considered Unique
Waziristan 1921–24[6] **North West Frontier 1930–31[9]**	7	Of the Utmost Rarity
Waziristan 1921–24[6] **Mohmand 1933[11]**	1	According to the roll as seen, can be considered Unique
Waziristan 1921–24[6] **North West Frontier 1935[12]**	3	Of the Utmost Rarity

Lieutenant Colonels: ~ (Bvt) A E C Burney[6] 26 Ind Mtn Bty, H G Carr[3,4&6] CRA, WFF thence Cmd. 25 & 11 Pk Art Bde.(s), G G W Corrie[1(Capt.)&3], (Bvt) A J T Farfan[3&6] 27 Mtn Bty, A C Fergusson[3] HQ, 9 Mtn Art Bde., J H Keogh[3] 8 Mtn Bty, L L Hepper[4], L K Stanbrough[6], A F E Stiffe[3] & (Bvt) W M Turner[4&6] 21 Mtn Bty

Majors: ~ C H Barker[3] 3 Mtn Bty, M D Bell[6] 26 Ind Mtn Bty, (Act) G F Campbell[4&6] 27 Ind Mtn Bty, D J M Champion[6&9(Lt. Col.)] 28 Mtn Bty, R H Clarke[4] SORA, WFF & Adjt 11 Pk Bde., A F Cole[3&6(32 Ind Mtn Bty)] 1 (Kashmir) Mtn Bty, C R Crowdy[3] 24 Ind Mtn Bty, M J Curry[3,4&5] 29 Ind Mtn Bty, L M Davies[6], (Act) C L Day[3] attch. 33 DSC, R M L Dutton[3,4&5], J H Edmond[1(Lt.),4,6&9(Lt. Col.)], C J Everard[6] 21 Ind Mtn Bty, R M N Forbes[4,6&11(Lt. Col.)] 12 Mtn Bty, E G Fowler[3,4&5] Bde. Maj. HQ, WFF & 11 Ind Pk Art Bde., (Act) D A Gardiner[3] 60 (H) Bty, A D Greig[6], G N Hill[3&6(33 Ind Mtn Bty)] 27 Ind Mtn Bty, W D Lindsay[6] 39 Ind Mtn Bty, E M Little[1(Lt.),6&9(Lt. Col.)] attch. HQ, 5 Bde., G S Low[4,5&6] 6 Mtn Bty, O M Lund[6] ADC to HE the CinC, G P R MacMahon[6] 13 (M) Bty, M E Mascall[3] 4 Mtn Bty, Bde. Maj HQ, WFF & (Act) J E F Montague[3&4] 3 Mtn Bty, C D O Pugh[6] 32 Ind Mtn Bty, H S K Snowdon[6], J A H B Somerville[6], P Thompson[4&6], J Way[4], E Le G Whitting[1(23 Ind Mtn Bty)&6] 35 Ind Mtn Bty, E R C Wilson[6] 34 Ind Mtn Bty & R G Wordsworth[6] 43 Ind Mtn Bty

Captains: ~ J Allen[3] 4 Mtn Bty, H V Allpress[3] 60 (H) Bty, J C Bowering[3] 22 Ind Mtn Bty, R M E Brady[3] 23 Ind Mtn Bty, (Act) E R W Bullen[3] 3 Mtn Bty, E G Campbell[3,4&6] 23 Ind Mtn Bty, R L O Carew[3&4] 33 Ind Mtn Bty, J F Carr[3] 28 Ind Mtn Bty, (Act) L S Coke[4,5&6(Act Maj.)] 27 Ind Mtn Bty, C R Cross[7&6] 10 Mtn Bty, G V Dreyer[3&9(Lt. Col.)] 29 Mtn Bty, K G Dymott[6] 29 Ind Mtn Bty, R A G Eales[3] 1 Mtn Bty, F E Elliot[6] 28 Ind Mtn Bty, J W English[3&6(33 Ind Mtn Bty)] 37 Ind Mtn Bty, D O Fardell[3,4&6] 6 Mtn Bty, H E Fooks[3,4&5] 6 Mtn Bty, A Fowler[3], L F Garratt[3] HQ, 2 Ind Pk Art Bde., F S B Grotrian[6], V R Guise[6] attch. 9 ACC, J C L Holman[3(Lt.)&4] 33 Ind Mtn Bty, J R Laurie[4&6] 26 Ind Mtn Bty, H S Lickman[4&6] 35 (Reserve) Ind Mtn Bty, A Macgregor[6] 43 Mtn Bty, M W M Macleod[6&9(21 Ind Mtn Bde.)] 34 Ind Mtn Bty, H M J McIntyre[3] 6 Mtn Bty, D Meston[3,4&5] 3 & 6 Mtn Bty(s), B S K Guise-Moores[6] 43 Ind Mtn Bty, W F Morgan[6], W H I Packington[3], D H Pearson[3] 27 Ind Mtn Bty, A A H Phillips[3] 4 Mtn Bty, C D O Pugh[6] 32 Ind Mtn Bty, S H Richardson[3] HQ, 2 Bde. RGA, C A Russell[3&9(Maj.)], F Steele[3] 3 Mtn Bty, R J M Saunders[4&5], A E Tawney[4&6] 21 Ind Mtn Bty, A Veitch[6], G W H Walker[3], G H Wateridge[3] 8 Mtn Bty, G F Willcox[3] & S H Wright[6&9(Maj.)]

Lieutenants: ~ C St. G E Alexander[3] 8 Mtn Bty, R W Allan[6] 34 Ind Mtn Bty, C S Allison[3] 60 (H) Bty, M T Annesley[4] 10 Mtn Bty, P L Babbage[4&6] 12 Mtn Bty, L C Ball[3] 6 Mtn Bty, C C Barrett[3&6(21 Ind Mtn Bty)] 33 Ind Mtn Bty, W J Barry[3] 60 (H) Bty, J W Beard[3] 37 Ind Mtn Bty, J Bee[3] 8 Mtn Bty, C G Bicknell[4&6] 12 Mtn Bty, E G Brine[6] 39 Ind Mtn Bty, W Broad[3&4] 35 Ind Mtn Bty, F F Capron[6], L H Carter[3] 23 Ind Mtn Bty, J A N Grant-Colquhoun[3] 9 Mtn Bty, W J Colyer[3&6] 33 Ind Mtn Bty, W J Cooper[6] 43 Ind Mtn Bty, A E Cunningham[7&6] 10 Mtn Bty, R A Curties[3,4&5(27 Ind Mtn Bty)] 28 Ind Mtn Bty, T B Davey[3] HQ, 3 Ind Pk Art Bde., F J Dillon[3,4,5&6] 6 Mtn Bty, H P D Dimmock[4&6] 13 (M) Bty, R D B Dupuis[6&12(Capt.)] 29 Ind Mtn Bty, P Edgar[3], R A S Edgecombe[3&6(32 Bty)] 37 Ind Mtn Bty, W Elliot[3&4], N M Fenton[3] 37 Ind Mtn Bty, E E French[6&9(Capt.)] 29 Ind Mtn Bty, T Gaskill[3] 6 Mtn Bty, W M Gayer[4&6] 26 Ind Mtn Bty, J B Gibbons[4] 33 Ind Mtn Bty, W J Goodman[3] 23 Ind Mtn Bty, I G G S Hardie[4&6] 26 Ind Mtn Bty, H A Hardy[4,5&6] 35 Ind Mtn Bty, L A Harris[3&6] 9&4 Mtn, Bty(s), E G Hayes[3] 60 (H) Bty, R L Herron[6&12(Capt.)] 26 Ind Mtn Bty, J G Hill[3&4] 2 DAC, R B Howard[4,5&6] 35 Ind Mtn Bty, K M James[4], A J Jenkins[3] 23 Ind Mtn Bty, S W Anketell-Jones[6] 34 Ind Mtn Bty, Q A Kennedy[6], J W Kenny[6], A H King[3], C G Lamb[3] 3 Mtn Bty, E G Lang[4&6] 33 Ind Mtn Bty, E F Lee[6], A C W Little[4] 10 (M) Bty, H D Lysons[6&11(Capt.)], (Originally Royal Air Force), I M MacDougall[3] 9 Mtn Bty, A O McCarthy[6], H P Maltby[3,4&6(26 Ind Mtn Bty)] 33 Ind Mtn Bty, H B Martini[6] HQ, 25 Ind Pk Art Bde., S Mason[3], G G Mears[3&6] 28 Ind Mtn Bty, R L Michaelis[3], K C Miller[4,5,6&9(Capt.)] 32 Ind Mtn Bty & Ord Off HQ, 11 Ind Pk Art Bde., R P Minchin[4&6(RTC)] 10 Mtn Bty, F K Morton[6], J W Mozley[3] 4 Mtn Bty, G D Munro[3] 60 (H) Bty, J C W Murie[3] 23 Ind Mtn Bty, M S Oxley[6], C E Page[3] 24 Ind Mtn Bty, W H A F Panton[3] 23 Ind Mtn Bty, A R E Parsons[6] 39 Ind Mtn Bty, R G Parsons[4] attch. 3 W/Sig Sqn, A Paton[3], E B Pigott[4&5] 6 Mtn Bty, W A Plummer[3] 23 Ind Mtn Bty, R H Poland[4&6] 26 Ind Mtn Bty, P G H Porter[3], F Pound[3] 8 Mtn Bty, E B Preston[3], H Redman[6] 6 Mtn Bty, C G Richards[4] 13 (M) Bty, J H W G Richards[4&6] 12 Mtn Bty, R J B Riches[3] 8 Mtn Bty, (Originally South African Forces), E W Rogers[3] 68 (H) Bty, R L M Rosenburg[4&6] 12 Mtn Bty, G Sherriff[5] 43 Ind Mtn Bty, S G Snatt[3] 23 Ind Mtn Bty, E H D Southgate[3] 6 Mtn Bty, W A Stephens[3], E M W Stevens[4,5,6&9(Maj.)] 6 Mtn Bty, A D Stonehouse[3] 23 Ind Mtn Bty, E I E Strong[6] 29 Ind Mtn Bty attch. 35 Ind Mtn Bty, T Sullivan[3] 8 Mtn Bty, R N Syme[6], F G S Thomas[4] 30 Ind Mtn Bty, F C Tilley[3] 23 Ind Mtn Bty, W Tuck[3] 6 Mtn Bty, L T Tully[3] 6 Mtn Bty, R S Wade[7&6] 10 Mtn Bty, G P Walsh[4&6] 21 Ind Mtn Bty, S Mc D Watson[3,4&6] 6 Mtn Bty, J Whelan[3] 23 & 35 Ind Mtn Bty, M Whelton[3&4], J M Whitside[3] 6 Mtn Bty, P Williams[6] 39 Ind Mtn Bty, C P B Wilson[6] 28 Mtn Bty, T M Witherow[4&5] 27 Ind Mtn Bty, L H de C Woodward[4,5&6] 35 Ind Mtn Bty & H L B Woodyatt[4,5&6(27 Bty)] 35 Ind Mtn Bty

Warrant Officers Class I: ~ (RSM) 16748 (1401678) W P Casey[3&6] attch. HQ, 25 Ind Pk Art Bde.

Warrant Officers Class II: ~ (Act BSM) 26774 J W Atkins[3,4&5] 6 Mtn Bty, 11989 H A Collis[1(Bdr.)&3], (Act BSM) 226248 R Dawson[3,4&5] 6 Mtn·Bty, (BSM) 1417946 R Frisby[4,11&12], (1400252) 291 J Kenneally[1(Bdr.),3,4&5] 6 Mtn Bty, (Act BSM) 31726 (1404838) T J Marryweather[3,7&6] 10 Mtn Bty & (BSM) 1402078 G G Price[4&6]

Battery Quartermaster Sergeants/Staff Sergeants: ~ (Act Fitter) (228850) 1416494 E G Bowler[4,5&6] 6 Mtn Bty, 1403926 S Passmore[4&6] 6 Mtn Bty, 26257 G H Willmott[3&4] attch. FGA Bannu & 24979 H Witney[3,4&5] 6 Mtn Bty

Quartermaster Sergeants / Sergeants: ~ 1408529 F B Asher[7&6] 10 Mtn Bty, 23040 (1402539) A Carter[3,4,5&6] 6 Mtn Bty, 16736 W H Flambard[1(Gnr.)&3], 36429 (1407241) S Flowers[3&6], 26691 (1403233) W Freeland[3&6] attch. 'B' DSC, 25020 E A Hurlock[1(Gnr.)&3], 1404374 F Hutson[4&6] 12 Mtn Bty, (Act) 34153 (1406026) J Kelly[3,4&5] attch. 49 PMC, 27655 G W Kyle[3,4&5] 6 Mtn Bty, 7000 F S Mattocks[6&(9 as Maj. RE)], 1403673 J McNamara[4&6] 6 Mtn Bty, 30342 C Mockford[1(Bdr.)&3], 1407795 M Mochan[4&6] 12 Mtn Bty, 22968 G Pearson[1(Gnr.)&3], 1403148 B W Pilfold[4&6] 6 Mtn Bty, 1404425 W A Price[4&6] 12 Mtn Bty, 1404249 R Ray[4&6] 12 Mtn Bty, (Act) 1403524 A Roberts[4&6], 1402850 W S Smith[4&6] 13 (Md) Bty, 1401549 F Stratton[4&6] 12 Mtn Bty, 1401489 S L Sullivan[4&6] 12 Mtn Bty, 33378 (1405641) W Thurtle[3&4], 301391 A Tomson[3,4&5] 6 Mtn Bty, 1405788 J Tourle[4&6] attch. 'B' Corps Sigs & 1402325 H R White[7&6] 10 Mtn Bty

Lance Sergeants/Corporals: ~ 1415872 D Adamson[7(Cpl.)&6] 10 Mtn Bty, 31318 W Brownhill[3,4&5] 6 Mtn Bty, 1405251 (32566) W J Burrough[1(Gnr.),3,4&6] 6 Mtn Bty, (1405005) 32070 J Fitzgerald[3,7&6] 10 Mtn Bty, 1409551 H W Gardiner[4&6] 12 Mtn Bty, 1405199 E Gaughran[4&6] 12 Mtn Bty, (Act) 1409869 T Griffiths[7(Bdr.)&6] 10 Mtn Bty, 1405995 C A Hadland[4&6] 12 Mtn Bty, 1402399 W G Hamilton[4&6] 12 Mtn Bty, 1407601 C E Hodge[4,6&(9 Sgt. R Sigs)] 12 Mtn Bty, 22288 J J Hughes[3,4,5&6] 6 Mtn Bty, 1410555 R J Laing[7(Cpl.)&6] 10 Mtn Bty, 30157 (1404040) F Lansbury[3,4&6] 6 Mtn Bty, 38125 A N Lever[3,4&5] 6 Mtn Bty, 1401391 C H Lovell[4&6] 12 Mtn Bty, 1415795 S Mappledoram[4&6] 6 Mtn Bty, (Temp) (1403073) 25820 A W Montague[3,4&6] 6 Mtn Bty, (Temp) 33530 T O'Connor[3,4,5&6] 6 Mtn Bty, 1410500 A A Russell[4&6] 12 Mtn Bty, (1403417) 27648 F W Tait[3,4(Act. Sgt.)&5(Act. Sgt.)] 6 Mtn Bty, 1408260 A S Traynor[4&6] 6 Mtn Bty, 38270 J J Vile[3,4&5] 6 Mtn Bty & 1409359 R N Wright[4&6] 12 Mtn Bty

Bombardiers: ~ 1409999 C E Attusol[4&6] 12 Mtn Bty, 32295 A Barrow[3,4&5] 6 Mtn Bty, 1415169 D Cartwright[7&6(Gnr.)] 10 Mtn Bty, 1410944 J H Cogger[4&6] 12 Mtn Bty, 1414838 J S Cole[7(Gnr.)&6] 10 Mtn Bty, (Act) 1409003 H Colgrave[4&6] 12 Mtn Bty, 1410375 W J Conduit[4&6] 12 Mtn Bty, 1412007 W H Congdon[7&6(Gnr.)] 10 Mtn Bty, 1409444 J Cracknell[4&6] 12 Mtn Bty, 1410186 A E Dale[4&6], (Act) 1404436 S H Davis[7&6] 10 Mtn Bty, 1410972 F Frost[4&6], 1403326 H A Halley[7&6] 10 Mtn Bty, 1411654 C Harriss[7(Gnr.)&6] 10 Mtn Bty, 1405190 J C Masters[4&6] 6 Mtn Bty, 1409099 G V Prescott[4&6] 12 Mtn Bty, 31670 (1404806) W R Shepherd[3,4&5] 6 Mtn Bty, 1406076 A E Smith[7&6] 10 Mtn Bty, 28058 H W Stanford[3,4&6], 1402070 F Stephens[4&6] 13 (Md) Bty, 1409858 H Tucker[7(Gnr.)&6] 10 Mtn Bty & (1416654) 229023 J Wilson[5] 9 Mtn Bty

Lance Bombardiers/Gunners: ~ 1413693 J Ackroyd[4&6] 12 Mtn Bty, 1410127 S A Aldridge[4&6] 12 Mtn Bty, 20988 C Allinson[3,4,5&6] 6 Mtn Bty, 1417488 F J Anderson[7&6] 10 Mtn Bty, 1418441 A E Andrews[4&6] 10 Mtn Bty, 1411700 H E Anscombe[7&6] 10 Mtn Bty, 1416785 R H Applebee[4&6] 6 Mtn Bty, 228576 R A Armstrong[3&6], 1418570 E H Ayling[7,6&12(Bdr.)] 10 Mtn Bty, 1412500 J Baker[4&6] 6 Mtn Bty, 22985 F Ballinger[3&4], 1410100 J Barkas[7&6] 10 Mtn Bty, 1419645 S J Barker[4&6] 6 Mtn Bty, 187328 J C Baron[3,4&5] 6 Mtn Bty, 1413403 A H Barstow[7(Gnr.)&6] 10 Mtn Bty, 1409030 W J Baxter[4&6] 6 Mtn Bty, 1410639 J P Beahan[4&6] 6 Mtn Bty, 37893 G C Berry[3,4&5] 6 Mtn Bty, 1410403 C E Blake[4&6] 6 Mtn Bty, 24121 P Bock[1(Tptr.)&3], 1406067 J Boreham[4&6] 12 Mtn Bty, 1416982 E Bottomley[4&6] 6 Mtn Bty, 28147 H J R Bowles[3,4,5&6] 6 Mtn Bty, 1411289 F Boxall[4&6] 6 Mtn Bty, 1410347 W J Brasher[4&6] 6 Mtn Bty, 1413881 A G Brown[4&6] 12 Mtn Bty, 1410150 R Brown[4&6] 12 Mtn Bty, 1417116 C P Browning[4&6] 12 Mtn Bty, 1415608 S Buffey[4&6] 6 Mtn Bty, 28425 S Carroll[3,4&5] 6 Mtn Bty, 1408936 T Chadwick[4&6] 12 Mtn Bty, 1403651 T H Channon[4&6] 12 Mtn Bty, 1410971 W G Chapman[4&6] 6 Mtn Bty, 1415359 A E Cheadle[4&6] 6 Mtn Bty, 39937 J Clapham[3&6], 1410511 R Clarke[7&6] 10 Mtn Bty, 1410785 R A Cleaver[4&6] 12 Mtn Bty, 1415968 W Cobb[4&6] 12 Mtn Bty, 148170 G Cocker[4&5] attch. IOD, 1415350 L le Cointe[7(Gnr.)&6] 10 Mtn Bty, 1405116 G Collins[4&6] 6 Mtn Bty, 33064 R Collis[3,4,5&6] 6 Mtn Bty, 28358 C Connolly[3,4,5&6] 6 Mtn Bty, (27995) 1403493 F Connolly[3,4&6] 12 Mtn Bty, 14206 T Connolly[3,4,5&6] 6 Mtn Bty, 1409329 C T Convey[4&6] 12 Mtn Bty, 1420994 J Cooper[4&6] 6 Mtn Bty, 1417109 H Copperwheat[4&6] 6 Mtn Bty, 1416055 H G Corp[4&6] 6 Mtn Bty, 31972 W J Cottam[3,4,5&6] 6 Mtn Bty, 1409341 D Cronin[4&6] 6 Mtn Bty, 26007 E Cross[3,4,5&6] 6 Mtn Bty, 1418144 J J Cullen[7&6] 10 Mtn Bty, 1415219 J Curtin[7&6] 10 Mtn Bty, 148607 (1412299) W E Dadswell[3,4,5,6&9] 6 Mtn Bty, 222007 H S Dalton[3&6], 1411012 M F Daniels[4&6] 12 Mtn Bty, 1417335 D Dann[4&6] 12 Mtn Bty, 1402505 C Dargan[4&6] 12 Mtn Bty, 5923 G H Davenport[3,4,5&6] 6 Mtn Bty, 1415578 A Dawson[7(Gnr.)&6] 10 Mtn Bty, 1419280 H E Day[4&6], 1409385 G H Derbyshire[4&6] 6 Mtn Bty, 1404024 B Dewey[4&6] 12 Mtn Bty, 1409252 M Doyle[4&6] 6 Mtn Bty, 34058 J Driscoll[3,4,5&6] 6 Mtn Bty, 23617 T Duck[1&3], 1414973 H Dukes[4&6] 13 (Md) Bty, 1410678 M Dunn[4&6] 12 Mtn Bty, 1421137 W G Dunn[4&6] 12 Mtn Bty, 1411461 G Durrant[4&9(Bdr.)], 30138 W Eastman[3,4,5&6] 6 Mtn Bty, 1407554 C Edwards[4&6], 1412513 G Edwards[4&6] 6 Mtn Bty, 1405265 M P Edwards[4&6] 12 Mtn Bty, 1409646 H Emm[4&6] 6 Mtn Bty, 36783 W Enright[3,4&5] 6 Mtn Bty, 25764 G Everton[1,3,4,5&6] 6 Mtn Bty, 25784 A Fane[3,4,5&6] 6 Mtn Bty, 29573 W Feetham[3,4&5] 6 Mtn Bty, 35787 F Fenton[3,4,5&6] 6 Mtn Bty, 1414952 R Ferguson[4&6] 6 Mtn Bty, 1415248 C S Fisher[4&6] 6 Mtn Bty, 28470 T Fitzpatrick[3,4,5&6] 6 Mtn Bty, 1413830 G H Flower[7(Tptr)&6] 10 Mtn Bty, 1411201 F W Ford[4&6] 12 Mtn Bty, (1410350) 43962 G Forester[4&6] 6 Mtn Bty, 1415373 W A Foxall[4&6] 13 (Md) Bty, 1417489 F H French[7(Gnr.)&6] 10 Mtn Bty, (51965) 1410890 W Frodsham[6&12] 10 Mtn Bty, 39219 A J Gates[3,4&5] 6 Mtn Bty, 1415036 A Golden[7&6] 10 Mtn Bty, 1409968 H J Gordon[4&6] 12 Mtn Bty, 33926 T Grady[3,4,5&6] 6 Mtn Bty, 1409636 J F Graves[4&6] 12 Mtn Bty, 1409134 C Gray[4&6] 12 Mtn Bty, 1417960 W G Greening[4&6] 12 Mtn Bty, 1409034 S A Greenoff[4&6] 6 Mtn Bty, 1411216 P Griffin[4&6] 6 Mtn Bty, 1410766 J F Gumbley[4&6] 12 Mtn Bty, 1405808 G T W Hale[4,6&9(Sgt.)] 12 Mtn Bty, 37444 E Hales[3,4&5] 6 Mtn Bty, 1414975 J Halligan[4&6] 13 Md Bty, 33987 J Harris[3,4,5&6] 6 Mtn Bty, 1409778 J Harrison[7(Bdr.)&6] 10 Mtn Bty, 1403333 S Harrison[4&6] 12 Mtn Bty, 1406925 A J Hay[4&6] 12 Mtn Bty, 33255 A Hazell[3,4,5&6] 6 Mtn Bty, 1409744 R C Hearn[4&6] 12 Mtn Bty, 32425 J Hennessy[3,4&5] 6 Mtn Bty, 1418126 W C Holbrooke[4&6] 6 Mtn Bty, 1418460 H Holt[4&6] 6 Mtn Bty, 1421138 F S Horwood[4&6] 12 Mtn Bty, 1418225 C H House[7&6] 10 Mtn Bty, 1417169 J H Huckstep[7,6&9] 10 Mtn Bty, 228371 (1416301) T H H Hunt[3&4], 1418444 W Hunt[7,6&9] 10 Mtn Bty, (222542) 1415663 A Hurd[7&6], 1410949 E Hutson[4&6] 6 Mtn Bty, 1409338 A V Ingram[4&6] 12 Mtn Bty, 1415360 J S Ingram[4&6] 6 Mtn Bty, 1409419 R Jackson[4&6] 6 Mtn Bty, 33613 F J Jefford[3,4&5] 6 Mtn Bty, 1401674 H E Jones[4&6] 6 Mtn Bty, 1410946 J H Jones[4&6] 12 Mtn Bty, 1409602 J J Jones[4&6] 12 Mtn Bty, 37775 W Jordan[3,4&5] 6 Mtn Bty, 1402421 M Kearney[7&6] 10 Mtn Bty, 1417412 J Kelly[7&6] 10 Mtn Bty, 1414626 H C Kent[4&6] 6 Mtn Bty, 1418516 P A Keywood[7&6] 10 Mtn Bty, 1405662 F Kidgell[4&6] 12 Mtn Bty, (1403427) 27686 G H Kilner[3,4&5] 6 Mtn Bty, 1415553 R King[4&6] 6 Mtn Bty, 29693 J Knight[3,4&5] 6 Mtn Bty, 30462 A T Knott[3&6], 1417485 H G Kyle[4&6] 12 Mtn Bty, 27973 M Lacey[3,4,5&6] 6 Mtn Bty, 1417081 H W Last[7&6] 10 Mtn Bty, 1409354 M Lawless[4&6] 6 Mtn Bty, (1403098) 25958 W Lawton[3,4,5&6] 6 Mtn Bty, 37793 E Legg[3,4&5] 6 Mtn Bty, 1410826 A J Lewis[4&6] 12 Mtn Bty, 1409556 F G Lilly[4&6] 12 Mtn Bty, 1416101 W J Littlechild[4&6] 12 Mtn Bty, 33331 R E Lloyd[3,4&5] 6 Mtn Bty, 1410792 E Lunn[4&6] 12 Mtn Bty, 1400150 B Magee[4&6] 12 Mtn Bty, (192190) 1409453 F T Mallett[4&6] 6 Mtn Bty, (1404931) 31905 A H Marshall[3,4&5] 6 Mtn Bty, 1410562 S Marshall[4&6] 6 Mtn Bty, 27967 F G Maskelyne[3,4,5&6] 6 Mtn Bty, 1416222 T S Maslen[4&6] 12 Mtn Bty, 27959 T Mason[3,4,5&6] 6 Mtn Bty, 23966 R Massey[3,4,5&6] 6 Mtn Bty, 5719688 W H Massey[4&6] 6 Mtn Bty, 1418353 J Matthews[4&6] 12 Mtn Bty, 1410910 S G Maybank[4&6] 12 Mtn Bty, 1409266 H McCarthy[4&6] 12 Mtn Bty, 300838 J G McCarthy[3,1&5] 6 Mtn Bty, 1415145 W J McCormick[4&6] 6 Mtn Bty, 38090 P McDonald[3,4&5] 6 Mtn Bty, 1408908 P J McHugh[4&6] 13 (Md Bty), 1415324 A McKirdy[4&6] 13 (Md) Bty, 40005 J McLean[3,4,5&6] 6 Mtn Bty, 36502 A R Mead[3,4&5] 6 Mtn Bty, 1409170 J E Meaker[4&6] 6 Mtn Bty, 9373 J Meath[3,4,5&6] 6 Mtn Bty, 1403074 A Melville[4&6] 12 Mtn Bty, 33852 A E Mew[3,4&5] 6 Mtn Bty, 1409657 F Milford[4&6] 12 Mtn Bty, 25796 S Minogue[1&3], 1410558 G Mittell[4&6] 12 Mtn Bty, 12226 D Molloy[1&3], 1401495 J Moran[4&6] 6 Mtn Bty, 1411952 S S Morris[4&6] 12 Mtn Bty, (1401222) 12862 T Mulhearn[3,4,5&6] 6 Mtn Bty, 1403578 J Mullen[4&6] 6 Mtn Bty, 1405533 E Murphy[4&6] 6 Mtn Bty, 1403546 T Murphy[4&6] 12 Mtn Bty, 1412538 G H Nichol[4&6] 12 Mtn Bty, 1414804 W F Noake[7&6] 10 Mtn Bty, 1410450 E G Noble[4&6] 12 Mtn Bty, 1403777 W Norman[7&6] 10 Mtn Bty, 1409520 F Norris[4&6] 6 Mtn Bty, 1418899

T North[7&6] 10 Mtn Bty, 37014 C O'Callaghan[3,4&5] 6 Mtn Bty, (36304) 1407167 R Page[3,4,5&6] 6 Mtn Bty, 1414494 P E Parkes[4&6] 6 Mtn Bty, 29956 A Paul[3,4&5] 6 Mtn Bty, 1410696 A J Pawson[4&6], 228600 F Peach[3,4&5] 6 Mtn Bty, 1409793 G E Peachment[4&6] 12 Mtn Bty, 202911 A Pearce[3,4&5] 6 Mtn Bty, 1420781 A Pearce[4,5&6] 6 Mtn Bty, 1410935 H J C Peckham[4&6] 12 Mtn Bty, 1409303 T C Pennell[4&6] 6 Mtn Bty, 1402198 G Phillips[4&6] 6 Mtn Bty, 1409591 F Pirouet[4&6] 6 Mtn Bty, 1406554 S L R Powell[4&6] 12 Mtn Bty, (1403486) 27979 M Power[3,4&5] 6 Mtn Bty, 32588 A Prosser[3,4,5&6] 6 Mtn Bty, 1422792 H J Prosser[6&9], 1058207 J Proudfoot[7&6] 10 Mtn Bty, 1408519 G G Puddy[4&6] 6 Mtn Bty, 38498 H Quinlan[3,4&5] 6 Mtn Bty, 1409812 F Rawle[4&6] 6 Mtn Bty, 1405817 G W J Reed[3&9], 1405590 T E Reed[4&6] 6 Mtn Bty, 1420812 A E Rice[4&6] 6 Mtn Bty, 1411110 G Richards[4&6] 12 Mtn Bty, 1415465 W Richardson[4&6] 12 Mtn Bty, 1404203 E Riley[4&6] 6 Mtn Bty, 1418582 W Rimmell[4&6] 12 Mtn Bty, 1403320 R Rimmer[4&6] 6 Mtn Bty, 34182 E Robins[3,4(Cpl.)&5(Cpl.)] 6 Mtn Bty, 1409994 W A Roper[4&6] 6 Mtn Bty, 1403309 A G Ross[4&6] 6 Mtn Bty, 1417067 W (J) Rowley[4&6] 12 Mtn Bty, 1407628 A J Russell[4&6] 12 Mtn Bty, 30733 H Russell[3,4,5&6] 6 Mtn Bty, 1403741 W Ryan[4&6] 12 Mtn Bty, 59737 R Scriven[3,4&5] 6 Mtn Bty, 1404079 J Shasby[7&6] 10 Mtn Bty, 37666 G Silcox[3,4&5] 6 Mtn Bty, 32841 C J Simmons[3,4,5&6] 6 Mtn Bty, (221981) 1415165 A L Sims[4&6] HQ, 25 Ind Pk Art Bde., 1595 J Simpson[1&3], 1409872 T Slade[4&6] 6 Mtn Bty, 1420876 T Smith[4&6] 12 Mtn Bty, 50839 W G Smith[3,4,5&6] 6 Mtn Bty, 1410787 J R Smithers[4&6] 12 Mtn Bty, 37825 H J Sparkes[3,4&5] 6 Mtn Bty, 28049 J Stansfield[3,4,5&6] 6 Mtn Bty, 1409159 W J Stapleton[4&6] 12 Mtn Bty, 1420987 W Stimson[4&6] 6 Mtn Bty, 1410166 A Stocker[4&6] 6 Mtn Bty, 1409947 F L Stone[4&6] 6 Mtn Bty, 37468 A T Stonesbridge[3,4&5] 6 Mtn Bty, 1410180 R Strade[4&6] 6 Mtn Bty, 1409890 F G Strafford[4&6] 12 Mtn Bty, 1402067 E Strain[4&6] 12 Mtn Bty, (22994) 1417466 G Suggitt[4,7&6] 10 Mtn Bty, 1402703 J Sullivan[4&6] 6 Mtn Bty, 1413635 S B Taylor[4&6] 12 Mtn Bty, 1414972 T Taylor[4&6] 13 (Md) Bty, (1403057) 25769 J Teear[1,3,4&5] 12 Mtn Bty, 1419736 F Thompson[6&9], 228880 A C Toner[3,4,5&6] 6 Mtn Bty, 31314 A Torrance[3,4,5&6] 6 Mtn Bty, (1411890) 204099 L Tough[4&6] 12 Mtn Bty, 24321 W Trigwell[1&3], 1415922 A S Tugwell[4&6] 12 Mtn Bty, 1417361 F A Turner[4&6] 6 Mtn Bty, 1406460 W W Tyrrell[4&6] 6 Mtn Bty, 1421034 A J Vallas[4&6] 6 Mtn Bty, 22971 S Vaughan[1&3], 1403475 J Walker[4&6] 6 Mtn Bty, 37057 N Walsh[3,4&5] 6 Mtn Bty, 1416467 F E Watkins[4&6] 6 Mtn Bty, 30827 F J Webster[3,4&5] 6 Mtn Bty, 1418538 N J Wells[4&6] 6 Mtn Bty, 22837 W Wetton[1&3], 1418202 W H Whitfield[4&6] 12 Mtn Bty, 1410634 W J Wilcox[4&6] 12 Mtn Bty, 1414612 F Williams[4&6] 6 Mtn Bty, 212629 A H Williamson[3,4&5] 6 Mtn Bty, 38456 E H Wimpress[3,4&5] 6 Mtn Bty, 1416507 W A C Window[4&6] 6 Mtn Bty, 1415460 J L Windsor[4&6] 12 Mtn Bty, 1415178 F Withnell[4&6] 6 Mtn Bty, 1419679 N C Wittleton[4&6] 6 Mtn Bty, 1412377 A M Wood[4&6] 6 Mtn Bty, 36466 A W Wood[3,4&5] 6 Mtn Bty, 1411155 C Woodman[4&6] 6 Mtn Bty, 1405366 S C S Worsley[4&6] 12 Mtn Bty, 1420795 F W Wortley[4&6] 12 Mtn Bty, 1417484 J C Wright[4&6] 12 Mtn Bty & 1413973 J W Young[4&6] 12 Mtn Bty

Trumpeters: ~ 1414401 L A Holloway[4&6] 12 Mtn Bty, 1414327 G A McCarthy[4&6] 12 Mtn Bty & 1038207 A Parker[7&6] 10 Mtn Bty

THE CORPS OF ROYAL ENGINEERS:

Note a.   *Roll of all commissioned personnel identified as eligible.*

Note b.   *Non-commissioned and other rank personnel multi clasp or non-Afghanistan 1919 / Waziristan single clasp recipients.*

Note c.   *The roll includes the names of Royal Engineer personal attached to the Indian Army Sappers & Miners and Military Works Service establishments. (From 1923 Military Engineering Service). Indian Army establishment personnel including Royal Engineers who transferred on either permanent or temporary loan to the Indian Signal Corps or Indian Unattached List have been omitted. Reference has been made to the relevant Medal Record Card to ensure, (as far as possible), that this is so.*

Note d.   *For reference, India General Service Medals 1919–24 to transferred British personnel serving with the Indian Army signals establishment were named either:*

         A.   Division designation followed by 'DIV. SIGS'

         B.   Company designation followed by 'SIG COY' e.g. '44 SIG COY'.

Note e.   *Personnel who's entire service was with the Indian Signal Corps would appear on rolls compiled by the Indian Army and might, therefore, be available for view at the India Office.*

Note f.   *The Royal (Corps) of Signals was formed in June 1920 from personnel transferred (principally) from the Royal Engineers Signal Service and on loan to the Indian Army signals establishment. This 'exchange' of personnel took some time to stabilise and consequently many medals bearing the clasps 'AFGHANISTAN N.W.F. 1919', 'WAZIRISTAN 1919-21' and/or 'MAHSUD 1919-20' are named as 'R.E.', while subsequent clasps were won as members of the Royal Signals. Some late claims might be named to the Royal Signals even though the initial entitlement was earned as a member of the Royal Engineers. (Refer to next section 'Royal Corps of Signals' if required).*

Single Clasp	No. Identified	Rarity
Afghanistan N.W.F. 1919[3]	In Strength	Not Rare
Mahsud 1919–20[5]	2	Of the Utmost Rarity
Waziristan 1919–21[4]	In Strength	Not Rare
Waziristan 1921–24[6]	In Strength	Not Rare

Combination Clasps	No. Identified	Rarity
North West Frontier 1908[1] Abor 1911–12[2] Afghanistan N.W.F. 1919[3]	1	According to the roll as seen, can be considered Unique
North West Frontier 1908[1] Afghanistan N.W.F. 1919[3]	1	According to the roll as seen, can be considered Unique
North West Frontier 1908[1] Waziristan 1919–21[4]	1	According to the roll as seen, can be considered Unique
Abor 1911–12[2] Mahsud 1919–20[5] Waziristan 1919–21[4]	1	According to the roll as seen, can be considered Unique
Abor 1911–12[2] Waziristan 1921–24[6]	2	Of the Utmost Rarity
Afghanistan N.W.F. 1919[3] Waziristan 1919–21[4]	18	Extremely Rare
Afghanistan N.W.F. 1919[3] Mahsud 1919–20[5] Waziristan 1919–21[4]	10	Of the Utmost Rarity
Afghanistan N.W.F. 1919[3] Mahsud 1919–20[5] Waziristan 1919–21[4] Waziristan 1921–24[6]	1	According to the roll as seen, can be considered Unique
Afghanistan N.W.F. 1919[3] Waziristan 1919–21[4] Waziristan 1921–24[6]	4	Of the Utmost Rarity
Afghanistan N.W.F. 1919[3] Waziristan 1919–21[4] North West Frontier 1930–31[9]	1	According to the roll as seen, can be considered Unique
Afghanistan N.W.F. 1919[3] Waziristan 1921–24[6]	14	Extremely Rare
Afghanistan N.W.F. 1919[3] Waziristan 1921–24[6] North West Frontier 1930–31[9]	1	According to the roll as seen, can be considered Unique
Afghanistan N.W.F .1919[3] North West Frontier 1930–31[9]	4	Of the Utmost Rarity
Afghanistan N.W.F. 1919[3] Burma 1930–32[10]	1	According to the roll as seen, can be considered Unique
Afghanistan N.W.F. 1919[3] Mohmand 1933[11]	1	According to the roll as seen, can be considered Unique
Afghanistan N.W.F. 1919[3] North West Frontier 1935[12]	1	According to the roll as seen, can be considered Unique
Mahsud 1919–20[5] Waziristan 1919–21[4]	31	Very Rare
Mahsud 1919–20[5] Waziristan 1919–21[4] Waziristan 1921–24[6]	19	Extremely Rare
Mahsud 1919–20[5] Waziristan 1919–21[4] Waziristan 1921–24[6] North West Frontier 1930–31[9]	2	Of the Utmost Rarity
Waziristan 1919–21[4] Waziristan 1921–24[6]	58	Rare
Waziristan 1919–21[4] Waziristan 1921–24[6] North West Frontier 1930–31[9]	4	Of the Utmost Rarity

Waziristan 1919–21[4] Waziristan 1921–24[6] Burma 1930–32[10]	1	According to the roll as seen, can be considered Unique
Waziristan 1919–21[4] North West Frontier 1930–31[9]	2	Of the Utmost Rarity
Waziristan 1919–21[4] North West Frontier 1930–31[9] Burma 1930–32[10]	1	According to the roll as seen, can be considered Unique
Waziristan 1919–21[4] North West Frontier 1930–31[9] North West Frontier 1935[12]	1	According to the roll as seen, can be considered Unique
Waziristan 1919–21[4] Burma 1930–32[10]	2	Of the Utmost Rarity
Waziristan 1921–24[6] North West Frontier 1930–31[9]	8	Of the Utmost Rarity
Waziristan 1921–24[6] North West Frontier 1930–31[9] Burma 1930–32[10]	3	Of the Utmost Rarity
Waziristan 1921–24[6] Burma 1930–32[10]	1	According to the roll as seen, can be considered Unique
Waziristan 1921–24[6] Mohmand 1933[11]	2	Of the Utmost Rarity
Waziristan 1921–24[6] North West Frontier 1935[12]	1	According to the roll as seen, can be considered Unique
Malabar 1921–22[7] Waziristan 1921–24[6] North West Frontier 1930–31[9]	1	According to the roll as seen, can be considered Unique

Lieutenant Colonels: ~ A H Bell[3,4&5], H J Donkin[3], G C V Fenton[4] DMW, J E G Festing[6], A F Garrett[3] CRE Peshawar, A R Gemmell[6], (Temp) J A Graeme[3] attch. MWS, A E Grasett[4&6] GSO2 HQ, 8 Bde., C H Haswell[3&6] ADMW, Kohat, (Bvt) H C Hawtrey[3] attch. 'A' DSC, G M Morrell[6], (Bvt) F P Nosworthy[3] GSO1 HQ, 4 Div., D Ogilvy[3&6(MES)] CRE 16 Div., E C Tylden-Patterson[1(Capt.),2(Maj.)&3], (Bvt) G L G Pollard[3,4,5&6] attch. ISC, W F(R M?) Powell[6], (Act) W H Roberts[4] CRE Wana Col, G Macleod Ross[4&6], R B Skinner[1(Capt.)&3] attch. MWS, B G Smith[3], W B Whishaw[6&11] & E de L Young[3] attch. MWS

Majors: ~ (Act) F E Buller[3] 71 Fld Coy, 3rd S&M, E F S Dawson[6] MES, R Maxwell-Everett[2(Lt.)&6] 21 Coy 3rd S&M, (Temp) G J Fearfield[4] attch. MES, C H Foulkes[4], H N G Geary[4&6(MES)] MWS, A E Grasett[4&6] GSO2 HQ, 8 Bde., (Act) C R Gurney[3], (Act) R N Hawes[3], P C S Hobart[1(Lt.)&4] GSO2 Wana Col, (Bvt) H B W Hughes[3,4&5], R G P Hunter[3&4], A S James[3], C L Kilcoin[4&6(MES)] MWS, (Act) J S Lethbridge[3] 57 Fld Coy, 1st KGO S&M, (Bvt) C G Lewis[3] attch. SI, G Llewellyn[3] Bde. Maj 3 Bde., J Macintyre[3], P H Maflin[3&4], A A McClelland[3] 2nd QVO S&M, J M McMullan[3], G H J G Morris[3], H T Morshead[2(Lt.)4&5] attch. SI, (Act) C Preedy[3&10(Lt. Col.)], (Temp) R Rayner[3] Staff, G Macleod Ross[4&6], E K Squires[3] 73 Fld Coy, 3rd S&M, C F Stoehr[6] 21 Coy 3rd S&M, (Act) P J R Watkins[3] attch. Rly Bn, S&M, J G O Whitehead[3,4&5] 55 Fld Coy, 1st KGO S&M & H J Wogan[3&6(Lt.? MES)] attch. MWS

Captains: ~ J E Barnes[4] Adv Eng Pk Tank, P G Barton[3] S&M, F H Batterbury[3] 1st KGO S&M, J R Bernal[4] attch. MWS as GE Tank, C F A Bird[3], W D Boyes[4&5] attch. MWS S. Waziristan Rlys, Bvt) E Bradney[4&6(Bvt. Maj.)] 13 Coy 2nd QVO S&M, R Brennan[4] attch. 44 DSC, G Browne[2&6], C G Cardew[6], W E Coltham[2(Cpl.)&6] MES, (Act) E A Crane[3&6(MES)] 57 Fld Coy 1st KGO S&M, R Cryan[4] attch. MWS, W J Dean[4], L C B Deed[3&6] attch. MWS, M J Dolan[3&6(19 Coy)] 74 Fld Coy, 3rd S&M, J H Dower[6] attch. MES, F E Eustace[4] 3rd S&M, T G B Forster[4], E B Fox[4], C de L Gaussen[6] 19 Coy 3rd S&M, F J P Gibson[3] 2nd QVO S&M, G R Gilpin[6&9] 2nd QVO S&M, H M Greathead[3], H F G Greenwood[6] 1st KGO S&M, H W R Hamilton[6] 19 Coy 3rd S&M, W Hamilton[6], A V St. G Harris[4], T W R Haycroft[6], D N Hill[3&4] attch. MWS, H L Hodgson[3], S H Holding[4], H E Horsfield[6] 22 Coy 3rd S&M, R H S Hounsell[4&6] attch. MES, E Ingram[4], E F Johnston[3], C J Kane[3], H A Kenyon[6] MES Roads & Posts, WFF, C J S King[3] 2nd QVO S&M, J H King[4&5] attch. 44 DSC, E H Knight[6] MES, W H Knox[3&9] 2nd QVO S&M, G H H Lee[6] MES, W J Lyall[4&5] 55 Fld Coy, 1st KGO S&M, A Mason[3], T K Mason[3], R M McNaught[3&4] S&M, A E Meredith[3&4] DADS Waz, C F Mulvany[6], W J Norman[6], J E F Paton[3] attch. 3/W Sig Sqn, G P Pavey[3,(4&5 R Sigs)] attch. 7 DSC, R D B Perrott[3,4&6] MWS Khyber Ropeways, E W Pert[4&6(MES)] MWS, C C Phipps[3], G R Pim[3&11(Maj.)] 53 Fld Coy, 1st KGO S&M, J A Pocock[4,5&6], L C Reid[3&6(MES)] attch. MWS, B H Robertson[6] 1st KGO S&M, T J Robson[4], E A Rogers[3], H R Sandford[3&4] attch. MWS, C R Simpson[6&9(Maj.)] MES, C A Skinner[4,5&6] attch. 3/W Sig Sqn, C Slater[3] 2nd QVO S&M, C Sleigh[4&6] 2nd QVO S&M, R G Stevens[3], R C R Stevenson[6] MES DIK, F H G Stockdale[4&5], R Swire[6], C H H Vulliamy[6&12(Lt. Col. 'A' Corps Sigs, R Sigs)], R H Walker[3] attch. 3 W/Sig Sqn, P J R Watkins[3&4] 26 Rly Coy, S&M, G D Watson[3], R A D Watson[3], C

C S White$^{3,4\&5}$, B F Whitestone$^{4\&6}$ 2nd QVO attch. ISC, C S Widdowfield^{3} S&M, W B Wishaw^{6} GE Derajat & (Act) P C Woolner$^{3\&6(Capt. MES)}$ 10 Works (Hutting) Coy

Lieutenants: ~ J B P Angwin^{6}, A E Armitage^{6}, A C Baillie$^{4\&5}$ 5 Fld Coy, 1st KGO S&M, W H Bay^{6} 2nd QVO S&M, C G Beicher^{6} 1st KGO S&M, A Bennetts^{6} 26 Rly Coy, E M Blake^{6} 19 Coy 3rd S&M, E A E Bolton$^{4\&6}$ S&M, G Bomford^{4} 14 Fld Coy, 2nd QVO S&M, D E Bostock^{4} attch. 3/W Sig Sqn, W M Broomhall$^{4,6(MES)\&9(Maj.)}$ S&M, W J Bull^{3}, H W Bush$^{4,6\&9(Capt.)}$, D M Christison$^{3\&9(Capt.)}$ 2nd QVO S&M, A R Churchill$^{6\&9(Capt.)}$ 1st KGO S&M, P A Clauson^{6} 26 Rly Coy, C F Clifton$^{4\&5}$ S&M, J E Clutterbuck^{3} 56 Fld Coy, 1st KGO S&M, C W Couchman^{3} 7 Fld Trp, RE, D S Cowie^{6} 22 Coy 3rd S&M, J J Cronin^{3} S&M, R St. C Davidson^{6} MWS Derajat & DIK, H H Daw$^{3,4\&6(Capt. MES)}$ MWS, T B L Disney$^{4\&6(R Sigs)}$, V Dykes^{4}, J H Eades$^{4\&6(MES)}$ MWS, T J Evans$^{4\&6}$, A E Fawcett^{3}, P J Fitzpatrick$^{3\&6(Capt. MES)}$ 46 Bde. KKF, G Ford^{3}, F H R French^{6} 2nd QVO S&M, P T Garner^{3}, A M Garnett$^{6\&10(Capt.)}$ 2nd QVO S&M, E H T Gayer^{6} S&M, R Le H Guiton$^{4\&6}$ S&M, J R Hainsworth^{6} MES, J Heenan$^{3\&6(Capt. MES)}$ MWS, W G Hole$^{3\&4}$ 40 DSC, R S Horner^{6} MES, M Hunter$^{3,4\&5}$ S&M, R I C Jacob^{6} 1st KGO S&M, J James$^{3\&9}$ 2nd QVO S&M, G J Jeffery^{3}, M R Jeffries$^{4\&9}$, S W Joslin^{3} 21 Coy 3rd S&M, L F R Kenyon$^{6,9\&10}$ 1st KGO S&M, H G Leigh^{3}, B H S Lloyd^{6} 19 Coy 3rd S&M, T E Longfield^{6} 1st KGO S&M, R H B Longland^{3}, D R Martin$^{3\&6}$ 1st KGO S&M, M F C Martin$^{6\&9(Capt.)}$ MES, S F Matheson^{3} S&M, A W McHeish^{4} attch. 3/W Sig Sqn, A Minnis^{3} attch. 26 Rly Coy S&M, A C Mitchell$^{3\&12(Maj.)}$, E J Murphy^{3} attch. 17 CBST, A H G Napier$^{6,9(Capt.)\&10(Capt.)}$ 1st KGO S&M, E Nixon^{3}, G H Osmaston^{3} attch. ISC, F W L Mc C Parker^{6} S&M, F L Parkinson^{3} RE Rlys, H Patterson^{3} S&M, E F J Payne$^{7,6\&9(Capt.)}$, A Phillips^{3} attch. MWS, F E Pool$^{6\&9(Capt.)}$, W Porter$^{3,4\&6}$, T J P Price^{3} S&M, W H Ray$^{6\&9}$ S&M, C D Reed^{6} 21 Coy 3rd S&M, J A Riccomini^{3} S&M, O L Roberts$^{3\&4}$, E E N Sandman^{6} 1st KGO S&M, W A Scott$^{4\&6(R Sigs)}$, E E G L Searight$^{4\&10(Capt.)}$ 2nd QVO S&M, W H Shaw^{3}, F E W Simpson^{3} 24 Fld Coy, 3rd S&M, B K Smith^{3} 1 KGO S&M, J F D Steedman$^{4\&9(Capt.)}$ 2nd QVO S&M, R Stillingfleet$^{4\&6}$, M R H Z Swinhoe^{6}, G Tayleur^{3} attch. ISC, R L Thompson^{6}, P A Tucker$^{3,4\&9(Capt.)}$ 2nd QVO S&M, C E F Turner$^{4\&6}$ S&M, F R Turner$^{4\&6}$ 2nd QVO S&M, P A Ullman^{6} MES, R C Walker^{6} 21 Coy 3rd S&M, A R F Webster^{6} 21 Coy(s) 3rd S&M, H R F Webster^{6} 19 Coy 3rd S&M. R P Wheeler^{6} 19 Coy 3rd S&M, P F White^{6}, J B Wilson^{4} attch. 77 Sig Coy, A J R Wishart$^{3,4\&5}$ 55 Fld Coy, 1st KGO S&M, H J Wogan$^{3\&6}$ attch. MES & H F Pipe-Wolferstan$^{4,(9(Lt. R Sigs)\&10(Capt. R Sigs)}$ 3rd S&M

Warrant Officers Class II: ~ (Act) 1852883 (R J) (A E) Burridge$^{4,6\&9(2 QVO S\&M)}$, (Temp) 23441 F G Craig$^{4\&5}$ 2 Sig Coy RE, attch. 'F' DSC, (Temp) (1851911) 14859 T Earwaker$^{3\&4}$ attch. No. 1 War Expense Store, Kalabagh, (Temp) (1850357) 10342 J H Haines$^{4\&6(R Sigs)}$, (Temp) (1850356) 14149 M Hepburn$^{4,5\&6(R Sigs)}$ & 1853065 F A Southam$^{4(57 Coy, 1 KGO S\&M)\&6}$ 19 Coy 3rd S&M

Quartermaster Sergeants/Sergeants: ~ (601962) 1850280 H F Cox$^{4,5\&6(R Sigs)}$ attch. 'F' DSC, (Act) 37671 G Drew$^{3\&4}$ attch. 38 DSC, (1851680) 13118 G Fairs$^{3,4,\&5}$, (Act) 14386 R H Gass$^{4\&6(54 Fld Coy 1 KGO S\&M)}$ MWS, (1850266) 23305 E R Hole$^{4\&5}$ attch. 40 DSC, (315028) 1856236 W Locke$^{4\&6(R Sigs)}$, 1852918 C B Logan$^{6\&11(WOII)}$, 1853663 E C Odell$^{6,9(WOII)\&10(WOII)}$, 1853077 F C Parsons$^{6\&9}$, 1856291 L O Sanford$^{4\&6(RASC)}$ attch. RASC & (1850377) 601942 J Sweeting$^{4,5\&6(R Sigs)}$ 2 Sig Coy

Lance Sergeants/Corporals: ~ (314763) 1850368 W J Bloomfield$^{4\&5}$ attch. 'F' DSC, (1850372) 344389 G Brill$^{4\&6(R Sigs)}$, 32299 L A Clarke$^{3\&4}$ attch. 2 LofC Sig Coy, 1858980 J Coppock$^{3\&(9 Cpl. R Sigs)}$, (344400) 1850373 D E A Godfrey$^{4,5\&6(R Sigs)}$, 1854281 A Greenhalgh$^{4,6\&10(WOII)}$ 2nd QVO S&M, (1850360) 24264 A G Hales$^{4,5\&6(R Sigs)}$, (25885) 1853039 E James$^{4\&5}$ attch. MWS, (1861342) 616082 W E King$^{6\&9(Sgt.)}$, 62065 J J Over$^{3\&4}$ attch. 38 DSC, (7752) 1850358 F W Rowland$^{3,4\&5}$ 5 Sig Trp, (32530) 1850419 E R P Stone$^{4,5\&6}$ & (230790) 315230 P R Symes$^{3\&6(R Sigs)}$

Lance Corporals/Sappers/Pioneers: ~ (344743) 1850374 B Abrahams$^{4,5\&6(Sgt. R Sigs)}$, (1850350) 624450 A Allen$^{4\&6(R Sigs)}$, 260056 E Archer$^{4\&5}$ attch. 'F' DSC, 37364 R G Bachelor$^{4\&6}$, (1850379) 622979 V H Bradshaw$^{4\&6}$ attch. 'B' DSC, 624677 F A Bruce$^{4\&6(R Sigs)}$, 601837 A G Bush$^{4\&5}$, (1850412) 624258 J Cassidy$^{4,5\&6}$ attch. 'B' DSC, 127305 C H G Charles$^{3\&4}$ attch. 38 DSC, (341196) 602080 F W Clarke$^{4\&5}$ attch. 'F' DSC, (510687) WR/199055 R G Coleman$^{3\&4}$ attch. 16 SSB, (343955) 1850370 C Conway$^{4,5,(6\&9 Sgt. R Sigs)}$, (2309555) 623852 A J Cowderoy$^{4\&6(R Sigs)}$, (1850408) 613713 A E Davis$^{4\&6}$ attch. 'B' DSC, (1857038) 10476 W J Dowie$^{3,(6\&9 Sgt. R Sigs)}$ attch. 3 W/Sig Sqn, (1860669) 624473 P R Dunn$^{4,(6\&9 Sgt. R Sigs)}$, (2311059) 625651 B J Eades$^{4\&6(R Sigs)}$, (1857465) 624685 H Faraday$^{4\&6(R Sigs)}$, 624495 H Fellows$^{4\&6(R Sigs)}$, 1856985 H Gasson$^{3\&6(R Sigs)}$, (2306664) 32705 A E Giles$^{4\&6(R Sigs)}$, (1850394) 344528 J A G Gilmour$^{4\&6(R Sigs)}$, (1856953) 314134 L Halstead$^{4\&5}$, (357757) 349046 F L G Haswell$^{4\&5}$ attch. 'F' DSC, (1850398) 344774 T Hooper$^{4\&6(R Sigs)}$, 4379181 W Horseman$^{4\&5}$, (601818) 1850401 A E Hull$^{4,5\&6}$ attch. 'B' DSC, 624987 R Hutchinson$^{40\&6(R Sigs)}$, (1850388) 314147 R W Kelly$^{4,5\&6(R Sigs)}$, (1856684) 613783 F R C Kenny$^{4\&6(R Sigs)}$, (1850276) 39740 H H Kitchen^{5}, ???995 C J (T J?) Lane$^{4\&5}$, 80533 T F Latham$^{3,4\&5}$, 344753 A E Lewis$^{4\&5}$ attch. 'F' DSC, (25559) 1850362 H J Lewis$^{4,5\&6(Cpl. R Sigs)}$, (1856960) 343994 J H Lister$^{4\&6(R Sigs)}$, (1850403) 601848 F Lodder$^{4\&5}$ attch. 'F' DSC, 237911 C C G Mason$^{3\&4}$ attch. 38 DSC, (1850434) 623231 E J McFarland$^{4\&6(R Sigs)}$, (1856906) 315310 G McKechnie$^{3,4\&6(R Sigs)}$ attch. 3 W/Sig Sqn, (1850442) 624395 F C Murphy$^{4\&6(R Sigs)}$, 254189 H Nailon$^{4\&5}$ attch. 40 DSC, 344719 R Naismith$^{4,5\&6}$ attch. 40 DSC, 1853201 J O'Neill$^{4\&6(R Sigs)}$, (39516) 1850418 F C Osborne$^{4\&6}$ attch. 'B' DSC, (1850438) 623946 T E Page$^{4\&6(R Sigs)}$, (1850444) 624623 W H Parkes$^{4\&6}$ attch. 'F' DSC, (1850423) 314743 W C Paskins$^{4,5\&6(R Sigs)}$, (623895) 1850437 D Philps$^{4\&6}$ attch. 'F' DSC, (1850429) 344057 B Poulton$^{4\&6(R Sigs)}$, (1850487) 344501 H E R Pulman$^{4\&5}$, (1857004) 344738 J H S Read$^{4\&5}$ attch. 3/W Sig Sqn, (1858992) 344674 J G Robertson$^{4\&5}$ attch. 40 DSC, 32690 S W Robinson$^{4,5\&6}$ attch. 'F' DSC, (623173) 1857326 W A Sharp$^{4\&6}$ attch. 'B' DSC, 3522218 H Simonds$^{4\&5}$, (344200) 1850430 R Singleton$^{4,5\&6(R Sigs)}$, (1850428) 315521 A Smith$^{4\&5}$, (624421) 1850347 J Smith$^{4\&6}$ attch. 'B' DSC, 1857387 W W Southon$^{4\&6}$, 625745 H C Spencer$^{4\&6(R Sigs)}$, (T1150) 502168 H H Stafford$^{3\&4}$, (25377) 1850361 S A Stevens$^{4,5,6(Cpl. R Sigs)\&9(Sgt. R Sigs)}$, (623942) 1857206 A E Templeman$^{4\&6}$ attch. 'B' DSC, 33977 B R Tucker$^{3\&4}$, 301782 R Tucker$^{4\&5}$ attch. 'F' DSC, 23550 N Turland$^{4,5\&6(R Sigs)}$ 1 Sig Trp, (1855209) 23667H B Walker$^{4\&5}$ attch. 'F' DSC, 32619 T S Wallace$^{4\&6(R Sigs)}$, (1856889) 314806

C W Warburton[4&5] attch. 3/W Sig Sqn, (1850450) 24580 A Webb[4&6(R Sigs)], (254598) 344675 G J Webb[4&5] attch. 'F' DSC, (1850454) 361620 H C Wells[4,5&6] attch. 'F' DSC, (624531) 1850457 G Windras[4&6] attch. 'F' DSC, (1858986) 343716 H R Winton[4&5] attch. 40 DSC, 625074 H Wise[4&6(R Sigs)], (1856406) 344817 E Woodcock[4&5] attch. 40 DSC & (1859197) 619539 E J Wyeth[4,(9&12 Sgt. R Sigs)]

Trumpeters: ~ (1750385) 25195 H E Cullum[4&6(Sgln. R Sigs)] 2 Fld Sqn

THE ROYAL CORPS OF SIGNALS:

Note a. Roll of all commissioned personnel identified as eligible.

Note b. Non-commissioned and other rank personnel multi clasp only.

Note c. The Royal Corps of Signals was formed in June 1920 from personnel transferred (principally) from the Royal Engineers Signal Service and those previously transferred or on loan to the Indian Army signals establishment. This 'exchange' of personnel took some time to stabilise and consequently many medals bearing the clasps 'AFGHANISTAN N.W.F. 1919', 'WAZIRISTAN 1919-21' and / or 'MAHSUD 1919-20' are named as 'R.E.', while subsequent clasps were won as members of the Royal Signals. Reference has been made to the relevant Medal Record Card to ensure, as far as possible, that only recipients with medals named to the Royal Corps of Signals are included in the roll below. Personnel with service on the Indian Army establishment and with medals identified as 'Issued by the Government of India' (or similar wording) have therefore been omitted. (Refer to previous section 'Royal Engineers' if required). Medals should not exist bearing the 'AFGHANISTAN N.W.F. 1919' or 'MAHSUD 1919-20' clasps named to the Royal Corps of Signals.

Note d. Medals to the Royal Corps) of Signals are named 'R. SIGNALS.'.

Note e. For reference, India General Service Medals 1919–1924 to transferred British personnel serving with the Indian Army signals establishment were named either:

    A. Division designation followed by 'DIV. SIGS'

    B. Company designation followed by 'SIG COY' e.g. '44 SIG COY'.

Note f. Personnel who's entire service was with the Indian Signal Corps would appear on rolls compiled by the Indian Army and might, therefore, be available for view at the India Office.

Single Clasp	No. Identified	Rarity
Afghanistan N.W.F. 1919[3]	0	Corps Not Formed
Mahsud 1919–20[5]	0	Corps Not Formed
Waziristan 1919–21[4]	?	Difficult to Verify From Medal Record Card Whether Named to Royal Engineers or Indian Army Signals Establishment
Waziristan 1921–24[6]	In Strength	Not Rare
Combination Clasps	No. Identified	Rarity
Malabar 1921–22[7] Waziristan 1921–24[6]	5	Of the Utmost Rarity
Malabar 1921–22[7] Waziristan 1921–24[6] Burma 1930–32[10]	1	According to the roll as seen, can be considered Unique
Waziristan 1921–24[6] North West Frontier 1930–31[9]	11	Of the Utmost Rarity
Waziristan 1921–24[6] Burma 1930–32[10]	2	Of the Utmost Rarity
Waziristan 1921–24[6] Mohmand 1933[11]	2	Of the Utmost Rarity
Waziristan 1921–24[6] Mohmand 1933[11] North West Frontier 1935[12]	2	Of the Utmost Rarity
Waziristan 1921–24[6] North West Frontier 1935[12]	2	Of the Utmost Rarity

Captains: ~ H D Beadon[6], A J Harris[6&10(Maj.)] & J C H Shaw[7(Lt.)&6]

Lieutenants: ~ F R L Goadby[4&6] (Possibly Named As Royal Engineers), A W McHeish[4] (Possibly Named As Royal Engineers), C L Morgan[6], T A R Scott[6] & C Spurway[6]

Lance Sergeants/Corporals: ~ 1858869 A Carney[6&9], 2312295 H A Evens[6&9], 2309066 J E Handby[6&9(Sgt.)] PDS, 1857466 A Hawley[6&9], 1857071 R Shaw[6&9(Sgt.)], 1857189 J P Swaine[6&9] & 2312416 A S P Szarkowski[6&9(Sgt.)],

Lance Corporals/Signalmen: ~ 2312093 W H Bonner[6&9(Cpl.)], 2310990 A Brown[6&12(Cpl.)], 2313988 L J Brown[6&11(Cpl.)], 2313656 E W J Collins[7&6], 5610844 C E Cummings[6&12(Cpl.)], 2309488 J Gildea[6&9(Cpl.)], 1857295 J Law[6&9(Sgt.)], 2314124 J Lawson[6&10(Sgt.)], 2309849 D Leyshon[7&6], (Originally Royal Navy Reserve), 2311312 H E Mott[6,11(Cpl.)&12(Cpl.)], (625510) 2310920 A Mowatt[6,11(Cpl.)&12(Cpl.)], 2312224 A Negro[6&9(Sgt.)], 2310828 J Peters[7(Sgln.),6&10(Cpl.)], 2313910 T W E Thomas[7&6(Cpl.)], 2314991 B G Thompson[6&11(Cpl.)] & (2310753) 625240 E R Turner[7&6]

THE INFANTRY:

~ 3rd Bn, The Coldstream Guards ~

Note a.   *Roll of all personnel identified as eligible.*
Note b.   *France August 1914 forward.*
Note c.   *Medals named in impressed in capitals: 'C GDS'.*

Single Clasp	No. Identified	Rarity
Afghanistan N.W.F. 1919[3]	1	According to the roll as seen, can be considered Unique.
Mahsud 1919–20[5]	0	None Identified.
Waziristan 1919–21[4]	0	None Identified.
Waziristan 1921–24[6]	1	According to the roll as seen, can be considered Unique.

Majors: ~ L M Gibbs[6], ADC to HE the CINC India
Lance Corporals/Privates: ~ 29893 W Johnson[3] attch. 2 N Stafford

~ 1st Bn, The Royal Scots (Lothian Regiment) ~

Note a.   *Roll of all personnel identified as eligible.*
Note b.   *India August 1914. France & Flanders December 1914, Salonika December 1915, Bulgaria September 1918, Salonika November 1918, India October 1919 forward.*
Note c.   *Medals named in impressed capitals: 'R. SCOTS'*

Single Clasp	No. Identified	Rarity
Afghanistan N.W.F. 1919[3]	0	None Identified
Mahsud 1919–20[5]	0	None Identified
Waziristan 1919–21[4]	7	Of the Utmost Rarity
Waziristan 1921–24[6]	4	Of the Utmost Rarity
Combination Clasps	**No. Identified**	**Rarity**
Mahsud 1919–20[5] Waziristan 1919–21[4]	1	According to the roll as seen, can be considered Unique
Waziristan 1919–21[4] Waziristan 1921–24[6]	1	According to the roll as seen, can be considered Unique

Majors: ~ I I E Stanley-Murray[4&5] attch. 2/150 Infantry, IA
Lieutenants: ~ J D Crawford[4] attch. RTE, Tank & A Drummond[6] attch. 7 ACC
Warrant Officers Class II: ~ (RQMS) 3044892 J B Sinclair[4&6] attch. 'F' DSC
Quartermaster Sergeants/Sergeants: ~ 3044900 J Reid[6]
Lance Corporals/Privates: ~ 3045925 F J Caine[4] attch. HQ, WFF, 3045732 J Campbell[4] attch. 34 DSC, 3045794 C W Cheyne[4] attch. 34 DSC, 3044721 D Cooper[6] attch. HQ, 9 & 10 Bde.s, 3045944 C J Fox[4], 3046309 A B Hamer[4] attch. HQ, WFF, 3045068 R J Kirby[6] & (70211) 3045845 A Peyman[4] attch. IAOC

1/5th Bn, The Royal Scots (Queen's Edinburgh Rifles), Territorial Force

Note a. *Roll of all personnel identified as eligible.*

Note b. *United Kingdom August 1914. Egypt April 1915, Gallipoli April 1915, Mudros October 1915, Egypt January 1916, France March 1916 forward.*

Note c. *Medals named in impressed capitals: 'R. SCOTS'*

Single Clasp	No. Identified	Rarity
Afghanistan N.W.F. 1919[3]	1	According to roll as seen, can be considered Unique
Mahsud 1919–20[5]	0	None Identified
Waziristan 1919–21[4]	0	None Identified
Waziristan 1921–24[6]	0	None Identified

Lieutenants: ~ A H Benson[3] attch. 1/4 Queen's

~ 1/7th Bn, The Royal Scots (Queen's Edinburgh Rifles), Territorial Force ~

Note a. *Roll of all personnel identified as eligible.*

Note b. *United Kingdom August 1914. Egypt June 1915, Gallipoli July 1915, Egypt January 1916 and France & Flanders April 1918.*

Note c. *Medals named in impressed capitals: 'R. SCOTS'*

Single Clasp	No. Identified	Rarity
Afghanistan N.W.F. 1919[3]	1	According to roll as seen, can be considered Unique
Mahsud 1919–20[5]	0	None Identified
Waziristan 1919–21[4]	0	None Identified
Waziristan 1921–24[6]	0	None Identified

Lieutenants: ~ (P) D S Wilson[3] attch. 287 Coy, MGC

~ 2nd Bn, The Queen's (Royal West Surrey Regiment) ~

Note a. *Roll of all commissioned personnel identified as eligible.*

Note b. *Non-commissioned and other ranks non-Waziristan series clasps. Verified 'single' clasp 'WAZIRISTAN 1919-21' and 'WAZIRISTAN 1921-24' medals are scarce and would only have been only won by time expired personnel, reinforcement drafts or those retired from the campaign due to sickness or other. The bars on many two-clasp specimens examined are not riveted leading to the frequent loss of the Waziristan 1921-24 award. This is primarily due to the latter clasp being issued some two to three years after receipt of the initial award and 'churn' of personnel back into civilian life.*

Note c. *South Africa August 1914. France & Flanders October 1914, Italy November 1917 forward. India September 1919 forward.*

Note d. *Title changed to The Queen's Royal Regiment (West Surrey) in 1920*

Note e. *Medals named in impressed capitals: '2 QUEEN'S RL. R.*^v*, '2 BN.*^{THE}* QUEEN'S R.*^{MG6}* or 'THE QUEEN'S R.*^{MG6}*

Single Clasp	No. Identified	Rarity
Afghanistan N.W.F. 1919[3]	4	Of the Utmost Rarity
Mahsud 1919–20[5]	0	None Identified
Waziristan 1919–21[4]	?	If verified, Scarce
Waziristan 1921–24[6]	?	If verified, Scarce
Combination Clasps	No. Identified	Rarity
Afghanistan N.W.F. 1919[3] Mahsud 1919–20[5] Waziristan 1919–21[4] Waziristan 1921–24[6]	1	According to the roll as seen, can be considered Unique

Afghanistan N.W.F. 1919[3] **Waziristan 1919–21**[4]	1	According to the roll as seen, can be considered Unique
Mahsud 1919–20[5] **Waziristan 1919–21**[4] **Waziristan 1921–24**[6]	1	According to the roll as seen, can be considered Unique
Waziristan 1919–21[4] **Waziristan 1921–24**[6]	Bn. Strength	Not Rare
Waziristan 1919–21[4] **Waziristan 1921–24**[6] **North West Frontier 1930–31**[9]	2	Of the Utmost Rarity
Waziristan 1921 – 24[6], **Mohmand 1933**[11] **North West Frontier 1935**[12]	1	According to the roll as seen, can be considered Unique

Lieutenant Colonels: ~ P J Fearon[4&6] & E B Matthew-Lannowe[4,6&(9 Brig. Gen. Staff)], GSO1 Mhow

Majors: ~ A N S Roberts[4&6] & S T Watson[4]

Captains: ~ J B Coates[4,5&6], H W Credland[3], D'Arcy H Dillow[3] attch. 28 Rly Coy, S&M, (QM) C J M Elliott[4&6], T C Filby[3&4] attch. 1/4 Queen's, R C G Foster[4], W F Holford[3] attch. 12 Cav Bde., F A Jacob[4], G K Olliver[4&6], R H Philpot[4&6], R K Ross[4&6] & W H Stacey[3,4,5&6] Fld Cashier, WFF

Lieutenants: ~ F T Badcock[4&6], A P Block[4], R F C Oxley-Boyle[4&6], R M Burton[4&6], H J Carpenter[4], H P Combe[4&6], E C W Cumberlege[4&6], L C East[4&6], N Eustace[4], B C Haggard[4&6], R A Harrild[4], I T P Hughes[4&6], M S Shuldham-Legh[4], P L Leighton[4], L E L Maxwell[4], E Mushett[4&6], C O W Morgan[4&6], A B Oliver[4], S Paddison[3] attch. 270 Coy, MGC, 57 Bde., J L P Paine[4], R E Pickering[4&6], F T Pope[6] attch. 'A' Corps Sigs, C C Prescott[4], J H Sillem[4] & R C Wilson[4&6]

Lance Corporals/Privates: ~ 6077914 C F Bowden[4], 6077517 H Snook[6,(11 Sgt. R Sigs)&(12 Sgt. R Sigs)] & 6077719 E W Wilson[4,6&9(L/Sgt. PDS, R Sigs)]

~ 1/4th Bn, The Queen's (Royal West Surrey Regiment), Territorial Force ~

Note a. *Roll of all commissioned personnel identified as eligible.*

Note b. *Non-commissioned and other ranks multi clasp only or non-Afghanistan 1919 single clasp.*

Note c. *United Kingdom August 1914. India December 1914 to September 1919.*

Note d. *Battle honour 'Third Afghan War 1919'.*

Note e. *Medals named in impressed capitals: '4 QUEEN'S RL. R.'*

Single Clasp	*No. Identified*	*Rarity*
Afghanistan N.W.F. 1919[3]	Bn. Strength	Not Rare
Mahsud 1919–20[5]	0	None Identified
Waziristan 1919–21[4]	0	None Identified
Waziristan 1921–24[6]	0	None Identified
Combination Clasps	*No. Identified*	*Rarity*
Afghanistan N.W.F. 1919[3] **Mahsud 1919–20**[5] **Waziristan 1919–21**[4]	1	According to the roll as seen, can be considered Unique
Afghanistan N.W.F. 1919[3] **Waziristan 1919–21**[4]	1	According to the roll as seen, can be considered Unique
Afghanistan N.W.F. 1919[3] **Waziristan 1919–21**[4] **Waziristan 1921–24**[6]	2	Of the Utmost Rarity
Mahsud 1919–20[5] **Waziristan 1919–21**[4] **Waziristan 1921–24**[6]	1	According to the roll as seen, can be considered Unique
Waziristan 1919–21[4] **Waziristan 1921–24**[6]	1	According to the roll as seen, can be considered Unique

Lieutenant Colonels: ~ H R Atkins[3] & (QM) J Greer[3]
Majors: ~ H J Gosney[3]
Captains: ~ A Dibdin[3], O K Caroe[3], E F Charlesworth[3] attch. MGC, O Featherstone[3], E G Frost[3], L L Gosney[3], G L Groves[3], M D Helps[3,4&6(RTC)], W S Hooker[4&6] attch. S&TC & W H Maud[3]
Lieutenants: ~ L Bates[3], A C Brandt[3], P H Cutler[3], W G Endley[3], N B Greener[3], R E Howell[3], F W T Hughes[3], W F Hurry[3], H Mason[3], J S Menhinick[3], W D B Read[3], M H Ridley[3], A J Sharpe[3] & H C Stone[3]
Quartermaster Sergeants / Sergeants: ~ 200421 A E Granger[4,5&6(R Sigs)] attch. 30 DSC & (6078190) 200376 A W Jeaner[3,(4&6 2 Queen's)]

Lance Corporals/Privates: ~ 200426 J Dunn[3&4] & 200728 G H Lane[3,4&5] attch. 'F' DSC

~ 1/5th Bn, The Queen's (Royal West Surrey Regiment), Territorial Force ~

Note a.   *Roll of all personnel identified as eligible.*
Note b.   *United Kingdom August 1914. India November 1914, Mesopotamia December 1915 to March 1919 thence To United Kingdom via India.*
Note c.   *Medals named in impressed capitals: '5 QUEEN'S RL. R.'.*

Single Clasp	No. Identified	Rarity
Afghanistan N.W.F. 1919[3]	108	Very Scarce
Mahsud 1919–20[5]	0	None Identified
Waziristan 1919–21[4]	0	None Identified
Waziristan 1921–24[6]	0	None Identified

Lieutenants: ~ A D McLean[3] attch. 1/25 London
Lance Sergeants/Corporals: ~ 240109 H J Corrigan[3] attch. 1 S Lanc, 240509 W Killick[3] & 240036 J A A Peters[3]
Lance Corporals/Privates: ~ 240452 F A Best[3] attch. 1 S Lanc, 240869 A Bignall[3] attch. 1 S Lanc, 241437 A Bishop[3] attch. 1 S Lanc, 241092 J W Bourn[3] attch. 1 S Lanc, 60516 G Breme[3] attch. 2 Som LI, 240468 W Bridger[3] attch. 1 S Lanc, 241103 W Brooks[3] attch. 1 S Lanc, 243572 R F Bryant[3] attch. 17 SSB, 241138 J Buckland[3] attch. 1 S Lanc, 240895 F Church[3] attch. 1 S Lanc, 240292 A H Cobbitt[3] attch. 1 S Lanc, 241174 F J Cole[3] attch. 1 S Lanc, 242318 J C Collins[3] attch. 33 SSB, 240493 A Cooper[3] attch. 1 S Lanc, 241133 H W Cornish[3] attch. 1 S Lanc, 240632 J Cripps[3] attch. 1 S Lanc, 243290 T Cunningham[3] attch. 2/6 Sussex, 240986 A W Cutten[3] attch. 1 S Lanc, 240535 G H Cutten[3] attch. 1 S Lanc, 241391 C Dallaston[3] attch. 1 S Lanc, 241392 G E Davis[3] attch. 1 S Lanc, 240651 M Driscoll[3] attch. 1 S Lanc, 241450 C H Eve[3] attch. 1 S Lanc, 243309 A E Feltham[3] attch. 1 S Lanc, 240580 W Foster[3] attch. 1 S Lanc, 241204 R Francis[3] attch. 1 S Lanc, 240650 H W Frome[3] attch. 1 S Lanc, 241001 R C Fry[3] attch. 1 S Lanc, 240718 F W Gates[3] attch. 1 S Lanc, 240700 F Giles[3] attch. 1 S Lanc, 241185 G Gill[3] attch. 1 S Lanc, 241130 G Gray[3] attch. 1 S Lanc, 240672 A P Hall[3] attch. 1 S Lanc, 240713 H G Harris[3] attch. 1 S Lanc, 240527 J T Hillman[3] attch. 1 S Lanc, 241406 A E Hillyer[3] attch. 1 S Lanc, 241521 E A Hine[3] attch. 1 S Lanc, 240836 F F Holden[3] attch. 1 S Lanc, 241055 H B Holden[3] attch. 1 S Lanc, 240786 W R Holden[3] attch. 1 S Lanc, 240467 J Holmes[3] attch. 1 S Lanc, 240553 A Howells[3] attch. 1 S Lanc, 240470 A Hubbard[3] attch. 1 S Lanc, 241589 W S Hughes[3] attch. 1 S Lanc, 241169 A V Hunt[3] attch. 1 S Lanc, 241072 F Hunt[3] attch. 1 S Lanc, 243355 R Jackson[3] attch. 1 S Lanc, 241008 A E Kent[3] attch. 1 S Lanc, 241454 F L Kilby[3] attch. 1 S Lanc, 240425 H Killick[3] attch. 1 S Lanc, 240985 J H King[3] attch. 1 S Lanc, 240445 P King[3] attch. 1 S Lanc, 241084 A R Kitchingside[3] attch. 1 S Lanc, 241362 W J Knight[3] attch. 1 S Lanc, 240848 E Lacey[3] attch. 1 S Lanc, 241010 F Lacey[3] attch. 1 S Lanc, 241457 A S Land[3] attch. 1 S Lanc, 241597 G A Langdell[3] attch. 1 S Lanc, G/81822 P B Langley[3] attch. 1 S Lanc, 240620 H C Ledger[3] attch. 1 S Lanc, 241233 C W Lenton[3] attch. 1 S Lanc, 241458 R Lewis[3] attch. 1 S Lanc, 240788 C F Luff[3] attch. 1 S Lanc, 241086 E Luff[3] attch. 1 S Lanc, 240722 L Nash[3] attch. 2 Som LI, 243345 F H Martin[3] attch. 1 S Lanc, 241114 C F Morris[3] attch. 1 S Lanc, 241218 J H Morris[3] attch. 1 S Lanc, 241461 H H Mortlock[3], 241416 F R C North[3] attch. 1 S Lanc, 240604 W Parrett[3] attch. 1 S Lanc, 241418 F J Payne[3] attch. 1 S Lanc, 243348 L T Pearse[3] attch. 1 S Lanc, 240455 A E Pobgee[3] attch. 1 Sussex, 241372 H Pocock[3] attch. 1 S Lanc, G/22509 A Procter[3] attch. 1 S Lanc, 243415 W J J Procter[3] attch. 1 S Lanc, 241459 A Quilton[3] attch. 1 S Lanc, 240782 W J Raymond[3] attch. 2/6 Sussex, 241198 C Robinson[3] attch. 1 S Lanc, 240483 A Rose[3] attch. 1 S Lanc, 240975 R Scogeing[3] attch. 1 S Lanc, 240690 A Simmonds[3] attch. 1 S Lanc, 240797 C H Simmons[3] attch. 1 S Lanc, 241216 D Smith[3] attch. 1 S Lanc, 241475 R F Smith[3] attch. 1 S Lanc, 241764 W Smith[3] attch. 2 Som LI, 240942 H A Steer[3] attch. 1 S Lanc, 240668 C G Stower[3] attch. Admin HQ, 241227 J L Sutton[3] attch. 1 S Lanc, 240563 E J Taylor[3] attch. 1 S Lanc, G/37674 A Thomas[3] attch. 1 S Lanc, 243281 W T Tilkner[3] attch. 1 S Lanc, 241121 F G Welland[3] attch. 1 S Lanc, 240996 A T Wells[3] attch. 1 S Lanc, 240696 A W West[3] attch. 1 S Lanc, 241478 G West[3] attch. 1 S Lanc, 240763 H F White[3] attch. 1 S Lanc, 241382 J W White[3] attch. 1 S Lanc, 240488 A E Whitmore[3] attch. 1 S Lanc, 240662 A E Williamson[3] attch. 1 S Lanc, 243353 G P Wingate[3] attch. 1 S Lanc, 241142 H Wood[3] attch. 1 S Lanc & 241188 E G Woods[3] attch. 1 S Lanc

~ 2nd Bn, The Buffs (East Kent Regiment) ~

Note a.   *Roll of all personnel identified as eligible.*
Note b.   *India August 1914. France and Flanders January 1915, Salonika November 1915, Turkey November 1918, India November 1919, Iraq December 1920, Kurdistan January 1921, Iraq October 1921, Aden March 1922 to April 1923.*
Note c.   *Medals named in impressed capitals: '2/BUFFS.'. Late claims may be named 'E. KENT. R.'.*

Single Clasp	No. Identified	Rarity
Afghanistan N.W.F. 1919[3]	3	Of the Utmost Rarity
Mahsud 1919–20[5]	0	None Identified
Waziristan 1919–21[4]	13	Extremely Rare
Waziristan 1921–24[6]	0	None Identified
Combination Clasps	**No. Identified**	**Rarity**
Afghanistan N.W.F. 1919[3] Waziristan 1919–21[4]	2	Of the Utmost Rarity
Mahsud 1920–21[5] Waziristan 1919–21[4]	3	Of the Utmost Rarity

Majors: ~ E C Norman[4&5] attch. 1/5 GR, IA
Captains: ~ A S Lowe[4] RTO, Kaur Bridge
Lieutenants: ~ A C Dolben[3&4] attch. MGC & G H Mitchell[4] RTE, Kaur Bridge
Company Quartermaster Sergeants/Staff Sergeants / Colour Sergeants: ~ L/6464 F Pepper[3] attch. NW Rly Vols, AFI
Quartermaster Sergeant /Sergeants: ~ (Act) L/11462 A Hicks[4] attch. 2 CSS
Lance Corporals/Privates: ~ L/10467 J Bailey[4], L/12970 G H W Daynes[3], L/8615 W J Deeks[4&5], L/12201 G E Fagg[4], L/12934 G Floate[3], L/12061 A Goddard[4] attch. 40 DSC, L/2173 E G Haimes[4] attch. 43 IGH DIK, L/12122 R T Hills[4], L/11547 G Hodgkin[4], L/11709 H R Holden[4], L/12571 S C Lambert[4] attch. 40 DSC, 16 Div., L/11665 H Statham[4&5], L/11668 F J Stubbing[4], L/6972 J Stubbings[4] & L/10807 E J Ward[3&4] attch. 36 ISS, Tank

~ 3rd (Reserve) Bn, The Buffs (East Kent Regiment) ~

Note a.   *Roll of all personnel identified as eligible.*
Note b.   *United Kingdom August 1914 forward.*
Note c.   *Medals named in impressed capitals: 'BUFFS.'*

Single Clasp	No. Identified	Rarity
Afghanistan N.W.F. 1919[3]	1	According to the roll as seen, can be considered Unique
Mahsud 1919–20[5]	0	None Identified
Waziristan 1919–21[4]	0	None Identified
Waziristan 1921–24[6]	0	None Identified

Lieutenants: ~ A Lambert[3]

~ 1/4th Bn, The Buffs (East Kent Regiment), Territorial Force ~

Note a.   *Roll of all personnel identified as eligible.*
Note b.   *United Kingdom August 1914. India November 1914, Aden August 1915 thence India February 1916 to October 1919.*
Note c.   *Medals named in impressed capitals: '1/4/BUFFS.' Late claims may be named 'E. KENT. R.'*

Single Clasp	No. Identified	Rarity
Afghanistan N.W.F. 1919[3]	48	Very Rare
Mahsud 1919–20[5]	0	None Identified

Waziristan 1919–21[4]	0	None Identified
Waziristan 1921–24[6]	0	None Identified

Captains: ~ G M Kingsford[3] Staff, HQ, Multan Bde. & J E Monins[3] Staff

Warrant Officers Class II: ~ (Act) 200333 H Wyles[3] attch. RE

Quartermaster Sergeants/Sergeants: ~ (Act) 200625 W C T Arnold[3], 200607 A E Attfield[3] attch. 44 DSC, (Act) 200043 R A Bailey[3], (Act) 200297 H H Barker[3] attch. RAMC, (Act) 200405 W J Clayson[3] attch. 68 PMC, 200214 S H Fairbrass[3] attch. HQ, Jamrud, 243005 R Gibb[3], (Originally 5th Bn), (Act) 200540 G Hall[3] attch. 43 PMC, 200065 A J Hubbard[3] attch. 3 ISS, 200433 C J Matthews[3] attch. 4 MMG Bty, MGC, (Act) 200539 C J Pidduck[3] attch. S&TC, 200612 G W F Rumney[3] attch. DA&QMG, (Act) 200869 E S Tarry[3] attch. MWS & (Act) 200194 W S Taylor[3] attch. 178 IFA

Lance Sergeants/Corporals: ~ 200038 A G Fowler[3] attch. 4 ISS, 203082 F H Penfold[3] attch. HQ, Derajat Bde., (Act) 201070 R Pilcher[3] attch. 2 MAC & (Act) 200235 F M Wood[3] attch. ACS

Lance Corporals/Privates: ~ 200619 H E Binfield[3] attch. 4 ISS, 200573 H H Bird[3] attch. S&TC, 201440 S J Brazier[3] attch. 40 DSC, G/21396 A E Brooks[3] attch. 3 ISS, 203179 H Burr[3], 200506 S Chancellor[3], 20047 F Christian[3], 200314 L L Crouch[3], L/10574 F A Emery[3] attch. 3/W Sig Sqn, (L/13164) 203346 L G Fellows[3] attch. 3 ISS, 200278 T Hannon[3], 201307 F W Hartstone[3] attch. 3/W Sig Sqn, 200657 F J Hickson[3], 200628 E A Hill[3] attch. 2 MT Coy, S&TC, 203187 H Hood[3], 200650 S J Luck[3] attch. 3 ISS, 203281 H Offen[3] attch. 44 DSC, 200516 J A Pettman[3] attch. 45 MAC, RASC, G/24369 H W Powell[3] attch. 3 ISS, 200784 A H Rose[3] attch. 3 ISS, 201249 F G Rouse[3] attch. 4 ACS, 200133 J W Sandy[3] attch. 3/W Sig Sqn, 201197 J A Scott[3] attch. 3 ISS, 201327 F Sills[3] attch. 40 DSC, 200545 N G Somerford[3] attch. 44 DSC, 200577 A G Tutt[3] attch. 2 LofC Sig Sect & 200401 T W Woolcott[3] attch. 4 MMG Bty, MGC

~ 1/5th (The Weald Of Kent) Bn, The Buffs (East Kent Regiment) ~

Note a.   *Roll of all personnel identified as eligible.*

Note b.   *United Kingdom August 1914. India December 1914, Mesopotamia December 1915 to December 1919.*

Note c.   *Medals named in impressed capitals: '1/5/BUFFS.' Late claims may be named 'E. KENT. R.'*

Single Clasp	No. Identified	Rarity
Afghanistan N.W.F. 1919[3]	134	Very Scarce
Mahsud 1919–20[5]	0	None Identified
Waziristan 1919–21[4]	1	According to the roll as seen, can be considered Unique
Waziristan 1921–24[6]	0	None Identified
Combination Clasps	**No. Identified**	**Rarity**
Afghanistan N.W.F. 1919[3] Waziristan 1919–21[4]	1	According to the roll as seen, can be considered Unique
Afghanistan N.W.F. 1919[3] Waziristan 1921–24[6]	1	According to the roll as seen, can be considered Unique

Captains: ~ R Walker[4] attch. RASC

Lieutenants: ~ M L Blaxall[3] attch. 1/25 London

Company Quartermaster Sergeants/Staff Sergeants/Colour Sergeants: ~ (Act) 240363 E Jarrett[3] attch. 1 MT Coy, S&TC

Quartermaster Sergeants / Sergeants: ~ 240687 W G Davis[3] attch. 2 Som LI, G/22333 A F Filby[3] attch. IOD, (Act) 240364 H G Ford[3] attch. 3/W Sig Sqn, 242831 J Fuller[3], 241486 A Hatley[3], (Act) G/21711 J Morton[3&4] attch. MT Est., S&TC & (Act) 243069 B G Rampe[3] attch. 4 SSB

Lance Sergeants/Corporals: ~ 242905 F Hall[3], 200627 J A Hewitt[3], 241149 W Lloyd[3], 200426 J Martin[3], 243011 A Mortimore[3], 240042 A J Packham[3], 240106 W A Partiss[3], 243065 C W Phipps[3], 241191 A C J Potkin[3], (Act) 240126 E J Poynter[3] attch. 8 SSB, (Act) 240442 G Surtees[3] attch. 3/W Sig Sqn & G/21794 C E Wren[3]

Lance Corporals/Privates: ~ G/21984 V E Baker[3], 240103 F Barling[3] attch. 1 DWR, 241850 F C Bartlett[3], 201079 D G Beard[3], G/21964 C Biggs[3], 241424 B Bingham[3], 201410 A J Blake[3], 201287 R Bligh[3], 242843 T W Botten[3], 242787 H C W Boyall[3], 241862 G F Briant[3] attch. 1 DWR, 241439 T Bruce[3] attch. 2/6 Sussex, 240375 J Burgess[3], 243039 E Burton[3], 240702 W G Chamberlain[3], 241388 P Cook[3], G/20291 O Cooper[3], 242792 A J Copper[3] attch. 1 DWR, 243194 F Cowley[3], 243039 J Cronelie[3], 201357 E Croucher[3], 243034 S C Croucher[3] attch. 1 DWR, 240451 H H Crump[3] attch. 1 MT Coy, S&TC, 200437 J Dawson[3], 241168 F Deakin[3], 240202 R Ditton[3] attch. 1 DWR, G/6705 V A Dodd[3], 200265 S L Drury[3], 243036 F Edwards[3], 241330 R Ellis[3], (7817688) 242707 G Erriera[3&6(RTC)], 243037 G L Euden[3], 201066 T Eve[3], 243038 A T Excell[3], 240431 A Forsdick[3], G/436 G Fox[3], 240505 H Fryer[3] attch. 4 SSB, 242861 W Gant[3], 242862 A Geal[3], 240213

A E E Gibbs[3], 243043 F G Gibbins[3], 241350 C H L Gilbert[3], 242929 C Green[3], 241188 H J Groves[3], G/21989 J Hamlyn[3] attch. HQ, NWFF, 243199 J Hawley[3], 201285 C Hewitt[3] attch. ISC, 200261 G T Hodges[3], 242798 H Hodsden[3], 240694 G Hogston[3], 240292 H Hook[3], 240745 W T Hope[3], 201111 G Houghton[3], 241283 F F Izzard[3] attch. 2 N Stafford, 241141 W Jackson[3], 241491 C Jacques[3], G/7532 C J James[3], 243006 P Jeffrey[3], 240111 J T Johnson[3], 242938 A Jones[3], 243051 B W Kemp[3], 293664 H Lampkin[3], 242872 H Langridge[3], G/1602 J H Lovett[3], 241102 T H Mahy[3], 20495 H E Marriott[3], 200078 S G Miller[3], 240277 E M Mills[3], 241100 B C Morris[3], G/21711 J Morton[3] attch. 692 Coy, RASC, 241879 P G Moss[3], 240129 T E Noakes[3] attch. 33 SSB, G/50 D Orgar[3], 241882 S T Ovenden[3], 241287 T Parrott[3], 240443 W G Perkins[3], 241372 W Philpott[3], 242879 F Phippard[3], 201220 G Phipps[3], 200673 R J Pitkin[3], 241509 W J Preston[3] attch. 2/6 Sussex, 242881 P A Prunty[3], 243068 J Ralph[3] attch. 1 DWR, 241409 G B B Rance[3] attch. 4 SSB, 241512 W J Randall[3], 241039 E Ratcliff[3], 240824 A Relf[3], 242815 G T Roberts[3], 240831 W H Santer[3], 201088 G Savage[3], 242886 A Sawyer[3], 243074 H Sayer[3], 241164 J Scott[3], 240475 J D Scott[3], 240463 D J Sharp[3], 242851 F Sharville[3], 241602 W Simons[3], 200542 A Simpson[3], 241522 E F Smith[3] attch., 1 DWR, 201421 F Smith[3], 241359 D Snelling[3], 241263 H Spicer[3], 200616 W Stevenson[3], 241107 W Stimpson[3], 241885 W H Strouts[3], G/21342 T O'Sullivan[3] attch. 1 DWR, 22304 W Symonds[3], G/7719 F Taylor[3], 240264 J A Thompson[3] 3/W Sig Sqn, 240429 W A Veale[3], 241535 A J Vincent[3], 241542 J Willis[3] attch. 18 SSB, 242827 J Wisden[3] & 200196 W Wood[3]

Drummers: ~ 240039 E J Blackwell[3] attch. 16 SSB

~ 6th (Service) Bn, The Buffs (East Kent Regiment) ~

Note a. *Roll of all personnel identified as eligible.*
Note b. *United Kingdom August 1914. France & Flanders June 1915.*
Note c. *Medals named in impressed capitals: 'BUFFS.'*

Single Clasp	No. Identified	Rarity
Afghanistan N.W.F. 1919[3]	2	Of the Utmost Rarity
Mahsud 1919–20[5]	0	None Identified
Waziristan 1919–21[4]	0	None Identified
Waziristan 1921–24[6]	0	None Identified

Lieutenants: ~ M de J Creswick[3] attch. 2 N Stafford & A L B Swaine[3] attch. 1/1 Kent

~ 9th (Reserve) Bn, The Buffs (East Kent Regiment) ~

Note a. *Roll of all personnel identified as eligible.*
Note b. *Formed October 1914. Remained United Kingdom throughout Great War period as Training Reserve supplying drafts and reinforcements.*
Note c. *Medals named in impressed capitals: 'BUFFS.'*

Single Clasp	No. Identified	Rarity
Afghanistan N.W.F. 1919[3]	1	According to the roll as seen, can be considered Unique
Mahsud 1919–20[5]	0	None Identified
Waziristan 1919–21[4]	0	None Identified
Waziristan 1921–24[6]	0	None Identified

Lieutenants: ~ E H Bonner[3]

~ 2nd Bn, The King's Own (Royal Lancaster Regiment) ~

Note a. *Roll of all personnel identified as eligible.*
Note b. *India August 1914. France & Flanders January 1915, Egypt October 1915, Salonika December 1915, Bulgaria 1918 thence Turkey. India November 1919 forward.*
Note c. *Title changed to 'The King's Own Royal Regiment (Lancaster) in 1920.*
Note d. *Medals named in impressed capitals: 'R. LANC. R.*

Single Clasp	No. Identified	Rarity
Afghanistan N.W.F. 1919[3]	1	According to the roll as seen, can be considered Unique.
Mahsud 1919–20[5]	0	None Identified
Waziristan 1919–21[4]	4	Of the Utmost Rarity
Waziristan 1921–24[6]	2	Of the Utmost Rarity

Combination Clasps	No. Identified	Rarity
Afghanistan N.W.F. 1919[3] Waziristan 1919–21[4]	1	According to the roll as seen, can be considered Unique
Waziristan 1919–21[4] Waziristan 1921–24[6]	3	Of the Utmost Rarity

Lieutenant Colonels: ~ O C Borrett[4&6(Col. Cmdt. 7 Ind Bde.)] Staff
Company Quartermaster Sergeants/Staff Sergeants/Colour Sergeants: ~ 3701418 J Hamilton[6] attch. 'C' DSC
Quartermaster Sergeants/Sergeants: ~ (3701458) 9778 E A Hall[3&4] attch. 39 DSC
Lance Sergeants/Corporals: ~ 3702519 G H Barker[4&6] attch. 'E' DSC, 3702892 S Finan[6] attch. 'C' DSC & 3702627 J G Plester[4] attch. HQ WFF
Lance Corporals/Privates: ~ 3701841 R Chalton[4&6], 3702499 J Hough[4] attch. 34 DSC, 3702721 T E Langley[4] attch. HQ, WFF, 3702788 T H Sims[4] attch. HQ WFF & (3701856) 177116 W White[3]

~ 2/4th (Reserve) Bn, The King's Own (Royal Lancaster Regiment) ~

Note a. *Roll of all personnel identified as eligible.*
Note b. *Formed February 1915. Remained United Kingdom throughout Great War Period supplying drafts and reinforcements.*
Note c. *Medals named in impressed capitals: 'R. LANC. R.'*

Single Clasp	No. Identified	Rarity
Afghanistan N.W.F. 1919[3]	2	Of the Utmost Rarity
Mahsud 1919–20[5]	0	None Identified
Waziristan 1919–21[4]	0	None Identified
Waziristan 1921–24[6]	0	None Identified

Lieutenants: ~ A Birkmyre[3] attch. 1 Yorkshire & H F Page[3] attch. 2/6 R Sussex

~ 2/5th Bn, The King's Own (Royal Lancaster Regiment) Territorial Force ~

Note a. *Roll of all personnel identified as eligible.*
Note b. *Formed September 1914. United Kingdom thence France & Flanders from February 1917 forward.*
Note c. *Medals named in impressed capitals: 'R. LANC. R.'*

Single Clasp	No. Identified	Rarity
Afghanistan N.W.F. 1919[3]	1	According to the roll as seen, can be considered Unique
Mahsud 1919–20[5]	0	None Identified
Waziristan 1919–21[4]	0	None Identified

Waziristan 1921–24[6]	0	None Identified

Lieutenants: ~ W J Williamson[3]

~ 6th (Service) Bn, The King's Own (Royal Lancaster Regiment) ~

Note a. *Roll of all personnel identified as eligible.*
Note b. *Formed August 1914. United Kingdom thence Gallipoli July 1915, Egypt January 1916, Mesopotamia February 1916 forward.*
Note c. *Medals named in impressed capitals: 'R. LANC. R.'*

Single Clasp	No. Identified	Rarity
Afghanistan N.W.F. 1919[3]	30	Very Rare
Mahsud 1919–20[5]	0	None Identified
Waziristan 1919–21[4]	0	None Identified
Waziristan 1921–24[6]	0	None Identified

Lieutenants: ~ L Beaumont[3] attch. 1/4 QORWK, H H Kingsley[3] attch. 2 King's & S C Roberts[3] attch. 2 Som LI
Quartermaster Sergeants/Sergeants: ~ (Act) 2652 J Beswick[3] attch. MFP
Lance Sergeants/Corporals: ~ 18204 J H Morris[3] attch. 2/6 Sussex
Lance Corporals/Privates: ~ 11688 W H Allday[3] attch. 2 Som LI, 25622 J W Bates[3] attch. 1 DLI, 17430 J Briggs[3] attch. 1 DLI, 34139 L Davis[3] attch. 2/6 Sussex, 12092 G Dimlow[3] attch. 2/6 Sussex, 22069 A Fletcher[3] attch. 2/6 Sussex, 19744 J T Kernick[3] attch. 2/6 Sussex, 36381 J Kirton[3] attch. 2 MT Coy, S&TC, 34118 E A Lawty[3] attch. 52 CFA, 2161 W Lees[3] attch. 2 Som LI, 23268 H Ledger[3] attch. 2/6 Sussex, 35655 H J Mullineaux[3] attch. 5 MT Coy, S&TC, 22304 H O'Neill[3] attch. 17 SSB, 25418 F Peskett[3] attch. 2/W Sig Sqn, 34225 J B Potter[3] attch. 2 MT Coy, S&TC, 36402 H J J W Rogers[3] attch. 2 MT Coy, S&TC, 202491 F Sanderson[3] attch. 2/6 Sussex, 36405 H H Shutt[3] attch. MT, S&TC, 32175 E Smart[3] attch. 1 DLI, (3701815) 12552 J Southward[3] attch. 17 SSB, 36434 J Steel[3] attch. 2 MT Coy, S&TC, 2490 F Sweeting[3] attch. 2 Som LI, 11598 J J Troy[3], 36424 J Waghorn[3] attch. MT, S&TC & 14789 R Ward[3] attch. 2/6 Sussex

~ 2nd Bn, The Northumberland Fusiliers ~

Note a. *Roll of all personnel identified as eligible.*
Note b. *India August 1914, France and Flanders January 1915 thence Salonika and back to France. Iraq 1919, Persia 1920 and India 1921.*
Note c. *Medals named in impressed capitals: 'NORTH'D. FUS.'*

Single Clasp	No. Identified	Rarity
Afghanistan N.W.F. 1919[3]	0	None Identified
Mahsud 1919–20[5]	0	None Identified
Waziristan 1919 21[4]	0	None Identified
Waziristan 1921–24[6]	2	Of the Utmost Rarity
Combination Clasps	*No. Identified*	*Rarity*
Mahsud 1919–20[5] Waziristan 1919–21[4]	1	According to the roll as seen, can be considered Unique
Waziristan 1919–21[4] Waziristan 1921–24[6]	1	According to the roll as seen, can be considered Uniqu.

Captains: ~ O H Mather[4&5] attch. 67 PMC, S&TC
Lieutenants: ~ F Brown[4&6(RTC)]
Lance Corporals / Privates: ~ 4257131 A Oldham[6] attch. HQ, DIK & 4256632 H Williamson[6] attch. 'G' DSC

~ 2/7ᵗʰ Bn, The Northumberland Fusiliers, Territorial Force ~

Note a.   *Roll of all personnel identified as eligible.*
Note b.   *Formed September 1914. United Kingdom thence Egypt from January 1917 forward.*
Note c.   *Medals named in impressed capitals: NORTH'D. FUS.'*

Single Clasp	No. Identified	Rarity
Afghanistan N.W.F. 1919[3]	1	According to the roll as seen, can be considered Unique
Mahsud 1919–20[5]	0	None Identified
Waziristan 1919–21[4]	0	None Identified
Waziristan 1921–24[6]	0	None Identified

Captains: ~ R Smales[3]

~ 2ⁿᵈ Garrison Bn, The Northumberland Fusiliers ~

Note a.   *Roll of all personnel identified as eligible.*
Note b.   *Formed October 1916. United Kingdom thence India from March 1916 forward.*
Note c.   *Medals named in impressed capitals: 'NORTH'D. FUS.'*

Single Clasp	No. Identified	Rarity
Afghanistan N.W.F. 1919[3]	49	Very Rare
Mahsud 1919–20[5]	0	None Identified
Waziristan 1919–21[4]	0	None Identified
Waziristan 1921–24[6]	0	None Identified

Captains: ~ G G Armstrong[3] attch. 1 S Lanc & E A Tregoning[3]
Warrant Officers Class I: ~ 49169 E Fitzgerald[3]
Warrant Officers Class II: ~ (Act) 206362 W J Howard[3]
Quartermaster Sergeants/Sergeants: ~ 206346 G S Davis[3] attch. 1/4 QORWK, 9101 A A Nix[3] attch. 2/6 Sussex & 63042 R L Toseland[3]
Lance Sergeants/Corporals: ~ (Act) 205869 W F Gate[3] attch. 17 SSB & 205941 B Johnson[3] attch. 2/6 Sussex
Lance Corporals/Privates: ~ 26473 W Allen[3], 57157 A M Bargeman[3] attch. 33 DSC, 4 Div., 63065 F Bircumshaw[3] attch. 1 Yorkshire, 56430 H E Bouck[3] attch. 2/6 Sussex, 63064 E Brutnall[3] attch. 1 Yorkshire, 56537 W Cann[3] attch. 2/6 Sussex, 53702 E Carr[3] attch. 1 Yorkshire, 26610 G E Cartledge[3] attch. 1 Yorkshire, 52577 S H Cheater[3] attch. 1 Yorkshire, 48775 A J F Cheeseman[3] attch. DFD, 53579 C C J Cummings[3] attch. 1 Yorkshire, 57114 C F Darbyshire[3], 21/1720 J W Dodds[3] attch. 1 MT Coy, S&TC, 77252 G F Edmunds[3], 26705 W T Gardiner[3] attch. 2/6 Sussex, 77052 H Glide[3], 26210 G Gray[3] attch. 39 DSC, 56462 M Hart[3] attch. 1 Yorkshire, 26571 J Hewines[3] attch. ITD, 206372 A A Holliday[3], 205812 E Holman[3], 56425 W V Hughes[3] attch. 2 Som LI, 205953 R W Hutton[3] attch. 1 Yorkshire, 49429 W Knowles[3] attch. 1 Yorkshire, 49387 H E Mattacks[3] attch. 1 Yorkshire, 50607 R McKelvey[3] attch. 1 Yorkshire, 26702 H Murphy[3] attch. 1 Yorkshire, 26768 A Nixon[3] attch. 1 Yorkshire, 205876 F Peverall[3] attch. 2/6 Sussex, 206268 W Prime[3] attch. 2/6 Sussex, 50449 J Quinn[3] attch. 1 Yorkshire, 64114 J Reilly[3] attch. 6 SSB, 53266 P C Richards[3] attch. 1 Yorkshire, 77081 W Richards[3], 50463 T Rockell[3] attch. 1 Yorkshire, 53609 J H Smith[3] attch. 1 Yorkshire, 53277 C W Sprigmore[3] attch. 41 ISS, 311060 F Stock[3] attch. 1 SSB, 49349 W Thornton[3] attch. 1 Yorkshire & 26628 J Wynne[3] attch. 1 Yorkshire

~ 2ⁿᵈ Bn, The Royal Warwickshire Regiment ~

Note a.   *Roll of all personnel identified as eligible.*
Note b.   *Malta August 1914. France & Flanders October 1914 thence Italy from November 1917 forward.*
Note c.   *Medals named in impressed capitals: 'R. WAR. R.'*

Single Clasp	No. Identified	Rarity
Afghanistan N.W.F. 1919[3]	1	According to the roll as seen, can be considered Unique
Mahsud 1919–20[5]	0	None Identified
Waziristan 1919–21[4]	19	Extremely Rare
Waziristan 1921–24[6]	25	Very Rare

Lieutenants: ~ R H Adams[4] attch. RTE & C W Nicholls[3] Staff, 43 Bde.

Warrant Officers Class II: ~ (Act Rly Tpt Sgt. Maj.) 5096570 W G Shorland[6] attch. RTE, DIK

Quartermaster Sergeants/Sergeants: ~ 5096314 F W Davis[4] attch. RTE WFF, 64022 J Fletcher[4] attch. RTE Tank, (43844) 5095233 H T Jilley[4] attch. BGH Tank, (64984) 5096703 S F Jones[4] attch. RTE & (Act) 5095249 W J Smith[4] attch. HQ, 9 Bde.

Lance Sergeants/Corporals: ~ (3234848) 5096098 W Eyers[6] attch. HQ, Razmak, 5096078 W Lewis[6] attch. RTE, DIK & 5096302 H S Short[6] attch. RTE, Waz Dist

Lance Corporals/Privates: ~ 5096261 W Allen[6] attch. 10 IGH, Bannu, (55629) 5095804 L P R Audrain[4] attch. 43 BGH, Tank, (60749) 5096144 J Barker[4] attch. RTE Kalabagh, (43864) 5095251 H Bird[4] attch. RTE, Bannu & Kalabagh, 5096353 G Britton[6] attch. 7 IGH, DIK, 5095903 E Caldicote[6] attch. 27 FA, Razmak, 5097594 G Chambers[6] attch. 39 ISS, (43911) 5095289 W Clark[4] attch. IGH Tank, (64968) 5096693 E Coates[4] attch. IGH Tank, 5096812 F H Cockbill[6] attch. 7 IGH, DIK, 5095371 C Collins[6] attch. 'G' DSC, 39866 C R Cook[4] attch. 7 ICCS Tank, (11276) 5094477 J T Gardner[4] attch. RTE DIK, (43892) 5095275 G Gillman[4] attch. RTE Tank, 5095971 L C Gorton[4] attch. Medical Est., Dardoni, (20475) 5094600 A Hallam[4] attch. RTE Khirgi, 5097595 G R Hayes[6] attch. 6 Bde., SS, 5096322 W Hopkins[6] attch. 'G' DSC, 5096079 A Horton[6] attch. 7 IGH, DIK, (61991) 5096330 T Johnstone[4] attch. LofC Sig Sect, 5096335 J Monk[6] attch. 'G' DSC, 5095396 W Moorcroft[6] attch. 'G' DSC, 5097461 W T Moreton[6] attch. 7 IGH, DIK, 5095957 T Nash[6] attch. 'G' DSC, 5097792 E A Neville[6] attch. 43 BSH, 5096092 W C Pane[6] attch. 'G' DSC, 63773 E Pidgeon[4] attch. RTE Kalabagh, 5097902 W H Plume[6] attch. 7 IGH, DIK, 5096166 H Powell[6] attch. 'G' DSC, (63755) 5096400 T Prince[4] attch. BGH Bannu, 5096271 A E Smith[6] attch. 'G' DSC, 5096263 J O'D W Stretton[6] attch. 7 IGH, DIK, 5096568 A Timms[6] attch. 39 ISS & 5096757 F Warren[6] attch. 7 IGH, DIK

~ 1/6th Bn, The Royal Warwickshire Regiment, Territorial Force ~

Note a.   Roll of all personnel identified as eligible.

Note b.   United Kingdom August 1914. France & Flanders March 1915, Italy November 1917 thence Austria and back to Italy in 1919.

Note c.   Medals named in impressed capitals: 'R. WAR. R.'

Single Clasp	No. Identified	Rarity
Afghanistan N.W.F. 1919[3]	1	According to the roll as seen, can be considered Unique
Mahsud 1919–20[5]	0	None Identified
Waziristan 1919–21[4]	0	None Identified
Waziristan 1921–24[6]	0	None Identified

Lieutenants: ~ F R Nield[3] attch. 1 S Lanc

~ 9th (Service) Bn, The Royal Warwickshire Regiment ~

Note a.   Roll of all personnel identified as eligible.

Note b.   Formed August 1914. Gallipoli July 1915, Mudros and Egypt January 1916. Mesopotamia February 1916 thence North Persia August 1918 and South Russia until August 1919 where the battalion was disbanded and remaining personnel transferred to 9th Bn, Worcestershire Regiment.

Note c.   Medals named in impressed capitals: 'R. WAR. R.'

Single Clasp	No. Identified	Rarity
Afghanistan N.W.F. 1919[3]	29	Very Rare
Mahsud 1919–20[5]	0	None Identified
Waziristan 1919–21[4]	0	None Identified

Waziristan 1921–24[6]	0	None Identified

Lance Sergeants/Corporals: ~ (Act) 37572 G H Barradell[3] attch. 1 Yorkshire & 330405 F I Page[3] attch. Officers Mess, HQ, Tank

Lance Corporals/Privates: ~ 15315 H Barber[3] attch. 1 Yorkshire, 28759 E Bates[3] attch. 1 Sussex, 20043 W C Breeden[3] attch. 1 Sussex, 31940 J Brown[3] attch. 2/6 Sussex, 24989 A J Bayliss[3] attch. 1 Yorkshire, 24931 A W Camp[3] attch. 1 Sussex, 203865 H E Cheeseman[3] attch. 36 ISS, Tank, 27556 C W Hallam[3] attch. 36 ISS, Tank, 22923 P J Herbert[3] attch. HQ, 62 Bde., 37604 C A J Jeal[3] attch. 1 Yorkshire, 26767 W H Kirk[3] attch. 1 Sussex, 203872 P J Lett[3] attch. 1 Yorkshire, 21819 C W Neil[3] attch. 1 Yorkshire, 25037 H Nicholls[3] attch. 1 Sussex, 25629 G A Parker[3] attch. 1 Yorkshire, 5163 A H Pitt[3] attch. 2/6 Sussex, 24353 H W Powell[3] attch. 1 Sussex, 22230 W J Rickett[3] attch. 1 Sussex, 16540 B Shemmonds[3] attch. 1 Sussex, 10710 E Sherriff[3] attch. 1/25 London, 25086 S Wagg[3] attch. 1 Yorkshire, 24964 J Walter[3] attch. 1 Yorkshire, 37606 F Weeks[3] attch. 1 Sussex, 2742 F Westwick[3] attch. 1 Sussex, 18557 W J Witchell[3] attch. 1 Yorkshire, 26717 A Woolfe[3] attch. 1 Yorkshire & 26010 Zealley[3] attch. 1 Yorkshire

~ 1st Bn, The Royal Fusiliers (City of London Regiment) ~

Note a. *Roll of all personnel identified as eligible.*
Note b. *United Kingdom August 1914. France & Flanders September 1914 forward. Ireland from September 1920 to February 1921 thence India from 1922.*
Note c. *Medals named in impressed capitals: 'R. FUS.'*

Single Clasp	No. Identified	Rarity
Afghanistan N.W.F. 1919[3]	0	None Identified
Mahsud 1919–20[5]	0	None Identified
Waziristan 1919–21[4]	1	According to the roll as seen, can be considered Unique
Waziristan 1921–24[6]	15	Extremely Rare

Combination Clasps	No. Identified	Rarity
Waziristan 1921–24[4] North West Frontier 1930–31[9]	1	According to the roll as seen, can be considered Unique

Captains: ~ A W Goddard[4] attch. 2/15 Sikhs, IA, Ft Sandeman

Quartermaster Sergeants/Sergeants: ~ 6449273 H Gardner[6] attch. 27 FA, 6454569 H E Harley[6] attch. 'B' DSC & 6448644 H G Tipping[6] attch. HQ, Razmak

Lance Corporals/Fusiliers: ~ 6454141 T Abbitt[6] attch. 27 FA, 6446255 T W Brown[6] attch. 27 FA, 6447790 E O Burkett[6] attch. 'G' DSC, 6446126 R H Doneathy[6] attch. HQ, Waz Dist, 6448585 H A Fisher[6] attch. 27 FA, 6446330 L T Da Fonseca[6] Staff, Kalabagh, 6454756 W H Howard[6] attch. Rest Camp, Mari Indus, 6454580 E N King[6] attch. 27 FA, 6446097 E A Laysell[6] attch. 27 FA, 1661265 W Matthews[6] attch. 27 FA, 6448633 H Prudence[6] attch. 'G' DSC, 6448654 J C Scrimgeour[6&9(Sgt.)] attch. HQ, Waz Dist & 6446152 A H W Vincent[6] attch. RTO, Tank

~ 2nd Bn, The Royal Fusiliers (City of London Regiment) ~

Note a. *Roll of all personnel identified as eligible.*
Note b. *India August 1914. Egypt March 1915, Limnos April 1915, Gallipoli April 1915, Egypt January 1916 thence France & Flanders March 1916 forward. India from 1919 to 1921 followed by Aden.*
Note c. *Medals named in impressed capitals: 'R. FUS.'*

Single Clasp	No. Identified	Rarity
Afghanistan N.W.F. 1919[3]	1	According to the roll as seen, can be considered Unique
Mahsud 1919–20[5]	0	None Identified
Waziristan 1919–21[4]	2	Of the Utmost Rarity
Waziristan 1921–24[6]	0	None Identified

Combination Clasps	No. Identified	Rarity
Waziristan 1919–21[4] Waziristan 1921–24[6]	1	According to the roll as seen, can be considered Unique

Lieutenants: ~ L A Mosely[3] attch. 1/25 London
Quartermaster Sergeants/Sergeants: ~ (Act) GS/128048 A N Sanders[4&6] attch. 21 MT Coy, S&TC
Lance Corporals/Privates: ~ G/127611 S W Curtis[4] attch. 4 ISS & G/128412 J S Putman[4] attch. 4 ISS

~ 2nd Bn, The King's (Liverpool Regiment) ~

Note a. *Roll of all commissioned personnel identified as eligible.*
Note b. *Non-commissioned and other ranks multi clasp only or non-Afghanistan 1919 single clasp.*
Note c. *India August 1914 forward to 1920.*
Note d. *Battle honour 'Third Afghan War 1919'.*
Note e. *Title changed to The King's Regiment (Liverpool) in 1920.*
Note f. *Medals named in impressed capitals: 'L'POOL. R.'*

Single Clasp	No. Identified	Rarity
Afghanistan N.W.F. 1919[3]	Bn. Strength	Not Rare
Mahsud 1919–20[5]	0	None Identified
Waziristan 1919–21[4]	0	None Identified
Waziristan 1921–24[6]	0	None Identified
Combination Clasps	**No. Identified**	**Rarity**
Afghanistan N.W.F. 1919[3] Malabar 1921–22[7]	1	According to the roll as seen, can be considered Unique
Afghanistan N.W.F. 1919[3] Waziristan 1921–24[6]	3	Of the Utmost Rarity
Waziristan 1919–21[4] Waziristan 1921–24[6]	1	According to the roll as seen, can be considered Unique

Lieutenant Colonels: ~ F Hyslop[3]
Majors: ~ G S Duckworth[3] attch. 281 Coy, MGC
Captains: ~ F C C Briggs[3], (QM) T H Caddy[3], E C Cross[3], F G Harden[3] & N Kynaston[3]
Lieutenants: ~ C S Agar[3], G C Capell[3], T H Cooper[3], R W Jones[3], C E Kent[3], R M Hewitt[3], H J Slynn[3], T H Treharne[3], J E T Webb[3&7(Dorset)] & A G Wrixon[3] attch. S&M
Warrant Officers Class II: ~ (3436818) 9733 H W R Sewerin[4&6(Lanc Fus)] attch. No. 1 War Expense Store Kalabagh
Lance Sergeants/Corporals: ~ (10140) 3757460 W Milam[3&6('G' DSC)]
Lance Corporals/Privates: ~ (M/16108) 9901 A Francis[3&6(Act. Sgt. RASC)] & (7817693) 9566 S Sines[3&6(7 ACC, RTC)]

~ 2nd Bn, The Norfolk Regiment ~

Note a. *Roll of all commissioned personnel identified as eligible.*
Note b. *Non-commissioned and other ranks multi clasp only or non-Waziristan 1919 single clasp.*
Note c. *India August 1914. Mesopotamia November 1914 captured Kut al Amara 29th April 1916.*
Note d. *Composite battalion of recovered wounded and drafts of Norfolks and Dorsets formed February 1916 while main battalion besieged – The Norsets. 2nd Battalion reformed July 1917. India November 1919 to November 1920 thence Iraq.*
Note e. *Medals named in impressed capitals: 'NORF. R.'*

Single Clasp	No. Identified	Rarity
Afghanistan N.W.F. 1919[3]	8	Of the Utmost Rarity

Mahsud 1919–20[5]	0	None Identified
Waziristan 1919–21[4]	Bn. Strength	Not Rare
Waziristan 1921–24[6]	1	According to the roll as seen, can be considered Unique
Combination Clasps	*No. Identified*	*Rarity*
Afghanistan N.W.F. 1919[3] Mahsud 1919–20[5] Waziristan 1919–21[4]	1	According to the roll as seen, can be considered Unique
Waziristan 1919–21[4] North West Frontier 1930–31[9]	2	Of the Utmost Rarity

Lieutenant Colonels: ~ W F L Gordon[4]

Majors: ~ F de W Harman[4]

Captains: ~ A C E Daniel[3] attch. 2/4 Border, R T Frere[4], E T Horner[4], E W Montgomerie[4], G N Paget[4], A J Shakeshaft[4] & J C Turner[3] attch. 1 S Lanc

Lieutenants: ~ S F Allen[3], J C Bowstead[4], J A Brawn[3] attch. 1/66 Punjabis, IA, F M E D Briscoe[4], H M Burton[4], T Campbell[4], C M Clode[4&9(Capt.)], S J Cozens[3] attch. 1 Yorkshire, F L Cubitt[4], F S H Farmer[3] attch. 17 SSB, (QM) J Haggar[4], B C King[4], C J D Maiden[3] attch. 2/6 Sussex, H C Mead[4], G A Mitchell[4], H L Peacocke[4], E C Prattley[4], G C Shorne[4], J N Sinclair[3] attch. Light Lorry Sect RASC, E W Sisson[4], T J C Weir[4], G P St. de Wilton[4&9(Capt.)], G H Winter[4] & E J Woolsey[3,4&5] attch. 1 DWR

Lance Corporals/Privates: ~ 3589806 A Sparkes[6]

~ 7th (Service) Bn, The Norfolk Regiment ~

Note a.   *Roll of all personnel identified as eligible.*

Note b.   *Formed August 1914. United Kingdom thence France & Flanders May 1915 forward.*

Note c.   *Medals named in impressed capitals: 'NORF. R.'*

Single Clasp	*No. Identified*	*Rarity*
Afghanistan N.W.F. 1919[3]	1	According to the roll as seen, can be considered Unique
Mahsud 1919–20[5]	0	None Identified
Waziristan 1919– 21[4]	0	None Identified
Waziristan 1921– 24[6]	0	None Identified

Captains: ~ B O F de C Fisher[3] attch. 1/25 London

~ 9th (Service) Bn, The Norfolk Regiment ~

Note a.   *Roll of all personnel identified as eligible.*

Note b.   *Formed September 1914. United Kingdom thence France & Flanders August 1915 forward.*

Note c.   *Medals named in impressed capitals: 'NORF. R.'*

Single Clasp	*No. Identified*	*Rarity*
Afghanistan N.W.F. 1919[3]	1	According to the roll as seen, can be considered Unique
Mahsud 1919–20[5]	0	None Identified
Waziristan 1919–21[4]	0	None Identified
Waziristan 1921–24[6]	0	None Identified

Lieutenants: ~ H R Glover[3] attch. 1/5 Hampshire, (Originally 27th Canadian Infantry)

~ 1st Garrison Bn, The Norfolk Regiment ~

Note a.   *Roll of all personnel identified as eligible.*
Note b.   *Formed September 1915. India December 1915 forward.*
Note c.   *Medals named in impressed capitals: 'NORF. R.'*

Single Clasp	No. Identified	Rarity
Afghanistan N.W.F. 1919[3]	93	Rare
Mahsud 1919–20[5]	1	According to the roll as seen, can be considered Unique
Waziristan 1919–21[4]	0	None Identified
Waziristan 1921–24[6]	0	None Identified
Combination Clasps	**No. Identified**	**Rarity**
Afghanistan N.W.F. 1919[3] Mahsud 1919–20[5] Waziristan 1919–21[4]	1	According to the roll as seen, can be considered Unique
Afghanistan N.W.F. 1919[3] Waziristan 1919–21[4]	2	Of the Utmost Rarity
Waziristan 1919–21[4] Waziristan 1921–24[6]	3	Of the Utmost Rarity
Waziristan 1919–21[4] North West Frontier 1930–31[9]	1	According to the roll as seen, can be considered Unique
Waziristan 1919–21[4] Waziristan 1921–24[6] North West Frontier 1930–31[9]	1	According to the roll as seen, can be considered Unique

Majors: ~ F R Day[3,4&] & R A Downs[3] DAAG, 2 Div.

Lieutenants: ~ L P Clarke[3] attch. 222 Coy, MGC

Company Quartermaster Sergeants/Staff Sergeants/Colour Sergeants: ~ 15111 W A Craske[3] attch. 1/1 Kent

Quartermaster Sergeants/Sergeants: ~ (Act) 26090 I S Burton[3] attch. 1/1 Kent, 7803 W Greengrass[3] attch. 1 DWR, 23028 D N Maconie[3] attch. S&TC, (Act) 8040 W H Morris[3], (Act) 8877 E V Morter[3] attch. 1 DWR, (Act) 72718 A A V Payne[3] attch. 2 Som LI, 8359 A A Raynsford[3] attch. 1 DWR, (Act) 21954 H A Small[3] attch. S&TC, (5764317) 10550 H J Stroud[3&4], (Act) 3/7825 A D Waterfield[3] attch. 46 BSS, (Act) 23128 T Wicks[3] attch. 1/1 Kent & (Act) 7285 W J Wilson[3] attch. HQ, 16 Div.

Lance Sergeants/Corporals: ~ 7840 S H Chapman[3] attch. 3/W Sig Sqn & 18473 C Moore[3] attch. 1/1 Kent

Lance Corporals/Privates: ~ 8418 A S Ansell[3] attch. 2 Som LI, 18881 G E Baines[3] attch. 1/1 Kent, 19335 W Baker[3] attch. 1/1 Kent, 30371 F W W Barber[3] attch. 2 Som LI, 8325 J D Barber[3] attch. 1 DWR, 10196 B Beales[3] attch. 1 DWR, 20066 G W Beales[3] attch. 1/1 Kent, 22092 F Beech[3] attch. 17 SSB, 7167 C A Bird[3] attch. 2 Som LI, 22512 P O Bramble[3] attch. 1 DWR, 19600 J Briggs[3] attch. 1 DWR, 28425 H Burling[3] attch. 2 Som LI, 72074 E H Cannings[4&6(RA)], 30101 W J Carpenter[3] attch. 36 DSC, 20202 W R Castleton[3] attch. 2 N Stafford, (5765062) 72538 C J Cleary[4,6&(9 Sgln. R Sigs)] attch. 'F' DSC, 43584 W F Clutton[3] attch. 1/1 Kent, 8019 W H Coburn[3] attch. 2 Som LI, (5764571) 72005 C Cooke[4&9(2 SS)], 26598 B J Cooper[3] attch. 2 Som LI, 72513 W G Dean[5] attch. HQ, Derajat Col, 20297 G R Denny[3] attch. 17 SSB, 7692 W Downes[3] attch. 1 DWR, 22619 A A Driver[3] attch. 2 Som LI, 7382 R Ducker[3] attch. ITD, 8922 C H Edge[3] attch. 17 SSB, 22465 G J Fabian[3] attch. 1/1 Kent, 29034 G Farnham[3] attch. 2 Som LI, 26989 W E Firman[3] attch. 1/1 Kent, 4815 C I Fisher[3] attch. 1 DWR, 72763 R H Fisher[3] attch. DFD, 31091 H J Forster[3] attch. 1/1 Kent, 7506 L C Fox[3] attch. 1 DWR, 21894 O R Game[3] attch. 1/1 Kent, 7281 S A George[3&4] attch. 2 Som LI, 72748 B Gess[3] attch. IOD, 3/7894 R B Greensides[3] attch. 36 DSC, 29040 H R Hall[3] attch. 1/1 Kent, 26019 H M Harmer[3] attch. 1/1 Kent, 22915 H L W Hayne[3] attch. 1 DWR, 8333 A G Hendra[3] attch. 1 DWR, 20173 C J Holman[3] attch. 2 N Stafford, 7497 F G Hood[3] attch. 1 DWR, 3/7898 J Horner[3], 22949 G V Jay[3] attch. 17 SSB, 22722 R Jermyn[3] attch. 2 Som LI, 30389 W Jermyn[3] attch. 2 Som LI, 35304 L John[3] attch. 2 Som LI, 28385 A T Joyce[3] attch. 2 Som LI, 26046 E W Kennedy[3] attch. 15 SSB, E D Kentish[3] attch. 14 PMC, 5811 J King[3] attch. 1 DWR, 26075 J Knights[3] attch. 2 N Stafford, 30220 H G Leak[3] attch. 17 SSB, 18885 J Leaman[3] attch. 2 N Stafford, 7632 F G Ling[3] attch. 1 DWR, 26084 T Lovick[3] attch. 1/1 Kent, 26682 J Lundy[3] attch. 1 DWR, 20395 E Mann[3] attch. 2 Som LI, 30341 G A G Meffan[3] attch. 1 DWR, 5763471 E J Misson[4&6(Suffolk)] attch. DFD, 26723 W C Murton[3] attch. 2 Som LI, 8375 G R Nobes[3] attch. 1 DWR, 7716 G E Osborne[3] attch. 1 DWR, 31078 A E Palmer[3] attch. 17 SSB, 3/7921 L W Read[3], 31114 W R Riley[3] attch. 1/1 Kent, 738083 R R Rowland[4&6(Suffolk)] attch. HQ, Waz Dist, 31032 A H Salton[3] attch. 1/1 Kent, 25332 H Savory[3] attch. 17 SSB, 29003 A J Selway[3] attch. HQ, KKF, 7522 F J Skipper[3] attch. 1 DWR, 19446 T E Smith[3] attch. 1/1 Kent, 7630 H A Stien[3] attch. ITD, 7122 W E Stolworthy[3] attch. 1 DWR, 26077 H A Strickland[3] attch. 2 N Stafford, 28320 S Summers[3] attch. 2 Som LI, 27237 A Tavley[3] attch. 2 Som LI, 8383 H O Thompson[3] attch. 36 DSC, 21315 P C Walsh[3] attch. 1 DWR, 9595 W Waller[3] attch. 2 Som LI, 7337 A Whitwood[3] attch. 1 DWR, 33756 J Windle[3] attch. 2 Som LI & 27257 H Yaxley[3] attch. 1 DWR (A Supplementary roll shows Yaxley as being attch. 2 Somerset LI)

~ 2nd Bn, The Lincolnshire Regiment ~

Note a.   Roll of all personnel identified as eligible.
Note b.   Bermuda August 1914. France & Flanders November 1914 thence India November 1919 to 1924.
Note c.   Medals named in impressed capitals: 'LINC. R.'

Single Clasp	No. Identified	Rarity
Afghanistan N.W.F. 1919[3]	0	None Identified
Mahsud 1919–20[5]	0	None Identified
Waziristan 1919–21[4]	2	Of the Utmost Rarity
Waziristan 1921–24[6]	1	According to the roll as seen, can be considered Unique
Combination Clasps	No. Identified	Rarity
Waziristan 1919–21[4] Waziristan 1921–24[6]	3	Of the Utmost Rarity
Waziristan 1919–21[4] North West Frontier 1930–31[9]	1	According to the roll as seen, can be considered Unique

Captains: ~ O Jackson[4] attch. RE, A E J Miller[4] attch. MWS Eng Pk Mari Indus and Kalabagh, R H Neale[6] attch. 'C' DSC & G C Winckley[4&9(R. Sigs)]
Quartermaster Sergeants/Sergeants: ~ (Act) (9603) 4794522 H M Beaumont[4&6(RA)] attch. 11 Pk Bty, RGA & 4793526 F E Hodgson[4&6] attch. RASC
Lance Corporals/Privates: ~ 4793132 C G Lynham[4&6] attch. 'B' Corps Sigs

~ 4th Bn, The Lincolnshire Regiment, Territorial Force ~

Note a.   Roll of all personnel identified as eligible.
Note b.   1/4th and 2/4th Battalions both disembodied in France 1918!
Note c.   Medals named in impressed capitals: 'LINC. R.'

Single Clasp	No. Identified	Rarity
Afghanistan N.W.F. 1919[3]	1	According to the roll as seen, can be considered Unique
Mahsud 1919–20[5]	0	None Identified
Waziristan 1919–21[4]	0	None Identified
Waziristan 1921–24[6]	0	None Identified

Lieutenants: ~ G Guyton[3] attch. 2 King's

~ 1st Garrison Bn, The Lincolnshire Regiment ~

Note a.   Roll of all personnel identified as eligible.
Note b.   Formed September 1915. India October 1915 forward.
Note c.   Medals named in impressed capitals: 'LINC. R.'

Single Clasp	No. Identified	Rarity
Afghanistan N.W.F. 1919[3]	12	Extremely Rare
Mahsud 1919–20[5]	0	None Identified.

Waziristan 1919–21[4]	0	None Identified
Waziristan 1921–24[6]	0	None Identified

Lieutenants: ~ E W Reed[3] attch. 1 Yorkshire

Quartermaster Sergeants / Sergeants: ~ 19636 L Athersmith[3] attch. S&TC, 65055 H Campion[3] attch. S&TC, (Act) 32415 R Green[3] attch. 1 MT Coy & (Act) 20131 E Madder[3] 7 IGH, DIK

Lance Sergeants / Corporals: ~ 19635 W P Arnold[3]

Lance Corporals / Privates: ~ 32478 J Carruthers[3] attch. 1 Div. Sply Coy, S&TC, 32479 J H Carry[3] attch. ITD, 64081 W Cutter[3] attch. S&TC, 32378 A Fleming[3] attch. 35 BGH, Peshawar, 19900 S Harris[3] attch. 4 IFA & 32491 C Liggett[3] attch. 6 MT Coy, S&TC

~ 2nd Bn, The Devonshire Regiment ~

Note a. *Roll of all personnel identified as eligible.*

Note b. *Egypt August 1914. France & Flanders November 1914 forward. Battalion virtually annihilated in May 1918 during the Battle of the Aisne. Reformed and posted India from September 1919 forward.*

Note c. *Medals named in impressed capitals: 'DEVON. R.'*

Single Clasp	No. Identified	Rarity
Afghanistan N.W.F. 1919[3]	11	Extremely Rare
Mahsud 1919–20[5]	0	None Identified
Waziristan 1919–21[4]	22	Very Rare
Waziristan 1921–24[6]	8	Of the Utmost Rarity
Combination Clasps	**No. Identified**	**Rarity**
Afghanistan N.W.F. 1919[3] Waziristan 1921–24[6]	1	According to the roll as seen, can be considered Unique
Waziristan 1919–21[4] Waziristan 1921–24[6]	5	Of the Utmost Rarity
Waziristan 1919–21[4] Waziristan 1921–24[6] North West Frontier 1930–31[9]	1	According to the roll as seen, can be considered Unique
Waziristan 1921–24[6] North West Frontier 1930–31[9]	1	According to the roll as seen, can be considered Unique
Waziristan 1921–24[6] North West Frontier 1930–31[9] Mohmand 1933[11]	1	According to the roll as seen, can be considered Unique

Lieutenants: ~ R E A G Badger[4] attch. 2/1 GR, IA, L W Bristowe[4&6(MGC)] & D E Elford[3] attch. 281 Coy, MGC

Warrant Officers Class I: ~ (Act Rly Tpt Sgt. Maj.) 5609722 S E Doney[4&6] & 5431197 F W Thornback[4]

Warrant Officers Class II: ~ 5608063 C Featherstone[6] attch. RTO, Bannu

Company Quartermaster Sergeants/Staff Sergeants/Colour Sergeants: ~ 5610501 P J Ware[4] attch. IAOC

Quartermaster Sergeants/Sergeants: ~ 5610529 J Barnes[4&6] attch. 'C' DSC, 5609770 W Craigie[4], (Act) 5609097 W Greedy[4] attch. CMSC, 5610548 L C Hillard[4] attch. 'A' DSC, 5608734 W Lee[4], 5763177 H J Newstead[3&6] attch. 'B' DSC (Was originally Norfolk Regt.), 5608496 W Pearce[4] & (Act) 5430402 W J Roberts[4] attch. 8 Bde.

Lance Sergeants/Corporals: ~ 5610124 J Bennett[6,(9&11Sgt. R Sigs)], 3271 C C Caynes[3] attch. 1/25 London, 5608956 J Cole[6], 5609816 G Hulland[4], 5608817 J E T Ivy[6&9 Sgt. R Sigs], 5609456 A W Lydamore[6], 5609548 G H Norman[6], 5609482 A W Phillips[6], 5430003 R Smyth[4,6&9] attch. 21 Bde., 5609017 D J Urquhart[6], 5609220 E L West[6] attch. 'B' DSC & (54977) 7809370 S E Weston[3] attch. 222 Coy, MGC

Lance Corporals/Privates: ~ 5609720 H J Butcher[4] attch. 42 ISS, 76790 C B Comber[3] attch. HQ, Peshawar, 5608811 W E C Goss[4], 76753 E E Hodge[3] attch. 2 Som LI, (5608287) 9980 D J Johnson[4] attch. IOD, 5609040 G F Lane[4] attch. 42 ISS, 5608951 H E Latham[4] attch. 42 ISS, (5610506) 02263 W J Ley[3] attch. 1/25 London, 01267 E Mallon[3] attch. 2 N Stafford, 5430409 W H Martin[4&6] attch. 'F' DSC, 5610140 R Middleton[4] attch. 52 FA, 5610068 H M Mills[4] attch. 42 SS, 5610167 W Norman[4] attch. 42 ISS, 5609835 W J Piper[4] attch. HQ, 10 Bde., 5609672 H F Pope[6] attch. RTE, 5429475 H Salter[4&6],

5608225 J T Sillince[3] attch. IOC, (5609708) 01327 R W Skelly[3] attch. 17 SSB, 5608492 E Stockwin[4] attch. IGH, Tank, 0150 W H Stokes[3] attch. ACC, 5610517 F H Stone[4], 01268 A J Tucker[3] attch. 1 S Lanc & (0966) 5609386 T Wollacott[4] attch. WFF

~ 3rd (Reserve) Bn, The Devonshire Regiment ~

Note a.   Roll of all personnel identified as eligible.
Note b.   United Kingdom August 1914 forward providing drafts and reinforcements.
Note c.   Medals named in impressed capitals: 'DEVON. R.'

Single Clasp	No. Identified	Rarity
Afghanistan N.W.F. 1919[3]	2	Of the Utmost Rarity
Mahsud 1919–20[5]	0	None Identified
Waziristan 1919–21[4]	1	According to the roll as seen, can be considered Unique
Waziristan 1921–24[6]	0	None Identified

Lieutenants: ~ D R Lysaght[3] attch. 1/25 London & L G White[3] attch. 1 DWR
Lance Corporals/Privates: ~ 3/7100 E Beazley[4] attch. 40 DSC

~ 1/4th Bn, The Devonshire Regiment, Territorial Force ~

Note a.   Roll of all personnel identified as eligible.
Note b.   United Kingdom August 1914. India November 1914, Mesopotamia March 1916 forward.
Note c.   Medals named in impressed capitals: 'DEVON. R.'

Single Clasp	No. Identified	Rarity
Afghanistan N.W.F. 1919[3]	154	Scarce
Mahsud 1919–20[5]	0	None Identified
Waziristan 1919–21[4]	0	None Identified
Waziristan 1921–24[6]	0	None Identified

Majors: ~ (Temp) A L M Lefroy[3] ADRTE
Lieutenants: ~ A M Scales[3] attch. 2/6 Sussex
Warrant Officers Class II: ~ 290164 F J Serle[3] attch. 1/25 London
Quartermaster Sergeants/Sergeants: ~ (Act) 200512 G Carter[3] attch. 1/25 London, 200239 A Dark[3] attch. 2 Som LI, 200183 R T Dart[3] attch. 1 S Lanc, 200095 T Earles[3] attch. 2 Som LI, 200028 C H Farrant[3] attch. 1 S Lanc, (Act) 200170 L G Hearn[3], (Act) 200408 H G Hillman[3] attch. 1/25 London, (Act) 202585 W H C Hobbs[3] attch. 1 S Lanc, 202588 F H Holman[3] attch. 2 Som LI, 202602 A G McPherson[3] attch. 17 SSB, 9436 F Ovey[3] attch. 2 Som LI, 200269 R J Stark[3] attch. 2 Som LI & (Act) 201467 E Trowbridge[3] attch. 1/25 London
Lance Sergeants/Corporals: ~ 200934 W Aldridge[3] attch. 2 Som LI, 200640 H Allen[3] attch. 2 Som LI, (Act) 201047 H C Blackmore[3] attch. 1 S Lanc, 290098 L C Chanter[3] attch. 1 S Lanc, (From 7th Cyclist Bn), 200198 E Connett[3] attch. 2 Som LI, 201061 J Coombes[3] attch. 1 S Lanc, 205954 W F Lewis[3] attch. 1/25 London, 200395 W Mansfield[3] attch. 2 Som LI, 200912 A Maxwell[3] attch. 2 Som LI, 200158 R W Mayers[3] attch. 2 Som LI, 200810 L Strong[3] attch. 1 S Lanc & 201227 D Wakeley[3] attch. 39 DSC
Lance Corporals/Privates: ~ 202530 F Adams[3] attch. 2 Som LI, 201772 F W Allen[3] attch. 17 SSB, 202617 G Anning[3] attch. 2 Som LI, 200128 E N Anniss[3] attch. 1 S Lanc, 202971 E T Arnold[3] attch. 4 ACS, 202369 D J A T Atkinson[3] attch. 17 SSB, 201583 B Baker[3] attch. 17 SSB, 200671 F L Baker[3] attch. 17 SSB, 200402 W Baker[3] attch. 2 Som LI, 201440 W Ball[3] attch. 1 S Lanc, 201337 W J Banting[3] attch. 1 S Lanc, 201277 J Barrett[3] attch. 2 Som LI, 200926 G Bastin[3] attch. 2 Som LI, 201074 T Beach[3] attch. 2 Som LI, 200167 P Beer[3] attch. 1 S Lanc, 202901 A Bishop[3] attch. 2 Som LI, 200157 F Boater[3] attch. 2 Som LI, 202633 A M Bonner[3] attch. 2 Som LI, 200195 R Braddon[3] attch. 2 Som LI, 200006 R G Braund[3] attch. 1 S Lanc, 200451 W Broome[3] attch. 2 N Stafford, 200415 W R Bruce[3] attch. 2 Som LI, 202943 F Burgoyne[3] attch. 2 Som LI, 201446 F Carter[3] attch. 1 S Lanc, 202872 H Chudleigh[3] attch. 2 Som LI, 201042 C Clarke[3] attch. 1 S Lanc, 202551 H J Clarke[3] attch. 2 N Stafford, 200878 J H Clarke[3] attch. 2 Som LI, 200947 J A L Conant[3] attch. 1 S Lanc, 200505 H F Copp[3] attch. ISC, 200862 H J W Court[3] attch. 1 S Lanc, 201675 E Cruse[3] attch. 17 SSB, 200837 L G Curtis[3] attch. 1/25 London,

200651 W Davis[3] attch. 2 Som LI, 201106 A Dimon[3] attch. 2 Som LI, 202710 W Doddridge[3] attch. 1 S Lanc, 201625 P R Dyble[3] attch. 1 S Lanc, 200768 E M Easton[3] attch. 17 SSB, 200501 E J Edwards[3] attch. 2 Som LI, 200535 F Emmett[3] attch. 1 S Lanc, 203760 G Ferridge[3] attch. 2 Som LI, 200995 M A Futcher[3] attch. 1 S Lanc, 200237 J Gibbings[3] attch. 1 S Lanc, 200216 L Gigg[3] attch. 2 Som LI, 200502 A F Glanville[3] attch. 17 SSB, 200495 F A Godsland[3] attch. 1 S Lanc, 202578 A W Graham[3] attch. 10 IMVS, 203962 J Green[3] attch. 2 Som LI, 201258 W Gush[3] attch. 2 Som LI, 203934 G Hadley[3] attch. 2 Som LI, 206005 H Halesworth[3] attch. 5 MT Coy, S&TC, 203106 W Hamlin[3] attch. 2 Som LI, 201823 E R Hart[3] attch. 17 SSB, 201726 S C Havill[3] attch. 17 SSB, 200421 A Hawkins[3] attch. 2 N Stafford, 200561 J Hayman[3] attch. 2 Som LI, 201566 W Heal[3] attch. 2 Som LI, 200732 M Henley[3] attch. 2 Som LI, 265081 C Hicks[3] attch. 1 S Lanc, 200187 C Hosegrove[3] attch. 2 Som LI, 266101 F Howard[3] attch. 2 N Stafford, 200925 H Hurd[3] attch. 2 Som LI, 200196 F Hutchings[3] attch. 1 S Lanc, 201275 J D Hutchings[3] attch. 2 N Stafford, 200366 R S Hyne[3] attch. 1 S Lanc, 202888 S Jago[3] attch. 2 Som LI, 203116 H Lewis[3] attch. 2 Som LI, 203792 W Lewis[3] attch. 2 Som LI, 202924 A Liversedge[3] attch. 2 Som LI, 200478 J Lonsdale[3] attch. 1/25 London, 202850 W Moore[3] attch. 2 Som LI, 200351 F Morgan[3] attch. 2 Som LI, 205447 F Morgan[3] attch. 2 Som LI, 202607 W Norman[3] attch. 2 Som LI, 202283 H Owen[3] attch. 2 Som LI, 201574 C A Pannell[3], 200909 W Parker[3] attch. 1/25 London, 201018 F Parsons[3] attch. 2 Som LI, 202611 C Pearce[3] attch. 2 Som LI, 200178 F Philliot[3] attch. 1 S Lanc, 200571 H Pickard[3] attch. 2 Som LI, 201782 R J Pomroy[3] attch. 17 SSB, 201492 R F Rennell[3] attch. 17 SSB, 203809 L A Rhodes[3] attch. 17 SSB, 201466 W Rice[3] attch. 2 Som LI, 203810 A E Ridgeon[3] attch. 1 S Lanc, 200213 A J Ridgeway[3] attch. 2 Som LI, 201192 T Richards[3] attch. 2 Som LI, 200860 B Rowe[3] attch. 1 S Lanc, 200078 C Rowland[3] attch. 2 Som LI, 201182 C Salter[3] attch. 2 Som LI, 200270 J Salway[3] attch. 2 Som LI, 200850 H T Sellick[3] attch. 2 Som LI, 201024 E J Skewers[3] attch. 1 S Lanc, 201423 H Smith[3] attch. 2 Som LI, 201019 J Spiller[3] attch. 2 Som LI, 202236 R B Spiller[3] attch. RE Sigs, 200192 F Start[3] attch. 2 Som LI, 201230 R Start[3] attch. 2 Som LI, 202948 W H Stephens[3] attch. 1 S Lanc, 200436 F Stone[3] attch. 2 Som LI, 200426 C Strong[3] attch. 2 Som LI, 202289 A Taylor[3] attch. 2 Som LI, 200570 W J Thomas[3] attch. 1 S Lanc, 201620 A Thorne[3] attch. 2 Som LI, 202633 S Thorpe[3] attch. 2 Som LI, 201369 I M Tonkins[3] attch. 2 Som LI, 201835 W F Tooze[3] attch. 2 Som LI, 01268 A J Tucker[3] attch. 2 N Stafford, 201394 E Tucker[3] attch. 1 S Lanc, 202916 H Tucker[3] attch. 1 S Lanc, 203743 C W Waldron[3] attch. 2 Som LI, 200254 E R W(h)alley[3] attch. 1 S Lanc, 201202 T Ware[3] attch. 1 S Lanc, 201622 J Warren[3], 201119 R Wattley[3] attch. 2 Som LI, 200249 C C Webber[3] attch. 1 S Lanc, 200318 W White[3] attch. 2 Som LI, 202644 G Wilcox[3] attch. 2 Som LI, 200668 F G Williams[3] attch. 9 MT Coy, S&TC, 200398 F Wills[3] attch. 2 Som LI, 201053 S Woodley[3] attch. 2 Som LI, 201482 C Wright[3] attch. 2 Som LI, 201427 G Youldon[3] attch. 2 Som LI & 200419 M Yeatman[3] attch. 2 Som LI

Buglers: ~ 200205 E Gillard[3] attch. 2 Som LI

~ 2/4ᵗʰ Bn, The Devonshire Regiment, Territorial Force ~

Note a.   *Roll of all personnel identified as eligible.*

Note b.   *Formed September 1914. India January 1915, Egypt October 1917 forward. Battalion disbanded in Egypt 17ᵗʰ August, 1918 and consequently I am at a loss as to why the roll refers to recipients from this battalion! The probable explanation is that prior to the disbandment of the battalion the recipients below were attached to the Indian Signal Corps and were still serving as such in 1919.*

Note c.   *Medals named in impressed capitals: 'DEVON. R.'*

Single Clasp	No. Identified	Rarity
Afghanistan N.W.F. 1919[3]	6	Of the Utmost Rarity
Mahsud 1919–20[5]	0	None Identified
Waziristan 1919–21[4]	0	None Identified
Waziristan 1921–24[6]	0	None Identified

Quartermaster Sergeants/Sergeants: ~ 200413 L C Dedman[3] attch. 3/W Sig Sqn & (Act) 201109 F Forsey[3] attch. 39 DSC

Lance Sergeants/Corporals: ~ 200782 P N Thomas[3] attch. 39 DSC, 201213 W E Upjohn[3] attch. 44 DSC, KKF & 200951 R L Waters[3] attch. 1 MT Coy, S&TC

Lance Corporals/Privates: ~ 201310 A R Lock[3] attch. 44 DSC, KKF

~ 1/5th (Prince Of Wales's) Bn, The Devonshire Regiment, Territorial Force ~

Note a.   *Roll of all personnel identified as eligible.*
Note b.   *United Kingdom August 1914. India November 1914, April 1917 Egypt, France & Flanders June 1918 forward.*
Note c.   *Medals named in impressed capitals: 'DEVON. R.'*

Single Clasp	No. Identified	Rarity
Afghanistan N.W.F. 1919[3]	3	Of the Utmost Rarity
Mahsud 1919–20[5]	0	None Identified
Waziristan 1919–21[4]	0	None Identified
Waziristan 1921–24[6]	0	None Identified
Combination Clasps	No. Identified	Rarity
Afghanistan N.W.F. 1919[3] Waziristan 1919–21[4]	1	According to the roll as seen, can be considered Unique

Company Quartermaster Sergeants/Staff Sergeants/Colour Sergeants: ~ 240254 A Grad[3] attch. 44 DSC, KKF
Quartermaster Sergeants/Sergeants: ~ 240643 H Tucker[3&4] attch. 43 BGH, Quetta
Lance Corporals/Privates: ~ 240723 F Hardisty[3] attch. 3/W Sig Sqn & 240237 W G Pearce[3] attch. 3/W Sig Sqn

~ 1/6th Bn, The Devonshire Regiment, Territorial Force ~

Note a.   *Roll of all personnel identified as eligible.*
Note b.   *United Kingdom August 1914. India November 1914, Mesopotamia January 1916 forward.*
Note c.   *Medals named in impressed capitals: 'DEVON. R.'*

Single Clasp	No. Identified	Rarity
Afghanistan N.W.F. 1919[3]	128	Very Scarce
Mahsud 1919–20[5]	0	None Identified
Waziristan 1919–21[4]	0	None Identified
Waziristan 1921–24[6]	0	None Identified

Lieutenants: ~ L C Jenkins[3]
Quartermaster Sergeants/Sergeants: ~ 266098 M A Arthur[3] attch. 1/25 London, 265064 S Bowden[3] attch. 1/25 London, 265025 E Clark[3], 267726 C Coniam[3] attch. 1/25 London, (Act) 265160 W M Dennis[3] attch. HQ, Peshawar, 267065 F J Gray[3] attch. 1/25 London, 268171 F G Hill[3] attch. 1/25 London, (Act) 266687 W H Kellaway[3] attch. 17 SSB, 265417 A T Newcombe[3] attch. 1/25 London, (Act) 266043 P A Norman[3] attch. 2 MT Coy, S&TC, (Act) 265354 H J Peardon[3] attch. 2 (Armd Train) SSB, (Act) 267331 T Pickford[3] attch. 1/1 Kent, (Act) 265869 P Willis[3] attch. HQ, Peshawar & (Act) 266954 A C Willmott[3] attch. 12 SSB
Lance Sergeants/Corporals: ~ (Act) 258253 E E Hungstone[3] attch. 1/25 London, (Act) 268245 H J Mayne[3] attch. 1/25 London, (Act) 266381 S H Oliver[3] attch. HQ, Peshawar & (Act) 267858 W T Whitehead[3] attch. 1/25 London
Lance Corporals/Privates: ~ 267744 L H Adams[3] attch. 1/25 London, 265662 W Balment[3] attch. 1/25 London, 265798 J H Bament[3] attch. 1/25 London, 267075 S Barnett[3] attch. 1/25 London, 265695 R Bartholomew[3] attch. 1/25 London, 266230 F C Beer[3] attch. 1/25 London, 265431 L Beer[3] attch. 1/25 London, 15985 E J Bowden[3] attch. 17 SSB, 20240 J H Bowden[3] attch. 1/25 London, 265457 H Burgess[3] attch. 1/25 London, 265523 T G Burrow[3] attch. 1/25 London, 265234 J Carder[3] attch. 1/25 London, 256748 C E Cawsey[3] attch. 1/25 London, (Originally 5th Bn), 265380 F W Chapple[3] attch. 1/25 London, 267754 J R Charlick[3] attch. 1/25 London, 33120 S G Cheffers[3] attch. 1/25 London, 266921 W A Child[3] attch. 1/25 London, 267058 W Chislett[3] attch. 1/25 London, 66573 J Chumley[3] attch. 1/25 London, (268344) 01644 G C Churchward[3] attch. 1/25 London, 265712 T J Cockram[3] attch. 1/25 London, 203733 W H Coles[3] attch. 2 Som LI, (Originally 4th Bn), 267081 B E Collins[3] attch. 1/25 London, 265973 T H Colliver[3] attch. 1/25 London, 267407 G R Coombe[3] attch. 17 SSB, 268266 A G Cory[3] attch. 40 DSC, 240489 C E Cosgrove[3] attch. 1/25 London, (Originally 5th Bn), 268259 E E Costin[3] attch. 1/25 London, 266568 W H Cox[3] attch. 1/25 London, (267034) 01964 H C Crocker[3] attch. 1/25 London, (Originally 3/6th Bn), 266734 C Crook[3] attch. 17 SSB, 267260 S Cuthbertson[3] attch. 1/25 London, 267871 W C Daniel[3] attch. 1/25 London, 267461 H Dash[3] attch. 17 SSB, 267504 (S) A Defren[3] attch. 1/25 London, 12571 J Doe[3] attch. 1/25 London, 267762 C H Dyer[3] attch. 1/25 London, 266522 J Eastman[3] attch. 1/25 London, 265954 E

Edwards[3] attch. 1/25 London, 267714 W J Field[3] attch. 1/25 London, 265575 D H Ford[3] attch. 1/25 London, 266014 L J B Fursman[3] attch. RE Sigs, 266654 W G Gidley[3] attch. 1/25 London, 268185 A G Hammett[3] attch. 1/25 London, 266248 F H Harding[3] attch. 1/25 London, 266515 F Harris[3] attch. 1/25 London, 290573 W H Hatherley[3] attch. 2 N Stafford, (Originally 7th Cyclist Bn), 268255 W T Haynes[3] attch. 1/25 London, 267719 F W Headon[3] attch. 1/25 London, 266534 R Heard[3] attch. 1/25 London, 267536 T Herrera[3] attch. 1/25 London, 268513 C Hooker[3] attch. 1/25 London, 267796 W H Jenkins[3] attch. 1/25 London, 268190 H Johns[3] attch. 1/25 London, 265425 R Johns[3] attch. 40 DSC, 265752 S Johns[3] attch. 1/25 London, 202661 W Jones[3] attch. 2 Som LI, 11108 W B Johns[3] attch. 1/25 London, 266627 P D Kingshott[3] attch. 1/25 London, 267805 A W Knapman[3] attch. 1/25 London, 266350 C Lane[3] attch. 1/25 London, 267589 F Legge[3] attch. 1/25 London, 266638 C Ley[3] attch. 1/25 London, 265487 F A Lile[3] attch. 1/25 London, 265445 W Lock[3] attch. 1/25 London, 265597 S Manning[3] attch. 1/25 London, 265505 R Marples[3] attch. 40 DSC, 266625 S Martin[3] attch. 1/25 London, 267943 R Maunder[3] attch. 1/25 London, 267345 A J May[3] attch. 1/25 London, 265170 C F May[3] attch. 1 S Lanc, 268388 E Metherall[3], 265297 F J Metters[3] attch. 1/25 London, 265665 P F Miles[3] attch. 1/25 London, 266341 W J L Millman[3] attch. 1/25 London, 268286 A J Mitchmore[3] attch. 1/25 London, 266601 H J Newcombe[3] attch. 1/25 London, 267315 F Newland[3] attch. 1/25 London, 265335 W H Norrish[3] attch. 17 SSB, 267362 S Passmore[3] attch. 1/25 London, 265770 W Passmore[3] attch. 1/25 London, 267708 H Pike[3] attch. 1/25 London, 265422 E Prouse[3] attch. 1/25 London, 267916 H Prowse[3] attch. 1/25 London, 266560 R Pugsley[3] attch. 1/25 London, 01328 S Rawle[3] attch. 17 SSB, 267917 E A Rhodes[3] attch. 1/25 London, 266324 S Rice[3] attch. 1/25 London, 266136 C E Rodd[3] attch. 1/25 London, 267921 J W Shillabeer[3] attch. 1/25 London, 266261 L G Short[3] attch. 1/25 London, 265245 S E Slee[3] attch. 1/25 London, 265263 W J Slee[3] attch. 1/25 London, 265558 C Spurway[3] attch. 1/25 London, 266579 R Spurway[3] attch. 1/25 London, 267343 A Stevenson[3] attch. 2 (Armd Train) SSB, 268234 E H Stott[3] attch. 1/25 London, 265807 G Taylor[3] attch. 1/25 London, 267042 W Thomas[3] attch. 1/25 London, 66580 F Townsend[3] attch. 1/25 London, 267840 C F Trick[3] attch. 1/25 London, 267953 B W Tucker[3] attch. 1/25 London, 265764 F Tucker[3] attch. 1/25 London, 267953 B W Turner[3] attch. 1/25 London, 267893 P Varcoe[3] attch. 1/25 London, 267929 C S Vogwell[3] attch. 1/25 London, 266930 M F Walsh[3] attch. 1/25 London, 267779 W J Wiffill[3] attch. 1/25 London & 265750 H Wrey[3] attch. 1/25 London

~ 2/6th Bn, The Devonshire Regiment, Territorial Force ~

Note a.   *Roll of all personnel identified as eligible.*

Note b.   *Formed September 1914. India January 1915, Mesopotamia September 1917 forward.*

Note c.   *Medals named in impressed capitals: 'DEVON. R.'*

Single Clasp	No. Identified	Rarity
Afghanistan N.W.F. 1919[3]	16	Extremely Rare
Mahsud 1919–20[5]	0	None Identified
Waziristan 1919–21[4]	0	None Identified
Waziristan 1921–24[6]	0	None Identified
Combination Clasps	No. Identified	Rarity
Afghanistan N.W.F. 1919[3] Waziristan 1919–21[4]	1	According to the roll as seen, can be considered Unique

Lieutenants: ~ N A Grose[3]

Quartermaster Sergeants/Sergeants: ~ (Act) 267456 E T Boon[3] attch. MAD & (Act) 266476 W L Cheffers[3] attch. 1/25 London

Lance Sergeants/Corporals: ~ 266323 H J Rice[3] attch. 1/25 London

Lance Corporals/Privates: ~ 268444 G H Blackmore[3] attch. 17 SSB, 266812 W T Bridle[3] attch. 17 SSB, 265731 J E Heal[3] attch. 3 SSB, 266809 F Hockin[3] attch. 17 SSB, 265460 M Jeffrey[3] attch. 3/W Sig Sqn, 267689 J Little[3] attch. 1 MT Coy, S&TC, 205917 A Lloyd[3] attch. 1/25 London, (Originally 4th Bn), 268388 E Metherell[3&4] attch. 2 N Stafford, 266785 W J Moore[3] attch. Dpty GOC Dept, Jamrud, 266156 A E Norman[3] attch. 17 SSB, 205483 G M Sturman[3] attch. 1/25 London, (Originally 4th Bn), 266810 A J Weeks[3] attch. 17 SSB & 265519 R A Whitaker[3] attch. 2 N Stafford

~ 3/6th Bn, The Devonshire Regiment, Territorial Force ~

Note a.   *Roll of all personnel identified as eligible.*
Note b.   *Formed March 1915. United Kingdom throughout Great War period.*
Note c.   *Medals named in impressed capitals: 'DEVON. R.'*

Single Clasp	No. Identified	Rarity
Afghanistan N.W.F. 1919[3]	1	According to the roll as seen, can be considered Unique
Mahsud 1919–20[5]	0	None Identified
Waziristan 1919–21[4]	0	None Identified
Waziristan 1921–24[6]	0	None Identified

Lance Corporals/Privates: ~ 267351 F J Pepall[3] attch. 17 SSB

~ Unidentified Bn, The Devonshire Regiment, Territorial Force ~

Note a.   *Roll of all personnel identified as eligible.*
Note b.   *Medals named in impressed capitals: 'DEVON. R.'*

Single Clasp	No. Identified	Rarity
Afghanistan N.W.F. 1919[3]	1	According to the roll as seen, can be considered Unique
Mahsud 1919–20[5]	0	None Identified
Waziristan 1919–21[4]	0	None Identified
Waziristan 1921–24[6]	0	None Identified

Captains: ~ G B Hole[3] attch. 1 DWR

~ 1st Bn, The Suffolk Regiment ~

Note a.   *Roll of all personnel identified as eligible.*
Note b.   *Sudan August 1914. France & Flanders January 1915, Egypt October 1915, Salonika November 1915 forward. India November 1919 to March 1924.*
Note c.   *Medals named in impressed capitals: 'SUFF. R.'*

Single Clasp	No. Identified	Rarity
Afghanistan N.W.F. 1919[3]	0	None Identified
Mahsud 1919–20[5]	0	None Identified
Waziristan 1919–21[4]	2	Of the Utmost Rarity
Waziristan 1921–24[6]	6	Of the Utmost Rarity
Combination Clasps	No. Identified	Rarity
Mahsud 1919–20[5] Waziristan 1919–21[4]	1	According to the roll as seen, can be considered Unique
Waziristan 1919–21[4] Waziristan 1921–24[6]	4	Of the Utmost Rarity
Waziristan 1921–24[6] Burma 1930–32[10]	1	According to the roll as seen, can be considered Unique

Majors: ~ P S Walker[4&5] attch. 2/5 GR, IA
Captains: ~ E Allen[4] attch. RTE
Lance Sergeants/Corporals: ~ 5820515 H J Steed[6&10(Sgt. R Sigs)] attch. 'B' DSC & 5820480 C C Twitchett[6] attch. 'D' DSC
Lance Corporals/Privates: ~ 5820221 C J M Clarke[6] attch. HQ, Waz Dist, (5819754) 10179 B Cohen[4&6] attch. HQ, Waz

Dist, (5819565) 9952 P W Huggins[4&6] attch. HQ, Waz Dist, 5820217 B Jarmyn[6] attch. Sply Depot, DIK, (5820461) 11485 S F Mayhew[4&6] attch. HQ, Waz Dist, 5820346 F W A Minns[6] attch. HQ, Waz Dist, 5820227 T G Newman[4] attch. 34 DSC, 5764857 B Powell[4&6] attch. HQ, Waz Dist, 5819925 F C Spraggins[6] attch. HQ, Waz Dist & 5819458 A Walker[6] attch. HQ, Waz Dist

~ 1/4ᵗʰ Bn, The Suffolk Regiment, Territorial Force ~

Note a. *Roll of all personnel identified as eligible.*
Note b. *United Kingdom August 1914. France & Flanders November 1914 forward.*
Note c. *Medals named in impressed capitals: 'SUFF. R.'*

Single Clasp	No. Identified	Rarity
Afghanistan N.W.F. 1919[3]	3	Of the Utmost Rarity
Mahsud 1919–20[5]	0	None Identified
Waziristan 1919–21[4]	1	According to the roll as seen, can be considered Unique
Waziristan 1921–24[6]	0	None Identified

Captains: ~ J G Frere[4] attch. 6 MMG Bty, MGC
Lieutenants: ~ K W Brown[3] attch. 5 LofC Sigs, L G Hayward[3] attch. 1/25 London, (Formally Royal Navy) & H R Scoggins[3]

~ 1/5ᵗʰ Bn, , The Suffolk Regiment, Territorial Force ~

Note a. *Roll of all personnel identified as eligible.*
Note b. *United Kingdom August 1914. Mudros, Imbros, Suvla Bay August 1915. Mudros thence Egypt December 1915 thence Palestine forward.*
Note c. *Medals named in impressed capitals: 'SUFF. R.'*

Single Clasp	No. Identified	Rarity
Afghanistan N.W.F. 1919[3]	1	According to the roll as seen, can be considered Unique
Mahsud 1919–20[5]	0	None Identified
Waziristan 1919–21[4]	0	None Identified
Waziristan 1921–24[6]	0	None Identified

Captains: ~ H Buck[3] Staff, 2 Bde.

~ ?/6ᵗʰ (Cyclist) Bn, The Suffolk Regiment, Territorial Force ~

Note a. *Roll of all personnel identified as eligible.*
Note b. *Medals named in impressed capitals: 'SUFF. R.'*

Single Clasp	No. Identified	Rarity
Afghanistan N.W.F. 1919[3]	1	According to the roll as seen, can be considered Unique.
Mahsud 1919–20[5]	0	None Identified
Waziristan 1919–21[4]	0	None Identified
Waziristan 1921–24[6]	0	None Identified

Majors: ~ M S Banks[3] attch. 287 Coy, MGC

~ Unidentified Service Bn, The Suffolk Regiment ~

Note a.   *Roll of all personnel identified as eligible.*
Note b.   *Medals named in impressed capitals: 'SUFF. R.'*

Single Clasp	No. Identified	Rarity
Afghanistan N.W.F. 1919[3]	1	According to the roll as seen, can be considered Unique
Mahsud 1919–20[5]	0	None Identified
Waziristan 1919–21[4]	0	None Identified
Waziristan 1921–24[6]	0	None Identified

Lieutenants: ~ J H Crisp[3]

~ 1st (Reserve) Garrison Bn, The Suffolk Regiment ~

Note a.   *Roll of all personnel identified as eligible.*
Note b.   *Formed March 1916. United Kingdom throughout Great War period.*
Note c.   *Medals named in impressed capitals: 'SUFF. R.'*

Single Clasp	No. Identified	Rarity
Afghanistan N.W.F. 1919[3]	1	According to the roll as seen, can be considered Unique
Mahsud 1919–20[5]	0	None Identified
Waziristan 1919–21[4]	0	None Identified
Waziristan 1921–24[6]	0	None Identified

Lieutenants: ~ W H Crutchley[3] attch. 1 DWR

~ 2nd Bn, The Prince Albert's (Somerset Light Infantry) ~

Note a.   *Roll of all commissioned personnel as identified.*
Note b.   *Non-commissioned and other ranks multi clasp only or non-Afghanistan 1919 single clasp.*
Note c.   *India August 1914 forward to October 1919 thence Palestine and Egypt returning to India December 1920 forward.*
Note d.   *Title changed to The Somerset Light Infantry (Prince Albert's) in 1920.*
Note e.   *Battle honour 'Third Afghan War 1919'.*
Note f.   *Medals named in impressed capitals: 'SOM. L. I.', '2/SOM. LT. INFY.' or '2 BN SOM. L.I.'*

Single Clasp	No. Identified	Rarity
Afghanistan N.W.F. 1919[3]	Bn. Strength	Not Rare.
Mahsud 1919–20[5]	0	None Identified.
Waziristan 1919–21[4]	2	Of the Utmost Rarity.
Waziristan 1921–24[6]	6	Of the Utmost Rarity.
Combination Clasps	No. Identified	Rarity
Afghanistan N.W.F. 1919[3] Mahsud 1919–20[5] Waziristan 1919–21[4] Waziristan 1921–24[6]	2	Of the Utmost Rarity.
Afghanistan N.W.F. 1919[3] Waziristan 1919–21[4]	8	Of the Utmost Rarity.
Afghanistan N.W.F. 1919[3] Waziristan 1921–24[6]	5	Of the Utmost Rarity.

Mahsud 1919–20[5] Waziristan 1919–21[4]	1	According to the roll as seen, can be considered Unique
Mahsud 1919–20[5] Waziristan 1919–21[4] Waziristan 1921–24[6]	1	According to the roll as seen, can be considered Unique
Waziristan 1919–21[4] Malabar 1921–22[7]	1	According to the roll as seen, can be considered Unique
Waziristan 1919–21[4] Waziristan 1921–24[6]	2	Of the Utmost Rarity

Lieutenant Colonels: ~ (Temp) E W Worrall[3]

Majors: ~ R J Lamb[3] attch. RTE, (Hon QM) D J Owens[3] & (Temp) W Roche[3] DA&AG, BFF

Captains: ~H H Broadmead[3] attch. 1 Yorkshire, H J Browne[3] attch. 1 Yorkshire, C W P Ludlow[3] attch. 1 Yorkshire, E O Milne[3] attch. 1/4 QORWK, C A Moat[3] attch. 1 Yorkshire, W Moger[3] attch. 1 Yorkshire, G N Molesworth[3], C R Spear[4&6] attch. 58 Rifles, IA, C A Williams[3] & (Act) N O Willis[3]

Lieutenants: ~ H B J Clarke[3], D H Cox[3], E G M Crocker[3], W Dowsett[3], W C Emery[3], J Galbraith[3], W H Jeffkins[3] attch. 1 Sussex, C W Jimby[3], O J Kind[3], F W Lias[3], D H G McCririck[3], G H Pratt[3], W J Ranger[3], F Seamark[3], A E Snow[3], J Woods[3] & S C G Young[3]

Warrant Officers Class II: ~ (Act) (01614) 5663846 W G Parrish[3&6] attch. Rest Camp, Tank

Company Quartermaster Sergeants/Staff Sergeants / Colour Sergeants: ~ (Act) 275019 D J Fryer[3&4(7 MT Coy, S&TC)]

Quartermaster Sergeants/Sergeants: ~ 5662970 H Andrews[4,5&6], attch. 'F' DSC, (Possibly Named To ISC), 5664755 A G Chivers[6] attch. 'B' DSC, 5119534 T M Crowther[6] attch. HQ, Waz Dist ICC, (5662101) 8277 A V Davey[3&4] attch. 'G' DSC, (5662087) 7752 G Harvey[3,4,5&6] attch. 'B' DSC, (5662111) 8418 W King[3&4], 5610528 F Perrett[3&6] attch. 'B' DSC, 34505 F H Robinson[3&4], 9333 J Salvidge[4] attch. S&TC, 5662097 A Scriven[6] attch. 'B' DSC, 5718294 H C Stainer[6] attch. 'G' DSC, 8121 E Ubank[3&4] attch. 11 MT Coy, S&TC & 19355 E D Webster[4] attch. S&TC

Lance Sergeants/Corporals: ~ 5662978 W Bull[4&6] attch. 'B' DSC, (5662089) 8014 F C Caines[3&6] attch. 'F' DSC, (Act) 5719534 F Crowther[4&5] attch. 43 Bde., 5676227 T C Walker[3&6] attch. 'G' DSC & 8490 E H Webb[3&4] attch. 40 DSC

Lance Corporals/Privates: ~ 5718075 C F Balne[6] attch. ISC, 8422 M Carney[3, (4&5 'F' Div. Sigs RE)&(6 R Sigs)], 5662103 R J Holland[6] attch. 'B' Corps Sigs, (5663845) 8813 C Preston[3&4], (5662291) 19970 S Spurgeon[3&6] attch. Rest Camp, Tank, 5719311 E H Thomas[4&7(Dorset)] & 25705 J Walker[3&4]

~ 1/4th Bn, The Prince Albert's (Somerset Light Infantry), Territorial Force ~

Note a. *Roll of all personnel identified as eligible.*

Note b. *United Kingdom August 1914. India November 1914, Mesopotamia January 1916 forward.*

Note c. *Medals named in impressed capitals: 'SOM L. I.', '1/4/SOM. LT. INFY.' or '1/4 BN SOM. L.I.'*

Single Clasp	No. Identified	Rarity
Afghanistan N.W.F. 1919[3]	71	Rare
Mahsud 1919–20[5]	0	None Identified
Waziristan 1919–21[4]	1	According to the roll as seen, can be considered Unique
Waziristan 1921–24[6]	0	None Identified

Warrant Officers: ~ (Temp) 241792 T Radford[3] attch. 14 MT Coy, S&TC (Originally 5th Bn)

Company Quartermaster Sergeants /Staff Sergeants / Colour Sergeants: ~ 240750 C C Harris[3] attch. 1 MT Coy, S&TC, (Originally 5th Bn)

Quartermaster Sergeants/Sergeants: ~ 240273 C Bishop[3] attch. 1 MT Coy, S&TC, (Originally 5th Bn), (Act) 240999 C T Doble[3] attch. DIG of Coms, (Originally 5th Bn), 202239 S V N Parfitt[3] attch. IOD, 209262 G Rich[3] attch. 2 Som LI, (Act) 200591 G Richards[3] attch. S&TC, 200796 A Silcox[3] attch. 2 Som LI & 200117 F A Willcox[3] attch. 2 N Stafford

Lance Sergeants/Corporals: ~ 200103 R E Andrews[3] attch. 1 DLI, (Act) 36980 A Boulton[3] attch. 1/25 London, 200634 A Broom[3] attch. 2 Som LI, (Act) 200257 F Kiddle[3] attch. 25 BSS, 200931 E Musgrave[3] attch. 2 Som LI, 200237 W Otridge[3] attch. 2 Som LI & 201467 W Smith[3] attch. 2 Som LI

Lance Corporals/Privates: ~ 200209 E Abbot[3] attch. 2 Som LI, 200780 G F Adams[3], 201019 E F Barnes[3] attch. 1 DLI, 200436 G Barrett[3] attch. 2 Som LI, 201694 E Barrow[3] attch. 2 Som LI, 201196 S Bell[3] attch. 2 Som LI, 202208 S Bookyer[3] attch. 2 Som LI, 200387 P Brimble[4] attch. 3/W Sig Sqn, 201245 L T Brodrip[3] attch. 2 Som LI, 200633 G Bullock[3] attch.

2 Som LI, 32162 E F Carter[3] attch. 17 SSB, 36755 H Carter[3] attch. 2 Som LI, 200276 C Catley[3] attch. 2 Som LI, 15309 S Charles[3] attch. 2 Som LI, 200166 R Chinnock[3] attch. 2 Som LI, 201512 W Clarke[3] attch. 2 Som LI, 201088 C V Dunford[3] attch. 2 MT Coy, S&TC, 200855 A W Fray[3] attch. 2 Som LI, 200370 J Gilbert[3] attch. 2 Som LI, 201111 A S Govard[3] attch. 17 SSB, 202068 F Grabham[3] attch. 2 Som LI, 200238 H W Griffin[3] attch. 17 SSB, 201006 S Harvey[3] attch. 2 Som LI, 190193 C Hawkins[3] attch. 2 Som LI, 201189 W Hayward[3] attch. 2 Som LI, 202830 A G House[3] attch. HQ, NWFF, 200545 H W Hulonce[3] attch. 2 Som LI, 240591 W Kellow[3] attch. 1 MT Coy, S&TC, (Originally 5th Bn), 201597 G B Lapham[3] attch. 2 MT Coy, S&TC, 201528 C Little[3] attch. 2 Som LI, 27344 F Lock[3] attch. 2 Som LI, 201462 B Miller[3] attch. 2 Som LI, 200465 H E Mitten[3] attch. 285 Coy, MGC, 200212 E Moger[3] attch. 2 Som LI, 242013 W M Mosley[3] attch. 2 Som LI, (Originally 5th Bn), 201608 E Newbury[3] attch. 2 Som LI, 203798 T H Nicholas[3] attch. 1 DLI, 203930 V R Noakes[3] attch. 18 IMVS, 200650 C Nott[3] attch. 2 Som LI, 201691 A Pasley[3] attch. 2 Som LI, 200714 S Peters[3] attch. 2 Som LI, 201595 F Phillips[3] attch. 2 Som LI, 200489 F Price[3] attch. 2 Som LI, 201627 W Puddy[3] attch. 2 Som LI, 201623 A Rose[3] attch. 2 Som LI, 201576 H Russ[3] attch. 2 Som LI, 240485 W Scriven[3] attch. 39 DSC, (Originally 5th Bn), 201393 J E Smith[3] attch. 17 SSB, 200861 H Stockman[3] attch. 2 Som LI, 200278 F E Tarrant[3], (4427) 201680 H N Toop[3] attch. 2 Som LI, 10821 T Tudball[3] attch. 2 Som LI, 201580 A J Uphill[3] attch. 17 SSB, 200484 W J White[3] attch. 17 SSB, 201638 T Wills[3] attch. 2 Som LI & 200623 A Young[3] attch. 2 Som LI

~ 2/4th Bn, The Prince Albert's (Somerset Light Infantry), Territorial Force ~

Note a.   *Roll of all personnel identified as eligible.*
Note b.   *Formed September 1914. India January 1915, Egypt September 1917, France & Flanders June 1918 forward.*
Note c.   *Medals named in impressed capitals: 'SOM. L. I.', '2/4/SOM. LT. INFY.' or '2/4 BN SOM. L.I.'*

Single Clasp	No. Identified	Rarity
Afghanistan N.W.F. 1919[3]	9	Of the Utmost Rarity
Mahsud 1919–20[5]	0	None Identified
Waziristan 1919–21[4]	0	None Identified
Waziristan 1921–24[6]	0	None Identified

Lance Corporals/Privates: ~ 202198 E G Brice[3] attch. 39 DSC, 201786 A J Coombs[3] attch. 44 DSC, 201328 D H Dicker[3] attch. 3/W Sig Sqn, 201892 J G Perkins[3] attch. 44 DSC, 201270 H R Senior[3] attch. 3/W Sig Sqn, 201072 A J Sweet[3] attch. 3/W Sig Sqn, 200960 W R E Tanner[3], 201227 H F Ward[3] attch. 3/W Sig Sqn & 201380 E V C Weston[3] attch. 3/W Sig Sqn

~ 1/5th Bn, The Prince Albert's (Somerset Light Infantry), Territorial Force ~

Note a.   *Roll of all personnel identified as eligible.*
Note b.   *United Kingdom August 1914. India November 1914, Egypt May 1917 thence Palestine forward.*
Note c.   *Medals named in impressed capitals: 'SOM. L. I.', '1/5/SOM. LT. INFY.' or '1/5 BN SOM. L.I.'*

Single Clasp	No. Identified	Rarity
Afghanistan N.W.F. 1919[3]	4	Of the Utmost Rarity
Mahsud 1919–20[5]	0	None Identified
Waziristan 1919–21[4]	0	None Identified
Waziristan 1921–24[6]	0	None Identified

Quartermaster Sergeants/Sergeants: ~ (Act) 240264 A A Coombes[3] attch. 14 MT Coy, S&TC, (Act) 240725 A Miller[3] attch. S&TC & (Act) 240227 L F Wilkins[3] attch. S&TC
Lance Corporals/Privates: ~ 240445 E Burrows[3] attch. 1/25 London

~ 2/5th Bn, The Prince Albert's (Somerset Light Infantry) ~

Note a. *Roll of all personnel identified as eligible.*
Note b. *Formed September 1914. India January 1915 forward.*
Note c. *Medals named in impressed capitals: 'SOM. L. I.', '2/5/SOM. LT. INFY.' or '2/5 BN SOM. L.I.'*

Single Clasp	No. Identified	Rarity
Afghanistan N.W.F. 1919[3]	41	Very Rare
Mahsud 1919–20[5]	0	None Identified
Waziristan 1919–21[4]	0	None Identified
Waziristan 1921–24[6]	0	None Identified

Warrant Officers Class II: ~ 203886 H H Chamberlain[3] attch. 139 Rly Const Coy, RE, (Originally 4th Bn) & (act) 241147 E Noonan[3] attch. 14 MT Coy, S&TC

Quartermaster Sergeants/Sergeants: ~ (Act) 36155 J W Allen[3] attch. S&TC, (Act) 241876 W E Bale[3] attch. 25 Div. Sply Coy, S&TC, (Act) 39606 L Cartwright[3] attch. S&TC, (Act) 240928 C J Coles[3] attch. 1 ARW, S&TC, (Act) 36044 B W H Just[3] attch. S&TC, (Act) 39624 H D Overton[3] attch. S&TC, (Act) 25178 C Porter[3] attch. S&TC, (Act) 241883 E Pym[3] attch. S&TC, (Act) 240996 H Routley[3] attch. 3/W Sig Sqn, (Act) 240559 C H Thorne[3] attch. S&TC, (Act) 10054 C Whittle[3] attch. S&TC, (Act) 240647 F Willis[3] attch. S&TC, 241269 A T Wood[3] attch. 66 PMC & (Act) 50705 C Woodward[3] attch. S&TC

Lance Sergeants/Corporals: ~ (Act) 241227 F C Abbott[3] attch. ISC, (Act) 36136 C C Burnham[3] attch. MAD, (Act) 241107 E V Haste[3] attch. 39 DSC, 240269 E J Larway[3] attch. 36 DSC, 8935 H H Morley[3] attch. 40 DSC, (Act) 241187 B G L Rendall[3] attch. 2 MT Coy, S&TC, (Act) 36053 F H Timmins[3] attch. 4 ACS & 240440 C S Whittington[3] attch. 2 MT Coy, S&TC

Lance Corporals/Privates: ~ 240184 E J Chinn[3] attch. 40 DSC, 41140 H Garvey[3] attch. ISC, 241322 F J Glover[3] attch. HQ, WFF, 241121 F C Hook[3] attch. 44 DSC, 241097 W D King[3] attch. 3/W Sig Sqn, 240782 E Lassiter[3] attch. 33 DSC, 240461 R Loram[3] attch. ISC, 36113 J McGulgan[3] attch. 38 DSC, 37067 E Nicholls[3], 241142 C Overd[3] attch. 40 DSC, 241388 H J Pike[3] attch. 40 DSC, 241307 C F Pym[3] attch. 40 DSC, 240991 C Sealey[3] attch. 33 DSC, 240917 C H Sharp[3] attch. 1 ARW, S&TC, 240359 C Staples[3] attch. 40 DSC, 240452 A Stevens[3] attch. 3/W Sig Sqn & 241244 R G Walbrin[3]

~ 1st Garrison Bn, The Prince Albert's (Somerset Light Infantry) ~

Note a. *Roll of all personnel identified as eligible.*
Note b. *Formed January 1917. India February 1917 forward.*
Note c. *Medals named in impressed capitals: 'SOM. L. I.'*

Single Clasp	No. Identified	Rarity
Afghanistan N.W.F. 1919[3]	33	Very Rare
Mahsud 1919–20[5]	0	None Identified
Waziristan 1919–21[4]	1	According to the roll as seen, can be considered Unique
Waziristan 1921–24[6]	0	None Identified
Combination Clasps	**No. Identified**	**Rarity**
Afghanistan N.W.F. 1919[3] Waziristan 1919–21[4]	1	According to the roll as seen, can be considered Unique

Warrant Officers Class II: ~ 6157 H Bowman[3] & (Act) 275508 H W H White[3] attch. 5 MT Coy, S&TC

Quartermaster Sergeants/Sergeants: ~ 275312 E Bradley[3] attch. Dir of Coms, (Act) 275048 J T Cooper[3&4] attch. S&TC, (Act) 275209 R Curtis[3] attch. S&TC, 34974 W W Gale[3] attch. IOD, 39760 G R Gill[3] attch. 1/4 Queen's, (Act) 39658 J S Hall[3] attch. HQ, 2 Div., (Act) 34556 A Jones[3] attch. 165 Sply Depot, S&TC, (Act) 275528 E W King[3] attch. S&TC, (Act) 275295 J King[3] attch. Derajat Sply Base, (Act) 275298 R H Martin[3] attch. S&TC, (Act) 275299 H A Oakman[3] attch. ITD, (Act) 33597 H H Pole[3] attch. S&TC, (Act) 275503 E E Schoelkope[3] attch. HQ, 2 Div., (Act) 33627 H Spencer[4] attch. S&TC & (Act) 33546 J Symonds[3] attch. S&TC

Lance Sergeants/Corporals: ~ 275340 W J Holden[3] attch. 25 & 144 IFA, (Act) 275123 W Moon[3] attch. 2 MT Coy, S&TC & 34501 W R Randall[3] attch. 1/4 Queen's

Lance Corporals/Privates: ~ 275343 R F Anker[3] attch. MAD, 275490 W G Berry[3] attch. 4 & 43 CFA, 275079 H Buckle[3] attch. 1/4 Queen's, 275494 W J Clark[3] attch. 43 CFA, 275250 C H Cream[3] attch. 15 IMVS, 275068 E Easy[3] attch. 1/4 Queen's, 204075 F Fitzpatrick[3] attch. BGH Peshawar, 275446 W T Flowers[3] attch. 1/4 Queen's, 275243 W H Hendy[3] attch. ADAS, 275319 D Hignett[3] attch. ITD, 39825 A D J Jones[3] attch. 1/4 Queen's, 34793 P J Lawes[3] attch. 15 IMVS, 35133 T Mahoney[3] attch. 1/4 Queen's, 34420 G Myers[3] attch. ITD & 34620 W Whiteway[3] attch. 1/4 Queen's

~ 2 Bn, The Prince of Wales's Own (West Yorkshire Regiment) ~

Note a.   *Roll of all personnel identified as eligible.*
Note b.   *Malta August 1914. France & Flanders November 1914 forward. India August 1919 thence Iraq January 1923.*
Note c.   *Title changed to The West Yorkshire Regiment (The Prince of Wales's Own) in 1920.*
Note d.   *Medals named in impressed capitals: 'W. YORK. R.'*

Single Clasp	No. Identified	Rarity
Afghanistan N.W.F. 1919[3]	7	Of the Utmost Rarity
Mahsud 1919–20[5]	0	None Identified
Waziristan 1919–21[4]	11	Extremely Rare
Waziristan 1921–24[6]	0	None Identified
Combination Clasps	**No. Identified**	**Rarity**
Mahsud 1919–20[5] Waziristan 1919–21[4] Waziristan 1921–24[6]	1	According to the roll as seen, can be considered Unique
Waziristan 1919–21[4] Waziristan 1921–24[6]	2	Of the Utmost Rarity

Majors: ~ C B Costin-Nian[4] attch. 11 Bn, MGC
Captains: ~ R B Leach[3] attch. 288 Coy, MGC
Lieutenant: ~ H P Cinnamond[3] attch. 150 Inf, IA
Warrant Officers Class II: ~ (Act Rly Tpt Sgt. Maj.) (64785) 4334263 S E Hawkes[4,5&6] attch. RTE & (Temp) 64630 J R Neville[3]
Quartermaster Sergeants/Sergeants: ~ (64609) 4524461 J Feather[4,5&6] attch. 'F' DSC, (Act) 64586 S P Phillips[3] attch. S&TC & (Act) 4525402 W T Spicer[4] attch. RTE
Lance Sergeants/Corporals: ~ (Act) 4524237 R Alder[4] attch. HQ, WFF & 54089 W L Cox[4] attch. RTO Tank
Lance Corporals/Privates: ~ 4525438 H Boydell[4] attch. 8 CCCS, 88156 F Connelly[4], 85845 T G Fairweather[3] attch. RTO Staff, Mari Indus, 87257 J C Forster[3] attch. RTE, 9058 J Frisby[3], 4524760 L Lawton[4] attch. 8 CCCS, (64476) 4524406 J McClay[4] attch. 34 DSC, 4525707 E Middleditch[4] attch. RTE, DIK, 4524932 H Moss[4] attch. HQ, WFF, 4682503 E Smith[4&6] attch. 'F' DSC & 4682006 J Smith[4] attch. ISC

~ ?/5th Bn, The Prince of Wales's Own (West Yorkshire Regiment), Territorial Force ~

Note a.   *Roll of all personnel identified as eligible.*
Note b.   *Medals named in impressed capitals: 'W. YORK. R.'*

Single Clasp	No. Identified	Rarity
Afghanistan N.W.F. 1919[3]	2	Of the Utmost Rarity
Mahsud 1919–20[5]	0	None Identified
Waziristan 1919–21[4]	0	None Identified
Waziristan 1921–24[6]	0	None Identified

Lieutenants: ~ C Crabtree[3] attch. 2 King's & A Stocker[3] attch. 1 DWR

~ ?/6th Battalion, The Prince of Wales's Own (West Yorkshire Regiment), Territorial Force ~

Note a.   *Roll of all personnel identified as eligible.*
Note b.   *Medals named in impressed capitals: 'W. YORK. R.'*

Single Clasp	No. Identified	Rarity
Afghanistan N.W.F. 1919[3]	1	According to the roll as seen, can be considered Unique.
Mahsud 1919–20[5]	0	None Identified
Waziristan 1919–21[4]	0	None Identified
Waziristan 1921–24[6]	0	None Identified

Lieutenants: ~ C Tomlinson[3] attch. 1 DWR

~ ?/7th Bn The Prince of Wales's Own (West Yorkshire Regiment), Territorial Force ~

Note a.   *Roll of all personnel identified as eligible.*
Note b.   *Medals named in impressed capitals: 'W. YORK. R.'*

Single Clasp	No. Identified	Rarity
Afghanistan N.W.F. 1919[3]	1	According to the roll as seen, can be considered Unique
Mahsud 1919–20[5]	0	None Identified
Waziristan 1919–21[4]	0	None Identified
Waziristan 1921–24[6]	0	None Identified

Lieutenants: ~ A (E) H Booth[3] attch. 1 Yorkshire

~ 2 Bn, The East Yorkshire Regiment ~

Note a.   *Roll of all personnel identified as eligible.*
Note b.   *India August 1914. France & Flanders January 1915, Egypt November 1915, Salonika December 1915 forward. India March 1919 to September 1920, thence to Iraq returning to India in 1921*
Note c.   *Medals named in impressed capitals: 'E. YORK. R.'*

Single Clasp	No. Identified	Rarity
Afghanistan N.W.F. 1919[3]	2	Of the Utmost Rarity
Mahsud 1919–20[5]	0	None Identified.
Waziristan 1919–21[4]	0	None Identified.
Waziristan 1921– 24[6]	1	According to the roll as seen, can be considered Unique

Lieutenants: ~ A M Mieville[3] attch. RTO, Bannu & D S Norman[6] attch. 1 Border
Company Quartermaster Sergeants/Staff Sergeants/Colour Sergeants: ~ (4334033) 7314 J W Bamford[3]

~ 3rd (Reserve) Bn, The East Yorkshire Regiment ~

Note a.   *Roll of all personnel identified as eligible.*
Note b.   *United Kingdom August 1914 forward throughout Great War period providing drafts and reinforcements.*
Note c.   *Medals named in impressed capitals: 'E. YORK. R.'*

Single Clasp	No. Identified	Rarity
Afghanistan N.W.F. 1919[3]	1	According to the roll as seen, can be considered Unique

	0	None Identified
Mahsud 1919–20[5]	0	None Identified
Waziristan 1919–21[4]	0	None Identified
Waziristan 1921–24[6]	0	None Identified

Lieutenants: ~ W C Valentine[3] attch. 1 DWR

~ ?/4th Bn, The East Yorkshire Regiment, Territorial Force ~
Note a. *Roll of all personnel identified as eligible.*
Note b. *Medals named in impressed capitals: 'E. YORK. R.'*

Single Clasp	No. Identified	Rarity
Afghanistan N.W.F. 1919[3]	1	According to the roll as seen, can be considered Unique
Mahsud 1919–20[5]	0	None Identified
Waziristan 1919–21[4]	0	None Identified
Waziristan 1921–24[6]	0	None Identified

Lieutenants: ~ G H Brewer[3] attch. MAD

~ 5th (Cyclist) Bn, The East Yorkshire Regiment, Territorial Force ~
Note a. *Roll of all personnel identified as eligible.*
Note b. *United Kingdom August 1914 forward throughout Great War period.*
Note c. *Medals named in impressed capitals: 'E. YORK. R.'*

Single Clasp	No. Identified	Rarity
Afghanistan N.W.F. 1919[3]	1	According to the roll as seen, can be considered Unique
Mahsud 1919–20[5]	0	None Identified
Waziristan 1919–21[4]	0	None Identified
Waziristan 1921–24[6]	0	None Identified

Majors: ~ A Woods[3] attch. MGC

~ 1st Garrison Bn, The East Yorkshire Regiment ~
Note a. *Roll of all personnel identified as eligible.*
Note b. *Formed October 1915. India February 1916 forward.*
Note c. *Medals named in impressed capitals: 'E. YORK. R.'*

Single Clasp	No. Identified	Rarity
Afghanistan N.W.F. 1919[3]	11	Extremely Rare
Mahsud 1919–20[5]	0	None Identified
Waziristan 1919–21[4]	0	None Identified
Waziristan 1921–24[6]	0	None Identified

Warrant Officers Class II: ~ (Act) 21322 A E Johnson[3]
Quartermaster Sergeants/Sergeants: ~ (Act) 21374 G Chamberlain[3], (Act) 18694 D Keld[3], 9717 E B Hart[3], (Act) 23269 J W Smailes[3], (Act) 20938 J F Teear[3] attch. S&TC & 20791 J T Wood[3]
Lance Sergeants/Corporals: ~ (Act) 9575 E Luxton[3] attch. RE
Lance Corporals/Privates: ~ 12/63 H A Carr[3], (4334539) 21362 J Dexter[3] attch. 19 IMVS & 36099 J Wilson[3] attch. 19 IMVS

~ 2nd Bn, The Bedfordshire Regiment ~

Note a.   *Roll of all personnel identified as eligible.*
Note b.   *South Africa August 1914. France and Flanders October 1914 forward. India from October 1919.*
Note c.   *Title changed to Bedfordshire and Hertfordshire Regiment in 1919.*
Note d.   *Medals named in impressed capitals: 'BEDF. R.' or 'BEDFS. & HERTS. R.' depending on period. (See Note 3 above).*

Single Clasp	No. Identified	Rarity
Afghanistan N.W.F. 1919[3]	2	Of the Utmost Rarity
Mahsud 1919–20[5]	0	None Identified
Waziristan 1919–21[4]	6	Of the Utmost Rarity
Waziristan 1921–24[6]	5	Of the Utmost Rarity
Combination Clasps	**No. Identified**	**Rarity**
Mahsud 1919–20[5] Waziristan 1919–21[4]	1	According to the roll as seen, can be considered Unique

Captains: ~ E R Bryan[3] attch. Base Depot, Quetta & R T Oldfield[4] attch. 2/15 Sikhs, IA, ZF
Lieutenants: ~ A Topley[3] attch. RTO
Quartermaster Sergeants/Sergeants: ~ (Act) 24151 E T Bradshaw[4&5] attch. S&TC & attch. 'C' DSC
Lance Sergeants/Corporals: ~ (Act) 5943671 H Bradley[4] attch. HQ, 10 Bde., 5942878 F W Chapman[6] attch. 'C' DSC, 7178326 C Gibbard[6] attch. 'C' DSC & 7177524 G Keogh[4] attch. 34 DSC (From Leinster R)
Lance Corporals/Privates: ~ 7177724 J Allen[6] attch. 'C' DSC, 5943844 S Boyd[4] attch. 52 FA, 5943894 H G B Keen[6] attch. 'A' Corps Sigs, 5943690 S G Linay[4] attch. 16 MMG Bty, 5942478 A Morley[4] attch. 21 Bde. & 5942900 H W Turner[6] attch. 'C' DSC

~ 1/5th Bn, The Bedfordshire Regiment, Territorial Force ~

Note a.   *Roll of all personnel identified as eligible.*
Note b.   *United Kingdom August 1914. August 1915 Mudros and Sulva Bay, December 1915 Mudros and Egypt. Palestine 1917 thence Syria returning to Egypt December 1918 to 1919.*
Note c.   *Medals named in impressed capitals: 'BEDF. R.'*

Single Clasp	No. Identified	Rarity
Afghanistan N.W.F. 1919[3]	1	According to the roll as seen, can be considered Unique
Mahsud 1919–20[5]	0	None Identified
Waziristan 1919–21[4]	0	None Identified
Waziristan 1921–24[6]	0	None Identified
Combination Clasps	**No. Identified**	**Rarity**
Waziristan 1921–24[6] & Burma 1931–32[10]	1	According to the roll as seen, can be considered Unique

Captains: ~ W A Shaw[6&10] attch. HQ, Waz Dist
Lieutenants: ~ F M Foster[3] attch. 1/5 Hampshire

~ 1ˢᵗ Garrison Bn, The Bedfordshire Regiment ~

Note a. *Roll of all personnel identified as eligible.*
Note b. *Formed December 1915. India February 1916 forward.*
Note c. *Medals named in impressed capitals: 'BEDF. R.'*

Single Clasp	No. Identified	Rarity
Afghanistan N.W.F. 1919[3]	7	Of the Utmost Rarity
Mahsud 1919–20[5]	0	None Identified
Waziristan 1919–21[4]	0	None Identified
Waziristan 1921–24[6]	0	None Identified

Warrant Officers Class I: ~ (Act) 32670 C G Lovejoy[3] attch. S&TC
Quartermaster Sergeants/Sergeants: ~ (Act) 206781 C A Parker[3] attch. RTO, Peshawar, 24025 M Richards[3] attch. 3 W/Sig Sqn & (Act) 32747 G A Seymour[3] attch. S&TC
Lance Corporals/Privates: ~ 210920 W E Childs[3] attch. 21 IMVS, 205560 H Crook[3] attch. 6 MT Coy, S&TC & 32589 R Mitchell[3] attch. 10 IMVS, 1 Div.

~ 2ⁿᵈ Garrison Bn, The Bedfordshire Regiment ~

Note a. *Roll of all personnel identified as eligible.*
Note b. *Formed December 1916. India February 1917 forward.*
Note c. *Medals named in impressed capitals: 'BEDF. R.'*

Single Clasp	No. Identified	Rarity
Afghanistan N.W.F. 1919[3]	16	Extremely Rare
Mahsud 1919–20[5]	0	None Identified
Waziristan 1919–21[4]	0	None Identified
Waziristan 1921–24[6]	0	None Identified

Warrant Officers Class II: ~ (Act) 205636 L A V Heath[3] attch. 107 Bde. Sply Sect, S&TC
Quartermaster Sergeants/Sergeants: ~ (Act) 205521 V H Eve[3] attch. S&TC & (Act) 204347 P H Thomas[3] attch. 2 MT Coy, S&TC
Lance Corporals/Privates: ~ 46118 W Branter[3] attch. 1 ARW, S&TC, 205472 A E Gaiger[3] attch. 14 MT Coy, S&TC, (5944353) 2052950 C E Hayward[3] attch. 40 DSC, 37617 A W Hewitt[3] Div. Staff, Quetta, 205733 J A Killeen[3] attch. HQ, 46 Bde., 205470 F N Lewis[3] attch. CMSC, 205432 J H Moore[3] attch. 4 LofC Sigs, 206603 J J Parsons[3] attch. 1 MT Coy, S&TC, 35647 E P Perkins[3] attch. 14 MT Coy, S&TC, 35099 P T Smith[3] attch. 17 MT Coy, S&TC, 35405 G S Tattersall[3] attch. 4 LofC Sigs, 205566 C Tizzard[3] & 205575 A Wiltshire[3] attch. DFD

~ 3ʳᵈ Garrison Bn, The Bedfordshire Regiment ~

Note a. *Roll of all personnel identified as eligible.*
Note b. *Formed January 1917. India February 1917 forward.*
Note c. *Medals named in impressed capitals: 'BEDF. R.'*

Single Clasp	No. Identified	Rarity
Afghanistan N.W.F. 1919[3]	5	Of the Utmost Rarity
Mahsud 1919–20[5]	0	None Identified
Waziristan 1919–21[4]	0	None Identified
Waziristan 1921–24[6]	0	None Identified

Quartermaster Sergeants/Sergeants: ~ 206580 E H Jepson[3] attch. 2 MT Coy, S&TC
Lance Corporals/Privates: ~ 205263 F A E Hancock[3] attch. 4 LofC Sigs, 206449 A C Parkins[3] attch. 4 LofC Sigs, 35686 A H R Simmons[3] attch. RAMC & 205235 F J Williams[3] attch. 4 LofC Sigs

~ 2nd Bn, The Leicestershire Regiment ~

Note a.   *Roll of all personnel identified as eligible.*
Note b.   *India August 1914. France & Flanders October 1914, Egypt November 1915, Mesopotamia December 1915, Egypt January 1918 thence India from September 1919 via Palestine and Syria. November 1923 Sudan.*
Note c.   *Medals named in impressed capitals: 'LEIC. R.'*

Single Clasp	No. Identified	Rarity
Afghanistan N.W.F. 1919[3]	9	Of the Utmost Rarity
Mahsud 1919–20[5]	0	None Identified
Waziristan 1919–21[4]	5	Of the Utmost Rarity
Waziristan 1921–24[6]	1	According to the roll as seen, can be considered Unique
Combination Clasps	**No. Identified**	**Rarity**
Waziristan 1919–21[4] Waziristan 1921–24[6]	1	According to the roll as seen, can be considered Unique

Captains: ~ G N Wykes[4]
Quartermaster Sergeants/Sergeants: ~ 62255 W H Boor[3] attch. RTO, (Act) 50038 R M Crichton[4] attch. 12 Div. Sply Coy, S&TC & (65198) 4850661 T Holden[4&6] attch. 'B' DSC
Lance Corporals/Privates: ~ 9439 G Baker[3] attch. 2 N Stafford, 4850588 C G Chapman[4] attch. Rest Camp, DIK, 9197 J Clarke[3] attch. 33 DSC, 4850752 C A Drake[4] attch. Rest Camp, DIK, 64904 J Drummond[3] attch. 2 N Stafford, 43153 J Holmes[3] attch. 1028 Coy, RASC, 69405 G Johnson[3] attch. 2 N Stafford, 4848871 H E Mitchell[6] attch. 'B' DSC, 4850684 G R Potter[4] attch. Rest Camp, DIK & Convoy Duties, Tank, 63294 V T Sheldrake[3] attch. 1 MT Coy, S&TC & 9170 C Skudder[3] attch. 2 N Stafford & 8276 J W Woodcock[3] attch. 3/W Sig Sqn

~ Unidentified Service Bn, The Leicestershire Regiment ~

Note a.   *Roll of all personnel identified as eligible.*
Note b.   *Medals named in impressed capitals: 'LEIC. R.*

Single Clasp	No. Identified	Rarity
Afghanistan N.W.F. 1919[3]	2	Of the Utmost Rarity
Mahsud 1919–20[5]	0	None Identified
Waziristan 1919–21[4]	0	None Identified
Waziristan 1921–24[6]	0	None Identified

Captains: ~ R Goody[3] attch. 2 King's
Lieutenants: ~ G R B Dixon[3] attch. 2/4 Border

~ 2nd Bn, The Royal Irish Regiment ~

Note a.   *Roll of all personnel identified as eligible.*
Note b.   *United Kingdom August 1914. France & Flanders October 1914 forward. India March 1920 to disbandment in 1922 upon formation of Irish Free State.*
Note c.   *Medals named in impressed capitals: 'R. IR. REGT.'*

Single Clasp	No. Identified	Rarity
Afghanistan N.W.F. 1919[3]	1	According to the roll as seen, can be considered Unique
Mahsud 1919–20[5]	0	None Identified
Waziristan 1919–21[4]	3	Of the Utmost Rarity
Waziristan 1921–24[6]	1	According to the roll as seen, can be considered Unique

Combination Clasps	No. Identified	Rarity
Waziristan 1919–21[4] Waziristan 1921–24[6]	1	According to the roll as seen, can be considered Unique

Lieutenants: ~ A Connors[3] attch. RTE & G R Lucas[6] attch. 7 ACC, RTC

Warrant Officers Class I: ~ (Temp) 7110475 A J Mauger[4] attch. RTE Darya Khan

Company Quartermaster Sergeants/Staff Sergeants/Colour Sergeants: ~ (7109088) 9333 B Harris[4&6]

Lance Corporals/Privates: ~ 7110528 T Power[4] attch. HQ, WFF & 7110547 P Scarry[4]

~ 1st Bn, Alexandra, Princess of Wales's Own (Yorkshire Regiment) ~

Note a.   *Roll of all commissioned personnel identified as eligible.*

Note b.   *Non-commissioned and other ranks multi clasp only or non–Afghanistan 1919 single clasp.*

Note c.   *India August 1914 forward throughout Great War period to March 1920 thence Egypt and Palestine returning to India December 1920 forward.*

Note d.   *Battle honour 'Third Afghan War 1919'.*

Note e.   *Title changed to The Green Howards (Alexandra, Princess of Wales's Own, Yorkshire Regiment) in 1920.*

Note f.   *Medals named in impressed capitals: '1 – YORK. R.' or 'YORK. R.'*

Single Clasp	No. Identified	Rarity
Afghanistan N.W.F. 1919[3]	Bn. Strength	Not Rare
Mahsud 1919–20[5]	0	None Identified
Waziristan 1919–21[4]	2	Of the Utmost Rarity
Waziristan 1921–24[6]	2	Of the Utmost Rarity

Combination Clasps	No. Identified	Rarity
Afghanistan N.W.F. 1919[3] Mahsud 1919–20[5] Waziristan 1919–21[4] Waziristan 1921–24[6]	1	According to the roll as seen, can be considered Unique
Afghanistan N.W.F. 1919[3] Waziristan 1919–21[4]	1	According to the roll as seen, can be considered Unique
Afghanistan N.W.F. 1919[3] Waziristan 1919–21[4] Waziristan 1921–24[6]	4	Of the Utmost Rarity
Afghanistan N.W.F. 1919[3] Waziristan 1921–24[6]	5	Of the Utmost Rarity
Mahsud 1919–20[5] Waziristan 1919–21[4] Waziristan 1921–24[6] North West Frontier 1930–31[9]	1	According to the roll as seen, can be considered Unique

Lieutenant Colonels: ~ (Act) M D Carey[3]

Majors: ~ J R F Errington[3] attch. 285 Coy, MGC & O G Grace[3,4&6]

Captains: ~ (Act) V J Barber[3], (Act) W D Clayton[3], (Act) P Clow[3], A W Craven[3], (QM) W T Howes[3] & G W E Maude[3]

Lieutenants: ~ G Ball[3], E Brewman[3], L M O'Callaghan[3], (Adjt) F Crowsley[3], R H Marr[3], F Hartley[3], E W Heckle[3], A Lyle[3], W H Mitchell[3], E B Newman[3], E Prestwich[3], A L Shaw[6] Staff, DIK, C F Turpin[3] & H O Ure[3] attch. Sig Coy, Peshawar

Company Quartermaster Sergeants/Staff Sergeants/Colour Sergeants: ~ (4379187) 9306 G C Greer[3&6] attch. IASC

Quartermaster Sergeants/Sergeants: ~ 4379457 G Hinchley[4,5,6&(9 Sgt. R Sigs)] attch. 'F' DSC, 66394 A Lazenby[4] attch. S&TC & (4379089) 8615 H Southwell[3,4&6] attch. 'F' DSC

Lance Sergeants/Corporals: ~ 9151 B F Grimbley[3,4,5&6(R Sigs)] attch. 2/W Sig Sqn & (4379395) 9790 S C E Lawson[3&6] attch. 33 DSC

Lance Corporals/Privates: ~ (7617567) 9247 H Creed[3&6(7 ACC, RTC)], 8251 J Dobson[3,(4&6) Queen's], 4380619 W Hassall[6] attch. MFO, DIK, (4379174) 9270 C Johnson[3&6] attch. MFO, DIK, (4379061) 8087 E Lane[3&6(RTC)], 4379135 T O'Neill[4] attch. 'F' DSC, 9903 A Purvis[3&4] attch. 40 DSC & (4379275) 9495 H W Willingdale[3,4&6] attch. 'C' DSC

~ 1st Garrison Bn, Alexandra, Princess of Wales's Own (Yorkshire Regiment) ~

Note a. *Roll of all personnel identified as eligible.*
Note b. *Formed October 1915. India January 1916 forward.*
Note c. *Medals named in impressed capitals: 'YORK. R.'*

Single Clasp	No. Identified	Rarity
Afghanistan N.W.F. 1919[3]	2	Of the Utmost Rarity
Mahsud 1919–20[5]	0	None Identified
Waziristan 1919–21[4]	0	None Identified
Waziristan 1921–24[6]	0	None Identified

Quartermaster Sergeants/Sergeants: ~ (Act) 40163 W E Browne[3] attch. S&TC
Lance Corporals/Privates: ~ 39966 P A Barrington[3] attch. 2 MT Coy, S&TC

~ 2nd Bn, The Lancashire Fusiliers ~

Note a. *Roll of all personnel identified as eligible.*
Note b. *United Kingdom August 1914. France & Flanders November August 1914 forward. India November 1919 forward.*
Note c. *Medals named in impressed capitals: 'LAN. FUS.'*

Single Clasp	No. Identified	Rarity
Afghanistan N.W.F. 1919[3]	0	None Identified
Mahsud 1919–20[5]	0	None Identified
Waziristan 1919–21[4]	7	Of the Utmost Rarity
Waziristan 1921–24[6]	8	Of the Utmost Rarity

Combination Clasps	No. Identified	Rarity
Afghanistan N.W.F. 1919[3] Waziristan 1919–21[4]	1	According to the roll as seen, can be considered Unique
Afghanistan N.W.F. 1919[3] Waziristan 1921–24[6]	2	Of the Utmost Rarity
Mahsud 1919–20[5] Waziristan 1919–21[4]	3	Of the Utmost Rarity
Waziristan 1919–21[4] Waziristan 1921–24[6]	3	Of the Utmost Rarity

Warrant Officers Class I: ~ (RQMS) 3436814 (1069) G Ryder[3&6] attch. 'F' DSC
Warrant Officers Class II: ~ (Act) (3434898) 65735 T J Reid[4] attch. HQ Mari Indus
Quartermaster Sergeants/Sergeants: ~ (Act) 3434847 H Atkins[4] attch. HQ Mari Indus, 3437093 J Clements[6] attch. 'B' DSC, (3436667) 72419 G V Currie[4] attch. IAOC, (Act) 3436681 A Hartington[4&6] (Alias H Stafford) attch. 2 MT Coy, S&TC, (68359) 3435136 H Kaye[4] attch. HQ Kalabagh, 3757456 J H Lodge[3&6] attch. 'B' DSC, (Act) 3434236 D McEvoy[4&6] (Rest Camp) attch. HQ Mari Indus & (Act) 3435011 C Wilkinson[4&6] attch. HQ Mari Indus
Lance Sergeants/Corporals: ~ 3436265 W J Glassey[6] attch. 27 FA, & 3434529 P Tobin[6] attch. HQ Mari Indus
Lance Corporals/Privates / Fusiliers: ~ 3436218 G Baldwin[6] attch. HQ Waz Dist, 69776 T Connett[4] attch. RTO, Tank, 3435483 W H Daniels[6] attch. 96/97 ISS, 3436310 G Gibbs[6] attch. HQ Waz Dist, 3435078 J E Greenall[4&6] attch. 'D' DSC, (68158) 3435056 G Parton[4&5] attch. 1 CSS, 3435723 J Redhead[4] attch. 'D' DSC, 3434610 E G Rowlinson[6] attch. 'D' DSC, 3435102 S Searson[6] attch. Int, Razani, (5056) 3434305 G Taylor[4&5] attch. 1 CSS & (71315) 3436213 A J Webb[4] attch. HQ Kalabagh

~ 4th (Extra Reserve) Bn, The Lancashire Fusiliers ~

Note a.   *Roll of all personnel identified as eligible.*
Note b.   *United Kingdom August 1914 forward throughout Great War period providing drafts and reinforcements.*
Note c.   *Medals named in impressed capitals: 'LAN. FUS.'*

Single Clasp	No. Identified	Rarity
Afghanistan N.W.F. 1919[3]	1	According to the roll as seen, can be considered Unique
Mahsud 1919–20[5]	0	None Identified
Waziristan 1919–21[4]	0	None Identified
Waziristan 1921–24[6]	0	None Identified

Captains: ~ I M B Oliphant[3] attch. 16 Rajputs, IA.

~ 3/6th Bn, The Lancashire Fusiliers, Territorial Force ~

Note a.   *Roll of all personnel identified as eligible.*
Note b.   *Formed March 1915. United Kingdom throughout Great War period.*
Note c.   *Medals named in impressed capitals: 'LAN. FUS.'*

Single Clasp	No. Identified	Rarity
Afghanistan N.W.F. 1919[3]	1	According to the roll as seen, can be considered Unique
Mahsud 1919–20[5]	0	None Identified
Waziristan 1919–21[4]	0	None Identified
Waziristan 1921–24[6]	0	None Identified

Lieutenants: ~ F D Woodcock[3] attch. 1/25 London.

~ 1/8th Bn, The Lancashire Fusiliers, Territorial Force ~

Note a.   *Roll of all personnel identified as eligible.*
Note b.   *United Kingdom August 1914. Egypt September 1914, Gallipoli May 1915, Mudros December 1915, Egypt January 1916, France & Flanders February 1917 forward.*
Note c.   *Medals named in impressed capitals: 'LAN. FUS.'*

Single Clasp	No. Identified	Rarity
Afghanistan N.W.F. 1919[3]	1	According to the roll as seen, can be considered Unique
Mahsud 1919–20[5]	0	None Identified
Waziristan 1919–21[4]	0	None Identified
Waziristan 1921–24[6]	0	None Identified

Lieutenants: ~ R Blanche[3] attch. 2/6 Sussex.

~ 18th (Service) Bn, The Lancashire Fusiliers ~

Note a.   *Roll of all personnel identified as eligible.*
Note b.   *Formed January 1915. France & Flanders January 1916 forward.*
Note c.   *Medals named in impressed capitals: 'LAN. FUS.'*

Single Clasp	No. Identified	Rarity
Afghanistan N.W.F. 1919[3]	2	Of the Utmost Rarity

Mahsud 1919–20[5]	0	None Identified
Waziristan 1919–21[4]	0	None Identified
Waziristan 1921–24[6]	0	None Identified

Lieutenant: ~ G M Grime[3] attch. 281 Coy, MGC & J F B Stevenson[3] attch. 22 Sqn, MGCC, (Formally NZEF)

~ 2nd Bn, The Royal Scots Fusiliers ~

Note a.   *Roll of all personnel identified as eligible.*
Note b.   *Gibraltar August 1914. France & Flanders October 1914 forward. India from November 1920.*
Note c.   *Medals named in impressed capitals: 'R. S. FUS.' or 'R. SCOTS FUS.'*

Single Clasp	No. Identified	Rarity
Afghanistan N.W.F. 1919[3]	3	Of the Utmost Rarity
Mahsud 1919–20[5]	0	None Identified
Waziristan 1919–21[4]	0	None Identified
Waziristan 1921–24[6]	3	Of the Utmost Rarity

Combination Clasps	No. Identified	Rarity
Waziristan 1919–21[4] Waziristan 1921–24[6]	1	According to the roll as seen, can be considered Unique
Waziristan 1921–24[6] North West Frontier 1930–31[9]	1	According to the roll as seen, can be considered Unique

Majors: ~ D S Davidson[3] Staff
Lieutenants: ~ W F Stewart[3] attch. RAF & D M Strachan[3]
Quartermaster Sergeants/Sergeants: ~ 3179421 W H Goodwin[4&6] attch. LofC Sigs
Lance Sergeants/Corporals: ~ 3179138 J Russell[6] attch. 'B' DSC & 3179748 W Wall[6&(9 Sgt. R Sigs)] attch. 'G' DSC
Lance Corporals/Fusiliers: ~ 3123050 W A Griggs[6] attch. Garrison Police, Tank, & 3122197 D Russell[6] attch. Garrison Police, Tank

~ 1st Garrison Bn, The Royal Scots Fusiliers ~

Note a.   *Roll of all personnel identified as eligible.*
Note b.   *Formed October 1915. India February 1916 forward.*
Note c.   *Medals named in impressed capitals: 'R. S. FUS.' or 'R. SCOTS FUS.'*

Single Clasp	No. Identified	Rarity
Afghanistan N.W.F. 1919[3]	8	Of the Utmost Rarity.
Mahsud 1919–20[5]	0	None Identified.
Waziristan 1919–21[4]	0	None Identified.
Waziristan 1921–24[6]	0	None Identified.

Quartermaster Sergeants/Sergeants: ~ (Act) 34191 A G Brettell[3] attch. 2 Div. Sply Coy, S&TC, (Act) 21670 F Higgs[3] attch. 2 Div. Sply Coy, S&TC, (Act) 34237 J Keir[3] attch. 52 PMC, S&TC, (Act) 21749 J Ness[3] attch. HQ, BFF & (Act) 26192 J Woods[3] attch. HQ, 60 Bde.
Lance Corporals/Privates: ~ 26158 G Brown[3] attch. HQ, 44 DSC, KKF, 21397 J M Grieve[3] & 21925 P Leadbetter[3]

~ 1st Bn, The Cheshire Regiment ~

Note a. *Roll of all personnel identified as eligible.*
Note b. *United Kingdom August 1914. France & Flanders August 1914, Italy December 1917, France & Flanders April 1918 forward. India April 1922 forward.*
Note c. *Medals named in impressed capitals: 'CHES. R.'*

Single Clasp	No. Identified	Rarity
Afghanistan N.W.F. 1919[3]	0	None Identified
Mahsud 1919–20[5]	0	None Identified
Waziristan 1919–21[4]	1	According to the roll as seen, can be considered Unique
Waziristan 1921–24[6]	2	Of the Utmost Rarity

Captains: ~ L V J Pogson[6] attch. FTCO, Razmak
Lieutenants: ~ G Hall[4] attch. RE
Lance Corporals/Privates: ~ 4114768 H Darlington[6] attch. HQ, Waz Dist

~ 2nd Bn, The Cheshire Regiment ~

Note a. *Roll of all personnel identified as eligible.*
Note b. *India August 1914. France & Flanders January 1915, Egypt October 1915, Salonika November 1915 forward. Turkey January 1919 forward.*
Note c. *Medals named in impressed capitals: 'CHES. R.'*

Single Clasp	No. Identified	Rarity
Afghanistan N.W.F. 1919[3]	1	According to the roll as seen, can be considered Unique
Mahsud 1919–20[5]	0	None Identified
Waziristan 1919–21[4]	0	None Identified
Waziristan 1921–24[6]	0	None Identified

Company Quartermaster Sergeants / Staff Sergeants / Colour Sergeants: ~ 8536 E B Miller[3]

~ 3rd (Reserve) Bn, The Cheshire Regiment ~

Note a. *Roll of all personnel identified as eligible.*
Note b. *United Kingdom August 1914 forward throughout Great War period providing drafts and reinforcements.*
Note c. *Medals named in impressed capitals: 'CHES. R.'*

Single Clasp	No. Identified	Rarity
Afghanistan N.W.F. 1919[3]	3	Of the Utmost Rarity
Mahsud 1919–20[5]	0	None Identified
Waziristan 1919–21[4]	0	None Identified
Waziristan 1921–24[6]	0	None Identified

Lieutenants: ~ F Handley[3] attch. 222 Coy, MGC
Lance Corporals/Privates: ~ 3/59300 A Gardiner[3] & 34778 P Tarpey[3]

~ 1/6th Bn, The Cheshire Regiment, Territorial Force ~

Note a. *Roll of all personnel identified as eligible.*
Note b. *United Kingdom August 1914. France & Flanders November 1914 forward.*
Note c. *Medals named in impressed capitals: 'CHES. R.'*

Single Clasp	No. Identified	Rarity
Afghanistan N.W.F. 1919[3]	2	Of the Utmost Rarity
Mahsud 1919–20[5]	0	None Identified
Waziristan 1919–21[4]	0	None Identified
Waziristan 1921–24[6]	0	None Identified

Lieutenants: ~ J Gibson[3] attch. 2 N Stafford & A P S Heron[3] attch. MAD

~ 8th (Service) Bn, The Cheshire Regiment ~

Note a. *Roll of all personnel identified as eligible.*
Note b. *Formed August 1914. Egypt June 1915, Gallipoli July 1915, Mesopotamia February 1916 forward.*
Note c. *Medals named in impressed capitals: 'CHES. R.'*

Single Clasp	No. Identified	Rarity
Afghanistan N.W.F. 1919[3]	28	Very Rare
Mahsud 1919–20[5]	0	None Identified
Waziristan 1919–21[4]	0	None Identified
Waziristan 1921–24[6]	0	None Identified

Quartermaster Sergeants/Sergeants: ~ (Act) 11378 F McKay[3] attch. 43 B(S)S, Manzai & 26171 F Smart[3]
Lance Sergeants/Corporals: ~ 11294 J Hamnett[3] & 44370 W W W Morgan[3] attch. BFF
Lance Corporals/Privates: ~ 8607 T Allen[3] attch. 43 B(S)S, Manzai, 62496 C Anderton[3] attch. 43 B(S)S, Manzai, 26739 S Barnes[3], 59453 C Benham[3] attch. 43 B(S)S, Manzai, 32849 C E Brown[3], 25691 H Chemsworth[3] attch. 43 B(S)S, Manzai, 36033 J Davie[3] attch. 43 B(S)S, Manzai, 32700 J T Davies[3], 64573 J C Donald[3] attch. 43 B(S)S, Manzai, 18158 J Evans[3], 62795 J T Fortune[3] attch. 43 B(S)S, Manzai, 62776 B J Hariman[3] attch. 43 B(S)S, Manzai, 28040 E J James[3] attch. 43 B(S)S, Manzai, 10104 S Melbourne[3], 64592 J Ormerod[3] attch. 43 B(S)S, Manzai, 33672 W H Quayle[3] attch. 43 B(S)S, Manzai, 10056 T Rowland[3] attch. 43 B(S)S, Manzai, 45791 A Sandland[3] attch. 43 B(S)S, Manzai, 26318 J Slavin[3] attch. 43 B(S)S, Manzai, 24354 J Smith[3] attch. 43 B(S)S, Manzai, 10636 S Smith[3], 34623 W Sutton[3] attch. 43 B(S)S, Manzai, 18348 T H Upton[3] attch. 43 B(S)S Manzai & 28252 W Wilson[3] attch. 43 B(S)S, Manzai

~ 9th (Service) Bn, The Cheshire Regiment ~

Note a. *Roll of all personnel identified as eligible.*
Note b. *Formed September 1914. France & Flanders July 1915 forward*
Note c. *Medals named in impressed capitals: 'CHES. R.'*

Single Clasp	No. Identified	Rarity
Afghanistan N.W.F. 1919[3]	1	According to the roll as seen, can be considered Unique
Mahsud 1919–20[5]	0	None Identified
Waziristan 1919–21[4]	0	None Identified
Waziristan 1921–24[6]	0	None Identified

Lieutenants: ~ H H Whiteside[3] attch. 1/4 QORWK

~ 12th (Service) Bn, The Cheshire Regiment ~

Note a.   *Roll of all personnel identified as eligible.*
Note b.   *Medals named in impressed capitals: 'CHES. R.'*

Single Clasp	No. Identified	Rarity
Afghanistan N.W.F. 1919[3]	1	According to the roll as seen, can be considered Unique
Mahsud 1919–20[5]	0	None Identified
Waziristan 1919–21[4]	0	None Identified
Waziristan 1921–24[6]	0	None Identified

Lieutenants: ~ E Martin[3] attch. 1/1 Kent

~ 14th (Reserve) Bn, The Cheshire Regiment ~

Note a.   *Roll of all personnel identified as eligible.*
Note b.   *Formed October 1914. United Kingdom for duration of Great War period providing drafts and reinforcements.*
Note c.   *Medals named in impressed capitals: 'CHES. R.'*

Single Clasp	No. Identified	Rarity
Afghanistan N.W.F. 1919[3]	1	According to the roll as seen, can be considered Unique
Mahsud 1919–20[5]	0	None Identified
Waziristan 1919–21[4]	0	None Identified
Waziristan 1921–24[6]	0	None Identified

Lance Corporals/Privates: ~ 33022 G H Mazier[3]

~ 23rd (Special) Bn, The Cheshire Regiment, Territorial Force ~

Note a.   *Roll of all personnel identified as eligible.*
Note b.   *Formed January 1917. France and Flanders May 1918 forward.*
Note c.   *Medals named in impressed capitals: 'CHES. R.'*

Single Clasp	No. Identified	Rarity
Afghanistan N.W.F. 1919[3]	2	Of the Utmost Rarity
Mahsud 1919–20[5]	0	None Identified
Waziristan 1919–21[4]	0	None Identified
Waziristan 1921–24[6]	0	None Identified

Lance Corporals/Privates: ~ 68912 J Bird[3] & 10827 A Wilcox[3]

~ 1st Bn, The Royal Welsh Fusiliers ~

Note a.   *Roll of all eligible commissioned personnel identified as eligible.*
Note b.   *Non-commissioned and other ranks non-Waziristan multi clasp. Verified 'single' clasp' WAZIRISTAN 1919–21' and 'WAZIRISTAN 1921–24' medals are scarce and would only have been only won by timeexpired personnel, reinforcement drafts or those retired from the campaign due to sickness or other. The bars on many two-clasp specimens examined are not riveted leading to the frequent loss of the Waziristan 1921-24 award. This is primarily due to thelatter clasp being issued some two to three years after receipt of the initial award and 'churn' of personnel back into civilian life.*
Note c.   *Malta August 1914. France & Flanders October 1914, Italy November 1917 forward. India November 1919 forward.*
Note d.   *Army Order 56 of 1920 authorised the spelling of the word 'Welsh' to be changed to 'Welch'.*
Note e.   *Medals named in impressed capitals: 'R. W. FUS.'*

Single Clasp	No. Identified	Rarity
Afghanistan N.W.F. 1919[3]	0	None Identified
Mahsud 1919–20[5]	0	None Identified
Waziristan 1919–21[4]	?	Scarce
Waziristan 1921–24[6]	?	Scarce

Combination Clasps	No. Identified	Rarity
Waziristan 1919–21[4] Waziristan 1921–24[6]	Bn. Strength	Not Rare
Waziristan 1919–21[4] Waziristan 1921–24[6] North West Frontier 1930–31[9]	1	Of the Utmost Rarity

Lieutenant Colonels: ~ C S Owen[4&6] & W G Holmes[4&6]

Majors: ~ E O Skaife[4&6]

Captains: ~ L A A Alston[4&6], Hon G R B Bingham[6], A M G Evans[4&6], J Edwardes-Evans[6], Hon D H W Kirby[6], S J Parker[6], C G H Peppe[4&6], H F Garnons-Williams[6] & E Wodehouse[4&6]

Lieutenants: ~ G E Cardwell[4&6], M B Dowse[4&6], D R Evans[4], W B Frank[6], E R C Freeman[6], H A Freeman[6], T S Griffiths[6], H B Harrison[6], H Hopkins[4&6], B E Horton[4&6], R G Davies-Jenkins[4&6], R A Johnson[6], S S O Jones[4&6], W P Kenyon[4&6], R E Lampen[6], H D'Oyly Lyle[4&6], H D T Morris[4&6], O L Richards[4&6] & (QM) G M Scofield[4&6]

Lance Sergeants/Corporals: ~ 4180019 W Phillips[4,6&(9 Sgt. 1 ACC, RTC)]

~ 8th (Service) Bn The Royal Welsh Fusiliers ~

Note a.   *Roll of all personnel identified as eligible.*

Note b.   *Formed August 1914. Mudros July 1915, Gallipoli August 1915, Egypt January 1916, Mesopotamia February 1916 to July 1919.*

Note c.   *Medals named in impressed capitals: 'R. W. FUS.'*

Single Clasp	No. Identified	Rarity
Afghanistan N.W.F. 1919[3]	33	Very Rare
Mahsud 1919–20[5]	0	None Identified
Waziristan 1919–21[4]	1	According to the roll as seen, can be considered Unique
Waziristan 1921–24[6]	0	None Identified

Combination Clasps	No. Identified	Rarity
Afghanistan N.W.F. 1919[3] Waziristan 1919–21[4] Waziristan 1921– 24[6]	1	According to the roll as seen, can be considered Unique

Lieutenant Colonels: ~ E A Stretch[3] attch. 1 SSB

Captains: ~ (Act) T Owen[3] attch. 17 SSB

Lance Sergeants/Corporals: ~ 19007 D R James[3] & 94673 W Phillips[3,4&6(RTC)]

Lance Corporals/Privates: ~ 12558 R J Barker[3], 49301 A G T Bartle[3], 12564 T Blackwall[3], 30316 W Cartwright[3] attch. 17 SSB, 30440 H Clegg[3], 13492 T J Davies[3], 30319 T Duffy[3], 30210 J Fanthorpe[3] attch. 25 SS, 70051 F Fisher[3], 11309 J L Franklin[4] attch. S&TC, 69465 A J Gooday[3], 40870 J H Hanks[3] attch. 17 SSB, 30025 G Harwick[3], 30372 C P Herd[3], 37936 T B Hicks[3], 49830 D E Hughs[3], 43705 H King[3], 30097 T Leathers[3], 44189 F G Lunt[3], 30345 F Martin[3], 59832 S Parker[3], 61597 D J Roberts[3], 41780 F Saunderson[3], 49846 C Slawson[3], 60647 R Smith[3], 315787 C H Symmons[3], 12168 H G Thomas[3] attch. 17 SSB, 9799 L G Tysall[3], 69975 C V Williams[3], 44394 D O Williams[3] & 200554 F Williams[3]

~ 2nd Bn, The South Wales Borderers ~

Note a. *Roll of all personnel identified as eligible.*
Note b. *China August 1914. Egypt March 1915, Mudros and Gallipoli April 1915, Egypt January 1916, France & Flanders March 1916 forward. India November 1919 forward.*
Note c. *Medals named in impressed capitals: 'S. WALES BORD.' or 'S. W. BORDRS.'*

Single Clasp	No. Identified	Rarity
Afghanistan N.W.F. 1919[3]	1	According to the roll as seen, can be considered Unique
Mahsud 1919–20[5]	0	None Identified
Waziristan 1919–21[4]	1	According to the roll as seen, can be considered Unique
Waziristan 1921–24[6]	1	According to the roll as seen, can be considered Unique
Combination Clasps	**No. Identified**	**Rarity**
Mahsud 1919–20[5] Waziristan 1919–21[4]	1	According to the roll as seen, can be considered Unique
Waziristan 1919–21[4] Waziristan 1921–24[6]	1	According to the roll as seen, can be considered Unique

Lieutenant Colonels: ~ (Bvt) L I G Morgan-Owen[4&5] AA&QMG WFF & (Bvt) W H Stanway[6], Adjt NW Rly Regt, AFI
Majors: ~ (Bvt) R L Petre[3] attch. Staff
Warrant Officers Class II: ~ 31529 E Poote[4] attch. RTE
Quartermaster Sergeants/Sergeants: ~ (Act) (3902621) 82303 R Owen[4&6] attch. IAOC

~ 1/1st Brecknockshire Bn, The South Wales Borderers, Territorial Force ~

Note a. *Roll of all personnel identified as eligible.*
Note b. *United Kingdom August 1914. Aden December 1914, India August 1915 forward to October 1919.*
Note c. *Medals named in impressed capitals: 'S. WALES BORD.' or 'S. W. BORDRS.'*

Single Clasp	No. Identified	Rarity
Afghanistan N.W.F. 1919[3]	65	Rare
Mahsud 1919–20[5]	0	None Identified
Waziristan 1919–21[4]	2	Of the Utmost Rarity
Waziristan 1921–24[6]	0	None Identified

Captains: ~ A C S Butcher[3] attch. 33 DSC & D J Williams[3] attch. HQ East Persian Cordon
Lieutenants: ~ F Wilson[3] attch. 285 Coy, MGC
Quartermaster Sergeants/Sergeants: ~ (Act) 200090 F E Bradley[3] attch. 1 S Lanc, (Act) 200603 A H Davies[3] attch. 52 PMC, (200103) 1225 T R Edwards[3] attch. 1 S Lanc, (Act) 200537 T Evans[3], (Act) 45534 F Hacking[3], (Act) 200304 R James[3] attch. 1/25 London, (Act) 200213 D J Jones[3] attch. 1 S Lanc, (Act) 201049 P Jones[4] attch. S&TC, (Act) 200522 W C Roberts[3] attch. 1 S Lanc & (Act) 200073 D Williams[3] attch. 1/25 London
Lance Sergeants / Corporals: ~ (Act) 200340 G A Edwards[3] attch. 1 S Lanc, 200010 L J Evans[3] attch. S&TC, (Act) 200225 G R Hawkes[3] attch. 1/25 London & (Act) 200359 W J Williams[3] attch. 1 S Lanc
Lance Corporals/Privates: ~ 45525 W Bibbing[4], 201077 H Brown[3], 201523 I J Clement[3] attch. 1 S Lanc, 200649 R W Colcombe[3], 200089 T S Colwell[3], 201529 I Davies[3], 201321 J J Davies[3] attch. 1/25 London, 200693 W T Davies[3], 201125 C H Duggan[3] attch. 1 S Lanc, 201411 A H Edwards[3] attch. 1 S Lanc, 201217 E C Evans[3], 201372 J W Games[3] attch. 1 S Lanc, 13072 F Gibbons[3], 200600 L J Glover[3], 201175 E Griffiths[3], 201303 P L Jarman[3] attch. 1/25 London, 201562 T J Jenkins[3] attch. 1 S Lanc, 201271 A Jenner[3] attch. 1 S Lanc, 201272 A E Jones[3] attch. 1 S Lanc, 201236 A J Jones[3] attch. 1 S Lanc, 201198 E Jones[3] attch. 1 S Lanc, 200915 J T Jones[3] attch. 1/25 London, 200535 M Lawrence[3] attch. 39 DSC, 201123 A H Lewis[3], 200952 B Lewis[3] attch. 1 S Lanc, 201570 M Marks[3] attch. 1/25 London, 201568 W G Marks[3], 200094 J E Mason[3], 201223 A W Meale[3] attch. 1 S Lanc, 201197 J I Meredith[3] attch. 1 S Lanc, 200539 R J Miller[3] attch. 1 S Lanc, 200152 L H C Morgan[3] attch. 1 S Lanc, 201185 E Morris[3], 200483 A Page[3], 201216 H Parry[3] attch. 1 S Lanc, 200278 E A Price[3] attch. 1 S Lanc, 201078 T Price[3] attch. 1/25 London, 201155 S Probert[3], 201349 T Roberts[3], attch. 1/25 London, 201526 D Simon[3], 200710 A G Stevenson[3] attch. 44 DSC, KKF, (2902963) 11572 E Sully[3] attch. 1 S Lanc, 200209 W D Thomas[3],

200325 G H Thorogood[3], 200489 G Wargent[3], 201451 W Weale[3] attch. 1/25 London, (3902879) 38754 G Williams[3] attch. 1/25 London, 201199 H Williams[3] attch. 1 S Lanc & 201481 R T Williams[3]
Drummers: ~ 200321 C Hellard[3]

~ 4th (Service) Bn, The South Wales Borderers ~

Note a.   *Roll of all personnel identified as eligible.*
Note b.   *Formed August 1914. Mudros and Gallipoli July 1915, Mudros and Egypt January 1916, Mesopotamia March 1916 and thence to Kurdistan 1918.*
Note c.   *Medals named in impressed capitals: 'S. WALES BORD.' or 'S. W. BORDRS.'*

Single Clasp	No. Identified	Rarity
Afghanistan N.W.F. 1919[3]	55	Rare
Mahsud 1919–20[5]	0	None Identified
Waziristan 1919–21[4]	1	According to the roll as seen, can be considered Unique
Waziristan 1921–24[6]	0	None Identified

Majors: ~ E P Bury[3] DAAG, KKF
Captains: ~ J W Foreman[4] attch. 7 MT Coy, S&TC
Lieutenants: ~ T R Graham[3] attch. 1/25 London & R C D Tovey[3] attch. 285 Coy, MGC
Quartermaster Sergeants/Sergeants: ~ (Act) 28886 J H Jones[3] attch. 47 B(S)S, BFF
Lance Corporals/Privates: ~ 19686 J W Blueman[3], 3/26893 G Bowler[3], 82623 T J Broome[3], 13163 W S Bull[3], 14394 D Butt[3] attch. 1/4 Queen's, (Originally 5th Bn), 31566 W J Cawley[3], 26413 L B Clack[3], 24896 J Conlan[3], 31673 W R Crowe[3], 30181 J Devonland[3], 3/19918 W Fields[3], 31404 E C Ford[3], 30035 W S G Fordham[3], 28770 N Fox[3] attch. 1/4 Queen's, 33091 H Hall[3], 31492 W J Harris[3], 202589 T E Iredale[3], 30531 R E L Johns[3], 28421 R Jones[3], 44805 T Jones[3], 31493 W Joseph[3], 31407 F Legge[3], 38971 D J Lewis[3] attch. 1 S Lanc, 22857 H Long[3], 31378 H Morgans[3], 31501 J H Morris[3], 27797 J Nicholls[3], 200191 H F Parsons[3], 31536 J Pearce[3], 26917 G H Reacher[3], 282762 W H Rees[3], 31331 O Roberts[3], 31562 R A Roberts[3], 24869 A Robertson[3], 4/19847 G Roscoe[3], 27506 W Rhys[3] attch. RASC, 44840 J Scott[3], 3/27037 V Season[3], 24197 W Simpson[3], 24815 R Snape[3], 31211 I C Southwoon[3], 31666 E Thomas[3], 12088 H Thomas[3], 30116 W Thomas[3], 3/13358 C E Townsend[3], 31398 W Turner[3], 12696 H Webber[3], 27503 R Williams[3] attch. RASC, 26986 J A Willis[3] attch. 1/4 Queen's, 19920 J Wilson[3] & 9/27584 A Wright[3]

~ 1st Bn, The King's Own Scottish Borders ~

Note a.   *Roll of all personnel identified as eligible.*
Note b.   *India August 1914. Egypt November 1914, United Kingdom, Egypt March 1915, Mudros and Gallipoli April 1915, Egypt January 1916, France & Flanders March 1916 forward. India November 1919.*
Note c.   *Medals named in impressed capitals: 'K.O.S.B.' OR 'K.O.SCO.BORD.'*

Single Clasp	No. Identified	Rarity
Afghanistan N.W.F. 1919[3]	3	Of the Utmost Rarity
Mahsud 1919–20[5]	0	None Identified
Waziristan 1919–21[4]	3	Of the Utmost Rarity
Waziristan 1921–24[6]	0	None Identified

Lieutenants: ~ A H Currie[3] attch. 2 King's
Quartermaster Sergeants/Sergeants: ~ (Act) 3178758 W Cooper[4] attch. RTE, Bannu & 9765 J McLarty[3] attch. 26 CFA
Lance Sergeants/Corporals: ~ 3179072 J Scott[4] attch. Pishin Det Sigs, Haji Khan Col
Lance Corporals/Privates: ~ 10857 W F Lawrence[3] attch. Fort Ali Masjid & (48367) 3179141 D Pollock[4] attch. MFO, WFF

~ 2ⁿᵈ (Scottish Rifles) Bn, The Cameronians (Scottish Rifles) ~

Note a.   *Roll of all personnel identified as eligible.*
Note b.   *Malta August 1914. France & Flanders November 1914 forward. India November 1919 to February 1922 thence to Iraq and Kurdistan returning to India in January 1924.*
Note c.   *Medals named in impressed capitals: 'SCO. RIF.' Specimens bearing the clasp 'WAZIRISTAN 1921-24' clasp are believed to be named 'CAMERONS.'*

Single Clasp	No. Identified	Rarity
Afghanistan N.W.F. 1919[3]	0	None Identified
Mahsud 1919–20[5]	1	According to the roll as seen, can be considered Unique
Waziristan 1919–21[4]	3	Of the Utmost Rarity
Waziristan 1921–24[6]	11	Extremely Rare

Combination Clasps	No. Identified	Rarity
Mahsud 1919–20[5] Waziristan 1919–21[4]	1	According to the roll as seen, can be considered Unique
Waziristan 1919–21[4] Waziristan 1921–24[6]	1	According to the roll as seen, can be considered Unique

Majors: ~ J S Millar[6] attch. 'B' DSC
Captains: ~ D G Moncrieff Wright[5]
Quartermaster Sergeants/Sergeants: ~ 3233672 W Ranson[4]
Lance Corporal /Privates/Riflemen: ~ 3234390 H J Broom[6] attch. ISH, Sararogha, 3233855 T Carr[6] 27 CCCS, Ladha, 3233716 W A Goodrich[4&6] attch. 'G' DSC, 3234952 T Jamieson[4&5] attch. 27 CCCS, Ladha, 3235039 T T Johnston[6] attch. HQ, 5 Bde., Manzai, 3235174 A H K Kell[6] attch. 43 B(S)S, Manzai, 3233602 W King[6] attch. 'G' DSC, 3234214 W Matthews[6] attch. IGH, Tank, 3233827 W McCracken[6] 27 CCCS, Ladha, 3234800 G Muir[6] attch. 'G' DSC, 3234855 H T Proud[4] attch. 'G' DSC, 3234758 R Robinson[4] attch. 'G' DSC, 3234187 G Saunders[6] attch. 27 CCCS, Ladha & 3233722 H Wilson[6] attch. HQ, Kohat

~ ?/5ᵗʰ Bn, The Cameronians (Scottish Rifles), Territorial Force ~

Note a.   *Roll of all personnel identified as eligible.*
Note b.   *Medals named in impressed capitals: 'SCO. RIF.'*

Single Clasp	No. Identified	Rarity
Afghanistan N.W.F. 1919[3]	1	According to the roll as seen, can be considered Unique
Mahsud 1919–20[5]	0	None Identified
Waziristan 1919–21[4]	0	None Identified
Waziristan 1921–24[6]	0	None Identified

Lieutenants: ~ N C Lamberton[3] attch. 1/25 London

~ 1ˢᵗ Garrison Bn, The Cameronians (Scottish Rifles) ~

Note a.   *Roll of all personnel identified as eligible.*
Note b.   *Formed February 1916. India February 1916 forward.*
Note c.   *Medals named in impressed capitals: 'SCO. RIF.'*

Single Clasp	No. Identified	Rarity
Afghanistan N.W.F. 1919[3]	9	Of the Utmost Rarity
Mahsud 1919–20[5]	0	None Identified
Waziristan 1919–21[4]	0	None Identified

Waziristan 1921–24[6]	0	None Identified

Lieutenants: ~ J H Clark[3] attch. 1 DWR, C N Barclay[3] attch. 1 Yorkshire & S J S Scoular[3] attch. 17 SSB
Quartermaster Sergeants/Sergeants: ~ 24516 D McKenzie[3]
Lance Sergeants/Corporals: ~ 24334 J Jenkins[3]
Lance Corporals/rivates: ~ 29567 S W Hayfield[3], attch. 118 ICCS, 12583 J Kerr[3] attch. 35 BGH, Peshawar, 24282 H Leigh[3] attch. 12 CFA, 4 Div. & 23969 W J Williamson[3] attch. 18 IMVS

~ 1st Bn, The Royal Inniskilling Fusiliers ~

Note a. *Roll of all personnel identified as eligible.*
Note b. *India August 1914. Mudros and Gallipoli April 1915, Egypt January 1916, France & Flanders March 1916 forward. India November 1919 to April 1924 thence to Iraq.*
Note c. *Medals with the clasp 'WAZIRISTAN 1919-21' as first award to enlisted men bear the rank designation 'PTE.'. Those with 'WAZIRISTAN 1921-24' bear the designation 'FUS'.*
Note d. *Medals named in impressed capitals: 'R. INNIS. FUS.'*

Single Clasp	No. Identified	Rarity
Afghanistan N.W.F. 1919[3]	0	None Identified
Mahsud 1919–20[5]	1	According to the roll as seen, can be considered Unique
Waziristan 1919–21[4]	4	Of the Utmost Rarity
Waziristan 1921–24[6]	4	Of the Utmost Rarity
Combination Clasps	No. Identified	Rarity
Afghanistan N.W.F. 1919[3] Waziristan 1921–24[6]	1	According to the roll as seen, can be considered Unique
Waziristan 1919–21[4] Waziristan 1921–24[6]	1	According to the roll as seen, can be considered Unique

Warrant Officers Class II: ~ (Act Rly Tpt Sgt. Maj.) 7042318 F Desmond[6] attch. RTE & 7040132 T E Johnston[4&6] attch. 'C' DSC
Lance Corporals/Privates/Fusiliers: ~ (6972109) 8204 S Brown[3&6] attch. 33 DSC, BFF, 6973279 R Buckley[6] attch. 'G' DSC, 6972711 J Dinsmore[4] attch. RTE, WFF, 6972918 A Lavelle[6] attch. 'G' DSC, 6973044 R McAnulty[4] attch. 4 BSS, 6972684 W Moody[4] attch. 43 B(S)S, Manzai, 6973215 R Morley[6] attch. 'G' DSC, 27261 R W Savage[4] & 6972538 A Sloan[5] attch. 27 CCCS, Ladha

~ 2nd Bn, The Gloucestershire Regiment ~

Note a. *Roll of all personnel identified as eligible.*
Note b. *China August 1914. France & Flanders December 1914, Salonika December 1915 forward. India from November 1919 forward.*
Note c. *Medals named in impressed capitals: 'GLOUC. R.'*

Single Clasp	No. Identified	Rarity
Afghanistan N.W.F. 1919[3]	4	Of the Utmost Rarity
Mahsud 1919–20[5]	0	None Identified
Waziristan 1919–21[4]	4	Of the Utmost Rarity
Waziristan 1921–24[6]	29	Very Rare
Combination Clasps	No. Identified	Rarity
Mahsud 1919–20[5] Waziristan 1919–21[4]	1	According to the roll as seen, can be considered Unique

Waziristan 1919–21[4] Waziristan 1921–24[6]	7	Of the Utmost Rarity

Majors: ~ Hon N F R Somerset[3] attch. MMG Bty, MGC

Captains: ~ G A Edwards[6] attch. 'B' Corps Sigs, A H Kidston[4] attch. S&TC & A J McCarthy[4] attch. 'A' Corps Sigs

Lieutenants: ~ C G Bound[3] attch. 44 DSC, KKF, R M M Davy[3] attch. HQ, BFF, C M Frank[3] attch. 263 Coy, MGC, P Devlin-Hamilton[4&6] Fld Cashier, WFF, G E Mirehouse[6] attch. 21 Bde. & F K Wilson[6] attch. 'C' DSC

Quartermaster Sergeants/Sergeants: ~ (Act) (55665) 5173846 A J Cook[4&6] attch. HQ, WFF, (Act) 5172080 C P Cunningham[6] attch. 8 ISS, Bannu, (Act) 5173669 W H Heaton[6] attch. RTE, Kalabagh, 5173289 S Higgins[6] attch. RTE, Mari Indus, (Act) 5173209 S G Howe[6] attch. RTE, Mari Indus, (5172127) 8938 H M Smith[4&5] attch. HQ, 68 Bde. & (Act) 5172273 W C Tanner[6] attch. RTE, Bannu

Lance Sergeants/Corporals: ~ 5172514 A J Nash[6] attch. Provo Staff, Bannu & 5172539 J Pallett[6] attch. 'B' Corps Sigs

Lance Corporals/Privates: ~ 5174729 W Aldridge[6] attch. Provo Staff, Bannu, 5172970 C Baillie[6] attch. 64 CFA, 5172632 F F Baker[6] attch. 8 ISS, Bannu, 5173248 G F Blakeway[6] attch. Provo Staff, Bannu, 5173623 A J Carroll[6] attch. 'G' DSC, 5172559 A E Cole[6] attch. 'A' Corps Sigs, 56495 W C Coles[4&6] attch. Ord Dept, Mari Indus, 5173664 J H Davis[6] attch. Provo Staff, Bannu, 5173510 W J Davey[6] attch. RTE, DIK, 5173113 T G Dunn[6] attch. LofC Sig, DIK, 5174204 C Emmett[6] attch. 27 CCCS, Ladha, 5173942 H F Hemmings[6] attch. Ord Dept, Mari Indus, 5172805 H Hill[4] attch. 2 MT Coy, S&TC, 5174122 W J Johnson[6] attch. 'G' DSC, 5173903 E H M Jones[6] attch. 'G' DSC, (40589) 5172976 E Knowlson[4&6] attch. Ord Dept, Mari Indus, 5173204 W Large[6] attch. 27 CCCS, Ladha, 5273735 E H Lewis[6] attch. 'B' Corps Sigs, (39518) 5172769 A E Lock[4&6] attch. Ord Dept, Mari Indus, 5173292 J W B Maddox[6] attch. 'G' DSC, 5173480 A S Palmer[4] attch. 2 MT Coy, S&TC, (55700) 5173881 H G Smith[4&6] attch. RTE, Mari Indus, 5172942 A C Snell[6] attch. 8 ISS, Bannu, (46582) 5172969 H H K Varcoe[4&6] attch. RTE, DIK, 5174989 R H Warren[6] attch. 8 SS & 5173470 C L E Watts[6] attch. HQ, 8 Bde., Bannu

~ 3rd (Reserve) Bn, The Gloucestershire Regiment ~

Note a.   *Roll of all personnel identified as eligible.*

Note b.   *United Kingdom August 1914. United Kingdom throughout Great War period providing drafts and reinforcements.*

Note c.   *Medals named in impressed capitals: 'GLOUC. R.'*

Single Clasp	No. Identified	Rarity
Afghanistan N.W.F.1919[3]	20	Extremely Rare
Mahsud 1919–20[5]	0	None Identified
Waziristan 1919–21[4]	5	Of the Utmost Rarity
Waziristan 1921–24[6]	0	None Identified

Lieutenants: ~ C G Bound[3] attch. 44 DSC, KKF, R M M Davy[3] attch. HQ, BFF & C M Frank[3] attch. 263 Coy, MGC

Quartermaster Sergeants/Sergeants: ~ 25902 S H Blackmore[4] attch. Ord Depot

Lance Sergeants/Corporals: ~ (Act) 34381 E A Batchelor[3] attch. 2 Som L I, (Formerly 1st Bn)

Lance Corporals/Privates: ~ (9967) 5172345 P E Barnett[3] attch. 10 IMVS, 30860 A G S Blake[3] attch. HQ, ZF, 2347 J H Cureton[3] attch. 1 IGC, NWFF, 25854 H A Dale[3] attch. 13 IMVS, 266776 F C Eastcott[3] attch. 46 BSS, (52845) 5173419 A E Elliott[4] attch. 1 CCCS, 22251 A N England[3] attch. HQ, ZF, 204291 W Fudge[4] attch. 20 IMVS, 22271 S Horniblow[3] attch. 10 IMVS, 22262 J E Howson[3] attch. 1 IGC, NWFF, (56347) 5174155 T M Matthews[4] attch. 2 MT Coy, S&TC NWFF, 55661 W H Monk[3] attch. RTE, 25507 W Oliver[3] attch. 2/6 Sussex, 16242 A Preston[3] attch. 2/6 Sussex, (56249) 5174077 R J Sadler[4] attch. 1 CCCS, 46550 M Smith[3] attch. RTE, 10596 C C Tower[3] attch. 2/6 Sussex, 21351 A Vaisey[3] attch. 2/6 Sussex, 33762 J Walkden[3] attch. 10 IMVS & 265107 W Walkley[3] attch. 10 IMVS

~ 7th (Service) Bn, The Gloucestershire Regiment ~

Note a.   *Roll of all personnel identified as eligible.*

Note b.   *Formed August 1914. Gallipoli July 1915, Egypt January 1916, Mesopotamia February 1916 forward. North Persia July 1918 forward.*

Note c.   *Medals named in impressed capitals: 'GLOUC. R.'*

Single Clasp	No. Identified	Rarity
Afghanistan N.W.F. 1919[3]	6	Of the Utmost Rarity
Mahsud 1919–20[5]	0	None Identified
Waziristan 1919– 21[4]	0	None Identified
Waziristan 1921–24[6]	0	None Identified

Corporals: ~ (Act) 33781 H Percival[3] attch. 2 Som LI
Lance Corporals/Privates: ~ 21463 W Boulton[3] attch. 2 Som LI, 24208 L Fisher[3] attch. 2 Som LI, 10556 H Higgins[3] attch. 2 Som LI, 10834 A Mills[3] attch. 2 Som LI & 291642 B Shelton[3]

~ 1st Bn, The Worcestershire Regiment ~

Note a. Roll of all personnel identified as eligible.
Note b. Egypt August 1914. France & Flanders November 1914, forward. India 1922 forward.
Note c. Medals named in impressed capitals: 'WORC. R.'

Single Clasp	No. Identified	Rarity
Afghanistan N.W.F. 1919[3]	0	None Identified
Mahsud 1919–20[5]	0	None Identified
Waziristan 1919–21[4]	10	Of the Utmost Rarity
Waziristan 1921–24[6]	6	Of the Utmost Rarity

Combination Clasps	No. Identified	Rarity
Afghanistan N.W.F. 1919[3] Mahsud 1919 – 20[5] Waziristan 1919–21[4] Waziristan 1921–24[6]	1	According to the roll as seen, can be considered Unique
Mahsud 1919–20[5] Waziristan 1919–21[4]	1	According to the roll as seen, can be considered Unique
Waziristan 1919–21[4] Waziristan 1921–24[6]	3	Of the Utmost Rarity
Waziristan 1921–24[6] Malabar 1921–22[7]	1	According to the roll as seen, can be considered Unique

Majors: ~ E L G Lawrence[4&5] attch. 2/5 GR, IA & (Bvt) G A Slaughter[3,4,5&(6 RTC)] 1 MMG Bty
Lieutenants: ~ T Ivor-Moore[4] attch. 10 ACC & L R Samut[4] attch. RTE, (Originally Malta Militia) & J E S Walford[6] attch. 'B' DSC
Lance Sergeants/Corporals: ~ 5239123 C W Muddiman[6&7(L/Cpl. R Sigs)] attch. 'B' Corps Sigs
Lance Corporals/Privates: ~ 5097780 G Barker[6] attch. HQ, Waz Dist, 5241989 J Bishop[4] attch. 18 BSS, 5241975 R J Bullock[4&6] attch. HQ, WFF, 5241540 L Gaul[4] attch. 43 B(S)S, Manzai, 5239745 J Goodwin[4] attch. 3/W Sig Sqn, 5240512 W G Guest[4&6] attch. 15 BSS, 5240876 J Guise[4&6(18 Coy RAMC)] attch. 43 B(S)S, 5241701 S R Holder[6] attch. ISH, Mari Indus, 5240159 B Millward[4] attch. 43 B(S)S, Manzai, 5240985 J K Pauncefort[4] attch. BGH Bannu, 5241979 F A Roberts[6] attch. 7 Bde., Dardoni, 5242691 C J Sodo[6], 5241206 A Tandy[4] attch. 7 IGH, DIK, 5240691 K G Taylor[4] attch. BGH, Bannu, 5240845 E Vivash[6] attch. 43 B(S)S, Manzai & 5240840 E Wilkes[4] attch. 43 B(S)S, Manzai

~ 3rd Bn, The Worcestershire Regiment ~

Note a. Roll of all personnel identified as eligible.
Note b. United Kingdom August 1914. France & Flanders August 1914 forward. India March 1920 to disbandment in 1922.
Note c. Medals named in impressed capitals: 'WORC. R.'

Single Clasp	No. Identified	Rarity
Afghanistan N.W.F. 1919[3]	1	According to the roll as seen, can be considered Unique

Mahsud 1919–20[5]	0	None Identified
Waziristan 1919–21[4]	6	Of the Utmost Rarity
Waziristan 1921–24[6]	0	None Identified
Combination Clasps	**No. Identified**	**Rarity**
Mahsud 1919–20[5] Waziristan 1919–21[4]	1	According to the roll as seen, can be considered Unique
Waziristan 1919–21[4] Waziristan 1921–24[6]	1	According to the roll as seen, can be considered Unique

Captains: ~ R H M Lee[4&5]

Lieutenants: ~ W G W Venn[3] attch. 2/6 R Sussex

Quartermaster Sergeants/Sergeants: ~ (Act) 5240212 G A Read[4] attch. HQ, WFF

Lance Corporals/Privates: ~ 5243241 C Cattle[4] attch. MFO, Wana Col, 5241080 J H Knott[4] attch. 1 CCCS, 5240955 G W Lane[4&6] attch. HQ, WFF, 5239518 W Lloyd[4] attch. RTE, DIK, 5241588 J Robinson[4] attch. RTE, DIK & 5240698 H F Smith[4] attch. HQ, WFF

~ 5th (Reserve) Bn, The Worcestershire Regiment ~

Note a.   *Roll of all personnel identified as eligible.*
Note b.   *United Kingdom August 1914. United Kingdom throughout Great War period providing drafts and reinforcements.*
Note c.   *Medals named in impressed capitals: 'WORC. R.'*

Single Clasp	No. Identified	Rarity
Afghanistan N.W.F. 1919[3]	1	According to the roll as seen, can be considered Unique
Mahsud 1919–20[5]	0	None Identified
Waziristan 1919–21[4]	0	None Identified
Waziristan 1921–24[6]	0	None Identified

Lieutenants: ~ J F Davis[3] attch. 1/25 London

~ 6th (Reserve) Bn, The Worcestershire Regiment ~

Note a.   *Roll of all personnel identified as eligible.*
Note b.   *United Kingdom August 1914. United Kingdom throughout Great War period providing drafts and reinforcements.*
Note c.   *Medals named in impressed capitals: 'WORC. R.'*

Single Clasp	No. Identified	Rarity
Afghanistan N.W.F. 1919[3]	1	According to the roll as seen, can be considered Unique.
Mahsud 1919–20[5]	0	None Identified
Waziristan 1919–21[4]	0	None Identified
Waziristan 1921–24[6]	0	None Identified

Lieutenants: ~ E S Pink[3] attch. 17 SSB

~ ?/7th Bn, The Worcestershire Regiment, Territorial Force ~

Note a.   *Roll of all personnel identified as eligible.*
Note b.   *Medals named in impressed capitals: 'WORC. R.'*

Single Clasp	No. Identified	Rarity
Afghanistan N.W.F. 1919[3]	1	According to the roll as seen, can be considered Unique
Mahsud 1919–20[5]	0	None Identified
Waziristan 1919–21[4]	0	None Identified
Waziristan 1921–24[6]	0	None Identified

Lieutenants: ~ C E Hardwicke[3] attch. MGC

~ ?/8th Bn, The Worcestershire Regiment, Territorial Force ~

Note a.   *Roll of all personnel identified as eligible.*
Note b.   *Medals named in impressed capitals: 'WORC. R.'*

Single Clasp	No. Identified	Rarity
Afghanistan N.W.F. 1919[3]	1	According to the roll as seen, can be considered Unique
Mahsud 1919–20[5]	0	None Identified
Waziristan 1919–21[4]	0	None Identified
Waziristan 1921–24[6]	0	None Identified

Lieutenants: ~ T E Lee[3] attch. 2/4 Border

~ 9th (Service) Bn, The Worcestershire Regiment ~

Note a.   *Roll of all personnel identified as eligible.*
Note b.   *Formed August 1914. Gallipoli July 1915, Egypt January 1916, Mesopotamia February 1916, North Persia Force October 1918, Southern Russia November 1918 to August 1919 and thence Turkey.*
Note c.   *Medals named in impressed capitals: 'WORC. R.'*

Single Clasp	No. Identified	Rarity
Afghanistan N.W.F. 1919[3]	37	Very Rare
Mahsud 1919–20[5]	0	None Identified
Waziristan 1919–21[4]	0	None Identified
Waziristan 1921–24[6]	0	None Identified

Lieutenants: ~ E M Dixon[3] attch. 2 N Stafford
Quartermaster Sergeant /Sergeants: ~ (Act) 26478 H S Crosbee[3] attch. 32 Bde. Sply Sect
Lance Sergeants/Corporals: ~ 45500 E McAffery[3] attch. 1 ARW, S&TC
Lance Corporals/Privates: ~ 38429 W C Ball[3] attch. 1 Yorkshire, 203895 P Bevington[3] attch. 1 Yorkshire, 49596 E A Bowd[3] attch. 1 Yorkshire, 49584 W T Cole[3] attch. 1 Yorkshire, 44517 E W Davis[3] attch. 1 Yorkshire, 31641 G Dulake[3] attch. 1 Yorkshire, 12922 A G Elmer[3] attch. 2/6 Sussex, 46861 A Fradgley[3] attch. 1 Yorkshire, 49541 C F Golding[3] attch. 1 Yorkshire, 204318 F A Griggs[3] attch. 1 Yorkshire, 17785 W Hackett[3] attch. 1 Yorkshire, 49543 H B Hall[3] attch. 1 Yorkshire, 35526 G Handoll[3] attch. 1 DLI, 14488 C H Hill[3] attch. 2/6 Sussex, 44562 C H Hill[3] attch. 2/6 Sussex, 49545 A Hillyard[3] attch. 1 Yorkshire, 204307 T H Hodges[3] attch. 1 DLI, 22504 W Hughes[3] attch. 1 Yorkshire, 44511 T E Humphries[3] attch. 36 & 37 SSs, 47992 T Jewell[3] attch. 1 Yorkshire, 45510 R S McKay[3] attch. 1 Yorkshire, 48247 F Milner[3] attch. 1 Yorkshire, 23636 A Moore[3] attch. 1 Yorkshire, 35672 A P Moore[3] attch. 2/6 Sussex, 49554 A Norris[3] attch. 1 Yorkshire, 47959 W Pearce[3] attch. 1 Yorkshire, 25527 W H Reynolds[3] attch. 1 DLI, 49558 A Rose[3] attch. 1 Yorkshire, 47302 P Schilling[3] attch. 1 DLI, 33782 W G Shepston[3] attch. 1 Yorkshire, 48887 R Smith[3] attch. 1 Yorkshire, 23360 W H Taylor[3] attch. 2/6 Sussex, 47994 J S Toye[3] attch. 1 Yorkshire & 46819 W D Watts[3] attch. 1 DLI

~ 6th (Service) Bn, The East Lancashire Regiment ~

Note a. *Roll of all personnel identified as eligible.*
Note b. *Formed August 1914. Egypt June 1915, Mudros and Gallipoli July 1915, Mudros December 1915, Egypt January 1916, Mesopotamia February 1916 to December 1918 and thence Kurdistan.*
Note c. *Medals named in impressed capitals: 'E. LAN. R.'*

Single Clasp	No. Identified	Rarity
Afghanistan N.W.F. 1919[3]	16	Extremely Rare
Mahsud 1919–20[5]	0	None Identified
Waziristan 1919–21[4]	0	None Identified
Waziristan 1921–24[6]	0	None Identified

Lieutenants: ~ J A Brothers[3] attch. 1/1 Kent, E W Croasdale[3] attch. 287 Coy, MGC, H E D Pearce[3] attch. 17 SSB & W Wallington[3] attch. 1 S Lanc
Quartermaster Sergeants/Sergeants: ~ (Act) 9300 H J Richards[3] attch. IUL & (Act) 22407 A Skelton[3] attch. 25 DSC
Lance Sergeants/Corporals: ~ 35893 A Cook[3] attch. 1 DLI
Lance Corporals/Privates: ~ 9159 A Brooks[3] attch. 33 DSC, 19811 G W Brownbridge[3] attch. Mushki MT Sect, S&TC, 38300 E Good[3] attch. 2 Som LI, 24150 W A F Mallinson[3] attch. 2 Som LI, 11745 H Steele[3] attch. 2 King's, 11099 E Taylor[3] attch. 2 Som LI, 37179 T Tattersall[3] attch. 2 Som LI, 11159 H Waring[3] & 21955 A Warwick[3] attch. 286 Coy, MGC

~ 1st Bn, The East Surrey Regiment ~

Note a. *Roll of all personnel identified as eligible.*
Note b. *United Kingdom August 1914. France & Flanders August 1914, Italy December 1917, France & Flanders April 1918 to August 1919 and thence North Russia.*
Note c. *Medals named in impressed capitals: 'E. SURR. R.'*

Single Clasp	No. Identified	Rarity
Afghanistan N.W.F. 1919[3]	1	According to the roll as seen, can be considered Unique
Mahsud 1919–20[5]	0	None Identified
Waziristan 1919–21[4]	0	None Identified
Waziristan 1921–24[6]	0	None Identified

Lieutenants: ~ H N Bousfield[3] attch. Staff

~ 2nd Bn, The East Lancashire Regiment ~

Note a. *Roll of all personnel identified as eligible.*
Note b. *India August 1914. France & Flanders January 1915, Egypt October 1915, Salonika December 1915, Turkey from November 1918 to April 1919 and thence ???.*
Note c. *Medals named in impressed capitals: 'E. SURR. R.'*

Single Clasp	No. Identified	Rarity
Afghanistan N.W.F. 1919[3]	1	According to the roll as seen, can be considered Unique
Mahsud 1919–20[5]	0	None Identified
Waziristan 1919–21[4]	0	None Identified
Waziristan 1921–24[6]	0	None Identified

Quartermaster Sergeants/Sergeants: ~ L/9417 A V Whittome[3] attch. S&TC

~ 1/5th Bn, The East Lancashire Regiment, Territorial Force ~

Note a. *Roll of all personnel identified as eligible.*
Note b. *United Kingdom August 1914. India December 1914, Mesopotamia December 1917 to May 1919 and thence Kurdistan.*
Note c. *Medals named in impressed capitals: 'E. SURR. R.'.*

Single Clasp	No. Identified	Rarity
Afghanistan N.W.F. 1919[3]	57	Rare
Mahsud 1919–20[5]	0	None Identified
Waziristan 1919–21[4]	2	Of the Utmost Rarity
Waziristan 1921–24[6]	0	None Identified.
Combination Clasps	**No. Identified**	**Rarity**
Afghanistan N.W.F. 1919[3] Waziristan 1919–21[4]	1	According to the roll as seen, can be considered Unique

Lieutenants: ~ D Grahame[3] attch. 222 Coy, E P Stevens[3] attch. MAD & MGC & A C Thompson[3]

Warrant Officers Class II: ~ (Act) 200449 G C Birch[3] attch. 36 BGH & 200029 L A Emms[3] attch. HQ, NWFF

Company Quartermaster Sergeants/Staff Sergeants/Colour Sergeants: ~ (Act) 200685 C J Browning[3] attch. CMSC, 200063 A H Coveley[3] attch. 1 ARW, S&TC, 200789 A E T Dendy[3] attch. 1 ARW, S&TC, 200344 W P Hamshar[3] attch. 1 ARW, S&TC, 200697 W T Piper[3] attch. 1 Bde. Spt Col, S&TC, 200447 H L Smith[3] attch. 1 Bde. Spt Col, S&TC & 200498 J E Woodward[3] attch. 1 ARW, S&TC

Quartermaster Sergeants/Sergeants: ~ (Act) 200656 H Elms[3] attch. 1/4 QORWK, 57 Bde., (Act) 200769 W T Fishleigh[3] attch. HQ, NWFF, (Act) 200668 J C Gibson[3] attch. 6 MT Coy, S&TC, 200180 A Gregory[3] attch. IOD, (Act) 200143 G W Joyce[3] attch. 45 Bde. Sply Coy, 200330 J W Lawrence[3] attch. 1 MT Coy, S&TC, 200238 C W H Mortiboy[3] attch. S&TC, (Act) 200100 P Trustam[3] attch. S&TC, (Act) 201901 A E S Venn[3] & 200433 H F Waller[3] attch. 1 MT Coy, S&TC

Lance Sergeants/Corporals: ~ 200244 W G Chick[3] attch. 2 MT Coy, S&TC, 201433 J W H Collins[3] attch. 2 MT Coy, S&TC, 201310 A Elliott[3] attch. 1 ARW, S&TC, 200648 A L Firth[3] attch. 38&39 DSC, 2 Div., 200223 C F Hill[3] attch. 3/W Sig Sqn, (Act) 200513 J H Martin[3] attch. 1 MT Coy, S&TC & (Act) 201889 G E Newland[3] attch. 1 ARW, S&TC, 200562 C J Owden[3] attch. AOC, 200227 R (C) Tillett[4] attch. ISC & 200432 E R Vine[3&4] attch. 5 MMG Bty, MGC

Lance Corporals/Privates: ~ 201277 H P Allwright[3] attch. 1/25 London, 45 Bde., 200736 R H Aplin[3] attch. LofC Sigs, 200185 W R Bell[3] attch. 44 DSC, KKF, 200267 G R F Boniface[3] attch. 2 MT Coy, S&TC, 206158 A C E Bosten[3] attch. 1/4 QORWK, 57 Bde., 200355 T L Driver[3] attch. 2 MAC, 201435 C E Edwards[3] attch. 3/W Sig Sqn, 201846 H Garbett[3] attch. 1/4 QORWK, 57 Bde., 201206 G E Grant[4] attch. ISC, 200412 W Green[3] attch. LofC Sigs, 201189 R W Halley[3] attch. 1/25 London, 200135 S E Haryett[3] attch. 40 DSC, 200723 F R Hogsden[3] attch. 44 DSC, KKF, 200838 L Hopper[3] attch. IOD, 201444 F J Hunt[3] attch. 1/4 QORWK, 201130 A Kent[3] attch. 1/25 London, 201282 E J Lancaster[3] attch. 40 DSC, 16 Div., 200931 C Langley[3], 200644 G W Marsh[3] attch. 1/4 QORWK, 201226 J Mew[3], 201267 D Mitchell[3] attch. 1/4 QORWK, 200713 G W Monard[3] attch. 40 DSC, 16 Div., 206178 H E Newman[3], 200229 A J Richards[3] attch. 38 DSC, 201452 F W Spencer[3] attch. 4 Corps Sigs Coy, 200281 H E Watts[3] attch. 2 LofC Sigs, 200594 H F White[3] attch. 1/4 QORWK & 203768 H S White[3] attch. 1/25 London

~ 1/6th Bn, The East Lancashire Regiment, Territorial Force ~

Note a. *Roll of all personnel identified as eligible.*
Note b. *United Kingdom August 1914. India December 1914, Aden February 1917, India January 1918 to October 1919.*
Note c. *Medals named in impressed capitals: 'E. SURR. R.'*

Single Clasp	No. Identified	Rarity
Afghanistan N.W.F. 1919[1]	44	Very Rare
Mahsud 1919–20[5]	0	None Identified
Waziristan 1919–21[4]	0	None Identified
Waziristan 1921–24[6]	0	None Identified
Combination Clasps	**No. Identified**	**Rarity**
Mahsud 1919–20[5] Waziristan 1919–21[4]	1	According to the roll as seen, can be considered Unique

Waziristan 1919–21[4] Waziristan 1921–24[6]	1	According to the roll as seen, can be considered Unique

Majors: ~ P Hallett[3] Staff, 16 Div.

Captains: ~ J E Barnby[3] attch. 1 DLI, H V R Bates[3] attch. 2 Som LI, C D Field[3] attch. RE & W A Dimoline[4&6] attch. 'B' Div. Sigs

Lieutenants: ~ E A Smedley[3] attch. RE & J P Williams[3] attch. 1 Yorkshire

Company Quartermaster Sergeants/Staff Sergeants/Colour Sergeants: ~ 240488 F N Simpson[3] attch. 1 MT Coy, S&TC

Quartermaster Sergeants / Sergeants: ~ (Act) 240760 W T Bell[3] attch. 32 Bde. Sply Sect, 240655 V H Bennett[3] attch. 43 Bde. Sply Sect, (Act) 240324 F G Browning[3] attch. 29 PMC, 241333 J F Chambers[3] attch. RTO, 240691 J D Daws[3] attch. RTE, (Act) 240092 G E O Eyles[3] attch. 210 Supt Sect, S&TC, (Act) 242490 E A Flewin[3] attch. RTE, (Act) 240200 F Fountain[3] attch. RTE, (Act) 241719 E M Franklin[3] attch. RTE, 241761 F C Grindrod[3] attch. RTO, (Act) 200367 A Harding[3] attch. 7 MT Sect, S&TC (Originally 5th Bn), (Act) 240699 S F Hathaway[3] attch. RTE, (Act) 240587 E W Parker[3] attch. RTE, 240606 G T Philpott[3] attch. RTE & (Act) 240484 W Smith[3] attch. 8 MT Coy, S&TC

Lance Sergeants/Corporals: ~ 240172 J H Gibson[4&5] attch. 71 PMC & 240788 W Heley[3] attch. 39 DSC, 2 Div.

Lance Corporals/Privates: ~ 240086 G H Allen[3] attch. 2 MT Coy, S&TC, 241637 G E Batt[3] attch. MFD, 240669 P Bell[3] attch. 5 LofC Sigs, 200382 V C Bentley[3] attch. 36 Div. Sply Coy, 240219 W E Bull[3] attch. 33 DSC, 4 Div., 240633 G H Buringham[3], 241264 J V Carrington[3] attch. MFD, 240384 E E Cole[3] attch. 3/W Sig Sqn, 241631 S F Constable[3] attch. RTO, 240937 G W Denyer[3] attch. RTO, 241006 A H Dicker[3] attch. 39 DSC, 2 Div., 240148 B G H Farrow[3] attch. RTO, 241707 J H Gadd[3] attch. RTE, 240502 W O Gilks[3] attch. 3/W Sig Sqn, 241341 B W Glassborow[3] attch. RTO, 31958 E Hyatt[3] attch. 36 DSC, 1 Div., 241709 F Matthews[3] attch. RTO, 240364 W R Nixon[3] attch. 3/W Sig Sqn, 240697 H R Sullivan[3] attch. 39 DSC, 2 Div., 240536 F G Weller[3] attch. RTE & 240534 J D Wiltshire[3]

~ 1st Bn, The Duke of Cornwall's Light Infantry ~

Note a.   Roll of all personnel identified as eligible.

Note b.   United Kingdom August 1914. France & Flanders August 1914, Italy December 1917, France & Flanders April 1918. India 1922 forward.

Note c.   Medals named in impressed capitals: 'D.C.L.I.'

Single Clasp	No. Identified	Rarity
Afghanistan N.W.F. 1919[3]	0	None Identified
Mahsud 1919–20[5]	0	None Identified
Waziristan 1919–21[4]	0	None Identified
Waziristan 1921–24[6]	1	According to the roll as seen, can be considered Unique

Lance Corporals/Privates: ~ 5430882 A H Stevens[6] Clk, 16 Bde., Manzai

~ 2nd Bn, The Duke of Cornwall's Light Infantry ~

Note a.   Roll of all personnel identified as eligible.

Note b.   Hong Kong August 1914. France & Flanders December 1914. Salonika December 1915, Southern Russia December 1918 to June 1919 thence India followed by Iraq September 1920 to 1921.

Note c.   Medals named in impressed capitals: 'D.C.L.I.'

Single Clasp	No. Identified	Rarity
Afghanistan N.W.F. 1919[3]	1	According to the roll as seen, can be considered Unique
Mahsud 1919–20[5]	0	None Identified
Waziristan 1919–21[4]	5	Of the Utmost Rarity
Waziristan 1921–24[6]	0	None Identified
Combination Clasps	No. Identified	Rarity
Mahsud 1919–20[5] Waziristan 1919–21[4]	1	According to the roll as seen, can be considered Unique

Lieutenants: ~ R Brown[4] attch. S&TC & G C S Rule[4] Staff & M E Grenop[3] attch. 1/4 QORWK
Quartermaster Sergeants/Sergeants: ~ (Act) 01334 T Maylam[4&5] & (Act) (5431094) 02313 W C Weeks[4] attch. IOD
Lance Sergeants/Corporals: ~ 201120 W T Tregonning[4]
Lance Corporals/Privates: ~ (5400536) 01457 F Ebbett[4]

~ 3rd (Reserve) Bn, The Duke of Cornwall's Light Infantry ~

Note a.   *Roll of all personnel identified as eligible.*
Note b.   *United Kingdom August 1914. United Kingdom throughout Great War period providing drafts and reinforcements.*
Note c.   *Medals named in impressed capitals: 'D.C.L.I.'*

Single Clasp	No. Identified	Rarity
Afghanistan N.W.F. 1919[3]	1	According to the roll as seen, can be considered Unique
Mahsud 1919–20[5]	0	None Identified
Waziristan 1919–21[4]	0	None Identified
Waziristan 1921–24[6]	0	None Identified

Lieutenants: ~ P W C S Lowe[3] attch. 2/6 Sussex

~ 2/4th Bn, The Duke of Cornwall's Light Infantry, Territorial Force ~

Note a.   *Roll of all personnel identified as eligible.*
Note b.   *Formed September 1914. India January 1915 to June 1919.*
Note c.   *Medals named in impressed capitals: 'D.C.L.I.'*

Single Clasp	No. Identified	Rarity
Afghanistan N.W.F. 1919[3]	31	Very Rare
Mahsud 1919–20[5]	0	None Identified
Waziristan 1919–21[4]	0	None Identified
Waziristan 1921–24[6]	0	None Identified
Combination Clasps	**No. Identified**	**Rarity**
Afghanistan N.W.F. 1919[3] Waziristan 1919–21[4]	2	Of the Utmost Rarity
Mahsud 1919–20[5] Waziristan 1919–21[4]	1	According to the roll as seen, can be considered Unique

Lieutenants: ~ A Dalgleish[3] & W F Penberthy[3] attch. 288 Coy, MGC
Warrant Officers Class I: ~ (Act) 201206 W Dowling[3&4] attch. RTE, (Act) 200453 D O Harding[3] attch. RTE, Peshawar & (Act) 200480 W H Hosking[3] attch. RTE
Warrant Officers Class II: ~ (Act) 200799 D Marshall[3] attch. 5 MT Coy, S&TC & (Act) 201100 W Yates[3]
Company Quartermaster Sergeants/Staff Sergeants/Colour Sergeants: ~ 200414 E F Bray[3] attch. 1 MT Coy, S&TC & 200466 C Chirgwin[3] attch. 1 ARW, S&TC
Quartermaster Sergeants/Sergeants: ~ (Act) 200148 R H C Edwards[3] attch. 2 MT Coy, S&TC, (Act) 201811 J H D Donovan[3] attch. S&TC, (Act) 200994 A J Ford[3] attch. RTE, (Act) 201648 H Maddaford[3] attch. 52 Wing, RAF, (Act) 201870 K H Snell[3] attch. HQ, NWFF & (Act) 36074 J D Snowden[3] attch. S&TC
Lance Sergeants/Corporals: ~ 200590 J Allen[3] attch. 41 CFA, 201025 W Best[3] attch. LofC Sigs, 200806 R C Congdon[3] attch. 3/W Sig Sqn, (Act) 201614 A W Warden[3] attch. 13 Armd Car Bde. & (Act) 200526 J Wilkinson[3] attch. S&TC
Lance Corporals/Privates: ~ 200967 H Barrett[3] attch. 3/W Sig Sqn, 201433 A Honey[3] attch. 1 York, 201549 C Hutchens[3] attch. ISC, 36011 W H King[3] Staff, 201758 P Matthews[3] attch. 40 DSC, 16 Lahore Div., 202083 A D S Morrison[3] attch. 44 DSC, KKF, 0321 G Poulton[3] attch. 1 MT Coy, S&TC, 0274 W Porter[3] attch. 1 MT Coy, S&TC, 200810 A Reed[4&5] attch. 'F' DSC, 45659 F Smith[3] attch. 1 MT Coy, S&TC, 200812 S R Truran[3&4], 201521 W J Warren[3] attch. 3 ISS, 200164 G P Webb[3] attch. 3/W Sig Sqn & 47027 J Wiseman[3] attch. 21 IMVS

~ 1/5th Bn, The Duke of Cornwall's Light Infantry, Territorial Force ~

Note a. *Roll of all personnel identified as eligible.*
Note b. *United Kingdom August 1914. France & Flanders May 1916 forward.*
Note c. *Medals named in impressed capitals: 'D.C.L.I.'*

Single Clasp	No. Identified	Rarity
Afghanistan N.W.F. 1919[3]	0	None Identified
Mahsud 1919–20[5]	0	None Identified
Waziristan 1919–21[4]	1	According to the roll as seen, can be considered Unique
Waziristan 1921–24[6]	0	None Identified

Captains: ~ E J Perks[4] attch. S&TC

~ 1st Bn, The Duke of Wellington's (West Riding Regiment) ~

Note a. *Roll of all commissioned personnel identified as eligible.*
Note b. *Non commissioned and other ranks multi clasp or non Afghanistan 1919 single clasp except those single Afghanistan specimens identified as having been named 'W. RID. R.' See Note 6 below.*
Note c. *India August 1914 forward to January 1920 thence Egypt and Palestine returning to India December 1920 forward.*
Note d. *Title changed to The Duke of Wellington's Regiment (West Riding) in 1920.*
Note e. *Battle honour 'Third Afghan War 1919'.*
Note f. *Medals for the clasp 'AFGHANISTAN N.W.F. 1919' issued from the initial 'battalion' role are named: '1/DUKE OF WELLINGTON'S REGT'. Recipients with claims listed on rolls processed (principally in York) from 1921 forward are named 'W. RID. R.' and as such are scarce. These are identified thus: (*). This list may not be exhaustive. The reason for this change is probably linked to the change in title identified in Note 4 above.*

Single Clasp	No. Identified	Rarity
Afghanistan N.W.F. 1919[3]	Bn. Strength	Not Rare
Afghanistan N.W.F. 1919[3] Named 'W RID R'	35	Very Rare
Mahsud 1919–20[5]	0	None Identified
Waziristan 1919–21[4] Named 'W RID R'	1	According to the roll as seen, can be considered Unique
Waziristan 1921–24[6]	0	
Combination Clasps	**No. Identified**	**Rarity**
Afghanistan N.W.F. 1919[3] Mahsud 1919–20[5] Waziristan 1919–21[4]	1	According to the roll as seen, can be considered Unique
Afghanistan N.W.F. 1919[3] Waziristan 1919–21[4]	1	According to the roll as seen, can be considered Unique
Afghanistan N.W.F. 1919[3] Waziristan 1919–21[4] Waziristan 1921–24[6] Named 'W RID R'	1	According to the roll as seen, can be considered Unique
Afghanistan N.W.F. 1919[3] Waziristan 1921–24[6]	1	According to the roll as seen, can be considered Unique
Afghanistan N.W.F. 1919[3] North West Frontier 1935[12]	2	Of the Utmost Rarity

Lieutenant Colonels: ~ E C Boutflower[3]
Majors: ~ R H W Owen[3(*)]
Captains: ~ W G Baker[3], A O L Davis[3], St. J T Faulkner[3], (QM) D Looney[3], C Rowland[3] & H S Sampson[3]

Lieutenants: ~ J N Allan[3], V W Allen[3], V H E Baker[3], H Brereton[3(*)], C C F Butler[3] attch. 222 Coy MGC, C R Carman[3], A V Field[3] attch. 72 GCC, F L Foster[3], G P Marsh[3], W A V Regan[3] attch. 286 Coy MGC, J W Scott[3], G C Tree[3] & R Wood[3] Staff, BFF

Quartermaster Sergeants/Sergeants: ~ (Act) 8839 A Beaney[3(*)] attch. S&TC, (Act) 9792 H Briggs[3(*)], (Act) 9793 H Briscombe[3(*)], 9148 W G Dowsing[3(*)] attch. 12 CFA, (4524391) 8980 W H Elder[3&4(IAOC)], 32834 J W Stevens[3,(4&5 7 Ind MT Coy)], 9763 A V Swithinbank[3(*)] attch. 9 BSS & (Act) 9807 J Yaxley[3(*)]

Lance Sergeants /Corporals: ~ (Act) 9811 D Coates[3(*)], 10213 S G Walter[4(*)] attch. 40 DSC & (Act) 9316 W Young[3(*)]

Lance Corporals/Privates: ~ 8765 R Anstey[3(*)] attch. 3/W Sig Sqn, 30904 R S Archer[3(*)], 8815 F L Bennett[3(*)], 30743 J Bristow[3(*)] attch. ISS, 9543 A H Button[3(*),(4&6 R Sigs)] attch. 44 DSC, 9602 W Carter[3(*)], 31090 F T Clough[3(*)], 9437 F Grange[3(*)] attch. 33 DSC, 31111 S Grayson[3(*)], 9350 D Grimsdick[3(*)], 8547 W Hudson[3(*)], 9841 A C Kemp[3(*)], 269383 F Lawrence[3(*)], 10003 F Marsden[3(*)] attch. ITD, 8910 G H Palmer[3(*)] attch. 42 CFA, (4334721) 64605 A Ruddiman[3&6 (KOYLI)], 14953 W Simpson[3(*)], 3-9797 E Smith[3(*)], 29855 J Smith[3(*)] attch. Nuski MT Sect, S&TC, 4687194 W Stone[3&12], 29134 E Tavener[3(*)], 9361 J Verrier[3(*)], 8804 F Wallbank[3(*)], 31194 A Walton[3(*)], 4686650 J Warburton[3&12], 31225 W Wearne[3(*)], 10146 J Whitham[3(*)], 16304 R Williamson[3(*)], 30854 P Wood[3(*)] & 9723 H Young[3(*)]

~ 1ˢᵗ Bn, The Border Regiment ~

Note a. *Roll of all commissioned personnel identified as eligible.*

Note b. *Non-commissioned and other ranks non-Waziristan multi clasps. Verified 'single' clasp 'WAZIRISTAN 1919-21' and 'WAZIRISTAN 1921-24' medals are scarce and would only have been only won by time expired personnel, reinforcement drafts or those retired from the campaign due to sickness or other. The bars on many two-clasp specimens examined are not riveted leading to the frequent loss of the Waziristan 1921-24 award. This is primarily due to the latter clasp being issued some two to three years after receipt of the initial award and 'churn' of personnel back into civilian life.*

Note c. *India (Burma) August 1914. Egypt March 1915, Mudros and Gallipoli April 1915, Mudros and Egypt January 1916, France & Flanders March 1916 forward. India November 1919 forward.*

Note d. *Medals named in impressed capitals: 'BORD. R.'*

Single Clasp	No. Identified	Rarity
Afghanistan N.W.F. 1919[3]	2	Of the Utmost Rarity
Mahsud 1919–20[5]	0	None Identified
Waziristan 1919–21[4]	?	Scarce
Waziristan 1921–24[6]	?	Scarce
Combination Clasps	**No. Identified**	**Rarity**
Afghanistan N.W.F. 1919[3] Waziristan 1919–21[4] Waziristan 1921–24[6]	1	According to the roll as seen, can be considered Unique
Afghanistan N.W.F. 1919[3] North West Frontier 1930–31[9]	1	According to the roll as seen, can be considered Unique
Mahsud 1919–20[5] Waziristan 1921–24[6]	1	According to the roll as seen, can be considered Unique
Waziristan 1919–21[4] Waziristan 1921–24[6]	Bn. Strength	Not Rare
Waziristan 1919–21[4] Waziristan 1921–24[6] North West Frontier 1930–31[9]	2	Of the Utmost Rarity
Waziristan 1919–21[4] Waziristan 1921–24[6] North West Frontier 1935[12]	1	According to the roll as seen, can be considered Unique
Waziristan 1921–24[6] North West Frontier 1930–31[9]	17	Extremely Rare

Lieutenant Colonels: ~ H Nelson[4&6]

Majors: ~ A J Ellis[4&6], H E Festing[4&6], G Darwell[4&6] & W O Lay[5&6] attch. 4/3 GR, IA

Captains: ~ H R Alexander[4&6], W F H Chambers[4&6], P R Dowding[4&6], F G Drayson[3,4&6] attch. 'F' DSC, P D W Dunn[4,6&9], G W O'Brien[4&6], G W B Tarleton[4&6], H J B Warren[4&6] & (QM) E O B White[4&6]

Lieutenants: ~ M A E Ashby[4&6], C C Blackwell[4&6], V Blomfield[4&6], E C Brewer[4&6], H S Cooper[4&6], M Elington[4&6], T E Flewitt[4,6&12(Capt.)], C M Craig-McFeely[4&6], W J Murphy[4&6], J S Nichols[4&6] attch. 2/21 Punjabis, IA, P J Kingston-Blair-Oliphant[4&6], F L Samut[4&6], D C A Shepard[4&6], H T Thompson[4&6] & A G Wilkinson[4,6&9(Capt.)]
Quartermaster Sergeants/Sergeants: ~ 3590863 S Entwistle[6&9], 3589491 H Peters[6&9(CQMS)] & 3590993 J Tinkler[6&9]
Lance Sergeants/Corporals: ~ 9823 H J Wood[3] attch. 36 DSC, 1 Div.
Lance Corporals/Privates: ~ 3591811 A Adams[6&9(Sgt.)], 3590472 D Adams[6&9], 9577 P J Adams[3] attch. 1 S Lanc thence Quetta Arsenal, 3591216 W A Anderson[6&9], 3590183 A Challis[6&9], 3591256 W H Cobb[6&9], 3591904 W Harrison[6&9], 3590999 W Martindale[6&9], 3592595 H Newton[6&9], 3590407 A Noble[6&9], 3589897 E Parish[6&9(Sgt.)], 3589787 E Phinn[6&9], 3590416 F Reynolds[6&9], 3589978 A E Tucker[6&9], 52554 (3590985) J Wannop[3&9] & 3592509 P Winstanley[6&9(Cpl.)].

~ 1/4th (Cumberland & Westmorland) Bn, The Border Regiment, Territorial Force ~

Note a. Roll of all personnel identified as eligible.
Note b. United Kingdom August 1914. India December 1914 forward.
Note c. Medals named in impressed capitals: '1-4 BORD. R.'

Single Clasp	No. Identified	Rarity
Afghanistan N.W.F. 1919[3]	14	Extremely Rare
Mahsud 1919–20[5]	0	None Identified
Waziristan 1919–21[4]	1	According to the roll as seen, can be considered Unique
Waziristan 1921–24[6]	0	None Identified

Quartermaster Sergeants/Sergeants: ~ (Act) 200743 B Burge[3] attch. S&TC & (Act) 201081 T C Hetherington[4] attch. 26 CFA, 200095 C McGeorge[3] attch. S&TC & 200614 C H Sellers[3] attch. 40 DSC, 16 Div.
Lance Sergeants/Corporals: ~ 201919 A Bolton[3] attch. 44 DSC, KKF, 203782 E Bull[3] attch. 1 MT Coy, S&TC & (Act) 200692 M Hall[3] attch. S&TC
Lance Corporals/Privates: ~ 200213 H T Bragg[3] attch. 46 Mbl Bde. Sig Sect, 200289 W Friend[3] attch. 35 BGH, 200703 H Grahame[3] attch. 39 DSC, 2 Div., 200714 F Holstead[3] attch. S&TC, 200204 I H Lamb[3] attch. 4 Div. Supt Coy, S&TC, 201905 J C Latimer[3] attch. 38 DSC, 201288 A E Simpson[3] attch. 40 DSC, 16 Div. & 200772 T Stephenson[3] attch. S&TC.

~ 2/4th (Cumberland & Westmorland) Bn, The Border Regiment, Territorial Force ~

Note a. Roll of all commissioned personnel identified as eligible.
Note b. Non-commissioned and other ranks multi clasp and non-Afghanistan 1919 single clasp.
Note c. United Kingdom August 1914. India March 1915 forward.
Note d. Battle honour 'Third Afghan War 1919'.
Note e. Medals named in impressed capitals: '2-4 BORD. R.'

Single Clasp	No. Identified	Rarity
Afghanistan N.W.F. 1919[3]	Bn. Strength	Not Rare
Mahsud 1919–20[5]	0	None Identified
Waziristan 1919–21[4]	2	Of the Utmost Rarity
Waziristan 1921–24[6]	0	None Identified
Combination Clasps	**No. Identified**	**Rarity**
Afghanistan N.W.F. 1919[3] Waziristan 1919–21[4]	2	Of the Utmost Rarity
Afghanistan N.W.F. 1919[3] Waziristan 1919–21[4] Waziristan 1921–24[6]	1	According to the roll as seen, can be considered Unique

Afghanistan N.W.F. 1919[3] Malabar 1921–22[7] Waziristan 1921–24[6]	1	According to the roll as seen, can be considered Unique

Lieutenant Colonels: ~ F W Halton[3] & (Bvt) V S Jones[3]

Majors: ~ E Bousfield[3], G H Heelis[3] & (Temp) H G Marshall[3]

Captains: ~ A Alexander[3] attch. MWS, (Act) A W Anderson[3], (Act) E H Ashburner[3], (Act) E H Barker[3], (QM) J Brooks[3], (Act) B F Chester[3], (Act) J Glasson[3], (Act) L MacGlasson[3], (Act) H C Grierson-Jackson[3], J Jackson[3] & (Act) P S Hamilton[3]

Lieutenants: ~ H S Abram[3], A A Brown[3] attch. 10 MT Coy, S&TC, P V Curtis[3], H Deuchars[3], O D Gibbings[3], C G Parker[3] attch. 281 Coy, MGC, W Pepperell[3], D G Perry[3], P M Rheam[3&4] attch. 10 MT Coy, S&TC, M Russell[3] attch. 2 Som LI, G H Snow[3] & C F Turnbull[3] attch. 285 Coy MGC

Lance Corporals/Privates: ~ 3589904 H Andrews[4] attch. 'F' DSC, (201289) 2665 H K Baldock[3,(4 RE)&(6 R Sigs)], (1863113) 39281 J W Brown[3,(7&6 L/Cpl. R Sigs)], 203609 E Henderson[3&4] attch. 1 BGH, Tank & 52843 H G Roome[4] attch. 'F' DSC, (Originally Imperial Camel Corps, Australian Imperial Force)

Bandsmen: ~ 3589714 A W Forster[3&6]

~ 1st Bn, The Royal Sussex Regiment ~

Note a.   *Roll of all commissioned personnel identified.*
Note b.   *Non-commissioned and other ranks multi clasp and non-Afghanistan 1919 single clasp.*
Note c.   *India August 1914 forward throughout Great War period to December 1920.*
Note d.   *Medals named in impressed capitals: 'R. SUSS. R.'*

Single Clasp	No. Identified	Rarity
Afghanistan N.W.F. 1919[3]	Bn. Strength	Not Rare.
Mahsud 1919–20[5]	0	None Identified.
Waziristan 1919–21[4]	0	None Identified.
Waziristan 1921–24[6]	0	None Identified.
Combination Clasps	**No. Identified**	**Rarity**
Afghanistan N.W.F. 1919[3] Waziristan 1919–21[4]	3	Of the Utmost Rarity.
Afghanistan N.W.F. 1919[3] Malabar 1921–22[7]	1	According to the roll as seen, can be considered Unique
Afghanistan N.W.F. 1919[3] Malabar 1921–22[7] Waziristan 1921–24[6]	1	According to the roll as seen, can be considered Unique
Afghanistan N.W.F. 1919[3] Waziristan 1921–24[6]	2	Of the Utmost Rarity
Afghanistan N.W.F. 1919[3] North West Frontier 1930–31[9]	9	Of the Utmost Rarity

Lieutenant Colonels: ~ B M Hynes[3] attch. 1/25 London & E L MacKenzie[3]

Majors: ~ (QM) G Gilpin[3]

Captains: ~ J E Calver[3], (Act) A G Cook[3] attch. Malaria Convalescence Depot, C C Hawkes[3], W Holderness[3], C C Malden[3], E D Perodeau[3] & F St. D Skinner[3]

Lieutenants: ~ H Berendt[3] attch. 285 Coy MGC, B Bryant[3], L A Cheeseman[3], E K Cormody[3&9(Capt.)], A R Ford[3], F H Haigh[3], W J Hook[3], A R Lawrence[3], W C A Linfield[3], J T Nixon[3], R F P Orme[3], W G Phillips[3], F C Platts[3], D H Richards[3], E V Taylor[3], F R Tyler[3] attch. 44 DSC, KKF, F T Watson[3] & R V Wilson[3]

Warrant Officers Class II: ~ 8593 H Bradford[3&4] attch. 40 DSC

Quartermaster Sergeants/Sergeants: ~ (Act) (6392497) L/13812 C W Butcher[3&9(WOI)]

Lance Corporals/Privates: ~ (7817838) L/13798 C A Attwater[3&7(8 ACC RTC)], (1850380) L/1369 A Bryant[3&4(Spr. RE)], L/8943 J Gander[3&6(R Berkshire)], (6392366) L/13640 W H R Gates[3&9], L/8318 C Guy[3&6(RTC)], (6392361) L/13635 W Hudd[3&9], (6392041)

L/13213 E Humphries[3&9], (6390272) L/9938 H Jones[3&9], (6390257) L/6711 W T Lovell[3&4], (7817811) L/13822 J Marner[3,(7&6 as 8 ACC RTC)], (6390733) L/10911 H Oakley[3&9], (6390375) L/9234 G A Ralph[3&9] & (6390472) L/9590 T R Tresize[3&9]

~ 2nd Bn, The Royal Sussex Regiment ~

Note a.   *Roll of all personnel identified as eligible.*
Note b.   *United Kingdom August 1914. France & Flanders August 1914 forward. West Indies November 1919, Malta November 1921, Turkey September 1922, Singapore October 1923.*
Note c.   *Medals named in impressed capitals: 'R. SUSS. R.'*

Single Clasp	No. Identified	Rarity
Afghanistan N.W.F. 1919[3]	0	None Identified
Mahsud 1919–20[5]	0	None Identified
Waziristan 1919–21[4]	1	According to the roll as seen, can be considered Unique
Waziristan 1921–24[6]	0	None Identified
Combination Clasps	*No. Identified*	*Rarity*
Afghanistan N.W.F. 1919[3] Waziristan 1919–21[4]	1	According to the roll as seen, can be considered Unique
Waziristan 1919–21[4] Waziristan 1921–24[6] North West Frontier 1930–31[9]	1	According to the roll as seen, can be considered Unique

Lieutenants: ~ R H Rohde[4,6&9(Capt.)] attch. 6 MMG Bty, MGC
Quartermaster Sergeants/Sergeants: ~ (Act) G/20850 J Pye[3&4] attch. RASC
Lance Corporals/Privates: ~ L/5215 A Goddard[4]

2/6th (Cyclist) Bn, The Royal Sussex Regiment, Territorial Force ~

Note a.   *Roll of all commissioned personnel as identified.*
Note b.   *Non-commissioned and other ranks multi clasp and non-Afghanistan 1919 single clasp.*
Note c.   *Formed November 1914. India February 1916 forward.*
Note d.   *Medals named in impressed capitals: '2-6 R. SUSS. R.'*

Single Clasp	No. Identified	Rarity
Afghanistan N.W.F. 1919[3]	Bn. Strength	Not Rare
Mahsud 1919–20[5]	0	None Identified
Waziristan 1919–21[4]	1	According to the roll as seen, can be considered Unique
Waziristan 1921–24[6]	0	None Identified

Lieutenant Colonels: ~ F W F Johnson[3] & A K Tennent[3]
Majors: ~ (Temp) T G Bennett[3] attch. 222 Coy, MGC & L Vaughan[3]
Captains: ~ N E Bannatyne[3], (QM) E J Glazebrook[3], C F Johnson[3] & A R G Roberson[3]
Lieutenants: ~ A J Benson[3], B Beringer[3], J H Crisp[3], H L King[3], H Souter[3] & W G W Venn[3]
Lance Corporals/Privates: ~ 266248 T A Williamson[4]

~ 1ˢᵗ Bn, The Hampshire Regiment ~

Note a.   *Roll of all personnel identified as eligible.*
Note b.   *United Kingdom August 1914. France & Flanders August 1914 forward. Turkey April 1920 thence Egypt December 1921.*
Note c.   *Medals named in impressed capitals: 'HAMPS. R.'*

Single Clasp	No. Identified	Rarity
Afghanistan N.W.F. 1919[3]	3	Of the Utmost Rarity
Mahsud 1919–20[5]	0	None Identified
Waziristan 1919–21[4]	2	Of the Utmost Rarity
Waziristan 1921–24[6]	0	None Identified

Combination Clasps	No. Identified	Rarity
Afghanistan N.W.F. 1919[3] Waziristan 1921–24[6] North West Frontier 1930–31[9]	1	According to the roll as seen, can be considered Unique

Captains: ~ D W Baring[3] attch. 260 Coy, MGC & G C Palmer[4] attch. 57 Sillader CC
Lieutenants: ~ J J Anderson[4] attch. 6 MMG Bty, MGC, R C Keller[3] attch. 222 Coy, MGC & W C Meiklejohn[3] attch. 1/5 Hampshire
Lance Corporals/Privates: ~ (5488598) 306720 G W Devenish[3,6&(9 Cpl. R Sigs)] attch. 'B' Corps Sigs

~ 3ʳᵈ (Reserve) Bn, The Hampshire Regiment ~

Note a.   *Roll of all personnel identified as eligible.*
Note b.   *United Kingdom August 1914. United Kingdom throughout Great War period providing drafts and reinforcements.*
Note c.   *Medals named in impressed capitals: 'HAMPS. R.'*

Single Clasp	No. Identified	Rarity
Afghanistan N.W.F. 1919[3]	2	Of the Utmost Rarity
Mahsud 1919–20[5]	0	None Identified
Waziristan 1919–21[4]	0	None Identified
Waziristan 1921–24[6]	0	None Identified

Lieutenants: ~ J Petty[3] & E F Whittington[3] attch. 1/5 Hampshire

~ 1/4ᵗʰ Bn, The Hampshire Regiment, Territorial Force ~

Note a.   *Roll of all personnel identified as eligible.*
Note b.   *United Kingdom August 1914. India November 1914, Mesopotamia March 1915 forward. Two companies captured Kut al Amara 29ᵗʰ April 1916. Composite battalion formed and reconstituted 2ⁿᵈ Battalion May 1916. South Russia August 1918 to October 1918 thence Northern Persia.*
Note c.   *Medals named in impressed capitals: 'HAMPS. R.'*

Single Clasp	No. Identified	Rarity
Afghanistan N.W.F. 1919[3]	87	Rare
Mahsud 1919–20[5]	0	None Identified
Waziristan 1919–21[4]	0	None Identified
Waziristan 1921–24[6]	0	None Identified

Captains: ~ G D Andrews[3] attch. 17 SSB & G A Capes[3]
Warrant Officers Class II: ~ (Act) 200235 E J Bowers[3] & (Act) 39856 W E J Gibbs[3] attch. 'B' Railhead Tpt Sect, S&TC

Quartermaster Sergeants/Sergeants: ~ (Act) 202212 W Bignell[3] attch. 26 Div. Sply Coy, S&TC, (Act) 200872 H J Brooks[3] attch. 2 N Stafford, 280037 P R Cutler[3] attch. 2 N Stafford, (Originally 6th Bn), (Act) 200758 A F Friend[3] attch. 2 N Stafford, (Act) 202097 R P Glanville[3] attch. S&TC, (Act) 40467 E W Hallard[3] attch. General Staff, (Act) 281151 C Hyett[3] attch. S&TC, (Originally 6th Bn), (Act) 200213 O Lane[3] attch. 2 N Stafford, 280325 E E Peters[3] attch. 1 Sussex, (Originally 6th Bn), 280171 E H Powell[3], (Originally 6th Bn), (Act) 39871 A Prangle[3] attch. 'K' Sect, S&TC & (Act) 200078 R Snow[3] attch. IOD

Lance Corporals/Corporals: ~ 355239 J Bastable[3] attch. S&TC, (Act) 200830 J Charters[3] attch. LofC Sigs, (Act) 203038 E H Le Cointe[3] attch. 27 CFA, 200623 D Groves[3] attch. 1 S Lanc, 357186 F D Roberts[3] attch. 39 DSC, (Originally 9th Cyclist Bn) & (Act) 200218 H Scrase[3] attch. 1 ARW, S&TC

Lance Corporals/Privates: ~ 201637 A E Andrews[3] attch. 1 S Lanc, 201908 A W Ayres[3] attch. 1 S Lanc, 202963 E Allen[3] attch. 2 N Stafford, 200300 E Barrett[3] attch. 2 N Stafford, 39917 A Barton[3] attch. HQ, Ambala Bde., 240637 A V Bartram[3] attch. 33 DSC, 4 Div., (Originally 5th Bn), 200548 C Blackmore[3] attch. 1 MT Coy, S&TC, 40040 S C Blackwell[3] attch. 1 MT Coy, S&TC, 200632 J Bone[3] attch. 2 N Stafford, 201773 W E Bramble[3] attch. 1 Sussex, 200519 E Brooks[3] attch. 38 DSC, 200609 A Bulpit[3] attch. 1 S Lanc, 204080 H G H Bunday[3] attch. 1 Sussex, 201436 W Butler[3] attch. 2 N Stafford, 200445 J H Chedd[3] attch. 2 N Stafford, 200325 I P W Coles[3], 200200 H Crowe[3] attch. 1 S Lanc, 201932 R Cryer[3] attch. 1 S Lanc, 240377 V Cummins[3] attch. 2 N Stafford, (Originally 5th Bn), 200660 J Daniels[3] attch. 1 S Lanc, 241792 G Davis[3] attch. 38 DSC, (Originally 5th Bn), 203002 C H Dowson[3] attch. 2 N Stafford, 201228 A E Elkins[3] attch. 2/6 Sussex, 201359 A French[3] attch. 2 N Stafford, 280936 W E Gammon[3] attch. 2 N Stafford, (Originally 6th Bn), 200836 D W Geddes[3] attch. 2 N Stafford, 200260 J T Goulding[3] attch. 1 S Lanc, 202100 L Grose[3] attch. 1 S Lanc, 355818 J H Hardey[3] attch. 1 S Lanc, (Originally 9th Cyclist Bn), 202007 G Hennessey[3] attch. 1 S Lanc, 201099 J H A Hill[3] attch. HQ, BFF, 200362 E P Holland[3] attch. 2 N Stafford, 202045 P Hore[3] attch. 1 Sussex, 241162 A T Horne[3] attch. Chakdina Bn, (Originally 5th Bn), 203021 F Hurst[3] attch. 1 S Lanc, 355460 W Jesse[3] attch. 44 DSC, KKF, (Originally 9th Cyclist Bn), 203267 C Kimber[3] attch. 2 N Stafford, 14851 H Kinge[3] attch. 1 Sussex, 201091 F T Levy[3] attch. 33 DSC, 201625 V E D C Martin[3] attch. 2 N Stafford, 201955 C R Masters[3] attch. 1 S Lanc, 203051 J A McGregor[3] attch. 2 N Stafford, 201697 C D Moody[3] attch. 1 S Lanc, 203165 C E Morris[3] attch. 2 N Stafford, 202137 W T Nicholls[3] attch. 2 N Stafford, 202140 W G Nile[3] attch. 1 S Lanc, 356287 E C Norkett[3] attch. 1 MT Coy, S&TC, 202034 J A O Parkman[3] attch. ACS, 200493 F Passingham[3] attch. 1 S Lanc, 201960 P S Penny[3] attch. 2 N Stafford, 9733 J E Pickett[3] attch. 1 S Lanc, 202151 W H Pounds[3] attch. 2 N Stafford, 202157 S Rickard[3] attch. 2 N Stafford, 202002 C E Smith[3] attch. 1 S Lanc, 23706 H Smith[3] attch. 2/6 Sussex, 241621 T J M Smith[3] attch. 3/W Sig Sqn, 355810 A Snelling[3] attch. 39 DSC, (Originally 9th Cyclist Bn), 202240 H F Stevens[3] attch. 1 Sussex, 280513 J E L Symes[3] attch. 1 S Lanc, (Originally 6th Bn), 200900 W J Thair[3] attch. 1 Sussex, 200157 P Thorner[3] attch. 44 DSC, KKF, 240372 H Townsend[3] attch. 17 SSB, (Originally 5th Bn), 204166 B Travers[3] attch. 2 N Stafford, 202192 P Trenoweth[3] attch. 1 S Lanc & 201698 F Vince[3] attch. 1 S Lanc

~ 2/4th Bn, The Hampshire Regiment, Territorial Force ~

Note a. *Roll of all personnel identified as eligible.*

Note b. *Formed September 1914. India January 1915 to April 1917 thence Egypt moving to France & Flanders in May / June 1918.*

Note c. *Medals named in impressed capitals: 'HAMPS. R.'*

Single Clasp	No. Identified	Rarity
Afghanistan N.W.F. 1919[3]	11	Extremely Rare
Mahsud 1919–20[5]	0	None Identified
Waziristan 1919–21[4]	1	According to the roll as seen, can be considered Unique
Waziristan 1921–24[6]	0	None Identified

Lieutenants: ~ D Cranton[3] attch. RE

Quartermaster Sergeants/Sergeants: ~ (Act) 201454 T Ball[3] attch. S&TC, (Act) 201151 A W Clark[3] attch. MFD, 201366 W Harris[3] attch. 33 DSC, 4 Div. & (Act) 200210 J W Mason[3] attch. CMSC

Lance Sergeants/Corporals: ~ (Act) 201283 J M Lewington[3] & (Act) 201572 E Vincent[3] attch. 5 MT Coy, S&TC

Lance Corporals/Privates: ~ 201771 W C Brown[3] attch. S&TC, 010205 H F Eyers[4] attch. 40 DSC, 010265 F E Ford[3] attch. 38 DSC, 280638 F Ridge[3] attch. 33 DSC, 4 Div., (Originally 6th Bn) & 280591 F W White[3] attch. 33 DSC, 4 Div., (Originally 6th Bn)

~ 1/5th Bn, The Hampshire Regiment, Territorial Force ~

Note a.   *Roll of all commissioned personnel identified as eligible.*
Note b.   *Non-commissioned and other ranks multi clasp and non-Afghanistan 1919 single clasp.*
Note c.   *United Kingdom August 1914. India November 1914 forward including Burma in 1918.*
Note d.   *Medals named in impressed capitals: 'HAMPS. R.'*

Single Clasp	No. Identified	Rarity
Afghanistan N.W.F. 1919[3]	Bn. Strength	Not Rare
Mahsud 1919–20[5]	0	None Identified
Waziristan 1919–21[4]	0	None Identified
Waziristan 1921–24[6]	0	None Identified
Combination Clasps	**No. Identified**	**Rarity**
Afghanistan N.W.F. 1919[3] Waziristan 1919–21[4] Waziristan 1921–24[6]	1	According to the roll as seen, can be considered Unique

Lieutenant Colonels: ~ H de S B Burford-Hancock[3]
Majors: ~ J C Dominy[3] & H P Hill[3]
Captains: ~ E W Andrews[3], (QM) S Baldwin[3], H J Harris[3], (Act) C A Lucas[3], R Mead[3] attch. 17 SSB & A F G Wharton[3]
Lieutenants: ~ N C Aldridge[3], H R Christmas[3], W A N Craven[3] attch. 1 DLI, W E Fishburn[3], A MacLeod[3], J B McGovern[3], M Napier[3], C P Norris[3], C N de W Palethorpe[3], P E Read[3], G H Stavert[3] & C W S Tatton-Winter[3] attch. 1 DLI
Lance Corporals/Privates: ~ 34187 J Burgan[3,(4&6 RASC)]

~ 2/5th Bn, The Hampshire Regiment, Territorial Force ~

Note a.   *Roll of all personnel identified eligible.*
Note b.   *Formed September 1914. India January 1915 to March 1917 thence Egypt.*
Note c.   *Disbanded in Palestine during August 1918 five officers and three hundred rank and file were transferred to 1/4th Battalion, Wiltshire Regt., consequently it is difficult to understand why the roll makes reference to this battalion.*
Note d.   *Medals named in impressed capitals: 'HAMPS. R.'*

Single Clasp	No. Identified	Rarity
Afghanistan N.W.F. 1919[3]	14	Extremely Rare
Mahsud 1919–20[5]	0	None Identified
Waziristan 1919–21[4]	0	None Identified
Waziristan 1921–24[6]	0	None Identified
Combination Clasps	**No. Identified**	**Rarity**
Afghanistan N.W.F. 1919[3] Waziristan 1921–24[6] North West Frontier 1935[12]	1	According to the roll as seen, can be considered Unique

Warrant Officers Class II: ~ (Act) 241609 S G Bellingham[3] attch. S&TC
Lance Sergeants/Corporals: ~ 240751 J Baker[3] attch. 38 DSC, 241256 J J Foss[3] attch. 3/W Sig Sqn, (Act) 241817 H J Long[3] attch. 1 MT Coy, S&TC & (Act) 241182 C G Piper[3] attch. 1 MT Coy, S&TC
Lance Corporals/Privates: ~ 240847 G A Allen[3] attch. 3/W Sig Sqn, 240481 J B Bartlett[3] attch. 3/W Sig Sqn, 241320 F C Binham[3] attch. 40 DSC, 16 Div., (5488595) 241198 A C Cummins[3,6(R Sigs)&12(Sgt. PDS, R Sigs)] attch. 'D' DSC, 241356 H J Franklin[3], 241388 E J Hurst[3] attch. 36 DSC, 1 Div., 280999 C C Lawrence[3] attch. 3/W Sig Sqn, 240719 A Miell[3] attch. 3/W Sig Sqn, 240805 J W Pattison[3] attch. 3/W Sig Sqn & 241178 D Randolph[3] attch. 44 DSC

~ 1/6th (Duke Of Connaught's Own) Bn, The Hampshire Regiment ~

Note a.   *Roll of all personnel identified as eligible.*
Note b.   *United Kingdom August 1914. India January 1915 to September 1917 thence Mesopotamia forward.*
Note c.   *Medals named in impressed capitals: 'HAMPS. R.'*

Single Clasp	No. Identified	Rarity
Afghanistan N.W.F. 1919[3]	137	Very Scarce
Mahsud 1919–20[5]	0	None Identified
Waziristan 1919–21[4]	0	None Identified
Waziristan 1921–24[6]	0	None Identified

Captains: ~ D C Breton[3] attch. 285 Coy, MGC

Lieutenants: ~ A D Johnson[3] attch. 282 Coy MGC

Warrant Officers Class II: ~ (Act) 280486 J A Beale[3] attch. S&TC, (Act) 26470 C Gibbs[3] attch. 1 Sussex, 6 Bde. & (Act) 45409 F Jenkins[3] attch. 17 SSB

Company Quartermaster Sergeants/Staff Sergeants/Colour Sergeants: ~ 280943 F Rands[3] attch. 17 SSB

Quartermaster Sergeants/Sergeants: ~ 280653 E A Baker[3] attch. S&TC, (Act) 38670 A H Barreau[3] attch. S&TC, (Act) 280237 C H Barton[3] attch. 2/6 Sussex, 280925 T V Bridger[3] attch. 2 N Stafford, 280147 W G Chandler[3] attch. 2 N Stafford, (Act) 281171 J Coward[3] attch. S&TC, (Act) 280285 P E James[3] attch. IOD, 280709 F Kerridge[3] attch. 17 SSB, 261694 W Light[3] attch. 21 IMVS, (Originally 5th Bn), 45410 J H Mycock[3] attch. 2 N Stafford, 280272 P S Papps[3] attch. 2 N Stafford, (Act) 281244 W Rayson[3] attch. 17 SSB, (Act) 280929 S Rowe[3] attch. S&TC, (Act) 280840 R P Simms[3] attch. 44 DSC, KKF & 280773 H H Waller[3] attch. DIG of C

Lance Sergeants/Corporals: ~ 280082 J H Baines[3] attch. 1 Sussex, (Act) 281278 V S Boorer[3] attch. 2 N Stafford, 280750 A Dukes[3] attch. S&TC, (Act) 280851 A G Eade[3] attch. 2 N Stafford, 280113 E A Edmiston[3] attch. 1 MT Coy, S&TC, 280982 L R C Fisher[3] attch. 263 Coy, MGC, (Act) 281335 G S Jervis[3] attch. 17 SSB, (Act) 280270 F G Rines[3] attch. 1 Sussex, (Act) 307007 G Sadler[3] attch. 10 IMVS, (Originally 7th Bn), 280132 G Smith[3] attch. 1 Sussex & 280693 W Wareham[3] attch. 1 MT Coy, S&TC

Lance Corporals/Privates: ~ 356094 T Andrews[3] attch. 2 N Stafford, (Originally 9th Cyclist Bn), 281169 W J Ansell[3] attch. 38 DSC, 281009 G Aylward[3] attch. 2 N Stafford, 356164 E A Ball[3] attch. 2 N Stafford, (Originally 9th Cyclist Bn), 355925 W H Barter[3] attch. 1 Sussex, (Originally 9th Cyclist Bn), 355263 H Bartlett[3] attch. 1 Sussex, (Originally 9th Cyclist Bn), 280801 R Bartlett[3] attch. 1 Sussex, 356122 L J Battersby[3] attch. 2 N Stafford, (Originally 9th Cyclist Bn), 45394 H V Beeston[3] attch. 1 SSB & RTO, 201589 J E Belcher[3] attch. 1 Sussex, (Originally 4th Bn), 281632 H C Betsworth[3] attch. 2 N Stafford, 280536 W Bond[3] attch. 44 DSC, KKF, 40839 E F Black[3] attch. 17 SSB, 281286 G E Blundell[3] attch. 2 N Stafford, 280412 C H Brett[3] attch. Malmiss Mission, 3/4054 M Bryan[3] attch. 1 Sussex, 356149 R V Bryant[3] attch. 17 SSB, (Originally 9th Cyclist Bn), 281446 B F Burden[3] attch. 2 N Stafford, 40874 H Burton[3] attch. 1 Sussex, 205401 H F Campling[3] attch. 1 Sussex, (Originally 4th Bn), 202080 T Carhart[3] attch. 1 Sussex, (Originally 4th Bn), 280953 J Carpenter[3] attch. 2/6 Sussex, 281341 H D Carter[3] attch. 2 N Stafford, 206003 G J Carver[3] attch. 2 N Stafford, (Originally 4th Bn), 280631 E E Clarke[3] attch. 1 Sussex, 356272 A D Clements[3] attch. 2 N Stafford, (Originally 9th Cyclist Bn), 356160 A Coleman[3] attch. 2 N Stafford, (Originally 9th Cyclist Bn), 355614 C Collett[3] attch. 17 SSB, (Originally 9th Cyclist Bn), 281227 F Collins[3] attch. 1 Sussex, 355874 J Connock[3] attch. HQ, 66 Bde., (Originally 9th Cyclist Bn), 355794 A J K Coombes[3] attch. 1 Sussex, (Originally 9th Cyclist Bn), 281595 P C Cornwell[3] attch. 1 Sussex, 281800 C O Coulbert[3] attch. 14 B(S)S, 280959 A J Cox[3] attch. 1 Sussex, 202679 W Cox[3] attch. 4 SSB, (Originally 4th Bn), 281801 G E Creasy[3] attch. 1 Sussex, 281409 A Cribb[3] attch. 2 N Stafford, 281506 W F J Dacombe[3] attch. 2 DLI, 211502 A J Day[3] attch. 1 Sussex, 281572 F G Drake[3] attch. 1 DLI, 355569 E C Edwards[3] attch. 1 Sussex, (Originally 9th Cyclist Bn), 205400 G Ellen[3] attch. 1 Sussex, (Originally 4th Bn), 281504 E Evans[3] attch. 1 DLI, 281259 W T Fairingside[3] 17 SSB, 203011 H Foard[3] attch. 1 Sussex, (Originally 4th Bn), 281467 H R Food[3] attch. 2 N Stafford, 45399 R W Fothergill[3] attch. 1 Sussex, 281351 J E Freestone[3] attch. 2 N Stafford, 281584 A E Gange[3] attch. 1 Sussex, 280367 W J Gregg[3] attch. 25 SS, 356028 S J Gregory[3] attch. 1 Sussex, (Originally 9th Cyclist Bn), 40867 E Griffith[3] attch. 1 Sussex, 40844 T Groom[3] attch. 2 N Stafford, 280266 A Grout[3] attch. 1 Sussex, 355233 C H Hall[3] attch. 2/6 Sussex, (Originally 9th Cyclist Bn), 356292 E Hall[3] attch. 17 SSB, (Originally 9th Cyclist Bn), 280903 H J Harris[3] attch. 2 MT Coy, S&TC, 355947 W Heard[3] attch. 1 Sussex, (Originally 9th Cyclist Bn), 281324 L A Hewitt[3] attch. 17 SSB, 355849 W J Holloway[3] attch. 1 Sussex, (Originally 9th Cyclist Bn), 355804 H C Holly[3] attch. 1 Sussex, (Originally 9th Cyclist Bn), 281438 S J Hooper[3] attch. 17 SSB, 280668 H Hudson[3] attch. 2 N Stafford, 205409 E R G Jackson[3] attch. 2 N Stafford, (Originally 4th Bn), 20939 H James[3] attch. 17 SSB, 281454 F J Jervis[3] attch. 17 SSB, 281806 G Joyner[3] attch. 1 Sussex, 281422 E A Jurd[3] attch. 2 N Stafford, 355791 A Kelley[3] attch. 2 N Stafford, (Originally 9th Cyclist Bn), 260636 G A Kent[3] attch. 3/W Sig Sqn, (Originally 5th Bn), 280374 H A Knocker[3] attch. 1 Sussex, 206006 P C Knott[3] attch. 2 N Stafford, (Originally 4th Bn), 281014 H A C Lambert[3] attch. 1 Sussex, 40617 F A Lapping[3] attch. 1 Sussex, 281247 H T Leggatt[3] attch. 1 Sussex, 38692 T H Lillington[3] attch. 17 SSB, 241253 A H Love[3] attch. 1 Sussex, 40849 W Lucas[3] attch. 2/6 Sussex, 281232 S H Mac Murray[3] attch. 1 Sussex, 280350 W Mc L McDonald[3] attch. 1 Sussex, 280485 F

J Mockford[3] attch. 1 Sussex, 355566 V Moxham[3] attch. 2 N Stafford, (Originally 9th Cyclist Bn), 281570 J V Mutlow[3] attch. 2 N Stafford, 40852 R G Nethercot[3] attch. 1 Sussex, 281253 E H Norris[3] attch. 17 SSB, 281473 H Oughton[3] attch. 17 SSB, (Originally 9th Cyclist Bn), 45427 J S Paling[3] attch. 1 Sussex, 356114 H T Paxton[3] attch. 2 N Stafford, 281394 F W Reiner[3] attch. 17 SSB, 280210 R F Riddett[3] attch. 1 Sussex, 281450 H A Saddler[3] attch. 3/W Sig Sqn, 281315 N Seager[3] attch. 17 SSB, 281499 C Short[3] attch. 2 N Stafford, 281387 S A Strong[3] attch. 17 SSB, 281352 T Teague[3] attch. 17 SSB, 281296 C Tindall[3] attch. 17 SSB, 280174 F Tipper[3], 280743 A S Varndell[3] attch. 3/W Sig Sqn, 40836 G R Virgo[3] attch. 1 Sussex, 31495 E G Wakeford[3] attch. 17 SSB, 281133 A Walker[3] attch. 1 Sussex, 355896 C Welsh[3] attch. 1 Sussex, (Originally 9th Cyclist Bn), 280623 E Wheatcroft[3] attch. 17 SSB, 201597 F T Wheeler[3] attch. 3/W Sig Sqn, (Originally 4th Bn) & 280120 G White[3] attch. 1 Sussex

~ 1/7th Bn, The Hampshire Regiment, Territorial Force ~

Note a.   *Roll of all personnel identified as eligible.*
Note b.   *United Kingdom August 1914. India November 1914 to January 1918 thence Aden forward.*
Note c.   *Medals named in impressed capitals: 'HAMPS. R.'*

Single Clasp	No. Identified	Rarity
Afghanistan N.W.F. 1919[3]	38	Very Rare
Mahsud 1919–20[5]	0	None Identified
Waziristan 1919–21[4]	0	None Identified
Waziristan 1921–24[6]	1	According to the roll as seen, can be considered Unique

Captains: ~ H A H Kemp-Welch[3] attch. 263 Coy, MGC
Warrant Officer Class I: ~ 306039 G A Pemberton[3] attch. 2 MT Coy, S&TC
Warrant Officer Class II: ~ 305083 A Stote[3] attch. 1 ARW, S&TC
Quartermaster Sergeants/Sergeants: ~ (Act) 306161 R Chisham[3] attch. HQ, 45 Bde., 307263 R G Dowling[3] attch. S&TC, (Act) 306646 W E Gray[3] attch. HQ, Bannu, (Act) 305274 F Gritt[3] attch. S&TC, 306163 D H Jenkins[3] attch. S&TC, (Act) 306168 A Lockyear[3] attch. S&TC, (Act) 305620 A Pring[3] attch. S&TC & 306104 R E Wilson[3] attch. S&TC
Lance Sergeants/Corporals: ~ 306055 A J Bailey[3] 1 ARW, S&TC, 305271 W J Dear[3] attch. 39 DSC, 2 Div., 5488893 S W Deventon[6] attch. ISC, (Act) 306526 W Hayter[3] attch. 44 DSC, KKF, 306327 L A Luff[3] attch. 2 MT Coy, S&TC, 307008 T Marquis[3] attch. S&TC, 306075 A D Mate[3] attch. 3/W Sig Sqn, 307148 G R Stickland[3] attch. 2 MT Coy, S&TC & 306093 F J Vivian[3] attch. 3/W Sig Sqn
Lance Corporals/Privates: ~305120 E P Ash[3] attch. 1 S Lanc, 306584 A E R Baggs[3] attch. 39 DSC, 2 Div., 306611 A Beckingham[3] attch. 3/W Sig Sqn, 305185 J Cole[3] attch. 1 ARW, S&TC, 305551 S Cushing[3] attch. 40 DSC, 16 Lahore Div., 305746 C Cutler[3] attch. 1 Sussex, 305435 O Colborne[3] attch. 1 S Lanc, 306748 W H Dominey[3] attch. 1 S Lanc, 306294 A Harrison[3] attch. 39 DSC, 2 Div., 307022 M J Hibberd[3] attch. 2 Indpt. Cable Sect, 305338 H Jones[3] attch. 39 DSC, 2 Div., 305825 A A Long[3] attch. 3/W Sig Sqn, 306094 G May[3] attch. 3/W Sig Sqn, 45318 A D Padfield[3] attch. 1 S Lanc, 306596 W J Ridout[3] attch. 3/W Sig Sqn, 305776 W V L Robins[3] attch. 3/W Sig Sqn, 306924 H Sherred[3] 1 S Lanc, 307268 J R P Talbot[3] & 305762 A J Vey[3] attch. 38 DSC

~ 2/7th Bn, The Hampshire Regiment, Territorial Force ~

Note a.   *Roll of all personnel identified as eligible.*
Note b.   *Formed September 1914. India January 1915 to September 1917 thence Mesopotamia forward to January 1919.*
Note c.   *Medals named in impressed capitals: 'HAMPS. R.'*

Single Clasp	No. Identified	Rarity
Afghanistan N.W.F. 1919[3]	45	Very Rare
Mahsud 1919–20[5]	0	None Identified
Waziristan 1919–21[4]	0	None Identified
Waziristan 1921–24[6]	0	None Identified

Quartermaster Sergeants/Sergeants: ~ 306347 H Alexander[3] attch. S&TC, 306362 A Brown[3] attch. 2 MT Coy, S&TC, (Act) 305232 F G Clist[3] attch. 44 DSC, KKF, 306574 A Duce[3] attch. S&TC, (Act) 306483 A H C Poole[3] attch. S&TC, (Act) 307045 C F Wayman[3] attch. S&TC & (Act) 307135 B M Wright[3] attch. S&TC

Lance Sergeants/Corporals: ~ (Act) 306582 J J Dayman[3] attch. 1 S Lanc, (Act) 205272 J H Folkes[3] attch. 1 S Lanc, (Originally 4th Bn), (Act) 306895 W Marshall[3] attch. 2 MT Coy, S&TC, (Act) 307321 W G Sartain[3] attch. 1 S Lanc, 306476 H R Scott[3] attch. 1 S Lanc & 305180 G A Stokes[3] attch. S&TC

Lance Corporals/Privates: ~ 305466 H J Arnold[3] attch. 1 S Lanc, 307040 F Bailey[3] attch. 3/W Sig Sqn, 307164 G T C Bonner[3] attch. 17 SSB, 205360 C M Clarke[3] attch. IS Office, (Originally 4th Bn), 206077 C Court[3] attch. 17 SSB, (Originally 4th Bn), 39613 G H Davis[3] attch. 1 S Lanc, 306995 P Fisher[3] attch. 39 DSC, 2 Div., 305922 W J S Fowler[3] attch. 1 S Lanc, 306297 A H Francis[3] attch. 39 DSC, 2 Div., 305547 G T Gates[3] attch. 2/6 Sussex, 39859 F Gill[3] attch. 17 SSB, 0823 H T Gillians[3] attch. 1/4 Hampshire, 206059 G W Hewitt[3] attch. 17 SSB, (Originally 4th Bn), 243354 T F Jones[3] attch. 1 S Lanc, (Originally 5th Bn), 205304 A Mee[3] attch. 1 MT Coy, S&TC, (Originally 4th Bn), 306075 T Mervyn[3] attch. 17 SSB, 243357 E W Mitchell[3] attch. 16 SSB, (Originally 5th Bn), 205326 W A V Moore[3] attch. 17 SSB, (Originally 4th Bn), 243197 A F S Moss[3] attch. 1 S Lanc, (Originally 5th Bn), 305835 W Moulem[3] attch. 17 SSB, 306962 W Oliver[3] attch. 17 SSB, 305847 T Powell[3] attch. 3/W Sig Sqn, 205273 W Sanford[3] attch. 1 S Lanc, (Originally 4th Bn), 386289 J J Sawyer[3] attch. 17 SSB, (Originally 17th Bn), 305804 J G Spratt[3] attch. 17 SSB, 306527 W E Taylor[3] attch. 40 DSC, 16 Div., 306076 M Tuffin[3] attch. 17 SSB, 205315 W Tyrrell[3] attch. BCCS, (Originally 4th Bn), 306356 W Ward[3] attch. 40 DSC, 16 Div., 41842 W C Webb[3] attch. 2 N Stafford, 306994 E Whitlock[3] attch. 39 DSC, 2 Div. & 35280 W D Williams[3] attch. 1 S Lanc

~ 1/8th (Isle Of Wight Rifles, Princess Beatrice's') Bn, The Hampshire Regiment, Territorial Force ~

Note a.   *Roll of all personnel identified as eligible.*

Note b.   *United Kingdom August 1914. Mudros and Gallipoli August 1915, Egypt December 1915 to March 1919 including tours of Palestine and Syria.*

Note c.   *Medals named in impressed capitals: 'HAMPS. R.'*

Single Clasp	No. Identified	Rarity
Afghanistan N.W.F. 1919[3]	1	According to the roll as seen, can be considered Unique
Mahsud 1919–20[5]	0	None Identified
Waziristan 1919–21[4]	0	None Identified
Waziristan 1921–24[6]	0	None Identified

Lieutenants: ~ L Hitchcock[3]

~ 1/9th (Cyclist) Bn, The Hampshire Regiment ~

Note a.   *Roll of all personnel identified as eligible.*

Note b.   *United Kingdom August 1914. India February 1916 to October 1918 thence Russia via Hong Kong.*

Note c.   *Medals named in impressed capitals: 'HAMPS. R.'*

Single Clasp	No. Identified	Rarity
Afghanistan N.W.F. 1919[3]	6	Of the Utmost Rarity
Mahsud 1919–20[5]	0	None Identified
Waziristan 1919–21[4]	0	None Identified
Waziristan 1921–24[6]	0	None Identified

Lieutenants: ~ G E Downs[3] attch. 260 Coy, MGC

Lance Sergeants/Corporals: ~ 39878 E M Kenway[3] attch. S&TC, (Originally 17th Bn)

Lance Corporals/Privates: ~ 39710 P Brewer[3] attch. 36 DSC, 1 Div., (Originally 17th Bn), 355483 A H Clarke[3] attch. 36 DSC, 1 Div., 355288 P V Hardwick[3] attch. 36 DSC, 1 Div. & 355645 P C Noss[3] attch. 38 DSC, 1 Div.

~ Unidentified Service Bn, The Hampshire Regiment ~

Note a. *Roll of all personnel identified as eligible.*
Note b. *Medals named in impressed capitals: 'HAMPS. R.'*

Single Clasp	No. Identified	Rarity
Afghanistan N.W.F. 1919[3]	5	Of the Utmost Rarity
Mahsud 1919–20[5]	0	None Identified
Waziristan 1919–21[4]	0	None Identified
Waziristan 1921–24[6]	0	None Identified

Lieutenants: ~ W E D'Angibau[3] attch. 288 Coy, MGC, H C Beere[3] attch. 1 DWR, R E Calloway[3] attch. 222 Coy, MGC, L H Helsdon[3] attch. 17 SSB & D C Leek-Roe[3] attch. 185 Coy, MGC

~ 1/5th Bn, The South Staffordshire Regiment, Territorial Force ~

Note a. *Roll of all personnel identified as eligible.*
Note b. *United Kingdom August 1914. France & Flanders March 1915, Egypt January / February 1916, thence France and Flanders forward.*
Note c. *Medals named in impressed capitals: 'S. STAFF. R.'*

Single Clasp	No. Identified	Rarity
Afghanistan N.W.F. 1919[3]	1	According to the roll as seen, can be considered Unique
Mahsud 1919–20[5]	0	None Identified
Waziristan 1919–21[4]	0	None Identified
Waziristan 1921–24[6]	0	None Identified

Captains: ~ F E Rowe[3] attch. 2 N Stafford.

~ 1/6th Bn, The South Staffordshire Regiment, Territorial Force ~

Note a. *Roll of all personnel identified as eligible.*
Note b. *United Kingdom August 1914. France & Flanders March 1915, Egypt January / February 1916 thence back to France and Flanders forward.*
Note c. *Medals named in impressed capitals: 'S. STAFF. R.'*

Single Clasp	No. Identified	Rarity
Afghanistan N.W.F. 1919[3]	1	According to the roll as seen, can be considered Unique
Mahsud 1919–20[5]	0	None Identified
Waziristan 1919–21[4]	0	None Identified
Waziristan 1921–24[6]	0	None Identified

Lieutenants: ~ S Dalgleish[3] attch. 2 N Stafford

245

~ 1ˢᵗ Garrison Bn, The Hampshire Regiment ~

Note a.   *Roll of all personnel identified as eligible.*
Note b.   *Formed January 1917. India from spring 1917 forward.*
Note c.   *Medals named in impressed capitals: 'S. STAFF. R.'*

Single Clasp	No. Identified	Rarity
Afghanistan N.W.F. 1919[3]	5	Of the Utmost Rarity
Mahsud 1919–20[5]	0	None Identified
Waziristan 1919–21[4]	0	None Identified
Waziristan 1921–24[6]	0	None Identified

Lieutenants: ~ A E Bryant[3] attch. 17 SSB
Quartermaster Sergeants/Sergeants: ~ 204738 A Gillies[3] attch. 41 PMC
Lance Corporals/Privates: ~ 47347 E Armstrong[3] attch. 2 N Stafford, 34751 J Potts[3] attch. 2 N Stafford & 204633 A W Whale[3] attch. 2 MT Coy, S&TC

~ 2ⁿᵈ Bn, The Dorsetshire Regiment ~

Note a.   *Roll of all personnel identified as eligible.*
Note b.   *India August 1914. Mesopotamia November 1914 forward.*
Note c.   *Captured at Kut al Amara on 29ᵗʰ April 1916. Survivors and non-deployed drafts were merged with similar 'odd' men of 2ⁿᵈ Bn, Norfolk Regt, to form the 'Norsets'. Re established as a functioning entity in July 1916, the new battalion moved to India in October 1919 via Egypt, Palestine and Syria thence Egypt again in January 1922.*
Note d.   *The battalion was present as a complete unit for the clasp 'MALABAR 1921-22'.*
Note e.   *Medals named in impressed capitals: 'DORSET. R.'*

Single Clasp	No. Identified	Rarity
Afghanistan N.W.F. 1919[3]	1	According to the roll as seen, can be considered Unique
Mahsud 1919–20[5]	0	None Identified
Waziristan 1919–21[4]	2	Of the Utmost Rarity
Waziristan 1921–24[6]	1	According to the roll as seen, can be considered Unique
Combination Clasps	**No. Identified**	**Rarity**
Afghanistan N.W.F. 1919[3] Mahsud 1919–20[5] Waziristan 1919–21[4]	1	According to the roll as seen, can be considered Unique
Mahsud 1919–20[5] Waziristan 1919–21[4]	1	According to the roll as seen, can be considered Unique
Waziristan 1919–21[4] Malabar 1921–22[7]	2	Of the Utmost Rarity
Waziristan 1919–21[4] Waziristan 1921–24[6]	2	Of the Utmost Rarity

Captains: ~ E L Stephenson[3] attch. 4/39 Garhwal Rifles, IA
Lieutenants: ~ G E Fielder[4&5] attch. S&TC & W T Toms[3,4&5] attch. 'F' DSC
Warrant Officers Class II: ~ 5718856 R J Lawless[4] (Originally Australian Imperial Force)
Quartermaster Sergeants/Sergeants: ~ (Act) 5718112 W J Butler[4&6] attch. Sigs & (Act) (0552) 5719217 A C Davis[4&7] attch. S&TC
Lance Corporals/Privates: ~ 5718329 W J Croft[6] attch. 'B' Corps Sigs, 5718338 B O Cutler[4&6], 5719277 A R J Darby[4&7] attch. S&TC & (5719126) 0453 T C Webb[4] attch. 'C' DSC

~ 3rd (Reserve) Bn, The Dorsetshire Regiment ~

Note a.   *Roll of all personnel identified as eligible.*
Note b.   *United Kingdom August 1914. United Kingdom throughout Great War period providing drafts and reinforcements.*
Note c.   *Medals named in impressed capitals: 'DORSET. R.'*

Single Clasp	No. Identified	Rarity
Afghanistan N.W.F. 1919[3]	1	According to the roll as seen, can be considered Unique
Mahsud 1919–20[5]	0	None Identified
Waziristan 1919–21[4]	0	None Identified
Waziristan 1921–24[6]	0	None Identified

Lieutenants: ~ H G Ardron[3] attch. 1 Sussex

~ 1/4th Bn, The Dorsetshire Regiment, Territorial Force ~

Note a.   *Roll of all personnel identified as eligible.*
Note b.   *United Kingdom August 1914. India November 1914 thence Mesopotamia February 1916 to November 1919.*
Note c.   *Medals named in impressed capitals: 'DORSET. R.'*

Single Clasp	No. Identified	Rarity
Afghanistan N.W.F. 1919[3]	159	Scarce
Mahsud 1919–20[5]	0	None Identified
Waziristan 1919–21[4]	3	Of the Utmost Rarity
Waziristan 1921–24[6]	0	None Identified
Combination Clasps	*No. Identified*	*Rarity*
Afghanistan N.W.F. 1919[3] Waziristan 1919–21[4]	1	According to the roll as seen, can be considered Unique
Mahsud 1919–20[5] Waziristan 1919–21[4]	1	According to the roll as seen, can be considered Unique

Lieutenant Colonels: ~ H L Kitson[3] attch. Base Depot, Quetta
Captains: ~ J E Ogle[3]
Lieutenants: ~ R H Cobb[3] attch. 2 King's, V Eastwood[3] attch. 8 GCC Res Bn, Quetta & C M S Missing[3] attch. 1 DWR
Warrant Officers Class II: ~ (Act) (5720366) 16949 A T Ryan[3] attch. S&TC & (Act) (5718196) 9593 F J Woollen[3] attch. S&TC
Company Quartermaster Sergeants/Staff Sergeants/Colour Sergeants: ~ (Act) 201267 H D Dunning[4] attch. 52 Wing RAF & 201426 J E Warren[3] attch. MT Coy Mushki, S&TC
Quartermaster Sergeants/Sergeants: ~ (Act) (5720329) 13273 J Beahan[3] attch. S&TC, (Act) (5720406) 31633 J R Bryant[3] attch. 'G' Sply Depot, Dugdap, S&TC, (Act) 15827 J V Calvert[4] attch. Derajat Sply Depot, S&TC, (Act) 29114 J Currie[3] attch. 1 Sussex, (Act) 200362 E N Dodge[3] attch. 39 DSC, 2 Div., (Act) 5983 R J Duncan[3] attch. Sig Sect, Quetta, (Act) 26501 E F Elliott[3&4] attch. BC, S&TC, (Act) 24394 M A Gallagher[3] attch. S&TC, 200974 R J Garland[3] attch. S&TC, (Act) 16965 G D Ginder[3] attch. S&TC, (Act) 24408 G O Grant[3] attch. 299 Sply Depot, S&TC, (Act) 201958 H M Legg[3] attch. Brit Mil Mis Meshed, (Act) 24392 H R McDermott[3] attch. S&TC, 203020 E Pictor[3] attch. 2 N Stafford, (Act) 31622 A Price[3] attch. 62 Bde., S&TC, (Act) 203908 J D Roberts[3] attch. 1/4 QORWK, (Act) (5720360) 16525 V E Sackett[3] attch. S&TC, (Act) 201611 E H J Sibley[3] attch. HQ, NWFF, (Temp) (5712039) 26512 A C Sullivan[3] attch. S&TC, (Act) 13275 W H Swindle[3] attch. S&TC, (Act) 201014 A C Talbot[3], 15848 P 'late[3] attch. 32 Bde. Sply Sect, S&TC, (Act) 201057 W J Tuck[3], 13043 F J Tucker[3] attch. 1/1 Kent & (Act) 26496 H R Vincent[4] attch. 13 Div. Sply Coy, S&TC
Lance Sergeants/Corporals: ~ 200621 A Cox[3] attch. 1 Sussex, (Act) 28207 E Y Miles[3] attch. 1 MT Coy, S&TC, 200170 R G Taylor[3] attch. 17 SSB, (5719383) 0728 S J Toms[3] attch. 1 S Lanc & (Act) 27235 A L Wolstenholme[3] attch. HQ, Insp Gen LofC
Lance Corporals/Privates: ~ 202253 H J Ackers[3] attch. 1 Sussex, 201541 L G Adams[3] attch. 1 DLI, 201752 F S Allner[3] attch. 17 SSB, 201709 H E Allwood[3] attch. 2 N Stafford, 200568 E F R Amey[3], 28987 W A Amy[3] attch. 17 SSB, 201688 A Arnold[3] attch. 2 LofC Sigs, 201828 A J Bagg[3] attch. 17 SSB, 201490 E G Barnes[3] attch. 2 N Stafford, 28965 J Baudains[3]

attch. 17 SSB, 28984 C F Blampied[3] attch. RE, 29777 A H Blason[3] attch. 19 MT Coy, S&TC, 201396 F Brown[3] attch. 2 N Stafford, (0588) 201019 F J Bryant[3] attch. 1/4 QORWK, 201563 A V Burgess[3] attch. 2 N Stafford, 202734 S Chance[3] attch. 17 SSB, 202268 A Child[3] attch. 1 Sussex, 201306 E Churchill[3] attch. 5 LofC Sig Coy, 200922 F Clarke[3] attch. 2 N Stafford, 201364 W J Coakes[3] attch. 40 DSC, 16 Div., (5719253) 0591 H Cobb[3] attch. 1/4 QORWK, 201237 R F Cobb[3] attch. ITD, Quetta, 200666 T Coey[3] attch. 3/W Sig Sqn, 201033 A Coke[3] attch. ITD, 201591 F H Cornick[3] attch. 17 SSB, 201389 W T Court[3] attch. 2 N Stafford, 201193 S Crumpler[3] attch. 3/W Sig Sqn, 202411 E G Dashper[3] attch. HQ, 65 Bde., 200513 A Dawe[3] attch. 1 DLI, 201346 E Day[3] attch. 2 N Stafford, 203417 F W Day[3] attch. 17 SSB, 200986 W Diffey[3] attch. 2 N Stafford, 201304 T Dowland[3] attch. 2 N Stafford, (5719252) 0590 F G Edmonds[3] attch. 1/4 QORWK, (571924) 0586 A Evans[3] attch. 1/4 QORWK, 201367 G W Farwell[3], attch. 1/4 QORWK, 200868 C H G Foord[3] attch. ITD, Quetta, 8430 J Foot[3] attch. 1 Sussex, 201238 F Fordham[3] attch. 2 N Stafford, 202570 F J Gardiner[3] attch. 1 S Lanc, 15303 H E Gibson[3] attch. 1 DLI, 200723 R J Gillard[3] attch. 39 DSC, 2 Div., 200994 W F Gillingham[3] attch. 2 N Stafford, 202757 A E Goatley[3] attch. 2 N Stafford, 201811 C E Goff[3] attch. 17 SSB, 200896 P H Gordge[3] attch. 2 N Stafford, 200430 J Green[3] attch. 1 Sussex, 201110 E F Guppy[3] attch. ITD, New Charman, 201401 A Guy[3] attch. 39 DSC, 201353 F Haggett[3] attch. 1/25 London, 201672 P W Hallett[3] attch. 17 SSB, 201699 P D Harrison[3] attch. 17 SSB, 202459 T W Harrison[4&5] attch. S&TC, 202763 W Hart[3] attch. 2 N Stafford, 200191 T Haskell[3] attch. 1/4 QORWK, 200707 A Haysom[3] attch. 1 Sussex, 200063 A J Herridge[3] attch. GHQ, NWFF, 201302 V Hoare[3] attch. 17 SSB, 203008 F E Horlock[3] attch. 17 SSB, 0592 R H Hoskins[3] attch. 1/4 QORWK, 201032 T V House[3] attch. ITD, Peshawar, 201667 H W Howe[3] attch. 1/1 Kent, 200434 T L Howes[3] attch. 2 N Stafford, 202951 F Ingram[3] attch. 2 N Stafford, 201384 E O Jewer[3], 24283 H Kay[3], 201275 E P Keynes[3] attch. 1 DLI, (5718303) 13265 W C Knight[3] attch. MAD, 201736 W W Lee[3] attch. 17 SSB, (5719255) 0594 G W Legg[3] attch. 1/4 QORWK, 201681 C M Lewis[3] attch. 17 SSB, 202586 G A Lewis[3] attch. 2 N Stafford, 201694 H Lock[3] attch. 17 SSB, 201404 F J Loder[3] attch. 39 DSC, 2 Div., 200252 E B Marsh[3] attch. 1/1 Kent, 201414 F A C Marshallsay[3] attch. 2 N Stafford, (5719677) 01074 F R Martin[3] attch. 1 DLI, 201666 H C Martin[3] attch. 17 SSB, 25943 C W McDonald[3] attch. 1/1 Kent, 201376 F G Middleton[3] attch. 2 N Stafford, 200306 A Miller[3] attch. 1/4 QORWK, 201443 W S Mitchell[3] attch. 2 N Stafford, 201150 W G Newport[3] attch. 2 N Stafford, 201916 F Norman[3] attch. 17 SSB, 202060 S E Pacello[3] attch. 2 LofC Sig Sect, 201444 W Paddock[3] attch. 38 DSC, 29397 H H Palmer[3] attch. 1 Sussex, 200604 W J Paul[3] attch. 17 SSB, 202716 S Pateman[3] attch. 1 Sussex, 202597 H G Penny[3] attch. 14 MT Coy, S&TC, 201338 W Penny[3] attch. 2 N Stafford, 202788 W Pope[3] attch. 2 N Stafford, 28920 W C Proper[3] attch. 17 SSB, 202681 S Rendall[3] attch. 1 DLI, (5719251) 0589 W J Richards[3] attch. 1/4 QORWK, 201595 R Riglar[3] 17 SSB, 203901 W Ritson[3] attch. 17 SSB, 201795 H J Rogers[3], 201630 W G J Samways[3] attch. 17 SSB, 200916 J Selby[3] attch. 17 SSB, 201889 A V Seller attch. ITD, 201749 E J Silcox[3] attch. 17 SSB, 202549 H G Simmonds[3] attch. 2 N Stafford, 200230 B Smith[3] attch. 14 MT Coy, S&TC, 7742 P V Smith[3] attch. ITD, Rawalpindi, 201438 S Stacey[3] attch. 2 N Stafford, 200948 W Stickley[3] attch. 44 DSC, KKF, 201796 E P Sue[3] attch. 3/W Sig Sqn, (5719402) 0750 A G Sweatland[3] attch. 1/5 Hampshire, 200781 C E Tarry[3] attch. 3/W Sig Sqn, 210272 W F Trim[3] attch. 2 N Stafford, 201779 A Voss[3] attch. 17 SSB, 201778 J P Waight[3] 2 LofC Sig Sect, 202694 A W Walker[3] attch. 2 N Stafford, 0605 A E Watkins[3] attch. 1/4 QORWK, 201801 J Way[3] attch. 2 N Stafford, 202399 F C Webb[3] attch. HQ, 45 Bde., 201633 S G Weller[3] attch. 17 SSB, (5719249) 0587 W H F West[3] attch. 1/4 QORWK, 201536 A R F Westmacott[3] attch. 2 N Stafford, 201605 S H White[3] attch. 17 SSB, 201516 T G White[3] attch. 2 N Stafford, 28321 F M Williams[3] attch. 1 MT Coy, S&TC, 201912 H Woodford[3] attch. 2 N Stafford & (5719994) 8613 W Woodhouse[3] attch. 3/W Sig Sqn

~ 1st Bn, The Prince of Wales's Volunteers (South Lancashire Regiment) ~

Note a.   Roll of all commissioned personnel identified as eligible.

Note b.   Non commissioned and other ranks multi clasp or non-Afghanistan 1919 single clasp except those single Afghanistan specimens identified as having been named 'S. LAN. R.'. See Note 6 below. These are identified thus: (*). This list may not be exhaustive.

Note c.   India August 1914 forward. Ireland March 1920 to 1922.

Note d.   Title changed to The Prince of Wales's Volunteers (South Lancashire) Regiment in 1920.

Note e.   Battle honour 'Third Afghan War 1919'.

Note f.   Medals for 'Afghanistan N.W.F. 1919' issued from the initial 'battalion' submission are named: '1 P. W. VOLS.'. Recipients with claims listed on rolls processed (principally in Preston) from 1922 forward are named: 'S. LAN. R.' and as such are rare. The reason for this change is unclear.

Single Clasp	No. Identified	Rarity
Afghanistan N.W.F. 1919[3]	Bn. Strength	Not Rare
Afghanistan N.W.F. 1919[3] Named 'S LAN R'	88	Rare
Mahsud 1919–20[5]	0	None Identified
Waziristan 1919–21[4] Named 'S LAN R'	1	According to the roll as seen, can be considered Unique
Waziristan 1921–24[6]	0	None Identified

Combination Clasps	No. Identified	Rarity
Afghanistan N.W.F. 1919[3] Mahsud 1919–20[5] Waziristan 1919–21[4] Waziristan 1921–24[6]	2	Of the Utmost Rarity
Afghanistan N.W.F. 1919[3] Waziristan 1919–21[4] Named 'S LAN R'	1	According to the roll as seen, can be considered Unique
Afghanistan N.W.F. 1919[3] Waziristan 1919–24[6]	1	According to the roll as seen, can be considered Unique

Lieutenant Colonels: ~ A de V Willoughby-Osborne[3]

Majors: ~ R H MacDonald[3&6] attch. 'G' DSC & (QM) T A Simon[3]

Captains: ~ R W Braide[3], F E D Campbell[3(*)], L H Curry[3], J L French[3], J F G Hislop[3], C A Jones[3], J H Whalley-Kelly[3] attch. MGC, K M Murray[3], R A Ransom[3], N Shaw[3] & W D Ward[3]

Lieutenants: ~ S Baker[3], G A Barker[3], H R Breething[3], J W Burghope[3], D Campbell[3], E J Earle[3] attch. 287 Coy, MGC, R S Ernst[3], G A Harker[3], H K Hyde[3], A J Jarman[3], D H Kerr[3], E D Lunn[3], R Makin[3], L H Shaw[3], W M Simon[3] & H E Wootton[3]

Warrant Officers Class II: ~ (Act) 8250 A V Wallbridge[3(*)]

Quartermaster Sergeants/Sergeants: ~ 39692 W B Armstrong[3(*)], (3436808) 8097 J H Clarkson[3,4,5&6(Lanc Fus)] attch. 33 DSC, 4 Div., (3436746) 8734 C Cross[3,4,5&6(Lanc Fus)] attch. 33 DSC, 4 Div., (Act) 9605 J Davies[3(*)], 6984 W Duggan[3(*)], (Act) 9716 F Farenden[3(*)] attch. 21 BSS, (Temp) 39657 F W Jackson[3(*)] attch. 11 Div. Sply Coy, (Act) 39313 G Tickle[3(*)] attch. 11 Div. Sply Coy, (Act) 16547 F C Upjohn[3(*)], (Temp) 16566 P C Young[3(*)&4(Lanc Fus)], (Act) 8415 H Wade[3(*)] attch. DFD & (Act) 9139 H Williams[3(*)]

Lance Sergeants/Corporals: ~ 9440 W Ashall[3(*)] attch. S&TC, (Act) 278976 A H Clarke[3(*)], 70608 J Crawford[3(*)] attch. 43CFA, 8746 J Hackwell[3(*)], (Act) 8709 J T Hall[3(*)], 9237 A Losh[3(*)] attch. 33 DSC, (Act) 18188 A Mason[3(*)], 8183 R McDermott[3(*)] (Act) 8494 J O'Reilly[3(*)] & 4248 G W Wardlow[3(*)]

Lance Corporals/Privates: ~ 23179 G H Bayuley[3(*)], 9737 P Bibby[3(*)], 90494 F Browne[3(*)], 9039 F W Buckingham[4(*)], 8707 P W Budd[3(*)] attch. 38 DSC, 9249 G C Burrows[3(*)] attch. 33 DSC, 9286 W Campbell[3(*)], 9169 F G Castle[3(*)], 42397 J Clare[3(*)], 9247 F J D Coe[3(*)], 9298 T Concannon[3(*)] attch. HQ, BF, 37838 T Cox[3(*)], 44028 W T Dashall[3(*)], 9552 J Dobson[3(*)], 8665 J Eaton[3(*)], 9541 J W Edwards[3(*)], 9457 J H Field[3(*)], 30048 T Finn[3(*)], 42330 W H Follows[3(*)], 8188 J Gallagher[3(*)] attch. 33 DSC, 8203 W Garrity[3(*)] attch. 3 W S/Sqn, 70727 J E Gatcliffe[3(*)], 8369 A Gibson[3(*)] attch. BGH, 265662 J J Graham[3(*)], 9782 J Green[3(*)] attch. 39 DSC, 40035 T Grice[3(*)], 8911 J Hale[3(*)], 43621 F R Harrison[3(*)], 8574 G A Harrison[3(*)], 9831 W Hewer[3(*)], 266051 E Hewitt[3(*)], 9190 F G Jenkins[3(*)], 9806 A B Jones[3(*)], 19876 J Kenny[3(*)], 37856 A Kenyon[3(*)] attch. HQ NWFF, 40742 J R Leather[3(*)], 8393 W J Mannerings[3(*)], 8222 J H Masters[3(*)], 8670 W McGain[3(*)], 50216 H McLenaghan[3(*)] attch. 2 MT Coy S&TC, 37861 W Mercer[3(*)], 8166 W Moneypenny[3(*)], 8466 C Myall[3(*)], 9694 A Parker[3(*)] attch. 33 DSC, 37870 A Pennington[3(*)] attch. 33 DSC, 29979 H Pennington[3(*)], 37896 W Platt[3(*)], 9567 W Polfrey[3(*)] attch. Govt. Dairy, 50065 W Read[3(*)], 39503 G R Redman[3(*)], 265088 J Rose[3(*)], 8246 W Rose[3(*)], 8600 E Rushton[3(*)] attch. 33 DSC, 9759 J Salisbury[3(*)], 8558 A Sanson[3(*)], 8986 A Shorter[3(*)], 70706 R J Sly[3(*)], 9275 J Stanley[3(*)], 39041 J Sudlow[3(*)], 9748 W G Swift[3(*)], 36260 E Taylor[3(*)], 9733 P Terry[3(*)], 8958 A Thompson[3(*)], 44006 W Thornton[3(*)], 9570 J Timperley[3(*)], 9783 J Walker[3(*)], 42342 F Wignall[3(*)], 30031 H Wilson[3(*)] & 266040 H Wrigley[3(*)]

~ 2nd Bn, The Prince of Wales's Volunteers (South Lancashire Regiment) ~

Note a. *Roll of all personnel identified as eligible.*

Note b. *United Kingdom August 1914. France & Flanders August 1914 forward. Egypt May to October 1922 thence India.*

Note c. *Medals named in impressed capitals: '2 P. W. VOLS.' or 'S. LAN. R.'*

Single Clasp	No. Identified	Rarity
Afghanistan N.W.F. 1919[3]	0	None Identified
Mahsud 1919–20[5]	0	None Identified
Waziristan 1919–21[4]	0	None Identified
Waziristan 1921–24[6]	3	Of the Utmost Rarity

Combination Clasps	No. Identified	Rarity
Waziristan 1919–21[4] Waziristan 1921–24[6]	1	According to the roll as seen, can be considered Unique

Captains: ~ W H Brooks[6] Staff, Jandola

Lance Sergeants/Corporals: ~ (Act) 3645163 J W Overend[6] attch. MFO, Idak & 3903916 A Peden[4&6] attch. 'F' DSC

Lance Corporals/Privates: ~ 3646551 F A Gagen[6] Clk, Mari Indus

~ 1/5th Bn, The Prince of Wales's Volunteers (South Lancashire Regiment), Territorial Force ~

Note a. Roll of all personnel identified as eligible.

Note b. United Kingdom August 1914. France & Flanders February 1915 forward.

Note c. Medals named in impressed capitals: '1-5 P. W. VOLS.' or 'S. LAN. R.'

Single Clasp	No. Identified	Rarity
Afghanistan N.W.F. 1919[3]	3	Of the Utmost Rarity
Mahsud 1919–20[5]	0	None Identified
Waziristan 1919–21[4]	0	None Identified
Waziristan 1921–24[6]	0	None Identified

Captains: ~ A L Corlett[3] attch. 1/9 Middlesex

Lieutenants: ~ R A Bigham[3] & R D Vowles[3] attch. 2 Som LI

~ 6th (Service) Bn, The Prince of Wales's Volunteers (South Lancashire Regiment) ~

Note a. Roll of all personnel identified as eligible.

Note b. Formed August 1914. Helles July 1915, Mudros and Gallipoli August 1915, Mudros December 1915, Egypt January 1916, Mesopotamia February 1916 to April 1919 thence to demobilisation.

Note c. Medals named in impressed capitals: 'P. W. VOLS.' or 'S. LAN. R.'

Single Clasp	No. Identified	Rarity
Afghanistan N.W.F. 1919[3]	8	Of the Utmost Rarity
Afghanistan N.W.F. 1919[3] Named S LANC R	3	Of the Utmost Rarity
Mahsud 1919–20[5]	0	None Identified
Waziristan 1919–21[4]	0	None Identified
Waziristan 1921–24[6]	0	None Identified

Quartermaster Sergeants/Sergeants: ~ (Act) 19078 H Alton[3] attch. 1 Yorkshire

Lance Sergeants/Corporals: ~ (Act) 42148 C H Barker[3] attch. RASC & 11223 J Devine[3] attch. 2 Som LI

Lance Corporals/Privates: ~ 42147 T H Brimlow[3] attch. RASC, 36527 S Carter[3] attch. 1 Yorkshire, 204090 C Hayes[3(*)] attch. 2 Som LI, 42199 J Killilea[3(*)] attch. 2 Som LI, 12215 G Pye[3] attch. 2 Som LI, 50065 W Read[3] attch. 2 Som LI, 42198 G Rutter[3] attch. RASC & 203924 P Scott[3(*)]

~ 1st Bn, The Welsh Regiment ~

Note a. Roll of all commissioned personnel identified as eligible.

Note b. Non-commissioned and other ranks multi clasp or non-Waziristan 1921 – 24 single clasp.

Note c. India August 1914. France & Flanders January 1915, Salonika November 1915 forward. India September 1919.

Note d. In 1920, the spelling of the word 'Welsh' was changed to 'Welch'.

Note e. Medals named in impressed capitals: 'WELSH. R.' or 'WELCH. R.' depending on when the claim was processed. (See Note 4 above).

Single Clasp	No. Identified	Rarity
Afghanistan N.W.F. 1919[3]	0	None Identified
Mahsud 1919 - 20[5]	0	None Identified
Waziristan 1919 – 21[4]	4	Of the Utmost Rarity
Waziristan 1921 – 24[6]	Bn. Strength	Not Rare

Combination Clasps	No. Identified	Rarity
Mahsud 1919 – 20[5] Waziristan 1919 – 21[4] Waziristan 1921 – 24[6]	2	Of the Utmost Rarity
Waziristan 1919 – 21[4] Waziristan 1921 – 24[6]	6	Of the Utmost Rarity
Waziristan 1921 – 24[6] North West Frontier 1935[12]	1	According to the roll as seen, can be considered Unique

Lieutenant Colonels: ~ C R Berkeley[6]

Majors: ~ (Bvt) W G Hewett[6], W M Hore[4,5&6] attch. 4/3 GR, IA & T G Mathias[6]

Captains: ~ C P Bayer[6], J A Daniel[6], F W Ford[6], F W Gransmore[6], W Guthrie[4], B T Phillips[6], P H Phillips[6] & W H Stitt[6]

Lieutenants: ~ M Bennetts[6], J W Lewis Bowen[6], S L Collier[6] attch. 'B' Corps Sigs, A C Cottell[6], H F A Dunn[6], (QM) H J M Edwards[6], J T Gibson[6], J K M Gordon[6], W D J Harris[6], R M Hill[6], G F Jones[6], I B S Lewin[6], W N Lewis[6], C H Schofield[6] & A Smedley[6]

Quartermaster Sergeants/Sergeants: ~ 3948381 D Bennett[4&6], 3949208 P F Burrows[4&6] & 3942888 G John[6&12(2 Welch)]

Lance Corporals/Privates: ~ 3948557 P G Chinnock[4&6], 3948326 W A Davies[4&6], (87709) 3950254 W J Ellis[4] attch. H WFF, 3949367 S C Ibbitson[4&6], 86587 H Mills[4] attch. MMP, 3949018 H Petherbridge[4,5&6] attch. Admin Staff, Jandola & HQ, WFF DIK, (3948869) 86949 H Shackleford[4&6] attch. HQ, Waz Dist & (87287) 3949167 C Turrington[4] attch. IOD

~ 1/4th Bn, The Welsh Regiment, Territorial Force ~

Note a.   Roll of all personnel identified as eligible.
Note b.   United Kingdom August 1914. Mudros and Gallipoli August 1915, Egypt December 1915 thence Palestine 1917 to 1918 thence?
Note c.   Medals named in impressed capitals: 'WELSH. R.'

Single Clasp	No. Identified	Rarity
Afghanistan N.W.F. 1919[3]	1	According to the roll as seen, can be considered Unique
Mahsud 1919–20[5]	0	None Identified
Waziristan 1919–21[4]	0	None Identified
Waziristan 1921–24[6]	0	None Identified

Captains: ~ J Tremaine[3] attch. Base Depot, Quetta

~ 1/5th Bn, The Welsh Regiment, Territorial Force ~

Note a.   Roll of all personnel identified as eligible.
Note b.   United Kingdom August 1914. Mudros and Gallipoli August 1915, Egypt December 1915 thence Palestine 1917 to 1918 thence?
Note c.   Medals named in impressed capitals: 'WELSH. R.'

Single Clasp	No. Identified	Rarity
Afghanistan N.W.F. 1919[3]	1	According to the roll as seen, can be considered Unique
Mahsud 1919–20[5]	0	None Identified
Waziristan 1919–21[4]	0	None Identified
Waziristan 1921–24[6]	0	None Identified

Lieutenants: ~ W T Gething-Jones[3] attch. 281 Coy, MGC

~ 8th (Service) Bn (Pioneers), The Welsh Regiment ~

Note a.   *Roll of all personnel identified as eligible.*
Note b.   *Formed August 1914. Mudros and Gallipoli August 1914, Egypt December 1915, Mesopotamia February 1916 forward.*
Note c.   *Medals named in impressed capitals: 'WELSH. R.'*

Single Clasp	No. Identified	Rarity
Afghanistan N.W.F. 1919[3]	44	Very Rare
Mahsud 1919–20[5]	0	None Identified
Waziristan 1919–21[4]	0	None Identified
Waziristan 1921–24[6]	0	None Identified

Captains: ~ H V Palin[3] attch. 17 SSB

Lieutenants: ~ T Anwyl[3] attch. 2 N Stafford, G M Jones[3] attch. 270 Coy MGC, R S Legge[3] attch. 1 Sussex, L Lloyd[3] attch. 2/4 Border, J T Raybould[3] attch. 286 Coy, MGC, J C Smith[3] attch. DLI & W Tickle[3] attch. 1 DLI

Lance Sergeants/Corporals: ~ (Act) 33073 E Crabbe[3] attch. 35 ISS

Lance Corporals/Privates: ~ 62529 A J Alderton[3], 200708 J Baker[3], (Originally 4th Bn), (87709) 3949279 C Bevan[3], 38237 E V Cole[3], 203346 T Cox[3], (Originally 4th Bn), 129416 S David[3], 44214 D G Davies[3], 27236 T Davies[3], 18451 H A Davis[3], 202891 J W Drew[3], (Originally 4th Bn), 10380 J A Hall[3], 48606 L T Headland[3], 33958 B James[3], 51070 A G Jones[3], 43842 W J Jones[3], 59558 C Kelly[3], 87266 F N Lowe[3], 87267 J MacDonald[3], 49765 E J MacIntyre[3], 47418 S Matthews[3], 48098 E W Nelms[3] attch. 35 ISS, 26989 T Nightingale[3], 58715 D Parfitt[3], 87328 A E Parr[3], 87310 J Phillips[3] attch. 1 S Lanc R, 19441 W D Phillips[3], 37423 W A Pink[3], 51087 M A Rilat[3], 46553 T J Roberts[3], 51150 J C Rose[3], 202901 E T Rowlands[3], 43856 J Simpson[3], 10869 C Springall[3], 61776 C Webb[3] & 59758 L Williams[3]

~ 1st Bn, The Black Watch (Royal Highlanders) ~

Note a.   *Roll of all personnel identified as eligible.*
Note b.   *United Kingdom August 1914. France & Flanders August 1914 forward. India September 1919 forward.*
Note c.   *Medals named in impressed capitals: 'BLACK WATCH', 'R. HIGHRS.' or '1/R. HDRS.'*

Single Clasp	No. Identified	Rarity
Afghanistan N.W.F. 1919[3]	5	Of the Utmost Rarity
Mahsud 1919–20[5]	0	None Identified
Waziristan 1919–21[4]	3	Of the Utmost Rarity
Waziristan 1921–24[6]	12	Extremely Rare
Combination Clasps	**No. Identified**	**Rarity**
Mahsud 1919–20[5] Waziristan 1919–21[4]	2	Of the Utmost Rarity
Waziristan 1919–21[4] Waziristan 1921–24[6]	1	According to the roll as seen, can be considered Unique

Majors: ~ N A B Bailie-Hamilton[6] attch. 2/18 Garhwal Rifles, IA

Captains: ~ L C Bell[3] attch. 36 DSC, 1 Div., E T L Gurdon[6] attch. 3/8 Punjab Regt, IA, R C MacPherson[6] attch. RAF, N McMicking[4], J E M Richard[6] attch. 1/17 Dogras, IA, R H Robertson[3] attch. MAD, 4 Div. & J W Telfer[3] attch. 287 Coy MGC

Lieutenants: ~ R Dick[3] attch. 1 Sussex, A L C Edwards[3] Staff Capt, Kohat & F I Gerrard[6] Staff Capt, 5 Bde., Razmak

Company Quartermaster Sergeants / Staff Sergeants / Colour Sergeants: ~ 2744760 A D Swan[4&6] attch. HQ, WFF

Quartermaster Sergeants / Sergeants: ~ (Act) 2745541 A Rose[6] attch. HQ, Waz Dist

Lance Sergeants / Corporals: ~ 2745059 G C Wilson[6] attch. 'B' DSC

Lance Corporals / Privates: ~ 2745995 T F Andison[6], 2746714 W Cunningham[6] attch. 'B' DSC, 2746148 W Garrigan[6] attch. ISH, Bannu, 30691 A Jackson[4&5], 2746061 W Lynch[4&5] attch. HQ, 68 Bde., 2746142 W Mathieson[4] attch. HQ, WFF & Wana Col, 274576 (30182) R N Preece[4] attch. 45 CFA, 274076? A F Thomas[6] attch. 64 FA & 2745852 A G Walker[6] attch. 'B' DSC

~ 2nd Bn, The Black Watch (Royal Highlanders) ~

Note a.   Roll of all personnel identified as eligible. Entry in roll not found but medal forms part of Black Watch Regimental Museum collection.

Note b.   India August 1914. France October 1914, Mesopotamia December 1915, Palestine January 1918 forward. .

Note c.   Medals named in impressed capitals: '2/R. HIGHRS.'

Single Clasp	No. Identified	Rarity
Afghanistan N.W.F. 1919[3]	1	If verified, can be considered Unique
Mahsud 1919–20[5]	0	None Identified
Waziristan 1919–21[4]	0	None Identified
Waziristan 1921–24[6]	0	None Identified

Lance Corporals/Privates: ~ 588 G Allan[3]

~ 1/4th (City of Dundee) Bn, The Black Watch (Royal Highlanders), Territorial Force ~

Note a.   Roll of all personnel identified as eligible. Entry in roll not found but medal forms part of Black Watch Regimental Museum collection.

Note b.   United Kingdom August 1914. France & Flanders March 1915 forward.

Note c.   Medals named in impressed capitals: '4/R. HIGHRS.'

Single Clasp	No. Identified	Rarity
Afghanistan N.W.F. 1919[3]	1	If verified, can be considered Unique
Mahsud 1919–20[5]	0	None Identified
Waziristan 1919–21[4]	0	None Identified
Waziristan 1921–24[6]	0	None Identified

Lieutenants: ~ G M Smith[3] attch. MGC Motors

~ 1st Bn, The Oxfordshire & Buckinghamshire Light Infantry ~

Note a.   Roll of all personnel identified as eligible.

Note b.   India August 1914. Mesopotamia November 1914 forward.

Note c.   Captured at Kut al Amara on 29th April 1916. Survivors and non-deployed drafts were concentrated as Lines of Communication troops along the River Tigris. 1st Battalion re-established October 1917. HQ Company and 'A' Company detached for service in North Russia. Balance to India in March 1919.

Note d.   Medals named in impressed capitals: 'OXF & BUCKS. L. I.'

Single Clasp	No. Identified	Rarity
Afghanistan N.W.F. 1919[3]	104	Very Scarce
Mahsud 1919–20[5]	0	None Identified
Waziristan 1919–21[4]	3	Of the Utmost Rarity
Waziristan 1921–24[6]	0	None Identified
Combination Clasps	No. Identified	Rarity
Afghanistan N.W.F. 1919[3] Mahsud 1919–20[5]	1	According to the roll as seen, can be considered Unique
Afghanistan N.W.F. 1919[3] Mahsud 1919–20[5] Waziristan 1919–21[4]	1	According to the roll as seen, can be considered Unique

253

Afghanistan N.W.F. 1919[3] Waziristan 1919–21[4] Waziristan 1921–24[6]	1	According to the roll as seen, can be considered Unique
Afghanistan N.W.F. 1919[3] Malabar 1921–22[7]	1	According to the roll as seen, can be considered Unique

Captains: ~ D A J Wilmot[3] attch. 28 SSB & R G Wilsdon[4] attch. Base Eng Pk, Tank

Lieutenants: ~ B L Hugh-Jones[3,4&5] attch. RASC & L R Watts[3] attch. 2 Som LI

Company Quartermaster Sergeants/Staff Sergeants/Colour Sergeants: ~ (Act) 23553 I Markson[3] attch. S&TC & (Act) 16685 F H Timms[3] attch. 1/1 Kent

Quartermaster Sergeants/Sergeants: ~ (Act) 44943 W E Atkinson[3] attch. S&TC, (Act) 38270 W H Averies[3] attch. S&TC, (Act) 38287 E H W Beale[3] attch. 693 Coy, RASC, (Act) 44947 H Bickley[3] attch. S&TC, 9648 R V J Caladine[3] attch. 1/1 Kent, (Act) 31262 C B Carr[4] attch. S&TC, (Act) 38280 R N Clapham[3] attch. S&TC, (Act) 234001 S Coote[3] attch. IOD, (Act) 38296 C A Cutler[3&5] attch. S&TC, 23478 G H Gainsford[3] attch. 1/1 Kent, (Act) 38334 H St. Gilby[3] attch. S&TC, 19885 H L Hill[3] attch. S&TC, 7751 H Jones[3] attch. 2 Som LI, 9010 W M Kirby[3] attch. 32 DSC, (Act) 37973 G R M Knowles[3] attch. 51 CFA, 17929 J T Launchberry[3] attch. 1/1 Kent, 27723 J Lewens[3] attch. 1/1 Kent, (Act) 38279 R M Mayes[3] attch. 45 CFA, (Act) 31263 L C Pacheco[3] attch. 2 Som LI, (Act) 8593 A A Payne[4] attch. S&TC, (Act) 21113 F J A Ross[3] attch. 2/6 Sussex, (Act) 38304 C B Smart[3] attch. S&TC, 9539 W Smith[3] attch. 1/1 Kent, (Act) 9481 J Stone[3] attch. 2 N Stafford, (Act) 38315 C L Walton[3] attch. S&TC & (Act) 23445 G A Wilson[3] attch. HQ, NWFF

Lance Sergeants/Corporals: ~ (Act) 23470 R H Bates[3] attch. 1/1 Kent, (Act) 21458 H J Davis[3] attch. 1/1 Kent, (Act) 20395 C W Drew[3] attch. 2 MT Coy, S&TC, 9502 A H Green[3] attch. 1/1 Kent, 38324 F Grogan[3] attch. 2 Som LI, 19480 A C Parsons[3] attch. 1/1 Kent, (Act) 17612 H Pitchford[3] attch. 1/1 Kent & 8727 S W H Wells[3] attch. 38 DSC

Lance Corporals/Privates: ~ 21833 G E Aldridge[3] attch. 1 MT Coy, S&TC, 19281 A Bagstaff[3] attch. 1/1 Kent, 20699 T E Baker[3] attch. 3 LofC Sig Sect, 19792 E Band[3] attch. 1/1/ Kent, 37883 J Banger[3] attch. 38 DSC, 19312 A H Barralet[3] attch. 1/1 Kent, 23423 H Barrow[3] attch. 1/1 Kent, 21672 G Battrick[3] attch. 2 Som LI, 9573 F Beckett[3] attch. 1/1 Kent, 21434 H P Broome[3] attch. 1/1 Kent, 18462 A W Buckingham[3] attch. 1/1 Kent, 20865 R T M Bushy[3] attch. 1/1 Kent, 9335 J Buxcey[3] attch. 2 Som LI, 8824 H Clarke[3] attch. 2 Som LI, 18875 S Clarke[3] attch. 1/1 Kent, 19731 A C Cobbett[3], 19280 A E Collier[3] attch. 1/1 Kent, 8320 W E Cook[3] attch. 1/1 Kent, 9264 G Davis[3] attch. 38 DSC, 9333 A Day[3] attch. 2 Som LI, 19054 L Farrar[3] attch. 1/1 Kent, 20004 J W G Faulkner[3] attch. 39 DSC, 2 Div., 18618 W F Fenemore[3] attch. 1/1 Kent, 7431 F E Fulbrook[3] attch. 1/1 Kent, 38311 N B Gifford[3] attch. IOD, 21617 W F Gomm[3] attch. 1/1 Kent, 21853 J Gosnell[3] attch. 1/1 Kent, 18324 T J Griffin[3] attch. 1/1 Kent, 23437 E J Griffiths[3] attch. 1/1 Kent, 22211 S Harmer[3] attch. 1/1 Kent, 23499 H G Hartnell[3] attch. 17 SSB, 9725 W Haynes[3] attch. 2 Som LI, 21554 O A Hodges[3] attch. 1/1 Kent, 7043 F Hull[3] attch. 1/1 Kent, 19024 E Innes[3] attch. 1/1 Kent, 23592 E I G St.John[3] attch. S&TC, 20431 J Lee[3] attch. 1/1 Kent, 9077 T Littlejohn[3] attch. 1/1 Kent, 23549 R H Lowman[3] attch. 17 SSB, 21948 G W A Major[3] attch. 1/1 Kent, 21868 S Marks[3] attch. 1/1 Kent, 23510 H Marsden[3] attch. 1/1 Kent, 20727 E W A Mealin[3,4&6] attch. 2 Som LI, 18719 T H Miller[3] attch. 1/1 Kent, 19342 A Moore[3] attch. 1/1 Kent, 19548 J Morgan[3] attch. 1/1 Kent, 27136 W W N Moss[3] attch. 2 Som LI, 9597 W Nash[3] attch. 1/1 Kent, 28181 J Payne[3] attch. 2/6 Sussex, 26895 J W Priestley[3] attch. 17 SSB, 21585 O Rawlings[3] attch. 1/1 Kent, 203219 W Rolle[3] attch. 1/1 Kent, (Originally 4th Bn), 19573 R M Scrivens[3] attch. 1/1 Kent, 23572 D Shearwood[3] attch. 1/1 Kent, 202516 C F Shipman[3] attch. 3/W Sig Sqn, (Originally 4th Bn), 23559 E Smith[3] attch. 17 SSB, 8739 G H Smith[3&(7 as Pte. Dorset R)] attch. 1/1 Kent, 19413 J Stanley[3] attch. 1/1 Kent, 23432 C A Stanton[3] attch. 17 SSB, 21994 J A Stott[3] attch. 1/1 Kent, 9209 J Stringer[3] attch. 2 Som LI, 21886 J Sykes[3] attch. 2/6 Sussex, 29205 A Taylor[3] attch. 2 Som LI, 30578 W R Wakeman[3] attch. HQ, Peshawar, 18339 F Wales[3] attch. 1/1 Kent, 9490 O Warrilow[3] attch. 17 SSB, 20652 T Wiggins[3] attch. 1/1 Kent, 29171 J Wilson[3] attch. 1/1 Kent, 18663 W H Woolford[3] attch. 1/1 Kent, 19463 W H Youens[3] attch. 1/1 Kent & 26839 C Young[3] attch. 1/1

~ 2nd Bn, The Oxfordshire & Buckinghamshire Light Infantry ~

Note a.   *Roll of all personnel identified as eligible.*

Note b.   *United Kingdom August 1914. France & Flanders August 1914 forward. Ireland July 1919 to July 1920, India April 1922 forward.*

Note c.   *Medals named in impressed capitals: 'OXF & BUCKS. L. I.'*

Single Clasp	No. Identified	Rarity
Afghanistan N.W.F. 1919[3]	0	None Identified
Mahsud 1919–20[5]	0	None Identified
Waziristan 1919–21[4]	0	None Identified
Waziristan 1921–24[6]	15	Extremely Rare

Majors: ~ J L Portal[6] Staff Capt, HQ, Waz Dist, DIK
Lieutenants: ~ W T Yeoman[6] attch. RTO, Kalabagh
Quartermaster Sergeants/Sergeants: ~ 5373136 W J Cramp[6] & 6837570 G Hancock[6]
Lance Corporals/Privates: ~ 5374527 A Ball[6], 5374728 F G Bishop[6], 5374516 E Brown[6], 5375832 W C Brown[6], 5373577 J A Butler[6], 5374429 G Cummings[6], 5374706 A J French[6], 5375833 T W Green[6], 5374641 J Grosert[6], 5374589 P Hunt[6] & 5373717 G W Jones[6]

~ 3rd (Reserve) Bn, The Oxfordshire & Buckinghamshire Light Infantry ~

Note a.   Roll of all personnel identified as eligible.
Note b.   United Kingdom August 1919 forward throughout Great War period providing drafts and reinforcements.
Note c.   Medals named in impressed capitals: 'OXF & BUCKS. L. I.'

Single Clasp	No. Identified	Rarity
Afghanistan N.W.F. 1919[3]	1	According to the roll as seen, can be considered Unique
Mahsud 1919–20[5]	0	None Identified
Waziristan 1919–21[4]	0	None Identified
Waziristan 1921–24[6]	0	None Identified

Lieutenants: ~ J H Brasher[3] attch. 1/25 London

~ 1st Garrison Bn, The Oxfordshire & Buckinghamshire Light Infantry ~

Note a.   Roll of all personnel identified as eligible.
Note b.   Formed September 1915. India February 1916 forward.
Note c.   Medals named in impressed capitals: 'OXF & BUCKS. L. I.'

Single Clasp	No. Identified	Rarity
Afghanistan N.W.F. 1919[3]	3	Of the Utmost Rarity
Mahsud 1919–20[5]	0	None Identified
Waziristan 1919–21[4]	0	None Identified
Waziristan 1921–24[6]	0	None Identified

Lance Sergeants/Corporals: ~ 200909 F Belshaw[3] attch. 52 Wing, RAF, (Originally 4th Bn) & (Act) 8400 P Edwards[3]
Lance Corporals/Privates: ~ 20004 J W C Faulkner[3] attch. 39 DSC & 19873 F J White[3] attch. 23 MAC

~ 2nd Bn, The Essex Regiment ~

Note a.   Roll of all personnel identified as eligible.
Note b.   United Kingdom August 1914. France & Flanders August 1914 forward. Malta September 1919, Turkey June 1920, Malta November 1920, Turkey November 1921 thence India March 1923 forward.
Note c.   Medals named in impressed capitals: 'ESSEX R.'

Single Clasp	No. Identified	Rarity
Afghanistan N.W.F. 1919[3]	0	None Identified
Mahsud 1919–20[5]	0	None Identified
Waziristan 1919–21[4]	0	None Identified
Waziristan 1921–24[6]	3	Of the Utmost Rarity

Lance Sergeants/Corporals: ~ 5999391 H A Davey[6] attch. RTE, Bannu & 5998166 A Piggott[6] Staff, Mari Indus
Lance Corporals/Privates: ~ 6002060 H J Baxter[6] attch. Provo Staff, Tank

~ 3rd (Reserve) Bn, The Essex Regiment ~

Note a.   *Roll of all personnel identified as eligible.*
Note b.   *United Kingdom August 1914 forward throughout Great War period providing drafts and reinforcements.*
Note c.   *Medals named in impressed capitals: 'ESSEX R.'*

Single Clasp	No. Identified	Rarity
Afghanistan N.W.F. 1919[3]	1	According to the roll as seen, can be considered Unique
Mahsud 1919–20[5]	0	None Identified
Waziristan 1919–21[4]	0	None Identified
Waziristan 1921–24[6]	0	None Identified

Lieutenants: ~ A T Ross[3] attch. 1 DWR

~ 1/8th (Cyclist) Bn, The Essex Regiment, Territorial Force ~

Note a.   *Roll of all personnel identified as eligible.*
Note b.   *United Kingdom August 1914 forward throughout Great War period providing drafts and reinforcements.*
Note c.   *Medals named in impressed capitals: 'ESSEX R.'*

Single Clasp	No. Identified	Rarity
Afghanistan N.W.F. 1919[3]	1	According to the roll as seen, can be considered Unique
Mahsud 1919–20[5]	0	None Identified
Waziristan 1919–21[4]	0	None Identified
Waziristan 1921–24[6]	0	None Identified

Majors: ~ G C R Taylor[3] Staff, 16 Div.

~ 2nd Garrison Bn, The Essex Regiment ~

Note a.   *Roll of all personnel identified as eligible.*
Note b.   *Formed January 1916. India February 1916 forward.*
Note c.   *Medals named in impressed capitals: 'ESSEX R.'*

Single Clasp	No. Identified	Rarity
Afghanistan N.W.F. 1919[3]	6	Of the Utmost Rarity
Mahsud 1919–20[5]	0	None Identified
Waziristan 1919–21[4]	0	None Identified
Waziristan 1921–24[6]	0	None Identified
Combination Clasps	**No. Identified**	**Rarity**
Afghanistan N.W.F. 1919[3] Waziristan 1919 – 21[4]	1	According to the roll as seen, can be considered Unique

Lieutenants: ~ J Dee[3] attch. IOD & K J Detmold[3] attch. ISC
Quartermaster Sergeants/Sergeants: ~ (Act) 33470 C R Luther[3&4] attch. 82 LTC, S&TC
Lance Sergeants/Corporals: ~ 25213 J W Woods[3] attch. 1 MT Coy, S&TC
Lance Corporals/Privates: ~ 33308 J R Davison[3] attch. IMVS, 20250 A J Everest[3] attch. 4 LofC Sigs & 25134 R MacDonald[3] attch. 40 DSC, 16 Div.

~ Unidentified Service Bn, The Essex Regiment ~

Note a.   *Roll of all personnel identified eligible.*
Note b.   *Medals named in impressed capitals: 'ESSEX R.'*

Single Clasp	No. Identified	Rarity
Afghanistan N.W.F. 1919[3]	1	According to the roll as seen, can be considered Unique
Mahsud 1919–20[5]	0	None Identified
Waziristan 1919–21[4]	0	None Identified
Waziristan 1921–24[6]	0	None Identified

Lieutenants: ~ W S Cornwell[3] attch. 1/1 Kent.

~ 1st Bn, The Sherwood Foresters (Nottinghamshire & Derbyshire) Regiment ~

Note a.   *Roll of all personnel identified as eligible.*
Note b.   *India August 1914. France & Flanders November 1914 forward. Ireland August 1919, India 1922 forward.*
Note c.   *Medals named in impressed capitals: 'NOTTS. & DERBY R.'*

Single Clasp	No. Identified	Rarity
Afghanistan N.W.F. 1919[3]	1	According to the roll as seen, can be considered Unique
Mahsud 1919–20[5]	0	None Identified
Waziristan 1919–21[4]	0	None Identified
Waziristan 1921–24[6]	9	Of the Utmost Rarity

Captains: ~ N A Mc Donald Walker[6]
Lieutenants: ~ V J Shea[3] attch. S&TC
Lance Sergeants/Corporals: ~ 4962193 H Bailey[6]
Lance Corporals/Privates: ~ 4965121 G Biddle[6] attch. ISH, Bannu, 4963410 J Buck[6], 4965337 A Hayes[6], 4965124 W Hayto[6] attch. ISH, Bannu, 4962165 A E Housley[6], 4738690 J W McHale[6] & 4964233 W H Swift[6]

~ 3rd (Reserve) Bn, The Sherwood Foresters (Nottinghamshire & Derbyshire) Regiment ~

Note a.   *Roll of all personnel identified as eligible.*
Note b.   *United Kingdom August 1914 forward throughout Great War period providing drafts and reinforcements.*
Note c.   *Medals named in impressed capitals: 'NOTTS. & DERBY R.'*

Single Clasp	No. Identified	Rarity
Afghanistan N.W.F. 1919[3]	1	According to the roll as seen, can be considered Unique
Mahsud 1919–20[5]	0	None Identified
Waziristan 1919–21[4]	0	None Identified
Waziristan 1921–24[6]	0	None Identified

Lieutenants: ~ C W C Braithwaite[3] attch. 1/25 London

~ ?/5th Bn, The Sherwood Foresters (Nottinghamshire & Derbyshire) Regiment, Territorial Force ~

Note a.   Roll of all personnel identified as eligible.
Note b.   Medals named in impressed capitals: 'NOTTS. & DERBY R.'

Single Clasp	No. Identified	Rarity
Afghanistan N.W.F. 1919[3]	1	According to the roll as seen, can be considered Unique
Mahsud 1919–20[5]	0	None Identified
Waziristan 1919–21[4]	0	None Identified
Waziristan 1921–24[6]	0	None Identified

Lieutenants: ~ L J W Millward[3] attch. 2/6 Sussex

~ ?/6th Bn, The Sherwood Foresters (Nottinghamshire & Derbyshire) Regiment, Territorial Force ~

Note a.   Roll of all personnel identified as eligible.
Note b.   Medals named in impressed capitals: 'NOTTS. & DERBY R.'

Single Clasp	No. Identified	Rarity
Afghanistan N.W.F. 1919[3]	1	According to the roll as seen, can be considered Unique
Mahsud 1919–20[5]	0	None Identified
Waziristan 1919–21[4]	0	None Identified
Waziristan 1921–24[6]	0	None Identified

Lieutenants: ~ S Stiles[3] attch. 1/5 Hampshire

~ Unidentified Service Bn, The Sherwood Foresters (Nottinghamshire & Derbyshire) Regiment ~

Note a.   Roll of all personnel identified as eligible.
Note b.   Medals named in impressed capitals: 'NOTTS. & DERBY R.'

Single Clasp	No. Identified	Rarity
Afghanistan N.W.F. 1919[3]	5	Of the Utmost Rarity
Mahsud 1919–20[5]	0	None Identified
Waziristan 1919–21[4]	0	None Identified
Waziristan 1921–24[6]	0	None Identified
Combination Clasps	No. Identified	Rarity
Afghanistan N.W.F. 1919[3] Waziristan 1919–21[4]	1	According to the roll as seen, can be considered Unique

Lieutenants: ~ R D Cooke[3] attch. 1/4 QORWK, A Crane[3] attch. 1/4 QORWK, H Hallam[3] attch. 1 Sussex, J Lee[3&4] attch. 53 GCC, C H Lloyd[3] attch. S&TC & W Smith[3] attch. 1/25 London

~ 2nd Bn, The Loyal North Lancashire Regiment ~

Note a.   Roll of all personnel identified as eligible.
Note b.   India August 1914. German East Africa November 1914, South Africa May 1916, East Africa August 1916, Egypt January 1917, France & Flanders May 1918 thence Ireland November 1919.
Note c.   Title changed to The Loyal Regiment (North Lancashire) in 1920.
Note d.   Medals with clasp 'AFGHANISTAN N.W.F. 1919' named in impressed capitals: 'L. N. LAN. R.' Waziristan series medals named in impressed capitals: 'LOYAL R.'

Single Clasp	No. Identified	Rarity
Afghanistan N.W.F. 1919[3]	7	Of the Utmost Rarity
Mahsud 1919–20[5]	0	None Identified
Waziristan 1919– 21[4]	0	None Identified
Waziristan 1921–24[6]	2	Of the Utmost Rarity

Majors: ~ (Temp) C B O'Connor, Staff[3]
Captains: ~ A F Cowdell[3]
Lieutenants: ~ H D Copeman[3] attch. 1 S Lanc & W Scholes[3] attch. 106 Hazard Pioneers, IA
Warrant Officers Class II: ~ 3846650 C E Lawrence[6] attch. 'G' DSC & 3846634 C McLoughlin[6] attch. 'C' DSC
Quartermaster Sergeants/Sergeants: ~ 9083 H J T Billinge[3] attch. 36 DSC, 1 Div. & (Act) 7633 C Landau[3] attch. ITD
Lance Corporals/Privates: ~ 9768 A Baker[3]

~ 6th (Service) Bn, The Loyal North Lancashire Regiment ~

Note a.   Roll of all personnel identified as eligible.
Note b.   Formed August 1914. Mudros July 1915, Hells and Gallipoli August 1915, Mudros December 1915, Egypt January 1916, Mesopotamia February 1916 forward.
Note c.   Medals named in impressed capitals: 'L. N. LAN. R.'.

Single Clasp	No. Identified	Rarity
Afghanistan N.W.F. 1919[3]	22	Very Rare
Mahsud 1919–20[5]	0	None Identified
Waziristan 1919–21[4]	0	None Identified
Waziristan 1921–24[6]	0	None Identified

Lieutenants: ~ H G Croft[3] attch. 17 SSB as QM & K Kinna[3] attch. 17 SSB
Quartermaster Sergeants / Sergeants: ~ (Act) 10189 W Culshaw[3] attch. 2 Som LI
Lance Sergeants / Corporals: ~ (Act) 39424 C A Carter[3] attch. 5 MT Coy, S&TC & 19847 J Robinson[3] attch. 2 Som LI
Lance Corporals / Privates: ~ 20000 A Bairsto[3] attch. 1 DLI, 11123 W Challoner[3] attch. 2 Som LI, 27333 G W Chaney[3] attch. 17 SSB, 39506 W Charnook[3] attch. 2 Som LI, 20285 P Cleworth[3] attch. 2 Som LI, 19458 J O'Donohue[3] attch. 2 Som LI, 24687 A W Garratt[3] attch. 1 DLI, 39799 S Greaves[3] attch. 2 Som LI, 39603 M Greenhalgh[3] attch. 2 Som LI, 39674 E Hickson[3] attch. 2 Som LI, 35812 J Huntington[3] attch. 694 MT Coy, RASC, 38385 J Laraway[3] attch. 2 MT Coy, S&TC, 39625 R Lilley[3] attch. 2 Som LI, 39821 J Litler[3] attch. 5 MT Coy, S&TC, 27542 G Mason[3] attch. 2 Som LI, 36355 F Thornley[3] attch. 1 DLI & 27094 J H Wiggin[3] attch. 1 DLI

~ 2nd Bn, The Northamptonshire Regiment ~

Note a.   Roll of all personnel identified as eligible.
Note b.   Egypt August 1914. France & Flanders November 1914 forward. India November 1919.
Note c.   Medals named in impressed capitals: 'NORTH'N. R.'

Single Clasp	No. Identified	Rarity
Afghanistan N.W.F. 1919[3]	0	None Identified
Mahsud 1919–20[5]	0	None Identified
Waziristan 1919–21[4]	4	Of the Utmost Rarity
Waziristan 1921–24[6]	11	Extremely Rare

Combination Clasps	No. Identified	Rarity
Mahsud 1919–20[5] Waziristan 1919–21[4] Malabar 1921–22[7] Waziristan 1921–24[6]	1	According to the roll as seen, can be considered Unique
Waziristan 1919–21[4] Waziristan 1921–24[6]	2	Of the Utmost Rarity

Lieutenants: ~ F C Papworth[6]

Quartermaster Sergeants/Sergeants: ~ (Act) 5875663 P H Cubitt[6] attch. HQ, Razmak

Lance Sergeants/Corporals: ~ 5875302 B L R Cheverton[4,5,(6&7 R Sigs)] attch. 3/W Sig Sqn & 5875149 F Lemon[4&6] attch. 3/W Sig Sqn

Lance Corporals/Privates: ~ 5875979 D G Brunger[6] attch. HQ WFF, 5719414 A H Busby[6] attch. 'A' Corps Sigs, 5876899 A Collett[4] attch. HQ, 23 Bde., Wana Col, 5876520 E G Foord[4] attch. 3/W Sig Sqn, 5876886 B R Gascoigne[4] attch. HQ, 9 Bde., 5875420 W J H Gregory[6] attch. 'G' DSC, 5875584 R H Lowe[6] attch. 'G' DSC, Razmak FF, 7110477 J T Mahon[4&6] attch. 3/W Sig Sqn, Razmak FF, (From Royal Irish Regiment), 5876672 H F Peckover[4] attch. HQ, WFF, 5876712 A E Turner[6] attch. 'G' DSC, Razmak FF, 5875305 J J Wayling[6] attch. 'G' DSC, Razmak FF, 5875268 J Webb[6] attch. 'G' DSC, Razmak FF, 5875268 H Wolfe[6] attch. HQ, WFF & 5876424 H F Youngs[6] attch. 'A' Corps Sigs

Unidentified Service Bn, The Northamptonshire Regiment ~

Note a. *Roll of all personnel identified as eligible.*
Note b. *Medals named in impressed capitals > 'NORTH'N. R.'*

Single Clasp	No. Identified	Rarity
Afghanistan N.W.F. 1919[3]	1	According to the roll as seen, can be considered Unique
Mahsud 1919–20[5]	0	None Identified
Waziristan 1919–21[4]	0	None Identified
Waziristan 1921–24[6]	0	None Identified

Lieutenants: ~ F W Ashton[3] attch. 1 DLI

~ 1st Bn, The Princess Charlotte of Wales's (Royal Berkshire Regiment) ~

Note a. *Roll of all commissioned personnel identified as eligible.*
Note b. *Non-commissioned and other ranks multi clasp or non-Waziristan 1921–24 single clasp.*
Note c. *United Kingdom August 1914. France & Flanders August 1914 forward. Iraq December 1919, North West Persia May 1920, Iraq May 1921, India November 1921 forward.*
Note d. *Medals named in impressed capitals: 'R. BERKS. R.'*

Single Clasp	No. Identified	Rarity
Afghanistan N.W.F. 1919[3]	1	According to the roll as seen, can be considered Unique
Mahsud 1919–20[5]	0	None Identified
Waziristan 1919–21[4]	1	According to the roll as seen, can be considered Unique
Waziristan 1921–24[6]	Bn. Strength	Not Rare
Combination Clasps	No. Identified	Rarity
Waziristan 1921–24[6] North West Frontier 1930–31[9]	3	Of the Utmost Rarity

Lieutenant Colonels: ~ S G Francis[6]

Majors: ~ A E F Harris[6]

Captains: ~ G L Blight[6], (QM) M A G Coombs[6], E F Eagar[6], P H Hight[6], H H R Hilliard[6], J H Sugrue[6] & M Wykes[6]

Lieutenants: ~ A P Aveline[6], H V Batchelor[4] attch. 6 MMG Bty, A D Brown[6], A W Dolby[6], F N Elliott[6], H du Pru Finch[6], D W Furlong[6], H S Hall[6], A A V Hoather[6], W E C Davidson-Houston[6], H E Rew[6], A L Taffs[6] & T G Watney[6]
Lance Corporals/Privates: ~ 5329016 A J S Kelly[6&9(Cpl.)], 5329386 A J Mansfield[6&(9 L/Sgt., R Sigs)], 5329205 L C Morton[6&(9 Sgt., Black Watch attch. 2 ATC (Mules) Kohat)] & 39758 F W Penny[3] attch. 1/4 QORWK

~ Unidentified Service Bn, The Princess Charlotte of Wales's (Royal Berkshire Regiment) ~

Note a.   *Roll of all personnel identified as eligible.*
Note b.   *Medals named in impressed capitals: 'R. BERKS. R.'*

Single Clasp	No. Identified	Rarity
Afghanistan N.W.F. 1919[3]	1	According to roll as seen, can be considered Unique
Mahsud 1919–20[5]	0	None Identified
Waziristan 1919–21[4]	0	None Identified
Waziristan 1921–24[6]	0	None Identified

Lieutenants: ~ G E Laughlin[3] attch. 2 Som LI

~ 1st Bn, The Queen's Own (Royal West Kent Regiment) ~

Note a.   *Roll of all personnel identified as eligible.*
Note b.   *United Kingdom August 1914. France & Flanders August 1914, Italy December 1917, France & Flanders April 1918 forward. India November 1919.*
Note c.   *Title changed in 1920 to The Royal West Kent Regiment (Queen's Own) and again in 1921 to The Queen's Own Royal West Kent Regiment.*
Note d.   *Medals named in impressed capitals: 'R. W. KENT R.'*

Single Clasp	No. Identified	Rarity
Afghanistan N.W.F. 1919[3]	3	Of the Utmost Rarity
Mahsud 1919–20[5]	3	Of the Utmost Rarity
Waziristan 1919–21[4]	11	Extremely Rare
Waziristan 1921–24[6]	12	Extremely Rare
Combination Clasps	**No. Identified**	**Rarity**
Afghanistan N.W.F. 1919[3] Mahsud 1919–20[5] Waziristan 1919–21[4]	1	According to the roll as seen, can be considered Unique
Afghanistan N.W.F. 1919[3] Waziristan 1919–21[4]	6	Of the Utmost Rarity
Afghanistan N.W.F. 1919[3] Waziristan 1919–21[4] Waziristan 1921–24[6]	1	According to the roll as seen, can be considered Unique
Mahsud 1919–20[5] Waziristan 1919–21[4]	6	Of the Utmost Rarity
Waziristan 1919–21[4] Waziristan 1921–24[6]	7	Of the Utmost Rarity

Lieutenant Colonels: ~ H D Buchanan-Dunlop[4&5] attch. 6 MMG Bty, MGC
Captains: ~ R L Travers[4&5] attch. 2/9 GR, IA
Lieutenants: ~ G Ingham[6] Adjt Rest Camp, Kalabagh, (Originally Royal Navy), W A Simpson[4] attch. 40 DSC & A J Wilson[6] attch. 'G' DSC
Warrant Officers Class II: ~ (Act) 6280117 E J Lewis[3,4&5]

Company Quartermaster Sergeants/Staff Sergeants/Colour Sergeants: ~ (Act) (L/10910) 6334387 E Barnes[4&6] attch. CMSC, HQ, WFF

Quartermaster Sergeant /Sergeants: ~ (Act) L/13905 R W Brenchley[3&4] attch. 101 PMC, S&TC, 6280152 H Burtenshaw[6] attch. 'B' Corps Sigs, (Act) 6390352 B Carman[6] attch. HQ, Waz FF, 6392045 S J Gibbons[6] attch. 'C' DSC, (L/7704) 6334167 A E Hannan[4&6] attch. 'B' Corps Sigs, (Act) (L/12947) 6280116 A R Must[4&6] attch. IASC, (L/9251) 6390452 F Norris[4&6] attch. 'B' Corps Sigs, (Act) 6336258 S Oram[6] attch. RTE, Mari Indus, 6334183 A Page[6] attch. 'B' Corps Sigs, (Act) G/25724 E C Pearce[3&4] attch. 101 PMC, S&TC, G/25684 H H Rees[4] attch. S&TC, (Act) (L/11129) 6334413 H M Smith[4&5] attch. HQ, 43 Bde., 6335350 M G Wainscott[6] attch. 'B' Corps Sigs, (Act) 6334959 W A Whitten[6] Clk HQ, 9 Bde. & (L/1348) 6335626 A G Wills[4&6] attch. 'B' Corps Sigs

Lance Sergeants/Corporals: ~ L/13269 R Stokes[3&4] RTE Daryakhan & (L/12136) 6334626 W F J Westlake[4] attch. Ord Depot Bannu

Lance Corporals/Privates: ~ L/8573 E J Adams[3], L/8677 W N Arnott[3], L/12949 E G Baker[5], L/13472 F W Benton[4], L/12925 T Borras[4] attch. RASC, L/13102 E S Buckett[5] attch. HQ, Maj. Gen. Skeen, L/12018 R D Buckingham[3&4] attch. 101 PMC, S&TC, L/12058 C Cousins[4], L/13666 A Davies[3], 6334789 E J Dunn[6], (6334504) L/12001 F A Gard[4&5], (9682) 6334239 D Gillespie[3,4&6(RE)], (L/13664) 6335785 S J M Glass[4] attch. HQ, WFF, (6634701) L/12216 P Habgood[4], 6335837 P Harmer[6] attch. HQ, Waz Dist, (6280101) L/13434 H E King[3&4] attch. 23 Bde. Sigs, Wana Col, 6279831 S S R Lee[4&6] attch. APM Bannu, (6335588) L/13445 E W Nutley[4&5], (6335654) L/13517 J Parish[4] attch. 694 MT Coy, RASC, (6334508) L/12005 F G Pentecost[4], 6336080 E D Price[6] attch. HQ, WFF, (6634641) L/12153 C W Roberts[4&6(RASC)], (6334805) L/12429 H Rolfe[4&5], G/39931 F W West[5], L/13391 J W A Williams[3&4] & (6334593) L/12097 J Wright[4] attch. 694 MT Coy, RASC

~ 2nd Bn, The Queen's Own (Royal West Kent Regiment) ~

Note a.   *Roll of all personnel identified as eligible.*

Note b.   *India August 1914. Mesopotamia February 1915 forward. 'B' & 'D' Companies captured at Kut al Amara in April 1916. Balance of battalion remained in theatre until March 1919 thence to India until July 1919.*

Note c.   *Medals named in impressed capitals: 'R. W. KENT R.'*

Single Clasp	No. Identified	Rarity
Afghanistan N.W.F. 1919[3]	31	Very Rare
Mahsud 1919–20[5]	0	None Identified
Waziristan 1919–21[4]	2	Of the Utmost Rarity
Waziristan 1921–24[6]	0	None Identified
Combination Clasps	*No. Identified*	*Rarity*
Afghanistan N.W.F. 1919[3] Mahsud 1919–20[5] Waziristan 1919–21[4]	1	According to the roll as seen, can be considered Unique
Afghanistan N.W.F. 1919[3] Waziristan 1919–21[4]	1	According to the roll as seen, can be considered Unique

Majors: ~ I Pilditch[3] attch. 1/1 Kent

Captains: ~ S R Carill[3] attch. 1/1 Kent & P E Wilberforce-Bell[3] attch. 1/4 QORWK

Lieutenants: ~ H M Barker[3] attch. 1 S Lanc

Warrant Officers Class II: ~ L/5956 A L Bellion[3]

Company Quartermaster Sergeants/Staff Sergeants/Colour Sergeants: ~ (Act) L/9494 J Hunt[3,4&5] attch. RASC

Quartermaster Sergeants/Sergeants: ~ (Act) G/25697 A R S Meredith[3], (Act) G/25672 M O'Mealey[3] attch. S&TC & (Act) G/26543 J A Saunders[3]

Lance Sergeants/Corporals: ~ L/9268 L E J Fannin[3] attch. 17 SSB, (Act) G/23669 E J Lomax[3] attch. 35 ISS & (Act) L/11470 F Matthews[3] attch. 17 SSB

Lance Corporals/Privates: ~ L/6627 T Baker[3] attch. 2 Som LI, G/3438 A T Banks[3] attch. 17 SSB, 240329 C Benson[3], L/5983 J Blackall[3] attch. 2 Som LI, L/3089 W Boreham[3] attch. 2 Som LI, (6334826) L/12450 A R Briant[4] attch. 694 MT Coy, RASC, L/8753 C W Carr[3] attch. 4 Corps Sigs, G/6259 J Duffy[3] attch. 2 Som LI, G/27861 F Elgar[3] attch. 2 Som LI, G/15403 J Fairway[3] attch. 17 BSS, 712 B French[3] attch. 2 Som LI, L/10354 C Green[3] attch. 2 Som LI, 23547 A Hill[3] attch. 2 Som LI, (633569) L/13563 A H Howard[4] attch. 694 MT Coy, RASC, G/4341 H Martin[3] attch. 17 SSB, G/1662 W G Matthews[3] attch. 2 Som LI, G/27898 G Ramplin[3] attch. 2 Som LI, SR/9052 A F Remmett[3] attch. 3 SSB, 8952 F

Simmonds[3] attch. 2 Som LI, (6336580) L/9276 C Strong[3&4] attch. 33 DSC, 4 Div., L/11202 A Tomkins[3] attch. S&TC, L/8781 F J Watson[3] & L/18766 H C Wood[3]

~ 1/4th Bn, The Queen's Own (Royal West Kent Regiment), Territorial Force ~

Note a.   Roll of all commissioned personnel identified as eligible.
Note b.   Enlisted personnel multi clasp or non–Afghanistan 1919 single clasp.
Note c.   United Kingdom August 1914. India December 1914 to November 1919.
Note d.   Battle honour 'Third Afghan War 1919'.
Note e.   Medals named in impressed capitals: 'R. W. KENT R.'

Single Clasp	No. Identified	Rarity
Afghanistan N.W.F. 1919[3]	Bn. Strength	Not Rare
Mahsud 1919–20[5]	0	None Identified
Waziristan 1919–21[4]	0	None Identified
Waziristan 1921–24[6]	0	None Identified
Combination Clasps	No. Identified	Rarity
Afghanistan N.W.F. 1919[3] Waziristan 1921–24[6]	1	According to the roll as seen, can be considered Unique
Waziristan 1919–21[4] Malabar 1921–22[7]	1	According to the roll as seen, can be considered Unique

Lieutenant Colonels: ~ C B Robb[3]
Majors: ~ A M Cohen[3] attch. HQ, BFF
Captains: ~ W B Bakewell[3] attch. 286 Coy, MGC, H A J Baker[3], A G Balbernie[4&7], O G R Barnes[3], G C Golding[3], A R Kelsey[3], J L Kirkham[3], W A Leach[3], I R Lovell[3], L O Melore[3], W F E Peareth[3], H W Styles[3], L Taylor[3], G F C Warry[3] & R D Watney[3]
Lieutenants: ~ E F Allnutt[3], J H Brown[3], A Cave[3], F H Etheridge[3], G T Hammond[3], K Hartree[3], G W Joel[3], J Lawton[3], F H Nuttall[3] attch. QORWK, A E Pedgrift[3], J W H Southerton[3], C E Stern[3], R Oliver Testaferrata[3], A Tindall[3] attch. 1 S Lanc, J J J Van Tromp[3], C W Weedon[3] & T (A) Wells[3]
Lance Corporals/Privates: ~ 204327 F W G Allaway[3&6(R Berkshire)]

~ 1/5th Bn, The Queen's Own (Royal West Kent Regiment), Territorial Force ~

Note a.   Roll of all personnel identified as eligible.
Note b.   United Kingdom August 1914. India December 1914 to December 1917 thence Mesopotamia until December 1919.
Note c.   Medals named in impressed capitals: 'R. W. KENT R.'

Single Clasp	No. Identified	Rarity
Afghanistan N.W.F. 1919[3]	27	Very Rare
Mahsud 1919–20[5]	0	None Identified
Waziristan 1919–21[4]	1	According to the roll as seen, can be considered Unique
Waziristan 1921–24[6]	0	None Identified
Combination Clasps	No. Identified	Rarity
Waziristan 1919–21[4] Waziristan 1921–24[6]	1	According to the roll as seen, can be considered Unique

Captains: ~ R E Satterthwaite[3] Staff, 11 Bde.
Company Quartermaster Sergeants/Staff Sergeants/Colour Sergeants: ~ 240644 C P Harvey[3] attch. 7 MMG Bty, MGC
Quartermaster Sergeants/Sergeants: ~ 240420 G Blacker[3] attch. 2 MT Coy, S&TC & (Act) 240731 S H Doughty[3]

Lance Sergeants/Corporals: ~ (Act) 240221 N Butler[3] attch. 40 DSC, 16 Div., (Act) 240728 H S Clarke[3] attch. HQ, NWFF, (Act) 240044 G H Dingwall[3] attch. 2 MT Coy, S&TC & 240683 W Kibble[3]

Lance Corporals/Privates: ~ 242523 A J Batliff[3], 240703 E C Bishop[3] attch. 39 DSC, 2 Div., L/12925 T Borras[4], L/12464 L Bottomley[4&6(RASC)], 240099 G Bowers[3], 240704 G H Brandon[3], 240611 J F Cahill[3] attch. 46 Mbl Bde. Sig Sect, RE, 240244 F Cullingham[3], 240325 J Friend[3], 240279 R C D Graves[3], 242505 T S Heron[3] attch. 17 SSB, 241096 A E Jeffery[3] attch. 40 DSC, 16 Div., 240302 F O'Brien[3] attch. RE Sigs, G/27537 F D Pennington[3], 240169 E J Pilcher[3] attch. 46 Mbl Sig Bde., TF/240472 P W Ribbe(o)ns[3], 241111 W Rollings[3] attch. 1 ARW, S&TC, 241476 R A Rothwell[3] attch. 36 DSC, 1 Div., 240330 A E Spooner[3] attch. 38 DSC, 1 Div., 240278 G W Thomas[3] attch. 33 DSC, 4 Div. & 240237 T Turner[3]

~ 1st Bn, The King's Own (Yorkshire Light Infantry) ~

Note a.   *Roll of all personnel identified as eligible.*
Note b.   *Singapore August 1914. France & Flanders January 1915, Salonika December 1915, France & Flanders July 1918 forward. India August 1919 to September 1920 thence Iraq.*
Note c.   *Medals named in impressed capitals: 'K.O.Y.L.I.' or 'YORK. L. INF.'*

Single Clasp	No. Identified	Rarity
Afghanistan N.W.F. 1919[3]	13	Extremely Rare
Mahsud 1919–20[5]	0	None Identified
Waziristan 1919–21[4]	0	None Identified
Waziristan 1921–24[6]	0	None Identified

Majors: ~ H Hall[3] attch. 9 MT Coy, S&TC & J B Saul[3] attch. MGC, (Possibly named MGC)

Captains: ~ R J Butler[3] attch. 2 Som LI & A G C Deuber[3] attch. 1 Yorkshire

Lieutenants: ~ G Abbott[3] attch. 1 Yorkshire, R Eden[3], W Dowland[3] attch. 1 Yorkshire, G A Kilner[3] attch. 1 DWR, A L Laskie[3] attch. 1 Yorkshire, E E Leacock[3] attch. MWS, H R Marr[3] attch. 1 Yorkshire, A R Munro[3] attch. 285 Coy, MGC & C J Taylor[3] attch. 1/5 Hampshire

~ 2nd Bn, The King's Own (Yorkshire Light Infantry) ~

Note a.   *Roll of all personnel identified as eligible.*
Note b.   *United Kingdom August 1914. France & Flanders August 1914 forward. Ireland December 1920 to December 1921 thence India March 1922 forward.*
Note c.   *Medals named in impressed capitals: 'K.O.Y.L.I.' or 'YORK. L. INF.'*

Single Clasp	No. Identified	Rarity
Afghanistan N.W.F. 1919[3]	0	None Identified
Mahsud 1919–20[5]	0	None Identified
Waziristan 1919–21[4]	0	None Identified
Waziristan 1921–24[6]	13	Extremely Rare

Lieutenants: ~ A D Mulligan[6]

Warrant Officers Class II: ~ 4334721 A E Turner[6] attch. 'B' DSC

Quartermaster Sergeants/Sergeants: ~ 4529726 W Fletcher[6] attch. 'B' Corps Sigs, 4680972 (53394) A Newbould[6] attch. 39 ISS & 4524463 A Parsons[6] attch. 'C' DSC

Lance Corporals/Privates: ~ 4681625 H Burgin[6] attch. 10 IGH, Bannu, 4960970 E Cohen[6] attch. 10 IGH, Bannu, 4681827 C Gray[6] attch. 10 IGH, Bannu, 4681246 H J Lee[6] attch. 8 ISS, Bannu, 4682610 G W Morton[6] attch. 8 ISS, Bannu, 4681407 W Redfern[6] attch. 8 ISS, Bannu, 4682992 J C Suter[6] attch. 10 IGH, Bannu & 4681633 R Wilford[6] attch. 8 ISS, Bannu

~ 1st Bn, The King's (Shropshire Light Infantry) ~

Note a. Roll of all personnel identified as eligible.
Note b. United Kingdom August 1914. France & Flanders September 1914 forward. Germany December 1918, Aden November 1919, India December 1920 forward.
Note c. Medals named in impressed capitals: 'K.S.L.I.'

Single Clasp	No. Identified	Rarity
Afghanistan N.W.F. 1919[3]	3	Of the Utmost Rarity
Mahsud 1919–20[5]	0	None Identified
Waziristan 1919–21[4]	1	According to the roll as seen, can be considered Unique
Waziristan 1921–24[6]	1	According to the roll as seen, can be considered Unique

Captains: ~ R Attoe[4] Staff Capt., 23 Bde., Southern Waziristan, J G Burnet[3] attch. 1 Armd Mtr Bde., MGC, A E Lawrence[3] Staff Capt., Ft. Jamrud, R H Shears[3] attch. 31 Sqn, RAF & R G Smithard[6] Staff Capt., 10 Bde.

~ 3rd Bn, The Duke of Cambridge's Own (Middlesex Regiment) ~

Note a. Roll of all personnel identified as eligible.
Note b. India August 1914. France & Flanders January 1915, Salonika December 1915 forward. Thrace November 1918 thence Silesia June 1921.
Note c. Title changed to The Middlesex Regiment (Duke of Cambridge's Own) in 1920.
Note d. Medals named in impressed capitals: 'MIDD'X. R.'

Single Clasp	No. Identified	Rarity
Afghanistan N.W.F. 1919[3]	2	Of the Utmost Rarity
Mahsud 1919–20[5]	0	None Identified
Waziristan 1919–21[4]	0	None Identified
Waziristan 1921–24[6]	0	None Identified

Combination Clasps	No. Identified	Rarity
Afghanistan N.W.F. 1919[3] Waziristan 1919–21[4]	1	According to the roll as seen, can be considered Unique
Waziristan 1919–21[4] Waziristan 1921–24[6]	1	

Majors: ~ (Bvt) A C Arnold[4&6] Bde. Maj., 7 Bde.
Lieutenants: ~ R L Hill[3&4] attch. 263 Coy, MGC
Quartermaster Sergeants/Sergeants: ~ L/9965 A E Wickham[3] attch. 2 Sig Eng Pk
Lance Corporals/Privates: ~ L/11976 W H Smith[3] attch. Sigs Det, Shelabach

~ 1/9th Bn, The Duke of Cambridge's Own (Middlesex Regiment), Territorial Force ~

Note a. Roll of all personnel identified as eligible.
Note b. United Kingdom August 1914. India December 1914, Mesopotamia November 1917 forward.
Note c. Medals named in impressed capitals: 'MIDD'X. R.'

Single Clasp	No. Identified	Rarity
Afghanistan N.W.F. 1919[3]	108	Very Scarce
Mahsud 1919–20[5]	0	None Identified
Waziristan 1919–21[4]	0	None Identified

Waziristan 1921–24[6]	0	None Identified

Lieutenant Colonels: ~ (Temp) G Beach[3] Staff

Captains: ~ L F Findlay[3] attch. MGC & V Holt[3]

Lieutenants: ~ W G Brown[3] attch. 1/4 QORWK

Warrant Officers Class I: ~ 265474 R E Patterson[3] attch. 1 MT Coy, S&TC & (Act) 265048 F H Spall[3] attch. 17 SSB

Warrant Officers Class II: ~ (Act) L/7373 R I Furman[3] attch. 1/25 London, (Act) 265030 W Hemington[3] attch. 17 SSB & (Act) 265796 J Skilton[3] attch. 11 MT Coy, S&TC

Quartermaster Sergeants/Sergeants: ~ (Act) 265464 J Birch[3] attch. 17 SSB, (Act) 265530 H S Dalley[3] attch. IOC, (Act) 265593 W C Day[3] attch. 1 ARW, S&TC, (Act) 267517 E J Fender[3] attch. SASMS, Peshawar, 265448 L H Helyar[3] attch. Northampton, 265694 H F Kiff[3] attch. 1 ARW, S&TC, (Act) 265441 H A King[3] attch. 1 ARW, S&TC, (Act) 265741 J Marks[3] attch. 17 SSB, 265647 W J Palmer[3] attch. IOD, (Act) 265328 A J Simmonds[3] attch. 1 Yorkshire, (Act) 267443 W J Stapleton[3] attch. 17 SSB & (Act) 265150 W E Templeman[3] attch. 1 Yorkshire

Lance Sergeants/Corporals: ~ (Act) 265849 T R Bennett[3] attch. 17 SSB, (Act) 265496 H Fidler[3] attch. 2 Som LI, (Act) 265211 H Franceis[3] attch. HQ, Peshawar, 265235 A G Garrett[3] attch. 39 DSC, 2 Div., (Act) 265676 S J Heavens[3] attch. 1 Yorkshire, 265431 R H Ketley[3] attch. 1 Yorkshire, (Act) 265307 F A Laslett[3] attch. 17 SSB, G/51774 J W Lee[3] attch. 39 DSC, 2 Div., (Act) G/57087 J R Peacock[3] attch. 17 SSB & 265302 E W Pearce[3] attch. 39 DSC, 2 Div.

Lance Corporals/Privates: ~ 266092 C H Atkins[3] attch. 17 SSB, 291544 C Bacon[3] attch. 17 SSB, 265622 J V Bailey[3] attch. 17 SSB, 267114 R Bartlett[3] attch. 17 SSB, 87731 F Blackwell[3] attch. 2 Som LI, 267471 C E Bolton[3] attch. 1 Yorkshire, 267505 B T Bowden[3] attch. 17 SSB, 200514 J E Bowles[3], (Originally 7th Bn), 265709 R J Brackstone[3] attch. 2 MT Coy, S&TC, 267488 J P Briggs[3] attch. 17 SSB, 291654 J Broadbeck[3] attch. 17 SSB, (Originally 10th Bn), 291450 J W Brooker[3] attch. 17 SSB, (Originally 10th Bn), 265724 D Brooks[3] attch. 1/1 Kent, 267454 E Butler[3] attch. 17 SSB, 265337 G R Champ[3] attch. 17 SSB, 291597 W Coombs[3] attch. 17 SSB, (Originally 10th Bn), 292742 C H Coster[3] attch. 17 SSB, (Originally 10th Bn), 291568 F A Cox[3] attch. 17 SSB, (Originally 10th Bn), 265454 A E Craggs[3] attch. 2 MT Coy, S&TC, G/57021 D Croy[3] attch. 1 Yorkshire, 267459 A S Day[3] attch. 17 SSB, 265866 H E Dean[3], 267509 W J Dennis[3] attch. 17 SSB, 290223 A H Dover[3] attch. 1 Yorkshire, (Originally 10th Bn), 267027 D E Drowley[3] attch. HQ, 16 Div., 265429 W J Franklin[3] attch. 2 MT Coy, S&TC, 266139 W H Giddins[3] attch. 17 SSB, 266055 J Gomm[3] attch. 17 SSB, 265785 T A B Green[3] attch. 3 SSB, 267085 H Hainton[3] attch. 1 Yorkshire, 266124 A E Hewes[3] attch. 17 SSB, 266164 C E Hilliger[3] attch. 17 SSB, 240103 J Holloway[3] attch. 1 Yorkshire, (Originally 8th Bn), 267494 B Holmes[3] attch. 2 Som LI, 267531 W Holmes[3] attch. 17 SSB, 265132 C Hosbach[3] attch. 39 DSC, 2 Div., 265723 L Hughes[3] attch. 40 DSC, 16 Div., 265452 W Jacques[3] attch. 1/1 Kent, 266148 F Jones[3] attch. 17 SSB, 266101 G W Jones[3] attch. IOD, G/51701 H W Kefford[3] attch. 1 Sussex, 265999 B Lacey[3] attch. 17 SSB, 265253 H A Lane[3] attch. HQ, Peshawar, 266202 W G Lee[3] attch. 17 SSB, 265721 F G Leech[3] attch. HQ, 2 Div., 265525 J Lewis[3] attch. 1/1 Kent, G/39077 P W Malone[3] attch. 2 Som LI, 266227 W H Mitchell[3] attch. 17 SSB, 267467 R Nash[3] attch. 17 SSB, G/57082 E J Newsum[3] attch. 1 Yorkshire, 265339 P O'Dea[3] attch. 1/1/ Kent, 265265 A E Park[3] attch. 1 Yorkshire, 265768 E J Pattle[3] attch. 1 Sussex, 267461 G Pryor[3] attch. 1 Yorkshire, G/57093 S C Randall[3] attch. 1 Yorkshire, G/57095 H J Richardson[3] attch. 17 SSB, 267480 W Rickett[3] attch. 17 SSB, 267523 J Robertson[3] attch. 1/1/Kent, 267481 H J Saunders[3] attch. 17 SSB, G/57105 J A Shaw[3] attch. 1 Yorkshire, 265737 A F E Short[3] attch. HQ, 16 Div., G/57108 R W Simpson[3] attch. 17 SSB, 291560 W Stansell[3] attch. 17 SSB, (Originally 10th Bn), 265747 C Stubbs[3], 265349 C Thompson[3], 265756 R K L Todd[3] attch. 1 Sussex, 266244 H T Viner[3] attch. 17 SSB, 265248 G A Wallis[3] attch. 40 DSC, 16 Div., 265274 O T Wallis[3] attch. 4 Corps Sigs, 266217 H V Ward[3] attch. 17 SSB, 265665 H Warren[3] attch. 40 DSC, 16 Div., 266219 F Webley[3] attch. 17 SSB, 266218 W Webley[3] attch. 17 SSB, 266245 G R Wells[3] attch. 17 SSB, 58345 W J Whiting[3] attch. 7 SSB, G/57121 G W Williams[3] attch. 17 SSB & 267464 T J Woodland[3] attch. 17 SSB

~ 1/10th Bn, The Duke of Cambridge's Own (Middlesex Regiment), Territorial Force ~

Note a. *Roll of all personnel identified as eligible.*

Note b. *United Kingdom August 1914. India December 1914 forward.*

Note c. *Medals named in impressed capitals: 'MIDD'X. R.'*

Single Clasp	No. Identified	Rarity
Afghanistan N.W.F. 1919[3]	64	Rare
Mahsud 1919–20[5]	0	None Identified
Waziristan 1919–21[4]	1	According to the roll as seen, can be considered Unique
Waziristan 1921–24[6]	0	None Identified

Combination Clasps	No. Identified	Rarity
Afghanistan N.W.F. 1919[3] Waziristan 1919 – 21[4]	1	According to the roll as seen, can be considered Unique

Majors: ~ P J Cowan[3] attch. RE, (Temp) C J Fisher[3], P C Lisle[3] attch. 263 Coy, MGC & S H White[3] Staff, 46 Bde.

Captains: ~ R E Coleman[3] attch. RE Sigs

Lieutenants: ~ P Gaillard[3] attch. 263 Coy, MGC, C A Grigg[3] attch. 270 Coy, MGC, W A Fickling[3] attch. 270 Coy, MGC, E W Holland[3] attch. 1 Sussex & W H Lloyd[3] attch. ISC

Quartermaster Sergeants/Sergeants: ~ (Act) 290182 L Allder[3] attch. HQ, Admin, Kohat, 201942 F M Bradfield[3] attch. Staff 46 Bde., (Originally 7th Bn), 290423 A F Cox[3] attch. 2 MT Coy, S&TC, (Act) 290086 L C Curd[3] attch. S&TC, (Act) 290516 R J Fittall[3] attch. 2 Div. Sply Coy, S&TC, 292275 H J Fordham[3] attch. 4 Corps Sigs, (Act) 290617 E T Griffith[3] attch. 2 MT Coy, S&TC, 290418 J A Higgins[3] attch. S&TC, (Act) 290593 H A R Iggulden[3] attch. S&TC, (Act) 290525 J H Laverty[3] attch. S&TC, 290034 W C Owen[3] attch. 3/W Sig Sqn & 291561 C G Vollrath[3] attch. 2 MT Coy, S&TC

Lance Sergeants/Corporals: ~ (Act) 290563 T W W Rowe[3] attch. Frontier Police, Kohat, (Act) 290406 J Snell[3] attch. 2 MT Coy, S&TC, 290773 S P Vaughan[3] attch. 4 Corps Sigs, 290697 R Wills[3] attch. Muski MT Sect, S&TC & (Act) 290735 J B Wood[3] attch. 4 LofC Sigs

Lance Corporal /Privates: ~ 291785 W H Baker[3] attch. 11 Div. Sply Coy, S&TC, 291671 E Barns[3] attch. S&TC, G/87549 H G Biggs[3] attch. 1 MT Coy, S&TC, 291582 E W Blaskett[3] attch. 44 DSC, KKF, PW-6105 F G Bolton[3] attch. 39 SS, G/87551 A J Brooks[3] attch. 1 MT Coy, S&TC, 290747 A G Brown[3] attch. 33 DSC, 4 Div., G/87566 P E Clarke[3] attch. HQ, Bannu Bde., G/87560 S F Claydon[3] attch. 1 MT Coy, S&TC, 291605 H C Cole[3] attch. 2 MT Coy, S&TC, 292053 S V Copley[3] attch. 40 DSC, 16 Div., L/22416 W Creighton[3] attch. 1/4 QORWK, G/87368 W E Eade[3] attch. 1 Sussex, 290783 W J Fairbrother[3] attch. ACS, 290734 W J Fitzgerald[3] attch. 2/W Sig Sqn, 290199 G T Fruin[3&4] attch. 37 DSC, G/67578 E C Gibson[3], 292265 V Holdford[3] attch. 39 DSC, 2 Div., 290555 G W Josling[3] attch. 40 DSC, 16 Div., G/39999 F Leitch[3] attch. 1 Sussex, 291536 A Mancey[3] attch. 20 B(S)S, 290597 A R Manning[3] attch. 40 DSC, 16 Div., 290510 E W Osborn[3] attch. S&TC, 290462 A E Parker[3] attch. S&TC, G/87855 C Pelham[3] attch. 39 DSC, 292811 J Petts[3] attch. 1 Sussex, G/49144 M A Potts[3] attch. 19 IMVS, 292796 J A Prew[3] attch. 1 Sussex, 290768 G A Rhodes[4], 290095 G H Rutty[3] attch. 3/W Sig. Sqn, 292234 F J Sanson[3] attch. HQ, 2 Div., 292825 A V Seamark[3] attch. 1 Sussex, G/87834 R F Sheppard[3] attch. 1 Sussex, 290706 F F J Sparksman[3] attch. 2 LofC Sigs, 290605 D C F Springett[3] attch. 38 DSC, 290204 W Titchener[3], G/87932 D Turner[3] attch. 1 Sussex, 292304 W T Tyler[3] & 86057 J Wicks[3] attch. 2/6 Sussex

~ 16th (Service) Bn (Public Schools), The Duke of Cambridge's Own (Middlesex Regiment) ~

Note a. *Roll of all personnel identified as eligible.*
Note b. *Formed September 1914. France & Flanders November 1915 forward. Battalion disbanded in France February 1918!*
Note c. *Medals named in impressed capitals: 'MIDD'X. R.'*

Single Clasp	No. Identified	Rarity
Afghanistan N.W.F. 1919[3]	1	According to roll as seen, can be considered Unique
Mahsud 1919–20[5]	0	None Identified
Waziristan 1919–21[4]	0	None Identified
Waziristan 1921–24[6]	0	None Identified

Lieutenants: ~ H O K Pope[3] attch. 1/4 Queen's

~ Unidentified Service Bn, The Duke of Cambridge's Own (Middlesex Regiment) ~

Note a. *Roll of all personnel identified as eligible.*
Note b. *Medals named in impressed capitals. 'MIDD'X. R.'*

Single Clasp	No. Identified	Rarity
Afghanistan N.W.F. 1919[3]	3	Of the Utmost Rarity
Mahsud 1919–20[5]	0	None Identified
Waziristan 1919–21[4]	0	None Identified

Waziristan 1921–24[6]	0	None Identified

Captains: ~ C H Ellis[3] & G Wicks[3] attch. 1 DWR
Lieutenants: ~ E G Shalless[3] attch. 1 Sussex

~ 3rd Bn, The King's Royal Rifle Corps ~

Note a.   *Roll of all personnel identified as eligible.*
Note b.   *India August 1914. France & Flanders December 1914, Salonika December 1915 forward. Bulgaria November 1918, Salonika January 1919, Turkey from February to May 1919 thence India. Disbanded February 1923.*
Note c.   *Medals named in impressed capitals: 'K.R.R.C.'*

Single Clasp	No. Identified	Rarity
Afghanistan N.W.F. 1919[3]	15	Extremely Rare
Mahsud 1919–20[5]	0	None Identified
Waziristan 1919–21[4]	1	According to the roll as seen, can be considered Unique
Waziristan 1921–24[6]	0	None Identified
Combination Clasps	No. Identified	Rarity
Afghanistan N.W.F. 1919[3] Mahsud 1919–20[5] Waziristan 1919–21[4] Waziristan 1921–24[6]	1	According to the roll as seen, can be considered Unique

Majors: ~ R Linton[3] attch. 9 MT Coy, S&TC & T H Powell[4] attch. IOC
Captains: ~ H N Burrell[3] attch. 2 King's
Lieutenants: ~ H Andrews[3] attch. 1 Sussex, V A Du May[3] attch. 2 Som LI, R W Kyle[3] attch. 2 Som LI, E Sands[3] attch. 36 DSC, 1 Div. & S Vickers[3] attch. 2 King's
Quartermaster Sergeants / Sergeants: ~ (1858931) 82501 J Beresford[3,4,5&6(Sgt. R Sigs)] attch. 3/W Sig Sqn, 8352 A W Rackstraw[3] attch. ITD & (Act) 8860 G Stubbs[3] attch. ITD
Lance Sergeants / Corporals: ~ 1595 J Brookes[3] attch. 5 LofC Sigs
Lance Corporals / Privates: ~ 8931 W J Giblin[3] attch. 44 DSC, KKF, 9670 B Moore[3] attch. ITD, 8136 T Handley[3] attch. ITD, 9674 C Senior[3] attch. ISC & 69383 A H Da Silva[3] attch. HQ WFF

~ 4th Bn, The King's Royal Rifle Corps ~

Note a.   *Roll of all personnel identified as eligible.*
Note b.   *India August 1914. France & Flanders December 1914, Salonika November 1915, France & Flanders July 1918 forward. India November 1919 forward.*
Note c.   *Medals named in impressed capitals: 'K.R.R.C.'*

Single Clasp	No. Identified	Rarity
Afghanistan N.W.F. 1919[3]	0	None Identified
Mahsud 1919–20[5]	0	None Identified
Waziristan 1919–21[4]	16	Extremely Rare
Waziristan 1921–24[6]	24	Very Rare
Combination Clasps	No. Identified	Rarity
Mahsud 1919–20[5] Waziristan 1919–21[4]	1	According to the roll as seen, can be considered Unique
Waziristan 1919–21[4] Waziristan 1921–24[6]	2	Of the Utmost Rarity

Waziristan 1921–24[6] North West Frontier 1935[12]	1	According to the roll as seen, can be considered Unique

Lieutenant Colonels: ~ C H N Seymour[4&5] attch. 3/11 GR, IA

Captains: ~ R E F G North[6] Staff, 9 Bde.

Lieutenants: ~ O S Owen[4]

Quartermaster Sergeants/Sergeants: ~ 6838374 T M Bowdler[6] attch. 'C' DSC, 7109059 J O'Donoghue[6] attch. 'B' DSC, (From R Irish Regt), 6737735 J A G Hemmings[4], 6837595 H F Hoad[4] & 6840252 T W Perkins[4]

Lance Sergeants/Corporals: ~5763746 A Ellerton-Long[6&12(Sgt. R Sigs)] attch. 'C' DSC & 6838416 H Warburton[4]

Lance Corporals/Privates/ Riflemen: ~ 6841000 P C Barton[6] attch. 9 ACC, Kotkai, 6840941 H Brooks[6], 6839897 C J Carter[6] attch. HQ, 9 Bde., 6839694 J Clayton[4] attch. 15 BSS, 6840714 J V Cooke[6] attch. 17 IGH, Razmak, 6841713 A Duckers[6] attch. Provo, DIK, 6840174 J Elliott[4] attch. 15 BSS, 6837715 J M Evans[6], 6838190 G E Eyre[4] attch. HQ, WFF, 6840581 J R Fillery[6] attch. 7 IGH, DIK, 6840613 A C Gillett[4], 6906873 J A Hodges[6], 6841837 H J Holdbrook[6] attch. Rest Camp, Mari Indus, 6840587 E Hubbard[4], 6838608 F Johnson[4] attch. 15 BSS, (R14781) 6838376 A Jolliffe[4], 6841052 O E Jones[6] attch. HQ, Waz Dist, 6838888 W Keegan[6] attch. 'B' DSC, 6838316 R Lee[6] attch. 'B' DSC, 6841968 W T Lewis[6] attch. 8 ISS, Bannu, 6831736 R F Mitchell[6] attch. HQ, Waz Dist, Razani, 6841982 G Peters[6] attch. RTE, Mari Indus, 6840204 W H Potter[4], 6840496 L Reeves[4], 6840472 B E Rogers[6] attch. 7 IGH, DIK, 6840133 F J Sears[4&6], 6839672 D Shepherd[4&6], attch. 'B' Corps Sigs, 6840653 A Thomas[6], 6840840 J Turner[6], 6841268 F le Valle[6] attch. Rest Camp, Mari Indus, 6840193 F Watkins[4], 6841128 J Weston[4] attch. 15 BSS, 6841696 T H Whetton[6], 6840527 W Williams[6] & (43487) 6839784 J R Wood[4] attch. 9 MT Coy, S&TC

~ 2nd Bn, The Duke of Edinburgh's (Wiltshire Regiment) ~

Note a. *Roll of all personnel identified as eligible.*

Note b. *Gibraltar August 1914. France & Flanders October 1914 forward. Hong Kong October 1919, India February 1922 forward.*

Note c. *Title changed to The Wiltshire Regiment (Duke of Edinburgh's) in 1920.*

Note d. *Medals named in impressed capitals: 'WILTS. R.'*

Single Clasp	No. Identified	Rarity
Afghanistan N.W.F. 1919[3]	0	None Identified
Mahsud 1919–20[5]	0	None Identified
Waziristan 1919–21[4]	0	None Identified
Waziristan 1921–24[6]	3	Of the Utmost Rarity

Lance Corporals/Privates: ~ 5563591 N L Benke[6] attch. HQ WFF, DIK, 5563541 E C Jacobs[6] attch. HQ WFF, DIK & 5563495 S R Saunders[6] attch. HQ WFF, DIK

~ 1/4th Bn, The Duke of Edinburgh's (Wiltshire Regiment), Territorial Force ~

Note a. *Roll of all personnel identified as eligible.*

Note b. *United Kingdom August 1914. India November 1914, Egypt September 1917 thence Palestine forward. Egypt December 1918, Sudan April 1919 thence Egypt August to October 1919.*

Note c. *Medals named in impressed capitals: 'WILTS. R.'*

Single Clasp	No. Identified	Rarity
Afghanistan N.W.F. 1919[3]	1	According to roll as seen, can be considered Unique
Mahsud 1919–20[5]	0	None Identified
Waziristan 1919–21[4]	0	None Identified
Waziristan 1921–24[6]	0	None Identified

Lance Corporals/Privates: ~ 201550 J Bray[3] attch. 44 DSC, KKF

~ 2/4th Bn, The Duke of Edinburgh's (Wiltshire Regiment) ~

Note a.   *Roll of all personnel identified as eligible.*
Note b.   *Formed October 1914. India from January 1915 forward.*
Note c.   *Medals named in impressed capitals: 'WILTS. R.'*

Single Clasp	No. Identified	Rarity
Afghanistan N.W.F. 1919[3]	31	Very Rare
Mahsud 1919–20[5]	0	None Identified
Waziristan 1919–21[4]	2	Of the Utmost Rarity
Waziristan 1921–24[6]	0	None Identified
Combination Clasps	No. Identified	Rarity
Afghanistan N.W.F. 1919[3] Waziristan 1919–21[4]	1	According to the roll as seen, can be considered Unique
Mahsud 1919–20[5] Waziristan 1919–21[4]	1	According to the roll as seen, can be considered Unique

Captains: ~ C T Lloyd[4] attch. RTO, Bannu & (Act) C A Young[3] attch. ISC

Lieutenants: ~ A T Griffiths[4] attch. Staff, WFF LofC

Quartermaster Sergeants/Sergeants: ~ (Act) 201113 J A Batten[3] attch. S&TC, (Act) 202494 W H Cole[3] attch. HQ, LofC Peshawar, (Act) 202090 E J Dicks[3&4] attch. 64 PMC, S&TC thence 11 Div. Sigs, 200047 E J King[3] attch. S&TC, (Act) 202526 L R Pearson[3] attch. 2 Div. Sply Coy, S&TC, (Act) 202434 H Saywood[3] attch. 8 BC, S&TC, (Act) 202395 J Slater[3] attch. 25 Div. Sply Coy, S&TC & 201641 L Smith[3] attch. IOD

Lance Sergeants /Corporals: ~ (Act) 200398 R J Ferris[3] attch. 39 DSC, 2 Div., (Act) 34743 J Keddie[3] attch. 19 IMVS & (Act) 200836 F Lye[3] attch. 2 MT Coy, S&TC

Lance Corporals/Privates: ~ 201235 R Boulter[3] attch. 40 DSC, 16 Div., 200186 M T Bray[3] attch. 3/W Sig Sqn, 202098 L J Buckland[3] attch. 33 DSC, 4 Div., 34678 A E Cardwell[3] attch. RE, 200818 R Chappell[3] attch. 40 DSC, 16 Div., 202581 A F Cleverly[3] attch. 1 MT Coy, S&TC, 25978 H Cook[3] attch. 19 MMG Bty, MGC, 201729 T P Dee[3] attch. 40 DSC, 16 Div., 200542 S W Edwards[3] attch. 60 CFA, 472760 G H A Gates[3] attch. Adm HQ, Kohat, 200599 G H L Gray[3], 47284 W O Jones[3] attch. Adm HQ, Kohat, 201059 A J Minto[3] attch. 40 DSC, 16 Div., 201897 A Noyle[3], 200911 J W Parsons[3] attch. S&TC, 200618 W G Riddle[4&5], 34741 W Robertson[3] attch. 2 MT Coy, S&TC, 201998 W F Street[3] 33 DSC, 4 Div., 201693 A C Webb[3] attch. 45 CFA, 200531 F H Wheeler[3] attch. 3/W Sig Sqn & 201029 F T Wiggins[3] 2 LofC Sigs

~ 5th (Service) Bn, The Duke of Edinburgh's (Wiltshire Regiment) ~

Note a.   *Roll of all personnel identified as eligible.*
Note b.   *Formed August 1914. Helles and Gallipoli July 1915, Egypt January 1916, Mesopotamia February / March 1916 forward.*
Note c.   *Medals named in impressed capitals: 'WILTS. R.'*

Single Clasp	No. Identified	Rarity
Afghanistan N.W.F. 1919[3]	43	Very Rare
Mahsud 1919–20[5]	0	None Identified
Waziristan 1919–21[4]	1	According to the roll as seen, can be considered Unique
Waziristan 1921–24[6]	0	None Identified

Quartermaster Sergeants/Sergeants: ~ (Act) 202035 O Adams[3] attch. 1 ARW, S&TC, (Originally 4th Bn), 200191 F J Savin[3] attch. 39 DSC, 2 Div., (Originally 4th Bn), (Act) 202484 S Smith[3] attch. MT Duties, S&TC, (Originally 4th Bn) & 200165 T R Thatcher[3], (Originally 4th Bn)

Lance Sergeants/Corporals: ~ 200831 W T Arnold[3] attch. 2 MT Coy, S&TC, (Originally 4th Bn), (Act) 202044 S H Couch[3] attch. 14 MT Coy, S&TC, (Originally 4th Bn), (Act) 201068 W E James[3] attch. 1 ARW, S&TC, (Originally 4th Bn), 34689 C J Robinson[3] attch. GHQ, RE Bde. & 31183 E G Thompson[3] attch. 2/6 Sussex

Lance Corporals/Privates: ~ 34263 R Applin[3] attch. 1 Sussex, 8675 W Ayliffe[3] attch. 1 Sussex, 22117 R W Bailey[3] attch. 1 Sussex, 20741 H Booth[3] attch. 1 Sussex, 22663 G G Bunce[3] attch. 1 Sussex, 8849 A Chapman[3] attch. 1 Sussex, 7755 E J Cooper[3] attch. 1 Sussex, 202923 C R Corey[3] attch. 1 Sussex, (Originally 4th Bn), 20955 W T Crook[3] attch. 1 Sussex, 11458

E Crookes[3] attch. 2/6 Sussex, 10017 W M Davey[3] attch. 1 Sussex, 25852 E Dudley[3] attch. 1 Sussex, 1175 R Eyers[4] attch. 40 DSC, 23193 R Fielder[3] attch. 1 Sussex, 25170 A E Goodall[3] attch. 17 SSB, 200605 A G Gray[3] attch. 39 DSC, 2 Div., (Originally 4th Bn), 34304 J Houilleberq[3] (Houiellebecq) attch. 1 Sussex, 11747 W T Ingersoll[3] attch. 1 Sussex, 26033 C D J Jones[3] attch. 1 Sussex, 20519 A MacKay[3] attch. 17 SSB, 34353 F Marks[3] attch. 1 Sussex, 32603 A Minear[3] attch. 1 Sussex, 35865 F Missen[3] attch. 1 Sussex, 6099 S J Monks[3] attch. 1 Sussex, 22089 G Myall[3] attch. 1 Sussex, 11577 F Orchard[3] attch. 2/6 Sussex, 8579 J Ponting[3] attch. 1 Sussex, 32653 E G Robbins[3] attch. 1 Sussex, 200288 E Sanger[3] attch. 3/W Sig Sqn, (Originally 4th Bn), 201279 E M Sloper[3] attch. 33 DSC, 4 Div., (Originally 4th Bn), 33339 R Sherrington[3] attch. 1 Sussex, 34665 A W Steadman[3], 26039 H B Trott[3] attch. 1 Sussex, 201071 B W Tyler[3] attch. 3/W Sig Sqn, (Originally 4th Bn), 202922 S F Wavell[3] attch. 1 Sussex, (Originally 4th Bn) & 20295 C L Wheeler[3] attch. 1 Sussex

~ 1st Bn, The Manchester Regiment ~

Note a.   Roll of all personnel identified as eligible.
Note b.   *India August 1914. France & Flanders September 1914, Mesopotamia January 1916, Egypt April 1918, Palestine June 1918 to August 1919. Ireland March 1920 to December 1922.*
Note c.   *Medals named in impressed capitals: 'MANCH. R.'*

Single Clasp	No. Identified	Rarity
Afghanistan N.W.F. 1919[3]	8	Of the Utmost Rarity
Mahsud 1919–20[5]	0	None Identified
Waziristan 1919–21[4]	2	Of the Utmost Rarity
Waziristan 1921–24[6]	0	None Identified

Majors: ~ B V Mair[3] Bde. Maj. 21 Bde.
Captains: ~ G R H Bailey[4] attch. 6 MMG Bty, MGC, Wana Col / Ladha & T S W Jarvis[3]
Lieutenants: ~ V A Albrecht[3] attch. 97 Sqn, RAF & R P Flint[3]
Lance Corporals/Privates: ~ 3612 J Collier[3] attch. 3/W Sig Sqn, 9285 T Hadfield[3] attch. 2 Som LI, 3513068 J Robinson[4] attch. 1 GH, Tank, (3512265) 1375 W C Slade[3] attch. 3 W/ Sig Sqn & 1737 W Woodward[3]

~ 2nd Bn, The Manchester Regiment ~

Note a.   Roll of all personnel identified as eligible.
Note b.   *United Kingdom August 1914. France & Flanders August 1914 forward. Ireland November 1919, Iraq March 1920, India from January 1921 to 1924.*
Note c.   *Medals named in impressed capitals: 'MANCH. R.'*

Single Clasp	No. Identified	Rarity
Afghanistan N.W.F. 1919[3]	0	None Identified
Mahsud 1919–20[5]	0	None Identified
Waziristan 1919–21[4]	0	None Identified
Waziristan 1921–24[6]	0	None Identified
Combination Clasps	**No. Identified**	**Rarity**
Waziristan 1921–24[6] North West Frontier 1930–31[9]	1	According to roll as seen, can be considered Unique

Lieutenants: ~ J J Dolan[6&9(Capt.)] Staff Capt., Kalabagh

~ 1/6th Bn, The Manchester Regiment, Territorial Force ~

Note a.   *Roll of all personnel identified as eligible.*
Note b.   *United Kingdom August 1914. Egypt September 1914, Gallipoli May 1915, Egypt January 1916, France & Flanders March 1917 forward.*
Note c.   *Medals named in impressed capitals: 'MANCH. R.'*

Single Clasp	No. Identified	Rarity
Afghanistan N.W.F. 1919[3]	1	According to the roll as seen, can be considered Unique
Mahsud 1919–20[5]	0	None Identified
Waziristan 1919–21[4]	0	None Identified
Waziristan 1921–24[6]	0	None Identified

Captains: ~ L A Whittaker[3]

~ 1/7th Bn, The Manchester Regiment ~

Note a.   *Roll of all personnel identified as eligible.*
Note b.   *United Kingdom August 1914. Egypt September 1914, Gallipoli May 1915, Egypt January 1916, France & Flanders March 1917 forward.*
Note c.   *Medals named in impressed capitals: 'MANCH. R.'*

Single Clasp	No. Identified	Rarity
Afghanistan N.W.F. 1919[3]	1	According to the roll as seen, can be considered Unique
Mahsud 1919–20[5]	0	None Identified
Waziristan 1919–21[4]	0	None Identified
Waziristan 1921–24[6]	0	None Identified

Lieutenants: ~ W G Bailey[3] attch. 1/25 London

~ 1/8th (Ardwick) Bn, The Manchester Regiment ~

Note a.   *Roll of all personnel identified as eligible.*
Note b.   *United Kingdom August 1914. Egypt September 1914, Gallipoli May 1915, Egypt January 1916, France & Flanders March 1917 forward.*
Note c.   *Medals named in impressed capitals: 'MANCH. R.'*

Single Clasp	No. Identified	Rarity
Afghanistan N.W.F. 1919[3]	2	Of the Utmost Rarity
Mahsud 1919–20[5]	0	None Identified
Waziristan 1919–21[4]	0	None Identified
Waziristan 1921–24[6]	0	None Identified

Lieutenants: ~ C L Bond[3] attch. 1/25 London & A T Cleere[3] attch. 1/25 London

~ Unidentified Service Bn, The Manchester Regiment ~

Note a.   *Roll of all personnel identified as eligible.*
Note b.   *Medals named in impressed capitals: 'MANCH. R.'*

Single Clasp	No. Identified	Rarity
Afghanistan N.W.F. 1919[3]	3	Of the Utmost Rarity

Mahsud 1919–20[5]	0	None Identified
Waziristan 1919–21[4]	0	None Identified
Waziristan 1921–24[6]	0	None Identified

Captains: ~ J Galloway[3] attch. 2 King's & R Hobkirk[3] attch. 1/4 QORWK
Lieutenants: ~ E F Phillips[3] attch. 1/4 Border

~ 1st Bn, The Prince of Wales's (North Staffordshire Regiment) ~

Note a.   *Roll of all personnel identified eligible.*
Note b.   *United Kingdom August 1914. France & Flanders September 1914 forward. Ireland July 1919, Gibraltar December 1921, Turkey / Thrace September 1922, India March 1923.*
Note c.   *Title changed to The North Staffordshire Regiment (The Prince of Wales's) in 1920.*
Note d.   *Medals named in impressed capitals: 'N. STAFF. R.'*

Single Clasp	No. Identified	Rarity
Afghanistan N.W.F. 1919[3]	1	According to the roll as seen, can be considered Unique
Mahsud 1919–20[5]	0	None Identified
Waziristan 1919–21[4]	0	None Identified
Waziristan 1921–24[6]	0	None Identified

Lieutenants: ~ F M K Harrison[3] attch. 263 Coy MGC

~ 2nd Bn, The Prince of Wales's (North Staffordshire Regiment) ~

Note a.   *Roll of all commissioned personnel identified as eligible.*
Note b.   *Non-commissioned and other ranks multi clasp or non-Afghanistan 1919 single clasp.*
Note c.   *India August 1914 forward to February 1920.*
Note d.   *Title changed to The North Staffordshire Regiment (The Prince of Wales's) in 1920.*
Note e.   *Battle honour 'Third Afghan War 1919'.*
Note f.   *Medals named in impressed capitals > 'N. STAFF. R.'*

Single Clasp	No. Identified	Rarity
Afghanistan N.W.F. 1919[3]	Bn. Strength	Not Rare
Mahsud 1919–20[5]	0	None Identified
Waziristan 1919–21[4]	1	According to the roll as seen, can be considered Unique
Waziristan 1921–24[6]	0	None Identified
Combination Clasps	No. Identified	Rarity
Afghanistan N.W.F. 1919[3] Waziristan 1919–21[4]	2	Of the Utmost Rarity
Afghanistan N.W.F. 1919[3] Waziristan 1919–21[4] Waziristan 1921–24[6]	1	According to the roll as seen, can be considered Unique
Afghanistan N.W.F. 1919[3] Waziristan 1921–24[6]	2	Of the Utmost Rarity
Afghanistan N.W.F. 1919[3] Waziristan 1921–24[6] North West Frontier 1930–31[9]	1	According to the roll as seen, can be considered Unique
Afghanistan N.W.F. 1919[3] North West Frontier 1930–31[9]	1	According to the roll as seen, can be considered Unique

Afghanistan N.W.F. 1919[3] **Malabar 1921–22[7]**	**1**	According to the roll as seen, can be considered Unique
Afghanistan N.W.F. 1919[3] **Burma 1930–32[10]**	**1**	According to the roll as seen, can be considered Unique

Lieutenant Colonels: ~ E V Fox[3]

Majors: ~ T E Lowther[3] & B E Nicholls[3] DAQMG, Peshawar

Captains: ~ E L G Beville[3], F Hatton[3], C B Blanche-Hearn[3], T J Stroud[3], S A Tuck[3] & J R Whyte[3]

Lieutenants: ~ W G N Birkett[3] attch. MAD, H Gibson[3], G G Goode[3], S Harris[3], G Hollinrake[3], H J Horncastle[3], E V Horseman[3], C Irwin[3], E J Keeling[3], R Lacey[3], J J Mumford[3] attch. MAD, J Munn[3], C G Pugh[3], R V Rice[3] attch. 18 SSB, A B Savory[3], L A Scantlebury[3], J H Sims[3] Staff, E A Squirrell[3], B E Thompson[3], C Vining[3] & C Ward[3]

Quartermaster Sergeants/Sergeants: ~ (4794439) 65507 W R Bromley[3&10(WOI (RSM) Upper Burma Bn, AFI)] & (Act) 32726 H L D Elkins[4] attch. S&TC

Lance Sergeants/Corporals: ~ (Act) 9572 G W Parton[3&4(Queens)]

Lance Corporals/Privates: ~ (4794441) 8574 J Barker[3&6(Lincolnshire attch. 'D' DSC)], (7817773) 9343 F Burns[3,(4&6 11 Bn MGC)], (68807) 47425 E N B Davis[3&(7 L/Cpl. Dorset)], 27034 (311950) F Draper[3&9(Sgt. R Sigs)], L/8591 (7817810) T Kitching[3&4(MGC)] & (4794471) 9399 G W Neal[3,(6 Cpl. Lincoln)&(9 Sgt. R Sigs)] attch. 'F' DSC

~ 7th (Service) Bn, The Prince of Wales's (North Staffordshire Regiment) ~

Note a. *Roll of all personnel identified as eligible.*

Note b. *Formed August 1914. Gallipoli July 1915, Egypt January 1916, Mesopotamia February 1916, North Persia July 1918, South Russia August 1918, North Persia September 1918 thence South Russia from November 1918 to June 1919.*

Note c. *Medals named in impressed capitals: 'N. STAFF. R.'*

Single Clasp	No. Identified	Rarity
Afghanistan N.W.F. 1919[3]	**6**	Of the Utmost Rarity
Mahsud 1919–20[5]	**0**	None Identified
Waziristan 1919–21[4]	**0**	None Identified
Waziristan 1921–24[6]	**0**	None Identified

Lance Corporals/Privates: ~ 18835 T Griffin[3], 61611 M Harrison[3], 32158 H Johnson[3], 45583 C W Matthews[3], 39459 O Wrenn[3] & 31981 J R Wright[3]

~ 2nd Bn, The York and Lancaster Regiment ~

Note a. *Roll of all personnel identified as eligible.*

Note b. *United Kingdom August 1914. France & Flanders September 1914 forward. Iraq and Persia via India from October 1919 to December 1921 thence India forward.*

Note c. *Medals named in thin impressed capitals: 'YORK & LANC. R.' or 'Y&L R.'*

Single Clasp	No. Identified	Rarity
Afghanistan N.W.F. 1919[3]	**0**	None Identified
Mahsud 1919–20[5]	**0**	None Identified
Waziristan 1919–21[4]	**0**	None Identified
Waziristan 1921–24[6]	**16**	Extremely Rare

Lance Corporals/Privates: ~ 4737219 J A Addy[6] attch. 7 IGH, DIK, 4739986 F Ashley[6] attch. 7 IGH, DIK, 4737804 R Baker[6] attch. 1 BGH, Tank, 4739097 J Bell[6] attch. 7 IGH, DIK, 4737587 T Bentley[6] attch. 7 IGH, DIK, 4738838 E Bolsover[6] attch. 7 IGH, DIK, 4737174 F R Butcher[6] attch. 4 IFA, DIK, 4738064 E Carter[6] attch. 7 IGH, DIK, 4737988 J Drury[6] attch. 7 IGH, DIK, 4737816 G Kenny[6] attch. 7 IGH, DIK, 4739194 M Killeen[6] attch. 7 IGH, DIK, 4737674 H T Marshall[6] attch. 7 IGH, DIK, 4739107 H T Marshall[6] attch. 7 IGH, DIK, 4736841 J Robinson[6] attch. 7 IGH, DIK, 4736401 L Thomas[6] attch. 4 IFA & 4737371 F J S Waller[6] attch. 7 IGH, DIK

~ Unidentified Service Bn, The York and Lancaster Regiment ~

Note a. Roll of all personnel identified as eligible.
Note b. Medals named in impressed capitals: 'YORK. & LANC. R' or 'Y&L R.'

Single Clasp	No. Identified	Rarity
Afghanistan N.W.F. 1919[3]	3	Of the Utmost Rarity
Mahsud 1919–20[5]	0	None Identified
Waziristan 1919–21[4]	0	None Identified
Waziristan 1921–24[6]	0	None Identified

Lieutenant: ~ C E Chatterton[3] attch. 1/5 Hampshire, J J W Fairbairn[3] attch. 1 Yorkshire & H B Hewitt[3] attch. 1 Yorkshire

~ 1ˢᵗ Bn, The Durham Light Infantry ~

Note a. Roll of all commissioned personnel identified as eligible.
Note b. Non-commissioned and other ranks multi clasp or non-Afghanistan 1919 single clasp.
Note c. India August 1914 forward to 1921.
Note d. Battle honour 'Third Afghan War 1919'.
Note e. Medals named in impressed capitals: 'DURH. L. I.'

Single Clasp	No. Identified	Rarity
Afghanistan N.W.F. 1919[3]	Bn. Strength	Not Rare
Mahsud 1919–20[5]	0	None Identified
Waziristan 1919–21[4]	0	None Identified
Waziristan 1921–24[6]	1	According to the roll as seen, can be considered Unique
Combination Clasps	**No. Identified**	**Rarity**
Afghanistan N.W.F. 1919[3] Waziristan 1919–21[4]	1	According to the roll as seen, can be considered Unique
Afghanistan N.W.F. 1919[3] Waziristan 1919–21[4] Waziristan 1921–24[6]	1	According to the roll as seen, can be considered Unique
Afghanistan N.W.F. 1919[3] Waziristan 1921–24[6]	4	Of the Utmost Rarity
Afghanistan N.W.F. 1919[3] N.W.F. 1930–32[9]	6	Of the Utmost Rarity

Lieutenant Colonels: ~ E du P H Moore[3]
Majors: ~ A J Clifton[3&6(RTC Experimental Section)], J O C Hasted[3] & H Richardson[3]
Captains: ~ P Hartridge[3], (Act) A Harwood[3], W McDonald[3], S V Mercer[3], C W Sibbald[3] & C Whiton[3]
Lieutenants: ~ K N Brown[3], G Callie[3], A Clark[3], H Critchley[3], G Curry[3], G W Daintree[3], C A Gill[3], A J Goldie[3], G T Goldschmidt[3] attch. 36 DSC, 1 Div., J H Hartigan[3], A W T Harwood[3], A G Henderson[3] attch. 39 DSC, 2 Div., (QM) W H Lowe[3], J Mahoney[3], F A Marks[3], A Peers[3] attch. 1/1 Kent, J M Ward[3], H M Wardle[3], E K Wyatt[3] attch. 36 DSC & F Taylor[3&9] attch. MGC
Warrant Officers Class II: ~ 9004 G Shields[3&9(As QM Lt.)]
Quartermaster Sergeants/Sergeants: ~ 10953 H McLean[3&6] attch. 'B' DSC & 10764T H McManus[3&4] attch. 40 DSC
Lance Sergeants/Corporals: ~ (Act) 4435150 A Aston[3&9(Sgt.)] & (Act) 4436980 W H Pickering[6] attch. HQ, Waz Dist
Lance Corporals/Privates: ~ (43347391) 9926 J Clark[3&6(KSLI)], 10109 T Connon[3&6(R Sigs)], (4438523) 52320 D Lawlor[3&9], (4435426) 11192 M Marrin[3&9], (4441728) 11425 T Sefton[3&9] & (M/4336896) 10150 N Tiesdell[3,(4&6 RASC)] attch. 1 MT Coy, S&TC

~ 2ⁿᵈ Bn, The Durham Light Infantry ~

Note a.   *Roll of all personnel identified as eligible.*
Note b.   *United Kingdom August 1914. France & Flanders September 1914 forward. South Russia October 1919, Turkey from July to November 1920 thence India forward.*
Note c.   *Medals named in impressed capitals: 'DURH. L. I.'*

Single Clasp	No. Identified	Rarity
Afghanistan N.W.F. 1919[3]	0	None Identified
Mahsud 1919–20[5]	0	None Identified
Waziristan 1919–21[4]	0	None Identified
Waziristan 1921–24[6]	0	None Identified
Combination Clasps	No. Identified	Rarity
Waziristan 1921–24[6] North West Frontier 1930–31[9]	1	According to the roll as seen, can be considered Unique

Captains: ~ R Jee[6&(9 R Sigs)] attch. 'B' DSC

~ 3ʳᵈ (Reserve) Bn, The Durham Light Infantry ~

Note a.   *Roll of all personnel identified as eligible.*
Note b.   *United Kingdom August 1914 forward throughout Great War period providing drafts and reinforcements.*
Note c.   *Medals named in impressed capitals: 'DURH. L. I.'*

Single Clasp	No. Identified	Rarity
Afghanistan N.W.F. 1919[3]	3	Of the Utmost Rarity
Mahsud 1919–20[5]	0	None Identified
Waziristan 1919–21[4]	0	None Identified
Waziristan 1921–24[6]	0	None Identified

Lieutenants: ~ L Brotherton[3] attch. 1/4 Queen's, S L Lincoln[3] attch. 1/4 Queen's & W Stones[3] attch. 1/4 Queen's

~ 18ᵗʰ (Service) Bn (1ˢᵗ County), The Durham Light Infantry ~

Note a.   *Roll of all personnel identified as eligible.*
Note b.   *Formed September 1914. Egypt December 1915 to March 1916 thence France and Flanders forward.*
Note c.   *Medals named in impressed capitals: 'DURH. L. I.'*

Single Clasp	No. Identified	Rarity
Afghanistan N.W.F. 1919[3]	1	According to the roll as seen, can be considered Unique
Mahsud 1919–20[5]	0	None Identified
Waziristan 1919–21[4]	0	None Identified
Waziristan 1921–24[6]	0	None Identified

Captains: ~ E Rasche[3] attch. 2 Som LI

~ 19th (Service) Bn (2nd County), The Durham Light Infantry ~

Note a.   *Roll of all personnel identified as eligible.*
Note b.   *Formed January 1915. France & Flanders February 1916 forward.*
Note c.   *Medals named in impressed capitals: 'DURH. L. I.'*

Single Clasp	No. Identified	Rarity
Afghanistan N.W.F. 1919[3]	1	According to the roll as seen, can be considered Unique
Mahsud 1919–20[5]	0	None Identified
Waziristan 1919–21[4]	0	None Identified
Waziristan 1921–24[6]	0	None Identified

Lieutenant: ~ T C S McGowan[3] attch. 1/1 Kent

~ 1st Bn, The Highland Light Infantry ~

Note a.   *Roll of all personnel identified as eligible.*
Note b.   *India August 1914. France & Flanders December 1914, Mesopotamia January 1916 to 1919 thence Egypt to November 1920.*
Note c.   *Title changed to The Highland Light Infantry (City of Glasgow Regiment) in 1923.*
Note d.   *Medals named in impressed capitals: 'H.L.I.'*

Single Clasp	No. Identified	Rarity
Afghanistan N.W.F. 1919[3]	1	According to the roll as seen, can be considered Unique
Mahsud 1919–20[5]	0	None Identified
Waziristan 1919–21[4]	0	None Identified
Waziristan 1921–24[6]	0	None Identified

Lieutenants: ~ G S M Mackay[3] attch. 2 King's

~ 3rd (Reserve) Bn, The Highland Light Infantry ~

Note a.   *Roll of all personnel identified as eligible.*
Note b.   *United Kingdom August 1914 forward throughout Great War period providing drafts and reinforcements.*
Note c.   *Medals named in impressed capitals: 'H.L.I.'*

Single Clasp	No. Identified	Rarity
Afghanistan N.W.F. 1919[3]	1	According to the roll as seen, can be considered Unique
Mahsud 1919–20[5]	0	None Identified
Waziristan 1919–21[4]	0	None Identified
Waziristan 1921–24[6]	0	None Identified

Lieutenants: ~ K J G Sugden[3] attch. 281 Coy, MGC

~ 1/5th (City Of Glasgow) Bn, The Highland Light Infantry, Territorial Force ~

Note a. *Roll of all personnel identified as eligible.*
Note b. *United Kingdom August 1914. Egypt June 1915, Mudros and Gallipoli July 1915, Mudros January 1916, Egypt February 1916, Palestine 1917, France & Flanders April 1918 forward.*
Note c. *Medals named in impressed capitals: 'H.L.I.'*

Single Clasp	No. Identified	Rarity
Afghanistan N.W.F. 1919[3]	1	According to the roll as seen, can be considered Unique
Mahsud 1919–20[5]	0	None Identified
Waziristan 1919–21[4]	0	None Identified
Waziristan 1921–24[6]	0	None Identified

Lieutenants: ~ S J Knight[3], attch. 17 SSB

~ 1/6th (City Of Glasgow) Bn, The Highland Light Infantry, Territorial Force ~

Note a. *Roll of all personnel identified as eligible.*
Note b. *United Kingdom August 1914. Egypt June 1915, Mudros and Gallipoli July 1915, Mudros January 1916, Egypt February 1916, Palestine 1917, France & Flanders April 1918 forward.*
Note c. *Medals named in impressed capitals: 'H.L.I.'*

Single Clasp	No. Identified	Rarity
Afghanistan N.W.F. 1919[3]	1	According to the roll as seen, can be considered Unique
Mahsud 1919–20[5]	0	None Identified
Waziristan 1919–21[4]	0	None Identified
Waziristan 1921–24[6]	0	None Identified

Lieutenants: ~ C A Pollock[3] attch. 1 S Lanc

~ 1st (Reserve) Garrison Bn, The Highland Light Infantry ~

Note a. *Roll of all personnel identified as eligible.*
Note b. *Formed May 1916. India from 1916 forward.*
Note c. *Medals named in impressed capitals: 'H.L.I.'*

Single Clasp	No. Identified	Rarity
Afghanistan N.W.F. 1919[3]	235	Scarce
Mahsud 1919–20[5]	0	None Identified
Waziristan 1919–21[4]	0	None Identified
Waziristan 1921–24[6]	0	None Identified

Quartermaster Sergeants/Sergeants: ~ 8767 A Anderson[3] attch. 2/6 Sussex, 3743 E Blackstock[3] attch. 2/6 Sussex, (Act) 14632 T Calder[3] attch. RASC, 187 L Crossley[3] attch. 2/6 Sussex, (Act) 19182 L Galbraith[3] attch. S&TC, 200979 R Gow[3] attch. 2/6 Sussex, (Originally 5th Bn), 200087 A P Ireland[3] attch. 1 DLI, (Originally 5th Bn), (Act) 56820 J Jamieson[3] attch. S&TC, (Act) 58804 H Miller[3] attch. S&TC, 20342 W Ovington[3] attch. 2/6 Sussex, 8250 J Peacock[3] attch. 2/6 Sussex, 33294 J Pollock[3] attch. 2/6 Sussex, 10467 W C Rae[3] attch. Ammo Col Rawalpindi - Peshawar, S&TC, 14669 G Ramage[3] attch. 1 DLI, 3976 G B Smith[3] attch. 1 DLI, 15787 R L Stark[3] attch. 2/6 Sussex, 56807 W S Taylor[3] attch. MT, S&TC & (Act) 34191 F H Wright[3] attch. 1 SSB & Post Cmd.'ts Staff Kacha, Garhi

Lance Sergeants /Corporals: ~ (Act) 40349 A L Allan[3] attch. 1 DLI, 21375 R Fraser[3] attch. 1 DLI, 330344 R Henderson[3] attch. 1 DLI, (Originally 9th Bn), 1178 K MacKenzie[3] attch. 2/6 Sussex, J McMillan[3] attch. 1 SSB, 38604 J Marshall[3] attch. 2/6 Sussex, 2900 J G Miller[3] attch. 1 DLI, 8895 A H J Mizen[3] attch. 2/6 Sussex, (Act) 3975 W Smith[3] attch. 1 DLI, B/21145 F A Valentine[3] attch. 2/6 Sussex, 20355 J G Whittles[3] attch. 2 Som LI, 1 Div. & 56817 T Wright[3] attch. 6 MT Coy, RASC

Lance Corporals/Privates: ~ 43212 G S Allan[3] attch. 1 DLI, 26325 J F Anderson[3] attch. 1 DLI, 18429 D Aitken[3] attch. 1 DLI, 33263 T Aitken[3] attch. 1 DLI, 50285 R Armstrong[3] attch. 2 Som LI, 37995 W Baird[3] attch. 1 SSB, 20013 D W Bangs[3] attch. MFP, 20732 A Barnes[3] attch. 1 DLI, 26941 W Beattie[3] attch. 1 DLI, 8721 P G Beck[3] attch. 2 Som LI thence 1 SSB, 40858 G Bell[3] attch. 1 DLI, 8896 J Bell[3] attch. 1 DLI, 56 A K Bennett[3] attch. 1 DLI, 26398 G Binns[3] attch. 1 DLI, 14333 G Boyd[3] attch. 1 DLI, 26418 E Brown[3] attch. 1 DLI, 282657 P Brown[3] attch. 1 DLI, (Originally 7th Bn), 21133 W Britten[3] attch. 1 DLI, 50364 J Bulman[3] attch. 2 Som LI, 4780 C Burden[3] attch. 1 DLI, 1239 T Burnett[3] attch. 2/6 Sussex, 40015 V Burns[3] attch. 2/6 Sussex, 33536 C Cahill[3] attch. 1 DLI, 21263 G Cameron[3], 21317 J Cameron[3] attch. 1 DLI, 34236 F Campbell[3] attch. 1 DLI, 32883 J A Campbell[3] attch. 1 DLI, 20309 W Capewell[3] attch. 1 DLI, 25228 J Carrol[3] attch. 1 DLI, 330306 D Carson[3] attch. 1 DLI, (Originally 9th Bn), 14345 A Chalmers[3] attch. 2/6 Sussex, 330692 T Chaplin[3] attch. 1 DLI, (Originally 9th Bn), 331985 M Clark[3] attch. 1 SSB, (Originally 9th Bn), 18325 J Clunie[3] attch. 1 DLI, 22539 J Cochrane[3] attch. 1 DLI, 35433 J Cockburn[3] attch. 1 DLI, 24382 T Connor[3] attch. 2/6 Sussex, 41996 J Coulthard[3] attch. 2/6 Sussex, 43354 G Coventry[3] attch. 1 DLI, 40139 R Crawford[3] attch. 1 DLI, 21213 J Cray[3] attch. 1 DLI, 203347 A Crowley[3] attch. 2 Som LI, 29578 C Cufflin[3] attch. 2/6 Sussex, 7955 S Curran[3] attch. 1 DLI, 16393 W Cutmore[3] attch. 2/6 Sussex, 1306 D Dempsey[3] attch. 1/1 Kent, 1078 J Derry[3] attch. 2/6 Sussex, 280960 A Dewar[3] attch. 1 DLI, (Originally 7th Bn), 50221 J Dewar[3] attch. 1 DLI, 34107 J Dodgson[3] attch. 1 DLI, 26452 T Donald[3] attch. 1 DLI, 21266 W Doogan[3] attch. 1 DLI, 40002 J Douglas[3] attch. 1 SSB, 20313 W Dowell[3] attch. 1 DLI, 24790 J Doyle[3] attch. 1 DLI, 35460 H A Edwards[3] attch. 1 SSB, 13848 R Egan[3] attch. 1 SSB, 40278 J W Elder[3] attch. 1 DLI, 21049 A J Eve[3] attch. 1 DLI, 20368 J Farrer[3] attch. 1 DLI, 20369 F Fisher[3] attch. 1 DLI, 43333 J Fisher[3] attch. 1 DLI, 10407 W Fitzgerald[3] attch. Amb Sect, 4259 P Fitzpatrick[3] attch. 1 DLI, 4188 P Flood[3] attch. 1 DLI, 40070 J Follen[3] attch. 1 DLI, 74752 A Fraser[3] attch. 1 DLI, 36468 W Fraser[3] attch. 2 Som LI, 34128 J Fyfe[3] attch. 1 DLI, 7889 T Gaffney[3] attch. 2/6 Sussex, 35465 G A M Galloway[3] attch. 1 DLI, 9466 J Gee[3] attch. 2/6 Sussex, 34162 A Gibson[3] attch. 2/6 Sussex, 43390 R Gilmour[3] attch. 1 DLI, 242737 J Glasgow[3] attch. 1 DLI, (Originally 6th Bn), 37990 T H Gosnell[3] attch. 1 DLI, 23445 A Graham[3] attch. 1 DLI, 1639 J Graham[3] attch. 1 DLI, 12454 H Gray[3] attch. 1 DLI, 20370 G Green[3] attch. 1 DLI, 39464 W K Hall[3] attch. 1 DLI, 8890 H Halliday[3] attch. 1 DLI, 40314 D Harris[3] attch. 2/6 Sussex, 21222 G Hastie[3] attch. 1 DLI, 1202 J Hay[3] attch. 1 DLI, 21220 J S Henderson[3] attch. 1 DLI, 331996 W Henderson[3] attch. 1 DLI, (Originally 9th Bn), 74735 W Hodge[3] attch. 11 BCCS, 4493 J Holligan[3] attch. 1 DLI, 42711 J W Honeyman[3] attch. 1 DLI, 21218 R Horne[3] attch. 1 DLI, 529 J Howitt[3] attch. 2/6 Sussex, 32702 R Hudson[3] attch. 2/6 Sussex, 33230 W Hume[3] attch. 1 DLI, 5967 C Hutchison[3] attch. 1 DLI, 28992 W Innes[3] attch. 2/6 Sussex, 1484 G Irving[3] attch. 2 Som LI, 1955 G James[3] attch. 1 DLI, 18850 W Jamieson[3] attch. 1 DLI, 20380 A Kearton[3] attch. 1 DLI, 37988 N Kelly[3] attch. 1 DLI, 24398 A Lamont[3] attch. 1 DLI, 35478 J Lavery[3] attch. 2/6 Sussex, 1184 A B Lawrence[3] attch. 1 DLI, 202008 G Lunn[3] attch. 2 Som LI, (Originally 5th Bn), 201643 A Lynch[3] attch. 1 DLI, (Originally 5th Bn), 240737 I A Mathison[3] attch. 33 DSC, 4 Div., (Originally 6th Bn), 50257 D H McCall[3] attch. 2 Som LI, 11124 J G MacDonald[3] attch. 2 Som LI, 34254 G MacInnes[3] attch. 1 DLI, 9007 G Mc A Neish[3] attch. 1 DLI, 8895 F McBeath[3] attch. 1 DLI, 25512 T McCrorie[3] attch. 1 DLI, 203357 D McCulloch[3] attch. 1 DLI, (Originally 5th Bn), 8757 J McDonald[3] attch. 1 DLI, 50348 J McDonald[3] attch. 2 Som LI, 37984 A McDougall[3] attch. 1 DLI, 15366 P McDougall[3] attch. 1 SSB, 14613 J McEllan[3] attch. 1 DLI, 201394 N McFadyen[3] attch. 1 DLI, (Originally 5th Bn), 21287 P McGauchran[3] attch. 1 DLI, 4359 T McGovan[3] attch. 2/6 Sussex, 31305 M McGurk[3] attch. 1 DLI, 33525 R McKay[3] attch. 1 DLI, 3855 W J McKintosh[3] attch. 1 DLI, 11919 P McLaughlin[3] attch. 2/6 Sussex, 10002 W McLaughlin[3] attch. 1 DLI, 18882 J McLaven[3] attch. 1 DLI, 33702 D McLellan[3] attch. 1 DLI, 32796 W McMurtrie[3] attch. 1 DLI, 6887 W McWilliams[3] attch. 1 DLI, 35502 J Malcolm[3] attch. 1 DLI, 1361 P Marshall[3] attch. 1 DLI, 4377 P Marshall[3] attch. 1 DLI, 242725 D Martin[3] attch. 1 DLI, (Originally 6th Bn), 9236 H Martin[3] attch. 1 DLI, 43394 G Millar[3] attch. 1 DLI, 200769 D Mitchell[3] attch. 1 DLI, (Originally 5th Bn), 26310 J F Mitchell[3] attch. 1 DLI, 26938 J Mooney[3] attch. 2/6 Sussex, 23258 D Moran[3] attch. 1 DLI, 4538 M L Morrison[3] attch. 2/6 Sussex, 16033 A Morton[3] attch. 1 DLI, 35068 A Mowat[3] attch. 1 DLI, 1814 J Mowat[3] attch. 1 DLI, 41040 H Mullen[3] attch. 1 DLI, 572 H Murray[3] attch. 1 DLI, 241710 M R Murray[3] attch. 39 DSC, 2 Div., 26387 J Naish[3] attch. 1 DLI, 8944 J Neil[3] attch. 2/6 Sussex, 14904 W Nimmo[3] attch. 1 DLI, 21382 R Johnstone[3] attch. 1 DLI, 16871 W O'Connor[3] attch. 1 DLI, 28405 H O'Donnell[3] attch. 1 DLI, 35518 P O'Fee[3] attch. 1 DLI, 37994 J O'Hara[3] attch. 2/6 Sussex, 50281 D A Pagan[3] attch. 1 DLI, 18506 T Parkes[3] attch. 1 DLI, 331928 J Paterson[3] attch. 1 DLI, (Originally 9th Bn), 7903 R Patrick[3] attch. 1 DLI, 14499 J E Perston[3] attch. 2/6 Sussex, 38004 G Peter[3] attch. 1 DLI, 19845 E Phillips[3] attch. 1 DLI, 26280 J Potter[3] attch. 1 DLI, 8030 J Purdie[3] attch. 1 DLI, 24050 A Rae[3] attch. 1 DLI, 5400 J Ramsey[3] attch. 1 DLI, 18908 W J Reid[3], 27473 F A Roberts[3] attch. WT Stn, Thal, 34180 J Rocks[3] attch. 1 DLI, 24877 J Ross[3] attch. 1 DLI, 34135 J Ross[3] attch. 1 DLI, 25043 C Sandeman[3] attch. 1 DLI, B/21143 G E Savage[3] attch. 2/6 Sussex, 20349 J Savage[3] attch. 1 DLI, 22328 T Scarr[3] attch. 1 DLI, 19588 C A Schofield[3] attch. 2/6 Sussex, 1278 J Scobie[3] attch. 1 DLI, 7592 J Sheridan[3] attch. 1 DLI, 3797 W Sheridan[3] attch. 1 DLI, 27808 P Shields[3] attch. 1 DLI, 11177 D Smith[3] attch. 1 DLI, 11391 J Smith[3] attch. Afghan Mission Hospital, Bannu, 330296 W Strachan[3] attch. 1 DLI, (Originally 5th Bn), D/21298 J Sutherland[3] attch. 2/4 Border, B/8076 G Taylor[3] attch. 11 BCCS, 27978 J Thompson[3] attch. 1 DLI, 18179 T Thompson[3] attch. 1 DLI, 29317 J N Todd[3] attch. 1 DLI, 22664 J Trotter[3] attch. 1 DLI, 330892 C Walker[3] attch. 1 DLI, 20398 F Walker[3] attch. 1 DLI, 19884 J Walker[3] attch. 1 DLI, 40447 J Walker[3] attch. 1 DLI, 25209 W Ward[3] attch. 1 DLI, 20048 W F Ward[3] attch. 2/6 Sussex, 3822 A Webb[3] attch. 1 DLI, 56147 J S Weir[3] attch. 1 DLI, 20664 J Welch[3] attch. 2 Som LI, 22094 T Welsh[3] attch. 1 DLI, 56779 A Wilson[3] attch. 1 DLI, 280430 J Wilson[3] attch. 1 DLI, (Originally 7th Bn), 56798 J Wood[3] attch. 1 DLI, 56791 B Worswick[3] attch. 2 Som LI & 21010 J J York[3] attch. 1 DLI

~ Unidentified Service Bn, The Highland Light Infantry ~
Note a.   *Roll of all personnel identified as eligible.*
Note b.   *Medals named in impressed capitals: 'H.L.I.'*

Single Clasp	No. Identified	Rarity
Afghanistan N.W.F. 1919[3]	1	According to the roll as seen, can be considered Unique
Mahsud 1919–20[5]	0	None Identified
Waziristan 1919–21[4]	0	None Identified
Waziristan 1921–24[6]	0	None Identified

Lieutenants: ~ A Watson[3] attch. 1 DWR

~ 2nd Bn, Seaforth Highlanders (Ross-Shire Buffs, The Duke of Albany's) ~
Note a.   *Roll of all personnel identified as eligible.*
Note b.   *United Kingdom August 1914. France & Flanders August 1914 forward. India November 1919 forward.*
Note c.   *Medals named in impressed capitals: 'SEAFORTH' or 'SEAFORTHS'.*

Single Clasp	No. Identified	Rarity
Afghanistan N.W.F. 1919[3]	1	According to the roll as seen, can be considered Unique
Mahsud 1919–20[5]	0	None Identified
Waziristan 1919–21[4]	4	Of the Utmost Rarity
Waziristan 1921–24[6]	3	Of the Utmost Rarity
Combination Clasps	**No. Identified**	**Rarity**
North West Frontier 1908[1] Waziristan 1919–21[4]	1	According to the roll as seen, can be considered Unique
Afghanistan N.W.F. 1919[3] Mahsud 1919–20[5]	1	According to the roll as seen, can be considered Unique
Afghanistan N.W.F. 1919[3] Waziristan 1919–21[4]	1	According to the roll as seen, can be considered Unique
Waziristan 1919–21[4] Waziristan 1921–24[6]	1	According to the roll as seen, can be considered Unique
Waziristan 1921–24[6] North West Frontier 1930–31[9]	2	Of the Utmost Rarity

Captains: ~ I C Barclay[6&9] Staff, Razmak FF & E C Dodgson[3] attch. 1 S Lanc
Lieutenants: ~ C J Shaw McKenzie[6] Staff Capt, Razmak FF & G S Rawstorne[4] attch. 9 GR, IA
Quartermaster Sergeants /Sergeants: ~ (Act) 2810507 A K Slesser[6&9] attch. 39 SS, 7 Bde.
Lance Sergeants /Corporals: ~ 2810503 J T Pearce[4&6] attch. 'B' thence 'F' DSC & 2809349 E Ward[6] attch. 'B' DSC
Lance Corporals/Privates: ~ 8427 A Brown[1&4] attch. S&TC LofC, (2810049) 30926 R Butler[3&5] attch. HQ, 43 Bde., 2809664 R Cavin[6] attch. HQ, Derajat Bde., 9459 W A Gray[3&4] 3/W Sig Sqn, 31329 J Hannan[4] attch. MFO, Khirgi, 31806 W McIntyre[4] attch. 2 CSS & 2809574 A O Peshkin[4] attch. 1 AOC

~ 3rd (Reserve) Bn, Seaforth Highlanders (Ross-Shire Buffs, The Duke of Albany's) ~
Note a.   *Roll of all personnel identified as eligible.*
Note b.   *United Kingdom August 1914 forward throughout Great War period providing drafts and reinforcements.*
Note c.   *Medals named in impressed capitals: 'SEAFORTH' or 'SEAFORTHS'.*

Single Clasp	No. Identified	Rarity
Afghanistan N.W.F. 1919[3]	1	According to the roll as seen, can be considered Unique
Mahsud 1919–20[5]	0	None Identified
Waziristan 1919–21[4]	0	None Identified
Waziristan 1921–24[6]	0	None Identified

Lieutenants: ~ D I Urquhart[3]

~ 1/5th (The Sutherland & Caithness Highland) Bn, Seaforth Highlanders
(Ross-Shire Buffs, The Duke of Albany's) ~

Note a. *Roll of all personnel identified as eligible.*
Note b. *United Kingdom August 1914. France & Flanders May 1915 forward.*
Note c. *Medals named in impressed capitals: 'SEAFORTH' or 'SEAFORTHS'*

Single Clasp	No. Identified	Rarity
Afghanistan N.W.F. 1919[3]	1	According to the roll as seen, can be considered Unique
Mahsud 1919–20[5]	0	None Identified
Waziristan 1919–21[4]	0	None Identified
Waziristan 1921–24[6]	0	None Identified

Lieutenants: ~ J White[3] attch. 44 DSC, KKF

~ 2nd Bn, The Gordon Highlanders ~

Note a. *Roll of all personnel identified as eligible.*
Note b. *Egypt August 1914. France & Flanders October 1914, Italy November 1917 to April 1919 thence to Ireland.*
Note c. *Medals named in impressed capitals: 'GORDONS'*

Single Clasp	No. Identified	Rarity
Afghanistan N.W.F. 1919[3]	1	According to the roll as seen, can be considered Unique
Mahsud 1919–20[5]	0	None Identified
Waziristan 1919–21[4]	0	None Identified
Waziristan 1921–24[6]	0	None Identified

Lieutenants: ~ A Mackie[3] attch. 270 Coy, MGC

~ 3rd (Reserve) Bn, The Gordon Highlanders ~

Note a. *Roll of all personnel identified as eligible.*
Note b. *United Kingdom August 1914 forward throughout Great War period providing reinforcement drafts.*
Note c. *Medals named in impressed capitals: 'GORDONS'*

Single Clasp	No. Identified	Rarity
Afghanistan N.W.F. 1919[3]	1	According to the roll as seen, can be considered Unique
Mahsud 1919–20[5]	0	None Identified
Waziristan 1919–21[4]	0	None Identified
Waziristan 1921–24[6]	0	None Identified

Lieutenants: ~ W J Grassick[3] attch. 2 King's

~ 9th (Service) Bn (Pioneers), The Gordon Highlanders ~

Note a.   *Roll of all personnel identified as eligible.*
Note b.   *Formed September 1914. France & Flanders July 1915 forward.*
Note c.   *Medals named in impressed capitals: 'GORDONS'*

Single Clasp	No. Identified	Rarity
Afghanistan N.W.F. 1919[3]	1	According to the roll as seen, can be considered Unique
Mahsud 1919–20[5]	0	None Identified
Waziristan 1919–21[4]	0	None Identified
Waziristan 1921–24[6]	0	None Identified

Lieutenants: ~ W B Kerr[3] attch. 1 Yorkshire

~ 1st Garrison Bn, The Gordon Highlanders ~

Note a.   *Roll of all personnel identified as eligible.*
Note b.   *Formed 1916. India from January 1917 forward.*
Note c.   *Medals named in impressed capitals: 'GORDONS'*

Single Clasp	No. Identified	Rarity
Afghanistan N.W.F. 1919[3]	211	Scarce
Mahsud 1919–20[5]	0	None Identified
Waziristan 1919–21[4]	3	Of the Utmost Rarity
Waziristan 1921–24[6]	0	None Identified
Combination Clasps	**No. Identified**	**Rarity**
Afghanistan N.W.F. 1919[3] Waziristan 1919–21[4]	1	According to the roll as seen, can be considered Unique

Majors: ~ W Home[3]

Captains: ~ G H Henderson[3], T E A Buchan-Hepburn[3], F H C McTavish[3], J T Peareth[3], S Sherwell[3] & A D Wood[3]

Lieutenants: ~ I W Astell[3], M M Burns[3], J C Cattanach[3], A R Gordon[3], C R S Jefferson[3], A H Kay[3&4] attch. 40 DSC, R D McLeod[3], J Mort[4] attch. S&TC & G D Pitcairn[3] Staff, 1 Div.

Warrant Officers Class I: ~ 12626 D H McMillan[3]

Warrant Officers Class II: ~ S/16870 A Anderson[3], S/16473 R W Brown[3], (Act) 12638 J M W Hart[3], 12699 J Howe[3], 3/7390 A MacRury[3] & S/16430 W T Ross[3]

Company Quartermaster Sergeants/Staff Sergeants/Colour Sergeants: ~ (Act) 241923 G Cullen[3], (Originally 5th Bn), (Act) 202224 H Emslie[3], (Originally 4th Bn), S/16004 J W Goodfellow[3], (Act) S16131 A McGregor[3], (Act) S/16008 A Miller[3] attch. HQ, NWFF, 16779 J H Wardlaw[3] & (Act) S/16741 A Wilkie[3]

Quartermaster Sergeants/Sergeants: ~ S/16937 G W Barclay[3] attch. 12 Div. Sply Coy, S&TC, (Act) S/98016 M Beaumont[3], (Act) 16784 W Connelly[3], S/16707 T A Davis[3] attch. 27 CCCS, Ladha, (Act) 13595 P E Eastough[3], 34138 J Fraser[3], (Act) S/16233 W C King[3], (Act) S/16411 J MacDonald[3], 3/7415 A Mancrieff[3] attch. 25 CFA, 12696 G McLennon[3], (Act) S/16683 D B Medlock[3] attch. 2/4 Border, (Act) S16793 D Murray[3], (Act) S/16375 A Newton[3], (Act) S/16366 W J Paterson[3], S/16333 A Rankin[3], (Act) S/16133 W S Renfrew[3], (Act) S/20883 R Scales[3], (Act) S/16915 G S Smith[3], (Act) 241496 J Smith[3], (Act) S/18861 W Steven[3] attch. 2/4 Border, 12698 R Westwater[3], (Act) S/16091 J G White[3] & (Act) S/16389 J Williams[3]

Lance Sergeants/Corporals: ~ S/18735 A Boyne[3] attch. 2/4 Border, (Act) S/17131 W Coutts[3], 291549 J Cowan[3], (Originally 7th Bn), S/16494 J Drummond[3], (Act) S/16562 J Garside[3], (Act) S/16519 H Grant[3] attch. HQ, 2 Div., S/167509 A Heritage[3], 12697 A W Hunt[3], (Act) S/16436 A McDonald[3], (Act) 3/7429 D McIver[3], S/16107 T McGregor[3], (Act) 12680 J McKay[3], (Act) S/17141 W O'Brian[3], (Act) S/16220 S S Page[3], (Act) S/16162 D Peters[3], (Act) S/16656 G W Robson[3], (Act) S/16428 C Stacey[3] attch. 2 ISS, (Act) S/16466 T Stevenson[3], S/8280 G Thomson[3] attch. 2 MT Coy, S&TC, (Act) S/16679 P E Turnbull[3] & (Act) S/16144 R Walker[3]

Lance Corporals/Privates: ~ 3/7391 J Allison[3], 203791 T A Arthur[3], S/8550 T J Ashworth[4] attch. 12 MT Coy S&TC, S/16316 A Austin[3], S/16907 F Bacon[3], S/16612 R Barr[3], S/16358 A Bennett[3], S/20121 P Black[3], 241332 A Boddy[3], S/16356

T Bowling[3], S/16062 D Brisbane[3], S/20111 A Brown[3], S/20104 E R Brown[3], 241765 G H Brown[3], (Originally 5th Bn), S/16364 H Brown[3], S/17114 J Brown[3], S/20125 J Brown[3], S/18684 P Brown[3], S/16245 R Brown[3], S/16218 A B Bruce[3], S/16271 G R Bruce[3], 241860 D Mc L Buchanan[3], (Originally 5th Bn), S/16374 J Callaghan[3], S/16261 J Cassidy[3], 34190 J Chaplin[3], S/16262 J Cheetham[3], 3/7413 C Conaghan[3], 12658 G H Cox[3], S/16248 R W M Craigie[3], S/18707 J Cull[3], S/16234 T S Cunningham[3], S/16633 M Darcy[3], S/16319 J Darroch[3], S/16535 D Davidson[3], S/16513 J Davidson[3], 3/7426 W Dawson[3], S/16859 G Dempsey[3], S/16338 G Dempster[3], S/16758 A Digweed[3], 200084 J Donald[3] attch. 25 CFA, (Originally 4th Bn), S/20166 H Drummond[3], 12629 W Drummond[3], 16129 D Drysdale[3], S/5785 A Duke[3], 16434 D Dunn[3] attch. IGH, Bannu, S/18643 J Flett[3], S/16940 M Gallacher[3], S/16621 G A S Gibson[3], S/16926 A Gordon[3], 202184 R Gordon[3], S/20902 A Greenhough[3] attch. 31 CFA, S/16748 F Haggas[3] attch. 1 DLI, S/18709 G Hanley[3], S/16914 W Hardell[3], S/19050 D Harper[3], S/16659 J Hay[3], S/16408 F Hendry[3], S/16191 L Hill[3], S/16251 J Hillis[3], S/20102 J Holloway[3], 3/7440 A Hunter[3], 12645 H Irvine[3] attch. S&TC, S/16511 G N Johnson[3], S/16435 G Johnston[3], S/16097 J Keown[3] attch. 2 SS, 291588 J Knight[3], (Originally 7th Bn), S/20103 R Lang[3], 2413(5)60 S Langley[3], (Originally 5th Bn), S/16316 A Lind[3], 240022 W Lunan[3], (Originally 5th Bn), S/16457 W G Mair[3], S/16458 W G Mair[3], S/16757 A Major[3], 290746 W Mayes[3], (Originally 7th Bn), S/16421 J McBride[3], S/16525 M McCluskey[3], S/16675 J McCormack[3], S/16209 J McFee[3], 203797 H McGill[3], (Originally 4th Bn), 12694 J McIntosh[3] attch. S&TC, 16249 J McIntyre[3] attch. 2/4 Border, S/16487 K McKenzie[3], S/16556 M McKune[3], 3/7398 P McLeod[3], S/16670 J McMillan[3], 16693 J McNeil[3], S/17122 T McQueen[3], S/16486 W Mercer[3], S/16554 A Millar[3], S/16101 A Millar[3], S/16371 J Millar[3], 29398 W T Milne[3], S/16558 T Mitchell[3], S/16765 R Morrison[3], 241292 J Morton[3], (Originally 5th Bn), S/15301 D S Napier[3], S/16549 A Nicholson[3], S/16363 W Oliver[3], S/18711 O'Neill[3], S/16317 G T Paton[3], 202126 J D Porter[3], S/19366 C Rae[3], S/16643 W Rennie[3], S/16592 R P Richardson[3] attch. HQ, 2 Div., S/16531 J G Rodger[3], S/19028 M Rourke[3], S/16584 A Scott[3], S/16736 O H Seagrave[3] attch. 9 BSS, RAMC, S/19351 C Shepherd[3], S/16183 T Shields[3], S/16609 J Smeaton[3], S/17120 R W Smith[3], S/16709 W Smith[3], S/23380 A Standen[3], 203791 J Stansfield[3], S/20045 G F J Steckham[3], S/19029 A W Stevens[3], 23728 J Stevenson[3] attch. 1/25 London, S/20108 C G Stewart[3], 12641 D Stoddart[3], 23709 D C Strachan[3], 241733 J Sugrue[3], (Originally 5th Bn), S/16628 G Sutherland[3] attch. 2 MT Coy, S&TC, S/16058 W Syme[3], S/20037 R J Symonds[3], S/16890 W E Tansley[3], 12701 G Taylor[3] attch. 2/6 Sussex, S/16949 G I Thomas[3] attch. 59 DPC, S/16398 D Thompson[3], S/16365 J Thompson[3], 266764 J Thompson[3], S/20114 W J Thompson[3], S/18159 H Wadsworth[3], S/16289 T Waldie[3], S/16208 J H Wallace[4] attch. 71 PMC, S/16983 J W Wallis[3] attch. HQ, 2 Div., S/16653 A Weir[3], S/20047 T Wellman[3], S/16734 A Will[3], S/16620 S Wilson[3] & 3/7394 R Wylie[3]

~ 1st Bn, The Queen's Own Cameron Highlanders ~

Note a. *Roll of all personnel identified as eligible.*
Note b. *United Kingdom August 1914. France & Flanders August 1914 forward. India September 1919 until 1924.*
Note c. *Medals named in impressed capitals: 'CAMERONS'.*

Single Clasp	No. Identified	Rarity
Afghanistan N.W.F. 1919[3]	4	Of the Utmost Rarity
Mahsud 1919–20[5]	0	None Identified
Waziristan 1919–21[4]	6	Of the Utmost Rarity
Waziristan 1921–24[6]	18	Extremely Rare

Lieutenants: ~ C M Barber[6] attch. HQ, 21 Bde., Serarogha, J C Farquharson[3] attch. 2/4 Border & W D Sladen[3] attch. 2/6 Sussex

Quartermaster Sergeants/Sergeants: ~ (Act) 2922479 A Boam[6] attch. 12 CFA

Lance Sergeants/Corporals: ~ 2922680 J K Murphy[6] attch. 'G' DSC & 2921145 R Stevenson[3] attch. DSC

Lance Corporals/Privates: ~ 2922908 J Bell[6] attch. 10 IGH, Bannu, 2923335 R Bridges[6] attch. 10 IGH, Bannu, 2923370 D Cossar[6] attch. 17 IGH, Razmak, 394816 A Crocker[6] attch. 10 IGH, Bannu, 2921999 J M Easton[6] attch. 17 IGH, Razmak, 2921815 J Ferguson[6] attch. ITD, DIK, 2921119 J Forrest[6] attch. HQ, 52 Wing RAF, DIK, 2922506 D L Grant[6] attch. 'G' DSC, 2921810 E Grant[6] attch. 'G' DSC, 2922617 J Grant[4] attch. HQ, WFF, 2922679 H J Hunt[4] attch. Tochi Col, 2921659 J Hutton[6] attch. ITD, DIK, 2921848 G McIntyre[6] attch. ITD, DIK, 2923030 J McKeown[4] attch. 12 thence 64 CFA, 2921958 J McKenzie[6] attch. ITD, DIK, (2922096) 34677 M McPhee[3] attch. 285 Coy, MGC, 2923400 W O'Neil[6] attch. 'G' DSC, (34346) 2922703 R Robertson[4] attch. IGH Tank, 2921880 E S Stewart[6] attch. 'C' DSC, 33386 P Strachan[4] attch. 19 BSS, 2921463 C Watson[6] attch. 'G' DSC & 2921797 J W Whitson[4] attch. 12 thence 64 CFA

~ 2ⁿᵈ Bn, The Royal Irish Rifles ~

Note a.   *Roll of all personnel identified as eligible.*
Note b.   *United Kingdom August 1914. France & Flanders August 1914 forward. Iraq October 1919, Egypt May 1921 thence India December 1923.*
Note c.   *Following the establishment of the Irish Free State in 1922, the title of the regiment changed to The Royal Ulster Rifles. (See Royal Ulster Rifles below).*
Note d.   *Medals named in impressed capitals > 'R. IR. RIF.'*

Single Clasp	No. Identified	Rarity
Afghanistan N.W.F. 1919[3]	1	According to the roll as seen, can be considered Unique
Mahsud 1919–20[5]	0	None Identified
Waziristan 1919–21[4]	0	None Identified
Waziristan 1921–24[6]	0	None Identified

Lieutenants: ~ W J Irwin[3] attch. 2 King's

~ 3ʳᵈ (Reserve) Bn, The Royal Irish Rifles ~

Note a.   *Roll of all personnel identified as eligible.*
Note b.   *United Kingdom August 1914 throughout Great War period providing reinforcement drafts.*
Note c.   *Medals named in impressed capitals: 'R. IR. RIF.'*

Single Clasp	No. Identified	Rarity
Afghanistan N.W.F. 1919[3]	1	According to the roll as seen, can be considered Unique
Mahsud 1919–20[5]	0	None Identified
Waziristan 1919–21[4]	0	None Identified
Waziristan 1921–24[6]	0	None Identified

Lieutenants: ~ H J L Stewart[3] attch. 1 DWR

~ 4ᵗʰ (Extra Reserve) Bn, The Royal Irish Rifles ~

Note a.   *Roll of all personnel identified as eligible.*
Note b.   *United Kingdom August 1914 throughout Great War period providing reinforcement drafts.*
Note c.   *Medals named in impressed capitals: 'R. IR. RIF.'*

Single Clasp	No. Identified	Rarity
Afghanistan N.W.F. 1919[3]	1	According to the roll as seen, can be considered Unique
Mahsud 1919–20[5]	0	None Identified
Waziristan 1919–21[4]	0	None Identified
Waziristan 1921–24[6]	0	None Identified

Captains: ~ T Thompson[3] attch. MGC

~ 1ˢᵗ Garrison Bn, The Royal Irish Rifles ~

Note a.   *Roll of all personnel identified as eligible.*
Note b.   *Formed November 1915. India February 1916 forward.*
Note c.   *Medals named in impressed capitals: 'R. IR. RIF.'*

Single Clasp	No. Identified	Rarity
Afghanistan N.WF 1919[3]	2	Of the Utmost Rarity
Mahsud 1919–20[5]	0	None Identified
Waziristan 1919–21[4]	0	None Identified
Waziristan 1921–24[6]	0	None Identified

Captains: ~ E O S Allen[3] attch. 17 SSB
Quartermaster Sergeants/Sergeants: ~ G821 M Reilly[3] attch. MAD

~ Unidentified Service Bn, The Royal Irish Rifles ~

Note a.   *Roll of all personnel identified as eligible.*
Note b.   *Medals named in impressed capitals: 'R. IR. RIF.'*

Single Clasp	No. Identified	Rarity
Afghanistan N.W.F. 1919[3]	2	Of the Utmost Rarity
Mahsud 1919–20[5]	0	None Identified
Waziristan 1919–21[4]	0	None Identified
Waziristan 1921–24[6]	0	None Identified

Lieutenants: ~ R W Kirkwood[3] attch. 1/1 Kent & F R White[3] attch. 2/4 Border

~ 2ⁿᵈ Bn, The Royal Ulster Rifles ~
(Formed From The Royal Irish Rifles In 1922 Upon The Establishment of The Irish Free State)

Note a.   *Roll of all personnel identified as eligible.*
Note b.   *Battalion in Egypt upon formation from 2ⁿᵈ Battalion, The Royal Irish Rifles thence to India December 1923.*
Note c.   *Medals named in impressed capitals: 'R.U.R.'*

Single Clasp	No. Identified	Rarity
Afghanistan N.W.F. 1919[3]	0	None Identified
Mahsud 1919–20[5]	0	None Identified
Waziristan 1919–21[4]	0	None Identified
Waziristan 1921–24[6]	0	None Identified
Combination Clasps	**No. Identified**	**Rarity**
Mahsud 1919–20[5] Waziristan 1919–21[4]	1	According to the roll as seen, can be considered Unique

Captains: ~ J S Steele[4&5]

~ 2nd Bn, Princess Victoria's (Royal Irish Fusiliers) ~

Note a.   *Roll of all personnel identified as eligible.*
Note b.   *India August 1914. France & Flanders December 1914, Salonika November 1915, Egypt September 1917, thence Palestine. Egypt from November 1918 forward to amalgamation with 1st Battalion in 1922 following reduction in the Irish establishment upon formation of the Irish Free State.*
Note c.   *Title changed to The Royal Irish Fusiliers (Princess Victoria's) in 1920.*
Note d.   *Medals named in impressed capitals: 'R. IR. FUS.'*

Single Clasp	No. Identified	Rarity
Afghanistan N.W.F. 1919[3]	2	**Of the Utmost Rarity**
Mahsud 1919–20[5]	0	**None Identified**
Waziristan 1919–21[4]	0	**None Identified**
Waziristan 1921–24[6]	1	**According to the roll as seen, can be considered Unique**

Lieutenants: ~ J L Kinnaird[3] attch. 287 Coy, MGC & J E Murphy[3] attch. 263 Coy, MGC
Lance Corporals/Fusiliers: ~ 7040382 J Kearns[6] attch. 'G' DSC

~ 1st Bn, The Connaught Rangers ~

Note a.   *Roll of all personnel identified as eligible.*
Note b.   *India August 1914. France & Flanders September 1914. 1st and 2nd Battalions amalgamated December 1914. January 1916 Mesopotamia, Egypt April 1918, thence Palestine. India November 1919 to disbandment in 1922 upon formation of the Irish Free State.*
Note c.   *Medals named in impressed capitals: 'CONN. RANG.'*

Single Clasp	No. Identified	Rarity
Afghanistan N.W.F. 1919[3]	2	**Of the Utmost Rarity**
Mahsud 1919–20[5]	0	**None Identified**
Waziristan 1919–21[4]	0	**None Identified**
Waziristan 1921–24[6]	1	**According to the roll as seen, can be considered Unique**

Lieutenant Colonels: ~ (Temp) W N S Alexander[3] attch. 2 Som LI
Major: ~ (QM) J T Gorman[6]
Lieutenants: ~ J T Cronin[3] attch. IASC

~ 1st Bn, Princess Louise's (Argyll & Sutherland Highlanders) ~

Note a.   *Roll of all personnel identified as eligible.*
Note b.   *India August 1914. France & Flanders December 1914, Salonika December 1915, Bulgaria September 1918 forward. Turkey December 1918, India November 1919 to December 1923 thence Egypt.*
Note c.   *Title changed to The Argyll and Sutherland Highlanders (Princess Louise's) in 1920.*
Note d.   *Medals named in impressed capitals: 'A.&S.H.'*

Single Clasp	No. Identified	Rarity
Afghanistan N.W.F. 1919[3]	0	**None Identified**
Mahsud 1919–20[5]	0	**None Identified**
Waziristan 1919–21[4]	1	**According to the roll as seen, can be considered Unique**
Waziristan 1921–24[6]	0	**None Identified**
Combination Clasps	**No. Identified**	**Rarity**
Mahsud 1919–20[5] Waziristan 1919–21[4]	1	**According to the roll as seen, can be considered Unique**

Waziristan 1921–24[6] Burma 1930–32[10]	1	According to the roll as seen, can be considered Unique
Waziristan 1921–24[6] North West Frontier 1935[12]	1	According to the roll as seen, can be considered Unique

Majors: ~ (Bvt) W G Campbell[6&10] Bde. Maj. 9 & 21 Bde.(s)
Lieutenants: ~ P Dean[4] attch. MGC
Lance Sergeants/Corporals: ~ 8167 T Brand[4&5] attch. HQ 67 Bde. Derajat Col at Taudi China & MWS, DIK
Lance Corporals/Privates: ~ 31237 (2967541) H Wilson[6&12(Cpl. R Sigs)] attch. 'B' Corps Sigs

~ 2nd Bn, Princess Louise's (Argyll & Sutherland Highlanders) ~

Note a.   *Roll of all personnel identified as eligible.*
Note b.   *United Kingdom August 1914. France & Flanders August 1914 forward. Ireland September 1920 to 1922.*
Note c.   *Medals named in impressed capitals: 'A.&S.H.'*

Single Clasp	No. Identified	Rarity
Afghanistan N.W.F. 1919[3]	0	None Identified
Mahsud 1919–20[5]	0	None Identified
Waziristan 1919–21[4]	1	According to the roll as seen, can be considered Unique
Waziristan 1921–24[6]	0	

Majors: ~ A W R Sprot[4] attch. 55 Coke's Rifles, IA

~ ?/5th (Renfrewshire) Bn, Princess Louise's (Argyll & Sutherland Highlanders), Territorial Force ~

Note a.   *Roll of all personnel identified as eligible.*
Note b.   *Medals named in impressed capitals: 'A.&S.H.'*

Single Clasp	No. Identified	Rarity
Afghanistan N.W.F. 1919[3]	1	According to the roll as seen, can be considered Unique
Mahsud 1919–20[5]	0	None Identified
Waziristan 1919–21[4]	0	None Identified
Waziristan 1921–24[6]	0	None Identified

Lieutenants: ~ M Russell[3] attch. 2/4 Border, (Originally Royal Air Force)

~ ?/6th (Renfrewshire) Bn, Princess Louise's (Argyll & Sutherland Highlanders), Territorial Force ~

Note a.   *Roll of all personnel identified as eligible.*
Note b.   *Medals named in impressed capitals: 'A.&S.H.'*

Single Clasp	No. Identified	Rarity
Afghanistan N.W.F. 1919[3]	1	According to the roll as seen, can be considered Unique
Mahsud 1919–20[5]	0	None Identified
Waziristan 1919–21[4]	0	None Identified
Waziristan 1921–24[6]	0	None Identified

Lieutenants: ~ J C Clyde[3] attch. 1 S Lanc

~ ?/7ᵗʰ Bn, Princess Louise's (Argyll & Sutherland Highlanders), Territorial Force ~

Note a.   *Roll of all personnel identified as eligible.*
Note b.   *Medals named in impressed capitals: 'A.&S.H.'*

Single Clasp	No. Identified	Rarity
Afghanistan N.W.F. 1919[3]	1	According to the roll as seen, can be considered Unique
Mahsud 1919–20[5]	0	None Identified
Waziristan 1919–21[4]	0	None Identified
Waziristan 1921–24[6]	0	None Identified

Lieutenants: ~ C F Gunn[3] attch. 1 DLI

~ ?/8ᵗʰ (Argyllshire) Bn, Princess Louise's (Argyll & Sutherland Highlanders), Territorial Force ~

Note a.   *Roll of all personnel identified as eligible.*
Note b.   *Medals named in impressed capitals: 'A.&S.H.'*

Single Clasp	No. Identified	Rarity
Afghanistan N.W.F. 1919[3]	1	According to the roll as seen, can be considered Unique
Mahsud 1919–20[5]	0	None Identified
Waziristan 1919–21[4]	1	According to the roll as seen, can be considered Unique
Waziristan 1921–24[6]	0	None Identified

Lieutenants: ~ J H Bowden[4] attch. 40 DSC & A A Knapman[3] attch. 2 King's

~ ?/9ᵗʰ (The Dunbartonshire) Bn, Princess Louise's (Argyll & Sutherland Highlanders) ~

Note a.   *Roll of all personnel identified as eligible.*
Note b.   *Medals named in impressed capitals: 'A.&S.H.'*

Single Clasp	No. Identified	Rarity
Afghanistan N.W.F. 1919[3]	1	According to the roll as seen, can be considered Unique
Mahsud 1919–20[5]	0	None Identified
Waziristan 1919–21[4]	0	None Identified
Waziristan 1921–24[6]	0	None Identified

Lieutenants: ~ R C Munro[3] attch. 1 Sussex

~ Unidentified Service Bn, Princess Louise's (Argyll & Sutherland Highlanders) ~

Note a.   *Roll of all personnel identified as eligible.*
Note b.   *Medals named in impressed capitals: 'A.&S.H.'*

Single Clasp	No. Identified	Rarity
Afghanistan N.W.F. 1919[3]	2	Of the Utmost Rarity
Mahsud 1919–20[5]	0	None Identified
Waziristan 1919–21[4]	0	None Identified
Waziristan 1921–24[6]	0	None Identified

Captains: ~ W R Maxwell[3] attch. HQ, 3 Bde.
Lieutenants: ~ E C Melville[3] attch. 1 Sussex

~ 1ˢᵗ Bn, The Prince of Wales's Leinster Regiment (Royal Canadians) ~

Note a.   *Roll of all personnel identified as eligible.*
Note b.   *India August 1914. France & Flanders December 1914, Salonika December 1915, Egypt September 1917 thence Palestine. India November 1919 to April 1922. Disbanded 1922 upon formation of the Irish Free State.*
Note c.   *Battalion qualified as a unit for the clasp 'MALABAR 1921-22'.*
Note d.   *Medals named in impressed capitals: 'LEINS. R.'*

Single Clasp	No. Identified	Rarity
Afghanistan N.W.F. 1919[3]	1	According to the roll as seen, can be considered Unique
Mahsud 1919–20[5]	0	None Identified
Waziristan 1919–21[4]	0	None Identified
Waziristan 1921–24[6]	1	According to the roll as seen, can be considered Unique

Combination Clasps	No. Identified	Rarity
Waziristan 1919–21[4] Waziristan 1921–24[6]	1	According to the roll as seen, can be considered Unique

Captains: ~ V A Haddick[3] attch. 256 Sply Coy, S&TC
Lance Sergeants/Corporals: ~ 7178120 J McKenna[6] attch. 'B' DSC
Lance Corporals/Privates: ~ (7178257) 40013 F Pender[4&6] attch. MWS

~ 2ⁿᵈ Bn, The Prince of Wales's Leinster Regiment (Royal Canadians) ~

Note a.   *Roll of all personnel identified as eligible.*
Note b.   *France & Flanders September 1914 forward. Upper Silesia June 1921 to March 1922. Disbanded 1922 upon formation of the Irish Free State.*
Note c.   *Medals named in impressed capitals: 'LEINS. R.'*

Single Clasp	No. Identified	Rarity
Afghanistan N.W.F. 1919[3]	0	None Identified
Mahsud 1919–20[5]	0	None Identified
Waziristan 1919–21[4]	0	None Identified
Waziristan 1921–24[6]	0	None Identified

Combination Clasps	No. Identified	Rarity
Mahsud 1919–20[5] Waziristan 1919–21[4] Waziristan 1921–24[6]	1	According to the roll as seen, can be considered Unique
Waziristan 1919–21[4] Malabar 1921–22[7] North West Frontier 1930–31[9]	1	According to the roll as seen, can be considered Unique

Majors: ~ L D Daly[4,7&(9 KOYLI)] GSO2, HQ, WFF & (Act) W F Morrogh[4,5&6] attch. 6 MMG Bty, MGC, Kot Kai

~ 1ˢᵗ Bn, The Royal Munster Fusiliers ~

Note a.   *Roll of all personnel identified as eligible.*
Note b.   *India (Burma) August 1914. Egypt February 1915, Mudros April 1915 thence Gallipoli. Mudros and Egypt January 1916, France & Flanders March 1916 forward. Silesia September 1921. Disbanded in 1922 upon formation of the Irish Free State.*
Note c.   *Medals named in impressed capitals: 'R. MUN. FUS'*

Single Clasp	No. Identified	Rarity
Afghanistan N.W.F. 1919[3]	1	According to the roll as seen, can be considered Unique
Mahsud 1919–20[5]	0	None Identified
Waziristan 1919–21[4]	0	None Identified
Waziristan 1921–24[6]	0	None Identified

Lieutenants: ~ I H Beattie[3] attch. 1/4 QORWK

~ 3ʳᵈ (Reserve) Bn, The Royal Munster Fusiliers ~

Note a.   *Roll of all personnel identified as eligible.*
Note b.   *United Kingdom August 1914 throughout Great War period providing reinforcement drafts.*
Note c.   *Medals named in impressed capitals: 'R. MUN. FUS'*

Single Clasp	No. Identified	Rarity
Afghanistan N.W.F. 1919[3]	1	According to the roll as seen, can be considered Unique
Mahsud 1919–20[5]	0	None Identified
Waziristan 1919–21[4]	0	None Identified
Waziristan 1921–24[6]	0	None Identified

Lieutenants: ~ J Geraghty[3] attch. 1 DLI

~ 2ⁿᵈ Bn, The Royal Dublin Fusiliers ~

Note a.   *Roll of all personnel identified as eligible.*
Note b.   *India August 1914. Egypt March 1915, Mudros and Gallipoli April 1915, Mudros and Egypt January 1916, France & Flanders March 1916 forward. Army of the Black Sea December 1919 thence Turkey. India December 1920 until disbandment in 1922 upon formation of the Irish Free State.*
Note c.   *Medals named in impressed capitals: 'R. D. FUS.'*

Single Clasp	No. Identified	Rarity
Afghanistan N.W.F. 1919[3]	0	None Identified
Mahsud 1919–20[5]	0	None Identified
Waziristan 1919–21[4]	1	According to the roll as seen, can be considered Unique
Waziristan 1921–24[6]	1	According to the roll as seen, can be considered Unique
Combination Clasps	**No. Identified**	**Rarity**
Waziristan 1919–21[4] Waziristan 1921–24[6]	1	According to the roll as seen, can be considered Unique

Lieutenants: ~ C Matson[4&6] attch. 6 MMG Bty, MGC, Kot Kai
Lance Corporals/Private /Fusiliers: ~ 7076033 P Cunningham[6] attch. IOD & 7076152 P Keough[4] attch. RTE, WFF

~ 6th (Service) Bn, The Royal Dublin Fusiliers ~

Note a.   Roll of all personnel identified as eligible.
Note b.   Formed August 1914. Gallipoli August 1915, Salonika October 1915, Egypt September 1917, Palestine January 1918, France & Flanders July 1918 forward.
Note c.   Disbanded in 1922 upon formation of Irish Free State.
Note d.   Medals named in impressed capitals: 'R. D. FUS.'

Single Clasp	No. Identified	Rarity
Afghanistan N.W.F. 1919[3]	10	Of the Utmost Rarity
Mahsud 1919–20[5]	0	None Identified
Waziristan 1919–21[4]	0	None Identified
Waziristan 1921–24[6]	0	None Identified

Lieutenants: ~ J G Dick[3] attch. RE, E J O'Donoghue[3] attch. 2/6 Sussex, E H Hare[3] attch. 1 Yorkshire, M J Keeshan[3] & R H Magill[3]
Lance Corporals/Privates/Fusiliers: ~ 44035 G Allsopp[3], 707714 F Cousins[3], 9689 D Rice[3] attch. ISC, 7077125 B J Thomas[3] & 5038882 L Tompkinson[3]

~ 1st Bn, The Rifle Brigade (The Prince Consort's Own) ~

Note a.   Roll of all personnel identified as eligible.
Note b.   United Kingdom August 1914. France & Flanders August 1914 forward. Iraq October 1919 to January 1923 thence India forward.
Note c.   Medals named in impressed capitals: 'RIF. BRIG.'

Single Clasp	No. Identified	Rarity
Afghanistan N.W.F. 1919[3]	2	Of the Utmost Rarity
Mahsud 1919–20[5]	0	None Identified
Waziristan 1919–21[4]	0	None Identified
Waziristan 1921–24[6]	6	Of the Utmost Rarity
Combination Clasps	No. Identified	Rarity
Waziristan 1919–21[4] Waziristan 1921–24[6]	2	Of the Utmost Rarity

Lieutenant Colonels: ~ W V L Prescott-Westcar[3] attch. 204 Coy, MGC
Lieutenants: ~ F E A Fulford[6] attch. HQ, 5 Bde. & A W Mead[3]
Quartermaster Sergeants/Sergeants: ~ (Act) 6905499 W Burrows[6] attch. HQ, Waz Dist, DIK & 6906176 H Doman[6] attch. 'B' DSC
Lance Corporals/Privates/Riflemen: ~ 6906530 E E Bernard[6] attch. 'F' DSC, 6907550 W Bolshaw[4&6] attch. 'F' DSC, 6907521 W Hands[4&6] attch. 'F' DSC, 6907389 R Prince[6] attch. 'B' DSC & 6907404 W Rodgers[6] attch. 'B' DSC

~ 4th Bn, The Rifle Brigade (The Prince Consort's Own) ~

Note a.   Roll of all personnel identified as eligible.
Note b.   India August 1914. France & Flanders December 1914, Salonika December 1915 forward. December 1918 Turkey, India November 1919 to November 1921.
Note c.   Medals named in impressed capitals > 'RIF. BRIG.'

Single Clasp	No. Identified	Rarity
Afghanistan N.W.F. 1919[3]	5	Of the Utmost Rarity
Mahsud 1919–20[5]	0	None Identified

Waziristan 1919– 21[4]	9	Of the Utmost Rarity
Waziristan 1921– 24[6]	0	None Identified

Combination Clasps	No. Identified	Rarity
Afghanistan N.W.F. 1919[3] Waziristan 1919–21[4]	2	Of the Utmost Rarity
Waziristan 1919–21[4] Waziristan 1921–24[6]	1	According to the roll as seen, can be considered Unique

Captains: ~ R D Baird[4] Staff, Wana Col & C Saunders[3] Staff

Quartermaster Sergeants/Sergeants: ~ 6905945 G F Dawson[4] attch. 2 Norfolk, 9483 A Scutcher[3] attch. 1 IOC, Quetta & 3098 C Thompson[3&4] attch. ITD, Kalabagh

Lance Sergeants/Corporals: ~ 6905868 W H F Minter[4] attch. 2 Norfolk & 39303 A Young[4] Staff, Wana Col Mari Indus and Tank

Lance Corporals/Privates/Riflemen: ~ 605 R Brown[3] attch. 2 Som LI, 6906342 W E Cheesley[4] attch. HQ, ZF, 6905140 W Edge[4] attch. HQ, WFF, 7814910 F C Forrester[4&6(MGC)], 6907311 G P Gilbert[4] attch. 1 BGH Tank, 6907491 H G Green[4] attch. 1 BGH, Tank, 6907359 A L Oger[4] attch. 53 FA, 4020 H T Smith[3] attch. ISC, 3098 C Thompson[3&4] attch. ITD, Kalabagh & 9606 A W Woodhouse[3] attch. ITD

~ 18th (London) Bn, The Rifle Brigade (The Prince Consort's Own), Territorial Force ~

Note a.   *Roll of all personnel identified as eligible.*

Note b.   *Formed November 1915 from existing Supernumerary Territorial Force Companies. India 1916 forward including tour in Burma.*

Note c.   *Medals named in impressed capitals: 'RIF. BRIG.'*

Single Clasp	No. Identified	Rarity
Afghanistan N.W.F. 1919[3]	3	Of the Utmost Rarity
Mahsud 1919–20[5]	0	None Identified
Waziristan 1919–21[4]	0	None Identified
Waziristan 1921–24[6]	0	None Identified

Quartermaster Sergeants/Sergeants: ~ (Act) 205442 F Hibbert[3] attch. S&TC, East Persian LofC & 200247 J H Tyler[3] attch. IOD, Tank

Lance Corporals/Private /Riflemen: ~ 200204 A Seabrook[3] attch. 2 MT Coy, S&TC

~ 23rd (North Western) Bn, The Rifle Brigade (The Prince Consort's Own), Territorial Force ~

Note a.   *Roll of all personnel identified as eligible.*

Note b.   *Formed November 1915 from existing Supernumerary Territorial Force Companies. India 1916 forward.*

Note c.   *Medals named in impressed capitals: 'RIF. BRIG.'*

Single Clasp	No. Identified	Rarity
Afghanistan N.W.F. 1919[3]	5	Of the Utmost Rarity
Mahsud 1919–20[5]	0	None Identified
Waziristan 1919–21[4]	0	None Identified
Waziristan 1921–24[6]	0	None Identified

Quartermaster Sergeants/Sergeants: ~ (Act) 212471 W T Cooper[3] attch. 694 MT Coy, RASC

Lance Sergeants/Corporals: ~ 210807 W A Collett[3]

Lance Corporals/Privates/Riflemen: ~ 212152 E Gardner[3], 212473 R J Martin[3] attch. Ord Dept Stores & 210787 P Stainton[3] attch. HQ RE, NWFF

~ 24th (Home Counties) Bn, The Rifle Brigade (The Prince Consort's Own), Territorial Force ~

Note a.   *Roll of all personnel identified as eligible.*
Note b.   *Formed November 1915 from existing Supernumerary Territorial Force Companies. India 1916 forward.*
Note c.   *Medals named in impressed capitals: 'RIF. BRIG.'*

Single Clasp	No. Identified	Rarity
Afghanistan N.W.F. 1919[3]	4	Of the Utmost Rarity
Mahsud 1919–20[5]	0	None Identified
Waziristan 1919–21[4]	1	According to the roll as seen, can be considered Unique
Waziristan 1921–24[6]	0	None Identified

Quartermaster Sergeant/Sergeants: ~ (Act) 206657 E G Markwick[4] attch. 12 Div. Sply Coy, S&TC, WFF
Lance Corporals/Privates/Riflemen: ~ 209690 C Daniels[3], 206345 W C Smithers[3], 211271 G Walker[3] & 206720 H C Young[3] attch. 2 MT Coy, S&TC

~ Honourable Artillery Company (Infantry) ~

Note a.   *Roll of all personnel identified as eligible.*
Note b.   *Medals named in impressed capitals: 'H.A.C. – INF.'*

Single Clasp	No. Identified	Rarity
Afghanistan N.W.F. 1919[3]	7	Of the Utmost Rarity
Mahsud 1919–20[5]	0	None Identified
Waziristan 1919–21[4]	0	None Identified
Waziristan 1921–24[6]	0	None Identified

Captains: ~ J D Canning[3] attch. 1 MMG Bty, MGC
Lieutenants: ~ H B Belder[3] attch. 2 Som LI, C J Newland[3] attch. 2 King's, F W Pillar[3] attch. 2 Som LI, H C Rowe[3] attch. 2 Som LI, R H L Scott[3] attch. 2 Som LI & R Thorburn[3] attch. 2 Som LI

~ 1/2nd Bn, The Monmouthshire Regiment ~

Note a.   *Roll of all personnel identified as eligible.*
Note b.   *United Kingdom August 1914. France & Flanders November 1914 forward.*
Note c.   *Medals named in impressed capitals: 'MONMOUTH. R.'*

Single Clasp	No. Identified	Rarity
Afghanistan N.W.F. 1919[3]	0	None Identified
Mahsud 1919–20[5]	0	None Identified
Waziristan 1919–21[4]	1	According to the roll as seen, can be considered Unique
Waziristan 1921–24[6]	0	None Identified

Lieutenants: ~ F N Dayson[4]

~ 1st Bn, The Cambridgeshire Regiment ~

Note a.   *Roll of all personnel identified as eligible.*
Note b.   *United Kingdom August 1914. France & Flanders February 1915 forward.*
Note c.   *Medals named in impressed capitals: 'CAMB. R.'*

Single Clasp	No. Identified	Rarity
Afghanistan N.W.F. 1919[3]	2	Of the Utmost Rarity
Mahsud 1919–20[5]	0	None Identified
Waziristan 1919–21[4]	0	None Identified
Waziristan 1921–24[6]	0	None Identified

Captains: ~ (QM) W W Carter[3] attch. 1/4 QORWK
Lieutenants: ~ A Diplock[3] attch. 2 King's

~ 2nd (City Of London) Bn (Royal Fusiliers), The London Regiment ~

Note a.   *Roll of all personnel identified as eligible.*
Note b.   *Medals named in impressed capitals: '2 - LOND. R.'*

Single Clasp	No. Identified	Rarity
Afghanistan N.W.F. 1919[3]	1	According to the roll as seen, can be considered Unique
Mahsud 1919–20[5]	0	None Identified
Waziristan 1919–21[4]	0	None Identified
Waziristan 1921–24[6]	0	None Identified

Captains: ~ W H Sendall[3] attch. 2/96 Berar Inf, IA

~ 4th (City Of London) Bn (Royal Fusiliers), The London Regiment ~

Note a.   *Roll of all personnel identified as eligible.*
Note b.   *Medals named in impressed capitals: '4 - LOND. R.'*

Single Clasp	No. Identified	Rarity
Afghanistan N.W.F. 1919[3]	0	None Identified
Mahsud 1919–20[5]	0	None Identified
Waziristan 1919–21[4]	0	None Identified
Waziristan 1921–24[6]	0	None Identified
Combination Clasps	No. Identified	Rarity
Mahsud 1919–20[5] Waziristan 1919–21[4]	1	According to the roll as seen, can be considered Unique

Majors: ~ E H Stillwell[4&5] attch. S&TC

~ 5th (City Of London) Bn (London Rifle Brigade), The London Regiment ~

Note a.   Roll of all personnel identified as eligible.
Note b.   Medals named in impressed capitals: '5 - LOND. R.'

Single Clasp	No. Identified	Rarity
Afghanistan N.W.F. 1919[3]	2	Of the Utmost Rarity
Mahsud 1919–20[5]	0	None Identified
Waziristan 1919–21[4]	0	None Identified
Waziristan 1921–24[6]	0	None Identified

Captains: ~ F D Charles[3] attch. 1 DLI & G C Kitching[3] attch. 1/1 Kent

~ 7th (City Of London) Bn, The London Regiment ~

Note a.   Roll of all personnel identified as eligible.
Note b.   Medals named in impressed capitals: '7 - LOND. R.'

Single Clasp	No. Identified	Rarity
Afghanistan N.W.F. 1919[3]	1	According to the roll as seen, can be considered Unique
Mahsud 1919–20[5]	0	None Identified
Waziristan 1919–21[4]	0	None Identified
Waziristan 1921–24[6]	0	None Identified

Lieutenants: ~ S J King[3] attch. 1/25 London

~ 8th (City Of London) (Post Office Rifles) Bn, The London Regiment ~

Note a.   Roll of all personnel identified eligible.
Note b.   Medals named in impressed capitals: '8 - LOND. R.'

Single Clasp	No. Identified	Rarity
Afghanistan N.W.F. 1919[3]	1	According to the roll as seen, can be considered Unique
Mahsud 1919–20[5]	0	None Identified
Waziristan 1919–21[4]	0	None Identified
Waziristan 1921–24[6]	0	None Identified

Lieutenant: ~ R P Alsop[3] attch. 1/25 London

~ 9th (County Of London) Bn (Queen Victoria's Rifles), The London Regiment ~

Note a.   Roll of all personnel identified as eligible.
Note b.   Medals named in impressed capitals: '9 - LOND. R.'

Single Clasp	No. Identified	Rarity
Afghanistan N.W.F. 1919[3]	1	According to the roll as seen, can be considered Unique
Mahsud 1919–20[5]	0	None Identified
Waziristan 1919–21[4]	0	None Identified
Waziristan 1921–24[6]	0	None Identified

Majors: ~ A Gordon[3] attch. Staff

~ 11th (County Of London) Bn (Finsbury Rifles), The London Regiment ~

Note a.   *Roll of all personnel identified as eligible.*
Note b.   *Medals named in impressed capitals: '11 - LOND. R.'*

Single Clasp	No. Identified	Rarity
Afghanistan N.W.F. 1919[3]	1	According to the roll as seen, can be considered Unique
Mahsud 1919–20[5]	0	None Identified
Waziristan 1919–21[4]	0	None Identified
Waziristan 1921–24[6]	0	None Identified

Lieutenants: ~ W W Gregg[3]

~ 14th (County Of London) Bn (London Scottish), The London Regiment ~

Note a.   *Roll of all personnel identified as eligible.*
Note b.   *Medals named in impressed capitals: '14 - LOND. R.'*

Single Clasp	No. Identified	Rarity
Afghanistan N.W.F. 1919[3]	1	According to the roll as seen, can be considered Unique
Mahsud 1919–20[5]	0	None Identified
Waziristan 1919–21[4]	0	None Identified
Waziristan 1921–24[6]	0	None Identified

Majors: ~ (Act) J C Murley[3] attch. 286 Coy, MGC

~ 15th (County Of London) Bn (Prince Of Wales Own Civil Service Rifles), The London Regiment ~

Note a.   *Roll of all personnel identified as eligible.*
Note b.   *Medals named in impressed capitals: '15 - LOND. R.'*

Single Clasp	No. Identified	Rarity
Afghanistan N.W.F. 1919[3]	3	Of the Utmost Rarity
Mahsud 1919–20[5]	0	None Identified
Waziristan 1919–21[4]	0	None Identified
Waziristan 1921–24[6]	0	None Identified

Captains: ~ A V James[3] attch. 2 King's
Lieutenants: ~ R M Briggs[3] attch. 1 DLI & S E Dabbs[3] attch. 2 King's

~ 16th (County Of London) Bn (Queen's Westminster Rifles), The London Regiment ~

Note a.   *Roll of all personnel identified as eligible.*
Note b.   *Medals named in impressed capitals: '16 - LOND. R.'*

Single Clasp	No. Identified	Rarity
Afghanistan N.W.F. 1919[3]	2	Of the Utmost Rarity
Mahsud 1919–20[5]	0	None Identified
Waziristan 1919–21[4]	0	None Identified
Waziristan 1921–24[6]	0	None Identified

Lieutenants: ~ E Brimelow[3] attch. 2 King's & G Smith[3] attch. 1/25 London

~ 17th (County Of London) Bn (Poplar & Stepney Rifles), The London Regiment ~

Note a.   *Roll of all personnel identified as eligible.*
Note b.   *Medals named in impressed capitals: '17 - LOND. R.'*

Single Clasp	No. Identified	Rarity
Afghanistan N.W.F. 1919[3]	2	Of the Utmost Rarity
Mahsud 1919–20[5]	0	None Identified
Waziristan 1919–21[4]	0	None Identified
Waziristan 1921–24[6]	0	None Identified

Lieutenants: ~ A Laithwaite[3] attch. 1 DWR & H H V Phelps[3] attch. 1 S Lanc

~ 19th (County Of London) Bn (St. Pancras), The London Regiment ~

Note a.   *Roll of all personnel identified as eligible.*
Note b.   *Medals named in impressed capitals: '19 - LOND. R.'*

Single Clasp	No. Identified	Rarity
Afghanistan N.W.F. 1919[3]	1	According to the roll as seen, can be considered Unique
Mahsud 1919–20[5]	0	None Identified
Waziristan 1919–21[4]	0	None Identified
Waziristan 1921–24[6]	0	None Identified

Lieutenants: ~ F H Henwood[3] attch. 1/25 London

20th (County Of London) Battalion (Blackheath & Woolwich):

Note a.   *Roll of all personnel identified as eligible.*
Note b.   *Medals named in impressed capitals: '20 - LOND. R.'*

Single Clasp	No. Identified	Rarity
Afghanistan N.W.F. 1919[3]	1	According to the roll as seen, can be considered Unique
Mahsud 1919–20[5]	0	None Identified
Waziristan 1919–21[4]	0	None Identified
Waziristan 1921–24[6]	0	None Identified

Lieutenants: ~ A E Pollard[3] attch. 1/25 London

25th (County Of London) (Cyclist) Battalion:

Note a.   *Roll of all commissioned personnel identified as eligible.*
Note b.   *Non-commissioned and other ranks multi clasp or non-Afghanistan 1919 single clasp.*
Note c.   *United Kingdom August 1914.India February 1916 to October 1919.*
Note d.   *Battle honour 'Third Afghan War 1919'.*
Note e.   *Medals named in impressed capitals: '1-25 LOND. R.'*

Single Clasp	No. Identified	Rarity
Afghanistan N.W.F. 1919[3]	Bn. Strength	Not Rare
Mahsud 1919–20[5]	0	None Identified
Waziristan 1919–21[4]	0	None Identified

Waziristan 1921–24[6]	0	None Identified
Combination Clasps	*No. Identified*	*Rarity*
Afghanistan N.W.F. 1919[3] Waziristan 1919–21[4]	1	According to the roll as seen, can be considered Unique

Majors: ~ W S Stafford[3] & H Swinnerton[3]

Captains: ~ C A Burt[3], C A Francis[3] & C N Paget[3]

Lieutenants: ~ N R C Frith[3], E J Macrostie[3] attch. SW Militia & J Smith[3]

Company Quartermaster Sergeants/Staff Sergeants/Colour Sergeants: ~ (Act) (GS/98346) 740136 S G Parkinson[3&4(R FUS)] attch. 8 MT Coy, S&TC

~ 1/1 Kent Bn, The Kent (Cyclist) Battalion ~

Note a.   *Roll below is for all personnel identified from the roll as 'serving' with 1/1 Kent Battalion and being entitled to the clasp 'AFGHANISTAN N.W.F .1919'. Cross referencing the official medal roll with the appropriate Medal Record Cards suggests a significant churn of personnel between the Kent Cyclist Battalion and the Royal West Kent Regiment during the Great War and immediately thereafter.*

Note b.   *Qualifying while 'cap badged' Kent Cyclist Battalion did not necessarily mean the recipient received a medal named to that unit. Indeed, specimens named 'KENT CYC. BN.' are rare. The majority of specimens are named 'R. W. KENT R.'. This can be very confusing and no doubt, many Kent Cyclist Battalion medals have been wrongly catalogued, in the past, as Royal West Kent Regiment medals. The inclusion of a British War Medal 1914 – 1918 named 'KENT CYC. BN.' in a pair with an India General Service Medal with clasp 'AFGHANISTAN N.W.F. 1919' named 'R. W. KENT R.' cannot be construed as proof the recipient qualified for the India General Service Medal whilst 'cap badged' Kent Cyclist Battalion due to the policy of naming British War Medals to the unit the recipient belonged to when first completing qualification for that award.*

Note c.   *To bring clarity to this situation I have compiled two separate registers below:*

Register One lists those 1/1 Kent Battalion personnel who's Medal Record Card shows they were 'cap badged' Kent Cyclists at the time they qualified for the clasp 'AFGHANISTAN N.W.F. 1919'.

Register Two lists those 1/1 Kent Battalion personnel who's Medal Record Card shows they were 'cap badged' Royal West Kent Regiment at the time they qualified for the clasp 'AFGHANISTAN N.W.F. 1919'.

Note d.   *A third register lists the names of (late) claimants shown on a supplementary roll compiled by the Hounslow (Army) Records Office in 1922. This roll states that the medals issued from it should be named 'KENT CYC. BN.' I list this separately because some of the men contain therein are shown on their Medal Record Card as being 'cap badged' Royal West Kent Regiment at the time they qualified for their medal! These examples are marked with an asterisk thus (*).*

Note e.   *United Kingdom August 1914. India from March 1916 to 1919.*

Single Clasp	No. Identified	Rarity
Afghanistan N.W.F. 1919[3]	Bn. Strength	See Notes Below
Register One	381	Not Rare
Register Two	247	Scarce
Register Three	21	Very Rare
Combination Clasps	*No. Identified*	*Rarity*
Register One Afghanistan N.W.F. 1919[3] North West Frontier 1930–31[9]	1	According to the roll as seen, can be considered Unique
Register Three Afghanistan N.W.F. 1919[3] Waziristan 1919–21[4]	1	According to the roll as seen, can be considered Unique

Register One - Name appears on 1/1 Kent Medal Roll. Medal Record Card shows recipient as being most likely 'cap badged' Kent Cyclist Battalion on qualification.

Lieutenant Colonels: ~ W G Moore[3]

Captains: ~ G L Dunn[3], T A Fuller[3], (Act) J A Harding[3] & R T W Smith[3]

Lieutenants: ~ E A Baillie, N Carlaw[3], F B Hancock[3] Staff, 44 Bde. & F H Hatton[3]

Warrant Officers Class II: ~ (Act) (TF342) 265041 A R Blackburn[3], (Act) (TF16) 265012 E H Burton[3] & (Act) (TF311) 265033 J Salter[3]

Company Quartermaster Sergeants/Staff Sergeants/Colour Sergeants: ~ (Act) (TF693) 265127 F E Jupp[3], 265109 E F J Pettett[3], (TF400) 265048 G H Price[3], (Act) (TF585) 265080 A E Richardson[3] & (Act) (TF391) 265047 F E Seckerson[3]

Quartermaster Sergeants/Sergeants: ~ (TF678) 265118 A A Assiter[3], (Act) (TF133) 268019 R Assiter[3], (Act) (TF1178) 265432 L W Barber[3], (Act) (TF868) 265238 H G Bettridge[3], (Act) (TF706) 265135 A G Brewer[3], 265379 A F Buckingham[3], (Act) (TF1988) 266103 J A Chambers[3], (Act) (TF162)265782 F B Day[3], (Act) (TF1352) 265575 C Easton[3], (Act) (TF1968) 266084 H Elphick[3], (TF741) 265155 E D Gouger[3], (Act) (TF691) 265126 E J Hancock[3], (Act) (TF845) 265222 G Horley[3], (Act) (TF1110) 265392 T A Lewis[3], (Act) (TF1577) 265741 J P Marsh[3], (TF6) 265003 J E Merralls[3], (Act) (TF750) 265161 P H Milner[3], (Act) (TF1424) 265636 H W Nicholson[3], (Act) (TF1398) 265614 F H Pearson[3], (Act) (TF495) 265061 A D Pellatt[3], (Act) (TF800) P265190 A P Pellatt[3], (Act) (TF1209) 265458 W Rodgers[3], (TF532) 265067 H Simmonds[3], (Act) (TF1077) 265362 S Tomei[3], (Act) (TF1607) 265766 A White[3] & (Act) (TF647) 265100 A S Wickens[3]

Lance Sergeants/Corporals: ~ (Act) (TF1940) 266057 P Edge[3], (Act) (TF1642) 265799 W S Halley[3], (Act) (TF1524) 265702 E J Humphrey[3], (Act) (TF2027) 266136 R F Lancaster[3], (Act) (TF1681) 265837 F W Neeves[3], (Act) (TF1813) 265948 G K Pharaoh[3], (Act) (TF651) 265102 H J Rodgers[3], (Act) (TF1164) 265422 G Styles[3], (Act) (TF1366) 265587 F S Styles[3], (Act) (TF1165) 265423 A M Terrell[3], (Act) (TF1761) 265905 F H Underdown[3], (Act) (TF840) 265217 H Vere[3] & (Act) (TF1496) 265683 R J Webb[3]

Lance Corporals/Privates: ~ (TF2150) 266232 F Adams[3], (TF1980) 266096 F Adley[3], 265665 S E Allen[3], (TF1885) 266009 H H Alexander[3], (TF2044) 266149 E J Appleton[3], (TF482) 265058 W E Archer[3], (TF1824) 265958 F G Arnold[3], (TF1700) 265854 H Ash[3], (TF1230) 265476 P A Ashby[3], (TF1565) 265732 A G Aylward[3], (TF1340) 265574 H M Aylward[3], (TF1699) 265853 E Baines[3], (TF1886) 266010 A E Baker[3], 265502 S Baker[3], (TF2354) 266320 A Bangs[3], (TF2016) 266126 H E Bantock[3], (TF1953) 266069 J Barnes[3], (TF1588) 265751 H W Barton[3], (TF1860) 265986 W H Batcup[3], (TF2032) 266140 F J Bateman[3], (TF1775) 265914 W A Bayliss[3], (TF1194) 265446 W J Beeching[3], 266250 A C Beer[3], (TF1928) 266047 W B Beer[3], 266516 C F Benstead[3], (TF1461) 265657 D Blake[3], 266418 E J Boast[3], (TF1217) 265464 L H Bolton[3], (TF1456) 265656 A H Bond[3], (TF1091) 265376 H A Bone[3], (TF1634) 265791 B Booth[3], (TF1093) 265377 E Boswell[3], (TF1214) 265462 V R Boswell[3], (TF2010) 266121 B Botting[3], (TF1025) 268340 A Boulding[3], (TF993) 265323 M Bourne[3], (TF/1066) 265352 W J Bowd[3], (TF895) 265259 H Bramley[3], (TF1918) 266038 F M Bridger[3], (TF1882) 266006 E H Brill[3], (TF1348) 265571 J Brisley[3], (TF1933) 266051 F P Bristow[3], 265827 A H Brocker[3], (TF1779) 265917 F A Brookes[3], (TF1620) 265777 R Brown[3], (TF1429) 265643 W H Brown[3], (TF1660) 265817 A E C Browne[3], (TF1903) 266026 A T Bugg[3], (TF1547) 265719 P T Buley[3], 265935 J A Bullemor[3], (TF1966) 266082 H H Burdett[3], (TF1278) 265520 F G Butcher[3], (TF898) 265261 E W Butler[3], (TF962) 265302 W H Calver[3], (TF1340) 265564 A R Cantle[3], (TF1553) 265724 L E Cassell[3], (TF708) 265136 A J Castle[3], 266503 W F Catton[3], 266014 R G E Chambers[3], (TF1717) 265869 J H Channon[3], (TF1499) 265686 H Chapman[3], (TF2012) 266122 H Chiddick[3], (TF727) 265148 G Chivers[3], (TF728) 265149 W Chivers[3], (TF2085) 266177 G Clapson[3], (TF1896) 266020 H Claridge[3], (TF693) 265257 T J Clark[3], (TF1734) 265885 A F Clarke[3], (TF1989) 266104 A Claydon[3], (TF723) 265145 A Clifton[3], (TF2110) 266200 S W Coates[3], 266294 W H Cockburn[3], (TF2122) 266211 E Coker[3], 266367 R J Collins[3], (TF1402) 265617 J Comber[3], (TF125) 265497 F R Constant[3], (TF1579) 265743 H A Coombs[3], (TF1834) 265965 T Cowell[3], (TF1103) 265385 S Critchlow[3], (TF1814) 265949 P Croucher[3], 265267 F Crowhurst[3], (TF1941) 266058 R E Crump[3], (TF1418) 265631 W G H Crump[3], (TF1978) 266094 C E Culver[3], 266513 R Dale[3], (TF1365) 265586 G W Dane[3], (TF1399) 265615 R H Daniels[3], 265563 H E Daw[3], (TF2001) 266112 T H Dawson[3], 266491 C W Delo[3], (TF2029) 266137 H Denman[3], 266154 N F Denning[3], 265144 E H Dibben[3], (TF1438) 265642 W Digance[3], (TF1032) 265345 L W Dinnage[3], 265315 A C Dorrell[3], (TF1667) 265824 A A Down[3], (TF1623) 265780 F T Drayson[3], (TF1878) 266002 P Durrant[3], (TF1264) 265506 J Easton[3], (TF1004) 265386 W Edmonton[3], (TF1523) 265701 A W Edney[3], (TF1671) 266261 W C Edwards[3], (TF930) 265280 L A Ellis[3], (TF1722) 265874 H Entickna(p)(o)[3], (TF1822) 265956 R S Epps[3], (TF1141) 265406 C H N Evans[3], TF/266727 N J Evenden[3], (TF1469) 265662 E T Fagan[3], (TF1347) 265570 H R Fairbrass[3], (TF1719) 265871 V Fairbrother[3], (TF1536) 265711 S A Farrier[3], (TF1361) 265582 D Faulkener[3], (TF1873) 265998 C H Finn[3], (TF2656) 265714 A V Flood[3], (TF1540) 265714 A V Flood[3], (TF1605) 265764 J E Foreman[3], (TF1575) 265740 E W Fox[3], (TF1894) 266018 A Friend[3], (TF/1442) 265646 T J Fullagar[3], (TF1897) 266021 W J Fuller[3], (TF2353) 266319 R C Galley[3], 266404 E T Gambrill[3], (TF2125) 266213 K J Garbutt[3], (TF1733) 265884 C Gibson[3], (TF1919) 266039 F Gilbert[3], 266421 E Gillett[3], 266037 G H Gillett[3], (TF1083) 265368 A Godden[3], (TF883) 265251 J H Godden[3], (TF1265) 265507 R G Godden[3], (TF1380) 265599 W G Godden[3], 265159 W Goldsmith[3], (TF2360) 266326 M Goldstein[3], (TF1384) 265603 R Goodhew[3], (TF1977) 266093 W C Gosling[3], (TF918) 265 F J Gower[3], (TF1590) 265752 A T Graves[3], (TF804) 265194 R W Griffiths[3], (TF1833) 265964 W O Griffiths[3], (TF1696) 265850 J Haley[3], (TF1181) 265435 J R Hall[3], (TF1180) 265434 R Hall[3], (TF2055) 266158 R Hall[3], (TF1962) 266078 G Hammett[3], 266220 A J Hammond[3], (TF1386) 265605 W C Hardeman[3], (TF1817) 265952 A Harlow[3], (TF1656) 265813 W J Harlow[3], (TF1897) 265757 E A J Harris[3], (TF1848) 265977 F L Harwood[3], (TF1507) 265692 C A Hawkes[3], 265497 A H Heath[3], (TF1671) 265828 C Heaysman[3] 266304 W J Hedgecock[3], (TF1784) 265921 A Hellier[3], (TF1865) (TF1842) 265972 W R Hill[3], 265991 W S Hill[3], (TF1235) 265481 J H Hills[3], (TF1515) 265696 R L Hodges[3], (TF1724) 265876 A G Holden[3], (TF1639) 265796 E C Homersham[3], (TF2155) 266235 A Hone[3], (TF2373) 266339 H A L Howard[3], (TF1341) 265565 K C Howard[3], (TF1621) 265778 F Humphrey[3], (TF830) 265210 R E Hyland[3], 265658 J W Ibbett[3], (TF1943) 266060 H R Jarvis[3], 266387 W Jeffrey[3], (TF1288) 265529 H Jenner[3], (TF1994) 266106 R Johnson[3], (TF1965) 266081 E C Jones[3], 266521 G W Jones[3], (TF887) 265254 W G Jordan[3], 266162 A W Kemp[3], (TF1315) 265548 G H W

Kennett[3], (TF1598) 265758 J F Kenward[3], (TF1148) 265411 H Kettle[3], (TF2016) 266163 A V King[3], (TF1362) 265554 G E J King[3], (TF1465) 265660 T W Kingsford[3], (TF1869) 265994 W F Knott[3], (TF484) 265059 H R Lamplugh[3], (TF1194) 265466 B Langton[3], (TF1275) 265517 H W Large[3], (TF2102) 266192 A J Lashmar[3], (TF799) 265189 G Lawrence[3], (TF1606) 265765 W R Lawrence[3], 266182 G Leach[3], 265983 A E Lemon[3], (TF1688) 265843 W T Levison[3], (TF1581) 265745 G A Lickorish[3], (TF1151) 265414 H G Linkins[3], (TF1951) 266070 F C Lucas[3], (TF1743) 265892 H Luck[3], (TF2388) 266354 E G Luke[3], 265495 S Mantle[3], (TF1765) 265908 W A Marchant[3], (TF1283) 265525 S Marsh[3], 265803 T G Marsh[3], (TF1290) 265531 H G Marshall[3], (TF1212) 265461 C H Matcham[3], (TF1887) 265750 F Matcham[3], (TF2364) 266330 C Mathews[3], (TF2037) 266145 T J Mathews[3], (TF1726) 265878 S J Maxwell[3], (TF1908) 266031 J E May[3], (TF1471) 265664 H Maynard[3], (TF2002) 266113 C A Medhurst[3], (TF1970) 266086 A W Millard[3], (TF1760) 265904 F W Mills[3], (TF2384) 266350 J Mills[3], (TF1666) 265823 R Milton[3], (TF1749) 265896 C Morris[3], (TF2043) 266148 W F Munday[3], (TF2004) 266115 W S N Munn[3], (TF1592) 265753 G W Neeve[3], (TF539) 265069 F E Newman[3], (TF1012) 265333 C Norton[3], (TF1893) 266017 A F Nunn[3], (TF2164) 266241 H N Orrom[3], (TF1560) 265729 A Osborne[3], 266372 W J Osborne[3], (TF1267) 265509 F E Oxley[3], (TF1926) 266045 C Parkin[3], (TF1226) 265472 R Parren[3], (TF802) 265192 S P Parry[3], (TF1452) 265652 P Partridge[3], (TF1619) 265776 P Partick[3], (TF1299) 265537 I G Penfold[3], (TF1729) 265881 S B Perry[3], (TF916) 265273 A E Pickard[3], (TF1391) 265609 W S Pocknell[3], (TF201) 266123 A G Pollard[3], (TF1911) 266033 C Proctor[3], (TF1370) 265590 L V Read[3], (TF2377) 266343 C A Reason[3], (TF1208) 265457 F G V Reeves[3], (TF1486) 265675 E H Renshaw[3], (TF1680) 265836 A Richardson[3], (TF1610) 265769 P E Rootes[3], (TF2366) 266332 A J Rose[3], (TF1999) 266110 A W Rowe[3], (TF2101) 266191 G Russell[3], (TF1529) 265706 P H Russell[3], (TF1279) 265521 V J Russell[3], (TF1866) 265992 S J Sayers[3], (TF899)265262 S Seale[3], (TF1484) 265673 A R Sharp[3], 265344 T Sherrell[3], (TF1772) 265911 R W Simpson[3], (TF1982) 266098 E R Skinner[3], 266409 H W Sladden[3], (TF1163) 265421 A W C Smith[3], (TF1746) 265894 F Smith[3], (TF1987) 266102 F Smith[3], (TF1995) 266107 F Smith[3], (TF2026) 266135 F H Smith[3], (TF779) 265178 G Smith[3], (TF1448) 265648 G H Smith[3], 266539 J D Smith[3], (TF1174) 265428 S Smith[3], (TF1490) 265678 W C Smith[3], (TF1805) 265370 G Spain[3], (TF1425) 265637 W Sparrow[3], (TF1679) 265835 W M Spillane[3], (TF1492) 265679 R Standenn[3], (TF1936) 266054 A C Stephen[3], (TF1644) 265801 H Stevens[3], 265115 S C Stevenson[3], (TF1320) 265550 A Stolton[3], (TF2112) 266202 H A Streater[3], (TF1029) 265343 A Surtees[3], 265957 S E G Swaine[3&9(RAF)], (TF1648) 265805 F Swan[3], (TF1626) 265783 A V Taylor[3], (TF1983) 266099 F Taylor[3], (TF1961) 266077 H J Taylor[3], (TF1256) 265499 W C A Taylor[3], (TF1379) 265598 J Tissington[3], (TF2107) 266197 C Tolhurst[3], (TF1600) 265760 H J Tree[3], (TF1527) 265704 P A C Tuff[3], (TF1963) 266079 E Turner[3], (TF796) 265188 A Unwin[3], (TF1684) 265840 P C Upton[3], (TF1441) 265645 T P Upton[3], (TF1191) 265443 B Varrier[3], (TF772) 265174 G Vaughan[3], (TF1277) 265519 C Wake[3], (TF1311) 265544 F Wanstall[3], (TF1406) 265620 W E Want[3], (TF1405) 265619 A E Ward[3], 265655 H Ward[3], (TF896) 265260 A Ware[3], (TF1622) 265779 F G Ware[3], (TF1566) 265733 F E Waterman[3], (TF1169) 265425 G Webster[3], (TF1292) 265533 F W West[3], (TF1314) 265547 R Wheeler[3], (TF2033) 266141 B C Whitcher[3], (TF942) 265289 F H White[3], (TF1861) 266005 P R White[3], (TF943) 265290 W V White[3], (TF1538) 265713 A E Whitnall[3], (TF1905) 266028 H Whittingstall[3], (TF2142) 266224 E Wickens[3], (TF2143) 266225 J Wickens[3], (TF1927) 266046 T J Wickham[3], (TF2379) 266345 A W Willmott[3], (TF1935) 266053 J H Wilkins[3], (TF1413) 265626 M A Willis[3], (TF1253) 265496 F P Wilson[3], (TF204) 266153 C F Wilson[3], (TF1488) 265677 C T Wilson[3], (TF2109) 266199 J S Wilson[3], (TF1608) 265767 E A Winder[3], (TF1945) 266062 F E Winder[3], (TF2380) 266346 W Wood[3], (TF2108) 266198 F E Woodland[3], 265759 W F Woolgar[3], (TF1857) 265985 G L Wraight[3], (TF1942) 266059 R W Wressell[3], (TF1770) 265910 W H Wright[3], 266381 S E Yeoman[3], (TF265888) F Young[3], 266366 E Youngman[3] & 265117 G A Yule[3]

Register Two - Name appears on 1/1 Kent Medal Roll. Medal Record Card shows recipient as being most likely 'cap badged' Royal West Kent Regiment on qualification.

Major: ~ A J A Oldendorff[3]

Captains: ~ T L Kendrick[3]

Lieutenants: ~ (QM) K D Bain[3], A L C Charman[3], J N le Fleming[3] & D E Sheffield[3]

Warrant Officers Class II: ~ (Act) G/6432 T R Chapman[3], L/4957 H Childs[3], 265013 T H Clifton[3], (Act) 265004 H Gates[3], (Act) 265054 S M Larkin[3] & (Act) 265043 C H Lord[3]

Quartermaster Sergeants/Sergeants: ~ L/13829 C S Atkinson[3], (Act) 265318 A Batchelor[3], (Act) 265350 E P Bird[3], 265018 W K Bushell[3], (Act) 265090 W E Button[3], 265082 W Chamberlain[3], (Act) 265184 E Darrell[3], 268099 C A Gilham[3], (Act) 265735 E A Hodges[3], (Act) 204289 P Lucas[3], (Act) 265942 F Miles[3], (Act) 265265 A T Ollerenshaw[3], 265568 R C Palmer[3], 265278 P Smithers[3], (Act) 265275 H C Thimbleby[3] & (Act) 265045 G H Wyatt[3]

Lance Sergeants/Corporals: ~ (Act) 265186 W E Allard[3], (Act) 265528 S H Allen[3], (Act) 265578 L G Bailey[3], (Act) G/27030 B B Barnadier[3], (Act) 266207 F Bridgeland[3], (Act) 265183 J Catt[3], (Act) 265833 J Chandler[3], L/13836 T Chapman[3], (Act) 265202 A L Fennell[3], (Act) 265613 F A Flint[3], (Act) 265220 J A French[3], (Act) 265157 C Groves[3], (Act) 266179 F J Hancock[3], (Act) 266277 R T Harris[3], (Act) 266176 A C Haywood[3], (Act) 265498 H D Hoare[3], (Act) 265694 P G Hunt[3], (Act) 265098 E G Johnson[3], (Act) 265288 W J Lego[3], 265268 F W Littlechild[3], (Act) 265314 F J MacKie[3], 265319 F M Marsden[3], (Act) 265243 E W Martin[3], (Act) 265927 J H Mordaunt[3], (Act) 265946 C F Morrison[3], (Act) 265240 J W Preston[3], 265978 A W Smith[3], (Act) 265285 W B Smith[3], (Act) 265639 F C Standen[3], (Act) 265601 J A Taylor[3], (Act) 265150 E W Wallis[3], (Act) 265512 A E Willey[3] & (Act) 265112 G Wyborn[3]

Lance Corporals/Privates: ~ G/30306 A T R Addison[3], G/27140 J Allan[3], G/27024 J Mc K Allan[3], G/27044 W Ambrose[3], G/27025 J Anderson[3], 265938 H J Archer[3], G/27042 E Attwell[3], G/27022 F G Attwell[3], L/13830 L H Attwood[3], G/30301 W A Bailey[3], 265800 F Baldock[3], G/27289 R Ballard[3], G/27085 P V Baker[3], G/27026 G Barnes[3], G/27086 F Barraclough[3], L/13833 B Beal[3], L/13831 W Bean[3], G/ 27027 W J Begley[3], G/27034 J Berry[3], L/13863 A Bigg[3], 265703 E A Birch[3], L/12794 T L Bradbury[3], 265518 E A J Bradley[3], G/27134 F Britcher[3], 265316 G Broadbridge[3], L/13834 A E Brockwell[3], 265932 H A Brown[3], G/27084 J Brown[3], 265293 S V Burchell[3], 266188 W E Burton[3], L/13832 F J Bussell[3], 265852 S V K Butchers[3], 265928 W W Butler[3], G/27196 B Callaghan[3], G/27093 D Canning[3], 265939 A Cave[3], G/27090 T B Chadwick[3], 265381 L G Chainey[3], L/13835 J P Chapman[3], 266542 R Chatfield[3], G/27087 E C Clarke[3], L/13767 F Clarke[3], G/27100 A J Collings[3], L/13837 C J Collins[3], 265384 G Cook[3], G/27092 R H Cooksey[3], G/27096 S S Copley[3], G/30302 E Coulson[3], G/27101 W Crummett[3], G/27197 A Davies[3], 265134 R W Davies[3], G/27193 S Day[3], G/27136 A H Dean[3], G/27194 D McC Dick[3], G/27287 A W Dove[3], G/27106 J F C Eaton[3], 266203 C Edmonds[3], G/6657 G Edwards[3], 265166 H T Edwards[3], G/27107 W Efford[3], 265794 W J Fagg[3], G/27041 R H Farrell[3], G/27075 C Felstead[3], 265841 J F Figgett[3], 265140 S Foster[3], G/27138 N Fox[3], 265798 V Fox[3], G/27162 J E Franklin[3], G/27109 S H Franklin[3], L/13840 H E Garner[3], 265926 S W Geering[3], L/13864 A J George[3], 265940 G H Godfrey[3], 265922 H E Goldfinch[3], G/30310 E H Green[3], L/13898 J W Griffiths[3], 265514 L W Griggs[3], G/27290 L Harrison[3], 265165 R P Harvey[3], G/27116 F H Hayes[3], G/27046 J Hayhurst[3], G27113 D Hedges[3], G/27288 W H Hiles[3], G/27280 H Hill[3], L/13841 L J Hogben[3], G/27115 W Holland[3], G/27145 G Homer[3], 265925 C S Hood[3], G/27147 J R Hooper[3], 265101 J Hope[3], 265708 A W Hover[3], 265143 E Howard[3], L/13842 A Hughes[3], G/27200 S Hurst[3], 265806 W A Irvin[3], 265867 F L Jagels[3], G/27153 C J R Johnson[3], G/30313 W Jolley[3], L/13843 H Jones[3], G/27125 F S Jordan[3], G/27127 J Kennedy[3], (TF/1862) L/13844 F Kernan[3], G/27204 F J Kilford[3], 265225 C A King[3], 265182 J King[3], G/27128 P King[3], G/30309 P G Kingsford[3], G/27126 E D Knowles[3], 265142 A Larcher[3], 265338 A Law[3], 265167 R A Lawrence[3], 265627 E Long[3], 265108 F G Marchant[3], 265185 L W Maskell[3], G/28235 P Mather[3], 265065 H W Maylam[3], G/30315 A E McEnvoy[3], G/28236 H W McKinney[3], G/27047 A Murray[3], G/27277 G H Murray[3], 265256 R Neaves[3], 265180 V Norris[3], G/27049 S Palmer[3], L/13847 S C A Palmer[3], 265269 C T Patten[3], 265248 E E Payne[3], G/27048 H W G Payne[3], 265592 C E Percival[3], G/27158 W Petterson[3], G/27055 H Pettie[3], G/28237 W C Phillips[3], 265947 H J V Phipp[3], 265244 F W K Picken[3], G/27050 H F M Piper[3], G/27056 G Plant[3], G/27053 W M Pollock[3], L/13865 E C Porter[3], L/13846 A E Prebble[3], L/13845 F E Prebble[3], 266447 A Price[3], 265929 G Pummell[3], 265160 E T Ralph[3], 266064 A J Rayner[3], G/27166 G E Richards[3], 265175 R Richardson[3], G/28240 A Robson[3], G/27170 J Mc K Rothwell[3], G/27171 T Rowell[3], G/27167 W H Rowland[3], 265295 A C Rule[3], G/28241 A L Russell[3], L/13939 J Saunders[3], G/27207 J Schofield[3], G/27060 D F Shotton[3], G/27210 T Silk[3], G/27059 W J Simmonds[3], G/27063 J A Slater[3], G/28164 W S Smith[3], 204814 J S P Smitherman[3], G/27061 E Snowden[3], L/13866 C F Spain[3], 265967 A R Stacey[3], 265932 H J Stalley[3], G/28244 A Stephens[3], G/28245 A T Stockting[3], 266380 C Sturges[3], G/27057 E Sylvester[3], 265347 G D Terry[3], 267134 F T Thomas[3], 200260 A Thompson[3] attch. RE, L/13899 S T Tutt[3], 265768 F W Tyler[3], 265173 C Vanner[3], 28246 T B Vickers[3] attch. RE, 266007 R G Wagg[3], L/13848 B Waters[3], 265436 A W Watson[3], 265229 F Westover[3], 265979 J Whitbread[3], L/13849 P J Wilkin[3], TF/265610 F Wilkins[3], G/27079 K L Williams[3], 265196 S L Wilson[3], 265277 G Woodger[3], 265062 G Wooldridge[3] & 266210 A Worsley[3]

Register Three - Name appears on Medal Roll for claims processed by Hounslow (Army) Records Office dated 15/10/1922 and shown 'to be' engraved 'KENT CYC BN'. (*) Indicates that Medal Record Card shows recipient as being most likely 'cap badged' Royal West Kent Regiment at time of Afghanistan 1919 qualification.

Quartermaster Sergeant/Sergeants: ~ (Act) L/13839 A W Greenwood[3](*)

Lance Sergeants/Corporals: ~ (Act) 265508 W G Blackley[3]

Lance Corporals/Privates: ~ 266035 H H Furley[3](*) attch. 3 W/Sig Sqn, 266034 R A Killick[3](*) & 266324 A E Turner[3](*)

Claims processed by Hounslow (Army) Records Office dated 15/5/1922 and shown 'to be' engraved 'KENT CYC BN'.

Quartermaster Sergeant/Sergeants: ~ (Act) 265456 F E Hart[3&4]

Claims processed by Hounslow (Army) Records Office dated 15/1/1923 and shown 'to be' engraved 'KENT CYC BN'.

Quartermaster Sergeants/Sergeants: ~ (Act) (TF577) 265079 W A Elkington[3]

Lance Sergeants/Corporals: ~ 265168 H J Foster[3]

Lance Corporals/Privates: ~ 265374 E Bennett[3] & 265460 J E Farrier[3]

Claims processed by Hounslow (Army) Records Office dated 16/4/1923 and shown 'to be' engraved 'KENT CYC BN'.

Quartermaster Sergeants/Sergeants: ~ (Act) (TF510) 265064 J F Russell[3]

Lance Corporals/Privates: ~ (TF1997) 266109 P Gillett[3] & 266408 G P Wright[3]

Claims processed by Hounslow (Army) Records Office dated 14/8/1923 and shown 'to be' engraved 'KENT CYC BN'.

Quartermaster Sergeants/Sergeants: ~ (Act) (TF697) 265130 S C Smith[3]

Lance Corporals/Privates: ~ (TF2070) 266167 F Arthur[3], 266489 A W Garwood[3], (TF998) 265327 S F Haywood[3], (TF1709) 265862 W A Mailey[3] & 265511 F G Oliver[3]

Claims processed by Hounslow (Army) Records Office dated 13/10/1923 and shown 'to be' engraved 'KENT CYC BN'.
Lance Corporals/Privates: ~ (TF1132) 265403 E G Ashdown[3] attch. 39 DSC, 2 Div. & (TF1247) 265490 J E Holley[3] attch. 3 W/Sig Sqn,
Claims processed by Hounslow (Army) Records Office dated 16/4/1924 and shown 'to be' engraved 'KENT CYC BN'.
Quartermaaster Sergeants/Sergeants: ~ (Act) (TF1074) 265359 S J Pledger[3]

THE CORPS:

~ The Royal Army Chaplains Department ~

Note a.   *The Indian Ecclesiastical Establishment, Indian Army, also provided Christian Chaplain support.*
Note b.   *Medals named in impressed capitals: 'R. A. Ch. D.'*

Single Clasp	No. Identified	Rarity
Afghanistan N.W.F. 1919[3]	0	None Identified
Mahsud 1919–20[5]	0	None Identified
Waziristan 1919–21[4]	0	None Identified
Waziristan 1921–24[6]	1	According to the roll as seen, can be considered Unique

Chaplains: ~ J M Clarke[6] attch. 9 Bde.

~ The Royal Army Service Corps ~

Orbit, including Indian Army Supply & Transport Corps units, is shown under Indian Army Establishment

Note a.   *Roll of all commissioned personnel as identified.*
Note b.   *Non-commissioned and other ranks multi clasp only or non–Afghanistan 1919 / Waziristan series single clasp.*
Note c.   *The Royal Army Service Corps (RASC) was formed in 1918 from the Army Service Corps (ASC).*
Note d.   *Many members of the Royal Army Service Corps (RASC) served on attachment to the Indian Army Supply & Transport Corps (S&TC). Personnel enlisted into the Indian Army and serving full time with the Supply & Transport Corps, or from 1923 the Indian Army Service Corps (IASC), are beyond the scope of this work and are therefore omitted from the roll below.*
Note e.   *Medals named in impressed capitals: 'R.A.S.C.'*

Single Clasp	No. Identified	Rarity
Afghanistan N.W.F. 1919[3]	In Strength	Not Rare
Mahsud 1919–20[5]	0	None Identified
Waziristan 1919–21[4]	In Strength	Not Rare, but Trending Scarce
Waziristan 1921–24[6]	In Strength	Not Rare, but Trending Scarce
Combination Clasps	*No. Identified*	*Rarity*
Afghanistan N.W.F. 1919[3] Mahsud 1919–20[5] Waziristan 1919–21[4]	3	Of the Utmost Rarity
Afghanistan N.W.F. 1919[3] Mahsud 1919–20[5] Waziristan 1919–21[4] Waziristan 1921–24[6]	4	Of the Utmost Rarity
Afghanistan N.W.F. 1919[3] Waziristan 1919–21[4]	21	Very Rare
Afghanistan N.W.F. 1919[3] Waziristan 1919–21[4] Waziristan 1921–24[6]	7	Of the Utmost Rarity

Afghanistan N.W.F. 1919[3] Waziristan 1921–24[6]	4	Of the Utmost Rarity
Mahsud 1919–20[5] Waziristan 1919– 21[4]	3	Of the Utmost Rarity
Waziristan 1919–21[4] Waziristan 1921–24[6]	82	Rare

Lieutenant Colonels: ~ (Bvt) E H Blamey[6], J C M Canny[6] 24 MT Coy, R P Crawley[6], G B Dartnell[6], A G Galloway[4&6], (Bvt) W T Hollins[6], (Temp) W P Robinson[3] DDT India, G L Rossiter[6] 4 MT Coy, C D E Upton[6] & A M Wilson[4&6] HQ, BMT Col

Majors: ~ A W Alexander[4], (Temp) H H Berridge[3,4,5&6] DADTMT HQ, WFF, H de Brath[6], A M Cockshott[6], E H Crispin[4], F R Dawes[4&6], D B R Dickery[6] 4 MT Coy, F W C Featherson-Godley[4], G E Goldsmith[6], J Gorman[3], J H Harris[4], A Herklots[6], A W Jones[4&6], (Bvt) G E Loefubee[6], F G McKim[3], F G G Moores[4&6] 2 MT Coy S W Morrison[4] 10 MT Coy, J H B Peyton[6], F K Puckle[6], H P Raymond[4], B Reyner[3], F E Simkin[3] attch. S&TC, (Bvt) C L St. J Tudor[6], J M Tweedie[4] & (Temp) L J de Burgh-Whyte[3&4] attch. S&TC

Captains: ~ A C Arden[4] 8 MT Coy, P W Attride[3], J H Barbor[4&6], E C Beale[3&4] 693 MT Coy, B C Bean[3], G V Bennett[4] 10 MT Coy, M Birch[4&6] 8 MT Coy, R G Breadmore[6], G A Beale-Browne[6], M J Cahill[3,4,5&6], T C W Carlyon[3&4], W H Clarke[4] 8 MT Coy, J E Cockshott[4&6] 11 MT Coy, J D Constable[6], H A Courtenay[4&6], L W W Davis[3], R V Doudney[3], F R L Downham[4] 11 MT Coy, T Evans[3], J H D Faithfull[4&6] 8 MT Coy, A J M Saville-Farr[4] 8 MT Coy, J T Field[3,4,5&6], H F Fraser[3], F W C Godley[4] 692 Coy, R L Hambly[3&4], H J C Hawkins[6], F W Hobday[4&6], A F B Hopwood[6], H J M Howard[6], E P Innocent[3], W Johns[4] 1 MT Coy, A H R M Laird[6], I A Lander[4], C Levy[4], F D Martin[6], J Maxwell[4], T O McEwan[4&6], E J R McWatters[4], H V McWatters[6] 18 MRU, J W Messenger[3], S U Nasmith[3], A A J G D O'Flynn[4], C R O'Neill[4], F S W Savill-Onley[4], S J Pearson[4] 8 MT Coy, W C Price[6], H P Raymond[4&6], C W Read[3&4], L Revell[3] 19 MAC & DAD S&T, C B Robertson[4&6], R S Ronald[4], M G Rowcroft[4], D P Sandilands[6], E Scott Snell[4] 8 MT Coy, R H Stewart[4] 1 MT Coy, H Sydney[4], R J Tench[4] 8 MT Coy, N S Thomas[6], C R Thompson[3], G Thompson[3], L J Walch[4&6], L W J Warren[3], W R V Warren[4] 27 MT Coy, J H Whitehouse[4&6] 7 MT Coy & 18 MRU, F G Winn[3] & G F Yard[6]

Lieutenants: ~ J N V Anderson[4] 8 MT Coy, J F Burchardt-Ashton[4] 1 MT Coy, C Avery[6] 14 MT Coy, S H Bailey[4], W L Baird[6], C G Baker[6], A S N Barron[3&4] 2 MT Coy, KW Brand[6], B C Brook[6], J J Brough[6], H E F L Brown[6], R Brydges[4&6], F J Burton[4], F E Carpenter[6], E King-Clifford[3&4], L E S Coleman[4], T N Collet[4], J C C Cooke[3,4&6] attch. S&TC, D E Cope[4] 8 MT Coy, R W Courtney[6] 7 MT Coy, C H Crews[3], D C C Crichton[3,4&6], H A Dartnall[3] attch. Combined MT Workshops, O Davies[6], H C Davis[6], C McIntyre Delf[6], R P Dent[6], V L Douglas[6], W Dunlop[6], G G Edgell[6], A L Ellison[6], F J K Ellison[4&6], L E Evans[3] attch. S&TC, B U Farrell[4], H B Finch[6], F C Green[6], G W F Gyll[3], D L Harbottle[3], T V Harrison[3], G H Hedley[6], R W W Hills[6], R K Holmes[4&6] 1 MT Coy, J M H Houghton[4], W H Hynes[4] 8 MT Coy, C E R Ince[6], L T E Ivy[6], P T James[6], W R Kellett[3], T C King[6], W A King[6], F W Latham[6], P L MacDermatt[6], J F Metcalfe[3&6], T L Minniece[4&6] 2 MT Coy, G Naylor[6], C S O'Dell[6], G R O'Neill[4&6], G L Ovens[3], W Prain[3], H B Rodgers[3], U D Sawman[6], H L Shipman[4] 2 MT Coy, E J Sleven[4] 8 MT Coy, W O Spafford[4] 9 MT Coy, C McKidd Stirling[3&4], J W Taylor[4] 2 MT Coy, W M W Thorn[6], G E Tolfree[3&4] 7 MT Coy, A Tredinnick[4], C de Vall[4] 8 MT Coy, S A Webb[4&6] 14 MT Coy, G J Welch[3], C P White[6] & F H E Whittaker[4&6]

Warrant Officers Class I: ~ (Act) EMT44490/M19479 E G English[4&6], (Act Mech) M/27693 R Forbes[4&6] 1 MT Coy & (Act Mech) M25234/M14217 A Oldridge[4&6] 18 IMRU

Warrant Officers Class II: ~ (Act) M17786/M14016 C H Carroll[4&6], (Act) M22715/M14139 T B Doherty[4&6], EMT64458/M21788 F Heun[4&6], (Act Mech) EMT43988/M19030 F H Jackson[4&6], (Act) EMT64698/M22981 J H Jennings[4&6], (Act) M23371/M14181 J E Legg[4&6], (Act Mech) M2-193737/M24996 G Lilley[3,4,5&6] 7 MT Coy, (Act) M2/101123 C W N Nichols[3&4], (Act) M/31308-M/14640 N A Parry[4&6] 12 MT Coy, (Act) M31637/M14681 P J Parsons[4&6], (Act) M14341 H Rowlands[4&6], (Act) M27103/M14291 A Sansom[4&6], (Act) M29411/M14486 C J Searle[4&6] 9 MT Coy, EMT43326/M18332 S S Thrush[3&4] & EMT64652/M21960 W Vorley[4&6] 1 MT Coy

Company Quartermaster Sergeants/Staff Sergeants: ~ (Act Mech) EMT43576/M18553 H J Blake[4&6], (Act Mech) M31646/M14684 H Bloxham[4&6], (Mech) EMT43081/M18113 G A Cherry[4&6], M15009/M37057 F W Dibble[3,4&6], (Act) M34071/M14938 H G Fogg[3&6], EMT43215/M18238 A Gray[3&4] 18 IMRU, (Act Mech) EMT43186/M18209 G Hallam[4&6], (Mech) M16316/M46994 J J Hargroves[4&6], (Mech) EMT46506/M20480 L E Kane[4&6], (Act Mech) M23976/M14185 W Laird[4&6], M378798 J W Lindow[3&4] attch. 18 IMRU & (Act Mech) EMT45977/M20060 A Mooney[4&6], M54184/M16908 H F Smith[4&6], EMT45976/M20059 T H Strickland[3,4&6] 18 IMRU & (Act) M24685/EMT43837 G W Swift[4&5]

Quartermaster Sergeants/Sergeants: ~ (Tmpt) M2/166640 A H Albon[4&5], M3233601/M23668 W Bain[4&6], (Act) EMT43031/M18067 S G Boatman[3&4] 18 IMRU, M20501/EMT46533 W Boycott[4&6] 1 MT Coy, M2/100937 A E Burden[3&4] 693 Coy, (Act) M17076/M56392 W E Burrows[4&6], EMT756863/M17251 W Butler[4&6], (Act) M15508/M45063 L C Capon[4&6] 27 MT Coy, EMT43123/M18152 J Costello[4&6] 1 MT Coy, M14848/M33501 E E Farmer[4&6], M24648/M14201 C Gee[4&5] 8 MT Coy, M18163/EMT43136 L E Harrison[4&6], (Act) M25315/M66254 E Hogan[4&6], M62963/M17331 A A Humphries[4&6], M16684/M53519 D C Ince[4&6], M31329/M08732 J W Kelly[4&6], (Act) M/4794436 A Lavender[4&6], (Act) M15886/M45500 F T Lindsay[3&6] 18 MRU, (Act) M29668/M14513 E Major[4&6], (Act) T21330/M955 G W Mosley[4&6], M17080/M56397 T Riches[4&6], EMT64661/M21969 W Thornton[4&6], M38942/M15107 F A Walter[4&6] & (Act) M23310/EMT61414 G A Williams[4&6] 18 IMRU

Lance Sergeants/Corporals: ~ M/456034 A Alder[4&6], (Act) M47011/M16331 H E J Downs[4&6], (Act) DM2/189092 J P Ewing[3&4], (Act) M2/166831 A W Setter[3&4] 692 Coy & M18039/EMT42999 G H Wood[3&4] attch. 18 IMRU

Lance Corporals /Privates: ~ M17445/M63100 J W Bounds[4&6], EMT43881/M18790 R G Clinton[4&6], M47701/M25003 G A Cook[4&6], (was RAF 251447), M/339106 J P Crook[3&4], M/16102 S H Dever[4&6], EMT/43920 T Dunbar[3&4] 18 IMRU, M17105/M56429 H C Dunham[4&6], (M/40312) 15232 W A Everitt[4&6(RTC)], M21758/EMT64423 G H Excell[3,4&6], EMT/43255 G Forsyth[3,4&6], M1036244/275787 F Hillier[4&6], M47184/M16467 W W Hyde[4&6], M/314812 E H Jones[3,4&5] 23 MAC, M322345/EMT64745 W J Lewsley[3&6], M16980/M154947 F J Locks[4&6], M16654/M53484 W McCann[4&6], M/5239772 R Powers[4&6] 18 IMRU, M16769/M53914 F T Reynard[4&6], M45519/M15903 W J Widdicombe[3,4&6] 7 MT Coy & M/22577 F L Wilson[4&6] attch. 10 ACC

~ The Royal Army Medical Corps ~

Note a.   Roll of all commissioned personnel identified as eligible.
Note b.   Non-commissioned and other ranks multi clasp only.
Note c.   Roll includes Dental Specialists until formation of Army Dental Corps (ADC) in 1921.
Note d.   Enlisted personnel multi bar recipients only or single clasp 'MAHSUD 1919 – 20'.
Note e.   Medals named in impressed capitals: 'R.A.M.C.'

Single Clasp	No. Identified	Rarity
Afghanistan N.W.F. 1919[3]	In Strength	Not Rare
Mahsud 1919–20[5]	0	None Identified
Waziristan 1919–21[4]	In Strength	Not Rare, But Trending Scarce
Waziristan 1921–24[6]	In Strength	Not Rare, but Trending Scarce

Combination Clasps	No. Identified	Rarity
Afghanistan N.W.F. 1919[3] Mahsud 1919–20[5] Waziristan 1919–21[4]	9	Of the Utmost Rarity
Afghanistan N.W.F. 1919[3] Waziristan 1919–21[4]	26	Very Rare
Afghanistan N.W.F. 1919[3] Waziristan 1919–21[4] North West Frontier 1930–31[9]	2	Of the Utmost Rarity
Afghanistan N.W.F. 1919[3] Waziristan 1921–24[6]	4	Of the Utmost Rarity
Afghanistan N.W.F. 1919[3] North West Frontier 1930–31[9]	1	According to the roll as seen, can be considered Unique
Afghanistan N.W.F. 1919[3] Burma 1930–32[10]	1	According to the roll as seen, can be considered Unique
Afghanistan N.W.F. 1919[3] North West Frontier 1935[12]	1	According to the roll as seen, can be considered Unique
Mahsud 1919–20[5] Waziristan 1919–21[4]	4	Of the Utmost Rarity
Mahsud 1919–20[5] Waziristan 1919–21[4] Malabar 1921–22[7]	1	According to the roll as seen, can be considered Unique
Mahsud 1919–20[5] Waziristan 1919–21[4] Waziristan 1921–24[6] Burma 1930–32[10]	1	According to the roll as seen, can be considered Unique
Waziristan 1919–21[4] Waziristan 1921–24[6]	10	Of the Utmost Rarity

Waziristan 1919–21[4] **Burma 1930–32**[10]	1	**According to the roll as seen, can be considered Unique**
Waziristan 1919–21[4] **Waziristan 1921–24**[6] **North West Frontier 1930–31**[9] **North West Frontier 1935**[12]	1	**According to the roll as seen, can be considered Unique**
Malabar 1921–22[7] **Waziristan 1921–24**[6]	1	**According to the roll as seen, can be considered Unique**
Waziristan 1921–24[6] **North West Frontier 1930–31**[9]	1	**According to the roll as seen, can be considered Unique**
Waziristan 1921–24[6] **Burma 1930–32**[10]	1	**According to the roll as seen, can be considered Unique**

Lieutenant Colonels: ~ E G Anthonisz[4&6], W Bennett[6], (Act) A G Biggam[3,4&5], G A Blake[3], (Act) W C Bosanquet[3], (Act) R A Bryden[4&6] 25 CFA, B B Burke[6], K Corbin[3], A Dawson[3] DADMS Northern Line, J N Fletcher[3&4], J E Folley[3], S O Hall[3], H Halton[3], (Act) W Harding[4] 8 CCCS, G W G Hughes[6], C M Ingoldby[4], T C C Leslie[3&4], F P Louder[4], J MacKenzie[3], C W Mainprise[3], (Act) R K Mallam[3&12], J Matthews[4], (Act) G R D McGeogh[3], H H Mulholland[3&4] 12 IGH, H D Packer[3], P E D Pank[3&4], (Act) R V Powell[3], (Act) W F O'Regan[3], F A Roddy[3&4] 27 CFA, (Bvt) A H Safford[3] ADMS KKF, (Act) W W S Sharpe[3], R M Skinner[3], W J D Smyth[3], W M Snodgrass[4] 34 CCCS, W H M Spiller[4&6], (Act) G H Stack[4&5] & C G Thompson[4] 2 IFA Wana Col

Majors: ~ A C Amy[6&9(Lt. Col.)], G A E Argo[4] 1 CSS, W Bird[6], (Act) H S Blackmore[3], R F Bridges[3&6], W H Bush[4], W M Cameron[4] DADMS WFF, W K Campbell[4&6] 18 BSS, E G S Cane[6], F A H Clark[3], C J Coppinger[3], W M Dickson[3], C M Drew[6], G G Drummond[4], T S Dudding[3], E F L'Estrange[3], H H J Fawcett[3], A N Fraser[3&6], W Frier[4&6] DADMS WFF, A C H Gray[6], D H Hadden[4] DADMS WFF, C H H Harold[3], F B Jefferies[3], H F Joynt[6], M Keane[3], J W Lone[3], E B Marsh[4&5] 3 CSS, W Mathieson[6], A A Meaden[3] DADMS ZF, W McNaughton[3], R W Murphy[3], R B Myles[3&4] DADMS Waz & LofC, T B Nicholls[3], E W M Paine[6], B G Patch[4&5], M P Power[4,6,9&12], P Power[3], J M B Rahilly[6], D Reynolds[3&4], J D Richmond[4], J J Ritchie[3], M M Russell[4], C Ryles[3], T W O Sexton[3] 35 BGH, W G Shakespeare[3&6], C G K Sharp[3], B C O Sheridan[4,5,6&10] 49 IGH, F R S Show[3&4], F R B Skrimshire[3], G K Stringer[6], G G Tabuteau[6&10], N D Walker[3], G S Wallace[3,4&5], R C Wilmot[3], J L Wilson[3], H C Winckworth[3], (Act) W B Wood[3] & H E Pierpoint-Yorke[4&5]

Captains: ~ G M Adam[3], E B Andreae[3] MO 25 Lond, F D Annesley[3] 8 CCFA Dakka, C F Anthonisz[3&9(Maj.)] 165 ISS, H D Apergis[3], J S Armstrong[3], F C K Austin[3] 21 BSS & 73 ISS, R A Austin[4] IGH Tank, J H Baird[3], H W Bennett[3], J W Bennett[3], G C Berg[3], H B Binks[3], W S Birch[3], W Bisset[3], A B Black[3&4], C J Blaikie[3&10(Maj.)], I Braun[3], G A Bridge[6], R F Bridges[3], B W Brown[3&4] 43 IGH, W Bruce[4&6] Tank Lines Wana Col, J B Burgess[3], W W Burt[3], J A G Burton[4] 49 IGH, W R Campbell[4&6], H L Carson[3], J C Collins[3], W P Cooney[3], D Cran[3], W P Croker[3], A B Cross[3], F K Daunt[3], L W Davies[3] MO 287 Coy MGC, T R Davies[3&4] MO 82 Punjabis, IA, J C Denvir[3] 24 BSH, A R C Doorly[3], J H Dove[3], M Dwyer[3], H A G Dykes[3&4] 18 BSS, H B Dykes[3], C L Emmerson[3], D G Evans[6], R R Evans[6], D Fettes[3], A E Finney[3], F G Flood[6], J S B Forbes[3] 49 IGH, M Foster[3] MO 1 S Lancs, W Foot[3], J B Fotheringham[3], G J Garraway[4] 49 IGH, F S Gillespie[3] 1 BSS, R H Graham[3], W N Greer[3], B Grellier[3], F Griffith[4] 49 IGH, G D Gripper[7&6], E H R Harries[3], C C Harrison[3&4], C W C Harvey[3], J R Hayman[3], T L Heath[3], P H Henson[4] 15 BSS, A J Herne[3], J Hewat[3], H W Hodgson[3], W E Hopkins[3], A Howes[3], J J Humell[3], R M Humphreys[3], L Hutchinson[3], E P Irving[3], R Isbister[3], A C Jebb[3], D W John[4] 1 CSS, D J H Jones[3], I W Jones[3], T Jones[3], J D Johnson[3], R Johnson[6], M B King[6], J E Kitchen[3], D A Laird[4], W J A Laird[3,4&5], E Lanzon[3], G T Longborough[3], R H Liscombe[3], J N Lyons[3], D MacFarlane[3] IGH Tank, J P MacNamara[3,4&9(Maj.)], J A Martin[3], W F Mason[3], R J Harley-Mason[3] MO 2 N Staffs, J L McBean[3], T McClurkin[3], G S McConkey[3,4&5] 23 MA thence 43 CFA thence 13 CSS, H D McCrossan[3], McEwan[3], G J McGorty[6], C R McIntosh[3], J W McKeggie[3], A J McNair[3], A F Milne[3], C T Milne[3] SMO Malakand FF, J B Minch[3] SMO Malakand FF, J S Moore[3], J A Musgrave[4] 49 IGH, E L F Nash[3,4&5], K M Nelson[4&6], W Neven[3] 13 IFH, F D Nicholson[3], F H B Norrie[3], K L O'Sullivan[4] 49 IGH, F C Ormerod[3], E Parker[3&4], A E S Pringle Patterson[3], H G Peake[3], J F Penman[3], M C Peterson[6], C H Phillips[3] attch. IFA G S Phillips[3], A D Pope[3], C Pophorn[3&4], M P Powel[4&6], W W Pratt[3] 100 ISS, R B Reed[3], M B Reichwald[3] 36 BGH, S W Rintoul[3], P D Ritchie[3], R L Ritchie[6], J G Ronaldson[4&6] IGH DIK thence 64 CFA thence IGH Tank, C Russell[3], C Rutherford[3], T H Sarsfield[3,4&5] 18 BSS, C Scales[3], A A B Scott[3,4&5] 18 BSS, D C Scott[6], G M Scott[3], C O Shackleton[3&4], G E L Simons[3] MO 1 Yorks, R G Simpson[4], G Smith[3], F G A Smyth[4] 49 IGH, T R Snelling[4], D B Spence[3], G R Spence[3], H R Stafford[6], C L Stewart[3] MO Troop Trains, H Stewart[3], R I Sullivan[4,5&7] 2 IFA, H S Swann[3], H V Swindale[3], S P Sykes[3], T B H Tabuteau[4&10] 12 IGH, C R Taylor[3] MO 2/33 Punjabis, IA, R T Taylor[3], W H Thomas[3], R H Thompson[3], R R Thompson[3,4&5], P Thornton[3], W O Tobias[3], J R Turner[3] MO 1/4 Queens, W G Verniquet[3], J H C Walker[3], G W Watson[3] MO 17 SSB, T T B Watson[3], M J Whelton[6], A G E Wilcock[3], G W Wood[3] 43 BGH, W C S Wood[3] & I H Woods[4]

Lieutenants: ~ F D Annesley[3&6], D G Carmichael[3], J M MacKenzie[3,4&9(Maj.)] DADMS Wana Col 1921, E Phillips[3] & J B Potter[3] MO 1 R Sussex

Warrant Officers Class II: ~ (Temp) 5372 J D O'Flaherty[3,4&5] 7 Coy

Lance Segeants /Corporals: ~ (Act) 83974 W Anderson[3&4] 23 MAC, (Act) 75408 D Hall[3&4] 23 MAC & (Act) 75401 W Whitley[3&4] 23 MAC

Lance Corporals/Privates: ~ 83931 H Barlow[3&4], 69135 H Conroy[3&4], 11204 S Furness[3&4] 23 MAC, 111383 W Gardiner[3&4], 114249 L G F Gully[3&4], 71697 F H Hawney[3&4] 23 MAC & 70123 A Ramsay[3&4] 23 MAC

~ The Royal Army Ordnance Corps ~

Note a.   *Roll of all commissioned personnel identified as eligible.*

Note b.   *Non-commissioned and other ranks multi bar only.*

Note c.   *Medals named in impressed capitals: 'R.A.O.C.'*

Single Clasp	No. Identified	Rarity
Afghanistan N.W.F. 1919[3]	In Strength	Not Rare
Mahsud 1919–20[5]	0	None Identified
Waziristan 1919–21[4]	In Strength	Note Rare, but Trending Scarce
Waziristan 1921–24[6]	In Strength	Note Rare, but Trending Scarce

Combination Clasps	No. Identified	Rarity
Afghanistan N.W.F. 1919[3] Mahsud 1920–21[5] Waziristan 1919–21[4]	1	According to the roll as seen, can be considered Unique
Afghanistan N.W.F. 1919[3] Waziristan 1919–21[4]	4	Of the Utmost Rarity
Waziristan 1919–21[4] Waziristan 1921–24[6]	6	Of the Utmost Rarity
Waziristan 1919–21[4] Malabar 1921–22[7]	1	According to the roll as seen, can be considered Unique

Lieutenant Colonels: ~ E S J Britton[4] & H J Shipman[3]

Majors: ~ S C R Chester[3] DADOS LofC, A G Dalimore[3], G F W Echlin[3&4], M R Fitzwilliam[3], P J Gibbs[4], H A Mills[3], J H B Mowels[3] & M T Smith[3]

Captains: ~ J Benfield[3], J E Clements[4], F W Farlie[4], J Grant[4], G W Johnson[3], J A Mackenzie[3], W R Marsh[3], M R Neale[3], G Paton[3,4&5], S N Pring[3], K F Farquharson-Roberts[3], H C Whitaker[3] & W White[3]

Lieutenants: ~ W Brown[3], J B Clarke[3&4], W Drew[4], H G Murdoch[3], C T Taylor[3] & R R Townsend[3]

Conductors & Warrant Officers Class I: ~ S/3447 H G Deane[4&6] attch. Ord Depot, Mari Indus

Sub Conductors & Warrant Officers Class II: ~ 7578660 L R Anderson[3&4] 34 Ord Mbl Wkshop

Quartermaster Sergeants/Staff Sergeants: ~ (Armt) 7578824 L E Baker[4&7(attch. 1 Suffolk)], (Act Armt) (7578591) A/1053 T Beard[4&6] attch. RTC, 7578838 C C Grimmer[4&6] attch. 2 Queen's, (Armt) 7579206 R E Lord[4&6] attch. 34 Ord Wks Shop Mari Indus, (Armt) 7578881 J A McMillan[4&6] attch. 1 RWF & (Armt) 7578842 E Webster[4&6] attch. Ord Depot, Mari Indus

Lance Sergeants/Corporals: ~ 06581 W MacMillan[3&4]

~ The Mounted Military Police ~

Note a.   *Roll of all eligible personnel identified 'cap badged' Mounted Military Police (MMP), as opposed to being shown on roll as 'attached Mounted Military Police'. (See rolls above).*

Note b.   *Medals named in impressed capitals: 'M.M.P.'*

Single Clasp	No. Identified	Rarity
Afghanistan N.W.F. 1919[3]	9	Of the Utmost Rarity
Mahsud 1919–20[5]	0	None Identified
Waziristan 1919–21[4]	0	None Identified
Waziristan 1921–24[6]	0	None Identified

Quartermaster Sergeants/Sergeants: ~ (Act) P11321 F E Critchell[3], (Act) P11320 J Green[3] & P14123 W J Ridler[3]
Lance Corporals/Privates: ~ P1601 P E Cranford[3], P14106 A Hawkins[3], P11336 W G Leighfield[3], P13231 H McCree[3], P1364 C Olson[3] & P13723 W C Samways[3]

~ The Military Foot Police ~

Note a. Roll of all eligible personnel identified 'cap badged' Military Foot Police (MFP), as opposed to being shown on roll as 'attached Military Foot Police'. (See rolls above).
Note b. Medals named in impressed capitals: 'M.F.P.'

Single Clasp	No. Identified	Rarity
Afghanistan N.W.F. 1919[3]	26	Very Rare
Mahsud 1919–20[5]	0	None Identified
Waziristan 1919–21[4]	0	None Identified
Waziristan 1921–24[6]	0	None Identified

Warrant Officers Class I: ~ P11239 G Berry[3]
Warrant Officers Class II: ~ (Act) P12766 H Burt[3]
Quartermaster Sergeants/Sergeants: ~ (Act) P5627 J Bardsley[3], P13272 T Brown[3], P13214 G Dyson[3], P11653 T A Mannerings[3] & (Act) P12642 H H Parsons[3]
Lance Sergeants/Corporals: ~ P13791 A V Dyer[3], P11163 J Kershaw[3], P13197 J L Murphy[3], (Act) P13721 A N Prior[3], (Act) P11240 F W Roy[3] & P13714 P Webb[3]
Lance Corporals/Privates: ~ P11463 F Bailey[3], P12752 C Clements[3], P11176 G J Cooney[3], P11167 J J Dobson[3], P12740 H W Dugdale[3], P12619 T J Field[3], (Act) P12591 W Glancey[3], P13223 J Holdon[3], P13227 A Jones[3], P12735 E Morris[3], P14109 C Papworth[3], (Act) P11153 C Quinn[3] & P11278 E W Trivett[3]

~ The Military Accounts Department ~

Note a. Roll of all eligible personnel identified 'cap badged' Military Accounts Department (MAD), as opposed to being shown on roll 'attached Military Accounts Department'. (See rolls above).
Note b. Medals named in impressed capitals: 'M.A.D.'

Single Clasp	No. Identified	Rarity
Afghanistan N.W.F. 1919[3]	2	Of the Utmost Rarity
Mahsud 1919–20[5]	0	None Identified
Waziristan 1919–21[4]	0	None Identified
Waziristan 1921–24[6]	0	None Identified

Lieutenants: ~ D M Barchard[3] & H A Keywood[3]

~ The Royal Army Veterinary Corps ~

Note a. Roll of all personnel identified as eligible.
Note b. Medals named in impressed capitals: 'R.A.V.CPS.'

Single Clasp	No. Identified	Rarity
Afghanistan N.W.F. 1919[3]	47	Very Rare
Mahsud 1919–20[5]	0	None Identified
Waziristan 1919–21[4]	8	Of the Utmost Rarity
Waziristan 1921–24[6]	10	Of the Utmost Rarity

Combination Clasps	No. Identified	Rarity
Afghanistan N.W.F. 1919[3] Mahsud 1919–20[5] Waziristan 1919–21[4]	2	Of the Utmost Rarity
Afghanistan N.W.F. 1919[3] Mahsud 1919–20[5] Waziristan 1919–21[4] Waziristan 1921–24[6] North West Frontier 1930–31[9] Mohmand 1933[11] North West Frontier 1935[12]	1	According to the roll as seen, can be considered Unique
Afghanistan N.W.F. 1919[3] Waziristan 1919–21[4]	3	Of the Utmost Rarity
Afghanistan N.W.F. 1919[3] Waziristan 1919–21[4] Waziristan 1921–24[6]	2	Of the Utmost Rarity
Afghanistan N.W.F. 1919[3] Malabar 1921–22[7]	2	Of the Utmost Rarity
Afghanistan N.W.F. 1919[3] Burma 1930–32[10]	1	According to the roll as seen, can be considered Unique
Mahsud 1919–20[5] Waziristan 1919–21[4] Waziristan 1921–24[6] North West Frontier 1930–31[9]	1	According to the roll as seen, can be considered Unique.
Waziristan 1919–21[4] Waziristan 1921–24[6]	2	Of the Utmost Rarity

Lieutenant Colonels: ~ (Bvt) J J Atkin[4&6] ADVS WFF, (Bvt) T E Burridge[6], A F Deason[4], H Greenfield[4], (Bvt) H S Mosley[6] & (Bvt) W H Nicol[3] HQ BFF

Majors: ~ D'A S Beck[3&4], R Cunningham[3] East Persian Cordon, H E Gibbs[3], M St. G Glasse[6], F B Hayes[3&10], J R Hodgkins[6], H J Holness[6], F R Roche-Kelly[6], G A Kelly[3] HQ, WFF, J R Stevenson[3&7(DADVS)], L M Verney[4] DADVS, E Wallace[3&4] & E C Webb[3]

Captains: ~ J Anderson[3], T F Arnold[4], G Atkinson[3], T Bannatyne[3], W E Barry[4], R Beattie[3], J Blackburn[3], T Le Q Blampied[3] attch. BFF, E C Bowes[3], C K Calder[4] HQ, NWFF, F Christopher[3], C S Conder[3], C Davenport[6], R T Davis[3] 14 MVS, L A F Dawson[3], W R Edwards[3,4&5], W P S Edwards[3,4,5,6,9(Maj.),11(Maj.)&12(Maj.)], T Gordon[3], W D Halfhead[3], J W Hayes[3], J L Heffron[3], S G M Hickey[3], T Hodgins[4&6], F Hogg[6], H J Hughes[6], T S Hunter[3], G C Lawrence[3], W F MacDougall[3], C Mackie[3], O McGuirk[3,4&5], G H Melck[3], J P A Morris[3], R E Murison[3], A V Nicholas[3] 11 IMVS, B J W Nicholas[4,5,6&9(Maj.)], S O'Donel[3&4], M G O'Gogarty[3], A O'Neill[4] 20 IMVS, B S Parkin[3], W S Petrie[3], J A Power[3], E B Reynolds[3], G K Shaw[3,4&6], S L Slocock[3&7] LofC Vet Hosp Nowshera, G K Shaw[3,4&6] C M Stewart[3] 3 Field Vet Hosp Peshawar, W Urquhart[3], R F Wall[3], F S Warburton[3], J H M White[3], J B Williams[3] & P F Woodland[3]

Lieutenants: ~ H J Jerrom[6]

Quartermaster Sergeants/Sergeants: ~ SE17047 T Bentley[3], (Temp) R993 P Matthews[3] & SE852 A Savage[3]

Lance Sergeants/Corporals: ~ SE17422 E A Boulton[3]

Lance Corporals/Privates: ~ SE22590 A E Halsey[3], SE11226 W G Hughes[3] & SE2803 C H White[3]

~ The Corps of Army Schoolmasters ~

Note a.   *Roll of all personnel identified as eligible.*
Note b.   *Corps re designated Army Education Corps (AEC) in 1920.*
Note c.   *Corps of Army Schoolmaster serial numbers not shown on roll.*
Note d.   *Medals named in impressed capitals: 'C. of A.S.'*

Single Clasp	No. Identified	Rarity
Afghanistan N.W.F. 1919[3]	4	Of the Utmost Rarity

Warrant Officers Class I: ~ (7720464 AEC) A V Boon[3] attch. 7 Bde. RFA, NW13291 S O Cox[3] attch. 2 N Stafford, (7720565 AEC) M J Gallagher[3] attch. 2 King's & A P G Hennessy[3] attch. 2 Som LI

~ The Army Education Corps ~

Note a.   *Roll of all personnel identified as eligible.*
Note b.   *Corps formed 1920.*
Note c.   *Medals named in impressed capitals: 'A.E.C.'*

Single Clasp	No. Identified	Rarity
Afghanistan N.W.F. 1919[3]	0	Corps not formed
Mahsud 1919–20[5]	0	None Identified
Waziristan 1919–21[4]	3	Of the Utmost Rarity
Waziristan 1921–24[6]	11	Extremely Rare

Combination Clasps	No. Identified	Rarity
Waziristan 1919–21[4] Waziristan 1921–24[6]	3	Of the Utmost Rarity

Captains: ~ F Rylands[4] attch. 2 Queen's & C A Wilson[6]
Lieutenants: ~ A E Buck[4&6] attch. 2 Queen's, J T Burgess[6] attch. 1 Berkshire, E A E C Hopkin[6] attch. 1 Border, C J Kennedy[6], J C Rowley[4&6] attch. 1 RWF & O Sutcliffe[4] attch. 2 Norfolk
Warrant Officers Class II: ~ 4180712 F Lambert[6] attch. 1 Welsh & 7720614 G A Wilde[4] attch. 2 Queen's
Quartermaster Sergeants/Instructor Sergeants: ~ 3758317 H D G Chalmers[6] attch. 10 ACC, 7254988 A Coleman[4&6] attch. 1 RWF, 5956 G Darkin[6] attch. 9 ACC, 5564399 A E Hall[6] attch. 'B' DSC, 5040614 A Rhodes[6], 4602137 T W Strange[6] attch. 9 ACC & 4792921 R L Walker[6]

~ The Army Dental Corps ~

Note a.   *Roll of all personnel identified as eligible.*
Note b.   *Formed in 1921 from Dental Specialist branch of the Royal Army Medical Corps (RAMC).*
Note c.   *Medals named in impressed capitals: 'A.D.CORPS.'. Examples to officers have been seen with no corps designation as per the practise employed on British War Medal 1914–1920 and Allied Victory Medal 1914–1919 when awarded to commissioned personnel.*

Single Clasp	No. Identified	Rarity
Afghanistan N.W.F. 1919[3]	0	Corps Not Formed
Mahsud 1919–20[5]	0	Corps Not Formed
Waziristan 1919–21[4]	1	According to the roll as seen, can be considered Unique
Waziristan 1921–24[6]	4	Of the Utmost Rarity

Combination Clasps	No. Identified	Rarity
Mahsud 1919–20[5] Waziristan 1919–21[4]	1	According to the roll as seen, can be considered Unique
Waziristan 1919–21[4] Waziristan 1921–24[6]	1	According to the roll as seen, can be considered Unique

Captains: ~ P E Brown[6], J P Duguid[4], A V Milnes[4&5], H K Oswald[4&6] & C Y Walker[6]
Lance Sergeants/Corporals: ~ 7249679 R Saville[6]
Lance Corporals/Privates: ~ 7249882 A G W Burman[6]

~ The Queen Alexandra's Imperial Military Nursing Service ~

Note a. *Roll of all personnel identified as eligible.*

Note b. *Medals named to civilian, temporary or locally recruited (Indian Army establishment) nursing personnel should not be confused with members of the British Regular, Reserve or Territorial Force Nursing Services.*

Note c. *There was a separate Queen Alexandra's Military Nursing Service Indian within the Indian Establishment.*

Note d. *Matron F M Hall is recorded on her Peshawar military cemetery grave as having died 'on active service at Peshawar 7 July 1919'. I have found no record of the India General Service Medal with clasp 'AFGHANISTAN N.W.F. 1919' having been authorised for issue but I include Matron Hall's name below due to the detail upon the grave headstone.*

Note e. *Medals named in impressed capitals: 'Q.A.I.M.N.S.'*

Single Clasp	No. Identified	Rarity
Afghanistan N.W.F. 1919[3]	3	Of the Utmost Rarity
Mahsud 1919–20[5]	0	None Identified
Waziristan 1919–21[4]	0	None Identified
Waziristan 1921–24[6]	0	None Identified

Matrons: ~ F M Hall[32]

Sisters: ~ F Meyer[3] & K Nichol[3]

~ The Queen Alexandra's Imperial Military Nursing Service Reserve ~

Note a. *Roll of all personnel identified as eligible.*

Note b. *Medals named to civilian, temporary or locally recruited (Indian Army establishment) nursing personnel should not be confused with members of the British Regular, Reserve or Territorial Force Nursing Services (TFNS).*

Note c. *Medals named in impressed capitals: 'Q.A.I.M.N.S.R.'*

Single Clasp	No. Identified	Rarity
Afghanistan N.W.F. 1919[3]	2	Of the Utmost Rarity
Mahsud 1919–20[5]	0	None Identified
Waziristan 1919–21[4]	0	None Identified
Waziristan 1921–24[6]	0	None Identified

Sisters: ~ A B Logan[3] & I Keeble[3]

~ The Territorial Force Nursing Service ~

Note a. *Roll of all personnel identified as eligible.*

Note b. *Medals named to temporary or locally recruited (Indian Army establishment) nursing personnel should not be confused with members of the British Regular, Reserve or Territorial Force Nursing Services (TFNS).*

Note c. *Medals named in impressed capitals: 'T.F.N.S.'*

Single Clasp	No. Identified	Rarity
Afghanistan N.W.F. 1919[3]	1	According to the roll as seen, can be considered Unique
Mahsud 1919–20[5]	0	None Identified
Waziristan 1919–21[4]	0	None Identified
Waziristan 1921– 24[6]	0	None Identified

Sisters: ~ E Rimmer[3] attch. QAIMNS

~ Regiment Not Inscribed ~

Note a.   *Roll of all personnel identified on the roll as having 'No Regiment Inscribed' thus following the practise adopted on the British War Medal 1914 – 1920 and Allied Victory Medal 1914 - 1919 when awarded to commissioned personnel.*

Note b.   *Units shown in brackets after name have been identified from Medal Record Card or Army List 1919 series.*

Lieutenant Colonels: ~ S S Butler[6] Asst Mil Sec N. Cmd. (RE), C L Flick[3] (Essex) attch. 2 (Armd Train) SSB & R P Yates[3] (Welsh Regt.) attch. 17 SSB

Majors: ~ W R Meredith[4] (R Innis Fus.) & C J Tribe[4] DADRT(RGA)

Captains: ~ J G A Adams[3] (General List) attch. 2/4 Border, F Coburn[3] (General List) Staff, A B M (H) Cole[3] attch. 5 CFA, L R Haydon[3] (Dental), A W W Kyle[3] attch. S. Persia Rifles, Mil. Mission, East Persia, H C V Porter[3], DAAG 1 Div., (Possibly Named as West India Regiment or 'Staff'), E D Preston[3] (R Sussex) Staff, S V Shrimpton[3] (RAMC) attch. SH, Quetta, S M Vidler[3] (General List) & R G Wilson[3,4&5]

Lieutenants: ~ G H Greenock[3] (General List) attch. 1 DWR, E H Jones[3] attch. 'F' DSC, G E Pennell[3] (General List) attch. 3/W Sig Sqn, H E Pinhey[3] (DCLI) attch. 17 SSB, J C Sims[3] (General List) attch. ISC & (QM) J Walsh[3] (General List)

DOMINION & EMPIRE FORCES (OTHER THAN INDIAN ARMY):

Australia

~ The Australian Army Staff Corps ~

Note a.   *Roll of all personnel identified as eligible.*

Note b.   *Australian officers were commissioned from the Royal Military College Duntroon into the Australian Staff Corps. Several were sent each year to India for attachment to both British and Indian Army units.*

Note c.   *Medals believed to be named: 'AUST. STAFF CORPS'*

Single Clasp	No. Identified	Rarity
Afghanistan N.W.F. 1919[3]	0	None Identified
Mahsud 1919–20[5]	0	None Identified
Waziristan 1919–21[4]	0	None Identified
Waziristan 1921–24[6]	0	None Identified
Combination Clasps	No. Identified	Rarity
Waziristan 1919–21[4] Waziristan 1921–24[6]	1	According to the roll as seen, can be considered Unique
Waziristan 1919–21[4] Malabar 1921–22[7]	1	According to the roll as seen, can be considered Unique

Lieutenants: ~ J F Roberts[4&7(Suffolk)] attch. 2 Queen's & J R Woldenden[4&6] attch. 2 Queen's

~ The Australian Army Nursing Service ~

Note a.   *Roll of all personnel identified as eligible.*

Note b.   *The Australian Army Nursing Service (AANS) deployed several detachments to India during the Great War.*

Note c.   *All of the personnel qualifying for the India General Service Medal with clasp 'Afghanistan N.W.F. 1919' were attached to No. 43, British General Hospital (BGH), Royal Army Medical Corps (RAMC), Quetta.*

Note d.   *Medals named in impressed capitals: 'A.A.N.S.'*

Single Clasp	No. Identified	Rarity
Afghanistan N.W.F. 1919[3]	7	Of the Utmost Rarity
Mahsud 1919–20[5]	0	None Identified

311

Waziristan 1919–21[4]	0	None Identified
Waziristan 1921–24[6]	0	None Identified

Sisters: ~ M L Craven[3] & A Hodson[3]

Staff Nurses: ~ E V I Foster[3], O S McKay[3], E B McKay[3], M M Rout[3] & I Pierce[3]

New Zealand

~ The New Zealand Staff Corps ~

Note a. *Roll of all personnel identified as eligible.*

Note b. *Medals named in impressed capitals. Believed: 'N.Z. STAFF CORPS'*

Single Clasp	No. Identified	Rarity
Afghanistan N.W.F. 1919[3]	0	None Identified
Mahsud 1919–20[5]	0	None Identified
Waziristan 1919–21[4]	4	Of the Utmost Rarity
Waziristan 1921–24[6]	0	None Identified

Lieutenants: ~ S F Allen[4] attch. 2 Norfolk, C H G Davis[4] attch. 2 Queen's, A K Lambly[4] attch. 2 Queen's & S C V W Sugden[4] attch. 2 Queen's

~ The Royal New Zealand Artillery ~

Note a. *Roll of all personnel identified as eligible.*

Note b. *Medals named in impressed capitals. Believed: 'R.N.Z.A.'*

Single Clasp	No. Identified	Rarity
Afghanistan N.W.F. 1919[3]	0	None Identified
Mahsud 1919–20[5]	0	None Identified
Waziristan 1919–21[4]	0	None Identified
Waziristan 1921–24[6]	0	None Identified
Combination Clasps	**No. Identified**	**Rarity**
Mahsud 1919–20[5] Waziristan 1919–21[4]	1	According to the roll as seen, can be considered Unique

Lieutenants: ~ A T Nevill[4&5] attch. 6 Mtn Bty, RGA

The West Indies:

~ The British West Indies Regiment ~

Note a. *Roll of all personnel identified as eligible.*

Note b. *Roll is not clear whether the medal is named > 'BR. W.I.R.', > 'STAFF', or no unit inscribed as per practise on British War Medal 1914-1920 and Allied Victory Medal 1914-1919 when awarded to commissioned personnel. (See 'Regiment Not Inscribed' entry).*

Single Clasp	No. Identified	Rarity
Afghanistan N.W.F. 1919[3]	1	If verified, could be considered Unique

Mahsud 1919–20[5]	0	None Identified
Waziristan 1919–21[4]	0	None Identified
Waziristan 1921–24[6]	0	None Identified

Captains: ~ H C V Porter[3] attch. Leicester, DAAG 1 Div.

MISCELLANEOUS:

~ The Army Remount Department ~

Note a.   *Roll of all personnel identified as eligible.*
Note b.   *Medals named in impressed capitals. Believed: 'A. REMT. DEPT.'*

Single Clasp	No. Identified	Rarity
Afghanistan N.W.F. 1919[3]	0	None Identified
Mahsud 1919–20[5]	0	None Identified
Waziristan 1919–21[4]	0	None Identified
Waziristan 1921–24[6]	0	None Identified
Combination Clasps	No. Identified	Rarity
Mahsud 1919–20[5] Waziristan 1919–21[4]	1	According to the roll as seen, can be considered Unique

Captains: ~ (Act) A E F Batchelor[4&5] attch. Advanced Remount Depots DIK, Tank, Jamlota & Kotkai

~ The Army Cycle Corps ~

Note a.   *Roll of all personnel identified as eligible.*
Note b.   *Medals named in impressed capitals: 'A. CYC. CORPS. Or A.C.C.'*

Single Clasp	No. Identified	Rarity
Afghanistan N.W.F. 1919[3]	2	Of the Utmost Rarity
Mahsud 1919–20[5]	0	None Identified
Waziristan 1919–21[4]	0	None Identified
Waziristan 1921–24[6]	0	None Identified

Lance Corporals/Privates: ~ 4748 H P Farrington[3] attch. 14 MT Coy, S&TC plus 3 MAC & 5851 H Wilmott[3] attch. 1 DLI

~ The Corps of Military Staff Clerks ~

Note a.   *Roll of all eligible personnel identified as 'cap badged' Corps of Military Staff Clerks', as opposed to being shown on roll as attached Corps of Military Staff Clerks'. (See rolls above).*
Note b.   *Corps primarily part of Indian Establishment but did exist in British Establishment. Recipient below listed in British roll and therefore it is believed this was a British Establishment award.*
Note c.   *Medals named in impressed capitals: 'C.M.S.C.'*

Single Clasp	No. Identified	Rarity
Afghanistan N.W.F. 1919[3]	1	According to the roll as seen, can be considered Unique
Mahsud 1919–20[5]	0	None Identified

Waziristan 1919–21[4]	**0**	**None Identified**
Waziristan 1921–24[6]	**0**	**None Identified**

Quartermaster Sergeants/Sergeants: ~ 8521 E A Waring[3]

~ The Military Farms & Conservancy Department(s) ~

Note a.   *The Military Farms and Conservancy Departments formed part of the Indian Army establishment; however, many British personnel were attached on temporary duty. It is thought that the majority of such medals were named to their 'parent' units and are thus listed in the rolls above.*

Note b.   *The recipient below received a medal named 'MILY. D. FARMS' while retaining his Royal Artillery rank and serial number.*

Single Clasp	*No. Identified*	*Rarity*
Afghanistan N.W.F. 1919[3]	**0**	**None Identified**
Mahsud 1919–20[5]	**0**	**None Identified**
Waziristan 1919–21[4]	**0**	**None Identified**
Waziristan 1921–24[6]	**1**	**According to the roll as seen, can be considered Unique**

Lance Bombardiers/Gunner: ~ 1049960 F W Devine[6] from 'K' Bty, RHA

FOREIGN

Poland

~ Polish Army ~

Note a.   *Roll of all personnel identified as eligible.*

Note b.   *Lieutenant Gotchalk was an Exchange Officer sponsored by the British Military Mission, Poland.*

Note c.   *It is not known how this medal is named.*

Single Clasp	*No. Identified*	*Rarity*
Afghanistan N.W.F. 1919[3]	**1**	**According to the roll as seen, can be considered Unique**
Mahsud 1919–20[5]	**0**	**None Identified**
Waziristan 1919–21[4]	**0**	**None Identified**
Waziristan 1921–24[6]	**0**	**None Identified**

Lieutenants: ~ T Gotchalk[3]

THE ROYAL AIR FORCE

Note a.   *The Royal Air Force was established on 1st April 1918 from the Royal Flying Corps (Army) and the Royal Naval Air Service (Navy).*

Note b.   *Initially the rank structure was a hybrid of RFC and RNAS designations. Thus: 2nd Lieutenant, Lieutenant, Flight Lieutenant, Major, Wing Commander, etc. Non-commissioned ranks followed the same practise. The most junior rank, Air Craftsman, was initially designated Airman. Additionally, Pilots were styled 'Flying Officers' and Observers were styled 'Observer Officers'. The 'current' rank structure was established from 1st August 1919 with initial references appearing in the London Gazette dated 5th September 1919. (Sergeant Majors were not designated Warrant Officers until 1933). This period of change straddled potential participation in the Afghanistan 1919, Mahsud 1919-20 and Waziristan 1919-21 operations. To bring clarity to this situation, I have compiled two separate registers below:*

        Register One *lists those personnel whose names are recorded under the 'old' rank system.*

        Register Two *lists those personnel whose names are recorded under the 'current' rank system.*

Note c.   *Criteria for personnel to be included in the following roll follows that set for the Army roll for the Frontier Campaigns of 1919 –1925 i.e. all identified eligible commissioned ranks plus multi bar other rank personnel. Mahsud 1919-20 is reproduced in full.*

Note d.   *Due to 'austerity' measures, it was determined in Air Ministry Order 643/26 of December 1926 that those personnel who qualified for both of the clasps 'WAZIRISTAN 1921–24' and 'WAZIRISTAN 1925' could only apply for one clasp. The 'WAZIRISTAN 1925' roll appears at the end of the next section.*

Note e.   *Medals named in impressed capitals: AFGHANISTAN N.W.F. 1919 named 'R.A. FORCE'; others named 'R.A.F.'*

Single Clasp	No. Identified	Rarity
Afghanistan N.W.F. 1919[3]	708	Not Rare
Mahsud 1919–20[5]	4	Of the Utmost Rarity
Waziristan 1919–21[4]	334	Not Rare
Waziristan 1921–24[6]	515	Not Rare
Combination Clasps	**No. Identified**	**Rarity**
Afghanistan N.W.F. 1919[3] Mahsud 1919–20[5]	6	Of the Utmost Rarity
Afghanistan N.W.F. 1919[3] Mahsud 1919–20[5] Waziristan 1919–21[4]	68	Rare
Afghanistan N.W.F. 1919[3] Mahsud 1919–20[5] Waziristan 1919–21[4] Waziristan 1921–24[6]	4	Of the Utmost Rarity
Afghanistan N.W.F. 1919[3] Mahsud 1919–20[5] Waziristan 1919–21[4] Waziristan 1921–24[6] North West Frontier 1930 – 31[9]	1	According to the roll as seen, can be considered Unique
Afghanistan N.W.F. 1919[3] Mahsud 1919–20[5] Waziristan 1919–21[4] North West Frontier 1930–31[9]	2	Of the Utmost Rarity
Afghanistan N.W.F. 1919[3] Mahsud 1919–20[5] Waziristan 1919–21[4] Waziristan 1911–24[6] North West Frontier 1930–31[9]	1	According to the roll as seen, can be considered Unique
Afghanistan N.W.F. 1919[3] Waziristan 1919–21[4]	53	Very Rare
Afghanistan N.W.F. 1919[3] Waziristan 1919–21[4] Waziristan 1921–24[6]	5	Of the Utmost Rarity
Afghanistan N.W.F. 1919[3] Waziristan 1919–21[4] North West Frontier 1930–31[9]	1	According to the roll as seen, can be considered Unique
Afghanistan N.W.F. 1919[3] Waziristan 1921–24[6]	1	According to the roll as seen, can be considered Unique
Afghanistan N.W.F. 1919[3] North West Frontier 1930–31[9]	2	Of the Utmost Rarity
Afghanistan N.W.F. 1919[3] North West Frontier 1930–31[9] Mohmand 1933[11]	1	According to the roll as seen, can be considered Unique
Mahsud 1919–20[5] Waziristan 1919–21[4]	73	Rare

Mahsud 1919–20[5] **Waziristan 1919–21[4]** **Waziristan 1921–24[6]**	6	**Of the Utmost Rarity**
Mahsud 1919–20[5] **Waziristan 1919–21[4]** **North West Frontier 1930–31[9]**	1	**According to the roll as seen, can be considered Unique**
Mahsud 1919–20[5] **Waziristan 1919–21[4]** **Mohmand 1933[11]**	1	**According to the roll as seen, can be considered Unique**
Waziristan 1919–21[4] **Waziristan 1921–24[6]**	24	**Very Rare**
Waziristan 1919–21[4] **Waziristan 1925[8]**	9	**Of the Utmost Rarity**
Waziristan 1919–21[4] **North West Frontier 1930–31[9]**	6	**Of the Utmost Rarity**
Waziristan 1921–24[6] **North West Frontier 1930–31[9]**	5	**Of the Utmost Rarity**
Waziristan 1921–24[6] **Mohmand 1933[11]**	1	**According to the roll as seen, can be considered Unique**
Waziristan 1921–24[6] **Mohmand 1933[11]** **North West Frontier 1935[12]**	2	**Of the Utmost Rarity**
Waziristan 1921–24[6] **North West Frontier 1935[12]**	3	**Of the Utmost Rarity**

Register One – Personnel with names are recorded under the 'old' rank system.

Majors: ~ D Cloete[3], E Greenwood[4] & J B Quested[3]

Captains: ~ W E Humphreys[3], P F J Kent[6], F J Phillips[3], G H Salaman[3], L J Stuart[3], H Tilley[3&4], G R Travis[3] & A C Upham[3]

Lieutenants: ~ P F Antelme[3], J L Bernard[3], R P A Crisp[3], A H Darnbrough[4&5], W H Dowling[3], ? Featherstone[3], B A Foord[3], B N Goudge[3], W V N Grant[3], L T M Griffin[3&4], A F Harris[3], J D Hewett[4], E N Hewitt[3], E T H Hill[3], F E Horley[3], W H Kingsland[3], J F Mead[3], G L Nicholson[3,4&5], R W Parkinson[3], A H Parsons[3], G Rogerson[3,4&5], D M Rooke[3], B E Sharwood-Smith[3], A D Sinclair[4], R J Smith[3], A V Street[3], R B Tapp[3,4&5], D E D Taylor[3], J E Truss[3], O S Waymouth[4&5], J A Wilson[3], L Wycherley[3] & H C Young[3]

2nd Lieutenants: ~ J R Astin[3], C D Ball[3&4], H E Foster[3,4&5], W E Harper[3], S E Hodgson[3], W A Manson[3], C S Millar[4&5], K Onyett[3], H G C Plumridge[3], W J Porter[3], J E Roberts[3], W J Sutherland[3,4&5], R Watson[3&9], A I Watts[3] & R C Williams[3]

Observer Officers: ~ H Alexander[3], W P Bingham[3], R A C Brie[4&5], A J Cox[3,4&5], E Cuthbert[3,4&5], J Davidson[3,4&5], N S Dougall[4&5], C N Ellen[4,5,8&11], R B Gordon[4], R Hamilton[4], P J Hayes[4], R Henderson[3], G E Hillman[3], G McCormack[3,4&5], W McGowan[3,4&5], B J Malyan[3,4&5], E G Munson[3], C H F Nesbit[4&5], A E Reynolds[3&4], R T Rich[4], E W Tyrrell[3], J S F Watson[3] & A L Willcox[3]

Register Two – Personnel with names are recorded under the 'current' rank system. (This Register includes Flying Officers who may technically have been designated as such because they were Pilots under the 'old' system. It is not possible to differentiate with the information currently available).

Air Commodore: ~ T I Webb-Bowen[4&5]

Wing Commanders: ~ J R F Barton[4&6], (Act) W W Hart[6], A C Maund[6], N D K McEwen[3], W G S Mitchell[4&6], E M Murray[6] & T S Rippon[3&4]

Squadron Leaders: ~ B F Beatson[6], W R Bruce[3], W A Coryton[6], C R Cox[3,4&5], A P V Daly[3], J Everidge[3], J B Graham[4], E N H Gray[4], A T Harris[6], T McClurkin[3], P C Maltby[6], E L Millar[2], R J Mounsey[6], A W Mylne[6], H S Powell[6], J C Russell[3&4], P C Sherren[6], B E Smythies[4], D E Stodart[3], J H S Tyssen[4], R P Whitehead[6], J T Whittaker[6], G A Williams[4] & W F Wilson[6]

Flight Lieutenants: ~ W R B Annesley[6], E L Ardley[6], J E M Atherley[4?], G Baker[4], P E Bishop[3,4&5], G F Blackburn[6], A G Bond[6], L C Boyd[3], A Briscoe[4], A F Brooke[4&9], E Burton[6], E I Bussell[3,4,5&6], W J Butler[3], L A K Butt[4], H C Calvey[6], D H M Carbery[3,4&(9 as Capt. RA, 4 Mtn Bty)], H V Champion De Crespigny[4,5,6&9], K D G Collier[4], J Cottle[3], D Craik[4&5], W N Cumming[6], P H Cummings[4&9], H Mc W Daniel[4&5], C J S Dearlove[6], P A De Fontenay[6], R J M De St. Ledger[6], W H Dolphin[3,4&5], D S Don[4&6], W H Dunn[4], C M Eastley[4], A B Ellwood[6], C E W Foster[3,4&5], J B Fox[4], A W F Glenny[4,5&6], R Graham[4], E O Grenfell[4&6], R Halley[3], H A Hamersley[6], S B Harris[6&9], G H Harrison[6], W E Hodgins[6], L N Hollinghurst[3,9&11], R T B

Houghton[6&12], F J W Humphreys[6], C R Keary[6], H P M Kesterton[3,4&5], H E King[3,4&5], H P Lale[3,4&5], L A Lavender[4], J D Leahy[6], V S E Linop[4&6], H P Lloyd[6,11&12], D F Massy[3], C H Masters[6], P N Melitus[6], H M Moody[6], C F Norris[4], C H N Nunn[4&5], J Oliver[6], E R B Playford[6], W H Poole[4], F J Powell[4&6], A D Prior[4&5], H G P Rees[4], C Y Roberts[6], P G Scott[6], W J Seward[3], R H Shears[3], C H Sherwin[3], G H Simister[3], F O Soden[4], W E Somervell[6], R De L Stedman[3], W E Theak[6], W D Thom[3&4], R L Thomas[3], T F W Thompson[4,5&6], W D Thorn[3], H A Tweedie[3], J L Vachell[4], F J Vincent[4], J G Walser[6] & F J Watts[3,4,5&6]

Flying Officers: ~ D S Allan[6], G H Allison[3], J L W Bacon[3], C G Barker[3], M W Baseden[4], J C Bedford[6], W Best[4,2&8], C H Bird[4], G L Blake[4&5], J F Blick[3,4&5], J H Body[3], J A Boret[6], C A Bouchier[4], J Bradbury[6], C F Brewerton[4&6], E A C Britton[3,4,5&9], W A D Brook[6], H J Brown[6], K H Brown[3], S P B De Moyse-Bucknell[3,4&5], N Burke[3], J H Butler[3,4&5], J P Cafferkey[3&4], D O Onslow-Carleton[4], N Carter[6&12], R F Casey[6], R Ivelaw-Chapman[4,5&6], J S Chick[4&6], F C Cogswell[3&4], E J Crichton[3], G M Cocker[4,5&6], R A Curry[3], J H Dand[4], M R D'Arcy[3], P H Davy[4&5], G V De Boissiere[3], E C Delamain[3,4,5&9], F V Devonshire[3], H A Dinnage[3], C Dollery[6], R B Dormor[3], G F Drudge[4], L B Duggan[3,4&5], J C Dunbar[4&5], D C Duncan[3,4&5], A L Courtnay-Dunn[4&5], I G G Edgar[4&5], E D Edwards[3], C A Elliot[3,4&6], G A Elliot[4], J A Elliott[4], E T H Ellis[4], W R Fairbairn[5], E N Fenton[4&5], A L Fiddament[4&5], N Fielden[3&5], M H Findlay[4&5], H Ford[6], R M Foster[4,5&6], O D Freeman[6], G W Gay[6&9], R A George[4&6], T Gilbert[3], J B V Glyde[6], R G R Godby[6], J M Godfrey[3,4&5], C F H Grace[6], H S Green[3], R S Greenslade[3,4&5], W Halford[4], B J O'Connor-Hanstock[6], J D I Hardman[6], B R Harris[3,4&5], L G Harvey[4&5], H S Hawkes[3], F L B Hebbert[4&6], D A P Heron[4&5], H W Heslop[4&6], G P F Hills[6], C A Hoy[4], G C Huggard[3&4], D J C Hutton[3], L H Bell-Irving[4], C Jackson[4&6], J D Jackson[4], N H Jay[4&6], E C N Jeffries[4], B P Jones[6], E G Keeping[3], J L Kirby[3,4&5], D M Lapraik[3], A G Lawe[3,4&5], E Lawson[3], J A Leonard[3], B A S Lewin[4,5&6], G F Lines[6], G D Longfellow[3], D G R Lord[3], R B Luard[6], H F Luck[6], E McGowen[3], C S McGregor[3], G F Mackay[6], S McKeever[6&9], G W K Mercer[4&9], J W F Merer[3,4,5&6], D R Mitchell[6], R P Mollard[6], M Moore[4&5], N V Moreton[6], S J Morrell[3], D R Mullan[3,4&5], P Murgatroyd[3], L Murphy[4&5], S G Newport[4], W G Nicholls[6], L G Nixon[6], T O Oakes[6], G R C Oliver[4], H G P Ovenden[3,4&5], J W Parkinson[3], H A L Pattison[3,4&5], N S Paynter[4], A L Pearce[6], J Pipe[3], A E Platford[6], A H Power[4&5], W E Purdin[3], R Pyne[6], G E Randall[3], R M Rankin[3], C H Ratcliffe[6], G J Rayner[6], W J Richards[6], E H Richardson[4?], G T Richardson[5], L H Ridley[6], T H R Riggs[6], F G A Robinson[4,5&9], T Rose[4&5], H J Saker[4&5], N C Saward[4], G Scarrott[4&5], G C Sclater[6], T J Shaw[6], F A Skoulding[6], F A R Smith[6], J K Smith[6], C R Smythe[4], E C Usher-Somers[4], W E Staton[4&5], C R Steele[4&6], G V Stewart[3], G W Sturman[4], J R Swanston[4&5], J Talbot[3&4], C N Thompson[3], D Thompson[3], C F Toogood[3,4&5], F E E Villiers[3], C Mc C Vincent[3], C Walker[4&6], R R S Waller[6], R S Walter[6], K E Ward[4&5], A L Watkins[3], S N Webster[4&6], P G Wells[3], H W Westaway[6], F N Whitehead[3,4&5], W Mahony-Whitton[4], G Winstanley[3], A M Wray[4&6] & F W Wrench[6]

Pilot Officers: ~ W J Allan[3], A M Anderson[3&4?], L W Beck[3], G A Body[3], C G Boothroyd[3], T R Breakell[6], D Mc D Calder[3], F G Carter[3], S G Davis[3], L C Dodkins[3], R B Fortune[4&5], F D D Gaussen[3], N P B Giddens[3], J E Goudey[3,4&5], D E Hall[3], L J Hoare[3], H R Junor[3,4&6], J H Low[3], S Moyles[3], R O Mullinger[3], J G Nagle[3], R E Nixon[3,4&5], G S Oddie[3], E S Oxley[3], J Platt[3,4&5], R Pughe[3], R F Ralph[3,4&5], G N Richmond[3,4&5], M St. J Ross[3], B H C Russell[3,4,5,6&9], J T O'Brien-Saint[3,4&5], W Stewart[3], P G White[3], H E Winch[4&5] & W Wright[3]

Sergeant Majors: ~ 2132 A W Ivey[3&4], 269 W P Parker[3,4&5], E Ramden[3&4] & 753 W J Southgate[5]

Flight Sergeants: ~ 254122 R H Garner[3,4&5], 6606 F G Hammond[3,4&5], 401704 L F Kingston[4&5], 313171 T F Mantle[4&5], 230 O R Rowe[3,4&6] & 410 A Springate[4&8?]

Technical Sergeants: ~ 55150 W S Simpson[4&5]

Sergeants: ~ 11175 J D Allan[3&5], 109253 S B Badsey[3&4], 8246 A E Clayson[3&4], 6409 S H Fereday[3,4&5], 99730 C R Haigh[3&4], 200697 F G McAllister[3&6], 205786 V G Macario[3&4], 206462 F H Pearce[4&6], 230436 C F Perkin[3&4], 211382 W H Pickering[4&5], 7392 A D Rutherford[4&8?], 20948 W Smith[3&4?], 55149 N Unett[4&5], 246000 S G Walker[4&5] & 82587 J Wood[3&4]

Corporals: ~ 340824 F L Bowman[4?&9], 248272 G F Cockell[4&9], 327793 A Fisher[6,11&12], (Act) 26505 A Fox[3&4], 877 S F Fraser[3,4&5], 48688 R E Gilling[3&4], 156537 S Gordon[4&6], 343586 L Hilton[6&11], 241197 F G Jones[4&6], 404265 W H Jones[3&4], 16911 W Morris[3,4&5], M J Roberts[3&4], 342046 C F Smith[6&9], 330751 T L Walters[4&8?] & 5951 R J A Webb[3&4]

Leading Air Craftsmen: ~ 157808 S Bounden[4&5], 341751 E A Bubb[6&9], 248608 A L Cockerline[4&6], 17189 T A Dewson[3&4], 250618 W G Donnan[4&5], 107500 W H Dowle[4&5], 136895 F T Geal[3,4&5], 7468 G E Harding[3&4], 54908 H G Hay[3,4&5], 247385 T R Hilder[3&4], 247939 W J Kelly[4&5], 49199 C E La Gallienne[4&5], 39185 E G Lewis[4&5], 329342 C E Littlewood[4&5], 995 A B McAllister[4&5], 355603 S F Mayhew[4&6], 9897 A J Orchiston[3,4&5], 340801 J Phelan[4&6], 63788 A Powell[4&5], 345405 V Tonkin[6&12], 64567 J Tweedle[3&4], 66582 H Warne[3&4] & 15284 J Watton[3&4]

(Airman) Air Craftsmen 1st Class: ~ 245537 T A H Adamson[4&5], 404259 G C Aldred[3,4&5], 78916 H H Allen[3&4], 158844 F E Beardsall[3&5?], 104683 C C Bedford[3,4&5], 191022 W L Boyd[3,4&5], 240768 W H Boyes[4&5], 156531 A J Craven[3,4&6], 343241 F Dunstan[4&8], 247230 H V Emery[3&4], 139211 H Farmer[4&5], S W Fenton[4&5], A W Fiske[4&8?], 158997 J M Fitzgerald[4&5], 86440 L C Hill[4&5], 334134 O S Hobbs[4&5], 114101 E E Honeywell[3&4], 13868 S C Kemp[3,4&5], 84069 J E Lockhurst[3&4], 59860 C A Loosemore[3,4,5&6], 252554 H J Ridgley[3&4], 329240 L Robinson[4&5], 16053 W Scarte[3&5?], 239481 L A Sparks[3&9], 341035 C E Styles[4&8], 338020 C R Thomas[4&5], 332574 W J Thomas[4&5], 78876 C C Toone[3&4], 334368 J Tumilty[4&5], 246164 J P Ward[4&5], 337911 A Wareham[4&5] & 240771 J F Young[3&4]

(Airman) Air Craftsmen 2nd Class: ~ 336654 W H Abbs[4?&9], 338081 R Adams[4&5], 211277 C Anderson[4&5], 281494 W J Anderson[3,4&5], 275068 H Andrews[3&4], 239583 F B Beaumont[3&4], 246844 J F D Beazer[3&4], 329347 G Blackwood[3,4&5], 156103 A Bradford[4&5], 244723 F J Brown[4&5], 81791 W G Brown[4&5], 241107 L P Bugh[3&4], 116187 J H Champion[4&5], 250538 C J Clow[5], 63604 J E P Clowes[3&4], 289142 J Connell[4&5], 329348 E E Cook[3,4&5], 248890 G Deacon[4&5], 245293 H J Deslandes[3,4&5],

191757 G C Dickson[3,4&5], 342857 T J Doyle[4&6], 132662 F C Dummett[3,4&5], 239399 T W Ellcock[3,4&5], 284237 L Elsom[3&4], 290520 S Ferris[3&4], 148720 A E Hawkins[3&5], 119053 J Hays[3&5], 166730 F Haywood[4&5], 18667 A E Howard[3&4], 329242 J Lawrence[4&5], 131158 W L Mallandain[3&4], 23727 E Manning[3,4&5], 59586 H H Mayo[3,4&5], 251458 S Millyard[3,4&5], 247869 A Mitchener[3&4], 333863 D Mounsey[4&5], 156309 O Orton[3,4&5], 107362 A Pedley[3,4&5], 326817 B R Rickerby[4&8?], 303943 I C Riley[3&4], 94060 A G Rosenheim[3,4&5], 163596 R J Ruggles[3&4], 409041 F S Sanderson[3&4], 122823 G N Scott[4&5], 343100 H Thorn[4&8], 406289 E F Warner[3&4?], 332454 J Watson[4&5], 332008 W F Weir[3,4&6], 120644 R H White[3,4&5], 408849 W J Wodhams[3,4&5] & 277318 W J Woodhouse[3,4&5]

~ Civilian Personnel ~

Note a. *Many civilian personnel qualified for Indian General Service Medals during the period 1919–1924 and beyond. Recipients ranged from civil servants of both the British and Indian Government establishments, to medical and nursing staff, communications staff (including railway engineers and train crew), administrators and press correspondents.*

Note b. *The names below should not be construed as a complete roll of eligible recipients but rather a sampling of medals seen.*

Note c. *Naming sometimes includes a relevant employment designation such as 'Clk', 'Dr.' or 'Ind Rlys'.*

General Category:
Civilian: ~ Mr. Wilson[3], Censer Dept

Medical Category:
Doctors: ~ Dr. A M Pennell[3] attch. BGH, Bannu
Nurses: ~ E Archard[3], E E Bott[3], M Dowling[3&4], A Holmes[3], A R I Lowe[3&4], N Newton[4&6] & A M Irvin[6]
British Red Cross: ~ Mrs. A H Bell[4&5] Secretary to the Assistant Red Cross Commissioner

Supply & Transport Category:
Civilian: ~ 77 H R Jennings

Communications Category:
Telegraphists: ~ RP1878 G R Matthews[3], RP1032 D H Reece[3] & RP2089 A Smith[3]
Clerks: ~ Mrs. Newberry[3]

In addition, many others whose names are recorded on unidentified rolls many of which would have been drawn up by the Indian Establishment.

INDIAN ESTABLISHMENT:
Qualifying Units Present

The Cavalry:
By 1922 Structure & Seniority
(Verified Clasp Entitlement Shown)

1922 Title	Pre 1922 Title
1st Duke of York's Own Skinner's Horse	1st Duke of York's Own Lancers (Skinner's Horse)[3] & 3rd Skinner's Horse[3]
2nd Lancers (Gardner's Horse)	4th Cavalry[3]
5th King Edward's Own Probyn's Horse	12th Cavalry[3]
6th Duke of Connaught's Own Lancers	13th Duke of Connaught's Lancers (Watson's Horse)[3] & 16th Cavalry[4]
7th Light Cavalry[6]	28th Light Cavalry[3&6]
8th King George's Own Light Cavalry	30th Lancers (Gordon's Horse)[3]
10th Queen's Own Corps of Guides Cavalry (FF)	Queen's Own Corps of Guides (FF) (Lumsden's) Cavalry[3]
11th Prince Albert Victor's Own Cavalry (FF)	21st Prince Albert Victor's Own Cavalry FF (Daly's Horse)[3,4&5] (1 Sqn Only For Waziristan / Mahsud) & 23rd Cavalry FF[3]
12th Cavalry (FF)	25th Cavalry FF[3]
13th Duke of Connaught's Own Bombay Lancers*	31st Duke of Connaught's Own Lancers[3&4]
15th Lancers	17th Cavalry[3] & 37th Lancers (Baluch Horse)[3] (1 Sqn)
16th Light Cavalry[6]	27th Light Cavalry[3,4&6]
17th Queen Victoria's Own Poona Horse[6]	33rd Queen Victoria's Own Light Cavalry[3&6]
18th King Edward's Own Cavalry	7th Hariana Lancers[4] (Individuals)
The Central India Horse (21st King George's Own Horse[6])*	38th King George's Own Central India Horse
Disbanded 1921	40th Cavalry[3]
Disbanded 1921	41st Cavalry[3]
Disbanded 1921	42nd Cavalry[3]

Note: * = *Disbanded 1923*

Imperial Service Cavalry:
Alwar Lancers[3], Bhopal Lancers[3&4], Navanagar Lancers[3], Patiala Lancers[3]

The Artillery:

Pre 1920 Changes	1920 Title	1921 Title	1922 > 1927
21 Kohat Mountain Battery (FF)	21 Kohat Pack Battery (FF)	101 (Kohat) Pack Battery	101 Royal (Kohat) Pack Battery (FF)
22 Derajat Mountain Battery (FF)	22 Derajat Pack Battery (FF)	102 (Derajat) Pack Battery	102 (Derajat) Pack Battery (FF)
23 Peshawar Mountain Battery (FF)	23 Peshawar Pack Battery (FF)	103 (Peshawar) Pack Battery	103 (Peshawar) Pack Battery (FF)
24 Hazara Mountain Battery (FF)	24 Hazara Pack Battery (FF)	104 (Hazara) Pack Battery	104 (Hazara) Pack Battery (FF)
26 Jacob's Mountain Battery	26 Jacob's Pack Battery	106 (Jacob's) Pack Battery	No Change
27 Mountain Battery	27 Pack Battery	107 (Gujarat) Pack Battery	107 (Bengal) Pack Battery
28 Mountain Battery	28 Pack Battery	108 (Lahore) Pack Battery	No Change
29 Mountain Battery	29 Pack Battery	109 (Murree) Pack Battery	No Change
30 Mountain Battery	30 Pack Battery	110 (Abbottabad) Pack Battery	No Change
32 Mountain Battery	32 Pack Battery	112 (Poonch) Pack Battery	No Change
33 (Reserve) Mountain Battery	33 Pack Battery	113 (Dardoni) Pack Battery	No Change
34 (Reserve) Mountain Battery	34 Pack Battery	114 (Rajputana) Pack Battery	No Change
35 (Reserve) Mountain Battery	35 Pack Battery	115 (Jhelum) Pack Battery	No Change
36 (Reserve) Mountain Battery	36 Pack Battery	116 (Zhob) Pack Battery	No Change
37 (Reserve) Mountain Battery	37 Pack Battery	117 Pack Battery	No Change
38 (Reserve) Mountain Battery	38 Pack Battery	118 (Sohan) Pack Battery	No Change
39 (Reserve) Mountain Battery	39 Pack Battery	119 (Maymyo) Pack Battery	No Change
43 (Reserve) Mountain Battery	43 Pack Battery	121 (Nowshera) Pack Battery	No Change
47 (Reserve) Mountain Battery	47 Pack Battery	Disbanded	Disbanded
50 (Reserve) Mountain Battery	50 Pack Battery	Disbanded	Disbanded

Post Guns
Chitral Pack Artillery Section

Imperial Service Artillery
No. 1 Bty, Kashmir Imperial Service Artillery & No. 2 Bty, Kashmir Imperial Service Artillery

The Sappers & Miners:
1923 Title...Pre 1923 Title
King George's Own Bengal Sappers & Miners...1King Georges Own Sappers & Miners
Nos. 1, 4, 5, 7''', 8, 53'', 55'', 56'', 57' & 58' Field Companies
Note: Disbanded 1920 1921** 1922****

Queen Victoria's Own Sappers & Miners...2 Queen Victoria's Own Sappers & Miners
Nos. 11, 12, 13, 14, 15, 63, 64'', 66'', 67', 68', 69''', 94'' & 96 Field Companies
Nos. 3 & 4''Photo-Litho Section

(In 1923 No. 3 Photo-Litho Section became No. 54 Photo Litho Section)
Note: Disbanded 1920* 1921** 1922***

Royal Bombay Sappers & Miners...3 Sappers & Miners
Nos. 17, 19, 20, 21, 24***, 71**, 73*, 74*, 75*, 76*** & 113 Field Companies
No. 6@ Photo-Litho Section No. 7@ Printing Section
4 Field Troop³*
Note: Disbanded 1919@ 1920* 1921** 1922***

Railway Sappers & Miners
26 Railway Battalion (Company) > To 3 Sappers & Miners in 1921

Military Works Service
(From 1923 Military Engineer Services)
Advance Engineer Parks: Nos. 1, 7 & 8 > Bannu, Kalabagh, Mari-Indus & Tank
No. 1 Survey Section
Railway Construction Companies Based At Bannu, Darya Khan, Mari Indus & Tank Sidings:
Nos. 122, 126, 127, 131 & 139
Decauville Railway DIK to Tank
E & M Works Depot: Detachment Nos. 9 & 12
Military Works Company: No. 11
Works Battalions: Nos. 3 Punjab, 4 Madras, 5 Madras & 6 United Provinces
(1 Wing) Labour Corps
Works Labour Corps & Camps: Nos. 13, 15, 99, 101, 103, 110, 112, 114, 118, 119, 120, 141 & 147 Khyber Arial Rope Way³

Signals Service Sappers & Miners
(From 1920 The Indian Signal Corps)
1921 Title..**Pre 1921 Title**
'A' & 'B' Corps Signals
Line Companies 'A' & 'B' Corps Signals
1 Cavalry Brigade Signal Squadron
3 Pack Wireless Station
16 Pack Wireless Station
Infantry Brigade Signals Troops

1920 GHQ (Baghdad)..No. 2 Wireless Signal Squadron
2 Wireless Company > 'A/B' Corps Signals.....................................No. 3 Wireless Signal Squadron
'B' Divisional Signals⁴ˆ⁶...33 Divisional Signal Company
'C' Divisional Signals⁴ˆ⁶...34 Divisional Signal Company
'D' Divisional Signals⁴ˆ⁶...35 Divisional Signal Company
'E' Divisional Signals⁴ˆ⁶...36 Divisional Signal Company
'F' Divisional Signals⁴ˆ⁶...38 Divisional Signal Company
'G' Divisional Signals⁴ˆ⁶...39 Divisional Signal Company
'H' Divisional Signals (From 1922 'A' Divisional Signals)....................40 Divisional Signal Company
Disbanded 1919..43 Divisional Signal Company
Merged With 35 Divisional Signal Company to form 'D' Divisional Signals..............44 Divisional Signal Company
Disbanded 1919..45 Divisional Signal Company
Disbanded 1919..46 Divisional Signal Company
Disbanded 1920..67 Divisional Signal Company
Disbanded 1920..68 Divisional Signal Company
Disbanded 1919..Draft Cable Sections
No. 1 L of C Signals Company...No. 1 L of C Signals Section
Disbanded 1919...No. 2 L of C Signals Section
Disbanded 1919...No. 3 L of C Signals Section
Disbanded 1919...No. 4 L of C Signals Section
Disbanded 1919...No. 5 L of C Signals Section
Cadres Only From 1920...2 Mobile Pigeon Lofts

The Pioneers:
1922 Title..**Pre 1922 Title**
1/1ˢᵗ Madras Pioneers (King George's Own)...1/61ˢᵗ King George's Own Pioneers
(Disbanded 1921)...2/61ˢᵗ King George's Own Pioneers
2/1ˢᵗ Madras Pioneers...1/64ᵗʰ Pioneers

10/1st Madras Pioneers	1/81st Pioneers
(Disbanded 1921)	2/81st Pioneers
1/2nd Bombay Pioneers	1/107th Pioneers
2/2nd Bombay Pioneers (Kelat-I-Ghilzai)	1/12th Pioneers (The Kelat-I-Ghilzai Regiment)
(Disbanded 1921)	2/12th Pioneers (The Kelat-I-Ghilzai Regiment)
4/2nd Bombay Pioneers	1/48th Pioneers
1/3rd Sikh Pioneers	1/23rd Sikh Pioneers
2/3rd Sikh Pioneers	1/32nd Sikh Pioneers
3 (Royal) / 3rd Sikh Pioneers	1/34th Royal Sikh Pioneers
(Disbanded 1921)	2/34th Royal Sikh Pioneers
(Disbanded 1921)	3/34th Royal Sikh Pioneers
10/3rd Sikh Pioneers	2/23rd Sikh Pioneers
1/4th Hazara Pioneers	1/106th Hazara Pioneers

The Infantry:
(Verified Clasp Entitlement Shown)

1922 Title	Pre 1922 Title
1/1st Punjab Regiment	1/62nd Punjabis[4] (Individuals)
2/1st Punjab Regiment[6]	1/66th Punjabis[3,4&6]
3/1st Punjab Regiment[6]	1/76th Punjabis[3&6] & 2/76th Punjabis[4,5&6]
4/1st Punjab Regiment[6]	1/1st Brahmans
5/1st Punjab Regiment[6]	1/82nd Punjabis[3,4,5&6]
1/2nd Punjab Regiment	1/67th Punjabis & 2/67th Punjabis[3]
2/2nd Punjab Regiment[6]	1/69th Punjabis[3&6] & 2/69th Punjabis[3,4&6]
3/2nd Punjab Regiment	1/72nd Punjabis & 2/72nd Punjabis[3]
1/3rd Madras Regiment[6]	73rd Carnatic Infantry[6]
1/4th Bombay Grenadiers[6]	1/101st Grenadiers & 2/101st Grenadiers[6]
2/4th Bombay Grenadiers[6]	1/102nd Grenadiers[3] & 2/102nd King Edward's Own Grenadiers[3,4&6]
4/4th Bombay Grenadiers[6]	1/109th Infantry[3,4,5&6]
5/4th Bombay Grenadiers (Disbanded 1923)	2/112nd (Infantry) Rifles[3,4&5]
10/4th Bombay Grenadiers[6]	2/113th Infantry[3,4&6]
1/5th Mahratta Light Infantry	1/103rd Mahratta Light Infantry[3,4&5]
3/5th Mahratta Light Infanty[6]	1/110th Mahratta Light Infantry[3&6]
1/6th Rajputana Rifles (Wellesley's)[6]	1/104th Wellesley's Rifles[4,5&6]
2/6th Rajputana Rifles (Prince of Wales's Own)[6]	1/120th (Prince of Wales's Own) Rajputana Infantry[3&6]
4/6th Rajputana Rifles (Outram's)[6]	2/123rd Outram's Rifles[3&6]
5/6th Rajputana Rifles (Napier's)[6]	125th Napier's Rifles[6]
1/7th Rajput Regiment (Queen Victoria's Own Light Infantry)[6]	1/2nd Queen Victoria's Own Rajput Light Infantry[6]
2/7th Rajput Regiment (Prince Albert Victor's)[6]	1/4th Prince Albert Victor's Rajputs[3,4&6] & 2/4th Prince Albert Victor's Rajputs[4&6]
5/7th Rajput Regiment	1/11th Rajputs[3]
10/7th Rajputs (The Lucknow Regiment)[6]	1/16th Rajputs (The Lucknow Regiment)[3&6]
1/8th Punjab Regiment	2/89th Punjabis[3]
2/8th Punjab Regiment[6]	1/90th Punjabis[3&4] & 2/90th Punjabis[3&4]
3/8th Punjab Regiment[6]	1/91st Punjabis
1/9th Jat Regiment (Light Infantry)[6]	1/6th Royal Jat Light Infantry[3&6]
2/9th Jat Regiment (Mooltan)[6]	2/119th Infantry (The Mooltan Regiment)[3&6]
3/9th Jat Regiment[6]	1/10th Jats[6] & 4/9th Jat Regiment[6]
1 (Duchess of Connaught's Own) / 10th Baluch Regiment	1/124th Duchess of Connaught's Own Baluchistan Light Infantry 2/124th Duchess of Connaught's Own Baluchistan Light Infantry/ 3/124th Duchess of Connaught's Own Baluchistan Light Infantry[3]
2/10th Baluch Regiment	1/126th Baluchistan Infantry[3]
3/10th Baluch Regiment (Queen Mary's Own)	1/127th Queen Mary's Own Baluchistan Light Infantry & 2/127th Queen Mary's Own Baluchistan Light Infantry[4&5]
4/10th Baluch Regiment (Duke of Connaught's Own)[6]	1/129th Duke of Connaught's Own Baluchis[3] & 2/129th Duke of Connaught's Own Baluchis[3&6]
5/10th Baluch Regiment (King George's Own Jacob's Rifles)[6]	130th King George's Own Baluchis (Jacob's Rifles)[6]
1/11th Sikh Regiment (KGO Ferozepore Own)	1/14th King George's Own Ferozepore Sikhs[3]
2/11th Sikh Regiment (Ludihana Sikhs)	1/15th Ludihana Sikhs[3]
4/11th Sikh Regiment[6]	1/36th Sikhs[6]
10/11th Sikh Regiment	1/35th Sikhs[3]
1/12th Frontier Force Regiment (Prince of Wales's Own Sikhs)[6]	1/51st Sikhs FF[6]

2/12th Frontier Force Regiment (Sikhs)[6]..1/52nd Sikhs FF[6]
3/12th Frontier Force Regiment (Sikhs)[6] ....1/53 Sikhs FF[6]
4/12th Frontier Force Regiment (Sikhs)[6]..1/54th Sikhs FF[4&6]
5/12th Frontier Force Regiment (Queen Victoria's Own Corps of Guides).......................1st Queen Victoria's Own Corps of Guides Infantry (Lumsden's)[3]
10/12th Frontier Force Regiment (Queen Victoria's Own Corps of Guides). ....2nd Queen Victoria's Own Guides Infantry[3]
1/13th Frontier Force Rifles (Coke's)..1/55th Coke's Rifles FF[3,4&5]
2/13th Frontier Force Rifles[6]...1/56th Punjabi Rifles FF[6]
4/13th Frontier Force Rifles (Wilde's)[6]...1/57th Wilde's Rifles[3,4,5&6]
5/13th Frontier Force Rifles (Vaughan's)[6]..1/58th Vaughan's Rifles[3,4&6]
10/13th Frontier Force Rifles..2/56th Punjabi Rifles FF[3]
1/14th Punjab Regiment[6]..1/19th Punjabis[3,4&6] & 2/19th Punjabis[4,5&6]
3/14th Punjab Regiment..1/22nd Punjabis[3]
5/14th Punjab Regiment (Pathans)..1/40th Pathans[3]
10/14th Punjab Regiment[6]...1/21st Punjabis & 2/21st Punjabis[4&6]
1/15th Punjab Regiment[6]...1/25th Punjabis & 2/25th Punjabis[4&6]
2/15th Punjab Regiment[6]...1/26th Punjabis[3] & 2/26th Punjabis[3&6]
3/15th Punjab Regiment.......................................1/27th Punjabis[4] (Individuals) & 2/27th Punjabis[3]
4/15th Punjab Regiment[6]...1/28th Punjabis[4&6]
1/16th Punjab Regiment[6]...1/30th Punjabis[3,4&6] & 2/30th Punjabis[4]
3/16th Punjab Regiment...1/33rd Punjabis[3] & 2/33rd Punjabis[3]
1/17th Dogra Regiment (Prince of Wales's Own)[6]..1/37th Dogras[3&6]
3/17th Dogra Regiment[6]..1/41st Dogras[3&6] & 2/41st Dogras[3,4&6]
2/18th Royal Garhwal Rifles[6]...2/39th Garhwal Rifles[4&6]
3/18th Royal Garhwal Rifles..3/39th Garhwal Rifles[3]
10/18th Royal Garhwal Rifles[6]...4/39th Garhwal Rifles[3,4,5&6]
1/19th Hyderabad Regiment (Russell's)..2/94th Russell's Infantry[4]
2/19th Hyderabad Regiment (Berar)..1/96th Berar Infantry[3]
3/19th Hyderabad Regiment..1/97th Deccan Infantry[3]
4/19th Hyderabad Regiment..1/98th Infantry[3]

Qualifying Line Regiments Disbanded Between 1919 – 1923
Disbanded 1919
3/30th Punjabis[3] & 1/154 Infantry[3]
Disbanded 1920
2/3rd Gaur Brahmans[3], 2/151st (Punjabi Rifles) Sikh Infantry[3] & 1/152nd Punjabis[3]
Disbanded 1921
2/2nd Queen Victoria's Own Rajput Light Infantry[3], 3rd Queen Victoria's Own Guides Infantry[3,4&5], 2/10th Jats[3], 2/11th Rajputs[3], 2/15th Ludihana Sikhs[3&4], 1/17th The Loyal Regiment[3], 2/35th Sikhs[3], 2/54th Sikhs FF[3], 3/124th Duchess of Connaught's Own Baluchistan Light Infantry[3], 1/150th Infantry[4], 2/150th Infantry[4&5], 3/150th Infantry[3], 3/151 (Punjabi Rifles) Sikh Infantry[3&4], 2/152 Punjabis[4&5], 3/152 Punjabis[4], 1/153 Punjabis[3], 2/153 Punjabis[3], 2/153 Punjabis[3] & 2/154th Infantry[4]
Disbanded 1922
1/5th Light Infantry[3] & 1/18th Infantry[6]
Disbanded 1923
2/50th Kumaon Rifles[6] >> 2nd Kumaon Rifles[6]

Gurkha Rifles (Verified Clasp Entitlement Shown)
1st King George V's Own Gurkha Rifles (The Malaun Regiment)..2nd Battalion[3,4&6]
2nd King Edward's Own Gurkha Rifles (The Sirmoor Rifles)..2nd Battalion[3,4&6]
3rd Queen Alexandra's Own Gurkha Rifles...1st Battalion[4&6] & 2nd Battalion[6]
4th Prince of Wales's Own Gurkha Rifles.....................................1st Battalion[3,4&6] & 2nd Battalion[3,4&6]
5th (Royal*) Gurkha Rifles (Frontier Force)...........................1st Battalion[3,4,5&6] & 2nd Battalion[4,5&6]
6th Gurkha Rifles..1st Battalion[4&6] & 2nd Battalion[6]
7th Gurkha Rifles...1st Battalion[4] & 2nd Battalion[3]
8th Gurkha Rifles..2nd Battalion[3&6]
9th Gurkha Rifles...1st Battalion[3&6] & 2nd Battalion[3,4,5&6]
10th Gurkha Rifles...2nd Battalion[3&6(1 Coy Only)]
*Note: * Granted 1921*

Qualifying Gurkha Regiments Disbanded Between 1919 – 1922
Disbanded 1920
3/2nd King Edward's Own Gurkha Rifles[3]
Disbanded 1921
3/1st Bn, King George's Own Gurkha Rifles (The Malaun Regiment)[3], 3/5th Bn, Royal Gurkha Rifles (Frontier Force)[3],
3/6th Bn, Gurkha Rifles[3&4], 3/7th Bn, Gurkha Rifles[3], 3/8th Bn, Gurkha Rifles[3], 3/9th Bn, Gurkha Rifles[3],
1/11th Bn Gurkha Rifles[3], 2/11th Bn, Gurkha Rifles[3]
Disbanded 1922
4/3rd Queen Alexandra's Own Gurkha Rifles[3,4&6] & 3/11Gurkha Rifles[3,4&5]

The Militia:

1920 Title	Pre 1920 Title
Tochi Scouts[4&6]	Northern Waziristan Militia[3,4&6]
South Waziristan Scouts[4&6]	Southern Waziristan Militia[3,4,5(100)&6]
Zhob Levy Corps[4&6]	Zhob Militia[3,4&6]
Tochi Scouts[4&6]	Mohmand Militia[3,4&6]

Kurram Militia[3,4&6] / Baluchistan Militia[3] / Khyber Rifles[3] (Disbanded 1919) / Chitral Scouts[3]
/ Gilgit Scouts[3] / Kahassadar Force[4&6]

Volunteers:
Indian Army Reserve of Officers / Auxiliary Forces India / Indian Territorial Force

1920 Title	Pre 1920 Title
The North West Railway Regiment[4&6]	24th North West Railway Volunteers[3,4&6]
The Great Indian Peninsular Railway Regiment13[th]	Great Indian Peninsular Railway Battalion[3]

The Baluchistan Company[4]

Imperial Service Infantry
Gwalior, Jhind, Karpurthala, Kashmir, Nabha, Nepalese & Patiala

The Indian Corps:
The Supply & Transport Corps:
From 1923 – Indian Army Service Corps
Supply Units
Force Supply & Transport Headquarters - No. 21
Divisional Supply Parks – Nos. 12 & 13
Supply Depot Headquarters - Nos. 22, 23 & 24
Divisional Supply Companies - Nos. 1, 2, 4, 11, 12, 13, 22 & 26
Brigade Supply Sections - Nos. 1, 7, 9, 33, 34, 35, 36, 37, 61, 62, 63, 76, 110 & 119
Supply Depot Sections - Nos. 162, 163, 164, 165, 166, 167, 168, 173, 174, 175, 176, 177 (1/2), 206, 207, 210, 256, 299, 312,
313 & 314
Divisional Area Troops Supply Section - No. 13
Butchery & Bakery Sections –
Nos. 63, 64, 71 (1/2), 77, 78, 157, 381, 384, 395 (1/2), 396 (1/2), 401, 402 & 675
Supply Workshop Sections - Nos. 22, 44 & 45
Supply Tally Sections - Nos. 77, 79, 80, 82 (1/2), 135 & 136
Cattle Depots Bannu & Dera Ismail Khan

Transport (Animal)
Horse
Horse Transport – No.1 Company
Mule & Pony
157th Pack Sub Division
Pack & Draft Mule Corps
Nos. 14, 19, 29, 41, 43, 45, 46, 48, 49, 52, 53, 58 (4 Troops For Waziristan), 59, 60 (4 Troops), 61, 62, 64, 65, 66, 67 (3 Troops),
68 (2 Troops), 69 (4 Troops), 70 (5 Troops), 71, 72 & 101 (6 Troops)
Camel
Government Camel Corps - Nos. 1, 2, 3, 5, 6, 7, 8 (Patiala), 53, 71 (3 Troops) & 72
Silladar Camel Corps – Nos. 52, 53, 55 & 57
Bullock & Local Transport Corps
Bullock Corps / Local Transport Corps – 2, 3, 4 (4 Troops), 6, 7, 8, 9 (4 Troops), 11, 12, 14 (4 Troops),
17, 18, 19 (4 Troops), 24, 30, 36, 37, 38, 40, 42, 49, 50, 54, 81 (6 Troops), 82, 83 & 99

Transport (Mechanical)
RASC & S&TC
RASC MT Companies
Nos. 630, 692, 693, 694 & 1028
Motor Ambulance Companies
Nos. 2, 3**, 19, 23** (Less 1 Section), 28 & 45
S&TC MT Companies
Nos. 1, 2, 3, 4, 5*, 6, 7 (FVC)****, 8 (FVC), 9 (FVC)**, 10 (FVC)**, 11 (FVC)***, 12 (FVC)***, 13**, 14, 15, 16, 17 (MRU),
18 (MRU), 19 (MRU), 20 (MRU), 21, 22, 23 (Became No. 13 in 1924), 24, 25 , 26, 27 (Became No. 7 in 1924) , 28*****, 29
(Became No. 9 in 1924), 30 (Became No. 10 in 1924), 31 (Became No. 11 in 1924), 32 (Became No. 12 in 1924), 33*****,
34******, 35 & 36

Note: * = Disbanded 1920, ** = Disbanded 1921, *** = Disbanded 1922, **** = Disbanded 1923, ***** = Disbanded 1924, MRU's
From 1920

Miscellaneous MT Related
Supply Depots - 36
Advanced Repair Shops - No. 1 (Peshawar)[3]
From 1923 Designated 'Heavy Repair Shop Class III' - Peshawar & Quetta
S&TC Mechanical Repair Units – Nos. 18

Miscellaneous S&TC
Khyber Ropeway Company from 1921 - 1926
Railway Companies – No. 28
'B' Railhead Transport Sections

The Combined Medical Establishment:
British:
Royal Army Medical Corps & Army Dental Corps > (From 1921)
Queen Alexandra's Imperial Military Nursing Service, Territorial Force Nursing Service,
Red Cross and Civilian Nursing Staff
Indian:
Indian Medical Service, Army Hospital Corps / Army Bearer Corps >
(From 1920 - The Indian Hospital Corps)
Queen Alexandra's Imperial Military Nursing Service India >
(From 1926 – The Indian Military Nursing Service)
Static Hospitals
British General Hospitals - Bannu, Gharial,
Jhansi, Kohat, Peshawar, Quetta, Rawalpindi & Tank
Indian General Hospitals - Nos. 6, 7, 10, 12, 17, 38''', 43'', 49''' & (Tank)
Combined General Hospitals – 58 Mashed & 59 Shusp
British Station Hospitals – 19, 23, 24 & 43
Indian Station Hospitals - Dardoni, Mari Indus & Sararogha
Casualty Clearing Stations
British – Nos. 11, 20, 27 & 38
Indian – Nos. 7, 8, 27 & 118''
Combined – 1, 7, 8, 34 & 36
Field Ambulances
Cavalry Field Ambulances – 6 (Loo Dakka) & 8[3]
British / Combined Field Ambulances - Nos. 4, 5, 7, 12, 16'',
14', 15, 25''', 26, 27''', 31, 41, 42''', 43, 45, 51, 52, 53, 60 & 64'''
Indian Field Ambulances - Nos. 2'', 4'', 25, 144 & 178
'B' Ambulance Train – Rawalpindi
Staging Sections
British Staging Sections – Nos. 11, 12, 13, 14, 15, 19, 20, 22, 41, 43, 46 & 47
Indian Staging Sections – Nos. 55, 59, 60, 66, 96 & 97
Combined Staging Sections – Nos. 1, 2 & 5'''
Sanitary Sections
British Sanitary Sections – Nos. 9, 12, 15, 17, 18, 19, 20, 21, 25 & 46
Indian Sanitary Sections – Nos. 2, 3, 4, 6, 8, 25, 35, 36, 37, 39, 41, 42, 73, 100 & 165

Combined Sanitary Sections – Nos. 2 & 3
Indian Bearer Units
Nos. 1 & 9

Miscellaneous
7 Company RAMC - Peshawar
Nos. 19 & 22 X-Ray Sections / Advance Depots, Medical Stores - Nos. 11 & 13
Bearer Units - No. 1 / Bleaching Laboratories - Nos. 1, 2, 3, 4" & 5

Note: * = Disbanded 1919, ** = Disbanded 1921, *** = Disbanded 1922

The Indian Army Veterinary Corps:
Veterinary Hospitals – Dera Ismail Khan, Razmak & Quetta
Camel Transport Sick Lines Ft. Sandaman
Base Depot Veterinary Stores - No. 4
Field Veterinary Sections – Nos. 5, 14, 21', 26 (Camels) & 27" (Camels)
Indian Mobile Veterinary Sections – 10, 11, 13, 15, 16, 17, 18, 19, 20 & 21

The Indian Ordnance Department:
(1922 Onwards: Indian Army Ordnance Corps)
Advanced Ordnance Depots – Bannu & Tank
Ordnance Transit Depot – Tank
34 Ordnance Mobile Workshop – Bannu

The Indian Army Corps of Clerks:

The Army Remount Department:
Remount Depots - Bannu, Dera Ismail Khan & Tank

The Military Farms Department:
Dairy & Grass Circles
Conservancy Departments

The Police, Judiciary & Intelligence:
Frontier Constabulary, Jail Department & Frontier Intelligence Corps

The Telegraph Department:

The Postal Department:

The Indian Ecclesiastical Department:

The Political & Civil Departments:

Medals Have Been Seen To:
Indian Railways & Burma Military Police

ROYAL AIR FORCE ORDER OF BATTLE FRONTIER CAMPAIGNS 1919-1924							
Squadron	1919	1920	1921	1922	1923	1924	Aircraft
5 Squadron[4,5&6]	Europe Disbanded	Quetta Reformed From 48 Sqn (Below)	Quetta	Ambala Dets. Saugor	Ambala Dets. Saugor	Dardoni	Bristol F2b
20 Squadron[3&4]	Risalpur, Parachinar & Bannu Dets. Sorarogha	Parachinar & Tank	Ambala	Quetta Dets. Loralai	Quetta Dets. Loralai	Quetta Dets. Loralai	Bristol F2b
27 Squadron[4,5&6]	Europe Disbanded	Mianwali & Risalpur Dets. Tank & Dardoni Reformed From 99 Sqn	Risalpur Dets. Tank & Dardoni	Dardoni	Risalpur Dets. Dardoni, Miranshah & Arawali	Risalpur Dets. Dardoni, Miranshah & Arawali	DeHavilland 9A
28 Squadron[4&6]	Europe Disbanded	Ambala Reformed From 114 Sqn (Below)	Kohat Dets. Dardoni & Tank	Parachinar Kohat & Dardoni	Tank & Peshawar Dets. Dardoni & Hassani Abdel	Peshawar Dets. Dardoni, Hassani Abdel & Tank	Bristol Fb2
31 Squadron[3,4&6]	Risalpur Dets. Bannu, Kohat & Tank	Mhow & Cawnpore	Peshawar Dets. Dardoni & Tank	Peshawar Dets. Dardoni & Tank	Dardoni	Ambala Dets. Quetta	Bristol F2b
48 Squadron[3]	Quetta Det. Loralai	Disbanded Used To Form 5 Sqn (Above)					
60 Sqn[4,5&6]	Europe	Disbanded Europe. Reformed Risalpur From 97 Sqn Dets. Juhu, Tank, Karachi, Rajkot, Dardoni & Mianwali	Risalpur Dets. Juhu, Tank, Karachi, Rajkot, Dardoni & Mianwali	Risalpur Dets. Juhu, Tank, Karachi, Rajkot, Dardoni & Mianwali	Risalpur Dets. Hassani Abdel, Quetta, Dardoni, Arawali, Delhi & Miranshah	Risalpur Dets. Hassani Abdel, Quetta, Dardoni, Arawali, Delhi & Miranshah	To March 1923 – DeHavilland 10/10A Thence – DeHavilland 9A
97 Squardon[4]	To India from Europe Allahabad Lahore	Risalpur Disbanded Used to Form 60 Sqn (Above)					DeHavilland 10
99 Squadron[4]	To India from Europe Ambala Mianwali	Mianwali Disbanded Used to Form 27 Sqn (Above)					DeHavilland 9A

114 Squadron[3]	Quetta, Lahore, Ambala Dets. Cawnpore, Kohat, Agra, Bannu & Loralai	Disbanded Used To Form 28 Sqn (Above)					Bristol F2b
The Aden Flight	Dispersed						

~ Waziristan 1925 ~

~ India General Service Medal 1908–1935 ~
WAZIRISTAN 1925
Issue 2: Calcutta Mint

The 'WAZIRISTAN 1925' clasp was sanction by Air Ministry Order 255 of 1926 to reward airmen employed under Wing Commander R.C.M. Pink, RAF, during operations in Waziristan between 9th March and 1st May 1925. This campaign was the first in which the Royal Air Force was deployed as an independent fighting force and its successful (cost effective) conclusion inspired significant debate in Whitehall regarding the future responsibility for 'policing' the Indian Frontier. In addition to those airmen eligible, Captain W.R. Hay, Indian Political Department and Mr. E.B. Howell, British Political Resident, received this award thus making 'Waziristan 1925' a campaign award not unique to the RAF as has been widely stated in the past.

Following the cessation of hostilities in May 1925, the Air Ministry stated that there had been insufficient casualties during the prosecution of the campaign to warrant the striking of a new clasp for the India General Service Medal 1908–1935. Air Marshal J. Salmond, RAF, Air Member for Personnel, determined that Wing Commander Pink's precedent-setting operations would not slip by unnoticed. Accordingly, he persistently lobbied the War Office to authorise the issue of a new 'Waziristan' clasp for award with the India General Service Medal 1908–1935. The Government only relented after Air Marshal Salmond likened the campaign to the Abyssinian War 1868 during which only two British deaths were sustained and yet some 14,000 medals had been struck for issue.

The final authorisation for the striking of the 'WAZIRISTAN 1925' clasp contained a restrictive caveat. Air Ministry Orders 642 and 643 of 1926 required eligible airmen who had already qualified for the 'WAZIRISTAN 1921–24' clasp to chose between either that or the clasp for 'WAZIRISTAN 1925'. Dual awards were not permitted.

*

During January and February 1925, several isolated British military installations across Waziristan began to experience an increase in the number of hostile contacts with militant tribesmen. The posts at Gomel and Manzai were singled out as particular targets. Intelligence reports suggested that the Abdur Rahman Khel, Guri Khel, Farida and Maresai Waziri were the principle perpetrators of these

~ Air Marchal J. Salmond, RAF ~

incursions. These peoples, residing in the remote Spli Toi, Shinkai Toi and Dre Alghad Valleys, had never officially submitted to the Government following the conclusion of the Waziristan campaign despite a specific *jirga* for that purpose held in Thal on 27th December 1924. Consequently, they had not been invited by the British to participate in the Kahassadar system or to be in receipt of any other Government allowance. In consequence, poverty was a major factor encouraging the tribesmen to continue raiding and kidnapping for ransom.

Anxious to contain the outbreak of hostility in a region already devastated by four years of bloodshed, the Government of India was quick to sanction outline planning for punitive action against the recalcitrant Waziri. Air Chief Marshal E. Ellington, RAF, Air Officer Commanding (India), was forthright in proposing that an operation conducted solely by the RAF in such a remote region would be both effective and financially efficient. This suggestion was readily accepted by the authorities and, much to the horror of many members of the Army General Staff, sanction was given for the execution of an independent RAF operation. Accordingly, No. 2 (Indian) Wing RAF, comprising 5, 27 and 60 Squadrons, was mobilised for activity duty.

On 20th February 1925, Flight Lieutenant J.W. Baker, RAF, of 60 Squadron, flew Wing Commander R.C.M. Pink, RAF, to Northern Command Headquarters at Rawalpindi where he attended a strategy meeting pertaining to the proposed punitive operations. A three-phase plan of campaign was agreed. Daylight raids would target settled areas and destroy specific targets, infrastructure and enemy *lashkars* (should they take to the field). An aerial blockade would be imposed by aircraft not engaged in offensive sorties with a view to disrupting inter tribal communications and collaborative action.

Wing Commander R.C.M. Pink, RAF, established his operational headquarters at Tank in late February 1925. Shortly thereafter No. 5 (Army Cooperation) Squadron, equipped with ten Bristol F2b fighters, deployed to this location from RAF Kohat. The sixteen DH9A bombers of 27 and 60 Squadrons were to be located at the isolated aerodrome adjacent to Fort Miranshah. The journey to Miranshah from RAF Risalpur was a long and arduous journey for the ground crews. Some 250 miles of ungraded road had to be traversed despite the two stations being only some 120 miles flying distance apart. The climatic conditions were by this juncture quite severe. The intense noonday heat gave way to daily thunderstorms during the afternoon. On more than one occasion, heavy bursts of hail rendered the Miranshah airstrip unserviceable. Forced landing sites were prepared at Razmak, Sorarogha, Sarwekai and Khirgi.

2 (Indian) Wing, RAF, was declared operational on 3rd March 1925. Meanwhile, the Indian Political Department sought one final opportunity to negotiate a satisfactory diplomatic solution to the situation. The following terms were issued for consideration to those resisting British authority on 5th March and a *jirga* at Jandola proposed to discuss their willingness to comply.

Terms For Consideration
Abdul Rahman Khel

- All warriors to attend a Government *jirga* in Jandola at 12 noon on 7th March 1925.
- Clan elders to deliver up safe and well to the British authorities all Hindu hostages captured during recent outrages and held for ransom.
- Non-compliance to result in the commencement of punitive military action from sunrise on 9th March 1925.

Guri Khel

- All warriors to attend a Government *jirga* in Jandola at 12 noon on 7th March 1925.
- Clan elders to deliver up to the British authorities a fine of Rs 1,600 in cash.
- Clan elders to deliver to the British authorities' five Government issue rifles and twelve local rifles.
- Clan elders to release all stolen livestock to their rightful owners by 7th March 1925.

Farida and Maresai

- All warriors to attend a Government *jirga* in Jandola by 12 noon on 7th March 1925.

With no agreement forthcoming, formal punitive operations began on the morning of 9th March 1925. Tribal settlements were harassed throughout the following days. Variation was achieved by interspersing desultory bombing with periods of intense attack. Fuse length and bomb type were varied depending on the timings and strengths of attack. The target area of some 50–60 square miles was an extremely mountainous region with peaks in excess of 6,000 feet. Most bomb releases were made from a height of only 3,000 feet. A payload of 8 x 20lb bombs and 2 x 112lb bombs was found to be the most efficient. Bombing sorties were generally followed up by a fighter sweep searching for warriors as they vacated their places of refuge.

Initial action focused on Abdur Rahman Khel concentrations in the Dre Algad area. They tended to live in small family groups and had few permanent physical structures that could be targeted. The tribesmen were quite unprepared for the speed and intensity of the assault. Having suffered several casualties, tribal elders used intermediaries to request a ceasefire during the second week of March 1925. These requests met with approval on condition that the Abdur Rahman Khel would comply with the original terms of submission, published by the authorities on 5th March. When a tribal delegation failed to attend Jandola on 13th March, operations were quickly resumed. This forthright action had the desired effect and shortly thereafter Abdur Rahman Khel elders delivered their various Hindu captives into the safekeeping of the Frontier Constabulary at Spli Toi thus triggering a second ceasefire. On 17th March, the elders reported to Captain W.R. Hay, the Political Agent at Jandola, and negotiations began in earnest. However, the discussions soon broke down and shortly thereafter hostilities were resumed.

Being shot down due to enemy small arms fire was a constant threat for all aircrew engaged in low altitude frontier operations. On 21st March 1925, Flying Officers E.J. Dashwood, RAF, and N.C. Hayter-Hames, RAF, of 27 Squadron were on patrol when enemy marksmen targeted their DH9A aircraft. The plane crashed and the two airmen were fatally injured. When the bodies of these two officers were eventually recovered by the authorities, it became evident that the Waziri had gone to some considerable trouble to succour the men in their final hours.

A Guri Khel delegation attended Jandola on 25th March 1925 and delivered up the fine in rifles but the poverty-stricken warriors had been unable to secure the cash required for the Rs 1,600 settlement in line with the terms required by the authorities. Captain W.R. Hay, however, agreed in lieu of the fine to hold as collateral a leading tribal *malik* thus enabling a conclusion of these operations.

Squadron Leader T.F. Hazell, RAF, the commanding officer of 60 Squadron, and his air gunner narrowly escaped death on 4th April 1925, when the engine cowling of their DH9A machine came adrift during a combat sortie that led to the pilot having to fly the aircraft blind. Guided by the air gunner, Squadron Leader Hazell managed to fly the stricken plane to the forced landing strip at Sorarogha and execute a crash landing. Though injured, both aviators survived the ordeal.

Meanwhile, intelligence sources suggested that a large number of Abdur Rahman Khel were preparing to escape across the frontier into Afghanistan. A swift resolution to the situation was considered necessary and, to that end, Wing Commander R.C.M. Pink, RAF, determined to add night operations to the range of tactics being employed. Two additional night flying machines joined No. 5 Squadron at Tank on 6th April 1925, and within three days, the fight had been taken to the enemy on a 24 hour basis. This manoeuvre had an extremely debilitating effect on the enemy clan. Constant disruption and further loses in both manpower and valuable livestock led to revised peace overtures being received by the authorities on 15th April 1925. Once again, the overtures were rejected as they did not comply with the Government's terms as published.

60 Squadron attacked a *lashkar* of Faridai warriors on 9th April 1925. Lack of fuel, however, forced the assault to be terminated prematurely. A follow-up mission was launched but storms forced the second flight to return to Miranshah before contact with the enemy could be achieved. Three days later, however, both the Faridai and Maresai decided to surrender leading to a cessation of operations against their settled areas. The Abdur Rahman Khel remained in the field until 28th April when Captain Hay in Jandola received three rifles as a token of good faith during a *jirga*. Tough negotiations resulted in a peace accord that was agreed on 1st May. Waziristan was once again 'officially' at peace.

*

The campaign had been a complete success. All belligerent clans had been subdued and an outbreak of prolonged rebellion prevented in a region already weary of conflict. The RAF, having been put to the test, had proved itself capable of conducting independent punitive operations beyond all expectations. Logistical problems and shortages of aircraft spares had been overcome by the tireless efforts of the ground crews. Bombing missions had been flown on 42 of the first 45 days of active duty. Some 2,070 hours of combat flying had been logged by 1st May 1925.

Air Chief Marshal E. Ellington, RAF, subsequently submitted proposals to the Government of India calling for the complete control of the frontier region by the RAF. Following a period of reflection, however, the Government determined not to adopt the Air Marshal's plan (a view significantly influenced by the Army General Staff). The principle reasons given were that:

- Solutions to tribal problems were dependent on 'civilizing' influences such as civil engineering works including irrigation and civil engineering schemes that require secure ground communications, which in turn require protection and maintenance.

- The Frontier Constabulary and the Frontier Scouts require regular ground support and training from the Regular Army and therefore a need for land garrisons would remain. (Note: The security of RAF installations at this time was also technically the responsibility of the Army).

- Public opinion in Britain was adverse to the concept of aerial bombardment against arguably 'civilian' targets.

Nevertheless, that the RAF continued to be actively involved in every post-1925 campaign on the Indian Frontier.

* * *

RAF ROLL OF HONOUR WAZIRISTAN 1925			
Date:	Person:	Unit:	Type Of Casualty:
1/3/1925	F/O J Dashwood	27 Sqn, RAF	DOW
1/3/1925	F/O Hayter-Hames	27 Sqn, RAF	DOW
19/5/1925	315022 LAC W G Eldridge	20 Sqn, RAF	Died

WAZIRISTAN 1925[8] ROLL

BRITISH ESTABLISHMENT
THE ARMY

No Recipients Qualified

THE ROYAL AIR FORCE

Note a.   *Roll of all personnel identified as eligible.*

Note b.   *Due to 'austerity' measures, it was determined in Air Ministry Order 643/26 of December 1926 that those personnel who qualified for both of the clasps 'WAZIRISTAN 1921 –24' and 'WAZIRISTAN 1925' could only apply for one clasp.*

Note c.   *Medals named in impressed capitals: 'R.A.F.'*

Single Clasp	No. Identified	Rarity
Waziristan 1925[8]	281	Scarce / Accepted as Rare.
Combination Clasps	No. Identified	Rarity
Waziristan 1919–21[4] Waziristan 1925[8]	9	Of the Utmost Rarity
Waziristan 1925[8] North West Frontier 1930–31[9]	2	Of the Utmost Rarity
Waziristan 1925[8] North West Frontier1935[12]	4	Of the Utmost Rarity

Wing Commanders: ~ F F Minchin[8], R C M Pink[8] & A A Walser[8]

Squadron Leaders: ~ L M Bailey[8], A J Capol[8], C B Cook[8] & T F Hazell[8]

Flight Lieutenants: ~ J W Baker[8], C P Barber[8], A G Bishop[8], C W Busk[8], J L M De C Hughes-Chamberlain[8], P R T Chamberlayne[8], C R Davidson[8], S Graham[8], R W M Hall[8], L S Hamilton[8], J A G Haslem[8], J A Hollis[8], F H Laurence[8], C A Lindup[8], A C Sanderson[8], R C Savery[8] & C A Stevens[8]

Flying Officers: ~ L W Aiken[8], C E H Allen[8], E L W H Alms[8], E V E Andrewartha[8], W Best[4?&8], H A Boniface[8], F Boston[8], N C Bretherton[8], G E Campbell[8], G N Carroll[8], W A Chase[8], J J C Cocks[8], E E F Colam[8], B R C Coope[8], L Darvall[8], E J Dashwood[8], C J A Delany[8], M C W C Flint[8], C Gardner[8], F F Garraway[8], J H Hargroves[8], N C Hayter-Hames[8], E T O'N Hogben[8], H B Holdway[8], T Humble[8], W J Hutchinson[8], A F James[8], A King-Lewis[8], R A R Mangles[8], F G S Mitchell[8], C C Musselwhite[8], C B R Pelly[8], G H Rawlinson[8], C W Rugg[8], E H D Spence[8], G R C Spencer[8], F W Todd[8], W H Vetch[8], C W Weedon[8], J G Western[8], G V Wheatley[8] & W P Wiltshire[8]

Pilot Officers: ~ D C Burnley[8], F E R Dixon[8], R W Holden[8], N W F Mason[8], J H A Mollison[8], C N A B Mumby[8], A E Paish[8&12], L R Shaw[8] & D L Thomson[8]

Sergeant Majors: ~ 737 J Greener[8]

Flight Sergeants: ~ 38 A E Attree[8], 314223 A Halstead[8], 343656 J Lynch[8], 410 A Springate[4&8?], 313923 E W Strudwick[8], 314406 F Thomsett[8], 4158 S T Towns[8] & 313303 J R Woollard[8]

Sergeants: ~ 240535 H E Blanche[8], 157159 E W Braund[8], 1344 S W Cockram[8], 651 F R J Cooper[8], 6428 B Crane[8], 342755 W H C Hampshire[8], 84631 R E Hawkins[8], 335127 D Kinnear[8], 245780 L Morgan[8], 337793 D J Munro[8] & 7392 A D Rutherford[4&8?]

Corporals: ~ 345329 C Adams[8&12], 343433 G G Angelo[8], 327584 R G Bartlett[8], 247225 W J Bowers[8], 341816 G B Bowes[8], 341153 T Cooper[8], 327978 E D Croft[8], 346379 J E Edwards[8], 24203 F L Fluellen[8], 341894 R T Forth[8], 338023 W Foster[8], 342593 E J Foyle[8], 345676 F Grigg[8], 330142 J Harman[8], 349205 E L C Hill[8], 249274 E T Hoole[8], 242657 J R Jamieson[8], 343873 J S Mason[8], 327410 W A Maude[8], 244493 J M Patrick[8], 341771 F E Pearce[8], 349798 W J Pond[8], 341034 H J Ramm[8], 337185 S L Reeve[8], 348053 C R Saunders[8], 159973 E S Sellek[8], 180857 J F Sigsworth[8], 334124 G R Small[8], 330751 T L Walters[4&8?], 340793 W F Welbourne[8], 343011 C W Wilson[8] & 291808 A G Woods[8]

Leading Air Craftsmen: ~ 342187 H W Atterbury[8], 292508 W Bain[8], A E Barley[8], 326247 C H Bennett[8], 327892 J Boniface[8], 328656 E W Bradley[8], 349715 W F Brighton[8], 344462 R W Broomhead[8], 347901 A O Burford[8], 346262 J W Burley[8], 344417 H S Butler[8], 343379 W H Cann[8], 350326 R E Castle[8], 342525 A J Clarke[8], 347465 F J Cobbold[8], 159596

F Collins[8], 330315 F W Collins[8], 313058 A E Colverson[8], 326987 S F Cooper[8], 344620 H Dickie[8], 327464 A Driver[8], 342314 O T Duncan[8], 9466 E J Dunford[8], 180029 L A Eades[8], 348728 A T Eccles[8], 315022 W G Eldridge[8], 327388 S G Ellis[8], 345349 G T Evans[8], 343548 H J Fagg[82], 350302 L T Fells[8], 344850 E Garnett[8], 356426 W R Gilmartin[8], 342257 B Glenfield[8], 342787 H F Goodwin[8], 341876 W Gordon[8], 342846 G Gray[8], 245777 A H Griffiths[8], 326138 T E Groves[8], 330080 A R B Hart[8], 328975 C Hawkins[8], 347122 J E Heppenstall[8], 159493 A F Hobbins[8], 345092 W J Holburn[8], 328048 A J E Hope[8], 342521 R Hope[8], 264545 H R Hutton[8], 346783 J S Jarvie[8], 345362 A J Jones[8], 342364 S F Jones[8], 343846 C Jupp[8], 342729 J B Kelly[8], 342611 A L Lancaster[8], 343350 A R Lloyd[8], 326587 H McNeil[8], 345547 F Manning[8], 347517 R J Meech[8], 332369 D Meredith[8&9], 342817 J W Miller[8], 347859 V R Milsom[8], 340965 J W Nicholson[8], 351933 W C Noble[8], 159113 H Norris[8], 9839 J S Osborne[8], 298949 N E Osborne[8], 343141 A C Pain[8], 349753 F Palliser[8], 343151 R T Palmer[8], 343644 S Parker[8], 328172 E M Piper[8], 326182 W C Preston[8], 248647 S M Rankine[8], 156588 D A Riches[8], 327656 J M Robb[8], 327686 P W Robins[8], 347635 L R Sadler[8], 334136 A B Scott[8&12], 330400 G A Scott[8], 352819 F H Smith[8], 326747 F Spooner[8], 243678 E E Suter[8], 159965 A T Turner[8], 251488 A J Waite[8], 341541 C Walsh[8], 314420 L W Walsh[8], 349696 S Warnt[8], 342818 C Watkinson[8], 341200 C F Webb[8], 159949 L Williamson[8], 347527 W S Wood[8] & 341607 S C Woodley[8]

(Airman) Air Craftsmen 1st Class: ~ 342298 H H Barrett[8], 326487 L H Beavan[8], 343845 E Bellamy[8], 330901 W G Boggis[8], 344350 A R Burley[8], 328540 F M Burman[8], 327394 S W Burrows[8], 347556 G Cairns[8], 330399 M Campbell[8], 326427 H V Capps[8], 341717 B C B Carter[82], 335151 L E Chappell[8], 344855 A Corry[8], 326637 E H Cutler[8], 326868 R P Douglas[8], 343012 F Duffan[8], 343241 F Dunstan[4&8], A W Fiske[4&8?], 511823 W F Fowle[8], 330345 E Gadd[8&12], 158716 H Garrett[8], 365848 L J Gibson[8], 330527 S R Gould[8], 326675 E M Harding[8], 326976 E H Harris[8], 335575 H J Hayter[8], 353225 C H Hill[8], 347002 H F Hill[8], 343652 T E Jones[8], 343733 F Kempthorn[8], 351442 S E Lee[8], 147133 A Mair[8], 347675 H A D Marsh[8], 349142 S W Marsh[8], 348469 J Martin[8], 327389 J F Mitchell[8], 344849 A W Newman[8], 343601 A N Owen[8], 349510 S G S Pound[8], 352712 J J C Redhead[8], 342699 A J Reed[8], 326590 J E Richardson[8], 342394 C Roy[8], M E H Short[8], 348471 S Skinner[8], 335159 C W Smith[8], 326803 A Spackman[8], 343124 H Stevens[8], 348651 F G Street[8], 341035 C E Styles[4&8], 327448 H V Taylor[8], 327189 J Tilston[8], 326336 C M Tye[8], 328022 W G Wade[8], 145516 A E Webb[8], 330634 J West[8], 335205 J Westwood[8&9], 345765 E Williams[8], 348199 G E Wise[8] & 346147 J Woods[8]

(Airman) Air Craftsmen 2nd Class: ~ 350263 A G L Baker[8], 345716 J Butler[8], 9466 E J Dunford[8], 248038 F J Golding[8], 341878 J Graves[8], 327682 R F Langdown[8], 350070 J C Morgan[8], 344856 P Murray[8], 326817 B R Rickerby[4&8?], 342226 W A J Robinson[8], 344305 A D Simmonds[8], 342999 J B Skene[8], 349573 R Soder[8], 343100 H Thorn[4&8] & 327021 S E Wood[8]

INDIAN ESTABLISHMENT

Qualifying Units Present (Officers Plus Known Individuals)

Political Department

Individual	Position
Capt. W R Hay	Political Agent, South Waziristan
Mr. E B Howell	British Resident, South Waziristan

4. MALABAR 1921–1922

~ India General Service Medal 1908–1935 ~
MALABAR 1921–22
WAZIRISTAN 1921–24
Issue 2: Calcutta Mint

The 'MALABAR 1921–22' clasp was sanctioned by Army Order 50 of 1924 to reward military and mobilised civil personnel employed with the Malabar Field Force under Major General J.T. Burnett-Stuart during the suppression of the Moplah Rebellion in the Malabar District of Madras, southwest India.

To qualify for the 'MALABAR 1921–22' clasp to the India General Service Medal 1908–1935 personnel had to be mobilised on active service between 20th August 1921 and 25th February 1922 inclusive in an area bounded as follows:

- To the west the Arabian Sea.

- To the south the River Ponnani.

- To the east by a north/south line extending due south from the town of Gudalur to the River Ponnani.

- To the north, an east/west line extending due west from the town Gudalur to the Arabian Sea.

No Royal Air Force personnel participated in the Malabar campaign.

Following the defeat of its native ruler, Tipu Sultan, by the Army of the British East India Company, Malabar became part of the Madras Presidency in 1799. This event was the culmination of a series of successful military campaigns that brought to a conclusion the Anglo Mysore Wars. Malabar was a sparsely garrisoned region in 1921. HQ Madras District was concentrated in the Madras Cantonment with outlying garrisons in the regional population centres of Bangalore and Wellington. The bulk of the Regular Army actually in Malabar comprised 'C' Company, and two platoons 'B' Company, 1st Bn, Leinster Regt., stationed on the coast at Calicut. Supporting the Regular Army were various local reserve formations of the Auxiliary Forces India including the Calicut Auxiliary Corps, the Southern Provinces Mounted Rifles and the South of India Railway Battalion. Local police units were extensively employed during the rebellion, as well as the infamous para military Malabar Special Police.

A detachment of ratings and marines from the cruiser HMS *Comus* came ashore at Calicut during the early stages of the campaign. These men were employed on humanitarian aide duties only and did not qualify for the India General Service Medal 1908–1935. The 1st Bn, Leinster Regt. was disbanded on 31ˢᵗ July 1922 upon the formation of the Irish Free State. Medals to this unit, the last southern Irish regiment to fight under British colours, are highly prized. During the period leading up to the disbandment of the Leinster Regt., some personnel desirous of remaining in the British Army transferred to other units stationed in India. Consequently, examples of medals named to the Leinster Regt. exist bearing additional clasps won after the regiment was disbanded.

Much of the Malabar campaign was fought during the tropical monsoon season. Torrential rainfall and swollen rivers seriously disrupted land communications especially in the densely forested foothills of the Western Ghats Mountains that ran north to south through eastern Malabar separating the area from the Coorg, Nilgiris and Coimbatore regions. The effective use of early wireless technology was widely employed by the fledgling Royal Corps of Signals to overcome these problems. Cavalry chargers and pack mules suffered greatly from the damp conditions resulting in the Queen's Bays composite squadron withdrawing prematurely from the order of battle. Unlike many previous operations conducted in monsoon conditions, fever and disease related mortality among the troops deployed was successfully kept to a minimum.

*

The Moplah were descended from maritime Arab merchants who had settled in the region from approximately 800AD onwards. Devout Muslims, the Moplah were anxious to overthrow British rule and establish an independent (Islamic) Khalifate state. Initially this desire was prosecuted via peaceful means. The London Khalifate Conference of 1920, which stemmed from post war pressure by the Allies to abolish the Turkish caliphate and dissolve the Ottoman Empire, led Muslim leaders in India to drive forward their own Islamic agendas. Charismatic individuals, such as Maulana Mohammad Ali Jouhar and his brother Maulana Shaukat Ali Jouhar, were highly vocal in espousing the cause of Islamic statehood for certain regions in Indian. Over time, this philosophy aligned itself with the wider Indian independence movement driven by the Indian National Congress under M.K. Gandhi.

A regional Khalifate congress held at Ponnani in 1921 enabled some local Moplah agitators to link an Islamic agenda to hatred of the landowning Hindu commercial community in Malabar as well as to long held anti-British sentiment. Initially M.K. Gandhi gave the Moplah tacit support, despite their overt anti-Hindu sentiment. The Congress leader blamed the subsequent slide towards violence on the British authorities for not allowing him to visit Malabar and preach his message of 'passive resistance' and 'non-cooperation'.

The fact that both the British and Indian Armies were heavily engaged in operations in the tribal regions of the Indian North West Frontier during the early 1920s no doubt encouraged the Moplah to launch their insurrection at this juncture. Many Moplah had in fact served in the Indian Army during World War One. Potential recruits with recent military experience and skills were thus readily available to support the Moplah cause.

*

During the summer of 1921, the British civil administration in Malabar began to note an ever-increasing number of Moplah openly bearing arms in public. Such behaviour was in direct contravention of the Malabar Offensive Weapons Act 1854 and as such, the authorities could not allow these offences to go unpunished. Seditious rhetoric and aggressive behaviour became commonplace leading to a rapid decline in civil order. When incidents of physical violence occurred, the District Commissioner placed all local civil police personnel on alert and gave instructions for Special Branch to gather information on known Moplah leaders with a view to taking these men into custody.

In August 1921, informants advised the Malabar Police that a militant Moplah gang, complete with several previously identified rebel leaders including the notorious Ali Musaliar, were concentrating in and around the large settlement of Tirurangadi. The Malabar District Magistrate, Mr. E.F. Thomas, thereupon determined that arrest warrants should be executed against these influential men with a view to quickly restricting the spread of any potential large scale Moplah violence. On the evening of 19th August 1921, a force of Malabar Special Police, under Superintendent Hitchcock, supported by 100 rifles of the 1st Bn, Leinster Regt., entrained at Calicut station and travelled south to Parappanangadi with a view to marching under cover of darkness from that location to Tirurangadi and engaging the rebel force. A stiff engagement was anticipated by the authorities. However, they were surprised to find that the Moplah offered no resistance and only three arrests were made.

Later the same day, a second police patrol advanced beyond Tirurangadi to conduct a 'sweep' in and around the mosque at Kishikkapalle. The police discovered no illegal contraband, or other incriminating evidence, and within the space of several hours, the patrol began to withdraw. Retracing its original route, the police fell into a Moplah ambush composed of rebels who had travelled to the area from Tanur with the express purpose of avenging the alleged desecration of their mosque. Surrounded, and with little or no knowledge of the local terrain, the police sepoys were forced to defend their position eventually fighting off the rebels at a cost of two constables killed and several wounded.

Emboldened by this success, the Moplah secured Tirurangadi and then advanced swiftly across country to Parappanangadi hoping to intercept the original British force before it entrained back to Calicut. Arriving at the railway station, they discovered the train had already left and, therefore, sought instead to incite anti-British feeling among the local population. Despite strenuous efforts from Muhammad Abdurrahman and other local Congress Party leaders to calm the situation down, a full-scale riot soon developed. Government buildings were set on fire in addition to the train station and associated infrastructure. The uprising spread rapidly during the ensuing days. Several more police sepoys were murdered in horrific circumstances and many European families came under threat and so evacuated their isolated plantations and related commercial interests, to flee west towards the coast. Having achieved the flight of the British, the Moplah turned their attention to the local Hindu population upon whom they committed appalling atrocities including decapitation, female violation and forced conversion to Islam.

At this juncture, the Moplah ruling council proclaimed Ali Musaliar to be Rajah of a new Khalifat kingdom fully independent of the British. With law and order disintegrating by the hour, Lord Willingdon, Governor of Madras, ordered Lieutenant General W. Marshall, GOC Southern Command, to mobilise all available forces in Bangalore and deploy them post-haste in support of the civil authorities in Malabar. Assets were limited due to operational commitments on the North West Frontier, combined with the ongoing reorganisation and reduction of the Indian Army. The need for the maintenance of a reserve to contain the possible spread of anti-British activity elsewhere in Madras was a further consideration. On 22nd August 1921, a small force under Major General J.T. Burnett-Stuart, set out in several special trains from Baird Barracks, Bangalore for Calicut. Designated the Malabar Field Force, the troops deployed consisted of a composite mounted squadron of the Queen's Bays, a section of 10 Pack Battery RGA, 2nd Bn, Dorset Regt, a platoon of 2nd Queen Victoria's Own Madras Sappers and Miners supported by the 64th Pioneers.

*

The 2nd Bn, Dorset Regt., arrived in southern Malabar on 23rd August 1921. Half the battalion detrained at Pattambi from where 'C' Company, commanded by Major E.S. Weldon, was despatched to quell an anti-British riot at Malathur, a village located a short distance north of Pattambi railway station. Meanwhile, a tactical reconnaissance was made of the South of India Railway Company track bed towards Kuttipputam in order to ascertain the extent of infrastructure damage reportedly wrought by local Moplah. The Sappers and Miners detachment conducted hasty repairs to the track enabling HQ Company to press on to Kuttipputam where it established a forming-up position for the balance of the wider Malabar Field Force. The second half of the battalion, under Major L.C. Hope, detrained at Shoranur Junction where it remained until 27th August when it also moved up to Kuttipputam.

Meanwhile, two platoons of 'C' Company, 1st Bn, Leinster Regt., supported by some 20 Malabar Special Police, advanced across country southeast from Calicut to the principle regional settlement of Malappuram with a view to discouraging the local population from rallying to the rebel cause. Enemy opposition in the region was more severe than had been anticipated, and the Leinster patrol became marooned at its objective following a hard march. Contact with the Moplah was vigorously maintained resulting in the deaths of Lieutenant R.W. Johnston and Superintendent Readman.

A relief column, commanded by Captain P. McEnroy, 1st Bn, Leinster Regt., consisting of some 100 rifles of the battalion, thereupon swiftly advanced towards Malappuram from Calicut. Moplah marksmen constantly harassed the relief force throughout its march. On 26th August 1921 a full-scale enemy ambush was sprung. More than 400 rebels swarmed from the dense jungle and in the ensuing firefight Assistant Superintendent C.B. Lancaster and two Leinster other ranks died. Lieutenant H.A.K. McGonigal and nine Leinster other ranks were wounded. Once this action concluded no further contacts occurred and Malappuram was successfully relieved the following day.

Over the ensuing days, floods of refugees from the Malabar hinterland began to arrive in Calicut seeking sanctuary from marauding gangs of Moplah rebels. Temporary accommodation for these souls was found at West Hill Barracks but it rapidly became apparent that the authorities were about to be overwhelmed. Lord Willingdon determined to evacuate all non-essential personnel by sea. HMS *Comus*, a Royal Naval light cruiser under Captain A. Cochrane RN, was despatched from Colombo, Ceylon, with orders to remove all European women and children to safety in Aden. All able-bodied males were formed into a makeshift 'town guard' known as the Calicut Auxiliary Corps thus enabling all regular and reserve military units to deploy into the field.

Towards the end of August 1921, Major General J.T. Burnett-Stuart decided that the Army should secure Tirurangadi and engage the Moplah force that remained active in and around the settlement. Two columns of the 2nd Bn, Dorset Regt. were detailed to spearhead this manoeuvre supported by troopers of the Queen's Bays and gunners of 10 Pack Battery, RGA. Unaware that the 1st Bn, Leinster Regt. patrol base in Malappuram had been relieved, Lieutenant Colonel F.W. Radcliffe of the Dorset Regt. determined to divide his command and despatched his own relief column towards Malappuram while simultaneously deploying Major L.C. Hope and the remaining rifle companies northwest to a forming-up position shy of Tirurangadi.

Leaving Kattippuram early on 27th August 1921, Lieutenant Colonel F.W. Radcliffe's force made good progress towards Malappuram arriving at its objective early the following day. Discovering that its services were no longer required, the column rested for the night before setting out along the road west towards Tirurangadi with a view to rendezvousing with Major L.C. Hopes' command. Good progress was made by Lieutenant Colonel Radcliff's force despite delays caused by crude roadblocks

~ Jungle fighters ~

and collapsed river bridges. Disaster was averted at one location only when Lieutenant A.L. Grindley swam across the obstacle and located a native boat that was subsequently employed to ferry the men to the opposite bank. Major Hope's column, meanwhile, avoided any significant delays and on 30th August, the two columns were reunited. The following morning Tirurangadi was secured without opposition.

Information gathered from prisoners taken at Tirurangadi suggested a party of some 500 Moplah were occupying a fortified position within the grounds of Kishikkapalle mosque. Not wishing to place his command in unnecessary danger, Lieutenant Colonel F.W. Radcliffe determined to use Major L.C. Hope's company to surround the rebel location and await the enemy's surrender while withdrawing his main force back towards Malappuram. A long, wet night ensued. By mid morning the following day, the sun was shining brightly and thirst began to get the better of the Moplah. Spasmodic firing aimed towards the 1st Bn, Dorset Regt. picquets began at approximately 10 a.m. This slowly intensified and then, at 1.30 p.m., the mosque doors were flung open and the desperate natives streamed out towards the adjacent river bank. The Army immediately opened fire and some 30 rebels were cut down in their tracks. A further 40 of the enemy were subsequently captured including the key Moplah leader Ali Musliar. The bulk of the rebel party, however, broke though the Dorset Regt. perimeter and escaped into the jungle whereupon it split into several small gangs. Some 12 members of the Dorsets were injured during the firefight including four men killed or mortally wounded. Major Hope's company withdrew to Malappuram the following day less one platoon employed to escort the prisoners to Tirur.

*

Following the action near Tirurangadi the Moplah avoided direct contact with the Army. They remained, instead, hidden deep in the jungle advancing into the open only to engage in terror attacks before escaping back to their remote camps long before the authorities could effectively pursue them. British military tactics altered accordingly from early September 1921. Mobile patrols using lorries and hastily requisitioned civil omnibuses from Calicut were established along the few passable rural roads and tracks with dismounted sweeps of more remote areas. These activities met with only limited success. Felled trees and damaged river bridges confronted the troops at every turn significantly raising the risk of ambush. Both vehicular and equine transport frequently had to turn back due to impassable waterlogged terrain infested with poisonous reptiles. Forest Agency elephants proved a much more resilient medium and were widely employed by the Army to clear roadblocks and help carve new routes from the virgin forest.

On 10th September 1921, a Moplah gang attacked the Government facilities at Nilambur in the Malabar sub-district of Erand. Troops were immediately deployed to the area but the rebels had dispersed by the time the authorities arrived at the scene. Two days later a party of rebels from Mannarghat incited the citizens of Palghat to lay siege to the local police station. Fires were set and important tax records destroyed. During the confusion, the police garrison succeeded in escaping unharmed to Malappuram.

At this time, the 1st Bn, Suffolk Regt., stationed in Wellington, was called upon to provide a rifle company in support of the Malabar Field Force. 'D' Company, commanded by Captain H P Sparkes, deployed on 13th September 1921. Initially the men were sent to Tirur to act as a special reserve where they assisted the police in the execution of several property searches. Thereafter the company was despatched to Malappuram. Battalion HQ, 'A' and 'B' Companies, 1st Bn, Suffolk Regt. remained in Wellington until 17th November 1921 when they were despatched to Malabar in relief of the 2nd Bn, Dorset Regt. ('C' Company, 1st Bn, Suffolk Regt., which was initially in Jubbulpore subsequently moved to Wellington to form a depot and did not deploy to Malabar).

By mid-September 1921, most Moplah gangs had been isolated in the sub-districts of Ernad and Walavand. When a rebel chieftain, Kunhi Tangal, died in Cannonore gaol on 18th September 1921, it was hoped this would finally sap the morale of the enemy. Moplah deputy leader V K Hadji, however, immediately declared himself the new champion of the Moplah cause and set about rallying the remaining rebels to pursue with vigour their vision of an independent Kaliphate kingdom in northern Malabar. The renewed sense of purpose demonstrated by the Moplah following the death of Kunhi Tangal caused the authorities a great deal of concern. Military patrolling intensified and hostile contacts significantly increased.

Towards the end of September 1921, Moplah gangs led by V K Hadji ambushed several civilian tea convoys in northern Malabar. A significant tonnage of product destined for export was destroyed and a number of Hindu coolies killed. After each incident, the Moplah retreated into the jungle long before the authorities could mount a pursuit. Little useful intelligence was gleaned from the survivors who were fearful of reprisal.

ACTIVITIES OF MILITARY COLUMNS, MALABAR, LATE SEPTEMBER 1921

20th September 1921
1st Bn, Suffolk Regiment
'D' Company - Capt. H P Sparkes
Deploy to Malappuram from Tirur and prepare to secure local district.
2nd Bn, Dorset Regiment
'B' Company - Lt. Col. G M Herbert
Return to Wandur having had a successful patrol of the region to the east of the town.
Ordered to advance on Nilambur located forty miles east of Calicut.
'C' Company - Maj. E S Weldon
Advance towards Tuvur with a view to establishing a patrol base in that location. Ambush set on known route of enemy travel resulting in death of twenty-four Moplah for loss of several wounded including one man mortally.
'D' Company - Lt. Col. F W Radcliffe
Ambushed. Succeed in repelling Moplah attack for the loss of two personnel wounded.

22nd September 1921 **1st Bn Suffolk Regiment** **'D' Company – Capt. H P Sparkes** Advance to Cherpulasseri some distance north of patrol base in Malappuram. Objective to occupy Mannarakkad where rebels reported to be engaged in destruction of Government facilities. **2nd Bn, Dorset Regiment** **'C' Company – Maj. E S Weldon** Occupy Tuvur.
23rd September 1921 **1st Bn Suffolk Regiment** **'D' Company – Capt. H P Sparkes** Occupy Kumaramputtur some miles west of their objective at Mannarakkad. No opposition encountered. Company position established and patrols despatched to reconnoitre the objective. **2nd Bn, Dorset Regiment** **'B' Company – Lt. Col. G M Herbert** Attacked one mile southwest of Nilambur. Assault fought off resulting in the death of some twenty Moplah for the loss of one Dorset killed. **'C' Company – Maj. E S Weldon** Advance from Tuvur towards Nenmini.
24th September 1921 **1st Bn Suffolk Regiment** **Two platoons 'D' Company – Capt H P Sparkes** Enter Mannarakkad. Forty-four Moplah taken into custody. **2nd Bn, Dorset Regiment** **'B' Company – Lt. Col. G M Herbert** Occupy Nilambur. Stout resistance encountered. Seven Dorset Regt. personnel wounded, one mortally.

The 2nd Bn, Dorset Regt. remained heavily committed throughout October 1921. A significant contact occurred on 1st October when a convoy under Lieutenant Colonel G.M. Herbert was attacked between Malappuram and Nilambur during which (Quartermaster) Lieutenant J.A. Hardy was mortally wounded. A platoon operating in the Vadapuram region suffered a casualty on 7th October while returning to its patrol base in Mampad. Five days later, 'C' Company was ambushed on the Perintalmanna-Nellatur road whilst acting as an escort to a survey officer of the Royal Engineers. During this incident, the company took fire from an abandoned farm building and became unable to extricate themselves to safety. With casualties mounting, Captain L.T. Woodhouse, accompanied by Corporal Collins and Private Alexander, succeeded in working his way around to the flank of the structure from whence the threesome launched a successful assault and carried the enemy position.

Early on 16th October 1921 intelligence was received suggesting a Moplah gang, under a man known as Seta Koya, was about to collapse a river bridge in the vicinity of Mannarakkad. 'D' Company, 1st Bn, Suffolk Regt. immediately deployed in pursuit, but the chase proved futile. The regiment mounted several further expeditions over the ensuing days that forced those responsible for the damage to break into smaller ineffective parties.

At this time, a squadron of armoured cars furnished by 8 Armoured Car Company, Tank Corps, reinforced the Malabar Field Force. Two additional infantry battalions were also deployed. (3/70th Burma Rifles and 2/8th GR appear to have been selected for service in Malabar because of their operational experience in jungle regions). Additional mules to replace those declared lame from foot rot and associated damp-induced injury were supplied by 20 Draught Mules Corps, RIASC. These animals were immediately put to work in support of two major area sweeps in the Manjeri region on 20th October 1921. During the first operation, 45 rebels were accounted for by a Gurkha patrol

~ Prisoners were often transported in overcrowded conditions ~

operating along the Manjeri-Calicut road. In the second action, 'A' Company, 2nd Bn, Dorset Regt. swept a suspect area in the Pukkatur region driving a sizable Moplah gang into an ambush set by the regiments' 'D' Company. During the ensuing firefight some 30 enemy were killed.

Following the successful operations of 20th October 1921, intelligence officers were advised of a large concentration of Moplah in and around the village of Malmury situated some miles west of Malappuram. Steps were therefore taken to seal off the region and an assault by the 2nd Bn, Dorset Regt. supported by 10 Pack Battery, RGA, was prepared for dawn on the 25th October. During the subsequent attack a party of Moplah took shelter in the village mosque. This structure was thereupon subjected to an intense artillery barrage with devastating results. The destruction of Malmury mosque and the subsequent razing of the adjacent village led to the deaths of some 250 locals including women, children and pensioners – a fact readily and not unreasonably used to advantage by the wider Indian Nationalist Movement especially M.K. Ghandi's Congress Party.

Active patrolling continued throughout late October and early November 1921. Several contacts were registered and the occasional Moplah killed. No major engagements occurred until mid-month when on 15th November a company strength patrol base of the 2/8th GR was attacked by a large rebel force at Pandikkad. The Moplah, led by V.K. Hadji and Chembrasseri Thangal, assaulted the Gurkha position from all directions. The Gurkha defence was robust, resulting in the death of several hundred enemy for the loss of four riflemen killed.

The balance of the 1st Bn, Suffolk Regt., less 'C' Company, arrived by train in Tirur from Wellington on 17th November 1921. Upon their arrival, the battalion was ordered to Malappuram in relief of 1st Bn, Dorset Regt. which was to be withdrawn from the field and retired back to Bangalore prior to being deployed to the Sudan. During the march from Tirur, (Quartermaster) Lieutenant M.S. Chase and the regimental catering staff advanced ahead of the main column in a motor van towards the 1st Bn, Leinster Regt. patrol base in Kottakkal with a view to preparing a night bivouac for the troops. While journeying along the road, the quartermaster's party came upon a group of about 100 dejected-looking Moplah who appeared agitated and relieved at the appearance of British troops. They were evidently intent on surrendering to the authorities and agreed to accompany Lieutenant Chase to Kottakkal whereupon they were taken into custody by two platoons of the Leinster Regt.

*

By mid-November 1921, an estimated 27,000 Moplah had surrendered to the security forces. Detention facilities in Malabar were unable to cope with them and consequently the authorities decided to relocate several thousand prisoners to facilities elsewhere in India. One such party, destined for Bellary Gaol, entrained at Tirur early on 19th November. During a routine locomotive watering halt at Podanir Station, the guard discovered 56 Moplah lying dead in a sealed freight car. The heat and cramped conditions had apparently resulted in their asphyxiation. Survivors were immediately evacuated to hospital in nearby Coimbatore where a further eight men subsequently died.

The incident at Podanir was dubbed a modern day 'Black Hole of Calcutta' by the Nationalist Press. A board of inquiry was convened by the Government, under the chair of Mr. A.R. Knapp, Special Commissioner for Malabar, to investigate the circumstances surrounding the deaths of the Moplah prisoners. Among those called to give evidence at the inquiry were General Gifford IA, Surgeon General of Madras, and Mr. Brown, Traffic Inspector of the South India Railway Company. A verdict of accidental death by suffocation was eventually determined. Unfortunately, attitudes pertaining to the living conditions of prisoners did not improve dramatically after this incident and riots, such as the incident at Cannamore Gaol on 5th December 1921, became commonplace and led to several further casualties.

*

Located some six miles northwest of Malappuram was a steep hill known as the Urakuth Mala. This feature, standing some 1,600 feet above sea level, dominated the countryside for 30 miles or so in each direction. When intelligence reports were received by 1st Bn, Suffolk Regt. suggesting that a large Moplah force was expected to assemble at the summit on 27th November 1921, a decision was made to intercept them. 'D' Company deployed to the area but the rebels determined instead to attack several 1st Bn, Leinster Regt. picquets at Kottakkal. 'A' Company, 1st Bn, Suffolk Regt. followed up this incident and a number of the enemy were killed. Meanwhile, 'D' Company secured the summit of Urakuth Mala where it went on to establish a signals station. The Royal Signals subsequently employed this position to direct wireless communications in support of future operations.

1st Bn, Suffolk Regt. remained active throughout December 1921 and participated in several large-scale sweeping operations in conjunction with 1st Bn, Leinster Regt., 1/39th Garhwal Rifles and 83rd Wallajahbad Light Infantry. The Army's kill rate steadily declined towards the end of December as more and more rebels, realising that they were fighting a lost cause surrendered in drones. Chembrasseri Thangal gave himself up to a patrol of 2/8th Gurkha Rifles on the 19th December while shortly thereafter V.K. Haji was also captured. These two men were subsequently tried and, having been found guilty of committing several capital offences, sentenced to death. Both were executed on the Malappuram police rifle range at dawn on 9th January 1922.

Most of Malabar had been secured by Christmas 1921. A few disparate Moplah groups remained active in the remote regions of Ernad, north of the Beypore River. These pockets of resistance were eradicated during operations in February 1922. With the civil situation once again under the control of the local authorities, it was determined that military assistance in Malabar was no longer required and on 25th February the Malabar Field Force was formally stood down by Lieutenant General W. Marshall. The campaign had been a complete success. Thousands of Moplah rebels had been killed or transported for the loss of some 43 British and Indian Army troops killed. The authorities learnt many valuable lessons regarding the use of military formations in jungle environments although it was to be almost a decade before the Army would be required to put such practises to the test while on active operations in Burma.

* * *

	BRITISH ROLL OF HONOUR MALABAR 1921–1922 (To Six Months Past Operational Conclusion)		
Date:	**Person:**	**Unit:**	**Comment:**
24th August 1921	Lt. R W Johnston	1st Bn, Leinster Regt.	KIA Tirur Area
24th August 1921	Supt. Readman	Malabar Police	KIA Tirur Area
26th August 1921	7178002 Pte. E Kennedy	1st Bn, Leinster Regt.	KIA Malapparum Area
28th August 1921	7178532 Pte. J Clancy	1st Bn, Leinster Regt.	KIA Malapparum Area
26th August 1921	Asst. Supt. Lancaster	Malabar Police	KIA Malapparum Area
31st August 1921	5719581 Pte. H Williams	2nd Bn, Dorset Regt.	KIA Tirurangadi Mosque
31st August 1921	5718896 Pte. J M (F) Eley	2nd Bn, Dorset Regt.	Mortally Wounded Tirurangadi Mosque 30/8/21
31st August 1921	5718762 Pte. H C Hutchings	2nd Bn, Dorset Regt.	Mortally Wounded Tirurangadi Mosque 30/8/21
1st September 1921	5718825 Pte Haycock	2nd Bn, Dorset Regt.	Mortally Wounded
23rd September 1921	5718453 Pte. P Hughs	2nd Bn, Dorset Regt.	KIA Nilambur Area
24th September 1921	5718825 Bdsm C M McGill	2nd Bn, Dorset Regt.	Mortally Wounded Pandikkad Area
28th September 1921	5719453 Pte. H Percy	2nd Bn, Dorset Regt.	KIA
29th September 1921	5718062 Pte. R White	2nd Bn, Dorset Regt.	Mortally Wounded
31st September 1921	5718787 L/Cpl M Broomfield	2nd Bn, Dorset Regt.	Mortally Wounded
1st October 1921	(QM) Lt. J A Hardy	2nd Bn, Dorset Regt.	Mortally Wounded Nilambur Area
1st October 1921	5719062 Pte. J H Sprake	2nd Bn, Dorset Regt.	Mortally Wounded Nilambur Area
26th December 1921	5719130 Pte. F J Allen	2nd Bn, Dorset Regt.	DOW / Disease?
Unknown	Asst. Supt. W J D Rowley	Malabar Police	Killed
13th March 1922	5820884 Pte E Wischusen	1st Bn, Suffolk Regt.	DOW / Disease?
6th February 1922	5820668 Pte. W P Beaumont	1st Bn, Suffolk Regt.	Mortally Wounded Calicut road DOW 26/1/22
16th March 1922	1403192 BQMS C A Murphy	10 Pack Bty, RGA	Died (Of Disease?)
Unknown	7177142 WO11 E Brereton	1st Bn, Leinster Regt.	?
Unknown	1039620 Dvr. J Webster	99 Bty, RFA	Died (Of Disease?)

MALABAR 1921–22[7] ROLL

BRITISH ESTABLISHMENT
THE ARMY

~ Staff Grade Officers ~

Note a.   *Only Officers of the British Army are listed. Officers of the Indian Establishment are beyond the scope of this work and are thus excluded.*

Note b.   *Medals named in impressed capitals.*

Major Generals: ~ Sir J B Stuart[7]
Colonels: ~ T D Broughton[7] CRE Malabar

THE CAVALRY:

~ 2nd Dragoon Guards (Queen's Bays) ~

Note a.   *Roll of all personnel identified as eligible.*

Note b.   *France & Flanders August 1914. Palestine July 1919 thence India from December 1920. A single composite squadron consisting of one troop 'A' Squadron and three troops 'B' Squadron qualified for the clasp 'MALABAR 1921–1922'.*

Note c.   *Medals named in impressed capitals: 'THE BAYS.'*

Single Clasp	No. Identified	Rarity
Malabar 1921–22[7]	114	Very Scarce
Combination Clasps	*No. Identified*	*Rarity*
Malabar 1921–22[7] North West Frontier 1930–31[9]	1	According to the roll as seen, can be considered Unique
Malabar 1921–22[7] North West Frontier 1930–31[9] Burma 1930–32[10]	1	According to the roll as seen, can be considered Unique

Majors: ~ E Stone[7]

Lieutenants: ~ G F Dale[7], G W C Draffen[7], O V Holmes[7], E L Ridley Thompson[7] & W J Watson[7]

Warrant Officers Class II: ~ (SSM) 390475 F Barber[7] & (SSM) 390486 B J Cornish[7]

Squadron Quartermaster Sergeants/Staff Sergeants: ~ (Farrier) 390477 F Collier[7]

Quartermaster Sergeants/Sergeants: ~ 389702 A G Brown[7], 391062 D G Burnside[7], 390896 W R Chamberlain[7], 390902 F G Cocking[7], 391152 T H A Godbold[7], 389628 L A Litchfield[7], 390901 T Reid[7], 389496 A J Smart[7] & 389677 G W Stevens[7]

Corporals: ~ 391194 J Bennett[7], 392147 C E Campbell[7], 391477 S Dalton[7], 389628 L J Litchfield[7], (Farrier) 391560 E W Mill[7], 391415 L J Toms[7] & 391173 G F Walker[7]

Lance Corporals/Troopers: ~ 392907 J W Abram[7], 392150 A Allen[7], 391024 E H M Archdale[7], 394119 G Armitage[7], 392798 A W Barclay[7], 391061 R Barclay[7], 394076 J Barrett[7], 392894 R T Bastin[7], 392655 D H Beattie[7], 393992 J Blyth[7], 392075 E Boole[7], 392219 A E G Bowles[7], 392747 F L Brookes[7], 391094 P Carters[7], 391302 C Challis[7], 394013 G S Chaplain[7], 392249 T N Clare[7], 392455 E T Davies[7], 394003 E H Deakin[7], 394359 J Devine[7], 393631 J Deurish[7], 391974 E Eccles[7], 394017 R W Ellison[7], 391346 J E Evans[7], 391129 F Featherston[7(9&10 Sgt. RE attch. KGO S&M)], 391960 J Fish[7], 393994 J B Freer[7], 392165 F Gibbs[7], 391704 A E Goddard[7], 391205 E Gough[7], 394116 T Grady[7], 394020 T Greenlay[7], 394112 F A S Guyatt[7], 394102 W R Hall[7], 393221 J Higgins[7], 394103 H Hinge[7], 394025 J W Hooper[7], 392381 F Huckell[7], 391095 G Hunter[7], 391986 J Hunter[7], 392404 J Hirst[7], 393508 J Jennings[7], 391434 F Johnston[7], 391155 G Jones[7], 392926 J R Jones[7], 392121 L Jones[7], 391919 R W Kennelly[7], 394114 A King[7], 391056 C H Knaggs[7], 393116 W le Lievre[7], 394370 E A Mason[7], 394068 J McCrea[7], 394081 T McFarland[7], 394090 D McInnes[7], 393051 V G Mills[7], 392351 J Mitchell[7], 391443

J T Mitchell[7], 391069 T Meran[7], 392875 C W Morris[7], 392903 G Nacy[7], 392704 J Nash[7], 394614 A Newell[7], 392173 J Newman[7], 390835 A Nichol[7], 393817 W R Parsons[7], 7817078 H Pike[7], 390228 L H Pollard[7], 390893 J Read[7], 393132 L F Reynolds[7], 391162 W Reeves[7], 391983 T W Ridley[7], 391252 H Self[7&(9 F/S/Sgt. 15/19H)], 393033 T Shead[7], 393052 A Shook[7], 392192 E Smith[7], 391059 G A Smith[7], 391989 J J Stove[7], 393044 W E Sturgeon[7], 394100 S H Sullivan[7], 392379 H M Sutton[7], 391676 F J Taylor[7], 393780 J Thomas[7], 391437 W H Vann[7], 391440 W H Walker[7], 392448 A E Walton[7], 392228 P Welsh[7], 391090 J E Wheelhouse[7], 391915 A H Wilde[7] & 393839 J Wright[7]

Trumpeters: ~ 390193 J E Cook[7] & 389731 H Whittaker[7]

~ 18th (Queen Mary's Own) Hussars ~

Note a.   Roll of all personnel identified as eligible.
Note b.   France & Flanders August 1914 forward. India December 1919 to 1922.
Note c.   Amalgamated in United Kingdom with 13th Hussars in 1922 to form the 13th/18th Royal Hussars (Queen Mary's Own).
Note d.   Medals named in impressed capitals: '18 HRS.'

Single Clasp	No. Identified	Rarity
Malabar 1921–22[7]	2	Of the Utmost Rarity

Quartermaster Sergeants/Sergeants: ~ 537372 W Curtis[7], Rly Tpt Sgt. Maj., Base Camp, Tirur
Lance Corporals/Privates: ~ 537387 C J Hicks[7] attch. HQ, Malabar Field Force (MFF)

~ 19th (Queen Alexandra's Own Royal) Hussars ~

Note a.   Roll of all personnel identified as eligible.
Note b.   France & Flanders August 1914 forward. India November 1919 to 1922.
Note c.   Amalgamated with 15th (The King's Hussars) in 1922 to form the King's Royal Hussars.
Note d.   Recipient served as Deputy Assistant Director of Auxiliary and Territorial Forces, Madras District.
Note e.   Medals named in impressed capitals: '19 HRS.'

Single Clasp	No. Identified	Rarity
Malabar 1921–22[7]	1	According to the roll as seen, can be considered Unique

Lieutenant Colonels: ~ H E MacFarlane[7]

THE TANK CORPS (ROYAL FROM 1922):
Sub Units Identified As Entitled:
Section 8 Armoured Car Company
Detachment 9 Armoured Car Company

Note a.   Roll of all personnel identified as eligible.
Note b.   The Tank Corps was formed in 1917 from the heavy branch of the Machine Gun Corps. Motorised Machine Gun units remained within the orbit of the MGC.
Note c.   Medals named in impressed capitals: 'TANK CORPS.'

Single Clasp	Company	No. Identified	Rarity
Malabar 1921–22[7]	8	23	Very Rare
Malabar 1921–22[7]	9	4	Of the Utmost Rarity
Combination Clasps	**Company**	**No. Identified**	**Rarity**
Waziristan 1919–21[4] Malabar 1921–22[7]	8	1	According to the roll as seen, can be considered Unique

Waziristan 1919–21[4] Malabar 1921–22[7] Waziristan 1921–24[6]	8	2	**Of the Utmost Rarity**
Waziristan 1919–21[4] Malabar 1921–22[7] Waziristan 1921–24[7]	9	1	**According to the roll as seen, can be considered Unique**
Malabar 1921–22[7] Waziristan 1921–24[6]	8	2	**Of the Utmost Rarity**
Malabar 1921–22[7] Waziristan 1921–24[6]	9	3	**Of the Utmost Rarity**
Malabar 1921–22[7] North West Frontier 1930–31[9]	8	1	**According to the roll as seen, can be considered Unique**

Majors: ~ G A Rosser[4(9ACC),6(9 ACC)&7]

Lieutenants: ~ P J Dawson[7]

Quartermaster Sergeants/Sergeants: ~ 1404390 A Holt[7]

Lance Sergeants/Corporals: ~ 4681200 J C Kay[7] & 7871330 W T Nightingale[7]

Lance Corporals/Privates: ~ 7807134 G J Baily[7] 9 ACC, 7811849 W Barr[7&6(10 ACC)], 7819462 J E Burns[7&6(9 ACC)], 7814338 R W Burton[4&7], 7868617 J C Chetwynd[7&9(Sgt. 1 ACC)], 7870082 A Chorlton[7], 7870241 G Condon[7], 7817708 A H Dall[7], 7812214 D Daly[7&6] 9 ACC, 7810861 J Gardner[4(10 ACC),6(10 ACC)&7], 7871062 J F Gibson[4,7&6] 9 ACC, 7817494 R Green[7], 7815560 J B Greer[7] 9 ACC, 7869884 P Hall[7], 7808583 L Healey[7] 9 ACC, 7817608 W Kennedy[7], 7868272 R Lambert[7], 7869367 F P Luck[7&6] 9 ACC, 7870223 W Morton[7] 9 ACC, 7871522 G H Norris[7], 7870639 J H Pass[7], 7871063 W E Pryor[7], 7871207 A W Reeves[7], 7869249 H J Roser[7], 7871302 R Sleet[7], 7870246 W H Smith[7], 7870509 W Straw[7], 7870275 F Temple[7&6] 9 ACC, 7813076 H Terry[7], 7869172 W Todd[7], 7868764 H Walker[7] & 7817537 W H White[7]

THE MACHINE GUN CORPS:

Note a.   *Roll of all personnel identified as eligible.*

Note b.   *Recipient attached 'E' Company, South of India Railway Battalion, Auxiliary Forces India (AFI).*

Note c.   *The Machine Gun Corps (MGC) was formed in 1915 with three branches – a. Machine Gun Corps Cavalry, b. Machine Gun Corps Infantry (From May 1918 included Guards Machine Gun Regiment), c. Motorised Machine Gun Service.*

Note d.   *A fourth branch, Heavy Machine Gun Corps, was formed in 1916 and became the nucleolus for the creation of the Tank Corps (TC) in 1917.*

Note e.   *The Machine Gun Corps was disbanded in 1922 with many non-demobilising personnel then transferring to the Tank Corps (TC).*

Note f.   *Medals named in impressed capitals: 'M.G.C.'*

Single Clasp	*No. Identified*	*Rarity*
Malabar 1921–22[7]	1	**According to the roll as seen, can be considered Unique**

Company Quartermaster Sergeants/Staff Sergeants: ~ 7808268 J Owen[7]

THE ARTILLERY:

~ The Royal Field Artillery ~
Sub Units Identified As Entitled:
67 Field Battery

Note a.   *Roll of all personnel identified as eligible.*
Note b.   *The Royal Field Artillery (RFA) and the Royal Garrison Artillery (RGA) merged in 1924 and re-adopted the simple title 'Royal (Regiment of) Artillery' (RA). (For further details, please see Royal Field Artillery introductory notes on page XYZ).*
Note c.   *Medals named in impressed capitals: 'R.A.'*

Single Clasp	No. Identified	Rarity
Malabar 1921–22[7]	48	Very Rare

Majors: ~ H G Lee Warner[7] GSO2, HQ Madras
Captains: ~ D S M Woodward[7]
Lieutenants: ~ B Pennefeather-Evans[7] attch. 1 Leinster, C Neville[7] ADC to GOC Southern Cmd., C F Tyson[7] & F L Underwood[7]
Quartermaster Sergeants/Sergeants: ~ 1039483 J Bond[7], 1017469 F P Harris[7], 1039450 W J Page[7], 1039451 H G Robinson[7] & 1039445 H J Robinson[7]
Bombardiers: ~ 1039524 T Lahy[7], 538229 A Shipman[7], 537023 G C K Shipman[7] & 1039537 H Shuter[7]
Lance Bombardiers/Gunners/Drivers: ~ 1039400 F J Bavestock[7], 1039551 W T Bennett[7], 1039487 N Boyle[7], 1039494 S Brown[7], 1039558 J Callear[7], 1039503 Duncan[7], 1039887 D H Elliot[7], 1039572 T Forth[7], 1039473 W E Fowler[7], 1039505 R Fuller[7], 1039510 E C Gardner[7], 1039317 T G Hanson[7], 1039532 W D Johnson[7], 1039522 T Keevin[7], 1039531 R E Knight[7], 1039587 J Locker[7], 1039589 G McLaren[7], 1039590 J Molloy[7], 1039600 S Pullen[7], 1039601 T Quinn[7], 1039602 T Richardson[7], 1039606 G H Rigden[7], 1039614 W Shepherd[7], 1039539 A E Sheridan[7], 1039542 R Shuttleworth[7], 1039615 S Skelding[7], 1039616 A T Smalley[7], 1039613 B Smith[7], 1039612 W J Stevenson[7], 1039543 G Topping[7], 1039546 F Watson[7] & 1039620 J Webster[7]
Shoeing Smiths: ~ 1039288 E Duffy[7]

~ The Royal Garrison Artillery ~
Sub Units Identified As Entitled:
8 Pack Battery – Individuals
10 Pack Battery

Note a.   *Roll of all personnel identified as eligible.*
Note b.   *In 1920, Mountain Batteries Royal Garrison Artillery (RGA) were designated Pack Batteries Royal Garrison Artillery (RGA).*
Note c.   *10 Pack Battery qualified for 'Malabar 1921–22' before 'Waziristan 1921–24'.*
Note d.   *During the period 1919–1921, the Royal Garrison Artillery (RGA) discontinued the use of the rank designation 'Corporal' and adopted the existing Royal Field Artillery (RFA) designation 'Bombardier' instead. This decision made necessary the remustering of existing Bombardiers as 'Lance Bombardiers'.*
Note e.   *The Royal Garrison Artillery (RGA) and the Royal Field Artillery (RFA) merged in 1924 and re-adopted the simple title 'Royal (Regiment of) Artillery' (RA).*
Note f.   *Medals named in impressed capitals: 'R.A.'*

Single Clasp	Battery	No. Identified	Rarity
Malabar 1921–22[7]	8	4	Of the Utmost Rarity
Malabar 1921–22[7]	10	51	Rare

Combination Clasps	Battery	No. Identified	Rarity
Afghanistan N.W.F. 1919[3] Malabar 1921–22[7] Waziristan 1921–24[6]	10	2	Of the Utmost Rarity

Waziristan 1919–21[4] Malabar 1921–22[7] Waziristan 1921–24[6]	10	1	According to the roll as seen, can be considered Unique
Malabar 1921–22[7] Waziristan 1921–24[6]	10	42	Very Rare
Malabar 1921–22[7] Waziristan 1921–24[6] North West Frontier 1930–31[9]	10	1	According to the roll as seen, can be considered Unique
Malabar 1921–22[7] Waziristan 1921–24[6] North West Frontier 1935[12]	10	1	According to the roll as seen, can be considered Unique

Majors: ~ G S Phillips[7]

Captains: ~ C R Cross[7&6]

Lieutenants: ~ A E Cunningham[7&6], W E Pengelly[7] & R S Wade[7&6]

Warrant Officers Class II: ~ (Act BSM) (1403048) 31726 T J Marryweather[3,7&6] & (BSM) 1402163 G Smyth[7]

Battery Quartermaster Sergeants/Staff Sergeants: ~ 1402186 H T Chandler[7] & 1403192 A Murphy[7]

Quartermaster Sergeants/Sergeants: ~ 1408529 F B Asher[7&6], 1403402 A E Dalton[7] & 1402325 H R White[7&6]

Corporals: ~ 1415872 D Adamson[7&6(L/Sgt.)], 1404543 R Emans[7], (1405005) 32070 J Fitzgerald[3,7&6] & 1410555 R J Laing[7&6(L/Sgt.)]

Bombardiers: ~ (Act) 1404436 S H Davis[7&6], 1048332 W Eldridge[7], (Act) 1404255 J French[7], 1409869 T Griffiths[7&6(Act L/Sgt.)], 1403326 H A Halley[7&6], (Act) 1409535 H E Harrison[7], (Act) 1409778 J Harrison[7&6(Gnr.)], 1409474 R James[7] & 1406076 A E Smith[7&6]

Lance Bombardiers/Gunners: ~ 1417488 F J Anderson[7&6], 1405258 L H Anderson[7], 1418441 A E Andrews[7&6], 1411700 H E Anscombe[7&6], 1418570 E H Ayling[7,6&12(Bdr.)], 1410100 J Barkas[7&6], 1413403 A H Barstow[7&6(L/Bdr.)], 1417973 L G Bastin[7], 1413953 T Bird[7], 1409944 R J Burgess[7], 1415169 D Cartwright[7Bdr.)&6], 1410927 T Chambers[7], 1417741 F Chown[7] 8 Mtn Bty, 1410511 R Clarke[7&6], 1415350 L le Cointe[7&6(L/Bdr.)], 1414838 J S Cole[7&6(Bdr.)], 1410126 E Coleing[7], 1412007 W H Congdon[7&6(Bdr.)], 1412524 J S Corney[7], 1418144 J J Cullen[7&6], 1415219 J Curtin[7&6], 1415578 A Dawson[7&6(L/Bdr.)], 1417666 P C Dennett[7], 1409543 W Dixon[7], 1410486 F Eggleton[7], 1411709 W Eyers[7], 1411405 J Ferguson[7], 1410988 T J Fiddy[7], 1417489 F H French[7&6(L/Bdr.)], 1408906 F J Gittins[7], 1404016 T Glass[7], 1415036 A Golden[7&6], 1410142 H A Griffin[7], 1409875 A Harper[7], 1411654 C Harriss[7&6(Bdr.)], 1416140 M Hehir[7], 1417782 L H Heron[7], 1410618 E J A Heseltine[7], 1418225 C H House[7&6], 1417169 J H Huckstep[7,6&9], 1418444 W Hunt[7,6&9], 1415663 (222542) A Hurd[7&6], 1417005 W E Ilott[7] 8 Mtn Bty, 1410584 H Jones[7], 1402421 M Kearney[7&6], 1417412 J Kelly[7&6], 1410905 F D Kewell[7], 1418516 P A Keywood[7&6], 1406556 F W Knowlden[7], 1417081 H W Last[7&6], 1405282 C Martin[7], 1409724 H Medlock[7], 1418363 E Morgan[7], 1409684 A Newman[7], 1414804 W F Noake[7&6], 1403777 W Norman[7&6], 1418899 T North[7&6], 1410837 A H Payne[7], 1412110 R S Paynter[7], 1411140 R Perks[7], 1058207 J Proudfoot[7&6], 1416381 H T Rogers[7], 1404079 J Shasby[7&6], 1415027 W C Shortman[7], 1411735 E J Spears[7] 8 Mtn Bty, 1410512 W A Staff[7], 1403283 R Stirrups[7] 8 Mtn Bty, (22994) 1417466 G Suggitt[4,7&6], 1418595 S Thomas[7], 1409858 H Tucker[7&6(Bdr.)], 1409417 J E Tucker[7], 1410016 E L Turner[7], 1418680 P G Walker[7], 1410176 F Wall[7], 1411935 T H Williams[7] & 1417579 S J Willis[7]

Trumpeters: ~ 1413830 G H Flower[7&6(Gnr.)] & 1038207 A Parker[7&6]

THE CORPS OF ROYAL ENGINEERS:

Note a. *Roll of all personnel identified as eligible.*

Note b. *Recipients attached 2nd Queen Victoria's Own Sappers & Miners.*

Note c. *Medals named in impressed capitals: 'R.E.'*

Single Clasp	No. Identified	Rarity
Malabar 1921–22[7]	1	According to the roll as seen, can be considered Unique

Combination Clasps	No. Identified	Rarity
Malabar 1921–22[7] Waziristan 1921–24[6] North West Frontier 1930–31[9]	1	According to the roll as seen, can be considered Unique

Captains: ~ A V Anderson[7]

Lieutenants: ~ E F J Payne[7,6&9(Capt.)]

THE ROYAL CORPS OF SIGNALS:
Sub Units Identified As Entitled:
6 Wirless Section, 2 Wireless Company, 'B' Corps Signals

Note a.   *Roll of all personnel identified as eligible.*
Note b.   *The Royal (Corps) of Signals was formed in June 1920 from personnel transferred (principally) from the Royal Engineers Signal Service and Indian Army signals establishment.*
Note c.   *Medals named in impressed capitals: 'R. SIGNALS.'*

Single Clasp	No. Identified	Rarity
Malabar 1921–22[7]	18	Extremely Rare

Combination Clasps	No. Identified	Rarity
Malabar 1921–22[7] Waziristan 1921–24[6]	5	Of the Utmost Rarity
Malabar 1921–22[7] Waziristan 1921–24[6] Burma 1930–32[10]	1	According to the roll as seen, can be considered Unique
Malabar 1921–22[7] Burma 1930–32[10]	1	According to the roll as seen, can be considered Unique

Lieutenants: ~ J C H Shaw[7&6(Capt.)]

Quartermaster Sergeants/Sergeants: ~ (Act) 1855026 W Blundell[7] & 7211227 F Ponder[7]

Lance Sergeants/Corporals: ~ (Act) 2309516 M Shadlow[7&10(Sgt.)]

Lance Corporals/Signalmen: 2310734 A Ayton[7], 1850317 S Bygrave[7], 2313656 E W J Collins[7&6], 2309814 W J Cornish[7], 2310976 A J Davis[7], 1857312 C M Edward[7], 2312168 E H Harding[7], 2313821 F C Jones[7], 2309773 C K Knight[7], 2309849 D Leyshon[7&6(L/Cpl.)], (Originally Royal Navy), 2309665 A J Loveridge[7], 2310936 A Murray[7], 2310828 J Peters[7,6(Sgln.)&10(Cpl.)], 2309455 J P Rippin[7], 2311041 E T Sanley[7], 2310989 J Sargeant[7], 2313910 T W E Thomas[7&6], 2309299 W Thompson[7], (2310753) 625240 E R Turner[7&6], 2310795 G Urwin[7] & 2310835 A C Wells[7]

THE INFANTRY:

~ 2nd Bn, The Lincolnshire Regiment ~

Note a.   *Roll of all personnel identified as eligible.*
Note b.   *Bermuda August 1914. France & Flanders November 1914 thence India November 1919 to 1924.*
Note c.   *Recipient attached 6 Wireless Section, 'B' Corps Signals.*
Note d.   *Medals named in impressed capitals: 'LINC. R.'*

Single Clasp	No. Identified	Rarity
Malabar 1921–22[7]	1	According to the roll as seen, can be considered Unique

Lance Corporals/Privates: ~ 4793284 J T Wadsworth[7]

~ 1st Bn, The Suffolk Regiment ~

Note a.   *Roll of all commissioned personnel identified as eligible.*
Note b.   *Non-commissioned and other rank personnel multi clasp only.*
Note c.   *Sudan August 1914. France & Flanders January 1915, Egypt October 1915, Salonika November 1915 forward. India November 1919 to March 1924.*
Note d.   *Battalion deployed to Malabar less 'C' Company, which was held in reserve and (believed) subsequently employed in Waziristan.*
Note e.   *Medals named in impressed capitals: 'SUFF. R.'*

Single Clasp	No. Identified	Rarity
Malabar 1921–22[7]	Partial Bn. Strength	Scarcer than standard Battalion Strength issues due to exclusion of 'C' Company

Combination Clasps	No. Identified	Rarity
Malabar 1921–22[7] Waziristan 1921–24[6]	1	According to the roll as seen, can be considered Unique

Lieutenant Colonels: ~ F S Cooper[7] & F T D Wilson[7]

Majors: ~ S J B Barnardiston[7]

Captains: ~ F C Berrill[7], C W Merison[7], N B Oakes[7], S W H Silver[7] & H P Sparkes[7]

Lieutenants: ~ S H Atkins[7], L J Baker[7], N A Bott[7], E A Pickard-Cambridge[7], H C Carrigan[7], (QM) M S Chase[7], S E Clarke[7], A A Johnson[7], J W Josselyn[7], F Maxwell-Lawford[7], I G Owen[7], A G Rumblow[7], H B Monier-Williams[7] & J Yates[7]

Quartermaster Sergeants/Sergeants: ~ (Act) 5819666 H H Young[7&6(RASC)]

~ 2nd Bn, The Royal Scots Fusiliers ~

Note a. Roll of all personnel identified as eligible.

Note b. Gibraltar August 1914. France & Flanders October 1914 forward. India from November 1920.

Note c. Recipient served as General Staff Officer Grade 2 (GSO2) at Headquarters (HQ) Madras District.

Note d. Medals named in impressed capitals: 'R. S. FUS.' or 'R. SCOTS FUS.'

Single Clasp	No. Identified	Rarity
Malabar 1921–22[7]	1	According to the roll as seen, can be considered Unique

Majors: ~ (Bvt.) R V G Horn[7]

~ 1st Bn, The Hampshire Regiment ~

Note a. Roll of all personnel identified as eligible.

Note b. United Kingdom August 1914. France & Flanders August 1914 forward. Turkey April 1920 thence Egypt December 1921.

Note c. Recipient served as Deputy Adjutant and Quartermaster General (DA&QMG), Madras District.

Note d. Medals named in impressed capitals: 'HAMPS. R.'

Single Clasp	No. Identified	Rarity
Malabar 1921–22[7]	1	According to the roll as seen, can be considered Unique

Majors: ~ R D Johnson[7]

~ 2nd Bn, The Dorsetshire Regiment ~

Note a. Roll of all commissioned personnel identified as eligible.

Note b. Non-commissioned and other rank personnel multi clasp only.

Note c. India August 1914. Mesopotamia November 1914 forward.

Note d. Captured at Kut al Amara on 29th April 1916 survivors and non-deployed drafts were merged with similar 'odd' men of 2nd Bn, Norfolk Regt, to form the 'Norsets'. Re-established as a functioning entity in July 1916, the new battalion moved to India in October 1919 via Egypt, Palestine and Syria thence Egypt again in January 1922.

Note e. Medals named in impressed capitals: 'DORSET. R.'

Single Clasp	No. Identified	Rarity
Malabar 1921–22[7]	Bn. Strength	Not Rare.

Combination Clasps	No. Identified	Rarity
Waziristan 1919–21[4] & Malabar 1921–22[7]	2	Of the Upmost Rarity
Malabar 1921–22[7] North West Frontier 1930–31[9]	1	According to the roll as seen, can be considered Unique
Malabar 1921–22[7] North West Frontier 1935[12]	1	According to the roll as seen, can be considered Unique

Lieutenant Colonels: ~ G M Herbert[7], F W Radcliffe[7] & E Saunders[7]

Majors: ~ L C Hope[7] & E S Welden[7]

Captains: ~ J Angell[7], E R U Bailey[7], W Barton[7], J Bessell[7], W H A Bishop[7] attch. Staff as GSO3, GSA E Hawkins[7], J S Hewick[7], C T Highett[7], J S Rendall[7], D A Simmons[7] & L T Woodhouse[7]

Lieutenants: ~ G J Bullard[7], R E C Goff[7], A L Grindley[7], (QM) J A Hardy[7], W H B Raif[7], H B Rathborne[7], J H Spencer[7], D R Stephens[7], M S Wheatley[7] & K W Wright[7]

Quartermaster Sergeants/Sergeants: ~ (Act) 5718740 R A Eaton[7&12(WOII)] & (Act) 5719217 A C Davis[4&7] attch. S&TC

Lance Sergeants/Corporals: ~ 5718882 D Heatley[7&(9 Cpl. 1 ACC, RTC)]

Lance Corporals/Privates: ~ 5719277 A R J Darby[4&7] attch. S&TC

~ 1st Bn, The Black Watch (Royal Highlanders) ~

Note a.   *Roll of all personnel identified as eligible.*

Note b.   *United Kingdom August 1914. France & Flanders August 1914 forward. India September 1919 forward.*

Note c.   *Recipient served on the Staff at Headquarters (HQ) Malabar Field Force (MFF).*

Note d.   *Medals named in impressed capitals: 'BLACK WATCH', 'R. HIGHRS.' or 'R. HDRS.'*

Single Clasp	No. Identified	Rarity
Malabar 1921–22[7]	1	According to the roll as seen, can be considered Unique

Captains: ~ D S Gordon Brown[7]

~ 1st Bn, The Queen's Own (Royal West Kent Regiment) ~

Note a.   *Roll of all personnel identified as eligible.*

Note b.   *United Kingdom August 1914. France & Flanders August 1914, Italy December 1917, France & Flanders April 1918 forward. India November 1919.*

Note c.   *Title changed in 1920 to The Royal West Kent Regiment (Queen's Own) and again in 1921 to The Queen's Own Royal West Kent Regiment.*

Note d.   *Medals named in impressed capitals: 'R. W. KENT. R.'*

Single Clasp	No. Identified	Rarity
Malabar 1921–22[7]	1	According to the roll as seen, can be considered Unique
Combination Clasps	**No. Identified**	**Rarity**
Waziristan 1919–21[4] Malabar 1921–22[7]	1	According to the roll as seen, can be considered Unique

Captains: ~ A G Balbernie[4(RWK)&7] & A C S Palin[7] attch. 1 Leinster

~ 4th Bn, The King's Royal Rifle Corps ~

Note a.   *Roll of all personnel identified as eligible.*

Note b.   *India August 1914. France & Flanders December 1914, Salonika November 1915, France & Flanders July 1918 forward. India November 1919 forward.*

Note c.   *Medals named in impressed capitals: 'K.R.R.C.'*

Single Clasp	No. Identified	Rarity
Malabar 1921–22[7]	1	According to the roll as seen, can be considered Unique

Lance Corporals/Privates: ~ ?????? A Bloomfield[7]

~ 2nd Bn, The Prince of Wales's (North Staffordshire Regiment) ~

Note a.   *Roll of all personnel identified as eligible.*

Note b.   *India August 1914 forward to February 1920.*

Note c.   *Recipient served as Adjutant (Adjt.) of the Southern Provinces Mounted Rifles, Auxiliary Forces India (AFI).*

Note d.   *Medals named in impressed capitals: 'N. STAFF. R.'*

Single Clasp	No. Identified	Rarity
Malabar 1921–22[7]	1	According to the roll as seen, can be considered Unique

Lieutenants: ~ J T Leese[7]

~ 1st Bn, The Durham Light Infantry ~

Note a.   *Roll of all personnel identified as eligible.*

Note b.   *India August 1914 forward to 1921.*

Note c.   *Recipient served as Barrack Department Clerk, Headquarters (HQ), Wellington Garrison, Madras District.*

Note d.   *Medals named in impressed capitals: 'DURH. L. I.'*

Single Clasp	No. Identified	Rarity
Malabar 1921–22[7]	1	According to the roll as seen, can be considered Unique

Company Quartermaster Sergeants/Staff Sergeants/Colour Sergeants: ~ 4435159 J H Creber[7]

~ 1st Bn, Princess Louise's (Argyll & Sutherland Highlanders) ~

Note a.   *Roll of all personnel identified as eligible.*

Note b.   *India August 1914. France & Flanders December 1914, Salonika December 1915, Bulgaria September 1918 forward. Turkey December 1918, India November 1919 to December 1923 thence Egypt.*

Note c.   *Title changed to The Argyll and Sutherland Highlanders (Princess Louise's) in 1920.*

Note d.   *Recipient served as General Staff Officer Grade 3 (GSO3), at Headquarters (HQ), Malabar Field Force (MFF).*

Note e.   *Medals named in impressed capitals: 'A.&S.H.'*

Single Clasp	No. Identified	Rarity
Malabar 1921–22[7]	1	According to the roll as seen, can be considered Unique

Majors: ~ A R G Wilson[7]

~ 1st Bn, The Prince of Wales's Leinster Regiment (Royal Canadians) ~

Note a. *Roll of all commissioned personnel identified as eligible.*
Note b. *Non-commissioned and other rank personnel multi clasp only.*
Note c. *India August 1914. France & Flanders December 1914, Salonika December 1915, Egypt September 1917 thence Palestine. India November 1919 to April 1922. Present in battalion strength for the clasp 'MALABAR 1921-1922'. Disbanded in 1922 upon the formation of Irish Free State.*
Note d. *Medals named in impressed capitals: 'LEINS. R.'*

Single Clasp	No. Identified	Rarity
Malabar 1921–22[7]	Bn. Strength	Scarcer than standard battalion strength issues. This potentially due to turmoil in Southern Ireland and disassociation with Britain during issue period
Combination Clasps	**No. Identified**	**Rarity**
Waziristan 1919–21[4] Malabar 1921–22[7] North West Frontier 1930–31[9]	1	According to the roll as seen, can be considered Unique
Malabar 1921–22[7] Waziristan 1921–24[6]	4	Of the Utmost Rarity

Lieutenant Colonels: ~ E T Humphries[7]
Majors: ~ L D Daly[4,7&(9 KOYLI)] attch. Calicut Aux Corps, AFI & J V Macartney[7&(6 10 ACC, RTC)]
Captains: ~ P Mc Enroy[7]
Lieutenants: ~ A Duncan[7], A S Dundas[7], H V T French[7], H A K Mc Gonigal[7], F C Hitchcock[7], H A Howes[7], J J MacDonald[7] attch. Staff & J R H Whitla[7]
Lance Corporals/Privates: ~ 717738 E Barrett[7&(6 Pte. Welch)], 717735 E J Hitchcock[7&(6 Pte. Welch)] & 7178325 P Shannon[7&(6 Pte. Welch)]

~ 4th Bn, The Rifle Brigade (The Prince Consort's Own) ~

Note a. *Roll of all personnel identified as eligible.*
Note b. *India August 1914. France & Flanders December 1914, Salonika December 1915 forward. December 1918 Turkey, India November 1919 to November 1921.*
Note c. *Recipient served as Aide de Camp (ADC) to the General Officer Commanding (GOC) Madras District.*
Note d. *Medals named in impressed capitals: 'RIF. BRIG.'*

Single Clasp	No. Identified	Rarity
Malabar 1921–22[7]	1	According to the roll as seen, can be considered Unique

Lieutenants: ~ E A R Ramsay-Fairfax-Lucy[7]

THE CORPS:

~ The Royal Army Service Corps ~

Note a. *Roll of all personnel identified as eligible.*
Note b. *Recipients attached 14 Motor Transport Company (MT Coy), Supply & Transport Corps (S&TC), unless shown otherwise.*
Note c. *The Royal Army Service Corps (RASC) was formed in 1918 from the Army Service Corps (ASC).*
Note d. *Medals named in impressed capitals: 'R.A.S.C.'*

Single Clasp	No. Identified	Rarity
Malabar 1921–22[7]	6	Of the Utmost Rarity

Lieutenants: ~ A W J Bavin[7]
Quartermaster Sergeants/Sergeants: ~ (Act) M/21657 W Langton[7]
Lance Sergeants/Corporals: ~ M/16828 J W H Marsh[7] attch. 3 MT Coy, S&TC
Lance Corporals/Privates: ~ M/22175 J W Blofield[7], M/16409 F W Broadhead[7], S&TC & M/53889 C N Ewing[7] attch. 8 ACC

~ The Royal Army Medical Corps ~

Note a. *Roll of all personnel identified as eligible.*
Note b. *Medals named in impressed capitals: 'R.A.M.C.'*

Single Clasp	No. Identified	Rarity
Malabar 1921 - 22[7]	5	Of the Utmost Rarity
Combination Clasps	**No. Identified**	**Rarity**
Mahsud 1919–20[5] Waziristan 1919–21[4] Malabar 1921–22[7]	1	According to the roll as seen, can be considered Unique
Malabar 1921–22[7] Waziristan 1921–24[6]	1	According to the roll as seen, can be considered Unique
Malabar 1921–22[7] North West Frontier 1930–31[9]	1	According to the roll as seen, can be considered Unique

Majors: ~ T T H Robinson[7], Malabar Base Hospital, Padanur
Captains: G D Gripper[7&6], R A Hepple[7], R I Sullivan[4,5&7] & T O Thompson[7&9(Maj.)]
Lance Corporals/Privates: ~ 7249321 P C Bird[7], 7249375 J C Scott[7] & 7249631 J A Starkie[7]

~ The Royal Army Ordnance Corps ~

Note a. *Roll of all personnel identified as eligible.*
Note b. *Medals named in impressed capitals: 'R.A.O.C.'*

Single Clasp	No. Identified	Rarity
Malabar 1921–22[7]	4	Of the Utmost Rarity
Combination Clasps	**No. Identified**	**Rarity**
Waziristan 1919–21[4] Malabar 1921–22[7]	1	According to the roll as seen, can be considered Unique

Warrant Officers Class II: ~ (Sub Cndtr) 7579070 J C Hogger[7]
Company Quartermaster Sergeants/Staff Sergeants: ~ (Armt) 7578824 L E Baker[4&7] attch. 1 Suffolk
Quartermaster Sergeants/Sergeants: ~ (Armt) 7578566 D Hepburn[7] attch. 2 Dorset.
Lance Sergeants/Corporals: ~ 7574570 H R Symonds[7]
Lance Corporals/Privates: ~ 7575350 D Frater[7]

~ The Royal Army Veterinary Corps ~

Note a. *Roll of all personnel identified as eligible.*
Note b. *Medals named in impressed capitals: 'R.A.V.C.'*

Single Clasp	No. Identified	Rarity
Malabar 1921–22[7]	0	None Identified

Combination Clasps	No. Identified	Rarity
Afghanistan N.W.F. 1919[3] Malabar 1921–22[7]	2	Of the Utmost Rarity

Majors: ~ J R Stevenson[3&7] DADVS
Captains: ~ S L Slocock[3&7]

~ The Army Educational Corps ~

Note a. *Roll of all personnel identified as eligible.*
Note b. *Recipient attached 2 Dorset Regt.*
Note c. *Medals named in impressed capitals: 'A.E.C.'*

Single Clasp	No. Identified	Rarity
Malabar 1921–22[7]	0	None Identified

Combination Clasps	No. Identified	Rarity
Malabar 1921–22[7] North West Frontier 1930–31[9]	1	According to the roll as seen, can be considered Unique

Lieutenants: ~ J C Wood[7&(9 Capt. attch. HQ 2 Bde.)]

DOMINION

~ The Australian Army Staff Corps ~

Note a. *Roll of all personnel identified as eligible.*
Note b. *Australian officers were commissioned from the Royal Military College Duntroon into the Australian Staff Corps. Several were sent each year to India for attachment to both British and Indian Army units.*
Note c. *Medals named in impressed capitals. Believed: 'AUST. STAFF CORPS'*

Single Clasp	No. Identified	Rarity
Malabar 1921–22[7]	1	According to the roll as seen, can be considered Unique

Combination Clasps	No. Identified	Rarity
Waziristan 1919–21[4] Malabar 1921–22[7]	1	According to the roll as seen, can be considered Unique

Lieutenants: ~ J F Roberts[4(attch. 2 Queen's)&7] attch. 1 Suffolk & C H Simpson[7] attch. 1 Suffolk

~ The New Zealand Staff Corps ~

Note a. *Roll of all personnel identified as eligible.*
Note b. *Recipient attached 1 Suffolk Regt.*
Note c. *Medals named in impressed capitals. Believed: 'N.Z. STAFF CORPS.'*

Single Clasp	No. Identified	Rarity
Malabar 1921–22[7]	1	According to the roll as seen, can be considered Unique

Lieutenants: ~ W Gonbry[7]

MISCELLANEOUS

~ The Corps of Military Staff Clerks ~

Note a.   *Roll of all eligible personnel identified as cap badged 'Corps of Military Staff Clerks', as opposed to being shown on roll as 'attached Corps of Military Staff Clerks'.*

Note b.   *Medals named in impressed capitals: 'C.M.S.C.'*

Single Clasp	No. Identified	Rarity
Malabar 1921–22[7]	1	According to the roll as seen, can be considered Unique

Quartermaster Sergeants/Sergeants: ~ 8804 A E Willsher[7] attch. 1 Leinster

INDIAN ESTABLISHMENT

Qualifying Units Present

The Cavalry:
None Identified

The Artillery:
None Identified

The Sappers & Miners:
2nd Queen Victoria's Own Sappers & Miners – One Platoon

Military Works Service

The Pioneers:
64th Pioneers – Detachment

The Infantry:

1922 Title	Pre 1922 Title
4/3rd Madras Regiment (Wallajahbad) Light Infantry	83rd Wallajahabad Light Infantry
1/18th Royal Garhwal Rifles	1/39th Royal Garhwal Rifles
3/70th (Kachin) Rifles (Burma Rifles)	Chin Kachin Battalion, Burma Rifles
2/3rd Queen Alexandra's Own Gurkha Rifles (No Change)	Bvt. Maj. E J Shearer, DAQMG (Only)
2/8th Gurkha Rifles (No Change)	
2/9th Gurkha Rifles (No Change)	

The Indian Army Reserve of Officers:

The Militia, Auxiliary Forces India & Indian Territorial Force:
The Southern Provinces Mounted Rifles, AFI
The Nilgiri Malabar Bn, AFI
South India Railway Bn, AFI
Calicut Auxiliary Bn, AFI

The Indian Corps:
The Indian Army Service Corps: (Including British Officers & NCO's)
Animal Transport
20th Mule Corps
Mechanical Transport
3 & 14 MT Companies

Medical Units:
Indian Medical Service - Indian Hospital Corps
Malabar Base Hospital, Padanur

The Judiciary:
Malabar Police, Malabar Special Police & Malabar Jail Department

The Postal Department:

The Indian Ecclesiastical Department:

The Political & Civil Departments:

5. NORTH WEST FRONTIER 1930–1931

~ India General Service Medal 1908–1935 ~
NORTH WEST FRONTIER 1930–31
Issue 3: Royal Mint

The 'NORTH WEST FRONTIER 1930–31' clasp to the India General Service Medal 1908–1935 was sanctioned by Army Order 94 of September 1933 with subsequent amendments under Army Orders 123 of 1933 and 15 of 1935. The clasp rewarded troops and certain war mobilised civilians employed during the suppression of the Red Shirt Rebellion and the subsequent Afridi uprising on the Indian North West Frontier. This was the first campaign clasp sanctioned for award with the third striking of the India General Service Medal 1908–1935.

To qualify for the 'NORTH WEST FRONTIER 1930–31' clasp to the India General Service Medal 1908–1935, Army and war mobilised civilian personnel had to satisfy one or more of the following criteria:

- Be engaged on active service in Kohat, Waziristan or Peshawar Districts between 23rd April and 30th September 1930 inclusive.

- Be engaged on active service within the area as follows between 1st October 1930 and 22nd March 1931:
  – North – Bazar River to the Khyber River bridge on the Peshawar/Jamrud road.
  – East – A line running from the Khyber River bridge on the Peshawar/Jamrud road to Narai Khwan post and thence to Frontier road as far as Fort Bara.
  – South & West – A line running from Aimal Chabutra through Point 2498 as far as the Indo Afghan frontier.

Royal Air Force personnel qualified under similar provisions.

During September 1930 a military column en route from Dargai to Fort Chitral in Tirah, became the first recorded formation to received air-to-ground logistics support. Fourteen Westerland Wapiti aircraft from No. 2 (India) Wing RAF were employed to deliver fresh rations via parachute. These early experiments proved highly successful and led to the eventual creation of the art of 'air despatch'.

*

The zealous drive towards Indian independence championed by both the Indian National Congress and the Muslim Khalifat movement had, by the late 1920s, been slow to gain momentum across the vast North West Frontier region. Disturbances among pro-independence activists during the early part of the decade had largely died down following the arrest and imprisonment of the charismatic and influential anti-imperialist Abdul Ghafar Khan. By the summer of 1929, however, Abdul Khan had been a free man for several years and was energetically engaged in the creation of the Frontier Youth League, a quasi-political organisation for those keen to create a new India based on self-determination, Hindu Islamic unity and education for all citizens.

Initially, the Frontier Youth League met in Abdul Khan's home village of Utmanzai, a farming settlement located some 20 miles northwest of Peshawar in the Charsadda Sub Division of British Administered India. Within a relatively short space of time interest in Khan's teachings soared. Committees and affiliated groups began to flourish throughout the Province, especially in the settled districts of Peshawar, Kohat, Bannu and Dera Ismail Khan. In time, Khan's popularity grew to such a level that it became virtually inevitable that he should be elected the North West Frontier's 'delegate in chief' to the December 1929 All-India Congress rally in Lahore. At the conference, Khan took a sternly anti-British position. He was eager to show solidarity with the wider Congress Movement and their ongoing objection to the potential imposition on India of the political reforms that were being created by the hated Simon Commission.

The global economic crisis that spiralled out of control following the 1929 Wall Street crash did not spare rural northern India. Unemployment among young men raised further the spectre of dissatisfaction with the status quo, resulting in a massive expansion in the membership of the Frontier Youth League during the spring of 1930. At this time the organisation began to adopt a distinctly military code. Former Indian sepoys, often augmented by Afghan subversives, were recruited to encourage military style discipline and solidarity. Unable to afford uniforms, members of the Frontier Youth League dyed their clothes with brick dust and water in an attempt to establish a sense of unity. Henceforth the group became known as the 'Red Shirts'.

~ Indian Pattern Crossley Armoured Car ~
North West Frontier 1930–31

*

Inevitably, he Government of India considered the Red Shirt movement, especially in its para-military form, to be a highly subversive organisation. In April 1930 the Chief Commissioner of the North West Frontier decided to take decisive action to prevent the spread of Red Shirt influence among the largely settled and generally pro-British population within the administered region. When intelligence was intercepted by the authorities indicating that Abdul Khan and eleven of his key subordinates would be visiting

Peshawar on 21st April with a view to attending a Congress Party rally at a school campus, the Deputy Commissioner, Mr. Metcalf, decided that arrest warrants should be drawn up and the men taken into 'protective' custody.

The old walled city of Peshawar was a difficult place to police effectively. Narrow streets and even narrower allies snaked their way from city gate to city gate. The local population were generally loyal to the British Indian Government but could easily be influenced by anti-British activists. The riots of 1919 during the early stages of the Third Afghan War were but recent memories for many officials and it was thus determined that should the authorities seize Abdul Khan and his associates there would, in all likely hood, be serious civil disturbances. Consequently, plans were drawn up to bolster the strength of the city police establishment by the creation of a City Disturbance Column mounted by troops from the Peshawar District Command under Lieutenant General Godwin.

1st (PESHAWAR) BRIGADE BATTLE GROUP, APRIL 1930

Peshawar Cantonment – Brig. H R Sandilands
1 Armoured Car Coy, Royal Tank Corps
2nd Bn, King's Own Yorkshire Light Infantry
2/11th Sikh Regiment, 4/11th Sikh Regiment & 2/18th Royal Garhwal Rifles

The City Disturbance Column consisted of a section of Indian pattern Crossley armoured cars from 1 ACC and three mounted troops of the Poona Horse, IA supported by 'B' Company, 2nd Bn, KOYLI, commanded by Major T.E.F. Penny, and a rifle company of the 2/18th Royal Garhwal Rifles. On 23rd April 1930, the City Disturbance Column fell under the operational command of Major Brunskill, 2/18th Royal Garhwal Rifles. Reinforcements in the form of an additional section of armoured cars, the balance of the Poona Horse and an additional rifle company from each of the two committed infantry battalions, were available. These troops remained in the British Cantonment area located a short distance northwest of Peshawar, but were kept at a high state of readiness to deployed should the need arise.

The police executed Mr. Metcalf's arrest warrants without incident, quickly securing ten of the twelve wanted men. The remaining two were eventually located at the Peshawar Congress Party offices where they gave themselves up without a struggle. However, news of the police action had spread rapidly throughout the walled city and a menacing crowd, including Red Shirt members, began to form on the streets. As the police convoy moved away from the Congress Party offices, the vehicles were confronted by the nationalists. Unable to proceed further, the stationary police vehicles were subjected to attack by the crowd. The situation deteriorated rapidly and, despite the efforts of the two wanted men to calm the crowd, the arresting party and their prisoners were forced to fight their way the length of Kissa Khani Bazaar road before gaining the relative safety of the 'A' Division Police Station compound situated adjacent to the Kabuli Gate. From this location the senior police officer present telephoned HQ Peshawar District to seek armed assistance from the Cantonment.

Rather than immediately deploying the City Disturbance Column, the Deputy Commissioner decided to review in person the severity of the situation. Moving from the Cantonment in his own private motorcar, Mr. Metcalf advanced towards the Kabuli Gate escorted by four armoured cars of 2 Section, 1 ACC. As the vehicles approached the city walls they were greeted by a hail of bricks and assorted rubble. This attack forced the convoy to halt just inside the gate with the rear vehicle a short distance from the 'A'

~ A Red Shirt rally, 1930 ~
Bottom right: Abdul Ghafar Khan

Divisional Police Station. At this juncture Private H Bryant, one of two despatch riders accompanying the party, was pulled from his motorcycle and stoned to death. Upon seeing Private Bryant lying prone in the road, the lead armoured car, 'Bethune' commanded by Lieutenant M. Synage, advanced along the street with a view to recovering the body. In making this manoeuvre, several rioters were knocked over and injured which incensed the crowd further. Mounted police officers attempted to clear the area but failed to achieve any positive result.

Shortly thereafter, the rioters produced a drum of gasoline and set 'Bethune' ablaze forcing the crew to evacuate the vehicle and take refuge in the police station compound. Thereupon the Deputy Commissioner gave orders for the three remaining military vehicles to open fire with their machine guns. This act succeeded in shocking the crowd into some semblance of order. Shortly after this incident Brigadier H R Sandilands, deployed the balance of the City Disturbance Column from the Cantonment area down to the Kabuli Gate.

The City Disturbance Column secured the various gates leading into the walled city prior to confronting the rioters on the streets. This manoeuvre took some seven hours to achieve under extremely hazardous conditions involving much close quarter contact and many serious injuries to Army personnel. At least 20 rioters lost their lives during these incidents. Red Shirt emissaries were quick to exploit the situation in the interests of their own cause and arranged for several 'washing baskets' of blood soaked clothing to be taken across the Administrative Border to demonstrate to the tribal regions the extent of the vicious wrath of the British yoke. Seventeen sepoys of 2/18th Royal Garhwal Rifles were so traumatised by what they had witnessed that several days later they mutinied and had to be disarmed by members of the 2nd Bn, KOYLI.

With the civil situation in Peshawar only barely controllable, Lieutenant General Godwin and the Chief Commissioner determined to seek the deployment of military reinforcements from Lieutenant General R.A. Cassels, the GOC Northern Command. Although resources for immediate deployment were scarce, HQ Company and two rifle companies of the 2nd Bn, Essex Regt. were quickly mobilised and deployed by rail from Nowshera. The 2/5th GR were likewise moved up from Abbottabad. The balance of the 2nd Bn, Essex Regt. was employed to guard Government facilities in Nowshera, Cherat and Risalpur in anticipation of rioting in those locations.

On 25th April 1930, a deputation of city elders met with the Chief Commissioner at Government House, Peshawar, seeking his agreement to withdraw the Army from the walled city area in an attempt to calm the pent-up mob. A plan was agreed and implemented but within days the civil situation had again deteriorated requiring the Army to reoccupy its previously held positions. This operation took place at dawn on 4th May. The Red Shirts were taken by complete surprise. Peshawar was completely sealed off within a matter of only a few hours. The enforced removal of a makeshift shrine, erected in the city centre by Red Shirts to commemorate 'patriots' killed on 23rd April, took away an obvious rallying point which, over the ensuing days, helped subdue local hostility. The lockdown of the city gradually resulted in the need for less repression. Riots in Kohat City during mid-May, however, slowed somewhat the resumption of normality in Peshawar.

The 31st May 1930 was a tragic day in Peshawar. A sentry at the Kabuli Gate, Corporal Cummings, 2nd Bn, KOYLI, apparently accidentally shot and killed two Sikh children following a most negligent discharge while cleaning his rifle. This incident prompted further aggression by Red Shirt youths. The streets rapidly filled with the aggrieved but prompt action by the authorities, including the deployment of 'A' Company, Essex Regt., under Captain C.J.E. Hopegood, made the crowd realise that nothing could be achieved by further action. Within days of this unfortunate event, Peshawar returned to 'normality'.

*

Red Shirt members had been active in the tribal regions west of the Indus River for some months. In Waziristan, they met with only limited success in their quest for militant support. The local population was, to one extent or another, still smarting from the impact of the 1919–1925 insurrection and was, therefore, not keen to embark on further operations especially at the behest of men who were not direct kinsmen. However, some Madda Khel and Khiddar Khel were prepared to support the Red Shirts which resulted in a significant investment against the Tochi Scout garrison at Datta Khel on 11th May 1930. The RAF razed several Waziri villages in an attempt to break the siege but to no avail. Only the deployment of the Razmak Column, including the 2nd Bn, DLI, proved sufficient threat for the tribesmen to disperse.

~ The Razmak Column returns to camp, 1930 ~

The Frontier Constabulary in areas close to the Administrative Border conducted several operations over the ensuing days. Some 21 arrests were made under the provisions of the recently extended Prevention of Seditious Meetings Act. Mindful of the violence experienced in Peshawar, the authorities sanctioned the deployment of the Risalpur Flying Column, under Brigadier J. Van der Byl, in support of the civil police. Armed raids were conducted against several villages from the 12th May 1930 culminating in the securing of Utmanzai on 14th May and Dargai on 16th May. These events encouraged the Red Shirts to embark upon a campaign to disrupt communications throughout the North West Frontier. Telegraph wires were severed and an attempt was made to derail an express train on the Nowshera to Mardan route. Nationalist sympathisers inflicted several fatal casualties during these endeavours including the killing of Assistant Superintendent D.B. Murphy at Mardan on 25th May 1930.

COMPOSITION RISALPUR FLYING COLUMN, MAY 1930

Brig. J Van der Byl
1 Squadron 15th / 19th Hussars
'E' Battery Royal Horse Artillery
6th Lancers, IA (From 6th June – 11th July)
Guides Cavalry, IA
20th Lancers, IA
1/1st Punjab Regiment
(Deployed from Jhelum 30th May 1930. To Peshawar 27th June 1930)
2/7th Rajput Regiment
(Deployed from Rawalpindi 30th May 1930. To Peshawar 27th June 1930)

The situation throughout the frontier region continued to deteriorate and, on 20th May 1930, the following official intelligence was released to the media:

Malakand Area	–	Rulers of Swat and Dir to offer Government of India use of their Imperial Service Troops to contain regional aggression.
Kurram Area	–	Quiet.
Kohat Area	–	Relatively calm.
Bajaur Area	–	Unrest.
Khyber Area	–	Unrest.
Waziristan	–	Sever potential of unrest severe.
Mahsud Area	–	Unrest.

On 27th May 1930, 2/13th Frontier Force Rifles were fired upon by angry Red Shirts while attempting to secure the village of Takkar, some distance northwest of Mardan. The Guides Cavalry was immediately deployed to the area to lend support. The use of firearms by the Red Shirts was a new and sinister development and prompted a decision by the authorities to mount blockades against key militant villages throughout the Charsadda Sub District. These blockades were successful, with all targeted settlements capitulating to British terms by 27th June.

During early June 1930, several attempts were made to dislodge from its mountain stronghold the Mohmand *lashkar* responsible for the killing of Superintendent Murphy. This force, under Badshah Gul I, son of Mullah Fazali-Wahid, the Haji of Turangzai, evaded an aerial assault and went on to ambush a RIASC convoy travelling between Michni Kando and Fort Shabkadar killing one driver and injuring several other sepoys. Accordingly, a 3.7" Howitzer Pack Battery was deployed from Shabkadar to Matta Post on 3rd June in order to shell the positions believed to be occupied by the enemy. The barrage achieved little of practical value and the battery was withdrawn later the same day.

Elsewhere, RAF reconnaissance patrols sighted war parties of Utman Khel warriors, under the Haji of Turangzai, moving eastward towards the Jindai Khwar from Bajaur. Several bombing raids were launched against these formations over the ensuing days including sorties directly targeting Utman Khel settlements in the Swat Valley region. These assaults were followed up on the ground by a force under Brigadier W.H. Fordham drawn from 1st (Abbottabad) Infantry Brigade.

COMPOSITION FORDHAM'S FORCE, JUNE 1930

Two Troops, Poona Horse, IA
8 Mountain Battery, Royal Artillery
One Section, Sappers and Miners
2nd Bn, King's Own Yorkshire Light Infantry
5/2nd Punjab Regiment
2/13th Frontier Force Rifles

*

In Waziristan and the Mahsud, the RAF and Razmak Column remained active at this time. Following the siege at Datta Khel, several further opportunistic Mahsud *lashkars* were raised. In July 1930 the Kahassadar garrison at Sorarogha Post, located east of Razmak, was besieged. Attempts were also made to capture the various small forts along the Tank Zam River including the site of 1920 fame at Ahnai Tangi. The Razmak Column was immediately deployed with a view to securing Mahsud submission. The Column visited the principle settlement at Tauda China on 9th July but it required several RAF bombing sorties to quell factions further to the west.

The Razmak Column made a significant contact on 12th July 1930 along the Tauda China–Ladha road. The firefight claimed the lives of at least 17 Mahsud; several British military casualties were also sustained. Total subjugation of the Mahsud in this affair was not achieved until 27th July when the Nazar Khel formally submitted. The Hathi Khel Waziri, who maintained an aggressive stance in their homeland northeast of Bannu, were subdued in late August following a bloody, close-range contact between their force and 2/9th Jats supported by a company of Frontier Constabulary. In the engagement the Waziri lost 42 warriors for the lost of nine Indian Army troops including Captain F. Ashcroft, 6/13th Frontier Force Rifles attached 2/9th Jats.

In the Kurram Valley region, the Ozakais had been causing concern to the authorities since early August 1930. Concerted action by the RAF culminated in regional elders seeking a *jirga* at Parachinar on 24th August to discuss peace terms. One hundred and fifty *maliks* attended upon the Kurram Political Agent during this meeting. Tension remained acute, however, and further RAF bombing sorties were required before the Kurram Valley tribesmen were subjugated.

*

During the winter months, most Afridi warriors moved their families and livestock down to the Kajauri Plain, Khyber Pass and Peshawar Plain regions in order to escape the worst effects of the harsh winter climate. Many tribal elders spent this period in Peshawar city. To that end, the political agenda of the Red Shirts was not lost on those elements of the Afridi who wielded influence and control beyond the Administrative Border.

Bad feeling in the tribal regions had been unintentionally exacerbated by the Peshawar City Coroner when the names of several Afridi notables killed in the riots of 23rd April 1930 were published in the local press. On 2nd May, Afridi elements, supported by both Red Shirt and Khalifat factions, held a war council in the western Khyber at Bagh. During this gathering, it was determined that direct support should be given to the 'oppressed' of Peshawar District. A *lashkar* was raised under the leadership of Sayed Kabir, a Malikdin Khel warrior of some reputation. By 10th May, this force had advanced some distance southeast and was formed up among the various hidden cave complexes that straddled the western boundary of the Kajauri Plain.

The desire for militant action caused some degree of consternation among many sections of the Afridi who were doubtless keen to avoid British military retribution should Sayed Kabir's *lashkar* advance across the Administrative Boundary. Nevertheless, over the ensuing days, the force was augmented by parties and individuals from sub-sections throughout the entire Afridi nation including the Zakka Khel. On 4th June 1930, the warriors, who by now numbered some 7,000, advanced towards Bara Fort but subsequently called off their intended attack following the reinforcement of that location by 1/3rd GR.

Sayed Kabir thereupon determined to direct his resources towards Peshawar and the seat of the Provincial Government. A two-pronged attack plan was devised. Warriors from the 'northern' Mohmand tribes would move north of the blockaded Bara military road with a view to attacking the British military cantonment and aerodrome. It was hoped that such action would tie up the military garrison enabling warriors from the 'southern' Mohmand tribes to sweep south and then north into the walled city. The moon-lit trek across the Kajauri Plain, however, took longer than anticipated and on 5th June 1930 both *lashkars* were forced to take shelter among the various villages and farms that were scattered across the Kajauri Plain. Telegraph lines were cut and barricades erected in an attempt to disrupt any possible military interference.

By now, the authorities in Peshawar were well aware of the Afridi threat. RAF reconnaissance flights had tracked the *lashkar*'s progress from Bara Fort on an almost hourly basis. The extent of local cooperation and succour afforded the warriors by the normally pro-British population of rural Kajaur was an unanticipated variable. The wide spread nature of enemy deployment, however, did require a change in established standing orders for the defence of Peshawar. Instead of a military force advancing to contact towards Bara it was decided instead to drive the scattered columns of warriors into a fixed firing line to be established by the Nowshera Brigade under Brigadier C.A. Milward.

Early on 5th June 1930, the Risalpur Flying Column, mounted by 1st Cavalry Brigade, was deployed post-haste to Bara Fort whereupon the troops turned about and began to advance back across the open country in extended order. Frequent fire was taken from warriors sheltering among the various dry watercourses that crisscrossed the region as well as from farmsteads and settlements. At each incident of significance, the Royal Artillery neutralised the threat and the drive moved forward again. By nightfall the Kajauri Plain had been largely cleansed of the Afridi and the British military force retired on Peshawar. The following day, RAF patrols reported evidence of numerous enemy stragglers retiring back across the Administrative Boundary.

COMPOSITION OF NOWSHERA COLUMN, JUNE 1930

'A' Echelon
Brigade HQ
Brigade Signals
1 Section, 31 Field Battery, Royal Artillery
1 Section, 1 Light Tank Company Royal Tank Corps
2nd Bn, Border Regiment (Less One Company)
1/3rd Ghurkha Rifles (Less One Company)
1 Section, 4 Field Company, King George's Own Bengal Sappers & Miners
'B' Echelon
1 Section, 58 Field Battery, Royal Artillery
2/5th Royal Ghurkha Rifles

*

The failure of the Afridi incursion towards Peshawar was the subject of bitter recrimination between those involved. Sectional *jirgas* went to great length to lay blame at the feet of other parties. Fearing British reprisals, tribal elders sought to persuade their more reactionary colleagues to now approach the authorities in an effort to represent their position in the most favourable light possible. This proposal received a largely hostile reception. Red Shirt activists under the guise of a Khalifat committee continued to exercise control of those wishing to pursue conflict with British India by overtly positioning the issue as a religious struggle.

The Khyber Political Agent agreed to meet those Afridi elders who sought a peaceful resolution to the current conflict, in *jirga* at Fort Jamrud on 13th July 1930. It was evident, however, that the representatives assembled were not in a position to agree terms for everyone. Indeed, limited aggressive incursions onto the Kajauri Plain by those not represented by the tribal elders had been occurring regularly for the previous two weeks. As a result the meeting broke up without resolution and the elders began to make their way back to their tribal homeland.

Meanwhile, the malcontents had held a religious *jirga* at Bagh in the western Khyber with a pan Indo Afghan Afridi congregation in attendance. The outcome of this meeting was a decision to seek recruitment for a new attack on Peshawar under the banner of *jihad* rather than general tribal unrest. This proposition met with some success and, despite the withholding of fighters by some groups, a new *lashkar* was eventually formed. By 7th August 1930, some 3,000 fully-armed and motivated tribesmen had assembled on the edge of the Aka Khel Plain south of the Bara River.

From 1st August 1930 forward, HQ Northern Command reviewed intelligence regarding the threat posed by the raising of a new Afridi *lashkar*. By the night of 5th–6th August the 1st Cavalry Brigade had formed up at Peshawar while both Fordham's Force and the Nowshera Column had been augmented. Arial confirmation of the Afridi movements was not achieved until late afternoon on 6th August. The information gathered was not specific enough, however, to delineate the Afridi plan of attack. Nevertheless, a decision was made to advance the cavalry towards Bara Fort while two battalions of the Nowshera Column were moved to a forward intercept position astride the Bara road. That evening the RAF began to bomb enemy villages in the Bara Valley in an attempt to persuade the warriors to break off their advance and return to their home settlements. With limited sophisticated communication, however, it is unlikely the Afridi were actively aware of the extent of this destruction.

COMPOSITION OF NOWSHERA COLUMN, AUGUST 1930

16 Mountain Battery, Royal Artillery
Two Troops, Poona Horse, IA
Section, Sappers and Miners
2nd Bn, Border Regiment
1/11th Sikh Regiment (PWO)
1/3rd Gurkha Rifles

The day of 7th August 1930 passed without incident. That night the Afridi advanced northeast under the cover of darkness and early the following day reports of contacts began to be received by the authorities from locations across the length and breadth of the Kajauri Plain. These were used to plot enemy concentrations and anticipated lines of advance. Before counterattacks could be launched, however, the Afridi retired. A British advance to contact was executed on 9th August. This manoeuvre drew troops away from Peshawar and thus enabled certain elements of the enemy to secure an advance on the city.

To the northeast of Peshawar lay an extensive military ordnance depot. 'K' Supply Depot was a strategic installation containing both ordnance and fuel, yet the authorities had, in the face of a potential Afridi incursion into the Peshawar district, determined to defend the facility with a guard consisting of one officer and 50 sepoys mounted by 4/11th Sikh Regt. All but nine of these men were maintained in barracks located some distance away from the main depot facilities.

At about 4.30 p.m. on 9th August 1930, the Sikh sentry at the Depot's Nowshera Gate observed a party of Afridi advancing upon his location from the cover of Shah Bagh village. Locking the gate behind him, this man immediately ran to the petroleum store where he advised the guard commander of the coming threat. Rather than fall back on the main garrison, the alert NCO led his small command to the roof of the storehouse where they set up a machine gun position and immediately began firing on the warriors who had smashed the Nowshera Gate and were in the act of flooding into the Depot compound. This robust action temporarily checked the Afridi advance and gave Jemadar Allah Ditta the opportunity to telephone HQ Peshawar Brigade for assistance.

Within a short space of time, the Afridi broke through the Depot's perimeter fencing and established firing positions that enabled some of their number to ebb their way forward towards the small detachment defending the petroleum store. Enfilade fire from the now mobilised main garrison did little to check this advance. Once within the compound, the enemy had a bountiful array of cover and vantage points from which to attack the defending sepoys. The defenders' situation rapidly became desperate.

Available troops in the Peshawar Cantonment were limited when news was received of the attack on 'K' Supply Depot. A section of armoured cars was deployed almost immediately while a cavalry force, composed of one squadron 15th/19th Hussars supported by elements of the Poona Horse, IA, and the 20th Lancers, IA, followed on shortly thereafter. 'B' and 'C' Companies, 2/11th Sikh Regt., were available but there was no means of getting these men to the scene quickly because the duty RIASC MT section was in the act of bringing the 2nd Bn, Border Regt back to the Cantonment from Bara Fort.

By 5 p.m., the armoured cars had entered the 'K' Supply Depot compound. Working their way along the interior perimeter line they flushed out many warriors who were then despatched by the machine guns of the defending Sikhs. As the enemy withdrew beyond the perimeter fence, the armoured cars gave chase and maintained a constant engagement. Air to ground support became available at this point enabling the destruction of enemy parties taking shelter among the many scattered orchards and bean fields.

During the evening, 2nd Bn, Border Regt., accompanied by the two available companies of 2/11th Sikh Regt., deployed up to the railway station, a short distance west of 'K' Supply Depot. Once in position, the infantry began to clear the enemy from the native villages that occupied the open countryside to the northeast and southwest. Several close contacts occurred and, on more than one occasion, additional support had to be sought from 20th Lancers, IA. As dusk fell that evening, the troops fell back on the Depot area with a view to securing the site for the night.

On 10th August 1930, mobile patrols operating west from Peshawar located several isolated groups of Afridi hidden among the region's network of dry riverbeds. These formations were destroyed by artillery fire. The Afridi *lashkars,* that had been so intent on entering Peshawar, had been effectively crushed. Individual snipers and small groups remained active over the coming weeks but the Army maintained constant vigilance and demonstrated a clear determination to force any surviving enemy combatants to retire without delay back into tribal territory.

Troop strengths in the region were augmented at this time with fresh reserves. A new infantry brigade was formed at Nowshera, while further to the south the Kohat garrison was reinforced by 1/8th Punjab Regt. from Multan and 4 Mountain Battery, Royal Artillery, from Abbottabad. Concerns that the strategically important railway line between Peshawar and Nowshera to the east and down to Attock in the south might be sabotaged led to the deployment of an armoured train from the railway depot at Lahore. The train, manned by a detachment of 2nd Northumberland Fusiliers from Napier Barracks, Lahore, supported by gunners from 12 Field Battery, Royal Artillery, and crewed by personnel of the North West Railway Battalion, AFI, maintained a daily presence along the route until being withdrawn on 3rd September 1930.

COMPOSITION RESERVE BRIGADE NOWSHERA, AUGUST 1930

Composition Reserve Brigade Nowshera August 1930
2/7th Rajput Regiment
1/1st Punjab Regiment
2/17th Dogra Regiment
2/5th Royal Gurkha Rifles

*

With the threat of insurgency significantly diminished, the Chief Commissioner of the North West Frontier Province was keen to restore the power of the civil police rather than depending on the presence of the military to maintain law and order. The Red Shirt threat had not completely evaporated, however, and the destabilising nature of this organisation's relations within the administered territories continued to raise concerns especially now an overt Islamic agenda appeared to have been adopted. Consequently, His Excellency the Viceroy, Lord Irwin, was requested to impose martial law in Peshawar District. This request was approved and subsequently a decree to this effect was promulgated on 15th August 1930.

In an attempt to prevent any further incursions from the tribal regions into the Administered Territory the Chief Commissioner convened a strategy meeting in Peshawar on 4th September 1930.

~ Fort Jamrud commanded the Gate Way to the Khyber Pass ~

Attending this conference were senior dignitaries including Mr. E.B. Howell, Foreign Secretary to the Government of India, Lieutenant General C. Deverall, CGS, Lieutenant General R. Cassels GOC Northern Command and Air Marshal G. Salmond, AOC India. Following this meeting it was determined that as a measure of 'active defence' the Kajauri Plain to the west of Peshawar and the Aka Khel Plain lying south of the Bara River should be occupied in force on an on-going basis thus forming a blockade between tribal and administered regions west of the Administered Border. This would be the first occasion that British troops had entered the Aka Khel region since a punitive expedition under Lieutenant Colonel J.H. Craigie visited the area in 1855. Responsibility for this operation was vested in Major General J.F.S.D. Coleridge.

The 'active defence' strategy was designed to deny the Afridi their traditional winter grazing land on the plains while also securing the extensive network of caves that ran north to south along the western extremity of the region. To deny this natural accommodation to Afridi families sheltering from the winter cold was considered a legitimate act so long as the region was also denied to warriors using the caves as forming-up positions for raids across the Administrative Border into British India. Permanent control of the region would be established by the creation of a network of military roads suitable for the rapid deployment of troops from one outpost to another as and when required. In essence the plan was very similar to the strategy adopted in Waziristan some six to seven years previously.

During late September 1930, staff planners proposed a three-stage plan for the occupation of the two regions. Initially extensive survey and reconnaissance work was required due to the relatively uncharted nature of the terrain. This operation was followed by road and infrastructure development and then finally the deployment of a permanent garrison of troops and frontier police. Three infantry brigades were detailed for the initial operation. These formations consisted of the 2nd (Rawalpindi) Infantry Brigade which was assigned the Aka Khel Plain objective, the 3rd (Jhelum) Infantry Brigade

~ Troops deploy onto the Kajauri Plain ~

which was assigned the central Kajauri Plain area and the 9th (Jhansi) Infantry Brigade which was assigned the western Kajauri Plain area. Air support was to be provided by 5 (AC) Squadron RAF at Kohat and 20 (AC) Squadron at RAF Peshawar.

Before any of these activities could be put into operation, however, the GOC Peshawar District, Lieutenant General Godwin, insisted that all existing frontier roads, especially those leading to Fort Jamrud at the mouth of the Khyber Pass and Fort Bara in the midst of the Kajauri Plain, should be repaired and upgraded. Deployment began on 11th October 1930 with the 2nd (Nowshera) Brigade initially securing a line along the Jamrud to Peshawar road thus preventing any possible interference from tribesmen who might attempt to infiltrate from the north. Troop numbers in and around Peshawar were rapidly increased and, on 14th October 1930, an advance was made by the Army onto the Kajauri Plain. A base camp was established on level terrain forward of Karwal Hill, enabling units to form up there over the ensuing days prior to deploying to their specific objectives.

*

Several weeks before the launch of 'phase one' of the Kajauri Plain blockade operation, a summons was sent out to all Afridi elders requiring them to attend a Government *jirga* at Fort Jamrud on 7th October 1930. Many senior *maliks* were keen to comply, but Red Shirt Islamists attempted to prevent compliance. Some representative from the Aka Khel evaded the Red Shirts and managed to reach Jamrud on 16th October, whereupon they were received by the Assistant Political Officer. Several days later, more elders arrived outside Jamrud having been allowed to do so by the Red Shirts on condition they place before the British authorities several demands including the immediate release from captivity of their leader Abdul Khan. The *jirga* was dismissed when it became apparent no tangible solutions could be negotiated. Several further meetings occurred in late November.

The Army spent much of October and November 1930 on surveying and constructing the planned road system. The routes fell into several categories: fully-metalled all-weather roads, graded tracks capable of taking motorised vehicles in fine weather, and non-vehicular 'camel' tracks. Construction and water divining parties were fired upon from time to time but, for the most part, well-placed defensive picquets succeeded in deterring open attack. Incidents of determined resistance did occur on occasion. 'A' Company, 1st Bn, KSLI, Captain R.B.L. Presse, were hard-pressed near Talao Pond on 22nd November while providing an escort to a Royal Engineers water divining party and required armoured car support to extricate themselves. On 3rd December, picquets of 9th Brigade came under fire from a large Afridi party near Miri Khel camp. The 2nd Bn, Seaforth Highlanders, came under significant pressure and had to be extricated by the 2/9th Jats. During the ensuing firefight, Captain H. St. C. Will, 3/11th Sikh Regt., was killed in action.

*

'Phase two' of the plan to control the Kajauri and Aka Khel Plains began in early December 1930 following an agreement by the military authorities as to the locations of the proposed new fortified camps. Several key considerations had to be considered at each potential site. These considerations not only included the availability of secure fresh water supplies, but also the proximity to the border cave complexes for the post-artillery engagement of potential enemy concentrations. A personal reconnaissance of the region was conducted at this time by the newly appointed CinC India, Field Marshal P. Chetwode accompanied by Lieutenant General C. Deverell CGS and General R. Cassels, GOC Northern Command.

The following sites were eventually selected for the location of the principal posts:

- Samghaki Kandao, commanding the route south from Jamrud onto the Kajauri plan

- Fort Salop (initially named 'Shropshire Post') 2 miles southwest of Karawal Hill.

- Jhansi Post on the north bank of the Bara River overlooking a proposed new road bridge and astride the road running northeast from Miri Khel Camp past Fort Bara and on to Peshawar.

- Fort Milward on the north bank of the Star River overlooking the ford.

Each of these locations serviced several satellite positions, blockhouses and watch-towers.

Construction of the facilities began almost immediately and, by early March 1931, most locations were almost complete. This fact enabled the military authorities to thin out the troop commitment in the region. The 9th Infantry Brigade battle group returned to its home station on 16th January and 3rd Infantry Brigade Battle Group departed for its home station on 9th March following which the GOC, 2nd Infantry Brigade Battle Group, took command responsibility for the ongoing operation. The RAF commitment was reduced to 20 (AC) Squadron only.

Throughout this period, the various troops deployed engaged in active patrols penetrating deep into the Afridi hinterland. Such manoeuvres prevented any concerted tribal interference against the construction projects on the plains. Suspect cave complexes were whitewashed for target identification enabling aircrew to bomb them more effectively. The enemy maintained a campaign of long-range sniping but were seldom engaged in open contact. Occasionally rudimentary improvised explosive devices were set by Afridi at locations along the burgeoning road system. These devices were generally fashioned from unexploded aerial ordnance and failed to pose a significant threat. More frequently, the Afridi would break into construction depots under cover of darkness and damage road-making plant. On 1st January 1931, four steamrollers were destroyed by Afridi bombs during one such incident near Ilm Gudr.

Several long-range punitive expeditions were undertaken, including the destruction of the principle Afridi settlement of Tauda China by the 3rd Infantry Brigade in February 1931. A similar operation, conducted by the 2nd Infantry Brigade at Spintigga on 11th March, resulted in robust interference by the enemy though no casualties were inflicted on the force engaged. A brigade-level reconnaissance operation on 18th March was not so fortunate. Nevertheless, the anticipated Afridi 'offensive', that had been rumoured to commence some weeks earlier after the Muslim festival of Id, failed to materialise.

COMPOSITION OF FORCE DEPLOYED TO SECURE SPINTIGGA, MARCH 1930

17 Light Battery, Royal Artillery
4 Field Company, KGO Bengal Sappers & Miners
Machine Gun Sections, 2nd Bn, Essex Regiment
1/11/ Sikh Regiment
2/13 Frontier Force Rifles
3/17 Dogra Regiment
1/1/Gurkha Rifles
2 Field Ambulance

On 27th February 1931 the base camp at Karawal began to be dismantled. A month later, on 23rd March, the GOC 1st Infantry Brigade was placed in command of both the Military and Frontier Constabulary units that were to form the permanent garrison across the Kajauri and Aka Khel Plains. The Nowshera Infantry Brigade returned to its peacetime station and it was hoped an element of routine frontier soldiering would envelope the area. This situation was maintained despite the fact the Afridi had not agreed terms with the Government. The Red Shirts were still using Islam as a means of influencing the tribe. By late summer, however, their power began to wan and, on 22nd September, a formal *jirga* met with the Khyber Political Agent to request terms. This was followed on 3rd October by a further meeting chaired by the Chief Commissioner of the North West Frontier Province at which the Afridi elders agreed to abide by the terms outlined below.

Terms Agreed By Afridi Elders, 3rd October 1931, Fort Jamrud
- Government of India, as an act of grace, will impose no fine or act of retribution on the Afridi tribe.

- Allowances will be granted on the same scale as before April 1930, subject to good conduct and acceptance of tribal and territorial responsibility.

- No changes will be made to the line of the current Administrative Border, but the Government of India reserves the right to take such measures as they consider necessary for the maintenance of roads and posts on the Kajauri and Aka Khel Plains and to employ such garrisons as may be considered desirable from time to time whether military or otherwise. Necessary steps for the maintenance of military control (including RAF over- flying of tribal regions) will be taken, but otherwise the plains will be available for the use by the tribes according to past precedent.

- Kahassadar will continue to be recruited according to requirements and, if found necessary, to assist in the control of the Kajauri and Aka Khel Plains.
- There is a recognition that the existence of outlaws (Red Shirts) is neither useful for Government or for ourselves and therefore the question as to how far the outlaws can be made harmless, in

*~ A.G. Khan and M.K. Ghandi
eventually established a working
relationship ~*

future, will be taken up with the Political Agent in accordance with past customs.

• Past restrictions and arrangements in force before April 1930 will be adhered to.

*

The Red Shirts were not, as yet, a completely spent force within the administered territories. Abdul Khan had been released from prison in March 1931 following the signing of the Irwin–Ghandi pact. He lost no time in reinvigorating his organisation. A strategy to spread a climate of fear and intimidation among native citizens loyal to the British Crown was rapidly progressed and in August, an 'alliance' was established with M.K. Ghandi's Congress Party. This led to more anti-British political activity and the eventual formation of a joint committee known as the Provincial Frontier *Jirga*.

By December 1931, the level of anti-Government sedition being preached by the Red Shirts had got to a point likely to cause a major breakdown in law and order. Thus finally a decision was made by the authorities to bring the organisation to heel. The Red Shirts were declared an illegal organisation on 24th December. All key leaders were arrested and deported from the North West Frontier Province. A violent reaction was anticipated and 2nd Bn, KOYLI, supported by elements of the City Disturbance Force, the occupied area around Peshawar. Elsewhere in the region, units were placed on alert but were subsequently stood down within days following only minor disturbances. Without any leaders, the Red Shirt rank and file simply faded away into obscurity.

* * *

COMMAND STRUCTURE, NORTH WEST FRONTIER 1930–1931

Commander Northern Command	
Gen. R A Cassels	
Commander 1st (Peshawar) Division	
Lt. Gen. Godwin	
Commander Kajauri Plain	
Maj. Gen. J F S D Coleridge (Thence Maj. Gen. C M Wagstaff)	
Brigade Commanders	
1st (Peshawar) Division	
Brig. J Van der Byl	1st Cavalry Brigade
Brig. H R Sandilands	1st (Peshawar) Infantry Brigade
Brig. C A Milward	2nd (Nowshera) Infantry Brigade
Brig. W K Venning	3rd (Rawalpindi) Infantry Brigade
Commander 2nd (Nowshera) Division	
Maj. Gen. E A Fagen	

Brig. W H Fordham	1st (Abbotabad) Brigade
Brig. E B Matthew-Lannowe	2nd (Rawalpindi) Brigade
Brig. R Gardiner	3rd (Jhelum) Brigade
(Kohat) Division?	
Brig. ?	9th (Jhansi) Brigade
Waziristan District Maj. Gen. H E Herdon	
Brig. A M Mills	Razmak Brigade
Brig. P H Keen	Bannu Brigade
Brig. M Saunders	Wana Brigade

Royal Air Force:		
No 1 (Indian) Group		
Squadron	**Location**	**Aircraft**
No. 5 (AC) Squadron 2 Wing	RAF Kohat det Miranshah	Bristol F2b Fighter
No. 11 Squadron	RAF Risalpur	Westerland Wapiti
No. 20 (AC) Squadron	RAF Peshawar	Bristol F2b Fighter
No. 27 Squadron 2 wing	RAF Kohat	Westerland Wapiti
No. 28 Squadron	RAF Risalpur (From 1/12/30 – Ambala)	Bristol F2b Fighter
No. 39 Squadron	RAF Risalpur det Miranshah	Westerland Wapiti
No. 60 Squadron 2 wing	RAF Risalpur det Miranshah	Westerland Wapiti

BRITISH ARMY & RAF ROLL OF HONOUR **NORTH WEST FRONTIER 1930–1931**			
Date:	**Person:**	**Unit:**	**Comment:**
?	1020109 Bdr J R Anderson	Royal Artillery	Z Ammo Col, Date Not Shown
?	Capt A M Barrett	2nd Bn, Essex Regt.	Died, Date Not Shown
?	6394580 Pte H Beard	2nd Bn, R Sussex Regt.	Died, Date Not Shown
19/3/31	6007036 Pte H Bently	2nd Bn, Essex Regt.	Died BMH Nowshera
5/6/30	3521840 Pte F Bertenshaw	2nd Bn, Border Regt.	Killed in Action Peshawar
?	4684564 Pte H Birch	2nd Bn, KOYLI	Died
22/1/31	7873867 Sgt W L Bolus	RTC	Died
?	Bdsm R J Braithwaite	2nd Bn, DLI	Died
?	2816281 Pte A F Brind	2nd Bn, Seaforth H	Died
?	2816281 Pte. A F Brind	2nd Bn, Seaforth H	Died
23/4/30	7876463 Pte H Bryant	1 ACC, RTC	Killed in Action
5/6/30	L/Cpl P Cadman	2nd Bn, Border Regt.	Killed in Action
6/6/30	3594155 Pte J Campbell	2nd Bn, Border Regt.	Killed in Action
14/5/30	363555 LAC H J Chapell	1 (Indian) GP HQ, RAF	
15/9/30	330150 Sgt (Pilot) O C Clarke	11 (B) Sqn, RAF	Killed, Accident, RAF Risalpur
1/5/30	401156 Tpr W D Clement	15/19th Hussars	Died
2/7/30	548546 Tpr S Cooke	15/19th Hussars	Drowned
?	2318895 Siglm F Cottam	Royal Signals	'B' Corps Signals
1931	4445336 L/Cpl H Croft	2nd Bn, DLI	Killed in Action
?	Capt. E F Crowdy	Royal Artillery	14 Light Battery
1930	4446922 Pte J P Dobson	2nd Bn, DLI	Died

?	363870 LAC E S East	RAF	Died
19/1/31	7873656 Sgt. F L Flake	1 ACC, RTC	Died, Peshawar
1/9/30	2815758 Pte. J Gemmell	2nd Bn, Seaforth H	Died Rawalpindi (Wounds?)
?	2Lt G Grayrigge	Royal Signals	
?	5998149 Sgt E Green	2nd Bn, Essex Regt.	Died
?	2815516 Pte J Gunn	2nd Bn, Seaforth H	Died
1/2/31	3594511 Pte. (J) (H) Hales	2nd Bn, Border Regt.	Died BMH Rawalpindi
?	6006167 Pte R Harrington	2nd Bn, Essex Regt.	Died
25/4/30	3128???? Pte. W Hart	2nd Bn, R Sussex Regt.	Died, Pesawar
?	6394166 Pte W E Hart	2nd Bn, R Sussex Regt.	Died
24/11/30	1040296 Bdr. A D Hawkins	RHA	Died, Peshawar
13/6/30	363654 Sgt (Pilot) E A Hindeling	60 (B) Sqn, RAF	Killed, Accident, RAF Kohat
?	6395926 Pte J Howell	2nd Bn, R Sussex Regt.	Died
?	4686130 Pte J Hudson	2nd Bn, KOYLI	Died
?/1/31	344812 Cpl T W P Jeffrey	39 (B) Sqn, RAF	Killed, Accident, RAF Risalpur
29/8/30	4686660 Pte J Jobling	2nd Bn, KOYLI	Killed Ft. Jamrud
?	4027327 Pte W H Jones	1st Bn, KSLI	Died
?	2559610 Cpl E K Kiddle	Royal Signals	'B' Corps Signals
?	6001886 Pte N Knott	2nd Bn, Essex Regt.	Died
?	Lt. A M Knox	Royal Engineers	Date
24/3/31	4030775 Pte L Lambert	1st Bn, KSLI	DOW?
13/6/30	335828 LAC W H Lansdell	60 (B) Sqn, RAF	Killed, Accident, RAF Kohat
?	6000619 Pte S Long	2nd Bn, Essex Regt.	Died
23/7/30	4687347 Boy W Lowe	2nd Bn, KOYLI	Killed
?	2812665 Sgt W MacLeod	2nd Bn, Seaforth H	Died
7/5/31	4029193 Pte A Miller	1 Bn, KSLI	DOW?
?	1020174 Gnr A R Palmer	Royal Artillery	58 Bty, Date Not Shown
18/9/31	4263290 Fus G E Peacock	2nd Bn, Northumberland F	Attch. 'T' Coy, Indian Signals DOW Peshawar
13/11/30	1409699 Bdr W J Perkins	Royal Artillery	Died
?	2815039 Pte G Porteous	2nd Bn, Seaforth H	Died
5/6/30	3594876 Pte J J Potts	2nd Bn, Border Regt.	Killed in Action Peshawar
10/4/31	402211 Tpr T Press	15/19th Hussars	DOW?
23/11/30	3184348 Gnr W Preston	Royal Artillery	Waz Md Sect / Died
?	1859011 S/Sgt C H Prince	Royal Signals	1 CBST
?	7110191 Pte M Roche	2nd Bn, Seaforth H	Died
?	6008365 Pte A Scott	2nd Bn, Essex Regt.	Died
?	2313800 Sgt H Shirley	Royal Signals	1 CBST
	4797615 L/Bdr. F J Staines	Royal Artillery	3 Light Battery, Died Rawalpindi (Wounds)
2/6/30	547107 T F Stone	15/19th Hussars	Killed in Action, Drowned
23/4/30	Lt T M Synge	RTC	1 ACC, Mortally Injured, Died 2/11/31
14/5/30	Flt. Lt. J C H Tavendale	RAF	
10/8/30	401537 Tpr R R Taylor	15/19th Hussars	Died
10/7/31	4187390 L/Cpl B Thomas	1st Bn, KSLI	DOW?

18/3/1931	777600 L/Bdr. A F E Thompson	Royal Artillery	17 Light Bty, KIA, Gandad Kotal
?	7878623 Pte W J Young	RTC	7 ACC, Died
15/9/30	365072 LAC F S Valentine	11 (B) Sqn, RAF	Killed, Accident, RAF Risalpur
30/8/30	4686790 Pte W Webb	2nd Bn, KOYLI	Killed, Ft Jamrud
2/11/31	7879841 Pte O Whawell	RTC	7 ACC, Died of Wounds
24/1/31	2318656 Sig J A Williams	Royal Signals	Died
?	2317546 Sig H G Wilson	Royal Signals	Waziristan District Signals,
?/1/31	345850 Sgt (Pilot) J E Wren	39 (B) Sqn, RAF	Killed, Accident, RAF Risalpur
18/3/31	Gnr ??????	Royal Artilery	17 Battery, KIA

NORTH WEST FRONTIER 1930–31[9] ROLL

BRITISH ESTABLISHMENT
THE ARMY

~ Staff Grade Officers ~

Note a.   *Only Officers of the British Army are listed. Officers of the Indian Establishment are beyond the scope of this work and are thus excluded.*

Note b.   *Medals named in impressed capitals.*

Major Generals: ~ C M Wagstaff[1(Capt. RE)6(Col.)&9] GOC 3 Bde.

Brigadiers: ~ E B Matthew-Lannowe[(4,6 Lt. Col. Queen's)&9] GOC 2 Bde.

Colonels: ~ A G Bayley[9] GSO1, HQ PD, W H Nicholson[9] AQMG, PD & H W Wynter[9] RA, GSO1, HQ Waz Dist

THE CAVALRY:

~ 1st Royal Dragoons ~

Note a.   *Roll of all personnel identified as eligible.*

Note b.   *Recipient attached 7 Field Ambulance (FA), Royal Army Medical Corps (RAMC), Razmak.*

Note c.   *Medals named in thin impressed capitals: 'THE ROYALS.'*

Single Clasp	No. Identified	Rarity
North West Frontier 1930–31[9]	1	According to the roll as seen, can be considered Unique

Lance Sergeants / Corporals: ~ 1055899 H G Bartlett[9]

~ 15th / 19th Hussars ~

Note a.   *Roll of all commissioned personnel identified as eligible.*

Note b.   *Non-commissioned and other rank personnel multi clasp only.*

Note c.   *Medals named in thin impressed capitals: '15-19 H.'*

Single Clasp	No. Identified	Rarity
North West Frontier 1930–31[9]	Regt. Strength	Not Rare
Combination Clasps	**No. Identified**	**Rarity**
North West Frontier 1930–31[9] Mohmand 1933[11]	1	According to the roll as seen, can be considered Unique

Lieutenant Colonels: ~ H F Brace[9]

Majors: ~ R H O Hanbury[9] & N W Leaf[9],

Captains: ~ T J Arnott[9], H McC B Bramwell[9], C Cokayne-Frith[9], W E H Grylls, W R N Hinde[9], (QM) H Jordison[9] & J Patrick[9]

Lieutenants: ~ N A Courage[9], D'A A Dawes[9], Hon W Edwardes[9], R B Hodgkinson[9], J H L Holford[9], E H G Moon[9], R H Baden-Powell[9], W Rankin[9] & A R A Dorrien-Smith[9]

Lance Corporals/Privates: ~ 548554 C R Gordon[9&11]

THE ROYAL TANK CORPS:
Sub Units Identified As Entitled:
1, 7 & 8 Armoured Car Companies

Note a.   *Roll of all personnel identified as eligible.*
Note b.   *Medals named in thin impressed capitals: 'R. TANK C.'*

Single Clasp	Company	No. Identified	Rarity
North West Frontier 1930–31[9]	1	119	Very Scarce
North West Frontier 1930–31[9]	7	100	Rare
North West Frontier 1930–31[9]	8	152	Scarce

Combination Clasps	Company	No. Identified	Rarity
Waziristan 1919–21[4] North West Frontier 1930–31[9]	7	1	According to the roll as seen, can be considered Unique
Malabar 1921–22[7] North West Frontier 1930–31[9]	1	1	According to the roll as seen, can be considered Unique
Waziristan 1921–24[6] North West Frontier 1930–31[9]	1	1	According to the roll as seen, can be considered Unique
Waziristan 1921–24[6] North West Frontier 1930–31[9]	7	1	According to the roll as seen, can be considered Unique
Waziristan 1921–24[6] North West Frontier 1930–31[9]	8	1	According to the roll as seen, can be considered Unique
North West Frontier 1930–31[9] Mohmand 1933[11]	7	1	According to the roll as seen, can be considered Unique
North West Frontier 1930–31[9] North West Frontier 1935[12]	1	2	Of the Utmost Rarity
North West Frontier 1930–31[9] North West Frontier 1935[12]	7	1	According to the roll as seen, can be considered Unique
North West Frontier 1930–31[9] North West Frontier 1935[12]	8	1	According to the roll as seen, can be considered Unique

Majors: ~ G P L Drake-Brockman[9] 1 ACC, A G Kenchington[9] 8 ACC & S J King[9] 1 ACC

Captains: ~ G W Chattey[9] 1 ACC, H F B Garrett[6(Lt.)&9] 1 ACC, A H Gatehouse[9] 1 ACC, A E P Hall[6(Lt. 9 ACC)&9] 8 ACC, A Joyce[9] 8 ACC, G R McCormick[9] 7 ACC & C H Montague[9] 8 ACC

Lieutenants: ~ T Baily[9] 8 ACC, E F G Bird[9] 7 ACC, H Cantrell[9&12] 7 ACC, R V Clifford[9] 8 ACC, J G S Compton[9] 8 ACC, H T B Cracroft[9] 1 ACC, A J Macalpine-Downie[9] 1 ACC, H C F V Dunbar[9] 7 ACC, G Gaisford[9] 7 ACC, J T Gough[9] 1 ACC, J Higginson[9] 8 ACC, R Hope-Kellsall[9] 8 ACC, E G B Moss[9] 7 ACC, A C H Newnham[9] 8 ACC, J A M du Port[9] 1 ACC, W A Rumsey[9] 7 ACC, R G Shaw[9] 8 ACC, R E S Skelton[9] 1 ACC, J G Stephens[9] 8 ACC, T M Synge[9] 1 ACC, C W M Timmis[9] 7 ACC & R A H Walker[9] 1 ACC

Warrant Officers Class II: ~ (CSM) 3758546 A W Barlow[9] 8 ACC, (RQMS) 7868447 H Brockshaw[9] 1 ACC, 7810036 S M Carey[9] 1 ACC, (RQMS) 7868539 F Doley[9] 8 ACC & 7871465 S Mear[9] 8 ACC

Company Quartermaster Sergeants/Colour Sergeants/Staff Sergeants: ~ 7875345 W G Blair[9] 1 ACC, 18349 H G Balderson[9] 8 ACC, 7809308 D Eaton[9] 8 ACC & 7868248 E Fowler[9] 1 ACC

Quartermaster Sergeants/Sergeants: ~ 7814842 G Allen[9] 7 ACC, 7873867 W L Bolus[9] 1 ACC, 7874620 J A Cakebread[9] 1 ACC, 7868329 R J Canary[9] 8 ACC, 4179370 P Charman[9] 1 ACC, 7868617 J C Chetwynd[7(Pte. 8 ACC)&9] 1 ACC, 7878846 W R Dean[9] 8 ACC, 10823 T C Duffin[9] 1 ACC, 7871379 J W Edmonds[4(Cpl.)&9] 7 ACC, 4115618 H Evans[9] 1 ACC, 7873656 F L Flake[9] 1 ACC, 7871315 G Giles[9] 1 ACC, 7813350 J Hill[9] 1 ACC, 7869378 T Johnson[9] 1 ACC, 7873473 A Jukes[9] 1 ACC, 7873942 W Murray[9] 8 ACC, 7813066 A Nunn[9] 8 ACC, 7870472 T Palmer[9] 8 ACC, 6448807 E S Shepherd[9] 1 ACC attch. Kohat DS, 7871075 A H Sinclair[9] 8 ACC, 7815208 H J Sparrow[9] 1 ACC, 7816966 W Tamkin[9] 1 ACC, (Act) 7879645 J Taylor[9] 7 ACC, 7869948 R Thomson[9] 1 ACC, 7875124 J Townsend[9] 8 ACC, 7869391 W White[9] 7 ACC attch. 8 ACC & 7874621 F Wyatt[9] 8 ACC

Lance Sergeants/Corporals: ~ 7874573 J R Atkinson[9] 7 ACC, 7875897 A R J Bateman[9] 1 ACC, 7876272 J H Billing[9] 1 ACC, 7875325 J S Blant[9] 8 ACC, 6337853 E G Clements[9] 8 ACC, 7875887 W F Coates[9] 7 ACC, 7871944 J T W Collings[9]

1 ACC, 22567 W C Crimes[9] 1 ACC, 7871659 E Davies[9] 8 ACC, 7871909 G E H Davis[9] 1 ACC, 7875759 T Eastham[9] 1 ACC, 4115618 H Evans[9] 1 ACC, 7873089 E C Ford[9] 8 ACC, 7875006 H Gaston[9] 8 ACC, 7878287 H A Giles[9] 1 ACC, 7811378 C Girvan[9] 1 ACC, 7876963 F A Green[9] 8 ACC, 7874991 S B Hamilton[9] 1 ACC, 7879213 C J Jennings[9] 1 ACC, 7876779 G G Levell[9] 1 ACC, 7877153 V N Mallinson[9] 7 ACC, 7876862 E E Myers[9] 1 ACC, 7869208 J H Pemberton[6(Pte.)&9] 7 ACC, 39722 L Poole[9] 8 ACC, 7874774 W H Rabson[9&11(Sgt.2LTC)] 7 ACC, 7873716 E F E Richards[9] 8 ACC, 7869474 J Robinson[9] 8 ACC, 7875309 F R Sanderson[9] 8 ACC, 7873088 A N Saunders[9] 7 ACC, 7874987 W R Stone[9] 1 ACC, 7879291 F G Swinburn[9] 1 ACC, 7874982 A H Upton[9] 1 ACC & 7876097 L Waters[9] 8 ACC

Lance Corporals/Privates: ~ 7879211 J Adamson[9] 8 ACC, 7880371 E Allen[9&12] 8 ACC, 7876360 G E Almonds[9] 8 ACC, 7877601 D B Anderson[9] 8 ACC, 7880647 D F Anderson[9] 1 ACC, 7879023 W B Anderson[9] 8 ACC, 7880360 T A Andrews[9] 1 ACC, 395050 A D Aris[9] 1 ACC, 7877977 C Arrowsmith[9] 1 ACC, 7868388 A Arundell[9] 8 ACC, 7880171 J Ashton[9] 1 ACC, 7864349 T A G Aslett[9] 8 ACC, 7878760 J Atkinson[9] 8 ACC, 7876449 E F Austin[9] 7 ACC, 6135856 W J Avery[9] 1 ACC, 7875021 A A J Baker[9] 1 ACC, 7877197 F Baker[9] 7 ACC, 7880581 V E Baker[9] 1 ACC, 7880503 M Barnes[9] 7 ACC, 7878619 J Barnett[9] 8 ACC, 7873246 E Barras[9] 1 ACC, 7880665 F Beardmore[9] 1 ACC, 7880225 C A Beattie[9] 1 ACC, 7876352 J S Beattie[9] 8 ACC, 4120765 A T Beaven[9] 8 ACC, 7876156 M Bermingham[9] 1 ACC, 7879034 H Bickerton[9] 8 ACC, 7877469 E Billyeald[9] 8 ACC, 4532270 H Bindon[9] 1 ACC, 7878176 J Binning[9] 8 ACC, 7880089 R J Birbeck[9] 1 ACC, 7873851 W Birkett[9] 8 ACC, 7876279 R F Bisset[9] 1 ACC, 7877681 A T Blair[9] 1 ACC, 2557514 G H Blanchette[9] 8 ACC, 7878063 F C Booth[9] 1 ACC, 746533 A G Bowen[9] 1 ACC, 7875888 H Bowie[9] 1 ACC, 7877378 J Bowman[9] 8 ACC, 7879243 E W Boyle[9] 8 ACC, 7879516 A R Bradley[9] 1 ACC, 4604806 C Bradley[9] 7 ACC, 7873152 P G Bradshaw[9] 8 ACC, 7880520 F L Bragg[9] 8 ACC, 7872291 E W Brehaut[9] 8 ACC, 2205188 J T Brevitt[9] 1 ACC, 7879036 C Bridger[9] 1 ACC, 7877413 H L Brightwell[9] 1 ACC, 7876461 S G N Brooks[9] 8 ACC, 7879348 L G W Broom[9] 1 ACC, 7877603 J Brown[9] 8 ACC, 7880706 J W Brown[9] 1 ACC, 5931948 W D Brown[9] 8 ACC, 7876463 H Bryant[9] 1 ACC, 7878912 C E Buffy[9] 8 ACC, 7877197 H E V Bunyard[9] 7 ACC, 7878549 F S Burston[9] 7 ACC, 7879229 E Busbridge[9] 8 ACC, 7877566 H W C Butler[9] 7 ACC, 7878083 B F Byworth[9] 1 ACC, 7876363 T C S Cake[9] 1 ACC, 7877316 G W Campbell[9] 7 ACC, 7878099 R W Cant[9] 7 ACC, 7878824 C W Carroll[9] 1 ACC, 7870674 A Cartwright[9] 7 ACC attch. 8 ACC, 7878630 C Cattaneo[9] 8 ACC, 7879201 T J C Channer[9] 8 ACC, 7878656 S A Chapman[9], 534046 F Clark[9] 1 ACC, 7879443 W Clark[9] 1 ACC, 7872304 A C Clarke[9] 1 ACC, 7872305 W C Clarke[9] 1 ACC, 7876259 C H Clench[9] 1 ACC, 7880433 E T Cluskey[9] 7 ACC, 7880916 S G Cole[9] 1 ACC, 7880163 E C Coles[9] 7 ACC, 7882221 L C Collins[9] 1 ACC, 7878959 W Cornell[9] 7 ACC, 7878818 T R Costello[9] 8 ACC, 7876493 J E Cotton[9] 1 ACC, 7876838 J Coulson[9] 7 ACC, 7874722 C J Crane[9] 8 ACC, 7878998 L Crossfield[9] 1 ACC, 7879445 C E Crosswell[9] 1 ACC, 7876256 P W Dams[9] 1 ACC, 7878961 A F Daniels[9] 8 ACC, 7878323 C Davies[9] 1 ACC, 782182 F T Davies[9] 1 ACC, 7879411 H Davies[9] 1 ACC, 7875146 L M Davies[9] 1 ACC, 7877818 W T Davies[9] 7 ACC, 7876903 F J Davis[9] 1 ACC, 7878975 H Dawson[9] 8 ACC, 7878149 L J Day[9] 1 ACC, 7874975 L W Debenham[9] 8 ACC, 7879069 C G Dennis[9] 7 ACC, 7879250 G S Dent[9] 7 ACC, 5666899 H J Dibble[9] 8 ACC, 7879549 A E Dodd[9] 8 ACC, 7880564 C R Doe[9] 1 ACC, 7880643 C S Donovan[9&12(2LTC)] 1 ACC, 7879218 R Drewery[9] 8 ACC, 211188 P H Dromey[9] 1 ACC, 7875964 C Dury[9] 1 ACC, 7878624 H A Easdown[9] 8 ACC, 7878677 T Edwards[9] 7 ACC, 7877437 A G Eke 8 ACC, 4341112 W Ellerington[9] 1 ACC, 7877596 R M English[9] 1 ACC, 7877610 A C Evans[9] 1 ACC, 7880465 E Evans[9] 1 ACC, 7876435 C Fee[9] 1 ACC, 7880563 B Fenwick[9] 1 ACC, 3180784 J Ferguson[9] 7 ACC, 7870963 J Fitzpatrick[9] 1 ACC, 7876062 R G H Fletcher[9] 8 ACC, 7873341 J F Fogarty[9] 8 ACC, 7879255 G D Ford[9] 7 ACC, 7876372 J A Ford[9] 1 ACC, 7876997 J Foreath[9] 8 ACC, 7877578 W W Forward[9] 8 ACC, 7874641 W C Fuller[9] 7 ACC, 7870668 P Furey[9] 1 ACC, 7880010 C Furness[9] 7 ACC, 7879779 E J Gallop[9] 1 ACC, 7880903 H Garvey[9] 7 ACC, 7876424 H E Gent[9] 7 ACC, 7880232 A George[9] 8 ACC, 7879400 R J Gibbons[9] 1 ACC, 7877604 G F V Gibbs[9] 8 ACC, 7880524 H F Giles[9] 1 ACC, 7877483 B T Goldstone[9] 8 ACC, 7880301 W J Goodall[9] 1 ACC, 7877372 T Gordon[9] 8 ACC, 7876060 F Gould[9] 1 ACC, 7876180 H Graham[9] 8 ACC, 7877076 T L Grant[9] 1 ACC, 7879390 R L Green[9] 7 ACC, 7878116 F T Greening[9] 1 ACC, 7880024 W Gregory[9] 7 ACC, 7881096 S A G Gresswell[9] 7 ACC, 5101718 J Griffin[9] 8 ACC, 7876677 F R Grout[9] 7 ACC, 5491214 G A Guest[9] 1 ACC, 7879834 F W Gwilliam[9] 1 ACC, 7878293 E R Hale[9] 1 ACC, 7875872 J Hall[9] 1 ACC, 7876633 R W Hallam[9] 1 ACC, 7880411 W Hamblin[9] 7 ACC, 7876373 C F Hampton[9] 8 ACC, 7880222 J W Hancock[9] 1 ACC, 7876944 H W Harbon[9] 8 ACC, 7879447 H Harding[9] 8 ACC, 6197513 J H Harmer[9] 1 ACC, 7876970 W G Harnden[9] 1 ACC, 7876447 A E Harris[9] 8 ACC, 7876071 G Harris[9] 1 ACC, 7879003 E Hawley[9] 8 ACC, 7877231 C Hayman[9] 1 ACC, 7879405 H Hayward[9] 7 ACC, 7876992 J Heather[9] 8 ACC, 7878622 A E Hesplop[9] 7 ACC, 7873353 H Higginbotham[9] 1 ACC, 7877165 J P Hill[9] 7 ACC, 7880261 W Hinton[9] 1 ACC, 7878268 N Hirst[9] 8 ACC, 7876397 W J Hoare[9] 8 ACC, 7877761 A Hodgson[9] 1 ACC, 3706183 W Hogg[9] 7 ACC, 7877083 F W Hollins[9] 1 ACC, 7875788 R S Hollinson[9] 8 ACC, 7877441 G J Howard[9] 1 ACC, 7878938 L F W Howe[9] 8 ACC, 7880274 R R Hudson[9] 1 ACC, 7878088 J A Hugh[9] 8 ACC, 7875797 P H Hughes[9] 7 ACC, 7876974 R Hughes[9] 7 ACC, 7880428 G Huish[9] 7 ACC, 7874645 J H Hunt[9] 7 ACC, 7879404 L Hutchinson[9] 7 ACC, 7877778 J Hyde[9] 1 ACC, 7876379 A C Illingworth[9] 8 ACC, 7878507 W H Jackman[9] 7 ACC, 7873960 P A Jackson[9] 8 ACC, 7877585 A G Jamieson[9] 1 ACC, 7872682 R S Jeffery[9] 1 ACC, 7880655 C Jenkins[9] 1 ACC, 7879094 F L Jones[9] 7 ACC, 7880271 A Jones[9] 8 ACC, 7680008 F Jones[9] 7 ACC, 2215442 H Jones[9] 8 ACC, 7877072 J Jones[9] 7 ACC, 2209670 J A Jones[9] 8 ACC, 7879230 L B Jones[9] 8 ACC, 7880502 W Jones[9] 1 ACC, 7873173 G H Kattenhorn[9&12(Cpl.)] 8 ACC, 7878145 C A Kearsey[9] 1 ACC, 7875277 T A Kemp[9] 7 ACC, 7873290 J F Kennedy[9] 7 ACC, 7877476 J Kesson[9] 7 ACC, 7880210 H Kimber[9] 7 ACC, 7878078 H H King[9] 1 ACC, 2208009 F J Kippox[9] 8 ACC, 7874939 H Knight[9] 7 ACC, 7876448 J Knight[9] 1 ACC, 7879363 S G Knight[9] 1 ACC, 7878028 G L Lamond[9] 1 ACC, 7876100 J Langton[9] 1 ACC, 7880512 A Leadbetter[9] 1 ACC, 5103672 A C Leatherbarrow[9] 1 ACC, 7877557 W Y Leggett[9] 1 ACC, 7876176 J H W Lennard[9] 1 ACC, 7880094 A Y Leslie[9] 1 ACC, 7880255 J Ling[9] 1 ACC,

7876188 W G Low[9] 1 ACC, 7873364 M (F) (P) W Lucas[9] 1 ACC, 7869367 F P Luck[9] 7 ACC, 7879784 L R Ludlow[9] 1 ACC, 7876399 J McBlaine[9] 7 ACC, 5566064 V W Macey[9] 7 ACC, 7877768 A Machin[9] 7 ACC, 7879068 H Macpherson[9] 7 ACC, 7878636 J Maitland[9] 7 ACC, 7877840 H Major[9] 7 ACC, 7876453 W Manyena[9] 1 ACC, 7877057 L E Marriner[9] 7 ACC, 7880071 B Mathieson[9] 8 ACC, 7877606 P V Mattock[9] 8 ACC, 7880560 H Maund[9] 1 ACC, 7878082 D S McColl[9] 1 ACC, 7870046 J McGrath[9] 1 ACC, 7877831 J E Mellors[9] 1 ACC, 7877643 A Miller[9] 1 ACC, 7874567 F Mills[9] 7 ACC, 7877772 F A Morgans[9] 1 ACC, 7876162 C Morris[9] 1 ACC, 7880293 G Morris[9] 1 ACC, 7880464 R Morris[9] 7 ACC, 7877560 I M Morrison[9] 7 ACC, 7887174 J C Morrough[9] 7 ACC, 7879515 T Morton[9] 1 ACC, 7877580 O S Muir[9] 8 ACC, 7875864 J Mummery[9] 1 ACC, 5489148 F Munday[9] 1 ACC, 7880047 D Murchison[9] 1 ACC, 7879480 S W Murrell[9] 1 ACC, 7876826 E E Myers[9] 1 ACC, 7880472 P A Napper[9] 1 ACC, 7872681 A E Newman[9] 8 ACC, 5246350 F Nibblett[9] 1 ACC, 7875899 J R Nicholis[9] 1 ACC, 4121699 F D Nield[9] 1 ACC, 7110246 M Noonan[9] 8 ACC, 7879508 J W Northcott[9] 1 ACC, 7875865 V C Okey[9] 1 ACC, 7877787 L J Orme[9] 1 ACC, 7876183 F Palmer[9] 1 ACC, 7811717 H Parker[9] 8 ACC, 4967033 C Parsons[9] 8 ACC, 4684562 T Patchett[9] 1 ACC, 7877637 E G Patten[9] 8 ACC, 7877607 E Patternoster[9] 8 ACC, 7339453 S L Paul[9] 1 ACC, 7880674 J Paterson[9] 8 ACC, 7880187 C W Pearce[9] 1 ACC, 7876456 F Percival[9] 7 ACC, 4910425 W H Perrens[9] 1 ACC, 7880597 J Perry[9] 1 ACC, 7873677 G Pinson[9] 8 ACC, 7872315 H G Port[9] 8 ACC, 5491175 A E Pragnell[9] 1 ACC, 7879470 A C Price[9] 7 ACC, 7876290 H Puttick[9] 8 ACC, 7880463 E W Pyemont[9] 1 ACC, 7876214 M J Quirke[9] 7 ACC, 7871830 T Quirke[9] 8 ACC, 7880016 A Randall[9] 8 ACC, 7878542 W L Rapson[9] 1 ACC, 7879295 J Reay[9] 8 ACC, 7873252 R Rennie[9] 7 ACC, 7877829 J Revell[9] 7 ACC, 8788944 S E Rhodes[9] 8 ACC, 7876495 H Richards[9] 1 ACC, 7878105 D B Ricketts[9] 7 ACC, 1856671 W R Rippon[9] 8 ACC, 7876696 I E Roberts[9] 1 ACC, 4188327 T Roberts[9] 8 ACC, 7879231 S Robinson[9] 8 ACC, 7876960 R Ronald[9] 8 ACC, 3707071 G J Ronksley[9] 8 ACC, 7877191 F W Rose[9] 7 ACC, 7880366 S J Russell[9] 1 ACC, 2217052 J G Sargent[9] 8 ACC, 401616 A Scott[9] 1 ACC, 5614840 P T N Scott[9] 1 ACC, 7876490 W Sebbage[9] 1 ACC, 7877820 E Shackleton[9] 1 ACC, 7879228 C Shakeshaft[9] 8 ACC, 5667388 H N Sheppard[9] 7 ACC, 7880436 G Sherbourne[9] 1 ACC, 7874095 P Shew[9] 8 ACC, 7878932 D Sims[9] 8 ACC, 7880386 J C Sims[9] 1 ACC, 7876390 P C Skinner[9] 8 ACC, 7880250 W Skleton[9] 1 ACC, 7877374 A Smith[9] 8 ACC, 7880278 E P Smith[9] 1 ACC, 7880167 H V Smith[9] 1 ACC, 7879773 W H Smith[9] 1 ACC, 7880690 H J Southam[9] 1 ACC, 5613964 F W Sparkes[9] 7 ACC, 7881078 S V Spicer[9] 7 ACC, 7878816 F Spiller[9] 8 ACC, 2871922 J Stephen[9] 7 ACC, 7874571 G Stephens[9] 8 ACC, 7879615 W G Stephens[9] 1 ACC, 7877644 H Sterling[9] 8 ACC, 7875143 A Stevenson[9] 7 ACC attch. 8 ACC, 7879216 A Stewart[9] 8 ACC, 7878966 C A Storr[9] 8 ACC, 7877558 L Stringer[9] 7 ACC, 7876836 S B Swan[9] 7 ACC, 7874750 W T Tanner[9] 1 ACC, 7880279 P Tew[9] 8 ACC, 7875854 C A Thompson[9] 1 ACC, 7879296 F M Thompson[9] 7 ACC, 7876523 J Thompson[9&12(2LTC)] 1 ACC, 7880397 J W Thompson[9] 1 ACC, 7870731 S A Thompson[9] 7 ACC, 7879245 E H W Thornton[9] 8 ACC, 7879524A M Tilbury[9] 1 ACC, 7877084 L S Tinsley[9] 7 ACC, 7878609 E M Tobin[9] 8 ACC, 7872687 C H Tong[9] 8 ACC, 751667 E Tonks[9] 7 ACC, 7879063 A J Torry[9] 7 ACC, 7879669 R S Tranter[9] 1 ACC, 5246562 A E Turner[9] 1 ACC, 7878697 T Turner[9] 8 ACC, 7876173 E P Tyrrell[9] 8 ACC, 7877305 S H Vass[9] 7 ACC, 7879013 M W Verrill[9] 1 ACC, 7877470 C W Vickery[9] 8 ACC, 7876419 E D Villiers[9] 1 ACC, 7879610 A E Walton[9] 1 ACC, 7878839 H G Waring[9] 8 ACC, 4072380 F J Watters[9] 1 ACC, 7877193 F R G Watts[9] 7 ACC, 7880359 H G Watts[9] 1 ACC, 7871868 J F Watts[9] 8 ACC, 7877377 N Watson[9] 8 ACC, 5245078 J H Weaver[9] 7 ACC, 7878540 A W Webster[9] 1 ACC, 7880466 A T Wedlake[9] 1 ACC, 7879436 O West[9] 1 ACC, 7876179 L A Weston[9] 8 ACC, 7879841 O Whawell[9] 7 ACC, 7880507 R Wheeler[9] 1 ACC, 5613199 V Wheeler[9] 1 ACC, 7877579 C White[9] 7 ACC, 7880380 A Whittaker[9] 1 ACC, 7879062 C A G Williams[9] 7 ACC, 7880384 E Williams[9] 8 ACC, 7878778 G H Williams[9] 1 ACC, 7876990 J Williams[9] 1 ACC, 7880447 J Williams[9] 1 ACC, 7880202 L Williams[9] 1 ACC, 7581017 W F Williams[9] 1 ACC, 7880066 W R Williams[9] 1 ACC, 7878814 F J Wood[9] 8 ACC, 4529578 W Wood[9] 8 ACC, 7878124 W H Woodward[9] 1 ACC, 7870227 A C Wreen[9] 1 ACC, 5045790 A Wright[9] 7 ACC, 7875878 E Wright[9] 1 ACC, 7874062 G Wright[9] 8 ACC, 7878278 F Wykes[9] 1 ACC, 3522725 A E Young[9] 1 ACC, 3183355 J R Young[9] 8 ACC, 7872855 W Young[9] 8 ACC & 7878632 W J Young[9] 7 ACC

THE ARTILLERY:

~ The Royal Horse Artillery ~
Batteries Identified As Entitled:
'E' Battery
1st Cavalry Brigade Ammunition Column

Note a.   *Roll of all personnel identified as eligible.*
Note b.   *Medals named in thin impressed capitals: 'R.A.'*

Single Clasp	No. Identified	Rarity
North West Frontier 1930–31[9]	181	Scarce

Major: ~ The Hon. T P P Butler[9]
Captains: ~ H M Stanford[9]

Lieutenants: ~ A B Davies[9] attch. 17/23 Ind Mtn Bde., H A Macouochie[9], R W McLeod[9], A G Stuart[9] attch. R H A Ammo Col, J T de H Vaizey[9], H E Collett-White[9] & M Yates[9] attch. 1 CBAC

Warrant Officers Class I: ~ (Farrier) 1039823 A H Peck[9]

Battery Quartermaster Sergeants/Staff Sergeants: ~ 1035975 R Ivey[9], 1020388 W Quinn[9] attch. 1 CBAC & 1413913 C V Webb[9]

Quartermaster Sergeants/Sergeants: ~ 1035595 A G Adams[9], 1034612 G W Cocks[9], 1029062 E W Edwards[9], 1022770 A Hicks[9], (Fwd Loc) 1054474 J E Hutchinson[9], 1035588 A T Marney[9], 1049920 L D Over[9], (P/L) 1062326 W Sharpe[9], 1050671 H T Smith[9], 1056343 S H Swain[9], 1047078 E J Warner[9], 1034797 A E Watson[9] & 1021880 W J Wilson[9]

Bombardiers: ~ 1061915 E Ainger[9], (Saddler) 1022925 F C Archer[9], 1035576 H V Beckett[9] attch. 1 CBAC, 6133888 H Green[9], 1061910 A Greenwood[9], (Farrier) 1049783 J J Henley[9] attch. 1 CBAC, 1063550 F Hiom[9], 1049917 W Hodgkinson[9], 1020156 F G Holmes[9], 1040273 P H Holness[9], 1062604 J J Hyde[9], 1063368 W Joice[9], 2607179 C H Peachey[9], 1024161 H T Steele[9] & 1035908 B L Wiss[9]

Lance Bombardiers/Gunners/Drivers: ~ 1068947 W Adamson[9], 7335457 P Allen[9], 3593662 H Atkinson[9], 786360 C W B Ayson[9], 1057379 J Bailey[9], 1066820 G E Barrett[9], 1063220 E Beasley[9], 1070620 A G Bedford[9], 1066623 S Benbow[9], 1064998 H W Bennett[9], 3851649 R Bennett[9], 1062896 F Beverstock[9], 1071985 H Bolton[9], 1068301 J Booth[9], 5490999 E Boswell[9], 1022800 H A Botell[9], 1061948 F C Botting[9], 759747 A V Brain[9], 4853313 G Butler[9], 4909400 G Butler[9], 1066627 C R Buttle[9], 1012340 F J S Carne[9], 1068296 A W Chambers[9], 2210091 J Chester[9], 1036014 E C Clare[9], 1066039 F Clarke[9], 1066304 S N Clarke[9], 786301 R J Cole[9], 1056541 F Coleman[9], 1071983 R Collins[9], (Sdlr) 1021791 H Connell[9], 1070393 W H Cotter[9], 786653 B Coupe[9] attch. 1 CBAC, 1068671 C C Cox[9], 1061912 A Cross[9], 1061930 W Davies[9], 763870 W A Dimock[9], 1066828 W Dixon[9], 1066730 T W Dobson[9], 1066592 D J Donald[9], 786646 E Dunne[9], 2211969 A J Edgeworth[9], 1069369 D H Evans[9], 6550246 H Farrer[9], 786581 K H Felsing[9], 786682 W A Franks[9], 1054808 A French[9], 4528865 A C George[9], 1066732 H W Giles[9], 1066916 A Gove[9], 750150 J Graham[9], 1060888 C W Green[9], 1071779 O J Green[9], 1061914 P W Greenwood[9], 1066835 W Grierson[9], 1065321 P Grieve[9], 1071719 L Griffiths[9], 1068534 H Gulliford[9], 1066565 F Harman[9], 1066864 A G Harvie[9], 734339 J Havercamp[9] attch. 1 CBAC, 1068561 A Hemingway[9], 1063389 W Hillier[9], 1018174 W H Hogben[9], 1064895 A A L Holland[9], 1065257 S A Horne[9], 770659 T Hunt[9], 1066223 L A H Jackson[9], 1066734 A John[9], 1066792 A Jordan[9], 1066579 B Keyte[9], 10786716 A L King[9], 1068324 S King[9], 6136864 T J A King[9], 5666768 G T Kingdom[9], 1066798 H A G Kirby[9], 5102309 L Kirkland[9], 1066594 T W Lambert[9], 1049308 G L Lambourne[9], 1066790 B Law[9], 777891 W Lloyd[9], 1066791 W D H Logan[9], 1020705 E W Long[9], 1068827 W C Longhurst[9], 106933 J Lovell[9], 1057380 L Madell[9], 1066021 D C Mather[9], 1064084 A Matthews[9], 1035334 D McKenzie[9], 1066633 H J Mills[9], 786487 J Morray[9], 1062584 R E Moss[9], 5878960 T F Murdin[9], 1065472 N Nash[9], 1066604 T Newitt[9], 1063227 R H Oakley[9], 1073773 C Page[9], 1062728 A Pagett[9], 3233082 A Patterson[9], 1070238 T Payne[9], 1069681 L L Pearce[9], 1066797 E J Phillips[9], 1066788 L W Potter[9], 1066815 G Purvis[9], 1056882 W Pyle[9], 1066833 N Rayne[9], 1066603 E B Richardson[9], 786181 W Richardson[9], 1063664 W H Russell[9], 1055588 R Ryles[9], 1073115 J B Senior[9], 1068318 J Sinclair[9], 1066037 C Slade[9], 1066020 J Smith[9], 1066584 J J Smith[9], 1062229 N Smith[9], 779008 R A Smith[9], 3764476 W D Smith[9], 1062077 R A Strong[9], 1071560 W C Tappenden[9], 1065341 W E Taylor[9], 1066442 R Tegg[9], 4909445 B Thompson[9], 1063064 A Toon[9], 1047945 T W Turner[9], 1057437 G Underwood[9], 1061772 J E Waters[9], 786393 G Watson[9], 790578 D R Webb[9], 1065451 B Wedge[9], 1062719 A E Weedman[9], 1068681 T White[9], 3954604 C C Williams[9], 544575 G Williams[9], 1064926 H Williams[9], 1066620 R Williams[9], 1059475 J Wilson[9], 786502 V Womersley[9], 1063685 A A Wood[9] & 1066821 C W Woodhouse[9]

~ The Royal Artillery ~
Batteries Identified As Entitled:
Field Artillery Batteries
3 (L), 4 (L), 6 (M), 8 (L), Det 12, 15 (M), 17 (L), 20 (M), 25, 31 (How) & 58 (How) Batteries

Post Artillery Group
Bannu, Chakdara, Ft. Jhansi, Kohat, Landi Kotal, Ft. Lockhart, Malakand, Ft. Milward, Peshawar, Ft. Salop, Ft. Sandeman and Thal – All Under Indian Mountain Brigade Command

Waziristan Medium Section – (See Below)

1 Indian Division Ammunition Column & 'Z' Field Ammunition Column

Mountain Batteries - Royal Artillery Officers Attached
20, 21, 22, 23, 24 & 25 Indian Mountain Brigades
1 Royal (Kohat), 3 (Peshawar), 4 (Hazara), 5 (Bombay), 8 (Lahore), 9 (Murree), 10 (Abbottabad), 12 (Poonch), 16 (Zhob) & 19 (Maymyo) Mountain Batteries

Note a. *Roll of all commissioned personnel identified as eligible.*

Note b. *Non-commissioned and other rank personnel multi clasp only. (See separate listing for Lahore Armoured Train and Waziristan Medium Section).*

Note c. *The suffix 'HOW' was added to Nos 1,3,4,5,6,7,10,13,16,18 & 19 Batteries from 1928 until 1932 by which time all batteries had been equipped with the 3.7" Howitzer.*

Note d. *Medals named in thin impressed capitals: 'R.A.'*

Single Clasp	*No. Identified*	*Rarity*
North West Frontier 1930–31[9]	In Strength	Not Rare
Combination Clasps	*No. Identified*	*Rarity*
North West Frontier 1908[1] Waziristan 1919–21[4] Waziristan 1921–24[6] North West Frontier 1930–31[9]	1	According to the roll as seen, can be considered Unique
North West Frontier 1908[1] Waziristan 1921–24[6] North West Frontier 1930–31[9]	1	According to the roll as seen, can be considered Unique
Afghanistan N.W.F. 1919[3] North West Frontier 1930–31[9]	9	Of the Utmost Rarity
Afghanistan N.W.F. 1919[3] Waziristan 1919 21[4] Mahsud 1919–20[5] Waziristan 1921–24[6] North West Frontier 1930–31[9]	1	According to the roll as seen, can be considered Unique
Waziristan 1919–21[4] North West Frontier 1930–31[9]	1	According to the roll as seen, can be considered Unique
Waziristan 1919–21[4] Mahsud 1919–20[5] Waziristan 1921–24[6] North West Frontier 1930–31[9]	1	According to the roll as seen, can be considered Unique
Waziristan 1919–21[4] Waziristan 1921–24[6] North West Frontier 1930–31[9]	1	According to the roll as seen, can be considered Unique

Waziristan 1921–24[6] Malabar 1921–22[7] North West Frontier 1930–31[9]	2	Of the Utmost Rarity
Waziristan 1921–24[6] North West Frontier 1930–31[9]	7	Of the Utmost Rarity
North West Frontier 1930–31[9] Mohmand 1933[11]	59	Rare
North West Frontier 1930–31[9] Mohmand 1933[11] North West Frontier 1935[12]	5	Of the Utmost Rarity
North West Frontier 1930–31[9] North West Frontier 1935[12]	35	Very Rare

Lieutenant Colonels: ~ (Bvt) W J Bell[3(Capt.)&9] 1 IDAC, H F Buke[9] Cmd. 23 Ind Mtn Bde., (Bvt) D J M Champion[6(Maj.)&9] Cmd. 22 Mtn Bde., G V Dreyer[3(Capt.)&9] HQ 23 Mtn Bde., J H Edmond[1(Lt.),4(Maj.),6(Maj.)&9] HQ 21 Ind Mtn Bde., (Bvt) W W Green[9] 25 Fld Bde., E M Little[1(Lt.),6(Maj.)&9] HQ 22 Mtn Bde., (Bvt) H R Pownall[9] 17 Lt. Bty, GSO1 HQ PD, (Bvt) H M M Robertson[9,11&12] 58 Bty & J Waring[9] HQ 20 Mtn Bde.

Majors: ~ E L Armitage[9&11] 10 Mtn Bty, L Browning[9] Bde. Maj., Landi Kotal, J S Heaton-Ellis[9] 5 Mtn Bty, M E Orr-Ewing[9] 12 Fld Bty, J L Forbes[9] HQ 21 Ind Mtn Bde., G E A Granet[9] 12 Mtn Bty, R P Landon[3(Maj.)&9] 9 Mtn Bty, H S MacDonald[9] 3 Mtn Bty, B L Marriner[3(Maj.)&9] 16 Mtn Bty, J C Meredith[9] 17 Md Bty, J C M Mostyn[9] 4 Lt. Bty, C A Russell[3(Capt.)&9] 15 Md Bty, J Scott[9] 19 Mtn Bty & S H Wright[6(Capt.)&9]

Captains: ~ J C Allardyce[9] 1 IDAC, G S Andeman[9], 1 Mtn Bty, J C D'Arcy[9] 17 Lt. Bty, J S Bateman[9], E D A Buttemer[9] 25 Fld Bty, E F Crowdy[9] 4 Lt. Bty, N R B Eddowes[9] 16 Mtn Bty, W E C Eliot[9] 17 Lt. Bty, C L Ferard[9] Svy Sect RA, S F Fisken[9&12(Maj.)] 8 Mtn Bty, E E French[6(Lt. 29 Mtn Bty)&9] 9 Mtn Bty, R V M Garry[9] HQ 23 Mtn Bde., P F Grant[9] 12 Mtn Bty, P W Greest[9] 58 Bty, H A Hounsell[9&11] 10 Mtn Bty, D H Lee[9] 12 Fld Bty, J G MacGeorge[9] 3 Mtn Bty, M W M McLeod[6&9] 21 Ind Mtn Bde., K C Miller[4(Lt.),5(Lt.),6(Lt.)&9] 20 Md Bty, J W Nelson[9] 15 Md Bty, J S L Norris[9] 31 Bty, C H L Penney[9] 'Z' Ammo Col, L W Roberts[9] 3 Mtn Bty, J R S Roper[9] HQ 23 Mtn Bde., F J C Rybot[9] SSO, Razmak Bde., A L Tidcombe[9&12] 15 Md Bty, T L G Tod[9] 19 Mtn Bty, V A Young[9&12(Maj.)] 5 Mtn Bty, J S Wilkins[9] 'Z' Ammo Col & 25 Fld Bde. & S Williams[9] 12 Fld Bty attch. HQ 25 Fld Bde.

Lieutenants: ~ W C Auld[9] HQ 23 Mtn Bde., J M Bannerman[9] 'Z' Field Ammo Col, G F A Barff[9] attch. HQ 22 Mtn Bde., M F Kemmis-Betty[9] 19 Mtn Bty, G P D Blacker[9], J E C Blunt[9] 12 Fld Bty, L T T Bowers[9] 58 Bty, G E Cave[9] 12 Fld Bty, A B S Chennells[9&12] HQ 21 Ind Mtn Bde., P J E Clapham[9] 58 Bty, J R Cochrane[9] 21 Mtn Bde., C P Collingwood[9] 58 Bty, C M Courage[9] 25 Fld Bty, D G C Cowie[9] attch. PDS, G P Cunningham[9] 25 Fd Bty, B Daunt[9] 3 Mtn Bty, J C Dent[9] attch. 1 IDAC, H G M Dunn[9&11] 12 Fld Bty, C T L Findlay[9] 25 Fld Bty, R V R Foster[9] 25 Fld Bty, H R E C Fraser[9] 5 Mtn Bty, A Galletti[9] HQ 23 Mtn Bde., T L Gilchrist[9] 12 Fld Bty, C J Gittings[9&11] 4 Mtn Bty, F N W Gore[9] 12 Fld Bty, F J F Graham[9] 1 Mtn Bty, C H Lyall-Grant[9] 8 Mtn Bty, R H Hewetson[9], G B S Hindley[9] 25 Fld Bde., T W R Hill[9] 23 Mtn Bde., E A Howard[9] 16 Mtn Bty, R E H Hudson[9] 15 Md Bty, ADC to GOC PD, B P Hughes[9&11] 4 Mtn Bty, W Kaye[9] 1 Mtn Bty, G Kellett[9] 15 Md Bty, J W Kelway[9] 15 Md Bty, E G D Kennedy[9] 58 Bty, F B B Knight[9] 12 Mtn Bty, L H Landon[9] 25 Fld Bty, J A MacRae[9] 4 Lt. Bty, G W Mansell[9] 12 Fld Bty attch. Armd Train, Lahore Jnct, J M W Martin[9] 8 Mtn Bty, R B Molesworth[9] HQ 22 Mtn Bde., H V S Muller[9] HQ 21 Ind Mtn Bde., C H O'Reilly[9] 12 Mtn Bty, D N E O'Stallorow[9] 12&58 Fld Btys, A R E Parsons[9] HQ 20 Ind Mtn Bde., C R Paul[9] attch. Post Group Malakand, J C B Peart[9] 10 Mtn Bty, R Richards[9&11] 15 Md Bty, F E Robinson[9] 9 Mtn Bty, G R Rowbottom[9] Svy Sect, 25 Fld Bty, J H L'E Schreiber[9] 1 Mtn Bty, J Y B Sharpe[9] 16 Mtn Bty, O St J Skeen[9&11], A C Smith[9], L N Smith[9] 4 Lt. Bty, N le M Stevenson[9] 17 Bty, G W F Stewart[9] HQ 21 Ind Mtn Bde., W B Stewart[9] 17 Bty, W T Temple[9] 1 IDAC, J Mc L W Titley[9] HQ 23 Mtn Bde., A C Todd[9] HQ 20 Ind Mtn Bde., H B Truscott[9] 19 Mtn Bty, O P Wagstaff[9] 58 Bty, A A Walker[9] 15 Md Bty, C H K Willians[9] 20 Md Bty attch. Waz Md Sect & F G Wintle[9] 4 Lt. Bty

Warrant Officers Class II: ~ 1030481 J T L Chapman[9&11] 58 Fld Bty,

Battery Quartermaster Sergeants/Staff Sergeants: ~ 1017539 W F Allen[3(Boy)&9] 58 Bty attch. RIASC, 61822 (1022884) A Broughton[3(Act. S/Sgt 90 Bty)&9] 25 Fld Bty & 1407950 H W E Bushell[9&12(WOII)] 15 Bty

Quartermaster Sergeants /Sergeants: ~ 1052090 W A Beed[9&11] 58 Bty, 1028147 A J Cherry[9,11(WOII)] 58 Fld Bty, 1053700 F E Davidson[9&11] 58 Fld Bty, 1407879 A C A J Ford[9,11&12(WOII)] 15 Bty & 1 IDAC, 1405808 G T W Hale[4(Gnr.),6(Gnr.)&9] 17 Bty, 1041890 A Hughes[9&11] 58 Bty, 1415253 L Orange[9&12] 15 & 20 Bty, 1028698 G A E Prescott[9&11] 12 Bty & 2558820 A Wethercill[9&11] 15 Md Bty

Lance Sergeants/Bombardiers: ~ 73549 (1041137) C E Collins[3(Bdr.)&9], 1411461 G Durrant[4(Gnr.)&9] 17 Bty, 6338421 T Foster[9&11] HQ 22 Mtn Bde., 1060358 G F J Gray[9&11] 58 Bty, 1417125 J A Hartfield[9&11(Sdle Sgt.)] 58 Bty, 1054055 J T Hay[9&11(Sgt.)] 1 IDAC, 1068459 J Hulme[9&11(Sgt.)] 58 Bty, 1414210 J C Irwin[9&12] 1 IDAC, 1409263 J C Kerridge[9&11] 15 Md Bty, 4446654 D L Moorfott[9&12] 15 Bty, 1414872 E H C Smith[9&12(Sgt.)] 15 Bty & 1058204 D E Young[9&11(Sgt.)] 58 Bty

Lance Bombardiers/Gunners/Drivers: ~ 779023 J F Bannerman[9&11] 58 Bty, 798244 S Bate[9,11&12] 58 Bty, 1070343 P Bayes[9&11] 58 Fld Bty, 781827 J Berry[9&11] 58 Bty, 794654 E G Blackwell[9&11] 58 Fld Bty, 1073960 H R Blackwell[9&12(Bdr.)] 15 Bty, 786006

G C Bohan[9&11] 58 Fld Bty, 5193584 H S Brotherton[9&12] 15 Bty, 784382 F W Burt[9&11] 58 Fld Bty, 781644 A E Crawford[9&11] 12 Bty, 736026 F L Crook[9&11] 58 Fld Bty, (148607) 1412299 W E Dadswell[3,4,5,6&9] 17 Bty, 794583 R Dixon[9&12] 15 Bty, 786062 J R Duff[9&11] 58 Bty, 165294 F J Efford[9&12] 15 Bty, 778708 C Elliott[9&11] 58 Bty, 1416201 J Fenton[9&12] 'Z' Ammo Col, 1061679 W G Ford[9&12] 15 Bty, 5722211 E L Frampton[9&11] 58 Bty, 788395 J Gascoigne[9&11], 5493637 H A Gillett[9&12] Waz Md Sect, 1073248 W E C S Gould[9&11] 58 Bty, 4384287 C Gresty[9&12] 1 IDAC, 790200 L Heightley[9,11&12] 15 Bty, 1073554 J Henry[9&11] 58 Bty, 1060273 B W Herbert[9&11] 58 Bty, 784274 A W Higginson[9&12] Waz Md Sect, 1417169 J H Huckstep[6,7&9] 4 Bty, 797469 A L Hunt[9&12] 31 Bty, 1418444 W Hunt[6,7&9] 17 Bty, 1024922 H Illingsworth[9&12] 25 Bty, 790115 H Jones[9&12] 15 Bty, 1073969 C H Kelly[9&12] 15 Bty, 1069968 L Loughlin[9&11] 58 Bty, 4968616 C Martin[9&12(Bdr.)] 15 Bty, 790498 W H Meehan[9&12] Waz Md Sect, 788353 C A Moon[9&11] 58 Bty, 1070267 J Morgan[9&11] 58 Bty, 780857 J Morris[9&11] 58 Bty, 1073602 S M Nevins[9&11] 58 Bty, 1422960 H Newton[9&12] 15 Bty, 4264370 J Noble[9&12] 31 Bty, 1417376 J W Norley[6(Gnr.)&9] 17 Bty, 777996 J P Ormondroyd[9&11] 58 Bty, 1020174 A R Palmer[9&11(Sgt.)] 58 Bty, 1057374 L E Palmer[9&11(Sgt.)] 58 Bty, 1070903 R W Pond[9&11], 1422303 H J Prosser[6&9] 17 Bty, 1426004 A J Raisborough[9&12] 15 Bty, 1405817 G W J Reed[3&9] 17 Bty, 788153 N Reid[9&11] 58 Bty, 788782 C E Roberts[9&12] Waz Md Sect, 790193 T W Round[9&12] 15 Bty, 777971 W R Sacre[9&11] 58 Bty, 5468593 D Skutt[9&11] 58 Bty, 781144 M Smith[9&12] 15 Bty, (1063487) 791335 W T Smith[9,11&12] 4 Bty, 1049772 A P South[9&11(Farrier)] 58 Bty, 790211 G T Spilling[9&12] 15 Bty, 4264781 A Stuart[9&11(Bdr.)] 58 Bty, 1073684 F Sutcliffe[9&11] 58 Bty, 1073550 P H Taylor[9&11] 58 Bty, 1070060 R Thomas[9&11(Bdr.)] 58 Bty, 1419736 F Thompson[6&9] 17 Bty, 1066544 M Toohey[9&12] 15 Bty, 796042 L A Trickle[9&12] 58 Bty, 777881 S J Trigg[9&11] 58 Bty, 781942 J H Turner[9&11] 58 Bty, 788351 W H Udy[9&11] 58 Bty, 783259 A G Walsh[9&11] 58 Bty, 779823 C R Ward[9&12(Bdr.)] 15 Bty, 1073878 A G Watts[9&11] 58 Bty & 794294 H R Watts[9&12] 15 Bty

Boys: ~ 1073143 F J Knowles[9&11(Gnr.)] 58 Bty

~ The Lahore Armoured Train ~

Note a. *Roll of all personnel identified as eligible.*

Note b. *All personnel drawn from 12 Field Battery, Royal Artillery.*

Note c. *Medals named in thin impressed capitals: 'R.A.'*

Single Clasp	No. Identified	Rarity
North West Frontier 1930–31[9]	12	Extremely Rare

Lieutenants: ~ G W Mansell[9]

Lance Bombardiers/Gunners/Drivers: ~ 763254 J W Beaumont[9], 1066617 W J Bevell[9], 1065815 C H T Brothers[9], 779024 J Clewley[9], 1069743 C G Cording[9], 4909920 F W Lewis[9], 1068071 T Manton[9], 1064973 F McNamee[9], 1059093 C Mortimer[9], 1068811 J Smith[9] & 1064229 W Smith[9]

~ Waziristan Medium Section Royal Artillery ~

Note a. *Roll of all personnel identified as eligible.*

Note b. *Medals named in thin impressed capitals: 'R.A.'*

Single Clasp	No. Identified	Rarity
North West Frontier 1930–31[9]	39	Very Rare

Combination Clasps	No. Identified	Rarity
North West Frontier 1930–31[9] North West Frontier 1935[12]	4	Of the Utmost Rarity

Lieutenants: ~ C H K Willans[9] 20 Md Bty attch. Waz Md Sect

Quartermaster Sergeants/Sergeants: ~ 1407825 V F Crispin[9] & 1415452 C Jones[9]

Lance Sergeants/Bombardiers: ~ 1057140 G J Aitken[9], 1061499 A Francis[9], 1405526 W Haydon[9], 444679 W T Jones[9] & 1058199 R Saunders[9]

Lance Bombardiers/Gunners/Drivers: ~ 4852723 B Adams[9], 784905 H Ball[9], 1020121 F C Barker[9], 773644 H C E Chatters[9], 1072531 A E Davies[9], 1070155 C L Davies[9], 779961 R A Emmerson[9], 779394 G E Ferbrache[9], 1410650 F J Flint[9], 5493637 H A Gillett[9&12], 781142 C E Godsmark[9], 784274 A W Higginson[9&12], 1065968 J P Hanrahan[9], 1068148 J W Holoman[9], 1061552 G E Hunt[9], 444679 T W Johnson[9], 1072537 F W Johnston[9], 1063392 W T Jones[9], 1073103 T P Maughan[9], 5719699 F Mayfield[9], 1070892 W McIntyre[9], 790498 W H Meehan[9&12], 1417245 H Miller[9], 779609 W

Morrison[9], 1069201 J P Nolan[9], 1062645 W Owens[9], 1064318 A E Palmer[9], 3184398 W Preston[9], 779214 G E Burton-Pye[9], 788782 C E Roberts[9&12], 1059906 S Simpson[9], 781357 D L Sullivan[9], 1060252 N Todd[9], 1065312 W F Wilkinson[9] & 1412875 F C Wrapson[9]

THE CORPS OF ROYAL ENGINEERS:
Sub Units Identified As Entitled:
Royal Engineers Officers – Military Engineering Services
Survey of India – 1 Indian Survey Section, 18 Air Survey Party, 49 Fort Company, RE
Royal Engineers Personnel Attached Indian Sappers & Miners
3 & 4 Field Companies King George's Own Bengal Sappers & Miners
10 Field Company, Queen Victoria's Own Sappers & Miners
22 Field Company, Royal Bombay Sappers & Miners

Note a.   *Roll of all personnel identified as eligible including Royal Engineer personnel attached Sappers & Miners (S&M).*
Note b.   *Medals named in thin impressed capitals: 'R.E.'*

Single Clasp	No. Identified	Rarity
North West Frontier 1930–31[9]	63	Rare.
Combination Clasps	**No. Identified**	**Rarity**
Afghanistan N.W.F. 1919[3] Waziristan 1919–21[4] North West Frontier 1930–31[9]	1	According to the roll as seen, can be considered Unique.
Afghanistan N.W.F. 1919[3] North West Frontier 1930–31[9]	3	Of the Utmost Rarity
Waziristan 1919–21[4] Waziristan 1921–24[6] North West Frontier 1930–31[9]	3	Of the Utmost Rarity
Waziristan 1919–21[4] North West Frontier 1930–31[9]	2	Of the Utmost Rarity
Waziristan 1921–24[6] Malabar 1921–22[7] North West Frontier 1930–31[9]	1	According to the roll as seen, can be considered Unique
Waziristan 1921–24[6] North West Frontier 1930–31[9]	8	Of the Utmost Rarity
Waziristan 1921–24[6] North West Frontier 1930–31[9] Burma 1930–32[10]	3	Of the Utmost Rarity
North West Frontier 1930–31[9] Burma 1930–32[10]	27	Very Rare
North West Frontier 1930–31[9] Burma 1930–32[10] Mohmand 1933[11]	3	Of the Utmost Rarity
North West Frontier 1930–31[9] Burma 1930–32[10] North West Frontier 1935[12]	1	According to the roll as seen, can be considered Unique
North West Frontier 1930–31[9] Mohmand 1933[11]	4	Of the Utmost Rarity
North West Frontier 1930–31[9] Mohmand 1933[11] North West Frontier 1935[12]	1	According to the roll as seen, can be considered Unique
North West Frontier 1930–31[9] North West Frontier 1935[12]	2	Of the Utmost Rarity

Lieutenant Colonels: ~ G H J G Morris[9] MES, P de Fonblanque[9] MES & J C Wickham[9] MES

Majors: ~ (Bvt) W M Broomhall[4(Lt.),6(Lt.)&9] 4 Fld Coy, KGO S&M, K B S Crawford[9] MES, C J E Greenwood[9&12(Lt. Col.)] Bde. Maj. Landi Kotal Bde., G H S Kellie[9] GE PD, C G Martin[9], C M Simpson[6(Capt.)&9] MES, F L Stroud[9] Staff Capt & C A West[9] attch. HQ Nowshera Bde.

Captains: ~ G D S Adami[9], J R T Aldous[9] 22 Fld Coy R Bombay S&M, R P G Anderson[9] AGE, Peshawar, W G Lang-Anderson[9] MES, A E Armstrong[9], E F E Armstrong[9&10] KGO S&M, H W Bush[4(Lt.),6(Lt.)&9] ACRE Peshawar & AGE Peshawar, R C G Chapman[9] MES, D M Christison[3(Lt.)&9] attch. S&M, A R Churchill[6(Lt.)&9] Fld Eng, Kajuri Plain, L O Clark[9] 3 Fld Coy, KGO S&M, R St. C Davidson[9,10&11], G R Gilpin[6&9] 10 Fld Coy, QVO S&M, M R Jefferis[4(Lt.)&9] attch. MES, H T S King[9] GE, Peshawar Area, W H Knox[3&9] attch. S&M, R G Lamb[9], Manzai, M F C Martin[6(Lt.)&9] MES, A H G Napier[6(Lt.),9&10], N E V Patterson[9] AGE, Bannu, E F J Payne[6(Lt.),7(Lt.)&9], R H Perry[9], F E Pool[6(Lt.)&9], W D Robertson[9], J F D Steedman[4(Lt.)&9], CRE PD Staff, P A Tucker[3(Lt.),4(Lt.)&9] QVO S&M & P G Wavish[9] MES

Lieutenants: ~ W F Anderson[9], S H M Battye[9&10] KGO Bengal S&M, R I C Blenkinsop[9&10] KGO S&M, C B Boulden[9] 10 Fld Coy, QVO S&M, J A Cameron[9] 10 Fld Coy, QVO S&M, W J Cardale[9&10] KGO S&M, G G S Clarke[9&10] 4 Fld Coy, KGO S&M, E H W Cobb[9], E F B Cook[9&10], D R Crone[9&11] 18 Air Survey Party, SofI, R S Dalby[9&11], D V Deane[9] MES, P A Easton[9] 4 Fld Coy KGO S&M, M du B Floyer[9&10], E J Graham[9] MES, L T Grove[9&10] KGO S&M, R H Havers[9] MES, L F Heard[9] Staff Capt RE NWFF, R E Holloway[9,10&11(Capt.)] KGO S&M, E H Ievers[9&10], J James[3&9] attch. S&M, L F R Kenyon[6,9&10], A W Kiggell[9&10] KGO S&M, A M Knox[9], S Lamplugh[9] GE, R E Lloyd[9&10] KGO S&M, I G Loch[9&10] KGO S&M, D R M Orchard MES[9,11&12(Capt.)], L A B Paten[9&10] KGO S&M, M C Perceval[9&10], G A T Pritchard[9&10] KGO S&M, W H Ray[6&9] 10 Fld Coy, QVO S&M, C D Reed[9] MES, W P Rendell[9] MES, R H Sams[9] 1 Ind Fld Survey Sect, C V Seagrim[9] MES, J Mc C Smith[9] 22 Fld Coy R Bombay S&M, E F R Stack[9] QVO S&M, E E Stenhouse[9&12(Capt.)] MES, J Stuart[9] MES, O Sturt[9] MES, J B Sutherland[9] 10 Fld Coy, QVO S&M, W L D Veitch[9] MES, J C Walkey[9&10] KGO S&M, J H Wite[9], J W White[9&11] MES & F J Wyatt[9]

Warrant Officers Class I: ~ 1852294 W A Bower[9] attch. MES

Warrant Officers Class II: ~ (Mech) 1852822 E Armstrong[9] 49 (Fort) Coy, (CSM) 1852883 (R J) (A E) Burridge[4,6&9] 10 Fld Coy, QVO S&M, (CSM) 1852688 R J Carron[9] 10 Fld Coy, QVO S&M, (CSM) 1855370 F J Godfrey[9&10] KGO S&M, (CSM) 1853663 E C Odell[6(Sgt.),9&10] KGO S&M & (CSM) 1849243 J W Walker[9&10] KGO S&M

Company Quartermaster Sergeants/Staff Sergeants: ~ (Mech) 1862181 E W Christmas[9] attch. MES, (Mech) 1861898 H A Cox[9] attch. MES, (Mech) 1858584 W J Dispain[9] attch. MES, (Mech) 1862966 S A Greenfield[9] attch. MES & (Mech) 1859461 A J Sergeant[9] attch. MES

Quartermaster Sergeants/Sergeants: ~ 1853109 H Aiken[9&10] KGO S&M, 1859998 W Budden[9,10&11] KGO S&M, 728950 H Creese[9], (Mech QMS) 1851886 F G Deveny[9] attch. MES, 4116748 W J Dixon[9], 1854464 J Fisher[9&10] KGO S&M, (QMS) 1859280 A W Hunt[9] attch. MES, 1862124 W H James[9] attch. 10 Fld Coy, QVO S&M, 1859817 T Jones[9&10] KGO S&M, (1861342) 616082 W E King[6(Cpl.)&9] 10 Fld Coy, QVO S&M, 1853204 E Letten[9&10] KGO S&M, 1853077 F C Parsons[6&9] 22 Fld Coy R Bombay S&M, 1852562 J W Rainey[9&10] KGO S&M, 1859593 H E Smith[9&10] KGO S&M, (Mech QMS) 1854549 L Tootell[9] attch. MES, 1863402 J Webb[9] 22 Fld Coy R Bombay S&M & 1860069 A Wilson[9&10] KGO S&M

Lance Sergeants/Corporals: ~ 1859547 J Baxter[9] attch. 10 Fld Coy, QVO S&M, 1863865 W Bradley[9] attch. 10 Fld Coy, QVO S&M, 1864132 J Brown[9,10&12(Sgt.)] KGO S&M, 1865401 E J Childs[9&11(Sgt.)] KGO S&M, 1862145 J V Patterson[9] 22 Fld Coy, R Bombay S&M, 5492083 W J L Plowman[9&10] KGO S&M, 1864000 H A Sammes[9] 10 Fld Coy, QVO S&M & 1865283 H G Wells[9&10] KGO S&M

THE ROYAL CORPS OF SIGNALS:
Sub Units Identified As Entitled:
'A' & 'B' Corps Signals
1, 2 3 & 4 Indian Divisional Signals
Kohat District Signals, Peshawar District Signals, Waziristan District Signals
1st Cavalry Brigade Signals Troop - Risalpur
Brigade Signals Including Razmak & Waziristan Bde.s
Post Signals Sections
Wireless Experimental Section

Note a. *Roll of all commissioned personnel identified as eligible.*
Note b. *Non-commissioned and other rank personnel Cavalry Brigade Signals Troop, (CBST), Wireless Experimental Section, (WE Sect) or multi clasp only.*
Note c. *Medals named in thin impressed capitals: 'R. SIGNALS.'*

Single Clasp	No. Identified	Rarity
North West Frontier 1930–31[9]	In Strength	Not Rare
North West Frontier 1930–31[9]	CBST = 33	Very Rare
North West Frontier 1930–31[9]	WE Sect = 2	Of the Utmost Rarity

Combination Clasps	No. Identified	Rarity
Waziristan 1919–21[4] Mahsud 1919–20[5] Waziristan 1921–24[6] North West Frontier 1930–31[9]	1	According to the roll as seen, can be considered Unique
Waziristan 1919–21[4] Waziristan 1921–24[6] North West Frontier 1930–31[9]	3	Of the Utmost Rarity
Waziristan 1919–21[4] North West Frontier 1930–31[9]	1	According to the roll as seen, can be considered Unique
Waziristan 1919–21[4] Waziristan 1921–24[6] North West Frontier 1930–31[9] Burma 1930–32[10]	1	According to the roll as seen, can be considered Unique
Waziristan 1919–21[4] Waziristan 1921–24[6] North West Frontier 1930–31[9] North West Frontier 1935[12]	1	According to the roll as seen, can be considered Unique
Waziristan 1921–24[6] North West Frontier 1930–31[9]	11	Extremely Rare
Waziristan 1921–24[6] North West Frontier 1930–31[9]	CBST = 1	According to the roll as seen, can be considered Unique
North West Frontier 1930–31[9] Burma 1930–32[10]	10	Of the Utmost Rarity
North West Frontier 1930–31[9] Mohmand 1933[11]	49	Very Rare
North West Frontier 1930–31[9] Mohmand 1933[11]	CBST = 1	According to the roll as seen, can be considered Unique
North West Frontier 1930–31[9] Mohmand 1933[11] North West Frontier 1935[12]	7	Of the Utmost Rarity
North West Frontier 1930–31[9], Mohmand 1933[11] North West Frontier 1935[12]	CBST = 1	According to the roll as seen, can be considered Unique

North West Frontier 1930–31[9] North West Frontier 1935[12]	7	Of the Utmost Rarity
North West Frontier 1930–31[9] North West Frontier 1935[12]	CBST = 1	According to the roll as seen, can be considered Unique

Majors: ~ R A Bagnold[9] Waz DS, G M H Henderson[9] PDS, R A C Henderson[9] Kohat DS, W T Howe[9] PDS, A E P Mudge[9] 'B' Corps Sigs attch. Khajuri Force & R F H Nalder[9] HQ Kohat Dist

Captains: ~ A B Bushby[9] 'B' Corps Sigs, J F Charlesworth[9&11] PDS, E L Farnall[9] CBST, W C V Galwey[9], G G Glanville[9], F P L Gray[9] 1 IDS, H P Hart[9], (QM) J Hawke[9] PDS, C A Murray[9] PDS & V J E Westropp[9] 'B' Corps Sigs

Lieutenants: ~ J N Barker[9] Kohat DS, J R Beeton[9] PDS, T W Boileau[9&11] PDS, F R Booth[9] 'B' Corps Sigs, F W P Bradford[9], D W Burridge[9], R L Carpenter[9&12] Waz DS & 'B' Corps Sigs, (QM) J T Cussens[9], G W Roney-Dougal[9], W J S Gray[9] Waz DS, G Grayrigge[9] PDS, D N van der Groot[9&12] attch. 4 IDS, J C Hardy[9&11] PDS, E J F Heap[9&12] 1 CBST, J M C Hoblyn[9&10(4 IDS)] Kohat DS, G F Houghton[9] 'B' Corps Sigs, D L Hyde[9] PDS, P R Hyde[9] 1 IDS, H L B Kealy[9] Kohat DS, G A MacMunn[9] PDS, A J G McNair[9] Kohat DS, F R B Moore[9] 1 CBST, H C B Rogers[9] 'B' Corps Sigs, F G Seely[9] PDS, L T Shawcross[9&11] PDS, W A K Stodart[9] & R Webb[9] 'B' Corps Sigs

Warrant Officers Class II: ~ 522944 E Saunders[9] attch. CBST

Company Quartermaster Sergeants/Staff Sergeants: ~ 1038999 W Potter[9&10] & 1859011 C H Prince[9] CBST

Quartermaster Sergeants/Sergeants: ~ 1858869 A Carney[6&9], 2319849 P Coates[9&11] PDS, 5095009 J Cooper[9&12], 2312295 H A Evens[6&9], 2311403 F S Handley[9,11&12] CBST, 2309066 J E Handby[6(Cpl.)&9] PDS, 2313907 G A Harper[9&11], 1857466 A Hawley[6&9] Kohat DS, 6278543 C Holloway[9] attch. Wireless Experimental Sect, 1857295 J Law[9(Sgln.)&9] 'B' Corps Sigs, 2312224 A Negro[6(Sgln.)&9], 313351 S J Peters[9] attch. CBST, 1857071 R Shaw[6(Cpl.)&9] attch. CBST, 2313800 H Shirley[9] attch. CBST, 312575 R F Standen[9] attch. CBST, 5820515 H Steed[9&10], 1406867 W J Squires[9&11] PDS & 2312416 A S P Szarkowski[6(Cpl.)&9]

Lance Sergeants/Corporals: ~ 2310372 G Bennet[9&11(Sgt.)] PDS, 2312093 W H Bonner[6(Sgln..)&9] PDS, 7991 C Cheeseman[9,11(Sgt.)&12(Sgt.)] PDS, 6390674 A E Clevett[9&11] PDS, 2310956 H A Coaten[9&11] PDS, 5999529 V R Cole[9&12(Sgt.)], 5610360 R Collins[9] attch. CBST, 2313842 B Coy[9&10(Cpl.)] Kohat DS, 6907860 E Field[9&10], 2316734 A Gerrish[9&10], 2309488 J Gildea[6(Sgln.)&9] PDS, 1860365 A Grant[8&11(L/Sgt.)] PDS, 313648 J Hall[9] attch. CBST, 2309379 J P Hayes[9&11(L/Sgt.)] PDS, 2209868 A Lee[9(Sgln.)&11] PDS, 2314251 W C Manning[9] attch. CBST, 1857173 M McCormack[9&12(Sgt.)], 2314250 P McLachlan[9&10] 'A' Corps Sigs, 1850437 J Nesbit[8&9] Kohat DS, & 1857189 J P Swaine[6&9]

Lance Corporals/Signalmen: ~ 2318695 P A Alexander[9&11] PDS, 771089 J T Ashenhurst[9] attch. Wireless Experimental Sect, 2219017 V H Ashwood[9] attch. CBST, 2317980 F Bailey[9] attch. CBST, 2318772 E E Bale[9] attch. CBST, 2318912 W C Barber[9&11] PDS, 7536073 E Baxter[9] attch. CBST, 5823033 C O Bayley[9&11(L/Cpl.)], 2316341 F C Beasley[9&11], 2316951 L C Beech[9] attch. CBST, 2319643 C Beeching[9&11] PDS, 2316730 W E Birkett[9&12], 2314919 E F Boughton[9] attch. CBST, 2318687 G E Boulton[9&11] PDS, 2319449 H J Brett[9&11] PDS, 2317902 J Cain[9&11] PDS, 2559005 A A Christie[9&11] 'B' Corps Sigs attch. PDS, 2318139 C Collyns[9&11] PDS, 1055165 E J Crawford[9] attch. CBST, 2316757 E Cree[9] attch. CBST, 2318182 F C Curtis[9&11] PDS, 2318562 S Dawes[9&11] PDS, 2318418 W Dawson[9&11] PDS, 2315408 W C Day[9&11] attch CBST, 2318834 J J Delaney[9&12], 2316414 J H Dirs[9] attch. CBST, 2315199 G Few[9] attch. CBST, 2319857 E R Gentle[9,11&12] PDS, 6283693 H L George[9&11] PDS, 2319701 W H Gigg[9&11] PDS, 2319228 J C Gladwin[9&11] PDS, 2319369 S Grattage[9,11&12] PDS, 2316709 G C Head[9] attch. CBST, 2214337 R G A Hill[9&11] PDS, 2315576 A L Hills[9&10] 'B' Corps Sigs, 2317914 M H Hodgson[9&11] PDS, 2316802 R J Holley[9] attch. CBST, 2319592 J Howarth[9&11] PDS, 2973766 J Howell[9&11] PDS, 2314510 F Hubbard[9] attch. CBST, 2319699 S A Huggett[9&11] PDS, 2319979 J W Ireland[9,11&12] PDS, 2316665 C F Jackman[9] attch. CBST, 2318035 W L Jarvis[9,11(L/Cpl.)&12] 'B' Corps Sigs attch. PDS, 2313889 J M Johns[9] attch. CBST, 2318579 A Kay[9] attch. CBST, 2319352 J C Lucas[9&11] PDS, 2316278 M W Mac Donald[9] attch. CBST, 2319256 C J Martin[9&11] PDS, 2318703 C Miller[9&11] PDS, 2319198 W Mitchell[9&11] PDS, 2565397 F J Murrell[9,11&12] PDS, 2318822 W Nicholson[9] attch. CBST, 2318679 G Norton[9&11] PDS, 2318250 J O'Connell[9&11] 'B' Corps Signals attch. PDS, 2318708 A Palmer[9&11] PDS, 5493709 V G Parker[9&11] PDS, 2319636 W I I Partington[9&11] PDS, 2315726 S A Potts[9&11] PDS, 2317824 T Pugh[9&10] 'B' Corps Sigs, 2316092 E A Ravenhall[9] attch. CBST, 754344 C G Roberts[9&10], 2320204 G Rumford[9,11&12] PDS, 2317826 I M Shaw[9] attch. CBST, 2316683 D Shewring[9] attch. CBST, 2318667 J A Shinn[9&11] PDS, 2316053 R A Thomas[9] attch. CBST, 2316677 W Titt[9] attch. CBST, 2315754 L R J Vine[9] attch. CBST, 2314610 W N Wathen[9] attch. CBST, 2318555 E S Wickes[9&11] PDS, 2319463 T Williams[9&11] 'B' Corps Signals attch. PDS, 2315969 D Wilson[9] attch. CBST, 2312546 P A Wink[9&11] PDS & 2318462 R J Yarnell[9&11] PDS

THE INFANTRY:

~ 1ˢᵗ Bn, The Queen's (Royal West Surrey Regiment) ~

Note a.   *Roll of all personnel identified as eligible.*
Note b.   *Recipient attached 'M' Supply Depot, Indian Army Service Corps (IASC).*
Note c.   *Medals named in thin impressed capitals: 'THE QUEEN'S R.'*

Single Clasp	No. Identified	Rarity
North West Frontier 1930–31[9]	1	According to the roll as seen, can be considered Unique

Quartermaster Sergeants/Sergeants: ~ 6077189 H Boutemy[9]

~ 1ˢᵗ Bn, The Buffs (East Kent Regiment) ~

Note a.   *Roll of all personnel identified as eligible.*
Note b.   *All recipients attached 'T' Company, Indian Signals Corps (ISC), Peshawar District Signals (PDS).*
Note c.   *Medals named in thin impressed capitals: 'THE BUFFS.'*

Single Clasp	No. Identified	Rarity
North West Frontier 1930–31[9]	2	Of the Utmost Rarity

Lance Corporals/Privates: ~ 6279244 F C Bean[9] & 6279990 S Keats[9]

~ 2ⁿᵈ Bn, The King's Own Royal Regiment (Lancaster) ~

Note a.   *Roll of all personnel identified as eligible.*
Note b.   *Recipient attached 'T' Coy, Indian Signals Corps (ISC), Peshawar District Signals (PDS) as Telegraphist, Government Telegraph Office Peshawar*
Note c.   *Medals named in thin impressed capitals: 'K O ROYAL R.'*

Single Clasp	No. Identified	Rarity
North West Frontier 1930 –31[9]	1	According to the roll as seen, can be considered Unique

Lance Corporals/Privates: ~ 3763911 F N Newcombe[9]

~ 2ⁿᵈ Bn, The Northumberland Fusiliers ~

Note a.   *Roll of all personnel identified as eligible.*
Note b.   *All recipients served with the Lahore Armoured Train unless shown otherwise.*
Note c.   *Medals named in thin impressed capitals: 'NORTH'D. FUS.'*

Single Clasp	No. Identified	Rarity
North West Frontier 1930 –31[9]	43	Very Rare

Captains: ~ R Trenam[9]
Quartermaster Sergeants/Sergeants: ~ 4257185 A Doy[9] & 7814332 J R A Tierney[9]
Lance Sergeants/Corporals: ~ 4263935 G Bolam[9], 4261824 W Lacey[9] & 4383877 R Winward[9]
Lance Corporals/Fusiliers: ~ 4263851 J Auld[9], 4265855 T Blackburn[9], 4266012 L Bone[9], 4265553 B Brockson[9], 4264053 H Bourne[9], 4260392 C Cleveland[9], 426???? T Clever[9], 4263947 J W Coates[9] attch. ISC, PDS, 4262756 R Dodds[9], 4265710 G Ferguson[9], 4265994 F Gardiner[9], 4266576 J Gibson[9], 4264414 T Gleaves[9], 4256488 W Hadaway[9], 4266487 E Hardy[9], 4264316 J Hayton[9], 4263735 T Hitcham[9], 4383142 J Hogg[9], 4265398 R Holdsworth[9], 767336 J Holliday[9], 4263952 S Jones[9], 4259881 J Mallon[9], 4263945 G Morris[9], 4263292 G E Peacock[9] attch. 'T' Coy, ISC, PDS, 4265648 W T Rackstraw[9], 4264769

R Reid[9], 4265387 J G Riley[9], 4264779 T Ruddy[9], 4264321 G T Scott[9], 5768858 J W Smith[9], 4266612 W Webb[9], 4261120 E Whitchurch[9], 4266713 T Wilkinson[9], 4263872 W Wilkinson[9], 4265989 S Wolstenholme[9], 4265318 H Woodward[9] & 4265640 A Younghusband[9]

~ 2nd Bn, The Royal Warwickshire Regiment ~

Note a.   *Roll of all personnel identified as eligible.*
Note b.   *Recipient attached 'M' Supply Depot, Indian Army Service Corps (IASC).*
Note c.   *Medals named in thin impressed capitals: 'R. WAR. R.'*

Single Clasp	No. Identified	Rarity
North West Frontier 1930–31[9]	1	According to the roll as seen, can be considered Unique

Lieutenants: ~ F R Williams[9]

~ 1st Bn, The Royal Fusiliers (City of London Regiment) ~

Note a.   *Roll of all personnel identified as eligible.*
Note b.   *Recipient attached Headquarters (HQ) Waziristan District (Waz Dist), Dera Ismail Khan (DIK).*
Note c.   *Medals named in thin impressed capitals: 'R. FUS.'*

Single Clasp	No. Identified	Rarity
North West Frontier 1930–31[9]	0	None Identified
Combination Clasps	**No. Identified**	**Rarity**
Waziristan 1921–24[6] North West Frontier 1930–31[9]	1	According to the roll as seen, can be considered Unique

Quartermaster Sergeants/Sergeants: ~ (Act) 6448654 J Scrimgeour[6(Fus)&9]

~ 1st Bn, The Norfolk Regiment ~

Note 1.   *Roll of all personnel identified as eligible.*
Note 2.   *Medals named in thin impressed capitals: 'NORF. R.'*

Single Clasp	No. Identified	Rarity
North West Frontier 1930–31[9]	7	Of the Utmost Rarity
Combination Clasps	**No. Identified**	**Rarity**
Waziristan 1919–21[4] North West Frontier 1930–31[9]	3	Of the Utmost Rarity

Captains: ~ C M Clode[4(Lt.)&9] Fld Cashier, Fort Bara & G P St. C de Wilt.on[4(Lt.)&9] DAPM & Admin Cmdt, Ft. Bara
Lance Sergeants/Corporals: ~ 5764146 J Darwent[9] 'B' Company attch. 2 SS, Fort Bara / Karawal Camp & 5765869 W Palmer[9] 'B' Company attch. 2 SS Fort Bara / Karawal Camp
Lance Corporals/Privates: ~ 5768380 H Batting[9] 'A' Company attch. 2 SS, Fort Bara/ Karawal Camp, 5768689 H Cole[9] 'HQ' Company attch. 2 SS, Fort Bara / Karawal Camp, (5764571) 72005 C Cooke[4&9] 'HQ' Company attch. 2 SS, Fort Bara, 5768368 G Gilbank[9] 'A' Company attch. 2 SS, Fort Bara, 5768806 G Huggins[9] 'HQ' Company attch. 2 SS, Fort Bara / Karawal Camp & 5768703 A J Nash[9] attch. 1 Ind Group, RAF Peshawar

~ 1st Bn, The Devonshire Regiment ~

Note a.   *Roll of all personnel identified as eligible.*
Note b.   *Medals named in thin impressed capitals: 'DEVON. R.'*

Single Clasp	No. Identified	Rarity
North West Frontier 1930–31[9]	3	Of the Utmost Rarity

Combination Clasps	No. Identified	Rarity
Waziristan 1919–21[4] Waziristan 1921–24[6] North West Frontier 1930–31[9]	1	According to the roll as seen, can be considered Unique

Quartermaster Sergeants/Sergeants: ~ (Act) 5611456 F Craze[9] attch. HQ Bannu Bde. & 5608461 T Tomlin[9] attch. Rest Camp facility, Manzai.
Lance Sergeants/Corporals: ~ 5430003 R Smyth[4,6&9]
Lance Corporals/Privates: ~ 7178813 M Mooney[9] attch. HQ Razmak Bde.

~ 1st Bn, The East Yorkshire Regiment ~

Note a.   *Roll of all personnel identified as eligible.*
Note b.   *All recipients attached 18 Field Ambulance (FA), Royal Army Medical Corps (RAMC) unless shown otherwise.*
Note c.   *Medals named in thin impressed capitals: 'E. YORK. R.'*

Single Clasp	No. Identified	Rarity
North West Frontier 1930–31[9]	6	Of the Utmost Rarity

Quartermaster Sergeants/Sergeants: ~ 4337386 C Almond[9]
Lance Corporals/Privates: ~ 4340051 J Carty[9], 4336811 G Gledhill[9] attch. HQ Bannu Bde., 4340693 E Kyle[9], 4340347 M Sedgwick[9] & 4340669 E Vint[9]

~ 1st Bn, The Bedfordshire & Hertfordshire Regiment ~

Note a.   *Roll of all personnel identified as eligible.*
Note b.   *Recipient attached Headquarters (HQ), North West Frontier Force (NWFF).*
Note c.   *Medals named in thin impressed capitals: 'BEDF. & HERTS. R.'*

Single Clasp	No. Identified	Rarity
North West Frontier 1930–31[9]	1	According to the roll as seen, can be considered Unique

Company Quartermaster Sergeants/Staff Sergeants/Colour Sergeants: ~ (Act) 5946158 D P Greenwood[9]

~ 1st Bn, The Leicestershire Regiment ~

Note a.   *Roll of all personnel identified as eligible.*
Note b.   *Medals named in thin impressed capitals: 'LEIC. R.'*

Single Clasp	No. Identified	Rarity
North West Frontier 1930–31[9]	4	Of the Utmost Rarity

Company Quartermaster Sergeants/Staff Sergeants/Colour Sergeants: ~ 4853402 T WMarriott[9] attch. 2 SS, Fort Bara
Quartermaster Sergeants/Sergeants: ~ (Act) 4852858 W D Bent[9] Army HQ India attch. HQ PD
Lance Corporals/Privates: ~ 4796778 T E W Burrell[9] attch. 2 SS, Fort Bara & 4853129 T Green[9] attch. CIMH, Kohat

~ 2nd Bn, The Lancashire Fusiliers ~

Note a. *Roll of all personnel identified as eligible.*
Note b. *Medals named in thin impressed capitals: 'LAN. FUS.'*

Single Clasp	No. Identified	Rarity
North West Frontier 1930–31[9]	3	Of the Utmost Rarity

Quartermaster Sergeants/Sergeants: ~ (Act) 4260917 H W Roseberry[9] attch. HQ 9 Bde.
Lance Sergeants/Corporals: ~ 3435004 F Starkey[9] attch. SSO, Bannu
Lance Corporals/Fusiliers: ~ 3442852 A Bela[9] attch. 'T' Coy, ISC, PDS

~ 1st Bn, The Cheshire Regiment ~

Note a. *Roll of all personnel identified as eligible.*
Note b. *Medals named in thin impressed capitals: 'CHES. R.'*

Single Clasp	No. Identified	Rarity
North West Frontier 1930–31[9]	1	According to the roll as seen, can be considered Unique

Lance Corporals/Privates: ~ 4120306 J Lawless[9]

~ The Royal Welsh Fusiliers ~

Note a. *Roll of all personnel identified as eligible.*
Note b. *Recipient attached Rest Camp facility, Ranzai, Waziristan.*
Note c. *Medals named in thin impressed capitals: 'R.W.FUS.'*

Single Clasp	No. Identified	Rarity
North West Frontier 1930–31[9]	1	According to the roll as seen, can be considered Unique

Quartermaster Sergeants/Sergeants: ~ (Act) 4179735 L Robert[9]

~ 1st Bn, The Worcestershire Regiment ~

Note a. *Roll of all personnel identified as eligible.*
Note b. *Recipient attached 4/11 Sikhs, IA, 1 Bde.*
Note c. *Medals named in thin impressed capitals: 'WORC. R.'*

Single Clasp	No. Identified	Rarity
North West Frontier 1930–31[9]	1	According to the roll as seen, can be considered Unique

Captains: ~ L R Cooper[9]

~ 1st Bn, The East Surrey Regiment ~

Note a.   *Roll of all personnel identified as eligible.*
Note b.   *Battalion held as a reserve at Rawalpindi and therefore did not deploy as a complete unit.*
Note c.   *Medals named in thin impressed capitals: 'E. SURR. R.'*

Single Clasp	No. Identified	Rarity
North West Frontier 1930–31[9]	5	Of the Utmost Rarity

Captains: ~ C D Armstrong[9], Staff Capt., Wana Bde.
Lieutenants: ~ D J Campbell[9] & D St. A Campbell[9], Bde. IO, Fordhams Force, Fort Shabkadar, PD
Quartermaster Sergeants/Sergeants: ~ 6132883 E Barham[9] attch. HQ 1 Bde., Fort Bara & (Act) 6136765 L J Berry[9] attch. HQ 1 Bde., Fort Bara

~ 1st Bn, The Duke of Cornwall's Light Infantry ~

Note a.   *Roll of all personnel identified as eligible.*
Note b.   *Recipient served as Post Storeman, Rest Camp facility Manzai.*
Note c.   *Medals named in thin impressed capitals: 'D.C.L.I.'*

Single Clasp	No. Identified	Rarity
North West Frontier 1930–31[9]	1	According to the roll as seen, can be considered Unique

Lance Corporals/Privates: ~ 5434182 H Wheeler[9]

~ 2nd Bn, The Border Regiment ~

Note a.   *Roll of all commissioned personnel identified as eligible.*
Note b.   *Non-commissioned and other rank personnel multi clasp only.*
Note c.   *Initially Nowshera Column thence to Peshawar District Troops.*
Note d.   *Medals named in thin impressed capitals: 'BORD. R.'*

Single Clasp	No. Identified	Rarity
North West Frontier 1930–31[9]	Bn. Strength	Not Rare
Combination Clasps	**No. Identified**	**Rarity**
Afghanistan N.W.F. 1919[3] North West Frontier 1930–31[9]	1	According to the roll as seen, can be considered Unique
Waziristan 1919–21[4] Waziristan 1921–24[6] North West Frontier 1930–31[9]	2	Of the Utmost Rarity
Waziristan 1921–24[6] North West Frontier 1930–31[9]	17	Extremely Rare
North West Frontier 1930–31[9] North West Frontier 1935[12]	2	Of the Utmost Rarity

Majors: ~ C G Carruthers[9], N M S Irwin[9] HQ Northern Cmd. attch. PD, G R Sanderman[9] & N D Williams[9]
Captains: ~ J G Campbell[9], P D W Dunn[4,6&9], H J Hayman-Joyce[9], G M F Prynne[9] & A G Wilkinson[4(Lt.),6(Lt.)&9]
Lieutenants: ~ H E Colbeck[9], C J Day[9], T L Fasson[9], R H Haswell[9], K L Herbert[9], R C Cottrell-Hill[9], H J Lord[9], (QM) T Mann[9], K E F Millar[9], W Y Kington-Blair-Oliphant[9], H S Olsen[9], C M R Spedding[9], H F Weld[9] & W J Winkfield[9]
Company Quartermaster Sergeants/Staff Sergeants/Colour Sergeants: ~ 3590863 S Entwistle[6&9] & 3589491 H Peters[6(Sgt.)&9]

Quartermaster Sergeants/Sergeants: ~ 3591811 A Adams[6(Pte.)&9], 3589897 E Parish[6(Pte.)&9] & 3590993 J Tinkler[6&9]
Lance Sergeants/Corporals: ~ 3590183 A Challis[6(Pte.)&9], 3591904 W Harrison[6(Pte.)&9] & 3592509 P Winstanley[6(Pte.)&9]
Lance Corporals/Privates: ~ 3590472 D Adams[6&9], 3591216 W A Anderson[6&9], 3591256 W H Cobb[6&9], 3590999 W Martindale[6&9], 3592595 H Newton[6&9], 3590407 A Noble[6&9], 3589787 E Phinn[6&9], 3590416 F Reynolds[6&9], 3595371 J Riley[9&12], 3589978 A E Tucker[6&9], 3595292 W B Uren[9&12] & 52554 (3590985) J Wannop[3&9]

~ 2nd Bn, The Royal Sussex Regiment ~

Note a. Roll of all commissioned personnel identified as eligible.
Note b. Non-commissioned and other rank personnel multi clasp only.
Note c. Medals named in thin impressed capitals: 'R. SUSS. R.'

Single Clasp	No. Identified	Rarity
North West Frontier 1930–31[9]	Bn. Strength	Not Rare

Combination Clasps	No. Identified	Rarity
Afghanistan N.W.F. 1919[3] North West Frontier 1930–31[9]	9	Of the Utmost Rarity
Waziristan 1919–21[4] Waziristan 1921–24[6] North West Frontier 1930–31[9]	1	According to the roll as seen, can be considered Unique
North West Frontier 1930–31[9] Mohmand 1933[11]	1	According to the roll as seen, can be considered Unique
North West Frontier 1930–31[9] North West Frontier 1935[12]	1	According to the roll as seen, can be considered Unique

Lieutenant Colonels: ~ J S Woodruffe[9]
Majors: ~ V E C Dashwood[9], T F V Foster[9] & A L Thomson[9]
Captains: ~ E C Barton[9], A C Clayton[9], E K Cormody[3(Lt.)&9], P E M Legallais[9], G F Osborne[9] & R H Rohde[4(Lt.),6(Lt.)&9]
Lieutenants: ~ C E B Catt[9], (QM) C F Cavell[9], T F S Church[9], T S Frowd[9], J R D Gilbert[9], F C F Goodhart[9], T A Halsey[9], J C Holmes[9], A K Mumford[9], A J Oldling-Smee[9], R O V Thompson[9], G E Thornton[9] & J H Wilson[9]
Warrant Officers Class I: ~ (RSM) (6392497) L/13812 C W Butcher[3(Sgt.)&9]
Quartermaster Sergeants/Sergeants: ~ (6390733) L/10911 H Oakley[3(Pte.)&9]
Lance Corporals/Privates: ~ (6392366) L/13640 W H R Gates[3&9], 264906(1) J G Hoare[9&11(Sgt.)], (6392361) L/13635 W Hudd[3&9], (6392041) L/13213 E Humphries[3&9], (6390272) (6390568) L/9938 H Jones[3&9], (6390375) L/9234 G A Ralph[3&9] & (6390472) L/9590 T R Tresize[3&9]
Boys: ~ 6396765 J H Tucker[9&(12 Pte. DWR)]

~ 1st Bn, The Hampshire Regiment ~

Note a. Roll of all personnel identified as eligible.
Note b. Recipient attached Tactical Advance Party, Razmak, 2 Durh LI.
Note c. Medals named in thin impressed capitals: 'HAMPS. R.'

Single Clasp	No. Identified	Rarity
North West Frontier 1930–31[9]	1	According to the roll as seen, can be considered Unique

Lieutenant: ~ I M Goff[9]

~ 1st Bn, The Dorsetshire Regiment ~

Note a.   *Roll of all personnel identified as eligible.*
Note b.   *Recipient served as Storeman, Headquarters (HQ), Waziristan District (Waz Dist), Dera Ismail Khan (DIK).*
Note c.   *Roll states 'Local Sergeant' Private. Therefore might be names as Private.*
Note d.   *Medals named in thin impressed capitals: 'DORSET. R.'*

Single Clasp	No. Identified	Rarity
North West Frontier 1930–31[9]	1	According to the roll as seen, can be considered Unique

Quartermaster Sergeants/Sergeants: ~ (Local) 5720035 D Grahame[9]

~ 1st Bn, The Black Watch (Royal Highlanders) ~

Note a.   *Roll of all personnel identified as eligible.*
Note b.   *Medals named in thin impressed capitals: 'BLACK WATCH' or 'ROYAL HIGHLANDERS'*

Single Clasp	No. Identified	Rarity
North West Frontier 1930–31[9]	2	Of the Utmost Rarity

Quartermaster Sergeants/Sergeants: ~ 5329205 L C Morton[9] attch. 1 BT Coy as IC
Lance Sergeants/Corporals: ~ 2966009 S Duff[9] attch. 'T' Coy, ISC, PDS

~ 2nd Bn, The Essex Regiment ~

Note a.   *Roll of all commissioned personnel identified as eligible.*
Note b.   *Non-commissioned and other rank personnel multi clasp only.*
Note c.   *Medals named in thin impressed capitals: 'ESSEX R.*

Single Clasp	No. Identified	Rarity
North West Frontier 1930–31[9]	Bn. Strength	Not Rare

Lieutenant Colonels: ~ H R Bowen[9]
Majors: ~ G Disney[9], G K Meares[9] & C C Spooner[9]
Captains: ~ A M Barrett[9], H L H Boustead[9], W G Cowley[9], F R Grimwood[9], C J I F Hopegood[9] 'A' Coy, S O'C Mallins[9], L A Newbold[9], G V L Prowse[9] & C L Wilson[9]
Lieutenants: ~ E G Hazelton[9], E H Hills[9], H F Howell[9], R H A Painter[9], G J Purcell[9], S C W W Rea[9], H G Ricketts[9], H R S Sanguinetti[9], G N H Sheffield[9], E B Smyth[9], F E Stockley[9], G H Walker[9] & M H Whyte[9]

~ 2nd Bn, The Sherwood Foresters (Nottinghamshire & Derbyshire Regiment) ~

Note a.   *Roll of all personnel identified as eligible.*
Note b.   *Medals named in thin impressed capitals: 'FORRESTERS'*

Single Clasp	No. Identified	Rarity
North West Frontier 1930–31[9]	2	Of the Utmost Rarity

Lance Corporals/Privates: ~ 5045212 A E Pawley[9] attch. HQ Kohat Bde. & 4965363 W Spencer[9]

~ 1ˢᵗ Bn, The Loyal Regiment (North Lancashire) ~

Note a.   *Roll of all personnel identified as eligible.*
Note b.   *Recipient attached Headquarters (HQ), Razmak Bde.*
Note c.   *Medals named in thin impressed capitals: 'LOYAL R.'*

Single Clasp	No. Identified	Rarity
North West Frontier 1930–31[9]	1	According to the roll as seen, can be considered Unique

Lieutenants: ~ N H W Joynson[9]

~ 2ⁿᵈ Bn, Princess Charlotte of Wales's (Royal Berkshire Regiment) ~

Note a.   *Roll of all personnel identified as eligible.*
Note b.   *Recipient attached 7 Field Ambulance (FA), Royal Army Medical Corps (RAMC).*
Note c.   *Medals named in thin impressed capitals: 'R. BERKS. R.'*

Single Clasp	No. Identified	Rarity
North West Frontier 1930–31[9]	0	None Identified

Combination Clasps	No. Identified	Rarity
Waziristan 1921–24[6] North West Frontier 1930–31[9]	1	According to the roll as seen, can be considered Unique

Lance Sergeants/Corporals: ~ 5329016 A J S Kelly[6(Pte.)&9]

~ 1ˢᵗ Bn, The Queen's Own Royal West Kent Regiment ~

Note a.   *Roll of all personnel identified as eligible.*
Note b.   *Medals named in thin impressed capitals: 'R. W. KENT. R.'*

Single Clasp	No. Identified	Rarity
North West Frontier 1930–31[9]	3	Of the Utmost Rarity

Captains: ~ A A E Chitty[9] Staff Capt. Kohat Dist
Lance Sergeants/Corporals: ~ 6334130 G Hollands[9] attch. 'T' Coy, ISC, PDS
Lance Corporals/Privates: ~ 6339671 T D Mills[9] attch. 2 DLI

~ 2ⁿᵈ Bn, The King's Own (Yorkshire Light Infantry) ~

Note a.   *Roll of all commissioned personnel identified as eligible.*
Note b.   *Non-commissioned and other rank personnel multi clasp only.*
Note c.   *Medals named in thin impressed capitals: 'K.O.Y.L.I.'*

Single Clasp	No. Identified	Rarity
North West Frontier 1930–31[9]	Bn. Strength	Not Rare

Combination Clasps	No. Identified	Rarity
North West Frontier 1930–31[9] Mohmand 1933[11]	1	According to the roll as seen, can be considered Unique

Lieutenant Colonels: ~ E A Beck[9]
Majors: ~ T E F Penny[9] 'B' Coy, (QM) F H Pryor[9] & W P Bradley-Williams[9]

Captains: ~ A W B Becher[9], R A I Brooke[9] 'B' Coy, J A J Farrell[9] 'C' Coy, C J Keegan[9] 'D' Coy, W Robb[9] & J F Walker[9]

Lieutenants: ~ M G Beckett[9], W D Bramley[9] 'C' Coy, A B Brown[9], H N Burr[9], W S F Hickie[9], H A Livock[9], I F Low[9], P J Power[9], J C Preston[9], R B Freeman-Thomas[9], T W A H Harrison-Topham[9] & B W Wood[9] 'C' Coy

Lance Corporals/Privates: ~ 4684322 O F May[9&11(Sgt.)]

~ 1st Bn, The King's (Shropshire Light Infantry) ~

Note a.   *Roll of all commissioned personnel identified as eligible.*

Note b.   *Non-commissioned and other rank personnel multi clasp only.*

Note c.   *Medals named in thin impressed capitals: 'K.S.L.I.'*

Single Clasp	No. Identified	Rarity
North West Frontier 1930–31[9]	Bn. Strength	Not Rare

Combination Clasps	No. Identified	Rarity
North West Frontier 1930–31[9] North West Frontier 1935[12]	1	According to the roll as seen, can be considered Unique

Lieutenant Colonels: ~ H A R Aubrey[9]

Majors: ~ C Dalton[9] 'C' Coy & H T Hewitt[9]

Captains: ~ H W Baker[9], R Bryans[9] 'B' Coy, J M L Grover[9], W L Leslie[9], D S A McKimm[9], R C Norton[9] 'D' MG Coy & R B L Presse[9] 'A' Coy

Lieutenants: ~ W P Careless[9], D Colville[9], R Deedes[9], W H Hulton-Harrop[9], Hon G R Howard[9], W F H Kempster[9], R B Longe[9], C H Lynes[9], H R Jones[9], R A Smailes[9], R L Taverner[9], E N Thursby[9], (QM) H A C Wallbank[9] & M J F Wilson[9]

Quartermaster Sergeants/Sergeants: ~ (Act) 4029605 D R Griffiths[9&12] Clk HQ 2 Bde.

~ 1st Bn, The King's Royal Rifle Corps ~

Note a.   *Roll of all personnel identified as eligible.*

Note b.   *Recipient attached 'T' Company, Indian Signals Corps (ISC), Peshawar District Signals (PDS).*

Note c.   *Medals named in thin impressed capitals: 'K.R.R.C.'*

Single Clasp	No. Identified	Rarity
North West Frontier 1930–31[9]	1	According to the roll as seen, can be considered Unique

Lance Corporals/Riflemen: ~ 1035547 R Wallace[9]

~ 2nd Bn, The Manchester Regiment ~

Note a.   *Roll of all personnel identified as eligible.*

Note b.   *Medals named in thin impressed capitals: 'MANCH. R.'*

Single Clasp	No. Identified	Rarity
North West Frontier 1930–31[9]	1	According to the roll as seen, can be considered Unique

Combination Clasps	No. Identified	Rarity
Waziristan 1921–24[6] North West Frontier 1930–31[9]	1	According to the roll as seen, can be considered Unique

Captains: ~ J J Dolan[6(Lt.)&9] SSO 1 Mari Indus

Lance Corporal/Privates: ~ 3520195 J Clowes[9] attch. 'T' Coy, ISC, PDS

~ 2nd Bn, The York and Lancaster Regiment ~

Note a.   *Roll of all personnel identified as eligible.*
Note b.   *Medals named in thin impressed capitals: 'YORK & LANC. R.' or 'Y&L R.'*

Single Clasp	No. Identified	Rarity
North West Frontier 1930–31[9]	2	Of the Utmost Rarity

Quartermaster Sergeants/Sergeants: ~ (Act) 4740300 T Foster[9] attch. HQ Kohat Dist & 4737752 W Strutt[9] attch. HQ Wana Bde.

~ 2nd Bn, The Durham Light Infantry ~

Note a.   *Roll of all commissioned personnel identified as eligible.*
Note b.   *Non-commissioned and other rank personnel multi clasp only.*
Note c.   *Medals named in thin impressed capitals: 'DURH. L. I.'*

Single Clasp	No. Identified	Rarity
North West Frontier 1930–31[9]	Bn. Strength	Not Rare
Combination Clasps	**No. Identified**	**Rarity**
Afghanistan N.W.F. 1919[3] North West Frontier 1930–31[9]	6	Of the Utmost Rarity
North West Frontier 1930–31[9] Mohmand 1933[11]	4	Of the Utmost Rarity

Lieutenant Colonels: ~ R V Turner[9]
Majors: ~ W A Grey-Wilson[9]
Captains: ~ R J Appleby[9], C W Beart[9], E Dryden[9], S Gibbons[9] (Adjt.), E H L Lysaght-Griffin[9], M M Hutchinson[9] & F Taylor[3&9]
Lieutenants: ~ A R Bond[9], H E F Fox Davies[9], J M Hamer[9], J Johnstone[9], H McBain[9] Staff Capt Waz Dist, E C Sebag-Montefiore[9], F Murphy[9], H G Orr[9], C E S Phillips[9], J H N Poett[9], A H G Ricketts[9], F W Sanders[9], (QM) G Shields[3(WOII)&9], A Sladden[9], C M Townsend[9] & R F Ware[9]
Quartermaster Sergeants/Sergeants: ~ 4435150 A Aston[3(Cpl.)&9]
Lance Corporals/Privates: ~ 4445637 J Boddy[9&11(L/Cpl.)], (4438523) 52320 D Lawlor[3&9], (4435426) 11192 M Marrin (Also listed as Brady)[3&9], 4446396 A Rice[9&11], (4441728) 11425 T Sefton[3&9], 4445713 A S Simpson[9&11] & 4445805 J J Watts[9&11]

~ 1st Bn, The Highland Light Infantry (City of Glasgow Regiment) ~

Note a.   *Roll of all personnel identified as eligible.*
Note b.   *Medals named in thin impressed capitals: 'H.L.I.'*

Single Clasp	No. Identified	Rarity
North West Frontier 1930–31[9]	3	Of the Utmost Rarity
Combination Clasps	**No. Identified**	**Rarity**
North West Frontier 1930–31[9] North West Frontier 1935[12]	1	According to the roll as seen, can be considered Unique

Lance Corporals/Privates: ~ 3307853 W Brown[9], 5664564 R Coomber[9] & 3306957 T Forbes[9] attch. 'T' Coy, ISC, PDS
Pipers: ~ 3300215 A Lewis[9&12(Cpl.)]

~ 2nd Bn, Seaforth Highlanders (Ross-Shire Buffs, The Duke of Albany's) ~

Note a.   *Roll of all commissioned personnel identified as eligible.*
Note b.   *Non-commissioned and other rank personnel multi clasp only.*
Note c.   *Medals named in thin impressed capitals: 'SEAFORTH.'*

Single Clasp	No. Identified	Rarity
North West Frontier 1930–31[9]	Bn. Strength	Not Rare

Combination Clasps	No. Identified	Rarity
Waziristan 1921–24[6] North West Frontier 1930–31[9]	2	Of the Utmost Rarity
North West Frontier 1930–31[9] Burma 1930–32[10]	1	According to the roll as seen, can be considered Unique

Lieutenant Colonels: ~ K A N Anderson[9]

Major: ~ R G Barlow[9], D M Dunlop[9] & J Muirhead[9]

Captains: ~ D B Aitkin[9], I C Barclay[6&9], C E Fordyce[9], I R L Fraser[9], J M Grant[9], D H Haugh[9&10(Staff)], W A A Leslie[9], C A R McRae[9], D M W Smith[9], (QM) A Sutherland[9] & J H Walford[9]

Lieutenants: ~ A J H Cassels[9], M J D Drummond[9], H R Hildreth[9], R D Horne[9], P J Johnston[9], K MacKessack[9], R W G Robertson-McIsaac[9], R Mc A Richardson[9], N Baillie-Stewart[9], G C Stockwell[9], J M Sym[9], I S Tailyour[9], The Viscount Tarbat[9] & A R Wilson[9]

Company Quartermaster Sergeants/Staff Sergeants/Colour Sergeants: ~ 2810507 A K Slesser[6(Act. Sgt.)&9]

~ 1st Bn, The Gordon Highlanders ~

Note a.   *Roll of all personnel identified as eligible.*
Note b.   *Medals named in thin impressed capitals: 'GORDONS.'*

Single Clasp	No. Identified	Rarity
North West Frontier 1930–31[9]	8	Of the Utmost Rarity

Combination Clasps	No. Identified	Rarity
North West Frontier 1930–31[9] Mohmand 1933[11]	1	According to the roll as seen, can be considered Unique

Lance Corporals/Privates: ~ 2870948 W Duthie[9] attch. HQ Landi Kotal Bde., 2872536 D P Grant[9] attch. SSO Bannu, 2872405 G F Howitt[9] attch. HQ Peshawar Dist, 2871199 R S Innes[9] attch. HQ Landi Kotal Bde., 4864171 W Mc Queen Kelly[9] attch. 2 KOYLI, 2873474 R MacKay[9&11] attch. HQ Peshawar Dist, 2870251 E Spratt[9] attch. 'T' Coy ISC, Landi Kotal, 2210727 A Thomson[9] attch. HQ Landi Kotal Bde. & 2873138 J M Webster[9] attch. HQ Landi Kotal Bde.

~ 1st Bn, The Queen's Own Cameron Highlanders ~

Note a.   *Roll of all personnel identified as eligible.*
Note b.   *Recipient served as Brigade Major (Bde. Maj.), Fordham's Force, 1 Brigade (1 Bde.)*
Note c.   *Medals named in thin impressed capitals: 'CAMERONS.'*

Single Clasp	No. Identified	Rarity
North West Frontier 1930–31[9]	1	According to the roll as seen, can be considered Unique

Captains: ~ D N Wimberley[9]

~ 2ⁿᵈ Bn, The Royal Ulster Rifles ~

Note a. *Roll of all personnel identified as eligible.*
Note b. *Recipient attached 2 Durh LI.*
Note c. *Medals named in thin impressed capitals: 'R.U.R.'*

Single Clasp	No. Identified	Rarity
North West Frontier 1930–31[9]	1	According to the roll as seen, can be considered Unique

Lance Corporals/Riflemen: ~ 7009992 D Peoples[9]

~ 1ˢᵗ Bn, Princess Victoria's (Royal Irish Fusiliers) ~

Note a. *Roll of all personnel identified as eligible.*
Note b. *Recipients attached Station Staff Office (SSO), Bannu.*
Note c. *Medals named in thin impressed capitals: 'R. IR. FUS.'*

Single Clasp	No. Identified	Rarity
North West Frontier 1930–31[9]	2	Of the Utmost Rarity

Quartermaster Sergeants/Sergeants: ~ 7042117 C Pascoe[9]
Lance Sergeants/Corporals: ~ 6975201 A Gray[9]

~ 1ˢᵗ Bn, The Rifle Brigade ~

Note a. *Roll of all personnel identified as eligible.*
Note b. *Medals named in thin impressed capitals: 'RIF. BRIG.'*

Single Clasp	No. Identified	Rarity
North West Frontier 1930–31[9]	13	Extremely Rare

Majors: ~ (Bvt)T H Massy-Beresford[9] Bde. Maj., 9 Bde.
Lance Corporals/Riflemen: ~ 6907124 A Bass[9] attch. SS Fort Bara, 6910750 S G Buttons[9] attch. 'T' Coy ISC, PDS, 6910613 A Collis[9] attch. SS Fort Bara, 6911153 A Francis[9] attch. SS Fort Bara, 6650448 W Good[9] attch. 20 (AC) Sqn, RAF Peshawar, Int Liason Sect, 6004769 H F Hall[9] attch. 'T' Coy ISC, PDS, 6910433 G T Howes[9] attch. HQ Landi Kotal Bde., 6911846 R Kelly[9] attch. SS Fort Bara, 6912166 J Leslie[9] attch. SS Fort Bara, 6905515 N H Moyce[9] attch. 'T' Coy ISC, PDS, 6911803 R Munroe[9] attch. SS Fort Bara & 6912128 A Oakenfall[9] attch. SS Fort Bara

THE CORPS:

~ The Royal Army Chaplains Department ~

Note a. *Roll of all personnel identified as eligible.*
Note b. *Recipient served as Chaplain to 2 Seaforth.*
Note c. *Medals named in thin impressed capitals: 'R.A.Ch.D.'*

Single Clasp	No. Identified	Rarity
North West Frontier 1930–31[9]	1	According to the roll as seen, can be considered Unique

Reverends To The Forces: ~ D T H McLellan[9]

~ The Royal Army Service Corps ~

Note a.   *Roll of all personnel identified as eligible.*
Note b.   *Medals named in thin impressed capitals: 'R.A.S.C.'*

Single Clasp	No. Identified	Rarity
North West Frontier 1930–31[9]	3	Of the Utmost Rarity

Lieutenant Colonels: ~ S Hutchins[9] ADST PD
Quartermaster Sergeants/Sergeants: ~ M/721238 E Caley[9] attch. 5 Div Sply Coy, IASC & M/21492 J McNulty[9] attch. 13 MT Coy, IASC

~ The Royal Army Medical Corps ~
Sub Units Identified As Entitled:
Unit Medical Officers Attached
British Military Hospitals – Nowshera, Peshawar, Risalpur,
Combined Military Hospitals – Bannu, Landi Kotal, Razmak
31 Company
2 Cavalry Field Ambulance
2, 7, 8, 11, 18 Field Ambulance
2 & 3 Sanitary Sections

Note 1.   *Roll of all personnel identified as eligible.*
Note 2.   *All enlisted personnel drawn from 31 Company, Royal Army Medical Corps (RAMC).*
Note 3.   *Medals named in thin impressed capitals: 'R.A.M.C.'*

Single Clasp	No. Identified	Rarity
North West Frontier 1930–31[9]	48	Very Rare
Combination Clasps	**No. Identified**	**Rarity**
Afghanistan N.W.F. 1919[3] North West Frontier 1930–31[9]	1	According to the roll as seen, can be considered Unique
Afghanistan N.W.F. 1919[3] Waziristan 1919–21[4] North West Frontier 1930–31[9]	2	Of the Utmost Rarity
Waziristan 1919–21[4] Waziristan 1921–24[6] North West Frontier 1930–31[9] North West Frontier 1935[12]	1	According to the roll as seen, can be considered Unique
Malabar 1921–22[7] North West Frontier 1930–31[9]	1	According to the roll as seen, can be considered Unique
Waziristan 1921–24[6] North West Frontier 1930–31[9]	1	According to the roll as seen, can be considered Unique
North West Frontier 1930–31[9] & Burma 1930–32[10]	4	Of the Utmost Rarity
North West Frontier 1930–31[9] Mohmand 1933[11]	2	Of the Utmost Rarity
North West Frontier 1930–31[9] Mohmand 1933[11] North West Frontier 1935[12]	1	According to the roll as seen, can be considered Unique

Lieutenant Colonels: ~ A C Amy[6(Maj.)&9], H H Blake[9] & J C L Hingston[9]
Majors: ~ C F Anthonize[3(Capt.)&9], J F Bourke[9], H A Boyle[9] OC BMH Risalpur, J K Gaunt[9] CO 1 Coy, IHC, Peshawar, H C Godding[9] attch. 9 (Jhansi) Bde., G G B Holroyde[9] CMH Bannu, W O Holst[9] CMH Landi Kotal, J H G Hunter[9] attch.

BMH Peshawar, J M Macfie[9] CO 2 FA Khajuri Force, 2 (Nowshera) Bde., J M MacKenzie[3(Lt.),4(Lt.)&9] DADMA Peshawar Dist, J P MacNamara[3(Capt.),4(Capt.)&9] 11 FA, J T McConkey[9] CMIH Razmak, M P Power[4,6,9&12] CO 2 CFA 1 (Risalpur) Cav Bde., A E Richmond[9&11] DADH Peshawar Dist, H G Robertson[9] BMH Peshawar, H A Rowell[9&10], J M Ryan[9] OC 8 FA Wana, Waz Dist, T Stanton[9], T O Thompson[7(Capt.)&9] attch. 7 FA, E M Townsend[9] OC 11 FA & T Young[9] DADH Peshawar Dist

Captains: ~ G Anderton[9] MO Ladha Colmn, Waz Dist, J Gordon-Black[9] attch. 11 FA, C L Day[9&10(14 San Sect)] attch. 2 Seaforth & 18 FA Khajori Force, W A D Drummond[9] MO 2 Seaforth, H A Ferguson[9] attch. BMH Nowshera, R V Franklin[9] MO Ladha Colmn thence MO Kajuri Force, P T Palmer[9] attch. 1 KSLI, W R C Spicer[9], M G de L'Isle Sturm[9] attch. 11 FA, Karawal Camp, 3 (Rawalpindi) Bde. thence 2 FA, 9 (Jhansi) Bde., thence 2 (Nowshera) Bde. as MO Kajuri Force

Lieutenants: ~ R R Leaming[9&11(Capt.)] attch. 18 FA, Khajuri Force, P V MacGarry[9] MO 2 Essex & K McNeill[9&10]

Company Quartermaster Sergeants/Staff Sergeants: ~ 7251372 J S Gillard[9&10(8 Gen Hospital)] attch. 3 SS, Fort Bara

Quartermaster Sergeants/Sergeants: ~ 7255177 C F Ansell[9] attch. 2 CFA, 1 Cav Bde., (QMS)7246188 W G Crossman[9] attch RAMC det Peshawar &7248772 J Gray[9] attch. 11 FA Bara Camp

Lance Sergeants/Corporals: ~ 7255895 M T S Bousfield[9] attch. 8 FA thence CMH Razmak & 7250331 A Reddin[9] attch. RAMC det Peshawar

Lance Corporals/Privates: ~ 7258544 F O Birtles[9] attch 2 SS, Peshawar, 4686083 W H Blythe[9] attch RAMC det Peshawar, 7258705 K H Burford[9] attch 11 FA Karawal Camp, 7257081 H N Dale[9] attch RAMC det Peshawar, 7257143 G J Green[9] attch 2 FA, 7258507 A Grey[9] attch. 11 FA, Kajouri Plain, 7258683 I de Groot[9] 11 FA, Peshawar, 7259040 L Knowles[9] 2 FA, Peshawar, 7258956 R F MacKay[9] attch. 2 FA, 7257409 T H Marnham[9] attch RAMC det Peshawar, Peshawar, 7257805 S C Nicholson[9] attch RAMC det Peshawar, 7258962 L H Ritchie[9] attch. 11 FA, Kajuri Plain, 7258829 F Ryde[9,11&12] attch. 11 FA, Kajuri Plain, 7258952 J Sexton[9] attch. 2 FA, Peshawar Dist, 7258591 W D C Smart[9] attch. RAMC det Peshawar, 7254917 J L Smith[9], 7258168 W F Tomlin[9] attch. 2 FA, Peshawar, 7258522 F Weatherall[9] attch. RAMC dets Razmak, Wana, Kohat and DIK & 5246139 C Williams[9] attch. 2 FA, Peshawar

~ The Royal Army Ordnance Corps ~

Note a.   Roll of all personnel identified as eligible.
Note b.   Medals named in thin impressed capitals: 'R.A.O.C.'

Single Clasp	No. Identified	Rarity
North West Frontier 1930–31[9]	16	Extremely Rare

Company Quartermaster Sergeants/Staff Sergeants: ~ (Armt) 7578955 W Brown[9] attch. 15/19 H, (Armt) 7574582 J Cardinal[9] attch. 2 Border, (Armt) 7578924 H Gough[9] attch. 2 DLI, 7581988 G Howitt[9] attch. 2 R Sussex, (Armt) 7578782 J Johnston[9] attch 1 ACC, RTC, (Armt) 7578834 E Pritchard[9] attch. 2 Essex, (Armt) 7578783 W Swain[9] attch. 2 KOYLI & (Armt) 7578804 E Warner[9] attch. 8 ACC, RTC Razmak

Quartermaster Sergeants/Sergeants: ~ (Armt) 7574627 A E Charles[9] attch. 1 KSLI

Lance Sergeants/Corporals: ~ 1660510 C H Burton[9] attch. 1 ACC, RTC, 7577818 R Gray[9] attch. 8 ACC, RTC Razmak & 7581783 P Heap[9] attch. 2 Seaforth

Lance Corporals/Privates: ~ 4969432 T Ball[9] attch. 8 ACC, RTC Razmak, 7873901 W Benford[9] attch. 8 ACC, RTC Razmak, 7583529 D E Parsons[9] attch. 1 ACC, RTC & 7582928 F Steele[9] attch. 1 ACC, RTC

~ The Royal Army Veterinary Corps ~

Note a.   Roll of all personnel identified as eligible.
Note b.   Medals named in thin impressed capitals: 'R.A.V.C.'

Single Clasp	No. Identified	Rarity
North West Frontier 1930–31[9]	5	Of the Utmost Rarity
Combination Clasps	**No. Identified**	**Rarity**
Afghanistan N.W.F. 1919[3] Waziristan 1919–21[4] Waziristan 1921–24[6] North West Frontier 1930–31[9] Mohmand 1933[11] North West Frontier 1935[12]	1	According to the roll as seen, can be considered Unique

Mahsud 1919–20[5] **Waziristan 1919–21[4]** **Waziristan 1921–24[6]** **North West Frontier 1930–31[9]**	1	According to the roll as seen, can be considered Unique
North West Frontier 1930–31[9] **Mohmand 1933[11]** **North West Frontier 1935[12]**	1	According to the roll as seen, can be considered Unique

Lieutenant Colonels: ~ R W Mellard[9] MVH Kohat & ADVS

Majors: ~ W P S Edwards[3(Capt.),4(Capt.),6(Capt.),9,11&12], G V Golding[9,11&12], B J W Nicholas[4(Capt.),5(Capt.),6(Capt.)&9], K S Simpson[9] & P S Sparling[9]

Captains: ~ J P Hegarty[9] VO Khajuri Force & L H B Poer[9]

~ The Army Educational Corps ~

Note a.   *Roll of all personnel identified as eligible.*
Note b.   *Medals named in thin impressed capitals: 'A.E.C.'*

Single Clasp	*No. Identified*	*Rarity*
North West Frontier 1930–31[9]	16	Extremely Rare

Combination Clasps	*No. Identified*	*Rarity*
Malabar 1921–22[7] North West Frontier 1930–31[9]	1	According to the roll as seen, can be considered Unique

Captains: ~ T M Gordon[9] attch. HQ Peshawar Dist, W B Metcalf[9], J C Wood[7(Lt. attch. Dorset R)&9] attch. HQ 2 Rawalpindi Bde. & DEO DIK

Warrant Officers Class I: ~ 7720696 W H Goodwright[9] attch. 2 Essex, 7720645 G P Robertson[9] attch. HQ Nowshera Bde. & 7720760 H Toomey[9] attch. 15/19 H

Warrant Officers Class II: ~ 7720748 H R MacDonald[9] attch. 2 KOYLI, 7720785 E McDonnell[9] attch. 2 DLI & 1018818 P R Mole[9] attch. 2 R Sussex

Quartermaster Sergeants/Sergeants: ~ 6157 R V Bissett[9] attch. 'E' Bty, RHA, 1040260 W J Cheek[9] attch. 4 Lt. Bty RA, 1860414 E C Day[9] attch. 1 ACC, RTC, 1021115 J W Fowler[9] attch. HQ Bannu Bde., 2319498 A Johns[9] attch. 2 Suffolk, 1862084 L J King[9] attch. Kohat DS, 1862170 C A Parris[9] attch. PDS & 7720764 G J Stubbs[9] attch. 8 ACC, RTC

~ The Army Dental Corps ~

Note a.   *Roll of all personnel identified as eligible.*
Note b.   *Medals named in thin impressed capitals: 'A.D.C.'*

Single Clasp	*No. Identified*	*Rarity*
North West Frontier 1930–31[9]	2	Of the Utmost Rarity

Majors: ~ F H W Beer[9] attch. BMH Peshawar & J L Garrard[9] attch. BMH Nowshera

~ The Queen Alexandra's Imperial Military Nursing Service ~

Note a.   *Roll of all personnel identified as eligible.*
Note b.   *Medals named in thin impressed capitals: 'Q.A.I.M.N.S.'*

Single Clasp	*No. Identified*	*Rarity*
North West Frontier 1930–31[9]	17	Extremely Rare

Sisters: ~ S F Davies[9] attch. BMH Nowshera, D Duncun[9] attch. BMH Peshawar, P J Gibbs[9] BMH Nowshera, L G Hughes[9] attch. BMH Peshawar, D Kerridge[9] BMH Peshawar, A M Price[9] BMH Peshawar, V Rowe[9] BMH Peshawar, A Rowlands[9] attch. BMH Peshawar, E Shaw[9] attch. BMH Peshawar, E J Stirling[9] BMH Nowshera, E Townend[9] attch. BMH Peshawar & A Whitworth[9] attch. BMH Peshawar

Staff Nurses: ~ D M Beazley[9] attch. BMH Peshawar, K B Davies[9] attch. BMH Peshawar, M L Hallows[9] BMH Nowshera, E McIntosh[9] BMHs Peshawar & Murree & P/206420 C Somerville[9]

THE ROYAL AIR FORCE

Note a. *Refer to Royal Air Force notes at end of 'Frontier Campaigns 1919–1924' section for guidance regarding early rank designations.*

Note b. *Ranks shown are those applicable at award of first clasp.*

Note c. *Criteria for personnel to be included in the following roll follows that set for the Army roll for the clasp North West Frontier 1930–1931 i.e. all identified as eligible commissioned ranks and multi bar enlisted recipients.*

Note d. *Medals named in impressed block capitals: 'R.A.F.'*

Single Clasp	No. Identified	Rarity
North West Frontier 1930–31[9]	1,148	Not Rare

Combination Clasps	No. Identified	Rarity
Afghanistan N.W.F. 1919[3] North West Frontier 1930–31[9]	1	According to the roll as seen, can be considered Unique
Afghanistan N.W.F. 1919[3] Mahsud 1919–20[5] Waziristan 1919–21[4] North West Frontier 1930–31[9]	2	Of the Utmost Rarity
Afghanistan N.W.F. 1919[3] Mahsud 1919–20[5] Waziristan 1919–21[4] Waziristan 1921–24[6] North West Frontier 1930–31[9]	1	According to the roll as seen, can be considered Unique
Afghanistan N.W.F. 1919[3] North West Frontier 1930–31[9] Mohmand 1933[11]	1	According to the roll as seen, can be considered Unique
Mahsud 1919–20[5] Waziristan 1919–21[4] Waziristan 1921–24[6] North West Frontier 1930–31[9]	1	According to the roll as seen, can be considered Unique
Mahsud 1919–20[5] Waziristan 1919–21[4] North West Frontier 1930–31[9]	1	According to the roll as seen, can be considered Unique
Waziristan 1919–21[4] North West Frontier 1930–31[9]	6	Of the Utmost Rarity
Waziristan 1921–24[6] North West Frontier 1930–31[9]	5	Of the Utmost Rarity
Waziristan 1925[8] North West Frontier 1930–31[9]	2	Of the Utmost Rarity
North West Frontier 1930–31[9] Mohmand 1933[11]	41	Very Rare
North West Frontier 1930–31[9] Mohmand 1933[1] North West Frontier 1935[12]	16	Extremely Rare
North West Frontier 1930–31[9] North West Frontier 1935[12]	32	Very Rare

Group Captains: ~ H Le M Brock[9]

Wing Commanders: ~ J O Archer[9], C C Darley[9], H Gordon-Dean[9] & C H Nicholas[9]

Squadron Leaders: ~ L O Brown[9], O C Bryson[9], R G H Neville[9] & F W Trott[9]

Flight Lieutenants: ~ D F Anderson[9], G M Anderson[9], B Ankers[9], R E Bain[9], P E Berryman[9], I A Bertram[9], C N H Bilney[9], A F Brooke[4&9], G M Bryer[9], H V Champion De Crespigny[4,5,6&9], C J Collingwood[9], S D Culley[9&12], P H Cummings[4&9], N L Desoer[9], W E Dipple[9], C Feather[9], J G Franks[9], F J Fressanges[9], J L F Fuller-Good[9], F F W Hall[9], R E Hall[9], C R Hancock[9], B W T Hare[9], S B Harris[6&9], R G Hart[9], E A McKinley-Hay[9], L N Hollinghurst[3,9&11], J Hutchieson[9], F H Isaac[9], J R Jones[9], E J Foulkes-Jones[9], R B Jordan[9], E C de V Lart[9], C L Lea-Cox[9&11], J W Lissett[9], C H Loughnan[9], A H H MacDonald[9], J McBain[9], J Magner[9], M D Ommanney[9], J F F Pain[9], R A P Roberts[9], E G H Russell-Stacey[9], N I Smith[9], G S Strachan[9], O B Swain[9], J C H Tavendale[9], J E G Thomas[9], A A Townsend[9], C F Le Poer-Trench[9], R G Veryard[9&12] & R W White[9]

Flying Officers: ~ R B Abraham[9], M J Adam[9&12], O D Allerton[9], J C Atkins[9], D Barclay[9], L V G Barrow[9], R J O Bartlett[9&11], D W Bayne[9,11&12], W R Bearman[9], V Q Blackden[9], W N Blain[9], E A C Britton[3,4,5&9], H Broadhurst[9], J H Brown[9], L S T Brown[9], W D Butler[9], B M Cary[9], R P Cauthery[9], G P Chamberlain[9], R W P Collings[9], H M B Collins[9], H A G Comerford[9], de L Cooke[9], D H V Craig[9], H J Cross[9], J C Cunningham[9], T J Davidson[9], E C Delamain[3,4,5&9], J S Douglas[9&11], H W Duffey[9], T W G Eady[9], D J Eayrs[9], E E Ellison[9], R C W Ellison[9], E N V Everett[9], W G H Ewing[9], H A Fenton[9], F G Ferrier[9], F W Foster[9], J H Manning-Fox[9&11], J B Fyfe[9], G W Gay[6&9], C H Glover[9], S H C Gray[9], R C Hancock[9], C E Hartley[9], J W Hawke[9], A Haywood[9], M L Heath[9], W S Hebde.n[9], B W Hemsley[9], P W Lowe-Holmes[9], G K Horner[9], G H G S Jenkins[9], J C A Johnson[9], G A G Johnston[9], M W Keey[9], D W Lane[9], J O H Lobley[9], H R Lowry[9], P B Lusk[9], A McKee[9], S McKeever[6&9], H S Martin[9], J R Mathews[9], R Menzies[9&11], W K Mercer[4&9], A O Molesworth[9], G W Monk[9], J Mote[9], F W Murison[9], L Newcombe[9], E G Northway[9], B Paddon[9], M G Parker[9], R F Part[9], A C Pearson[9], R L Phillips[9], W J Pickard[9], C V J Pratt[9], H G Richards[9], A C Richardson[9], G N Roberts[9], F G A Robinson[5,4&9], E Rotheram[9], D W R Ryley[9], M S Shapcott[9], L F Sinclair[9], H D Spreckley[9], W A Stagg[9], F W Stannard[9], J A C Stratton[9], R W A Stroud[9], W P J Thompson[9], R E de T Vintras[9], E F Wain[9], C D G Welch[9], J G W Weston[9], H G Wheeler[9&12], G N E Tindal-Carill-Worsley[9], C C D Williams[9] & D H G Wood[9]

Pilot Officers: ~ L W C Bower[9], H M Lyons[9], P F Canning[9], H F Clayton-Daubeny[9], A M Cowell[9], J Grierson[9], N Kirkham[9], J A Nicholson[9], B H C Russell[3,4,5,6&9], F F Wicks[9] & W Wynter-Morgan[9]

Flight Sergeants: ~ 4383 A B Collins[9&11]

Sergeants: ~ 245551 A E Miller[9&12], 133214 H Pinchen[9&11], 334337 E R Skingsley[9&11] & 82908 E E R Williams[9,11&12]

Corporals: ~ 157978 W S Berry[9&12], 340824 F L Bowman[4&9], F W Boyles[9&11], 560557 E J Brandon[9&12], 248272 G F Cockell[4&9], 347149 A H Croombes[9&12], 560327 W R Cumbers[9,11&12], 327112 J R Hicks[9&12], 330149 J H Jones[9&12], 155057 F H Keirl[9,11&12], 336309 F G Loades[9&12], 364132 C E Mitchell[9&11], 342046 C F Smith[6&9], N W Turner[9&12] & 347181 W W Wright[9&11]

Leading Air Craftsmen: ~ 508577 H F Brittain[9&12], 341751 E A Bubb[6&9], 565670 F W Bullen[9,11&12], 506176 W F Coulson[9&11], 364547 A P Crowley[9&11], 364063 R P Gilmour[9&11], 365376 J D How[9&12], 508026 R Johnston[9&11], 358082 J G Kendall[9,11&12], 506148 S W Lipscomb[9&11], 365104 H G Martin[9&11], 332369 D Meredith[8&9], 370350 J A Mulford[9&12], 364735 R A Palmer[9&11], 507720 R Pleasants[9&11], J V J Reynolds[9&12], 365932 W R Rose[9&11], 507328 J Rutherford[9,11&12], F T Salmon[9&11], 364762 C F Smart[9&12], 365815 I G Stewart[9&12], 507671 G H Tice[9&12], 505376 J E Tilley[9&11], 506486 E J Wallis[9&12], 505953 A W White[9&11], 364393 E Williams[9&11] & 361747 A C Wood[9&12]

(Airman) Air Craftsmen 1st Class: ~ 507218 G K Barker[9&11], 506786 R C Bashford[9&11], 509293 J P Conway[9&11], 508252 P C Davies[9&11], 366078 P W E Dent[9,11&12], 364071 M J W Dunworth[9&11], 506197 J J English[9&11], 364643 W M Evans[9&11], 505959 W E Flitter[9&11], 507977 J C Irwin[9,11&12], 506188 D Laing[9,11&12], 364124 J H Lepper[9&11], 508683 W Mack[9&11], 508564 G McKeand[9&11], 363677 G Morris[9&11], 560898 H S Salmon[9,11&12], 506985 J H Simpson[9&11], 506119 H E Slark[9&11], 239481 L A Sparks[3&9], 335205 J Westwood[8&9], 508783 C J Woodhouse[9&12], 506286 D R Woolnough[9,11&12] & 506438 H J Van Zeller[9&12]

(Airman) Air Craftsmen 2nd Class: ~ 336654 W H Abbs[4&9], 507683 J J Blackwood[9&11], 506742 T I Bowen[9&11], 507733 A H Cairns[9,11&12], 510616 W Crabtree[9&12], 510647 W Edwards[9&12], 508838 W H Hattrick[9,11&12], 509995 G E Mead[9&12], 511815 W Middlemist[9&12], J P Murphy[9,11&12], 508333 V Palin[9&12], 511928 T J Parry[9&12], 511982 T M Parry[9&12], 511455 W E Sanderson[9,11&12], 508386 F H Street[9&11], 511590 P R West[9&12] & 510466 H W Why[9&12]

INDIAN ESTABLISHMENT

Qualifying Units Present (Officers Plus Known Individuals)

The Cavalry:

Hodson's Horse (4th Duke of Cambridge's Own Lancers)..Detachment Only
6th Duke of Connaught's Own Lancers (Watson's Horse)...1st Cavalry Brigade
The Guides Cavalry (10th Queen Victoria's Own Frontier Force)..1st Cavalry Brigade
The Poona Horse (17th Queen Victoria's Own Cavalry)...1st Cavalry Brigade
20th Lancers..1st Cavalry Brigade

The Artillery:
20, 21, 22, 23, 24 & 25 Indian Mountain Brigades
1 Royal (Kohat) Mtn Bty RA (FF), 3 (Peshawar) Mtn Bty RA (FF), 4 (Hazara) Mtn Bty RA (FF),
5 (Bombay) Mtn Bty RA, 8 (Lahore) Mtn Bty RA, 9 (Murree) Mtn Bty RA, 10 (Abbottabad) Mtn Bty RA, 12 (Poonch)
Mtn Bty RA, 16 (Zhob) Mtn Bty RA & 19 (Maymyo) Mtn Bty, RA

The Sappers & Miners:
King George V's Own Bengal Sappers & Miners
Nos. 3, 4 & 5 Field Companies
Royal Bombay Sappers & Miners
No. 22 Field Company
Queen Victoria's Sappers & Miners
No. 10 Field Company

Military Engineering Services

Survey of India
1 Indian Survey Section

The Indian Signal Service:

The Pioneers:
2nd Bombay Pioneers

The Infantry:
1/1st Punjab Regiment......................................Attached Risalpur Flying Column From Jhelum Thence 2 (Rawalpindi) Brigade
3/1st Punjab Regiment..? Brigade
5/2nd Punjab Regiment...Attached Fordham's Force – 1 (Abbottabad) Brigade
6/2nd Punjab Regiment..2 (Rawalpindi) Brigade
2/6th Rajput Regiment (PWO)..? Brigade
2/7th Rajput Regiment (PAV)...2 (Rawalpindi) Brigade
1/8th Punjab Regiment..To Kohat From Multan
3/8th Punjab Regiment...(Jhansi) Brigade
2/9th Jat Regiment (Mooltan)..(Jhansi) Brigade
1/10th Baluch Regiment (DCO)..? Brigade
2/10th Baluch Regiment...? Brigade
3/10th Baluch Regiment (QMO)..? Brigade
5/10th Baluch Regiment (KGO) (Jacob's Rifles)...? Brigade
1/11th Sikh Regiment (KGO) (Ferozepore Sikhs)...................................Peshawar District Troops Nowshera Column Thence
2 (Nowshera) Brigade
2nd Royal Battalion, 11th Sikh Regiment (Ludhiana Sikhs)...1 (Peshawar) Brigade
3/11th Sikh Regiment (Rattray's Sikhs)..(Jhansi) Brigade
4/11th Sikh Regiment..1 (Peshawar) Brigade
5/11th Sikh Regiment (DCO)..? Brigade
2/12th Frontier Force Regiment (Sikhs)...? Brigade
2/13th Frontier Force Rifles..2 (Nowshera) Brigade
6th Royal Bn, 13th Frontier Force Rifles (Scinde)...Waziristan
1/14th Punjab Regiment..? Brigade
1/15th Punjab Regiment..? Brigade

1/16th Punjab Regiment..? Brigade
2/17th Dogra Regiment...3 (Rawalpindi) Brigade
3/17th Dogra Regiment..2 (Nowshera) Brigade
2/18th Royal Garhwal Rifles..1 (Peshawar) Brigade
1/1st KGO Gurkha Rifles (The Malaun Regt.)...Support Battalion 2 (Nowshera) Brigade
1/3 Queen Alexandra's Own Gurkha Rifles..........................Peshawar District Reinforcement Nowshera Column Thence Fort Bara
2/4th Prince of Wales's Own Gurkha Rifles..? Brigade
2/5th Gurkha Rifles (Frontier Force)......................................Peshawar District From Abbottabad Nowshera Column Thence
2 Rawalpindi Brigade

The Indian Army Reserve of Officers:

The Militia, Auxiliary Forces India & Indian Territorial Force:
Kurram Militia
South Waziristan Scouts
Tochi Scouts
North West Railway Bn, AFI

The Indian Corps:
The Royal Indian Army Service Corps: (Including British Officers & NCO's)
'K' Supply Depot & 'M' Supply Depot (Individuals)
5 Divisional Supply Company
4 IBT Company
Nos. 2 & 29 Animal Transport Companies (Mules)
13 Motor Transport Company
MT Repair Shop Peshawar
18 DTT Company
21 DTT Company

Medical Units:
The Indian Medical Department / The Indian Hospital Corps /
The Queen Alexander's Military Nursing Service India
British Military Hospitals Peshawar & Nowshera – Individuals
Combined Military Hospitals Razmak, Bannu & Landi Kotal
Combined Indian General Hospital – Kohat
Indian Station Hospital – Jamrud
No. 1 Company, Indian Hospital Corps
2 Cavalry Field Ambulance, 1 Cavalry Brigade
Nos. 2, 7, 8, 11 & 18 Field Ambulances
Post Sanitary Sections
Brigade Casualty Clearing Stations

The Indian Army Veterinary Corps:

The Indian Army Ordnance Corps:

The Indian Corps of Clerks:

The Military Farms Department:
Grass Circles & Conservancy

The Police, Judiciary & Intelligence:
Frontier Constabulary, Jail Department & Frontier Intelligence Corps

The Postal Department:

The Indian Ecclesiastical Department:

The Political & Civil Departments:

6. BURMA 1930–1932

~ India General Service Medal 1908–1935 ~
BURMA 1930–32
Issue 3. Royal Mint

The 'BURMA 1930–32' clasp was sanctioned by Army Order 94 of September 1933. The clasp rewarded troops and certain war mobilised civilians employed under the command of Major General F.E. Coningham during the suppression of the Saya San Rebellion. Examples of The India General Service Medal 1908–1935 bearing the 'BURMA 1930–32' clasp named to Royal Air Force personnel are extremely rare. Some personnel from both the British and Indian establishments qualified for both the 'NORTH WEST FRONTIER 1930–31' and the 'BURMA 1930–32' clasps.

To qualify for the 'BURMA 1930–32' clasp to the India General Service Medal 1908–1935, personnel had to satisfy the following criteria:

- Be engaged on active service in the Province of Burma within the following civil districts between 22nd December 1930 and 25th March 1932 inclusive:

  Bassein, Hanthawaddy, Henzada, Insein, Kyaukse, Lower Chindwin, Mandalay, Maubin, Mawe, Meiktila, Minbu, Myaungmya, Myingyan, Pakokku, Pegu, Prome, Pyapon, Sagaing, Shan States North, Shan States South, Shwebo, Thayetmyo, Tharrawaddy, Toungoo and Yamethin.

In 1930 Burma was a remote and largely underdeveloped province of British India. The region had fallen to British rule in stages between 1853 and 1889 following the conclusion of several successful military campaigns against local rulers. Vast tracts of wilderness separated the populated areas of Lower Burma from the main Indian hinterland. This situation often gave rise to a feeling of isolation from mainstream Indian society and politics. Upper Burma was sparsely populated. Offshore, in the Bay of Bengal, lay the Andaman and Nicobar Islands. The Burmese were more oriental in both culture and religious practices than were the citizens of India. Buddhism was the principle faith rather than Islam or Hinduism.

During the period under review, much of central Upper Burma remained largely unexplored. British influence in the remoter regions was largely restricted to trade routes along the Irrawaddy and Chindwin Rivers combined with the immediate environs of the strategic railway route that ran northeast from Rangoon to Myitkyina via Mandalay. A second mainline railway route ran northwest from Rangoon to

~ The charismatic Saya San ~

Prome on the west coast. Road communications beyond Rangoon were treacherous. A principal feature of the 1930–32 campaign was the wide spread use of both river craft and trains for patrolling purposes.

There are two main seasons in Burma, the wet and the dry. The monsoon generally lasts from the end of April until October during which significant rainfall can be experienced. As much as 200 inches can fall on the central uplands, while coastal regions, such as Rangoon, can receive as much as 90 inches. The damp environment, combined with an average mean temperature of 82° F, which frequently soars above 100° F, engenders malarial infestation and often leads to fever-induced death among European residents and visitors. During military operations in the nineteenth century, disease was the principle cause of mortality among European troops deployed. For this reason, the medical authorities invested substantial resources during the operations of 1930–32 to prevent a repeat of previous circumstances. This investment proved to be only partially successful. In 1930, dengue fever broke out among the men of 1st Bn, Ox and Bucks LI. While most personnel suffered a mild form of infection the commanding officer, Lieutenant Colonel A.E. Sanderson, was eventually invalided back to Britain where he subsequently died.

Sir Charles Innes, Governor of Burma, maintained his administration in the capital Rangoon. In 1930, Burma was sparsely garrisoned compared with the average Indian Province. This was an anomaly considering Burma's strategic position on the frontier between British India and China. The GOC Burma Independent District, Major General F.E. Coningham, had at his immediate disposal a limited force consisting of the (Rangoon) Infantry Brigade, Brigadier General C.F. Watson, supported by 7 (Bengal) Mountain Battery, RA, a field company of 2nd Queen Victoria's Own of Madras Sappers and Miners and details including Burma District Signals. Several battalions of the Burma Military Police augmented this force. Not all troops could be committed on operations, however, due to the need to defend the established military stations and arsenals at, in, and around Mingaladon Cantonment near Rangoon. Further, a company level garrison furnished by the Rangoon Brigade was permanently committed to the Andaman Islands in the Bay of Bengal while two battalions of the Burma Rifles were permanently deployed outside the province. A token RAF presence was maintained at Mingaladon aerodrome by units from Singapore. Military hospitals were located at Mingaladon, Mandalay and Maymyo. The movement of casualties between these locations by rail was established practice.

*

The principle catalyst for the troubles in Burma during the early 1930s was the economic recession that had spread rapidly throughout the globe following the 1929 Wall Street Crash. This crisis was combined simultaneously by a growing desire on the part of Burmese intellectual groups for separation from British India under a new constitutional arrangement establishing a 'direct' relationship with London. The Burmese had been disillusioned by the deliberations of the Simon Commission (1927–30) pertaining to Indian legislative reform and self-government. Consequently, professional and mercantile classes held high expectations when a delegation of Burmese politicians was invited to accompany Governor Innes to the 1930 India Round table Conference in London.

The discussions in London were frank. The Burmese were no longer prepared to be controlled by the Government of India on matters of taxation, commercial tariffs and the burden of a defence budget largely consumed by constant conflict on the Indian North West Frontier. Burma's principle export commodities consisted of hard wood forest products and rubber goods. These industries had increasingly fallen into decline as the global slump took hold. The scarcity of employment led to serious antipathy on the part of the indigenous Burmese towards the vast population of Indian, Chinese and Malay migrant workers who traditionally formed a large part of the nation's workforce. When these 'foreign' workers were used to break labour strikes in urban areas, such as Mandalay and Rangoon, the Burmese resorted to violent demonstrations.

On 2nd December 1930, the chair of the India Round Table Conference, Lord Sankey, agreed to the creation of a Burma Sub Committee, under the leadership of Lord Russell. This committee was charged with agreeing a solution for Burma. The outcome of these deliberations was a recommendation that Burma should indeed be established as an entity separate from India. Direct representation in the British Government would be established via a new Secretary of State for India and Burma. Dominion status would eventually be granted although a separate parliamentary commission would be required to determine the shape and process of this transition. The British Prime Minister, Ramsey MacDonald, however, determined to defer his support for this motion and the conference broke up with no firm plan in place.

The lack of resolution in London was received with vehement condemnation in Rangoon by the General Council of All Burmese Associations. This influential Buddhist professional organisation was dominated by the educated elite and for some years had been affiliated with the Indian Congress Movement led by M.K. Ghandi. The lack of official ratification for Burmese separation from India led many leading members of the Association to believe that Britain would stall the creation of a Burmese Constitution. Without a credible deal on this matter, it was easy to speculate that the conferring of Dominion Status would never materialise. It was therefore widely believed that the only solution for the long-term future of Burma was full independence from Britain along the same lines as the settlement that Ghandi was seeking for India.

*

In 1924, the General Council of Burmese Associations appointed a man called Saya San from Amherst District, to establish a rural affairs committee and report on the plight of the peasantry in central Burma. Evidence suggests that Saya San determined to manipulate this worthy Commission for personal advantage. Over time, it seems that his influence among the uneducated and poverty-stricken residents of Insein and Tharrawaddy Districts became so intense that they willingly agreed to appoint him as their 'sovereign' and defender of the Buddhist faith.

In this (deluded) mindset, Saya San styled himself the 'Only Golden Crow' following a mock 'coronation' at the Myasein Taung-Yo Pagoda on 28th October 1930. Employing a blend of religious mysticism and sorcery, he succeeded in raising a force of warriors charged with attacking British interests and encouraging acceleration along the road to independence. These men were perceived by the British as being little more than brigands. They possessed few weapons and relied on opiates and mystical charms to ward off the threat of 'government bullets'. Volunteers in Saya San's 'army' received a tattoo of the Gallon Hawk on their wrist. This practice led to the authorities designating the force the 'Black Hawks'.

The Burmese rice harvest of 1930 was one of the most bountiful in living memory. Unfortunately, the already depressed world market found it impossible to carry such a surplus and prices fell to below cost. This placed further strain on the Burmese rural economy. Already behind on their annual Land Revenue payments, farmers the length and breadth of the country petitioned their village elders to seek postponement of tax enforcement by their local distict authorities. The situation was not helped when reports were published in the Rangoon press suggesting that a consortium of British rice millers had been actively depressing the market for their own purposes. To postpone the collection of any tax would have had serious financial implications for the virtually bankrupt Government of Burma. Consequently, Governor Innes refused to endorse any revenue concessions, preferring instead to review the matter once he had returned from the India Round Table conference in London.

In late November 1930, Saya San relocated his rudimentary headquarters to a remote location deep in the Yomas Forest of Tharrawaddy District. A wooden 'citadel' was built on the summit of Alaungtaung Hill and several outposts established in the surrounding area. Emissaries were despatched to local settlements and villages to gauge likely support for the Black Hawk agenda. This period coincided with official notification from the Provincial Government that revenue inspectors were to enforce the gathering of Capitation Tax on 1st January 1931. Consequently, Saya San's intelligence gathering suggested that if an insurrection against the British was to be initiated, now would be a good time to begin.

*

On 23rd November 1930, Mr. H.V.W. Fields-Clarke, a government forest conservancy engineer, was reported missing in the Weywa area of the Yomas Forest. A routine investigation by the civil police discovered the smouldering remains of Mr. Fields-Clarke's bungalow combined with evidence suggesting forced abduction. Further investigation by a patrol of the Burma Military Police under Captain Rust led to a brief but indecisive engagement with a party of Black Hawks. Meanwhile, a second Black Hawk force laid siege to the civil police post at Yedaik. Intelligence gathered from prisoners taken during these incidents gave the authorities their first appreciation of the seriousness of recent rumours that an insurrection was being planned.

~ British Burmese troops 1930 ~

These were not isolated acts. Police Headquarters in Tharrawaddy received several reports of terror incidents throughout the region over the ensuing 48 hours. Villages were razed to the ground and populations massacred if they refused to recognise Saya San as their 'sovereign'. British commercial installations and forestry camps were particularly singled out as targets. By 26th December 1930, concerns that the growing violence might spread to urban areas led to a decision calling for Major General F.E. Coningham to deploy part of his command in aid of the civil power. The Rangoon Infantry Brigade at Mingaladon Cantonment was thereupon mobilised with immediate effect. The Maymyo Brigade was initially only placed on alert but ultimately deployed men ahead of the Rangoon Brigade.

On 28th December 1930, all District Commissioners and their deputies received a signal from HQ Burma District advising them that the insurrection appeared to be contained in southeast Tharrawaddy and northeast Insein Districts. Military resources were about to deploy and further troop movements were expected. An estimated 1,500 rebels were at large. Civil police officers and local officials were to advise all village headmen that anyone found guilty of aiding and abetting a member of the Black Hawks would be severely punished.

Intelligence gathered from subsequent prisoners during police operations gave the authorities the impression they were not dealing with fanatics but rather the impressionable and ignorant, many of whom were openly disillusioned, if not surprised, by the lack of protection their lucky charms had afford them. The captives identified the location of Saya San's position on Alaungtaung Hill. On 30th December 1930, a mixed force of 2/20th Burma Rifles and 3/20th Burma (Kachin) Rifles, was despatched to the Yomas Forest region under Major Hare with a view to destroying the Black Hawk camp and breaking up the rebel threat. The dense forest made this manoeuvre more difficult than anticipated and the key element of surprise was lost when 500 Black Hawks stumbled across the striking forces' forming-up position. During the ensuing firefight the Army accounted for over 100 of the enemy. Several survivors escaped the battle and succeeded in alerting Saya San of the approaching troops. When the enemy position was captured on 1st January 1931, the area was found to be deserted. During the ensuing sweep of the area, various items of personal property belonging to Mr. H.V.W. Fields-Clarke were recovered. Following the capture of Alantaung Hill, Lieutenant Colonel C. de M. Wellborne, Deputy Inspector General of Police, reported to the Government of Burma that the rebellion had been crushed. This assertion proved to be premature. The loss of Alantaung Hill did not prove to be a decisive blow to Saya San and the rebels, who had established a supplementary position some time previously on the summit of Taungbyat Mountain, as San reformed and began planning renewal acts of terrorism.

On 3rd January 1931, 'A' Company, 1st Bn, Ox and Bucks LI, under Captain H. Vernon, entrained for Shwebo District with a view to maintaining a moveable column in the region. Three days later the 2/15th Punjab Regt. deployed into the field from Rangoon followed shortly thereafter by 'A' Company, 1st Bn, Buffs, commanded by Major N.S. Hart. Mobility for this small force came in the form of six hastily requisitioned Rangoon Corporation omnibuses. (The Buffs remained in the field for only two days before returning to Rangoon to assist in the quelling of riots that had broken out between refugees from the Burman interior and the local unemployed). Meanwhile, the Provincial Government imposed stringent press censorship following inflammatory articles in the *Rangoon Times* calling for the population to employ 'Ghandi' style tactics to secure their freedom from Britain.

Saya San, who had by now had elevated himself to 'King of the Dragons', issued a proclamation on 7th January 1931 stating that he had declared war on all Englishmen for the benefit of the Rahan (the Buddhist priesthood's 'philosophical' foundation) and the religious health of the nation. His statement said that Indian, Chinese, Shan or Karen inhabitants were not to be molested. All Burmese citizens in the pay of the British would be pardoned if they surrendered themselves to Saya San's authority.

Rebel activity intensified in the days following the assault on Alantaung Hill. In the Dedaye area, the civil police succeeded in fending off several conserted attacks directed towards villages considered by the Black Hawks to be loyal to the Government. Elsewhere the 2/15th Punjab Regt. divided itself into company and platoon strength columns deployed to aggressively sweep tracts of forest for potential enemy patrol bases. The level of resistance encountered, combined with ongoing rebel assaults against civilian targets, led the Provincial Government to recognise the need to prepare for a longer-term campaign than had been predicted. On 8th January 1931 notification of an offer to pay a reward of Rs 5,000 for the capture of Saya San was circulated to all district authorities and police units.

On 13th January 1931, the day Governor Innes returned to Burma from the India Round Table Conference, rebel gangs began targeting remote sections of the Burmese railway network. The strategically important station at Zibyugan was particularly singled out for an attack that left several railway staff dead. To counter such activity the military authorities established the running of an armoured train north from Rangoon along the route to Mandalay and thence to Myitkyina. Manned by men of 1st Buffs, under Lieutenant G.L.B. Oliver and crewed by a detachment of the Burma Railway Battalion, AFI. The train did a grand job of 'flying the flag' for the Government of Burma but seldom, if ever, actually prevented any enemy activity.

Coordinated police raids were conducted against all 150 branches of the General Council of Burmese Associations including the organisation's Rangoon headquarters. No arrests were made, although significant quantities of documents were seized in an attempt to verify (alleged) links between sections of the GCBA and Saya San. Further, possible sponsorship and funding by Congress Party supporters in India required investigation and verification.

U So Nynn, an influential Burma Legislative Council member, had for some weeks realised that there were two distinct issues at play in Burma each of which affected different segments of society but which could, at the same time, encourage bloodshed on a national basis. Thus, in an attempt to end the stalemate regarding Burma's political future and at the sametime bring recognition to the national rice market crisis and its role in facilitating support for Saya San, U So Nynn determined to place before the Legislative Council session on 30th January 1931 several key draft resolutions. These proposals called on the British Government to immediately commence the drafting of a constitution for a separate Burma with an opt-out clause if at some stage in the future the Burmese electorate decided they would rather remain affiliated to India once the latter's political future had been determined. The proposals also called for immediate restrictions on Indian migration into Burma and sought the establishment of an impartial committee to investigate the alleged manipulation of the rice market by British millers. Unfortunately, no specific consensus of opinion was achieved in council, although a month later a resolution was passed forcing further debate about land tax reform.

On January 31st 1931, the Viceroy of India, Lord Willingdon, signed into law a special decree known as Ordnance 1 of 1931. This was designed to assist the Government of Burma in the delivery of swift justice for all persons found guilty of seditious behaviour or actively supporting the ongoing insurrection by empowering all District Commissioners to authorise arrests and property searches without warrant. Upon receipt of this decree in council, Governor Innes proscribed the General Council of Burmese Associations which, following the sifting of intelligence obtained during the earlier police raids on its offices, was alledged to be in league with the current insurrection.

February 1931 saw the spread of anti-British activity west from Tharrawaddy into the coastal province of Henzada. Minor contacts between the security forces and Black Hawk sympathisers steadily increased. On 22nd February, some 400 villagers attacked a Burma Military Police patrol near Ingwa. The military police, under Assistant Superintendant Smart, responded robustly and killed 25 enemy.

~ Armoured train, Burma 1930–32 ~

Unfortunately, reports of excessive brutality on the part of the authorities during some of these engagements began to appear in the Rangoon press. Several officers were committed to trial, but it was difficult to substantiate the charges as witnesses feared arrest should they come forward.

Military activities in March and early April 1931 were concentrated along the boundary between Tharrawaddy and Insein Districts. A sharp firefight near Okkan on 7th April lead to the death of at least one Burma Military Police sepoy and the serious wounding of an Inspector. Several days later, during a confrontation at Okpo, 12 Black Hawks were killed including the alleged rebel strategist General Boh San Htu. In mid-April the uprising spread further north and crossed into Thayetmyo District where, on 15th April, Superintendant H.C. Smith was injured in an ambush. The Government forestry camp at Yenatha in Tharrawaddy District was targeted by a large force of Black Hawks on 22nd April. The facility, managed by Mr. F. Tait, was subjected to a prolonged assault despite the area being allegedly under the protection of a detachment of Burma Military Police under Assistant Superintenant F. Bestall. The enemy fled only after Government reinforcements arrived.

The Burmese media was clearly divided between support for the insurrection, under the guise of reform, and support for the Government. Apart from lengthy articles ridiculing assertions regarding the strength and determination of the Black Hawks, most called for reform rather than bullets. Pressure was directed against both London and Delhi to rcome to a long-term political settlement. Fear that separation would lead to Crown Colony status being imposed rather than the desired option of Dominion Status being adopted was a subject openly debated. On one thing, all editors were agreed. Unless more troops were committed into the Burmese hinterland to quell the rising tide of support for Saya San there would eventually be a national bloodbath.

During early May 1931, Back Hawk violence spread to Prome District. A detachment of civil police under District Superintendant W.H. Austin was massacred by rebels on 5th May near the village of Myoma. Only two police officers escaped. The mutilated and burnt bodies of the slain were recovered some days later. Further incidents throughout the troubled regions over the ensuing days were met with tough responses from the over stretched security forces. In an attempt to kerb the spread of militancy, Headquarters Burma Independent District established a blockade line radiating west from Meiktila to the Bay of Bengal. This strategy proved futile despite the deployment of reinforcements into the region in the form of 1/17th Dogra Regt. from Jubbulpore and 'A' Company, 1st Bn Ox and Bucks LI from Wetwin Camp.

DISPOSITIONS 1ST BN, OXFORDSHIRE & BUCKINGHAMSHIRE LIGHT INFANTRY, 5TH MAY 1931

A Company	B Company	C Company	HQ Company
Meiktila	HQ Burma District, Sale Bks, Rangoon	Mandalay	Maymyo

By mid May 1931, the authorities finally decided there were simply insufficient troops in Burma to effectively quell the insurrection. Intelligence suggesting that rebels under the command of Aung Galog Myo were actively recruiting support in Lashio and throughout the Northern Shan Sates resulted in urgent requests for further reinforcements to be despatched from India. These received a positive response from Field Marshal P. Chetwode, Commander-in-Chief India, and on 26th May, the 12th Infantry Brigade, Brigadier H.E.R.R. Braine, was mobilised for active duty in Burma while a further two Indian Army infantry battalions were instructed to prepare for deployment at short notice.

The 12th Infantry Brigade arrived in Rangoon in stages by steamer from Calcutta. The 3/16th Punjab Regt. disembarked on 1st June 1931 followed several days later by 2nd Bn, Manchester Regt. and finally 3/10th Baluch Regt. accompanied by support units such as 28 Field Ambulance, RAMC from Lucknow. The troops were immediately deployed by train to Mandalay in an attempt to stop the northerly spread of violence. No cavalry units had been deployed due to fear of infection from the deadly equine Surra disease. Instead, an irregular corps of mounted infantry was raised from volunteers employing local Burmese ponies who were virtually immune to the Surra infection. To facilitate effective communication between civil and military commands the District Commissioner of Pegu, Mr. Booth-Gravely, was appointed Special Liaison Commissioner. (Further reinforcements from India in the form of the 2/5th Mahratta LI and the 3/6th Rajputana Rifles arrived in July).

OFFICIAL CASUALTY RETURNS CORRECT TO 10TH JUNE 1931

	Killed	Wounded
Army	5	5
Burma Military Police	12	41
Burma Civil Police	32	27

Operations in southern Burma intensified during late May and early June 1931. The 2/15th Punjab Regt. conducted themselves admirably throughout, especially during difficult operations in Prome District. On 5th June, however, a regrettable incident occurred following the pursuit of an enemy party. A patrol of the regiment, commanded by Captain Lane, surprised a party of Black Hawks in a poorly defended patrol base. Shots were exchanged and some 22 rebels were killed. Mr. Stevenson, a civilian intelligence officer attached to Captain Lane's command, thereupon requested that all of the corpses be transported to brigade headquarters for identification. This request was somewhat unrealistic given the small number of troops available. By way of compromise, Captain Lane misguidedly agreed to simply decapitate each of the bodies and have his troops carry the severed heads home in several large sacks. A court of inquiry was eventually convened to review the circumstances of these events but Captain Lane and Civil Officer Stevenson were acquitted because of their previous exemplary conduct.

During mid-June 1931, the Government of Burma came under increasing pressure from various civic leaders, as well as the media, to grant amnesty to all Black Hawks willing to submit themselves to the authorities. This followed the sentencing to death of 12 captured rebels in Rangoon on 11th June. Governor Innes found merit in this proposal since all of the prisons in both Rangoon and Mandalay were experiencing severe overcrowding. An initial amnesty proclamation was found wanting. A revised version was published on 29th June granting a more liberal and practical solution.

Terms of Amnesty Dated 29th June 1931
- The Government of Burma to grant a free pardon to all rebels who surrender themselves to Government forces within one month of the amnesty being posted in their home district.

- Persons wishing to surrender to swear never again to take up arms against the British Crown.

- No rebel accused of murder or similar outrage to be granted amnesty until tried and acquitted by an appropriate court.

- A roll of all known rebels ineligible for amnesty to be posted in each district.

On 5th July 1931, the Provincial Government declared that the insurrection had officially spread to the Northern Shan States. Army patrolling in the region increased and diplomatic ties with the local semi-autonomous Sawbwas chieftains improved. A Burma Military Police force, under Captain Forbes, was deployed along the Nam Yao River and came into contact with an enemy formation near Nalu Ferry located some 40 miles from Hsipaw. The ensuing engagement was vicious with neither side prepared to yield. The Burma Military Police eventually carried the position, recovering 40 Black Hawk corpses and taking prisoner several wound rebels.

The fanaticism demonstrated by Aung Myo's men at Nalu Ferry surprised the military authorities. Superintendant Grose, commander of police units in the Northern Shan States, immediately requested the deployment of more troops to the region. The strategically important Mandalay–Lashio railway was considered a prime target for enemy interference and accordingly the route was thereupon picqueted by men of the Lashio Battalion, Burma Military Police under Captain Cartmel. Particular attention was paid by this force to the protection of the Gokteik viaduct and, accordingly, men of the Taunggyi Battalion, Burma Military Police under Captain Wallace and 2/20th Burma Rifles, supported by a platoon of 1st Bn, Ox and Bucks LI, under Lieutenant J D Palmer, were deployed to provide additional coverage. Offensive action in the Northern Shan States was coordinated by Superintendant Grouse from Police Headquarters in Nawnghkia and, within a relatively short space of time, the Black Hawk threat had been contained in an area north of the Shweli River.

Although a significant number of Black Hawks took advantage of the Government's amnesty terms in Prome District, the general uptake elsewhere was poor. Widespread skirmishes and outrages persisted. On 14th July 1931, a patrol of Burma Military Police, under Captain L V Dart, was attacked while searching an abandoned settlement in Pegu District. Two sepoys were killed during this incident. Captain Dart was seriously wounded and needed to be evacuated to the military hospital in Rangoon. Some time later, three platoons of Burma Rifles, under Captain Balding, accompanied by a detachment of Burma Military Police, under Captain McCarthy, were engaged while patrolling in the Ton Hills region of Thayetmyo District. The enemy eventually fled after a brisk fight leaving four of its number dead and several wounded.

On 24th July 1931, the Government of Burma sanctioned attempts by five influential Buddhist monks, led by a priest named Aletawaya Sayadaw, to mediate between rebel factions and the security forces in both Insein and Tharrawaddy Districts. For several weeks, the monks roamed the forests preaching a message of forgiveness for those willing to surrender. Unfortunately, this mission met (initially) with only limited success.

The apparent lack of desire on the part of the rebel rank and file to surrender during July 1931 prompted the Government to take a firmer stance. The Burma Emergency Powers Ordnance was signed into law by the Viceroy of India on 2nd August. This legislation extended further the special powers available to Governor Innes to curb the insurrection. Henceforth it would be a criminal offence for any Burmese citizen to have any communication what-so-ever with a suspected Black Hawk. Anyone with any information regarding the whereabouts, or activities, of persons connected with the insurrection was required to surrender that information fully to the nearest magistrate, police or military representative. The withholding of any information liable to be of use to the authorities would be considered a criminal act.

Saya San was captured during a Burma Military Police operation on the Mandalay–Southern Shan States border on 3rd August 1931. He had apparently escaped a military attack on his position only days previously. The rebel leader did not resist arrest and upon identification was despatched to Rangoon for trial. Many rebel lieutenants, wary of possible government propaganda, were reluctant to believe the news of his arrest. Moreover, as some of them, were only loosely aligned with Saya San, they were more than content to continue their activities. Saya San was executed by the authorities in Rangoon during late November.

By mid-August 1931, the General Council of Burmese Associations, recognising that their tacit support for the rebellion had seriously damaged their wider political appeal, declared that in future all of their members would seek improvements in Burma's political settlement via constitutional consensus. They would no longer accept that violence was a medium for change. This decision may have been due to the fact that post the capture of Saya San, the rebels that remained in the field became even more ferocious in their attacks upon their compatriots. Alternatively, it may have been that Whithall had declared its intent to hold a Burma Round Table Conference in London with the express purposes of agreeing the long-awaited Burmese Constitution.

With the end of the 1931 monsoon season, the authorities anticipated an increase in rebel activity. This failed to materialise due to infighting among the few Black Hawk leaders still at large. Those attacks that did occur now tended to be related to the stealing of food and the kidnapping of women. On 23rd October 1931, the religious mission led by Aletawaya Sayadaw let it be known that they would excommunicate all Black Hawks who failed to surrender by the end of the month. This had a salutary effect on those remaining in the field and, on 18th November, the principal remaining Black Hawk leader, Saya Mya, instructed his men to bury their weapons and return peacefully to their villages.

Although rebel activity had all but ended by November 1931, it took several months before the rural Burmese civil population recovered their confidence in the ability of the authorities to protect them. Normality returned in degrees. On 7th January 1932, for example, Governor Innes presented 1st Bn, Buffs with new Colours during a formal public review in Rangoon. Active operations continued, including several long river patrols by 'C' Company, 1st Bn, Ox & Bucks LI up the Chidwin during February. It was not until 22nd March, however, that all of the troops deployed to crush the insurrection were stood down and the civil police once again resumed total responsibility for law and order.

* * *

COMMAND STRUCTURE, BURMA 1930–1931

Commander Burma
Maj. Gen. F E Coningham
Brigade Commanders
Brig. C F Watson
(Rangoon) Brigade
Brig. H E R R Braine
12 (Secunderabad) Brigade

Royal Air Force:		
Detachment From Far Eastern Command - Singapore		
Squadron	Home Station	Aircraft
No. 36 Squadron	RAF Seletar	Torpedo Bomber Sqn
No. 205 Squadron	RAF Seletar	Flying Boat

BRITISH ARMY ROLL OF HONOUR
BURMA 1930–1932

Date:	Person:	Unit:	Comment:
26/11/31	3520208 Pte T Bennett	2nd Bn, Manchester Regt.	Died
?	6282598 Pte F W Dibble	1st Bn, Buffs	Died
?	6284168 Pte M S Drew	1st Bn, Buffs	Died
?	6282768 Pte A Hill	1st Bn, Buffs	Died
?	6282328 Pte P Jenner	1st Bn, Buffs	Died
?	6282759 L/Cpl G W Legg	1st Bn, Buffs	Died
1/9/32	2564210 L/Cpl F Mc Manus	2nd Bn, Manchester Regt.	Died of Wounds / Injury?
?	6283097 Pte A Mansfield	1st Bn, Buffs	Died
?	6282795 Pte S Moverley	1st Bn, Buffs	Died
?	6188525 CQMS T E J Pratt	1st Bn, Buffs	Died
Jan 1933	Lt Col A E Sanderson	1st Bn, Ox & Bucks LI	From Dengue Fever In UK
?	Lt A B Slessor	1st Bn, Ox & Bucks LI	Died
?	6282419 Pte J E Tyrell	1st Bn, Buffs	Died
	1849243 CSM J W Walker	Royal Engineers	Died

BURMA 1930–32[10] ROLL

BRITISH ESTABLISHMENT
THE ARMY

~ Staff Grade Officers ~

Note a.   *Only Officers of the British Army are listed. Officers of the Indian Establishment are beyond the scope of this work and are thus excluded.*

Note b.   *Medals named in thin impressed capitals.*

Brigadiers: ~ H E R R Braine[1(Lt.)&10] Cmd. 12 Bde. & C F Watson[10] Cmd. Rangoon Bde. Area

Colonels: ~ P R C Commings[10] 2ic Rangoon Bde. Area, M C Festing[10] Staff HQ Burma Indpt. Dist, P J Hanafin[10] Staff HQ Burma Indpt. Dist, J P Lynch[10] BMH Maymyo & J W West[10] ADMS Burma Indpt. Dist

THE ROYAL TANK CORPS:

Note a.   *Roll of all personnel identified as eligible.*

Note b.   *Medals named in thin impressed capitals: 'R. TANK C.'*

Single Clasp	No. Identified	Rarity
Burma 1930–32[10]	1	According to the roll as seen, can be considered Unique

Lieutenant: ~ J C B Shearer[10]

THE ROYAL ARTILLERY:
Batteries Identified As Entitled:
7 (Bengal) Mountain Battery

Note a.   *Roll of all British personnel identified as eligible.*

Note b.   *All recipients served with 7 Mountain Battery, Royal Artillery, (RA) unless shown otherwise.*

Note c.   *Medals named in thin impressed capitals: 'R.A.'*

Single Clasp	No. Identified	Rarity
Burma 1930–32[10]	4	Of the Utmost Rarity
Combination Clasps	**No. Identified**	**Rarity**
Burma 1930–32[10] North West Frontier 1935[12]	2	Of the Utmost Rarity

Majors: ~ B J Bewley[10]

Captains: ~ G W Courtenay[10&12] & C H P Jeffery[10] attch. HQ 12 Indpt. Bde.

Lieutenants: ~ J H B Evatt[10] attch. Staff Burma Indpt. Dist, J H H Willans[10&12(Capt.)] & A W Woodrooffe[10]

THE CORPS OF ROYAL ENGINEERS:
Sub Units Identified As Entitled:
Royal Engineer Officers Attached Military Engineering Services
King George's Own Bengal Sappers and Miners
Queen Victoria's Own Sappers and Miners

Note a.   *Roll of all personnel identified as eligible.*
Note b.   *Medals named in thin impressed capitals: 'R.E.'*

Single Clasp	No. Identified	Rarity
Burma 1930–32[10]	19	Extremely Rare

Combination Clasps	No. Identified	Rarity
Afghanistan N.W.F. 1919[3] Burma 1930–32[10]	1	According to the roll as seen, can be considered Unique
Waziristan 1919–21[4] Waziristan 192–24[6] Burma 1930–32[10]	1	According to the roll as seen, can be considered Unique
Waziristan 1919–21[4] Burma 1930–32[10]	2	Of the Utmost Rarity
Waziristan 1921–24[6] North West Frontier 1930–31[9] Burma 1930–32[10]	3	Of the Utmost Rarity
Waziristan 1921–24[6] Burma 1930–32[10]	1	According to the roll as seen, can be considered Unique
North West Frontier 1930–31[9] Burma 1930–32[10]	27	Very Rare
North West Frontier 1930–31[9] Burma 1930–32[10] Mohmand 1933[11]	3	Of the Utmost Rarity
North West Frontier 1930–31[9] Burma 1930–32[10] North West Frontier 1935[12]	1	According to the roll as seen, can be considered Unique

Lieutenant Colonels: ~ C Preedy[3(Maj.)&10] MES

Majors: ~ R Briggs[10] MES GE Burma Indpt. Dist & I Simson[10] MES

Captains: ~ E F E Armstrong[9&10], T C W Bowen[10], G K Cassels[10] QVO S&M, R St. C Davidson[9,10&11] KGO S&M, A M Garnett[6(Lt.)&10] QVO S&M, S G Hudson[10] GE attch. 12 Bde., R C P James[10], MES, A H G Napier[6(Lt.),9&10], W E C Pettman[10] MES, E E G L Searight[4(Lt.)&10] QVO S&M & W D A Williams[10] GE Maymyo Dist

Lieutenants: ~ S H M Battye[9&10] KGO S&M, R I C Blenkinsop[9&10] KGO S&M, W J Cardale[9&10] KGO S&M, G G S Clarke[9&10] KGO S&M, E F B Cook[9&10] QVO S&M, M du B Floyer[9&10] QVO S&M, L T Grove[9&10] KGO S&M, A B Hayden[10] attch. Burma Public Works Dept Irrigation Branch Minbu & Thayetmyo Dists, R E Holloway[9,10&11(Capt.)] KGO S&M, S G Hudson[10], E H Ievers[9&10], L F R Kenyon[6,9&10], A W Kiggell[9&10] KGO S&M, R E Lloyd[9&10] KGO S&M, I G Loch[9&10] KGO S&M, H M O'Donnell[10] QVO S&M, L A B Paten[9&10] KGO S&M, M C Perceval[9&10], G A T Pritchard[9&10] KGO S&M, F. R Rowbotham[10] QVO S&M, J M Seagert[10] QVO S&M, D G H Tuite[10] 12 Fld Coy, QVO S&M & J C Walkey[9&10] KGO S&M

Warrant Officers Class II: ~ 1835370 F J Godfrey[9&10] KGO S&M, 1854281 A Greenhalgh[4(Cpl.),6(Cpl.)&10] QVO S&M, 1853663 E C Odell[6(Sgt.),9&10] KGO S&M, 1853555 F C Rowe[10] QVO S&M & 1849243 J W Walker[9&10] KGO S&M

Quartermaster Sergeants /Sergeants: ~ 1853109 H Aiken[9&10] KGO S&M, 1859998 W Budden[9,10&11] KGO S&M, 1862808 R W Edwards[10] QVO S&M, 1854464 J Fisher[9&10] KGO S&M, 1859817 T Jones[9&10] KGO S&M, 1853204 E Letten[9&10] KGO S&M, 1860132 R O'N Lyth[10] QVO S&M, 1852562 J W Rainey[9&10] KGO S&M, 1859593 H E Smith[9&10] KGO S&M, 1856641 C E H Ward[10] QVO S&M & 1860069 A Wilson[9&10] KGO S&M

Lance Sergeants/Corporals: ~ 1864132 J Brown[9,10&12(Sgt.)] KGO S&M, 1859987 G M Crimp[10] QVO S&M, 5492083 W J L Plowman[9&10] KGO S&M & 1865283 H G Wells[9&10] KGO S&M

THE ROYAL CORPS OF SIGNALS:
Sub Units Identified As Entitled:
4 Indian Divisional Signals – Ex 'F' & 'G' Sections (Remained India)
1 Pack Wireless Section – 'A' Corps Signals (From Karachi)
8 Pack Wireless Section – 'B' Corps Signals (From Rawalpindi)
1 Heavy Pack Cable Section – 3 Divisional Signals (From Meerut)
Burma Independent Brigade Signals Section
Burma Military Police Wireless Group

Note a.   *Roll of all personnel identified as eligible.*
Note b.   *Medals named in thin impressed capitals: 'R. SIGNALS'*

Single Clasp	No. Identified	Rarity
Burma 1930–32[10]	113	Very Scarce

Combination Clasps	No. Identified	Rarity
Waziristan 1919–21[4] Waziristan 1921–24[6] North West Frontier 1930–31[9] Burma 1930–32[10]	1	According to the roll as seen, can be considered Unique
Waziristan 1919–21[4] Waziristan 1921–24[6] Burma 1930–32[10]	1	According to the roll as seen, can be considered Unique
Malabar 1921–22[7] Waziristan 1921–24[6] Burma 1930–32[10]	1	According to the roll as seen, can be considered Unique
Malabar 1921–22[7] Burma 1930–32[10]	1	According to the roll as seen, can be considered Unique
Waziristan 1921–24[6] Burma 1930–32[10]	2	Of the Utmost Rarity
North West Frontier 1930–31[9] Burma 1930–32[10]	10	Of the Utmost Rarity
Burma 1930–32[10] Mohmand 1933[11]	4	Of the Utmost Rarity
Burma 1930–32[10] North West Frontier 1935[12]	1	According to the roll as seen, can be considered Unique

Majors: ~ A J Harris[6(Capt.)&10], P A Hitchcock[10] & W M Miller[10&11]

Captains: ~ A J A Schofield[10&12(Maj.)] & L V Younie[10] 4 IDS

Lieutenants: ~ L C C Harrison[10], J M C Hoblyn[9&10], H L Lewis[10&11] 'A' Corps Sigs attch. 4 IDS, H D Mountford[10] 4 IDS, L de M Thuillier[10] & R G Yolland[10] 'B' Corps Sigs attch. 4 IDS

Warrant Officers Class II: ~ 1856091 G F Mayes[10]

Company Quartermaster Sergeants/Staff Sergeants: ~ 1038999 W Potter[9&10]

Quartermaster Sergeants/Sergeants: ~ 2306277 P H R Batchelor[10], 534340 J D Fairman[10], 2311587 H Hamlin[10], 2311194 J Lawson[10], 2314124 J Lawson[6(Sgln.)&10], 5096526 R C Moult[10], 2309516 M Shardlow[7(Cpl.)&10] 'A' Corps Sigs attch. 4 IDS, 5820515 H Steed[9&10] 'A' Corps Sigs & 2312884 W H Winter[10] 4 IDS

Lance Sergeants/Corporals: ~ 2309558 W Bridge[10] 'A' Corps Sigs attch. 4 IDS, 2311334 C A Clance[10], 2311334 C A Clarke[10], 6449448 H S Cooper[10], 2313842 B Coy[9(L/Sgt.)&10] 'A' Corps Sigs attch. 4 IDS, 2315396 J V Evens[10], 6907860 E Field[9&10], 2316734 A Gerrish[9&10], 2314155 W M Hawkes[10], 2314450 J Knowles[10], 3123511 W MacDonald[10], 2314250 P McLachlan[9&10] 'A' Corps Sigs attch Wireless Group, Burma MP, 1417236 A Oates[10], 539712 A J Page[10], 2306662 S G Palmer[10], 2310828 J Peters[6(Sgln.-),7(Sgln.-)&10] 'B' Corps Sigs attch. 4 IDS, 2306779 C A Smith[10] 'B' Corps Sigs attch. 4 IDS & 2315203 J L Tanner[10] 'B' Corps Sigs attch. 4 IDS

Lance Corporals/Signalmen: ~ 2318324 P C G Andrews[10], 2316892 S R Attrill[10], 2318792 G Bailey[10], 2319117 G Barnett[10], 2317648 T S Barney[10], 2319489 T Beadmore[10] 'B' Corps Sigs attch. 4 IDS, 2318246 A F Bean[10], 2318264 J A Bennett[10], 2318581 B A Birley[10], 2317408 W Booth[10], 2316728 R H G Broom[10], 2562224 A Brown[10], 2318288 C A Chapman[10],

2563556 W J Church[10], 2317165 A M Clutton[10], 2318750 A C Cole[10], 2318646 H Constantine[10], 2316886 G Coop[10] 'A' Corps Sigs, 2316886 A Cooper[10] 'A' Corps Sigs, 2316747 J Costello[10], 2319804 J Crompton[10] 'A' Corps Sigs attch. 4 IDS, 2317942 G Dalton[10] 'A' Corps Sigs attch. 4 IDS, 2318249 A S H Daniels[10], 2310300 S Dean[10] 'A' Corps Sigs attch. 4 IDS, 2318380 S G Dean[10] 'A' Corps Sigs attch 4 IDS, 2319923 A E Dines[10&11] 'B' Corps Sigs attch. 4 IDS, 2318880 F Dixon[10] 'B' Corps Sigs attch. 4 IDS, 772350 T Edwards[10] 'A' Corps Sigs attch. 4 IDS, 2319111 L Francis[10], 5946032 A J Frith[10], 2319427 S W Furniss[10] 'B' Corps Sigs attch. 4 IDS, 2315414 R F Gilding[10], 2318932 D Given[10], 2317012 A Golding[10] 'A' Corps Sigs attch. 4 IDS, 1863581 W Gooding[10] 'A' Corps Sigs attch. 4 IDS, 2316210 K G Gray[10], 2319286 R F Green[10], 2314133 A Hamilton[10], 2317438 R Hardie[10] 'B' Corps Sigs attch. 4 IDS, 28953 G T Harvey[10], 2319647 A Hawkins[10], 2318345 J Hewett[10] 'A' Corps Sigs attch. 4 IDS, 2315576 A L Hills[9&10] 'B' Corps Sigs attch. 4 IDS, 2319725 J R Holt[10], 2319343 H Howell[10] 'A' Corps Sigs attch. 4 IDS, 2320150 R Irving[10&11] 'B' Corps Sigs attch. 4 IDS, 2319641 H Jamieson[10] 'A' Corps Sigs attch. 4 IDS, 2319069 R F Jamison[10], 2320028 H Johnson[10], 2309973 E R Jones[10], 2211824 F C Jones[10], 2317812 L Jones[10] 'A' Corps Sigs attch. 4 IDS, 2317182 L O R Jones[10], 2319854 R E Jones[10], 2318961 A Juniper[10], 2317570 W F Kent[10], 2317265 C H S Knight[10] 'A' Corps Sigs attch. 4 IDS, 2317282 S G Levick[10], 776683 H Levitt[10] 'B' Corps Sigs attch. 4 IDS, 2317935 P C MacDonald[10], 2318372 W Mair[10], 2319015 A McGuinness[10] 'A' Corps Sigs attch. 4 IDS, 2319296 J Milburn[10], 6196279 S V Missen[10], 2316722 A Morgan[10], 2319277 L North[10] 'B' Corps Sigs attch. 4 IDS, 2317866 W Parker[10], 2560178 A Parrington[10] 'B' Corps Sigs attch. 4 IDS, 2319017 A S Phillips[10], 2317465 C R Port[10], 2317824 T Pugh[9&10] 'B' Corps Sigs attch. 4 IDS, 2316122 G J Ray[10], 754344 C G Roberts[9&10], 2318323 F Robinson[10], 2320046 J W Scrivener[10], 2317022 J Shillitto[10] 'B' Corps Sigs attch. 4 IDS, 2319390 D Spare[10], 2319885 J Stanton[10], 2320042 A W Stringer[10], 2318341 R J Stuart[10], 2320184 G Thorpe[10], 2554867 H Walker[10], 2317210 E Ward[10] 'A' Corps Sigs attch. 4 IDS, 2317210 F J Ward[10] 'A' Corps Sigs attch. 4 IDS, 2320017 W Ward[10], 1413363 A Watkins[10], 2317307 G S Welchman[10] 'A' Corps Sigs attch. 4 IDS, 2317787 A F Wells[10], 2564381 T E Williams[10], 2317527 C Woodgate[10] 'B' Corps Sigs attch. 4 IDS, 2318404 A D W Woollett[10] & 2320113 B Wright[10] 'B' Corps Sigs attch. 4 IDS

THE INFANTRY:

~ 1ˢᵗ Bn, The Buffs (East Kent Regiment) ~

Note a. *Roll of all commissioned personnel identified as eligible.*
Note b. *Non-commissioned and other rank personnel multi clasp only.*
Note c. *Medals named in thin impressed capitals: 'THE BUFFS.'*

Single Clasp	No. Identified	Rarity
Burma 1930–32[10]	Bn. Strength	Not Rare

Lieutenant Colonels: ~ J V R Jackson[10] & L H Smith[10]
Majors: ~ G F Hamilton[10], N S Hart[10] & F Whitaker[10]
Captains: ~ E H Allen[10] attch. HQ Burma Indpt. Dist, E B Backhouse[10], L M S Essell[10], P R H Fox[10], N E Hoare[10], F A J E Marshall[10] Bde. Maj. Rangoon Bde., H P P Robertson[10], H F G d'Arcy Symonds[10], A F St. A Turner[10], R W M Webster[10] & J R Willows[10]
Lieutenants: ~ M G F Alexander[10], V Boucher[10], E P C Bruce[10], (Adjt.) D C Coates[10], B H Craig[10], M P D Dewar[10], J H N Foster[10], C G Hill[10], A G Jelf[10], (QM) H J Martin[10], R J Murphy[10], G E F Oliver[10], G L B Oliver[10] & G E Sankey[10] 'A' Coy

~ 2ⁿᵈ Bn, The Suffolk Regiment ~

Note a. *Roll of all personnel identified as eligible.*
Note b. *Recipients attached Headquarters (HQ), 12 Brigade (12 Bde.)*
Note c. *Medals named in thin impressed capitals: 'SUFF. R.'*

Single Clasp	No. Identified	Rarity
Burma 1930–32[10]	2	Of the Utmost Rarity

Lance Sergeants/Corporals: ~ (Act) 5823680 S J Cain[10]
Lance Corporals/Privates: ~ 5823631 W J Bray[10]

~ 2nd Bn, The Bedfordshire & Hertfordshire Regiment ~

Note a.   *Roll of all personnel identified as eligible.*
Note b.   *Medals named in thin impressed capitals: 'BEDF. & HERTS. R.'*

Single Clasp	No. Identified	Rarity
Burma 1930–32[10]	0	
Combination Clasps	**No. Identified**	**Rarity**
Waziristan 1921–24[6] Burma 1930–32[10]	1	According to the roll as seen, can be considered Unique

Captains: ~ W A Shaw[6&10]

~ The Royal Welsh Fusiliers ~

Note a.   *Roll of all personnel identified as eligible.*
Note b.   *Recipient attached 2 Manchester.*
Note c.   *Medals named in thin impressed capitals: 'R.W.FUS.'*

Single Clasp	No. Identified	Rarity
Burma 1930–32[10]	1	According to the roll as seen, can be considered Unique

Lieutenants: ~ H M ap R Pryce[10]

~ 1st Bn, Duke of Cornwall's Light Infantry ~

Note a.   *Roll of all personnel identified as eligible.*
Note b.   *Recipient attached Indian Army Ordnance Corps (IAOC).*
Note c.   *Medals named in thin impressed capitals: 'D.C.L.I.'*

Single Clasp	No. Identified	Rarity
Burma 1930–32[10]	1	According to the roll as seen, can be considered Unique

Quartermaster Sergeants/Sergeants: ~ 5432230 R S Payne[10]

~ 2nd Bn, The Royal Sussex Regiment ~

Note a.   *Roll of all personnel identified as eligible.*
Note b.   *Medals named in thin impressed capitals: 'R. SUSS. R.'*

Single Clasp	No. Identified	Rarity
Burma 1930–32[10]	1	According to the roll as seen, can be considered Unique

Lance Corporals/Privates: ~ 6397146 W H Bond[10]

~ 2nd Bn, The South Staffordshire Regiment ~

Note a. *Roll of all personnel identified as eligible.*
Note b. *Recipient attached Indian Army Corps of Clerks (IACC), Headquarters (HQ), Burma Indpendent District, Maymyo.*
Note c. *Medals named in thin impressed capitals: 'S. STAFF. R.'*

Single Clasp	No. Identified	Rarity
Burma 1930–32[10]	1	According to the roll as seen, can be considered Unique

Warrant Officers Class II: ~ (Sub Cndtr) 4907053 S Jones[10]

~ 2nd Bn, The Oxfordshire & Buckinghamshire Light Infantry ~

Note a. *Roll of all commissioned personnel identified as eligible.*
Note b. *Non-commissioned and other rank personnel multi clasp only.*
Note c. *Medals named in thin impressed capitals: 'OXF. & BUCKS L.I.'*

Single Clasp	No. Identified	Rarity
Burma 1930–32[10]	Bn. Strength	Not Rare

Lieutenant Colonels: ~ A E Sanderson[10] & G E Whittall[10]
Majors: ~ K Horan[10] 'A' Coy, J J Powell[10] 'HQ' Coy, W G Tolson[10] & E H Whitfield[10]
Captains: ~ P Booth[10] 'C' Coy, (QM) F Clare[10], D C Colvill[10] 'B' Coy, A B Hamilton[10], C R Horley[10] 'MG' Coy, D S Newton-King[10], (Adjt.) J A Theobalds[10], J Thorne[10] 'MG' Coy, H Vernon[10] 'A' Coy & T J W Winterton[10]
Lieutenants: ~ K Bayley[10], M Darell-Brown[10], C A R Campbell[10], R H Cooke[10] 'A' Coy, A P Godman[10], L L Falkiner[10], H J C Ducat-Hamersley[10], J A G R H Harden[10], P J Luard[10], P F Metcalfe[10] 'A' Coy, H E Montgomery[10], J D Palmer[10] 'A' Coy, E C Richards[10], A B Slessor[10], H G Temple[10], C L C Ward[10] & G C H Wykeham[10]

~ 1st Bn, The Loyal Regiment (North Lancashire) ~

Note a. *Roll of all personnel identified as eligible.*
Note b. *Recipient attached Indian Army Corps of Clerks (IACC), Headquarters (HQ), Burma Indpendent District, Maymyo.*
Note c. *Medals named in thin impressed capitals: 'LOYAL. R.'*

Single Clasp	No. Identified	Rarity
Burma 1930–32[10]	1	According to the roll as seen, can be considered Unique

Quartermaster Sergeants/Sergeants: ~ (Act) 3850413 W Smith[10]

~ 1st Bn, The Queen's Own Royal West Kent Regiment ~

Note a. *Roll of all personnel identified as eligible.*
Note b. *Recipient served as Private Secretary to His Excellency (HE), The Governor of Burma.*
Note c. *Medals named in thin impressed capitals: 'R.W.KENT.R.'*

Single Clasp	No. Identified	Rarity
Burma 1930–32[10]	1	According to the roll as seen, can be considered Unique

Captains: ~ B L Clay[10]

~ 2nd Bn, The King's Own (Yorkshire Light Infantry) ~

Note a. *Roll of all personnel identified as eligible.*
Note b. *Recipient served as Adjutant (Adjt.), Upper Burma Battalion, Auxiliary Forces India (AFI).*
Note c. *Medals named in thin impressed capitals: 'K.O.Y.L.I.'*

Single Clasp	No. Identified	Rarity
Burma 1930–32[10]	1	According to the roll as seen, can be considered Unique

Captains: ~ J Hassell[10]

~ 1st Bn, The King's Royal Rifle Corps ~

Note a. *Roll of all personnel identified as eligible.*
Note b. *All recipients attached 14 Sanitary Section (SS), Royal Army Medical Corps (RAMC).*
Note c. *Medals named in thin impressed capitals: 'K.R.R.C.'*

Single Clasp	No. Identified	Rarity
Burma 1930–32[10]	5	Of the Utmost Rarity

Lance Corporals / Riflemen: ~ 6842627 F Betts[10], 6843369 L Hubble[10], 6843036 G Morgan[10], 6843251 M Smith[10] & 6843139 T Stothard[10]

~ 2nd Bn, The Manchester Regiment ~

Note a. *Roll of all commissioned personnel identified as eligible.*
Note b. *Non-commissioned and other rank personnel multi clasp only.*
Note c. *Medals named in thin impressed capitals: 'MANCH.R.'*

Single Clasp	No. Identified	Rarity
Burma 1930–32[10]	Bn. Strength	Not Rare

Lieutenant Colonels: ~ E L Musson[10]
Majors: ~ R F G Burrows[10], (Bvt) K S Torrance[10], C S Tuely[10] & O H Warne[10]
Captains: ~ F C Egan[10], H R C Green[10], C H Keitley[10], A J Morris[10] SSO Rangoon, A Orwin[10], S K Pembroke[10], E A K Robinson[10] & C C Whyte[10]
Lieutenants: ~ J M T F Churchill[10], T B L Churchill[10], L Cromwell[10], E F Gale[10], N C Robertson-Glasgow[10], G D E B Harvey[10], C H R Hyde[10], C K Mott[10], R W Palk[10], W A Provan[10], F Snow[10], G A Tod[10], W A Venour[10] & E F Woolsey[10]

~ 2nd Bn, The Seaforth Highlanders (Ross-Shire Buffs, The Duke of Albany's) ~

Note a. *Roll of all personnel identified as eligible.*
Note b. *Recipient attached Headquarters (HQ), Burma Indpendent District, Maymyo.*
Note c. *Medals named in thin impressed capitals: 'SEAFORTHS'.*

Single Clasp	No. Identified	Rarity
Burma 1930–32[10]	0	None Identified

Combination Clasps	No. Identified	Rarity
North West Frontier 1930–31[9] Burma 1930–32[10]	1	According to the roll as seen, can be considered Unique

Captains: ~ D H Haugh[9&10]

~ 1ˢᵗ Bn, The Queen's Own Cameron Highlanders ~

Note a.   Roll of all personnel identified as eligible.
Note b.   Recipients attached Indian Army Corps of Clerks (IACC), Headquarters (HQ), Burma Indpendent District unless shown otherwise.
Note c.   Medals named in thin impressed capitals: 'CAMERON(S)'

Single Clasp	No. Identified	Rarity
Burma 1930–32[10]	4	Of the Utmost Rarity

Captains: ~ E P B Cameron[10] GSO3 HQ Burma Indpt. Dist Maymyo
Quartermaster Sergeants/Sergeants: ~ (Act) 3760032 J A M Walker attch. IACC
Lance Corporals/Privates: ~ 2925410 R Hall[10] & 2925998 D M Squire[10]

~ The Argyll & Sutherland Highlanders (Princess Louise's) ~

Note a.   Roll of all personnel identified as eligible.
Note b.   Medals named in thin impressed capitals: 'A.&S.H.'

Single Clasp	No. Identified	Rarity
Burma 1930–32[10]	0	None Identified
Combination Clasps	No. Identified	Rarity
Waziristan 1921–24[6] Burma 1930–32[10]	1	According to the roll as seen, can be considered Unique

Majors: ~ W G Campbell[6&10] GSO2 HQ Burma Indpt. Dist Maymyo

THE CORPS:

~ The Royal Army Medical Corps ~
Sub Units Identified As Entitled:
Unit Medical Officers Attached
British Military Hospitals – Mandalay, Maymyo & Mingalodan
8 British General Hospital - Meiktilla
Detachment 31 Company
28 Field Ambulance – 12 (Secunderbad) Brigade
14 Sanitary Section – 12 (Secunderbad) Brigade

Note a.   Roll of all personnel identified as eligible.
Note b.   All enlisted personnel drawn from 31 Company, Royal Army Medical Corps (RAMC).
Note c.   Medals named in thin impressed capitals: 'R.A.M.C.'

Single Clasp	No. Identified	Rarity
Burma 1930–32[10]	39	Very Scarce
Combination Clasps	No. Identified	Rarity
Afghanistan N.W.F. 1919[3] Burma 1930–32[10]	1	According to the roll as seen, can be considered Unique
Waziristan 1919–21[4] Mahsud 1919–20[5] Waziristan 1921–24[6] Burma 1930–32[10]	1	According to the roll as seen, can be considered Unique

Waziristan 1919–21[4] **Burma 1930–32**[10]	1	According to the roll as seen, can be considered Unique
Waziristan 1921–24[6] **Burma 1930–32**[10]	1	According to the roll as seen, can be considered Unique
North West Frontier 1930–31[9] **Burma 1930–32**[10]	4	Of the Utmost Rarity
Burma 1930–32[10] **Mohmand 1933**[11]	1	According to the roll as seen, can be considered Unique
Burma 1930–32[10] **Mohmand 1933**[11] **North West Frontier 1935**[12]	3	Of the Utmost Rarity

Lieutenant Colonels: ~ W H O'Riordan[10] OC 28 FA & SMO 12 Bde. & G G Tabuteau[6&10]

Majors: ~ C J Blaikie[3(Capt.)&10] BMH Mandalay, G F Carr[10] attch. BMH Mingaladon, A H T Davis[10], W L E Fretz[10] Surgical Specialist Burma Indpt. Dist, H A Rowell[9&10], B C O Sheridan[4,5,6&10], H N Stafford[10] DADH Burma Indpt. Dist & F Worthington[10]

Captains: ~ C L Day[9(18 FA)&10] 14 SS, R A M Humphrey[10] & T B H Tabuteau[4&10]

Lieutenants: ~ E J Curran[10] MO Troops Shwebo, G F Harrison[10&11(Capt.)] 8 BGH, C A Levy[10], K McNeill[9&10] & V C Verbi[10] 28 FA

Company Quartermaster Sergeants/Staff Sergeants: ~ 7251372 J S Gillard[9(3 SS)&10] 31 Coy attch. 8 GH, 7251253 S Harris[10] 31 Coy attch. 14 SS, 7255861 E D Harvey[10] 31 Coy attch. RAMC det Maymyo & 7246469 H Shoney[10] 31 Coy attch. RAMC det Mingaladon

Quartermaster Sergeants/Sergeants: ~ 7256925 B A McDermott[10] 31 Coy attch. 14 SS, 7249052 L Parnell[10] 31 Coy attch. 14 SS & 5987357 C J Wheeler[10] 31 Coy attch. RAMC det Mingaladon,

Lance Sergeants/Corporals: ~ 7257877 G Henney[10] 31 Coy attch attch. RAMC det Mingaladon & 7248310 S G Watson[10] 31 Coy attch. RAMC det Maymyo

Lance Corporals/Privates: ~ 7259837 J Allen[10] 31 Coy attch. 8 BGH Mandalay, 7259952 T Anthony[10] 31 Coy attch. 8 BGH, 7247217 J H Ashcroft[10] 31 Coy attch. 14 SS, 7258313 J W Bradley[10] 31 Coy attch. RAMC det Rangoon, 7259219 A Clarkson[10] 31 Coy attch. 14 SS, 7258344 D C Crick[10] 31 Coy attch. 28 FA, 6745754 H V Dredge[10] 31 Coy attch. RAMC det Rangoon, 725924 A J Duncan[10] 31 Coy attch. 14 SS, 7259247 S A Dyke[10] 31 Coy attch. 14 SS, 5104364 H G Fowler[10] 31 Coy attch. 14 SS, 7257908 R Gamble[10] 31 Coy attch. RAMC det Mingaladon, 6780270 H Jelfs[10,11&12] 31 Coy attch. 8 BGH, 5667526 J H Jones[10] 31 Coy attch. 28 FA, 7259668 L A Keene[10] 31 Coy attch. 8 BGH, 7259118 J McGhee[10] 31 Coy attch. 8 BGH , 7258620 J Parry[10] 31 Coy attch. RAMC det Maymyo, 7258708 H L Saffery[10] 31 Coy attch. RAMC det Mingaladon, 7259479 B Shaw[10] 31 Coy attch. 14 SS Mingaladon, 7259135 A Sutcliffe[10,11&12] 31 Coy attch. 8 BGH, 7249200 H Taylor[10] 31 Coy[10] attch. 8 BGH, 7249664 T I Thomas[10] 31 Coy attch. 8 BGH, 7249202 H Thorpe[10,11&12] 31 Coy attch. 8 BGH, 7258374 W W Whatley[10] 31 Coy attch. 28 FA & 7257840 P H Wilson[10] 31 Coy attch. BMH Maymyo

~ The Royal Army Ordnance Corps ~

Note a.   *Roll of all personnel identified as eligible.*

Note b.   *All recipients attached Indian Army Ordnance Corps, (IAOC), at Rangoon Arsenal unless shown otherwise.*

Note c.   *Medals named in thin impressed capitals: 'R.A.O.C.'*

Single Clasp	*No. Identified*	*Rarity*
Burma 1930–32[10]	12	Extremely Rare

Warrant Officers Class I: ~ 7579220 W R Hodge[10]

Warrant Officers Class II: ~ 7578882 A A Evans[10], 7578888 A G Heath[10] Forman Mingaladon Arsenal, 7579275 R Jones[10] & 758923 E McGeevor[10] attch. 2 Ox & Bucks LI

Company Quartermaster Sergeants/Staff Sergeants: ~ 7575593 L Gavin[10] attch. 2 Manchester & 7578820 W T Hubbard[10] attch. 1 Buffs

Quarter Master Sergeants/Sergeants: ~ 7581292 H Chilllingworth[10], 5432230 S R Payne[10] & 7578740 R E Warry[10]

Lance Sergeants/Corporals: ~ 7582378 C E Jones[10] attch. 1 Buffs & 7582897 J Westley[10] attch. 2 Manchester

~ The Royal Army Veterinary Corps ~

Note a. *Roll of all personnel identified as eligible.*
Note b. *Medals named in thin impressed capitals: 'R.A.V.C.'*

Single Clasp	No. Identified	Rarity
Burma 1930–32[10]	0	None Identified

Combination Clasps	No. Identified	Rarity
Afghanistan N.W.F. 1919[3] Burma 1930–32[10]	1	According to the roll as seen, can be considered Unique

Majors: ~ F B Hayes[38&10]

~ The Army Educational Corps ~

Note a. *Roll of all personnel identified as eligible.*
Note b. *Medals named in thin impressed capitals: 'A.E.C.'*

Single Clasp	No. Identified	Rarity
Burma 1930–32[10]	5	Of the Utmost Rarity

Captains: ~ J P Brown[10] attch. Burma Indpt. Dist
Lieutenants: ~ R A Morrison[10]
Warrant Officers Class I: ~ 7720713 R C Rowe[10] attch. 2 Manchester & 7720731 E L Skelly[10] attch. 1 Buffs
Warrant Officers Class II: ~ 7720778 A M Dodds[10] attch. 2 Ox & Bucks

~ The Army Dental Corps ~

Note a. *Roll of all personnel identified as eligible.*
Note b. *All recipients attached 31 Company, Royal Army Medical Corps (RAMC), British Military Hospital (BMH), Maymyo.*
Note c. *Medals named in thin impressed capitals: 'A.D.CORPS.'*

Single Clasp	No. Identified	Rarity
Burma 1930–32[10]	3	Of the Utmost Rarity

Captains: ~ D A McGeorge[10]
Quartermaster Sergeants / Sergeants: ~ (Act) 7536036 D F Herlihy[10]
Lance Corporals / Privates: ~ 7536119 H D Williams[10]

~ The Queen Alexandra's Imperial Military Nursing Service ~

Note a. *Roll of all personnel identified as eligible.*
Note b. *Medals named in thin impressed capitals: 'Q.A.I.M.N.S.'*

Single Clasp	No. Identified	Rarity
Burma 1930 32[10]	6	Of the Utmost Rarity

Sisters: ~ E M B Dyson[10] attch. BMH Maymyo, M B Fullalove[10] attch. BMH Mingaladon, B Jackson[10] attch. BMH Mingaladon, R M C Nind[10] attch. BMH Maymyo, F M Percival[10] attch. BMH Maymyo & L M Pickering[10] attch. BMH Mingaladon

THE ROYAL AIR FORCE

Note a. *Refer to Royal Air Force notes at end of 'Frontier Campaigns 1919–1924' section for guidance regarding early rank designations.*
Note b. *Ranks shown are those applicable at award of first clasp.*
Note c. *Roll of all personnel identified as eligible.*
Note d. *Medals named in thin impressed capitals :'R.A.F.'*

Single Clasp	No. Identified	Rarity
Burma 1930–32[10]	14	Extremely Rare

Squadron Leaders: ~ G E Livock[10]
Flight Lieutenants: ~ W N Plenderleith[10]
Flying Officers: ~ J R Ayling[10], L Crocker[10] & B A Oakley[10]
Flight Sergeants: ~ 201227 R L Bell[10]
Sergeants: ~ 365630 T H Farnsworth[10] & 363975 J Hart[10]
Corporals: ~ 364539 W H A Bourne[10], 364024 L E King[10] & 157962 J Yeoman[10]
Leading Air Craftsmen: ~ 359705 W Middleton[10] & 365959 C K Street[10]
Air Craftsmen 2nd Class: ~ 505891 S Groves[10]

INDIAN ARMY

Qualifying Units Present Or Known Individuals

The Cavalry:
No Presence Identified

The Artillery:
7 (Bengal) Mtn Bty, Royal Artillery

The Sappers and Miners:
King George's Own Bengal Sappers & Miners
Queen Victoria's Own Madras Sappers & Miners

Military Engineering Services

Survey of India

The Pioneers:
No Presence Identified

The Infantry:
2/5th Mahratta Light Infantry..From Poona
3/6th Rajputana Rifles.....................................12 Secunderabad Brigade
3/10th Baluch Regiment (QMO)........................12 Secunderabad Brigade
2/15th Punjab Regiment...Rangoon Brigade
3/15th Punjab Regiment..Individuals
2/16th Punjab Regiment..Individuals
3/16th Punjab Regiment....................................12 Secunderabad Brigade
1/17th Dogra Regiment (POWO)....................................From India
2/20th Burma Rifles...Maymyo Brigade
3/20th Burma Rifles (Kachin)..Maymyo Brigade
Unidentified Gurkha Battalion

The Burma Military Police:

The Indian Army Reserve of Officers/The Auxiliary Forces India / The Indian Territorial Force
III (Rangoon) Field Bde Artillery, AFI
No.2 (Rangoon) Field Company Engineers, AFI
The Mandalay Battalion, AFI
The Rangoon Battalion, AFI
The Upper Burma Battalion, AFI
The Burma Railway Battalion, AFI
Individuals

The Indian Corps:
The Indian Army Service Corps: (Including British Officers & NCO's)
Cantonment Supply Depots
Nos. 17 & 18 Animal Transport Companies

Medical Units:
The Indian Medical Department / The Indian Hospital Corps /
The Queen Alexander's Military Nursing Service India
British Military Hospitals Mandalay & Maymyo
No. 3 Indian General Hospital – From India
No. 28 Field Ambulance
No. 14 Sanitary Section

The Indian Army Ordnance Corps:
Mingaladon & Rangoon Arsenals

The Indian Army Corps of Clerks:

Military Conservancy Department:

Police, Judiciary & Intelligence:
Frontier Constabulary, Jail Department & Frontier Intelligence Corps

The Postal Department:

The Political & Civil Departments:

7. MOHMAND 1933

~ India General Service Medal 1908–1935 ~
MOHMAND 1933
Issue 3. Royal Mint

The 'MOHMAND 1933' clasp was sanctioned by Army Order 186 of 1933. The clasp was issued to reward troops, and war mobilised civilians employed under the command of Brigadier General C.J.E. Auchinleck and Brigadier General W.D. Croft during the suppression of the Mohmand uprising. Airmen serving under the command of Group Captain B.E. Sutton, RAF, AOC 1 (Indian) Group, were engaged in both the Mohmand and Bajaur regions and also qualified.

Examples of The India General Service Medal 1908–1935 bearing the 'MOHMAND 1933' clasp named to British personnel are scarce. This is due to a decision made by the Indian High Command exempting the British battalions in both 1st and 2nd Infantry Brigades from deploying with their respective brigade battle groups in an attempt to restrict incidents of heatstroke in the field. Royal Artillery, Royal Tank Corps and Royal Signals personnel were present as well as several men on detached duty including those assigned to No. 1 Provost Section.

Units engaged deployed in four formations: The Mohmand, (or Gandab Column), the Mohmand Blockade Line, Lines of Communication, and the Reserve.

To qualify for the 'MOHMAND 1933' clasp personnel had to satisfy one, or more, of the following criteria:

- Be engaged on active service with the Mohmand Column, including Lines of Communication and Reserve, advancing beyond Pir Kala into Mohmand territory between 28th July and 3rd October 1933 inclusive.

- Form part of the Mohmand Blockhouse Line between 28th July and 3rd October 1933 inclusive.

- Be engaged in active aerial support of land operations in Mohmand territory between 28th July and 3rd October 1933 inclusive.

- Be engaged in the prosecution of air operations over Bajaur between 24th July and 10th August inclusive.

*

~ Upper Mohmand warriors at a jirga ~

Of Yusuf Pathan extraction, the Mohmand were divided into Upper and Lower Mohmands each with distinct social and cultural attitudes. The Upper Mohmand were fiercely independent and had been the subject of several previous punitive expeditions. *Lashkars* from the tribe under their titular leader Mullah Fazali-Wahid, the Haji of Turangzai, and his three sons were veteran campaigners against British Indian authority and as such had been active during the frontier problems of 1930–31.

The Lower Mohmand, on the other hand, had accepted the authority of the Government and to that end received various official allowances including funding for Khassadari. As a direct result of these subsidies, the financial position of the Lower Mohmand was significantly more stable than that of their northern neighbours. (For a more detailed account of the Mohmand tribal structure and hinterland see: 1. North West Frontier Campaigns 1908).

*

~ Mohmand Operations ~

The Upper Mohmand took any opportunity to interfere with and molest the Lower Mohmand, especially the relatively peaceful Halamazai who occupied much of the Gandab Valley region. Upper Mohmand incursions into the Gandab Valley had been repulsed by aerial bombardment during the late 1920s. Further alleged incidents during the summer of 1932 were inspired by Upper Mohmand support for the Red Shirt movement. An appeal to the political authorities by Halamazai elders for British military protection resulted in a declaration by the Government of India proclaiming punitive retribution would be forthcoming unless the Upper Mohmand disbanded their *lashkars* and retired back to their homeland.

During January 1933, an anti-British 'zealot' dubbed the 'Crazy Faqir' attempted to ferment a 'new' insurrection among the frontier tribes beyond the Administrative Boundary of the North West Frontier. A joint Waziri/Mahsud rebellion would unite these peoples on both sides of the Indo-Afghan frontier with a view to driving back the relentless advance of British influence. Several *lashkars* were raised but enthusiasm waned after a relatively short space of time. By the end of February 1933, virtually all of the warriors who had originally taken to the field had retired to the relative safety of Afghanistan. The Haji of Turangzai, however, residing in the remote Chararmung Valley of Bajaur, was unrepentant.

In May 1933, a man claiming to be a relative of ex-King Amanullah of Afghanistan and therefore 'Pretender' to the Afghan throne, slipped across the Indo-Afghan frontier and took refuge in the home of the Khan of Kotkai in Bajaur. When it became apparent that this man intended to raise *lashkars* with a view to fermenting rebellion against King Nadir Khan, the incumbent King of Afghanistan, the Afghan Government called upon the British Indian Government to take steps to expel him. This interference in 'local affairs' enabled the Haji of Turangzai to use local sentiment for his own ends and thus persuaded the Upper Mohmand to declare war on their Lower Mohmand Halamazai brethren on the pretext that the Halamazai were interfering with established caravan routes in and out of Afghanistan through the strategically important Toratigga Valley. On 22nd July 1933, an Upper Mohmand *lashkar* numbering a 1,000 rifles invaded Halamazai territory.

*

The British military response to the unfolding situation within the Mohmand tribal region was initially limited to air action over Bajaur with a view to encouraging the Khan of Kotkai to surrender the 'Pretender' to the political authorities for 'relocation'. To that end, the political authorities advised residents of Kotkai that unless the 'Pretender' was surrendered by midnight on 29th July 1933, they would become subject to aerial retribution. The decision to employ the RAF in such a manner provoked serious controversy in Government circles. The morality of aerial assault against civilian targets had been strenuously debated when deployed on previous occasions. The topic was now in even greater focus following the recent destruction wrought on Chinese cities by the Imperial Japanese airforce and the fear of German rearmament in Europe including the potential for German involvement in the burgeoning Spanish situation. The relevant Whitehall ministers guardedly granted Government sanction of such operations only after a detailed review of the cost benefit.

The Upper Mohmand invasion of Halamazai territory intensified the magnitude of the problem. Consequently, the Viceroy, Lord Willingdon, approved a request from the Chief Commissioner R. Griffith of the North West Frontier to honour the Government's previous promise to protect the Halamazai. On 25th July 1933, Lieutenant General J.F.S.D. Coleridge, GOC Northern Command, received orders at Muree to mobilise a military column for deployment into the Gandab Valley which, in turn, following a period of staff planning, was forwarded to both Major General W. Dent, GOC Peshawar District and Group Captain B.E. Sutton, commanding 1 (Indian) Group RAF.

*

The Gandab Column was tasked with preserving peace on the Frontier and assisting the Halamazai (and others prepared to live under the tutelage of British India) when required. The force was also authorised to construct an all-weather spur from the existing Michni–Abazai road north from Pir Kala as far as Ghalanai in the Gandab Valley, thereby facilitating the rapid deployment of troops to the region as required. Further, the expedition was to ensure that the Haji of Turangzai, accompanied by his retinue of anti-British sympathisers and three sons (each called Badshah), vacated British India post-haste. Additionally, an agreement was also sought from the Upper Mohmand that they would in future co-existence peacefully with the Halamazai. No incursions into Afghanistan by land or air were to be permitted.

The plan of campaign required the reoccupation of the former Great War period Mohmand Blockade Line positioned along the line Abazai–Shabkadar–Michni. This manoeuvre was completed on 29th July 1933 under the auspices of Lieutenant Colonel C. O'B. Daunt commanding 18th KEO Cavalry, IA. Headquarters Blockade Line was established at Fort Shabkadar. The following morning

1st Infantry Brigade, under Brigadier C.J.E. Auchinleck, advanced towards Ghalanai via Pir Kala and Dand. The route north from Dand proved particularly trying due to the condition of the ungraded track. No enemy contacts were encountered. Meanwhile 2nd Infantry Brigade, under Brigadier W.D. Croft, having concentrated at Peshawar, moved up to Pir Kala on 31st July where a base operating camp was established. Elements of 2nd Brigade occupied Dand on 3rd August at which juncture the Brigade became responsible for the Lines of Communication from the forward operating area back to Pir Kala. The 3rd Infantry Brigade, under Brigadier Hon H.R.L.G. Alexander, assumed the duties of both the Peshawar and Nowshera Brigades in the Peshawar District order of battle.

On 31st July 1933, the Deputy Commissioner of Peshawar District attended a Lower Mohmand *jirga* at Fort Shabkadar. Some 300 warriors and local Kahassadar attended. The tribal elders thanked the Government for deploying a 'peace keeping' force so promptly and reiterated that the troops engaged were welcome in their region. The warriors surrendered valuable intelligence some of which suggested that several Upper Mohmand *lashkars* had formed up north of the Khapak and Nahakki Passes with a view to repelling the anticipated British 'invasion' of Mohmand territory. Aerial reconnaissance flights, however, failed to observe any enemy activity for several days. On 10th August a patrol of 18th KEO Cavalry, IA, was attacked during a recconasance of the foothills leading up to the Khapak Pass. Later the same day an Upper Mohmand war party attacked the Halamazai settlement of Skirmiah Toratigga located some miles east of Ghalanai

On 12th August 1933, the infantry at Ghalanai advanced north in an attempt to break up the now verified Upper Mohmand *lashkars* in and around the Khapak Pass area. A brief contact ensued, but the engagement was broken off before significant casualties could be inflicted upon the enemy. Several long-range patrols were subsequently deployed with a view to seeking out opportunities for further encounters. Some 300 warriors at Katsai were dispersed by artillery fire on 16th August. Several less

~ Road construction in the Upper Mohmand did bring some economic benefits to the region ~

435

significant firefights also took place. Air support was now sought from 1 (Indian) Wing RAF with a view to bombing specified enemy settlements. Permission to embark on such raids could not, however, be granted until bombing notices had been circulated among the target villagers. Further, many of the optimum targets were found to lie in the prohibited zone beyond the Indo-Afghan border.

Notice of the RAF's intent to bomb settled areas was circulated to target villages via an air-delivered leaflet drop on 17th August 1933. This action prompted a delegation of Upper Mohmand elders to enter into 'unofficial' dialogue with several influential Halamazai *maliks*. The Halamazai agreed to petition the Political Agent for a withdrawal of troops from the region in exchange for guarantees pertaining to the future ongoing sovereignty of the Lower Mohmand. The Upper Mohmand, who maintained their demand for ascendancy over their southern brethren, found this stipulation unacceptable. Consequently, the *jirga* broke up with out accord.

Road construction proceeded throughout August 1933. Snipping was spasmodic and the Sappers and Miners incurred no significant casualties. Towards the end of August, the authorities determined to extend the road beyond Ghalanai all the way to Yusuf Khel at the mouth of the Nahakki Pass. Anticipating Upper Mohmand resistance to this development Brigadier C.J.E. Auchinleck deployed several mobile columns to reinforce the domination of the Army and thus, potentially, dissuade enemy interference. Thus, on the 23rd August, an expedition was despatched towards Langham in the Pindiali Valley and a week later, an examination in force was made of the Nahakki Pass. (Several staff officers were in favour of a road extension beyond the Nahakki Pass to facilitate rapid deployments into Upper Mohmand territory as and when required. Although this proposal was considered to have merit, the Government eventually vetoed the idea due to lack of financial resources.)

The GOC Northern Command and the Agent to the Governor General, North West Frontier Province, invited representatives of all Mohmand clans to attend a Government *jirga* at Ghalanai on 3rd September 1933. During this meeting, terms for a Government sanctioned peace were promulgated. These included formal notification that should the Upper Mohmand fail to submit to published terms, the Government of India reserved the right to extend the Gandab Valley road as far north as it deemed appropriate. Political Officers would in future regularly observe the Gandab Valley region and if any tribe was deemed to be intimidating the Halamazai, military action would be employed to resolve the situation. The Upper Mohmand absented themselves from this *jirga* and therefore the Government was forced to take further steps to gain a compliance commitment.

On 5th September 1933, Brigadier General W.D. Croft moved 2nd Infantry Brigade up to Ghalanai from Dand. Lines of Communication security was henceforth vested in the Frontier Constabulary. One infantry battalion, however, remained in the Dand area to protect the newly constructed Rattroy Camp facility. This deliberate manoeuvre, combined with publication of Government terms that were unacceptable to the Upper Mohmand, led to a marked increase in enemy activity in the area north of Ghalanai over the ensuing days. At this juncture, however, the Afghan Government decided to give sanction to British operations west of the political border on condition that non-combatants were not to be targeted. Bombing notices were thus widely distributed throughout the region.

With a strengthened military position, the Deputy Commissioner invited the Upper Mohmand to attend a special *jirga* at Ghalanai on 12th September 1933. Representatives of Khwaezai, Musa Khel and Utman Khel groups attended the meeting but the Badshah Khel and Safi remained resolutely opposed and continued offensive operations against both the Halamazai and the British for several more weeks. The Deputy Commissioner informed the tribal elders that the military column would not be withdrawn until the Government of India was satisfied that the Upper Mohmand were prepared to coexist peacefully with the Lower Mohmand. Work parties would be employed to maintain the new road and Political Officers would be active in the region. These activities may or may not be supplemented by military patrols. The protection of the Halamazai remained a Government priority.

Negotiations continued until 18th September 1933 when those in attendance agreed to comply on condition their trade caravans could in future use the newly constructed road system to access the bazaars of Peshawar. Further, it was requested that the Government of India would stand as arbitrator in any possible future inter-tribal feuds. The political authorities found these requests acceptable. Therefore, following the dispersal of the *jirga*, tribal elders sent out instructions calling for the disbandment of all Upper Mohmand *lashkars*. Several *maliks* had to exert special pressure on both the Badshah Khel and Safi before they could extract a guarantee of compliance from these peoples. The Haji of Turangzai refused to accept this subjugation to Government authority and continued to preach anti-British sentiment at every opportunity.

*

Brigadier C. J.E. Auchinleck withdrew 1st Infantry Brigade from the Gandab Valley on 28th September 1933. Rather than return the force direct to Peshawar, the authorities decided that a final show of British resolve would be beneficial and thus the Brigade took a circular route via Langham and the Burjina Pass. Simultaneously, troops at Fort Shabkadar were withdrawn leaving behind them a garrison of Frontier Constabulary. On 3rd October, Brigadier General W.D. Croft evacuated Ghalanai and retired 2nd Infantry Brigade back via the new road to Peshawar from whence a train subsequently conveyed the men to their peacetime station in Nowshera. This date marked the official conclusion of the campaign to expel the Upper Mohmand from the Gandab Valley region.

***

~ Bajaur Operations ~

The ultimatum to surrender the 'Pretender' to the Afghan throne to the authorities was ignored by the Khan of Kotkai. On 30th July 1933, bombing notices were dropped on Kotkai Village advising the residents that in light of their unwillingness to comply with the Government's legitimate demands they would be subjected to an aerial assault from dawn on 1st August to sunset on 10th August. Time limitations were put in place to enable the action to be terminated without giving the enemy the impression that the RAF had lost its resolve.

A force of twelve Westerland Wapiti bombers drawn from 27 and 60 Squadrons at RAF Kohat were made available for these operations. Several Hawker Hart aircraft from 11 and 39 Squadrons at RAF Risalpur augmented these aircraft. Significant destruction was wrought on Kotkai during several sorties flown between 1st–4th August 1933. Group Captain B.E. Sutton, RAF, commanding 1 (Indian) Group RAF, then decided that for the rest of the offensive aggressive patrolling only would be employed. These measures, however, failed to deliver the required submission. Consequently, the military authorities determined that a land invasion of Bajaur would be required in order to ensure the capture of the 'Pretender'.

The 1st (Abbottabad) Brigade, under Brigadier General W.H. Fordham, was mobilised on 8th August 1933 with a view to moving up to Balambat from whence any incursion into the Bajaur would be launched. The threat of land action, however, proved to be too much for the Khan of Kotkai and on 13th August 1933 the 'Pretender' was officially expelled from Bajaur. In view of this development, the force assembling at Balambat was stood down and therefore did not qualify for the India General Service Medal 1908–1935 with clasp 'MOHMAND 1933'.

***

COMMAND STRUCTURE, MOHMAND 1933	
General Office Commanding Maj. Gen. W Dent	
Brigade Commanders	
Brig. E de Burgh	1st (Risalpur) Cavalry Brigade
Brig. C J E Auchinleck	1st (Peshawar) Infantry Brigade
Brig. W D Croft	2nd (Nowshera) Infantry Brigade
Brig. Hon. H R L G Alexander	3rd (Rawalpindi) Infantry Brigade
Air Officer Commanding 1 (Indian) Group, RAF G/Capt. B E Sutton	

BRITISH ARMY ROLL OF HONOUR MOHMAND 1933			
Date:	Person:	Unit:	Comment:
?	2313907 Sgt. G A Harper	R Signals	Cause Unknown

MOHMAND 1933 INDIAN ARMY CASUALTY RETURN	
Killed	Wounded
9	9

MOHMAND 1933[11] ROLL

BRITISH ESTABLISHMENT
THE ARMY

~ Staff Grade Officers ~

Note a. *Only Officers of the British Army are listed. Those on the Indian Establishment are beyond the scope of this work and are thus excluded.*

Note b. *Medals named in small impressed block capitals.*

Brigadier: ~ W D Croft[11&12] Cmd. 2 Bde.

THE CAVALRY:
~ 15th/19th King's Royal Hussars ~

Note a. *Roll of all personnel identified as eligible.*

Note b. *Recipient attached Headquarters (HQ), Peshawar District (PD).*

Note c. *Medals named in small impressed block capitals: '15-19 H.'*

Single Clasp	No. Identified	Rarity
Mohmand 1933[11]	0	None Identified
Combination Clasps	**No. Identified**	**Rarity**
North West Frontier 1930–31[9] Mohmand 1933[11]	1	According to the roll as seen, can be considered Unique

Lance Corporals / Privates: ~ 548554 C R Gordon[9&11]

THE ROYAL TANK CORPS:
Sub Units Identified As Entitled:
6 Armoured Car Company
(1 Vehicle) 2 Light Tank Company

Note a. *Roll of all personnel identified as eligible.*

Note b. *The Officer Commanding, (OC) 6 Armoured Car Company (ACC), Maj. H M Heyland, removed several names from the original roll including himself.*

Note c. *All 6 ACC unless shown otherwise.*

Note d. *6 ACC attached Mohmand Blockade Line.*

Note e. *Medals named in small impressed block capitals: 'R. TANK. C.'*

Single Clasp	Company	No. Identified	Rarity
Mohmand 1933[11]	6 ACC	99	Rare
Combination Clasps	**Company**	**No. Identified**	**Rarity**
Waziristan 1921–24[6] Mohmand 1933[11]	6 ACC	1	According to the roll as seen, can be considered Unique
North West Frontier 1930–31[9] Mohmand 1933[11]	6 ACC	1	According to the roll as seen, can be considered Unique

Mohmand 1933[11] North West Frontier 1935[12]	2 LTC	3	Of the Utmost Rarity

Captains: ~ J L C Napier[11]

Lieutenants: ~ E D Coyle[11], J Hall[11], T K D Pritchett[11], R H O Simpson[11], F W Skey[11] & D St. C Thorn[11&12] 2 LTC

Quartermaster Sergeants/Sergeants: ~ 7872632 J Cowe[11], 7869420 A Quirk[11], 7874774 W H Rabson[9(L/Sgt. 7 ACC)&11] & 7869533 R E Turner[11&12] 2 LTC

Lance Sergeants/Corporals: ~ 7879238 S G Harding[11], 7880894 G S Langham[11], 7874969 A G Maddison[11], 7874745 C E Seaford[11], 7880891 W E G Stroud[11], 7876935 T H Taylor[11], 7876626 H J Weeks[11], 7812621 W S Wiggett[11] & 3953273 G Witheridge[11]

Lance Corporals/Privates: ~ 7882452 A L Appleton[11], 7881748 W H Armstrong[11], 7879267 W Arthur[11], 5493094 F W C Ballard[11], 7882408 A M Barnard[11], 7882370 G H Barnet[11], 7881354 P N Bartleman[11], 7882396 A Bell[11&12] 2 LTC, 7880182 J G Bell[11], 5492935 C W H Bellenie[11], 7879091 J H Bourne[11], 5614360 W H Bowden[11], 7880378 T H Bridgwater[11], 4121366 F D Broadhurst[11], 4074872 A Brown[11], 7882813 T E Butler[11], 7882310 W R Calder[11], 7882415 J M Chalmers[11], 7880549 W Chapman[11], 7881725 S Clarkson[11], 7881367 P Clifford[11], 1425904 F A S Cloake[11], 6340224 F G Cooper[11], 7882822 W Cooper[11], 7882455 P H Cousens[11], 37641 M J Crawford[11], 7880177 A Dagnall[11], 7880540 T W Dale[11], 7882840 G C Dance[11], 7882494 G David[11], 7879658 L Dodds[11], 4610379 W Dronsfield[11], 4263973 J Duddin[11], 2564677 R Dye[11], 7879477 G J Elliot[11], 7882165 H Evans[11], 7881585 F Grainger[11], 7879726 F W Green[11], 7880061 T Hanlon[11], 7882810 C Haylor[11], 7879084 G H Henry[11], 7879759 R Hildreth[11], 7880602 N Horsefield[11], 7880582 I F Hughes[11], 4185930 R E Hughes[11], 7881032 A H Hume[11], 7880443 A D Iving[11], 7880393 L Jones[11], 882819 S F Keating[11], 5098347 C G Kennedy[11], 7882311 V Lamb[11], 7879791 A L Larner[11], 7880946 A Lathwell[11], 7882483 W Lea[11], 7881048 S J H Linton[11], 7880718 A Little[11], 782227 T H Lohrenz[11], 7879696 C Lomas[11], 7879611 W J Lomas[11], 7882623 J E Long[11], 7880747 W J Lugg[11], 4971330 D J Mackenzie[11], 5105993 H A Madeley[11], 7879396 L Mellor[11], 7880170 A Munton[11], 7879820 E Ogle[11], 7880417 R H Phillips[11], 7875568 G W Plaice[11], 7880168 H Powell[11], 7871250 J Quigg[6(Cpl.)&11], 7880454 D L Roberts[11], 769291 A Robertson[11], 7880070 A G Roden[11], 7879212 G Rumble[11], 7881030 A W G Ryder[11], 7880304 A J Southam[11], 7882689 E Sparkes[11], 7880189 W Stainthorpe[11], 7880860 R L Stevens[11], 4740906 E Tinsdale[11], 7880459 E G Vare[11], 7882207 A Waterhouse[11], 7880640 W E Wells[11] & 7075004 W Young[11]

THE ROYAL ARTILLERY:
Batteries Identified As Entitled:
Field Artillery:
3 (L), 4 (L)(Two Recipients), Det 12 attch. HQ Nowshera Bde.,
31 (Single Recipient attch. HQ Nowshera Bde.), Sect 15 (M) & 58 Batteries

Anti Aircraft Artillery:
8 Battery

Mountain Artillery:
HQ 22 Mountain Brigade
2 (Derajat), 4 (Hazara) & 10 (Abbottabad) Mountain Bateries

Note a.   *Roll of all British personnel identified as eligible including Royal Artillery (RA) officers of the Indian Mountain Artillery.*
Note b.   *2 Mountain Battery attached Reserve Subhan Khwar.*
Note c.   *4 Mountain Battery and 10 Mountain Battery attached Mohmand Column.*
Note d.   *58 Field Battery attached Mohmand Blockhouse Line – Fort Shabkadr.*
Note e.   *Medals named in small impressed block capitals: 'R.A.'*

Single Clasp	Battery	No. Identified	Rarity
Mohmand 1933[11]	4	1	According to the roll as seen, can be considered Unique
Mohmand 1933[11]	8	68	Rare
Mohmand 1933[11]	12	4	Of the Utmost Rarity

Mohmand 1933[11]	15	12	Extremely Rare
Mohmand 1933[11]	58	83	Rare
Mohmand 1933[11]	Other Inc. Mtn Bty	6	Of the Utmost Rarity

Combination Clasps	Battery	No. Identified	Rarity
Waziristan 1919–21[4] Waziristan 1921–24[6] Mohmand 1933[11]	Other Inc. Mtn Bty	1	According to the roll as seen, can be considered Unique
Waziristan 1919–21[4] Mohmand 1933[11] North West Frontier 1935[12]	Other Inc. Mtn Bty	1	According to the roll as seen, can be considered Unique
Waziristan 1921–24[6] Mohmand 1933[11]	Other Inc. Mtn Bty	1	According to the roll as seen, can be considered Unique
North West Frontier 1930–31[9] Mohmand 1933[11]	Other Inc. Mtn Bty	7	Of the Utmost Rarity
North West Frontier 1930–31[9] Mohmand 1933[11]	8	2	Of the Utmost Rarity
North West Frontier 1930–31[9] Mohmand 1933[11]	12	1	According to the roll as seen, can be considered Unique
North West Frontier 1930–31[9] Mohmand 1933[11]	15	3	Of the Utmost Rarity
North West Frontier 1930–31[9] Mohmand 1933[11]	58	46	Very Rare
North West Frontier 1930–31[9] Mohmand 1933[11] North West Frontier 1935[12]	Other Inc. Mtn Bty	1	According to the roll as seen, can be considered Unique
North West Frontier 1930–31[9] Mohmand 1933[11] North West Frontier 1935[12]	4	1	According to the roll as seen, can be considered Unique
North West Frontier 1930–31[9] Mohmand 1933[11] North West Frontier 1935[12]	15	2	Of the Utmost Rarity
North West Frontier 1930–31[9] Mohmand 1933[11] North West Frontier 1935[12]	31	1	According to the roll as seen, can be considered Unique
Mohmand 1933[11] North West Frontier 1935[12]	Other Inc. Mtn Bty	3	Of the Utmost Rarity
Mohmand 1933[11] North West Frontier 1935[12]	8	6	Of the Utmost Rarity
Mohmand 1933[11] North West Frontier 1935[12]	15	12	Extremely Rare
Mohmand 1933[11] North West Frontier 1935[12]	58	2	Of the Utmost Rarity

Lieutenant Colonels: ~ R M N Forbes[4(Maj.),6(Maj.)&11] HQ 22 Mtn Bde. & (Bvt) H M M Robertson[9,11&12] 4 Mtn Bty

Majors: ~ E L Armitage[9&11] 10 Mtn Bty & W B Mackie[11&12] 2 Mtn Bty

Captains: ~ M Lea-Cox[11&12] attch. HQ PD, R M V Denton[11] 58 Fld Bty, E J H Douch[11] 15 Md Bty, J C Fergusson[11] 4 Mtn Bty, H A Hounsell[9&11] 10 Mtn Bty & H D Lysons[6(Lt.)&11]

Lieutenants: ~ J T B Sylvester-Bradley[11&12] 15 Md Bty, H G M Dunn[9&11] 58 Fld Bty, J C Edlmann[11] 10 Mtn Bty, A S Ellis[11&12] 2 Mtn Bty, C J Gittings[9&11] HQ 22 Mtn Bde., A T J Graham[11] 58 Fld Bty, B P Hughes[9&11] 4 Mtn Bty, E R G St. John[11] 58 Fld Bty, W S King[11&12] 8 AA Bty attch. HQ PD as Fld Cashier, R Richards[9&11] HQ 22 Mtn Bde., O St. J Skeen[9&11] Col Orderly Officer, Nowshera Col, W H Skrine[11] 15 Md Bty, J S W Tremenheere[11] 2 Mtn Bty & W J N Walker[11] 10 Mtn Bty

Warrant Officers Class I: ~ 1426428 E C Atkins[11] attch. HQ 22 Mtn Bde.

Warrant Officers Class II: ~ 1030481 J T L Chapman[9&11] 58 Fld Bty, 1417946 R Frisby[4,11&12] HQ 22 Mtn Bde., 1026034 H Hewitt[11] 8 AA Bty & 1411460 F W Pavey[11] 15 Md Bty

Battery Quartermaster Sergeants/Staff Sergeants: ~ 1030734 G Carlow[11] 15 Md Bty & 1028147 A J Cherry[9(Sgt.)&11] 58 Fld Bty

Quartermaster Sergeants/Sergeants: ~ 1048744 W Anderson[11] 58 Fld Bty, 1052090 W A Beed[9&11] 58 Fld Bty, (QMS(F)1418468 C F Cornish[11] 58 Fld Bty, 1053700 F E Davidson[9&11] 58 Fld Bty, 1407879 A C A J Ford[9,11&12(WOII)] 15 Md Bty, (Sdlr) 1417125 J A Hartfield[9(Bdr.)&11] 58 Fld Bty, 1054055 J T Hay[9(Bdr.)&11] 15 Md Bty, 1054324 C Head[11] 58 Fld Bty, 1041890 A Hughes[9&11] 58 Fld Bty, 1068459 J Hulme[9(Bdr.)&11] 58 Fld Bty, 1662499 C L Miles[11] 4 Bty, 1028698 G A E Prescott[9&11] 58 Fld Bty, 2558820 A Wetherill[9&11] 15 Md Bty & 1058204 D E Young[9(Bdr.)&11] 58 Fld Bty

Bombardiers: ~ 1066484 C C J Cook[11&12] 58 Fld Bty, 1423774 A H Corlett[11&12] 15 Md Bty, 6338421 T Foster[9&11] HQ 22 Mtn Bde., 1060358 G F J Gray[9&11] 58 Fld Bty, 1423060 P J Gregory[11] 8 AA Bty, 28913 L Greensmith[11] 58 Fld Bty, 1055787 S J Ham[11] 8 AA Bty, 1000027 L H P Harvey[11] 8 AA Bty, 1068459 J Hulme[11] 58 Fld Bty, 1031329 C A Jackson[11&12(Sgt.)] 58 Fld Bty, 1409263 J C Kerridge[9&11] 15 Md Bty, 1052203 W Kettles[11&12(Sgt.)] 15 Md Bty, 1064857 H King[11&12] 15 Md Bty, 1064083 J McCullagh[11] 8 AA Bty, 800259 G H Medley[11] 8 AA Bty, 1020174 A R Palmer[9(Gnr.)&11] 58 Fld Bty, 1057374 L E Palmer[9(Gnr.)&11] 58 Fld Bty, 815094 G E Raw[11] 58 Fld Bty, 1021008 W H Scrivens[11] 58 Fld Bty, 1071434 A A Silk[11] 15 Md Bty, 4264781 A Stuart[9(Gnr.)&11] 58 Fld Bty, 1070060 R Thomas[9(Gnr.)&11] 58 Fld Bty & 1061612 W Todd[11] 8 AA Bty

Lance Bombardiers/Gunners/Drivers: ~ 806871 F Alford[11] 8 AA Bty, 794651 H H Askins[11] 58 Bty, 779023 J F Bannerman[9&11] 58 Fld Bty, 786936 A Bartholomew[11] 58 Fld Bty, 7782788 C E Barton[11] 58 Fld Bty, 5103805 G H Barton[11] 8 AA Bty, 798244 S Bate[9,11&12] 31 Fld Bty attch HQ Nowshera Bde., 805296 C H Bates[11] 58 Fld Bty, 805087 S Barker[11] 58 Fld Bty, 1070343 P Bayes[9&11] 58 Fld Bty, 5946102 W Beadle[11] 8 AA Bty, 779363 K Beardwell[11] 58 Fld Bty, 816932 F E Bell[11] 8 AA Bty, 781827 J Berry[9&11] 58 Fld Bty, 809046 B S Bishop[11] 58 Fld Bty, 794654 E G Blackwell[9&11] 58 Fld Bty, 786006 G C Bohan[9&11] 58 Fld Bty, 797476 A Bonnett[11] 8 AA Bty, 799042 F P Boodell[11] 58 Fld Bty, 797441 E Boulton[11&12] 15 Md Bty, 809969 W C Bowden[11] 8 AA Bty, 790389 R Bowes[11&12] 8 AA Bty, 800772 V Brennan[11] 8 AA Bty, 800428 S W Brown[11] 58 Fld Bty, 808781 J P Bryne[11&12] 8 AA Bty, 806156 F Burford[11] 58 Fld Bty, 790433 C V G Burgess[11] 58 Fld Bty, 784382 F W Burt[9&11] 58 Fld Bty, 828310 D J Carberry[11] 58 Fld Bty, 808550 E Cartwright[11] 8 AA Bty, 815981 R D L Chugg[11] 58 Fld Bty, 767798 F Clark[11] 15 Md Bty, 777380 R J Couch[11] 58 Fld Bty, 781644 A E Crawford[9&11] 12 Fld Bty, 1072730 E P Croke[11] 8 AA Bty, 736026 F L Crook[9&11] 58 Fld Bty, 808888 A Crooks[11] 8 AA Bty, 800405 F Culley[11] 58 Fld Bty, 797280 F Davey[11&12] 15 Md Bty, 816023 I G Dean[11] 8 AA Bty, 6139137 I G H Dean[11] 12 Fld Bty, 4385281 E C Deighton[11] 15 Md Bty, 791824 H Devall[11] 58 Fld Bty, 790870 A T Diston[11] 15 Md Bty, 791086 W Dodd[11] 8 AA Bty, 1072818 H Donelly[11] 58 Fld Bty, 5880842 W H Downing[11] 8 AA Bty, 786062 J R Duff[9&11] 58 Fld Bty, 790809 R Duke[11] 58 Fld Bty, 809014 A S Edgeley[11] 58 Fld Bty, 778708 C Elliott[9&11] 58 Fld Bty, 1664017 J J Ferdinando[11] 58 Fld Bty, 7542506 C L Le Flem[11] 58 Fld Bty, 786500 J Foggin[11] 58 Fld Bty, 31855 W Forde[11] 8 AA Bty, 5722211 E L Frampton[9&11] 58 Fld Bty, 790482 G E Gardner[11] 58 Fld Bty, 788395 J Gascoigne[9&11] 8 AA Bty, 791447 J Goldsborough[11] 58 Fld Bty, 1073248 W E C S Gould[9&11] 58 Fld Bty, 790968 J Gourlay[11] 58 Fld Bty, 794877 J Green[11] 8 AA Bty, 781757 L Griffin[11] 58 Fld Bty, 808785 R Hainsworth[11] 8 AA Bty, 788169 W H Hambleton[11] 58 Fld Bty, 788950 L Hamden[11] 15 Md Bty, 31932 H Hardwick[11] 58 Fld Bty, 800250 W H Hare[11] 8 AA Bty, 781244 F G Harris[11] 58 Fld Bty, 808409 A R Hartland[11] 8 AA Bty, 805586 R A Heaps[11] 8 AA Bty, 777572 J E Hedge[11] 8 AA Bty, 790200 L Heightely[9,11&12] 15 Md Bty, 1073554 J Henry[9&11] 58 Fld Bty, 784206 F Heppenstall[11] 58 Fld Bty, 1060273 B W Herbert[9&11] 58 Fld Bty, 796574 G W Hogg[11] 58 Fld Bty, 808804 A J Hooper[11&12] 8 AA Bty, 798591 J Houlbrock[11] 58 Fld Bty, 815023 S Howarth[11] 58 Fld Bty, 786796 E R Jeffries[11] 58 Fld Bty, 797455 A J Johnson[11] 8 AA Bty, 1065907 J A Johnson[11] 58 Fld Bty, 812637 R W Johnson[11] 58 Fld Bty, 797325 S A Jupp[11] 8 AA Bty, 1073143 F J Knowles[9(Boy)&11] 58 Fld Bty, 800824 C B Lavan[11] 58 Fld Bty, 5823996 F H Lawes[11&12] 15 Md Bty, 802600 W G Lawrence[11&12] 8 AA Bty, 1069968 L Loughlin[9&11] 58 Fld Bty, 798141 W MacDonald[11&12] 15 Md Bty, 802863 T A Mc Gregor[11] 58 Fld Bty, 805182 J Mc Kechnie[11] 8 AA Bty, 1421458 J Mc Ilree[11] 8 AA Bty, 798903 T Maddocks[11] 58 Fld Bty, 1670758 J W Marsh[11] 58 Fld Bty, 806631 G H Martin[11] 58 Fld Bty, 816015 J Merson[11] 58 Fld Bty, 808891 J N S Miles[11] 8 AA Bty, 794874 W Millburn[11] 8 AA Bty, 809088 L R Millie[11] 58 Fld Bty, 788353 C A Moon[9&11] 58 Fld Bty, 1072891 A J Morey[11] 15 Md Bty, 1070267 J Morgan[9&11] 58 Fld Bty, 780857 J Morris[9&11] 58 Fld Bty, 808987 S R Mundy[11] 8 AA Bty, 791832 W J Myers[11&12] 15 Md Bty, 780765 E Netherclift[11&12] 15 Md Bty, 1073602 S M Nevins[9&11] 58 Fld Bty, 786077 H R Newens[11] 58 Fld Bty, 818027 F Norman[11] 8 AA Bty, 777996 J P Ormondroyd[9&11] 58 Fld Bty, 4341190 J H Oxendale[11] 8 AA Bty, 4122112 J Palin[11] 58 Fld Bty, 784121 L Palin[11] 58 Fld Bty, 781251 A W Park[11] 58 Fld Bty, 779251 A Parker[11] 58 Fld Bty, 786350 G T Parkinson[11] 58 Fld Bty, 808837 H Pearce[11] 8 AA Bty, 37432 J Pentland[11] 8 AA Bty, 5668174 W F Perry[11] 58 Fld Bty, 788287 J Pickering[11] 58 Fld Bty, 809049 H Platt[11] 58 Fld Bty, 777967 W J Platten[11] 58 Fld Bty, 1070903 R W Pond[9&11] 8 AA Bty, 4909723 B Poole[11] 8 AA Bty, 788522 F Potts[11] 8 AA Bty, 806198 M Price[11] 58 Fld Bty, 1073071 T W Quinn[11] 58 Fld Bty, 806347 R S Rees[11] 58 Fld Bty, 788153 N Reid[9&11] 58 Fld Bty, 779172 S P Rendell[11] 8 AA Bty, 1069465 O J Riley[11] 58 Fld Bty, 777428 W H Riley[11] 8 AA Bty, 4075189 C Roberts[11] 58 Fld Bty, 794286 S Roberts[11&12] 15 Md Bty, 800043 A C Russell[11] 8 AA Bty, 802590 S Russell[11] 8 AA Bty, 777971 W R Sacre[9&11] 58 Fld Bty, 779434 O J Sampson[11] 58 Fld Bty, 800554 J Schofield[11] 8 AA Bty, 779902 J H Scott[11] 12 Fld Bty, 806325 C Shentall[11] 58 Fld Bty, 777700 W Sheppard[11] 58 Fld Bty, 779741 A Simcock[11] 15 Md Bty, 797334 T Simpson[11] 8 AA Bty, 5468593 D Skutt[9&11] 58 Fld Bty, 805990 A Smart[11] 58 Fld Bty, 752318 A H Smith[11] 8 AA Bty, 786234 E J Smith[11] 58 Fld Bty, 791865 F J Smith[11&12] 15 Md Bty, 4531613 H Smith[11] 58 Fld Bty, 3443258 J H Smith[11] 58 Fld Bty, 794035 P Smith[11] 8 AA Bty, 806593 S Smith[11] 8 AA Bty, 791335 W T Smith[9,11&12] attch. HQ PD, 800954 J Sneddon[11] 58 Fld Bty, 773903 R P Soutar[11] 8 AA Bty, 1069128 H A Stanton[11] 58 Fld Bty, 786931

J Stanton[11] 12 Fld Bty, 772171 E E Steele[11] 58 Fld Bty, 1068493 G E Stevens[11] 8 AA Bty, 802477 W Sturdy[11] 58 Fld Bty, 786836 G H Sturgeon[11] 12 Fld Bty, 1073684 F Sutcliffe[9&11] 58 Fld Bty, 1070389 H J W Sutton[11] 8 AA Bty, 777134 R Tait[11] 8 AA Bty, 1073550 P H Taylor[9&11] 58 Fld Bty, 1073959 W H Thompson[11] 8 AA Bty, 1419699 B F Timewell[11] 8 AA Bty, 805149 T Topping[11] 8 AA Bty, 777881 S J Trigg[9&11] 58 Fld Bty, 781942 J H Turner[9&11] 58 Fld Bty, 788351 W H Udy[9&11] 58 Fld Bty, 1072654 J E Vatcher[11] 8 AA Bty, 808530 C W Waites[11] 8 AA Bty, 783259 A G Walsh[9&11] 58 Fld Bty, 1073878 A G Watts[9&11] 58 Fld Bty, 797728 G F Webb[11] 8 AA Bty, 803550 A H West[11] 58 Fld Bty, 806668 J L West[11] 8 AA Bty, 816049 A E Westcott[11] 58 Fld Bty, 808964 H Weston[11] 8 AA Bty, 1073519 W Whalley[11] 8 AA Bty, 781145 E White[11] 58 Fld Bty, 805944 B Williams[11] 8 AA Bty, 808968 I M Williams[11] 8 AA Bty, 808988 T J Williams[11] 8 AA Bty, 1071144 J Wilson[11] 15 Md Bty, 816686 C Winmill[11] 8 AA Bty, 777395 W Wise[11] 8 AA Bty, 1073978 W Witts[11] 12 Fld Bty, 790947 H E Wood[11] 58 Fld Bty, 5824453 E B Wright[11&12] 8 AA Bty & 805122 J Young[11] 8 AA Bty

Farrier: ~ 1049772 A P South[9(Gnr.)&11] 58 Fld Bty

THE CORPS OF ROYAL ENGINEERS:
Sub Units Identified As Entitled:
RE Officers Attached Military Engineering Services – Corps of Indian Engineers
King George's Own Bengal Sappers & Miners
Royal Bombay Sappers & Miners – Individual
Advanced Engineer Dump & Park – Peshawar, Pir Kala and Dand

Note a. *Roll of all personnel identified as eligible.*
Note b. *'2 Field Company', Sappers & Miners – Ghalanai*
Note c. *'3 Field Company', Sappers & Miners – Dand*
Note d. *MES (Buildings & Roads) – Pir Kala and Dand*
Note e. *MES (Electrical & Mechanical) – Ghalanai*
Note f. *Medals named in small impressed block capitals: 'R.E.'*

Single Clasp	*No. Identified*	*Rarity*
Mohmand 1933[11]	11	**Extremely Rare**
Combination Clasps	*No. Identified*	*Rarity*
Afghanistan N.W.F. 1919[3] Mohmand 1933[11]	1	**According to the roll as seen, can be considered Unique**
Waziristan 1921–24[6] Mohmand 1933[11]	2	**Of the Utmost Rarity**
North West Frontier 1930–31[9] Burma 1930–32[10] Mohmand 1933[11]	3	**Of the Utmost Rarity**
North West Frontier 1930–31[9] Mohmand 1933[11]	4	**Of the Utmost Rarity**
North West Frontier 1930–31[9] Mohmand 1933[11] North West Frontier 1935[12]	1	**According to the roll as seen, can be considered Unique**
Mohmand 1933[11] North West Frontier 1935[12]	4	**Of the Utmost Rarity**

Lieutenant Colonels: ~ A V T Wakely[11] CRE
Majors: ~ G R Pim[3(Capt.)&11] KGO S&M, N A Coxwell Rogers[11&12(Lt. Col.)] & W B Whishaw[6&11]
Captains: ~ D R Crone[9(Lt.)&11] SI, R S Dalby[9(Lt.)&11], R St. C Davidson[9,10&11] KGO S&M, R E Holloway[9(Lt.),10(Lt.)&11] KGO S&M & A G Wyatt[11]
Lieutenants: ~ B M Archibald[11] MES Peshawar Asst Fld Engineer Royal, Bombay S&M, I H F Boyd[11], T Burrowes[11&12] KGO S&M, G A R Fawcus[11] KGO S&M, M C A Henniker[11] KGO S&M, D R M Orchard[9,11&12(Capt.)] MES, S R G Scott[11&12(Capt.)] KGO S&M, W H C Travers[11] KGO S&M, J W White[9&11] & T Wright[11&12] KGO S&M
Warrant Officers Class II: ~ 1852918 C B Logan[6(Sgt.)&11] KGO S&M
Company Quartermaster Sergeants/Staff Sergeants: ~ (Mech)1859413 L Marsh[11] MES

Quartermaster Sergeants/Sergeants: ~ 1859998 W Budden[9,10&11] KGO S&M, 1865401 E J Childs[9(Cpl.)&11] KGO S&M, 1863913 E T Emmings[11] KGO S&M & 1853596 H Ginger[11] KGO S&M

Lance Sergeants/Corporals: ~ 1863597 K J Leslie[11] KGO S&M

THE ROYAL CORPS OF SIGNALS:
Sub Units Identified As Entitled:
1 Indian Division Signals
3 Indian Division Signals
'B' Corps Signals Detachment Attached Peshawar District Signals
Peshawar District Signals
Brigade Signals Sections

Note a.   *Roll of all commissioned personnel identified as eligible.*

Note b.   *Non-commissioned and other rank personnel multi clasp only except 'B' Corps Signal Detachment, which is listed in full.*

Note c.   *Medals named in thin impressed capitals: 'R. SIGNALS.'*

Single Clasp	No. Identified	Rarity
Mohmand 1933[11]	In Strength	Not Rare
Mohmand 1933[11]	'B' Corps Signals = 30	Very Rare
Combination Clasps	**No. Identified**	**Rarity**
Waziristan 1921–24[6] Mohmand 1933[11]	2	Of the Utmost Rarity
Waziristan 1921–24[6] Mohmand 1933[11] North West Frontier 1935[12]	2	Of the Utmost Rarity
North West Frontier 1930–31[9] Mohmand 1933[11]	47	Very Rare
North West Frontier 1930–31[9] Mohmand 1933[11]	'B' Corps Signals = 3	Of the Utmost Rarity
North West Frontier 1930–31[9] Mohmand 1933[11] North West Frontier 1935[12]	7	Of the Utmost Rarity
North West Frontier 1930–31[9] Mohmand 1933[11] North West Frontier 1935[12]	'B' Corps Signals = 1	According to the roll as seen, can be considered Unique
Burma 1930–32[10] Mohmand 1933[12]	2	Of the Utmost Rarity
Burma 1930–32[10] Mohmand 1933[11]	'B' Corps Signals = 2	Of the Utmost Rarity
Mohmand 1933[11] North West Frontier 1935[12]	34	Very Rare

Majors: ~ W M Miller[10&11] PDS

Captains: ~ J F Charlesworth[9&11] PDS & G S Hurst[11]

Lieutenants: ~ T W Boileau[9&11] PDS, J C Hardy[9&11] PDS, H L Lewis[10&11] PDS, W A Purser[11&12] PDS, L T Shawcross[9&11] PDS & R C Yule[11] PDS

Company Quartermaster Sergeants/Staff Sergeants: ~ (Fitter) 1411848 G E Agar[11&12]

Quartermaster Sergeants/Sergeants: ~ 2310372 G Bennett[9(Cpl.)&11] PDS, 7991 C Cheeseman[9(Cpl.),11&12] PDS, 2311403 F S Handley[9,11&12] PDS, 2313907 G A Harper[9&11] 'B' Corps Sigs, 1406867 W J Squires[9&11] PDS & 2311826 A W Walker[11&12] PDS & 2306507 C Warren[11] 'B' Corps Sigs attch PDS

Lance Sergeants/Corporals: ~ 2315566 T Barry[11(Cpl.)&12] PDS, 2316730 W E Birkett[11] 'B' Corps Sigs attch. PDS, 2313988 L J Brown[6(Sgln.)&11] PDS, 769959 W Burton[11] 'B' Corps Sigs attch. PDS, 2311017 A B Clarke[11] 'B' Corps Sigs attch. PDS,

6390674 A E Clevett[9&11] PDS, 2310956 H A Coaten[9&11] PDS, 6336253 H W Dadswell[11&12] PDS, 1860365 A Grant[9(Cpl.)&11] PDS, 2309379 J P Hayes[9(Cpl.)&11] PDS, 2311312 H E Mott[6(Sgln.)11&12(Cpl.)] PDS, (625510) 2310920 A Mowatt[6(Sgln.),11&12(Cpl.)] PDS, 2311336 F G Sherrington[11&12] PDS, 2315091 F I E Stockton[11&12] PDS & 2314991 B G Thompson[6(Sgln.)&11] PDS

Lance Corporals/Signalmen: ~ 2318695 P A Alexander[9&11] PDS, 3383435 D A Alinutt[11&12] PDS, 2320890 G F Atkin[11] 'B' Corps Sigs attch. PDS, 2319895 W F Baker[11&12] PDS, 2320754 G E Ball[11] 'B' Corps Sigs attch. PDS, 2318912 W C Barber[9&11] PDS, 2319590 R G F Barker[11&12(Sgt.)] PDS, 5823033 C O Bayley[9&11], 2316341 F C Beasley[9&11], 2318661 W Becconsall[11] 'B' Corps Sigs attch. PDS, 2319643 C Beeching[9&11] PDS, 2313288 R C Blaikie[11&12] PDS, 2319291 J Blyth[11] 'B' Corps Sigs attch. PDS, 550117 D Bolton[11] 'B' Corps Sigs attch. PDS, 2318687 G E Boulton[9&11] PDS, 547471 V C Brassfield[11&12(Cpl.)] PDS, 2319449 H J Brett[9&11] PDS, 2321433 J M Brown[11] 'B' Corps Sigs attch. PDS, 5434915 J R Brown[11] 'B' Corps Sigs attch. PDS, 2319460 W B Brown[11] 'B' Corps Sigs attch. PDS, 2317902 J Cain[9&11] PDS, 2322467 J Cannot[11] 'B' Corps Sigs attch. PDS, 2320536 A J V Catt[11&12(Cpl.)] PDS, 2559005 A A Christie[9&11] 'B' Corps Sigs attch. PDS, 796278 A L T Cloke[11] 'B' Corps Sigs attch. PDS, 2319849 P Coates[9&11] PDS, 2318139 C Collyns[9&11] PDS, 2320490 L Coombes[11] 'B' Corps Sigs attch. PDS, 2318182 F C Curtis[9&11] PDS, 2321826 J Cutter[11] 'B' Corps Sigs attch. PDS, 2318562 S Dawes[9&11] PDS, 2318418 W Dawson[9&11] PDS, 2315408 W C Day[9&11] PDS, 2319923 A E Dines[10&11] 'B' Corps Sigs attch. PDS, 2320151 J Doherty[11] 'B' Corps Sigs attch. PDS, 2322025 J Done[11] 'B' Corps Sigs attch. PDS, 2322197 W Doris[11] 'B' Corps Sigs attch. PDS, 2319948 H Dumville[11&12] PDS, 2319094 R Durkin[11] 'B' Corps Sigs attch. PDS, 2318840 H Dyke[11] 'B' Corps Sigs attch. PDS, 2318669 G Eccleshall[11] 'B' Corps Sigs attch. PDS, 2320947 C J Ewer[11] 'B' Corps Sigs attch. PDS, 6084169 A C Fenwick[11] 'B' Corps Sigs attch. PDS, 2320474 S Fox[11&12] PDS, 2023843 J A Garnett[11] 'B' Corps Sigs attch. PDS, 2316209 E Gear[11] 'B' Corps Sigs attch. PDS, 2319857 E R Gentle[9,11&12] PDS, 6283693 H L George[9&11] PDS, 2319701 W H Gigg[9&11] PDS, 2319228 J C Gladwin[9&11] PDS, 2319369 S Grattage[9,11&12] PDS, 2319631 C I Griffin[11&12] PDS, 2320651 G Hale[11&12] PDS, 4911791 E S Hardwick[11&12] PDS, 2321571 C R Harrod[11&12] PDS, 2321389 W A Hearn[11] 'B' Corps Sigs attch. PDS, 2317182 A A Heighton[11&12] PDS, 2310806 R Henshall[11&12] PDS, 2214337 R G A Hill[9&11] PDS, 2317914 M H Hodgson[9&11] PDS, 2319812 J Holmes[11] 'B' Corps Sigs attch. PDS, 2320627 L R Holt[11&12] PDS, 2320387 H Horsman[11&12] PDS, 2319592 J Howarth[9&11] PDS, 2973766 J Howell[9&11] PDS, 2319699 S A Huggett[9&11] PDS, 2321335 G E Ide[11&12] PDS, 2319979 J W Ireland[9,11&12] PDS, 2320150 R Irving[10&11] 'B' Corps Sigs attch. PDS, 2313385 H F Jackson[11&12] PDS, 2318035 W L Jarvis[9,11&12] 'B' Corps Sigs attch. PDS, 2320100 D Jones[11] 'B' Corps Sigs attch. PDS, 2319994 J J Kelly[11&12] PDS, 1070674 J Lambert[11&12] PDS, 2209868 A Lee[9&11(L/Sgt.)] PDS, 2319352 J C Lucas[9&11] PDS, 2321209 H S Mangnall[11&12] PDS, 2319256 C J Martin[9&11] PDS, 2320571 C E Mason[11&12] PDS, 2318703 C Miller[9&11] PDS, 2319198 W Mitchell[9&11] PDS, 2565397 F J Murrell[9,11&12] PDS, 2320541 S Nesbit[11] 'B' Corps Sigs attch. PDS, 3185128 G Noble[11] 'B' Corps Sigs attch. PDS, 2318679 G Norton[9&11] PDS, 2318250 J O'Connell[9&11] 'B' Corps Sigs attch. PDS, 2318708 A Palmer[9&11] PDS, 5493709 V G Parker[9&11] PDS, 2319636 W H Partington[9&11] PDS, 2320227 L F Phipps[11&12] PDS, 2320199 F A Pike[11&12] PDS, 2315726 S A Potts[9&11] PDS, 2321008 S G Purkiss[11&12] PDS, 2313373 A T Roberts[11&12] PDS, 2320204 G Rumford[9,11&12] PDS, 2318667 J A Shinn[9&11] PDS, 3522516 H Walsh[11&12] PDS, 2318555 E S Wickes[9&11] PDS, 2319463 T Williams[9&11] 'B' Corps Sigs attch. PDS, 2312546 P A Wink[9&11] PDS & 2318462 R J Yarnell[9&11] PDS

THE INFANTRY:

~ 1st Bn, The Leicestershire Regiment ~

Note a.   *Roll of all personnel identified eligible.*
Note b.   *Recipients attached Moforce Provost Company.*
Note c.   *Medals named in small impressed block capitals: 'LEIC. R.'*

Single Clasp	No. Identified	Rarity
Mohmand 1933[11]	3	Of the Utmost Rarity

Warrant Officers Class II: ~ (CSM) 4848599 A E Clifford[11]
Lance Corporals/Privates: ~ 4855225 C W Hodgkinson[11] & 4853016 J Stead[11]

~ 1st Bn, The Cheshire Regiment ~

Note a.   *Roll of all personnel identified as eligible.*
Note b.   *Recipients attached 1 Field Ambulance (FA), Royal Army Medical Corps (RAMC).*
Note c.   *Medals named in small impressed block capitals: 'CHESHIRE. R.'*

Single Clasp	No. Identified	Rarity
Mohmand 1933[11]	2	Of the Utmost Rarity

Lance Corporals/Privates: ~ 4121091 H Cartwright[11] & 4122595 J Eagleson[11]

~ 1st Bn, The Cameronions (Scottish Rifles) ~

Note a.   *Roll of all personnel identified as eligible.*
Note b.   *Recipient attached 4 Sanitary Section (SS), Royal Army Medical Corps (RAMC).*
Note c.   *Medals named in small impressed block capitals: 'CAMERON'*

Single Clasp	No. Identified	Rarity
Mohmand 1933[11]	1	According to the roll as seen, can be considered Unique

Quartermaster Sergeants/Sergeants: ~ 3238280 A Peaple[11]

~ 2nd Bn, The Royal Sussex Regiment ~

Note a.   *Roll of all personnel identified as eligible.*
Note b.   *Recipient attached Headquarters (HQ), 2 Brigade (2 Bde.)*
Note c.   *Medals named in small impressed block capitals: 'R. SUSS. R.'*

Single Clasp	No. Identified	Rarity
Mohmand 1933[11]	0	None Identified

Combination Clasps	No. Identified	Rarity
North West Frontier 1930–31[9] Mohmand 1933[11]	1	According to the roll as seen, can be considered Unique

Quartermaster Sergeants/Sergeants: ~ (Act) 264906(1) J G Hoare[9(Pte.)&11]

~ 1st Bn, The Hampshire Regiment ~

Note a.   *Roll of all personnel identified as eligible.*
Note b.   *Medals named in small impressed block capitals: 'HAMPS. R.'*

Single Clasp	No. Identified	Rarity
Mohmand 1933[11]	8	Of the Utmost Rarity

Combination Clasps	No. Identified	Rarity
Mohmand 1933[11] North West Frontier 1935[12]	9	Of the Utmost Rarity

Lieutenants: ~ J H Dyas[11&12(Capt.)] & T G Tucker[11&12]
Sergeants: ~ 5485330 W Box[11] & 5486758 E Holden[11]
Lance Corporals/Privates: ~ 5494194 K Broadley[11], 5494201 C E Budworth[11&12], 5494066 E G Galpin[11&12], 5493790 A Hinks[11], 5494011 R Lane[11&12], 5495037 S Limburn[11], 5485832 H J Pottle[11&12(Cpl.)], 5493852 G Raggatt[11], 5494073 R Richards[11&12], 5494669 R H Robinson[11&12], 54943331 L Rundle[11], 6911271 J Starkey[11] & 5494135 A Wellstead[11&12]

~ The Prince of Wales Volunteers (South Lancashire) ~

Note a.   *Roll of all personnel identified as eligible.*
Note b.   *Recipient attached Headquarters (HQ), Peshawar District (PD).*
Note c.   *Medals named in small impressed block capitals: 'S. LAN. R.'*

Single Clasp	No. Identified	Rarity
Mohmand 1933[11]	1	According to the roll as seen, can be considered Unique

Lance Corporals/Privates: ~ 7872615 J W Boardman[11]

~ 2nd Bn, The Essex Regiment ~

Note a.   *Roll of all personnel identified as eligible.*
Note b.   *Medals named in small impressed block capitals: 'ESSEX. R.'*

Single Clasp	No. Identified	Rarity
Mohmand 1933[11]	1	According to the roll as seen, can be considered Unique

Company Quartermaster Sergeants/Staff Sergeants/Colour Sergeants: ~ 6003074 W Larcher[11]

~ 1st Bn, The Sherwood Foresters (Nottinghamshire & Derbyshire) Regiment ~

Note a.   *Roll of all personnel identified as eligible.*
Note b.   *Recipient attached Headquarters (HQ), 2 Brigade (2 Bde.)*
Note c.   *Medals named in small impressed block capitals: 'FORRESTERS'*

Single Clasp	No. Identified	Rarity
Mohmand 1933[11]	1	According to the roll as seen, can be considered Unique

Quartermaster Sergeants/Sergeants: ~ (Act) 4967156 J Barnett[11]

~ 1st Bn, The Loyal Regiment (North Lancashire) ~

Note a.   *Roll of all personnel identified as eligible.*
Note b.   *Recipient attached 4 Sanitary Section (SS), Royal Army Medical Corps (RAMC).*
Note c.   *Medals named in small impressed block capitals: 'LOYAL R.'*

Single Clasp	No. Identified	Rarity
Mohmand 1933[11]	1	According to the roll as seen, can be considered Unique

Quartermaster Sergeants/Sergeants: ~ 3848231 W Shaxon[11]

~ 2nd Bn, The King's Own (Yorkshire Light Infantry) ~

Note a.   *Roll of all personnel identified as eligible.*
Note b.   *Recipient attached Headquarters (HQ), 2 Brigade (2 Bde.)*
Note c.   *Medals named in small impressed block capitals: 'K.O.Y.L.I.'*

Single Clasp	No. Identified	Rarity
Mohmand 1933[11]	0	None Identified

Combination Clasps	No. Identified	Rarity
North West Frontier 1930 –31[9] Mohmand 1933[11]	1	According to the roll as seen, can be considered Unique

Quartermaster Sergeants/Sergeants: ~ (Act) 4684322 O F May[9(Pte.)&11]

~ 2nd Bn, The York and Lancaster Regiment ~

Note a.   *Roll of all personnel identified as eligible.*
Note b.   *All recipients attached Moforce Provost Company.*
Note c.   *Medals named in thin impressed capitals: 'YORK & LANC. R.' or 'Y&L R.'*

Single Clasp	No. Identified	Rarity
Mohmand 1933[11]	6	Of the Utmost Rarity

Quartermaster Sergeants/Sergeants: ~ 4740741 T Scamadine[11]
Lance Corporals/Privates: ~ 4744103 A Bothamley[11], 4743206 J M Culliney[11], 4743018 J H Dearden[11], 4742798 A Headley[11] & 4742641 J W Jacklin[11]

~ 2nd Bn, The Durham Light Infantry ~

Note a.   *Roll of all personnel identified as eligible.*
Note b.   *Medals named in thin impressed capitals: 'DURH. L. I.'*

Single Clasp	No. Identified	Rarity
Mohmand 1933[11]	2	Of the Utmost Rarity
Combination Clasps	**No. Identified**	**Rarity**
North West Frontier 1930–31[9] Mohmand 1933[11]	4	Of the Utmost Rarity

Lance Corporals/Privates: ~ 4445637 J Boddy[9&11], 4447150 C Graham[11], 4446396 A Rice[9&11], 4445713 A S Simpson[9&11], 4447153 J Tolliday[11] & 4445805 J J Watts[9&11]

~ 1st Bn, The Gordon Highlanders ~

Note a.   *Roll of all personnel identified as eligible.*
Note b.   *Medals named in thin impressed capitals: 'GORDONS.'*

Single Clasp	No. Identified	Rarity
Mohmand 1933[11]	46	Very Rare
Combination Clasps	**No. Identified**	**Rarity**
North West Frontier 1930–31[9] Mohmand 1933[11]	1	According to the roll as seen, can be considered Unique

Captains: ~ H I Bradshaw[11] attch. HQ Peshawar Bde. & P T Pirie[11]
Lieutenants: ~ P Bell[11] attch. HQ Peshawar Bde., H E Clements[11] attch. HQ Peshawar Bde., G F C Halden[11] attch. HQ Peshawar Bde., J M Hay[11] attch. HQ Peshawar Bde. & R W M de Winton[11] attch. HQ Peshawar Bde.
Quartermaster Sergeants/Sergeants: ~ 2868425 D Cormack[11] attch. HQ Peshawar Bde., 2866658 J Fraser[11] attch. HQ Peshawar Bde., 2867407 J Hull[11] attch. HQ Peshawar Bde., 2869506 J McIntosh[11] attch. HQ Peshawar Bde., 2869641 D Stewart[11] attch. HQ Peshawar Bde. & 2866093 G Wisley[11] attch. HQ Peshawar Bde.
Lance Sergeants/Corporals: ~ 2873152 F Brown[11] attch. HQ Nowshera Bde., 6447554 J Laming[11] attch. HQ Peshawar Bde. & 4532184 F Waterfield[11] attch. HQ Peshawar Bde.

Lance Corporals/Privates: ~ 2873144 T Anderson[11] attch. HQ Nowshera Bde., 2875414 J Angerson[11] attch. HQ Nowshera Bde., 2871933 J Arnott[11] attch. HQ Nowshera Bde., 2873904 J Beattie[11] attch. HQ Peshawar Bde., 2871588 G Christie[11] attch. 2 FA, RAMC, 2873329 A Clark[11] attch. HQ Peshawar Bde., 2873457 A Duff[11] attch. HQ Nowshera Bde., 2873966 A Gatherer[11] attch. 4 SS, RAMC, 2872812 S Glass[11] attch. HQ Nowshera Bde., 2873597 W Haddan[11] attch. HQ Peshawar Bde., 2873799 R Hunter[11] attch. HQ Peshawar Bde., 2874114 J Hutchinson[11] attch. HQ Nowshera Bde., 2873278 A Kemp[11] attch. HQ Peshawar Bde., 2867701 P Kimpkin[11] attch. 4 SS, RAMC, 2871258 W Mackie[11] attch. HQ Peshawar Bde., 2873474 R MacKay[9&11] attch. HQ Peshawar Bde., 2873893 J Malone[11] attch. HQ Nowshera Bde., 2872748 A Michie[11] attch. HQ Peshawar Bde., 2874561 G Moir[11] attch. 58 Fld Bty RA, 2872482 J Nish[11] attch. HQ Nowshera Bde., 2873333 A Redmond[11] attch. HQ Peshawar Bde., 2874396 J Restorick[11] attch. HQ Nowshera Bde., 2872047 A Runciman[11] attch. HQ Peshawar Bde., 2865915 A Stewart[11] attch. HQ Peshawar Bde., 2873905 J Sutherland[11] attch. HQ Peshawar Bde., 2873790 F Taylor[11] attch. HQ Nowshera Bde., 3051175 P Thorburn[11] attch. 2 FA, RAMC, 2873220 W Walker[11] attch. 4 SS, RAMC, 2873556 G Weatherhead[11] attch. 2 FA, RAMC, 2873990 H Webster[11] attch. 4 SS, RAMC & 2873077 G Yates[11] attch. 4 SS, RAMC

THE CORPS:

~ The Royal Army Medical Corps ~
Sub Units Identified As Entitled:
Unit Medical Officers Attached
31 Company
1 & 2 Field Ambulances
4 Sanitary Section

Note a.   *Roll of all personnel identified as eligible.*

Note b.   *Non-Commissioned and other rank personnel all drawn from 31 Company, Royal Army Medical Corps (RAMC), Peshawar.*

Note c.   *'A' Company, 1 Field Ambulance (FA), attached Lines of Communication > Dand, 'B' Company, 1 Field Ambulance (FA), attached Reserve > Sunhan Khwar.*

Note d.   *2 Field Ambulance (FA), attached Mohmand Column.*

Note e.   *4 Sanitary Section (SS), Royal Army Medical Corps (RAMC), attached Lines of Communication Depot – Dand.*

Note f.   *Medals named in thin impressed capitals: 'R.A.M.C.'*

Single Clasp	No. Identified	Rarity
Mohmand 1933[11]	6	Of the Utmost Rarity
Combination Clasps	**No. Identified**	**Rarity**
North West Frontier 1930–31[9] Mohmand 1933[11]	2	Of the Utmost Rarity
North West Frontier 1930–31[9] Mohmand 1933[11] North West Frontier 1935[12]	1	According to the roll as seen, can be considered Unique
Burma 1930–32[10] Mohmand 1933[11]	1	According to the roll as seen, can be considered Unique
Burma 1930–32[10] Mohmand 1933[11] North West Frontier 1935[12]	3	Of the Utmost Rarity
Mohmand 1933[11] North West Frontier 1935[12]	23	Very Rare

Lieutenant Colonels: ~ L T Poole[11] DAMS, Mohmand FF

Majors: ~ A P Draper[11&12] MO, 18 KEO Cavalry, IA, F R H Mollan[11&12] OC 1 FA & A E Richmond[9&11]

Captains: ~ S W K Arundell[11] attch. 2 FA, G F Harrison[10(Lt.)&11] attch. 4 SS, W G Harvey[11] attch. 2 FA, R R Leaming[9(Lt.)&11] DADMS, 1 Ind Div. & A Sachs[11] Director of Pathology, PD Hospital attch. 2 FA

Lieutenants: ~ T M R Ahern[11&12] SMO Blockade Lines, N P Breden[11&12(Capt.)] MO 18 K E O Cavalry, IA, Ft. Shabkador, W B F Brennan[11&12(Capt.)] attch. 1 FA, L T Furnivall[11] attch. 1 FA & J B MacFarlane[11] attch. 1 FA

Quartermaster Sergeants/Sergeants: ~ 7254709 A Brooker[11&12]

Lance Sergeants/Corporals: ~ 7258604 J C Farmer[11&12], 7251528 P H W Harris[11&12] & 7255271 T Kitching[11&12]

Lance Corporals/Privates: ~ 7261049 R H Burfield[11&12], 7260675 L A Cook[11&12], 4910812 J N Cooper[11&12], 7259519 W C Cosnett[11&12], 7260722 H Doyle[11&12], 7260728 H Henry[11&12], 5103165 A Hitchcox[11&12], 7260716 J Inglis[11&12], 6780270 H Jelfs[10,11&12], 7260654 I W J Martin[11&12], 7260660 T H Mattox[11&12], 7258829 F Ryde[9,11&12], 7259135 A Sutcliffe[10,11&12], 7259202 H Thorpe[10,11&12], 7260701 F W Totty[11&12], 7260686 S R Whitehall[11&12], 7259463 A J Wignell[11&12] & 7259129 R T Wilson[11&12]

~ The Royal Army Ordnance Corps ~

Note a.   *Roll of all personnel identified as eligible.*

Note b.   *Recipients marked thus (*) were removed from the 6 Armoured Car Company (ACC) Roll dated 21st January 1925 by Maj. H M Heyland. It is not known whether this was because the names were added to a supplementary 'lost' Royal Army Ordnance Corps (RAOC) roll or whether the men were in fact found to be ineligible.*

Note c.   *Medals named in small impressed block capitals: 'R.A.O.C.'*

Single Clasp	No. Identified	Rarity
Mohmand 1933[11]	4	If verified, of the Utmost Rarity

Company Quartermaster Sergeants/Staff Sergeants: ~ (Armt) 7574656 G I Simpson[11] attch. 6 ACC, RTC *

Lance Corporals/Privates: ~ 7583056 C Jones[11] attch. 6 ACC, RTC, 1669117 J Leppard[11] attch. 6 ACC, RTC* & 7575831 H Pennington[11] attch. 6 ACC, RTC*

~ The Royal Army Veterinary Corps ~

Note a.   *Roll of all personnel identified as eligible.*

Note b.   *Medals named in thin impressed capitals: 'R.A.V.C.'*

Single Clasp	No. Identified	Rarity
Mohmand 1933[11]	0	None Identified
Combination Clasps	**No. Identified**	**Rarity**
Afghanistan N.W.F. 1919[3] Waziristan 1919–21[4] Waziristan 1921–24[6] North West Frontier 1930–31[9] Mohmand 1933[11] North West Frontier 1935[12]	1	According to the roll as seen, can be considered Unique
North West Frontier 1930–31[9] Mohmand 1933[11] North West Frontier 1935[12]	1	According to the roll as seen, can be considered Unique
Mohmand 1933[11] North West Frontier 1935[12]	1	According to the roll as seen, can be considered Unique

Majors: ~ W P S Edwards[3(Capt.),4(Capt.),6(Capt.),9,11&12], G V Golding[9,11&12] ADVS PD & J Leigh[11&12]

THE ROYAL AIR FORCE

Note a.   *Roll of all personnel identified as eligible.*

Note b.   *Refer to Royal Air Force notes at end of 'Frontier Campaigns 1919 – 1925' section for guidance regarding early rank designations.*

Note c.   *Ranks shown are those applicable at award of first clasp, which probably accounts for the lack of any awards in the rank of Squadron Leader.*

Note d.   *Medals named in thin impressed block capitals: 'R.A.F.'*

Single Clasp	No. Identified	Rarity
Mohmand 1933[11]	61	Rare

Combination Clasps	No. Identified	Rarity
Afghanistan N.W.F. 1919[3] North West Frontier 1930–31[9] Mohmand 1933[11]	1	According to the roll as seen, can be considered Unique
Waziristan 1919–21[4] Mahsud 1919–20[5] Mohmand 1933[11]	1	According to the roll as seen, can be considered Unique
Waziristan 1921–24[6] Mohmand 1933[11]	1	According to the roll as seen, can be considered Unique
Waziristan 1921–24[6] Mohmand 1933[11] North West Frontier 1935[12]	2	Of the Utmost Rarity
North West Frontier 1930–31[9] Mohmand 1933[11]	41	Very Rare
North West Frontier 1930–31[9] Mohmand 1933[11] North West Frontier 1935[12]	16	Extremely Rare
Mohmand 1933[11] North West Frontier 1935[12]	55	Rare

Group Captains: ~ B E Sutton[11]

Flight Lieutenants: ~ J L Airey[11&12], D F W Atcherley[11&12], C L Lea-Cox[9&11], A Harvey[11], L N Hollinghurst[3,9&11], G H Huxham[11], H P Lloyd[6,11&12], J Norwood[11&12], A C H Sharp[11] & V H Tompkins[11&12]

Flying Officers: ~ R J O Bartlett[9&11], D W Bayne[9,11&12], C N Carpenter[11&12], G F K Donaldson[11], J S Douglas[9&11], J H Manning-Fox[9&11], R B Harrison[11], P Haynes[11], W R Monro-Higgs[11], W M Keddie[11], R Menzies[9&11], W T H Nichols[11], E F Porter[11&12], A Pyke[11&12], A M Watts-Read[9&11], E B Waddy[11&12] & W G S Wood[11]

Observer Officer: ~ C N Ellen[4,5&11]

Warrant Officers Class II: ~ 332470 W Morgan[11], 3929 C Oakley[11&12]

Flight Sergeants: ~ 4383 A B Collins[9&11], 86948 V C Terry[11] & 81374 R C Woodthorpe[11]

Sergeants: ~ 335589 R W Baldwin[11&12], 345573 M O Davis[11], 364019 L E Farrell[11&12], 303543 F Florence[11&12], 352215 H C Greenhill[11], 133214 H Pinchen[9&11], 364446 A G Sancto[11], 334337 E R Skingsley[9&11], 343269 L Welch[11] & E E R Williams[9,11&12]

Corporals: ~ 333747 G S Anderson[11], 341147 S P Baker[11], 355033 F W Boyles[9&11], 352862 L R Collins[11&12], 560327 W R Cumbers[9,11&12], 359091 R C Dent[11], 327793 A Fisher[6,11&12], 363932 R A Godsell[11], 343586 L Hilton[6&11], 159941 W E Judson[11], 155057 F H Keirl[9,11&12], 356835 L V Mallinson[11], 560365 E H Maule[11&12], 239011 W H May[11&12], 364132 C E Mitchell[9&11], 358659 S E Nightingale[11&12], 505543 R D Parker[11], 349323 J Preston[11&12], 357129 A H J Smith[11], 350972 W R Squirrell[11], 362219 C H Tibbles[11], 366230 V G B White[11&12] & 347181 W W Wright[9&11]

Leading Aircraftsmen: ~ 365182 J W Ball[11], 363960 R A Bell[11], 510655 C V D Bolton[11&12], 506998 F Brooke[11], 565670 F W Bullen[9,11&12], 363796 R C Burge[11], 510424 J L Callaghan[11&17], 514437 J A Chandler[11&12], 506176 W F Coulson[9&11], 509318 P W K Crisp[11], 364547 A P Crowley[9&11], 365712 J C Daniel[11], 509983 B A Dorrell[11&12], 364614 K G Drury[11&12], 364082 A A J Fulford[11&12], 364063 R P Gilmour[9&11], 590036 F A Gosling[11], 506687 C C Halliday[11], 510388 H C Harris[11&12], 510377 G S Heard[11&12], 366362 E C Hogg[11], 364674 S W H Hutchinson[11], 508026 R Johnston[9&11], 562160 L Jowitt[11], 590099 G H Judge[11], 510730 C W Kearley[11&12], 366327 A P Kelly[11], 358082 J G Kendall[9,11&12], 506148 S W Lipscomb[9&11], 561274 G Mason[11&12], 366354 A McDonald[11&12], 364195 D McEwan[11&12], 513440 V Morton[11&12], 370350 J A Mulford[9&11], 506416 J L Newitt[11], 507513 D O'Connor[11], 364735 R A Palmer[9&11], 365936 W H Parker[11], 561849 F L Payne[11&12], 508331 R W

Penny[11&12], 561339 N V Phillips[11&12], 366442 R H Phillips[11], 507720 R Pleasants[9&11], 510950 W C Quennell[11&12], 510983 L H Reynolds[11&12], 510090 T G Roberts[11], 365932 W R Rose[9&11], 508932 T A Rowe[11&12], 507328 J Rutherford[9,11&12], 363326 F T Salmon[9&11], 356602 A G Scott[11], 506750 A Skinner[11], 560912 E L Spoors[11&12], 510174 H Swift[11], 505376 J E Tilley[9&11], 365031 E J W Walker[11&12], 513667 D A Warnett[11], 505953 A W White[9&11], 364393 E Williams[9&11], 365562 B H Willmott[11], 509026 A T Wilson[11], 511190 F Wilson[11&12] & 363311 H Wright[11]

Aircraftsmen 1st Class: ~ 513170 A Aitken[11&12], 507218 G K Barker[9&11], 506786 R C Bashford[11&12], 509293 J P Conway[9&11], 512957 E T Davies[11&12], 508252 P C Davies[9&11], 366078 P W E Dent[9,11&12], 364071 M J W Dunworth[9&11], 511417 C H Ellett[11], 506197 J J English[9&11], 364643 W M Evans[9&11], 506928 F T Farebrother[11], 505959 W E Flitter[9&11], 509633 C A Golding[11], 511582 C D Grieve [11&12], 507751 L W Holland[11], 507977 J C Irwin[9,11&12], 364111 T J Lade[11], 506188 D Laing[9,11&12], 364124 J H Lepper[9&11], 508683 W Mack[9&11], 508564 G McKeand[9&11], 562790 A McLoughlin[11&12], 511388 F Morgan[11], 363677 G Morris[9&11], 506471 L I Newman[11], 510190 H G Ranson[11&12], 509160 H Riley[11&12], 510029 G Rolfe[11&12], 560898 H S Salmon[9,11&12], 510988 H E Sandys[11&12], 506985 J H Simpson[9&11], 506119 H E Slark[9&11], 511930 S L Smith[11], 506286 D R Woolnough[9,11&12] & 508883 E Young[11&12]

Aircraftsmen 2nd Class: ~ 512470 E P Baldwin[11&12], 507683 J J Blackwood[9&11], 506742 T I Bowen[9&11], 507733 A H Cairns[9,11&12], 509221 A J Harpur[11&12], 508838 W H Hattrick[9,11&12], 512630 W R S Madgwick[11&12], 365506 J P Murphy[9,11&12], 513844 W J Reardon[11&12], 511455 W E Sanderson[9,11&12], 508386 F H Street[9&11] & 512771 H West[11&12]

INDIAN ESTABLISHMENT

Qualifying Units Present (Officers Plus Known Individuals)

The Cavalry:
18th King Edwards Own Cavalry...Mohmand Column & Blockhouse Line

The Artillery:
22 Indian Mountain Brigade
22 Mountain Brigade Ammunition Column
2 (Derajat) Mountain Battery (FF)...Reserve Subhan Khwar
4 (Hazara) Mountain Battery (FF)...Mohmand Column
10 (Abbottabad) Mountain Battery..Mohmand Column

The Sappers & Miners:
King George's Own Bengal S&M
No. 2 Field Company..Road Construction Ghalanai
No. 3 Field Company..Road Construction Dand
Advanced Engineer Park...Peshawar
Advanced Engineering Dumps...Pir Kala & Dand

Military Engineering Services

Survey of India

The Indian Signal Corps:

The Infantry:
1/7th Rajput Regiment Queen Victoria's Own Light Infantry..Peshawar Brigade
3/10th Baluch Regiment..Individuals
5/10th Baluch Regiment (King George's Own)..Peshawar Brigade
3/14th Punjab Regiment..Peshawar Brigade
5/12th Frontier Force Regiment (Queen Victoria's Own Corps of Guides).....................Nowshera Brigade attch. Peshawar Brigade
1/11th Sikh Regiment (King George's Own)...Nowshera Brigade
3/2th Punjab Regiment..Nowshera Brigade
3/11th Sikh Regiment..Reserve Subhan Khwar
1/1st Hyderabad Regiment...Individuals

The Indian Army Reserve of Officers / The Auxiliary Forces India / The Indian Territorial Force

The Indian Corps:
The Royal Indian Army Service Corps:
No. 37 Animal Transport Company (Camels)..Two Troops Mohmand Column & Two Troops Dand
Nos. 1, 27, 30, 32, 34 & 39 Animal Transport Companies (Mules)........................Split Mohmand Column and Dand
No. 2 Mechanical Transport Company...Fort Shabkadar
No. 14 Motor Ambulance Company...Fort Shabkadar

Medical Units:
The Indian Medical Service / The Indian Hospital Corps /
The Queen Alexander's Military Nursing Service India
British & Indian Military Hospitals...Peshawar & Nowshera
No. 1 Field Ambulance...Mohmand Column Peshawar Brigade
No. 2 Field Ambulance..Lines of Communication Dand
No. 4 Sanitary Section...Lines of Communication Dand

The Indian Army Veterinary Corps:

The Indian Army Ordnance Corps:
Artillery and Mechanical Transport Workshops

The Indian Corps of Clerks:

The Military Farms Department:

The Police, Judiciary & Intelligence:
Frontier Constabulary, Jail Department & Frontier Intelligence Corps

The Postal Department:
Nos. 1 and 2 Field Post Offices

The Indian Ecclesiastical Department:

The Political & Civil Departments:

Royal Air Force:			
1 (Indian) Group RAF			
1 (Indian) Wing RAF			
Squadron	Operation	Location	Aircraft
No. 27 (B) Squadron	Bajaur	RAF Kohat	Westerland Wapiti
No. 60 (B) Squadron	Bajaur	RAF Kohat	Westerland Wapiti
2 (Indian) Wing RAF			
Squadron	Operation	Location	Aircraft
No. 11 (B) Squadron	Bajaur	RAF Risalpur	Hawker Hart
No. 20 (AC) Squadron	Mohmand	RAF Risalpur	Westerland Wapiti
No. 39 (B) Squadron	Bajaur	RAF Risalpur	Hawker Hart

8. NORTH WEST FRONTIER 1935

~ India General Service Medal 1908–35 ~
NORTH WEST FRONTIER 1935
Issue 3: Calcutta Mint

The 'NORTH WEST FRONTIER 1935' clasp to the India General Service Medal 1908–1935 was sanctioned by Army Order No. 51 of 1936 amended by No. 111 of 1936. The clasp rewarded troops, airmen and war mobilised civilians employed during the Loe Agra Campaign in the Malakand Agency under Brigadier Hon H.R.L.G. Alexander and the subsequent subjugation of the Upper Mohmand under Major General S.F. Muspratt. This was the last campaign clasp sanctioned for award with the India General Service Medal 1908–1935.

To qualify for the 'NORTH WEST FRONTIER 1935' clasp to the India General Service Medal 1908–1935 personnel had to satisfy one or more of the following criteria:

~ Loe Agra Campaign ~

- Be mobilised with the 2nd Infanty Brigade battle group, or supporting organisations including elements of the 1st Infanty Brigade and 20 Squadron, RAF, and be engaged on active service in the Malakand Agency, north of the Administrative Boundary between 12th January and 12th June 1935 inclusive.

~ Mohmand Campaign ~

- Be mobilised with the 1st Infantry Brigade or 2nd Infantry Brigade battle groups, or supporting organisations, and be engaged on active service into the Gandab Valley along a line north of the Michni–Abazai road via Pir Kala and Fort Shabkadar between 15th August and midnight 3rd November 1935 inclusive.

- Be mobilised with the 'Mohforce' battle group, or supporting organisation, and be engaged on active service along a line north the Michni–Abazai road via Pir Kala and Fort Shabkadar between 7th September and 3rd November 1935 inclusive.

- Be mobilised and engaged on active service with an RAF formation supporting operations against Upper Mohmand tribes between 15th August and midnight 3rd November 1935 inclusive.

The severe climatic conditions endured by troops engaged during the early stages of the Mohmand Campaign 1935 were the worst encountered by an army in the field for many years. Heat exhaustion and fever significantly reduced the fighting strength of some units. Following a review of casualty rates during the campaign a decision was made requiring the issue of additional salt rations to British personnel engaged in frontier warfare.

Lieutenant Colonel G.G.F.F.Greville, commanding officer 2nd Bn, HLI, was rendered incapable of command immediately prior to his battalion's deployment with 2nd Infantry Brigade following a fall from his charger. Major H.P.M. Berney-Ficklin, the battalion's second in command, was on leave in the United Kingdom when he received a signal to return to India immediately. Using great initiative Major Berney-Ficklin sought out an enterprising pilot and flew directly back to Peshawar in what is believed to be the first ever instance of an aircraft being used to return an officer to urgent duty on the Indian Frontier from Europe.

*

~ The Loe Agra Campaign ~

The North Western Railway ran north from the garrison town of Nowshera via Mardan to a railhead at Dargai in the tribal region known as the Malakand Agency. From Dargai communication with the principle regional settlement at Malakand north to Chitral was, in 1935, by means of a metalled road that crossed the mighty Swat River at Chakdara. The Swat River flowed evenly east to west across northern Malakand before arcing south and slightly east to join the Kabul River at Charsadda. The Malakand Protected Area lay within the boundary formed by the arc of the Swat and a line west of the road Dargai, Malakand, Swat and north of the line Dargai due west to Swat.

Though situated beyond the Administrative Boundary of British India, the region owed its 'Protected' status to the vitally important Upper Swat Canal that flowed south towards the plains of Peshawar District where it supplied life-giving moisture to the region's agriculture. Further, the Swat River provided a natural first line of defence against hostile tribes from the region north of the river many of whom wished to cause difficulties to British interests south of the Administrative Boundary. Government treaties with local tribes guaranting protection from hostile elements in return for accepting subjugation to the British Crown dated from 1900. In 1907, further amendments to these protocols were published. These arrangements were not widely enforced and few troops were permanently present in the region save the para-military Swat Levies and a handful of Frontier Constabulary. Political Officers under the Political Agent, Mr. L.W.H.D. Best, maintained dialogue between local elders and the North West Frontier Provincial Government.

*

Extending north beyond the Swat River lay the lawless Bajaur region. The Bajaur had been the focus of anti British agitation for some years and had been the subject of punitive action by the RAF during August 1933. Following the conclusion of these operations Faqir Shah, also known as the Faqir of Alingar, crossed into the Malakand Protected Area from Bajaur with a view to consolidating anti British sentiment among the local tribes. Establishing himself in the principle village of Loe Agra during early 1935, Faqir Shah soon gathered a sizeable following from the Agra, Khanori and Buri Tutai peoples. This intrigue culminated in a *jirga* during which local elders pledged their future allegiance to him rather than the British Administration.

Upon receipt of reliable intelligence, pertaining to Faqir Shah's incursion into the Malakand Protected Area, Mr. L.W.H.D. Best deployed a force of Swat Levies to Loe Agra with a view to

455

~ British Officers plan their next manoeuvre, 1935 ~

encouraging the Faqir to retire back from whence he had come. The Levies proved no match for their opponents and quickly withdrew with casualties. Following several aggressive sorties by the RAF, however, the Faqir decided to retire north. As a precaution, thereafter, 1/4th GR were deployed into the region with rifle companies located at the southern town of Kot and the northern village of Kalangai.

During late January 1935, the Government of India determined to reaffirm the 1907 agreement made with the Agra *jirga* in respect of their inclusion within the Malakand Protected Area. The tribe received notice that a Swat Levy post was to be constructed in Loe Agra and that Lines of Communication to support this facility were to be established by the Government in a southerly direction to Kot via Bargholai. On 18th February, HQ, Northern Command received instructions from Army Headquarters India, requiring the mobilisation of a brigade level force to support the political authorities in the execution of this plan. Additionally, AOC 1 (Indian) Group, RAF, Group Captain N.H. Bottomley, RAF, received instructions to provide air to ground assistance as and when required.

When news of the proposed military deployment came to the attention of Faqir Shah, he immediately declared the operation to be a precursor to a British invasion of Bajaur. Appeals were made to the Shamozai section of the Utman Khel, located on the north bank of the Swat River, to raise a *lashkar* to defend the independence of not only the Agra but also the regional Khanori and Buri Tutai tribal areas. It would appear that the peoples of these areas were in fact more frightened of the Faqir's long-term intent and passion for extreme Islamic fundamentalism than the wrath of the British Indian Army. Consequently, in return for their immediate submission to Government terms, Mr. L.W.H.D. Best secured agreement with the military authorities for the deployment of 2/15th Punjab Rifles to Kot from where they would be available to support local interests from potential molestation by tribesmen loyal to the Faqir.

*

On 19th February 1935, the balance of 2nd Infantry Brigade, Brigadier General Hon H.R.L.G. Alexander, deployed by train to the Dargai railhead and thence by road to Bat Khela via Malakand town. From Bat Khela the column advanced on foot to Kalangai at the northern end of the track that led south from the Swat River to Loe Agra. It had been determined that the brigade would march south from Kalangai to Kot via Loe Agra in a simple show of force thus ensuring all local tribesmen would henceforth be fearful of Government retribution should they contemplate aligning themselves with the Faqir of Alingar. Throughout these manoeuvres 20 Squadron, RAF, maintained air to ground and reconnaissance support.

Brigadier Hon H.R.L.G. Alexander, accompanied by his principle staff officers, rendezvoused with the company commander of 1/4th GR at Kalangai on 22nd February 1935. The Gurkhas had completed a full survey of the region and advised Brigadier Alexander that prior to any large-scale advance south, it would be advisable for strong picquet positions to be established covering the route through the Hurmala Pass. To save valuable time it was thereupon determined that two platoons of the incumbent Gurkha force would undertake this mission early the following day.

Unfortunately, the manoeuvre to secure the selected picquet positions did not go according to plan. Intelligence suggesting the absence of hostile tribesmen in the area proved incorrect and the Gurkhas came under sustained attack while only halfway to their objective. Within a short space of time, they became trapped in a rocky ravine and were unable to advance any further.

The unfolding situation was observed from the ramparts of the Kalangai levy post and consequently Brigadier Hon H.R.L.G. Alexander determined to deploy the lead company of 5/12th Frontier Force Regt. from the main column in support of the threatened Gurkhas. The fresh troops, with a section of 4 Mountain Battery, Royal Artillery, in support, deployed as quickly as practical but they too became marooned while under enemy fire. With the situation on the ground deteriorating rapidly, a decision was made to seek RAF assistance and mount a battalion level attack by the balance of 5/12th Frontier Force Regt. Two rifle companies of 2nd Bn, DWR were also committed with a view to eliminating the anticipated threat from any hostile concentrations that might form up in the dead ground on the left flank of the attacking battalion. The operation proved successful and the Sappers and Miners constructed a permanent picquet on the summit of Point 4020 once the various other objectives were secured.

Early on 24th February 1935, a force was despatched from Kalangai to reconnoitre the route south through the Hurmalo Pass. The high ground on either side of the rough track was picqueted by troops drawn from 3/2nd Punjab Regt. and 5/12th Frontier Force Regt. The column encountered no opposition and withdrew back to Kalangai in the early evening having penetrated the entire length of the narrow pass. Confidant that the route towards Loe Agra was now secure Brigadier Hon H.R.L.G. Alexander ordered the column to resume its march at dawn the following day.

For the advance from Kalangai to Loa Agra, 2nd Bn, DWR acted as the vanguard. South of the Hurmalo Pass area, the terrain was found to be exceedingly arduous. The track clung to the side of precipitous cliffs that fell away steeply. Thirty pack mules were lost over the edge before the column reached the comparative safety of the Inzargai Pass. Between this location and Loe Agra, the route became less severe and the lead elements of the column succeeded in securing their objective just before noon.

It was reported that the villagers appeared friendly and seemed relatively pleased to see the troops. Mr. L.W.H.D. Best assembled a *jirga* of local elders on the afternoon of 26th February 1935, during which the tribesmen reaffirmed their loyalty to the British Crown and agreed to the establishment of a permanent garrison. The village offered the Political Agent a selection of local youths for recruitment as scouts for the Swat Levy contingent accompanying the column.

Meanwhile, the Sappers and Miners worked on track improvement schemes south of Loe Agra towards Bargholai via the Haspur Notra Pass. By 27th February 1935, the route towards Kot was declared open and the column, less the new levy post garrison, began its march south with a view to rendezvousing with 2/15th Punjab Regt. On 1st March, 2nd Infantry Brigade withdrew from the Malakand region via the Dargai railhead. By 3rd March, all previously deployed units were once again in barracks. However, Nos. 22 and 39 Animal Transport Companies (Mule), RIASC, remained at Dargai. A small rapid reaction force, dubbed 'Flycol', was created and held in readiness at Nowshera for deployment back into the Malakand Protected Area should the need arise.

COMPOSITION 'FLYCOL', MARCH 1935

Commander – Maj. H P Radley 3/2nd Punjab Regiment
One Section, 4 Mountain Battery, Royal Artillery
One Section 15 Medium Battery, Royal Artillery
One Section Field Company, King George's Own Bengal Sappers and Miners
One Rifle Company, 3/2nd Punjab Regiment
1 Machine Gun Section, 1/4th (Prince of Wales Own) Ghurkha Rifles
Details Including Peshawar District Signals Detachment

---

*

On 4th March 1935, the Loe Agra levy post commander sent an urgent signal to HQ Peshawar District stating that the Faqir of Alingar was imminently expected to advance a significant sized *lashkar* across the Swat River. Intelligence had been intercepted suggesting that the planned incursion was designed to punish the Agra for its recent submission to British authority. Westerland Wapiti aircraft of 20 Squadron, RAF, immediately deployed to the region but did not sight any enemy movement. As a precaution, however, the levy post commander deployed the bulk of his command to guard the Swat River rope bridges at Qaragh, Katwai and Tatar. The enemy force, meanwhile, crossed into the Malakand Protected Area via the more southerly Kajurai Kabar River crossing and pressed home its attack on Loe Agra from a south-westerly direction. This manoeuvre led to the Swat Levies evacuating their position and fleeing north to Kalangai. Loe Agra fell to the enemy without a fight on the night of 5th March.

The military authorities immediately declared the Malakand Protected Area a prohibited zone. As a result, 20 Squadron, RAF, conducted extensive sweeps of the Loe Agra area but this show of force did not deter Faqir Shah and, on the evening of 6th March 1935, a *jirga* of local tribal elders was hosted by him in Loe Agra. During this meeting, the Faqir organised the regional opposition and promised extensive support was on its way from the Bajaur hinterland.

'Flycol' deployed by motor transport direct to Kot and arrived during the early hours of 6th March 1935. The artillery and machine-guns remained in Kot while the remainder of the small force, led by the 3/2nd Punjab Regt. contingent, moved on to Bargholai where it established a forming-up position for 2nd Infantry Brigade. Meanwhile, Kot was reinforced by the balance of 2/15th Punjab Regt. which, in conjunction with a section of 15 Medium Battery, Royal Artillery, subsequently engaged several enemy war parties in the vicinity of Jindai Knwar before moving up to Bargholai to establish a forming-up position. Enemy snipers were active during the hours of darkness but this threat greatly diminished following a courageous platoon level action launched by 2/15th Punjab Regt.

The main column arrived in Kot on 8th March 1935, where it paused for two days before continuing its advance north. At Bargholai, Brigadier Hon H.R.L.G. Alexander determined to employ 2nd Bn, DWR as camp garrison, placing 2/15th Punjab Regt. in the strike force. Forward of the forming-up position, the column maintained a steady pace and by mid-afternoon on 10th March, Loe Agra was once again under British control. The Faqir of Alingar and his principle followers had fled. The ensuing days were restricted to the provision of intelligence gathering patrols and the establishment of defensive picquets. The Sappers and Miners busied themselves in the construction of a more substantial levy post at a strategic location on the village outskirts. A more direct rout south to Bargholai was forged enabling faster and more defendable Lines of Communication.

By 16th March 1935, the military authorities determined that the force had completed its mission and 2nd Infantry Brigade, less 2nd Bn, DWR and a section of 4 Mountain Battery, Royal Artillery at Bargholai, withdrew back to Kot. Here 3/2nd Punjab Regt. and the balance of artillery support, were held while the remainder of the force returned to Nowshera. After a period of several days, the garrisons of Kot and Bargholai exchanged duty stations.

*

Following his 'enforced' evacuation of Loe Agra, the Faqir of Alingar, accompanied by a co-conspirator nomad Faghjur, retired north into the Bajaur where he once again attempted to form a *lashkar*. Anxious that lest the British launch an invasion of his kingdom in Upper Bajaur, Mullah Fazali-Wahid, the Haji of Turangzai, additionally pledged Faqir Shah his support. To this end, the Haji's son, Badshah Gul I, advanced a small Utman Khel force to Sulai where it rendezvoused with the Faqir on or about 16th March 1935. These men then attempted to mobilise further material support from among the Shamozai and Asil peoples.

The Loe Agra levy post was subjected to sustained long-range rifle fire on 21st March 1935. Intelligence was simultaneously received by HQ Peshawar District suggesting that enemy forces were about to cross the Swat River southwest of Kot and invest loyal villages in the Khanori area. The Kot garrison, less two rifle companies of 2nd Bn, DWR, immediately deployed north to Bargholai to relieve 3/2nd Punjab Regt., which in turn advanced from that location to secure the strategically important ridge overlooking the new track up the Haspur Notra to Loe Agra.

A fortified picquet was established at Point 4768 from where machine gun fire could be brought to bear on Loe Agra if required. Aggressive patrols were conducted over the ensuing days but no contacts were achieved. On the night of 30th March 1935, however, an attempt was made by several tribesmen to rush the Point 4768 picquet. The 2nd Bn, DWR rifle company that was occupying the position fought off the assault without loss but was extremely hard pressed. When dawn broke the following morning, several enemy dead were discovered caught up in the barbed wire defences forward of the company position.

Despite constant aerial reconnaissance, a significant enemy force succeeded in penetrating the northern Malakand Protected Area during the night of 3rd April 1935. By the afternoon of 4th April, Loe Agra and its surrounding hamlets were effectively cut-off following infiltrations across the Swat River. On 5th April, machine gunners at Point 4768 engaged several enemy parties to positive effect. This action prompted a second and more determined attack against that location by several hundred tribesmen during the night of 5th April. The troops held their ground but not without loss.

Reinforcements were despatched to Bargholai from Kot during the early hours of 6th April 1935. One hundred heavily laden pack mules, escorted by 'B' Company, 2nd Bn, DWR, brought up ammunition and defensive wiring supplies. The troops spent the ensuing days consolidating the perimeter defences at

~ Mountain Battery prepares to cover an Infantry assault, 1935 ~

both Bargholai and Point 4768. Meanwhile, the balance of 2nd Infantry Brigade deployed to Kot from its concentration point in Mardan and 5/12th Frontier Force Regt. deployed a rifle company direct to Bargholai to bolster the force there with a pool of fresh reserves. Meanwhile, 1/4th GR, accompanied by sections 15 and 66 Medium Batteries, Royal Artillery, went up to Kalangai with a view to forming a northern blockade and a fire position from which targets both north and south of the Swat River could, with RAF guidance, be engaged. On 8th April, 1/4th Bombay Grenadiers, detached from 1st Infantry Brigade, occupied Kot in relief of the balance of 2nd Infantry Brigade which was then free to advance north to a form-up position in Bargholai.

At this stage, the Political Department distributed warning notices to all hostile elements advising the tribesmen to disperse back to their home villages forthwith. Faqir Shah held a *jirga* at Naranji Banda to discuss these developments but the outcome of this meeting was uncompromising. Poor weather restricted RAF observation flights at this time and this enabled the Faqir's men to significantly improve their dispositions. Consequently, by 11th April 1935, a *lashkar* of some 800 warriors had occupied the Agra region. This force was subdivided into two principle formations: the Shamozai, under Faqir Shah, took up a position north and west of Loe Agra, while the Asil and Utman Khel contingent, under Badshah Gul I, occupied the Naranji Banda.

Brigadier Hon H.R.L.G. Alexander's plan for the relief of Loe Agra on 11th April 1935 consisted of six integrated manoeuvres. Before dawn 2nd Bn, DWR was to advance from Bargholai and secure the Waruki Ridge southwest of Point 4768 thus re-securing the track up the Haspur Notra. The battalion would establish picquets along this line including a position at the western extremity of the ridge overlooking the mouth of the Haspur Valley. Having achieved these objectives, 2/15th Punjab Regt. was to advance towards the enemy formation at Naranji Banda and then swing north to secure Point 4870. Meanwhile, 5/12th Frontier Force Regt. was to sweep across the Agra Pass and reform on the by then 'secured' Point 4870. A twenty-minute artillery barrage launched simultaneously from both Bargholai and Kalangai would precede an assault by the infantry. Covering fire during the actual attacks would be provided by the machine guns of the DWR. To exploit the situation, 3/2nd Punjab Regt. would follow up any enemy retirement to within a mile of the Swat River at which point aircraft of 20 Squadron, RAF, would strife any tribal formations encountered.

Loe Agra was captured before dusk on 11th April 1935. Casualties were light and the plan of campaign executed well. The only reported British death was Mr. L.W.H.D. Best, killed in action while leading a party of his Swat Levies in support of 2/15th Punjab Regt. west of the Stargai Pass.

Further consolidation of the position in Loe Agra occurred the following day. Fighting patrols were deployed towards the Ghund, Inzargai and Stargai Passes to flush out any remaining enemy stragglers. Contacts occurred but by 13th April 1935, it seemed that all enemy combatants had crossed the Swat River into Bajaur and dispersed. On 14th April, HQ, 2nd Infantry Brigade withdrew back to Bargholai accompanied by 3/2nd Punjab Regt. Long-range artillery support for the brigade was withdrawn from both Kalangai and Kot although new close support in the form of 3 Light Battery, Royal Artillery, was immediately deployed to Bargholai. The troops in Loe Agra remained until the new fortified levy post was completed and communications back to Kot were improved to an acceptable standard.

Towards the end of April 1935, several Shamozai elders approached the new Political Agent with a view to securing a formal settlement. At Chakdora on 5th May, a political *jirga* met with only limited success. Most of the tribal representatives were clearly nervous of possible repercussions from Faqir Shah should they agree to reaffirm the maintenance of the Malakand Protected Area in general and the sovereignty of the Agra region in particular. Over the coming weeks, these fears slowly dissipated and all parties eventually achieved a workable consensus.

The first two weeks of May 1935 proved peaceful. There was an absence of sniping into British positions and no infiltrators from north of the Swat River were apprehended. Consequently, a decision was made by the military authorities calling for the thinning out of the remaining units deployed north of Bargholai. Thus on 14th May, the Loe Agra force was reduced to a permanent Swat Levy garrison plus 5/12th Frontier Force Regt., one rifle company 1/4th GR and one section 4 Mountain Battery, Royal Artillery, in support. At the same time, the Bargholai garrison was reduced to 2/15th Punjab Rifles and the balance of 4 Mountain Battery, Royal Artillery. To facilitate the ongoing maintenance of law and order throughout the region, the Political Agent agreed with all key local tribal leaders that two companies of the Frontier Constabulary would augment the presence of the Swat Levy garrison. The police were to deploy in stages from mid-May with platoons stationed at Kot, Loe Agra and Point 4870. With tacit tribal support a decision was made to further develop communications within the Malakand Protected Area. (The first combustion powered vehicle to reach Bargholai arrived from Kot on 6th May).

On 12th June 1935, the last British troops withdrew from the Malakand Protected Area and returned to their peacetime locations thus officially concluding the Loe Agra Campaign.

*

~ The Mohmand Campaign 1935 ~

The Mohmand operations of 1933 brought only short-term relief to the Mohmand Frontier. The failure of the Upper Mohmand to gain ascendancy over their southern brethren had not discouraged the militant attitude of Mullah Fazali-Wahid, the Haji of Turangzai, or his retinue of sons. While the air operations over Kotkai between 1ˢᵗ and 10ᵗʰ August 1933 had secured the expulsion of the Afghan 'Pretender', the Haji considered the Government's lack of resolve to follow up these operations via a land invasion as a sign of weakness.

Following the conclusion of military operations in October 1933, the Haji of Turangzai determined to offer open sanctuary to any criminal or political opponent sought by the British Indian Government. (The Haji's support of the Fair of Alingar's special ambitions in the Malakand Protected Area is reviewed in the first part of this chapter). Overtime, many of those taking advantage of this sanctuary were encouraged to participate in raids into British India where they targeted civilians loyal to the Crown. Suich an individual by the name of Chimnai secured a position of power among the militant Safi tribe and developed a notorious reputation for promoting murder and mayhem across the Charsadda and Mardan areas of Peshawar District. Police action in these areas during January and March 1935 led to the arrest of some 35 Safis, though Chimnai, himself, remained at large.

Safi elders soon became outraged at the number of 'innocent' warriors incarcerated by the Government and petitioned the Haji of Turangzai to mobilise an Upper Mohmand *lashkar* to affect the release of their kin from the Peshawar city jail. A tribal *jirga* convened at Lakarai on 11ᵗʰ May 1933, to discuss the situation but the Haji was reluctant to commit material support to any significant degree due to the failure of his recent ambitions allied to the Faqir of Alingar.

*

During July 1935, the Burham Khel and Isa Khel areas enter into a feud over the subsidies paid to them by the Government for accepting the presence of the 'new' Gandab Valley road between Ghalanai and Yusuf Khel. This dispute led to war parties interfering with the security of road maintenance personnel. One such party of road contractors came under fire and was forced to retire back to Dand on 29ᵗʰ July. As a direct consequence of this lawless behaviour, a force of some 200 Frontier Constabulary and local Kahassadar deployed to guard the road. These civil forces were augmented by a mechanised military column from the Peshawar Cantonment which was concentrated daily at Pir Kala on the old Mohmand Blockade Line. The deployment of this force was abandoned on or about 5ᵗʰ August.

At this time Badshah Gul I, eldest son of the Haji of Turangzai, advanced a small force of warriors from the Nahakki and Khazana Sar *lashkars* into Isa Khel territory with a view to encouraging the Upper Mohmand clans to demand, once again, the subjugation of the Lower Mohmand. This action was also designed to appease the Safi for the Haji of Turangzai's prior lack of tangible support in the prosecution of their dispute with the British authorities. Badshah Gul II remained in Nahakki village with a reserve *lashkar* while his father toured the Musa Khel region seeking additional fighters. A *jirga* convened early on 14ᵗʰ August 1935 during which most northern clans pledged to support Badshah Gul in provoking a British military incursion into the region. To achieve this objective a plan was set in motion to interfere with the infrastructure of the Gandab road. This proposal was implemented with immediate effect and thus on the night of 14/15ᵗʰ August, some 1,600 warriors from across the region descended on the Gandab Valley and began tearing up the road between Dand and the Karappa Pass.

The tribesmen were well organised. The Burhan Khel and Isa Khel concentrated their efforts on wrecking culverts, destroying retaining walls, and digging trenches across the carriage way. Where possible, they placed large boulders to obstruct the passage of wheeled vehicles. Throughout these activities, Safi riflemen picqueted the high ground extending north to south on either side of the road. Realising that such action would indeed prompt a British military response, the tribesmen also invested resources in establishing a series of defensive lines. The first of these positions was located at the mouth of the Karappa Pass south of Ghalanai, while the second position was at the mouth of the Alikandi Pass on the track running north from Matta Mughal Khel towards Langham in the Pindiali Valley.

1st BRIGADE COLUMN, 15th AUGUST 1935

Brig. C J E Auchinleck
Thence Lt. Col. A P Cadell & Then Brig. D S S O'Connor
2 Mountain Battery, Royal Artillery
One Squadron, 18th Cavalry, IA
One Section, 8 Armoured Car Company, Royal Tank Corps
One Section 3 Filed Company, Bengal Sappers & Miners
Brigade Signals, Royal Corps of Signals
½ Bn, 2nd Bn, Highland Light Infantry
5/1st Punjab Regiment
1/4th Bombay Grenadiers
5/10th Baluch Regiment
One Company, 3 Field Ambulance
6 Animal Transport Company (Mules), Royal Indian Army Service Corps
35 Animal Transport Company (Mules), Royal Indian Army Service Corps

HQ Peshawar District became aware of the unfolding situation in the Gandab Valley early on 15th August 1935. At 5.30 pm that afternoon in heavy rain, 1st Infantry Brigade, Brigadier General C.J.E. Auchinleck, was immediately mobilised for active service and deployed to Michni Kando and thence to a forming-up position at Pir Kala where 'D' Company, 2nd Bn, HLI secured a firm perimeter. (A portion of the HLI temporarily remained in Peshawar to aid the civil authorities lest disorder breakout in support of the Upper Mohmand). Patrols were despatched in the direction of Hafiz Kor but no contact achieved. Intelligence gathered from friendly Halamazai suggested that both Chimnai and the Haji of Turangzai were present among those investing the road north of Ghalanai.

The authorities appointed Group Captain N.H. Bottomley, RAF, operational commander and gave permission for 1 (Indian) Group, RAF, to commence operations to clear the enemy from the Gandab Valley. Only those concentrations of tribesmen actively engaged in belligerent behaviour were initially targeted. This directive was subsequently modified to enable the targeting of Upper Mohmand reinforcements that were flooding into the operational zone. Elders of the Burhan Khel and Isa Khel peoples, received terms stating that they should withdraw otherwise villages in both the Pindiali Valley and the Danish Kol areas would be selected for aerial attack from dawn on 19th August 1935. To facilitate the efficient execution of these air operations it was determined that No. 1 Wing at RAF Kohat would be given the responsibility for bombing predetermined targets, while No. 2 Wing at RAF Risalpur would be tasked with aggressive day and night patrolling. Great care was taken, however, to minimise casualties among women and children. To this end aircraft were fobbiden to fly at an altitude of less than 3,000 feet.

2ⁿᵈ BRIGADE COLUMN, 21ˢᵗ AUGUST 1935

Brig. Hon H R L G Alexander
4 Mountain Battery, Royal Artillery
66 Field Battery, Royal Artillery
Detachment 5 Field Company, Bengal Sappers & Miners
Brigade Signals, Royal Corps of Signals
2ⁿᵈ Bn, Duke of Wellington's Regiment
5/12ᵗʰ Frontier Force Regiment
3/2ⁿᵈ Punjab Regiment
2/15ᵗʰ Punjab Regiment (From 31ˢᵗ August)
Once Company, 3 Field Ambulance, Royal Army Medical Corps
22 Animal Transport Company (Mules), Royal Indian Army Service Corps
39 Animal Transport Company (Mules), Royal Indian Army Service Corps

On 19ᵗʰ August 1935, General K. Wigram circulated a warning order from HQ Northern Command for a proposed advance along the Gandab Valley road to Ghalanai. Reconnaissances occurred over the next two days during which long range rifle fire was exchanged with small parties of the enemy. To support this manoeuvre, 2ⁿᵈ Infantry Brigade was mobilised and brought to a forming-up position at Mile Post 5, some miles northeast of Pir Kala on the banks of the Subhan Khwar River. Additional resources, including 15 Medium Battery, 4 Field Battery and 7 Mountain Battery, Royal Artillery accompanied by a section of 2 Light Tank Company, Royal Tank Corps and the balance of No. 3 Field Company, Bengal Sappers and Miners, deployed to both column locations over the ensuing days. The assembled formations were designated 'Mohforce' from 20ᵗʰ August and placed under the operational command of Brigadier General C.J.E. Auchinleck. (From the 23ʳᵈ August, the AOC was placed under the direction of the Army).

*

The RAF action over the Pindiali Valley and Danish Kol areas met with only limited success. Many warriors ceased their exertions on the Gandab road and retired to their villages. The numeric strength of the enemy force did not diminish, however, due to the arrival in theatre of several hundred Baezai and Khwaezai warriors under the Faqir of Alingar, accompanied by a large contingent of additional Safi riflemen. As a result, the military authorities decided to expand the RAF mission to incorporate attacks on Safi interests. On 21ˢᵗ August 1935, the RAF distributed warning notices over proposed target areas. Operations began two days later with 1 (Indian) Wing assigned the entire mission.

With 'Mohforce' fully assembled, plans were prepared for an advance on Dand. So it was that 1ˢᵗ Infantry Brigade were tasked with securing a line astride the Gandab road north west of the 'abandoned' Kahassadar post at Kilagai. Once established, 2ⁿᵈ Infantry Brigade were to pass through 1ˢᵗ Infantry Brigade and occupy Dand. Lines of Communication defence from Kilagai back to Pir Kala was the responsibility of 1ˢᵗ Infantry Brigade. Defence of the route from Kilagai forward to Dand was the responsibility of 2ⁿᵈ Infantry Brigade. To assist in the execution of this operation, Nowshera Brigade was augmented, on a temporary basis, by a battalion of the Peshawar Brigade. Several companies of Frontier Constabulary would move up to secure the line Abazai-Michni Kando once the position at Dand had been consolidated by the striking force.

The advance towards Dand commenced at 05.15 hours on 23ʳᵈ August 1935. The manoevre took the enemy completely by surprise, because the formal notification of the Government's intent to retake the Gandab Valley road all the way to Yusuf Khel and beyond was only due to be published by the political authorities that afternoon. Contacts were made early in the day by the lead battalion, 2ⁿᵈ Bn, HLI, and the warriors in the foothills north of Pir Kala were driven north at no great risk to the Army. Within a few hours, 1ˢᵗ Infantry Brigade had secured its objective and 2ⁿᵈ Infantry Brigade in turn became the vanguard.

By this juncture, the Mohmand had rallied and consequently the Royal Artillery had to employ a creeping barrage to protect the general advance. Enemy fighters offered stout resistance, killing Lieutenant A.C.S. Moore, 5/12ᵗʰ Frontier Force Regt. and several Indian officers and other ranks. Before the position could be stabilised and a night bivouac established on the hills overlooking Dand, 2ⁿᵈ Infantry Brigade committed all available reserves. Tribesmen pressed this position hard throughout the night and a picquet occupied by elements of 2ⁿᵈ Bn, DWR, came under particular pressure before being relieved by a counterattack mounted by a force drawn from 5/12ᵗʰ Frontier Force Regt.

The troops at Dand spent much of the following day reconnoitring the route north towards the Karappa Pass. Several enemy warriors followed up the withdrawal of the reconnaissance patrol but the force sustained no casualties. Officers of the Sappers and Miners conducted an inspection of the road infrastructure. This led to the deployment of work details by all units not engaged on picqueting or patrolling. The worst of the trenching damage had been repaired by mid-afternoon. Debris were removed and sections liable to collapse were reinforced. Several hours later the road back to Pir Kala was opened to mechanised transport enabling HQ 'Mohforce' to move up to Dand.

Later the same day Brigadier C.J.E. Auchinleck issued orders for 'stage two' of the advance on Ghalanai. The 2ⁿᵈ Infantry Brigade was to advance from Dand early on 25ᵗʰ August 1935 to an east/west line from Point 4524 to Point 4423 (2ⁿᵈ Bn, DWR to retire on Kilagai). From this position, the brigade would then become responsible for Lines of Communication defence all the way back to Hafiz

~ Indian Army troops marching north ~

Kor. Upon securing this objective, 1ˢᵗ Infantry Brigade Column would pass through 2ⁿᵈ Infantry Brigade forward position and secure the Karappa Pass with a view to continuing an advance to contact all the way to Ghalanai.

Also, 20 Squadron, RAF, covered 2ⁿᵈ Infantry Brigade as it moved cautiously north from Dand. Some random shots were exchanged with enemy stragglers, but the presence of air cover prompted most of the tribesmen to remain out of sight. With its objective secured, 2ⁿᵈ Infantry Brigade signalled permission for 1ˢᵗ Infantry Brigade to move up and through its position. This manoeuvre commenced at about 08.30 hours. On the left flank were 1/4ᵗʰ Bombay Grenadiers and on the right flank were 5/10ᵗʰ Baluch Rifles.

The 2nd Bn, HLI moved astride the road behind several tanks furnished by the armoured vehicles of 2 Light Tank Company, Royal Tank Corps. The troops encountered little opposition and within a short space of time, the mouth of the Karappa Pass was in British hands.

With the entrance to the Karappa Pass secured, a decision was made enabling a patrol of 18th Cavalry, IA to advance at the gallop through the narrow pass and on towards Ghalanai in the hope of acquiring targets among any retiring enemy force. Finding its objective abandoned, the cavalry established a loose perimeter. This area was promptly reinforced by the arrival of 2 Light Tank Company, Royal Tank Corps detachment. By dusk, the road back to Dand was open and HQ echelons of both 'Mohforce' and 1st Infantry Brigade were camped at Ghalanai. The 2nd Infantry Brigade, less units of Lines of Communication defence, remained concentrated at Dand for the night. (28 MT Company, RIASC, successfully ran a supply convoy from Peshawar Cantonment direct to Ghalanai on 27th August 1935).

*

Air operations against targets in Safi territory had begun on 23rd August 1935. The tactics employed were the same as those used during the pre-existing missions against the Burhan Khel and Isa Khel tribes. The Safi, however, proved more obdurate than their cousins and failed to abandon their property promptly and withdraw their families from settled areas. To encourage compliance, the military authorities took a decision to destroy the residences of Upper Mohmand leaders considered to be particularly belligerent. The home of the Haji of Turangzai was, after some debate, exempted from attack due to its location adjacent to an important regional mosque. Several alternative properties were identified and subsequently attacked by the RAF with devastating effect. These low altitude operations were exceedingly hazardous for the aircrew employed due to the potential for enemy small arms fire to damage aircraft when flying at such low altitude.

*

Towards the end of August 1935, a group of Musa Khel elders, several of whom had been instrumental in securing the cessation of hostilities that marked the end of the 1933 campaign, presented themselves to the political authorities in Ghalanai. They requested safe passage to Fort Shabkadar with a view to entering into negotiations with Captain R. Bacon, the Political Agent. These men sought a Government commitment to cancel any planned extension of the Gandab Valley road beyond Yusuf Khel. In return for such a commitment, the *maliks* pledged to bring in a fully representative *jirga* of the Upper Mohmand people

Upon detailed examination by Captain R. Bacon, however, it became apparent that the assembled elders did not have a wide enough mandate. Accordingly, the delegation was dismissed and given instructions by the Political Department to return to Ghalanai only after having gained such a mandate. (To drive home this message Isa Khel villages in the Danish Kol were subjected to a short, albeit intense, attack by the RAF.) An inter-tribal *jirga* was held at Mahaban to review the Government's demands. Younger elements, enthusiastic for the Haji of Turangzai's rhetoric, vetoed all the proposals placed before the assembled *jirga* by the older, tribal *maliks*. They voted instead to maintain the fighting capability of the *lashkars* already committed to the field and returned to these formations post-haste.

Having suffered significant loses in battle, the Haji of Turangzai and other Upper Mohmands, devoted much of late August 1935 to the task of regrouping. Reinforcements were urgently required if the campaign to expel 'Mohforce' was to continue. To this end, Badshah Gul I and the Faqir of Alingar were despatched on a recruiting mission along the Indo Afghan Frontier. Badshah Gul III meanwhile, toured the Afghan Province of Ningrahar in the hope of securing material support from, among others, the independent Khwaezai tribe. A key ally was denied the Haji at about this time when an unknown assassin killed Chimnai.

The protection of the 'Mohforce' Lines of Communication from Kilagai to Dand was a major drain on the resources of 2nd Infantry Brigade. A vast region extended on either side of the Gandab Valley road and this area required effective control day and night to deny the enemy access to the road infrastructure. Accordingly, the brigade area was subdivided into two defensive zones. Each zone contained a robustly constructed permanent fortification garrisoned by an infantry battalion supported by a company level satellite position. These posts were located at Dand, Sikander, Kilagai and the former Rattray Camp. Daily patrols and ambushes were mounted from these locations supported by artillery with pre co-ordinated fire points. Kilagai was located in an unhealthy region and Summer Fever reduced many 2nd Infantry Brigade units in strength. For example, 2nd Bn, DWR was eventually reduced to only 310 fit men despite having been recently reinforced by the battalion's 'A' Company from Cherat.

Meanwhile, 1st Infantry Brigade began to probe forward from Ghalanai. The Upper Mohmand had withdrawn from the town's immediate environs and established new concentration points among the Khapak Mountains that formed both the demarcation between Upper and Lower Mohmand territory and the northern heights of the Toratigga Valley. A strong force also remained on the plains beyond the Nahakki Pass. Patrols initially ventured north towards Katsai. These manoeuvres were followed up by expeditions east of Khair-ud-din-Kandao and on towards the Pindiali Valley. On 29th

August 1935, elements of the brigade picqueted an armoured reconnaissance made by Brigadier Hon H.R.L.G. Alexander along the Toratigga Valley during which an assessment of enemy troop strength was attempted.

Conclusive intelligence gathered during the Toratigga Valley expedition, indicated that warriors from the Khapak Mountains were regularly coming down from their positions at night to abuse local Halamazi villages. Consequently, at dawn on 3rd September 1935, 1/4th Bombay Grenadiers, intending to sweep the area of potential opposition, launched an offensive operation. In support of the assault force were 5/10th Baluch Regt. and a section of 2 Light Tank Company, RTC. Troopers of 18th Cavalry, IA, were positioned strategically to pursue any tribesmen intent on fleeing from the area. Many casualties were were inflicted on the opposition before the troops began to withdraw. By this juncture enemy reinforcements had assembled and the Army's withdrawal was followed up in force. Long-range artillery from Katsai was brought into action, but as the rear guard approached the

~ An Indian Army scout gathers intelligence, 1935 ~

Ghalanai perimeter, held by 2ⁿᵈ Bn, HLI, the use of shelling had to be abandoned. Several platoon picquets were hard pressed including the location held by 2ⁿᵈ Lieutenant Milman, 5/1ˢᵗ Punjab Regt, which had been kept as brigade reserve.

For some hours that night, the troops inside the Ghalanai perimeter were subjected to very accurate sniper fire from the tribesmen who had just advanced along the Toratigga Valley. This prompted a further military operation on 4ᵗʰ September 1935. The 5/12ᵗʰ Frontier Force Regt. was attached to 1ˢᵗ Infantry Brigade from the Lines of Communication reserve to lend additional firepower to this manoeuvre. The operational plan called for the cordon and search of specific villages in conjunction with the political authorities. It was anticipated that the enemy would mount a robust defence of the Toratigga area but upon execution of the operation, only slight resistance was encountered. Several villages were successfully searched by the troops but little contraband recovered or useful intelligence gleaned.

*

With the Gandab Valley road fully functional as far as Ghalanai and mechanised forces able to operate north to Katsai, the Government was faced with a dilemma. Should 'Mohforce' now be restricted solely to consolidation, thus enabling the tentative peace overtures, already in play from the various *jirgas,* run their course? Alternatively, should plans be put in place enabling an extension of the road through the Nahakki Pass and beyond? The Upper Mohmand had been a constant irritant to the British Indian Government from the middle to late nineteenth century. Between 1908 and 1935, several significant campaigns had been prosecuted in the area. On each occasion, however, agreements and terms made between British Political Officers and Upper Mohmand elders had come to nought.

On 7ᵗʰ September 1935, the Government officially sanctioned the extension of the Gandab Valley road to Nahakki. In pursuance of this policy the military authorities sought first to consolidate the position of 'Mohforce' north of Katsai to the mouth of the Nahakki Pass. This consolidation was to include the upgrade of the road to mechanised standard as far forward as any selected operating position.

With Government approval, Army Headquarters India authorised the GOC Northern Command, General K. Wigram, to restructure the North West Frontier Province military order of battle. 'Mohforce' was removed from the Peshawar District orbit and became an independent entity reporting directly to Northern Command. The force was immediately augmented by the deployment to theatre of 3ʳᵈ Infantry Brigade, Brigadier C.D. Noyes, and 9ᵗʰ Infantry Brigade, Brigadier C.W. Frizell, combined with suitable levels of supporting arms. The southern extremity of the 'Mohforce' operational area was shrunk back to Kilagai. From this location south, the Lines of Communication defence back to the Peshawar Cantonment was to become the responsibility of Peshawar District under Brigadier D.K. McLeod. Political control of the region north of Kilagai was to be delegated to the GOC 'Mohforce' with the Political Agent acting in an advisory role on civil matters. Group Captain N.H. Bottomley, RAF, was instructed to continue to provide ongoing aerial support as and when required in a vastly expanded area of operations. However, this support was to be based upon a joint strategy of 'concentrate and destroy', as opposed to one of the 'dispersal' of enemy formations.

During this period, Brigadier Hon H.R.L.G. Alexander was invalided from the field suffering from the effects of malaria. Command of 2ⁿᵈ Infantry Brigade was thereupon transferred, on a temporary basis, to Lieutenant Colonel J.D. Fulton. Brigadier C.J.E. Auchinleck resumed command of 1ˢᵗ Infantry Brigade on 24ᵗʰ September 1935 following the return from home leave of Major General S.F. Muspratt, GOC 'Mohforce'.

The restructure of 'Mohforce' took place without loss although long range sniping was a constant menace. At each location, defences were consolidated and further picquets constructed on commanding ground. The Nowshera Brigade conducted an advance to contact along the Toratigga Valley on 14ᵗʰ September 1935. Several further Halamazi villages were searched but no significant contacts made. During this operation, survey work was begun on a fair weather track into the region.

MOHFORCE DISPOSITIONS, 17ᵗʰ SEPTEMBER 1935

1ˢᵗ (Peshawar) Infantry Brigade	Striking Force Ghalanai
2ⁿᵈ (Nowshera) Infantry Brigade	Striking Force Katsai
3ʳᵈ (Rawalpindi) Infantry Brigade	Lines of Communication North of Kilagai
3ʳᵈ (Jhelum) Brigade	Reserve Ghalanai

Upper Mohmand elders seeking a peaceful resolution to the unfolding situation greeted the news of the Government's intent to force a road through the Nahakki Pass with extreme dismay. Any chance of their influence being employed to calm the more implacable tribal elements would be dashed by such an 'invasion'. Several *maliks* approached the Political Agent at Ghalanai on 15ᵗʰ September 1935, but the *jirga* was unrepresentative of the whole Upper Mohmand areaand as such was turned away.

Upon receiving the order to advance north, Brigadier C.J.E. Auchinleck's immediate priority was the capture of the Nahakki Pass and the establishment of a forward operating base beyond this objective at Nahakki Village. Preparations to facilitate this manoeuvre were put into place on 17ᵗʰ September 1935. The following morning 1ˢᵗ Infantry Brigade advanced from Ghalanai to seize the high ground at Khazana Sar thus protecting the flank of any approach towards the mouth of the Nahakki Pass. Simultaneously, 2ⁿᵈ Infantry Brigade moved up from Katsai and secured the left flank approaches to the objective. The 3ʳᵈ Jhelum Infantry Brigade maintained flank security. Once these manoeuvres had been completed, 2ⁿᵈ Bn, HLI, advanced through the Nahakki Pass and captured the village of Sro, which was located several hundred yards beyond the exit of the pass. Once this location was secured and consolidated by men of 1/4ᵗʰ Bombay Grenadiers, troopers of 18ᵗʰ K E O Cavalry, IA, moved through Sro at the gallop and forward to a previously identified elevated position a mile or so further north towards Badshah Gul I's headquarters at Nahakki. Several tribesmen were encountered during the advance of the cavalry but these men were killed without loss to the Army. Shelling by 22 Mountain Battery, Royal Artillery, and 15 Medium Battery, Royal Artillery, kept the principal enemy formations at bay. (Several Northern Command Staff Officers, including the DCGS Major General E. de Burgh and the PMO, Brigadier Hartley, observed these operations).

With the Nahakki Pass and its immediate environs in British hands, the balance of 1ˢᵗ Infantry Brigade was deployed forward and a camp established on the plain beyond. Several strategic picquets were constructed, including those christened Assaye, Number 7 and Glasgow. Meanwhile 2ⁿᵈ Infantry Brigade consolidated itself at Wucha Jawar where it was co-located with 'Mohforce' HQ. The ensuing days saw further consolidation while the Sappers and Miners pushed the road forward from Yusuf Khel. By 28ᵗʰ September 1935, sufficient progress had been made to the existing track to enable a section of 2 Light Tank Company, Royal Tank Corps, to move up to the forward operating position from Ghalanai.

A major exercise was undertaken to ensure the ongoing availability of fresh water and to that end elements of 2nd Infantry Brigade sought out reserves west towards Zanawar China. Without a good supply, the deployment of adequate numbers of pack mules was severely restricted. A pipeline was laid forward from Wucha Jawar to ensure 1st Infantry Brigade was adequately supplied with water. (Mechanised contract water tenders operating from Peshawar supplied the balance of water for 'Mohforce' daily). Sappers attached to 3rd Jhelum Infantry Brigade hewed a camel track over the Khair-ud-din Kando into the Pindiali Valley.

Defensive picquets in both brigade locations were constantly subjected to attack by night. During the day several small parties of tribesmen were encountered by patrols mounted by 18th K E O Cavalry, IA, operating on the plain well forward of the Nahakki Pass. Contacts on the 19th and 21st September 1935 led to a brigade level operation by 1st Infantry Brigade designed to cleanse the region immediately forward of its brigade position. The enemy was surprised by this manoeuvre but maintained a stout resistance and even followed up the Army's withdrawal back to Sro resulting in several British casualties being sustained.

On 22nd September 1935, a fully representative *jirga* presented itself at Wucha Jawar. Previously uncooperative elders now appeared anxious to engage in dialogue. However, representatives of the Safi remained hesitant. Fines were paid and several hostages released. Intelligence was gathered from tribal representatives suggesting that Badshah Gul I had fled to Kabul at the suggestion of several Afghan mullahs. Following the surrender of these parties, the AOC was instructed to cancel bombing missions against villages of some of those present. The *jirga* was granted safe passage to travel south to Ghalanai for more detailed negotiations with the Political Agent.

Unfortunately, these compromises and delays did not influence the younger anti-British elements who formed the bulk of the remaining fighters in the field. The Khapak Mountains and Pass region remained firmly in tribal possession and its capture by the British was imperative if the Toratigga Valley was to be permanently denied as a conduit for any possible flanking movement to isolate the Peshawar Brigade Column. Additionally, the *lashkar* located in the region forward of 1st Infantry Brigade had been reinforced and needed to be neutralised as quickly as possible. Consequently, on 29th September 1935, a major offensive was launched with a view to encouraging a thinning out of enemy positions along the Khapak Pass by forcing them to support their brethren forward of Nahakki.

Major General S. F. Muspratt's operational plan called for 1st Infantry Brigade, supported by 2nd Light Tank Company, Royal Tank Corps and 18th K E O Cavalry, IA, to secure a wider perimeter

~ Some Tribal Elders engaged in dialogue ~

in the vicinity of Muzikor and then to sweep the region west to east raising several local settlements in the process. To lend flank support, 2nd Infantry Brigade was detailed to secure positions along the Khapak ridge between Point 2450 and Muzi Kor, enabling it to engage targets on the plains below. Protection of the exposed left flank of 2nd Infantry Brigade along the Toratigga Valley was assigned to 3rd Jhelum Infantry Brigade.

The advance to contact of 1st Infantry Brigade was checked soon after crossing the start line. Enemy positions in and around Kasai proved to be significant obstacles while long-range fire from across the Nashkul Khwar River also wrought damage to the advancing troops. The 2nd Bn, HLI and 1/4th Bombay Grenadiers secured their objectives but only after a difficult fight. Kasai was eventually captured by 5/10th Baluch Regt. after which some degree of consolidation for the wider operation was achieved. Meanwhile 2nd Infantry Brigade became bogged down while advancing on its various objectives. The lead battalion, 5/12th Frontier Force Regt., lost contact with the main formation while attempting to secure Point 4080 and was unable to effectively withdraw after coming under overwhelming and sustained attack. Serious casualties were sustained, including both Captain G. Meynell and Lieutenant A.P.S. Rendall killed. In total, 136 officers and men of 5/12th Frontier Force Regt. were wounded during this engagement and 31 killed. The use of artillery firepower to help in the Battalion's extrication was limited due to the lack of direct communications with the forward positions. (Captain G. Meynell was subsequently awarded a posthumous Victoria Cross for his part in this action).

The 2/15th Punjab Regt., wqhich was hitherto acting as left flank guard to 1st Infantry Brigade's right flank battalion, eventually broke forward and lent support to the retirement of the surviving Frontier Force men. This action forced the premature retirement of the Peshawar Brigade back towards Sro. Upon reaching its established operating base perimeter, Brigadier C.J.E. Auchinleck released 1/4th Bombay Grenadiers to provide additional support to the balance of 2nd Infantry Brigade in its attempt to secure the Khapak ridge and the final withdrawal of 5/12th Frontier Force Reg.

Survivors of the incident at Point 4080 reported that the advancing tribesmen had captured many of their wounded. This prospect caused considerable concern throughout 'Mohforce'. The repatriation of military prisoners by tribesmen was not unknown. However medical care of the prisoners was virtually non-existent and, of equal concern, was the fact that the injured sepoys were captives of intransigent opponents who may well feel less loyalty to established tribal practices. Consequently, the safe release of these men now became a major objective for Major General S.F. Muspratt.

To this end the principle Political Officer, Captain R. Bacon, immediately made contact with several Halamazai elders who were en-route to Lakai with a view to escorting to Ghalanai the Upper Mohmand representative *jirga* located there. Asked to divert their mission, the Halamazai instead made contact with the *lashkar* west of the Khapak Pass with a view to negotiating the release of the captured sepoys. This intervention proved successful and, on the morning of 30th September 1935, Major General S.F. Muspratt received a signal advising him that the prisoners would be released and moved down to the British lines over the ensuing few days.

On 1st October 1935, Major General S.F. Muspratt and Captain R. Bacon received in Katsai a fully representative *jirga* consisting of elders from the Baezai, Khwaezai, Kamalai Halamazai, Utmanzai, Dawezai and Safi peoples. At this meeting, the Political Agent stipulated the Government terms for tribal submission. These included the requirement for an immediate ceasefire on the part of the Upper Mohmand, the dispersal of all assembled *lashkars* and that henceforth the Ghalanai Agreement of 1933 was void. Notice was also given that the Gandab Valley road project was to be completed to plan and that the Upper Mohmand should fully respect its security at all times. The Government also advised those assembled that the RAF would maintain observation flights over the region for as long as deemed necessary to verify the execution of these mandates.

The *jirga* broke up on 3rd October 1935, albeit with notice that those present were to reassemble on 15th October at Yusuf Khel for an interview with Chief Commissioner R. Griffith and General K. Wigram, the GOC Northern Command. The terms presented to the tribesmen on 1st October were reiterated in detail during this subsequent meeting. Hostility towards the further extension of the Gandab Valley road was somewhat diluted by the Government undertaking not to patrol the road on an ongoing basis or maintain Kahassadar Posts along its route. Frontier Constabulary and Political Officers would, however, be expected to have free access to the region at will. The Governor went on to outline several clear warnings pertaining to the future conduct of the Upper Mohmand. Military force would be utilised to re-establish the rule of law and order should the Upper Mohmand rebel against British authority or give succour to 'criminal' elements responsible for illegal activities in settled regions of British India. From this date forward political control of the region reverted to the Political Agent.

The 700 or so assembled tribal elders were respectful and accepted responsibility for tribal military activity in their areas. Several requests were made of the Government, one of which sought military assistance in the clearing of unexploded ordnance from settled areas and tracks. The Governor accepted this responsibility and accordingly on 27th October 1935, an RAF bomb disposal unit embarked upon a tour of the region.

With terms now accepted by all parties, the gradual break up of 'Mohforce' began. The 3rd Jhelum Infantry Brigade retired to Peshawar from Ghalanai on 18th October 1935, from where ir returned to its peacetime station by rail. Two weeks later 1st Infantry Brigade withdrew from Nahakki back to Ghalanai and thence, in stages, to the Peshawar Cantonment. The 2nd Infantry Brigade evacuated Wucha Jawar on 1st November after which 3rd Infantry Brigade rolled back the Lines of Communication all the way down to Pir Kala. (Due to a lack of available transport, 1st Bn, Hampshire Regt. was compelled to march the 155 miles from Peshawar to Rawalpindi. This feat of endurance was considered a significant achievement because Brigadier C.D. Noyes had awarded the battalion a poor fitness score during their initial deployment). 'Mohforce' was officially stood down from midnight on 3rd/4th November 1935.

* * *

COMMAND STRUCTURE, NORTH WEST FRONTIER 1935

Commander Moforce
Maj. Gen. S F Muspratt

Commander Peshawar District
Brig. D K Mcleod

Brigade Commanders
Brig. C J E Auchinleck
1st (Peshawar) Infantry Brigade

Brig. Hon H R L G Alexander
2nd (Nowshera) Infantry Brigade

Brig. C D Noyes
3rd (Rawalpindi) Infantry Brigade

Brig. C W Frizell
3rd (Jhelum) Infantry Brigade

	BRITISH ARMY & RAF ROLL OF HONOUR NORTH WEST FRONTIER 1935		
Date:	Person:	Unit:	Comment:
4/9/1935	3310018 Pte. S Heaton	2 HLI	Died Peshawar
6/9/1935	3906922 Pte. Brow	2 South Wales Borders	Killed Accident RAF Abbottabad – No Medal!
6/9/1935	344714 Sgt. G W Brerton	5 Sqn, RAF	Killed Accident RAF Abbottabad
6/9/1935	561987 LAC R A Ayers	5 Sqn, RAF	Killed Accident RAF Abbottabad
29/9/1935	107269 Gnr. A E Mundin	3 Lt Bty, RA	KIA, Winchar Jawar
2/10/1935	2313007 Sgt. G A Harper	'B' Corps Signals, Royal Signals	Died Peshawar

NORTH WEST FRONTIER 1935 INDIAN ARMY CASUALTY RETURN	
Loe Agra	
Killed & DOW	Wounded
3	16
Mohmand	
Killed & DOW	Wounded
53	97

NORTH WEST FRONTIER 1935[12] ROLL

BRITISH ESTABLISHMENT
THE ARMY

~ Staff Grade Officers ~

Note a.   *Only Officers of the British Army are listed. Those on the Indian Establishment are beyond the scope of this work and are thus excluded.*

Note b.   *Medals named in thin impressed block capitals.*

Brigadier: ~ W D Croft[11&12] Cmd. 2 Bde. & C W Frizell[12] Cmd. 3 Bde.

THE CAVALRY:

~ 14th/20th Royal Hussars ~

Note a.   *Roll of all personnel identified as eligible.*

Note b.   *Medals named in thin impressed capitals: '14-20 H.'*

Single Clasp	No. Identified	Rarity
North West Frontier 1935[12]	2	Of the Utmost Rarity

Captains: ~ R H Hannay[12]

Lance Corporals/Troopers: ~ ??0638 G F Gramson[12] attch. RAF

THE ROYAL TANK CORPS:
Sub Units Identified As Entitle:
Armoured Car Companies
No. 6 ACC (Single Recipient) & No. 8 ACC
Light Tank Companies
No. 2 LTC & Det No. 11 LTC

Note a.   *Roll of all personnel identified as eligible.*

Note b.   *8 Armoured Car Company (ACC), Force Troops Mohmand.*

Note c.   *2 Light Tank Company (LTC), Force Troops Mohmand.*

Note d.   *Medals named in thin impressed capitals: 'R. TANK. C.'*

Single Clasp	Company	No. Identified	Rarity
North West Frontier 1935[12]	6 ACC	1	According to the roll as seen, can be considered Unique
North West Frontier 1935[12]	8 ACC	114	Very Scarce
North West Frontier 1935[12]	2 LTC	116	Very Scarce
North West Frontier 1935[12]	11 LTC	3	
Combination Clasps	*Company*	*No. Identified*	*Rarity*
Waziristan 1921–24[6] North West Frontier 1935[12]	8 ACC	1	According to the roll as seen, can be considered Unique

Waziristan 1921–24[6] North West Frontier 1935[12]	2 LTC	2	Of the Utmost Rarity
North West Frontier 1930–31[9] North West Frontier 1935[12]	8 ACC	2	Of the Utmost Rarity.
North West Frontier 1930–31[9] North West Frontier 1935[12]	2 LTC	2	Of the Utmost Rarity.
North West Frontier 1930–31[9] North West Frontier 1935[12]	11 LTC	1	According to the roll as seen, can be considered Unique.
Mohmand 1933[11] North West Frontier 1935[12]	2 LTC	3	Of the Utmost Rarity.

Majors: ~ H J Harvey[12] 8 ACC

Captains: ~ G H Brooks[6(Lt.)&12] 8 ACC, C I Lee[12] 2 LTC, H T de B Lipscomb[12] 8 ACC, M D B Lister[12] 2 LTC, E J O'Connor[12] 11 LTC attch. 2 LTC & G W Quinn-Smith[6&12] 2 LTC

Lieutenants: ~ A W Brown[12] 2 LTC, E N H Bryant[12] 2 LTC, H Cantrell[9&12] 11 LTC attch. 2 LTC, G C Hopkinson[12] 8 ACC, J H G Ievers[12] 8 ACC, R C D Kite[12] 8 ACC, A R de H Mallock[12] 2 LTC, D St. C Thorn[11&12] 2 LTC, A C Tute[12] 8 ACC, G M Warren[12] 8 ACC, R A C Wellesley[12] 2 LTC, F I C Wetherell[12] 8 ACC & S P Wood[12] 2 LTC

Warrant Officers Class II: ~ 7869341 A O Bennett[12] 2 LTC & 7868093 A C Clark[12] 2 LTC

Company Quartermaster Sergeants/Staff Sergeants/Colour Sergeants: ~ 7868491 A F Barron[12] 2 LTC & 7874606 F L Highfield[12] 2 LTC

Quartermaster Sergeants/Sergeants: ~ 814167 W H Blestone[12] 8ACC, 7870786 E Bolton[12] 2 LTC, 7873855 W Bosward[12] 8 ACC, 7877343 B T Burch[12] 2 LTC, 2308711 G Cawley[12] 2 LTC, 7814991 H J Down[12] 2 LTC, 7869759 P Harrison[12] 11 LTC, 7868030 E S Moxley[12] 8 ACC, 7872450 A J Petitt[12] 8 ACC, 7869533 R E Turner[11&12] 2 LTC, 7873226 A R Warren[12] 2 LTC, 7874934 A W Wilson[12] 8 ACC, 7877304 H Wilson[12] 2 LTC, 7874732 S J W Wilson[12] 2 LTC, 7875587 E G Winter[12] 8 ACC & 7879367 H E Wittington[12] 2 LTC

Lance Sergeants/Corporals: ~ 724651 R J Client[12] 2 LTC, 6653260 E Dodd[12] 8 ACC, 760009 R H Harding[12] 2 LTC, 7878946 G E W Harrison[12] 2 LTC, 7880179 L Harvey[12] 8 ACC, 7873173 G H Kattenhorn[9(Pte.)&12] 8 ACC, 7879061 E A F Webb-Morris[12] 8 ACC, 7881044 J Pond[12] 8 ACC, 2203390 H Stewart[6(7ACC Pte.)&12] 2 LTC, 30024 F J Thompson[12] 8 ACC & 7881361 E Wilshaw[12] 8 ACC

Lance Corporals/Privates: ~ 7882650 J C Ackroyd[12] 2 LTC, 7880371 E Allen[9&12] 8 ACC, 7880298 W F Allen[12] 2 LTC, 7883863 L Almond[12] 2 LTC, 2817421 F G Archibald[12] 8 ACC, 777941 F Andrews[12] 8 ACC, 7881112 E W Austin[12] 2 LTC, 7883118 W E Avery[12] 8 ACC, 4856724 F Barber[12] 2 LTC, 7881868 H F Barker[12] 2 LTC, 7884168 E Barnett[12] 2 LTC, 7877071 R W Bartle[12] 2 LTC, 7883690 E B Bateman[12] 2 LTC, 7880090 A G Beckett[12] 8 ACC, 7883457 H Beckett[12] 2 LTC, 7882396 A Bell[11&12] 2 LTC, 7883676 D F Bennett[12] 8 ACC, 7883082 J W Bennett[12] 2 LTC, 7586659 R Benwell[12] 2 LTC, 7883141 R W Bevan[12] 2 LTC, 7883824 W Bond[12] 2 LTC, 4970569 A W Bover[12] 8 ACC, 7883351 D R Black[12] 8 ACC, 7883778 P Broadbent[12] 2 LTC, 4854586 H Broughton[12] 8 ACC, 7883108 T Brownhill[12] 8 ACC, 7883356 E A Cairns[12] 8 ACC, 2565852 J Campbell[12] 8 ACC, 7883465 G C le Care[12] 2 LTC, 7882164 L E Challis[12] 2 LTC, 7883114 C Chaplin[12] 8 ACC, 7879293 J R Chapman[12] 2 LTC, 7882203 W Chatterton[12] 2 LTC, 5104702 D Chesterman[12] 8 ACC, 7883193 A L Cleaver[12] 2 LTC, 7881814 A J Clift[12] 2 LTC, 4912093 J Cockayne[12] 2 LTC, 7882268 J Cochrane[12] 8 ACC, 7883020 C L Collier[12] 2 LTC, 7881720 A Collinson[12] 8 ACC, 7883117 H Connal[12] 2 LTC, 7882291 A R Cox[12] 8 ACC, 7881087 H J Croft[12] 8 ACC, 7882372 J Cross[12] 2 LTC, 7880448 J Cummins[12] 2 LTC, 7883800 F C Davies[12] 2 LTC, 7878107 W Dealtry[12] 2 LTC, 7880643 C S Donovan[9(1ACC)&12] 2 LTC, 7881727 F Dowling[12] 8 ACC, 7883379 G Doyle[12] 8 ACC, 7880488 G H E M Drury[12] 2 LTC, 7882618 J A S Durns[12] 8 ACC, 7883925 L F Eagle[12] 2 LTC, 7883926 T N Ecclestone[12] 2 LTC, 7882205 E J Eustace[12] 2 LTC, 7884170 J H H Falvey[12] 2 LTC, 7883881 J H Farnell[12] 2 LTC, 7883838 D Farrar[12] 2 LTC, 7883140 R Fell[12] 8 ACC, 5333034 K V Fidler[12] 8 ACC, 4124006 H Fielden[12] 8 ACC, 7881591 R F Fishlock[12] 8 ACC, 403637 J E C Fraser[12] 8 ACC, 7882063 E A Fryer[12] 8 ACC, 7883047 S Gibbon[12] 8 ACC, 3025733 L H E Ginman[12] 2 LTC, 7884452 E G Gordon[12] 8 ACC, 7880302 J Granton[12] 2 LTC, 7884183 H Green[12] 2 LTC, 7882666 S Grundy[12] 8 ACC, 7882602 H C Hall[12] 8 ACC, 7883361 W Harknes[12] 8 ACC, 7881314 C W Harper[12] 2 LTC, 7883392 L Harsburgh[12] 2 LTC, 7883721 G Hawkins[12] 2 LTC, 7883839 V R F C Hawkins[12] 8 ACC, 4799758 P Heath[12] 8 ACC, 7881306 E J Hebblethwaite[12] 8 ACC, 7882880 B Hobbs[12] 2 LTC, 7888744 J Hodgson[12] 2 LTC, 7881090 D G Hounsome[12] 8 ACC, 7883748 H S Houston[12] 2 LTC, 2024122 A S Hudson[12] 8 ACC, 6396417 W J Hunt[12] 2 LTC, 7883483 R Hunter[12] 2 LTC, 7881807 E H Hyde[12] 2 LTC, 7881094 T Hyland[12] 8 ACC, 7883491 W B Ingram[12] 8 ACC, 7342137 G A Innocent[12] 8 ACC, 7883899 R A Irish[12] 8 ACC, 7883662 D W James[12] 8 ACC, 7882320 W James[12] 2 LTC, 7880572 F Jarvis[12] 2 LTC, 7881815 A P Jones[12] 2 LTC, 7881102 H C Jones[12] 8 ACC, 7883757 W Kershan[12] 2 LTC, 7881518 L G Kimberley[12] 2 LTC, 7883943 J C Lanyon[12] 8 ACC, 7882356 F Lawrence[12] 8 ACC, 7883808 G T Lawson[12] 8 ACC, 7881728 W G Lawson[12] 8 ACC, 7882256 S Lawton[12] 8 ACC, 7882276 T W Lee[12] 8 ACC, 7883405 G Leslie[12] 8 ACC, 7883843 C E Lings[12] 8 ACC, 7882968 T J W Lloyd[12] 2 LTC, 4190485 J Loftus[12] 2 LTC, 7883818 J Lomas[12] 2 LTC, 7881794 M L De Luc[12] 2 LTC, 7882302 H MacDonald[12] 8 ACC, 2926929 H D MacDonald[12] 8 ACC, 7883372 A B McKay[12] 8 ACC, 7882112 W A Marsden[12] 8 ACC, 7883832 A J Marshall[12] 2 LTC, 7882196 W J Marshall[12] 8 ACC, 7883011 J Maskell[12] 2 LTC, 7882284 E Mercer[12] 2 LTC, 7881818

G W Meyrick[12] 8 ACC, 7881810 E S Morgan[12] 2 LTC, 7882607 H M Morris[12] 8 ACC, 7883494 W H J Mundy[12] 2 LTC, 7883844 R H Newman[12] 8 ACC, 7881822 C North[12] 2 LTC, 7583870 M J O'Connor[12] 2 LTC, 7884191 G O'Sullivan[12] 8 ACC, 7884442 S G Osborne[12] 2 LTC, 7881942 D R Oyston[12] 2 LTC, 7883677 G J Palmer[12] 8 ACC, 7881109 G H Parker[12] 8 ACC, 7883826 I C Parkinson[12] 2 LTC, 7883849 R E Parsons[12] 8 ACC, 7883753 W Patterson[12] 2 LTC, 4267918 G Peebles[12] 2 LTC, 7883987 W Pennycook[12] 8 ACC, 7881704 R H Peryman[12] 8 ACC, 7882982 J W Pilmoor[12] 8 ACC, 7883499 A J Plummer[12] 2 LTC, 7863779 J F Pont[12] 11 LTC, 7883402 W J Powell[12] 8 ACC, 4122153 E Prescott[12] 8 ACC, 7881040 H Proudlove[12] 2 LTC, 7883485 F J Prouse[12] 2 LTC, 7884178 G Purves[12] 8 ACC, 7883781 W J Quinlan[12] 8 ACC, 7882487 G Richards[12] 2 LTC, 7882852 C Ricketts[12] 2 LTC, 4187927 H R O Ridge[12] 8 ACC, 7883197 J Rieley[12] 2 LTC, 7882009 R R Robbins[12] 2 LTC, 7881301 D E Roberts[12] 6 ACC, 7883878 R W Roberts[12] 2 LTC, 7880506 J Robinson[12] 2 LTC, 7883717 J T Rushbury[12] 2 LTC, 7880919 J E Rymer[12] 2 LTC, 7880078 W A Scorgie[12] 2 LTC, 7883124 J W Sidell[12] 2 LTC, 7881575 W Simpson[12] 8 ACC, 3053406 R Skene[12] 2 LTC, 7881759 B Smith[12] 8 ACC, 7884203 K Spackman[12] 8 ACC, 7882223 N L Stagg[12] 2 LTC, 7881293 H Straker[12] 2 LTC, 7883493 W J Sutherland[12] 2 LTC, 7882609 A Swan[12] 8 ACC, 7882178 D J Sweeney[12] 8 ACC, 7881731 O S D Swift[12] 8 ACC, 7883952 W S Styles[12] 8 ACC, 7883720 G L Tatler[12] 8 ACC, 7884217 A S Taylor[12] 8 ACC, 7883395 J Taylor[12] 8 ACC, 7882649 N W Taylor[12] 8 ACC, 7883922 E G Thomas[12] 8 ACC, 7882345 J Thomas[12] 8 ACC, 7876523 J Thomson[9&12] 2 LTC, 7876523 J Thompson[12] 2 LTC, 7883637 J Thompson[12] 2 LTC, 7883496 F Tipping[12] 2 LTC, 7883663 W J Trimm[12] 8 ACC, 7882627 H Tucker[12] 8 ACC, 7884218 V Mc C Turner[12] 2 LTC, 7882193 D J Vaughan[12] 8 ACC, 7883791 R J Venn[12] 2 LTC, 7884223 L Wakefield[12] 8 ACC, 7883647 W J C Walters[12] 8 ACC, 7884431 G E Ward[12] 2 LTC, 7881826 T Watkins[12] 2 LTC, 7880936 J H Watson[12] 8 ACC, 3768124 F R Waumsley[12] 2 LTC, 7881118 A White[12] 8 ACC, 7882611 S T Whittaker[12] 2 LTC, 1069998 A Williams[12] 8 ACC, 7880423 A Williams[12] 8 ACC, 5247095 J O M Williams[12] 8 ACC & 7881045 F L Winn[12] 8 ACC

THE ROYAL ARTILLERY:
Batteries Identified As Entitled:
Field Artillery:
HQ 4 Field Brigade
3, 4, 7, 14, 15, 66, 73, 78 & 81 Batteries
Anti Aircraft Artillery:
8 Battery (Individuals Only)
Mountain Artillery:
HQ 22 & 25 Mountain Brigades
2 (Derajat), 4 (Hazara) & 13 (Dardoni) Mountain Batteries
Post Guns:
Dand / Mohmand
1 Divisional Ammunition Column

Note a.   *Roll of all commissioned personnel identified as eligible.*

Note b.   *Non-commissioned and other rank personnel 8 Anti Air Craft Battery, 73 Field Battery, 78 Field Battery or multi clasp only.*

Note c.   *2 Mountain Battery – Peshawar Brigade. – Mohmand.*

Note d.   *4 Mountain Battery – Loe Agra / Nowshera Brigade. – Mohmand.*

Note e.   *13 Mountain Battery – Jhelum Brigade.*

Note f.   *3 Light Battery – District Troops Loe Agra / Force Troops Mohmand.*

Note g.   *4 Field Battery – Force Troops Mohmand.*

Note h.   *7 Field Battery – Force Troops Mohmand.*

Note i.   *8 Anti Aircraft Battery – Force Troops Mohmand.*

Note j.   *15 Medium Battery – District Troops Loe Agra / Force Troops Mohmand.*

Note k.   *66 Field Battery – District Troops Loe Agra / Nowshera Bde. Col – Mohmand.*

Note l.   *Medals named in thin impressed capitals: 'R.A.'*

Single Clasp	Battery	No. Identified	Rarity
North West Frontier 1935[12]	8	13	Extremely Rare
North West Frontier 1935[12]	73	1	According to the roll as seen, can be considered Unique
North West Frontier 1935[12]	78	1	According to the roll as seen, can be considered Unique

North West Frontier 1935[12]	All Other	In Strength	Not Rare
Combination Clasps	*Battery*	*No. Identified*	*Rarity*
Afghanistan N.W.F. 1919[3] North West Frontier 1935[12]	All Other	1	According to the roll as seen, can be considered Unique
Waziristan 1919–21[4] Mohmand 1933[11] North West Frontier 1935[12]	All Other	1	According to the roll as seen, can be considered Unique
Waziristan 1919–21[4] Mahsud 1919–20[5] Waziristan 1921–24[6] North West Frontier 1935[12]	All Other	1	According to the roll as seen, can be considered Unique
Waziristan 1921–24[6] North West Frontier 1935[12]	All Other	4	Of the Utmost Rarity
Waziristan 1921–24[6] Malabar 1920–22[7] North West Frontier 1935[12]	All Other	1	According to the roll as seen, can be considered Unique
North West Frontier 1930–31[9] Mohmand 1933[11] North West Frontier 1935[12]	All Other	5	Of the Utmost Rarity
North West Frontier 1930–31[9] North West Frontier 1935[12]	All Other	35	Very Rare
Burma 1930–32[10] North West Frontier 1935[12]	All Other	2	Of the Utmost Rarity
Mohmand 1933[11] North West Frontier 1935[12]	8	4	Of the Utmost Rarity
Mohmand 1933[11] North West Frontier 1935[12]	All Other	19	Extremely Rare

Lieutenant Colonels: ~ (Bvt) H M M Robertson[9,11&12] 4 Mtn Bty & G F R Wingate[12] Cmd. 25 Mtn Bde., CRA Mohmand FF

Majors: ~ R A Armstrong[12] 14 Bty, D A Buchan[12] 7 Bty, H N N Dudding[12] HQ 4 Fld Bde., S A J Grehan[12] 3 Bty, S F Fisken[9(Capt.)&12] 2 Mtn Bty, A S C Kennedy[12] 13 Mtn Bty, H B Latham[12] 81 Bty, W B Mackie[11&12] 2 Mtn Bty, E M W Stevens[4(Lt.),5(Lt.),6(Lt.)&12] 66 Bty, V A Young[9(Capt.)&12] 15 Bty & E T Weigall[12] 7 Bty

Captains: ~ M F T Baines[12] 13 Mtn Bty, F W N Bannaytyne[12] 66 Bty, G W Courtenay[10&12] 2 Mtn Bty, M Lea-Cox[11&12] DAQMG PD, R D B Dupuis[6(Lt.)&12] attch. HQ 22 Mtn Bde., M H A Fletcher[12] 4 Mtn Bty, R L Herron[6(Lt.)&12] 14 Bty, R H Fielding-Mould[12] 4 Bty, J W Palmer[12] 4 Mtn Bty, F N C Rogers[12] 7 Mtn Bty, J G S Ross[12] 15 Bty, J D Shapland[12] attch. HQ 3 Bde., N Skentelbery[12] 8 Bty attch. HQ PD as GSO3, A L Tidcombe[9&12] attch. HQ 25 Mtn Bde. as Staff Officer & J H H Willans[10(Lt.)&12] attch. HQ 22 Mtn Bty

Lieutenants: ~ A G Atkinson[12] 15 Bty, attch 20 Sqn RAF, J F Bassett[12] 14 Bty, J H Beattie[12] 2 Mtn Bty, D L Betts[12] 7 Mtn Bty, J T B Sylvester-Bradley[11&12] 15 Bty, A D G Braithwaite[12] 4 Mtn Bty, T G Brennan[12] 14 Bty, E M de Brett[12] 13 Mtn Bty, A Cameron[12] 4 Bty, N St. C Campbell[12] 7 Bty, A B S Chennells[9&12] attch. HQ 22 Mtn Bde., A E Chessels[12] 66 Bty, J O Cochrane[12] 15 Bty, H G Croly[12] 7 Mtn Bty, C A M Cumberledge[12] 13 Mtn Bty, D H Dumbell[12] 7 Bty, A S Ellis[11&12] 2 Mtn Bty, W J Fletcher[12] 66 Bty, T D Forsyth[12] 14 Bty, R A R Franshawe[12] 2 Mtn Bty, P C M A Gompertz[12] 7 Bty, J Grose[12] 4 Bty, G R L Hawks[12] 4 Mtn Bty attch. HQ Nowshera Bde. as Orderly Officer, R J Holland[12] 66 Bty, J H Hooper[12] 15 Bty, attch. 20 Sqn RAF, R W Jelf[12] 4 Mtn Bty, A F Johnson[12] 4 Bty, R E T Keelan[12] 15 Bty, W S King[11&12] 8 Bty attch. MF as Fld Cashier, D St. L Moore[12] ADC Cmd. PD, J L Ord[12] attch. HQ 14/4 Bde., J H Pallot[12] 15 Bty, G M Palmer[12] 4 Bty, D J Robertson[12] 7 Mtn Bty, A G Disney-Robuck[12] 3 Bty, J W P Saunders[12] 7 Bty, J D Sharpland[12] attch. HQ 3 (Jhelum) Bde., R W Sorabie[12] 3 Bty, W M D Turner[12] 66 Bty & J N D Tyler[12] 3 Bty

Warrant Officers Class II: ~ (BSM) 1407950 H W E Bushell[9(S/Sgt.)&12] 15 Bty, 1407879 A C A J Ford[9(Sgt.),11(Sgt.)&12] 15 Bty, 1417946 R Frisby[4,11&12] attch. HQ 22 Mtn Bde., (1028640) 110142 F Hill[3(Dvr.)&12] 3 Bty & (1039070) 910057 J N G Nelson[6(Sgt.)&12] 66 Bty

Battery Quartermaster Sergeants/Staff Sergeants: ~ 1028530 W H N Coole[12] 8 Bty attch Mohmand FF HQ

Quartermaster Sergeants/Sergeants: ~ 1031329 C A Jackson[11(Bdr.)&12] 66 Bty, 1052203 W Kettles[11(Bdr.)&12] 15 Bty, 1415253 L Orange[9&12] 15 Bty, 1414872 E H C Smith[9(L/Sgt.)&12] 15 Bty & 1421397 H H White[12] 8 Bty attch. HQ Peshawar Bde.

Bombardiers: ~ 1418570 E H Ayling[6(Gnr.),7(Gnr.)&12] 3 Bty, 1073960 H R Blackwell[9(Gnr.)&12] 15 Bty, 797654 E W Colly[12] 78

Bty attch. 3 Bde. Int Liason Sect, 1066484 C C J Cook[11&12] 58 Fld Bty, 1423774 A H Corlett[11&12] 15 Md Bty, 1414210 J C Irwin[9&12] 66 Bty, 1064857 H King[11&12] 15 Bty, 4968616 C Martin[9(L/Bdr.)&12] 14 Bty, 4446654 D L Moorfoot[9&12] 15 Bty, 1064258 A C Phillips[12] 8 Bty attch. HQ Peshawar Bde. & 779823 C R Ward[9(L/Bdr.)&12] 15 Bty

Lance Bombardiers/Gunners/Drivers: ~800493 W W Aldrich[12] 8 Bty attch. Mohmand FF HQ, 798244 S Bate[9,11&12] 66 Bty, 797441 E Boulton[11&12] 15 Bty, 790389 R Bowes[11&12] 8 Bty attch. HQ Peshawar Bde., 800350 E A Boyt[12] 8 Bty attch. HQ Peshawar Bde., 5193584 H S Brotherton[9&12] 15 Bty, 833242 G G Bruce[12] 8 Bty attch. HQ Peshawar Bde., 808781 J P Bryne[11&12] 15 Bty, 797280 F Davey[11&12] 15 Bty, 794583 R Dixon[9&12] 15 Bty, 818721 S J Edwards[12] 73 Bty attch. 20 Sqn RAF, 165294 F J Efford[9&12] 15 Bty, 1416201 J Fenton[9&12] 4 Bty, 1061679 W G Ford[9&12] 15 Bty, (51965) 1410890 W Frodsham[6&12] 7 Bty, 5493637 H A Gillett[9&12] 15 Bty, 806667 R Graham[12] 8 Bty attch. HQ Peshawar Bde., 4384287 C Gresty[9&12] 14 Bty, 6198825 A G Haward[12] 8 Bty attch. Mohmand FF HQ, 5495727 K J H Hayter[12] 8 Bty attch. HQ Peshawar Bde., 790200 L Heightley[9,11&12] 15 Bty, 784274 A W Higginson[9&12] 15 Bty, 808804 A J Hooper[11&12] 8 Bty attch. HQ P Bde., 797469 A L Hunt[9&12] 3 Bty, 1024922 H Illingsworth[9&12] 14 Bty, 790115 H Jones[9&12] 15 Bty, 1073969 C H Kelly[9&12] 15 Bty, 4800438 F Kirk[12] 8 Bty attch. HQ Peshawar Bde., 802600 W G Lawrence[11&12] 8 Bty attch. Mohmand FF HQ, 5823996 F H Lawes[11&12] 15 Bty, 798121 W MacDonald[11&12] 15 Bty, 790498 W H Meehan[9&12] 15 Bty, 809029 T Morgan[12] 8 Bty attch. HQ Peshawar Bde., 791832 W J Myers[11&12] 15 Bty, 780765 E Netherclift[11&12] 15 Bty, 1422960 H Newton[9&12] 15 Bty, 4264370 J Noble[9&12] 3 Bty, 1426004 A J Raisborough[9&12] 15 Bty, 788782 C E Roberts[9&12] 15 Bty, 794286 S Roberts[11&12] 15 Bty, 790193 T W Round[9&12] 66 Bty, 791865 F J Smith[11&12] 15 Bty, 781144 M Smith[9&12] 15 Bty, (1063487) 791335 W T Smith[9,11&12] 4 Bty, 790211 G T Spilling[9&12] 15 Bty, 1066544 M Toohey[9&12] 15 Bty, 796042 L A Trickle[9&12] 3 Bty, 794294 H R Watts[9&12] 15 Bty, 5824453 E B Wright[11&12] 15 Bty & 806231 S G Young[9] 8 Bty attch. Mohmand FF HQ

THE CORPS OF ROYAL ENGINEERS:
Sub Units Identified As Entitled:
RE Individuals
King George's Own Bengal Sappers & Miners

Note a.   *Roll of all personnel identified as eligible.*
Note b.   *'3 Field Company' – Peshawar Brigade Column – Mohmand.*
Note c.   *'5 Field Company' – Nowshera Brigade Column – Mohmand.*
Note d.   *Medals named in thin impressed capitals: 'R.E.'*

Single Clasp	No. Identified	Rarity
North West Frontier 1935[12]	15	Rare

Combination Clasps	No. Identified	Rarity
Afghanistan N.W.F. 1919[3] North West Frontier 1935[12]	1	According to the roll as seen, can be considered Unique
North West Frontier 1930–31[9] Burma 1930–32[11] North West Frontier 1935[12]	1	According to the roll as seen, can be considered Unique
North West Frontier 1930–31[9] Mohmand 1933[11] North West Frontier 1935[12]	1	According to the roll as seen, can be considered Unique
North West Frontier 1930–31[9] North West Frontier 1935[12]	2	Of the Utmost Rarity
Mohmand 1933[11] North West Frontier 1935[12]	4	Of the Utmost Rarity

Lieutenant Colonels: ~ C J E Greenwood[9(Maj.)&12] CRE PD & (Bvt) N A Coxwell Rogers[11(Maj.)&12] CRE 'Mohforce'

Majors: ~ E E Nott-Bower[12] 3 Fld Coy, K W Merrylees[12] & A C Mitchell[3(Lt.)&12] Bde. Maj., RE

Captains: ~ E W H Clarke[12], J V Corbet[12], R N Foster[12], R A Milne[12], D R M Orchard[9(Lt.)11(Lt.)&12] Staff Capt 'Mohforce', S R G Scott[11(Lt.)&12] 5 Fld Coy & E E Stenhouse[9(Lt.)&12] 3 Fld Coy

Lieutenants: ~ T Burrowes[11&12], J R Connor[12], R C N Jenny[12] attch. SofI 'Mohforce', O J R Orr[12], H A H Radcliffe-Smith[12] 5 Fld Coy, J C Winchester[12] 5 Fld Coy & T Wright[11&12]

Quartermaster Sergeants/Sergeants: ~ 1864132 J Brown[9(Cpl.),10(Cpl.)&12]

Lance Sergeants/Corporals: ~ 1862506 W Browning[12] 5 Fld Coy, 1866305 F G W Gammon[12] 5 Fld Coy, 1863770 C S Govier[12] 3 Fld Coy & 1865499 J Wood[12] 5 Fld Coy

THE ROYAL CORPS OF SIGNALS:
Sub Units Identified As Entitled:
Divisional & Brigade Signals
'A' Corps Signals & Det. 'B' Corps Signals
1 Divisional Signals & Det. 2 Indian Divisional Signals
Peshawar District Signals & Det. Waziristan District Signals

Note a. *Roll of all commissioned personnel identified as eligible.*

Note b. *Non-commissioned and other rank personnel 'B' Corps Signals Detachment, 2 Indian Divisional Signals Detachment, Waziristan District Signals Detachment or multi clasp only.*

Note c. *Medals named in thin impressed capitals: 'R. SIGNALS.'*

Single Clasp	No. Identified	Rarity
North West Frontier 1935[12]	In Strength	Rare
North West Frontier 1935[12]	'B' Corps Sigs = 6	Of the Utmost Rarity
North West Frontier 1935[12]	2 IDS = 1	According to the roll as seen, can be considered Unique
North West Frontier 1935[12]	Waziristan DS = 4	Of the Utmost Rarity

Combination Clasps	No. Identified	Rarity
Waziristan 1919–21[4] Waziristan 1921–24[6] North West Frontier 1930–31[9] North West Frontier 1935[12]	1	According to the roll as seen, can be considered Unique
Waziristan 1921–24[6] Mohmand 1933[11] North West Frontier 1935[12]	2	Of the Utmost Rarity
Waziristan 1921–24[6] North West Frontier 1935[12]	2	Of the Utmost Rarity
North West Frontier 1930–31[9] Mohmand 1933[11] North West Frontier 1935[12]	8	Of the Utmost Rarity
North West Frontier 1930–31[9] North West Frontier 1935[12]	1	According to the roll as seen, can be considered Unique
North West Frontier 1930–31[9] North West Frontier 1935[12]	7	Of the Utmost Rarity
Burma 1930–32[10] North West Frontier 1935[12]	1	According to the roll as seen, can be considered Unique
Mohmand 1933[11] North West Frontier 1935[12]	34	Very Rare

Majors: ~ E P C Collins[12] PDS, P A Chubb[12] & (Bvt) A J A Schofield[10(Capt.)&12]

Captains: ~ W M Clapp[12] PDS & L R Hall[12] PDS

Lieutenants: ~ A V Benton[12] PDS, E P Blake PDS attch. HQ Nowshera Bde., E C R Blaker[12], R L Carpenter[9&12], M A Charlton[12] 1 IDS attch. PDS, S J Dagg[12], D Van der Groot[9&12] PDS, N M Hay[12], E J F Heap[9&12] 1 IDS attch. PDS, P M P Hobson[12] 1 IDS attch. PDS, E Y Nepean[12] PDS attch. HQ Nowshera Bde. & W A Purser[11&12] PDS

Company Quartermaster Sergeants/Staff Sergeants: ~ (Fitter) 1411848 G E Agar[11&12] attch. PDS & 5095009 J Cooper[9&12] 'B' Corps Sigs

Quartermaster Sergeants/Sergeants: ~ 2319590 R G F Barker[11(Sgln..)&12] PDS, 7991 C Cheeseman[9(Cpl.),11&12] PDS, 5999529 V R Cole[9(Cpl.)&12] 'A' Corps Sigs, 2319240 R O Edwards[12] Waz DS, 2311403 F S Handley[9,11&12] PDS, 1857173 M McCormack[9(Cpl.)&12] 'B' Corps Sigs, 1413241 H J Sneddon[12] 'B' Corps Sigs & 2311826 A W Walker[11&12] PDS

Lance Sergeants/Corporals: ~ 2315566 T Barry[11&12]PDS, 547471 V C Brassfield[11(L/Cpl.)&12] PDS, 2310990 A Brown[6(Sgln.)&12], 2320536 A J V Catt[11(Sgln.)&12] PDS, 5610844 C E Cummings[6(Sgln.)&12] 1 IDS attch. PDS, 6336253 H W Dadswell[11&12] PDS, 2311312 H E Mott[6(Sgln.),11(Cpl.)&12] PDS, (625510) 2310920 A Mowatt[6(Sgln.),11(Cpl.)&12] PDS, 2311336 F G Sherrington[11&12] PDS, 2315091 F I E Stockton[11&12] PDS & 2318227 L A Whalebelly[12] Waz DS attch. 2 LTC

Lance Corporals/Signalmen: ~ 3383435 D A Alinutt[11&12] PDS, 2319895 W F Baker[11&12] PDS, 2316730 W E Birkett[9&12]

PDS, 2313288 R C Blaikie[11&12] PDS, 2320464 G H Carter[12] Waz DS attch. 2 LTC, 2318834 J J Delaney[9&12], 2319948 H Dumville[11&12] PDS, 2320474 S Fox[11&12] PDS, 2319857 E R Gentle[9,11&12] PDS, 2319369 S Grattage[9,11&12] PDS, 2319631 C I Griffin[11&12] PDS, 2320651 G Hale[11&12] PDS, 4911791 E S Hardwick[11&12] PDS, 2321571 C R Harrod[11&12] PDS, 2317182 A A Heighton[11&12] PDS, 2310806 R Henshall[11&12] PDS, 2320627 L R Holt[11&12] PDS, 2320387 H Horsman[11&12] PDS, 2321335 G E Ide[11&12] PDS, 2319979 J W Ireland[9,11&12] PDS, 2313385 H F Jackson[11&12] PDS, 2318035 W L Jarvis[9,11(L/Cpl.)&12] 'B' Corps Sigs, 2319994 J J Kelly[11&12] PDS, 1070674 J Lambert[11&12] PDS, 2320411 G T Leigh[12] 2 IDS, 2321209 H S Mangnall[11&12] PDS, 2319320 J L Martin[12] Waz DS attch. 2 LTC, 2320571 C E Mason[11&12] PDS, 2565397 F J Murrell[9,11&12] PDS, 2320227 L F Phipps[11&12] PDS, 2320199 F A Pike[11&12] PDS, 2321772 C Pulling[12] 'B' Corps Sigs, 2321603 A R Purdue[12] 'B' Corps Sigs, 2321008 S G Purkiss[11&12] PDS, 2321643 J Rankin[12] 'B' Corps Sigs, 2321460 H N Ransome[12] 'B' Corps Sigs, 2313373 A T Roberts[11&12] PDS, 2320204 G Rumford[9,11&12] PDS, 2320829 W F Thompson[12] 'B' Corps Sigs & 3522516 H Walsh[11&12] PDS

THE INFANTRY:

~ 2nd Bn, The Royal Scots (The Royal Regiment) ~

Note a.   *Roll of all personnel identified as eligible.*
Note b.   *Recipients attached 3 Sanitary Section (SS), 11 Field Ambulance (FA), Royal Army Medical Corps (RAMC).*
Note c.   *Medals named in thin impressed capitals: 'R. SCOTS.'*

Single Clasp	No. Identified	Rarity
North West Frontier 1935[12]	9	Of the Utmost Rarity

Quartermaster Sergeants/Sergeants: ~ 1665462 A Campbell[12] & 2561106 W M Robertson[12]
Lance Corporals/Privates: ~ 792922 C G Crawford[12], 3310141 J Ellison[12], 3053710 J Hammond[12], 3053779 K O P Hammond[12], 3053482 A Nelson[12], 3052868 A B Purves[12] & 3052924 W Somerville[12]

~ 1st Bn, The Leicestershire Regiment ~

Note a.   *Roll of all personnel identified as eligible.*
Note b.   *Medals named in thin impressed capitals: 'LEIC. R.'*

Single Clasp	No. Identified	Rarity
North West Frontier 1935[12]	6	Of the Utmost Rarity

Captains: ~ W P Deane[12] Staff Capt., 1 (Peshawar) Bde.
Lance Sergeants/Corporals: ~ 4852456 H S Newell[12] attch. 20 Sqn RAF Int Liaison
Lance Corporals/Privates: ~ 4855075 G H Adams[12] attch. 1 FA, RAMC, 4855503 W J Alexander[12] attch. 1 FA, RAMC, 4855946 A D Chilcott[12] attch. 1 FA, RAMC & 4855216 H Waltham[12] attch. 1 FA, RAMC

~ 1st Bn, The South Wales Borders ~

Note a.   *Roll of all personnel identified as eligible.*
Note b.   *Medals named in thin impressed capitals: 'S. WALES BORD.'*

Single Clasp	No. Identified	Rarity
North West Frontier 1935[12]	2	Of the Utmost Rarity

Captains: ~ R I Sugden[12] Staff Capt. 2 (Rawalpindi) Bde.
Lieutenants: ~ R O Crewe-Read[12] Cipher Officer, HQ Mohmand FF

~ 2nd Bn, The Duke of Wellington's Regiment (West Riding) ~

Note a. *Roll of all commissioned personnel identified as eligible.*
Note b. *Non-commissioned and other rank personnel multi clasp only.*
Note c. *Present for both the 'Loe Agra' & the 'Mohmand' operations.*
Note d. *Medals named in thin impressed capitals: 'D.W.R.'*

Single Clasp	No. Identified	Rarity
North West Frontier 1935[12]	Bn. Strength	Not Rare
Combination Clasps	No. Identified	Rarity
Afghanistan N.W.F. 1919[3] North West Frontier 1935[12]	2	Of the Utmost Rarity

Lieutenant Colonels: ~ M N Cox[12]
Majors: ~ (Bvt) F H Fraser[12], H R Kavanagh[12] & O Price[12]
Captains: ~ V C Green[12], S B Kington[12], A E H Sayers[12] & A H G Wathen[12]
Lieutenants: ~ R N H C Bray[12] Bde. IO, F R P St. Bunbury[12], R G Collins[12], M M Davey[12], R K Exham[12], J B Fallon[12], R A H Gerrard[12], K Gregory[12], J T Rivett-Karnac[12], J H S Lane[12], F J Laurder[12], C J MacLaren[12], J F Maffett[12], R R F Marett[12], (QM) T W Milner[12], R de la H Moran[12], H P Skinner[12], W A Waller[12] & F H V Wellesley[12]
Lance Corporals/Privates: ~ 4687194 W Stone[3&12] & 4686650 J Warburton[3&12]

~ 2nd Bn, The Border Regiment ~

Note a. *Roll of all personnel identified as eligible.*
Note b. *Recipients attached 11 Field Ambulance (FA), Royal Army Medical Corps (RAMC), Ft. Ghalanai unless shown otherwise.*
Note c. *Medals named in thin impressed capitals: 'BORD. R.'*

Single Clasp	No. Identified	Rarity
North West Frontier 1935[12]	4	Of the Utmost Rarity
Combination Clasps	No. Identified	Rarity
Waziristan 1919–21[4] Waziristan 1921–24[6] North West Frontier 1935[12]	1	According to the roll as seen, can be considered Unique
North West Frontier 1930–31[9] North West Frontier 1935[12]	2	Of the Utmost Rarity

Captains: ~ T E Flewitt[4(Lt.),6(Lt.)&12] Staff Capt 'Mohforce'
Lance Corporals/Privates: ~ 3592663 J Addison[12], 3595360 J Bowerbank[12], 3596192 C H Foster[12], 3596408 E S Hughes[12] attch. RAF, 3595371 J Riley[9&12] & 3595292 W B Uren[9&12]

~ 1st Bn, The Hampshire Regiment ~

Note a. *Roll of all commissioned personnel identified as eligible.*
Note b. *Non-commissioned and other rank personnel multi clasp only.*
Note c. *Medals named in thin impressed capitals: 'HAMPS. R.'*

Single Clasp	No. Identified	Rarity
North West Frontier 1935[12]	Bn. Strength	Not Rare
Combination Clasps	No. Identified	Rarity
Mohmand 1933[11] North West Frontier 1935[12]	9	Of the Utmost Rarity

Majors: ~ W H Day[12], H C Westmorland[12] & E G Wheeler[12] as Acting Officer Commanding
Captains: ~ G D Browne[12], J H Dyas[11(Lt.)&12], H C C Newnham[12], C E V Sams[12], V D L Talbot[12] & J W Watts[12]
Lieutenants: ~ R G F Frisby[12], C A T Halliday[12], (QM) H Herrington[12], D J Keen[12], C J Kinna[12], R C G Langrishe[12], T G Tucker[11&12] & E C Yeldham[12]
Lance Sergeants/Corporals: ~ 5485832 H J Pottle[11(L/Cpl.)&12]
Lance Corporals/Privates: ~ 5494201 C E Budworth[11&12], 5494066 E G Galpin[11&12], 5494011 R Lane[11&12], 5494073 R Richards[11&12], 5494669 R H Robinson[11&12] & 5494135 A F Wellstead[11&12]

~ 1st Bn, The Dorsetshire Regiment ~

Note a.   *Roll of all personnel identified as eligible.*
Note b.   *Recipients attached 1 Provost Section unless shown otherwise.*
Note c.   *Medals named in running script: 'DORSET. R.'*

Single Clasp	No. Identified	Rarity
North West Frontier 1935[12]	9	Of the Utmost Rarity

Combination Clasps	No. Identified	Rarity
Malabar 1921–22[7] North West Frontier 1935[12]	1	According to the roll as seen, can be considered Unique

Majors: ~ S W Miller[12] DAQMG, PD
Warrant Officers Class II: ~ 5718740 R A Eaton[7(Sgt.)&12]
Lance Sergeants/Corporals: ~ 5723459 S Newton[12]
Lance Corporals/Privates: ~ 5667728 M H Dominey[12], 5107243 G W Hall[12], 6700458 C King[12], 5722651 W J Lovell[12], 799989 J A Pike[12], 5723991 S B Ritson[12] & 5723973 E W Stevenson[12]

~ 2nd Bn, The Welch Regiment ~

Note a.   *Roll of all personnel identified as eligible.*
Note b.   *Recipients attached Cipher Staff, Headquarters (HQ), Mohmand Field Force (MFF) unless shown otherwise.*
Note c.   *Medals named in running script: 'WELCH R.'*

Single Clasp	No. Identified	Rarity
North West Frontier 1935[12]	11	Extremely Rare

Combination Clasps	No. Identified	Rarity
Waziristan 1921–24[6] North West Frontier 1935[12]	1	According to the roll as seen, can be considered Unique

Captains: ~ R M Phillips[12] DAPM Mohmand FF
Lieutenants: ~ F H Brooke[12] attch. 20 Sqn RAF & J S B Gaskell[12] Cipher Officer Mohmand FF
Quartermaster Sergeants/Sergeants: ~ 3949288 G John[6&12] attch. No. 1 Provo Sect
Lance Corporals/Privates: ~ 3957223 A T Arthur[12], 3957097 W J Davies[12] attch. No. 1 Provo Sect, 3956509 E G Downing[12] attch. No. 1 Provo Sect, 3957687 W H Hillman[12], 3957663 M D O'Connell[12], 3957615 R Thomas[12], 3957382 H Verrier[12] attch. No. 1 Provo Sect & 3956759 G N C Welch[12]

~ 1st Bn, The Northamptonshire Regiment ~

Note a. *Roll of all personnel identified as eligible.*
Note b. *Eligible recipients deployed on detached duty under Lt. McNally to Peshawar from Dalhousie. All personnel except Lt. McNally, deployed with Mohforce attached to 4 Sanitary Section (SS), Royal Army Medical Corps (RAMC), on hygiene and water cleansing duty. Lt. McNally remained Peshawar as Adjutant (Adjt.) of the Reinforcement Depot.*
Note c. *Medals named in running script: 'NORTH'N. R.'*

Single Clasp	No. Identified	Rarity
North West Frontier 1935[12]	8	Of the Utmost Rarity

Lance Sergeants/Corporals: ~ 5881239 C W Reynolds[12] & 5880700 S Smith[12]

Lance Corporals/Privates: ~ 5881564 P Barker[12], 5882887 A W Bradshaw[12], 5883771 J A E Davis[12], 5882278 S Hazel[12], 5882014 G W McCauley[12] & 5881804 W Willerton[12]

~ 1st Bn, The King's Shropshire Light Infantry ~

Note a. *Roll of all personnel identified as eligible.*
Note b. *Recipient served as a Clerk at Headquarters (HQ), 2 Brigade (2 Bde.)*
Note c. *Medals named in thin impressed capitals: 'K.S.L.I.'*

Single Clasp	No. Identified	Rarity
North West Frontier 1935[12]	0	None Identified
Combination Clasps	No. Identified	Rarity
North West Frontier 1930–31[9] North West Frontier 1935[12]	1	According to the roll as seen, can be considered Unique

Quartermaster Sergeants/Sergeants: ~ (Act) 4029605 D R Griffiths[9&12]

~ 2nd Bn, The Highland Light Infantry (City of Glasgow Regiment) ~

Note a. *Roll of all commissioned personnel identified as eligible.*
Note b. *Non-commissioned and other rank personnel multi clasp only.*
Note c. *A single detachment attached District Troops for the 'Loe Agra' operations.*
Note d. *Medal to Lt. Col. H P M Berney-Ficklen may be named as 'Maj.'*
Note e. *Medals named in thin impressed capitals: 'H.L.I.'*

Single Clasp	No. Identified	Rarity
North West Frontier 1935[12]	Bn. Strength	Not Rare
Combination Clasps	No. Identified	Rarity
North West Frontier 1930–31[9] North West Frontier 1935[12]	1	If verified can be considered Unique

Lieutenant Colonels: ~ H P M Berney-Ficklin[12]
Majors: ~ H A Adams[12], A C Bruce[12], F A Hawkins[12] & J D Russell[12]
Captains: ~ J MacGregor[12], J W M Patterson[12], (QM) P Shaw[12] & D G Thorburn[12]
Lieutenants: ~ W N P Anett[12], J F Brand[12], R A Bramwell-Davis[12], R W F Johnson[12], A H Fownes-Luttrell[12], J A R Milman[12], D C Mullen[12], F B B Noble[12] & H I G Stewart[12]
Corporals: ~ 3300215 A Lewis[9(Piper)&12]

~ 2nd Bn, The Argyll and Sutherland Highlanders (Princess Louise's) ~

Note a.   *Roll of all commissioned personnel identified as eligible.*
Note b.   *Non-commissioned and other rank personnel multi clasp only.*
Note c.   *Medals named in thin impressed capitals: 'A.&S.H.'*

Single Clasp	No. Identified	Rarity
North West Frontier 1935[12]	Bn. Strength	Not Rare

Lieutenant Colonels: ~ J Hay-Young[12]
Majors: ~ J C Cunningham[12], R G Moir[12] & A Mac Donald Ritchie[12]
Captains: ~ R M T Baker-Carr[12], D Darroch[12], F N Elliot[12], A W Gibbon[12], (QM) S C McKay[12] & L B Robertson[12] attch 20 Sqn RAF
Lieutenants: ~ F W Clark[12], F C C Graham[12], E Maxwell[12], E K L Melville[12], K Muir[12], I D Murray[12], E J D Snowball[12], D V S J Stewart[12] & J W Tweedie[12]

THE CORPS:

~ The Royal Army Chaplains Department ~

Note a.   *Roll of all personnel identified as eligible.*
Note b.   *Recipient served as Chaplain to 3 Light Battery, Royal Artillery, (RA).*
Note c.   *Medals named in thin impressed capitals: 'R.A.Ch.D.'*

Single Clasp	No. Identified	Rarity
North West Frontier 1935[12]	1	According to the roll as seen, can be considered Unique

Reverands To The Forces: ~ J Styles[12]

~ The Royal Army Medical Corps ~
Sub Units Identified As Entitled:
Unit Medical Officers Attached
31 Company
1, 3 & 11 Field Ambulance

Note a.   *Roll of all personnel identified as eligible.*
Note b.   *All Enlisted personnel drawn from 31 Company, Royal Army Medical Corps (RAMC), Peshawar.*
Note c.   *Medals named in thin impressed capitals: 'R.A.M.C.'*

Single Clasp	No. Identified	Rarity
North West Frontier 1935[12]	26	Very Rare
Combination Clasps	**No. Identified**	**Rarity**
Afghanistan N.W.F. 1919[3] North West Frontier 1935[12]	1	According to the roll as seen, can be considered Unique
Waziristan 1919–21[4] Waziristan 1921–24[6] North West Frontier 1930–31[9] North West Frontier 1935[12]	1	According to the roll as seen, can be considered Unique
North West Frontier 1930–31[9] Mohmand 1933[11] North West Frontier 1935[12]	1	According to the roll as seen, can be considered Unique

Burma 1930–32[10] **Mohmand 1933**[11] **North West Frontier 1935**[12]	3	**Of the Utmost Rarity**
Mohmand 1933[11] **North West Frontier 1935**[12]	23	**Very Rare**

Lieutenant Colonels: ~ R K Mallam[3&12] 1 FA

Majors: ~ R A Bennett[12] 3 FA, A P Draper[11&12] MO, 18 KEO Cavalry, IA, F R H Mollan[11&12] 1 FA, M P Power[4,6,9&12] OC 3 FA & C A Slaughter[12] 11 FA

Captains: ~ W M E Anderson[12] MO, 2 HLI, N P Breden[11(Lt.)&12] 3 FA, W B F Brennan[11(Lt.)&12] 3 FA, G W Crimmin[12] MO, 1 Hampshire, P T L Day[12] 1 FA, C King[12] MO, 2 DWR, E H P Lassen[12] MO, 2 A&SH, A D Low[12] MO, 2 HLI, A N T Meneces[12], P O'Shea[12] 1 FA, C B R Pollock[12] 3 FA & W H Scriven[12] 1 FA

Lieutenants: ~ T M R Ahern[11&12] SMO Blockade Line & J A D Johnston[12] 11 FA

Company Quartermaster Sergeants/Staff Sergeants / Colour Sergeants: ~ 7254343 E Clay[12]

Quartermaster Sergeants/Sergeants: ~ 7249316 G E Andrews[12] & 7254709 A Brooker[11&12]

Lance Sergeants/Corporals: ~ 7259229 L H Bryson[12], 7259489 W J Couchman[12], 7258604 J C Farmer[11&12], 7251528 P H W Harris[11&12] & 7255271 T Kitching[11&12]

Lance Corporals/Privates: ~ 7260652 S Bassett[12], 7261049 R H Burfield[11&12], 7260675 L A Cook[11&12], 4910812 J N Cooper[11&12], 7259519 W C Cosnett[11&12], 7260722 H Doyle[11&12], 7261996 L Eden[12], 7261683 E Hatton[12], 7260728 H Henry[11&12], 5103165 A Hitchcox[11&12], 7260716 J Inglis[11&12], 6780270 H Jelfs[10,11&12], 7260641 B S Lipsett[12], 7259204 A F Martin[12], 7260654 I W J Martin[11&12], 7260660 T H Mattox[11&12], 7261636 P A Moriarty[12], 7262094 H Owen[12], 7258829 F Ryde[9,11&12], 7259135 A Sutcliffe[10,11&12], 7259202 H Thorpe[10,11&12], 7260701 F W Totty[11&12], 7261403 J Travers[12], 7260686 S R Whitehall[11&12], 7259463 A J Wignell[11&12], 7259129 R T Wilson[11&12] & 7261384 J Wray[12]

~ The Royal Army Ordnance Corps ~

Note a. *Roll of all personnel identified as eligible.*

Note b. *Medals named in thin impressed capitals: 'R.A.O.C.'*

Single Clasp	No. Identified	Rarity
North West Frontier 1935[12]	9	Of the Utmost Rarity

Company Quartermaster Sergeants/Staff/Sergeants: ~ (Armt) 7574702 H J C Deane[12] attch. 2 DWR & 7582388 C Erskine[12] attch. 2 HLI

Quartermaster Sergeants/Sergeants: ~ 7876211 O C Lloyd[12] attch. 1 Hamps

Lance Sergeants/Corporals: ~ 7582939 R Duell[12] attch. 2 HLI & 758283 C D Robinson[12] attch. 2 LTC

Lance Corporals/Privates: ~ 7586659 R Bennell[12] attch. 2 LTC, 7585428 R Golding[12] attch. 2 LTC, 7583521 R A Hale 2 LTC & 7583055 G Thomas[12] attch. 2 DWR

~ The Royal Army Veterinary Corps ~

Note a. *Roll of all personnel identified as eligible.*

Note b. *Medals named in thin impressed capitals: 'R.A.V.C.'*

Single Clasp	No. Identified	Rarity
North West Frontier 1935[12]	6	Of the Utmost Rarity
Combination Clasps	**No. Identified**	**Rarity**
Afghanistan N.W.F. 1919[3] **Waziristan 1919–21**[4] **Waziristan 1921–24**[6] **North West Frontier 1930–31**[9] **Mohmand 1933**[11] **North West Frontier 1935**[12]	1	**According to the roll as seen, can be considered Unique**

North West Frontier 1930–31[9] Mohmand 1933[11] North West Frontier 1935[12]	1	According to the roll as seen, can be considered Unique
Mohmand 1933[11] North West Frontier 1935[12]	1	According to the roll as seen, can be considered Unique

Majors: ~ W P S Edwards[3(Capt.),4(Capt.),6(Capt.),9,11&12], G V Golding[9,11&12] DADVS, J Leigh[11&12] & W St. J F Macartney[12]
Captains: ~ L W Coulden[12]
Lieutenants: ~ J L Dalzell[12], J Clabby[12] 2 (Nowshera) Bde., Loe Agra, I Mclaren[12] & P A Reeves[12] 2 (Nowshera) Bde., Loe Agra

~ The Army Educational Corps ~

Note a. Roll of all personnel identified as eligible.
Note b. Medals named in thin impressed capitals: 'R.A.E.C.'

Single Clasp	No. Identified	Rarity
North West Frontier 1935[12]	2	Of the Utmost Rarity

Majors: ~ (Bvt) E I G Richards[12] DEO 1 (Peshawar) Dist
Sergeants: ~ 6082581 A E Stuart[12] attch. PDS

~ The Army Dental Corps ~

Note a. Roll of all personnel identified as eligible.
Note b. Recipient attached 31 Company, Royal Army Medical Corps (RAMC), Peshawar.
Note c. Medals named in thin impressed capitals: 'A.D.CORPS.'

Single Clasp	No. Identified	Rarity
North West Frontier 1935[12]	1	According to the roll as seen, can be considered Unique

Lance Corporals / Privates: ~ 7536311 R J Wheeler[12]

DOMINION

~ The Australian Army Staff Corps ~

Note a. Roll of all personnel identified as eligible.
Note b. Australian officers were commissioned from the Royal Military College Duntroon into the Australian Staff Corps. Several were sent each year to India for attachment to both British and Indian Army units.
Note c. Medals are believed to be named in thin impressed capitals: 'AUST. STAFF CORPS.'

Single Clasp	No. Identified	Rarity
North West Frontier 1935[12]	4	Of the Utmost Rarity

Lieutenants: ~ L J Bruton[12] attch. 1 IDS attch. PDS, S J Hill[12] attch. 'A' Corps R Sigs, A D Molloy[12] attch. PDS & C C F Spry[12] attch. 2 DWR

THE ROYAL AIR FORCE

Note a.   *Refer to Royal Air Force notes at end of 'Frontier Campaigns 1919–1925' section for guidance regarding early rank designations.*

Note b.   *Ranks shown are those applicable at award of first clasp.*

Note c.   *Criteria for personnel to be included in the following roll follows that set out for the Army roll for the clasp North West Frontier 1935 i.e. all identified eligible commissioned ranks and multi bar enlisted recipients.*

Note d.   *Medals named in thin impressed block capitals: 'R.A.F.'*

Single Clasp	No. Identified	Rarity
North West Frontier 1935[12]	818	Not Rare

Combination Clasps	No. Identified	Rarity
Waziristan 1921–24[6] North West Frontier 1935[12]	3	Of the Utmost Rarity
Waziristan 1921–24[6] Mohmand 1933[11] North West Frontier 1935[12]	2	Of the Utmost Rarity
Waziristan 1925[8] North West Frontier 1935[12]	4	Of the Utmost Rarity
North West Frontier 1930–31[9] Mohmand 1933[11] North West Frontier 1935[12]	16	Extremely Rare
North West Frontier 1930–31[9] North West Frontier 1935[12]	32	Very Rare
Mohmand 1933[11] North West Frontier 1935[12]	55	Rare

Group Captains: ~ N H Bottomley[12]

Wing Commanders: ~ W B Farrington[12], J W B Grigson[12] & A Lees[12]

Squadron Leaders: ~ T J D Craig[12], J MacG Fairweather[12], P F Fullard[12], K H Riversdale-Elliott[12] & G H Shaw[12]

Flight Lieutenants: ~ J L Airey[11&12], T J Arbuthnot[12], D F W Atcherley[11&12], H F V Battle[12], H G Brookman[12], J W Buchanan[12], P B H Butler[12], B A Chacksfield[12], J M Cohu[12], F C Cole[12], L M Corbet[12], S D Culley[9&12], T H Downes[12], P H Dutton[12], A W Elias[12], A E Evans[12], F G H Ewens[12], C W Gore[12], R K Hamblin[12], H F Harvey[12], C M Heard[12], R T B Houghton[6&12], E C Hudleston[12], A F Hutton[12], R O Jones[12], W J H Lindley[12], H P Lloyd[6,11&12], M B Mackay[12], P L P Marett[12], J Norwood[11&12], G R O'Sullivan[12], R Reay-Jones[12], H R McL Reid[12], J F Sandow[12], L R Stokes[12], F C Sturgiss[12], V H Tompkins[11&12], C H Turner[12], G W Tuttle[12], G H Vasse[12], R G Veryard[9&12], J L Walsh[12] & H M S Wright[12]

Flying Officers: ~ T M Abraham[12], M J Adam[9&12], J S L Adams[12], W D Anderson[12], R A C Barclay[12], D W Bayne[9,11&12], B H Becker[12], J A B Begg[12], A J Biggar[12], I W Braye[12], W R Brotherhood[12], C Broughton[12], R P H Carew[12], C N Carpenter[11&12], N Carter[6&12], R A C Carter[12], W G A Coulson[12], A O D Cox[12], W J Craig[12], E B C Davies[12], W G Devas[12], H M T Eversfield[12], W H Forbes-Mitchell[12], T G L Gale[12], D W H Gardner[12], A H Garland[12], R J Gosnell[12], W M Graham[12], P H Hamley[12], C C House[12], R S Howe[12], J Y Humphreys[12], A D Isemonger[12], W G R Jarman[12], N C Jones[12], A J Kennedy[12], D J P Lee[12], W A Lee[12], J S Leslie[12], C R D I Lloyd[12], C H E Lyster[12], W Macey[12], W B Murray[12], S P A Patmore[12], C F Pearce[12], J C Pope[12], E F Porter[11&12], A Pyke[11&12], A S Q Robins[12], T U Rolfe[11&12], W S P Simonds[12], E T Smith[12], C M Stewart[12], F A A H Strath[12], J N Tandon[12], J B P Thomas[12], G R Thwaite[12], E B Waddy[11&12], E L A Walter[12], C H T Warner[12], R G Watson[12], J J Watts[12], H G Wheeler[9&12] & G P Woodhouse[12]

Pilot Officer: ~ H Y Alloway[12], J R Gillman[12], C C Hodder[12], W T King[12], J E Kirk[12], R C F Lister[12], A E Paish[8&12], D G H Spencer[12], J A H Tuck[12] & C L Y Wright[12]

Warrant Officers Class II: ~ 3929 C Oakley[11&12]

Sergeants: ~ 335589 R W Baldwin[11&12], (Act) 351062 S A Eveleigh[11&12], 364019 L E Farrell[11&12], 303543 F Florence[11&12], 245551 A E Miller[9&12] & 82908 E E R Williams[9,11&12]

Corporals: ~ 345329 C Adams[8&12], 157978 W S Berry[9&12], 560557 E J Brandon[9&12], 352862 L R Collins[11&12], 347149 A H Croombes[9&12], 560327 W R Cumbers[9,11&12], 327793 A Fisher[6,11&12], 327112 J R Hicks[9&12], 330149 J H Jones[9&12], 155057 F H Keirl[9,11&12], 336304 F G Loades[9&12], 560365 E H Maule[11&12], 239011 W H May[11&12], 358603 S E Nightingale[11&12], 349323 J Preston[11&12], 560449 N W Turner[9&12] & 366230 V G B White[11&12]

Leading Aircraftsmen: ~ 510655 C V D Bolon[11&12], 508577 H F Brittain[9&12], 565670 F W Bullen[9,11&12], 510424 J L Callagan[11&12], 514437 J A Chandler[11&12], 509983 B A Dorrell[11&12], 364614 K G Drury[11&12], 364082 A A J Fulford[11&12], 510388

H C Harris[11&12], 510377 G S Heard[11&12], 365376 J D How[9&12], 510730 C W Kearley[11&12], 358082 J G Kendall[9,11&12], 509794 H E Leclere[12], 366354 A McDonald[11&12], 364195 D McEwan[11&12], 365104 H G Martin[9&12], 561274 G Mason[11&12], 513440 V Morton[11&12], 561849 F L Payne[11&12], 508331 R W Penny[11&12], 561339 N V Phillips[11&12], 510950 W C Quennell[11&12], J V J Reynolds[9&12], L H Reynolds[11&12], 508932 T A Rowe[11&12], 507328 J Rutherford[9,11&12], 334136 A B Scott[8&12], 364762 C F Smart[9&12], 560912 E L Spoors[11&12], 365815 I G Stewart[9&12], 507671 G H Tice[9&12], 345405 V Tonkin[6&12], 365031 E J W Walker[11&12], 506486 E J Wallis[9&12], 511190 F Wilson[11&12] & 361747 A C Wood[9&12]

Aircraftsmen 1st Class: ~ 513170 A Aitken[11&12], 512957 E T Davies[11&12], 366078 P W E Dent[9,11&12], 330345 E Gadd[8&12], 511582 C D Grieve[11&12], 507977 J C Irwin[9,11&12], D Laing[9,11&12], 562790 A McLoughlin[11&12], 510190 H G Ranson[11&12], 509160 H Riley[11&12], 510029 G Rolfe[11&12], 560898 H S Salmon[9,11&12], 510988 H E Sandys[11&12], 508783 C J Woodhouse[9&12], 506286 D R Woolnough[9,11&12], 508883 E Young[11&12] & 506438 H J Van Zeller[9&12]

Aircraftsmen 2nd Class: ~ 512470 E P Baldwin[11&12], 507733 A H Cairns[9,11&12], 510616 W Crabtree[9&12], 510647 W Edwards[9&12], 509221 A J Harpur[11&12], 508838 W H Hattrick[9,11&12], 512630 W R S Madgwick[11&12], 509995 G E Mead[9&12], 511815 W Middlemist[9&12], 365506 J P Murphy[9,11&12], 508333 V Palin[9&12], 511928 T J Parry[9&12], 511982 T M Parry[9&12], 513844 W J Reardon[11&12], 511455 W E Sanderson[9,11&12], 512771 H West[11&12], 511590 P R West[9&12] & 510466 H W Why[9&12]

INDIAN ESTABLISHMENT

Qualifying Units Present (Officers Plus Known Individuals)

The Cavalry:
6th Duke Of Connaught's Own Lancers..Maj. T Scott GSO2 'Mohforce' (Only)
18th King Edward's Own...Cavalry 'Mohforce' Force Troops

The Artillery:
22 & 25 Indian Mountain Brigades
2 (Derajat) Mountain Battery (FF)...Loe Agra Operations > ? / Mohmand Operations >Yes
4 (Hazara) Mountain Battery (FF)...Loe Agra Operations > Yes / Mohmand Operations > Yes
7 (Bengal) Mountain Battery..Loe Agra Operations > No / Mohmand Operations > Yes
13 (Dardoni) Mountain Battery...Loe Agra Operations > No / Mohmand Operations > Yes

The Sappers & Miners:
King George's Own Bengal S&M
No. 3 Field Company...Loe Agra Operations > No / Mohmand Operations > Yes
No. 5 Field Company...Loe Agra Operations > Yes / Mohmand Operations > Yes

Advanced Engineer Park > Peshawar

Military Engineering Services

Survey of India
18 Air Survey Party

The Indian Signal Corps:

The Infantry:
5/1st Punjab Regiment...Loe Agra Operations > No / Mohmand Operations > Yes / Peshawar Brigade
2/2nd Punjab Regiment.......................................Loe Agra Operations > No / Mohmand Operations > Yes / Rawalpindi Brigade
3/2nd Punjab Regiment.............................Loe Agra Operations > Yes / Mohmand Operations > Yes / Both Nowshera Brigade
1/4th Bombay Grenadiers......................Loe Agra Operations 'Yes' District Troops / Mohmand Operations > Yes / Peshawar Brigade
5/10th Baluch Regiment King (George V's Own) (Jacobs Rifles)...........................Loe Agra Operations > No / Mohmand Operations Yes > Peshawar Brigade
2/11th Sikh Regiment...............................Lt. W G D Sealy Asst Peshawar Brigade Transport Officer (Only) 'Moforce'
3/11th Sikh Regiment (Rattray's).............................Loe Agra Operations > No / Mohmand Operations > Yes / Rawalpindi Brigade
1/12th Frontier Force Regiment (Prince of Wales' Own Sikhs)................Maj. K A Garrett Brig Maj Rawalpindi Brigade (Only) Peshawar Brigade 'Moforce'
5/12th Frontier Force Rifles (Queen Victoria's Own Corps of Guides)..............Loe Agra Operations > Yes / Mohmand Operations > Yes / Both Nowshera Brigade
6/13th Frontier Force Rifles (Scinde)....................Capt. J B P Seccombe Cmd Det Frontier Intelligence Corps & DI (Only) 'Moforce'

1/14th Punjab Regiment...Loe Agra Operations > No / Mohmand Operations > Yes / Jhelum Brigade
1/15th Punjab Regiment..................................Loe Agra Operations > No / Mohmand Operations > Yes / Rawalpindi Brigade
2/15th Punjab Regiment.............................Loe Agra Operations > Yes / Mohmand Operations > Yes / Both Nowshera Brigade
4/15th Punjab Regiment....................................Loe Agra Operations > No / Mohmand Operations > Yes / 'Moforce' Troops
4/16th Punjab Regiment...................................Loe Agra Operations > No / Mohmand Operations > Yes / Jhelum Brigade
19th Hyderabad Regiment (1st Kumaon Rifles)...Maj. J B Macdonald Staff Capt (Only) 'Moforce'
4/19th Hyderabad Regiment.......................................Maj. G G Bull Staff Capt HQ Nowshera Brigade (Only) Both Operations
2/1st King George's Own Gurkha Rifles...........................Loe Agra Operations > No / Mohmand Operations > Yes / 'Force Troops'
1/3rd Queen Alexandra's Own Gurkha Rifles....................Maj. A D P Campbell Bde Maj HQ Nowshera Brigade (Only) Loe Agra
2/3rd Queen Alexandra's Own Gurkha Rifles..........................Maj. C H Boucher Bde Maj Peshawar Brigade (Only) 'Moforce'
1/4th (Prince of Wales' Own) Gurkha Rifles................Loe Agra Operations > Yes Nowshera Brigade / Mohmand Operations > No
2/4th (Prince of Wales' Own Gurkha Rifles)...Capt. J J L Mackirdy Staff Capt (Only) 'Moforce'
1/5th Royal Gurkha Rifles...Staff Capt Peshawar Brigade (Only) 'Moforce'
1/9th Gurkha Rifles...Maj. R M E King Bde Maj HQ Nowshera Brigade (Only) Both Operations

The Indian Army Reserve of Officers / The Auxiliary Forces India / The Indian Territorial Force

The Indian Corps:
The Royal Indian Army Service Corps:

Nos. 26 & 27 Supply Depots..Loe Agra > No / Mohmand > Yes
Nos. 2, 5, 13, 15 & 16 Supply Issue Sections...Loe Agra > No. 5 Only
No. 37 Animal Transport Company (Camels)...Loe Agra > No / Mohmand > Yes
Nos. 1 (Part), 6, 7, 18, 19, 22 & 29 (Det), 35 & 39 Animal Transport Companies (Mules)................Loe Agra > Nos. 1 (Part), 6 (Det.),
22, 35 (Det.) & 39
Nos. 2 (Det.), 4 (Det.) 20 (Det.), 27 (Det.) & 28 MT Companies......................Loe Agra > 28 MT Coy Dist Troops

Medical Units:
The Indian Medical Service / The Indian Hospital Corps /
The Queen Alexander's Military Nursing Service India
British & Indian Military Hospitals Peshawar & Nowshera
Convalescent Depot Cherat
Main Dressing Station Ghalanai
Nos. 3 & 4 Sanitary Sections
Nos. 1, 3 & 11 Field Ambulance (RAMC)

The Indian Army Veterinary Corps:
3 Mobile Veterinary Section

The Indian Army Ordnance Corps:
Artillery and Mechanical Transport Workshops

The Indian Corps of Clerks:

The Military Farms Department:
Grass Circles & Conservancy

The Police, Judiciary & Intelligence:
Frontier Constabulary, Jail Department & Frontier Intelligence Corps

The Postal Department:

The Indian Ecclesiastical Dept:
Rev. A J McDonald attch. 2 HLI

The Political & Civil Departments:
Political Officers & Swat Levies

ROYAL AIR FORCE:			
1 (Indian) Group RAF			
1 (Indian) Wing RAF			
Squadron	Operation	Location	Aircraft
No. 27 (B) Squadron	Mohmand	RAF Kohat	Westland Wapiti
No. 60 (B) Squadron	Mohmand	RAF Kohat	Wapiti
2 (Indian) Wing RAF			
Squadron	Operation	Location	Aircraft
No. 5 (AC) Squadron	Mohmand	RAF Risalpur	Wapiti
No. 11 (B) Squadron	Mohmand	RAF Risalpur	Hawker Hart
No. 20 (AC) Squadron	Loe Agra / Mohmand	RAF Risalpur	Wapiti
No. 39 (B) Squadron	Mohmand	RAF Risalpur	Hawker Hart

ABBREVIATIONS AND GLOSSARY

Jihad	Holy War
Jigra	Assembly of Tribal Elders
Lashkar	Tribal Army
Mullah	Religious Leader/Holy Man
Malik	Headman
Sangar	Breastwork built of stone or boulders
Sepoy	Indian Army Private Soldier
Sowar	Indian Army Mounted Trooper
(AC)	Army Cooperation (RAF)
AC	Air Craftsman
(H) Bty	Heavy Battery
1/1 Kent	Kent (Cyclist) Bn
AA&QMG	Assistant Adjutant & Quartermaster General
AANS	Australian Army Nursing Service
ABC	Army Bearer Corps
ACC	Armoured Car Company
ACRE	Assistant Commander Royal Engineers
ACS	Army Corps Signals
Act	Acting
ADC	Aide de Camp
AD CORPS	Army Dental Corps
Adjt	Adjutant
ADMS	Assistant Director of Medical Services
ADMW	Assistant Director of Military Works
ADRTE	Assistant Director Railway Transport Establishment
ADST	Assistant Director of Supply & Transport
Adv Eng Pk	Advanced Engineering Park
ADVS	Assistant Director of Veterinary Services
AEC	Army Education Corps
AEF	Abor Expeditionary Force
AFI	Auxiliary Forces India
AGE	Assistant Garrison Engineer
AHC	Army Hospital Corps
AM	Air Marshal
Ammo	Ammunition
AMP	Assam Military Police
AOC	Air Officer Commanding
(R)AOC	(Royal) Army Ordnance Corps
APC	Army Pay Corps
APD	Army Pay Department
APO	Assistant Political Officer
AQMG	Assistant Quartermaster General
AR	Assam Rifles
Armd Train	Armoured Train

Armt	Armament
Art	Artillery
ARW	Advanced Repair Workshop
ASC	Army Signal Corps (Indian Army)
(R)ASC	(Royal) Army Service Corps
ATC	Animal Transport Company
Attch	Attached
(R)AVC/CPS	(Royal) Army Veterinary Corps
AVM	Air Vice Marshal
B(S)S	British Staging Section
BC	Bullock Corps
BCCS	British Casualty Clearing Station
Bde	Brigade
Bde Sply Sect	Brigade Supply Section
Bedfs & Herts	Bedfordshire & Hertfordshire Regt
Berkshire	Berkshire Regt
BFF	Baluchistan Field Force
BFH	British Field Hospital
BGH	British General Hospital
BMH	British Military Hospital
Bmdr	Bombardier
BMP	Burma Military Police
Bn	Battalion
Border	Border Regt
BRCS	British Red Cross Society
Brig Gen	Brigadier General
BR WIR	British West India Regt
BSH	British Station Hospital
BSM	Battery Sergeant Major
BSO	Brigade Supply Officer
BSS	British Sanitary (Staging) Section
Bty	Battery
BVFF	Bazaar Valley Field Force
Bvt	Brevet
C&TS	Cable & Telegraph Section
C of Dns	Corps of Dragoons
C of Hrs	Corps of Hussars
C of Lcrs	Corps of Lancers
Capt	Captain
Cav	Cavalry
C of AS	Corps of Army Schoolmasters
CBAC	Cavalry Brigade Ammunition Column
Cbl & Telph Sect	Cable & Telegraphic Section
CBSS	Cavalry Brigade Signal Section
CBST	Cavalry Brigade Signal Troop

CC	Camel Corps
CCCS	Combined Casualty Clearing Station
CCS	Casualty Clearing Section
CFA	Combined Field Ambulance
CGS	Chief of the General Staff
CIGH	Combined Indian General Hospital
CinC	Commander in Chief
Clk	Clerk
Cmd	Commander
Cmdt	Commandant
CMH	Combined Military Hospital
CMSC	Corps of Military Staff Clerks
Col	Colonel
Colmn	Column
Condr	Conductor
Const	Construction
Coy	Company
Cpl	Corporal
CPO	Chief Political Officer
CRA	Commander Royal Artillery
CRE	Commander Royal Engineers
CRO	Commander Royal Ordnance
CSS	Combined Sanitary Section
CSM	Company Sergeant Major
CSO	Chief Staff Officer
D of C	Director of Communications
Div Sply Cpy	Divisional Supply Company
DA&QMG	Deputy Adjutant & Quartermaster General
DAAG	Deputy Assistant Adjutant General
DAC	Divisional Ammunition Column
DADA&TF	Deputy Assistant Director of Auxiliary & Territorial Forces
DADH	Deputy Assistant Director of Hygiene
DADMA	Deputy Assistant Director of Military Affairs
DADMS	Deputy Assistant Director of Medical Services
DADS	Deputy Assistant Director of Signals
DAMS	Director Army Medical Services
DAPM	Deputy Assistant Provost Marshal
DCGS	Deputy Chief of the General Staff
DCLI	Duke of Cornwall's Light Infantry
DDMS	Deputy Director of Medical Services
DD Works	Deputy Director of Military Works
DEO	Divisional Education Officer
Dep	Deputy
Dept	Department
Det	Detachment
DFD	Dairy Farms Department

DIG of C	Department of the Director General of Communications
DIK	Dera Ismail Khan
Dist	District
Div	Division
DLI	Durham Light Infantry
DMW	Director of Military Works
DPC	Draft Pack Company (Mules or Ponies)
DS	Director of Supply
DS&T	Director of Supply & Transport
DSC	Divisional Signal Company
DSO	Divisional Signals Officer
DT	Director of Transport
DWR	Duke of Wellington's Regt
Eng	Engineering
Eng Pk	Engineering Park
Essex	Essex Regt
FA	Field Ambulance
FC	Field Cashier/Frontier Constabulary
FF	Field Force/Frontier Force
FF Regt	Frontier Force Regt
FF Rifles	Frontier Force Rifles
FGA	Frontier Garrison Artillery
F/Lt (Lieut)	Flight Lieutenant
Fld Coy	Field Company
Flight	Flight
FM	Field Marshal
FO	Flying Officer
F/Sgt	Flight Sergeant
FTCO	Forward Transport Coordinating Office
Fus	Fusilier
FVS	Field Veterinary Section
G/Capt	Group Captain
GCC	Government Camel Corps
GE	Garrison Engineer
Gen	General
GH	General Hospital
GHQ	General Headquarters
GR	Gurkha Rifles
GSO1	General Staff Officer Grade 1
GSO2	General Staff Officer Grade 2
Hampshire	Hampshire Regt
HE	His Excellency
Hon	Honourable
HQ	Headquarters
Hrs	Hussars

I(S)S	Indian Staging Section
IA	Indian Army
IACC	Indian Army Corps of Clerks
IAOC	Indian Army Ordnance Corps
IARO	Indian Army Reserve of Officers
IAS	Indian Army Staff
IASC	Indian Army Service Corps
IC	Inspector of Communications
ICCS	Indian Casualty Clearing Station
ICS	Indian Civil Service
IDAC	Indian Divisional Ammunition Column
IDS	Indian Divisional Signals
I ECC EST	Indian Ecclesiastical Establishment
IFA	Indian Field Ambulance
IG	Inspector General
IGH	Indian General Hospital
IHC	Indian Hospital Corps
ILC	Indian Labour Company
IMD	Indian Medical Department
IMRU	Indian Mobile Repair Unit
IMS	Indian Medical Service
IMVS	Indian Mobile Veterinary Section
Ind	Indian
Indep	Independent
Inf	Infantry
Insp	Inspector
Int	Intelligence
IO	Intelligence Officer
IOD	Indian Ordnance Department
IPS	Indian Postal Service
I REMT D	Indian Remount Department
IS	Internal Security
ISC	Indian Signal Corps
ISH	Indian Station Hospital
ISMD	Indian Subordinate Medical Department
ISS	Indian Sanitary Section
ITD	Indian Telegraph Department
IUL	Indian Unattached List
KDG	King's Dragoon Guards
KGO S&M	King George's Own Sappers & Miners
King's	King's Liverpool Regt
KKF	Khost Kurram Force
KOYLI	King's Own Yorkshire Light Infantry
KRRC	King's Royal Rifle Corps
KSLI	King's Shropshire Light Infantry
LAC	Leading Air Craftsman
L of C	Lines of Communication
L/Bmdr	Lance Bombardier

L/Cpl	Lance Corporal
Lanc F	Lancashire Fusiliers
LAT	Lahore Armoured Train
Lcrs	Lancers
London	London Regt
Lt/Lieut	Lieutenant
LTC	Light Tank Company/Local Transport Corps
(M)	Medium
M Bty	Mountain Battery
MA	Motor Ambulance
MAC	Motor Ambulance Convoy/Column
MAD	Military Accounts Department
Maj	Major
Mbl	Mobile
MC	Mule Corps
MD	Medical Doctor
MES	Military Engineering Service
MFD	Military Farms Department
MFF	Mohmand/Malabar Field Force
MFO	Military Forwarding Officer
MFP	Military Foot Police
MG	Machine Gun
MGC	Machine Gun Corps
MGCC	Machine Gun Corps Cavalry
Mil	Military
Mis	Mission
MMGC	Motor Machine Gun Corps
MMP	Mounted Military Police
MO	Medical Officer
MRU	Mobile Repair Unit
MT	Motor Transport
Mtd	Mounted
Mtn	Mountain
Mtr	Motor
MWS	Military Works Service
N Stafford	North Staffordshire Regt
NF	Northumberland Fusiliers
NFH	Native Field Hospital
NIL MAL BN	Nilghal & Malabar Battalion
NIL VOL RIFLS	Nilghal Volunteer Rifles
Norfolk	Norfolk Regt
Northamt'n	Northamptonshire Regt
NW Rly Vol	North West Railway Volunteers
NWFF	North West Frontier Force
NWFP	North West Frontier Province
NZEF	New Zealand Expeditionary Force

OC	Officer Commanding		RTE	Railway Transport Establishment
OO	Orderly Officer		RTO	Railway Transport Office/Officer
OPC	Official Press Correspondent		RWF	Royal Welsh (Welch) Fusiliers
Ord Dep	Ordnance Depot		RWK	Royal West Kent Regt
			RY BN S&M	Railway Battalion Sappers & Miners
P BTY (FF)	Pack Battery (Frontier Force)			
PDS	Peshawar District Signals		S/Ldr	Squadron Leader
PISA	Peshawar Internal Security Area		SCO RIF	Scottish Rifles
Pk Bty	Pack Battery		S Lanc	South Lancashire Regt (Prince of Wales's Volunteers)
PM	Provost Marshal			
PMC	Pack Mule Corps		S&M	Sappers & Miners
PMO	Principal Medical Officer		S&TC	Supply & Transport Corps
PO	Pilot Officer		Seaforth	Seaforth Highlanders
POLITICAL IA	Political Department Indian Army		Sect	Section
Provo	Provost		Ser	Service
PS	Private Secretary		Sgln	Signalman
Pte	Private		Sgt	Sergeant
PWO	Prince of Wales's Own (West Yorkshire Regt)		SofI	Survey of India
			Sigs	Signals
PWO S&M	Prince of Wales's Own Sappers & Miners		SMO	Senior Medical Officer
			SO	Signals Officer
			Som LI	Somerset Light Infantry
QAIMNS(R)	Queen Alexandra's Imperial Military Nursing Service (Reserve)		SORA	Staff Officer Royal Artillery
			Sply	Supply
QM	Quartermaster		Sqn	Squadron
QORWKR	Queen's Own Royal West Kent Regt		SS	Sanitary Section
Queen's	Queen's (Royal West Surrey Regt)		SSB	Special Service Battalion
QVO S&M	Queen Victoria's Own Sappers & Miners		SSO	Station Staff Office/Officer
			STAFF	Staff (Corps)
			Stn	Station
R Sigs	Royal Corps of Signals		Supt	Superintendent/Support
RA	Royal Artillery		Sussex	Sussex Regt
RAF	Royal Air Force		SVO	Senior Veterinary Officer
RAMC	Royal Army Medical Corps			
RASC	Royal Army Service Corps		TCO	Treasure Chest Officer
RAVC	Royal Army Veterinary Corps		TEL DEPT	Telegraph Department
RC	Roman Catholic		TFNS	Territorial Force Nursing Service
RE	Royal Engineers		Tpr	Trooper
Regt	Regiment		Tptr	Trumpeter
REMT DEPT	Remount Department		TRF	Thai Relief Force
RFA	Royal Field Artillery			
RFLS	Rifles		VOLS	Volunteers
RGA	Royal Garrison Artillery			
RHA	Royal Horse Artillery		W/Cmdr	Wing Commander
Rly	Railway		WE Sect	Wireless Experimental Section
RMF	Royal Munster Fus		W/Sect	Wireless Section
RR OF CAV	Reserve Regiment of Cavalry		W/Sigs	Wireless Signals
R S FUS	Royal Scots Fusiliers		Warwick	Warwickshire Regt
RSM	Regimental Sergeant Major		Waz Dist	Waziristan District
RTC	Royal Tank Corps		Waz DS	Waziristan District Signals
			West Yorks	West Yorkshire Regt

WFF	Waziristan Field Force	Yorkshire	Yorkshire Regt (Green Howards)
WO	Warrant Officer		
Worcester	Worcester Regt	ZF	Zhob Force
WT	Wireless Telegraph	ZL Police	Zhob Levy Police
WTO	Water Transport Officer		

Selected Bibliography

Barthorp M, *The North-West Frontier, A Pictorial History 1839-1947*. New Orchard Editions, 1986.

Duckers P, *1 KSLI on the North West Frontier of India 1929–1931*. Shropshire Regimental Museum, 2003.

Dunbar G, *Other Men's Lives*. London, 1938.

Gordon L, *British Battles & Medals*. 4th Edition. Spink & Son, 1971.

Gould R, *Locations of British Cavalry, Infantry & Machine Gun Units 1914–1924*, Heralden, 1977.

Hamilton A, *In Abor Jungles*. G Bell & Sons, 1912.

India General Service Medal Roll 1908–1935 to the RAF. The Naval & Military Press, Date Unknown.

James E A, *British Regiments 1914-18*. 4th Edition. The Naval & Military Press, 1993.

Jefford G G, *RAF Squadrons*. Airlife, 1988.

Kempton C, *A Register of Titles of the Units of the HEIC & Indian Armies 1666–1947*. British Empire & Commonwealth Museum, 1997.

Miller C, *Khyber*. Macdonald & Janes, 1977.

Molesworth G N, *Afghanistan 1919*. Unknown

Nevill H L, *Campaigns on the North-West Frontier*. The Naval & Military Press, 2005.

The Official History of Operations Parts I, II & III: N W Frontier of India 1920-35. The Naval & Military Press in association with The Imperial War Museum, Date Unknown

The London Times. Contemporary Editions.

Regimental Histories/Journals and Magazines. Various.

Private Correspondence: Various.

Lightning Source UK Ltd.
Milton Keynes UK
UKOW02n1522080414

229481UK00001BA/2/P